THE YEAR'S WORK
IN ENGLISH STUDIES 1984

The Year's Work in English Studies

Volume 65 · 1984

English Association

Edited by
LAUREL BRAKE

and
SUSAN BROCK
DAVID DANIELL
OWEN KNOWLES
MAUREEN MORAN
(associate editors)

JACQUELINE HOOI
(editorial assistant)

Published for
THE ENGLISH ASSOCIATION

by
JOHN MURRAY, LONDON
HUMANITIES PRESS, ATLANTIC HIGHLANDS, N.J.

© The English Association 1987

Typeset by Fakenham Photosetting Ltd,
Fakenham, Norfolk
Printed and bound in Great Britain by
Biddles Ltd, Guildford and King's Lynn

British Library Cataloguing in Publication Data

The Year's work in English studies.—Vol. 65
1. English literature—History and criticism
—Periodicals
820.9   PR1
ISBN 0–7195–4348–7

The Library of Congress has cataloged this
serial publication as follows:

The Year's work in English studies.   v. [1]-   1919/20-
London. Published for the English Association
by John Murray [etc.]

v.   23 cm.

Annual.
ISSN 0084-4144 = Year's work in English studies.
ISBN 0–391–03501–0

1. English philology—History.   2. English philology—
Bibliography.   3. English literature—History and criticism.
4. English literature—Periodicals.
I. English Association.
PE58.E6   22-10024
                                                           MARC-S

Library of Congress   [8503r80]rev4

Preface

The *YWES* is a selective, comprehensive, and evaluative narrative bibliography of scholarly writing in the field of literature in English in Britain, America, Africa, Australia, Canada, the Caribbean, and India.

It may help the user of this work to remember that books are sometimes published a year later in the U.S.A. than they are in the U.K. and vice versa, that the year of publication is not always that which appears on the title-page of the book, and that the inevitable inadvertent omissions of one year are made good in the next; thus the search for a notice of a book or article may have to extend to the volume after the expected one and sometimes to that which precedes it. Reports of important omissions are welcomed.

Offprints of articles are always useful, and editors of journals that are not easily available in the U.K. are urged to join the many who already send us complete sets. These should be addressed to The Editor, *YWES*, The English Association, 1 Priory Gardens, London W4 1TT. We are grateful to the authors and publishers who have made our task easier by supplying books and articles for Volume 65, and to the editors of *ASE* and *MLA International Bibliography* for proof of their annual bibliographies. In drawing the reader's attention at the beginning of chapters to the main bibliographical aids, we presuppose in each case a reference to the *MLA International Bibliography*, and the *Annual Bibliography of English Literature* published by the MHRA.

We dedicate this volume to Professor Beatrice White, a distinguished editor of *YWES* between 1950 and 1963, who died on Easter day, 1986.

Laurel Brake
University College of Wales
Aberystwyth

for the Editorial Board

Susan Brock (The Shakespeare Institute)
David Daniell (University College, London)
Owen Knowles (University of Hull)
Maureen Moran (West London Institute of HE)

The English Association

This bibliography is an English Association publication. It is available through membership of the Association; non-members can purchase it through any good bookshop.

The object of the English Association is to promote the knowledge and appreciation of English language and literature.

The Association pursues these aims by creating opportunities of co-operation among all those interested in English; by furthering the recognition of English as essential in education; by discussing methods of English teaching; by holding lectures, conferences, and other meetings; by publishing a journal, books, and leaflets; and by forming local branches overseas and at home.

Publications

The Year's Work in English Studies. An annual bibliography. Published by John Murray (U.S.A.: Humanities Press).

Essays and Studies. An annual volume of essays by various scholars assembled by the collector covering usually a wide range of subjects and authors from the medieval to the modern. Published by John Murray (U.S.A.: Humanities Press).

English. The journal of the Association, *English* is published three times a year by the Oxford University Press.

News-Letter. A *News-Letter* is issued three times a year giving information about forthcoming publications, conferences, and other matters of interest.

Benefits of Membership

Full members receive copies of *The Year's Work in English Studies, Essays and Studies, English* (3 issues), three *News-Letters* and the Presidential Address.

Ordinary Membership covers *English* (3 issues), three *News-Letters* and the Presidential Address.

Schools Membership covers two copies of each issue of *English*, one copy of *Essays and Studies* (optional), three *News-Letters*, the Presidential Address and preferential booking for Sixth Form Conference places.

Occasional Publications

The Association has published many occasional publications including *A Guide to Degree Courses in English* (Sixth Edition 1982), *The English Association Handbook of Societies and Collections*, *English Short Stories of Today*, *Poems of Today*, Presidential Address, and many pamphlets.

For further details write to The Secretary, The English Association, 1 Priory Gardens, London W4 1TT.

Contents

Abbreviations

1. Journals and Series

A&E	*Anglistik und Englischunterricht*
ABäG	*Amsterdamer Beiträge zur Älteren Germanistik*
ABC	*American Book Collector*
ABELL	*Annual Bibliography of English Language and Literature*
ABMR	*Antiquarian Book Monthly Review*
ABR	*Australian Book Review*
ABSS	*Annual of Bernard Shaw Studies*
ACLALSB	*ACLALS Bulletin*
ACOLIT	*Association for Commonwealth Literature Studies*
ADS	*Australasian Drama Studies*
AEB	*Analytical and Enumerative Bibliography*
AF	*Anglistische Forschungen*
AH	*Art History*
AHR	*American Historical Review*
AI	*American Imago*
AJES	*Aligarh Journal of English Studies*
AKML	*Abhandlungen zur Kunst-, Musik- und Literaturwissenschaft*
AL	*American Literature*
ALASH	*Acta Linguistica Academiae Scientiarum Hungaricae*
AlexS	Alexander Shakespeare
ALLCB	*Bulletin of the Association for Literary and Linguistic Computing*
ALR	*American Literary Realism, 1870–1910*
ALS	*Australian Literary Studies*
ALT	*African Literature Today*
AmerP	*American Poetry*
AmerS	*American Studies*
AmLS	*American Literary Scholarship: An Annual*
AMon	*Atlantic Monthly*
AN	*Acta Neophilologica*
AN&Q	*American Notes and Queries*
ANF	*Arkiv för Nordisk Filologi*
AnL	*Anthropological Linguistics*
AnM	*Annuale Mediaevale*
AntigR	*Antigonish Review*
AQ	*American Quarterly*
AR	*Antioch Review*

ArAA	*Arbeiten aus Anglistik und Amerikanistik*
Archiv	*Archiv für das Studium der Neueren Sprachen und Literaturen*
ARCS	*American Review of Canadian Studies*
ArdenS	Arden Shakespeare
ArielE	*Ariel: A Review of International English Literature*
ArL	*Archivum Linguisticum*
ArlQ	*Arlington Quarterly*
ArP	*Aryan Path*
ArQ	*Arizona Quarterly*
ARS	Augustan Reprint Society
AS	*American Speech*
ASch	*American Scholar*
ASE	*Anglo-Saxon England*
ASInt	*American Studies International*
ASoc	*Arts in Society*
ASPR	*Anglo-Saxon Poetic Records*
ATQ	*American Transcendental Quarterly: A Journal of New England Writers*
AuBR	*Australian Book Review*
AUMLA	*Journal of Australasian U Language and Literature Assoc.*
AWR	*The Anglo-Welsh Review*
BAASB	*British Association for American Studies Bulletin*
BAP	British and American Playwrights 1750–1920
BaratR	*Barat Review*
BASAM	*BASA Magazine*
BB	*Bulletin of Bibliography*
BBCS	*Bulletin of the Board of Celtic Studies*
BBCSh	BBC Shakespeare
BBSIA	*Bulletin Bibliographique de la Société Internationale Arthurienne*
BC	*Book Collector*
BCS	*B. C. Studies*
BDEC	*Bulletin of the Department of English* (Calcutta)
BDP	*Beiträge zur Deutschen Philologie*
BFLS	*Bulletin de la Faculté des Lettres de Strasbourg*
BGDSL	*Beiträge zur Geschichte der Deutschen Sprache und Literatur*
BHI	*British Humanities Index*
BHL	*Bibliotheca hagiographica latina antiquae et mediae aetatis*
BHR	*Bibliothèque d'Humanisme et Renaissance*
BI	*Books at Iowa*
BIQ	*Blake: An Illustrated Quarterly*
BIS	*Browning Institute Studies: An Annual of Victorian Literary and Cultural History*
BJA	*British Journal of Aesthetics*
BJDC	*British Journal of Disorders of Communication*
BJECS	*British Journal for Eighteenth-Century Studies*
BJHS	*British Journal for the History of Science*
BJPS	*British Journal for the Philosophy of Science*
BJR	*Bulletin des Jeunes Romanistes*
BJRL	*Bulletin of the John Rylands Library*

BlakeS	*Blake Studies*
BLJ	*British Library Journal*
BLR	*Bodleian Library Record*
BMQ	*British Museum Quarterly*
BN	*Beiträge zur Namenforschung*
BNB	*British National Bibliography*
BNL	*Blake Newsletter*
BNYPL	*Bulletin of the New York Public Library* (now *Bulletin of Research in the Humanities*)
Boundary	*Boundary 2: A Journal of Postmodern Literature*
BP	*Banasthali Patrika*
BRH	*Bulletin of Research in the Humanities*
BRMMLA	*Bulletin of the Rocky Mountain Modern Language Association*
BSE	*Brno Studies in English*
BSEAA	*Bulletin de la Société d'Etudes Anglo-Américaines des xviie et xviiie siècles*
BSLP	*Bulletin de la Société de Linguistique de Paris*
BSNotes	*Browning Society Notes*
BST	*Brontë Society Transactions*
BSUF	*Ball State University Forum*
BuR	*Bucknell Review*
BWVACET	*The Bulletin of the W. Virginia Assoc. of College English Teachers*
ByronJ	*Byron Journal*
CahiersE	*Cahiers Élisabéthains*
CAIEF	*Cahiers de l'Association Internationale des Études Françaises*
C&L	*Christianity and Literature*
C&M	*Classica et Medievalia*
Camobs	*Camera obscura*
CamR	*Cambridge Review*
CanD	*Canadian Drama*
CanL	*Canadian Literature*
CanP	*Canadian Poetry*
CapR	*Capilano Review*
CARA	Centre Aixois de Recherches Anglaises
CarR	*Caribbean Review*
Carrell	*The Carrell: Journal of the Friends of the University of Miami Library*
CBEL	*Cambridge Bibliography of English Literature*
CCRev	*Comparative Civilizations Review*
CCrit	*Comparative Criticism: A Yearbook*
CDCP	*Comparative Drama Conference Papers*
CE	*College English*
CEA	*CEA Critic*
CEAAN	*Center for Editions of American Authors Newsletter*
CEAfr	*Cahiers d'Etudes Africaines*
CE&S	*Commonwealth: Essays & Studies*
CentR	*The Centennial Review*
CFM	*Canadian Fiction Magazine*
ChauR	*The Chaucer Review*

ChildL	*Children's Literature*
ChiR	*Chicago Review*
ChLB	*Charles Lamb Bulletin*
CHLSSF	*Commentationes Humanarum Litterarum Societatis Scientiarum Fennica*
CHum	*Computers and the Humanities*
CI	Critical Idiom
CITAP	Columbia Introductions to Twentieth-Century American Poetry
Cithara	*Cithara: Essays in the Judaeo-Christian Tradition*
CJ	*Classical Journal*
CJE	*Cambridge Journal of Education*
CJIS	*Canadian Journal of Irish Studies*
CJL	*Canadian Journal of Linguistics*
CL	*Comparative Literature* (Eugene, Oregon)
CLAJ	*College Language Association Journal*
ClarkN	*Clark Newsletter*
CLC	*Columbia Library Columns*
ClioI	*Clio: A Journal of Literature, History, and the Philosophy of History*
CLJ	*Cornell Library Journal*
CLQ	*Colby Library Quarterly*
CLS	*Comparative Literature Studies*
CMCS	*Cambridge Medieval Celtic Studies*
CML	*Classical and Modern Literature*
CN	*Chaucer Newsletter*
CNE	*Commonwealth Novel in English*
ColF	*Columbia Forum*
CollG	*Colloquia Germanica*
CollL	*College Literature*
ColQ	*Colorado Quarterly*
CompD	*Comparative Drama*
CompL	*Comparative Literature*
ComQ	*Commonwealth Quarterly*
ConL	*Contemporary Literature*
ConnR	*Connecticut Review*
ContempR	*Contemporary Review*
CornLC	Cornell Linguistic Contributions
CP	*Concerning Poetry*
CQ	*The Cambridge Quarterly*
CR	*The Critical Review*
CRCL	*Canadian Review of Comparative Literature*
CRev	*The Chesterton Review*
Crit	*Critique: Studies in Modern Fiction*
CritI	*Critical Inquiry*
Critique	*Critique* (Paris)
CritQ	*Critical Quarterly*
CSHVB	*Computer Studies in the Humanities and Verbal Behavior*
CSR	*Christian Scholar's Review*
CTR	*Canadian Theatre Review*

CVE	Cahiers Victoriens et Edouardiens
CWAAS	Transactions of the Cumberland and Westmorland Archaeological and Antiquarian Society
DA	Dictionary of Americanisms
DAE	Dictionary of American English
DAEM	Deutsches Archiv für Erforschung des Mittelalters
DAI	Dissertation Abstracts International
Daphnis	Daphnis: Zeitschrift für Mittlere Deutsche Literatur
DHLR	The D. H. Lawrence Review
Diac	Diacritics
DicS	Dickinson Studies
DiS	Dickens Studies
DLB	Dictionary of Literary Biography
DLessingN	Doris Lessing Newsletter
DM	The Dublin Magazine
DNB	Dictionary of National Biography
DOE	Dictionary of Old English
DownR	Downside Review
DQ	Denver Quarterly
DQR	Dutch Quarterly Review of Anglo-American Letters
DQu	Dickens Quarterly (formerly DSN)
DR	Dalhousie Review
DRev	Drama Review
DSA	Dickens Studies Annual
DU	Der Deutschunterricht: Beiträge zu Seiner Praxis und Wissenschaftlichen Grundlegung
DubR	Dublin Review
DUJ	Durham University Journal
DVLG	Deutsche Vierteljahrsschrift für Literaturwissenschaft und Geistesgeschichte
EA	Études Anglaises
EAL	Early American Literature
E&S	Essays & Studies
EAS	Essays in Arts and Sciences
EB	Euralex Bulletin
EC	Études Celtiques
ECCB	Eighteenth Century: A Current Bibliography
ECent	The Eighteenth Century: Theory and Interpretation
ECLife	Eighteenth-Century Life
ECr	L'Esprit Créateur
ECS	Eighteenth-Century Studies
ECW	Essays on Canadian Writing
EDAM	Early Drama, Art, and Music Newsletter
EDH	Essays by Divers Hands
EdL	Études de Lettres
EdN	Editors' Notes: Bulletin of the Conference of Editors of Learned Journals
EDSL	Encyclopedic Dictionary of the Sciences of Language
EHR	English Historical Review
EI	Études Irlandaises (Lille)

EIC	*Essays in Criticism*
EIL	*Essays in Literature*
EinA	*English in Africa*
EiP	*Essays in Poetics*
Éire	*Éire-Ireland*
EiT	*Essays in Theatre*
EJ	*English Journal*
ELang T	*English Language Teaching*
ELC	*English Literature in Canada*
ELH	*Journal of English Literary History*
ELN	*English Language Notes*
ELR	*English Literary Renaissance*
ELS	*English Literary Studies*
ELSMS	English Literary Studies Monograph Series
ELT	*English Literature in Transition*
ELWIU	*Essays in Literature* (Western Illinois University)
EM	*English Miscellany*
EPS	*English Philological Studies*
ERC	*Explorations in Renaissance Culture*
ES	*English Studies*
ESA	*English Studies in Africa*
ESC	*English Studies in Canada*
ESQ	*Emerson Society Quarterly*
ESRS	*Emporia State Research Studies*
EWIP	*Edinburgh University, Department of Linguistics, Work in Progress*
EWN	*Evelyn Waugh Newsletter*
EWW	*English World-Wide*
Expl	*Explicator*
FCEMN	*Mystics Quarterly* (formerly *Fourteenth-Century English Mystics Newsletter*)
FDP	*Four Decades of Poetry 1890–1930*
FDT	Fountainwell Drama Texts
FH	*Frankfurter Hefte*
FLang	*Foundations of Language*
FLH	*Folia Linguistica Historica*
FMLS	*Forum for Modern Language Studies*
FolL	*Folia Linguistica*
ForumH	*Forum* (Houston)
FR	*Feminist Review*
FrS	*French Studies*
FS	*Feminist Studies*
GaR	*Georgia Review*
GEFR	*George Eliot Fellowship Review*
GeM	*Genealogists' Magazine*
GHJ	*George Herbert Journal*
GissingN	*Gissing Newsletter*
GJ	*Gutenberg-Jahrbuch*
GL	*General Linguistics*
GLL	*German Life and Letters*

Glossa	Glossa: An International Journal of Linguistics
GR	Germanic Review
GRM	Germanisch-Romanische Monatsschrift
GSB	Garland Shakespeare Bibliographies
GSE	Gothenberg Studies in English
GUP	Georgetown University Papers on Language and Linguistics
HamSt	Hamlet Studies
HAR	Humanities Association Review
HC	The Hollins Critic
HistJ	Historical Journal
HJ	Hibbert Journal
HL	Historiographia Linguistica
HLB	Harvard Library Bulletin
HLQ	Huntington Library Quarterly
HOPE	History of Political Economy
HPT	History of Political Thought
HQ	Hopkins Quarterly
HRB	Hopkins Research Bulletin
HSE	Hungarian Studies in English
HSELL	Hiroshima Studies in English Language and Literature
HSJ	Housman Society Journal
HSL	University of Hartford Studies in Literature
HSN	Harvard Studies and Notes
HSSN	Henry Sweet Society Newsletter
HT	History Today
HTR	Harvard Theological Review
HudR	Hudson Review
HumLov	Humanistica Lovaniensia
HUSL	Hebrew University Studies in Literature
HW	History Workshop
HWS	History Workshop Series
I&C	Ideology & Consciousness
IF	Indogermanische Forschungen
IFR	International Fiction Review
IJES	Indian Journal of English Studies
IJSL	International Journal of the Sociology of Language
IJWS	International Journal of Women's Studies
IndL	Indian Literature
IowaR	Iowa Review
IRAL	International Review of Applied Linguistics in Language Teaching
IS	Italian Studies
ISh	Independent Shavian
ISJR	Iowa State Journal of Research
IUR	Irish University Review
JA	Jahrbuch für Amerikastudien
JAAC	Journal of Aesthetics and Art Criticism
JAAR	Journal of the American Academy of Religion
JAF	Journal of American Folklore
JAMS	Journal of the American Musicological Society

ABBREVIATIONS

JAmS	Journal of American Studies
JBeckS	Journal of Beckett Studies
JBS	Journal of British Studies
JCanL	Journal of Canadian Literature
JCC	Journal of Canadian Culture
JCF	Journal of Canadian Fiction
JChL	Journal of Child Language
JCL	Journal of Commonwealth Literature
JCS	Journal of Canadian Studies
JCSA	Journal of the Catch Society of America
JDJ	John Donne Journal
JEGP	Journal of English and Germanic Philology
JEH	Journal of Ecclesiastical History
JEn	Journal of English (Sana'a University)
JEngL	Journal of English Linguistics
JENS	Journal of the Eighteen Nineties Society
JEP	Journal of Evolutionary Psychology
JEPNS	Journal of the English Place-Name Society
JES	Journal of European Studies
JFI	Journal of the Folklore Institute
JGE	Journal of General Education
JGH	Journal of Garden History
JHI	Journal of the History of Ideas
JIES	Journal of Indo-European Studies
JIL	Journal of Irish Literature
JIPA	Journal of the International Phonetic Association
JIWE	The Journal of Indian Writing in English
JJB	James Joyce Broadsheet
JJQ	James Joyce Quarterly
JL	Journal of Linguistics
JLP	Journal of Linguistics and Politics
JLS	Journal of Literary Semantics
JLVSG	Journal of the Loughborough Victorian Studies Group
JMH	Journal of Medieval History
JML	Journal of Modern Literature
JMRS	Journal of Medieval and Renaissance Studies
JNT	Journal of Narrative Technique
JP	Journal of Philosophy
JPC	Journal of Popular Culture
JPhon	Journal of Phonetics
JPrag	Journal of Pragmatics
JPRS	Journal of Pre-Raphaelite Studies
JQ	Journalism Quarterly
JRH	Journal of Religious History
JRSA	Journal of the Royal Society of Arts
JRUL	Journal of the Rutgers University Libraries
JSA	Journal of the Society of Archivists
JSAS	Journal of Southern African Studies
JVLB	Journal of Verbal Learning and Verbal Behavior
JWCI	Journal of the Warburg and Courtauld Institutes

JWMS	*Journal of the William Morris Society*
JWSL	*Journal of Women's Studies in Literature*
KanQ	*Kansas Quarterly*
KN	*Kwartalnik Neofilologiczny* (Warsaw)
KPAB	*Kentucky Philological Association Bulletin*
KR	*Kenyon Review*
KSJ	*Keats-Shelley Journal*
KSMB	*Keats-Shelley Memorial Bulletin*
KUKA	*KUKA: Journal of Creative and Critical Writing* (Zaria, Nigeria)
LA	*Linguistic Analysis*
L&C	*Language and Communication*
L&H	*Literature and History*
L&P	*Literature and Psychology*
L&S	*Language and Speech*
Lang&S	*Language and Style*
LangS	*Language Sciences*
LangQ	*USF Language Quarterly*
LanM	*Les Langues Modernes*
LaS	*Louisiana Studies*
LB	*Leuvense Bijdragen*
LC	*The Library Chronicle* (Philadelphia, Pa.)
LCrit	*The Literary Criterion* (Mysore, India)
LCUT	*Library Chronicle of the University of Texas*
LeedsSE	*Leeds Studies in English*
LETS	Liverpool English Texts and Studies
LFQ	*Literature/Film Quarterly*
Lg	*Language*
LHR	*Lock Haven Review*
LHY	*Literary Half-Yearly*
Lib	*The Library*
Ling&P	*Linguistics and Philosophy*
LingB	*Linguistische Berichte*
LingI	*Linguistic Inquiry*
LingInv	*Lingvisticæ Investigationes*
Lings	*Linguistics*
Linguistique	*La Linguistique*
LitR	*Literary Review* (Madison, N.J.)
LJGG	*Literaturwissenschaftliches Jahrbuch im Auftrage der Görres-Gesellschaft*
LMag	*London Magazine*
Lore&L	*Lore & Language*
LR	*Les Lettres Romanes*
LRB	*London Review of Books*
LSE	Lund Studies in English
LSoc	*Language in Society*
LTP	*LTP: Journal of Literature, Teaching, Politics*
LWU	*Literatur in Wissenschaft und Unterricht*
MÆ	*Medium Ævum*
M&H	*Medievalia et Humanistica*

M&L	*Music and Letters*
MarkhamR	*Markham Review*
MASJ	*Midcontinent American Studies Journal*
MBL	*Modern British Literature*
MCJNews	*Milton Centre of Japan News*
McNR	*McNeese Review*
MCW	Methuen Contemporary Writers
MD	*Modern Drama*
MED	*Middle English Dictionary*
METh	*Medieval English Theatre*
MFS	*Modern Fiction Studies*
MHRev	*Malahat Review*
MichA	*Michigan Academician*
MiltonQ	*Milton Quarterly*
MiltonS	*Milton Studies*
MinnR	*Minnesota Review*
MissQ	*Mississippi Quarterly*
MJLF	*Midwestern Journal of Language and Folklore*
MLAIB	*Modern Language Assoc. International Bibliography*
MLJ	*Modern Language Journal*
MLN	*Modern Language Notes*
MLNew	*Malcolm Lowry Review* (formerly *Malcolm Lowry Newsletter*)
MLQ	*Modern Language Quarterly*
MLR	*Modern Language Review*
MLS	*Modern Language Studies* (a publication of the Northeast Modern Language Association)
MMD	Macmillan Modern Dramatists
ModA	*Modern Age*
ModSp	*Moderne Sprachen*
MP	*Modern Philology*
MPHJ	*Middlesex Polytechnic History Journal*
MPR	*Mervyn Peake Review*
MQ	*Midwest Quarterly*
MQR	*Michigan Quarterly Review*
MR	*Massachusetts Review*
MRDE	*Medieval and Renaissance Drama in England*
MRTS	Medieval and Renaissance Texts and Studies
MS	*Mediaeval Studies*
MSE	*Massachusetts Studies in English*
MSh	Macmillan Shakespeare
MSpr	*Moderna Språk*
MSR	Malone Society Reprints
MT	*Musical Times*
MTJ	*Mark Twain Journal*
MW	*The Muslim World* (Hartford, Conn.)
NA	*Nuova Antologia*
N&Q	*Notes and Queries*
NCaS	New Cambridge Shakespeare
NCBEL	*New Cambridge Bibliography of English Literature*
NCC	New Canadian Criticism

NCF	*Nineteenth-Century Fiction*
NCS	New Clarendon Shakespeare
NCTR	*Nineteenth Century Theatre Research*
NDEJ	*Notre Dame English Journal*
NDQ	*North Dakota Quarterly*
NegroD	*Negro Digest*
Neoh	Neohelicon
Neophil	*Neophilologus*
NEQ	*New England Quarterly*
NGC	*New German Critique*
NH	*Northern History*
NL	*Nouvelles Littéraires*
NLB	*Newbury Library Bulletin*
NLH	*New Literary History*
NLR	*New Left Review*
NLRev	*New Literature Review*
NLWJ	*The National Library of Wales Journal*
NM	*Neuphilologische Mitteilungen*
NMAL	*Notes on Modern American Literature*
NMer	New Mermaids
NMQ	*New Mexico Quarterly*
NMS	*Nottingham Medieval Studies*
NOB	*Namn och Bygd*
NoP	*Northern Perspective*
Novel	*Novel: A Forum on Fiction*
NPS	New Penguin Shakespeare
NR	*New Republic*
NRF	*Nouvelle Revue Française*
NS	*Die Neueren Sprachen*
NSS	New Swan Shakespeare
NT	New Testament
NTM	*New Theatre Magazine*
NWR	*Northwest Review*
NYH	*New York History*
NYLF	*New York Literary Forum*
NYRB	*New York Review of Books*
NYTBR	*New York Times Book Review*
OA	Oxford Authors
OB	*Ord och Bild*
OBSP	*Oxford Bibliographical Society Proceedings*
OED	*Oxford English Dictionary*
OENews	*Old English Newsletter*
OET	Oxford English Texts
OHEL	Oxford History of English Literature
OhR	*Ohio Review*
OL	*Orbis Litterarum*
OLR	*Oxford Literary Review*
OpL	*Open Letter*
OPLL	*Occasional Papers in Linguistics and Language Learning*
OR	*Oxford Review*

OS	Oxford Shakespeare
OSS	Oxford Shakespeare Studies
OT	Old Testament
PA	*Présence Africaine*
PAAS	*Proceedings of the American Antiquarian Society*
P&L	*Philosophy and Literature*
P&P	*Past and Present*
PAPA	*Publications of the Arkansas Philological Association*
PAPS	*Proceedings of the American Philosophical Society*
ParisR	*The Paris Review*
PaterN	*Pater Newsletter*
PAus	*Poetry Australia*
PBA	*Proceedings of the British Academy*
PBSA	*Papers of the Bibliographical Society of America*
PCLAC	*Proceedings of the California Linguistics Association Conference*
PCLS	*Proceedings of the Comparative Literature Symposium* (Texas)
PCP	*Pacific Coast Philology*
PELL	*Papers on English Language and Literature* (Japan)
PIL	*Papers in Linguistics*
PJCL	*Prairie Journal of Canadian Literature*
PLL	*Papers on Language and Literature*
PLPLS	*Proceedings of the Leeds Philosophical and Literary Society*
PMLA	*Publications of the Modern Language Association of America*
PN	*Poe Newsletter*
PNotes	*Pynchon Notes*
PNR	*PN Review*
POAS	Poems on Affairs of State
PoeS	*Poe Studies*
PoetryR	*Poetry Review*
PoT	*Poetics Today*
PowysR	*Powys Review*
PP	*Philologica Pragensia*
PPMRC	*Proceedings of the International Patristic, Mediaeval and Renaissance Conference*
PQ	*Philological Quarterly*
PQM	*Pacific Quarterly* (Moana)
PR	*Partisan Review*
Praxis	*Praxis: A Journal of Culture and Criticism*
Prépub	*(Pré)publications*
PRIA	*Proceedings of the Royal Irish Academy*
PRIAA	Publications of the Research Institute of the Åbo Akademi Foundation
PRMCLS	*Papers from the Regional Meetings of the Chicago Linguistics Society*
PRR	*Pre-Raphaelite Review* (now *Journal of Pre-Raphaelite Studies*)
PS	*Prairie Schooner*
PSt	*Prose Studies*
PsyculR	*Psychocultural Review*

PTL	PTL: A Journal for Descriptive Poetics and Theory
PULC	Princeton University Library Chronicle
PVR	Platte Valley Review
QI	Quaderni d'Italianistica
QJS	Quarterly Journal of Speech
QL	Quantitative Linguistics
QQ	Queen's Quarterly
QR	Quarterly Review
RAL	Research in African Literatures
R&L	Religion and Literature
RCEL	Revista Canaria de Estudios Ingleses
RCF	Review of Contemporary Fiction
RDN	Renaissance Drama Newsletter
ReAL	Re: Artes Liberales
RECTR	Restoration and Eighteenth-Century Theatre Research
RedL	Red Letters
REEDN	Records of Early English Drama Newsletter
Ren&R	Renaissance and Reformation
RenD	Renaissance Drama
RenP	Renaissance Papers
RenQ	Renaissance Quarterly
RES	Review of English Studies
Rev	Review (Blacksburg, Va.)
Revels	Revels Plays
RevelsCL	Revels Plays Companion Library
RH	Recusant History
Rhetorik	Rhetorik, ein internationales Jahrbuch
RHL	Revue d'Histoire Littéraire de la France
RHT	Revue d'Histoire du Théâtre
RLC	Revue de Littérature Comparée
RLMC	Rivista di Letterature Moderne e Comparate
RLV	Revue des Langues Vivantes
RMR	Rocky Mountain Review of Language and Literature
RMS	Renaissance and Modern Studies
RN	Renaissance News
RomN	Romance Notes
ROO	Room of One's Own: A Feminist Journal of Literature and Criticism
RORD	Research Opportunities in Renaissance Drama
RPT	Russian Poetics in Translation
RQ	Riverside Quarterly
RRDS	Regents Renaissance Drama Series
RRestDS	Regents Restoration Drama Series
RS	Research Studies
RUO	Revue de l'Université d'Ottawa
RuskinN	Ruskin Newsletter
SAB	South Atlantic Bulletin
SAC	Studies in the Age of Chaucer
SAF	Studies in American Fiction
SagaB	Saga Book of the Viking Society for Northern Research

SAntS	*Studia Anthroponymica Scandinavica*
SAP	*Studia Anglica Posnaniensia*
SAQ	*South Atlantic Quarterly*
SatR	*Saturday Review*
SAU	Studia Anglistica Upsalensia
SB	*Studies in Bibliography*
SBHC	*Studies in Browning and His Circle*
SBHT	*Studies in Burke and His Time*
SBL	*Studies in Black Literature*
SCB	*South Central Bulletin* (now *South Central Review*)
SCER	*Society for Critical Exchange Report*
SCJ	*The Sixteenth Century Journal*
SCL	*Studies in Canadian Literature*
ScLJ	*Scottish Literary Journal: A Review of Studies in Scottish Language and Literature*
ScLJ(S)	*Scottish Literary Journal Supplement*
SCN	*Seventeenth-Century News*
SCR	*South Carolina Review*
SCRev	*South Central Review* (formerly *South Central Bulletin*)
ScS	*Scandinavian Studies*
SDR	*South Dakota Review*
SECC	*Studies in Eighteenth-Century Culture*
SED	*Survey of English Dialects*
SEL	Studies in English Literature
SEL	*Studies in English Literature 1500–1900* (Rice University)
SELing	*Studies in English Linguistics* (Tokyo)
SELit	*Studies in English Literature* (Japan)
SF&R	Scholars' Facsimiles and Reprints
SFQ	*Southern Folklore Quarterly*
SFR	*Stanford French Review*
SFS	*Science-Fiction Studies*
SH	*Studia Hibernica* (Dublin)
ShakS	*Shakespeare Studies* (Tennessee)
ShFN	*Shakespeare on Film Newletter*
ShN	*Shakespeare Newsletter*
SHR	*Southern Humanities Review*
ShS	*Shakespeare Survey*
ShStud	*Shakespeare Studies* (Tokyo)
SIcon	*Studies in Iconography*
SIHoLS	Studies in the History of the Language Sciences
SIM	*Studies in Music*
SIR	*Studies in Romanticism*
SJH	*Shakespeare-Jahrbuch* (Heidelberg)
SJS	San José Studies
SJW	*Shakespeare-Jahrbuch* (Weimar)
SL	*Studia Linguistica*
SLang	*Studies in Language*
SLitI	*Studies in the Literary Imagination*
SLJ	*Southern Literary Journal*
SLSc	*Studies in the Linguistic Sciences*

SM	*Speech Monographs* (now *Communication Monographs*)
SMC	*Studies in Medieval Culture*
SMed	*Studi Medievali*
SMLit	*Studies in Mystical Literature* (Taiwan)
SMy	*Studia Mystica*
SN	*Studia Neophilologica*
SNL	*Satire Newsletter*
SNNTS	*Studies in the Novel* (North Texas State University)
SOÅ	*Sydsvenska Ortnamnssällskapets Årsskrift*
SoAR	*South Atlantic Review*
SoQ	*The Southern Quarterly*
SoR	*Southern Review* (Louisiana)
SoRA	*Southern Review* (Adelaide)
SP	*Studies in Philology*
Sphinx	*The Sphinx: A Magazine of Literature and Society*
SpM	*Spicilegio Moderno*
SPSRA	*Sel. Papers of the Shakespeare and Renaissance Assoc. of W. Va.*
SQ	*Shakespeare Quarterly*
SR	*Sewanee Review*
SRen	*Studies in the Renaissance*
SRO	*Shakespearean Research Opportunities*
SRS	Salzburg Renaissance Studies
SSAA	Salzburgur Studien zur Anglistik und Americanistik
SSE	Swiss Studies in English
SSELER	Salzburg Studies in English Literature: Elizabethan and Renaissance
SSELJDS	Salzburg Studies in English Literature: Jacobean Drama Series
SSELPDPT	Salzburg Studies in English Literature: Poetic Drama and Poetic Theory
SSELRR	Salzburg Studies in English Literature: Romantic Reassessment
SSEng	*Sydney Studies in English*
SSF	*Studies in Short Fiction*
SSL	*Studies in Scottish Literature*
SSMP	*Stockholm Studies in Modern Philology*
STC	*Short-Title Catalogue*
StHum	*Studies in the Humanities*
StIn	*Studi Inglesi*
StQ	*Steinbeck Quarterly*
StrR	*Structuralist Review*
StTCL	*Studies in Twentieth Century Literature*
SUAS	Stratford-upon-Avon Studies
SUS	*Susquehanna University Studies*
SVEC	*Studies on Voltaire and the Eighteenth Century*
SWR	*Southwest Review*
TA	*Theatre Annual*
TC	*The Twentieth Century*
TCBS	*Transactions of the Cambridge Bibliographical Society*
TCL	*Twentieth Century Literature*

TD	*Themes in Drama*
TDR	*The Drama Review*
TEAS	Twayne's English Authors Series
Text	*Text: Transactions of the Society for Textual Scholarship*
THA	*Thomas Hardy Annual*
ThC	*Theatre Crafts*
THES	*Times Higher Education Supplement*
ThHS	*Theatre History Studies*
THIC	*Theatre History in Canada*
THL	Theory and History of Literature
Thought	*Thought: A Review of Culture and Ideas*
Thph	*Theatrephile*
ThR	*Theatre Research International*
ThS	*Theatre Survey*
THSR	*Thomas Hardy Society Review*
THY	*The Thomas Hardy Yearbook*
TJ	*Theatre Journal*
TJS	*Transactions of the Johnson Society*
TkR	*Tamkang Review*
TLS	*Times Literary Supplement*
TN	*Theatre Notebook*
TN/DU	*True North/Down Under*
TP	*Terzo Programma*
TPLL	*Tilbury Papers in Language and Literature*
TPS	*Transactions of the Philological Society*
TQ	*Texas Quarterly*
TRB	*Tennyson Research Bulletin*
TRHS	*Transactions of the Royal Historical Society*
TriQ	*TriQuarterly*
TSAR	*Toronto South Asian Review*
TSB	*Tolkien Society Bulletin*
TSE	Tulane Studies in English
TSL	Tennessee Studies in Literature
TSLang	Typological Studies in Language
TSLL	*Texas Studies in Literature and Language*
TSWL	*Tulsa Studies in Women's Literature*
TTR	*Trinidad and Tobago Review*
TUSAS	Twayne's United States Authors Series
TWR	*Third World Review*
TYDS	*Transactions of the Yorkshire Dialect Society*
UCTSE	*University of Cape Town Studies in English*
UDQ	*University of Denver Quarterly*
UDR	*University of Dayton Review*
UE	*Use of English*
UEAPL	*UEA Papers on Linguistics*
UES	*Unisa English Studies*
ULR	*University of Leeds Review*
UMSE	*University of Mississippi Studies in English*
UOQ	*University of Ottawa Quarterly*
UR	*University Review* (Kansas City)

URev	*University Review* (Dublin)
USFLQ	*University of South Florida Language Quarterly*
USSE	*University of Saga Studies in English*
UTQ	*University of Toronto Quarterly*
UWR	*University of Windsor Review*
VEAW	Varieties of English Around the World
VN	*Victorian Newsletter*
VP	*Victorian Poetry*
VPR	*Victorian Periodicals Review*
VQR	*Virginia Quarterly Review*
VS	*Victorian Studies*
VSB	*Victorian Studies Bulletin*
VWQ	*Virginia Woolf Quarterly*
WAL	*Western American Literature*
W&L	*Women and Literature*
W&W	World and Word
WascanaR	*Wascana Review*
WC	World's Classics
WC	*Wordsworth Circle*
WCR	*West Coast Review*
WCWR	*William Carlos Williams Review*
WF	*Western Folklore*
WHR	*Western Humanities Review*
WLT	*World Literature Today* (formerly *Books Abroad*)
WLWE	*World Literature Written in English*
Wolfen-büttelerB	*Wolfenbütteler Beiträge: Aus den Schätzen der Herzog August Bibliothek*
WPCS	*Working Papers in Cultural Studies*
WQ	*Wilson Quarterly*
WS	*Women's Studies: An Interdisciplinary Journal*
WSCL	*Wisconsin Studies in Contemporary Literature*
WSJ	*The Wallace Stevens Journal*
WTW	Writers and their Work
WVUPP	*West Virginia University Philological Papers*
WWR	*Walt Whitman Quarterly Review*
XUS	*Xavier Review*
YCC	*Yearbook of Comparative Criticism*
YER	*Yeats Eliot Review*
YES	*Yearbook of English Studies*
YFS	*Yale French Studies*
YNS	York Notes Series
YPL	*York Papers in Linguistics*
YR	*Yale Review*
YSE	Yale Studies in English
YULG	*Yale University Library Gazette*
YWES	*The Year's Work in English Studies*
ZAA	*Zeitschrift für Anglistik und Amerikanistik*
ZCP	*Zeitschrift für Celtische Philologie*
ZDA	*Zeitschrift für Deutsches Altertum und Deutsche Literatur*
ZDL	*Zeitschrift für Dialektologie und Linguistik*

ZGL — *Zeitschrift für Germanistische Linguistik*
ZPSK — *Zeitschrift für Phonetik, Sprachwissenschaft und Kommunikationsforschung*
ZS — *Zeitschrift für Sprachwissenschaft*

2. Publishers

AAAH	Acta Academiae Åboensis Humaniora, Åbo, Finland
A&B	Allison & Busby, London
A&R	Angus & Robertson, North Ryde, N.S.W., Australia
A&U	Allen & Unwin, London
A&UA	Allen & Unwin, North Sydney, Australia
A&W	Almqvist & Wiksell Int'l, Stockholm
AberdeenU	Aberdeen University, Aberdeen, Scotland
Abhinav	Abhinav P, New Delhi
Abingdon	Abingdon Press, Nashville, Tenn.
ABL	Armstrong Browning Library, Baylor U, Texas
Åbo	Åbo Akademi, Åbo, Finland
Abrams	Harry N. Abrams Inc., New York
Academic	Academic Press, London
Academy	The Academy Press, Dublin
ACS	Assoc. for Canadian Studies, Toronto
Addison-Wesley	Addison-Wesley, Reading, Mass.
Adosa	Adosa, Clermont-Ferrand, France
AF	Akademisk Forlag, Copenhagen
AFP	Assoc. Faculty P, London and Port Washington, N.Y.
Africana	Africana Pub. Co., New York
AK	Akademiai Kiado, Budapest
Al&Ba	Allyn & Bacon, Boston, Mass.
Albion	Albion, Appalachian State U, Boone, N.C.
Allen	W. H. Allen, London
AM	Aubier Montaigne, Paris
AMAES	Association des Médiévistes Anglicistes de l'Enseignement Supérieur, Paris
AmberL	Amber Lane, Oxford
AMSP	AMS Press Inc., New York
AMU	Adam Mickiewicz U, Posnan
Anansi	Anansi Press, Toronto
Anvil	Anvil Press, London
APA	APA, Maarssen, Holland
Appletree	Appletree Press, Belfast, N.I.
APS	American Philosophical Society, Philadelphia, Pa.
Aquarian	The Aquarian Press, Wellingborough, Northants.
Archon	Archon Books, Hamden, Conn.
Ariel	c/o BBC Publications, London
Arnold	Edward Arnold, London
Aslib	Aslib, London
ASLS	Assoc. for Scottish Literary Studies
ASP	Applied Science Publishers Ltd, London
ASU	Arizona State U, Tempe, Arizona
ATCAL	Association for the Teaching of Caribbean and African Literature
Athlone	Athlone Press, London
AUG	Acta Universitatis Gothoburgensis, Sweden

AUP	Associated University Presses, London
AUPG	American University Publishers Group Ltd, London
AUU	Acta Universitatis Umensis, Umeå, Sweden
AUUp	Acta Universitatis Upsaliensis Uppsala, Sweden
Avebury	Avebury Press, Amersham, Bucks.
Avero	Avero Pubns, Newcastle upon Tyne
BA	British Academy, London
Bagel	August Bagel Verlag, Düsseldorf
B&B	Boydell & Brewer, Woodbridge, Suffolk
B&E	Buchan & Enright, London
B&H	Bell & Hyman, London
B&J	Barrie and Jenkins, London
B&N	Barnes & Noble, Totowa, N.J.
B&O	Burns & Oates, Tunbridge Wells, Kent
B&S	Benskin and Samuels, Edinburgh
BAR	British Archaeological Reports, Oxford
Bardavon	Bardavon Books, Rhinebeck, New York
Barnes	A. S. Barnes, San Diego, Calif. and London
Batsford	B. T. Batsford, London
BBC	British Broadcasting Corporation, London
BClark	Bruccoli Clark P, Columbia, S.C.
BCP	Bristol Classical Press, Bristol
Beacon	Beacon P, Boston, Mass.
Beck	C. H. Beck'sche Verlagsbuchhandlung, Munich
Belknap	Belknap Press, Cambridge, Mass.
Bellflower	Bellflower P, Case U, Cleveland, Ohio
Benjamins	John Benjamins, Amsterdam
Benn	Ernest Benn Ltd, London
BFI	British Film Institute, London
BGU	Bowling Green UP, Bowling Green, Ohio
BibS	Bibliographical Society, London
Bilingual	Bilingual Press, Ypsilanti, Michigan
Bingley	Clive Bingley, London
Binnacle	Binnacle P, London
BL	British Library, London
Black	Adam & Charles Black, London
Blackie	Blackie & Son, Glasgow
Black Moss	Black Moss, Windsor, Ontario
Blackstaff	Blackstaff P, Belfast
Blackwell	Basil Blackwell, Oxford
Blackwood	William Blackwood, Edinburgh
Bl&Br	Blond & Briggs, London
Bloodaxe	Bloodaxe Books, Newcastle upon Tyne
BM	Bobbs-Merrill, Indianapolis, Idaho
BMP	British Museum Publications, London
Bodleian	The Bodleian Library, Oxford
Bodley	The Bodley Head, London
Bogle	Bogle L'Ouverture, London
BoiseU	Boise State UP, Boise, Ind.
Borealis	Borealis Press, Ottawa

Borgo	Borgo P, San Bernardino, Calif.
Bowker	R. R. Bowker Co., New York
Boyars	Marion Boyars, London and Boston, Mass.
Boydell	The Boydell Press, Woodbridge, Suffolk
Breakwater	Breakwater P, St John's, Newfoundland
Brewer	D. S. Brewer, Cambridge (an imprint of Boydell & Brewer and Rowman & Littlefield)
Brill	E. J. Brill, Leiden
Brilliance	Brilliance Books, London
Browne	Sinclair Browne, London
BrownU	Brown UP, Providence, Rhode Island
BS	Black Swan Books, London
BSU	Ball State UP, Muncie, Ind.
BuckU	Bucknell UP, Lewisburg, Pa.
Burnett	Burnett Books, London
CAAS	Connecticut Academy of Arts and Sciences, New Haven, Conn.
Cairns	Francis Cairns, Liverpool
Calder	Calder Press, London
C&G	Carroll & Graf, New York
C&W	Chatto & Windus, London
Cape	Jonathan Cape, London
Carcanet	The New Carcanet Press, Manchester, Lancs.
Carleton	Carleton UP, Ottawa
Cass	Frank Cass, London
Cassell	Cassell & Co., London
Cave	Godfrey Cave Associates, London
CBA	Council for British Archaeology, London
CCP	Canadian Children's P, Guelph, Ont.
CDSH	Centre de Documentation Sciences Humaines, Paris
Century	Century P Co, London
Ceolfrith	Ceolfrith Press, Sunderland, Tyne and Wear
CESR	Société des Amis du Centre d'Etudes Superieures de la Renaissance, Tours
CFA	Canadian Fed. for the Humanities
C–H	Chadwyck–Healey, Cambridge
CH	Croom Helm, London
Champion	Librairie Honoré Champion, Paris
Chand	S. Chand, Madras
Christendom	Christendom Publications, Front Royal, Va.
Chronicle	Chronicle Books, San Francisco, Calif.
Clarendon	The Clarendon Press, Oxford
Clarion	Clarion State College, Clarion, Pa.
Clark	T. & T. Clark, Edinburgh
CMERS	Center for Medieval and Early Renaissance Studies, Binghamton, N.Y.
CML	William Andrews Clark Memorial Library, Los Angeles
CMST	Centre for Medieval Studies, Toronto
Collins	William Collins & Sons, London
ColU	Columbia UP, New York

Comedia	Comedia Publishing Group, London
Compton	The Compton Press, Tisbury, Wilts.
Constable	Constable & Co. Ltd, London
Corgi	Corgi Books, London
Cormorant	Cormorant Press, Victoria, B.C.
CornU	Cornell UP, Ithaca, N.Y.
Crossroad	Crossroad, New York
CSS	Charles Scribner's Sons, New York
CSU	Cleveland State University, Cleveland, Ohio
Cuff	Harry Cuff Publications, St John's, Newfoundland
CUP	Cambridge University Press, Cambridge
CVK	Cornelson-Velhagen & Klasing, Berlin
CWU	Carl Winter Universitätsverlag, Heidelberg
Da Capo	Da Capo Press, New York
Dalkey	Dalkey Archive P, Elmwood Park, Ill.
D&C	David & Charles, Newton Abbot, Devon
Dangaroo	Dangaroo P, Mundelstrup, Denmark
Dawson	William Dawson, Folkestone, Kent
DBP	Drama Book P, New York
De Graaf	De Graaf, Nieuwkoup, Netherlands
Dent	J. M. Dent, London
DentA	Dent Australia, Vic.
Deutsch	André Deutsch, London
Didier	Didier Erudition, Paris
Doaba	Doaba House, Delhi
Dobson	Dennis Dobson, Durham
Dolmen	Dolmen Press, Dublin
Donald	John Donald, Edinburgh
Doubleday	Doubleday, Garden City, New York
Dove	Dove, Sydney, Australia
Dover	Dover Publications, New York
Duckworth	Gerald Duckworth, London
DukeU	Duke UP, Durham, N.C.
Duquesne	Duquesne UP, Pittsburgh, Pa.
Dutton	E. P. Dutton, New York
DWT	Dr Williams's Trust, London
EA	English Association, London
ECW	ECW Press, Downsview, Ontario
Eden	Eden Press, St Albans, Vt, and Montreal
EdinU	Edinburgh University Press, Edinburgh
Eerdmans	Eerdmans, Grand Rapids, Mich.
EETS	Early English Text Society, Oxford
Ember	Ember Press, Furzeham, Brixham, South Devon
Enitharmon	Enitharmon P, London
EPNS	English Place-Name Society, Notts.
Eriksson	Paul Eriksson, Middlebury, Vt.
ESI	Edizioni Scientifiche Italiane, Naples
ESL	Edizioni di Storia e Letteratura, Rome
EUL	Edinburgh University Library, Edinburgh
Europa	Europa Publications, London

Eyre	Eyre Methuen, London
Faber	Faber & Faber, London
F&S	Feffer & Simons, London and Amsterdam
F-B	Ford-Brown, Houston, Texas
FDU	Fairleigh Dickinson UP, Madison, N.J.
Fine	Donald Fine Inc., New York
Fink	Fink Verlag, Munich
Flammarion	Flammarion, Paris
FlindersU	Flinders U of South Australia
Folger	The Folger Shakespeare Library, Washington, D.C.
Fontana	Fontana Books, London
FordU	Fordham UP, New York
Foris	Foris Publications, Dordrecht
Fortress	Fortress Press, Philadelphia, Pa.
Francke	Francke Verlag, Berne, Switzerland
Franklin	Burt Franklin, New York
Freundlich	Freundlich Books, New York
Fromann-Holzboog	Fromann-Holzboog, Stuttgart, W. Germany
FWP	Falling Wall Press, Bristol
Gale	Gale Research Co., Detroit, Mich.
Galilée	Galilée, Paris.
Gallimard	Gallimard, Paris
G&M	Gill & Macmillan, Dublin
Garland	Garland Publishing Co., New York
Girasole	Edizioni del Girasole, Ravenna
GlasU	Glasgow UP, Glasgow
Gleerup	C. W. K. Gleerup, Lund, Sweden and Melbourne
GMP	Gay Men's Press, London
Gollancz	Victor Gollancz, London
Granada	Granada Publishing, St Albans, Herts.
Grasset	Grasset, Paris
Grassroots	Grassroots, London
Greenhalgh	M. J. Greenhalgh, Eastcote, Middlesex
Greenwood	Greenwood Press, Westport, Conn.
Groos	Julius Groos Verlag, Heidelberg
Grüner	Verlag B.R. Grüner, Amsterdam
Gruyter	Walter de Gruyter, Berlin
Hale	Robert Hale, London
Hall	G. K. Hall, Boston, Mass.
H&I	Hale & Iremonger, Melbourne
H&M	Holmes & Meier, London and New York
H&S	Hodder & Stoughton, London
H&W	Hill & Wang, New York
Harbour	Harbour P, Madeira Pk, B.C.
Harper	Harper & Row, New York
Harrap	Harrap Ltd, London
Harvard	Harvard UP, Cambridge, Mass.
Harvester	Harvester Press, Brighton, Sussex
HBJ	Harcourt, Brace, Jovanovich, New York and London

Heath	D. C. Heath & Co., Lexington, Mass.
Heinemann	William Heinemann, London
HeinemannA	William Heinemann, Vic., Australia
Herbert	Herbert P, London
HH	Hamish Hamilton, London
HM	Harvey Miller, London
Hogarth	Hogarth Press, London
Howard	Howard UP, Washington, D.C.
HRW	Holt, Rinehart & Winston Inc., New York
HUL	Hutchinson University Library, London
Humanities	Humanities Press, Atlantic Highlands, N.J.
Huntington	Huntington Library, San Marino, Calif.
Hutchinson	Hutchinson & Co. Ltd, London
IAP	Irish Academic Press, Dublin
IHA	IHA, Waterloo, Ontario
Imago	Imago Imprint Inc., New York
IndU	Indiana UP, Bloomington, Ind.
IntUP	International U Presses, New York
IP	In Parenthesis, London
ISU	Iowa State UP, Ames, Iowa
IUP	Indiana U of Pennsylvania P, Indiana, Pa.
Ivon	Ivon Publishing House, Bombay
Jacaranda	Jacaranda Wiley, Milton, Queensland, Australia
JadavpurU	Jadavpur U, Calcutta
James CookU	James Cook U of North Queenland
JHall	James Hall, Leamington Spa, Warks.
JHU	Johns Hopkins UP, Baltimore, Md.
Joseph	Michael Joseph, London
Journeyman	The Journeyman Press, London
JT	James Thin, Edinburgh
Junction	Junction Books Ltd, London
Jupiter	Jupiter P, Lake Bluff, Ill.
JyväskyläU	U of Jyväskylä, Jyväskylä, Finland
Kaibunsha	Kaibunsha, Tokyo
K&W	Kaye & Ward, London
Karnak	Karnak House, London
Kardo	Kardo, Coatbridge, Scotland
Karoma	Karoma P, Ann Arbor, Mich.
Kenkyusha	Kenkyusha, Tokyo, Japan
Kennikat	Kennikat P, Port Washington, N.Y.
Kensal	Kensal P, Windsor Forest, Berks.
KenyaLB	Kenya Literature Bureau, Nairobi
Kestrel	Viking Kestrel, London
Kinseido	Kinseido, Tokyo, Japan
Klostermann	Vittorio Klostermann, Frankfurt am Main
Kraus	Kraus Int'l Publications, White Plains, N.Y.
LA	Library Assoc., London
Lake View	Lake View P, Chicago, Ill.
LAm	Library of America, New York
L&W	Lawrence and Wishart, London

Lane	Allen Lane, London
LaneA	Allen Lane, Ringwood, Victoria, Australia
Lang	Peter D. Lang, Frankfurt am Main and Bern
LC	Library of Congress, Washington, D.C.
LCP	Loras College Press, Dubuque, Iowa
LeuvenU	Leuven UP, Leuven, Belgium
Lexik	Lexik House, Cold Springs, N.Y.
LH	Percy Lund Humphries & Co. Ltd, London
Liberty	Liberty Classics, Indianapolis, Ind.
Liveright	Liveright Co., New York
Longman	Longman Group Ltd, London
LSU	Louisiana State UP, Baton Rouge, La.
LUP	Loyola UP, Chicago, Ill.
Lymes	The Lymes Press, London
MAA	Medieval Academy of America, Cambridge, Mass.
Macdonald	Macdonald, Edinburgh
MacdonaldCo	Macdonald & Co., London
McGraw-Hill	McGraw-Hill, New York
Macmillan	Macmillan, London
MacNutt	R. MacNutt Ltd, Tunbridge Wells, Kent
Mc-Q	McGill-Queen's UP, Kingston and Montreal
Mainstream	Mainstream P, Edinburgh
M&E	Macdonald & Evans, Estover, Plymouth, Devon
Maney	W. S. Maney & Sons, Leeds, Yorks.
Mansell	Mansell Publishers Ltd, London
ManU	Manchester UP, Manchester, Lancs.
MarloweB	Marlowe Books, London
Mayflower	Mayflower Books, London
MB	Mitchell Beazley Ltd, London
ME	M. Evans, New York
Methuen	Methuen, London
MH	Michael Haag, London
MHRA	Modern Humanities Research Association, London
MidNAG	Mid Northumberland Arts Group, Ashington, Northumberland
Milner	Milner, London
Minuit	Editions de Minuit, Paris
MIP	Medieval Inst. Pubs, WMU, Kalamazoo, Mich.
MITP	Massachusetts Inst. of Technology Press, Cambridge, Mass.
MLA	Modern Language Association of America, New York
MLPP	Manchester Literary and Philosophical Publications
Moonraker	Moonraker Press, Bradford-on-Avon, Wilts.
Moreanum	Moreanum, Angers, France
Morrow	William Morrow & Co., New York
Mouton	Mouton & Co., The Hague, Paris and New York
MR	Martin Robertson, Oxford
MRS	Medieval and Renaissance Society, North Texas State U, Denton, Texas
MRTS	MRTS, Binghamton, N.Y.

MS	Malone Society, c/o Kings College, London
MSU	Memphis State UP, Memphis, Tenn.
MtAllisonU	Mount Allison U, Sackville, N.B.
Muller	Frederick Muller, London
Murray	John Murray, London
NAL	New American Library, New York
Narr	Gunter Narr Verlag, Tübingen
NBB	New Beacon Books, London
ND	New Directions, New York
NDT	Nottingham Drama Texts, c/o U of Nottingham
NEL	New English Library, London
NeWest	NeWest P, Edmonton, Alberta
NH	New Horizon P, New York
N-H	Nelson Hall, Chicago, Ill.
NHPC	North Holland Publishing Co., Amsterdam and New York
Niemeyer	Max Niemeyer, Tübingen
Nijhoff	Martinus Nijhoff, The Hague
NIU	Northern Illinois UP, De Kalb, Ill.
NLB	New Left Books, London
NLP	New London Press Inc., Dallas, Texas
NorthU	Northeastern University, Boston, Mass.
Northwestern	Northwestern UP, Evanston, Ill.
Norton	W. W. Norton & Co. Inc., New York and London
NPP	North Point P, San Francisco
NSP	New Statesman Publishing Co., New Delhi
NSWUP	New South Wales UP, Kensington, N.S.W., Australia
NUP	National U Pub., Kennikat P, Port Washington, N.Y.
NUU	New U of Ulster, Coleraine
NYPL	New York Public Library, New York
NYU	New York UP, New York and London
O&B	Oliver and Boyd, Edinburgh
Oasis	Oasis Books, London
O'Brien	The O'Brien Press, Dublin
OBS	Oxford Bibliographical Society, Bodleian Library, Oxford
Octopus	Octopus Books, London
OdenseU	Odense U, Odense
OEColl	Old English Colloquium, Berkeley, Calif.
Offord	John Offord Pubs., Eastbourne, Sussex
OhioU	Ohio UP, Athens, Ohio
Olschki	Leo S. Olschki, Florence
Open Books	Open Books Pub. Ltd, Shepton Mallet, Somerset
OpenU	Open University Education Enterprises Ltd, Milton Keynes
OPP	Oxford Polytechnic P, Oxford
Orbis	Orbis Books, London
Oriel	Oriel Press (RKP), Stocksfield, Northumberland
Oryx	Oryx Press, Phoenix, Arizona
OSU	Ohio State UP, Columbus, Ohio
OTP	Oak Tree Press, London
OUP	Oxford University Press, Oxford
OUPM	OUP, Melbourne

Owen	Peter Owen, London
Pacifica	Press Pacifica, Waipahu, Hawaii
Paladin	Paladin Books, London
Pan	Pan Books Ltd, London
Pandora	Pandora P, London
Pantheon	Pantheon, New York
Paulist	Paulist Press, New York
Pavilion	Pavilion Books, London
Peachtree	Peachtree P, Atlanta, Ga.
Penguin	Penguin Books, Harmondsworth, Middx.
PenguinA	Penguin, Ringwood, Victoria, Australia
Penumbra	Penumbra P, Moonbeam, Ontario
Pergamon	Pergamon Press, Oxford
Permanent	Permanent P, Sag Harbor, N.Y.
Perpetua	Perpetua P, Oxford
PH	Prentice-Hall Inc., Englewood Cliffs, N.J.
Phaidon	Phaidon P, Oxford
PHI	Prentice-Hall International, Hemel Hempstead, Herts.
Pickwick	Pickwick Pubs., Allison Park, Pa.
Pilgrim	Pilgrim Books, Norman, Okla.
PIMS	Pontifical Institute of Mediaeval Studies, Toronto
Pinter	Frances Pinter (Pubs) Ltd, London
Plenum	Plenum Press, London and New York
Pluto	Pluto P, London
Polity	Polity P, Oxford
Polter	Clarkson N. Polter, New York
Popular	Popular Press, Bowling Green, Ohio
Porcepic	Press Porcepic, Victoria and Toronto
Princeton	Princeton UP, Princeton, N.J.
PRO	Public Record Office, London
Profile	Profile Books, Windsor, Bucks.
ProgP	Progressive Publishers, Calcutta
PSU	Pennsylvania State UP, University Park, Pa.
Pucker	Puckerbrush Press, Orono, Maine
PUF	Presses Universitaire de France, Paris
PurdueU	PurdueU Press, Lafayette, Ind.
Pustet	Friedrich Pustet, Regensburg
PWP	Poetry Wales P, Ogmore by Sea, Mid Glam.
Quartet	Quartet Books, London
RA	Royal Academy, London
R&B	Rosenkilde & Bagger, Copenhagen
R&L	Rowman & Littlefield, Totowa, N.J.
RandomH	Random House, New York
Ravan	Ravan P, Johannesburg
Rebel	The Rebel Press, Bideford, Devon
Reference	Reference P, Toronto
Regents	Regents Press of Kansas, Lawrence, Kansas
Reidel	D. Reidel Publishing Co., Dordrecht, Boston and London
Remak	Remak, Alblasserdam, The Netherlands
RH	Ramsay Head Press, Edinburgh

Richarz	Hans Richarz, Sankt Augustin
RKP	Routledge & Kegan Paul, London
Robson	Robson Books, London
Rodopi	Rodopi, Amsterdam
RoehamptonI	Roehampton Institute, London
RS	The Royal Society, London
RSL	Royal Society of Literature, London
RSVP	Research Society for Victorian Periodicals, Leicester
Rutgers	Rutgers UP, New Brunswick, N.J.
SA	Sahitya Akademi, New Delhi
SAI	Sociological Abstracts Inc., Ann Arbor, Mich.
Salamander	Salamander Books, London
S&D	Stein & Day, Briarcliff Manor, N.Y.
S&M	Sun and Moon P, College Pk, Md.
S&P	Simon & Pierre, Toronto, Ontario
S&S	Simon & Schuster, New York
S&W	Secker & Warburg, London
Sangsters	Sangsters Book Stores, Kingston, Jamaica
SAP	Scottish Academic Press, Edinburgh
S–B/Francke	Schwann–Bagel/Francke, Düsseldorf
Scarecrow	Scarecrow Press, Metuchen, N.J.
Scolar	Scolar Press, London
Seafarer	Seafarer Books, London
Seuil	Editions du Seuil, Paris
SF&R	Scholars' Facsimiles and Reprints, Delmar, N.Y.
SH	Somerset House, Teaneck, N.J.
Shearwater	Shearwater P, Hobart, Tasmania
Sheldon	Sheldon P, London
Shinozaki	Shinozaki, Tokyo
Shire	Shire P, Princes Risborough
Shoe String	Shoe String P, Hamden, Conn.
SIU	Southern Illinois UP, Carbondale and Edwardsville, Ill.
Skilton	Charles Skilton Ltd, Edinburgh
Sleepy Hollow	Sleepy Hollow P, Tarrytown, N.Y.
SLG	SLG Press, Oxford
Smythe	Colin Smythe, Gerrards Cross, Bucks.
SNLS	Society for New Language Study, Denver, Colorado
SOA	Society of Authors, London
SonoNis	SonoNis P, Victoria, B.C.
Souvenir	Souvenir P, London
SPCK	SPCK, London
Spokesman	Spokesman P, Nottingham
SSA	Steinbeck Society of America, Muncie, Ind.
SSAB	Sprakförlaget Skriptor AB, Stockholm
Stanford	Stanford UP, Palo Alto, Calif.
Star	Star Books, W. H. Allen, London
Starmont	Starmont House, Mercer Island, Washington
Station Hill	Station Hill, Barrytown, N.Y.
StDL	St Deiniol's Library, Hawarden, Clwyd
Steiner	Franz Steiner, Wiesbaden

Sterling	Sterling, New York
Sterling ND	Sterling P, New Delhi
St Martin's	St Martin's P, New York
Stockwell	Arthur H. Stockwell Ltd, Ilfracombe, Devon
StPB	St Paul's Bibliographies, Godalming, Surrey
STR	Society for Theatre Research, London
Strauch	R.O.U. Strauch, Ludwigsburg
Suhrkamp	Suhrkamp Verlag, Frankfurt am Main
SUNY	State University of New York Press, Albany and Binghamton, N.Y.
Sutton	Alan Sutton, Gloucester, Glos.
S-W	Shepheard-Walwyn P, London
Swallow	Swallow P, Athens, Ohio
SydneyU	Sydney UP, Sydney, Australia
Syracuse	Syracuse UP, Syracuse, N.Y.
Tabb	Tabb House, Padstow, Cornwall
T&H	Thames & Hudson, London
Tantivy	Tantivy P, London and San Diego, Calif.
Tavistock	Tavistock Press, London and New York
TCP	Three Continents P, Washington, D.C.
TCUP	Texas Christian UP, Fort Worth, Texas
Tecumseh	Tecumseh P, Ottawa
Telos	Telos P Ltd, St Louis, Mo.
TexA&M	Texas A & M UP, College Station, Texas
Thimble	Thimble P, Stroud
Thornes	Stanley Thornes, Cheltenham
Toucan	Toucan Press, St Peter Port, Guernsey, C.I.
Touzot	Jean Touzot, Paris
TPF	Trianon Press Facsimiles, London
Tragara	Tragara P, Edinburgh
Transaction	Transaction, New Brunswick, N.J.
Transcendental	Transcendental Books, Hartford, Conn.
TrinityU	Trinity UP, San Antonio, Texas
TTP	Texas Technical Press, Lubbock, Texas
TulaneU	Tulane UP, New Orleans, La.
TurkuU	Turku U, Finland
Twayne	Twayne Publishers, Boston, Mass.
UAB	University of Aston in Birmingham, Warks.
UAdelaide	U of Adelaide, Australia
UAla	U of Alabama P, University, Ala.
UBarcelona	U of Barcelona, Spain
UBC	U of British Columbia, Vancouver
UBergen	U of Bergen, Norway
UBrno	J. E. Purkyne U of Brno, Brno, Czechoslovakia
UCal	U of California P, Berkeley, Calif.
UChic	U of Chicago P, Chicago, Ill.
UCopen	U of Copenhagen P, Copenhagen
UDel	U of Delaware P, Newark, Del.
UDur	U of Durham

UEssex	U of Essex P, Colchester, Essex
UExe	U of Exeter P, Exeter, Devon
UFlor	UP of Florida, Gainesville, Fla.
UFlorS	U of Florida State, Tallahassee, Fla.
UGal	U College Galway, Galway
UGeo	U of Georgia P, Athens, Ga.
UGhent	Rijksuniversiteit, Ghent
UGoth	U of Gothenburg, Sweden
UHull	U of Hull, Hull
UIll	U of Illinois P, Urbana, Ill.
UKan	U of Kansas P, Lawrence, Kansas
UKen	U of Kentucky P, Lexington, Kentucky
ULaval	Les Presses de l'Université Laval, Quebec
ULeeds	U of Leeds P, Leeds, Yorkshire
ULeics	U of Leicester P, Leicester
ULeiden	Leiden U, The Netherlands
ULille	U de Lille, Villeneuve d'Ascq, France
ULiv	U of Liverpool P, Liverpool, Lancs.
Ulster	U of Ulster, Northern Ireland
UMass	U of Massachusetts P, Amherst, Mass.
Umeå	Umeå Universitetsbibliotek, Umeå
UMI	University Microfilms International Ltd, Ann Arbor, Mich.
UMich	U of Michigan P, Ann Arbor, Mich.
UMinn	U of Minnesota P, Minneapolis, Minn.
UMIRes	UMI Research P, Ann Arbor, Mich.
UMiss	U of Missouri P, Columbia, Missouri
UMissip	UP of Mississippi, Jackson, Miss.
UMysore	U of Mysore P, Mysore
UNancy	Presses Universitaires de Nancy, France
UNC	U of North Carolina P, Chapel Hill, N.C.
UND	U of Notre Dame, Notre Dame, Ind. and London
Undena	Undena Publications, Malibu, Calif.
UNeb	U of Nebraska P, Lincoln, Nebr.
Ungar	Frederick Ungar, New York
UNM	U of New Mexico, Albuquerque, N.Mex.
UNott	U of Nottingham P, Nottingham
UOkla	U of Oklahoma P, Norman, Okla.
UOslo	U of Oslo, Norway
UOttawa	U of Ottawa P, Ottawa
UPA	UP of America, Lanham, Maryland
UParis	U of Paris, France
UPenn	U of Pennsylvania P, Philadelphia, Pa.
UPitt	U of Pittsburgh P, Pittsburgh, Pa.
UPNE	UP of New England, Hanover, N.H. and London
Uppsala	U of Uppsala, Uppsala, Sweden
UProvence	U de Provence, Aix-en-Provence
UPValery	U Paul Valery, Montpelièr, France
UQueen	U of Queensland, St Lucia, Queensland
USalz	U of Salzburg, Salzburg
USC	U of South Carolina P, Columbia, S.C.

USheff	U of Sheffield
USussex	U of Sussex, Brighton, Sussex
USzeged	U of Szeged, Hungary
UTas	U of Tasmania, Hobart
UTenn	U of Tennessee, Knoxville, Tenn.
UTex	U of Texas P, Austin, Texas
UTor	U of Toronto P, Toronto
UVerm	U of Vermont, Burlington, Vt.
UVict	U of Victoria, Victoria, B.C.
UWales	U of Wales P, Cardiff
UWash	U of Washington P, Seattle, Wash.
UWisc	U of Wisconsin P, Madison, Wisc.
UWiscM	U of Wisconsin, Milwaukee, Wisc.
Valentine	Valentine Publishing & Drama Co., Rhinebeck, N.Y.
Vantage	Vantage P, New York
Vehicule	Vehicule P, Montreal
Verso	Verso Books, London
Viking	Viking Press, New York
Virago	Virago Press, London
Virginia	Virginia UP, Charlottesville, Va.
Vision	Vision Press, London
VLB	VLB, Montreal
VR	Variorum Reprints, London
Vrin	Vrin, Paris
W&N	Weidenfeld & Nicolson, London
Waterloo	Waterloo UP, Waterloo, Ontario
WB	Wissenschaftliche Buchgesellschaft, Darmstadt
W/B	Woolmer/Brotherson Ltd, Revere, Pa.
Webb&Bower	Webb & Bower, Exeter, Devon
Wedgestone	Wedgestone Press, Winfield, Kansas
Wesleyan	Wesleyan UP, Middletown, Conn.
West	West, St Paul, Minn.
Whiteknights	Whiteknights P, U of Reading, Berks.
Whitston	Whitston Publishing Co. Inc., Troy, N.Y.
Whittington	Whittington P, Andoversford, Glos.
WHP	Warren House Press, North Walsham, Norfolk
Wildwood	Wildwood House, London
Wiley	John Wiley & Sons, Melbourne
Wilson	Philip Wilson, London
Windward	Windward Press, London
Winthrop	Winthrop Publishers Inc., Cambridge, Mass.
WLU	Wilfrid Laurier UP, Waterloo, Ont.
WMU	Western Michigan U, Kalamazoo, Mich.
WMP	World Microfilms Publications, London
Wo&No	Wolters & Noordhoff, Groningen
Wolfhound	Wolfhound Press, Dublin
Wombat	The Wombat Press, Wolfville, Nova Scotia
Woolf	Cecil Woolf, London
WP	Women's P, London
WSU	Wayne State UP, Detroit, Mich.

WVU	West Virginia UP, Morgantown, W. Va.
WWU	Western Washington University, Bellingham, Wash.
Yale	Yale UP, New Haven, Conn.
Yamaguchi	Yamaguchi, Kyoto, Japan
York	University of York, Yorks.
YorkP	York P, Fredricton, N.B.
Zomba	Zomba Books, London

Literary History and Criticism: General Works

PETER DAVISON

Dr Philip Gaskell's two major contributions to learning about bibliography and editorial method, *A New Introduction to Bibliography* (1972) and *From Writer to Reader* (1978), were given too rough a ride by some critics. It is therefore very pleasing to see that Robert Cross of St Paul's Bibliographies has taken over the sheets of OUP's *From Writer to Reader*[1] and issued the book in paperback at a very reasonable price – fifteen per cent less at face value than when the book was first issued. There is, to boot, a neat example of a cancel title-page, and the whole enterprise perfectly fits Gaskell's description of re-issue in his *A New Introduction*, pp. 315–16. Although G. Thomas Tanselle's measured strictures in *Lib* (1980) must have been troubling to Dr Gaskell, and too-ready ammunition for the average academic (and I must share blame for that untoward effect as I commissioned and published the review), Tanselle wrote out of professional concern and I think the opportunity might have been taken to include the review as an appendix together with some reflections by Dr Gaskell on the issues raised. It is however, just as it is, thoroughly desirable that this volume should be made readily available to aspiring editors. It is very warmly welcomed.

The older bibliographic journals make no claim to being interdisciplinary but managed in 1984 to include an item or two from other than English and American culture, *Lib* ranging as far afield as eighteenth-century Calcutta. *SB* prints nineteen articles. Of these, half a dozen are fairly lengthy, and the remainder, in the manner to which readers are accustomed, take up points which, in the main, arise from individual works but which may have more general application. G. Thomas Tanselle yet again opens the volume. Having cogently advanced reasons for not writing about the arrangement of descriptive bibliographies he sets out to do just that, his prefatory remarks providing a context for the good sense he deploys (though I demur at 'most basic'). Harold Love also offers practical help in his discussion of the ranking of variants in the course of analysing moderately contaminated manuscripts. From a study of *The Dunciad*, David L. Vander Meulen considers how papers lacking water-marks may be distinguished. James McLaverty, also taking *The Dunciad* as a starting point, takes up F. W. Bateson's challenge that if the Mona Lisa is in the Louvre, where are *Hamlet* and *Lycidas*? His response, supported from writers on aesthetics, is to claim that 'the existence of works of art as print and

---

1. *From Writer to Reader: Studies in Editorial Method*, by Philip Gaskell. StPB. pp. xiii + 268. pb £8.50.

paper is not less but more important than bibliographers have generally taken it to be' and that 'a richer understanding of the relation of author, book trade, and public may lead to better interpretation of literary works'. D. F. McKenzie, with considerable lightness of touch, drives a coach and horses, or rather, a coach and six compositors, through too-complacent analysis of compositorial stints by type analysis and setting practice – an essay that must be read by those so labouring. Last of the longer articles is D. C. Greetham on 'Models for the Textual Transmission of Translation: The Case of John Trevisa'. Of the shorter articles, one of the briefest deserves to be singled out. This is 'Misconceptions about the Geneva Bible' by Naseeb Shaheen. This shows, despite fairly commonly held belief, that the Geneva Bible did not immediately become the most popular English Bible, getting off to a rather slow start; that most editions were not printed in roman rather than black-letter but, marginally, the reverse (between 1560 and 1616 forty-six black-letter and forty-four roman type editions were published in England); and it was not the Bible of the Puritans alone, being much favoured by Anglicans, including bishops and archbishops.

Lib published thirteen major articles, eleven bibliographical notes, and four dozen reviews, some long and detailed, in 1984. Two of the *SB* contributors appear, D. F. McKenzie on 'The Sociology of a Text' and James McLaverty, who writes on 'The Concept of Authorial Intention in Textual Criticism'. I find McLaverty helpful to my current concerns, wrestling with what Orwell intended but didn't do, or was prevented from doing, or was undermined from doing by publishers and compositors, though I find that I am unable to dissociate myself from the role of co-author (however modest that function is) as readily as one is advised to do if the author's stated intentions (not those implied) are to be carried out. Of that problem I write in my contribution to the *Lib*, 'Editing Orwell: Eight Problems'. There is also an article on paper and another on translations, as in *SB*: B. J. McMullin, 'Paper Quality Marks and the Oxford Bible Press, 1682–1717', and D. N. Griffiths, 'Prayer-Book Translations in the Nineteenth Century'. The remaining major articles consider 'Thomas Marsh, Henry Marsh, and the Roman Emperors' by A. R. Braunmuller, also a contributor to *Text* (see below); Thomas Southerne's *The Disappointment* by Peter W. M. Blayney (printed, perforce, without the benefit of the author returning his corrected proofs); Rudolph Ackermann's *History of the Colleges* by Jill Ford, which includes an identification of authors; 'Keats and His Editor: The Manuscript of *Endymion*' by Margaret Ketchum Powell; 'The Revisions of Emily Brontë's Poems of 1846' by Derek Roper; '*The maner to Lyue Well* and François Regnault's Primers' by Mary C. Erler; 'Ligature Shortage and Speech-Prefix Variation in *Julius Caesar*' by John Jowett; and 'William Michael Rossetti's Transcriptions and William Bell Scott's Tracings and Blake's Notebooks' by Mark L. Greenberg.

In his Presidential Address to the first conference of the newly formed Society for Textual Scholarship, G. Thomas Tanselle argued that 'when learned societies and journals proliferate ... they focus on more and more specialized subjects and help to accelerate the fragmentation of scholarly endeavour'. There is truth in this although I am far from certain that the countertrend, burgeoning interdisciplinarity, isn't a shibboleth. But then, perhaps I am to be numbered with the Ephraimites. What is certain is that to call a course, or a society, or a volume of essays, 'interdisciplinary' is false if, as here, one has no more than a gathering together of approaches in discrete packages without the essential interpenetration of disciplines that reveals the idea of one discipline working with and on that of another.

I have chased this hare through the pages of *RES*, so I mention merely that a new journal, *Text*, the organ of the Society of Textual Scholarship, comes no closer to its claim to be interdisciplinary than the annual run of *Lib* (which makes no such claim, of course, but does occasionally justify that description). Tanselle, as one would expect of him, raises a number of issues for discussion. He also puts firmly in its place the new, fast-convenience, guideline 'that every situation is unique and that general guidelines will prove unsatisfactory in handling individual cases'. The first paper, 'The Lachmann Method: Merits and Limitations' by the society's second president, Paul Oskar Kristeller, is low-key, appropriate for an undergraduate bibliography course. Jerome J. McGann throws a dash of cold water over the society he has just joined. As the academic world is 'currently dominated by structuralist and post-structuralist theory and practice', one would expect a new interdisciplinary society concerned with 'text' to show Derridean influence but 'a glance at the editorial and advisory board' shows no such thing. There is a curiously unbalanced presentation of 'The Editor and the Question of Value' by Claire Badaracco and Fredson Bowers, made more curious by an editorial footnote that states that the expansion of the former's conference paper was deemed 'philosophically inappropriate for *Text*' so that her position, expressed in a line or two over two pages, is answered by Professor Bowers in twenty-nine pages, ten and a half in considerably smaller type than the rest. To add to the uncertainty we are told that Dr Badaracco's proposal as printed '*might not*' (my italics) 'fully represent [her] current position on the issues at debate'. It is interesting to think of an interdisciplinary paper that is 'philosophically inappropriate'. Dr Badaracco's thesis is that there are two approaches to editing depending upon value. There is the 'textual editor' whose role is 'to ascertain the author's intention with regard to the semantically autonomous text' (which may be a construct) and to 'relate the outcome to the author's latter-day audience who are the editor's contemporaries'. Secondly, there is the 'documentary editor' who 'proceeds from the assumption that only the document is knowable'. Such an editor's audience is contemporaneous with the document and he does not interpret his text. Professor Bowers's rejoinder is detailed and he makes important distinctions between the ways 'text' seems to be being used by Dr Badaracco (as 'a conceptual abstraction that exists in its own right', independently of the document, for example) and in his analysis stresses how far he is from laying down laws. This is an important debate, aborted though it is here, and it will need more attention, perhaps via this new society and the Association for Documentary Editing.

The remaining articles are well defined by their titles, and, though not particularly interdisciplinary, may be of interest to those concerned with the matters they discuss. They are: John Miles Foley, 'Editing Oral Epic Texts: Theory and Practice'; Gunilla Iversen, 'Problems in the Editing of Tropes'; Marjorie Curry Woods, 'Editing Medieval Commentaries'; Paul F. Watson, 'The Illustrators of a 1427 *Decameron*'; John L. I. Fennell, 'Textology as a Key to the Study of Old Russian Literature and History'; Stanley Boorman, 'The Uses of Filiation in Early Music'; A. R. Braunmuller, 'Editing Elizabethan Letters'; John McClelland, 'Critical Editing in the Modern Languages';

David S. Hewitt, 'Burns and the Argument for Standardisation'; Donald H. Reiman, 'The Four Ages of Editing and the English Romantics'; Robert Stephen Becker, 'Challenges in Editing Modern Literary Correspondence: Transcription'; Ulla E. Dydo, 'How to Read Gertrude Stein'; Hans Walter Gabler, on the critical edition of *Ulysses*; and A. S. G. Edwards, 'Some Problems in Modern Enumerative Bibliography'.

John Miles Foley's article would perhaps bear comment in the light of issues raised below in noticing Martin Mueller's *The Iliad* (p. 6). Foley follows the work of Milman Parry and Albert Lord, seemingly without question: 'oral poetry, wherever it occurs, employs similar procedures of composition and performance' but, according to Mueller, Ruth Finnegan has demolished this argument. Foley has elsewhere written on this subject and has produced an annotated bibliography on oral-formulaic theory, so must know the field well. It would surely have been desirable had he brought that knowledge to bear here and mentioned that the theory he was advancing had been seriously challenged. This is particularly important when writing for those unfamiliar with controversial aspects of one's discipline.

The last article discusses, as well as other matters, retrieval. Most journals, says Edwards, produce indexes. Alas, not this serial! This is the more surprising in a journal purporting to serve an interdisciplinary community. An index is, surely, quintessentially interdisciplinary.

Like the pun, the proverb has experienced oscillations in its fortunes, can claim erudite support and inspiration, has suffered contempt, and yet has maintained its popularity. *The Concise Oxford Dictionary of Proverbs*[2], edited by J. A. Simpson takes as its starting point *The Oxford Dictionary of English Proverbs* (1970), ed. F. P. Wilson, but it concentrates on a thousand or so proverbs current in the twentieth century and is more new work than simple abridgement. It will be noted that 'English' is not included in the title; the dictionary takes account of proverbs originating in the United States and Commonwealth countries. The editor has contributed a short introduction in which he describes succinctly three classes of proverb and comments on fashions in their use. The dictionary is sensibly arranged by alphabetical ordering of the first significant word of each proverb, but with ample cross-referencing. There is a useful selection of earlier uses of each proverb and an indication of their origins. The bibliography is a little thin. As John Heywood's *Dialogue* of 1546 is included, one might have expected Erasmus's *Adagia* and perhaps also Martin Tupper's *Proverbial Philosophy* to be listed. Is there not a case for giving a pretty full list of 'foundation works' to supplement any *selection*, preferably annotated?

Professor George Hunter, neatly and, in the light of the task being undertaken here, somewhat ironically, sums up the problem of reviewing volumes of 'Essays by divers hands' in a review of just such a book contributed to *YES*. His problem is how to respond to a collection of twenty articles in a mere five hundred words. *YES* has as many articles and fifty-seven reviews and a few words should be allotted to give some account of its contents. The majority of the reviews are of books published in 1980 and they provide a useful conspectus of the scholarly study of English for that year, the year covered by *YWES*

2. *The Concise Oxford Dictionary of Proverbs*, ed. by J. A. Simpson. OUP (1982). pp. xiv + 256. £8.50.

61 published in 1982. There are two review articles. One is devoted to *The Literary Persona* (1982) by Robert C. Elliott, to whose memory this number of *YES* is dedicated. The second is Heinz-Joachim Mullenbrock's 'The English Landscape Garden in the Eighteenth Century and its Literary Context: Tendencies in Recent Research', reviewing what has been a significant rise in this field (if that can be the word in this context) in recent years. How appropriate that Garrick and Colman's *The Clandestine Marriage* is currently being reviewed, satirizing alleged 'improvement' in gardens and fortunes.

The first of the review articles gives a clue to the main contents of the volume. *YES* is subtitled 'Satire Special Number'. The result is a cohesive body of articles that with but the briefest of additions – a short introduction by Claude Rawson, the editor, and a fairly slim index – has been issued as a book in its own right, *English Satire and the Satiric Tradition*[3]. After a note on Robert C. Elliott by Alvin Kernan there are seventeen articles. These range from Aristophanes to Jorge Luis Borges. It is noticeable how different are the authors and works selected for discussion in this volume from the French collections also reviewed in this chapter, especially the two edited by Alain Morvan (although *Gulliver's Travels* recurs). The *YES*/Blackwell volume is not quite restricted to major undergraduate texts and authors, but the exceptions stand out: J. A. Burrow on 'Chaucer's *Sir Thopas* and *La Prise de Nuevile*', in which he shows the former as deriving in part from the Flemish poem, cannot be said to be course-related; 'reading' Hogarth is not now so uncommon as once it was, thanks largely to the pioneering work of Ronald Paulson, author of the article 'Hogarth's "Country Inn Yard at Election Time": A Problem in Interpretation', but Hogarth is hardly set for most eighteenth-century courses; and perhaps Wyndham Lewis ('The Satirist as Barbarian' by Hugh Kenner) is not central to too many twentieth-century courses. The remaining fourteen articles will all prove grist to the undergraduate mill. I say that not pejoratively. Indeed, this is a very good collection for that purpose. In addition to the subjects and authors mentioned above, the articles deal with Aristophanic satire (Stephen Halliwell); Dunbar's flytings and Skelton's invective (a useful broadening of the scene by Douglas Gray); Jonson (Ian Donaldson); Donne (Arnold Stein); Rochester (Ken Robinson); Restoration satire (Raman Selden); *Gulliver's Travels* (John Traugott and, contrasted with Horace, by William S. Anderson); Pope and Horace (Niall Rudd); Pope and Wordsworth (Howard Erskine-Hill); Hazlitt (Marilyn Butler); Conrad (Martin Price); *Sweeney Agonistes* (Barbara Everett); and Borges (John Sturrock).

So many bibliographies and checklists have been produced in recent years that there would seem a place for a guide to what is available. This *Literary Criticism Index*[4] tries to fill. What it offers is a quantitative listing, not a qualitative assessment. An assessment of each of the eighty-five bibliographies upon which the index is based would have made the volume more helpful. That they are not all of the same quality would be worth pointing out. The editors have listed by author, or for anonymous works by title, works to which

3. *English Satire and the Satiric Tradition*, ed. by Claude Rawson, assisted by Jenny Mezciems. Blackwell. pp. xiii + 289. hb £22.50, pb £7.50.

4. *Literary Criticism Index*, ed. by Alan R. Weiner and Spencer Means. Scarecrow. pp. xvii + 686. $49.50.

reference is made in the more readily available American bibliographies. These are chiefly those published by Gale Research (which provides over one-third of the list from its Guide to Information Sources series), Shoe String and Scarecrow Presses; AHM, Sallow, and Garland. A few cursory checks revealed no errors in listing and the index gives the impression of being thoroughly compiled. What would be a desirable addition, apart from a qualitative essay, would be the inclusion in the listings of references to the Gale Dictionary of Literary Biography series and an introduction giving some account of major works of reference such as *NCBEL*, the revised *Oxford Companion to English Literature*, and similar guides to theatre, French, and classical literature, and Martin Seymour-Smith's *Modern World Literature*.

Volumes in the Unwin Critical Library are each devoted to a single work and can normally be noticed in the chapter devoted to the period to which that work belongs. They are thus reviewed by someone *au fait* with that text, its background, and its criticism. *The Iliad*[5] has, perforce, to be included in Chapter 1 and it would be dishonest, and unconvincing, were I to claim anything more than an amateur's interest. Mueller's account of the vexed question of the supposed origin of the Iliad in oral tradition, coupled with his excellently annotated bibliography, seems to give a lucid and convincing interpretation of the current position. For the kind of reader for whom the book is intended, this is precisely what is required. Mueller's book has seven sections. The first discusses the history of the poem and oral poetry. There follow chapters on the plot, fighting, simile, the Gods, the poem's composition, and its life. There is an index.

Robert C. Holub's contribution to the New Accents series edited by Terence Hawkes, *Reception Theory: A Critical Introduction*[6], is doubly useful. It gives a good, critical, account of reception theory; and it also provides a remarkably clear résumé of the influences and precursors that have led to its evolution. The book is designed especially for those who have no German. Dr Holub begins, in the frankest possible manner, by admitting that his central difficulty is 'determining exactly what the term means'. A fundamental dilemma is posed by the extent to which *Rezeption* and *Wirkung* ('response' or 'effect') differ from one another: 'the most frequent suggestion has been to view *Rezeption* as related to the reader, while *Wirkung* is supposed to pertain to textual aspects' (xi), and this, he remarks with studied innocence, 'is not entirely satisfactory'. He sees reception theory as an umbrella term to refer to 'a general shift in concern from the author and the work to the text and the reader'. His starting point (though he makes references back in time) is Hans Robert Jauss's essay, 'The change in the paradigm of literary scholarship', which, of course, took up Thomas Kuhn's use of paradigm shift in *The Structure of Scientific Revolutions* – I say, 'of course', because not a few of us about that time were applying, perhaps less justly than was appropriate, Kuhn's theory to aspects of literary and textual studies. Holub pinpoints inherent problems in transferring Kuhn's theory from science to humanities and very interestingly demonstrates how unease with the current paradigm for literary studies broke down in the train of events of the late 1960s in our universities,

    5. *The Iliad*, by Martin Mueller. Unwin Critical Library. A&U. pp. xi + 210. £15.
    6. *Reception Theory: A Critical Introduction*, by Robert C. Holub. Methuen. pp. xiv + 189. hb £9.95, pb £3.95.

exemplified by *Ansichten einer künftigen Germanistik* (1969; 'Views of a Future Germanistik' – Holub translates all German titles). This was signed by some of the most important critics in the first stages of the development of reception theory, including Jauss, Wolfgang Iser, and Siegfried J. Schmidt. What rapidly developed was a technique for re-evaluating the literature of the past and for taking account of subliteratures and mass media. Holub, lucidly but without undue oversimplification, then analyses the work of those who prepared the way for reception theory: the Russian Formalists, Roman Ingarden, the Prague Structuralists, Hans-Georg Gadamer, and the development of a sociology of literature. He explains in detail the work of Jauss and Iser and goes on to discuss alternative models and controversies: levels of text–reader interaction; the east–west debate; and actual responses to texts. His last chapter deals with 'Problems and Perspectives', the last section of which, 'Renewing the provocation', has, tucked away on the last page of the text, its very own little time-bomb. German scholars, he writes, 'have been slow to take up the challenges implicit in French and American critical discourse'; the major works of Iser and Jauss 'contain no mention of Derrida or Lacan; and Foucault is included only in a passing footnote by Iser'. Thus, reception theorists have 'generally avoided the very issues that have proved most provocative outside Germany'. What reception theory now requires is a productive relationship with the work of other contemporary theorists. This is a most useful book and can be warmly recommended. There are odd moments when I thought a slightly broader perspective might have helped. Peter Handke's *Offending the Audience* is trotted out again as a play which attempts 'to break down traditional barriers between viewer and stage' with no reference to the long tradition behind such an approach (at least in England). Not everyone has taken texts at face value – he refers to 'the seemingly simple notion of the literary text'. To some of us the simple text has long been a myth. But these are personal quibbles.

A *YWES* reviewer of Geoffrey Hill's *The Lords of Limit: Essays on Literature and Ideas*[7] cannot but be disarmed by its publisher's puff. Of the nine lectures and articles reprinted in this collection, one, the dust-jacket puff tells us, Professor Hill's Inaugural Lecture at Leeds University, was described by Martin Dodsworth in *English* as being 'a characteristically dense and scrupulous meditation on the religious intensities of post-romantic poetry'. Another, 'Redeeming the Time', was said in *YWES* 53 to be 'by far the most stimulating and suggestive comment on Hopkins this year'. The other items gathered here are concerned with Robert Southwell, Jonson's *Sejanus* and *Catiline* (by far the earliest piece, being first published in 1960), *Cymbeline*, Swift, T. H. Green, John Ransome, and 'Our Word is Our Bond', which is not a dissertation on the Stock Exchange (whose motto this is), but on the exchange of the stock of language – the word hoard: 'words as being of "excellent use" when rightly understood and as powers only in a dark and negative sense when they "impose on the understanding"'. This last is a typical densely argued essay drawing on a wide range of authors and intellects: Sidney, Pound and Berkeley, Whichcote, Hobbes, Wordsworth, Austin and Green, Coleridge and Nettleship. The essay is marked not only by its intellectual toughness but by

7. *The Lords of Limit: Essays on Literature and Ideas*, by Geoffrey Hill. Deutsch. pp. xi + 203. £12.95.

literary, almost poetic, elegance. Hill's teasing out of Ezra Pound's defence when declared unfit to stand trial for treason in 1945 is particularly good in these respects, troubling the reader intellectually and morally: 'Pound's error was to confuse [judicial and legislative or executive acts], to fancy that poets' "judicial sentences" are, in mysterious actuality, legislative or executive acts. But poets are not legislators . . . The "world's" revenge . . . was unwittingly to pay him back, confusion for confusion, with legislative or executive acts presuming to be true verdictives.' Indeed 'mysterious actuality'.

The title of Professor John Fraser's reprint of some of his essays, *The Name of Action*[8], is presumably intended to suggest to us that they are 'enterprises of great pith and moment'. Certainly they have their moments. Professor Fraser is a master of the sly insult and he seems unable to get cracking without denigrating someone: 'Regrettable as was that famous note of T. S. Eliot'; 'when one considers the commentaries of such critics as Henry Nash Smith, Kenneth S. Lynn, Tony Tanner, and Leo Marx, it is hard not to feel momentarily sympathetic towards mavericks like William Van O'Connor and Martin Green . . .' If your fancy inclines to such knock-about stuff, well and good, but even addicts of abuse will become bored and wish Professor Fraser would get to his text, when he is often stimulating and invariably interesting. Northrop Frye's approach to criticism is not only given lengthy and hostile analysis – perhaps justifiable – but there is so much denigration of Frye that the reader might well feel it is personal animus that motivates Professor Fraser rather than concern with matters critical. The essay on Frye begins by invoking the Leavis–Snow controversy. The anti-Leavisians, he says, thought the errors Dr F. R. Leavis perceived in Sir Charles Snow's argument should have been corrected 'in the spirit of debate between fellow professionals'. However, he argues, Dr Leavis acted convinced that 'Snow as a would-be sage was preposterous, that the deference being accorded him was even more preposterous'. Professor Fraser, who has a good turn of phrase, correctly says that this kind of approach 'does not usually make for urbanity', but goes on to complain, quite deviously I think, that 'to seek to deny it utterance' is 'a denial of the ultimate seriousness of the intellectual life'. Fine, but who sought to deny Leavis utterance? The trick here is the footnote. The reader is directed to footnote 1, a hundred or so pages on. Professor Fraser has a right to expect his academic readers to check, but he can probably rely upon few doing so, not so much out of laziness but from an assumption that the footnote will show a denial of utterance challenging 'the ultimate seriousness of the intellectual life'. One hardly needs to check: the call to the barricades to defend academic licence is irresistible. Now, what the footnote to 'seek to deny it utterance' says is: 'As in, for instance, the curiously schoolmarmish pronouncement of Mr Lionel Trilling that "There can be no two opinions about the tone in which Dr Leavis deals with Sir Charles. It is a bad tone, an impermissible tone."' Saying your tone is lousy is not the same as denying utterance and 'an impermissible tone' means no more than that. Further, Trilling was writing in 1963 (Fraser gives the reprint date, 1965), a year *after* Leavis's attack was published in the *Spectator* (9 March 1962). How Trilling proposed thus to deny utterance of something published a year earlier beats me. But, says Professor Fraser, there

8. *The Name of Action: Critical Essays*, by John Fraser. CUP. pp. xi + 260. hb £25, pb £8.95.

are 'higher goods than decorum', a somewhat materialistic view of human relationships. Or does he mean 'Gods'? The urge to denigrate Frye (and Snow) is given rein elsewhere. The essay on *The Story of O* begins by invoking Frye's name three times in the first two dozen lines (Frye is a trifle complacent here) and Snow is insulted *en passant* by a comparison with Geoffrey Household and Donald Hamilton two pages later.

I have deliberately started in the manner of Fraser, as it were, partly because I want in this way to deplore the technique, partly because I want to warn prospective readers of Professor Fraser's book who may not be familiar with his style – and to tell them not to be put off, for something more worthy follows – and partly because he would not wish it otherwise. There is, he says, a 'flabby gentility that is far too common in the academic world today'; at least I have the dubious distinction of being short on gentility, academic, flabby, and otherwise. Now, if you can resist the tedium of Professor Fraser's passé digs and skip through to the meat you will be rewarded by incisive criticism, an original turn of mind, and still-fresh responses to literature. Professor Fraser wrote the essays over two decades and, in a number of instances, has added afterwords, one quite long. The subjects discussed are: *The Tempest*, *The Great Gatsby*, *Huckleberry Finn*, *Othello*, *Wuthering Heights*, *The Red Badge of Courage*, *The Death Ship*, *The Story of O*, Yvor Winters, Northrop Frye, 'Swift and the Decay of Letters' (published for the first time and the earliest of the essays), *The Village Labourer* by J. L. and Barbara Hammond, 'George Sturt's Apprenticeship' (the latter two both very handy essays), Eugene Atget's photographs of Paris, and 'Reflections on the Organic Community', which was initiated by the author's experience of spending eight months 'in the much anthropologized community of Tepoztlan', some fifty miles south of Mexico City. One serious production weakness is the absence of any of Atget's photographs. If Salzburg can produce illustrations, surely Cambridge can. It is no good Professor Fraser extolling and describing them if we are not shown anything more than the one used for the cover design.

Cambridge University Press has also reprinted twenty-two of Professor John Bayley's essays[9]. Like Fraser's volume, one, that on Pushkin, has not previously been published, but there the similarity ends. Professor Fraser's essays first appeared in academic-style journals whereas those of Professor Bayley appeared in *TLS*, *NYRB*, *The Guardian*, and the like; Professor Fraser devotes the first part of his book to set-text-type books and then ranges more broadly but chiefly in the Anglo-American tradition, with two excursions to France, and is mainly concerned with prose; Professor Bayley devotes most of his attention to poetry, offers nothing of the set-book variety, and explores especially Russian and East European literature. And Professor Bayley doesn't knock anyone about. Curiously, that doesn't make him a less vigorous critic. Perhaps the differences in approach might most easily be seen by contrasting Fraser on Frye with Bayley on Bloom (the alliteration is fortuitous). What Professor Bayley offers on Bloom strikes me as every bit as sharply analytical as Fraser on Frye and, lacking denigration, is the more effective essay. Another comparison, of a happier kind, might be made between their approaches to 'literature on the fringe' (though whether the author of *Church Poems* would have relished being so lumped with 'Pauline Reage' is

9. *Selected Essays*, by John Bayley. CUP. pp. vi + 217. hb £19.50, pb £7.95.

another matter). When Professor Fraser wrote on *The Story of O* twenty years ago it was scarcely a topic likely to win the critic much academic kudos. Betjeman's poetry as a subject for serious criticism by a scholar can today raise the odd eyebrow or two. Professor Fraser's essay reveals his critical strengths, his ability to cut through cant, and the power of his argument; Professor Bayley reveals directness, force, and delicacy of discrimination:

> Larkin has, rather oddly, referred to Betjeman as a 'committed writer', an adjective which might seem as beside the point as 'serious' would be. And yet perhaps not. A committed writer is more concerned with what he says than how he says it; and that, oddly enough, is both what impresses about the bulk of Betjeman's work, and what goes wrong. It takes a committed poet to express his convictions and feelings with such forcible flatness.

Professor Bayley's other subjects are Walt Whitman; 'State of the Nation: American Poetry'; the poetry of John Ashbery, Robert Lowell, John Berryman, e. e. cummings, W. H. Auden, and Philip Larkin. There is also an essay on Edward Mendelson's *Early Auden*. The second half of the book is given over to Eastern European authors, the Russians, Alexander Pushkin, Aleksandr Blok, Nikolai Gogol, Anna Akhmatova, Osip Mandelstam, Marina Tsvetaeva, and Vladimir Nabokov's *Lectures on Russian Literature*. These are followed by essays on the Bulgarian-born Elia Canetti, who writes chiefly in German; the Polish critic and philosopher, Czeslaw Milosz; and the Serbian poet, Vasco Popa. These are intelligent, perceptive, and elegantly written essays.

Esther Menascé seems to echo the title Isaac Rosenberg gave to the pamphlet of his poetry which he published himself in 1912 – *Night and Day*. Her study, *Guerra e pace nell'opera di Isaac Rosenberg (1890–1918)*[10], is in six sections, each title being further defined by a quotation from Rosenberg's writings:

1. La fortuna: 'I am afraid my public is still in the womb'
2. Un sognatore del ghetto: 'I wanted to write a battle song for the Judaens (sic) but can think of nothing strong and wonderful enough yet'
3. Le lettere: 'I believe I am a poet'
4. 'Moses': 'The real voice'
5. Sul Fronte Occidentale: 'Nothing can justify war'
6. Le immagini: 'The roots of a torn universe are wrenched'

Apart from a fairly full use of quotation, the book is in Italian and that, unfortunately, will mean that its readership and influence will be restricted.

Conformité et Déviances[11] and *La Peur*[12] reproduce, respectively, almost entirely in French, papers given at seminars held at the University of Lille III between 1981 and 1983 and at a conference held there in 1983. The former

10. *Guerra e pace nell'opera di Isaac Rosenberg (1890–1918)*, by Esther Menascé. Liviana Editrice, Padua. pp. vi + 295; 8 pl. L 30,000.

11. *Conformité et Déviances*, ed. by Alain Morvan. Actes du Seminaire, Centre de Recherches sur l'Angleterre des Tudors à la Régence, ULille III. ULille. pp. 109. Ffr 55.

12. *La Peur*, ed. by Alain Morvan. Actes du Colloque, Centre de Recherches sur l'Angleterre des Tudors à la Régence, ULille III. ULille. pp. 165. Ffr 70.

contains eight papers and these are devoted to English literature and institutions from the seventeenth to the nineteenth centuries. They consider the education of women (Paul Denizot); *la délectation morose* (as lengthily defined in the *Dictionnaire de Théologie catholique*, Paris 1911) in the English romantic poets (Jean-François Gournay); Inigo Jones as architect (Bernard Hibon); anti-urbanization and the development of the city at the time of the industrial revolution (Jean-Paul Hulin); 'Sexualité, amour et féminité dans *Gulliver's Travels*: les ambiguïtés swiftiennes' (Alain Morvan); conformity and deviance as exemplified by Lord John Hervey (Françoise Pavlopoulos); an account of novelettes featuring unusual women, chiefly of the eighteenth century, such as Anne Bonny, Mary Read, Maria Knowles, Mrs Christian Davies, and Mary Ann Talbot (Françoise du Sorbier): and ambiguity and deviance in the prose style of the mid-eighteenth-century novel (Serge Soupel).

The second collection, also edited by Alain Morvan, reprints eleven papers of which the last, in English, is an entertaining piece by Joel Weinsheimer on 'The Fear of Books'. This discusses the nature of pedantry and plagiarism and very amusingly shows Thomas Warton defining plagiarism by plagiarizing Samuel Johnson (not the last time that has been done!). The papers discuss the topic, fear, with respect to the Puritans, making wide references which provide an excellent introduction to the subject (Jean Delumeau); John Bunyan's *Grace Abounding* (Jean-François Camé); rhetoric from the Restoration to the mid eighteenth century (Paul Denizot); *Robinson Crusoe*, *Gulliver's Travels*, Samuel Brunt's *Voyage to Cacklogallinia*, Peter Longueville's *The English Hermit*, and Robert Paltock's *Peter Wilkins* (Jean Devoize); conscience in *Colonel Jack* and *Roxana* (Jean-Claude Dupas); the fear of papism among English travellers to France in the eighteenth century (Marc Leroy); Shakespeare and the terrors of the night (Jean-Marie Maguin); the fear of the French and the French Revolution in the novels of John Moore, especially his *Edward* and *Mordaunt* (Alain Morvan); aspects of fear in eighteenth-century novels (Serge Soupel); and the fear of Enthusiasm with particular reference to John Locke (Jean-Michel Vienne).

None of the contributions to either of the volumes is long, but they are often packed with detail. The subjects taken for discussion touch on a good many out-of-the-way aspects of life and literature in these centuries but their interest is not limited to the works selected for discussion. They suggest the depth and ramifications of the seminars and the conference and the documents of both are fresh and lively. *L'implicite dans la littérature et la pensée anglaises*[13] has been edited by N.-J. Rigaud for CARA, and is the product of a colloquium held in 1984. In a short introduction the editor briefly defines 'l'implicite': 'c'est ce qui est "dans les plis" ' – and 'les plis' are illustrated on the cover – 'ce qui n'est pas devoile'. Whether that one gets very far seems open to doubt but there is much more specific detail of the topic and its implications from Maurice Abiteboul in 'Rituel et stratégie de l'implicite dans la tragédie jacobéenne', which illustrates what the topic is (and isn't) from Jacobean plays. The quotations are given in French translations in the text of the article but in their English form in the notes. This article is preceded by a theoretical

13. *L'implicite dans la littérature et la pensée anglaises*, ed. by N.-J. Rigaud. CARA 5. UProvence (distr. by Jeanne Laffitte, Marseille). pp. ix + 164. pb Ffr 60.

account of 'L'implicite dans le discours poétique' by Gilles Mathis and this is
the longest contribution to the collection. The remaining nine articles focus on
specific texts with the exception of Felix Paknadel's discussion of portraits
painted between 1660 and 1780. The topics (with their authors) are: Ben
Jonson's Horatian poems, with reference to *The Alchemist* (Simone
Dorangeon); Henry Vaughan's *Silex Scintillans* (J. Pironon); Thomas
Middleton's *Women Beware Women* (N.-J. Rigaud); Hetty Sorrel of George
Eliot's *Adam Bede* (Jean-Pierre Garces); D. H. Lawrence (Sylvain Floc'h);
the short story with particular reference to T. F. Powys's *Fables* and Patrick
White's 'Willy-Wagtails by Moonlight' (Michel Pouillard); dialogue in Ivy
Compton-Burnett's novels (Josette Leray); and Harold Pinter's *The Room*
(Daniel Salem).

A just appraisal of the 1981 conference papers, *Espaces et Représentations
dans le Monde Anglo-Américain aux XVIIe et XVIIIe Siècles*[14] cannot be
gained from an account of individual articles. The papers reproduced are well
orientated round the central theme and one supports the other. However, as
the papers sometimes focus on less well-worn topics, it might be helpful were
their subjects to be noted here, though dispensing with their full titles which, in
the best French tradition, are often long enough to grace a book of the period
with which they are concerned. Robert Ellrodt writes on Donne and Traherne;
Alain Bony on Addison's periodical essays; there are then two articles of
particular interest to those concerned with 'Landscape and Literature': on
major gardens – Kew, Stowe, Stourhead, and Hagley – discussed by Jacques
Gury, and landscape in the eighteenth-century novel, touching on lesser-
known examples, by Suzy Halimi. There are two articles, by Marie-Madeleine
Martinet and Michel Jouve, on '*espace pictural*', followed by three articles
relating drama to the theme of the conference: Nadia J. Rigaud writes on
Thomas Middleton's *The Old Law*, Jean Fuzier on theatre-space within the
theatre in Philip Massinger's *The Roman Actor* (and I might interject that
Richard Brome's *The Antipodes* would have provided some even more in-
teresting points of focus), and unity of place in William Wycherley's *The Plain
Dealer* (Gilbert Schricke). Jina Politi writes on 'The Hell of Paradise' in
Rasselas; Pierre Morère discusses David Hume, Michèle Plaisant poetry, and
interstellar space with particular reference to James Thomson and William
Cowper, and finally Michel Baridon relates scientific theory to the conference
theme, particularly via the work of Sir Isaac Newton and James Thomson's
The Seasons. There is a vigorous sense uniting all these articles to the theme of
the conference so that the total effect is greater than that of the individual
parts. It is all rather imaginative.

Fabula appears twice a year and its third and fourth issues (for 1984) were
devoted to *Écrire du roman, aujourd'hui* (No. 3), and *Image Récit* (No. 4). The
articles are mainly in French – entirely so in *Image Récit* – but they should not
be overlooked by English scholars. *Écrire du roman, aujourd'hui* is divided
into four parts. It starts with two short extracts in English from the work of
Robert Coover and Christine Brooke-Rose (a member of the editorial committee). The former, from *The Adventures of Lucky Pierre*, is 'Man Walking at
24 Frames per Second' (the traditional speed at which sound ciné film is

14. *Espaces et Représentations dans le Monde Anglo-Américain aux XVIIe et XVIIIe
Siècles*. Actes du Colloque, Paris, 22–4 October 1981. UParis-Sorbonne. pp. 191.

projected) and would not be inappropriate in issue 4 of *Fabula*. The second piece of fiction, from *Amalgamemnon*, delves into our current despairs framed by the Agamemnon myth. The opening lines tell much: 'I shall soon be quite redundant at last despite of all ...'. There are five substantial articles, the longest of which, 'John Barth and Imitation: The Case for a Post-Structuralist Mimesis', is in English and by another member of the editorial committee, Robert Con Davis. Although he considers briefly mimesis as understood by Erich Auerbach, Ian Watt, Northrop Frye, and Wayne Booth, his concern is with self-referential fiction approached via P. F. Strawson's 'referring' and post-structuralist 'signification'. This is a doubly useful article for it succinctly reviews earlier interpretations of mimesis and explores the interplay between contemporary American fiction and post-structuralist theory. It bridges gaps in understanding and it points forward. The succeeding articles, all in French, are 'Impostures' (Jean Decottignies), which focuses on Jorge Luis Borge; 'Jean Rhys: Perte, retour. Egarements' (Chantal Delourme), concerned principally with the early *After Leaving Mr Mackenzie* and the much later *The Wide Sargasso Sea*; 'Norman Mailer et le discours sur le roman' (Claudine Thomas); and '*Gravity's Rainbow* à la carte: notes de lecture' (Simone Vauthier), which approaches Thomas Pynchon's novel under the appropriate menu headings. The third section of this issue is a series of three short 'Explorations' by two of the editors (Régis Durand and Henri Quéré) and, again, Christine Brooke-Rose – so that the association of editorial direction and contents is very close. Finally there are two interviews, one in French (of Hélène Cixous, the Algerian-born critic and novelist), and in English, of Anthony Burgess.

Fabula 4, *Image Récit*, is entirely in French. There are eleven articles and these are not arranged in subsections. As the title suggests, it is an issue concerned with reading images – classical pictures, (e.g. Giorgione's 'La Tempête'), modern painting (e.g. Paul Delvaux's 'Trains du soir'), book illustration (such as that to Jules Verne's *Round the World in Eighty Days*), Henry Cartier-Bresson's photography, and Hollywood films. The first essay, 'Focalisations cinématographiques: de la théorie à l'analyse textuelle' by François Jost, lays out a theoretical approach; the final article, 'La scène joycienne: la grille et le fantasme' by André Topia, interprets Joyce through scenario and image. As with *Fabula* 3 there is a close association between content and editorial direction.

A six-hundred page volume[15] containing forty-nine conference papers and reports (fifty were submitted so the fate of one is intriguing) cannot adequately be reviewed within the constraints of a survey of this kind. The book begins with a paper by Graham Caie on the editing of the OE *Judgement Day* and concludes with his short imitation of McGonagall's verse. All the papers are in English and most of the authors are Scandinavian. Twenty papers are devoted to literature; all the rest but one to language, including three each on OE and the teaching of English as a foreign language, one on the influence of the English language on contemporary Swedish over the past forty years (e.g. the use of English plural forms). The language articles are comparative (e.g. of English and Finnish, sex differentiation, written and spoken usage) or semantic (e.g. the Preterite and Perfect Tenses in BBC News Bulletins);

15. *Proceedings of the Second Nordic Conference for English Studies*, ed. by Hakan Ringbom and Matti Rissanen. PRIAA 92. Abo. pp. vii + 611.

characteristics of sentences (e.g. An Anatomy of Secular, Doctrinal and Supernatural Illocutionary Acts) or of conversation; the range of papers extends to body language: 'The Transferred Epithet and Body Language'. This last article takes as its starting point 'the Wodehouse effect' (p. 256) – that is the use of the transferred epithet by P. G. Wodehouse, as in 'I pronged a moody forkful'. The articles devoted to literature consider aspects of individual works – Mary Wollstonecraft's last novel, the ballad of 'Little Son Hugh', *Macbeth*, *Paradise Lost*, *Tess of the D'Urbervilles*, *A Pair of Blue Eyes*, *The Rainbow* – and individual authors: Otway, Coleridge, Hans Andersen (as an English writer), D. H. Lawrence, and Tom Stoppard. There are papers on Indian and South African writing, on current controversies over literary theory, and the applicability of traditional and more recent concepts of comedy to twentieth-century drama. Finally, there is a paper on 'Guides to English Literature', a brief, handy, and intelligent review of the products of the 'unique publishing phenomenon . . . that famous symbiosis between the egghead and the paperback'. If a reader knows to look in this book for what is wanted, he or she might find something useful, but the collection might be better served by some sense of point and direction. There is no index.

E&S has been collected by Raymond Chapman. In his preface he explains that he has pointedly avoided the associations which '1984' might bring to mind: to wit, 'tributes to George Orwell, or studies of futuristic and dystopic fantasies'. Being, for the time being at least, somewhat involved with George Orwell and what he wrote, I have an interest to declare. If it were tributes that 1984 suggested to the compiler, he did well to resist temptation. However, I am inclined to think that intelligent and searching scholarship prompted by that date might not have come amiss rather than 'no single theme . . . from Old English to a theme in which reference is made to Allen Ginsberg'. The disadvantage of such a loose approach is that however good are individual essays the lack of focus means they may easily be overlooked, or, even if read, too easily lost sight of. In fact, a slim volume such as this would have been about the right size for half a dozen penetrating essays prompted by this occasion and might then have brought together more that was worth while than any other assemblage we have been offered.

Lest their light be too successfully hid, it can be revealed that three of the seven essays will be of particular interest to those concerned with the relationship of literature and religion. Professor G. B. Tennyson writes on 'Victorian Biblical Typology', taking as his starting point Patrick Fairbairn's *The Typology of Scripture* (1845). One of its two illustrations is the fascinating 'Plan of the Poetic Cathedral' from Isaac Williams's *The Cathedral* (1838). Professor Arthur Pollard considers 'The Brontës and their Father's Faith'. He takes a vigorous line with those who have taken Patrick Brontë's faith, and his daughters' acceptance thereof, too simply. This is an illuminating essay (and rather good fun, to boot). The third essay on this theme is by the Rev Martin W. R. Jarrett-Kerr. This points to 'Indian Religion in English Literature, 1675–1967' and though it begins by referring to Ginsberg, it devotes most attention to the nineteenth century, especially to S. T. Coleridge, Robert Southey, Shelley, and Matthew Arnold. It attempts to cover too much ground in too slight a compass – Arnold to Ginsberg is singularly empty. Of the other four essays, the first two are from King's College, London. Janet Bately writes on 'Time and the Passing of Time in "The Wanderer" and Related OE Texts' and Richard Proudfoot on '*Love's Labour's Lost*: Sweet Understanding and the Five Worthies'. James R. Bennett considers 'Scenic Structure of Judgement in *Middlemarch*' and there is an entertaining and instructive piece by Pat Rogers, 'Diversions of the *DNB*'.

NLH is organized around themes and, I think, much the better for that. Furthermore, most of the themes are subject to discussion in immediately following articles. There are three issues a year: for the first, autumn 1983, eight critics write on 'Literature and/as Moral Philosophy' and there are seven responses, two by contributors to the first section. D. D. Raphael begins by asking 'Can Literature Be Moral Philosophy?' He attempts to show, from specific examples, how a work of moral philosophy can also be a work of literature, how moral philosophy can feed literature, and how, to some extent, a work of literature can also be a work of moral philosophy – the crux being what we are prepared to call moral philosophy. He takes as his first example the *Oresteia* of Aeschylus (finding, incidentally, *Agamemnon* the most dramatic play in the study but *Choephoroe* the most moving on stage, at least in the complete National Theatre production). He also discusses *Tom Jones* and *Erewhon*. Raphael is taken up by Cora Diamond, who also discusses Maurice Natanson's 'The Schematism of Moral Agency' and Martha Craven Nussbaum's 'Flawed Crystals: James's *The Golden Bowl* and Literature as Moral Philosophy'. She refers to the 'limiting assumptions in Raphael's account' and asks such questions as: What is the relevance of literary weakness to philosophical aims? Diamond is in turn answered by Raphael, who points to what he takes to be their essential difference in approach. A work of literature may have 'moral interest' and be 'morally significant', but, to Raphael, that 'does not make the work become a piece of moral philosophy'. Among other contributors to this issue are Nathan A. Scott Jr and Murray Krieger.

The winter 1984 issue is devoted in the main to ten contributions on 'Interrelation of Interpretation and Creation' and these are followed by two responses from Wolfgang Iser and Albert Rothenberg. The initial contributors include Richard Wollheim ('Art, Interpretation and the Creative Process'), Umberto Eco ('Metaphor, Dictionary, and Encyclopaedia'), Richard Shiff ('Representation, Copying, and the Technique of Originality'), and Norman Holland ('The Brain of Robert Frost'). After the discussion there is an article by David Punter, under the section heading, 'Literary Theory in the University', entitled 'Theory, Writing, Experience'. This was requested by the editor because of the author's connection with the Development of University English Teaching (DUET) project, centred on the University of East Anglia, which draws on the tradition of group study developed by the Tavistock Institute. There is no response to Punter's article, which is a pity. I don't mean by that that Punter needs putting right, but rather that what he says would have stimulated productive discussion.

The spring 1984 issue takes for its theme, 'Image/Imago/Imagination'. There are, again, ten articles (one, 'Blake, Trauma and the Female', being by David Punter) but on this occasion only a single response, Tom C. Conley's 'Images of Regression', which, while reviewing the whole issue, takes Yves Bonnefoy's inaugural lecture at the Collège de France ('Image and Presence') as 'the optical center of the journal, both its central focus and its vanishing point'. I wrote warmly of *NLH* last year; 1983–4 is even better.

CCrit is concerned chiefly with translation in theory and practice. There are three formal divisions to the volume: I, Translation in theory and practice; II, Translations; and III, Essay reviews. To these should be added the editor's introduction, 'Translation as metamorphosis and cultural transmission', in which he effectively sets out his wares, and the two bibliographies – of the translation of literature (compiled by L. G. Kelly) and of comparative literature in Britain and Ireland, 1981 (compiled by Glyn Tegai Hughes). The first section is made up of eight articles. These include 'Joyce translates Joyce' (Jacqueline Risset), Hölderlin's 'Pindar fragments' (Jeremy Adler), 'Ortega y Gasset's critique of method' (Nelson R. Orringer), theoretical essays and, of the latter, a very interesting and sharply focused piece by Gideon Toury, 'Translation, literary translation and pseudotranslation'. His account of the 'famous example' of pseudotranslation, Papa Hamlet, is amusing, enlightening and not, I dare say, too widely known. The idea of change being introduced into a national literature by means of pseudotranslations, tucked away in a footnote and deriving from a thesis in Hebrew, deserves much wider attention.

The translations, which occupy not too far short of half the volume, are of poetry (with a separate section on European Romantic poetry), short fiction, and of Bertolt Brecht's *The Horatians and the Curiatians*: a play for schools (preceded by a note on 'Brecht's "Chinese" peforming style' by Antony Tatlow). The play was written in 1934 but 'still represents a theatrical challenge . . . as it provides the impetus for a performance style yet to be devised'. The translator, Anthony Vivis, was, with Keith Bosley (whose work is also reproduced), a winner of the First Annual Translation Competition arranged by the British Comparative Literature Association. The two essay reviews are by Donald Davie, who considers 'The franglais of criticism; the English for translation', and by Stephen Bann, who writes of the history (or histories?) of *Tel Quel*. This all goes to make a particularly valuable volume; its different approaches and its re-creative examples, are imaginative, scholarly, and lively.

MPHJ is a new journal that might easily be missed by those concerned with English literature. There is a supplement to Volume I No. 4 (spring 1984), entitled 'Becoming a Dragon. George Orwell and Propaganda' by Clive Fleay and Michael Sanders, and I note that Volume II No. 1 devotes 180 pages to proletarian writing, focusing on Jack Hilton.

Richard Harter Fogle is celebrated in the *Festschrift*, *Reconciliations*[16], as much as anything for his influence as a teacher. He cannot but be delighted by the kick-off to this collection, given by a former secretary and part-time undergraduate, Harriett Hawkins, now a Senior Research Fellow at Oxford. The essay's title, 'Critical Counter-Interpretations of Shakespearian Drama: Some Results of the Dialectical Process', is its weakest feature: rather pretentious, and, despite its length, limiting, for it is concerned with much more than Shakespeare. What follows is, however, a splendid Counterblast to Silliness and, simultaneously, a marvellously lucid and down-to-earth guide to the tyro and warning to grey-beards. The whole volume was worth publishing to make this essay available and it should be issued separately as a pamphlet and widely disseminated. From its start – boredom as a crucial factor in instituting change in critical attitudes (to which she might have added the academic idleness of those who prefer ennui to the effort involved in tilling fresh fields of study) – to

16. *Reconciliations: Studies in Honor of Richard Harter Fogle*, ed. by Mary Lynn Johnson and Seraphia D. Leyda. SSELRR (1983). pp. ix + 261.

its conclusion, which questions the too-ready relationship of fraudulent literary 'approaches' with Thomas Kuhn's paradigms, it offers good, lucid sense. It would make admirable reading for anyone about to venture on the study of English literature at college or university and of those who teach them; only those too set, too comfortable, too idle in their ways could fail to benefit.

The article that immediately follows is also unusual: *Hamlet* as interpreted through twentieth-century poetry. Here, Ejner J. Jensen offers a stimulating variation on 'Shakespeare Our Contemporary', drawing on the work of poets of different traditions. With the exception of the last article, Malcolm Magaw on Saul Bellow's *Humboldt's Gift*, the bulk of this *Festschrift* is concerned with English and American poets and prose writers from Blake to Yeats. Mary Lynn Johnson (one of the editors) writes on 'Blake's Judgment on the Book of Judges' and, aided by half a dozen black-and-white plates, argues for Blake's watercolour designs as biblical commentary. This shows a good knowledge of critical work on Blake. Another nine illustrations are used to enable Richard E. Johnson to explore the way Blake responds 'as audience or reader when he reads a poet of empire', i.e. Thomas Gray, taking as his starting point the 'Ode on the Death of a Favourite Cat' and its illustrations. In a footnote he argues that 'Blake does not seek identity with this "poet of empire". Instead, he becomes sympathetic toward the text only after an act of correction, or deconstruction and repair of the text.' Daniel M. McVeigh writes on 'Reconciliations in Coleridge's Politics' and there are two articles on Keats. Seraphia D. Leyda (the other of the joint editors) argues that the structure of 'I stood tip-toe upon a little hill' is designed to show the interrelationship between nature and poetry, and W. Paul Elledge considers 'From Sonship to Fatherhood' through the medium of 'Sleep and Poetry'. There is a short article by Gerald Hoag on the last, one-line, paragraph of Herman Melville's 'Bartleby the Scrivener', and Tom H. Towers discusses the 'unity and failure' of Nathaniel Hawthorne's 'Alice Doane's Appeal'. Mary Rohrberger offers a surrealist reading of *Wuthering Heights* in an attempt to justify Virginia Woolf's description of her predecessor as 'a uniter of disorder'. D. H. Lawrence's interrelation of the Absolute and Relative are explained via eastern philosophies by William A. Gordon and, finally, James Lovic Allen asks the question 'Why Drumcliffe Churchyard?' as Yeats's choice for his last resting-place; he gives particular attention to the significance St Columba had for Yeats. This *Festschrift* should delight the man it honours. It is darkened only by the death of one contributor, Richard Blessing, who offers a preliminary parody, 'On First Looking into Norton's *Anthology of Poetry* (Revised)'.

In an interesting contribution to *On Poets & Poetry*[17], James Hogg (the editor of the series), takes up the cudgels on behalf of Roy Campbell ('An Outsider on the Right'). Maria Emanuela Eisl's book in German , *Lyrische und satirische Elemente in Roy Campbells Dichtung* (1979), 'failed to attract critical attention, as hardly any of the scholars who touch on Campbell's poetry know sufficient German to utilise it', and doubtless that kind of ignorance explains the neglect of studies on Campbell written in French and Spanish. Hogg's defence of Campbell springs from Robert Richman's review in *The*

17. *On Poets & Poetry*, ed. by James Hogg. Sixth series. SSELPDPT 27:6: *A Salzburg Miscellany: English and American Studies 1964–84*. USalz. Vol. 1, pp. 240; Vol. 2, pp. 214.

New Criterion (September 1983) of Peter Alexander's *Selected Poems* and *Critical Biography* of Campbell (both 1982), a review 'which surpasses in its vituperative vitriol the animosity of Campbell's own contemporaries'. Dr Hogg also writes on Browning's debt to Vasari. I wish his quotations from Vasari and Baldinucci had been rendered in English. The comparison of the claims by these two that Fra Lippo Lippi was a precursor of realism and the founder of a school of painters would then carry meaning.

The contents of *On Poets & Poetry* are strangely mixed. The pair of volumes are part of a series titled 'Poetic Drama and Poetic Theory'. Appropriately there are articles on Browning's *Strafford* (Derek de Silva); 'Three Notes on Middle English Poetry and Drama' (Michael G. Sargent), which considers the skewed symmetry of *Sir Gawain and the Green Knight* (analysing afresh the use of capitals of different sizes), *Wisdom* and the implications of fourteenth-century mysticism for a fifteenth-century audience, and 'Religious Form, Amorous Matter: Chaucer's *Legend of Good Women* and Gower's *Confessio Amantis*'; Gabriele Abermann writes on natural symbolism in Larkin's poetry; Sabine Foisner discusses William Morris's early poems; there is a lengthy article in German (the joint work of three authors) on T. S. Eliot's cat poem, 'The Rum Tum Tugger'; Hanna Nowak and Dorothea Steiner discuss the poetry of Alice Walker and Marianne Moore, respectively; Yeats's 'Crossways' and 'The Rose' are considered by Renate Thallinger; Ritamarie Sargent explores Puritan theological aesthetic and the personal uses of poetry through the elegies of Anne Bradstreet and Edward Taylor; and Erwin A. Sturzl writes on 'Lord Byron – Ein Polyglott?' If there is no strongly shaping hand, these contributions may be said to come under the aegis of either the volume or series titles, though quite what their relationship is, is uncertain. However, these two volumes also contain four poems (one for Dr Hogg) and six articles on prose and prose writers. Perhaps Leo Truchlar's *'On Being Blue*: Zum poet(olog)ischen Diskurs von William Gass' gets in because, despite declaring himself 'a rotten poet', he has tried to adapt symbolist technique to his prose, and Dr Hogg's subject, Ronald Duncan's autobiographies, are those of a man who was, among other things, a poet, but both articles stretch the limits. Who will think of looking in this series or these volumes for essays on Poe's tales (Katrina E. Bachinger), detective and crime fiction (Sieglinde Reschen, in German); William Oxley's 'The Sick Novel'; or Maria Schubert's 'The Use of Irony in Aldous Huxley's Short Fiction'? Surely a separately titled, if slightly expanded, prose volume was called for?

Volume 30 of *WVUPP*[18] is a special issue devoted to 'Deceit and Deception in Modern Literature'. It brings together fifteen papers – 'a refereed selection' – from a conference held in 1982 devoted to modern literature and film. Not much remains of whatever was offered on film (chiefly an interesting account of Michelangelo Antonioni's *Blow-Up* and Julio Cortázar's short story, 'Las babas del diabolo'). The remaining articles refer to a wide range of, in the main, less well-known authors and works. The articles tend to be on the short side (no bad thing) and they are inclined to be descriptive rather than exploratory. For those seeking something on Marguerite Yourcenar, Guillaume Apollinaire, Audrey Bely, Clemente Palma, Günter Eich, Bruno Apitz, Jurek

18. *WVUPP*. Vol. 30: *Deceit and Deception in Modern Literature*, ed. by Armand Singer and John Luchock. WVU. pp. 108.

Becker, Wolfgang Kolhaase (the last three discussed by Helen L. Cafferty under the title 'Survival under Fascism'), Julio Cortázar, and Guillermo Cabrera Infante, the journal is worth seeking out. Better-known authors considered are Stéphane Mallarmé, Friedrich Nietzsche, André Gide, Jean Giradoux, Bertolt Brecht, Philip Larkin, Alain Robbe-Grillet, and Günter Grass – a rich diet to compress into 108 pages. It is not surprising that one does not feel sufficiently extended even though much that is novel (to me, at least) is being introduced. *WVUPP* makes a greater demand on one's linguistic abilities than on one's intellect. A knowledge of French, German, and Spanish is essential to a reading of eight of the fifteen papers and quite handy for three others, though the reader is not expected to know Russian. This is paradoxical at this level.

David Constantine studies the 'eighteenth-century world of enthusiasm for Greece' in *Early Greek Travellers and the Hellenic Ideal*[19]. His aim, as he states in his introduction, is to introduce those who travelled to Greece and published accounts of what they found there, and 'to define and discuss the idea of Greece held by the travellers themselves and by certain contemporary men of letters who never made the journey'. Although he defines his period as 'the first century of revived European interest in Greece', his account runs for a considerably longer period, beginning with George Sandys, who visited Greece in 1610, and concluding with Jean Baptiste Lechevalier, who went 175 years later. Two dozen travellers and their published reports are listed in the handy Chronology of Travellers which prefaces the introduction. I shall not, I imagine, be alone in finding their names unfamiliar, in contrast to the names of such as Goethe, Schiller, and Hölderlin, frequently mentioned, and such as Byron and Gray, Büchner and Gibbon. That contrast suggests one of the merits of Dr Constantine's book for it not only illustrates how the interest in ancient Greece grew, developed, and changed, but provides the links to those it greatly influenced. These include not only great creative writers but men like Winckelmann, the great critic of Greek art, who never managed to steel himself to visit Greece. Indeed, one of the most intriguing sections of the book discusses Winckelmann's ambivalence about visiting Greece: his curious mixture of passionate longing and marked indifference towards the actual journey. Most of the quotations and phrases in foreign languages are given in their original tongue and translated, although there are a few puzzling exceptions. A great deal of matter is compressed and this is coupled with a style more involved than it need be. In happier contrast there are some quite sharply expressed observations:

> The modern Greeks have always had a hard time of it satisfying the largely inappropriate hopes of Western enthusiasts, particularly those from English public schools. If the view is that the modern Greeks are vile, then how else should one expect them to behave but vilely? Yet when they do – like Hyperion's men at Mistra – their detractors feel a terrible rage and disappointment.

There are eight illustrations, an interesting appendix on Homer's tomb, and a graceful tribute to the late Terence Spencer's *Fair Greece Sad Relic*.

19. *Early Greek Travellers and the Hellenic Ideal*, by David Constantine. CUP. pp. xii + 241; sketch-maps and 8 illus. £25.

Pierre J. Payer's study of the development of a sexual code during the period A.D. 550–1150, *Sex and the Penitentials*[20], takes its starting point in the prepenitential literature of Wales before considering the penitentials of Vinnian and Columbanus (the former undated, the latter being of about A.D. 591), and the ensuing spread of these manuals to continental Europe. When private penance succeeded the awesome public penance of the early church in the sixth century, there arose a need for guidance on theory and practice – precise penances for specific sins – to which the priest-confessor could turn. Basing his argument on the persistence and development of a tradition traceable through these manuals over a long period, Payer assumes that these handbooks were used in pastoral ministry. In this he disagrees with Nora Chadwick, who claimed that they, and what they described, were the products of 'the casuistry of the monkish brain ... thought up in the cloister by the tortuous intellect of the clerical scribe'. Neither she nor L. Bieler (who also cannot accept that these books were put to practical use) provide evidence to support their argument, says Payer (and the language used by Chadwick undermines conviction). Secondly, he assumes that the penances give a rough indication of the relative gravity with which sins were perceived. On this foundation Payer develops a detailed and, I sense, a convincing picture of what the church regarded as acceptable and what was to be prohibited in sexual relations: in fact, deviance and conformity in a period earlier than that which is the subject of the seminar papers edited by Alain Morvan (see pp. 11–12 above). The text is very fully supported by evidence from the penitentials; there are detailed notes, an index of references, and a general index. Direct relationships with English literature must be a little removed, but in drawing a picture of the sexual life of the time, and of the foundations upon which later attitudes were built, this is a rewarding study. It might almost be read as a counterpart to Roy Ladurie's *Montaillou*.

It is difficult to find words adequate in praise of Peter Dronke's *Women Writers of the Middle Ages: A Critical Study of Texts from Perpetua (†203) to Marguerite Porete (†1310)*[21]. It is, quite simply, a joy to read – and, of course, scholarly, informative, critical, and so on. It is a model of how to open up a little-known subject, especially in a field that (for proper-enough reasons) has become fashionable: the creative work of women, especially in writing and painting. Three of the women's names, and some of their writing, will not be unfamiliar, at least to some readers: Hrotsvitha, Heloise, and Hildegard of Bingen. Even a modest acquaintance with medieval drama will have led the more serious student to Hrotsvitha, perhaps, I fear, to pass her plays by as mere curiosities – Terence in Christian guise. But after Peter Dronke's analysis of her work, his delicate probing, wit, and gift for bringing out characteristics of the use of language that a reader's weakness in Latin might cause him or her to miss, that should no longer be its fate. Nowhere have I read so convincingly of 'a feminist triumph'.

The same qualities are deployed in bringing to our attention a truly obscure writer, the eighth-century nun, Berthgyth. Her three letters to her brother

20. *Sex and the Penitentials: The Development of a Sexual Code, 550–1150*, by Pierre J. Payer. UTor. pp. xi + 219. Can $24.95.

21. *Women Writers of the Middle Ages: A Critical Study of Texts from Perpetua (†203) to Marguerite Porete (†1310)*, by Peter Dronke. CUP. pp. xii + 338. hb £27.50, pb £10.95.

Balthard, the only relative remaining to her (and he living in her homeland, England), were written from her place of exile, Thuringia. These are shown off to full advantage without exaggerated claims being made for them. There is, for example, a subtle demonstration of the near-relation of one passage to the kind of 'song for a lover' (the *winileodas*) forbidden to the convent-dweller. There are generous quotations, often of texts never previously translated or discussed, the significance of which is carefully pointed out to the reader. The book has an overall purpose that goes well beyond giving belated attention to little-known writers and their work for it explains 'the ways women helped to shape the earliest Christian writing in a western language'.

The Tremulous Private Body[22] begins by quoting an entry from Samuel Pepys's *Diary*. Francis Barker tells us that it is a discourse shorn of its ornaments: 'a plain style for our bourgeois times. At least, that is how we have been taught to read Pepys' text by those commentators who have identified its significance for us in a way characterized by nothing so much as its plainness ...' However, the 'text employs massive means ... of diversion: we are asked to look "by the way" at "other things" ', and thus the 'text itself rehearses the situation it discloses as it inlays seclusion within seclusion'. Francis Barker evolves these statements from a detailed, very sharp, analysis of the entry he quotes. He goes on to argue that what he has shown is 'By no means the tortured predicament of a single, aberrant individual ... the situation is the result of the revolutionary process that preceded it.' We are, at one leap, like the hero of a nineteenth-century serial for boys, on to a broader stage that will fascinatingly be filled with scenes from Jacobean drama, *Areopagitica*, Philip Henslowe's *Diary*, the *Discourse on Method*, Rembrandt's *The Anatomy Lesson of Dr Nicolaas Tulp* – which is illustrated – 'an act of penal and sovereign domination which is exemplary and substantive, symbolic and material, at one and the same time', for Rembrandt is anatomized just as was Dr Tulp's subject. Thence to Andrew Marvell, 'who let aggressivity write in his poem', 'To His Coy Mistress'. Though divided into three sections, the third is just over a page long and the whole work is a seamless argument, so much so that Mr Barker precedes his text by listing the works to which he has referred, so ensuring his flow is maintained unhindered. What he says is infused by the work of Michel Foucault, Jacques Derrida, Jacques Lacan, and Louis Althusser, Sigmund Freud, Walter Benjamin, and others. The argument is complex and intricate as changes in the way corporeality is represented are described, with, ever present in the background, the title-word Subjection. The final aim? To undo the structure so exemplified: 'do these fragments not begin to figure the outline of a historical fable, even a structure: at the foundation of our own epoch a conjunction of themes and powers which it is still ours to live, and if enough time remains, undo, today?' Let me now return to Mr Barker's starting point. He first analyses the entry from Pepys's *Diary* and extrapolates broadly therefrom – one might say, extrapolates extravagantly. Pepys is in his beginning and at his end. Thus, five lines before his final paragraph (which has just been quoted) he selects various aspects which he has earlier discussed and melds one into another. Something, is found 'risible and haunting', something else 'salutary', something 'revealing in men driven blind by writing'. Despite

22. *The Tremulous Private Body*, by Francis Barker. Methuen. pp. xi + 116. hb £8.95, pb £4.95.

the plural, reference must be being made in this last statement to Pepys, for all the references are to characters with which he has peopled his little stage. But, you will say, Pepys did *not* go blind. True. But Mr Barker thinks he did and, further, that it was writing his *Diary* that caused his blindness. Examine the rhetoric within which this statement is embedded, as Mr Barker explains how Pepys's plain style works as a mask:

> The material history of the text ought to provide a converse image of this mystificatory clarity. A text ciphered and partly coded, hidden in a difficult early seventeenth-century shorthand, written in secret and kept locked away during Pepys' lifetime (and him driven blind by it), bequeathed, lost for so long a period to the *public* domain. Against what odds of obscurity has all this imputed transparency been achieved. And at what risk or perhaps promise, of truncation of the bourgeois soul it has come to represent.

Much could be commented upon, but consider simply whether the 'code' really was so difficult to decipher. It was a well-known, well-used shorthand (Sir Isaac Newton also used it) and although Pepys feared blindness, he most certainly never went blind. Indeed, he wrote four more diaries after giving up the one we remember him by, the longest being his Tangier journal of 1683–4 (see, conveniently, Robert Latham's *The Illustrated Pepys*, 1978, p. 230). But, much more important, what of the passage Barker quotes and upon which so much of his seamless garment hangs? If Barker's choice of text for Henslowe is slightly surprising (although perfectly acceptable), his choice for his Pepys quotation is astonishing. It is taken from an out-of-date text, designed in the main for schools, James Gibson's *John Evelyn and Samuel Pepys: Selections from the Diaries* (1957). Why ever not R. Latham and W. Matthews's eleven volume edition (1970–83) or, failing that, *The Illustrated Pepys*? A check reveals that Gibson, understandably having in mind his time and audience, omitted a line directly relevant to Barker's topic, which undermines the fanciful interpretation put on Barker's bowdlerized version.

The Western Humor and Irony Serial Yearbook (WHIMSY). Volume II: *Humor and Metaphor*[23] reports the proceedings of the society's 1983 conference. There are 125 contributions, defying summary. Most items are little more than a page or two in length; some are but a few lines. I imagine at first we were in the world of 'Pataphysical Academe: Conference as Serious Hoax – but I doubt if there is anything here rivalling the College of 'Pataphysics. The clue to what is going on may be the demand in the announcement of the next conference (an interdisciplinary one, bless the word), that $35 be sent in advance. This will ensure the right to attend the conference (in Tel Aviv) and enable those who pay 'to have your presentation (sic) excerpted in the conference proceedings and to a coy (sic) of the *WHIMSY IV* proceedings', This is neat. The organizers net upwards of four-and-a-half thousand dollars in advance and the participants can submit something to list in their annual return to their Dean. Or am I being cynical? Despite all this, there are a few interesting items though some of the stuff is at the level of the schoolboy howler. I enjoyed Kyoko Narita's 'A Pitfall of English Idioms for Japanese ESL Students'. To

---

23. *The Western Humor and Irony Serial Yearbook (WHIMSY).* Vol. II: *Humor and Metaphor*, ed. by Don L. F. Nilsen. English Dept, ASU (1984). pp. 320. $10.

describe a man as left-handed implies to a Japanese that he is a boozer; to 'let one's hair down', applied to a woman, means she has become a nun. The longest contribution is that of the Keynote Presentation by Warren Shibles: 'Teaching Humor in Schools'. This has an ingenious list of seventy categories of answer, with examples of each, to the diner's complaint that there is a fly in his soup. The limitations of this address, and perhaps of the whole enterprise, is strikingly illustrated by the way one is encouraged to extract humour in the classroom from the student error, $2 + 2 = 5$. This ignores (is ignorant of?) Sterne, Dostoievsky, Strindberg, Eugene Lyons, Ionesco, and Orwell.

In the first chapter of *Die englisch-schottische Volksballade*[24] Wolfgang G. Müller defines the object of his study as the popular ballad with an essentially oral tradition as opposed to the frequently written street-ballad or broadside or, indeed, to the separate class of songs. The text refers to the various collections of ballads and to the progress of critical research on ballads in the twentieth century. Following a chapter on the genre problems associated with the ballad the principal characteristics of the English and Scottish form are more closely defined: an oral, narrative composition in many versions, concentrating on the climax of a conflict and presenting this with dramatic means in which the voice of the narrator recedes behind the narrative. The following chapters address the history of the popular ballad, its formal characteristics and its typical impersonality and tragic moment. The text includes a bibliography and an index of ballads discussed. [M.H.]

24. *Die englisch-schottische Volksballade*, by Wolfgang G. Müller. Francke (1983). pp. 223. pb Sfr 24.80.

II

English Language

RICHARD COATES, DAVID DENISON, VIVIAN SALMON and
KATHLEEN WALES

1. Introduction

The chapter has ten sections: 1. Introduction; 2. General; 3. History of
English Linguistics; 4. Dialectology and Sociolinguistics (Including Creolistics); 5. Phonetics, Phonology, and Orthography; 6. Morphology; 7. Syntax; 8.
Vocabulary and Semantics; 9. Onomastics; 10. Stylistics. Responsibilities for
review of the year's work of 1984 lie mainly, but not exclusively, as follows:
sections 1, 2, 4–6, 9, Coates; section 3, Salmon; sections 7, 8, Denison; section
10, Wales. Inevitably we have treated some works under one heading which
might just as well have gone under another; we hope we have cross-referenced
these adequately. We have, as usual, systematically excluded work in psycholinguistics and applied linguistics, largely on the grounds that these receive
adequate coverage elsewhere and not on the grounds that they are of no
interest or relevance to scholars of the English language. Our only new policy
is to give explicit mention to creolistics in section 4; we therefore deem
English-derived languages to be English for our purposes.

2. General

This year we have come across no exceptionally interesting *Festschriften* for
persons best known as English scholars, and only two sets of conference
proceedings of general relevance to the English language. The volume edited
by Norman F. Blake and Charles Jones[1] is the proceedings of a conference
held in Durham as long ago as 1979 and delayed by unfortunate circumstances
in the publishing world. Papers from this will be followed by the abbreviation
(*EHL*). Those from André Crépin's collection of anglistic papers[2], some of
which were delivered at the Sheffield English Historical Linguistics conference
in 1983 (the next-but-one return of Blake and Jones's conference!) will be
marked (*LSSME*).

One of the more remarkable statistics about 1984 concerns the number
of general books devoted to the English language. Most of them have a sociolinguistic slant, but it seems appropriate to deal with them in this preliminary
section rather than along with the narrowly sociolinguistic works in section 4.
We have the distinct impression that a market has opened up for books about

1. *English Historical Linguistics: Studies in Development*, ed. by Norman F. Blake
and Charles Jones. CECTAL Conference Papers Series 3. USheff. pp. 313. pb £10.
2. *Linguistic and Stylistic Studies in Medieval English*, ed. by André Crépin.
AMAES 10. AMAES. pp. 132. pb.

English-outside-the-British-Isles – perhaps stimulated by John C. Wells's three-volume epic from CUP, *Accents and Dialects of English*, in 1982 and by the first edition, published in the same year, of Peter Trudgill and Jean Hannah's *International English* (Arnold); for both see *YW* 63.29–30. John Platt, Heidi Weber, and Ho Mian Lian publish *The New Englishes*[3], which details certain features of the English current in several Third World countries. They comment on the sociolinguistic and political problems which the existence of alternative English gives rise to and the educational dilemmas which follow from them, e.g. where British English has held a position of sociolinguistic prestige and/or where an English-derived creole is one of the languages in an area's linguistic repertoire. It is a useful sourcebook to complement the inevitably more disparate information scattered in the individual volumes of Benjamins's Varieties of English around the World series. Braj B. Kachru's *The Other Tongue*[4] went into its first British edition in 1983 and was missed in *YW* 64. It covers much the same ground as the book by Platt, Weber, and Ho just mentioned, but consists of papers by separate authors at a much more technical level. The focus is especially on English as a second language, with all that that implies for its functions in multilingual societies. The four sections of the book deal with the nature of the local varieties, the sociolinguistics of their nativization, the relation of local varieties to standards, and the nature of non-Anglo-American literatures. Kachru himself provides an epilogue pleading for utterances in 'other' Englishes to be understood in the context in which they are uttered, pointing out the perils, for instance, of trying to apply a general theory of second language acquisition across a range of situations where the sociolinguistic aspects of the process are very different. This is a stimulating and absorbing book. It should make us question, for instance, whether we as academics interested in enrolling African students at our universities and colleges have a practical linguistic policy that takes account of English-learning in an African context; are our requirements that they reach proficiency (or some other) level in some non-Third-World English realistic, coherent and politically aware?

Another book which first appeared in the U.S.A. in 1982 (*YW* 63.26) is Richard W. Bailey and Manfred Görlach's collection of papers *English as a World Language*[5], now published in Britain. Its contributors give a historical account of the emergence of English in thirteen areas and a description of its formal and sociolinguistic characteristics in those areas. The resulting work appears to be aimed at the non-native-speaker market. It is difficult to give any judgement beyond saying that the essays are necessarily brief and partial, and that within that limitation they are accurate and well written. There is a partial overlap with the essays in Peter Trudgill's large volume *Language in the British Isles*[6] Indeed Michael V. Barry contributes to both volumes: on Hiberno-English in the Bailey–Görlach book and on the English of the Isle of Man in

3. *The New Englishes*, by John Platt, Heidi Weber, and Ho Mian Lian. RKP. pp. viii + 225. pb £5.95.
4. *The Other Tongue: English across Cultures*, ed. by Braj B. Kachru. Pergamon Institute of English (1983). pp. xv + 358. pb £9.10.
5. *English as a World Language*, ed. by Richard W. Bailey and Manfred Görlach. CUP. pp. viii + 496. hb £22.50.
6. *Language in the British Isles*, ed. by Peter Trudgill. CUP. pp. 587. hb £37.50, pb £12.95.

Trudgill's. *Language in the British Isles* is somewhat differently organized from *English as a World Language* in that it has a separate section devoted to the sociolinguistic situations involving one or more varieties of English. Glanville Price has a smaller, handier book covering essentially the same ground in the same kind of way[7], though his is much more heavily weighted towards the traditional non-English languages of the British Isles and is strongest on the earliest centuries of the first millennium. It is of considerable interest that neither Trudgill's nor Price's book offers us a chapter on the structure of, say, Cypriot Greek, Bengali, Urdu, or Italian as spoken in England. Trudgill says it is because next to nothing is known about these. Why this is so invites rather bleak speculation. Both books have sections on languages that are poorly known by outsiders, for instance the various 'gipsy' or traveller languages and argots, and the casual anglicist is more likely to be arrested by these than by the sections on English. Price deliberately levels the coverage of English (including Scots) down to or below the dimensions of the pieces on the major Celtic languages (most salutary), while English looms larger with Trudgill, several regional varieties being described.

How many changes can one ring on the many-timbred bells of English? How many different ways can the scissors be wielded and the paste splurged? We have a selection of good compilations in 1984, but let us hope that the market has not been opened up to such an extent that we are swamped in 1985 by much more of the same type of thing, or this section of the English Language chapter will become a tedious procession of passing mentions of handsome books for the linguist's coffee table.

There are also two general works purporting to be about English etymology. The first one is, while the second does not fulfil its promise to an acceptable level. Louis Heller, Alexander Humez, and Malcah Dror write about *The Private Lives of English Words*[8]. This is one of those perennially fascinating bran-tubs of information where few of the parcels contain any novelties, though the information used is reasonably up to date (cf. the entry on *God*). Good stories including vast semantic shifts are favoured, as might be expected (thus *treacle*, *shambles*, *buxom*, *melancholy*, *hussy*, *forlorn hope* were predictable inclusions); contentious words figure prominently (*nice*, *alibi*); and words of high cultural interest abound (*jingo*, *sphinx*, *villain/-ein*). It is interesting that Geoffrey Leech, in his introduction to the book, picks on a subset of those I had independently selected for a mention! The book is decidedly predictable, but capable of selling philology and linguistics to interested outsiders, I hope. I have opposite hopes of James McDonald's *Wordly Wise*[9]. I hope no potential linguist buys it, for it is full of information that ought to be of the highest interest, but beset with so many philological inaccuracies, especially in the citation of foreign-language forms, as to make it both a dangerous firework and a damp squib (*tetragrammation*, *Kobald*, Latin *malificarum* 'of witches', Latin *neger* 'black', Anglo-Saxon *ough* 'elf' . . .; 'Spanish words such as *doña* or as we would spell it DONNA'). The lame old etymology of expletive *bloody*

---

7. *The Languages of Britain*, by Glanville Price. Arnold. pp. 245. hb £17.50, pb £9.95.

8. *The Private Lives of English Words*, by Louis Heller, Alexander Humez, and Malcah Dror. RKP. pp. xxx + 333. hb £13.95.

9. *Wordly Wise*, by James McDonald. Constable. pp. x + 293. hb £9.95.

from *by Our Lady* resurfaces again, believe it or not. McDonald wrote it because he found no such work existed, according to the dust-jacket; I would still prefer to send people to Ernest Weekley or Mario Pei, or even Ivor Brown.

We have decided to exclude this year all references to bibliographical aids, including work-in-progress lists, which relate to the year in question. The most complete ones tend to appear a couple of years after the relevant year and at roughly the same time as this one; and we feel there is no use whatever in reviewing the annual bibliographies *published* in 1984 since this pushes back our horizon by another two years or even more. Moreover, it is our experience that work-in-progress lists are rarely very full and are best given the status of handy guides which do not deserve the modest immortality which their mention here would confer. Accordingly, our practice of last year is discontinued. Major bibliographies of particular fields will, of course, be mentioned if they appear to deserve it.

Mention will still be made of interesting books in general linguistics. We find two more introductory textbooks, this time by Keith Brown[10] and Richard A. Hudson[11]; from a position of poverty in such books a very few years ago we now find several on the market written by reputable scholars, and there is no longer any excuse for university candidates to come for interview without having read a word about the subject (if there ever was). Brown's is largely biased towards English syntax and therefore in one sense mistitled – but not in another since its title reflects the bias in the field. Hudson's is characterized by an imaginative do-it-yourself or fieldwork approach with lots of examples from other languages, largely Beja and French. Phonology is well served by new textbooks from Roger Lass[12] and Peter Hawkins[13]. Ralph Fasold's *The Sociolinguistics of Society*[14] is billed as the first of a pair of textbooks. It consists of eleven essays each devoted to a major issue in sociolinguistics, very clearly written and arranged with well-flagged subsections which enable even the most casual reader to follow with ease the argument's overall line of development. Lastly, let us note Esa Itkonen's *Causality in Linguistic Theory*, missed in its year of publication[15]. It is a work in the philosophy of science which addresses the question of what status arguments in a linguistics autonomous of other disciplines might have, and argues that explanation in linguistics must be of a different kind from those employed in such disciplines as are uncontroversially called 'sciences'. Linguistic explanations cannot, he argues, proceed without an appeal to human reasoning processes, i.e. without seeing the language user as causally involved in his or her own behaviour. The notion of explanation that emerges is thus very different from the one implied in

10. *Linguistics Today*, by Keith Brown. Fontana. pp. 283. pb £3.95.

11. *Invitation to Linguistics*, by Richard A. Hudson. MR. pp. x + 182. hb £14.50, pb £5.50.

12. *Phonology*, by Roger Lass. Cambridge Textbooks in Linguistics. CUP. pp. xix + 363. hb £27.50, pb £7.95.

13. *Introducing Phonology*, by Peter Hawkins. Hutchinson. pp. 326. hb £20, pb £8.95.

14. *The Sociolinguistics of Society*, by Ralph Fasold. Blackwell. pp. xiii + 335. hb £22.50, pb £8.50.

15. *Causality in Linguistic Theory*, by Esa Itkonen. CH Linguistics Series. CH (1983). pp. x + 332. hb £19.95.

Roger Lass's book *On Explaining Linguistic Change* (*YW* 61.26); Lass seeks to defend a concept of explanation akin to the 'scientific' one, i.e. the deductive–nomological.

We conclude this section with two brief notes: we welcome the new journal *English Today*, appearing for the first time in 1985, but the appetizer for the series arrived before the new year; and we regret that *StudAngPos* arrived just too late for review, but this omission will be rectified in *YW* 66.

3. History of English Linguistics

We note as one of this year's most important publications, and a prime source of papers in linguistic historiography, *Matériaux pour une Histoire des Théories Linguistiques*[16] (cited below as *MHTL*). It is a collection of sixty-three papers first delivered at the Second International Congress of the History of the Language Sciences (Lille, 1981). Some of these items are of special interest to historians of English linguistics, and these will be noted below, while there are hardly any which do not have some degree of relevance.

However, we begin with an item on problems of linguistic historiography in Japanese with an English summary entitled 'An Approach to the History of English Linguistics' (*SELL*). Here T. Hayashi discusses the balance between external and internal histories, aims, and appropriate fields, arguing for the inclusion not only of phonology, semantics, and lexicography, but also of related fields such as the history of rhetoric, elocution, and biblical translation – a conclusion which will be heartily endorsed by scholars working in these areas who have discovered the impossibility of restricting their inquiries to self-contained compartments of knowledge.

The work of medieval British linguists whose medium of written discourse was Latin has again attracted some attention. One number of *HEL*, which is devoted to *Logique et grammaire*, contains a paper on Roger Bacon. 'Grammaire, Logique, Sémantique, Deux Positions Opposées au XIIe Siècle. Roger Bacon et les Modistes', in which Irène Rosier claims that Bacon and the Modistae give contradictory answers to the important linguistic questions of the later thirteenth century. She explains their differences by pointing out that the Modistae were dealing with universal and stable logical and grammatical properties of language, while Bacon was concerned with the variability of language and the individual speaker's freedom to alter the meaning of both lexical and syntactic items and, consequently, to inaugurate linguistic change. A second essay on Bacon, by Ch. Brousseau-Beuermann (*MHTL*[16]), deals with 'La Construction Figurée dans la *Summa Grammatica* de Roger Bacon'. The *Summa*, composed about 1240–5, is an early work largely neglected by previous scholars, but important because it is one of the rare witnesses to a linguistic tradition against which the Modistae erected their formal grammars. The author links it with the work of Bacon's countrymen, Kilwardby and Grosseteste. Another paper which refers to the *Summa* is P. O. Lewry's 'Grammar, Logic and Rhetoric 1220–1320' in *The Early Oxford Schools*[17].

16. *Matériaux pour une Histoire des Théories Linguistiques*, ed. by S. Auroux *et al.* ULille. pp. xv + 683. pb Ffr250.

17. *The Early Oxford Schools*, ed. by J. I. Catto. *The History of the University of Oxford*, Vol. I, ed. by T. H. Aston. Clarendon. pp. xliii + 684. hb £60.

Lewry illustrates not only the conceptual approach to language as a kind of mental grammar, which attends to meaning rather than to expression, but also notes some surprisingly sophisticated insights into the properties of language, both on the phonological and the syntactic level. The major work on medieval grammatical theory is by Michael A. Covington[18], who provides an impressive and illuminating account of the origins and development of Modistic grammar, using insights from contemporary theory where appropriate, though not in any consistent sense attempting to compare it with that of the Modistae. Although the development of theories of signification which gave the Modistae their name is associated with Paris (*c.* 1270–1310), this study also refers to the British scholars cited above, as well as to William of Ockham and William of Sherwood. Altogether, this book is a most welcome and clear account of theories which are not always easy to comprehend, and the translations of the Latin originals are a splendid bonus.

Although its subject matter is practical Latin teaching rather than theoretical grammar, David Thomson's important edition of the ME grammars of Latin[19] is most appropriately noted here. Thomson describes teaching grammars of Latin which were written in English towards the end of the fourteenth century; before about 1360, French was the medium of school instruction in Latin, but after the Black Death English was introduced by a grammar master in Oxford, and some of the existing texts are in all likelihood the work of one of his Oxford colleagues, John Leylond. An important conclusion is the demonstration of continuity within these manuscript grammars; even the earliest printed grammars in English were not an innovation but simply supplied what 'the market had shown it wanted for the last hundred or so years'. Continental grammatical influences in elementary education became dominant only with the royal sponsorship, in 1540, of Lily's Latin grammar. Since these ME grammars provide English translations of the Latin terminology and examples, they are an important source of information not only about the historiography of linguistics but also about the English language itself, including the phonology and orthography of the later Middle Ages, although the editor limits himself here mainly to comments on syntax.

Turning now to the history of grammars of the vernacular, we find commentaries on texts from the sixteenth century onwards. A comprehensive survey by T. Frank, 'I Primi Grammatici Inglesi 1586–1688' (*StIn*) has unfortunately not been accessible, but Frank's other publications are a guarantee of its value. Another treatment of our earliest vernacular grammarian, in R. E. Argemí's 'La Primera Gramática del Inglés: "Pamphlet for Grammar de William Bulloker"' (*RevEL*) has not previously been noticed, although it was published in 1983. Of seventeenth-century grammars there is an extremely valuable survey in A. P. R. Howatt's pioneering work *A History of English Language Teaching*[20], in a section called 'On "Fixing" the Language'. He also surveys the work of early orthoepists and lexicographers, and provides more detailed

18. *Syntactic Theory in the High Middle Ages*, by Michael A. Covington. Cambridge Studies in Linguistics 39. CUP. pp. viii + 163. hb £27.50.

19. *An Edition of the Middle English Grammatical Texts*, ed. and intro. by David Thomson. Garland. pp. xxxii + 287. hb $50, £55.25.

20. *A History of English Language Teaching*, by A. P. R. Howatt. OUP. pp. xiv + 394. pb £7.50.

accounts of the grammars of Ben Jonson and John Wallis. Jonson was the major source of John Evelyn's English grammar, an edition of which is supplied by A. C. Cook (*LeedsSE*) as a companion-piece to his earlier edition of the manuscript grammar of Thomas Tonkis (1982). Little of Evelyn's work proves to be original, but it is useful to have the material easily available so that we can judge for ourselves whether his merits as a linguist are comparable with those as a diarist. The answer, unfortunately, is 'No'. Moving on to the next century, we find an interesting study by Frances Austin of 'Double Negatives and the Eighteenth Century' (*EHL*[1]). Austin argues that, contrary to general belief, academic grammarians like Lowth and Priestley did not proscribe sentence element negation; there was no need to do so, because it had in any case become generally stigmatized as non-standard since the early seventeenth century. Academic grammarians devoted their attention to proscribing a different kind of negative structure – conjunctive (resumptive) negation. But provincial grammarians like Ann Fisher and James Gough, and grammarians writing for schools and non-academic institutions, continued to stigmatize such negation, and Austin argues that they did so because it was still current among the less well educated and thus called for 'correction'. She cites examples from eighteenth-century correspondence in confirmation of her view. The second item relating to eighteenth-century English grammar is Jarmila Tárnyîková's study of 'James White's Attempt at a Systemic Analysis of the English Verb' (*PP*), a very welcome account of a grammarian whose work has an unusually modern title – *The English Verb* (1761). Studies of specific grammatical phenomena of English can be traced back no earlier than the mid eighteenth century, and White appears to have been one of the first to examine one for its theoretical importance, and not for practical purposes. He was concerned with demonstrating that mood is a category denoted in different languages by different means, such as 'signs' in English and 'terminations' in the classical languages, but the function of mood is provided for in all. He deals with verbal moods, such as indicative and subjunctive, finite verb moods, and modality (necessity, possibility, and, marginally, volition) and in each case illustrates his system with genuine examples from literary sources. Perhaps his most penetrating observation is that 'The Verb in all Languages is of so important a nature, and all other parts of speech so connected with it, or dependant upon it, that, without a full comprehension of it, no Language can be Grammatically understood, nor any Syntax form'd'. No doubt he was indebted to unknown predecessors, but the study, as described in this article, certainly appears to be a major and innovative contribution to the linguistic thought of its time.

We return to prescriptive grammars with Lindley Murray, who is the subject of the summary of a paper read by David Reibel at the inaugural colloquium of the Henry Sweet Society (*HSSN*), 'Lindley Murray's Grammar: A Reassessment'. Reibel comments on the way in which Murray makes use of an integrated etymology and syntax to decide matters of propriety, and employs a sophisticated syntactic argumentation which draws far more on an unprejudiced attention to objective analysis than has recently been assumed. William Cobbett's *A Grammar of the English Language*[21] appears in a paper-

21. *A Grammar of the English Language*, by William Cobbett, intro. by Robert Burchfield. OUP. pp. xx + 179. pb £3.50.

back edition for the second time in two years. The format is preferable to that of the edition of 1983 (*YW* 64.36), and the introduction, by Robert Burchfield, is much more professional though unfortunately lacking an assessment of Cobbett's originality as a linguist. Nevertheless, the work itself is to be recommended as 'a period piece in the tradition that later produced ... George Orwell'. We may mention here another treatment of early English grammar which was unfortunately omitted in 1983. This is Risto Hiltunen's 'Phrasal Verbs in English Grammar Books before 1800' (*NM*), an enlightening account of how grammarians devoted to a part-of-speech approach to linguistic analysis came to acknowledge the existence of constructions consisting of verb + adverb/preposition as single units. Not until Miège (1688) is there any genuine understanding of this lexical type, and Maittaire's (1712) comprehensive account is not bettered until the nineteenth century – although Lowth had noticed the semantic distinction between *cast* and *cast up*, the latter in the sense of 'compute'.

The history of English phonetics is the subject of only two items this year, both from the Henry Sweet Society colloquium (*HSSN*). The first, 'Phonetics and Medicine in the Early Nineteenth Century', is summarized by Michael MacMahon. He compares German and British phonetic scholarship at this period, pointing out the greater attention paid by the former to the anatomical and physiological bases of speech, and attributing this to the greater interest taken in the subject by German medical scientists. Yet it was a paper by a physicist, Ernst Chladni, which came closest to establishing a general articulatory phonetic theory. Another paper, dealing with 'The Modernity of Henry Sweet', was written jointly by John Kelly and John Local, and is printed in full. Assessing Sweet's contribution to phonetics, Kelly and Local argue that his achievements as a phonetician are much more relevant to the needs of modern information technology and pragmatics than is the work of more traditional language teachers, aimed at foreign students, which culminated in the manuals of Daniel Jones and his colleagues. What is required now, they argue, is a means – not provided for by the I.P.A. – of recording the total phenomena of naturally occurring conversation. The authors show that Sweet's claim that the 'fixity of our conventional word-division ... blinds us to the real complexity of the questions involved in it' is much more important than it at first appeared. Nevertheless, Sweet makes full acknowledgement of his indebtedness to Ellis and Bell, whose aims differ in some respects and are more practical. The authors conclude 'the auditory system and the speech perception system are jointly sensitive to a great quantity of detail previously thought irrelevant'. Sweet thought nothing irrelevant; as the authors argue, if 'the tradition of practical linguistic phonetics that he founded had been seriously and rigorously pursued and developed, workers such as the one we have just quoted would not be in the position of having to make new beginnings'.

There are several studies in the history of English lexicography, beginning with John McNair's rediscovery of a 'hard-word' list which antedates Cawdrey (1604). In 'An Early Hard-Word List: Stephen Batman's *A Note of Saxon Wordes*' (*Neophil*) McNair describes the list and discusses its possible sources, some of which seem to be in legal terminology. It might be appropriate to mention here M. S. Hetherington's *The Beginnings of Old English Lexicography*, which, although published in 1980, has not received the attention which is its due because it was privately printed at Spicewood, Texas; it is reviewed by

A. Lutz in *Archiv*. Another overlooked item worth noting is Peter Rickard's 'Le "Dictionnaire" Franco-Anglais de la Langue Française (1611)' (*CAIEF*, 1983). Rickard is more concerned with the French entries in Cotgrave's dictionary, but he offers a critical evaluation of the work as a whole, regarding it as admirable for its time – particularly in using an alphabetical, rather than an etymological, ordering of entries. Johan Kerling provides a most interesting account of 'Franciscus Junius, Seventeenth-Century Lexicography and Middle English'[22], known to all students of OE literature through the eponymous manuscript. Kerling now draws our attention to a relatively unknown aspect of his work, his study of ME. Among the eighty-odd manuscripts which Junius collected, and which are now in the Bodleian Library, is an undated glossary to Chaucer (MS Junius 6) which Kerling describes as the 'first attempt at a scholarly glossary to Chaucer's works'. A possible rival, Stephen Skinner's dictionary of 1671, differs because it was not restricted to Chaucer, and its aim was etymological rather than explanatory. Kerling concludes, on good evidence, that Junius' glossary represents 'an important step in the growth and development of lexicographical techniques'. Another important contribution in this section is T. Hayashi's study of 'Methodological Problems of 18th-Century English Lexicography' (*MHTL*[16]). Hayashi classifies these problems as (i) grammatical, (ii) encyclopaedic, and (iii) orthoepical. He points out that the grammatical classification of entrywords was first consistently undertaken by John Kersey (1702), in his distinction between nouns and verbs, with a complete categorical classification first occurring in Dyche–Pardon's *New General English Dictionary* (1735), which also pioneered the inclusion of a brief grammar. 'Encyclopaedic' questions concern the gradual inclusion in dictionaries of the type of encyclopaedic material first published in France in the seventeenth century, and in England in the eighteenth. Finally, under 'orthoepical' problems, Hayashi deals with the systematic inclusion of pronunciation marking, from Bailey's universal English dictionary (1727) onwards. The first number of a new publication, *Euralex Bulletin* (*EB*), contains two relevant notes, one by N. E. Osselton on 'Lexicography; Or, the Art of Escaping Reproach', as an introduction to the new Euralex enterprise, founded two hundred years after Johnson's death. Osselton's note is a brief tribute to Johnson, and a second, short contribution, by Thomas Lavelle, 'On Celebrating the *OED*', is another tribute to past lexicographers. Lavelle notes that the anniversary has been mentioned frequently in the press; *The Times*, for example, devoted sixteen column inches to 'commemorate the centenary of the publication of the first section of the ... greatest book in the English language'. However, Lavelle goes on to inquire what exactly it is that we are celebrating, and he answers his own question in the rest of the paper. The new *EB* is to be greatly welcomed by historians of linguistics; although the association of which it is the organ, the European Association for Lexicography, is mainly concerned with contemporary lexicography, it also provides a forum for those who are primarily interested in the history of dictionary making.

Theory and practice in relating the written to the spoken word have tended to be the province of the amateur, and often anonymous, linguist, but since

---

22. *LEXeter '83 (Proceedings): Papers from the International Conference on Lexicography at Exeter, 9–12 September 1983*, ed. by R. R. K. Hartmann. Lexicographia, series maior 1. Niemeyer. pp. vii + 452. DM 132, £36.70.

Johnson's attempt at 'fixing' the orthography of English is involved, reference may be made here to N. E. Osselton's 'Informal Spelling Systems in Early Modern English' (*EHL*[1]); this is more fully discussed in section 5. More relevant here is a detailed account of the history of punctuation theory in English provided by Greta Little, who describes herself as 'concerned with punctuation for its own sake: its history, foundations, uses and controversies'[23]. The history is dealt with under three headings: the rhetorical, the grammatical, and the typographical tradition. Unfortunately, the early history is all too briefly related, and most of the author's attention is focused on nineteenth- and twentieth-century theories. Nevertheless, it is a valuable reference tool for those interested in examining in detail the punctuation theory of early English grammarians. A specific aspect of English punctuation, the use of the apostrophe, is provided with a historical explanation by S. Levin in 'The Greek Diacritical Marks and their Application to Other Languages in the Renaissance' (*GL*) – a study of surprisingly general interest. One rather different aspect of the written form may be mentioned – the possible historical iconicity of letter forms. In 'Letterforms as an Articulatory Notation' (*Open Letter*) Peter Mayer writes an informal account of the possible connection between letter shapes and the shapes of the articulating organs, and cites a number of British linguists who have seen some connection between them in the past, among them Bulwer, Nelme, Jones (for Devanāgari), and Paget.

Several papers deal with general attitudes to and theories about the English language and language study. Jane Donawerth examines Shakespeare's dramatic use of contemporary ideas on language, dealing in Chapters 1 and 3, respectively, with 'The Nature, History, and Powers of Language' and 'Attitudes towards Language'[24]. The remaining chapters show how ideas about language are used in each of the five plays examined. Donawerth points out that there is no history of English linguistics and linguistic philosophy in the sixteenth century, and admits that it is not her intention to write one. Nevertheless, she brings together a good deal of valuable information about the study of language in Shakespeare's day which will be of undoubted interest to historians of linguistics. In 'Bacon's Hieroglyphs and the Separation of Words and Things' (*PQ*) Martin Elsky argues that Bacon's views on the relationship between language and reality differed from those of many of his Renaissance predecessors, and he illustrates his thesis by reference to Alexander Top's views on the hieroglyphic, or allegorical, nature of the letters of the alphabet. He regards all alphabets as descendants of Hebrew, claiming that when God created the world, he simultaneously created Hebrew letters as hieroglyphs of his handiwork. Bacon, on the contrary, totally separated 'the order of language from the order of reality', and in this respect his views represented a departure from the prevailing opinion. Other Baconian ideas on language proved a source of inspiration to John Wilkins, first secretary of the Royal Society; one of those ideas – the possibility of devising a universally comprehensible universal character – was exploited by Wilkins in a section of an early

23. *Research in Composition and Rhetoric: A Bibliographical Sourcebook*, ed. by M. G. Moran and R. F. Lunsford. Greenwood. pp. 640. hb $55.

24. *Shakespeare and the Sixteenth-Century Study of Language*, by Jane Donawerth. UIll. pp. xi + 279. hb £18.75.

work, *Mercury*, of which a facsimile edition, together with a splendidly detailed commentary, is provided by B. Asbach-Schnitker[25]. On eighteenth-century English linguistic thought Patrice Bergheaud contributes 'Tensions Paradigmatiques et Objets Polémiques' (*MHTL*[16]), with special reference to Adam Smith and Lord Monboddo; and Thomas Frank surveys, in 'La Riflessione Linguistica nel '700 Inglese', the ideas of Harris, Priestley, Monboddo, Adam Smith, and Lowth, and deals among other topics with eighteenth-century theories on the origin of language (*Belfagor*). This is a subject also examined by R. Schreyer in 'Evidence and Belief: Arguments in the Eighteenth-Century Debate on the Origins of Language' (*MHTL*[16]). Although Schreyer refers to the 'surging interest' in the eighteenth century (shown by Condillac, Rousseau, and Herder among others) in the question of glottogenesis, his attention is directed more particularly to 'the constant application of the genetic method in order to explain all aspects of human culture' – a method employed by British philosophers like Bernard Mandeville, David Hume, Adam Ferguson, and Lord Kames. Schreyer argues that eighteenth-century anthropology saw the newly discovered savage cultures as exemplifying the origin and development of language; thus the 'great chain of being', originally hierarchical and ahistorical, became temporalized in the seventeenth and eighteenth centuries. Monboddo is also a central figure in a study of the beginnings of comparative philology by J. C. Müller, who writes on 'Saumaise, Monboddo, Adelung: Vers la Grammaire Comparée' (*MHTL*[16]). Müller discusses Monboddo's conclusion, in his immense work *Of the Origin and Progress of Language*, that in view of the similarities in certain items of vocabulary, Greek is derived from 'Teutonic', Persian, and Latin; or those are derived from Greek; or that all are derived from one parent language. Monboddo based his views on an existing tradition which depended in large measure on the work of Saumaise (1588–1658), a French Huguenot emigrant to Leyden who postulated a relationship between German and Persian. Müller points out that Sir William Jones could have derived his ideas in part from Monboddo, whom he is known to have met on at least one occasion.

Not strictly relevant to the history of English linguistics, but meriting brief reference as testimony to the persistence of linguistic attitudes from the seventeenth century, is Steven Blakemore's 'Burke and the Fall of Language: The French Revolution as Linguistic Event' (*ECS*). Like Bacon, Burke was disturbed by the potential confusion of word with thing, language with reality; he was also distressed by the 'Babel' arising from the Revolution, in which words like *nature*, *property*, and *liberty* had been deprived of their prelapsarian meanings and supplied with 'deformed' ones in the new Fall of Man. While Burke was lamenting the 'Babelization' of language due to a European revolution, a linguist affected by the American Revolution was setting out on a different course. In 'Noah Webster's Linguistic Thought and the Idea of an American National Culture' (*JHI*) Vincent Bynack describes how Webster aimed at creating a national language as early as his spelling-book of 1783, under the influence of views expressed in the Berlin Academy about the 'national' character of languages, and, in particular, by Michaelis's prize essay

---

25. *Mercury: or the Secret and Swift Messenger*, by John Wilkins, ed. and intro. by B. Asbach-Schnitker. Benjamins. pp. cix + viii + v + 184. Fl 82, $33, £20.35.

of 1759 which aimed to show, contrary to the opinion of the time, that human beings perceived reality in different ways, and hence created different forms of language to express that reality. Later, after a religious conversion, Webster came to believe that language was God-given, and that, in spite of Babel, it was possible to discover principles of linguistic change which would account for the differences between the language-groups derived from Shem, Ham, and Japhet. This article provides a new and stimulating approach to Webster, who is more usually regarded as an eminent lexicographer than as a linguist interested in wider issues.

An exception is made here to our rule of excluding texts on applied linguistics for what must be the first comprehensive treatment of the history of English language teaching. A. P. R. Howatt's attractively produced and illustrated paperback[20] contains four sections, on: (1) practical language teaching up to 1800, (2) 'fixing' the language, mentioned above, (3) language teaching in the nineteenth century, and (4) the making of a profession. There is a useful chronology of relevant dates and, among other interesting items, a translation of Wilhelm Vietor's *Der Sprachunterricht muss umkehren*. One of the major attractions of this work is its wide range of interests: and while the topics which it covers are well known to historians of the English language, their presentation in relation to an unusual context – the teaching of the vernacular – provides them with fresh interest.

The remaining items are noticed here because, although not specifically concerned with the history of British linguistics, they provide background material relevant to the understanding of its tradition. Most important is the study by Hans Arens of *Aristotle's Theory of Language and its Tradition*[26], which consists of (1) the Greek text of the relevant section of *Peri Hermeneias*, together with Arens' translation and commentary, (2) translations and discussions of seven Greek or Latin commentaries on this work, written between the sixth and seventeenth centuries A.D., and (3) a commentary on James Harris's *Hermes* (1750). This short Aristotelean text exerted a vitally important influence on the development of linguistic theory, and the author deserves our warmest thanks for what must have been an enormous expenditure of time and energy in providing us with the basic text. Individual papers which historians of British linguistics should find of interest and at least marginally relevant, noted in chronological order of subject matter, include the following: P. Swiggers, 'Cognitive Aspects of Aristotle's Theory of Metaphor' (*Glotta*); W. K. Percival, 'The Reception of Hebrew in Sixteenth-Century Europe: The Impact of the Cabbala' (*HL*); Manfred Peters, 'Theodore Bibliander. *De ratione communi omnium linguarum et literarum commentarius*, Zürich 1548' (*Archiv*) – an extremely valuable account of sixteenth-century views on language relationships; M. L. Breva-Claramonte, 'The Semiotic Aspects of Sanctius' *Minerva*' (*HL*); E. F. K. Koerner, 'French Influences on Saussure' (*GJL*) and 'Karl Bühler's Theory of Language and Ferdinand de Saussure's *Cours*' (*Lingua*). Finally, the 'Chomskian revolution' continues to provide a subject for debate. One view is represented by H. Bracken, who argues in 'Chomsky's Cartesianism'[27] that Chomsky has 'illuminated a segment of

26. *Aristotle's Theory of Language and its Tradition*, by Hans Arens. SiHoLS 29. Benjamins. pp. v + 525. hb Fl 150, $60, £37.35.

27. *Mind and Language*, by H. Bracken. PiLS 14. Foris. pp. xiv + 154. hb Fl 58, pb Fl 38.

our intellectual history'. This is true enough, even if different opinions are held about the accuracy of the illumination. E. F. K. Koerner, on the other hand, reiterates in 'The "Chomskyan Revolution" and Its Historiography'[28] his argument that there was no such thing as a 'revolution' in linguistics in the 1960s and 1970s. Koerner's argument is detailed and persuasive, but no doubt most linguistic scholars will go on believing that Chomsky heralded a new era.

4. **Dialectology and Sociolinguistics (Including Creolistics)**

Three major studies which might well have been placed in this section are dealt with in the first paragraphs of the following section because they are specifically phonological, and because they exemplify different approaches which are of major importance to theoretical phonology. Ralph Fasold's new textbook is discussed in section 2 above. In a general paper of great methodological interest, 'Linguistic Variation in English: Idealization, Varieties and Linguistic Items' (*ES*), F. G. A. M. Aarts reviews the history of attempts to incorporate mechanisms for describing variability into overall grammatical descriptions of languages, from the idealizationist position of abstracting away from variation to the realists' rejection of the possibility of writing grammars for varieties (or indeed for anything superordinate to the idiolect).

Many of the other sociolinguistics works this year narrowly concern the speech of North America. In *AS* Lee Pedersen, Susan Leas McDaniel, and Marvin Bassett report on the completion of 'The *LAGS* [= *Linguistic Atlas of the Gulf States*] Concordance'. The Canadian scene is discussed in 'Linguistic Insecurity in Winnipeg' (*LinS*) by Thompson W. Owens and Paul M. Baker, who replicate some findings of Labov's classic work on the question, and discover that although Americanization of the Canadian speech of the city is proceeding apace, citizens will nevertheless stigmatize relevant forms when asked for judgements of them. 'The Scotch–Irish Influence on American English' is investigated by Alan Crozier (*AS*), who finds some lexical items of putative Ulster origin on the eastern fringes of East Midlands U.S. English in Pennsylvania.

Two papers look at possible novelties in U.S. English, in addition to those reported in sections 6 and 8 on new words from the columns of *AS*. Alleen Pace Nilsen notes, in 'Greetings and Salutations in a New Age' (*LinS*), that there is evidence of experimentation with sex-neutral usage in salutations in personal letters, while James W. Hartman observes 'Some Possible Trends in the Pronunciation of Young Americans (Maybe)' (*AS*). He identifies these latter as being geographically widespread, non-prestigious and having known historical precedents, and he ascribes their supraregional occurrence in the speech of young people to the density of their communication networks. Halfway between the U.S.A. and England we find Linda Shockey's paper 'All in a Flap: Long-Term Accommodation in Phonology' (*JPhon*). She investigates the phenomenon of 'undoing' the effects of the U.S. English intervocalic flapping of coronal stops which occurs repeatedly in her experience in the speech of Americans in England, and attributes it, mildly controversially, to that

---

28. *Diacronia, Sincronia e Cultura: Saggi Linguistici in Onore di Luigi Heilmann*, ed. by Enrico Arcaini *et al*. Brescia: La Scuola.

aspect of accommodation theory which deals with the desire to be understood.

The major paper of the year to my mind is Suzanne Romaine's 'The Sociolinguistic History of T/D Deletion' (*FLH*). Romaine argues that this phenomenon is one of very great time-depth and is stably variable like the syntactic phenomenon she studied in her *Socio-historical Linguistics* (see *YW* 63.35). The consequence of the truth of her contention is a revision of the assumption that the further back one goes in time, the more phonological convergence should be apparent: that is, more generally, that the notions of parenthood and filiation in historical linguistics, as they are usually understood, cannot be taken for granted any more. A further, much more modest paper showing the utility of sociolinguistic-style research in a medieval and literary context is Urs Dürmüller's 'Sociostylistics and the Study of Medieval English' (*LSSME*[2]), where he gives a demonstration on the hapless body of the *Pardoner's Tale*.

As for the modern cis-Atlantic dialects, James Milroy presents evidence that is now familiar from several of his works on the sociolinguistics of the mergers involving front vowel phonemes in Belfast English ('Present Day Evidence for Historical Change', *EHL*[1]). John Harris uses syntactic divergence data from Hiberno-English to argue (in 'Syntactic Variation and Dialect Divergence', *JL*) that certain changes involve such radical restructuring in the dialects in question, that it is unrealistic to attempt to write single (panlectal) grammars for the totality of Hiberno-English. Much more than mere low-level rule-addition to grammars is at issue, he claims. In 'Death of a Dialect: Historical Implications of Sound-Change in a Devon Family' (*EHL*[1]) Alexander Baird argues that sound-change depends on the availability of variants among which to select, i.e. he implicitly supports a view of sound-change based on social network theory. He then sees a variety of changes observed in Devon as being consequences of the shifting of the typical realization of a central reference point in the vowel quadrilateral.

There are a number of works on BE vernacular and English creoles this year. The most welcome is John Holm's paper 'Variability of the Copula in Black English and its Creole Kin' (*AS*), which has burrowed around the underground since 1976. Holm compares the 'deletability' of the BE copula with the variability patterns of comparable units in other creoles and in Yorùbá, and puts forward the idea that similarity in such patterns enhances the possibility of genetic relationship. In particular, Holm finds the variety of copulas in Yorùbá suggestively reminiscent of preferred patterns of copula selection in BE. Zygmunt Frajzyngier gives a historical treatise 'On the Origin of *say* and *se* as Complementizers in Black English and English-Based Creoles' (*AS*). These, he holds, do not descend from the English verb of comparable shape as such, or from the Asante Twi verb *se* meaning 'say' (coincidentally), but involve an English relexification of the common West African (e.g. Twi, Gã) pattern involving complementation with a verb meaning 'say'. His thesis is persuasive despite its counterintuitive look on cold paper here. More complementizers are seen in Francis Byrne's 'FI and FU: Origins and Functions in Some Caribbean English-Based Creoles' (*Lingua*). He sees the /fi/-forms arising in creoles (e.g. Saramaccan) that exhibit vowel-harmonic assimilation, and then being disseminated to Jamaica, rather than springing up independently in Jamaica. I did not find this persuasive. Ronald R. Butters demands to know 'When Is English "Black English Vernacular"?' (*JEngL*). He denies that an appropriate definition of BE vernacular can follow from an observation of the application rate of certain variable rules stereotypically held to typify it. He provides data that does not fit the supposed characteristic application rate but which is nevertheless evaluated as BE vernacular by native speakers. Patricia Jones-Jackson provides an interesting perspective on language death by treating decreolization as an example of it in her paper 'On Decreolization and Language Death in Gullah' (*LinS*). She finds that in the post-creole continuum she is studying, different morphosyntactic features elaborate (i.e. decreolize) at different rates. We note briefly that David Sutcliffe's *British Black English*[29] goes into a paperback edition. And finally in this section we note Nicholas Faraclas's paper 'Rivers Pidgin English (South Eastern Nigeria): Tone, Stress or Pitch-Accent Language?' (*SILS*). Faraclas comes to the conclusion that it is a pitch-accent language with lexical tone on certain items borrowed from substrate languages. English words are allotted single tones and other tones are 'filled in' by rules at the level of the phonological word.

5. Phonetics, Phonology, and Orthography

Among the more noteworthy events this year are two quite extensive phonetic/phonological studies of individual English dialects in England, and a set of six descriptions of contrasting British English ones. David J. North publishes, in a monograph overlooked last year, his *Studies in Anglo-Cornish Phonology*[30], and Beat Glauser his *A Phonology of Present-Day Speech in Grassington (North Yorkshire)* [31]. The two works are extremely interesting for the methodological contrast which they exemplify, and this difference is the reason why I am treating them in the phonology section rather than as works of dialectology or sociolinguistics (section 4). North works in a structuralist tradition of linguistic geography, while Glauser attempts a generative treatment of his subject matter. North points to inadequacies in the data base provided by the *Survey of English Dialects* in Cornwall and adds a substantial amount of material collected by himself. On the basis of this enhanced data, he takes issue with Martyn Wakelin's published work on Cornish English (especially *Language and History in Cornwall*; see *YW* 56.36) in a number of particulars concerned with the chronology of the East Cornwall Fronting of high back vowels. In general, the work shows an impressive attention to phonetic detail of extreme refinement, though the structural notion of a *diaphoneme* to which he appeals appears to me to be a dubious construct. He describes it as 'a common functional unit with various local realizations'; that is, he is engaged in a process of data idealization which sits ill with his attention to the notion of contrast and to allophonic detail if the quoted words are indeed an ontological claim. It seems to me that his *diaphoneme* is merely a phonological equivalence class over lexical sets, whose reality, within the borders he

29. *British Black English*, by David Sutcliffe. Blackwell (1983). pp. 224. pb £6.95.
30. *Studies in Anglo-Cornish Phonology*, by David J. North. Institute of Cornish Studies, UExe (1983). pp. vi + 80. pb. £2.50.
31. *A Phonology of Present-Day Speech in Grassington (North Yorkshire)*, by Beat Glauser. Cooper Monographs 32. Francke. pp. 310. pb.

sets to it, could be guaranteed only if its users produced sociolinguistically governed variation among its various realizations. It is not clear what becomes of a diaphoneme when one of its realizing phonemes, in some dialect, merges with another representing some other supposed diaphoneme. Despite these remarks, this is very good work as a descriptive study. Glauser's study deals with a dialect expected to show both northern and midland features, though what he finds most salient is tension between a local and a standardizing form of speech. He pays special attention, as might be expected, to features which show phonetic variation. This redresses the balance against the older currently much-criticized tactic of ignoring local variability in the quest for a supposed authentic local speech. Prominence is also given to the relation between phonologically defined lexical sets in the standard and the non-standard dialect. His desire to produce a description treating morpho-phonemic relations in a reified way leads him into mild segment abstraction, e.g. he postulates an //x// underlying diphthongs in /-i/ with a front first element; and sequence abstraction in seeing an invisible voiced stop in cases where a nasal precedes a consonant not homorganic with it. He uses archi-phonemic-style representations for such nasals without going into the theoretical problems attached to such representations. He has used generative phonology as a tool, rather than sought to make his dialect yield insights into the mysteries of theoretical principles. Whatever one's view of descriptive tactics like this, he seems to have done a good job at the level of phonetic detail, and provides a pronouncing lexicon/onomasticon of his dialect, which is most welcome.

In *JEngL* David L. Shores gives a straightforward structural description of 'The Stressed Vowels of the Speech of Tangier Island, Virginia', his native dialect which is remarkable as showing virtually none of the typical features of Virginian vowel systems. David North, in addition to the work on Anglo-Cornish mentioned above, has worked on 'The Development of Middle English ā, ai and ī in Surrey, Kent and Sussex' (*LeedsSE*). Again this is careful work, using geographical distribution of forms as a tool in unwinding the history of diaphonic variety. He identifies the diffusion channels of innovations originating in London (the routes to Portsmouth, Brighton, and Dover) and shows that a wave of [æi] pronunciations in such words as *day* has been succeeded by a wave showing a higher and more central nucleus. In passing he gives some new credibility to the slightly discredited but intuitively appealing notion of 'phonological space'. K. R. Lodge's *Studies in the Phonology of Colloquial English*[32] presents six dialects (five of them urban) in the form of continuous naturally occurring texts in slightly modified I.P.A. transcription. Consonantal aspects of the transcriptions seem to be rather narrower than vocalic ones; a comparison with North's vowel representation is very revealing. Lodge's main interest is in investigating allegro or rapid-speech rules within a generative phonological framework; readers of this chapter are likely to find most interesting his conclusion that such processes are far from universal across the different dialects he investigates. He is somewhat sceptical about the desirability of formulating a unified phonology to underlie the linguistic behaviour of all speakers of some language; a position espoused

32. *Studies in the Phonology of Colloquial English*, by K. R. Lodge. CH. pp. vii + 160. hb £13.95.

more vigorously by John Harris in his paper 'Syntactic Variation and Dialect Divergence' (*JL*; see section 4). Lodge illuminates the phonological side of his findings by showing ways in which the insights of non-linear and especially dependency phonology can improve the statement of his rapid-speech rules.

Raymond Hickey (*Word*) attacks the problem of describing 'Syllable Onsets in Irish English'. He attempts to juggle with the processes of /j/-deletion and assibilation before /j/ on the one hand and the surface phones [ç] and [ʋʋ] on the other in such a way that the latter are analysable as sequences of /h/ and a semivowel. Another paper having goals going beyond mere description is Norio Yamada's 'Characterizing the Great Vowel Shift' (*Lingua*). Using a framework that in the end resembles that of dependency phonology, she explains the Great Vowel Shift as a cluster of linked fortitions. The system emerging at the end is one said to be characterized by increased articulatory and perceptual clarity. Donna M. Farina's 'The Morphological Rule of Learned Backing and Lexical Phonology' (*SLSc*) is, as the title implies, an attempt to clarify where the morphological subregularity named can be made to fit into the rule battery of a current lexicalist model. In *JPhon* Jerzy Rubach writes on 'Segmental Rules of English and Cyclic Phonology', in which he re-analyses some of the 'phonological rules' familiar from *The Sound Pattern of English* (cf. *YW* 50.52) into cyclic and post-cyclic ones, these terms being understood in terms of word-formational cycles *à la* Lexical Phonology. His analysis uses abstract representations; indeed he is one of the leading crusaders for the cause of such analyses. He re-interprets some alleged intermediate stages in the derivation of (e.g.) velar-softening forms in the light of his theoretical assumptions.

Die englische Sprache in den USA[33] is the first part of a study of American English and the variation in it. It covers phonology, and Part 2 will cover grammar and vocabulary. The work turns aside from the techniques of mainstream structural linguistics in favour of the Laborian methodology of seeking structure within phonological variation. The problems of definition of standard pronunciation and norms in both British and American English are addressed and the variations discernible in one speaker of standard American English analysed. Here and in the subsequent chapters the results are related, with extensive examples, to non-linguistic categories of region, age, ethnic origin, class, and status. The study concludes with a theoretical consideration of the notion of variation. Each chapter ends with a number of exercises for student use and a tape recording of the examples of speech usage is also available. [M.H.]

Leigh Lisker and Thomas Baer give a detailed phonetic analysis of the problem of 'Laryngeal Management at Utterance-internal Word-boundaries in American English' (*L&S*). They identify at least five different relationships between what is going on in the larynx and what is going on at the lips, thereby demonstrating that there are tensions between the articulatory and the conventional phonological descriptions of the supposedly homogeneous voiced/voiceless distinction in English. Lisker also has a letter to the editor of *L&S* properly protesting that aspiration should not be analysed, as it often is, as a feature whose value depends on that of voicing, but rather the reverse. Thomas Walsh argues, in 'Modelling Temporal Relations within English

---

33. *Die englische Sprache in den USA: Variation und Struktur*, Teil 1, by Ursula Domen. Niemeyer (1982). pp. x + 182. pb DM 24.

Syllables' (*JPhon*), that a given speaker maintains a fixed ratio between the duration of the CV- and the -C in a given CVC syllable, which has interesting ramifications for the conventional division of syllables into onset and coda. A further ostensibly phonetic paper is that by Raymond Hickey in *JL*, 'Coronal Segments in Irish English'. He presents and interprets phonologically data from that dialect and then uses it to argue that the Chomsky–Halle feature system is incapable in its classical form of handling (especially) certain morphophonemic relations. He argues further, with data from Irish, that phonetic features can, language-specifically, be associated with different levels of linguistic organization.

This has been a stressful year. In fact there are two whole new books on *English Word Stress*, by Ivan Poldauf[34] and Erik C. Fudge[35], and that is indeed the title of both, give or take a hyphen. We also have an article by B. O. Baptista entitled 'English Stress Rules and Native Speakers' (*L&S*). Poldauf's book, edited by William R. Lee, gives an essentially morphological/lexical account of stress placement, distinguishing under other labels the now-familiar stress-neutral and stress-affecting affixes. There is a great deal of prominence given to the diachronic origins of the words in question, which means that the book is of most use either to a cosmopolitan learner of English with a large encyclopaedic knowledge or to a linguist not very interested in the synchronic theory of the lexicon. Either way one could have hoped for something more interesting from Pergamon than this. It turns out as a catalogue of more or less minute lexical subcategories, many beset with exceptions. The only authority with a cited publication since 1979 is L. Guierre, which is regrettable in view of the very large relevant literature on metrical and lexical phonology published since then. Poldauf agrees with Guierre, though, on the importance of spelling in stress placement, and this is a welcome development. Guierre is also implicated in Baptista's work; here we are shown that Guierre's morpheme-based stress rules are a better predictor of English native speakers' behaviour with nonsense words having English phonotactic characteristics than the rules given in Chomsky and Halle's *The Sound Pattern of English* (cf. *YW* 50.52). It is doubtful whether this conclusion will surprise anybody.

Fudge's book also is short on recent developments in the field, but he has set himself the much more modest, albeit very difficult, goal of converting abstract principles of stress placement into a usable tool for learners of English. I shall therefore treat it as a textbook. As such it is clearly written – a great deal more intelligible than Poldauf's – and it helpfully includes both exercises and comparisons of the predictions of his stress-rules with actual pronunciations. In both books there are pronunciations recorded which had me reaching for a reputable dictionary (I won against Poldauf, Fudge won against me), and some minor points which seemed to me to represent self-inflicted difficulties; but this review is not the place for such minutiae. Both books make concessions to varieties of English spoken outside England. Poldauf's is fuller on the stressing of compounds than Fudge's.

By far the most massive contribution to the study of English suprasegmentals is Elisabeth O. Selkirk's *Phonology and Syntax: The Relation between*

34. *English Word Stress*, by Ivan Poldauf, ed. by William R. Lee. Pergamon Institute of English. pp. ix + 169. pb £15.95.
35. *English Word-Stress*, by Erik C. Fudge. A&U. pp. xiii + 240. hb £15, pb £7.50.

Sound and Structure[36]. It is a theoretical work from the MIT school of linguistics, and therefore almost exclusively dependent upon English, despite the title. It presents a novel way of solving the problem of how to arrive at a statement of the stress contours of English sentences from the syntactic surface structures output from the higher reaches of the grammar. Selkirk proposes the intermediaryship of what we might call an intonational subcomponent, which provides (i) stresses for the appropriate syntactic elements, (ii) analyses of surface structures, augmented with information about certain aspects of informational structure in terms of 'breath groups' (her term is 'intonational phrases'), and (iii) melodic contours. The important departure from 'classical' MIT positions is the idea that surface structure does not fully determine the accentual or tonal characteristics of utterances. To the amusement of this writer, some works dating from the 1960s by Michael Halliday are cited in defence of this view. Also novel is the view that intonation determines certain aspects of stress and rhythm. Much of the book is devoted to the defence of particular positions within current metrical theory; an indicative one is the rejection of Liberman and Prince's view of the so-called Rhythm Rule (alias Stress Retraction) as an operation on metrical trees in favour of a more generally stated rule of Beat Movement defined on the notion of prominence expressed in terms of the metrical grid. Selkirk also proposes a theory of English word-stress that I have not felt able to compare with those of Poldauf and Fudge discussed above. The essential proposal revolves around the notion that so-called stress-neutral affixes have a syntactic characterization different from that of other affixes, and that these others alone may be incorporated into the 'root', which is the domain over which word-stress rules operate. Bruce Hayes, in 'The Phonology of Rhythm in English' (*LingI*), gives an essentially theoretical account, using English as a model, of the nature of rhythm. His theory eliminates the familiar 'stress clash' as a motivation for the so-called 'rhythm rule' of stress retraction, and steers a middle way in current metrical theory by retaining both the tree and the grid, the former to handle linguistic stress and the latter to handle rhythmic structure. His appendix on 'eurhythmic principles' brings him up against one of those controversies that will not go away: that concerning the alleged tendency of English to stress-isochrony. He believes his model will account for it.

In the domain of intonation, in 'A Semantico-Pragmatic Analysis of Fall–Rise Intonation' (*PRMCLS*), Julia Hirschberg and Gregory Ward attempt to revivify and make more precise the claim, challenged in recent work by Robert Ladd, that the English fall–rise intonation has an essentially attitudinal meaning and as such makes an independent pragmatic contribution to utterances.

Phonological papers on the older phases of English are this year more or less confined to the conference proceedings mentioned in the introduction. Roger Lass has one of his usual perceptive critiques of current theory in 'Reflections on Rule Loss' (*EHL*[1]). He uses data largely from OE to show that rule loss (as conceived in the generative phonological paradigm current in 1979) is not a consequence of any straightforward functional principle like non-learnability, unnaturalness, or opacity of environment. In other papers in OE it is vowels which dominate the field. Lisbeth Strøjer argues, also in *EHL*, that OE

36. *Phonology and Syntax: The Relation between Sound and Structure*, by Elisabeth O. Selkirk. MITP. pp. xvi + 476. hb £33.25.

breaking is, like retraction of /æ:/ and back-mutation, a response to an auditory feature [grave] represented in the adjacent phonetic environment. She feels that it is unlikely that the latter two changes were auditorily based assimilatory ones, as previously argued by N. Davidsen-Nielsen and H. Ørum, while breaking had a straightforward articulatory basis. 'Old English ⟨ie⟩ and its phonetic identification' is the theme of Suksan Kim's contribution to *EHL*[1]; his arguments are much too complex to summarize here, but the upshot is that short ⟨ie⟩ resulting from palatal diphthongization or *i*-mutation or occurring before certain clusters with *r* as the first member is to be interpreted as [I], while those short ⟨ie⟩ due to palatal umlaut or failure of back umlaut, as well as some instances of reverse spelling, are [i]. Seiichi Suzuki offers 'A New Interpretation of the Development of Pre-OE *eaC$_0$ {¦} in Non-West Saxon' (*FLH*). For Suzuki, the traditional view of this as a one-stage operation forming part of *i*-mutation is incorrect. Rather, the *i*-mutation of *ea* applies to the product of a monophthongization which was also implicated in Anglian Smoothing of short vowels and 'failure of Breaking'. The fact that the *i*-mutation of *ea* also turns up as a mid vowel is accounted for by observing that *ǣ* was impervious to *i*-mutation but could have been raised by the process which attacked the Anglian reflex of Gmc *ǣ*. Suzuki finds confirmation of his views in certain forms in the Moore manuscript of Bede. Richard Coates settles 'On an Early Date for Old English *i*-Mutation' (*LSSME*[2]). He attempts to show that a category of traditional exceptions to *i*-mutation, including certain place-names, can be laid aside on the historically justifiable assumption that they are not formations of the first settlement period, and that their formation must post-date *i*-mutation, which must thus be relatively early. His view returns to that of Karl Luick, expressed over sixty years ago. In a paper 'Old English short vowels before nasals' (*EHL*[1]) Niels Davidsen-Nielsen interprets graphic alternations of vowel letters before nasals as representing phonological neutralizations, and attributes this state of affairs to a controversial scenario whereby nasals tend to raise adjacent vowels, one simple consequence of which could be the neutralization of contrasts. Nasals are, of course, usually held to lower vowels. Patrick Stiles, in 'The Attestation of Early Old English *wudu* "Wood"' (*NM*, 1983), shows that so-called combinative back-mutation in Northumbrian is found independently of and prior to ordinary back-mutation (though only in the word *wudu*). That the changes appear to be contemporaneous in Mercian entails a dialect difference in their relative chronology. Angelika Lutz, in a paper from the Ghent conference of Anglo-Saxonists reported in *OENews* and printed as 'Spellings of the *waldend* Group – Again' in *ASE*, uses the variation *waldend/wealdend* in West Saxon texts to argue that traditions of prose and poetic speech co-existed in the OE period.

The only paper noted on OE consonants is 'Remarks on Assimilation in Old English' (*FLH*) by Raymond Hickey. He endeavours to give a characterization of the regularity or otherwise of these processes in OE and to establish whether the form which they eventually take falls out naturally from any overriding principles of OE phonology. He demonstrates that they do given his own particular characterization of suitable strength and resonance hierarchies for English. Some constraints on the processes flow from morphological considerations such as the maintenance of inflectional transparency.

Three papers on the phonology of Early ME are to be noted. Donka

Minkova pursues reasons for 'Early Middle English Metric Elision and Schwa Deletion' in *EHL*[1]. She sees such elisions – in natural speech as well as in metrical writing – as partly accounting for eventual shwa-loss in ME, in addition to the panoply of other factors appealed to by ME scholars. They follow from general principles of rhythmic organization: elisions are most likely in hiatus and as a precondition for cliticization. Minkova is scathing about Luick's earlier attempt to account for such elisions in terms of speech tempo acceleration. Also in this collection is Veronika Kniezsa's 'On the Phonology of Compounded Words from Late Old English to Early Middle English'; the author takes the data of the *Peterborough Chronicle* and establishes a typology of juncture features in compounds. Her conclusion relates the developments at this period to those which have produced present-day obscured compounds in English. Gillis Kristensson[37] argues that ME /ø/ and /ø:/ did not persist in their rounded state in the west Midlands as long as their high counterparts.

In 'On Late Middle English Word Stress' (also *EHL*[1]) Toshio Nakao gives rather good phonological arguments for double stressing of Romance end-stressed borrowings. He proceeds to argue for a difference of degree in these stresses, with final stressed syllables being less heavily stressed than prefinal ones, and concludes by arguing that his analysis does not require the *ad hoc* assumptions about the placement of morpheme boundaries necessary to *The Sound Pattern of English* in order to sustain its cyclic stress allocation rules. He then has an inconclusive rider about the reasons for stress change.

We followed the custom in *YW* 64 that orthographical matters should be treated in this section. The only papers outside published conference proceedings noted this year are by R. I. Page, who in *MA* offers a new system for 'The Transliteration of English Runes' which is closer than Bruce Dickins's conventions are to the practices used for Scandinavian runes; and by Thomas Cable, who argues that punctuation in OE manuscripts can be used in conjunction with intonation patterns inferred from metre to reconstruct the musical settings of certain texts (paper delivered to the First International Conference of the Society of Anglo-Saxonists, reported and abstracted in *OENews*). N. E. Osselton, in 'Informal Spelling Systems in Early Modern English 1500–1800' (*EHL*[1]), starts from the observation that even Johnson observed public and private spelling 'norms' and goes on to chart the nature of private spelling systems in use in the period in question, concluding that the apparent chaos in such systems may be reducible to some kind of order by taking into account the acknowledged existence of different standards, the register in which particular spellings are recorded (and therefore implicit sociolinguistic variable rules), and a general time-lag in the introduction of printers' forms into the domain of private writing. A paper by S. Levin on punctuation is noted in section 3, for reasons which will be evident on cross-referring. On a practical level, Marcy S. Powell offers advice on good orthographic practice in relation to 'Word Division' (*ES*), the target being writers and printers of reports and papers.

---

37. *Historical and Editorial Studies in Medieval and Early Modern English for Johan Gerritsen*, ed. by Mary-Jo Arn and Hanneke Wirtjes, with Hans Jansen. Wo&No. pp. 229. DGlds 60,00.

6. Morphology

In comparison with the very extensive studies reported last year (*YW* 64), the products of this year on morphology are very limited, and show a morbid preoccupation with the bizarre and abnormal, which tends to make them more entertaining than usual. The only general work on English morphology noted is one missed in 1982, namely Steven L. Strauss's *Lexicalist Phonology of English and German*[38], which is as the title implies a comparative study of word-formational regularities in the light of the new generative theory of Lexical Phonology. The most salient characteristic of this new approach is to see what have in the generative tradition been called 'phonological rules' as functions of word-constructing operations, i.e. the application of such rules is restricted to particular levels defined by processes of (largely) affixation. Strauss reviews the earlier theories in the field, and in his sections 3.1 and 4.2 applies the new theory to the description of English. The exceptions which are acknowledged still lead me to question whether sufficient prominence has been given to the role of the idiosyncratic in the lexicon and to wonder what reality a theoretically parsimonious lexicon corresponds to. A further, purely theoretical, work from the same stable is Sergio Scalise's *Generative Morphology*[39], in which Scalise tries to unify the various strands of generative thinking on morphology into a single cogent whole and to chart the rise of morphology as a central concern in theoretical grammar. Several issues with which he deals are also covered by Strauss, e.g. the so-called 'level-ordering' of rules. Unfortunately, Alfred Bammesberger's *A Sketch of Diachronic English Morphology*[40] has not been seen.

Now to the papers promised at the beginning of this section, in several of which we can see the idiosyncratic acting in all its garish glory. In a paper which is actually a piece of Germanistik, but highly relevant for OE 'OE *sind(on)*: Its Germanic and Indo-European Origins' (*AmB*), Kenneth Shields argues that *sind(on)* is a form showing a binary history of person/number marking. It represents a **sinði* > **sind* with the hypercharacteristic addition of the **-un* suffix, the secondary third person plural suffix, as a consequence of there being no overt person/number marking on **sind*. The only other paper specifically on historical morphology is Juliette De Caluwé-Dor's 'Chaucer's Derivational Morphemes Revisited' (*LSSME*[2]), where she lists a whole battery of such things as part of her ongoing study of borrowings in Chaucer.

On the boundaries between morphology and syntax, H. F. W. Stahlke investigates 'Independent and Clitic Pronouns in English' (*PRMCLS*). He finds that the choice among variant forms of personal pronouns is governed by their discourse functions and not by their sentence-syntactic functions; he isolates independent, subject-focus, subject-topic clitic and object-given clitic paradigms. We can agree that the traditional case analysis is inappropriate for present-day English without going all the way with him. Gina Richardson asks 'Can *y'all* Function as a Singular Pronoun in Southern Dialect?' (*AS*) and answers with a resounding 'No', explaining away apparent cases of such a

38. *Lexicalist Phonology of English and German*, by Steven L. Strauss. PiLS 9. Foris (1982). pp. 180. hb Fl 64, pb Fl 44.
39. *Generative Morphology*, by Sergio Scalise. SiGG 18. Foris. pp. x + 237. pb.
40. *A Sketch of Diachronic English Morphology*, by Alfred Bammesberger. Eichstätter Materialien 7, Abteilung Sprache und Literatur. Pustet. pp. 94. DM 19.80.

function as due to hypercorrection or other entertaining deviances of usage. Garland Cannon pillages American desk dictionaries to find 544 words of Japanese origin, largely unfamiliar to me, and reports, in *AS*, that 'Zero Plurals among the Japanese Loanwords in English' are a stable phenomenon. Also in *AS*, Walt Wolfram examines the usage of English tense markers among American Indians. He claims, *inter* a lot of *alia*, that usage of marked and unmarked tense forms in relation to past time has been re-interpreted as expressing non-habituality and habituality, respectively ('Unmarked Tense in American Indian English'). Also on a matter of tense, Erik Jørgensen answers his own question ('Ought: Present or Past Tense?' (*ES*)) by supporting Zandvoort's analysis of the form mentioned as a modal preterite (i.e. not a present tense form; see below, p. 58).

Göran Kjellmer asks 'Why *great*:*greatly* but Not *big*:**bigly*? On the Formation of English Adverbs in *-ly*' (*SL*). His conclusion from a modest testing of corpus material is that the crucial factor is dynamicness and that most adjectives which can form *-ly* adverbs are either inherently dynamic or are basically stative but co-occur characteristically with dynamic nouns or clauses. Wim Zonneveld returns to the matter of the quasi-morphological process commonly referred to in the technical literature on the matter (available under plain wraps in the Tottenham Court Road) by the delicate name of *fucking*-insertion. In 'Expletive Insertion in English' (*LA*) he tidies up the typologically peculiar properties of this construction by arguing that it is extragrammatical, a language game, and not a morphological process at all. He compares it with 'middle-name' usage of the *Nat 'King' Cole* type.

A paper of greater importance than it might appear at first sight is Sterling Eisiminger and John L. Idol Jr's 'The Origin of Brand Names' in *AS*. They study popular etymologies for brand names, the importance of which lies in providing direct evidence for the kind of untrained etymologizing that people do, and hence, I submit, evidence for what they do in relation to morphology in general, i.e. for the kind of morphological theories they are capable of constructing. 'Among the New Words' in *AS*, Mary Gray Porter and I. Willis Russell include analyses of new forms in (among other elements) *-gate*, *-speak*, *Euro-* and *Cabbage* (as in *Patch Kid*).

7. Syntax

The full crop in 1983 and the major works already visible in 1985's harvest make 1984 look rather a lean year, although there is still in truth a quite substantial list of publications in this long-standing boom area. I keep the rough chronological arrangement used in *YW* 64.

(a) Old English

Much of this year's historical syntax appears in a collection of that title[41], cited hereafter as *HistSynt*, including three papers on word-order change. Marinel Gerritsen's is called 'Divergent Word Order Developments in Germanic Languages: A Description and a Tentative Explanation'. She suggests that embraciation (= verb-final) was lost in English because of an alleged late

---

41. *Historical Syntax*, ed. by Jacek Fisiak. Trends in Linguistics Studies and Monographs 23. Mouton. pp. xii + 636. DM 198.

development of periphrastic verb forms, and she hypothesizes that loss of inversion (= verb-second) is due either to creolization or to direct French influence in ME. Robert P. Stockwell's speculations 'On the History of the Verb-Second Rule in English' are characteristically crisp and stimulating. He finds some modern inversion types to be retained from OE, others to be innovations, and he supports the now-common claim that progressive, passive, and equational BE are the same verb, their predicates forming a separate constituent. Theo Vennemann's piece, whose title begins 'Verb-Second, Verb Late, and the Brace Construction', is clear, plausible, but not specifically or extensively on English. A more technical piece of Chomskian linguistics is Ans van Kemenade's 'Verb Second and Clitics in Old English'[42], which argues that OE – treated as a single *état de langue* (cf. *YW* 64.52) – is a verb-second language for main clauses, a position that can be strengthened by analysing personal pronouns as clitics.

Leena Kahlas-Tarkka focuses 'On the Syntactic Types "Every Man" and "Each of Men" in Old English'[43], rather than on the lexical items themselves, though there is inevitably some overlap with her earlier article (*YW* 64.63). Four more pieces from the same conference proceedings are mentioned below, and there are a further twenty or so short items on linguistic themes.

In 'The Origin of Old English Conjunctions: Some Problems' (*HistSynt*[41]), Bruce Mitchell argues, as often in rebuttal of another scholar (this time D. Carkeet, *YW* 57.16), that the majority of OE conjunctions do indeed derive from adverbs. Michiko Ogura discusses seven 'OE Temporal Conjunctions Denoting "When" or "While": With Special Regard to the Gospels and the Psalter' (*NM*). There is considerable semantic overlap, it seems, but there appear to be syntactic, stylistic, and dialectal differences, established mainly by comparison with Latin originals and presented diligently with the aid of tables. Possible forerunners of PE [Present-day English] sentence adverbs are Toril Swan's main quarry in 'Adverbial Usage in Ælfric's *Lives of Saints*' (*Nordlyd*). Thankfully she can't find many types in OE, though certain PE types show up in full or at least in apparent embryo. Based on the same text is another in the series of pieces by Ruth Waterhouse, 'Sentence Determination in Ælfric's *Lives of Saints*' (*NM*). A problem familiar to translators of medieval texts is how best to represent the original, given the rigid sentence boundaries of written ModE. Ruth Waterhouse identifies Ælfric's sentences by punctuation and capitalization in the manuscripts, by consistent correlation between sentence-opening and beginning of 'verse' line (cf. here *Beowulf*, for example), and by the use of *hwæt þa* and other overt markers, especially plain *þa*; much of this interesting paper is devoted to correlative and independent use of *þa*.

In *FLH* Leiv Egil Breivik has 'The Diachrony of Introductory *there*: A Rejoinder' (to D. Nagashima, cf. *YW* 53.44), a minor reworking of one section of his monumental book, on which see *YW* 64.55–6. Raymond Hickey presents 'A Valency Framework for the Old English Verb' (*HistSynt*[41]), without any new facts or generalizations to justify the elaborate notation.

42. *Linguistics in the Netherlands 1984*, ed. by Hans Bennis and W. U. S. van Lessen Koeke. PiLS 17. Foris. pp. 205. pb F1 32.50.

43. *Proceedings from the Second Nordic Conference for English Studies: Hanasaari/ Hanaholmen, 19–21 May, 1983*, ed. by Håkan Ringbom and Matti Rissanen. PRIAA 92. Åbo. pp. vii + 611. pb.

(b) Middle English

Cynthia L. Allen is also concerned to promote a particular linguistic framework, in her case Lexical Functional Grammar, but she has important things to say 'On the Dating of Raised Empty Subjects in English' (*LingI*), as in *to think it less to be lamented*, with salutary warnings of the dangers of reliance on Visser, plus useful data of her own. A paper by Sandor Rot (*EHL*[1]) is both more vague and decidedly more opaque. It is a general report on research, especially on Aktionsart/aspect matters in OE and ME. One could be forgiven for failing to spot its relation to its title, 'Inherent Variability and Linguistic Interference of Anglo-Old Scandinavian and Anglo-Norman French Language Contacts in the Formation of Grammatical Innovations in Late Old English and Middle English'. I did not spot a word of French in it.

John M. Anderson writes a demanding piece on 'The Natural History of Dative Sentences', also in *EHL*[1], treating the notion of subject-formation mainly in case grammar terms, while Ariane von Seefranz-Montag writes on '"Subjectless" Constructions and Syntactic Change' (*HistSynt*[41]). This is in effect a précis of her book[44], which came to my attention too late for *YW* 64. Her discussion of English impersonals is not convincing by comparison with the analysis given by Fischer and van der Leek (*YW* 64.54): it takes the Jespersen–Lightfoot account – already dubious, at least for the RUE verbs – and imposes a typological explanation on the data.

In 'Predicative Complements and Predicative Attributes: A Note on Middle English Usage in Coordinate Structures' (*NM*) Urban Ohlander returns to the subject matter of a book he published nearly fifty years ago. Here we have detailed analysis of a number of examples, without any overall direction except to demonstrate syntactic freedom and indeterminacy. Lilo Moessner takes a meandering path through 'Some English Relative Constructions' (*Linguistique*), citing texts from OE to Katherine Mansfield, but especially early ME, picking complex or ambiguous types, and scattering some sensible structural analyses in passing. F. N. M. Diekstra contributes a careful, traditional analysis of 'Ambiguous *That*-Clauses in Old and Middle English' (*ES*), namely those lumped together by Mustanoja and others as *that . . . he* = 'who'. Diekstra claims that not all are the same, and that sometimes *that* is a conjunction and not a pronoun (a recurrent Dutch concern?). Ruta Nagucka conducts some tame 'Explorations into Syntactic Obsoleteness: English *a-X-ing and X-ing*' (*HistSynt*[41]), trying to prove that the middle voice (*Supper is cooking*, etc.) derives historically from a type *Supper is a-cooking*.

(c) Modern English

Once again relative clause formation makes a big showing ('Visiting relatives can be a nuisance'? – not always). The most important and general article is Suzanne Romaine's essay 'Towards a Typology of Relative-Clause Formation Strategies in Germanic' (*HistSynt*[41]), in which the 'mixed' English strategy for relativization (namely invariant relativizing particle versus use of interrogative pronouns) is put in a wider Germanic and perhaps general typological perspective. 'Some Historical and Social Dimensions of Syntactic

44. *Syntaktische Funktionen und Wortstellungveränderung: Die Entwicklung 'subjektloser' Konstruktionen in einigen Sprachen*, by Ariane von Seefranz-Montag. Fink (1983). pp. 288. pb DM 40.

Change in Middle Scots Relative Clauses' (*EHL*[1]), by the same author, is an early piece by the same author on such matters as stylistic variation, the Case Hierarchy, and long-term competition between the strategies mentioned just above, now mostly rehashed in her book-length study (*YW* 63.35). Xavier Dekeyser's 'Relativizers in Early Modern English: A Dynamic Quantitative Study' (*HistSynt*[41]) presents simple statistics to document the rise of the zero relative and the development of constraints on *who*(*m*), *which*, and *that*, while Matti Rissanen, in 'The Choice of Relative Pronouns in 17th Century American English', also in *HistSynt*[41], claims that the spread of *wh*-forms can be related to the degree of looseness of link between antecedent and relative clause.

Still in the same collection but moving on a century we find Mats Rydén calling for more attention to be paid to 'The Study of Eighteenth Century English Syntax', with useful references to existing work that supplement those in his 1979 book (*YW* 60.33). Frances Austin arranges some examples from the Clift family correspondence with comments by contemporary grammarians for 'Double Negatives and the Eighteenth Century' (*EHL*[1]), filling a gap in Jespersen's collections of sentence element double negation.

There are a handful more historical items to consider. Johan van der Auwera offers 'More on the History of Subject Contact Clauses in English' (*FLH*), a survey of different accounts of the changing frequencies of contact clauses with zero subject. That such clauses are now colloquial he puts down to the colloquiality of focus constructions which allow them and that the colloquial register has been least affected by the growing requirement for overt subjects. Xavier Dekeyser's 'Diachronic Dimensions of Subject and Object Complement Clauses' (*EHL*[1]) suffers perhaps from the time-lag in publication. The data come from Visser, the ModE analysis NP → (Det) N (S) from Peter S. Rosenbaum, and the finding is that the rules remain constant over time but that obligatoriness varies. Richard C. DeArmond's piece in the same collection, 'On the Development of the Verb Phrase Node in English Syntax', seems even more to be a contribution to an outdated theory rather than to the history of English (OE doesn't have a VP node, ModE does). The history of DO for one thing is somewhat garbled. In 'Is the Passive Really Passive?' (*EHL*[1] yet again) Graham Nixon attempts to do away with voice as a systemic choice by viewing passive participles as deverbal adjectives. On the way there is an alarming misuse of conventional terminology (e.g. 'phrasal-prepositional verb') in a discussion of re-analysis of group-verbs. David Denison's 'On *Get it over with*' (*Neophil*) is both a case history of syntactic blending and a sigh of relief at the completion of a thesis on group-verbs. 'Syntactic Reconstruction' (*HistSynt*[41]) by Herbert Pilch is a bland and unhelpful assertion that all syntactic change is easy to describe in terms of productivity, shrinkage, contraction, and restructuring of syntactic systems. He certainly oversimplifies one concrete example, the English medio-passive so elaborately worried over by Ruta Nagucka in the preceding contribution (see above, p. 48).

(d) Present-day English and Linguistic Theory
    Firstly, a *pot-pourri* mainly on the NP. Ruth Seppänen and Aimo Seppänen discuss '*Two Dozen, Several Hundred*: An English Construction and its Non-English Parallels' (*ZPSK*). The claim is made that the *dozen*-word is plural in Germanic languages and singular in Finnic, and the real point of the article is a

Swedish dialect which follows the Finnic pattern in these constructions. There is good discussion of the English facts, including a brief historical synopsis. Erik Jørgensen 'explains' patterns like *the parents of them*, *the thinness of her*, as having strong emotional overtones lacking in the unmarked *their parents*, *her thinness*, and so on in ' "*Of* + Personal Pronoun" Used as Possessive and Subjective Genitives about Persons' (*ES*).

Several items address the question of reflexives, on the borders of syntax and semantics. Bengt Jacobsson's 'Simple Personal Pronouns and Compound Pronouns in *Self/Selves*' (*SN*) is a critical review of attempts (mostly) since his 1968 article in *MSpr* to account for the choice of pronoun in, e.g. *He took it upon him(self) to* . . . Jacobsson effectively acknowledges a nugget of truth in all the approaches reviewed but finds each one inadequate or incomplete. 'On Reflexivity' (*ZAA*) by L. M. Kovalyova concerns the semantics especially of personal reflexives and shows – not surprisingly – that referential identity between antecedent and anaphor is often incomplete; this point reappears in Paul Werth's book, noted below, p. 52. I have been unable to see Piotr Ruszkiewicz's book on reflexives[45]. 'Points of Modern English Syntax LXVI' (*ES*), the first contribution to the series by H. Chr. Wekker, addresses the old problems of the 'wrong' use of subjective and objective personal pronouns, journalistic omission of determiners, and the choice of predicative *of stone* as against just *stone*. Graham Shorrocks merely lists some examples of resumptive and other 'otiose' pronouns in 'The Syntax of the Dependent Pronoun in the Dialect of Farnworth and District (Greater Manchester County, formerly Lancashire)' (*TYDS*).

Krista Varantola's dissertation *On Noun Phrase Structures in Engineering English*[46] examines a variety of English which is generally thought to be distinguished by its high information content, particularly in the NP. She subjects two journalistic corpora of modest size (one on engineering, one more general) to an extensive and careful computer analysis at syntactic and textual levels. The results are probably of greatest interest for the teaching of English. 'An Aspect of Term-Formation in Engineering English' which she considers in a separate article is the before-the-noun chain compound[43]. I have not seen Rosemary Leonard's description of a computer program for interpreting noun phrases which lack explicit internal structure[47].

Jacqueline Guéron and Robert May discuss 'Extraposition and Logical Form' (*LingI*), a Government-Binding account of sentences like *Too many books have been published recently for me to be able to read them all*. (The example is theirs.) Edwin Williams returns to the problem of '*There*-Insertion' (*LingI*) in a clearly set-out transformational account, very much dealing with sentences in isolation (cf. Breivik, *YW* 64.56), in which he argues that *there* is a scope marker and that both *there* and post-copular material are NPs. He does at least mention focusing.

The whole business of focusing on particular constituents has become a major research topic, and I count some half-dozen items which are explicitly

45. *Aspects of Reflexivization in English*, by Piotr Ruszkiewicz. Prace Naukowe Uniwersytetu Śląskiego w Katowicach 637. Uniw. Śląski, Katowice. pp. 133. pb zł 107.

46. *On Noun Phrase Structures in Engineering English*, by Krista Varantola. Annales Universitatis Turkuensis, ser. B, 168. TurkuU. pp. 252. pb.

47. *The Interpretation of English Noun Sequences on the Computer*, by Rosemary Leonard. N-H Linguistic Series 51. N-H. pp. xii + 436. hb Fl 150.

on topicalization and kindred processes. Alice Davison's 'Syntactic Markedness and the Definition of Sentence Topic' (*Lg*) is an important theoretical discussion, based largely on English data. John Oakeshott-Taylor writes 'On the Location of "Tonic Prominence" in English' (*LingB*), not making any grand claims but providing a useful review of different approaches: syntactic, given/new, contrastive, identification (*THAT's the one to buy*), topicalization, default, and affective (= emphatic). Pertti S. Hietaranta, in 'A Functional Note on Topicalization' (*ES*), points out that it is 'not exclusively or even primarily' a contrastive or affective device in *Excellent food they have here*, but that both properties may follow from the role of topicalization as a textual linking device. 'Some Functional Aspects of the *Tough* Construction' (*SN*) by the same author consists of obvious comments to the effect that the choice of the construction *That man is impossible to understand* can involve topicalization or structural symmetry (it creates an adjective phrase), both of which can be cohesive devices. There is a nice paper by Gregory L. Ward called 'A Pragmatic Analysis of Epitomization: Topicalization It's Not' (*PIL*), on what I take to be an American locution, which Ward claims to be distinct both from topicalization and from the delightfully named 'Yiddish-Movement'.

From here we can move to cleft sentences. Renaat Declerck has much more to say on a fairly infrequent version of the construction in 'Some Restrictions on Clefts that Highlight Predicate Nominals' (*JL*), in addition to his justifiably long survey of 'The Pragmatics of *it*-Clefts and *wh*-Clefts' (*Lingua*). All this material (cf. *YW* 64.59) should be edited into a single book. The title of B. Brömser's piece, 'Towards a Functional Description of Cleft Constructions' (*Lingua*), is a fair one, this being an interesting discussion using Functional Sentence Perspective as its guiding principle. What I find in Göran Kjellmer's piece 'On the Grammatical Number of Relative *What*' (*ES*) is a long preamble, data from the Brown and LOB corpora, a simple questionnaire given to eight informants, but not enough crispness. Kjellmer finds slight evidence of a trend to use the singular. A squib in *LingI* by Randall B. Sparks is called 'Here's a Few More Facts' and lists some factors which permit singular *is* to be used with a plural subject.

Now a group of studies on complex sentences of various kinds. Y. G. Birenbaum's 'Complex Sentences of Comparison' (*PP*) is itself complex in its terminology and its diagrams (two of them three-dimensional), but then structures of comparison can vary enormously in what is compared and how (e.g. *Mrs Tracy's grief was greater than she could bear*). The random-looking corpus, never described, is certainly a fault. Bengt Altenberg takes a very wide field in 'Causal Linking in Spoken and Written English' (*SL*), using the London–Lund and LOB corpora for British spoken and written material, respectively. There are lots of data and tables to cover the wide variety of linguistic devices involved. One of the simplest and most striking conclusions is that in both speech and writing, the result clause more often precedes than follows the cause. *Conjunction-Headed Abbreviated Clauses*[48], that is non-finite or verbless ones, are studied in three major corpora and especially the Brown corpus by Ingegerd Bäcklund. The efficient survey of their properties is purely descriptive apart from a brief essay into Functional Sentence Perspec-

---

48. *Conjunction-Headed Abbreviated Clauses in English*, by Ingegerd Bäcklund. AUUp, SAU 50. A&W. pp. 197. Skr 120.

tive. While both written corpora show fifty-six per cent of eligible clauses abbreviated, the spoken material has just fifteen per cent; within temporal clauses the ratio is fifty-three or fifty per cent to eight per cent. Johan Elsness asks '*That* or Zero? A Look at the Choice of Object Clause Connective in a Corpus of American English' (*ES*). This is a statistical computer analysis with unsurprising results. Elsness claims to have evidence that the zero connective marks a closer clause juncture. Certain factors like the complexity of the following NP subject encourage the choice of zero. Peter Freckleton's 'Des "That Clauses" prépositionelles en anglais' (*LingInv*) is a descriptive account, failing to mention Radford, *TPS* 1979, which merely testifies to it that a preposition may be retained before a *that*-clause so long as *it* intervenes. Aimo Seppänen's rejoinder to Hietaranta, 'On an Analysis of the "for-NP-to-V" Structure' (*NM*), has already been mentioned (*YW* 64.59); Seppänen shows that the problem still awaits a solution, which he promises for the near future. He also has a note 'On the Marking of Subordination in English' (*MSpr*), where he examines (in)direct questions in (sub)standard English in order to suggest improvements to Quirk *et al.*'s formulation, namely to add that *whether* is the only interrogative *wh*-element that marks subordination, that *lack* of inversion can be an indicator of subordination (*How the book sells depends on the author*), and that there is no marker of subordination in cases like *He didn't know who had written it*.

Juhani Rudanko's long article 'On Some Contrasts between Infinitival and *That* Complement Clauses in English' (*ES*) gives a partial explanation of differences of meaning and acceptability between, e.g. *claim to be . . .* and *claim that one is . . .*, except that CLAIM is an admitted exception to the rules given. The framework used is standard theory TG.

Auxiliaries get their usual share of attention. Yehuda N. Falk's contribution is 'The English Auxiliary System: A Lexical-Functional Analysis' (*Lg*), in which he proposes that the modal/main verb distinction plus LFG is enough to account for all known properties. Anthony Warner has criticized this approach: more next year. Jonathan Owens has 'A Note on Constraining Syntactic Features' (*Word*), which makes cogent criticisms of G. Gazdar, G. K. Pullum and I. A. Sag's account (*YW* 63.37) on the grounds that the features they use are unconstrained. Owens's preferred analysis is based on Daughter-Dependency Grammar, now disavowed by Hudson – see below – but Owens admits that his coverage of data is incomplete. Paul Schachter has a squib, 'Auxiliary Reduction: An Argument for GPSG' (*LingI*), citing such examples as *What do you think's been happening?*, on which cf. *YW* 64.57. From the same journal we have C. L. Baker's 'Two Observations on British English *Do*', which claims as British such sentences as *I'm not sure that John checked out a book (sic) but he may have done*. The data are similar to those offered by Butters (*YW* 64.57); the argument here is that the BrE DO forms are elliptical.

Samuel Jay Keyser and Thomas Roeper write clearly 'On the Middle and Ergative Constructions in English' (*LingI*), illustrated, respectively, by *Bureaucrats bribe easily* and *The ice melted*. Although their piece is primarily theoretical, they present interesting data, especially on the relation of word-formation to syntax. There is a surprising amount of English data in Edward L. Keenan's 'Semantic Correlates of the Ergative/Absolutive Distinction' (*Lings*), given that it is a cross-linguistic survey.

I haven't noticed so much on discourse this year. The major contribution is Paul Werth's *Focus, Coherence and Emphasis*[49], in which a number of properties, notably anaphora and stress, are discussed in terms of coherence of discourse structure and its mediation by emphasis. There is up-to-date reference to work on text linguistics, psycholinguistics, and hard-line sentential syntax (e.g. Government-Binding theory), and Werth's attempt to give semiformal expression to a common-sense, functionalist view of language use is to be applauded in principle, though it remains somewhat vague in practice. Anna-Brita Stenström's *Questions and Responses*[50] is one of those Scandinavian dissertations on a ModE corpus, here mainly London–Lund. The approach is pragmatic and functional, concerned with question, response, and follow-up as elements of an exchange, and the text is readable. I have not seen Paul Kay's 'The *Kind of/Sort of* Construction', published as a working paper by the Program in Cognitive Science at Berkeley, but the London–Lund corpus is also used by Karin Aijmer for her attack on the same constructions in '"Sort of" and "Kind of" in English Conversation' (*SL*). To quote one of her not deeply theoretical conclusions about *sort of*, 'it makes spoken interaction easier, more pleasant and more efficient'. All this sort of work is reflected in *Corpus Linguistics*[51], a collection of fourteen short papers whose authors include several mentioned above. What comes out very strongly is that computer analysis of English – all the specific examples discussed are ModE – is making particular advances in the study of syntax. An excellent survey and bibliography can be found in 'Computers in English Language Research' (*Language Teaching*) by Geoffrey Leech and Andrew Beale.

Finally, some more general works. Rodney Huddleston's *Introduction to the Grammar of English*[52] uses the term 'introduction' rather modestly. This will surely become one of the standard textbooks, as it is discursive rather than a reference work (cf. Quirk and Greenbaum's *University Grammar*, 1973), and at a more advanced level than Leech, Deuchar, and Hoogenraad (*YW* 64.62). Huddleston justifies his structural, non-transformational analyses with some care, and he maintains a useful distinction between language-particular and general definitions. The care that has gone into this systematic treatment of English grammar comes out in the remarkably small amount of cross-reference which is necessary. Despite a rather similar title, *Introducing English Grammar*[53] by David J. Young is indeed at a very elementary level. Whether David Kilby's *Descriptive Syntax and the English Verb*[54] is a textbook, an exploration of semantic conditions on English verbal syntax, or a methodological critique of theoretical syntacticians remains unclear.

49. *Focus, Coherence and Emphasis*, by Paul Werth. CH. pp. 293. hb £16.95.
50. *Questions and Responses: In English Conversation*, by Anna-Brita Stenström. LundSE 68. Gleerup. pp. viii + 296. pb Skr 124.
51. *Corpus Linguistics: Recent Developments in the Use of Computer Corpora in English Language Research*, ed. by Jan Aarts and Willem Meÿs. Rodopi. pp. ii + 229. pb Fl 50.
52. *Introduction to the Grammar of English*, by Rodney Huddleston. Cambridge Textbooks in Linguistics. CUP. pp. xvi + 483. hb £30, pb £9.95.
53. *Introducing English Grammar*, by David J. Young. Hutchinson. pp. 125. pb £4.95.
54. *Descriptive Syntax and the English Verb*, by David Kilby. CH. pp. 198. hb £15.95, pb £8.95.

Nevertheless, the book poses interesting problems and offers a methodology of sorts. Frank Palmer's well-known little book on *Grammar*[55] is now in a bigger format, with the old chapter on structural linguistics split into 'Morphology' and 'Sentence Structure', the transformational generative material updated, and numerous changes of detail. Richard Hudson's *Word Grammar*[56] cheerfully does away with sacred cows and straw men of all kinds, including constituent structure (except in co-ordination), his own Daughter-Dependency Grammar (see *YW* 57.31–2), and the distinctions between competence and performance, phonology and morphology, linguistics and cognitive structure. This is a plainly written theoretical work which aims to offer a generative syntax and semantics with the word as the largest unit of analysis; compare Werth's book, moving away from the sentence ostensibly in the opposite direction. Hudson's networks of various kinds of association and relation are intuitively appealing, although I wonder how well the many loose ends will resist the unravelling of our sentence-fixated generativists. I find myself much in tune with a writer who can refer to 'the speaker themself'.

8. Vocabulary and Semantics

(a) Old English

The very useful microfiche concordance produced by the Dictionary of Old English team (*YW* 61.35–6) has now been supplemented by one for the high-frequency words[57]. Perhaps I should have noted this research tool in section 7, as its greatest utility will be for syntactic studies. A brief 'Dictionary of Old English: 1983 Progress Report' by Ashley Crandell Amos, the new editor, appears in *OENews*.

Paula Simmonds, in 'Nautical Terms in the Brussels Glossary'[58], gives a transcript of one section of the glossary, a meticulous comparison with, especially, Isidore's *Etymologies*, and a list of corrections for Bosworth–Toller. I note too an edition and discussion by Karl Toth of 'Altenglische Interlinearglossen zu Prospers *Epigrammata* und *Versus ad coniugem*' (*Anglia*). I have not seen Siegfried Wyler's paper on what ought to be an interesting topic, 'Old English Colour Terms and Berlin and Kay's Theory of Basic Colour Terms[59]. Smaller items include two by Phillip Pulsiano: 'A new Anglo-Saxon Gloss in the *Liber Scintillarum*', namely *detestor*: *ascunige*, and 'The Blickling Psalter: *aqua vel is*' (both *N&Q*); Bernhard Diensberg on 'The Etymology of Modern English *Girl*: An Old Problem Reconsidered' (*NM*), supporting a derivation from OE **gyrela/e* (?) 'young of an animal, child' < IE **ĝhr-* 'short, small, slight'; and two onomastic pieces by Gillis Kristensson noted in section 9, p. 60.

55. *Grammar*, by Frank Palmer. Second edn. Penguin. pp. 205. pb £2.95.

56. *Word Grammar*, by Richard Hudson. Blackwell. pp. vi + 267. hb £22.50.

57. *A Microfiche Concordance to Old English: The High Frequency Words*, by Richard L. Venezky and Sharon Butler. PIMS/Brill. pp. 201 + 253 microfiches. Can $150.

58. *Literature and Learning in Medieval and Renaissance England: Essays Presented to Fitzroy Pyle*, ed. by John Scattergood. IAP. pp. 233. hb £17.50.

59. *Modes of Interpretation: Essays Presented to Ernst Leisi on the Occasion of his 65th Birthday*, ed. by Richard J. Watts and Urs Weidmann. Tübinger Beiträge zur Linguistik 260. Narr.

Risto Hiltunen publishes some of his material 'On the Semantics and Lexical Development of the "Phrasal Verb" in Old and Early Middle English'[2] (cf. *YW* 64.53). I have not seen Marie-Line Groussier, 'Le système des prépositions dans la prose en vieil-anglais' (*Bulletin des Anglicistes Médiévistes*), nor articles on modal verbs, UNDERSTAND, and *cwyst þu* in a Japanese *Festschrift*, for details of which see *OENews* 18.2 (1985), 'Old English Bibliography 1984'.

(b) Middle English

The *Middle English Dictionary* enters a new editorship with a *Supplement* to the original *Plan and Bibliography*, and 1984 sees three more parts issued, ending in the middle of *rēd* 'advice'[60]. T. F. Hoad has a somewhat rambling survey of possible Scandinavian and Low German influence, sometimes advocating 'mixed' etymologies, in 'English Etymology: Some Problematic Areas in the History of the Middle English Period' (*TPS*), which emphasizes what is uncertain. It is a kind of interim report on his revision of *ODEE*, in the course of which he laments the lack of consistency among the etymological solutions offered in different supposedly authoritative works. Tim William Machan, '*Forlynen*: A Ghost Word Rematerializes' (*N&Q*), defends *OED* against *MED*'s charge of recording a ghost word in Chaucer's *Boece*.

Two articles are at pains to associate morphosyntactic change in the modals with semantic and functional factors, both of them rather delayed responses to versions of Lightfoot's purely syntactic account (1974 and 1979, see *YW* 60.33 and cf. 64.54). A paper by Louis Goossens in *EHL*[1], 'The Interplay of Syntax and Semantics in the Development of the English Modals', is economically stated and by and large convincing. Frans Plank's semi-review, 'The Modals Story Retold' (*SLang*), makes some similar points (e.g. that dynamic modals have always been syntactically distinguished from deontic/epistemic modals) but has more of them, in greater detail, and within a wider linguistic context. The piece is amusingly sarcastic, overlong, and important.

(c) Modern and Present-day English

There is a little historical material remaining to be discussed. A. M. Simon-Vandenbergen's 'Deontic Possibility: A Diachronic View' (*ES*), using previous articles (*YW* 64.67), advances the claims that MAY has developed from dynamic > subject oriented > neutral oriented > absence of actual prohibitions > permission > deontic, and that the acquisition of a deontic possibility meaning for CAN is due to the facts that CAN is following the same path as MAY and that dynamic MAY is on the decline. Utterly unrelated to this is Mats Rydén's inaugural work in a project on early ModE herbals and floras, *The English Plant Names in The Grete Herball*[61]. There is matter of interest here both in the content, if you like herbals, and in a technical register with such a long history. The book is well provided with lists, frequencies, and provenances. I note too the same author's article on 'The Contextual Significance of Shakespeare's Plant Names' (*SN*).

60. *Middle English Dictionary*, parts *P.8*, *Q*, *R.1* and *Supplement 1* to *Plan and Bibliography* (1984), Editor-in-Chief Robert E. Lewis, Review Editor John Reidy, and five Associate Editors. UMich.

61. *The English Plant Names in The Grete Herball: A Contribution to the Study of English Plant-Name Usage*, by Mats Rydén. Stockholm Studies in English 61. A&W. pp. 110. pb Skr 92.

Also primarily historical is Eric Partridge's *Dictionary of Slang*. Paul Beale's eighth edition[62] preserves the emphases and lightly worn pedantry of earlier editions and enhances the work's usefulness with a single alphabetical listing, more systematic internal arrangement of entries, and of course more recent material. Alfred Bammesberger's *English Etymology*[63] is an introductory textbook which provides scholarly information, rather curtly, for a reader who is not assumed to be familiar with linguistics or with the history of English. Although I am unsure just who would use the whole book in an academic context, scholars and students may find individual portions useful for their summaries of phonology, morphology, or lexical history, for Bammesberger's critical reviews of existing etymological dictionaries, or for the thirty specimen entries of his own. Christian J. Kay reports on 'The Historical Thesaurus of English'[22]. Bennett A. Brockman's 'O.E.D. "Tonsword", Robert Laneham's Letter, and the Character of Captain Cox' (*ELN*) is on a single lexical item from the sixteenth century. Thomas E. Murray's '*Poppy Show*' (*AS*) is turn of the twentieth. As usual Fred R. Shapiro goes looking for earliest attestations: of *bibliography* and related terms, of geographical terms, of (professorial) *chair* (all *N&Q*); of English folk-dance terms (with Jane Garry, also *N&Q*); and of *executive privilege* (with a computer, *AS*).

With the last-named item we are chillingly in the late twentieth century. Thomas E. Murray appears again with 'The Language of Bodybuilding', and Mary Gray Porter and I. Willis Russell, now plus assistants, are still delving 'Among the New Words' (all *AS*, and indeed all-American speech; for the last-named see also section 6, p. 46). Horst Mühlmann's piece 'Zum Gebrauch von Germanismen in der englischen Presse am Beispiel des OBSERVER 1981' (*ZGL*) is a diligently classified list of germanisms in *The Observer*.

Licht- und Glanzwörter im modernen Englisch[64] analyses the meaning and use of twenty-eight English verbs associated with effects of light (see YW 64.66). [M.H.]

This is a year for discussion of dictionary-making. William Card, Raven I. McDavid Jr, and Virginia McDavid set out 'Dimensions of Usage and Dictionary Labeling' (*JEngL*), a system of usage labels originally written nearly twenty years ago. Michael I. Miller's 'Arrant Solecisms' (*AS*) analyses the past tense variants *ran/run* and *dived/dove* in speakers who are broken down statistically by age, sex, and other debilitating factors like education, in order to criticize the inadequacy of usage rules in commercial dictionaries. Gabriele Stein alleges that '*Traditio Delectat* or No Change at OUP' (*Anglia*), a review of the seventh edition of the *Concise Oxford Dictionary* (and here and there of the *Supplement* to *OED*) which convicts it of great inconsistency. Barbara Ann Kipfer has compiled a *Workbook on Lexicography*[65], a welcome, clear, and

62. *A Dictionary of Slang and Unconventional English . . .*, by Eric Partridge. Eighth edn., ed. by Paul Beale. RKP. pp. xxix + 1400. hb £45.

63. *English Etymology*, by Alfred Bammesberger. Sprachwissenschaftliche Studienbücher 1. CWU. pp. 163. hb DM 50, pb DM 29.

64. *Licht- und Glanzwörter im modernen Englisch*, by Jörg Waldvogel. Francke (1983). pp. 336. Sfr 48.

65. *Workbook on Lexicography: A Course for Dictionary Users with a Glossary of English Lexicographical Terms*, by Barbara Ann Kipfer, with Jennifer Robinson (glossary) and six linguists and lexicographers (exercises). Exeter Linguistic Studies 8. UExe. pp. 218. pb £4.50.

even elementary introduction to the subject, showing a very slight American emphasis. As the title implies, its main rationale is the exercises it sets. Ulf Bäcklund's *'Realize' and 'Recognize'*[66] is hard going, very long, and idiosyncratic (over fifty per cent of the short bibliography is Bäcklund himself). It is an exhaustive study of the meanings of two verbs by means of their collocates in the Brown corpus and some novels. The theoretical relevance of Aimo Seppänen's piece, 'Lexical Integrity or Semantic Diversity: *Good, great, and well'* (*ES*), is easier to see. It is an argument, against Hines (*LACUS 5,* 1979), that the adjectives of the title are semantically diverse, with the claim of polysemy justified by ambiguous examples and syntactic differences, among others. Beatrice Warren's *Classifying Adjectives*[67] reports with pleasing clarity a research project on 291 adjectives in the Brown corpus; the title is an intentional play on words. Despite some unfortunate paraphrases (e.g. of *fundamental*), she sustains her claim that such adjectives have an overt referential meaning plus one of a limited number of regularly recurring (covert) relational meanings. The same author gives 'A Nervous Report: The Transferred Epithet and Body Language'[43], an analysis of *sad news, an unhappy home*, and so on.

What D. J. Allerton means by 'Three (or Four) Levels of Word Cooccurrence Restriction' (*Lingua*) is that three levels are unquestionably needed, namely syntactic, semantic (including his notion of 'tailoring' of, e.g. RUN by *child* or *nose* as subject), and 'locutional' (for the arbitrary choice of, e.g. prepositions). Whether a fourth, pragmatic level is needed is addressed in a rather anecdotal conclusion. Strangely he doesn't mention Angus McIntosh's 1961 'Patterns and Ranges' (*YW* 42.35), with which his ideas overlap a little. The dissertation by Ann-Mari Fåhræus, *Two Kinds of Syntactic-Semantic Value-Loading in English*[68], is on the pervasive phenomenon whereby apparent truisms and contradictions become meaningful by 'supercharging' (*She has taste*) or 'pregnancy' (*That's what I call a sea*). The work is based on written corpora (Brown and LOB) and is rather given to listing.

A fifth article by Aimo Seppänen this year, 'The Generic Indefinite Article in English: A Re-examination' (*SL*), is a characteristically careful study of the semantics of one use of $a(n)$, illustrated by the first word in *A whale is a mammal*. Aleš Klégr has a densely written paper, 'Hawkins' Location Theory and the Use of Articles in *of*-Genitive Headnouns' (*PP*), which attempts to account for the high frequency of *the* in a small corpus in such patterns as *the angle of fall*.

Dennis R. Preston looks at a surprising usage of 'Take and Bring' (*Word*) in American English, where BRING may sometimes be used without the speaker/writer's presence at the destination. 'Goal orientation' is said to be responsible, and ultimate German influence is possible.

Chung-yu Chen dislikes the attribution of time structure to VPs and larger units and prefers to discuss the 'Time Structure of English Verbs' (*PIL*). The right test frame for the admissibility of the progressive is claimed to be the use

66. *'Realize' and 'Recognize': A Study in Immediate Contextual Dependency*, by Ulf Bäcklund. Umeå Studies in the Humanities 63. AUU (distributed by A&W). pp. 299. pb Skr 107.

67. *Classifying Adjectives*, by Beatrice Warren. GSE 56. UGoth. pp. 318. pb Skr 120.

68. *Two Kinds of Syntactic-Semantic Value-Loading in English*, by Ann-Mari Fåhræus. AUUp, SAU 54. A&W. pp. 184. pb Skr 98.

of perfect + progressive, and plus/minus durative is the only distinction which can be made. This criticism of the Vendler–Dowty analysis is somewhat vitiated by dubious linguistic judgements. I have not seen Béla Hollósy's article 'On Aspectual Classes of Verb Phrases' (*HSE*, 1983), but the title already shows disagreement with the previous item. The answer to the question ' "Ought". Present or Past Tense?' (*ES*) is plausibly argued by Erik Jørgensen to be that *ought* is (still) past tense, thus with Zandvoort, against most other synchronic descriptions, and tangential to those generative syntaxes which treat modals as lacking tense altogether (cf. above, p. 46).

Ought is, mostly, a modal, and last year we had major books by Jennifer Coates and Michael Perkins on the semantics of the modals (*YW* 64.66–7). This year they get less systematic attention, apart from a three-part article by M. M. Zdrenghea, 'Towards an Analysis of Modal Verbs and Modal Expressions' (*RRL*) which is a theoretical piece on pragmatics, logic, and speech-act theory. Georgia Magnera's article on 'Semantic and Grammatical Aspects of Hypothetical Verbs' (*Lingua*) is reminiscent of Jennifer Coates's work, but less impressive. A bland and not especially original survey is followed by experimental evidence for the semantic clustering of 'hypothetical verbs' (essentially the modals, some quasi-modals, and some verbs of desire). A hierarchy running from Possibility to Permission/Ability, derived from the cluster experiment, is used to explain order of verbs within a sentence, from more to less hypothetical. There is too much of the arbitrary here. Elsewhere some minor facets of modal behaviour come under scrutiny. Gunnel Tottie and Gerd Övergaard search the Brown and LOB corpora for 'The Author's *would* – A Feature of American English' (*SL*). The use of *would* in the sense of 'destiny' of a character is fairly infrequent, nineteen American to one British in their data. Inger Krogvig and Stig Johansson get bigger numbers out of the same corpora by carrying out '*Shall* and *Will* in British and American English: A Frequency Study' (*SL*), but their findings merely flesh out what we knew before, e.g. that *should* is more frequent in British English, especially in the first person. Karin Aijmer looks for harmonic semantic properties of '*Go to* and *Will* in Spoken English'[43], basing her claims on data from the London–Lund corpus. Richard J. Watts makes 'An Analysis of Epistemic Possibility and Probability' (*ES*), which sounds grander than it is, being a comparison of CAN and MAY aimed at German-speaking learners of English and their teachers.

' "Pure Future" *Will* in *If*-Clauses' (*Lingua*) is a typically long, nine-way classification by Renaat Declerck of 'exceptions' to the 'rule' that the simple present is used in *if*-clauses. Declerck's solution is to claim that it is *will* that is normal and the simple present which needs explaining, which he then does. Bengt Jacobsson also provides a lot of data on, mainly, the use of BE GOING TO and non-volitional *will/would* in *if*-clauses, but his 'Notes on Tense and Modality in Conditional *if*-Clauses' (*SL*) are more cautious about giving explanations. Explanations rather than data are the concern of Liliane Haegeman and Herman Wekker. Their account of 'The Syntax and Interpretation of Futurate Conditionals in English' (*JL*) tries to capture the facts by syntactic means, analysing the WILL-futures as more peripheral than other *if*-clauses. They are confident that their X̄ account is the basis of a satisfactory explanation, but this seems doubtful to me. Another rather special kind of conditional mentioned also by Declerck (because WILL can occur there) is the 'utterance-conditional', e.g. . . . *if you know what I mean.* Liliane Haegeman treats both syntax and semantics in 'Pragmatic Conditionals in English'. If you're interested (and I was), the paper is in *FolL*.

John Oakeshott-Taylor introduces the concept of 'factuality', to do with 'the extent to which the propositional content of a sentence . . . conforms with the speaker's perception of the world'. His article 'Factuality and Intonation' (*JL*) addresses some of the prosodic, syntactic, and pragmatic correlates of the concept. The analysis is extended to comparatives, and sentence pairs like *John thinks/*I think Mary is older than she is* are discussed in his interesting and elegant piece, 'Factuality, Tense, Intonation and Perspective: Some Thoughts on the Semantics of "think"' (*Lingua*).

9. Onomastics

There is no doubt that the publishing event of 1984 in English name-studies is the appearance of Margaret Gelling's *Place-Names in the Landscape*[69]. It is a discursive catalogue of all name-elements denoting topographical features, with extensive analysis of all names in English-speaking Britain supposed to contain each one. It is a major achievement, serving to correct misleading impressions about element frequency which could be gleaned from Ekwall's *Dictionary* and Smith's *Elements*, and offering substantial new insights into several elements, e.g. especially those implicated in names like Ansty and (Build-)was. By its nature it is not as straightforwardly readable as her earlier volume *Signposts to the Past* (*YW* 59.58), but all future work in the area will need to look to it as a point of departure. By contrast with this massive endeavour, Edward Harrington's *The Meaning of English Place-Names*[70] is little more than an unanalysed list with no discussion or qualification; it is vastly inferior as a popularizing work to John Field's *Discovering English Place-Names*[71], the best short introduction to the subject, this year into its third edition.

An English Place-Name Society county volume, the fifty-fifth, appeared in 1984. It is J. P. Oakden's first volume on Staffordshire[72], long in the making. A detailed critique should not be given by those like me who do not know the county well, but there is room for comment from a purely linguistic point of view. I selected at random the first twenty-five pages of those devoted to West Cuttlestone half-hundred (pp. 128–53). The editor's use of the Domesday Book (DB) as a source appeared inconsistent; he rejects the inconvenient DB form in interpreting the name High Onn, but apparently allows another one to outweigh a whole raft of evidence pointing in a different direction in the case of Brineton. If the DB form is discounted, surely Barton is derivable from a personal name Beorhthere; but Oakden finds the forms 'too varied for any certainty'. Two interpretations appeared unconvincing, or to raise problems not even mentioned, on the evidence presented (Shredicote and Aqualate). A

69. *Place-Names in the Landscape*, by Margaret Gelling. Dent, pp. ix + 326. hb £15.

70. *The Meaning of English Place-Names*, by Edward Harrington. Blackstaff. pp. xi + 156. pb £2.95.

71. *Discovering English Place-Names*, by John Field. Third edn. 'Discovering' Books 102. Shire. pp. 72. pb £1.25.

72. *The Place-Names of Staffordshire*, Vol. I, by J. P. Oakden. EPNS 55. EPNS. pp. li + 186. £20.

phonological peculiarity required by Oakden's interpretation of Gnosall should have been discussed with a similar one affecting Blymhill. The watchword, if these twenty-five pages are truly representative, is: handle with care. Klaus Dietz reviews the county volumes of the twenty years from the mid 1960s in his 'Zur englischen Ortsnamenforschung' (*Anglia*). We note with regret, at this point, the death of the last survivor (Gover) of the amazingly productive trio of A. H. Mawer, F. M. Stenton, and J. E. B. Gover, who edited many of the county volumes which appeared annually in the 1920s and 1930s.

   Three early place-name elements which are neither demonstrably British nor English in origin are studied by Richard Coates in 'Remarks on Pre-British in England' (*JEPNS*). The same author records the tentative claim that some English place-names in *amber* may contain a reference to persons perceived as Ambrones ('Place-name Evidence for Ambrones in England?' (*BNF*)). There are new attempts by Gillis Kristensson to etymologize certain English place-names by reference to unattested elements, the latest being 'Old English *glīse "a Bright Place" and Cognates' (*N&Q*) and 'Old English *cēo "a Clearing" ' (*NM*). The former appeals to both a *glīse and a *glǣse as ablaut relatives of each other. The application of the word *burh* in toponymy is discussed in J. Klein's abstract 'Hillfort Reuse in Gloucestershire, AD 1–700' (*OENews*). Rune Forsberg, in his 'OE *burnstōw* and *merestōw*: Two Appellative Compounds in *-stōw* with a Topographical First Element' (*SN*), argues completely convincingly for a meaning 'site of something periodic or intermittent', i.e. here 'bed of a winterbourne' and 'place where a pond forms in wet weather'. 'Two *walh* Names in the Fields of Kingston' have turned up and are added by J. Wakeford (*Surrey Archaeological Collections*) to the corpus established by Kenneth Cameron (*YW* 61.38–9). The evergreen topic of pagan place-names is returned to in a Cambridge dissertation by Lance J. Bronnenkant, abstracted in *Nomina*; he rejects the notion that any of these names adhere to Anglo-Saxon pagan religious sites as such. Margaret Faull uses place-name evidence in her essay on 'Late Anglo-Saxon Settlement Patterns in Yorkshire' in her *Studies in Late Anglo-Saxon Settlement*[73]. Allan Warmington breathes new life into the forgotten identification of Domesday *Langeberge* with Longborough in Gloucestershire ('The Domesday Manor of Langeberge cum Mene' in *JEPNS*), and K. Harrison attempts yet another identification of Brunanburh (*DAJ*). Karl-Inge Sandred turns his attention to 'A River-Name, a Linguistic Change and the Importance of Non-Linguistic Evidence' in his quest to elucidate the controversial place-name Weybourne (Norfolk)[74]. Gillian Fellows Jensen argues ('Place-names and settlements: some problems of dating as exemplified by place-names in *-by*', *Nomina*) that most names in *-by* in England represent land already in use and taken over, rather than newly colonized, by Scandinavian settlers; and that the name-element provides little clue about the precise date of origin of the place bearing it – an important methodological problem of the moment which has its roots in the controversy about the dating of *-ingas* names. T. F. Hoad, in a ME lexical study ('English Etymology: Some Problematic Areas in the Vocabulary of the Middle English

Period[1] in *TPS*; cf. also section 8), comments on some applications of the ancestor of the word *groove* in place-names. The recurrent place-name *Coldharbour*, contentious for 150 years, is argued by Richard Coates (*Nomina*) to be usually of early-seventeenth-century origin, and to be transferred from the name of a notorious London slum. There are two interesting field- and minor-name studies: by R. W. Standing on a group of parishes in coastal West Sussex[75] and by Kenneth Kirkham on Woodhall in Pinner, Middlesex (*JEPNS*). Two articles in *Nomina* discuss place-names in Scotland with some slight reference to names in Scots and to the process of anglicization, but we regard these as beyond our brief. Over the water, we find a re-issue of W. A. Read's fifty-year-old *Indian Place-Names in Alabama*[76], on whose findings I can offer no informed comment; the etymologies are drawn largely from Creek and Choctaw.

L. G. Pine has produced a *DictionaryNicknames*[77], which is a really woeful ragbag of information – not all devoid of interest in itself, of course – thrown together with no systematization whatever and with no clear overall conception of what a nickname is. We find, nose to tail, surnames of (alleged) nickname origin (Pettifer), titles of (alleged) nickname origin (Pharisees), names for objects (Big Ben), epithets (Ivan 'The Terrible'), assorted journalistic kennings (Ornament of the Palace for Mumtaz Mahal; but not Golden Bear for Jack Nicklaus), casual nonce insults (Flanders Mare), unequivocal nicknames (Prinney (*sic*)), and things that I am quite unable to comprehend as nicknames even on the most liberal interpretation (Conservative, Order of Preachers, Theosophy, Belial). Rarely can a *pot* have been so *pourri*.

An interesting essay which has both toponymic and anthroponymic aspects is Cecily Clark's 'Starting from Youlthorpe (East Riding of Yorkshire): An Onomastic Circular Tour' (*JEPNS*). She considers the possible etymologies of the personal-name element of the place-name in the light of known patterns of late OE/OScand and Norman naming and gives special cultural reasons for apparent inconsistencies in the chain of forms from DB to the present. This essay treats the variety in the source documents with a loving care which ought to satisfy Alexander R. Rumble, who discusses 'The Status of Written Sources in English Onomastics' (*Nomina*). He concludes, *inter alia*, that name-researchers ought to be more conscious of certain biases inherent in written sources, of the precise diplomatic status of documents from which forms are cited, and of the social bias in the corpus of recorded personal names.

Nearly every year brings forth a non-mainstream paper on the nature of naming, and this year's application is to modern English building names, most of which never quite were, by J. M. Carroll ('The Name Game: Creative and Practical Names for a Building' (*L&S*)). This is an attempted typology of naming strategies, set up with a view to answering the question of whether the same principles are at work in the two putative categories named in the paper's title. He concludes that 'creative' naming is slightly more lexically innovative and less directly descriptive than 'practical' naming.

75. *Field Names of Angmering, Ferring, Rustington, East Preston and Kingston (West Sussex)*, by R. W. Standing. English Field-Name Studies 2. EPNS. pp. iv + 50. pb £2.50.
76. *Indian Place-Names in Alabama*, by William A. Read, rev'd with a foreword by James B. McMillan. UAla (distrib. by Eurospan). pp. xviii + 107. pb £8.50.
77. *A Dictionary of Nicknames*, by L. G. Pine. RKP. pp. viii + 207. hb £9.95.

10. Stylistics

The title of Norman Page's 'Casebook' for Macmillan, *The Language of Literature*[78], suggests an appropriate place to start a survey of 1984 publications in stylistics. However, this anthology is somewhat disappointing, mainly because it appears curiously dated. Part 1 ('Beginnings') presents a range of pieces from Sidney (1595) to A. E. Housman (1933); Part 2 ('Language and Style: General Considerations') ranges from I. A. Richards (1924) to Jonathan Culler (1975) (briefly on parody). Part 3 is the longest section ('Authors and Texts'), ranging from Shakespeare to Pinter; but seven of the eighteen pieces are pre-war, and there is only one from the 1980s (Stanley Wells). Page's own introduction provides some explanation for the basis of his selections, in his extremely general account of critical theory in the twentieth century. After a brief reference to Saussure, he adds: 'At one time it looked as though linguistics might provide valuable tools and useful terminology for literary analysis; but with a few notable exceptions (not cited) the marriage . . . has been neither happy nor fruitful'. Clearly in his selection he has chosen mainly 'literary critics' rather than 'linguists'; but equally clearly, these same critics seem to find the 'tools' and terminology of linguistics indispensable.

Surprisingly, perhaps, a similar pessimism is found in Talbot J. Taylor and Michael Toolan's survey article in *JLS* on 'Recent Trends in Stylistics'. One of their theses is that stylistic theory has really 'progressed little since the publication, in 1909, of Charles Bally's *Traité de Stylistique Française*'. On the basis of their review of book publications between 1980 and 1983, they obviously believe that 'salvation' for stylistics lies on the path of a kind of 'prescriptivism' they see embodied in Stanley Fish's *Is There A Text In This Class?* (*YW* 62.27) and hinted at in Walter Nash's *Designs in Prose* (1980). This is not the place to criticize Fish's rather vague tenets; but suffice it to say that Talbot and Taylor do less than justice to the alignment of stylistic theory and 'rhetoric'. It is also, of course, very difficult to define the discipline narrowly anyway . . .

Joseph Adams obviously can, for despite the title of his book (*Yeats and the Masks of Syntax*[79]), he states that it is 'not a study in stylistics': 'the purpose is not to describe or define Yeats' poetic style'. None the less, this is precisely what is achieved, both by the explicit comments he occasionally makes about Yeatsian characteristics, and (most of all) by his very analysis of his syntactic ambiguities (the 'masks'). Ostensibly his theoretical framework is poststructuralist, drawing on Gilles Deleuze; but beyond the introductory chapter this makes little impact, and he instead draws considerably on Halliday's early work of the 1960s. By disclaiming associations with stylistics Adams obviously believes it is enough to 'show language operating in a text'. But his comments on ambiguities of determiner and relative clause, etc., however interesting, suffer considerably as a result from lack of contextualization and summary, and overall produce a 'model' of little explanatory power.

From one point of view, no one can complain of slightness in Raymond Chapman's book, *The Treatment of Sounds in Language and Literature*[80]. Written in the same lucid style of his earlier books, it is likewise packed with

78. *The Language of Literature*, by Norman Page. Macmillan, pp. 209. £13.
79. *Yeats and the Masks of Syntax*, by Joseph Adams. Macmillan. pp. viii + 111. hb £20.
80. *The Treatment of Sounds in Language and Literature*, by Raymond Chapman. Blackwell/Deutsch. pp. 262. hb £19.50.

illustrative quotations. But strangely, only a quarter of the forty texts from which he chiefly draws are poetry, precisely where one would expect phonic awareness, and problems in representation to be crucial. Only in the penultimate chapter does Chapman consider the special implications of his subject for poetry. Some of the methods of representation deserve more detailed scrutiny, e.g. 'tags', or what he calls 'external comments' ('he snarled', 'she said in a cold voice', etc.), especially in respect of the reading process, and their potential prosodic scope. Some interesting implications of their use (and non-use) happen to be outlined in Marianne Shapiro's 'How Narrators Report Speech' (*Lang&S*), in particular their relation to the control of rhythm and narrative time.

It is interesting to relate Chapman's treatment of onomatopoeia to Derek Attridge's discussion of it in *MLN* ('Language as Imitation: Jakobson, Joyce, and the Art of Onomatopoeia'). Both writers stress the conventionality of it; but Attridge emphasizes from a semiotic perspective how important illusions are for literary effect. (The contradictions of the sign in general are exposed by Ann K. Clark in 'Style and the Sign: Conditions for a Theory of Style', in *Lang&S*.) A painstaking analysis of Bloom's body noises, Attridge's article is, as Joyce might have said, a splendid 'tour de farts'.

The body is the prime concern of Max Atkinson's *Our Masters [sic] Voices*[81], an extensive exercise in 'political man-watching', as he puts it. His aim is to compare the vocal and gestural rhetoric of present-day politicians with classical oratory, and concludes on the basis of audio-visual evidence that there is a narrower, if effective, repertoire of strategies which audiences respond to, notably contrasts and three-part lists.

Non-literary language is also the subject of Michael P. Jordan's book, *Rhetoric of Everyday English Texts*[82]. He argues for a basic informational 'metastructure' of 'Situation', 'Problem', 'Solution' and 'Evaluation', from a corpus of mainly technical but journalistic texts. Although his approach derives from the work of Eugene Winter on 'contextual grammar', the signalling devices he analyses tend to be lexical rather than syntactic. He provides, however, a useful introduction to textual analysis for native and foreign students of English. Winter's work does actually provide the framework for one stylistic study this year, namely Winifred Crombie's ' "To Enter in These Bond is to be Free": Semantic Relations and the Baroque Prose Style of John Donne', in *Lang&S*.

Informational and functional metastructures as generic characteristics are also the concern of two articles in *NLC*. Ruqaiya Hasan develops her own previous work in 'The Nursery Tale as Genre' to produce a convincing structural formula involving obligatory, optional, and iterative elements realized by specific lexico-grammatical features for stories as various as those of the Grimms and *Thomas the Tank Engine*. Eija Ventola, however, in 'The Dynamics of Genre', has found Hasan's earlier studies problematic for her own analysis of what are termed 'service encounters', i.e. shopping interchanges, and so proposes a more dynamic network model.

81. *Our Masters [sic]Voices: The Language and Body Language of Politics*, by Max Atkinson. Methuen. pp. xix + 203. hb £10.50, pb £4.95.
82. *Rhetoric of Everyday English Texts*, by Michael P. Jordan. A&U. pp. xiv + 160. hb £15, pb £5.95.

The overlap between stylistics and text linguistics (as well as discourse analysis) in matters of description and text typology is discussed by Willie Van Peer in his 'Pulp and Purpose: Stylistic Analysis as an Aid to a Theory of Text' (*TPLL*; also *DQR*). His particular concern is with potential linguistic differences between so-called 'pulp' fiction and 'quality' literature, but his computer-assisted analysis is limited to only a few selected features. His 'open' versus 'closed' distinction echoes Eco's, but no reference is made to the latter's work.

Three other general articles can be noted, all on literary narrative. Chris Hutchison's title 'The Act of Narration: A Critical Survey of Some Speech-Act Theories of Narrative Discourse' (*JLS*) indicates its purpose; but he also provides his own carefully worked out hypothesis based on the notion that narrative is a natural and typical use of ordinary language. In the same journal Uri Margolin catalogues possible relations of person, space, and time using a deictic or 'indexical' model ('Narrative and Indexicality: A Tentative Framework'). In a slighter piece, Douglas Messerli ponders the question of supposed 'objectivity' and authorial 'omniscience' in 'The Role of Voice in Nonmodernist Fiction' (*ConL*).

Twentieth-century fiction is the subject of many articles this year. Marie Maclean in *SFS* categorizes the different ways in which 'signifier–signified' is defined in SF, which increasingly reflects an understanding of language, human and artificial ('Metamorphoses of the Signifier in "Unnatural" Languages'). More specifically, Graham Good in *PSt* is concerned to show the essentially 'dialogic' nature of Orwell's prose style, and its relations with his political and linguistic views, in 'Language, Truth and Power in Orwell'. D. M. Roskies (*Neophil*) similarly identifies Sillitoe's strengths in a prose which is dynamically angry and tense ('"I'd Rather Be Like I Am"': Character, Style, and the Language of Class in Sillitoe's Narratives'). Lindsey Tucker (*ConL*) argues that for Heller linguistic disorder is deliberately form and content ('Entropy and Information Theory in Heller's *Something Happened*'). Much the same view is taken by Andrew Gibson in *SoR* about 'Eumaeus' in Joyce's *Ulysses*. If this has been argued before, Gibson's plausible slant is that the episode is identified with forms of life that are hopeless failures ('"Broken Down and Fast Breaking Up": Style, Technique and Vision in the "Eumaeus" Episode in *Ulysses*'). Using the logical systems of modality Jean-Jacques Weber in *NLC* carefully traces the main plot actions in a Greene novel ('Deontic, Axiological and Epistemic Distance in Graham Greene's *The Honorary Consul*').

Studies of prose writers in earlier periods begin with Richard Rolle. Gunnel Cleve's thesis in *NM* that certain linguistic features might shed light on the style of mystical experience needs much more substantiation than her own slight piece provides ('Some remarks on Richard Rolle's Prose Style'). In 'Ethical Style in Milton's *The Readie and Easie Way*', John Banschbach correlates different sentence structures with a 'monarchy' style and a 'commonwealth' style (*Lang&S*). Ian Small in *PSt* speaks generally of the lack of attention paid to the formal characteristics of non-fictional prose. His particular concern is the discrepancy between critical pronouncements about the lexis of writers like Pater, and his own (computer-assisted) analysis ('Computational Stylistics and the Construction of Literary Readings: Work in Progress'). Also in the nineteenth century, Kathleen Wales (*Lang&S*) examines the first paragraph of *Edwin Drood* in particular relation to the themes of the novel ('Dickens and Interior Monologue: The Opening of *Edwin Drood* Reconsidered'). Dickens's manipulation of speech representation is one aspect of his general creativity considered by Knud Sørensen in 'Charles Dickens: Linguistic Innovator' (*ES*).

Studies of poetic texts loom large this year. Those on OE style, if competent, add little to what is not already known about the '*Mod–Mægen* Balance in *Elene, The Battle of Maldon* and *The Wanderer*' (Norma J. Engberg, *NM*), and 'Varieties of Repetition in Old English Poetry, Especially in *The Wanderer* and *The Seafarer*' (Muriel Cornell, *Neophil*). Christopher B. McCully, in 'On Old English Verse Rhythm: A Reply' [to Ida Masters Hollowell, *ES* 63 (1982)], supports the traditional view of OE metre that it is based on four accents to a line, and rejects the notion of a primary stress on the first lift with a fall thereafter as definitionally incoherent (*ES*). James Noble traces the survival of 'Variation in Layamon's *Brut*' (*NM*). William McColly in '*The Book of Cupid* as an Imitation of Chaucer: A Stylo-Statistical View' (*ChauR*) supports the general opinion that the poem isn't Chaucer's; and statistics also confirm 'intuitions' in M. W. A. Smith's 'The Authorship of *A Lover's Complaint*: An Application of Statistical Stylometry to Poetry' (*CHum*). 'Shakespeare's Sonnet 29: An Aspectual Analysis' by Kathryn R. Urbonya (*Lang&S*) is a complex and detailed study based on the work of Ronald Clayton Taylor. Archie Burnett discusses the stylistic effect of ' "Wandering Steps and Slow" and "Vast Profundity Obscure": Two Miltonic Adjective Formations' (*ELN*), tabulating the two structures in poems from the fourteenth to the seventeenth centuries and showing that they are neither invented by Milton nor unEnglish.

Metaphysical poetry is the focus of Colin Martindale's article in *CHum* on hypotheses of stylistic change using vocabulary as data ('Evolutionary Trends in Poetic Style: The Case of English Metaphysical Poetry'). Alison R. Rieke in 'Donne's Riddles' (*JEGP*) interestingly examines the enigmatic features of his poetry in the context of contemporary literary riddle types. Sidney Greenbaum (*JEngL*) presents a detailed comparison of 'Three English Versions of Psalm 23' from 1611, 1970, and 1978 with the original Hebrew text in respect of imagery and sound patterning, etc.

W. Hutching's 'Syntax of Death: Instability in Gray's *Elegy Written in a Country Churchyard*' (*SP*) highlights the extent and significance of syntactic ambiguity in the poem. Syntactic ambiguity is also touched on in Peter Verdonk's 'Poetic Artifice and Literary Stylistics' (*DQR*), a study of Blake's *London*. His focus, however, is the poem's lexical patterning.

Wordsworth's distinctive and philosophical use of metaphor is the subject of Keith Hinchcliffe's discriminating article in *SIR* ('Wordsworth and the Kinds of Metaphor'). Steven Connor writes a lively, if inconclusive piece, on ' "Speaking Likenesses": Language and Repetition in Christina Rossetti's *Goblin Market*' (*VP*).

The development of Eliot's verse rhythms are described straightforwardly in J. M. Reibetanz's 'Accentual Forms in Eliot's Poetry from *The Hollow Men* to *Four Quartets*' (*ES*). In contrast, Thomas Elwood Hart in 'Frost's *The Road Not Taken*: Text-Structure and Poetic Theory' (*Lang&S*) discovers through elaborate series of patternings a cryptogram of Edward Thomas. Elaboration is also a feature of David Butt's 'systemic' approach to the analysis of two short poems by Stevens ('Perceiving as Making in the Poetry of Wallace Stevens',

NLC). The exploitation of lineation and spacing is the subject of Eleanor Berry's 'Language Made Fluid: The Grammetrics of George Oppen's Recent Poetry', in *ConL*.

Studies of dramatic texts appear to be few. The popular stylistic thesis of 'language as theme', 'form as content', appears in Lawrence D. Green's ' "We'll dress him up in voices": The Rhetoric of Disjunction in *Troilus and Cressida*' (*QJS*); in Mary W. Bledsoe's 'The Function of Linguistic Enormity in Ben Jonson's *Bartholomew Fair*' (*Lang&S*); and in Lois E. Bueler's 'The Rhetoric of Change in *The Changeling*' (*ELR*). In contrast, discourse analysis provides the inspiration and insights in Rei Noguchi's 'Style and Strategy in *Endgame*' (JBeckS), a sensitive and convincing dissection of the play's power struggle strategies.

Finally let us note specialist works on particular registers of non-literary English: the book and article on engineering English by Krista Varantola (see section 7), and articles on legal English by Risto Hiltunen who makes a careful analysis of 'The Type and Structure of Clausal Embedding in Legal English' (*Text*) and 'Some Complex Types of Embedding in Legal English'[43]. In the latter piece, his clear taxonomy of embedding helps to disentangle some remarkable convolutions of legal drafting.

III

Old English Literature

JOYCE HILL

In the preparation of this year's survey I have been greatly helped by the editors of *Anglo-Saxon England*, who kindly gave me access to the uncorrected proof copy of the bibliography for 1984, which will appear in *ASE* 14. Once again, therefore, I must record my thanks.

This chapter has the following sections: 1. Bibliography; 2. Social, Cultural, and Intellectual Background; 3. Vocabulary; 4. Literature: General; 5. Beowulf; 6. The Junius Manuscript; 7. The Poems of the Vercelli Book; 8. The Exeter Book; 9. Other Poems; 10. Prose.

1. Bibliography

Three comprehensive annual bibliographies continue to provide an invaluable service for students of OE literature. That in *ASE*, prepared this year by Carl T. Berkhout, Martin Biddle, Mark Blackburn, C. R. E. Coutts, David Dumville, and Simon Keynes, is a classified list of all 1983 publications in the entire field of Anglo-Saxon studies. The *International Medieval Bibliography*[1] likewise sets out to be comprehensive in its coverage of the previous year, although its scope is far greater than *ASE* since it is concerned with the whole field of medieval studies in the period A.D. 500–1500. It is a classified bibliography, however, so that it is easy to find one's own areas of interest.

The *OENews* which, like *ASE*, provides comprehensive coverage of the Anglo-Saxon period alone, performs a service of a different kind for, with commendable speed, a bibliography of the previous year's work is published annually in the spring issue, and this is followed in the fall by a second issue in which the publications are reviewed and summarized. In addition, the first part of each issue carries information about conferences, the availability of suitable computer hardware, notices about special publications, and occasional short articles and reports. For example, the spring issue for this year included a progress report on the Dictionary of Old English by Ashley Crandell Amos, and an article on the library of the Dean and Chapter of Durham by Roger C. Norris. In the fall issue David Yerkes discussed f. 115r of BL Ms. Cotton Otho C i vol. 2, where there are characteristic glosses by at least two of the early active readers of the OE *Dialogues*. A photograph of the folio is published facing Yerkes's discussion.

The *Medieval Sermons Studies Newsletter*, normally published twice a year

1. *International Medieval Bibliography*, ed. by Richard J. Walsh. ULeeds. 2 vols. pp. lv + 279; xxxi + 219. hb £65.50, pb £60.

by the English Department at the University of Warwick, can be a useful additional source of information for scholars working with homiletic literature, although it is not as systematic as the main bibliographies, and this year there was no autumn issue. However, the separate publication of the report of the Fourth Medieval Sermon Studies Symposium held in Oxford in July includes abstracts of two papers of particular interest: 'Ælfric the Catechist' by Fr Eugene Green, and 'Anonymous OE Homilies – Background and Themes' by James E. Cross.

Carl T. Berkhout's list of 'Old English Research in Progress 1983–1984' (*NM*) is hardly a bibliography in the conventional sense, but it is a useful source of information about what work is being done where and by whom. It would be even better if more people would remember to send in details.

All of the bibliographies so far mentioned are published annually, but this year has also seen the publication of a specialist bibliography and two manuscript catalogues. The specialist bibliography is Leonard E. Boyle's *Medieval Latin Palaeography: A Bibliographical Introduction*[2], an indispensable guide for anyone working in the medieval period. Despite its title, it is not concerned simply with manuscripts written in Latin, but with the Latin tradition of palaeography throughout Western Christendom, whether exemplified in its various forms in Latin texts, or in vernacular manuscripts whose hands derive, immediately or ultimately, from Latin models. The heart of Boyle's book is the collection of bibliographies grouped under the heading of 'Cultural Setting' (pp. 67–202), which deal directly with scripts. But there are several other sections which cover issues such as libraries, the technology of manuscript production, the training of scribes, and the transmission of texts. Yet others direct one's attention to scholarly tools in the form of bibliographies, manuals, and particularly useful periodicals, and there is also a section largely given over to the preparation of an edition. Moreover, the classified lists have brief but helpful introductions and there are many references clarified by a short explanatory note or word of comment as to the usefulness – or otherwise – of the item cited. As further aids to the user there are also two indexes, one of places, names, and things, and one of manuscripts. In his preface Boyle notes, all too modestly, that the book is 'a working bibliography for beginners' (p. xiv), but even the most-experienced scholar will find, from time to time, that he or she has been led into unfamiliar territory, so that Boyle's idea of a beginner should not be interpreted too narrowly. It is inevitable in a bibliography of this size and scope that there will be the occasional error, such as the dating of the Royal 7 C xii manuscript of Ælfric's First Series of *Catholic Homilies* to A.D. 900 [item 748, p. 113], but they scarcely detract from the immense value of the book as a whole.

There are relatively few Anglo-Saxon manuscripts in Andrew G. Watson's *Catalogue of Dated and Datable Manuscripts c. 435–1600 in Oxford Libraries*[3] but it is nevertheless a catalogue that Anglo-Saxonists will be glad to consult when dealing with an Oxford manuscript. The manucripts are described in

2. *Medieval Latin Palaeography: A Bibliographical Introduction*, by Leonard E. Boyle, O.P. Toronto Medieval Bibliographies 8. UTor. pp. xvi + 399. hb. $35, pb $15.

3. *Catalogue of Dated and Datable Manuscripts c. 435–1600 in Oxford Libraries*, by Andrew G. Watson. Vol. I: *The Text*. Vol. II: *The Plates*. Clarendon. pp. xxiv + 176; 818 pl. £120.

Volume I, beginning with the Bodleian manuscripts in alphabetical order of collections and by numbers within collections, followed by the college collections in alphabetical order, with the manuscripts listed numerically. Volume II is given over entirely to photographs from the manuscripts, arranged chronologically and cross-referred to the descriptive catalogue. Of these, the first thirty-six illustrate hands from England and the continent before 1100.

The second catalogue is Thomas Smith's *Catalogue of Manuscripts in the Cottonian Library, 1696*, edited by Colin Tite[4], which I have regrettably not had the opportunity to inspect closely. It has been reprinted from Sir Robert Harley's copy, which was annotated by Humfrey Wanley. Tite has included in his edition documents relating to the fire of 1731.

2. Social, Cultural, and Intellectual Background

Perhaps the most important Anglo-Saxon publication this year from a national standpoint was the first volume in what will eventually be a complete archive of surviving stone sculpture from the pre-Conquest period, a large and detailed record published by the British Academy under the general editorship of Rosemary Cramp. The first volume of the *Corpus of Anglo-Saxon Stone Sculpture*[5], devoted to the counties of Durham and Northumberland, is by Professor Cramp herself and, since it is the first of a ten-year cycle of definitive publications, the main body of Part I is preceded by an independently paginated general introduction to the series in which, for the first time, we are provided with a systematic vocabulary for the description of stone-types, carving techniques, and decorative ornaments. Part I proper begins with a number of interpretative chapters on the historical background to the sculpture, the circumstances of production, the sequence of ornament, and the chronology and schools of carving. Then follows the comprehensive catalogue first of County Durham, then of Northumberland, and finally a form and motif table showing types of monuments and decorative elements against sites in alphabetical order. The complete photographic record is contained in Part II. Subsequent volumes will use the same format.

As 1984 is the year in which one series of definitive publications is launched, so it is also the year in which another is brought to an end. Volume 3 of *The Sutton Hoo Ship-Burial*[6] by Rupert Bruce-Mitford, edited by Angela Care Evans, completes the British Museum's comprehensive study of the Sutton Hoo ship-burial and its rich collection of artefacts. This volume, in two parts, deals with the late Roman and Byzantine silver, the hanging bowls, drinking vessels, cauldrons and other containers, textiles, the lyre, pottery bottle, and other small miscellaneous items. As with Volumes 1 and 2, published in 1975 and 1978, the material is generously presented, with ample detailed discussion and an excellent collection of drawings, radiographs, and photographs, many of which are of objects that are not generally familiar since they have not been

4. *Catalogue of Manuscripts in the Cottonian Library, 1696, by Thomas Smith*, ed. by Colin Tite. B&B. pp. 530. £75.

5. *Corpus of Anglo-Saxon Stone Sculpture*, ed. by Rosemary Cramp. Vol. I: *County Durham and Northumberland*, ed. by Rosemary Cramp. 2 parts. OUP for the British Academy. pp. 404; 290 (1406 illus.). £95.

6. *The Sutton Hoo Ship-Burial*, by Rupert Bruce-Mitford. Vol. 3, ed. by Angela Care Evans. 2 parts. BMP. pp. lxiv + xix + 998. £100.

on display nor been included in the various editions of the museum's *Hand-book*. Of particular interest to students of OE poetry is the detailed discussion of lyres on pp. 611–757, which is well illustrated with pictures of lyre fragments and reconstructed lyres from England and the continent. Contrary to the original intention, it has been decided not to publish a fourth volume made up of interpretative essays.

Another important undertaking by the British Museum this year was the mounting of an exhibition on Anglo-Saxon art between 966 and 1066 to mark the death, one thousand years ago, of Bishop Æþelwold. The catalogue of the exhibition, entitled *The Golden Age of Anglo-Saxon Art 966–1066*[7] and edited by Janet Backhouse, D. H. Turner, and Leslie Webster, with contributions by Marion Archibald, Martin Biddle, Michael Borrie, Richard Gem, Catherine Haith, Simon Keynes, Dominic Tweddle, and Jeffrey West, deserves notice in its own right. An extraordinarily rich collection of items was put on display and for each the catalogue gives a brief factual description, a short but authoritative discussion, and a bibliography, which is sufficiently up to date to anticipate imminent publications. Although the focus of the exhibition was 966–1066, there was a section devoted to the legacy of Alfred, and another to the period after the Conquest. In the catalogue these sections are treated in Parts I and III, bracketing the main part (Part II), which is devoted to the Golden Age itself. The artistic achievements of the Benedictine Reform are thus given a chronological and artistic context. There are good introductory essays on the major groups of artefacts (manuscripts, metalwork, sculpture, coins) and broader surveys of the three stages of the exhibition – the Alfredian legacy, the Benedictine Reform, and the post-Conquest period. There is also an informative essay on Literature, Learning and Documentary Sources, which provides a background for the manuscripts, and an essay on Anglo-Saxon architecture of the tenth and eleventh centuries which, of course, could not be presented in the exhibition. There are black-and-white photographs throughout (including some excellent ones of Anglo-Saxon churches) and, at the end, a collection of very attractive colour photographs. The three editors and their contributors are to be congratulated on producing a scholarly and yet lively and attractive catalogue which offers a glowing testimony to what was indeed the Golden Age of Anglo-Saxon art.

Women in Anglo-Saxon England[8] by Christine Fell, with Cecily Clark and Elizabeth Williams, is an attractive semi-popular book whose publication was timed to coincide with the exhibition. The subject is intrinsically interesting and certainly important, but the insurmountable difficulty facing anyone who attempts a broadly based study of the woman's role throughout the period and at all levels of society is the dearth of hard evidence and a shortage of suitable illustrative material. Thus in the chapter on daily life, for example, there is a sense that Professor Fell is grasping at straws, while the illustrations that support the text, here and elsewhere, of necessity include allegorical and biblical women, there being all too few direct representations of Anglo-Saxon

7. *The Golden Age of Anglo-Saxon Art 966–1066*, ed. by Janet Backhouse, D. H. Turner, and Leslie Webster, with contributions by Marion Archibald, Martin Biddle, Michael Borrie, Richard Gem, Catherine Haith, Simon Keynes, Dominic Tweddle, and Jeffrey West. BMP. pp. 216. £10.

8. *Women in Anglo-Saxon England and the Impact of 1066*, by Christine Fell, with Cecily Clark and Elizabeth Williams. BMP. pp. 208. £15.

women and their activities in the extant manuscripts. These problems, however, are inherent in the subject and Professor Fell cannot be held accountable for them. In her text she exploits intelligently the often scrappy evidence and shows a healthy tendency to make an unprejudiced scrutiny of the wording of any given OE text in an attempt to determine what it really meant to the Anglo-Saxons themselves. Indeed, the re-examination of words relating to females and female concerns is one of the valuable contributions that the book makes to the subject. Valuable too are the concluding chapters by Cecily Clark and Elizabeth Williams, since their respective analyses of how the woman's role changed in society and in its literary representation following the Norman Conquest is not only a subject of interest in itself, but also helps to sharpen our sense of the female role in Anglo-Saxon England. There is a useful Select Bibliography and readers are directed to the relevant works in a paragraph on further reading at the end of each chapter. It is not, however, an entirely satisfactory method; I was unable to find in the bibliography a number of items that are briefly mentioned as further reading and yet, in the absence of full bibliographical details (which 'further reading' does not provide), I found it impossible to follow them up. I sympathize with the wish to avoid footnotes in a book of this kind, but surely those likely to read their way through a fairly serious work on Anglo-Saxon women would find a few footnotes more of a help than a hindrance.

Another book whose publication was timed to coincide with the exhibition is David M. Wilson's *Anglo-Saxon Art*[9], although it deals with the whole of the Anglo-Saxon period, unlike the exhibition itself. The format of the book is that of a popular work, generously laid out, with many lavish illustrations. But it is in fact an up-to-date survey of Anglo-Saxon art, the first in more than thirty years to rival Kendrick's two-volume synthesis. Recent finds, such as those from Coppergate in York, the Brandon plaque, and the Pentney brooches, are discussed and excellently illustrated, and the rephotographing of many familiar objects encouraged this reader at least to look at them with renewed interest and sharpened perception. Typically, Wilson's text is honest about what we do not know and sceptical about comfortable theories which, through sheer repetition, harden into 'fact'. The theories of modern scholars are examined, even to the extent of taking due note of 'the latest Ph.D. thesis' on the Reculver fragments (p. 71), but Wilson's scepticism is just as evident in his assessment of the work of modern scholars as it is of the work of older ones. The theory that the Vespasian Psalter is earlier than the Leningrad Bede, for example, is dismissed as 'nonsense' (p. 63). The survey is organized, reasonably enough, on a broad chronological basis, but a looser frame of reference is adopted in Chapter 4, which discusses the artistic influences to which the Anglo-Saxons were subject and those which they exerted. What is particularly memorable about the chapter is its illustration of objects from outside England, which dramatically support Wilson's arguments, but which are all too rarely reproduced in books on Anglo-Saxon art.

Among the new and unfamiliar items which are discussed and illustrated in Wilson's book are the Coppergate helmet, unearthed by chance during construction work in York in May 1982, and the Maaseik embroideries, which

9. *Anglo-Saxon Art from the Seventh Century to the Norman Conquest*, by David M. Wilson. T&H. pp. 224; 285 illus. £25.

have been largely ignored by scholars of Anglo-Saxon art and crafts until modern times. For each there is an accessible independent study. A well-illustrated popular but scholarly account of the helmet is provided by Dominic Tweddle in a booklet published for the York Archaeological Trust, *The Coppergate Helmet*[10], and the Maaseik embroideries are discussed by Mildred Budny and Dominic Tweddle in a joint article simply titled, 'The Maaseik embroideries' (*ASE*). Their approach is broad as well as detailed. Not only do they describe the embroideries (the earliest extant), but they also discuss how and when they arrived at Aldeneik before being moved to Maaseik in 1571, what characteristics make them Anglo-Saxon, their approximate date and place of origin, and where they stand within the corpus of Anglo-Saxon art in general and of Anglo-Saxon embroidery in particular. Unusually for *ASE* there are accompanying photographs, some in colour.

With Francis Wormald's studies of English and continental art from the sixth to the twelfth centuries, now collected and edited by J. J. G. Alexander, T. J. Brown, and Joan Gibbs, and reprinted under the general title *Studies in Medieval Art from the Sixth to the Twelfth Centuries*[11], we return to familiar territory. The essays are arranged according to the chronology of Anglo-Saxon art, and at the end of each the editors have provided a note giving information about its original publication and a list of relevant work produced since that date. Such was Wormald's breadth of vision and reference that this simple matter of re-arranging his articles conveys to the reader a sense of the history of the art of the period, but one which is firmly rooted in close analysis of individual works. It is a pity that the 190 plates following the essays are all in black and white; it greatly reduces their impact and, in some cases, destroys important detail.

Another re-issue that I am pleased to note this year is the publication in paperback form of Volume III of H. M. Taylor's *Anglo-Saxon Architecture*[12]. The format has been reduced considerably from that of the 1978 hardback edition so that it matches the convenient size of the 1980 paperback versions of Volumes I and II.

With *The Making of Britain: the Dark Ages*[13], edited by L. H. Smith, we move away from art, archaeology, and architecture to the historical development of Anglo-Saxon England. The book is made up of a series of essays by scholars who are well known in their respective fields so that the pitfalls of a bland popular survey are avoided, yet the topics are arranged chronologically, which enables the reader to build up a sense of the development of the period as a whole while being simultaneously introduced to the living issue of modern historical research. It can be safely recommended to beginning students, who might well enjoy the idea that they are reading a book which had its origins in a London Weekend Television series for Channel 4.

10. *The Coppergate Helmet*, by Dominic Tweddle, photography by Mike S. Duffy, drawings by Helen Humphreys and Dick Raines. Cultural Resource Management Ltd, Jorvik Viking Centre, for the York Archaeological Trust. pp. 22. £1.25.

11. *Francis Wormald. Collected Writings.* Vol. I: *Studies in Medieval Art from the Sixth to the Twelfth Centuries*, ed. by J. J. G. Alexander, T. J. Brown, and Joan Gibbs. HM/OUP. pp. 253. £34.

12. *Anglo-Saxon Architecture.* Vol. III, by H. M. Taylor. CUP. pp. xvi + 383. £12.95.

13. *The Making of Britain: the Dark Ages*, ed. by L. H. Smith. Macmillan. pp. ix + 190. £6.95.

H. R. Loyn's *The Governance of Anglo-Saxon England 500–1087*[14] also deals with the whole of the Anglo-Saxon period, but it is sharply focused on one issue and is aimed at an altogether different readership. Loyn sets out to analyse how, in practice, Anglo-Saxon England was governed, and what it meant to be a king at different times in Anglo-Saxon history. For the literary scholar, who needs to know about the changing role of the king, aristocracy, and church, but who lacks the particular skills needed to engage with the detailed arguments of current historical research, it is a useful guide. Loyn's description of the increasingly sophisticated governmental structures demonstrates by implication just how archaic the society of *Beowulf* must have seemed in the late tenth century, and the treatment of the church and of military organization in late Anglo-Saxon England (pp. 154–61, 163–9) casts an interesting light on the Benedictine Reform and *The Battle of Maldon*. It is refreshing to find that Loyn makes substantial use of vernacular writings, even to the extent of showing, from time to time, how words familiar in poetry come to mean different things as the period progresses. But he can be faulted in his handling of *Maldon*: the name of the Northumbrian hostage is not Ælscferth, as he twice states; the poet of *Maldon* is hardly an 'epic-poet' since *Maldon*, even complete, would not be an epic poem, and there was time for Loyn to replace his reference to the 1976 re-issue of E. V. Gordon's edition with a reference to the 1981 edition by D. G. Scragg; or at least to correct Scragg's initials, when naming him as the compiler of the supplementary bibliography to the 1976 re-issue of Gordon.

The shadowy period of the decline of Roman Britain and the beginning of Anglo-Saxon England is the subject of C. J. Arnold's *Roman Britain to Saxon England: An Archaeological Study*[15]. The usefulness of the survey for our purposes is that, without inflicting too much technical detail upon the non-specialist, it communicates the nature and significance of modern archaeological discoveries relating to this period of transition and indicates the ways in which the overall picture of the decline of Roman Britain is to be seen as more complex and more extended in time than some earlier scholarship would have had us believe.

Another book dealing with this same period is *Gildas: New Approaches*[16], a collection of scholarly and detailed essays by various contributors. As David Dumville notes in the General Editor's foreword (p. viii), our grasp of the period as a whole remains insecure and, as a result, Gildas and his immediate context are insufficiently understood. The purpose of the volume is to make Gildas and his work more intelligible through a variety of textually based approaches. Not all contributors are able to offer firm conclusions, but our understanding of Gildas's work is significantly advanced by these essays, which are models of their kind. Readers of this chapter of *YW* are most likely to be interested in Ian Wood's 'The end of Roman Britain: Continental evidence and parallels', a sensitive examination of how the end of Roman

14. *The Governance of Anglo-Saxon England 500–1087*, by H. R. Loyn. Arnold. pp. xvii + 222. £7.95.

15. *Roman Britain to Saxon England: An Archaeological Study*, by C. J. Arnold. CH. pp. x + 179. £14.95, $29.95.

16. *Gildas: New Approaches*, ed. by Michael Lapidge and David Dumville. Studies in Celtic History V. Boydell. pp. xii + 244. £25.

Britain was perceived by contemporaries, and by the two papers directly concerned with Gildas's education and literary skills, discussed by Michael Lapidge in 'Gildas's education and the Latin culture of sub-Roman Britain', and by Neil Wright in 'Gildas's prose style and its origins'. Lapidge and Wright support the view that Gildas's literary skills developed out of a knowledge of late Antique rhetoric and both therefore reject the older tendency to group him stylistically with writers such as Aldhelm or the seventh-century Irish writers of the *Hisperica Famina*.

At the other end of the period R. Allen Brown's *The Norman Conquest*[17] allows us to see this crucial event through the eyes of English and Norman contemporaries. The collection of texts is drawn from Latin, OE, and Anglo-Norman sources, but all are translated into readable modern English. Brief introductions and references to editions are provided for each item and there are informative footnotes that identify for the modern reader people and places referred to in a cryptic or casual way. The texts are grouped according to type and within these divisions are further grouped according to language and country of origin. Although obviously intended chiefly for students of history, it is a valuable resource for the non-historian who has an interest in late Anglo-Saxon England.

Before the Normans came on the scene, however, the English kingdoms had to come to terms with their northern neighbours, with whom they often fought and by whom Northumbria was converted. Alfred P. Smyth's *Warlords and Holy Men: Scotland AD 80–1000*[18] is a highly readable account of a country that had an important impact on Anglo-Saxon life. The most immediately relevant chapters are three and four, which deal with Iona under Columba and Adomnan and its influence on northern Christianity.

By far the best book this year on an ecclesiastical subject is Nicholas Brooks's *The Early History of the Church of Canterbury: Christ Church from 597 to 1066*[19], which has the distinction of being not just the first full study of the church of Canterbury in Anglo-Saxon times, but the first study that has been attempted on this scale for any major Anglo-Saxon church. In presenting us with a searching analysis of the fortunes of Christ Church, its achievements, failures, and influences over a five-hundred-year period, Brooks deploys an impressive range of evidence sensitively drawn from narrative and record sources, archaeology, architecture, numismatics, palaeography, liturgy, and art-history. We see how the archbishops were involved in the power politics of Anglo-Saxon England, how the standards of scholarship and manuscript production rose and fell, how individuals, such as Plegmund in the reign of Alfred, or Sigeric the dedicatee of Ælfric's *Catholic Homilies*, could make their mark; we have traced for us the land-holdings and the library-holdings of the church, and we are given a judicious assessment of Canterbury's response to the Benedictine Reform. I have to admit, by way of conclusion, that I have rarely enjoyed a work of scholarship so much.

17. *The Norman Conquest*, by R. Allen Brown, Documents of Medieval History 5. Arnold. pp. xix + 181. £12.50.
    18. *Warlords and Holy Men: Scotland AD 80–1000*, by Alfred P. Smyth. The New History of Scotland 1. Arnold. pp. viii + 279. £6.95.
    19. *The Early History of the Church of Canterbury: Christ Church from 597 to 1066*, by Nicholas Brooks. ULeics. pp. xiv + 402. £28.

Charters, which Brooks uses extensively in his study of the land-holdings of Canterbury and the careers of the archbishops, are the subject of this year's Jarrow Lecture, given by Patrick Wormald. In *Bede and the Conversion of England: The Charter Evidence*[20] he surveys in a typically vigorous and challenging way the possible formative influences on the early Anglo-Saxon charter and demonstrates that what was produced in England drew upon diverse models, thus producing an English charter-form that was *sui generis*. He demonstrates clearly the fundamentally important role played by the church in the production, use, and preservation of charters before the tenth century, and in particular focuses on the way in which large-scale gifts of land to the church confirmed by charter altered the pattern of land ownership in the early Anglo-Saxon period, attenuated the king's resources, and indirectly fostered family monasteries led, in many cases, by the sort of worldly half-reeve, half-abbot that Bede stigmatized in his famous letter to Bishop Egbert of York. The general cultural point that Wormald's lecture makes is that the unique nature of the Anglo-Saxon charter is a reflection of the variety of religious traditions from which the Anglo-Saxons derived their faith; his more specific point is that study of the early charters, despite the fact that they are southern documents, enables us to glimpse just how very rich was the endowment of Bede's *Ecclesia Anglorum* and why he disapproved so strongly of the form it was taking.

Twenty-five years ago the Jarrow Lecturer was Peter Hunter Blair who, in a productive scholarly life, did so much to advance our understanding of the early history and intellectual achievement of Northumbria. As a fitting memorial to his work, Michael Lapidge and Pauline Hunter Blair have published twelve of his articles and lectures in a book entitled *Anglo-Saxon Northumbria*[21]. The studies, which span a forty-year period, are arranged in order of their original publication. A general index has been provided, but the editors have not supplemented the bibliographical information with more up-to-date references.

With Susan Rankin's article 'From memory to record: musical notations in manuscripts from Exeter' (*ASE*) we move back to the Benedictine Reform when, as she shows us, the practice of recording chants in musical notation was introduced. By the late tenth century there were two systems of neumes in use, one related to northern French notations, especially those of Corbie, and the other to notations of Breton provenance. It was the northern French system which predominated, and within 150 years English musical practice changed from being a wholly oral tradition to one of mixed oral and written transmission. The period of transition is exemplified in Rankin's essay by manuscripts from Exeter which, incidentally, cast an interesting light on the impact of Leofric's episcopacy.

Since the maintenance of scholarship was a function of the church, it is appropriate to note here that the most recent issue of *Medievalia*, for 1981 but not published until this year, includes a list by J. D. A. Ogilvy of addenda and corrigenda to his *Books Known to the English, A.D. 597–1066* (*YW* 48.54).

20. *Bede and the Conversion of England: The Charter Evidence*, by Patrick Wormald. Jarrow Lecture. Distributed by The Parish of Jarrow, St Paul's House, 1 York Avenue, Jarrow. pp. 32. £1.40.

21. *Peter Hunter Blair: Anglo-Saxon Northumbria*, ed. by Michael Lapidge and Pauline Hunter Blair. VR. pp. vii + 263. £26.

The main sources of his additions and corrections are his own interim list (originally printed on pp. 295–300 of *Books Known*, but now incorporated into the revised list), the notes of errors and omissions in reviews (principally of Helmut Gneuss and, to a lesser extent, of Luitpold Wallach), the private communications of other scholars, and Ogilvy's own attempts to note scholarship up to 1981 and to make good his shortcomings in dealing with the provenance of manuscripts. It is essential reading for anyone who consults Ogilvy's book. The paper is to be published separately next year by *OENews* as *Subsidia* 11.

It cannot be denied, however, that for all our attention to the world of learning, what mattered more to most Anglo-Saxons was the teaching of the church on the affairs of everyday life. Pierre J. Payer, in an interesting book, *Sex and the Penitentials: The Development of a Sexual Code 550–1150*[22], teases out from an impressive body of penitential texts the sexual ethic that the penitentials defined and promulgated. Payer is not directly concerned with Anglo-Saxon England except through the penitentials attributed to Bede and Egbert, but the sexual code that Payer identifies must be regarded as having been generally applicable in England. He notes that there was an official move away from penitentials in the ninth century and that their creative period ended by the tenth. On the continent, however, much of their substance was thereafter transmitted through canons. The chapter divisions reflect these stages in the development of the penitential tradition, but although most of the book is given over to this discursive analysis, the substantial appendixes provide a wealth of detailed information about how the penitentials deal with particular aspects of sexual behaviour and the language that they employ. The book is impressive in its systematic clarity, a characteristic all the more commendable when one considers how much basic work still has to be done with penitentials, the majority of which are not yet adequately edited.

Just as typical of the early Middle Ages, though not at all practical in its focus, is the concept of the six ages of the world. It is the subject of a study by Hildegard L. C. Tristram, which I regret that I have not yet seen: '*Sex aetates mundi*': die Weltzeitalter bei den Angelsachsen und den Iren (*AF*).

In contrast with Payer's and Tristram's highly specialized books, C. H. Lawrence's *Medieval Monasticism: Forms of religious life in Western Europe in the Middle Ages*[23] is a publication that could well be of use to students who, in studying the intellectual history of England, would benefit from a clear account of the forms of monasticism prevalent in early medieval society and the changes that took place. Chapter 4 is devoted to England and the continent in the seventh and eighth centuries and Chapter 6 to the Age of Cluny, culminating in a section on the English revival of the tenth century. Other chapters in this half of the book provide a broad context for Anglo-Saxon monasticism and emphasize variety and change in monastic life, which is a valuable corrective to the tendency that some literary scholars show of equating monasticism with Benedictinism.

Another useful book with a broad chronological base is G. R. Evans's *The*

---

22. *Sex and the Penitentials: The Development of a Sexual Code 550–1150*, by Pierre J. Payer. UTor. pp. xi + 219. $24.95.

23. *Medieval Monasticism: Forms of religious life in Western Europe in the Middle Ages*, by C. H. Lawrence. Longman. pp. x + 260. hb £12, pb £5.95.

Language and Logic of the Bible: The Earlier Middle Ages[24]. The period dealt with is from the fall of the Roman Empire to the thirteenth century and the main focus is on the exegetical traditions of western Christianity, but although the earlier Middle Ages is Evans's declared scope, his chief concern is with the new intellectual developments between the eleventh and thirteenth centuries. However, he naturally makes some use of those earlier patristic works which formed the basis for exegesis in Anglo-Saxon England and, where he does so, he characterizes their approach with admirable clarity. A less obvious but equally valuable benefit for those interested in prescholastic exegesis is the way in which the earlier traditions are defined by implicit and explicit contrast.

The small but steady flow of articles on Anglo-Saxon scholarship in the sixteenth century is maintained this year by John R. McNair, who writes on 'An Early "Hard Word" List: Stephen Batman's "A Note of Saxon Wordes"' (*Neophil*), and Carl T. Berkhout, whose unexpected topic is 'William Lambarde's Old English Ex Libris' (*N&Q*). Batman's list of twenty-one 'Saxon Wordes' noted in his manuscript commonplace book in fact includes some words having their roots in Norman, Old French, and Latin, as well as identifiable OE words and others which are presumably meant to be OE but which are garbled beyond recognition. However, the list itself and the definitions that Batman supplies are enough to allow McNair to speculate on Batman's source, although he is not able to reach any firm conclusions beyond the general supposition that he got the list from his antiquary associates. William Lambarde's knowledge of the language was apparently better than Batman's, to judge from his ability to compose three 'Old English' *ex libris* although, as Berkhout shows, it was far from perfect. What is particularly noteworthy, however, is his use in one of the *ex libris* of the rare word *lamwyrhte*, which occurs only in the Rushworth and Lindisfarne Gospels. Berkhout notes that Lambarde uses the Mercian spelling, which means that the balance of probabilities is in favour of Rushworth as his source. If so, it might be a slender clue towards determining the whereabouts of the Rushworth Gospels in the 1560s.

I conclude this section with Michael Swanton's *Three Lives of the Last Englishmen*[25]: translations into English of the Latin lives of Harold Godwinsson, Hereward the Wake, and Wulfstan of Worcester. There are no notes to the translations, but there is a bibliography and a good introduction dealing with the contemporary history of England and the relative value of each work. The *Lives* gain from being juxtaposed, for by reading them in succession one can see clearly how the writer's purpose determined his structure and style. Hereward's *Life*, which may well be based ultimately on personal recollection, is the most vigorous and matter-of-fact; Harold's biographer seems to have attempted sanctification by the force of style alone; William of Malmesbury, in translating into Latin the OE *Life of Wulfstan*, preserves Coleman's nice balance between hagiography and homely detail. As saints go, Wulfstan seems quite human; at least his hagiographer attributes to him some good jokes.

24. *The Language and Logic of the Bible: The Earlier Middle Ages*, by G. R. Evans. CUP. pp. xix + 199. £18.50.
25. *Three Lives of the Last Englishmen*, trans. and intro. by Michael Swanton. Garland Library of Medieval Literature, Series B. Volume 10. Garland. pp. xxx + 156. $26.

3. Vocabulary

Ernst S. Dick and Kurt R. Jankowsky edited, in 1982, a large collection of essays on diverse subjects as a *Festschrift* for Karl Schneider[26] (hereafter *Schneider*). It was not noted in the 1982 or 1983 surveys in *YW*, but it deserves attention for the contributions it makes to OE word studies. Kurt R. Jankowsky, in 'Old English Time Concepts and Their Germanic and IE Cognates', tackles three apparently synonymous OE words relating to the concept of time, *fæc*, *first*, and *hwīl*, in an attempt to discover whether, beyond the seeming identity or similarity of meaning, there is any evidence of the particular meaning of each term. Analysis of *fæc* in surviving OE texts and a study of its Germanic cognates lead Jankowsky to conclude that, before acquiring its temporal meaning, it related to space in some way that was tied to the structural components of the house and their functional use. *First*, which is submitted to a similar analysis, seems to have a similar origin, but in this case Jankowsky is able to postulate how the transfer from spatial to temporal meaning took place. *Hwīl*, on the other hand, appears to have had a rather different origin, one concerned somehow with 'resting place' and hence to a notion of time whose duration, its beginning and end, is determined by fate. In conclusion he notes how, since the meaning of words is inseparable from the cultural context in which they take shape, analysis of the semantic history of OE words will add to our understanding of Old Germanic life. The erosion of the semantic distinctions between *fæc*, *first*, and *hwīl*, he believes, was hastened by the impact of Christianity, which changed the cultural foundations of the community. By contrast, Ernst S. Dick's purpose in 'AE. *Drēam*: Zur Semantik der Verbalbeziehungen in der Dichtung' is not to consider *drēam* as an isolated word, but to pay attention to the subtle changes of function and sense when the word collocates with the verbs 'to be' and 'to have'. The essay by Helmut Gneuss, 'Some Problems and Principles of the Lexicography of Old English', has an altogether broader approach in that it discusses some examples of what recent historical and philological research have contributed towards the making of the new dictionary of OE, and what, in return, the lexicographer will have to offer the historian and the philologist. Although the new dictionary will not be treating etymologies in any detail, Gneuss discusses the value of at least giving some etymological indication of loan words, despite the difficulty of deciding in some cases whether a word is a loan-formation or a native word. Another kind of information that the dictionary could provide is an indication whether a word has regional or stylistic restrictions, but here also, as Gneuss notes, modern research has complicated the issue by showing that the boundaries between regional forms and between poetic and prosaic language are not as firm as was once thought. The final problem that he discusses is definition of meaning, a particularly acute problem with some of the historical and legal terms that Gneuss brings forward (e.g. *fyrd*, *folcland*, *genēat*). The question that underlies Gneuss's paper is: how encyclopaedic could or should a dictionary entry become? He ends on the warning note that, although the dictionary will make use of modern historical research, and although the philological expertise used in drawing up the dictionary entries will be valuable to the historian, no one should

---

26. *Festschrift für Karl Schneider*, ed. by Ernst S. Dick and Kurt R. Jankowsky. Benjamins (1982). pp. xx + 595. Fl. 165, $66.

expect the lexicographers to perform miracles: many definitions will be tenuous.

The value of computers in furthering our understanding of the semantic field of OE words is examined in a clearly argued paper by Victor L. Strite, 'Semantic Field Analysis for Old English Poetry' (*In Geardagum*, 1983). He draws attention to the relative lack of work on OE semantics in the past and the consequent limitations of information already in print, and in conclusion outlines the beginnings of his own work on the large group of sea-words in OE poetry. It will be interesting to read in future publications of the results of Strite's approach.

By contrast with Strite, who is concerned with poetic vocabulary, Michiko Ogura deals with the demanding question of the semantic range of a group of common words: *þa, þonne, mid þam (þe), mid þy (þe), þa hwile (þe), swa lange swa*, and *þenden*. In 'OE Temporal Conjunctions Denoting "When" or "While"', with special regard to the Gospels and the Psalter' (*NM*) she analyses their occurrence in the psalter and gospel interlinear glosses in an attempt to discover whether the glossators' choices reveal any significant distinctions between them. Ogura's body of material, though large in bulk, is too homogeneous for us to be sure that her findings are an accurate representation of how these words were generally used in Anglo-Saxon England. Furthermore, there are severe limitations in using glosses as evidence for nuances in the meaning and use of conjunctions since glossing is not idiomatic and may be conditioned by stereotyped glossing and translating techniques. Even so, any steps that can be taken to refine our understanding of the syntactical words in the OE lexicon are to be welcomed. In this case, Ogura reaches the conclusion that the 'when' and 'while' conjunctions are semantically difficult to distinguish, but that their uses can be characterized syntactically, dialectically, or stylistically.

If the definition of common words is problematic, so too in a different way is the definition of the many *hapax legomena* in the OE lexicon. *Locbore* is one of these. It occurs only in Chapter 73 of the laws of Ethelberht, which survive only in the early-twelfth-century *Textus Roffensis*. Whatever this particular law may mean, it clearly refers to a woman, and *locbore* has usually been interpreted as a descriptive adjective, 'with long hair'. Christine Fell, in 'A *friwif locbore* revisited' (*ASE*), proposes a new interpretation of the law and, as part of her case, argues that *locbore* means 'in control of the keys', thus denoting the woman's position of responsibility within the household. Two other rare forms in this law, *friwif* and *leswæs*, are also discussed.

Lexicographers' attempts to define rare words cannot always be trusted and Paula Simmonds's article in the *Festschrift* for Fitzroy Pyle[27] (hereafter *Pyle*), 'Nautical Terms in the Brussels Glossary', offers some corrections to Bosworth–Toller. She prints in full the untitled section on ships (items 76–148) from the eleventh-century Brussels Glossary and demonstrates that two sections (items 76–122, 134–48) depend ultimately on the *Etymologies* of Isidore, while the third (items 123–36) shows a notable affinity with the Corpus, Épinal, and Erfurt Glossaries. It is these comparisons that provide her with a clear point of departure for re-assessing the dictionary definitions.

27. *Literature and Learning in Medieval and Renaissance England: Essays Presented to Fitzroy Pyle*, ed. by John Scattergood. IAP. pp. 233. £17.50.

Two new words are added to the lexicon by Gillis Kristensson. In 'Old English *cēo "a clearing"' (NM) Kristensson uses place-name evidence in charters to posit the existence of an otherwise unrecorded OE *cēo, 'a clearing', formed on the verb cēowan 'to chew'. It certainly sounds more plausible as an etymology for the place-name element Chew than Ekwall's rather desperate derivation from OE cēo 'the gill of a fish'. Kristensson's other new word, *glīse, 'a bright place', discussed in a short paper in N&Q, 'Old English *Glīse "A Bright Place" and Cognates', is drawn from the place-names Glyse and Glysenhall, recorded in fourteenth-century documents. Kristensson argues that the existence of OE *glīse, from IE *ghleis-, strengthens the case for an OE *glǣse, 'bright, clear, shining', first suggested by Ekwall and later taken up by A. H. Smith.

Phillip Pulsiano also adds to our knowledge of OE vocabulary by deciphering a gloss on f. 107r of British Library Ms. Royal 7 C iv, which he reports in 'A New Anglo-Saxon Gloss in the Liber Scintillarum' (N&Q). On the other hand, it may be necessary to remove from the record certain ghost-readings, as Pulsiano shows in another paper, 'The Blickling Psalter: aqua uel is' (N&Q). In 1963 Rowland Collins noted what appeared to be a strange gloss, īs 'ice' to Latin aqua 'water' in the Blickling Psalter (YW 44.78), but Pulsiano points out that, far from offering an idiosyncratic vernacular gloss at this point, the glossator was using his customary method of noting a variant Latin reading (i.e. aquis as an alternative to aqua, as found in the Paris, Bosworth, and Cambridge Psalters). It is a salutary reminder that the habits of glossators need to be understood before their glosses can be read correctly.

Glosses and glossaries have been the subject of several articles by Sherman M. Kuhn which have been published between 1939 and 1979. To mark his retirement these are now published in collected form, along with his rather smaller number of essays on OE literature, under the title Studies in the Language and Poetics of Anglo-Saxon England[28].

Finally, I am happy to recommend for students Alfred Bammesberger's admirably clear account of the bound morphemes in English, A Sketch of Diachronic English Morphology[29]. The focus is on OE, but each of the four main chapters, dealing respectively with the noun, the adjective, the pronoun, and the verb, begins with a relatively brief survey of what came before the Anglo-Saxon period and ends with an equally business-like summary of developments in ME and ModE, so that the characteristics of OE morphology are discussed in detail within a developmental context. The bibliography, though extensive, is not overwhelming, and is organized with the student very much in mind, listing works in order of decreasing relevance for the beginner.

4. Literature: General

After a flood of books on general literary topics last year, this year we have only two although, as always, there are some articles which are broadly based. Before reviewing them, however, I must return to the riches of last year in

---

28. Studies in the Language and Poetics of Anglo-Saxon England, by Sherman M. Kuhn. Karoma. pp. xviii + 236. $15.50.

29. A Sketch of Diachronic English Morphology, by Alfred Bammesberger. Eichstätter Materialien 7. Abteilung Sprache und Literatur. Pustet. pp. 94. DM 19.80.

commenting upon a book that was missed: Alexander Callander Murray's *Germanic Kinship Structure: Studies in Law and Society in Antiquity and the Early Middle Ages*[30]. In fact Murray's chief concern is with Frankish kinship and the *Lex Salica*, but Part I, which examines theories of Germanic kinship structure in Antiquity and the Early Middle Ages, and the first two sections of Part II, focusing on the evidence in Cæsar's *Bellum Gallicum* [*sic*] and Tacitus's *Germania*, are directly relevant for OE literature. Murray draws attention to the function of cognatic kindred groupings within Germanic society (groupings which allow for a sense of relationship through males or females) and argues vigorously against what he sees to be a modern emphasis on unilinealism, in which major corporate functions were carried out by descent groups. The *Germania* is shown to be a reliable testimony to cognatic relationships in early Germanic society and, indeed, to be a text that is generally trustworthy, unlike Cæsar's *Bellum Gallicum*. Murray's careful reading of what Tacitus really says – as opposed to what he is often too readily assumed to have said – is revealing and is, of course, helpful in our understanding of the kinship structures that operate in *Beowulf* and other poems. Murray recognizes this and discusses *Beowulf* in a series of extended footnotes on pp. 61–3.

Jeffrey Burton Russell's *Lucifer: The Devil in the Middle Ages*[31], is one of the two books this year, and it is a wide-ranging study of the figure of the devil in medieval Christianity. Much of Chapter 6, 'Lucifer in Early Medieval Art and Literature', is devoted to the treatment of the devil in Anglo-Saxon England, chiefly in the vernacular poems, but with some comment also on homilies and saints' lives. It is interesting to have the diabology of OE poetry examined in the broad context that Russell's book provides, and it is gratifying that so much space is devoted to it, but the value of the discussion is undercut in that it is often difficult to sort out at any given point what text Russell is writing about, or even whether it is poetry or prose. For example, his persistent use of the out-dated title *The Harrowing of Hell* for the Exeter Book poem *The Descent into Hell* leads to confusion between it and the OE prose accounts of this event, and the problem is exacerbated by his frequent reference to W. H. Hulme's work on *The Harrowing of Hell*, without making it clear that this is concerned with the OE prose tradition and not with Russell's poetic *Harrowing*. And yet, for all his use of Hulme, he appears to know only the article in *PMLA* 13 (1898) and not the equally important study in *MP* 1 (1903–4). A similar muddle occurs in the same paragraph on p. 136 where Russell summarizes a Harrowing scene which concludes with Christ's words: 'Lo, death, I am your death, and hell, I am your sting', translated, as the footnote tells us, from f. 154r of Ms. Junius 121 via an article by Luiselli Fadda. Russell claims that this is a poem (though he does not name it), but apart from the fact that Christ's words are not in poetic metre, Fadda's quotation is from an Easter Day homily on the Harrowing of Hell, and Junius 121, which records the homily on ff. 148v–54v, is not a poetic manuscript. The discussion of *Beowulf*

30. *Germanic Kinship Structure: Studies in Law and Society in Antiquity and the Early Middle Ages*, by Alexander Callander Murray. PIMS Studies and Texts 65. PIMS (1983). pp. xii + 256. $21.

31. *Lucifer: The Devil in the Middle Ages*, by Jeffrey Burton Russell. CornU. pp. 356. $24.95.

causes problems of a different kind. At one point we are invited to consider the possibility that Beowulf's three monster-enemies may hint at the unholy Trinity that some Christian Fathers had opposed to the divine Trinity, but there is no examination of how this works (or not) in the text: is Beowulf to be imagined as a representation of the holy Trinity and, if so, on what textual basis? Other assertions which are perhaps useful to Russell's argument but ill-founded in the text include the statement that the dragon has 'obvious association with the serpent of Eden' (p. 149), and an altogether too facile equation of Grendel as *sceadngenga* [*sic*] with the supposed role of Satan as 'shadow of God' (whatever that may mean). Matters are hardly improved by the bibliography. Krapp's edition of the Junius manuscript is cited as if it includes only *Genesis A*, when in fact it prints the conflated *A* and *B* texts as found in the manuscript; the second part of *Genesis A* in Krapp's edition begins on p. 28, not p. 29; and it is surely misleading to say that '*Genesis B* is consistent logically with *Genesis A* but gives greater color' (p. 319). In sum, Russell's book is useful more for the general picture it paints than for its handling of particular detail, at least with regard to the Anglo-Saxon tradition.

Margaret Enid Bridges's book, *Generic Contrast in Old English Hagiographical Poetry* (*Anglistica*), on the other hand, inspires confidence throughout. It is a commonplace in the literary criticism of OE that contrast is a dominant constructive principle; it is equally a commonplace to note that the saint's life tends to deal in polarities. Bridges's careful and systematic study of *Juliana, Guðlac A* and *B, Andreas*, and *Elene* attempts to determine the extent of their complex contrastive patterns, the structural, imagistic, and linguistic means by which these are achieved in each case, and finally to identify which elements are inherent in the hagiographical genre and which are attributable to the Anglo-Saxon poet's modification of his material. She chooses, inevitably, the long poetic saints' lives, but accident of survival means that these poems provide her with a good sampling of hagiographical types: *passio, vita, acta, conversio*. To some extent they overlap in the OE poems under discussion, but their mutual influences enable Bridges all the more readily to identify the constants within the genre as a whole. In Chapter 1 the contrastive plot-structure of each poem is discussed in turn; in Chapter 2 the poems are re-examined in the same order for their stylistic contrast. Two of the commonest ways in which polarization is achieved is through the exploitation of the sapiential motif and the imagery of (spiritual) warfare, but other polarizations are also present in several poems: habitat, mood, light, love, and so on. The survey, which is both thorough and sensitive, leads Bridges into a detailed consideration of the language of the poems and their thematic complexities. She sweeps away the generalities that so often fog the critical appreciation of the poetic saints' lives and, while avoiding any suggestion that they are great literature, she shows just how thoroughly the Anglo-Saxon poets understood the genre in which they were composing and how, in varying degrees, they succeeded in reflecting the genre in the native idiom.

For anyone interested in allusions to Mary in OE vernacular literature, Mary Clayton's study, 'Feasts of the Virgin in the liturgy of the Anglo-Saxon church' (*ASE*) will be essential reading, for, in a systematic chronological survey, she traces the establishment of Marian feasts in the Western Church, their adoption in Anglo-Saxon England, and their development throughout the period. Her analysis of primary sources demonstrates that the Roman feasts of the Purification, Annunciation, Assumption, and Nativity were introduced gradually and with some initial confusion in the seventh and eighth centuries and that by the end of the period they were observed throughout the country, at which time, c. 1030, the Eastern practices of celebrating the Purification and Conception were introduced in Winchester, spreading from there to Exeter and Canterbury. Surprisingly, these were the only churches in Western Europe to celebrate the Conception and Purification at this date, which is a striking testimony to Marian devotion in England.

'Falconry in Anglo-Saxon England' (*Medievalia*, 1984 for 1981) by Robin S. Oggins is useful in precisely the same way as Mary Clayton's study of Marian devotion. By providing us with a detailed account of a particular element in Anglo-Saxon life, he gives us a much clearer idea of what certain allusions conveyed to a contemporary audience. The instances that he discusses in the vernacular literature are those in *The Battle of Maldon*, *The Gifts of Men*, *The Fates of Men*, *Riddles*, and Ælfric's *Colloquy*.

The exploitation by Anglo-Saxon poets of the contrasting lexical collocations *mod* (mental ability) with its synonyms and *mægen* (physical ability) with its synonyms is the subject of Norma J. Engberg's '*Mod–Mægen* Balance in *Elene*, *The Battle of Maldon* and *The Wanderer*' (*NM*). Starting from the premise that the ideal human character has a balance of *mod* and *mægen*, she examines some instances in *Elene*, *Maldon*, and *The Wanderer* where, at a given moment, one or other predominates linguistically, and she shows how this linguistic weighting is an indication of what the poet is trying to convey about the satisfactory or unsatisfactory nature of the character's behaviour. It is a study that casts an interesting light on Byrhtwold's famous statement at the end of *Maldon* that the *mod* of the Anglo-Saxon warriors must increase as their *mægen* diminishes.

Important questions of editorial practice are raised by Alfred Bammesberger in 'Hidden glosses in manuscripts of Old English poetry' (*ASE*). In the present climate of conservative editing, few scholars are likely to respond enthusiastically to a method of textual criticism that may well lead to emendation or excision, yet the case put forward by Bammesberger is so reasonable and persuasive that it cannot easily be dismissed. He reminds us that Gollancz identified *Genesis* ll. 1546–48 as a late addition to the text, made when, at some stage in transmission, a scribe incorporated a marginal gloss into the body of the poem, with consequent disturbance of sense and metre. Taking this as his model, and admitting the possibility that marginal glosses may have found their way into other texts in the course of transmission, Bammesberger reconsiders *Genesis* ll. 1124b–7, *The Dream of the Rood* ll. 9b–10a, *Beowulf* ll. 59–63, 331b–2, and *Widsið* l. 35. In all of these cases, as Bammesberger demonstrates, the awkwardness that editors have regularly noticed may have been caused by additional or substitutional glosses. We are left with the tantalizing thought that there may be other examples in the corpus as yet unidentified.

Scribal activity is also a concern of Angelika Lutz's 'Spellings of the *waldend* group – again' (*ASE*). She shows that, whereas scribes writing in standard LWS use the expected spelling (with breaking) for the agent-noun *wealdend* in prose texts, in poetic texts, by contrast, they show a marked preference for unbroken *waldend*, a spelling that is normal in Anglian, but archaic for a LWS speaker. She argues that this choice was a deliberate one, that it indicates a perception that *waldend* was regarded as a word with 'poetic potential' (p. 62), and that the archaic spelling and consequent archaic pronunciation when the text was read aloud, contributed to the solemn and exalted nature of OE alliterative poetry, just like the exclusively poetic words and the uncontracted morphological forms which Sisam noted as distinctive characteristics in poetic style.

The remaining topic of general relevance is OE poetic metre. This year there are three articles, each of which approaches the subject from a markedly different viewpoint. Christopher B. McCully's 'Old English Verse Rhythm: A Reply' (*ES*) is the most general. He takes up a position contrary to that of Ida Masters Hollowell in her paper on 'Old English Verse Rhythm' published in *ES* two years ago (*YW* 63.53–4) when he argues that what matters in rhythmical patterns of speech is not the *actual* acoustic energy expended on syllabic sounds, but what the auditor seems to *perceive*. He therefore takes issue with Hollowell's statement that the verse-lifts of each line could not have been equal in force on the grounds that, although they are indeed unequal from the point of view of acoustic and experimental phonetics, they are *perceived* to be equal by the auditor, which is all that matters. He also objects to her remarks on falling rhythm because if, as he believes, rhythm is apprehended as a series of accents occurring in time, it cannot 'fall'. What does fall is the intonational contour, which is quite a different thing. Not surprisingly, McCully concludes his paper by rejecting Hollowell's suggestion that for OE poetry we must envisage a stress pattern probably contradictory to that of ordinary OE speech. As McCully notes, 'it is difficult to conceive of a troop of *heorðgenēatas* listening with much patience to a long recited narrative whose artificial rhythmical nature . . . needed to be learned in order to be appreciated . . .' (p. 390). It is a delight to find common sense being allowed to play its part in the discussion of a subject that often stimulates immensely elaborate theories.

Klaus R. Grinda, in 'Pigeonholing Old English Poetry: Some Criteria of Metrical Style' (*Anglia*), attempts to put metrical analysis to practical use by subjecting all OE poems of five hundred lines or more (plus *Maldon* as a datable poem) to nine criteria of metrical style and producing a series of tables to show what percentage of lines in each poem meets each criterion. The tables indicate that there is no significant difference between the various parts of *Beowulf*, which he is therefore inclined to think is by one author, not two. More generally, the stylistic affinities between certain texts and the differences between others, which are instinctively perceived by many readers of OE poetry, are uncannily reflected in Grinda's tabular hierarchy, which gives a statistical basis for what had hitherto been unconscious perceptions.

Finally, there is Eric Stanley's 'Alliterative Ornament and Alliterative Rhythmical Discourse in Old High German and Old Frisian Compared with Similar Manifestations in Old English' (*BGDSL*). Stanley is more concerned with illuminating our understanding of OHG and OFr patterns of rhythm and alliteration than the OE but, having noted metrical licences in the OHG texts, he raises the question of what constitutes traditional (i.e. common Germanic) metrical licence and whether such licences can be identified in *Beowulf* and *The Finnsburg Fragment*. If they could be, it may be a form of evidence for the 'Germanic lay' theory of their origins. But a note of caution is sounded since the examples are few and since any heroic lays that may have existed in OE are likely to have been much changed by the sophisticated poet of *Beowulf*, thus eliminating most of the metrical indications.

5. Beowulf

In last year's report, in summarizing a paper on *Beowulf* by Bernard F. Huppé (*YW* 64.104), I noted that his interpretation of the poem was soon to be set out more fully in a book-length study. It has now been published under the title *The Hero in the Earthly City: A Reading of Beowulf*[32]. Those who know Huppé's work will not be surprised to learn that the frame of reference used for the reading is Augustinian. His interpretation of the poem is thus emphatically Christian and moralistic: Beowulf and the society he moves in are doomed to failure because both are flawed in exalting heroic life above life in Christ. Huppé justifies this reading on the grounds that it 'forestall[s] mistaking the poem as a primitive work of art' (p. ix). But why should Huppé assume that non-Augustinian approaches to the poem make it seem primitive? On the contrary, Huppé's reading underplays the complex sophistication of the text, for he wishes us to believe that the poet is operating within a black-and-white world in which there is apparently no place for the emotional tensions, pathos, and profound tragedy which give *Beowulf* its powerful dynamism and which engage the audience on many levels. Indeed, if the audience were to regard the protagonists as mistaken, and their world and their deeds as sinful failures, the response throughout would necessarily be one of moral and emotional dissociation springing from a sense of spiritual superiority. But if Huppé's reading of the poem as some kind of admonitory exemplum presents me with a different *Beowulf* from the one I know and enjoy, so too does his translation, which constitutes half of the book. Like the interpretative arguments, the translation deserves more attention than I can give it here, but my general response, after going through it line by line, is that, while it might be a reliable guide to Huppé's personal conception of the poem, it is a thoroughly unreliable guide to the surviving OE text. Personal judgement always has a part to play in translation, and it is notoriously difficult to capture accurately the full meaning of an OE poetic line. But when all due allowance is made, the case is not altered. Throughout Huppé ignores details of grammar and syntax, thus altering the relationship between one clause and another, with considerable distortion of the meaning; he substitutes proper names for pronouns, even when there is at least as good a case for a different referent; he paraphrases in order to change the emphasis; he gives his own meaning to words and phrases whose sense is well established; he adds explanatory glosses as if they are part of the text; and he shows a tendency to elaborate without justification. In the preface (p. x) Huppé noted that a translation reveals wrong or misguided perceptions more readily than an involved argument can do and his version of the poem is therefore offered as integral to his case. He is thus hoist with his own petard, for the demonstrable unreliability of Huppé's translation must be a reflection of the unreliability of his interpretation.

At this point, before going on to consider the rest of this year's books on *Beowulf*, it is instructive to turn to an altogether different approach to the

32. *The Hero in the Earthly City: A Reading of Beowulf*, by Bernard F. Huppé. MRTS 33. SUNY. pp. x + 201. $15.

question of *Beowulf* and Christianity, Edward B. Irving's article 'The nature of Christianity in *Beowulf*' (*ASE*), which is a study characterized by sound common sense and faithfulness to the text. At the outset Irving vigorously disposes both of the old idea of the Monkish Interpolator and of the more modern method of interpretation via the *Patrologia Latina* and focuses his attention instead on the apparently simple matter of the distribution of Christian references in the poem, which is shown, on a statistical analysis, to be strikingly uneven as between speakers (including the poet-narrator) and as between different parts of the poem. In the discussion which follows Irving explores the implications of these findings, sensitively defining the different Christian sentiments of poet-narrator, Hroðgar, and Beowulf, and the impact that the distribution and nature of the Christian references have on the poem's mood and world-view.

With Helen Damico's *'Beowulf's' Wealhtheow and the Valkyrie Tradition*[33] we return to this year's book-length studies. Professor Damico attempts to solve the enigma of the otherwise unknown Wealhþeow by providing her with a literary context and a legendary origin. Comparative analysis of Wealhþeow's presentation in *Beowulf* and the presentation of women in OE and ON poetry lead Damico to conclude that the literary type to which Wealhþeow is related is that of the valkyrie-bride, best exemplified in Eddic poetry by such personages as Sigrun, Svava, Brynhild, and Guðrun. In her search for Wealhþeow's legendary origins Damico focuses on Scandinavian prose versions of Scylding history, in particular on the *Uppsalafǫr þáttr* of *Hrólfs saga Kraka*, and makes a case for the identity of Wealhþeow and Yrsa. On the face of it they are an unlikely pair, for our first impression of Wealhþeow is that she is a woman of great virtue, whereas Yrsa is notorious for her sexual impropriety. But, on the basis of the manuscript reading *suna minum* (l. 1227), usually emended to plural *sunum minum*, Damico argues that Wealhþeow's relationship to Hroþulf is the incestuous one of aunt–mother, and that her plea to Beowulf is on behalf of her son Hroþulf and not on behalf of her two sons by Hroðgar. There is, of course, much more to Damico's case than this, but acceptance of the manuscript reading is crucial and leads to a radical reconsideration of Wealhþeow's role, particularly in her second speech. In Chapter 1 the close analysis of the poet's presentation of the Danish queen is firmly based on the text and is valuable in its contradiction of the assumption that Wealhþeow is yet another hapless, elegiac woman, but the arguments that the book develops about her literary and legendary associations are highly speculative and will not convince every reader. Damico herself is, of course, well aware that there are difficulties in elucidating an Anglo-Saxon poetic figure largely on the basis of evidence drawn from later ON literature, but she presses ahead nevertheless.

In an altogether different class from the books by Huppé and Damico is *Approaches to Teaching 'Beowulf'*[34], edited by Jess B. Bessinger and Robert F. Yeager. It is geared specifically to the teaching of *Beowulf* in American

33. *'Beowulf's' Wealhtheow and the Valkyrie Tradition*, by Helen Damico. UWisc. pp. xiii + 270. $35.
34. *Approaches to Teaching 'Beowulf'*, ed. by Jess B. Bessinger and Robert F. Yeager. Approaches to Teaching Masterpieces of World Literature 4. MLA. pp. xvii + 214. hb $25, pb $12.50.

universities, where teachers may well not have Anglo-Saxon studies as their primary interest, and where the poem will be dealt with in translation, perhaps even in the short space of one or two hours. It is no doubt a useful practical guide in its home territory, but it will have little to offer teachers or students in the British system. However, on pp. 107–22 Fred C. Robinson gives a good survey of the historical background to the poem, and that at least has general value.

The *Beowulf* translation industry has been maintaining its usual high productivity levels. In addition to Huppé's translation (see above, p. 85), there are two translations which claim to be into modern English verse. I have not seen Marijane Osborn's version[35], and so cannot comment on the success of her attempt. In favour of that by Gildas Roberts, *Beowulf: A New Translation into Modern English Verse*[36], it must be said that it at least has the advantage of being fairly close to the OE original, although the notion that Beowulf uttered a boast 'before he climbed into his bed' (l. 676, p. 19) set me wondering what kind of cosy domestic image the student reader would have of the inside of Heorot. The notes are rather banal and the idiosyncratic bibliography could be more accurate: the *Germania*, for example, is cited in Mattingly's Penguin translation of 1948 without any mention of S. A. Handford's 1970 revision, and he cites Bruce Mitford's second edition of the Sutton Hoo *Handbook* (1972) without mention of the third edition of 1979. Bibliographical accuracy is not the main point at issue here; there were significant advances made throughout the 1970s in the interpretation of the Sutton Hoo treasure, and it is important to give the bibliographical information that will allow students to have the benefit of the most recent scholarship, albeit in the *Handbook*'s simplified form.

The question of how one should set about translating *Beowulf* is certainly a topic that merits discussion and it is the subject of an article by Raymond P. Tripp Jr in the 1983 issue of *In Geardagum*, ' "Like It or Lump It": Thematic Remarks Toward An *Accurate* Translation of *Beowulf*'. Tripp's opening position, that the translator should be sensitive to the true meaning of the words from which he is translating, can hardly be faulted, but I part company with him when, in discussing how the translator determines the true meaning, he states that 'in the last analysis, language is the greatest of democracies, and every man must rely upon his own subjective resources in deciding what a word means' (p. 15). The translator must, of course, make an independent decision about how to represent his perception of the word's meaning in the vocabulary of another language, but Tripp's statement goes much farther than this in allowing the meaning itself to be subjectively determined. It takes one to the top of a slippery slope and Tripp cheerfully slides down it when he discusses *Beowulf* ll. 733b–34a. Puns abound, so it seems, in almost every word, although it is *ālumpen* and *wēn* that are most exhaustively explored. At the end, in a continuation of the punning, we are invited to 'like it or lump it . . .'. My own response to the invitation was unhesitating.

Kevin S. Kiernan, in 'The state of the *Beowulf* manuscript 1882–1983'

35. *Beowulf: A Verse Translation with Treasures of the Ancient North*, by Marijane Osborn, with an intro. by Fred C. Robinson. UCal (1983). pp. xix + 141. $29.95.

36. *Beowulf: A New Translation into Modern English Verse*, by Gildas Roberts. Breakwater. pp. xii + 99. $6.95.

(*ASE*), takes us firmly back to the physical reality of the poem's survival. Under fibre-optic light Kiernan has been able to see between three and four hundred letters or part-letters that were not visible to Zupitza when he prepared his facsimile, and they are all listed in the article, in line order. Although the manuscript is not in a significantly worse shape than it was when Zupitza worked on it in 1882, Kiernan judges that it may soon be expedient for the British Library to provide a safer method of preserving it. The most conservative step would be rebinding, but if the opportunity were taken to separate the Southwick and Nowell codices, the new binding alone would provide significantly more protection than the present one because the covers would close properly.

Most of the remaining articles on *Beowulf* fall into three groups: textual elucidation, discussion of the monsters, and essays dealing in various ways with the poem's structure.

The elucidations of particular lines and longer passages are most conveniently dealt with in order of their occurrence in the text, beginning with Göran Kjellmer's 'On a New Reading of *Beowulf*' (*NM*), which was prompted by an essay in *ES* in which James B. Spamer offered a new interpretation of the poem's opening lines (*YW* 62.95). In his note, Kjellmer examines three possible ways of interpreting the plural genitive in *Gar-Dena* (l. 1) but comes to the conclusion that each, including Spamer's, has its own difficulty. He therefore expresses the opinion that, for the time being at least, it would be wise to reserve judgement.

A particularly popular crux – if that is not too bizarre a description of it – is the *gifstōl* passage in ll. 168–9, and in the 1983 issue of *In Geardagum* S. M. Riley offers yet another attempt to solve this *locus desperatus*. There is the usual listing of previous arguments and a scrutiny of each word, leading finally to the translation: 'he [Hrothgar] could not come near the gift-thorne [*sic*], the treasure, because of Fate; he knew not its favor' (p. 52).

The next article, 'The Coastwarden's Maxim in *Beowulf*: a Clarification' (*N&Q*) by R. E. Kaske, has its origins not in a textual crux, but in an editorial blunder. When Kaske's *SP* article '*Sapientia et Fortitudo* as the Controlling Theme of *Beowulf*' (*YW* 39.71) was anthologized, the editor translated *Beowulf* ll. 287–9 in such a way that it seemed to be at variance with Kaske's carefully argued interpretation, and the innocent author has recently been taken to task for the discrepancy. In this article Kaske defends his original position and re-examines the coastguard's statement about words and deeds, concluding, as he had done earlier, that the maxim is a gnomic generalization about human conduct applied by the coastguard – no doubt wryly – to himself. On this occasion, however, Kaske offers his own paraphrase of the *Beowulf* text, one which this time harmonizes with his interpretation.

Klaeber's interpretation of l. 804 as 'Grendel had laid a spell on swords' is rejected by H. L. Rogers in '*Beowulf*, line 804' (*N&Q*). He shows convincingly that Klaeber's alleged sense of *forswerian* is a lexicographical ghost and, with the ghost safely laid, the way is clear for Rogers to propose the sense of 'renounce', with Beowulf as the subject. In conclusion Rogers brings broader considerations into play to provide further justification for his reading.

The final article offering textual elucidation is Theodore M. Andersson's 'The Thief in *Beowulf*' (*Speculum*). In an attempt to discover what would have been the response of the Anglo-Saxon audience to this story of theft, the earliest extant in Germanic literature, Andersson considers the Scandinavian attitudes to thieves as expressed in legal terms in *Grágás* and, more emotively, in the sagas. He argues that the fuller evidence from the Norse parallels can deepen our understanding of the thief in *Beowulf*, although he also acknowledges that the Anglo-Saxon figure differs in some important respects from the Norse ones. Nevertheless, he feels that the similarities are sufficiently close to suggest that the completion of the manuscript lacuna in l. 2223b is more likely to be *þēow* or *þēof* than *þegn*, since the evidence of the Norse texts indicates that *þegn* would confer unwarrantable status on a man who steals and conceals.

The four studies of the Beowulfian monsters are all from this year's *In Geardagum*, which had this subject as its unifying theme. The first essay in the collection is Paul Beekman Taylor's 'Grendel's Monstrous Arts', which shows how Grendel's various attributes parallel those of the giant (*þurs*) of Norse mythology, a creature kin to the gods, a creator and artificer, whose crafts and skills, in a diabolic way, rival those of gods and men. Beowulf conceives of Grendel as a *þyrs* in l. 426 and Taylor believes that this hints at the poet's use of the tradition of giant figures. Alexandra Hennessey Olsen produces arguments against Taylor's interpretation, however. In her essay ' "Þurs" and "Pyrs": Giants and the Date of *Beowulf*' (*In Geardagum*) she questions what she sees to be Taylor's unspoken assumptions that *Beowulf* is early and that poet and audience were aware of the mythical Germanic past, and she claims, by contrast, that if *Beowulf* is a late poem, as may be the case, then *þyrs* would not have aroused connotations of mythical giants at all. Her analysis of *þurs* in *Egils Saga* suggests, rather, that by the early thirteenth century the semantic shift had been so great in Iceland that the word could be used for humorous effect as a kind of nickname for men of large stature. Olsen proposes that the one use of *þyrs* in *Beowulf* should also be taken in this humorous way. She notes that it is used by Beowulf only when he makes what she calls his 'cocky speech' upon his arrival in Heorot.

Raymond Tripp's approach to Grendel is quite different from Taylor's or Olsen's. In 'Grendel Polytropos' (*In Geardagum*) he assembles all the nominal characterizations of Grendel and arranges them in three lists: order of occurrence, alphabetical order, and order of frequency. It would be surprising if the exercise produced any new perceptions of the way in which Grendel is portrayed, but the lists are at least useful in demonstrating that the poet gives us a being who is decidedly more human than monstrous. They also allow us to see at a glance that he is an amalgam of traditions. I have never before thought of Grendel as a 'mongrel', least of all as a 'portmanteau monster', and I am not sure that I want to begin now, but it is in these terms that Tripp lightheartedly sums him up.

The other essay in the collection, 'Grendel's Heroic Mother', by Kevin Kiernan, shows how the idea of perversion is as important a clue to the understanding of Grendel's mother as it is of Grendel himself. He examines her many attributes and circumstances of life which parallel those of the heroic world, but demonstrates that in all of these details there is a warping element, with the result that her very being and her behaviour turn out to be an indictment of the kind of heroism she represents.

Sylvia Huntley Horowitz, in 'The Interrupted Battles in *Beowulf*' (*NM*), deals with the puzzling question of the relationship of the fitt-divisions to the structure of the poem, in particular the apparently arbitrary way in which, on nine occasions, they interrupt battle narratives. She notes that in four cases (the Breca incident, the mere-battle, and two in the dragon-battle) the division occurs just as the hero is in great danger and seems likely to fail – a suspense technique reminiscent of cliff-hanger movies. In four other cases (the Grendel fight, the Finnsburg episode, Beowulf's account of the Heathobard feud, and Beowulf's reflections on the Geatish–Swedish wars) the division occurs when the antagonists are locked in stasis; after the fitt-division, stasis continues, but then time passes and revenge is achieved. The ninth interrupted battle (the Messenger's narration) has elements of both patterns. Whether the fitt numbers are original to the composition or are a later addition, Horowitz's structural analysis indicates that they are not arbitrarily positioned, at least in relation to the battle scenes where, on a more superficial level, they might seem particularly ill-placed.

A structural element in the poem which has often been commented upon is the complex use of parallelisms and contrasts. Constance B. Heiatt, in 'Modþryðo and Heremod: Intertwined Threads in the *Beowulf*- Poet's Web of Words' (*JEGP*), explores the subtle ways in which the Heremod and Modþryðo allusions contribute to this thematic web of similarities and differences. She demonstrates that in the first Heremod allusion there is a tripartite set of parallelisms and contrasts involving Heremod, Beowulf, and Sigemund, and that in the second allusion, in Hroðgar's 'sermon', there is also a tripartite set, this time between Heremod, Beowulf, and Hroðgar. The Modþryðo passage is also not simply a case of a contrast between Modþryðo and Hygd, but is part of a web of similarities and differences involving Heremod (to whom she is a reverse-parallel – someone initially bad who turns out well) and Beowulf himself (who, like her, has an unpromising start but who, unlike her, was never guilty of the blood of his companions).

There are structural implications also in David Tandy's 'Evidence for Editing in *Beowulf*' (*NM*) since he discusses apparent parallelisms of word and phrase, but his primary concern is with finding clues to the prehistory of the extant text. He proposes that *Beowulf* should be seen as a 'transitional' text, composed orally but edited for the benefit of a more alert, sophisticated, and literate segment of the audience. In support of this he cites two areas where he believes he has detected signs of poetic editing: (i) the exploitation of the formulaic *þæt (þa) wæs god/an/frod cyning* which, in its six occurrences, refers once to Scyld, three times to Hroðgar, and twice to Beowulf, and which Tandy believes is evidence of the poet's conscious desire to identify Hroðgar and Beowulf, and (ii) correspondences between *mildust, monðwærust*, and *liðost* in ll. 3180–2 and the same or related words, *milde, geþwære, liðe*, in ll. 1172a, 1230, and 1220, all spoken by Wealhþeow. Tandy is convinced that these correspondences could only have been achieved by editing. The evidence seems to me to be remarkably slight for such a conclusion. The theory that the poet set out to establish a specific identity between Hroðgar and Beowulf through a half-line formula used over more than 2000 lines makes much of little and in any case requires that we drop the first of the six examples (Scyld). As for the supposed parallels between ll. 3180–2 and Wealhþeow's speeches about 2000 lines earlier, one is obliged to ask whether the audience would have made the connection on the basis of three not quite identical word-forms and whether they would have recognized that verbal similarity carried any significance; there were, after all, only a limited number of words available to describe what the *Beowulf* poet has in mind throughout the poem: the necessary humane aspects of kingship.

Finally, there is one article this year, by Patricia Bethel, specifically on the metre of *Beowulf*. In a short piece in *N&Q*, 'On the Combination of A-Types into Lines in *Beowulf*', she examines the instances in *Beowulf* where both half-lines are of the A-type, and notes that the poet shows a marked tendency in such cases to favour a disproportionately large number of rare subtypes. Taken together with the already established fact that the poet generally seems to have avoided using a pair of A-types in the same line wherever possible, she deduces that he was a man of some metrical sensitivity, who sought to avoid identical cadences, either by the expedient of not combining A-types, or by varying them if combined.

6. The Junius Manuscript

Once again the poems of the Junius manuscript have attracted little attention, but Barbara Raw has made an important contribution to our understanding of the codex itself. In 'The Construction of Oxford, Bodleian Library, Junius 11' (*ASE*) she reports the results of her careful re-examination of the manuscript's collation, stitching, binding, pricking, and ruling, and follows this with some important deductions concerning the production and history of the manuscript. The most significant of her conclusions are that the manuscript has been restitched and that the binding dates from the time of the restitching (perhaps in the early thirteenth century); that the end of *Daniel* has almost certainly been lost; and that *Christ and Satan* was not originally a separate manuscript, but was copied partly on vellum prepared in connection with the end of *Daniel*. She also considers the question of missing folios and the dates of their loss, and argues that the losses from the second gathering are not related to the interpolation of *Genesis B*. Diagrams, charts, and tables accompany the essay, which is an essential reference point for anyone interested in the Junius manuscript poems in particular, or the history of Anglo-Saxon manuscripts in general.

As for the contents of the manuscript, each poem has been the subject or part-subject of one article. In 'Satan's Injured Innocence in *Genesis B*, 360–2; 390–2: A Gregorian Source' (*ES*) Thomas D. Hill makes the plausible suggestion that the ultimate source for Satan's protestation of innocence after his fall is to be found in Gregory's exegesis of the Leviathan in his *Moralia in Job*. In a detailed discussion Gregory explores the idea that Satan, even after the fall, had no sense that he had done wrong. As Hill points out, a lamenting Satan is common enough, but a Satan who persists in protesting his innocence is an oddity.

With regard to *Exodus* Charles D. Wright, in 'Moses, *Manna Mildost* (*Exodus* 550a)' (*N&Q*), is able to demonstrate that the description of Moses as 'the mildest of men' is not a detail at odds with his portrayal as a *folctoga* and *herewisa*, but is a description which has biblical authority and which, in the Christian era, came to have almost proverbial status. In conclusion he notes some examples of early medieval insistence that mildness was an appropriate characteristic for kings, for whom Moses, as leader of the Israelites, was often cited as an Old Testament model. The phrase is thus shown to be rich in associations and singularly apt.

In a lengthy and at times strained study of *Daniel*, 'The Old English *Daniel*. The King and His City' (*NM*), Robert Emmett Finnegan attempts to demonstrate that Babylon, in the OE poem, becomes for a time the physical symbol of the heavenly Jerusalem and its king, for the duration of his conversion, a Job-like figure pleasing to God. We are invited to view the tension between Jerusalem and Babylon 'through the glass provided by Augustine's *De Civitate Dei* and *Enarratio in Psalmum 64*' (p. 195). Finnegan does not succeed in convincing me, however, that there is any real justification in the OE text for the Augustinian reading, and I remain distinctly uneasy about the weight he gives to the presence or absence of the name of Babylon at particular points in the poem. When one considers the demands of the narrative and the need for variation, it is inevitable that the word will appear frequently, but unevenly distributed, without this being in any way indicative of a subtle ulterior motive on the poet's part. Finnegan emphasizes Nabuchodonosor's conversion and believes that, in addition to revealing to the audience the character of a just but loving God, one of the major aims of the poem is to demonstrate how even notorious heathens, under God's tutelage, might be converted and perhaps saved.

Christ and Satan is only part of the subject of E. G. Stanley's 'Notes on the Text of *Christ and Satan*; and on *The Riming Poem* and *The Rune Poem*, chiefly on *wynn*, *wēn* and *wenne*' (*N&Q*), but what Stanley has to say makes an important contribution to the study of the poem's textual problems since he provides forty-five detailed notes to half-lines, lines, or groups of lines. His comments on the other two poems will be noted below, pp. 96–7.

7. The Poems of the Vercelli Book

The year, 1984, has likewise been poor for publications on the Vercelli Book poems, although I admit that my inability to obtain a copy of Julia Bolton Holloway's ' "The Dream of the Rood" and Liturgical Drama' (*CompD*) deprives this survey of what would have been one of its longer contributions. Holloway's article apart, there is only one publication that I have to report on *The Dream of the Rood*: 'Stylistic disjunctions in *The Dream of the Rood*' (*ASE*) by Carol Braun Pasternack. In a detailed and extended study Pasternack convincingly demonstrates that the large-scale disjunctions in the poem at ll. 27, 78, 121, and 147, along with the frequency of chiasmus, would have been recognized by the audience as a stylistic pattern complementing the poem's system of echoic repetitions and parallels. She goes on to argue that the poet's exploitation of these complementary patterns is indicative of his overall purpose in composing the *Dream*, which was not primarily to relate an individual's visionary experience, nor to give a striking account of the historical crucifixion, but was to explore the idea of the cross according to several different perspectives. Thus the disjunctions act as stylistic circumscriptions defining the limitations of each perspective, while the echoic repetitions and parallels have a unifying effect in signalling that each perspective is merely a facet of the cross's complex and absolute reality. Despite the reference to disjunction in the title of the essay, one of the clear and satisfying implications of Pasternack's study is that *The Dream of the Rood*, as it now exists, is a well-crafted unity, in which ll. 78 ff. are as integral to the poet's purpose as the more dramatic first half.

Lisa J. Kiser offers a contribution to the elucidation of *Andreas* by examining street and path imagery as a clue to the spiritual message of the poem. In her essay '*Andreas* and the *Lifes Weg*. Convention and Innovation in Old English Metaphor' (*NM*) she sets out to show how original the Anglo-Saxon poet is throughout the poem in his exploitation of the central Christian metaphor of the 'Way' and how, in using it as he does, he achieves a sophisticated and constantly shifting relationship between the poem's literal level and its spiritual dimension. However, since the words for street and path that Kiser discusses have the thoroughly prosaic function of denoting streets and paths along which Andreas and others necessarily move in the given narrative, some readers will no doubt feel sceptical about whether the poet really intended them to carry special metaphorical weight as images of the Christian Way. Yet the reading is a coherent one and the deductions that Kiser makes about the poet's didactic aims are certainly not inappropriate for vernacular hagiography.

Richard Cleasby's notes on the Vercelli Codex are the subject of a continuing series of articles by Christine Fell. Three years ago, in *LeedsSE* (*YW* 62.100), she published Cleasby's notes on the short poems, and in this year's issue she gives us his meditations on *Elene*, under the title 'Richard Cleasby's Notes on the Vercelli Codex (Continued)'; his notes on *Andreas* are promised for a future date. Taken as a whole the notes contribute to our understanding of the early development of OE textual scholarship; on a more intimate level they testify to Cleasby's excellent command of languages and his perception in providing conjectural readings or emendations. Anyone with a close interest in the text of *Elene* will find Cleasby's observations a stimulation and a challenge.

These three articles, with the addition of the study of *Andreas* and *Elene* in Bridges's *Generic Contrast in Old English Hagiographical Poetry*, reviewed above on p. 82, are the only 1984 publications that I have read on the Vercelli poems, but I should also mention an article by Douglas D. Short in last year's issue of *In Geardagum* (1983), a journal which is often slow to reach its subscribing libraries in Britain. In a business-like paper entitled 'Another Look at a Point of Old English Grammar: *Elene* 508 and *Psalm* 77: 27' Short offers two possible explanations for the lack of congruence between *wif oððe wer* as the subject and its verb *cendan* in l. 508 of *Elene*. The first suggestion is that the scribe wrote *oððe* in place of *ond*, influenced perhaps by *oðer* which stands immediately above *oððe* as the first word of a line in the manuscript's prose-lineation of the *Elene* text. The second suggestion, which involves a discussion of Psalm 77.27, is that, as in later English, poets were sometimes undecided between the use of 'and' and 'or' when the relationship between co-ordinate structures was segregatory but not specifically alternate. Short believes, therefore, that in the case of *Elene* l. 508 one could envisage the poet choosing *oððe* as a stylistic variant of *ond*, while still maintaining a sense in his own mind that the subject of *cendan* was a combined plural.

8. The Exeter Book

Schneider[26] also contains essays on literary topics, among which is 'The Non-Narrative Structure of "The Wife's Lament": A Reconsideration of its

Lyric Elements' by Uwe Böker. Böker takes issue with the idea that *The Wife's Lament* is essentially a narrative and argues rather that it is an expression of mood and that appreciation of the poem requires a thorough analysis of its formal aspects and of the aesthetic function of the poem's stylistic devices. The particular aspect of the poem that Böker deals with at length is the time-sequence. Lines 1–5 are regarded as stating the poem's content and presenting the reason for the lament; ll. 6–26 are interpreted as describing the events leading up to the woman's present plight; and ll. 27 ff. are taken to evoke her immediate situation, which is the poem's primary concern. The case is clearly presented, but I was left wondering why it was argued at all since, as far as I am aware, *The Wife's Lament* has been accepted as a mood-piece for many years, with the necessary consequence that the structure must be something like the one that Böker describes here.

Another popular elegy is *The Wanderer*. Elizabeth Hait's 'The Wanderer's Lingering Regret: A Study of Patterns of Imagery' (*Neophil*) draws attention to the speaker's fluctuations between vivid and less-vivid recollections of his past, which she interprets as a sign of his ageing – a time-based diminution of memory rather than a conscious rejection of it. She explores in some detail the poem's changes between past and present, between motion and stasis, and its images of diminishment, and she notes that, as the poem progresses, the past tends to become less vivid, while the present becomes more real. Her understanding of the wanderer's emotional and spiritual state is that, although he has come to realize that security rests with God, his distancing from his past happiness is as much the result of increasing old age as of spiritual transformation, so that some of his memories have a nostalgic hold on him and he cannot be said fully to embrace the vision of God.

The title of Janet Bately's article 'Time and the Passing of Time in "The Wanderer" and Related OE Texts' (*E&S*) might lead one to expect a similar approach to Hait's, but in fact the perspective is quite different. Professor Bately's study of the skilfully ambiguous handling of time in *The Wanderer* is presented in the context of some interesting observations about the Anglo-Saxon attitude to time in general and the treatment of time in a number of other OE poems, notably *The Seafarer* and *The Ruin*, where she finds, as in *The Wanderer*, a striking exploitation by the poets of the flexibility of time-reference which is inherent in OE syntax and lexis.

Deor is the subject of only one brief note this year. In 'Deor: The Refrain' (*Expl*) Jacqueline Banerjee proposes the following translation of the refrain: 'In that situation he overcame [or 'she' in the case of strophes referring to women]; in these circumstances, in the same way, I can' (p. 4). It is a radical re-interpretation of what has usually been regarded as an impersonal construction, but the flimsy evidence that Banerjee offers in its support is hardly likely to effect a dramatic conversion of *Deor* readers.

Joyce Hill's ' "Widsið" and the Tenth Century' (*NM*) considers what the poem would have meant to a tenth-century audience who listened to it in the form in which it is extant in the Exeter Book. Above all she attempts to identify what kind of appeal the poem's catalogues would have had for a late-Anglo-Saxon audience. Examination of the names listed in the poem leads her to conclude that, from the point of view of Germanic legend cycles, many *Widsið*-names have little or no significance and that some may well be spurious. As a consequence the audience must be imagined as responding to the total impression created by the catalogues, rather than to the evocative force of each 'allusion' in turn, with the result that the oriental and biblical names, which for many must have been equally lacking in suggestive force, would have been readily accepted as contributing to the cumulative effect of the impressively encyclopaedic lists.

Last year I noted some books that dealt with the entire collection of riddles in the Exeter Book (*YW* 64.110–11). This year I note one, by Reinhard Gleissner, which deals with a specialist group, the *double-entendre* riddles which, as Gleissner notes, have not received the scholarly attention they deserve. In *Die »zweideutigen« altenglischen Rätsel des 'Exeter Book' in ihrem zeitgenössischen Kontext*[37] Gleissner examines the riddles in the cultural context of the Benedictine Revival, the context in which they were preserved in the extant manuscript, and concludes that, given the norms of Christian sexual morality then prevailing (which he carefully identifies), the *double-entendre* riddles must have been understood as obscene. In this he takes his stand against those scholars who, while acknowledging the sexual allusions, have attempted to remove all traces of obscenity from them. Riddles 25, 42, and 46 (Krapp's numbering) are exhaustively examined, but in a lengthy appendix there is discussion of several other riddles which, at one time or another, have been regarded as *double-entendre* riddles and/or obscene. In the course of his discussions Gleissner proposes alternative interpretations to riddles 12 (pig-[skin]), 44 (writing quill or reed), and 62 (tool for tapping a smelting oven). He also accepts the recent solution 'urine' for riddles 75+76 and proposes a philological correction to *superne secg* in riddle 62. Gleissner argues that since the medieval mind did not locate the south at the bottom of the map, the phrase cannot be interpreted as 'the man who works from below'. Instead he proposes that the *superne secg* be taken to refer to the man living and working to the south of the medieval cloister, an interpretation which would be as apt for the innocent solution as for the obscene one. The close examination of riddle 25 suggests that the topos 'the wanton woman' exists alongside the innocent meaning of 'onion' and that riddle 46, 'Lot and his children', on the evidence of contemporary sources also had obscene connotations at the time of the Benedictine Revival. His analysis of this riddle indicates, further, that the immediate source is not the Bible, as is usually thought, but rather rabbinical and perhaps other medieval Latin versions of the riddle. Whether or not one agrees with Gleissner's interpretations – and the riddles are notoriously productive of disagreement – it is undeniably a stimulating exercise to look at them afresh in the cultural context of the Benedictine Revival when, whatever their prior history, they were committed to parchment for the last time and preserved first in an episcopal household and then in a cathedral library.

Two of the riddles discussed by Gleissner also figure in James E. Anderson's 'Two Spliced Riddles of the *Exeter Book*', which is one of the articles in last year's *In Geardagum*. Anderson points out that more than one hundred years of scholarship has not succeeded in fixing the numbering of the OE riddles, the boundaries of many of their texts, nor the difficult readings. The two (or four?)

37. *Die »zweideutigen« altenglischen Rätsel des 'Exeter Book' in ihrem zeitgenössischen Kontext*, by Reinhard Gleissner. Regensburger Arbeiten zur Anglistik und Amerikanistik. Sprache und Literatur 23. Lang. pp. xxiv + 450. Sfr 76.

riddles to which Anderson turns his attention are 42/43 and 47/48, which are 'palaeographically spliced' (p. 57) in the manuscript. Anderson attempts to show that their intricate wordplay combines humble and lofty themes in order to attain a well-hidden spiritual end. Well-hidden too is the name of the Latin poet who composed the *Tinea* riddle (cf. riddle 42, 'bookworm'); he is here introduced under the newly created pseudonym of Symphonis.

At this point, since Anderson is involved, it is appropriate to refer to N. F. Blake's 'Reflections on Old English Scholarship', which concluded *In Gearda-gum* for 1983. Blake was invited to comment on three of the articles in that issue, but since they are all dealt with in this chapter, Anderson's immediately above, Riley's on p. 88 and Short's on p. 93, it would be somewhat repetitive to summarize Blake's 'Reflections' in any detail. I therefore simply note it for the benefit of those who would like a second opinion on the essays in question.

I conclude with one other article from *In Geardagum* for 1983, 'The Sea of Life and the Ending of *Christ II*', by Phillip Pulsiano, which examines Cynewulf's elaboration in *Christ II*, ll. 850–66, of the seafaring image that he found in his Gregorian source as a metaphor for the journey of life. If this were Pulsiano's main purpose, the paper would be unexceptional, if also unoriginal. But Pulsiano's main aim is to demonstrate that the ship metaphor in *Christ II* 'redefines ordinary modes of human cognition and communication as mediary elements expressive of the epistemological relationship between God and man' (p. 10). Pulsiano's chief method of building up evidence for his case is to attempt to demonstrate that other sea-passages in OE poetry also deal with communication in some way, and to allow the light of these interpretations to illuminate the Cynewulf passage. Perhaps, in a well-defined homiletic tradition, there is some justification for this kind of lateral approach, but here the interpretation of the supporting examples seems to me to be as unconvincing as the interpretation of the *Christ* passage itself. The supposed ship/language relationship that Pulsiano sees in riddle 32 depends upon his idiosyncratic interpretation 'pen', which he claims co-exists with the usual interpretation 'ship', although in arguing his way through the 'pen' interpretation he avoids explaining how 'muð wæs on middan' (l. 9a) is supposed to fit. The other main example, *Guðlac B*, ll. 1326b–45a, is supposed to show how a relationship is set up between the boat and the sorrow of Beccel through the poet's device of alternating descriptions of them and how, in consequence, we are to under-stand the disciple's journey as being one from sorrow to understanding and the communication of that understanding through language. It does not communi-cate that to me, however many times I reread the lines. As for the discussion of the *Christ II* image itself, if the translations of the OE and the Latin are meant to show Pulsiano's understanding of the texts, one would wish that they were more accurate. We are told, for example, that Gregory's image is less definite than Cynewulf's (which it is), but Pulsiano exaggerates the difference by ignoring *patria* in his discussion of Gregory's image, perhaps because he confuses it with *pater*. In any event, he mistranslates 'in aeternam patriam' as 'in the Eternal Father' (p. 5). It is the worst but not the only instance that I could produce.

Two items already referred to also need to be mentioned again here: Bridges's *Generic Contrast in Old English Hagiographical Poetry*, which deals in part with *Juliana* and *Guðlac* (see above, p. 82), and E. G. Stanley's 'Notes on the Text of *Christ and Satan*; and on *The Riming Poem* and *The Rune Poem*, chiefly on *wynn*, *wēn* and *wenne*' (*N&Q*). The discussion of *The Riming Poem* is divided between comments on the metrical patterns and the origin and interpretation of individual words, notably *wennan* (l. 7), and *wencyn* (l. 61a).

9. Other Poems

The recent edition of *The Rune Poem* reviewed last year (*YW* 64.111–12) prompted E. G. Stanley to reconsider a number of textual and interpretative problems, which he presented in an essay already noted, 'Notes on the Text of *Christ and Satan*; and on *The Riming Poem* and *The Rune Poem*, chiefly on *wynn*, *wēn* and *wenne*' (*N&Q*). He concentrates on the interpretation of the *w*-rune in l. 22 which, in this context, he takes to be *wēn* followed by the negative particle *ne*, rather than the more usual *wyn* plus inflexion -*ne*, which is how Halsall reads it.

Of the poems that survive outside the four major codices, however, it is *The Battle of Maldon* that is most regularly studied, and this year is no exception since there are three articles to be noted. Mary P. Richards in '*The Battle of Maldon* in its Manuscript Context' (*Medievalia* 1984 for 1981) reconsiders the contents of the now badly burned *Maldon* manuscript in an attempt to discover if there is a topical relationship between the various items and hence, by implication, a clue to the significance of the poem for the compiler, or more properly the compilers, since the codex took shape over a period of approximately 100 years. Professor Richards ignores the items which were in a separate volume in the eleventh and twelfth centuries (Asser and the OE charms), but concludes from the rest of the items that the original codex evolved as part of a post-Conquest effort to record the deeds of local heroes and to respond to the Norman challenges regarding the authenticity of English saints. She is able to show that successive additions to the codex perpetuated this topical connection between the items and she argues, therefore, that the implied purpose of the collection (and hence of individual items within it, such as *Maldon*) was well understood over a long period.

John Scattergood's '*The Battle of Maldon* and History' in *Pyle*[27] begins with a discussion of the now commonly held view that the poem was composed in the reign of Cnut, *c.* 1020 or soon after. Scattergood challenges the validity of one of the major pieces of evidence for this, however, by pointing out that *eorl* need not be interpreted as the late OE territorial title parallel to Scandinavian *jarl*, but could well be a survival of *eorl* 'warrior' from the OE poetic vocabulary. He proposes that the poem should be seen as a work originating in the reign of Æþelred and that it had a propagandist function in defining how the Danes should be opposed. To judge from the description of English resistance in the *Chronicle*, from which Scattergood quotes extensively, some such propaganda was needed, though equally certainly it had no real effect.

The third *Maldon* article, by Alan J. Fletcher, '*Cald Wæter, Scir Wæter*. A Note on Lines 91 and 98 of "The Battle of Maldon"' (*NM*) takes up the point that, while the metaphoric implications of *cald* in the description of the river Pant (l. 91) have regularly been noted, the possibility that there is also a metaphoric force in the poet's use of *scir* (l. 98) has been overlooked in favour of a naturalistic interpretation. Fletcher examines the uses of *scir* in OE and of its ON parallel *skýrstr* and comes to the conclusion that it too had metaphoric connotations, although antonymous to *cald* in being indicative of joy, splendour, illustriousness, victory. He therefore makes the convincing suggestion that the poet deliberately used these two descriptions of the river within a few lines in order to contribute to his foreshadowing technique. In this case the river is *cald* for the doomed Byrhtnoð but *scir* for the soon to be victorious vikings.

Günter Kellermann and Renate Haas, in an article entitled 'Magie und Mythos als Argumentationsmittel in den AE. Dialoggedichten *Salomon und Saturn*', published in *Schneider*²⁶, examine the extent to which *Solomon and Saturn I* and *II* show evidence of Germanic traditions re-interpreted from a Christian perspective. The particular focus of their attention in *Solomon and Saturn I* is the Pater Noster runes, which they examine in the light of Augustine's comments on heathen gods in *De Civitate Dei*; in *Solomon and Saturn II* they attempt to assess how much the discussion of fate is affected by the Christian concept of divine order and providence.

Joseph A. Dane's ' "On Folce Geþeon": Note on the Old English "Maxims II," ' lines 43–45' (*NM*) proposes a new interpretation of three lines in *Maxims II*, based on his re-examination of the meaning of *geþeon* in poetry when collocated with *on folce* (as here), or *on þeode* (which Dane admits as an equivalent). For the phrase as a whole he proposes the meaning 'to flourish openly (as a rumour)' (p. 62) and thus translates the passage: 'A woman seeks out her lover with secret craft, if she does not wish it rumored that she is bought with rings' (p. 62).

A poem offering wisdom of a different kind is Bede's *Death Song*, the subject this year of an article by David Yerkes. Soon after A. H. Smith printed the West Saxon version of Bede's *Death Song* from BL Ms. Cotton Tiberius A ii in his *Three Northumbrian Poems* (*YW* 14.78), it was realized that the 'scribe' responsible for entering the poem on f. 20 was in fact Archbishop Parker's secretary, John Joscelyn (1529–1603). In 'Joscelyn's Text of *Bede's Death Song*' (*N&Q*) Yerkes sets about finding Joscelyn's source, after first demonstrating that it was not any of the surviving copies of the poem nor, in all probability, any of the four hitherto identified lost copies of the *Epistola Cuthberti*. However, as Yerkes points out, there was another copy of the *Epistola Cuthberti* in BL Ms. Cotton Otho A viii, which was probably written out by the same scribe who copied out the *Life of Machutus* in this manuscript. Since there are correspondences in spelling between the *Life of Machutus* in Otho A viii and Joscelyn's *Death Song* text in Tiberius A ii, Yerkes postulates that Joscelyn copied the song from the *Epistola Cuthberti* in the Otho A viii manuscript. If so, Joscelyn's Tiberius A ii text derives from a manuscript copied fully a century earlier than any of the extant witnesses of the West Saxon version of the *Death Song*. By means of indirect evidence Yerkes comes to the conclusion that Joscelyn copied this text faithfully; direct evidence is, of course, not available, since the Otho A viii manuscript was badly burned in the fire of 1731 and the leaves containing the *Epistola Cuthberti* were destroyed.

Peter S. Baker, in 'A Little-Known Variant Text of the Old English Metrical Psalms' (*Speculum*), edits, for the first time since 1889, a fragment of OE poetry in the Eadwine Psalter. This Psalter, which follows the Roman text, has a contemporary verbatim OE interlinear gloss throughout, except for Psalms 90.16–95.2, where the gloss is a metrical paraphrase. Baker raises some interesting questions about the reasons for this strange departure from normal practice but is not able to produce any firm answers. However, comparison of this piece of text with its parallel in the Paris Psalter provides the basis for a brief but challenging discussion of the faithfulness of OE scribes to their exemplars and the weight that should be given to the date of a manuscript when assessing its likely authority.

Another article concerned with metrical psalms is Patrick O'Neill's 'The Lost Tabernacle of Selom: A Proposed Emendation in the Paris Psalter 77: 60' (*N&Q*). When faced with an apparently inexplicable *swa gelome* in the Paris Psalter 77.60, Holthausen proposed that it should be omitted from the edited text; he also advocated adding *sinum* to the same OE verse since he believed that the vernacular text had nothing to correspond to *suum* in the Latin source. O'Neill's approach to the same verse exemplifies the difference between high-handed early editorial scholarship and the more conservative modern approach. He quickly dismisses the proposal that *sinum* should be added to the OE since the *suum* of the source is in fact faithfully translated as *his agen*, though Holthausen appeared not to notice this. The puzzle of *swa gelome* is harder to solve, but O'Neill finds the clue he needs in the Latin, where the tabernacle is named as *silon* (Paris Psalter). In the Vulgate this is *Selo*, and *Selom* in the best manuscript of the Romanum Psalter. O'Neill proposes that the OE text originally had the inflected form *Selome* and that a later scribe, unfamiliar with the Romanum *Selom*, garbled the text by changing the first letter to produce the familiar *gelome*, beside which he then wrote *swa* to complete the phrase.

It is a short step from the metrical psalms to the *Metres of Boethius*. Denise Cavanaugh, in 'A Note on *Metre 29* of the Old English *Metres of Boethius*' (*N&Q*), questions Krapp's presentation of *Metre 29*, ll. 67–72, in particular the status and function of *forð* in *forðbrengeð* (l. 69), the meaning of *hit* (l. 70), and the consequential editorial punctuation. Krapp appears to have regarded *forð* as an unstressed separable prefix, but Cavanaugh's analysis of the metre of this passage and of other poetic lines where *forð* occurs shows that stress is an inalienable feature of *forð* so that it is ill-suited for use as a verbal prefix. *Hit*, usually regarded as a rather awkward pronoun, is convincingly shown to be a verb here, from *hydan* 'hide', thus making it parallel with *eowað* and *nimð* in the two following lines. As a result Cavanaugh is able to re-edit the passage, with *forð* standing as an independent word and with changes in punctuation to allow *hit* to function verbally. The awkwardness of the lines is thus neatly removed. 230/70

10. Prose

The continuing steady interest in OE prose has once again produced a number of interesting articles as well as two important editions.

In recent years an increasing amount of work has been done on the medical texts which survive from Anglo-Saxon England, and it is therefore particularly satisfying to be provided this year with a good edition of the OE *Herbarium and Medicina de Quadrupedibus*[38] which, as it happens, are preserved in the same four manuscripts. De Vriend's edition of both works prints the OE versions in BL Mss. Cotton Vitellius C iii (Ms. V, also printed by Cockayne) and Harley 6258B (Ms. O, here printed for the first time). Since both works

38. *The English Herbarium and Medicina de Quadrupedibus*, ed. by Hubert Jan de Vriend. EETS OS 286. OUP for EETS. pp. xc + 403. £25.

are translations of Latin compilations dating from the fourth and fifth centuries of the Christian era, he also prints a parallel Latin text for both the *Herbarium* and *Medicina*, but with no suggestion that these are the actual texts used by the OE translators. As is usual in an EETS edition, there is careful discussion of the history of the texts and their manuscript tradition, and detailed comment on language. There are also extensive textual and explanatory notes, a full glossary (which, by the nature of the texts, is a treasure-house of unusual OE words) and appendixes of plant names, and of parallel cures in *Læceboc*, *Lacnunga* and a range of Latin texts, one of which is chiefly noteworthy as marking the depth of futility to which 'medicine' descended. The OE texts might not sink quite so low, but they hardly inspire confidence. De Vriend notes that the OE translator omitted some cures apparently because he was incapable of understanding the Latin, and his examination of the crucially important factor of weights and measures suggests that the Anglo-Saxons had difficulty both in translating and interpreting what the Latin text prescribed. As the editor fairly remarks, 'we can only hope that the Anglo-Saxon constitution was able to cope with wrongly dosed drugs administered by physicians who took their prescription from the OE medical texts' (p. lxxxi). Perhaps more important for us – though certainly not for the Anglo-Saxon patient – is De Vriend's conclusion that both works were translated into the vernacular probably during the eighth century and that the extant text of the *Medicina* is closely connected with the early Anglian version, but that the extant text of the *Herbarium* is either a new translation made directly from Latin, or a descendant of the Anglian text which, in the course of frequent copying, has been modernized and adapted to the LWS standard. All that survives, however, are three apparently interrelated manuscripts from the eleventh century (of which De Vriend prints V) and one from the twelfth century (De Vriend's O) which seems to be of a slightly different tradition.

Another significant contribution to our understanding of medical texts is Audrey L. Meaney's 'Variant versions of Old English medical remedies and the compilation of Bald's *Leechbook*' (*ASE*). She focuses attention on the relationships of the hundred or so remedies which have been preserved, usually in different manuscripts, in two or three versions so close that they obviously derive from the same original or are copied one from the other. Her purpose is to draw some conclusions about the method of compilation of Bald's *Leechbook*, in which almost all of the remedies in question are found, at least once. The evidence is systematically laid out in a series of manuscript descriptions and tables of correspondences. She deduces that *Leechbook* (BL Ms. Royal 12 D xvii), *Lacnunga* (BL Ms. Harley 585), and Nowell (BL Ms. Add. 43703, a copy of a now lost portion of Cotton Otho B xi) form a closely related group, with the *Leechbook* and *Lacnunga* more alike than either is to Nowell. Meaney finds it difficult to go beyond this, however, since the observable relationship can be accounted for in more than one way.

The second edition that I have to report is *The Old English Life of Machutus*[39], edited by David Yerkes from the charred remains of BL. Ms. Cotton Otho A viii (ff. 7–34), plus f. 66 of Cotton Otho B x, a fragment originally belonging to Otho A viii. The manuscript was written in the eleventh

39. *The Old English Life of Machutus*, ed. by David Yerkes. UTor. pp. xlvi + 186. $54, £38.

century and translates Bili's ninth-century *Vita Sancti Machuti*, a saint better known as Malo or Maclou. Before the Cotton fire, the OE version comprised forty-four folios, but now only twenty-eight remain and these are all damaged, some badly. Yerkes's text is therefore difficult to read comfortably, but it gives us, for the first time, a fragmentary text of some 9000 words. The OE is printed with the manuscript lineation, punctuation, and accents, and on the facing page is printed a diplomatic text of the appropriate portion of the Latin from Oxford Ms. Bodley 535, the one of the two surviving Latin copies to which the OE is closest. There is a full discussion of the manuscript in the introduction, and of the language, date, and place of origin of the translation. Yerkes concludes that, although the immediate provenance of the damaged manuscript could well be St Augustine's Canterbury, the Machutus story first became popular in Winchester, which may be the provenance of Ms. Bodley 535 and which is probably the place where the OE translation was made. The *Vita* perhaps came to England in the early tenth century when Scandinavian attacks on Brittany caused some emigration to Wessex.

In addition to the two book-length editions, there are also three editions of short texts which are published as articles. Karl Toth's 'Altenglische Inter-linearglossen zu Prospers *Epigrammata* und *Versus ad Coniugem*' (*Anglia*) is a full critical edition of ff. 165–6 of BL Ms. Cotton Tiberius A vii, the only two leaves of this copy of Prosper's *Epigrammata* and *Versus ad Coniugem* to survive the Cotton fire. What is especially important about this copy is that it is the only one to have been glossed in OE; all other extant Prosper manuscripts from Anglo-Saxon England are glossed in Latin. Toth's edition includes a brief discussion of the dissemination of Prosper's two works in the early Middle Ages and some detailed comment on all surviving texts from Anglo-Saxon England. There is also a careful analysis of the language of the OE Tiberius gloss and a photograph of f. 165v showing how the fire darkened the parchment. Toth's treatment is a model response to R. I. Page's plea, noted in *YW* 64.80, that glosses should be studied in their textual context rather than in the form of editorially created lists.

Another presentation of glosses in context is Hans Sauer's edition of the Latin text and OE glosses on ff. 163v–64r of BL Ms. Cotton Tiberius A iii, published in *Anglia* under the title 'Die Ermahnung des Pseudo-Fulgentius der Benediktregel und ihre altenglische Glossierung'. The passage, which is extremely short, is an injunction to follow the Benedictine Rule, which it immediately follows in the manuscript. In his introduction Sauer draws attention to the fact that this text is one of a group of four brief 'supplements' to the Rule which are found in varying combinations in five of the extant manuscripts of the Benedictine Rule from Anglo-Saxon England.

The third article-length edition is of an early- or mid-seventeenth-century copy of a hitherto unknown but apparently authentic charter of 963. It is published in full by Nicholas Brooks, Margaret Gelling, and Douglas Johnston under the title 'A new charter of King Edgar' (*ASE*). The text is supported by a detailed study of its form and content.

With Janet M. Bately's inaugural lecture, *The Literary Prose of King Alfred's Reign: Translation or Transformation*[40], we move to literary criticism.

40. *The Literary Prose of King Alfred's Reign: Translation or Transformation*, by Janet M. Bately. *OENews* Subsidia 10. CMERS. pp. 26. $3.

Professor Bately examines the prose of Alfred's reign in the light of its frequent summary dismissal as 'mere translation' and reaches the conclusion that the translators transformed the Latin texts into independent English prose since they did not simply translate but significantly reshaped their sources.

The development of an English prose style is also the subject of an article by Robert D. Smith, although his concern is to identify the characteristics of two different transitional stages in the development of ME prose in the east Midlands. In the first half of his paper 'The Peterborough Chronicle: the Development of a Prose Style'[41] he analyses the extent to which each Continuator departs from the regular grammar of OE, his movement towards fixed word order, and his use of French loan words. In all these the Final Continuator is shown, not surprisingly, to be more 'advanced' than the First; he is also shown to be more consistent, which Smith believes may reflect an increasing stability in the language as a whole. In the second half of the paper Smith turns his attention to the Continuators' stylistic differences, evident in the fact that there is a marked change of style at the point where each Continuator begins. What emerges gradually from the stylistic analysis is that each had his own concept of the kind of history he was writing. The claim that Smith ultimately makes for the Final Continuator is that he 'becomes compositional rather than annalistic' (p. 18) and his conclusion is that he is a writer who differs from the First in kind rather than in quality.

The remaining articles in this section are all concerned with homiletic texts and most of those with the work of Ælfric, although J. E. Cross makes two additions to his valuable series of articles on the OE *Martyrology*. In 'Antoninus of Apamea and an Image in the *Old English Martyrology*' (*N&Q*) he grapples with the problem of which Antoninus and what text or texts the martyrologist had in mind when he wrote the notice for 2 September. Since he places his Antoninus 'in Assiria mægðe' it seems an obvious deduction that he intended to relate the *passio* of the Syrian Antoninus. But the *passio* of Antoninus of Apamea, Syria, seems to have provided material for the *passio* of Antoninus of Apamea or Pamiers near Toulouse. Comparison of the notice in the OE *Martyrology* with the earliest texts of the Latin *passiones* shows that the OE account is substantially that of the Syrian saint, but with some elements drawn from the *passio* of the Gallic saint. What is impossible to unravel, in the absence of a corpus of suitable early Latin versions of the *passiones*, is whether this contamination is attributable to the OE writer, or whether it was already present in his exemplar. As an appendix, Cross gives the complete unedited text of the *passio* of Antoninus of Syria from a Vienna manuscript of the ninth century, with variants from Latin manuscripts of the twelfth and thirteenth centuries. The two Genesius entries are the subject of his other paper, also published in *N&Q*: 'Genesius of Rome and Genesius of Arles'. After an examination of the various Latin texts that could have served as a source for the OE obit of Genesius of Rome (25 August), he concludes that the Anglo-Saxon writer saw a text which was essentially that of the ninth-century Brussels manuscript, Bollandists' Library Codex 14, ff. 89r–v, but that it probably had small linguistic variants such as are found in the tenth-century Vienna Ms. Österreichische Nationalbibliothek 357, a recension which is of the same

41. *Studies in Early Middle English Literature*, ed. by Johan Kerling and Judith C. Perryman. ULeiden. pp. vi + 180. Fl. 8.

family as the Bollandists' Codex 14. For Genesius of Arles (24 October), Herzfeld's original identification of the source as BHL 3304 is accepted as correct, but Cross refines on this by taking into account more recent work on the Latin *passio*. There are, however, two details in the OE notice for which the known Latin tradition provides no source.

Remaining with the saints, but moving on to the end of the period, Bernadette Moloney's '*Be Godes Halgum*: Ælfric's Hagiography and the Cult of Saints in England in the Tenth Century' in *Pyle*[27] gives a brief survey of the popularity of saints in Anglo-Saxon England and brings together a number of references from a variety of vernacular and Latin texts from the tenth and eleventh centuries to show how the cult of saints was fostered by the Benedictine Reform. Her sketch thus provides a general context for Ælfric's production of his *Lives of Saints*.

It is not so much the content as the style of the *Lives of Saints* that concerns Ruth Waterhouse, however. In 'Sentence Determination in Ælfric's *Lives of Saints*' (*NM*) she shows how Ælfric generally signalled his sentence-boundaries very clearly by exploiting the rhythmical and alliterative patterns of his prose style and by his use of clear sentence-opening markers, such as *þa*, *hwæt*, *nu*, etc., the distribution of which Professor Waterhouse carefully analyses and, in the case of *þa*, discusses at some length. She demonstrates, however, that the sentence-boundaries in the *Life of Martin* (*Lives of Saints* XXXI) are far less distinct. The exceptional nature of *Martin* in this respect leads Waterhouse to speculate finally whether there were some special factors relating to its composition, or whether the text has been subject to some sort of scribal corruption which has not affected the rest. Whatever may be the explanation, there is no doubt that Ruth Waterhouse's study has produced yet more detail to support the common claim that Ælfric is a sensitive stylist.

Marcia A. Dalbey, in 'The Good Shepherd and the Soldier of God. Old English Homilies on St. Martin of Tours' (*NM*) is also concerned with one of Ælfric's Lives of St Martin, but in this case with that in the second series of *Catholic Homilies*, which she compares with the anonymous Lives preserved in the Blickling and Vercelli collections and, in fragmentary form, in Junius 86. Ælfric's version in the *Lives of Saints* is left out of account because it is a hagiographic *vita* rather than a homily. What emerges very clearly from Dalbey's interesting study is that the anonymous homilists, by a process of selection and carefully weighted emphasis, characterize St Martin as being very human, a teacher, and good shepherd, who interacts with other men. Ælfric, on the other hand, by a similar process of selection and emphasis, presents a saint who is a *miles Christi* and who is set apart from other men by his miraculous powers and his skills in exorcism. The inescapable conclusion is that Ælfric's didactic aims were quite different from those of the slightly earlier anonymous homilists, though whether Dalbey is right in tracing the cause of this difference to external factors such as the renewed Danish invasions which, as it were, divide the anonymous homilists and Ælfric is a moot point.

In Homily IX of Pope's *Supplementary Homilies* Ælfric describes the king as 'Christ's vicar'. In 'Ælfric's Designation of the King as "Cristes Sylfes Speligend"' (*RES*) M. J. Silverman shows that the source of the phrase was probably not Sedulius Scottus, as Pope had thought, nor Carolingian texts directly, but rather the contemporary Anglo-Saxon theory of Christ-centred kingship, which flourished in the tenth century.

One of Ælfric's acknowledged sources was Smaragdus, and this year there is a rare opportunity to read an essay on him. Jean Leclercq's 'Smaragdus', translated by John J. Mellenski, is one of fourteen original essays on various writers in a book edited by Paul E. Szarmach under the title *An Introduction to the Medieval Mystics of Europe*[42]. The useful bibliographical note on pp. 50–1 lists the significant works on Smaragdus from the 1970s.

The response of Anglo-Saxon homilists and particularly of Ælfric to an image that they found in their source-texts is the subject of Stephen Morrison's 'The Figure of *Christus Sponsus* in Old English Prose' (*BDP*). Although the bridal imagery was readily available, he shows that even Ælfric, when writing about female saints, tends to avoid the obvious opportunities for exploiting the image, and he suggests that the reluctance of Christian teachers to explore the literal bases of the metaphor is evidence that the theme of love, *per se*, was inimical to their literary sensibility. It thus contrasts with the exile image, which was also common in Christian teaching, but which was extensively used by Anglo-Saxon writers and often imaginatively developed by them because it corresponded to a secular (and heroic) literary *topos*.

In another essay, Morrison looks forward instead of back as he shows how Ælfric himself came to influence at least one post-Conquest homilist. In 'Orm's English Sources' (*Archiv*) he notes that Ælfric and Orm, alone among early medieval homilists, adopt the exegetical method as their norm and that, as far as is known, they alone compose prefaces to their collections, in which they name themselves and their patrons, and exploit established rhetorical *topoi* to lend authority to their works. Taking this similarity as his starting point, Morrison analyses certain commonplace modes of expression in the homilies of Ælfric and Orm and deduces that Ælfric's work, through repetition and recopying, had achieved the status of models for subsequent writers and that Orm, in general terms, was familiar with and responsive to this vernacular tradition. Further evidence for the influence of Ælfric (even if indirect) is provided by Morrison's comparison of Ælfric's and Orm's treatment of the Trinity. It is an appropriate item with which to conclude since it postulates a link between OE and ME prose and thus leads us directly into Chapter IV.

---

42. *An Introduction to the Medieval Mystics of Europe*, ed. by Paul E. Szarmach. SUNY. pp. vi + 376. hb. $39.50, pb $14.95.

Middle English: Excluding Chaucer

T. P. DOLAN, A. J. FLETCHER, and S. POWELL

The chapter has eleven sections: 1, 4, and 10 by T. P. Dolan; 3, 8, and 11 by
A. J. Fletcher; and 2, 5, 6, 7, and 9 by S. Powell. Sections are as follows: 1.
General and Miscellaneous Items; 2. Alliterative Poetry; 3. The Gawain-Poet;
4. Piers Plowman; 5. Romances; 6. Gower, Lydgate, Hoccleve; 7. Middle
Scots Poetry; 8. Lyrics and Miscellaneous Verse; 9. Malory and Caxton; 10.
Other Prose; 11. Drama.

1. General and Miscellaneous Items

Some outstanding books have been published in this category, and we shall
begin with the most striking of these. A. J. Minnis[1] has produced a splendid
book on the medieval contribution to the history of literary theory. A truly
pioneering work, it casts an entirely new light on our understanding of the
perception medieval writers had of themselves as *auctores*, eschewing
anachronistic theorizing based on non-contemporary sources. Petrarch,
Boccaccio, Chaucer, and Gower, as well as a host of other authors who
flourished in the period extending roughly from 1100 to 1400, are subjected
to minute analysis, in the light of scholastic literary attitudes. Minnis's sources
are the 'glosses and commentaries on the authoritative Latin writers, or
auctores . . . in particular, the prologues to these commentaries', which feature
'the commentators' preoccupation with authorial role and literary form'.
There are five chapters, dealing respectively with academic prologues to
auctores, prologues to scriptural *auctores*, authorial roles in the 'literal sense',
literary forms in the 'literal sense', and, finally, with literary theory and literary
practice. In the twelfth century there were three main types of prologues
employed in introducing an *auctor*. These were originally classified by R. W.
Hunt ('The Introductions to the Artes in the Twelfth Century' in *Studia
medievalia in honorem R. M. Martin*) in 1948. A key to the medieval scholars'
understanding of authorial role is provided by their attitude to the roles of God
and man in producing Holy Scripture. Minnis paraphrases Aquinas – 'God is
sole *auctor* of things and can use things to signify, whereas human *auctores* are
auctores of words and use words to signify'. Of crucial importance in the
development of the new conceptions of authorial role was the 'new method of
thinking and techniques of study which late-medieval scholars derived from
Aristotle', in particular their view of the human *auctor* as the efficient cause in

1. *Medieval Theory of Authorship*, by A. J. Minnis. Scolar. pp. xviii + 324. £35.

scriptural exegesis. A human *auctor* was inspired and 'engaged in a series of literary roles (*auctor*, *compilator*, *collector*, *editor*, etc.) and a series of moral roles, one of the most important of which was (in the cases of David and Solomon) the role of penitent sinner and ethical example'.

For scholars of medieval English literature, the most useful chapter of Minnis's book is the one entitled 'Literary Theory and Literary Practice' in which he deals with the practical application of the literary attitudes described in the preceding chapters. Here he concentrates on the writings of John Gower and Geoffrey Chaucer, both of whom exhibited interest in the major theoretical issues of their day. Gower, for instance, in the general prologue of the *Vox Clamantis*, perceived himself to have an authorial role similar to that of St John in the Apocalypse, in so far as both men composed works in the form of visions. 'Naturally,' as Minnis points out, 'Gower does not presume to claim the same *auctoritas* as that enjoyed by the *auctor* of the Apocalypse.' From his analysis Minnis concludes that 'academic prologues provided Gower with models for the composition of his own prolegomena'. It would be impossible to summarize the wealth of reasoning in this book. Suffice it to say that Minnis copiously proves his thesis: that the medieval perception of *auctor* went far beyond the mere notion of authorship and involved not only the *auctor*'s subject-matter, but also his moral pedigree, as well as his status in relation to God, the chief *auctor* of everything.

The third series of J. A. W. Bennett Memorial Lectures, held in Perugia (November 1982–April 1983), has been published under the engaging title *Medieval and Pseudo-Medieval Literature*, edited by Piero Boitani and Anna Torti[2]. There is a wide range of interests covered. Laura Mancinelli contrasts the prologue of Wolfram von Eschenbach's *Parzival* with that of Gottfried von Strassburg's *Tristran* from the point of view of their respective approaches to moral and philosophical questions. Siegfried Wenzel's lively and memorable paper takes most, if not all, medievalists to task for mouthing platitudes about the value of medieval sermons without actually reading them and thus missing the important relationship between homiletic and imaginative literature. Vittore Branca celebrates Boccaccio's role in the renewal of literary genres and the creation of new ones – for instance, with his *De vita et moribus . . . Francisci Petracchi* and his *De origine et vita . . . Dantis* 'he creates the exemplary biography, a genre with new heroes: not warriors, men of action or saints any more, but men of letters, moral teachers and reformers of personal and social behaviour'. In another striking paper André Crépin bristles with Gallic pride about Chaucer's debt to French culture and explains, with alarming conviction, how French critics have viewed Chaucer over the centuries and also 'why Chaucer has never exerted any creative influence on French literature'. Derek Pearsall's lecture deals primarily with what he perceptively calls 'epidemic irony in modern approaches to Chaucer's *Canterbury Tales*', but his salutary advice should be taken to heart by critics of any medieval literature which tempts the unwary to apply ironic interpretation. John Stevens writes about the relationship between music and poetry as perceived by Machaut, Deschamps, and Chaucer. Dieter Mehl considers Henryson's Moral Fables as

2. *Medieval and Pseudo-Medieval Literature: The J. A. W. Bennett Memorial Lectures, Perugia, 1982–3*, ed. by Piero Boitani and Anna Torti. Tübinger Beiträge zur Anglistik 6. Narr/Brewer. pp. 198. £17.50.

'experiments in didactic narrative' and points out what a startling variety of presentation they exhibit. The 'Pseudo-Medieval' part of this anthology's title is presumably covered by the following two papers – one by Marinella Salari on 'Ivanhoe's Middle Ages' which analyses Scott's version of the historical and geographical reality of thirteenth-century England – 'a completely new departure for Scott' – and one by Clara Bartocci on Mark Twain's *A Connecticut Yankee in King Arthur's Court*. The last paper in this stimulating book is not medieval at all, pseudo- or otherwise, but it is a good read, none the less: Alastair Fowler defends the style and 'adventurous' achievement of *Paradise Regained*.

Peter Dronke's book *Women Writers of the Middle Ages* is subtitled 'A Critical Study of Texts from Perpetua (†203) to Marguerite Porete (†1310)'[3]. Its purpose is to 'explore the ways women helped to shape the earliest Christian writing in a western language, and observe their particular contributions to western literature over a millennium'. There are seven chapters dealing with a host of famous and not-so-famous women, as well as with anonymous writings. Full attention is paid to, among others, Perpetua, Dhuoda, Hrotsvitha, Heloise, Hildegard of Bingen, Mechthild of Magdeburg, Grazida Lizier, and Marguerite Porete, who was publicly burnt in Paris in June 1310. The chapter on Heloise concludes with an interesting excursus entitled 'Did Abelard Write Heloise's Third Letter?' (No, says Dronke.) After the main chapters, Dronke adds a series of texts in the original Latin from Hildegard of Bingen, followed by a selection of women's testimonies from the Register of Jacques Fournier, also in Latin, and, in the original French, some 'lyrical moments' from Marguerite Porete's *Le mirouer des simples ames*. From this selection of texts Dronke sensitively discloses the way the women express their awareness of themselves and their world or 'construct imaginative worlds of their own'. Thanks to his rigorous process of selection, the quotations seem to reveal genuinely personal reactions and opinions: they wrote because they had something to say, not because it was an intellectually desirable thing to get something down in writing for others to admire. We read here, for instance, of Perpetua's conflict with her father, Hrotsvitha's notorious justification for her rewriting of Terence, and a masterly exposition of Heloise's changing and developing reactions. Much space is devoted to the 'overpowering, electrifying presence' of Hildegard of Bingen and her visions in the chapter devoted to her and also in the appendix, in which the bulk of the selected Latin texts come from her writings. As can be seen, this book abounds in ramifications for students of medieval literature: for instance, for students of drama, the chapter on Hrotsvitha will prove indispensable, and for students of dream-visions the section on Hildegard's use of *visio* will be especially useful. All in all, it would be difficult to overpraise this book.

The well-known remark *Non est consenescendum in artibus* does not suggest that the liberal arts should be discarded when students reach maturity, rather, it celebrates their fundamental importance in the education of man, says Ralph McInerny, who contributes the final essay in an enterprising book which 'presents a synthesis of existing scholarship'[4]. We may assume that all

3. *Women Writers of the Middle Ages*, by Peter Dronke. CUP. pp. xii + 338. £27.50.
4. *The Seven Liberal Arts in the Middle Ages*, ed. by David L. Wagner. IndU. pp. xiv + 282. $25.

medieval authors had some degree of exposure to this curriculum. This book lucidly describes each art, explains its history, and traces its emergence into the received curriculum. Each chapter commences with a summary of the following discussion and concludes with an up-to-date bibliography. The chapters on Grammar, Rhetoric, Dialectic, Arithmetic, Music, Geometry, and Astronomy are contributed by Jeffrey F. Huntsman, Martin Camargo, Eleonore Stump, Michael Masi, Theodore C. Karp, Lon R. Shelby, and Claudia Kren, respectively. David L. Wagner introduces the volume with a useful paper which illustrates the role played by classical scholarship in the development of the Seven Liberal Arts. This is followed by an essay written by Karl F. Morrison who poses and attempts to answer the question 'Why study the liberal arts?' (answer: position, wealth, fame, the understanding of holy scripture, and so forth). Indiana University Press is to be congratulated on publishing such a handsome, informative, and stimulating anthology of essays (see the translation of Martianus Capella's work on the Seven Liberal Arts, YW 58.76).

John A. Burrow has brought together twelve of his articles on medieval literature in a single publication[5] which deals with the Rawlinson lyrics, the *Knight's Tale* and the ages of man, irony in the *Merchant's Tale*, *Sir Thopas*, the action of Langland's second vision, the audience of *Piers Plowman*, honour and shame in *Sir Gawain and the Green Knight*, fantasy and language in the *Cloud of Unknowing*, Henryson's *The Preaching of the Swallow*, the poet as petitioner (which concerns the personal details that individual medieval poets put into their works: see Minnis[1], reflections on the medieval proverbs which warn youth not to cultivate the holiness reserved for age, and, finally, the laws governing allegorical fictions (see Chapter 4 of his *Medieval Writers and Their Work*, YW 63.74–5). It was a singularly helpful exercise for the Clarendon Press to publish this book because so many of its constituent essays are already classic pieces of medieval literary criticism.

John Scattergood has edited an interesting selection of papers entitled *Literature and Learning in Medieval and Renaissance England*[6]. More of the essays relate to the Renaissance than to the medieval period, but even those relating to later authors underpin some of their utterances with references to medieval concepts. For instance, Eiléann ni Chuilleanáin's paper on 'Time, Place and the Congregation in Donne's Sermons' contrasts the Anglicans' bare use of the liturgy in sermons for the dead with that of medieval Catholic iconography, and Harden Jay's essay on 'Innocence, Restoration Comedy and Mrs. Pinchwife' is informed by a grasp of the medieval sense of sin. The book has four specifically medieval papers. Scattergood convincingly argues for a return to the traditional dating of *The Battle of Maldon*, nearer the date of the battle, which challenges John McKinnell's argument for 1020 or thereabouts (*YW* 56.78). Bernadette Moloney presents a convincing paper on Ælfric's hagiography and its influence on the cult of the saints in subsequent centuries. Paula Simmonds discusses nautical terms in the Brussels Glossary (that is, ff. 50–50v and 94–95v of Brussels, Bibliothèque Royale de Belgique Ms. 1828–30

5. *Essays on Medieval Literature*, by John A. Burrow. Clarendon. pp. vi + 218. £17.50.

6. *Literature and Learning in Medieval and Renaissance England*, ed. by John Scattergood. IAP. pp. 234 + frontispiece. £17.50.

[185]). The fourth medieval essay is by Gerald Morgan who writes a powerfully well-supported case for the lovers in *Troilus and Criseyde* having free will. As can be seen, the book is something of a *pot-pourri*, but underlying it is the conviction that 'the literature of the past is best approached through a detailed knowledge of the historical, philosophical, ethical and doctrinal contexts in which it was produced'.

Fred C. Robinson's Presidential Address to the Medieval Academy of America deals in a magisterial and salutary way with the terms 'Medieval, the Middle Ages' (*Speculum*) which, he says, are in a sorry semantic state today.

Henrik Specht's seductively titled paper 'The Beautiful, the Handsome, and the Ugly: Some Aspects of the Art of Character Portrayal in Medieval Literature' (*SN*) shows how beauty and ugliness were correlated with virtue and evil respectively, basing his argument on a series of authorities, including Vincent of Beauvais's *Speculum doctrinale* (*c*. 1250), Matthew of Vendome, John of Garland, as well as Priscian and Cicero. Coincidentally, there is another paper on a similar theme, but in no sense constituting a duplication, by Jan Ziolkowski, entitled 'Avatars of Ugliness in Medieval Literature' (*MLR*) which considers the different themes implied in such tags as *memento mori* and *memento senescere*.

Word, Picture, and Spectacle is the title given to a selection of useful papers published by the Medieval Institute[7]. Karl P. Wentersdorf produces a lively piece, accompanied by a host of lurid illustrations, on the symbolical significance of *Figurae Scatalogicae* in Gothic manuscripts. Roger Ellis analyses the 'word', with its attendant symbols of book and pen, in religious art, pointing out the important distinction between the spoken and written word. Clifford Davidson tackles some difficult phenomenological questions related to the medieval understanding of space and time. The final paper, by R. W. Hanning, examines conceptions of creation both human and divine in the twelfth century – 'how the twelfth century understood the actuality of divine Creation, and how it assessed the possibilities of human creativity'.

Medievalists will welcome a re-issue of a translation by Mark Musa and Peter Bondanella of Boccaccio's *Decameron*[8] which they claim is the first English version of the work based on an authoritative and reliably edited Italian text – that done by Vittore Branca in 1975 for the Accademia della Crusca. Their translation is boisterous and demotic in an American way ('She asked Gioseto what he wanted her to fix for dinner'). Boccaccio's significance for ME literature cannot be overstressed (see Piero Boitani's *English Medieval Narrative in the 13th & 14th Centuries, YW* 63.75–6), and this translation effortlessly recalls the brilliance, humour, and skill of this famous narrative. The translators announce that they plan a companion volume which will include a full critical and aesthetic commentary. The present translation includes only a few explanations or historical footnotes.

The main portion of Ms. Lansdowne 285 is a paper book, containing English, French, and Latin items, which once belonged to the bibliophile Sir

7. *Word, Picture, and Spectacle*, ed. by Clifford Davidson. Early Drama, Art, and Music Monograph Series 5. MIP. pp. viii + 155 + frontispiece + 56 illus. + 2 text figures. hb $17.95, pb $10.95.
    8. *Giovanni Boccaccio: The Decameron*, trans. by Mark Musa and Peter Bondanella. Norton. pp. xiv + 690. £24.50.

John Paston (1442–79), for whom it was (mainly) written and compiled by William Ebesham. As G. A. Lester shows in his massively detailed description of this *Boke*[9], its contents reflect Sir John's tastes and interests, which seem to be warmly concerned with knightly matters such as pageantry, jousts, ordinances governing war and judicial combat. Thanks to Dr Lester's painstaking research, we know a good deal about the genesis of the book and, in particular, about the role played by Ebesham, whose letter and bill requesting a single payment for a major part of the extant volume survives. The *Grete Boke* is mentioned in the Paston Letters which tell us much about the life and character of Sir John and his relations with people like Sir John Fastolf and Anthony Woodville. Lester's book is divided into two parts. The introduction contains a checklist of the contents, a description of the manuscript, which is in quite good condition, a list of related manuscripts (there are no fewer than seventy-eight manuscripts containing part of the *Grete Boke*, and of these, fifteen contain more than one item in common with Lansdowne 285), and a very interesting section entitled 'Sir John Paston, William Ebesham, and the Making of the "Grete Boke"'. Lester goes on to describe the development of the *Grete Boke* and its generic connection with other heraldic books of the fifteenth century. He also records the ownership of the book up to 1630. The second part of the volume contains the Descriptive Catalogue itself, which explains the individual texts. According to Lester, the *Grete Boke* is not a 'mass-produced' book: it never existed in 'booklet' form or as anything other than a substantial codex. It may be described as a type of commonplace book. Lester's is an impressive and, above all, very honest piece of research, since it presents every conceivable item of evidence for the reader to appreciate the contents, construction and milieu of Sir John's *Grete Boke*.

Two excellent works concerned with medieval manuscripts have been published, one by CMERS and the other by Clarendon. Both will prove indispensable for medievalists.

The first volume of the *Catalogue of Medieval and Renaissance Manuscripts in the Beinecke Rare Book and Manuscript Library of Yale University* has been compiled by Barbara A. Shailor[10]. The library encompasses two distinct bodies of material – the general collection (at present 640 items, and still expanding) and the Marston manuscripts (234 items). Volume II will deal with Mss. 251–500, and the third volume with the Marston manuscripts. Each entry describes the textual contents, including incipits and explicits, parchment or watermarks, foliation, flyleaves, dimensions, binding, and provenance. After the main catalogue there are seven indices which provide access to information in the descriptions (e.g. manuscripts arranged by country or region of origin and by century, dated manuscripts, general index to persons, places, authors, etc.) These are followed by thirty-two plates, of which the first concisely explains binding terms. This is a welcome volume and both the compiler, who handsomely praises the pioneering work of Cora Lutz, to whom she dedicates her book, and her publishers are to be warmly congratulated.

9. *Sir John Paston's 'Grete Boke' A Descriptive Catalogue with an Introduction of British Literary MS Lansdowne 285*, by G. A. Lester. B & B. pp. 198. £17.50.

10. *Catalogue of Medieval and Renaissance Manuscripts in the Beinecke Rare Book and Manuscript Library Yale University*. Vol. I: *MSS 1–250*, by Barbara A. Shailor. MRTS 34. CMERS. pp. xxii + 420; frontispiece + 32 pls. $26.

Andrew G. Watson has compiled, in two volumes, a *Catalogue of Dated and Datable Manuscripts c. 435–1600 in Oxford Libraries*[11]. There are 882 entries, and 818 plates. His work displays (and also celebrates, in its modest way) the medieval holdings of the institutions in Oxford. It is much more, though, than a mere catalogue – it is a distillation of Oxford's cultural contribution to medieval studies. All the classical authors are represented, as are most late Latin writers (Donatus, Jerome, Gregory, Bede, and so forth), as well as late authors such as Johannes Duns Scotus, John of Salisbury, Petrus Riga, Petrus Comestor, Jacobus de Voragine, Innocent III, Nicholas of Lyra, Richard FitzRalph, Ralph Strode, and a host of others – all this, in addition to the famous vernacular holdings such as Alfred the Great's translation of Gregory's *Cura Pastoralis* (Ms. Hatton 20), *The Peterborough Chronicle* (Ms. Laud Misc. 636), Langland's *Piers Plowman* (Mss. Digby 145 and Douce 104), the Chronicle of 'Florence of Worcester' (Ms. Corpus Christi College 157), and much more. As well as English, Latin, and French manuscripts, there are also texts in Irish, German, Gaelic, Greek, Italian, Netherlandish, Spanish, and Welsh. Bodleian manuscripts are listed in alphabetical order of collections and by writers within collections, and are followed by college collections in alphabetical order, with manuscripts in numerical order. The individual entries include the name of the collection and the number, with date and place of origin in abbreviated form, the author and title, a physical description of the manuscript, evidence of date and origin, evidence of later history, bibliographical references, and references to the plates. The *Catalogue* is prefaced with an introduction which concisely describes the fortunes and development of the Bodleian and college libraries at Oxford, and also explains the scope, arrangement, and layout of the *Catalogue*. After the main entries there is a list of manuscripts which Watson rejects, since they have been claimed in published statements, directly or by implication, as dated or datable, whereas he challenges such certainty. There is also an index of the languages other than Latin found in the collections, a date index (running from 'After 435 or 442' to 1598), a name index, an index of Oxford manuscripts in the list of rejected manuscripts and of all manuscripts referred to in the text and, finally, a list of eleven addenda (dating from the thirteenth, fourteenth, and fifteenth centuries). Volume II is given over to the plates, which are beautifully clear. Indeed, the printing here constitutes a technical masterpiece in its own right – it makes the book very useful for the teaching of palaeography. All in all, this *Catalogue* is an awesome feat of scholarship in every respect.

2. Alliterative Poetry

A number of articles on alliterative metre have appeared in 1984. Traditional received opinion on the alliterative long line, as well as specific critical comment, is reviewed by A. T. E. Matonis in 'A re-examination of the Middle English alliterative long line' (*MP*). The title of Elichi Suzuki's '"Mold" in Middle English Alliterative Poetry: A Reconsideration' (*Poetica*) refers (American spelling) to R. A. Waldron's definition of alliterative poetry as

11. *Catalogue of Dated and Datable Manuscripts c. 435–1600 in Oxford Libraries*, by Andrew G. Watson. Vol. I: *The Texts*. Vol. II: *The Plates*. Clarendon. pp. xxiv + 176; 818 illus. £120.

'"empty" rhythmical-syntactical "moulds" ready to be filled with meaning'. Suzuki argues for the addition of an essential semantic requirement to the criteria of rhythm and syntax. Also in *Poetica*, Arthur Wayne Glowka's 'Prosodic Decorum in Layamon's *Brut*' runs on similar lines, arguing for a rhetorical, rather than purely metrical, scansion of the poem. Examples of this 'prosodic decorum' ('the seeming dance of meter and meaning'), which occurs especially in direct speech, suggest that the poem is 'grand experiment in English poetry'. Again on the *Brut*, James Noble criticizes J. S. P. Tatlock's dismissal of 'Variation in Layamon's *Brut*' (*NM*), pointing out that the types of formal variation and chiasmus found in the *Brut* are significant in showing the continuity of rhetorical practices between OE and early ME.

Writing on '*The Awntyrs off Arthure* and the Arthurian History' (*Poetica*), Takami Matsuda takes up the argument for the unity of the poem propounded by A. C. Spearing (*RES*, 1982). As Spearing has shown a structural poise between the two episodes of the poem, Matsuda suggests that the two episodes are not at variance with each other but 'are essentially the two aspects [religion and chivalry] of chivalric world in the heyday of the Round Table'.

Thorlac Turville-Petre's interest is primarily in alliterative poetry and it is worth reading his paper given to the First York Conference on Fifteenth-Century Manuscript Studies, 'Some Medieval English Manuscripts in the North-East Midlands'[12] (hereafter *York*). His analysis of Mss. Middleton O1 and Advocates 19.31, together with his investigation of the literary taste of manuscript owners, Thomas Chaworth of Wiverton and the Finderns of Findern, provides preliminary material for a planned study of literature in provincial society, which is to be based on the north-east Midlands. Already Turville-Petre would suggest that literary taste was national rather than local, and his work promises interesting and significant information in a dark area.

3. The Gawain-Poet

The crop this year has been altogether more abundant, and includes two books. The first of these, a guide to *Gawain* scholarship by R. J. Blanch, deserves honourable mention, for it will prove a convenient research tool for students both of the poem and of its critical history[13] One of its particular strengths is its fairly full summary of each listed item. In a short introduction, Blanch traces the development of *Gawain* studies from their earliest days with the appearance of an excerpt of the poem in Thomas Warton's *The History of English Poetry* (1824), and takes us judiciously through the hectic scholarly activity which the poem attracted from the 1950s onwards until his cut-off point in 1978. He suggests that when new work on place-names and ME dialects has been completed, philological study of the poem can be undertaken which will provide the cornerstone of any critical commentary worth its salt. *Gawain*, he says, should be studied further in its literary context, especially that provided by the northern Arthurian romances, and in its social context

12. *Manuscripts and Readers in Fifteenth-Century England: The Literary Implications of Manuscript Study: Essays from the 1981 Conference at the University of York*, ed. by Derek Pearsall. Brewer (1983). pp. 146. £22.50.
13. *Sir Gawain and the Green Knight: A Reference Guide*, by R. J. Blanch. Whitston. pp. iv + 298. $22.50.

too. To these general suggestions for further research he adds a few more specific ones, such as a proposal that further work might be undertaken on the theme of judgement in the poem. His introduction carefully describes the guide's scope and limitations.

The second book, a four-chapter study of *Gawain* by R. A. Shoaf[14], could be said to have caught up one of Blanch's enthusiasms, for it is the network of commercial imagery in the poem that fascinates him. We might begin on a positive note, and declare that his work is worth reading on account of the many provocative and stimulating points it raises. Chapter One contends that *Gawain* is proposing, through its vision of man's estate as lying somewhere between personal loyalties and abstract market forces, its own reconciliation between the old chivalric virtues on the one hand and the hardier economic realities of the fourteenth century on the other. The second chapter makes much of the theology of the circumcision, the date of Gawain's beheading match, and suggests that the feast, a fertile source of some of the poem's significance and imagery, is the ground of the poem's commercial vision. The final chapters analyse those parts of the poem where commercial vocabulary predominates, especially in the wooing scenes in the bedroom, and at the Green Chapel. Locally, Shoaf advances many sensible, and indeed, subtle, readings of the text, but on these is built an ornate edifice of a critical interpretation, both impressive and unreal, 'pared out of papure purely'. There are too many elusive and undemonstrable arguments in this book for it to be finally satisfying.

Some reference to the social and literary context of the poem is the common denominator of several of this year's articles on *Gawain*. The express purpose of 'Medieval Contracts and Covenants: The Legal Coloring of *Sir Gawain and the Green Knight*' (*Neophil*) by R. J. Blanch and J. N. Wasserman is to illustrate briefly the traditions underlying the legal vocabulary of *Gawain*. They claim that Gawain's verbal promises, which in all respects are modelled on medieval contractual tradition, entail a careful prescription of responsibility as well as of penalties for its violation, and they emphasize the importance of the spoken bond in medieval culture. Their documentation of this background is most useful, and sharpens our awareness of an important dimension in the poem. Nevertheless, their position is sometimes tendentious, for their analysis of Gawain's confession before leaving Hautdesert shows them unhesitatingly taking sides with the 'flawed confession' party.

The time when Gawain sets out on his quest for the Green Chapel has provoked a fair deal of commentary. 'Travelling in November: Sir Gawain, Thomas Usk, Charles d'Orléans and the *De Re Militari*' (*MÆ*) by M. Stokes and J. Scattergood suggests that to a medieval audience, that Gawain left Camelot in November would primarily have signalled the importance of his mission and the magnitude of the constraint under which he found himself. They support their argument by illustrating the recommendations against November travel, unless in dire necessity, in the works of Usk, Charles d'Orléans, and Vegetius. P. F. Reichardt begins his 'Gawain and the Image of the Wound' (*PMLA*) with an engagingly shame-faced apology that although he returns to a chestnut of *Gawain* criticism, the nature of Gawain's fault,

---

14. *The Poem as Green Girdle: Commercium in Sir Gawain and the Green Knight*, by R. A. Shoaf. UFlor. pp. xi + 105. $12.

there is more to be said about the flesh wound that the Green Knight inflicts. He believes that the image of the 'wound' throughout this poem has not received due attention. While the attention he proceeds to lavish upon it in recompense is perhaps a little too elaborate, his material on medieval wound imagery is worth while, and of interest irrespective of the finer details of its mooted application to the poem. H. Wirtjes argues that it is enlightening to regard Bertilak as sharing in the tradition of the literary vavasour in his article 'Bertilak de Hautdesert and the Literary Vavasour' (*ES*). While his adversion to the literary tradition is indeed enlightening, for one can readily assent to the idea that to a degree, Bertilak and his castle belong to a topos of romantic narrative, some of his literary conclusions are not impregnable, and he seems to show no awareness of the *Gawain* analogues in which the knight's chastity is assailed by a married woman. Consequently, to assert that the *Gawain*-poet 'consciously transformed the virgin daughter of the vavasour and the knight who feels attracted to her into the sophisticated lady and the unwilling Gawain' betrays dangerous disregard for the analogues.

There are two articles on *Pearl*, finally. I. Bishop, who has written on this poem so fluently, adds a note on '*Solacia* in *Pearl* and in Letters of Edward III Concerning the Death of His Daughter Joan' (*N&Q*), in which he illustrates the various topoi of the *consolatio mortis* tradition appearing in three letters, sent by Edward III in 1348 on the death of his daughter Joan to the king of Castile, his queen, and the Infante Pedro to whom Joan had been betrothed. The appearance of the topoi in such letters as these shows their use in a real-life context, and outside the more literary context of *Pearl*. '*Pearl*, Inexpressibility, and Poems of Human Loss' (*PMLA*) are considered by A. C. Watts. She begins with a reflection on what are the hallmarks of the literary manifestation of the 'inexpressibility topos', and these she finds pre-eminently in paradox, when words say that they are unable to say. She moves on to argue that treatment of the topos in *Pearl* is unusual, and to survey its nature, how other poets, and not just medieval ones, use the topos, and what historical influences may bear upon its use in *Pearl*.

4. Piers Plowman

Some very good work has been written on Langland this year, but we shall start with a book-length study[15] which seems to discover more to denigrate than to praise in his work. 'I decline to accept any of the modern printed editions' says John Norton-Smith in his polemical, iconoclastic strictures on both Langland and most of his critics. Only J. A. W. Bennett merits his unqualified approval and his book ends with support for C. S. Lewis's lofty verdict on the poet: 'He is confused and monotonous, and hardly makes his poetry into a poem'. Norton-Smith lashes most textual critics with a pitiless scourge. For example, on the Kane–Donaldson edition (*YW* 56.88–9) he comments: 'Kane and Donaldson have turned themselves into another set of scribes. We now have a strange and expensive anachronism: a printed copy of MS. KD (xx *saec.* ¾)'. Most of his debunking, though, is reserved for Langland himself: 'His art belongs to the engrafting, scissors-and-paste amalgamating side of the creative process of medieval imaginative activity.' Lang-

15. *William Langland*, by John Norton-Smith. pp. 144. Brill (1983). Fl 48.

land's sense and use of history is unintellectual, and he is 'little better as an ecclesiastical historian'. He has a 'penchant for moral superficiality'. On these and similar grounds Norton-Smith has no time for what he disparagingly calls 'most modern salvationists of Langland's literary writing' who 'may be classified as "coat-tailers" or "bandwaggoners"'. Still, he does find patches of great poetry in the work, for instance, in his detailed analysis of Passus I, ll. 43–70, from which emerges the claim that 'the stylistic range of these lines can be called characteristic of Langland's artistic method'. He instances Langland's 'intuitive appreciation of the force of verbs' in the phrases 'egged to ille' and 'iaped with silver'. There is a very fine discussion on Langland's deliberate choice of the satiric register for some passages (e.g. the Prologue). The powerful satiric emphasis of the Prologue is exchanged for the didactic mode in Passus I and brought back again for the Meed episode. Later, Passus V shows Langland's powers as a narrative poet, as also does Passus XVIII. The final two chapters of this arresting, controversial book deal respectively with what the author calls Langland's 'psychological vocabulary and images of mental processes' and with the visual form or mode of the poem. This is a book that J. A. W. Bennett would probably not have approved.

In stark contrast to the tone of Norton-Smith's criticism, an exhilarating paper by Malcolm Godden concentrates on the shifting status of 'Plowmen and Hermits in Langland's *Piers Plowman*' (*RES*). He invites us to contrast A Prol. ll. 1–4 and 20–30 with A VIII 99–113, over which period in the poem Langland seems to change his mind about hermits. This ostensible change of mind is given further explication in the B version, in which he similarly discards the ideal of productive labour for something approaching the reverse. Godden's article thus addresses some of the fundamental problems and contradictions in *Piers Plowman* and ends with a fascinating comparison which he perceives between Langland who, he says, 'was actually a kind of hermit, like his narrator', and Richard Rolle, who 'for immediate posterity' was 'Richard the hermit'.

In a formidable paper entitled '"A Covenant More than Courtesy": A Langlandian Phrase in Its Context' (*N&Q*) A. V. C. Schmidt demonstrates affinities between Langland and the author(s?) of *St. Erkenwald* and *Pearl*, in their respective views on the salvation of the heathen. Frederick M. Biggs offers a convincing explanation as to why virginity is identified as 'aungeles peeris' in *Piers Plowman* B XVI 67–72 and C XVIII 85–100, where there is a pun on 'pears/peers': virgins become a corruptible fruit. 'Virginity is the state from which Adam and Eve fell and the state to which the blessed will return' (*Anglia*).

Carol F. Heffernan suggests some possible origins for 'Piers Plowman B. I. 153–158' (*ELN*), six lines in which the poet takes us all the way from the Incarnation to the Crucifixion and Resurrection. Passages from the *Rorate Celi* ('aperiatur terra et germinet salutorem') and the *Ecce Lignum*, as well as other liturgical readings, may have been the source for these richly allusive lines. Gordon Whatley looks at the Ymaginatif's lines on the salvation of the 'justus' in his interesting paper entitled 'Piers Plowman B 12. 277–94: Notes on Language, Text, and Theology' (*MP*). Lines 290 and 291 are particularly difficult to construe, but they seem to affirm the just man's salvation.

In a closely argued paper Judson Boyce Allen, working on the Z text (*YW* 64.125–6) confidently asserts that a glossary in the Psalter Commentary of

Hugh St Cler was Langland's source for the Pardon Passus and that Hugh, who condemns lawyers and merchants, is also the source for Langland's doubts about the status of such people. This paper, which is entitled 'Langland's Reading and Writing: *Detractor* and the Pardon Passus' (*Speculum*), also presents a marvellously lively picture of the poet looking up the few books in his library while he was composing one or other versions of his poem. John A. Alford supplements his important earlier work (*YW* 56.91) with 'More Un-identified Quotations in *Piers Plowman*' (*MP*), arranged according to the version of the poem in which they make their first appearance (A, B, or C). The quotations identified here include the famous 'Whanne alle tresours arn triȝed treuþe is þe beste', which is taken from the *Secreta Secretorum*.

Denise Baker offers a full-scale analysis of 'The Pardons of *Piers Plowman* (*NM*), where the plural form of the keyword in the paper's title anticipates her contention that Langland's Pardon changes its form and significance as the poem progresses – from the Pardon of the *Visio* to the acquittance which Patience gives Haukyn in *Dowel* (XIV 180–95), to the patent which Love sends to Peace in *Dobet* (XVIII 182–7) and so on, finally, to the Pardon which Christ grants to Piers in *Dobest* (XIX 183–90). Seemingly exhausted by her endeavours with all this close analysis, Dr Baker resorts to a familiar explana-tion for such confusing changes of mind on Langland's part – the poem's structure is spiral. Her final remarks seem more desperate still: 'Langland's poem does have a design, and that is a design upon its reader.'

Two critics have sat in judgement on the recent edition of the Z text (*YW* 64.125–6). In 'The Z-Text: A New Version of *Piers Plowman*?' (*MÆ*) Hugh White agrees that the passages which are unique to the Z version seem to point to Langland's authorship, but wonders if Z may be post-A. A. V. C. Schmidt's paper entitled 'The Authenticity of the Z-Text of *Piers Plowman*: A Metrical Examination' (*MÆ*) studies the metre of the lines that are unique to this version 'using a schema based on an exhaustive study of the metrical structure of every line in the acknowledged three versions of the poem, A, B and C'. In conclusion, he agrees with the Z version's editors that in the text of Ms. Bodley 851 we have 'a version of the poem anterior to the A-text' and 'a new tool for assessing not only the textual traditions of the A, B, and C texts, but also Langland's development as a poet'.

Robert A. Wood identifies William Palmere, rector of St Alphage, Cripple-gate 1397–1400, as 'A Fourteenth-Century London Owner of *Piers Plowman*' (*MÆ*), and notes that 'Langland's work appealed to the thoughtful cleric as well as the educated layman'.

LeedsSE (1983) was subtitled 'Essays in Memory of Elizabeth Salter' and contains some very important studies of *Piers Plowman*. David Aers's paper on '*Piers Plowman* and Problems in the Perception of Poverty: A Culture in Transition' covers much new ground, since it shows that in the early part of the poem Langland toys with the 'new' ethos voiced by, among others, Richard FitzRalph, who tendentiously draws attention to the value of possessions because they were, he alleges, instituted by God. Langland shifts from some tolerance for this ethos (witness his condemnation of able-bodied vagrants and beggars) to a single-minded care for the poor in a series of statements attrib-uted to different speakers in the *Vita* section (especially Passus IX–XV).

E. Talbot Donaldson's lively illustration of the 'Apocalyptic Style in *Piers Plowman* B XIX–XX' concentrates on Langland's use of time sequence. A good instance of this manipulation is the fast work done by Life in taking a mistress, and then begetting Sloth who later marries Wanhope, all within the space of thirteen lines. Finally, A. C. Spearing (in marked contrast to the critical stand taken by John Norton-Smith, noted at the beginning of this section) presents a refreshing celebration of Langland's achievements as a poet. He addresses himself to the way Langland uses words in a close analysis of selected passages (I 179 ff., V 135 ff., XII 131 ff.), showing the poet's consummate use of alliteration and his memorably concrete realization of abstract ideas.

5. Romances

For his study of 'The Middle English Arthurian Romance'[16], Jörg O. Fichte compares *Lybaeus Desconus* and *Sir Perceval of Galles* with the 'classical Arthurian verse novel' of Chrétien and his followers. Formal differences link the two romances with the popular, rather than the classical, romance tradition, which Fichte then investigates in terms of authorship and presentation, content and meaning, and authorial intent and reception.

Geraldine Barnes's two 1984 articles, though on different romances, share a common theme. In an interesting analysis of *Floris and Blauncheflur* compared with its French source, she argues for the greater emphasis on 'Cunning and ingenuity in the Middle English *Floris and Blauncheflur*' (*MÆ*). Where the French poet uses the technique of imagery for sentimental and pious effect, the English poet focuses on episodes of direct speech in his development of the theme of intrigue, as revealed by his more frequent use of keywords and formulas involving *counseil, red(e), (en)gin*. A similar approach is adopted in Barnes's 'Deception and Game in *The Earl of Toulouse*' (*Poetica*) – 'the outstanding feature of the language of the work is its extensive terminology of secrecy and deception'. The article usefully treats various aspects of the 'structure of games' in the work, a structure which reveals itself in the shaping of bargains, secrecy/disguise/role-playing, and finally deception/trickery/fraud.

Nicolas Jacobs contributes two articles further to his note on *Sir Degarré* and an 'Auchinleck bookshop' (*N&Q*, 1982). In the one article he looks at 'The Second Revision of *Sir Degarré*: The Egerton Fragment and Its Congeners' (*NM*) and, as evidence for rewriting, meticulously analyses the agreements in unoriginal readings in the Egerton and Rawlinson manuscripts and the early printed version of the romance. In the second article he has taken the opportunity of the facsimile publication of Ms. Cambridge University Library Ff.2.38 to investigate 'The Processes of Scribal Substitution and Redaction: A Study of the Cambridge Fragment of *Sir Degarré*' (*MÆ*). Since there is no simple theory of group transmission of the ten romances in the manuscript, the textual transmission of each must be investigated. Jacobs's interest is in *Sir Degarré* and he has looked at the Cambridge fragment, which bears comparison with Auchinleck, for support of his argument that Auchinleck variants are the product of revision in a London bookshop. Unfortunately, a painstaking

---

16. In *Literature in Fourteenth-Century England: The J. A. W. Bennett Memorial Lectures, Perugia, 1981–2*, ed. by Piero Boitani and Anna Torti. Tübinger Beiträge zur Anglistik 5. Narr/Brewer (1983). pp. 221. £15.

record of substantive variants from '(i) lexical grouping' to '(xvii) casual errors' reveals that, though there is evidence of 'a good deal of rewriting at a fairly low level', there was no systematic revision and no confirmation of his 'Auchinleck bookshop' theory.

Three manuscript studies will be of interest to readers of this section. In an ambitious-sounding article on 'Middle English Popular Romances: The MS Evidence' (*Manuscripta*), Harriet Hudson uses brief descriptions of some of the major romance collections to draw a number of conclusions on the literary and cultural context of the romances. Less wide-ranging are two essays in *York*[12]. In 'The Compiler at Work: John Colyns and BL MS Harley 2252' Carol M. Meale discusses the format, date, contents and compiler of the manuscript which contains unique copies of *Ipomydon* and the stanzaic *Morte Arthur*. In an equally conscientious analysis, here of the Thornton manuscript, John J. Thompson elicits evidence on 'The compiler in action: Robert Thornton and the "Thornton romances" in Lincoln Cathedral MS 91'.

Norman Daniel has written a very readable book on the attitude to Islam and the Arab revealed by the *chansons de geste*[17]. Neither in social nor religious life was there any attempt to represent the Arab realistically. In social life (Part I, 'The People') Arab and French have the same customs and goals; equally crudely, and incorrectly, in religious life (Part II, 'The Gods') they are poles opposed. Dr Daniel has read widely in the area and writes fluently, but he is an Arab, rather than medieval, expert, and the lack of a medieval perspective may jar.

Finally, *Middle English Prose: A Critical Guide to Major Authors and Genres*[18] includes a wide-ranging review of the romances by George R. Keiser.

6. Gower, Lydgate, Hoccleve

It is again those working in manuscript studies who have currently most of interest to say in this area. In *York*[12] Kate Harris writes well on 'John Gower's *Confessio Amantis*: the virtues of bad texts'. Harris refers to the eight manuscripts of extracts and the two manuscripts of abridged texts, which she closely analyses in terms of syntactical and metrical revision in order to draw convincing conclusions about 'what the *Confessio* meant to its first readers in their own time'. In the same collection Jeremy Smith has useful things to say on the effect of Gower's language on a prolific copyist of the early fifteenth century, responsible for eight Gowers, as well as a Trevisa, a *Piers Plowman*, and two *Canterbury Tales*. On the subject of Lydgate, A. S. G. Edwards, in a paper on 'Lydgate manuscripts: some directions for future research', argues for research into the manuscripts as evidence of fifteenth-century literary taste and suggests numerous potential research topics. One of these is in the area of manuscript decoration, dealt with by Lesley Lawton in 'The illustration of late medieval secular texts with special reference to Lydgate's *Troy Book*'. This is a well-illustrated and informative article which attempts to define the function of the miniatures in a work intended for fashionable reading. Her careful

17. *Heroes and Saracens: A Reinterpretation of the Chansons de Geste*, by Norman Daniel. EdinU. pp. 349. £15.
18. *Middle English Prose: A Critical Guide to Major Authors and Genres*, ed. by A. S. G. Edwards. Rutgers. pp. xi + 440. $50.

analysis of six miniatures found in various forms in the eight fully illustrated manuscripts suggests that the decoration formed a system of visual punctuation, unlike that of the *Confessio Amantis*, where the miniatures stress elements of intellectual, rather than structural, importance. In addition, Lawton has interesting comments to make on the involvement of the commissioner of Ms. Royal 18 D II, Sir William Herbert, in the production of the miniatures of that manuscript.

By contrast, there is a certain sameness, if not staleness, about other contributions to this area. Judith Shaw writes on 'John Gower's illustrative tales' (*NM*, 1983) and emphasizes the function of the tales as illustrations of the vices and virtues by a study of Gower's treatment of the source for the Trump of Death *exemplum* in Book I of the *Confessio Amantis*. Paul Strohm provides 'A note on Gower's persona'[19] which attempts to relate E. Talbot Donaldson's threefold scheme of the Chaucer *persona* to Gower. Chaucer and Gower get together too in an article on 'Aspects of gluttony in Chaucer and Gower' (*SP*), in which R. F. Yeager goes over familiar penitential ground to demonstrate an unconvincing tradition encompassing within the sin of gluttony 'not only excessive eating and drinking, but also great swearing and blasphemy, sorcery and witchcraft, and devil worship (understood in two ways) as well'.

In Hoccleve studies Kate Harris points out in a note on 'The Patron of BL MS Arundel 38' (*N&Q*) that this manuscript is not the presentation copy for Prince Henry, later Henry V, that it has been thought to be, but a closely contemporary copy for John Mowbray, second Duke of Norfolk. If Ms. Arundel 38 is the copy, rather than Ms. BL Harley 4866, as has previously been assumed, the latter needs new investigation.

In a typically fascinating lecture on 'Autobiographical poetry in the Middle Ages: the case of Thomas Hoccleve' (*PBA*, 1982), J. A. Burrow as usual makes one think about many things besides the mere text. He both explains and criticizes the assumption that 'convention and autobiographical truth are in general to be taken as incompatible alternatives' and argues for a 'conventional fallacy' to offset George Kane's familiar 'autobiographical fallacy'. He analyses three key autobiographical passages, arguing against recent critical dismissal of them as conventional. Since Hoccleve's poetry is 'above all a poetry of address' and his addressees are numerous, he naturally adopts different roles for different addressees and, while these are not fictional roles, 'one should not look in Hoccleve's poetry for the simple truth about him'.

I have not yet been able to obtain access to what is clearly an important collection of essays on writers of the fifteenth century[20]. These will be reviewed in *YW* 66 but the titles may be usefully listed here. R. F. Yeager, the editor, writes on 'The Poetry of John Gower: Important Studies, 1960–83'; on Lydgate there is an article by A. S. G. Edwards on 'Lydgate Scholarship: Progress and Prospects' and one by A. C. Spearing on 'Lydgate's Canterbury Tale: *The Siege of Thebes* and Fifteenth-Century Chaucerianism'; Jerome

---

19. In *Acts of Interpretation: The Text in Its Contexts, 700–1600: Essays on Medieval and Renaissance Literature in Honor of E. Talbot Donaldson*, ed. by Mary J. Carruthers and Elizabeth D. Kirk. Pilgrim (1982). pp. xi + 385. $32.95.

20. *Fifteenth-Century Studies: Recent Essays*, ed. by Robert F. Yeager. Archon. pp. xi + 364. $39.50.

Mitchell surveys 'Hoccleve Studies, 1965–81' and John Burrow writes on 'Hoccleve's *Series*: Experience and Books'.

7. Middle Scots Poetry

Two excellent essays relevant to this section commence *Literature of the North*[21]. In the first, Matthew P. McDiarmid argues for 'The Northern Initiative: John of Fordun, John Barbour and the author of the "Saints' Legends"'. All three held office in Aberdeen Cathedral, and McDiarmid argues incisively for their recognition as the founders of a Scottish school of history-writing. In the next essay, on 'Richard Holland's "Buke of the Howlat"', Flora Alexander acknowledges McDiarmid's article on the *Buke of the Howlat* (*MÆ*, 1969) as the inspiration for her defence of the poem's structure, arguing cogently that the juxtaposition of the owl fable and the Douglas material has precedent in fourteenth-century English poetry, particularly the dream-vision. 'Far from being inept', the poem's construction is skilful in its symmetry, number symbolism, and use of the bird allegory to create parallels between birds and human society.

Critical opinion tends currently to place the *Moral Fables* above Henryson's *Testament of Cresseid*, but in 'Henryson's Masterpiece' (*RES*) Peter Godman produces a carefully worded defence of the *Testament* in the light of what he sees as fastidious criticism by the late J. A. W. Bennett (*ScLJ*, 1974). In 'Cresseid and her narrator: a reading of Robert Henryson's "Testament of Cresseid"' (*SMed*) Kevin J. Harty deals with the somewhat overworked *persona* issue, arguing that, while Cresseid achieves a Boethian salvation at the end of the poem, the narrator (who is not Henryson) remains intransigent, pitiless, and unsaved. Also on 'Henryson's Cresseid' (*Poetica*), Haruhiko Fujii narrates the events of Cresseid's downfall in order to emphasize the modernity, rather than medievalism, of Henryson's characterization of her.

In 'Henryson's *Moral Fables* as Experiments in Didactic Narrative', in Boitani and Torti[2], Dieter Mehl counters recent critical opinion on the *Moral Fables* by arguing for their disparity rather than unity. Useful comparisons are made with both Chaucer and Lydgate in an article which stresses the 'astonishing individuality' of the *Fables*, each one 'a new start, not a repeat performance' in which the moral applications 'almost read like exercises in ingenious explication'. Two less substantial notes also relate to the *Fables*. In 'Henryson, *Fables* 2193' (*RES*) R. G. Poole argues for the conjectural emendation of 'efterwart' by 'a stewart' in the difficult line in Henryson's *Fable* of *The Fox, the Wolf and the Cadger*. In a slight contribution to scholarship, 'George Buchanan and "The Lion and the Mouse"' (*N&Q*), Sally Mapstone points out the context of Buchanan's two references to the lion and the mouse and suggests that it is 'not altogether unlikely' that Buchanan had Henryson's *Fable* in mind and so did not feel, as contemporary critics suggest, that the fable could refer only to James III. Also on the subject of James III is Robert L. Kindrick's 'Politics and Poetry at the Court of James III' (*SSL*). Kindrick supports traditional historical criticism which sees James III's political ineptitude reflected in the poetry of the period. It is directly due to James's failures

21. *Literature of the North*, ed. by David Hewitt and Michael Spiller. AberdeenU (1983). pp. viii + 211. hb £9, pb £4.90.

as king that the heroic and romantic poetry of the previous two reigns gave way to the political and social satire which Kindrick investigates in his article.

In 'Dunbar's *The Golden Targe*: a Chaucerian Masque' (*SSL*) Pamela M. King focuses on the 'metaphoric' rather than the 'strictly metonymic' relation to masque of Dunbar's poem. Parallels in Chaucer and Lydgate and contemporary descriptions of court entertainments are usefully cited, and King concentrates in particular on the meaning of the four stanzas of disembarkation, where the two courts are opposing male and female tournament audiences. The message of the allegory is contained in the near-triumph of the antimasque, so that 'whatever Dunbar's poetic masque celebrates it is not the "court of love" per se'. Alasdair MacDonald deals with Dunbar's *The Testament of Maister Andro Kennedy* in 'William Dunbar, Andro and Walter Kennedy, and Hary's *Wallace*' (*Neophil*), which concentrates on elucidating ll. 35–40 of *The Testament* as a parody of Blind Harry's *Wallace* and explaining the manuscript confusion between Andro Kennedy and the better-known Walter. In an entertaining and wide-ranging essay on 'Rough Music: Some early invectives and flytings' (*YES*), Douglas Gray analyses *The Flyting of Dunbar and Kennedie* and sees in it the positive qualities of Dunbar's more appreciated satires – 'though it is "rough music", it really is a kind of music'.

Three articles on Henryson and two on Dunbar have appeared in a collection of essays which I have not yet been able to see, *Fifteenth-Century Studies*[20]. Louise O. Fradenburg reviews 'Henryson Scholarship: The Recent Decades', while C. David Benson writes on 'O Moral Henryson' and Denton Fox on 'The Coherence of Henryson's Work'. A review of Dunbar and Douglas is carried out by Florence H. Ridley in 'Studies in Douglas and Dunbar: The Present Situation', and Edmund Reiss investigates 'The Ironic Art of William Dunbar'.

8. Lyrics and Miscellaneous Verse

Robert Mannyng's *Handlyng Synne* is enjoying a bout of popularity. An edition of it by I. Sullens is, unfortunately, something of a poor show[22]. Certainly she has put a deal of work into it, but some of this could have been better employed. Her transcription of the version of Mannyng's poem preserved in Ms. Bodley 415 is prefaced by a brief introduction of the standard sort, in which are presented such things as manuscript descriptions and editorial method. This in itself would be perfectly acceptable, were it not for its superficiality. The linguistic commentary is weak, assertive and outdated; for example, no cognizance is taken of McIntosh's important work in 1976 on the language of the Havelok manuscripts (see *YW* 57.70). The manuscript descriptions are somewhat unscientific, and their undisciplined presentation leads to unevenness in their content. However, some of the information they contain is useful, and Sullens's speculation (p. xxii), based on the quality of some of the manuscripts, that the sort of reading public that *Handlyng Synne* had was not altogether that envisaged by its author, is very interesting. The stages in the deduction of the *stemma codicum* are never discussed, and its presentation as a *fait accompli* is quite unsatisfactory. Sentences like the following: 'Using F and

22. *Robert Mannyng of Brunne: Handlyng Synne*, ed. by I. Sullens. MRTS 14. CMERS. pp. xlvi + 387. $25.

H as resources to correct readings in B [the manuscript she has chosen to edit] is sometimes hazardous . . .' become incomprehensible in the light of her *stemma* which presents F and H as direct descendants of B, and therefore of no use whatsoever in determining B readings. Again in this section, there is scant attention paid to recent secondary literature. One wonders after reading this edition how much further forward we really are.

A second work, this time a large-scale study of *Handlyng Synne* in five chapters by F. Kemmler, is a much more rigorous affair[23]. The first chapter describes the cultural and literary background of the *Manuel des Péchés* and *Handlyng Synne*, and is concerned to illustrate both the preoccupations of a selection of thirteenth-century English synodalia and also the doctrinal emphases which constitute the thematic framework of selected *Summae confessorum* and *Manualia curatorum*. Chapter Two considers ostensible definitions of the word *exemplum* in selected *artes predicandi*, and the meaning of the word in actual practice. The third and longest chapter investigates the use of a selection of Mannyng's *exempla* in their immediate context, *Handlyng Synne* itself, and also considers their relationship to the wider social context. Chapter Four is a concise critical survey of studies on the *exemplum*, and the final chapter presents a general theory on the use of illustrative narrative. On reading Kemmler's work, we are both grateful for his detailed explanations of the stages of his procedure and also wearied by their crippling overstatement. This is a graceless book in many respects. Nevertheless, it seems reliable, with a fairly scrupulous attention to secondary criticism, and that, if that alone, should commend it.

Two excellent articles have been written by S. Morrison on the *Ormulum*. The first presents his evidence for 'New Sources for the *Ormulum*' (*Neophil*) and makes a good case that Orm consulted Isidore's *De Natura Rerum*, integrating some of its material with material taken from the *Glossa Ordinaria*. He also finds evidence of the use of Isidore's *Etymologiae*. In the second, 'Orm's English Sources' (*Archiv*), he stresses Orm's importance in the tradition of English homiletic writing, stating that alone among the English homilists, only Ælfric and Orm adopted the exegetical method as their norm. He identifies in the *Ormulum* selected syntactic units of formulaic currency in OE homilies, and claims for Orm a closer relationship with earlier homiletic tradition than has previously been recognized, especially in his use and treatment of word groups characteristic of Ælfrician phraseology. Orm, he believes, was frequently recollecting earlier vernacular phraseology, rather than constantly drawing upon Latin.

The *South English Legendary* features prominently in *LeedsSE* this year. S. Lavery locates 'The Source of the St Brendan Story in the *South English Legendary*' in the Hiberno-Latin *Navigatio Sancti Brendani*, rather than in the Anglo-Norman poetic version written by one 'danz Benedeiz'. O. S. Pickering's article, 'The *Southern Passion* and the *Ministry and Passion*: The Work of a Middle English Reviser', is a study of one of the many processes of revision that the *South English Legendary* attracted. Ten extracts from its *Southern Passion*, now declared to be a careful revision of the *Ministry and Passion*, are analysed to demonstrate their manipulation of the *Ministry* text. In the same periodical R. Copeland writes on 'The Middle English "Candet

---

23. *'Exempla' in Context*, by F. Kemmler. Narr. pp. 246. DM 68.

Nudatum Pectus" and Norms of Early Vernacular Translation Practice', explaining that the literary strategy employed in the ME poem's ultimate source, an eleventh-century meditation by John of Fécamp, seems frequently to have been unavailable as guidance for early ME poets in search of a voice. Because the *Candet nudatum pectus* was normally excerpted from the longer meditation and circulated separately, ME poets had to discover their own means of rendering it effectively. She illustrates some of these renditions and suggests that many of them have found their inspiration in contemporary art, in certain iconographical techniques of which these renditions are the literary counterparts.

A group of articles print new poems for the first time. T. F. S. Turville-Petre prints 'A Poem on the Nine Worthies' (*NMS*, 1983) from Ms. 2 Tennyson D'Eyncourt K/1, a roll in the Lincoln Archives Office containing a genealogical tree of the kings of England to Henry VI and his son Prince Edward. He dates the roll between 1453 and 1461, and plausibly suggests the poem may have been composed to be spoken in a pageant, or else to be inscribed under portraits of the Worthies. 'Two Middle English Lyrics in the Bibliothèque Mazarine' (*N&Q*) are printed with a short commentary by A. Barratt. The first, on f. 104v of Ms. Mazarine 469, is a translation into a rhyme royal stanza of the first two verses of the hymn *Stella celi extirpavit*. The second, on f. 7v of Ms. Mazarine 514, is in sixteen lines, a devotion to the Name of Jesus and possibly an epitome of the longer poem 'Swete Ihesu now wol I synge'. It is unfortunate that P. Whiteford's perfunctory note entitled 'Unnoticed Verses from a Fifteenth-Century Sermon Collection' (*N&Q*) was not more carefully researched. The lyric he prints from Bodleian Library Ms. e Museo 180, f. 181r, was printed in *N&Q* in 1976 (see *YW* 57.76), and his line 'Vita qua vinis . . .', which begins the same lyric is, as it stands, nonsensical; it ought more correctly to read 'Vita qua vivis . . .'.

J. J. Lamberts attempts a reconstruction of the spelling system of 'The "Prolowg" to *Cursor Mundi*, vv. 1–270' (*Neophil*), and supplies notes. The study would have been sounder had it taken into account the articles on scribal practice coming out of the Middle English Dialect Project over the past few years. F. Newman makes a careful and convincing argument in '*Christ Maketh to Man*, Stanza Four: A Case for Interpolation' (*NM*) that the fourth stanza of this lyric is an interpolation which mars the lyric's poetic integrity. R. H. Osberg's study of 'Alliterative Technique in the Lyrics of MS Harley 2253' (*MP*) sets itself the multifold task of deducing scansion rules for application to both alliterative and non-alliterative Harley lyrics, of demonstrating rhythmical kinships between alliterative lyrics and devotional alliterative prose, and finally of analysing the variety and occurrence of those rhythms in alliterative lyrics.

9. Malory and Caxton

Although the most important Caxton publication of 1984 should be James W. Spisak's edition of *Caxton's Malory*[24], it will be as well to begin with an

---

24. *Caxton's Malory: A New Edition of Sir Thomas Malory's Le Morte Darthur Based on the Pierpont Morgan Copy of William Caxton's Edition of 1485*, ed. by James W. Spisak, with a Dictionary of Names and Places by Bert Dillon. 2 vols. UCal. pp. 600, 320. £92.

article on 'Caxton's Malory again' by Shunichi Noguchi (*Poetica*). Noguchi follows up an earlier article (*Poetica*, 1977) which argued that the Roman War episode was revised by Caxton, rather than by Malory, by looking at Caxton's variants in the rest of the *Morte Darthur* as confirmation of his earlier thesis. Towards the end of the article, Noguchi looks forward to Spisak's edition, whose title-page affirms that it is 'based on work begun by the late William Matthews', expresses the hope that the edition will include the full text of Matthews's paper arguing for revision by Malory, and expects the remedying of two deficiencies in Oskar Sommer's 1889 edition, the out-dated critical apparatus and the transcriptional errors.

It must be said at once that Noguchi's hopes and expectations have not been realized. Volume I of *Caxton's Malory* contains the preface, Caxton's prologue, Caxton's table of contents and the text itself ('light modern punctuation and modern paragraphing' with no inverted commas or apostrophes); Volume II contains a brief and uncontroversial introduction (which mentions the Roman War controversy), notes which are almost entirely textual rather than explanatory, a glossary which should be described as select, a useful Dictionary of Names and Places (by Bert Dillon), and two appendixes (one is of the reset sheets in the Pierpont Morgan and John Rylands copies, the other is a transcription of the Winchester manuscript Roman War episode). Matthews's unpublished 'Who Revised the Roman War Episode in Malory's *Morte Darthur*?' is not published. There is a magisterial criticism of the edition in 'Caxton's Malory Re-edited' by Toshiyuki Takamiya which, despite its 1985 publication (*Poetica*), must be mentioned now for its thorough, objective, and damning comments.

An appendix to Spisak's limited discussion of the Roman War episode is provided by him in 'Malory Revises his Vocabulary' (*Poetica*). The assertion is that a dozen listed locutions were revised by Malory, not Caxton.

To deal with Malory alone, Stephen Knight's *Arthurian Literature and Society*[25] includes a chapter on 'Sir Thomas Malory's Arthuriad' in the course of its dynamic progress from Celtic legend to Mark Twain. The chapter title indicates Knight's decision to have his cake and eat it – 'Malory actually wrote a long narrative which contains both medieval looseness and, towards the end, a more modern type of unity.' Knight steers us through the *Morte Darthur*, directing our attention to landmarks such as wars, policing methods, the *devotio moderna*, and so on. In the course of our journey he is sometimes a little glib but always readable.

Derek Brewer is always a good read too, though a more conventionally academic one. In his study of 'The Presentation of the Character of Lancelot: Chrétien to Malory'[26], his interest is in the treatment of traditional folk elements. While Chrétien amplifies the core and increases realism, Malory summarizes and reduces realism – in Brewer's terms, he stresses the 'vertical' rather than the 'horizontal' references and shows 'the same blurring of the fictional border between narrative and commentary as we find in traditional writing between fiction and actuality'. In the same collection of essays Irene Joynt deals with 'Vengeance and Love in "The Book of Sir Lancelot and

25. *Arthurian Literature and Society*, by Stephen Knight. Macmillan (1983). pp. xvi + 229. £20.
26. *Arthurian Literature III*, ed. by R. Barber. Brewer/B&N. pp. 224. £17.50.

Queen Guinevere"'. The title of the paper indicates the prevalent themes which Malory, by careful arrangement of his material and modification of his sources, united in that book in preparation for the destruction and tragedy of the final book.

In an interesting though not always convincing exposition of *Arthur's Kingdom of Adventure*[27], Muriel Whitaker deals with the iconographical significance of the images of the *Morte Darthur*, the sword, the castle, the forest, and so on. The *Tale of the Sankgreal* is the pivot of the work, shifting attention from *la chevalerie terrienne* to *la chevalerie celestienne*, altering the iconography of the elements, changing the *genre* from romance to tragedy, and turning the treatment of the pattern of time (this last a stimulating final chapter) from cyclical to linear.

J. F. Cartwright has written on 'Journeys towards Self-Knowledge: The Quests of Gawain, Torre and Pellinor in *Malory's Tale of King Arthur*' (*UCTSE*, 1983). The quests are narrated at length in order to show that, in contrast to the Grail quest (which was 'uncongenial' to Malory), the external quest is 'only the framework for the more important action of the quest, which is an inner action' – 'what Buddhists call "mindfulness"'.

In Caxton studies Norman Blake provides an authoritative and comprehensive review of Caxton scholarship in *Middle English Prose: A Critical Guide to Major Authors and Genres*[18]. Two articles have appeared on *Reynard the Fox*. In 'Between Two Languages: Caxton's Translation of Reynaert de Vos'[28] Wytze and Lotte Hellinga explain why Caxton's translation is less pedestrian than is usually thought. In 'Reflections on William Caxton's "Reynard the Fox"'[29], Norman Blake also challenges common assumptions about the translation, usually seen as an aberration among his other translations (French in origin and moral or religious in tone). He argues discursively but effectively for the moral, rather than satiric, tone of the work and for its natural place in the animal moralizing tradition exemplified by Lydgate. Finally, John H. Fisher's article on 'Caxton and Chancery English' in *Fifteenth-Century Studies*[20] will be reviewed in *YW* 66.

10. Other Prose

As often happens these days, the main interest in this section lies with the mystical tradition, but two very fine studies draw attention to the excellent achievements of early ME prose. First, however, there is an invaluable book which covers the whole field, edited with great sensitivity and intuition by A. S. G. Edwards. Eighteen scholars contribute chapters to *Middle English Prose: A Critical Guide to Major Authors and Genres*[18]. The aim of the book is 'to produce systematic critical overviews', but this modest statement belies the

27. *Arthur's Kingdom of Adventure: The World of Malory's Morte Darthur*, by Muriel Whitaker. Arthurian Studies IX. Brewer/B&N. pp. 136. $35.

28. In *Studies in Seventeenth-Century English Literature, History and Bibliography: Festschrift for Professor T. A. Birrell on the Occasion of his Sixtieth Birthday*, ed. by G. A. M. Janssens and F. G. A. M. Aarts. Rodopi. pp. vii + 268. Ffr 60.

29. In *Le Roman de Renard: On the beast epic*, ed. by Adrian van den Hoven. Revue canadienne d'études ñeerlandaises/Canadian Journal of Netherlandic Studies IV, i. Association par l'Avancement des Etudes Ñeerlandaises/Association for the Advancement of Netherlandic Studies (1983). pp. vi + 90.

eruition and authority of the individual chapters. Each chapter, as will be noted from the following description of the contents, is written by an acknowledged specialist in the relevant field. Roger Dahood writes on *Ancrene Wisse*, the Katherine Group and the *Wohunge* Group, John A. Alford on Richard Rolle and related works, Alastair Minnis on *The Cloud of Unknowning* and Walter Hilton's *Scale of Perfection*, Barbara Nolan on Nicholas Love, Christina von Nolcken on Julian of Norwich, John C. Hirsh on Margery Kempe, Ralph Hanna III on Mandeville, Anthony S. G. Edwards on John Trevisa, Michael G. Sargent on minor devotional writings, Thomas J. Heffernan on sermon literature, Lister M. Matheson on historical prose, Anne Hudson on Wycliffite prose (see *YW* 64.137–8), George R. Keiser on the Romances, Traugott Lawler on Chaucer, Linda Ehrsam Voigts on medical prose, Laurel Braswell on utilitarian and scientific prose ('a comparatively uncharted area'), and Norman Blake on William Caxton. The final chapter, by Alexandra Barratt, is entitled 'Works of Religious Interest' and deals with treatises which cover 'the official teaching curriculum for the laity of the medieval Church'. This is a singularly useful book, and a copy of it should be on the shelves of every medievalist.

The introduction and Part I of *Ancrene Riwle* have been edited and translated, with a commentary, by the late Robert W. Ackerman and Roger Dahood[30]. The base text is BL Ms. Cleopatra C.VI. Ackerman contributed the introduction, and the text and translation are the work of Dahood. Ackerman's contribution can stand as an introduction to the whole of *Ancrene Riwle* or *Ancrene Wisse* since it deals with, among other topics, the whole anchorite tradition and contains an abstract of all eight parts. Dahood's text is authoritative, and his translation is fluent, elegant, and accurate. It is to be hoped that he will now turn his attention to Part VIII which, like Part I, also tends to be neglected because of the predominant interest shown in the much more glamorous Inner Rule, Parts II–VII.

Bella Millett's contribution to the Dobson *Festschrift*[31] re-opens the question as to whether or not stylistically idiosyncratic works such as *Hali Meiðhad* and *Sawles Warde* are landmarks in the 'continuity of English prose'. She offers strong reservations about the affirmative beliefs of J. R. R. Tolkien (*YW* 10.140–1) and R. W. Chambers (*YW* 13.18–20), and argues, instead, that the styles of these two works, with their affected two-stress rhythms, strongly reflect the influence of their Latin sources (see also her edition of *Hali Meiðhad*, *YW* 63.88–9). Note her controversial reference to the 'authors' – perhaps she should fully elaborate elsewhere on her theories about the authorship of these two texts.

Marion Glasscoe has edited another fine set of papers on the medieval mystical tradition in England[32]. Ritamary Bradley draws our attention to the use of the mirror image in mystical writings (see *YW* 63.75). Rosamund Allen illustrates the paradox that the solitary longs for a union with God that is also

---

30. *Ancrene Riwle Introduction and Part I*, ed. and trans. with Commentary, by Robert W. Ackerman and Roger Dahood. MRTS 31. CMERS. pp. xii + 114. $12.

31. *Five Hundred Years of Words and Sounds*, ed. by E. G. Stanley and D. Gray. B&B (1983). pp. 256. £25.

32. *The Medieval Mystical Tradition in England*, ed. by Marion Glasscoe. B&B, pp. 191. £15.

communal. Rita Copeland considers Rolle's theoretical assumptions about literary style based on an examination of the classical and medieval literary traditions. Malcolm Moyes discusses the importance of the much copied and frequently printed *Expositio super novem lectiones mortuorum* by Richard Rolle. James Hogg looks at the Latin version of the *Cloud of Unknowing* in Cambridge, Pembroke College Ms. 221. Franz Wöhrer outlines an approach to the mystographical work of the *Cloud*-author through Carl Albrecht's psychological consciousness. Anna P. Baldwin describes how the *Scale of Perfection* and *Piers Plowman* use the Platonic and Augustinian concept of the tripartite segmentation of the soul as a structural principle. Susan Dickman compares Margery Kempe and the continental tradition of the pious woman, pointing out the differences between thirteenth-century and fourteenth-century women (the latter seem to have been more politically active). The final paper, by David Wallace, presents a very interesting set of comparisons and contrasts between Margery Kempe and St Catherine of Siena.

Robert Boenig has done a modern English translation of some Latin works by Richard Rolle – his treatment of Psalm 20 from the *Commentary on the Psalms*, his *Comment on the First Verses of the Canticle of Canticles*, and his *Commentary on the Apocalypse*[33]. There is a short introduction which convincingly points out the significance of these three texts in the development of Rolle's writings and also indicates his individualistic manipulation of biblical sources. The translations themselves seem competent and keep close to the original. This book is useful as far as it goes, but annotations would have been helpful.

John Philip Daly has produced a critical text of Rolle's *Judica Me Deus* which is accompanied by a helpful translation[34]. Part I of the introduction deals with the contents, source (the *Oculus Sacerdotis*), and background of *Judica Me Deus*, and Part II discusses the eighteen extant manuscripts of the work (one of which, the Castle Howard manuscript, has been lost since 1944), the authorship, and date. In this section the editor closely follows the work of Hope Emily Allen (*YW* 8.96–8). This is followed by the edition itself which is based on Ms. Laud Misc. 528. The capitalization, punctuation, and paragraphing are all modern, and the *apparatus criticus* accompanying the text includes all rejected variants and subvariants where they have not been eliminated, as well as the omissions and additions of any branch of a tradition. The edition and translation are useful in themselves, but annotation would have helped to clarify the many difficult points. Finally, it seems from the bibliography, which contains no recent work on Rolle, that this edition was completed long ago.

Gunnel Cleve offers some very odd remarks on Richard Rolle's prose style (*NM*): 'the choice of the passive as the means of conveying mystical experience and experience of things divine seems a deliberate one'. J. P. H. Clark concentrates on the *Incendium Amoris* and the *Emendatio Vitae* in his enlightening paper on 'Richard Rolle: A Theological Reassessment' (*DownR* 1983),

33. *Richard Rolle Biblical Commentaries: Short Exposition of Psalm 20, Treatise on the Twentieth Psalm, Comment on the First Verses of the Canticle of Canticles, Commentary on the Apocalypse*, by Robert Boenig. SSELER 92.13. USalz. pp. vi + 194.
34. *An Edition of the Judica Me Deus of Richard Rolle*, by John Philip Daly. SSELER 92.14. USalz. pp. lvi + 126; 2 tables + 3 illus.

which contains a lucid explanation and analysis of the famous 'fervor, dulcor, and canor' experiences, as felt by someone he describes as 'a joyful and fulfilled Catholic'. The section on the *Emendatio Vitae* supplies a careful examination of what Rolle means by 'insuperabilis, inseparabilis, singularis' which, he says, are ultimately derived from Richard of St Victor's *De IV Gradibus Violentae Charitatis*. He concludes that Rolle is theologically sound, but his earlier enthusiasm may have caused some commentators to be (unnecessarily) suspicious about him.

Michael G. Sargent has produced a very interesting study of James Grenehalgh as a textual critic[35]. Grenehalgh, who originally came from Lancashire, was an English Carthusian monk who was born about 1465, professed in the Charterhouse at Sheen by November 1499, and who died at the Charterhouse at Kingston-upon-Hull before May 1530. According to Sargent, his annotations and distinct monogram have been found in manuscripts and early prints of Walter Hilton's *Scale of Perfection* and the contemporary Latin translation of the *Scale* made by the Carmelite Thomas Fishlake; of Hilton's short treatise *Of Mixed Life*; of the anonymous *Cloud of Unknowing*; of the ME translation of Margaret Porete's *Mirror of Simple Souls*; of *The Seven Points of True Love and Everlasting Wisdom*; of Richard Rolle's *Incendium Amoris*, *Emendatio Vitae*, and *Contra Amatores Mundi*; and of several other texts as well. In the present study, Sargent sets out to detail Grenehalgh's life, and to describe and evaluate his work as a textual critic of the literature of late medieval English spirituality. In other words, here for the first time Grenehalgh is brought centre-stage. The introductory section contains an informative discussion of the Carthusian order's concern for the correctness of texts, for the writing and copying of books generally, and also for keeping registers of all books in their libraries. Their favourite authors included Jan van Ruusbroec and Hugh of Balma, but students of ME will be drawn most of all to their interest in the writings of Richard Rolle and Walter Hilton, and also the *Cloud of Unknowing*. Twelve manuscripts have been identified as Grenehalgh's. In these there are some 1800 textual annotations by Grenehalgh which Sargent carefully distinguishes according to type – critical, philological, explanatory, and so forth. In the Douce Ms. 262 of the *Cloud*, for instance, Grenehalgh made about three hundred critical annotations. Many are simply corrections of the spellings used by William Tregooze, the Douce *Cloud* scribe – for example, the varying use of 'w' spellings. Sargent reserves two full chapters for Grenehalgh's work on the text of Walter Hilton's *Scale of Perfection*, and these are particularly interesting. Overall, both in its content and in its methodology, this book is a pleasure to study, and is highly recommended.

J. P. H. Clark surveys the sixteen extant manuscripts of the *Stimulus Amoris* (*DownR*) and, after a cautious examination of the arguments for attributing it to Hilton, comes down in favour of Hilton's having translated it into *The Pryckynge of Love*. He demonstrates that there is a closer similarity between these two texts than between the *Scale of Perfection* and *The Pryckynge*. Clark has also addressed 'The Problem of Walter Hilton's Authorship: *Bonum Est*, *Benedictus*, and *Of Angels*' (*DownR*, 1983) by examining 'how far the theological content of *Bonum Est* corresponds with Hilton's characteristic

35. *James Grenehalgh as Textual Critic*, by Michael G. Sargent. *Analecta Cartusiana* 85. 2 vols. pp. 590.

theology as shown in those works that are undoubtedly his'. He concludes that the authorship of *Bonum Est* remains unclear, the author of *Benedictus* is unknown, and Hilton wrote *Of Angels*.

Judith Lang writes on 'The Godly Wylle' which Julian of Norwich refers to in Chapter 37 of her book (*DownR*). Man's will is naturally disposed to good but often fails through lack of faith in God's grace. In 'The Motherhood of God in Julian of Norwich's Theology' (*DownR*, 1982) Paul S. Datsko Barker attempts to explain the apparent contradiction which Julian perceives between fear of God and love of God in the life of the Christian on earth through the imagery which she uses of the motherhood of God. The explanation which he offers here is not entirely clear.

M. F. Wakelin has recently found a vernacular version of a nun's profession, together with a vernacular 'charge' to the abbess, in the margins of BL Ms. Add. 6157 (*N&Q*), of which the material of interest here is written in a secretary hand of the mid fifteenth century, which he dates 'before 1470'. His paper concludes with an edition of the relevant marginalia.

Björn Wallner continues his great and seemingly never-ending task of editing the ME translation of Guy de Chauliac's *Great Surgery*[36]. Recent volumes include one which supplies notes, glossary, and marginalia for the Treatise on Ulcers (Book IV of the *Great Surgery*) and another which supplies notes, glossary, and a Latin appendix for the Treatise on Wounds (Book III of the *Great Surgery*).

In a useful paper Sarah M. Horrall furnishes missing sources for sections of a recent edition of Capgrave's *Abbreuiacion of Cronicles* (*N&Q*), YW 64.136) which disclosed sources for the second and third parts of the work, but not for the first part (dealing with history before the birth of Christ). According to Dr Horrall, Capgrave used Petrus Comestor's *Historia Scholastica* and also two of the sources which Comestor himself used – Josephus's *Jewish Antiquities* for the discussion on the longevity of the patriarchs and the account of the descendants of Noah, and also the *Revelations* of Methodius, referred to at I 15/18.

11. Drama

(a) Editions and General Studies

It was inevitable that the large compendium of references to dramatic texts and records, put together by I. Lancashire, would be out of date as soon as it was printed, what with the activity of such enterprises as the *REED* project constantly bringing new material to light, but for all of that, his is a very substantial, useful, and conveniently organized work[37]. It is, in Lancashire's words, 'less than a full descriptive calendar and more than a finding list', in

---

36. *The Middle English Translation of Guy de Chauliac's Treatise on Wounds*, Part II. Notes, Glossary and Latin Appendix: Book III of *The Great Surgery*, ed. by Björn Wallner. A&W (1979), pp. 114. *The Middle English Translation of Guy de Chauliac's Treatise on Ulcers*, Part II. Notes, Glossary, Marginalia: Book IV of *The Great Surgery*, ed. by Björn Wallner. A&W. pp. 48.

37. *Dramatic Texts and Records of Britain: A Chronological Topography to 1558*, by I. Lancashire. CUP. pp. lxxi + 633. £39.50.

which there has been collected a wide variety of references to dramatic activity dating from earliest times in these islands up until the accession of Elizabeth I. The introduction carefully prescribes its scope and aims, and includes a very brief history on the development of drama (the only lapse noticed here being the unfounded assertion that the *Interludium de Clerico et Puella* dates from the early thirteenth century). A chronological list of dramatic texts is followed by a topographical list of dramatic records. This lists dramatic sites, the records of dramatic activity in England, Wales, Scotland, and Ireland, the records from a few places outside the British Isles, and finally a list of texts and records over which there hangs some doubt. Appended is an index of playing companies, playwrights, playing places, and a chronological list of salient dates. Although it will inevitably be superseded, for the moment it is to be thoroughly welcomed.

A collection of essays edited by P. Neuss offers the student of medieval drama surprises reminiscent of a mystery tour with stops at nine places to admire a different view[38]. Even if, as the editor claims, the fruits of *REED* research and experimental modern productions 'form the basis of this book', the final impression it conveys is of a singularly varied mélange. R. Rastall's essay is a welcome and informative survey of the use of music in vernacular religious drama, and it attempts to explain the rationale of its use. P. Meredith addresses the important questions provoked by the play manuscripts themselves, with selected examples from those of York, N-Town, and Chester. His speculations on Chester are particularly interesting. It is high time that more attention be paid to 'the archaeology of the book', as it might be termed, a field of research which at last shows signs of coming more generally into fashion. M. Twycross is, as usual, eminently readable, and this time on the subject of clothing in the mystery plays. She convincingly queries received orthodoxy which holds that clothing in the plays more or less reproduces that of the contemporary medieval scene. R. Beadle considers, in a somewhat unevenly presented piece, the eighth play of the York cycle, performed by the Shipwrights, and illustrates the range and implication of its technical language. The comparative study by J. Cowen of the treatment of the Annunciation and Nativity in the plays is fluent and thoughtful, though unfortunately a gremlin in the press has printed the wrong picture as her plate 5. D. Grantley speculates on the staging of miraculous effects, and rightly stresses how important, but difficult, it is to understand their mechanics. R. Proudfoot ambles half-heartedly through a grey account of what some of the morality plays are about, but manages to get up a little steam when discussing *The Castle of Perseverance*. T. Davenport's article is lively and stimulating. It investigates the stereotype of the gallant in medieval drama, its flexibility, and uses. The final essay by R. Potter adroitly teases out some of the themes of justice in medieval plays and considers these themes' dramatic potential.

A second collection of essays, this one in two parts, edited by P. Happé, reprints a selection of early documents of dramatic interest, followed by articles reprinted from periodicals or, in some cases, excerpted from books[39]. The early documents comprise a short extract of the *Treatis of Miraclis Pleyinge*, Robert Mannyng's lines about plays in his *Handlyng Synne*, the 1433

38. *Aspects of Early English Drama*, ed. by P. Neuss. B&N. pp. xv + 195. $42.50.
39. *Medieval English Drama*, ed. by P. Happé. Macmillan. pp. 222. £15.

York Mercers' pageant waggon list, and the famous description of Chester waggons from Rogers's *Breviary*. The articles in Part Two deal with Corpus Christi plays, Moralities and Interludes, and aspects of performance. All of these have been reviewed already in the *YW* volume for the appropriate year, apart from the articles by P. Neuss and S. Lindenbaum. Consideration of its text and stage directions leads Neuss to the verdict that the Cornish *Creacion* play was not performed in quite the same way as were other Cornish plays, and she suggests a more intimate, though in its way equally elaborate, sort of staging for it. She also offers an explanation of the role of the play's 'Conveyour', and identifies him as one William Jordan. S. Lindenbaum reviews the presentation of the York cycle at Toronto in 1977, illustrating some of the ways in which practical production can illuminate our understanding of a text.

The Cornish *Creacion of the World* is indeed, in the words of P. Neuss, 'of great interest to students of mediaeval theatre', and she has made great strides in bringing it back before their attention in her new edition[40]. Her introduction discusses the relationship of the *Creacion* to the mainstream of vernacular religious drama, arguing that though its characters are mainly biblical rather than allegorical, in both tone and structure it in fact resembles a morality play. She traces the action of the play in which the good characters, at first somewhat bland and unsympathetic, gradually gain the audience's approval, while the evil characters suffer the reverse process. Also there is a discussion of the nature of the relationship of the *Creacion* to the *Origo Mundi* (the first of the Cornish *Ordinalia* trilogy), in which Neuss postulates a common ancestor lying behind both versions, and an examination of how the *Creacion* may have been staged. In a section on the playwright, she is categorical that 'William Jordan ... was almost certainly *not* the "conveyor"', although she has changed her mind about this in her article in Happé's collection (see the previous review above; it is unfortunate that the discrepancy was not noted). Dating the composition of the play is difficult, but sometime in the first half of the sixteenth century seems likely. The introduction concludes with a description of the unique manuscript and explanation of editorial method. The text itself is provided with a facing translation.

R. W. Vince has produced 'a compromise between theoretical historiography and bibliography' in his book on *Ancient and Medieval Theatre*[41]. In Chapter Four, which is the one most nearly concerning us, the first three dealing for the most part with classical theatre, he begins by tracing the shifts in scholarly attention given to medieval drama, from the narrow focus upon the text itself to the circumstances of play performance and an accompanying widening of the definition of theatre to include civic pageantry, tournaments, and so forth. He sees the data-collecting of the eighteenth- and early-nineteenth-century antiquarians yielding to its organization and explanation in terms of an evolutionary model by the later nineteenth-century critics: a pupating theatre was slowly emerging from its carapace to achieve full maturity in the Renaissance. The thesis proposed in H. C. Gardiner's *Mysteries' End*, that the Reformation put the plays down, is seen as the first important check to this earlier school which had considered their decay to be genetic.

40. *The Creacion of the World: A Critical Edition and Translation*, by P. Neuss. Garland. pp. lxxxii + 249. $50.

41. *Ancient and Medieval Theatre*, by R. W. Vince. Greenwood. pp. xi + 156. £27.95.

Practical revivals and the work of Salter, Southern, and Wickham, all helped shift the perception of early drama, so that today it is attracting substantial investigation in its own right, and is no longer considered an embarrassing prelude to a golden age. It is impossible to do justice to the rest of the chapter here, for it ranges widely over a variety of matters, including the diversity of play texts, the meaning of stage plans (curiously, no mention is made of N. C. Schmitt's important work when the stage plan of *The Castle of Perseverance* is being discussed), the difficulty of interpreting staging circumstances, folk drama, and use of the visual arts as evidence for dramatic practice. Vince's ambitious book is valuable as a quick point of reference, though its scope is so vast that it is inevitably severely selective, and for all its lip-service to Continental traditions, it is skewed towards readers with an interest in medieval British theatre. It is to those interested in the British dimension that it will prove the most worth while.

Devils have the last word. A. W. Divett prints a rare item from the Nottingham court rolls in 'An Early Reference to Devil's-Masks in the Nottingham Records' (*METh*). It concerns the disputed possession of a devil-mask in 1372. M. Collins prints 'An Early Sixteenth-Century Comment on Audience Reaction to the Impersonation of Devils' (*N&Q*) mentioned in an *Ars moriendi* written by one Richard Whitford. The reaction is twofold. Children and women, in particular, are first terrified, then upon realizing that all is done in play, delight in the impersonation.

(b) Chester

K. Tamburr considers that the episode of 'The Dethroning of Satan in the Chester Cycle' (*NM*) during the play of *The Fall of Lucifer* provides a prototypical illustration of the defeat of wilful disobedience, a theme which will be repeated in subsequent plays by further acts of dethronement (later in *Christ's Descent into Hell* and lastly in *The Coming of Antichrist*). The placing of these three episodes before, during, and after the life of Christ reinforces traditional typology and acts as a unifying factor in the cycle.

(c) Wakefield

The arguments mustered in J. Helterman's study of the plays of the Wakefield Master are, by and large, clear, unpretentious, and stimulating[42]. He believes that the Wakefield Master had discovered that the inept imitation of some ideal is a close parody of its fulfilment in symbolic form, and that the emphasis in the plays is on how such imitation differs from the ideal, rather than on what is being figured through typology. Parody in the hands of the Master tends to be a symbolic medium, while typology tends to be an allegorical one. Helterman devotes a chapter to each play in the canon. *Mactacio Abel* is said to present a Cain character whose actions are both humanly intelligible and symbolically significant, and that these values never clash. *Processus Noe*, on the other hand, allows human and figural values to play against each other in a complex fashion. *Prima pastorum* is said to illustrate the process of transition from the literal to the symbolic mode of perception in its case-history of the development of three foolish shepherds into prophets of Christ. The

---

42. *Symbolic Action in the Plays of the Wakefield Master*, by J. Helterman. UGeo. pp. iv + 202. $18.50.

essay on *Secunda pastorum*, though generally sensible, sometimes over-reaches itself, as when we hear that in the scene of Mak's casting in a canvas, '"cast" has special significance in reference to abortion ... With the tossing of Mak, all things he symbolizes become stillborn ...' *Magnus Herodes* is seen as embodying the Master's most traditional use of allegory. Herod, as an Anti-christ figure, is a constant reminder of Christ whose behaviour he parodies. Thus, through parody Christ, who is physically absent from the stage, is always invisibly present to an audience. The last essay on *Coliphizacio*, before a brief concluding chapter, suggests that this play is the reverse of *Prima pastorum* in its illustration of a regression into spiritual blindness. The continued insistence of the tormentors that Christ the Word speak manifests their blindness to the fact that his presence is itself his message.

In 'Daw's Tennis Ball: A Topical Allusion in the *Secunda Pastorum*' (*ELN*) L. Lepow suggests that Daw's offering of a tennis ball to the Christ child may be a calculated reminiscence of an alleged incident in 1414, when the French dauphin is supposed to have made a gift of a tun of tennis balls to Henry V as a mock at his youth and inexperience. Even if the play's reference be admitted as an allusion to the story of the dauphin's gift, a little too much is made out of the 'richly connotative function' Lepow proposes for it in the play.

C. Davidson, in 'Jest and Earnest: Comedy in the Work of the Wakefield Master' (*AnM*, 1982), builds his argument upon the principle derived by Curtius of *ridendo dicere verum*, of 'speaking the truth through laughter'. Davidson ably contends that the Wakefield Master mingles mirth with serious-ness in such a particular way as to produce in his plays a variety of comic distortion which, while it provokes laughter, simultaneously through the dis-tortion turns the mind towards the unimpugned reality of spiritual things.

(d) York

C. Davidson's book on the York cycle is stoutly buttressed by his rich acquaintance with the medieval art of York[43]. His work examines the whole cycle pre-eminently from the point of view of iconography. His awareness of the possible pitfalls inherent in looking to art as a means of informing our understanding of the drama ensures their avoidance. The result is a balanced appraisal and attempted reconstruction of the visual dimension of the cycle. Davidson begins by tracing the shift which occurred within the medieval period towards particularity and realism, a shift which saw the introduction of illusionistic techniques into drama, but which did not entirely lead to a break with the older (that is, roughly, pre twelfth century) 'iconic' mode of presenta-tion. The York Realist is seen as being very much in touch with the spirit of his age in this respect. Davidson considers that the Realist subjects the traditional iconographic core of his plays to a realistic elaboration and psychological probing in order to present familiar matter, perhaps wearily so, in a fresh guise to his audience. He regards the growing taste for particularity and detail in art as being related to the nominalist philosophical tradition and that tradition's finding of the quality of existence only in things individual by virtue of them-selves. It is unfortunate that this book, which relies so heavily on allusions to art, could not have found still more room for photographic reproductions than it did, for it is a distinct contribution to our understanding.

43. *From Creation to Doom*, by C. Davidson. AMSP. pp. ix + 256. $32.50.

In 'The Weight of Sin in the York *Crucifixio*' (*LeedsSE*) P. Willis argues that the scene in which the soldiers stagger and complain under the weight of Christ and the cross, a scene unique to York, is a dramatic metaphor of the atonement. Since Christ on the cross took upon himself the burden of the world's sin, this metaphorical, spiritual burden is turned into a literal, physical one in the play. He supports his argument by reference to the wide currency of the sin-as-burden metaphor in religious writings.

(e) Moralities and Non-Cycle Plays

The Macro plays fared well this year, with three articles. A. J. Fletcher explains what 'The Meaning of "Gostly to Owr Purpos" in *Mankind*' (*N&Q*) is, demonstrating how this phrase is in fact a formula derived from the language of contemporary preaching, and moreover that it is used at l. 459 of *Mankind* with a particularly scandalous twist. 'The Scribal Problem in the Macro Manuscript' (*ELN*) is set out by R. Beadle: is the scribe who copied the play *Wisdom* the same as the one who copied the bulk of the play *Mankind*? After consideration of the arguments for and against, he triumphantly vindicates the school of thought which believes they are the same, and proposes as the scribe's identity a monk of the name of Hyngham. M. Eccles brings his 1969 edition of 'The Macro Plays' (*N&Q*) more up to date in a useful article which covers new developments in the study of the plays, and includes a survey of recent performances. He also writes a note on '"Halfe a Yard of Rede Sea"' (*N&Q*), showing how this item in the accounts of the Coventry Cappers, which has since acquired an almost legendary stature, in fact referred to a length of red *say*, a fine-textured cloth resembling serge, and not to the Red Sea at all.

'Staging the Digby *Mary Magdalen*' (*METh*) stemmed from J. McKinnell's 1982 production of the play, and from it he reconstructs the essentials of the play's *mise-en-scène*. He establishes the minimum number of staging structures and their location relative to each other, and these are illustrated in a hypothetical staging plan. McKinnell conjectures that there may have existed a traditional idea of a particular sort of staging plan which dramatists who wrote large-scale plays intended for performance in the half-round were expected to use. D. Grantley argues cogently from several examples that the *South English Legendary*, rather than the *Legenda Aurea*, was an important source of the *Mary Magdalen* play in 'The Source of the Digby *Mary Magdalen*' (*N&Q*).

The first part of J. Dutka's valuable article on 'The Lost Dramatic Cycle of Norwich and the Grocer's Play of *The Fall of Man*' (*RES*) discusses the newly discovered Kirkpatrick manuscript, the third eighteenth-century transcription now known of the Norwich Grocers' play, and considers its relationship to the copies used by Fitch and Waterhouse for their own transcriptions. She goes on to support the Norwich cycle against charges of 'artistic difficulties' brought by Kolve, and to suggest that the city knew a religious drama equal in treatment of its material to the better-known plays of York, Chester, and Coventry. D. Taylor argues that 'The Tyres that Were Lost' (*METh*) in the Coventry Smiths' Account of 1450 do not necessarily refer to wheel rims as the *REED Coventry* volume takes them to be, but could more than well refer to caps or hats lost in that year's performance.

(f) Interludes

N. Davis begins 'The Meaning of the Word "Interlude": A Discussion' (*METh*) by first tracing the history of the modern critical use of the word 'Interlude' before turning to its early meaning and history. His attempt to find some common ground in the early usages leads him to suggest that a conceptual distinction operated in the word 'Interlude', and that it originally would have evoked the idea of a dramatic performance with a very particular and intimate sort of *mise-en-scène*, one in which players and audience occupied the same space. In the same issue of *METh*, he also continues his findings list of 'Allusions to Medieval Drama in Britain (4): Interludes'.

In 'Tudor Interludes and the Winter Revels' (*METh*) T. Pettitt argues that it is to household revels of late medieval times that we should look when trying to understand the genesis of the interlude. He believes that elements of various sorts of Christmas games presented there were absorbed into the mummers' performance (a genre which he suggests had no actual play component in medieval times) to produce the more fully dramatic mummers' plays, and also co-ordinated sequences of games became the seasonal interludes which, in turn, when amplified with more substantial matter, became the hybrid interludes represented in the surviving corpus of texts.

P. Meredith attempts to make sense of the mock joust in *Fulgens and Lucres* in an eye-catching piece entitled ' "Farte Pryke in Cule" and Cock-Fighting' (*METh*). First he closely examines what can be made of the episode from the text, and then subjects the results to some practical theatrical experiment to see what will best accommodate them.

Middle English: Chaucer

DAVID MILLS and DAVID BURNLEY

This chapter has four sections: 1. General Works; 2. Canterbury Tales; 3. Troilus and Criseyde; 4. Other Works.

1. General Works

Lorrayne Y. Baird-Lange and Cynthia Dobrich Myers have compiled 'An Annotated Chaucer Bibliography, 1982' (*SAC*). Thomas A. Kirby has published his annual reports, 'Chaucer Research, 1983: Report No. 44' (*ChauR*), and 'Chaucer Research' (*NM*). James D. Johnson has compiled a most useful reference-study, 'Identifying Chaucer Allusions, 1953–1980: An Annotated Bibliography' (*ChauR*), and Traugott Lawler provides a survey of scholarship on Chaucer's prose works[1].

Editing Chaucer: The Great Tradition[2] (reviewed by E. G. Stanley, *N&Q*, 32.3) is a collaborative history of the editors and editing of Chaucer in printed form. Each essay is filled with detail which it is impossible to reproduce in a brief review, and the following is the merest outline. Beverley Boyd commences the collection with a largely bibliographical account of Caxton as printer and publisher, and is followed by James E. Blodgett, who shows how William Thynne reflected the Renaissance concern for linguistic improvement, but also played an important role in establishing the canon. Ann Hudson's judgement of John Stow's role is rather negative, since she believes that most of his experience of Chaucer manuscripts dates from after his (1561) edition. By the time of Speght Chaucer had achieved 'classic' status, writes Derek Pearsall and, accordingly, he seeks to establish some of Speght's critical attitudes to the established author. Speght continued a tendency to augment the canon, but his major contribution lies in his glossary. William W. Alderson, in the only reprinted essay, deals with Urry's ill-starred edition, revealing how the expansion of the canon continued, and work on the glossary prospered, but despite a growing awareness of the importance of manuscripts linguistic insufficiencies hampered the editor. One experiences a warm glow of approval from B. A. Windeatt's account of Thomas Tyrwhitt, whose balance between respect for the manuscripts and individual judgement, scholarly reticence and great learning, marked the first pinnacle in Chaucer editing. As

1. In *Middle English Prose: A Critical Guide to Major Authors and Genres*, ed. by A. S. G. Edwards. Rutgers. pp. xi + 452. $50.
2. *Editing Chaucer: The Great Tradition*, ed. by Paul G. Ruggiers. Pilgrim. pp. vii + 301. $34.95.

well as his penetrating notes and more adequate glossary, Tyrwhitt marks
something of a watershed in that his scholarly scepticism brought about a
reversal of the tendency indiscriminately to add to the existing canon. As
revealed by Thomas W. Ross, the contribution of Thomas Wright to Chaucer
editing is slight; nevertheless, although he made an unfortunate choice to
demonstrate it, he developed the 'best text' method of editing, and provided a
glossary which Skeat found useful. Skeat's own edition is discussed by A. S. G.
Edwards, who, after a brief historical introduction, goes on to criticize Skeat
for the arbitrariness of his choice of base manuscript, his faith in his own
authority, and his pursuit of a neat and consistent text in company with a tale
order dependent upon the assumption of Chaucerian realism. As with others
before him, Skeat's achievement is said to lie in his glossary, notes, and work
on the canon. Ralph Hanna's account of R. K. Root begins with high praise,
but develops into a criticism of his editorial practices which leaves the now-
customary praise of his notes sounding rather lame. In the case of Manly and
Rickert, the sole value of their edition rested from the start on the validity of its
text, and this George Kane subjects to ruthless dissection, concluding that it
will be 'judicious to abstain from using the propositions of this edition as bases
of further argument, especially about the prehistory of the manuscript tradition of *The Canterbury Tales* or about the superiority of this or that manuscript'. George F. Reinecke's account of F. N. Robinson's edition is partly a
personal memoir of the editor and is occasionally somewhat defensive, yet
admits the shortcomings of the text and again praises the notes, seeking also to
moderate criticism aimed at the glossary. It is amusing to learn that Robinson
did not like the format of the second edition, apparently protesting that it
looked like a schoolbook. An essay by D. C. Baker on Furnivall raises the
question of coverage, since figures like H. Bradshaw, A. Brusendorff, J.
Koch, W. McCormick, R. Morris, and the editors of the Globe Chaucer are
consigned to the shadows. In these circumstances, the inclusion of Furnivall
results in some uncertainty as to whether the book is about personalities or the
textual tradition. Some fluctuation in emphasis between contributors is evident on this question too. Usually, however, the emphasis falls appropriately,
and the more recent editions receive the more technical textual treatment. The
historical perspective, which is epitomized in a brief introductory essay by Paul
Ruggiers, emerges strongly, giving an overview of the shifts in methods and
opinions over five hundred years, and also a wealth of entertaining and
informative detail. If any counsel emerges from history for the aspiring editor,
it is to pay due attention to his notes and glossary: laurels are not to be earned
from the text.

As the title of George Kane's brief, tight, and challenging study, *Chaucer*[3]
(reviewed by Bernard O'Donoghue, *TLS* 4280.416 and Derek Pearsall, *THES*
647.21), suggests, its focus is as much on the writer as upon his writings. The
poet's personal circumstances and his social milieu recur from the opening
outline of his life and times onwards, while discussions of individual poems
reach out into the literary and philosophical contexts that inform them. Inevitably, in a chronologically ordered and biographically focused study, there is
much that is familiar, but the real value of this book lies in its clarity of

3. *Chaucer*, by George Kane. Past Masters Series. OUP. pp. vi + 122. hb £7.95,
pb £1.95.

structure and its precise and apposite formulations – its simplicity is deceptive. Central to its thesis are Chaucer's interdependent concerns with the nature of vernacular art and with the poet's potential as a moral philosopher; the innovatory aspects of both are stressed. This view provides an avowedly selective account of the *Tales*, isolating several topics but concentrating primarily upon instances in which the ideal harmony of personality is denied by sexual or acquisitive urges; the *Tales* are Chaucer's response to 'the eschatological crises' of medieval Christianity and reflect his concern with the reasons for people making wrong moral choices. The discussion of *Troilus* indicates the ways whereby the reader is involved in the creation of the characters, and also the various frames of evaluation – 'poetic, philosophical and Christian' – to which the narrative is subjected. Chaucer perceived the tragic dimension in Boccaccio in a modern rather than a medieval sense; the rigorous judgement which may lead us to condemn tendencies to cloak the lower, irrational instincts in deceptive sublimation is qualified by compassion evoked by our awareness of the complex factors involved in human choice. Though questionably assertive on occasion, this is a stimulating and provocative book, to be trusted only to the thoughtfully critical reader.

Derek Brewer's *An Introduction to Chaucer*[4] (reviewed by Bernard O'Donoghue, *TLS* 4280.416 and Derek Pearsall, *THES* 647.21) is based upon – and at times draws directly from – the author's earlier books [*YW* 34.57; 44.93]. Though newly written, it provides the expected 'Brewer' virtues of clarity and allusive range within the chronological frame of the poet's life. Criticism of poems combines paraphrase of the work with accompanying commentary. The book attempts no new critical initiatives, challenges, or theses, but seeks to demonstrate the accessibility of Chaucer's poetry and its value to the receptive modern reader, who is invited to share Professor Brewer's sense of Chaucer as a congenial, wise, and humane colleague. A second book by the same author, *Chaucer: The Poet as Storyteller*[5] (reviewed by T. A. Shippey, *THES* 617.17), reprints six of his essays together with two new essays. In the first, 'The Poetry of Chaucer's *Fabliaux*', Chaucer's *fabliaux* are set against the antiromance French *fabliaux* and within a concern for the individual in tension with the group; Chaucer introduces a number of anti-*fabliau* elements into the genre – metonymy of detail and style to extend narrative resonance, and rhetorical devices which enrich the plots and personalize the narratives. In the second new essay, 'The Rationalism of Chaucer', Professor Brewer suggests Chaucer's interest in 'the new spirit of rational enquiry', seen in his empiricism and scepticism; this scepticism was not directed against Christianity, and the appeal of Boethius to Chaucer was his emphasis upon the rationalism within the Christian tradition – a point substantiated in a brief discussion of *Troilus*. Derek Brewer's article, 'Chaucer and Arithmetic' [*YW* 64.146], has been reprinted[6].

In 'Geoffrey Chaucer: The Critics and the Canon' (*Archiv*) N. F. Blake considers the meaning of 'incomplete' when applied to a number of Chaucer's works, including the *Astrolabe* and *Equatorie*, which are usually ignored by

4. *An Introduction to Chaucer*, by Derek Brewer. Longman. pp. vii + 263. £5.95.
5. *Chaucer: The Poet as Storyteller*, by Derek Brewer. Macmillan. pp. x + 150. £25.
6. In *Medieval Studies Conference Aachen 1983. Language and Literature*, ed. by Wolf-Dietrich Bald and Horst Weinstock. Lang. pp. 243. (Hereafter Bald–Weinstock.)

critics. With Norton-Smith (*YW* 62.142) he considers *Anelida* complete without its final stanza, and postulates manuscript damage for the *House of Fame* and *Legend of Good Women*. The *Monk's Tale* may be complete, *Thopas* is wilfully incomplete – in contrast to the *Cook's Tale*, where the scribes looked for a continuation, and the *Squire's Tale*, where none was expected. The prose works, stopping at a structural division, present problems different from the incomplete poems. Blake stresses the fallacies and dangers of theories that seek to account for incompleteness on the basis of circulating drafts, patronal interference or concern, date, or wilful incompleteness, and urges more attention for the 'incomplete' prose works. Kate Harris is concerned with 'The Origin and Make-up of Cambridge University Library MS Ff.1.6' (*TCBS*) – the 'Findern Manuscript'. She finds no good evidence for an early association with the Findern family, although it originated in south Derbyshire. The manuscript seems to have been put together over a period of more than fifty years by various scribes, whose work began in the mid fifteenth century. These compilers had access to Chaucer manuscripts related to the 'Oxford group'.

D. W. Robertson Jr, whose influence pervades David Lyle Jeffrey's anthology of original essays, *Chaucer and Scriptural Tradition*[7], provides the opening general context for 'Chaucer and Christian Tradition'. Illustrated with a wide range of examples, this erudite and readable essay makes only occasional direct reference to Chaucer as it stresses the importance of studying the lives and concerns of Chaucer's contemporaries and the corresponding relevance to them of their Christian heritage. Particular examples from the *Tales* illustrate Chauncey Wood's discussion of 'Artistic Intention and Chaucer's Uses of Scriptural Allusion' and Edmund Reiss's essay on 'Biblical Parody: Chaucer's "Distortions" of Scripture'. A section on 'Glosses and Contemporary Commentary' starts with Lawrence Besserman's account of Chaucer's concern with the uses and abuses of *glosynge*, '*Glosynge is a Glorious Thyng*: Chaucer's Biblical Exegesis', which sets the practice in the contexts of antifraternalism and of impulses to Bible translation, and concludes with examples of Chaucer's use of the Bible to 'gloss' his own fictional creations. Graham D. Caie focuses his discussion in 'The Significance of Marginal Glosses in the Earliest Manuscripts of *The Canterbury Tales*' on the glosses to the *Man of Law's Tale*, and concludes that, while giving the source of a textual allusion, the major effect of such glosses is to interrupt the teller's rhetoric and to alert the reader to possible flaws in the logic. Douglas Wurtele takes examples mainly from the Sergeant of Law and the Wife of Bath to support a connection between 'Chaucer's *Canterbury Tales* and Nicholas of Lyre's *Postillae Litteralis et moralis super totam Bibliam*', arguing that the concern with literal text, the sensible and charitable links made between it and its figural levels, and the intellectual curiosity of this widely influential Franciscan would have appealed to Chaucer. David Lyle Jeffrey's essay, 'Chaucer and Wyclif: Biblical Hermeneutic and Literary Theory in the XIVth Century', analyses Wyclif's literary approach to the Bible and its implicit theory of reading; an appendix indicates nine areas in which the affinities between Wyclif and Chaucer might be pursued. The '*Canterbury Tales*' section includes a reprint of Theresa Coletti's article on the *Shipman's Tale* (*YW* 62.137). Russell A. Peck

7. *Chaucer and Scriptural Tradition*, ed. by David Lyle Jeffrey. UOttawa. pp. xvi + 242. Can. \$20.

juxtaposes the Nun's Priest's citation of St Paul in support of fable with the Parson's citation of St Paul for the rejection of fable in favour of truth at the start of his contribution, 'Biblical Interpretation: St. Paul and *The Canterbury Tales*'. He argues that throughout Fragment B Chaucer uses Pauline views on language and truth to alert the reader to his critical responsibility while, in the Parson's Prologue, the pilgrimage is redefined in spiritual rather than social terms – a shift signalled by a preceding nexus of Pauline themes of time and the need to make a good end. Related Pauline themes of the *vetus homo* and of the human body are also linked to the overall structure of the *Tales*. This article, under the title 'St. Paul and the *Canterbury Tales*', also appears in *Mediaevalia* (1984, for 1981). In 'Gospel Asceticism: Some Chaucerian Images of Perfection' John V. Fleming examines Chaucer's poetic adaptation of formal documents of ascetic theology in the *Tales*, such as the resonant detail of the Pardoner's purse and the appropriation – probably directly – of details from Peter Damian in the Monk's portrait. John A. Alford's account of the revenge of the 'letter' over the 'gloss' in the *Summoner's Tale*, 'Scriptural Testament in *The Canterbury Tales*: The Letter Takes Its Revenge', centres upon the Friar's unwitting and parodic re-enactment of primitive Jewish oath-taking practice in the Tale. In a final section, David Lyle Jeffrey argues that *The House of Fame* expresses Chaucer's belief that an act of will and inspiration from the reader is necessary if the past is to serve as an authority for the present. In 'Sacred and Secular Scripture: Authority and Interpretation in *The House of Fame*' he points to the problem of individual interpretation posed alike by the Troy story and by Christian historiography. Tracing structural affinities between the poem and the *Book of Ezekiel*, he suggests that Chaucer may be introducing into a historicist hermeneutic a design suggested by *Ezekiel* but geared to faculties of mind. Though frustration of the poem's ending returns each reader to his own speculations, the introduction of the Man of Great Authority, God, offers the hopeful assurance that all will be revealed in the fullness of time.

André Crépin's account of 'Chaucer and the French'[8] looks in turn at the historical and cultural circumstances of Chaucer's contact with France and its literature; the evidence for the nature of literary interchange provided by Deschamps's *ballade* to Chaucer; and the comparative neglect of Chaucer in France thereafter, with reasons and exceptions. Judith Davis Shaw compares the attitudes to '*Lust* and *Lore* in Gower and Chaucer' (*ChauR*). While Gower believes that literature is primarily valid as a means of imparting moral *lore*, which must be judiciously balanced with lawful *lust*, Chaucer emphasizes the responsibility of the audience in the perception (or non-perception) of *lore* and, in figures such as the Host and the Parson, suggests simultaneously the desire for literary *lust* and its dangerous distraction from moral sobriety. In 'Late Medieval Images and Self-Images of the Poet; Chaucer, Gower, Lydgate, Henryson, Dunbar'[9] Robert O. Payne argues that Chaucer manipulates his self-image in his attempt to define the poetic process and in so doing both offers the reader the model of his own difficulties in reading the poetry of

8. In *Medieval and Pseudo-Medieval Literature: The J. A. W. Bennett Memorial Lectures. Perugia, 1982–3*, ed. by Piero Boitani and Anna Torti. Narr/Brewer. pp. 198. £17.50. (Hereafter Boitani–Torti.)

9. In *Vernacular Poetics in the Middle Ages*, ed. by Lois Ebin. SMC 12. WMU. pp. xv + 293. $24.95. (Hereafter Ebin.)

MIDDLE ENGLISH: CHAUCER 141

the past and also handles material explicitly assigned to voices from a distant past. In these respects Chaucer's self-image differs from that bestowed upon him by the other writers here discussed as they create their own self-images. J. D. Burnley relates the phrase 'Picked Terms' (*ES*) to the awareness in the fourteenth century of verbal selection as a concept and practice in literary style, and gives particular prominence to the contrast between *lemman* and *lady* (H.203–20) among his examples from Chaucer. Chauncey Wood argues for the valuable interaction of 'Affective Stylistics and the Study of Chaucer' (*SAC*). 'The Beautiful, the Handsome, and the Ugly: Some Aspects of the Art of Character Portrayal in Medieval Literature' (*SN*) are considered by Henrik Specht in an article which ranges beyond Chaucer to Chrétien's *Yvain* and the Latin tradition of *descriptio*. Concentrating on the types of the 'handsome youth' (where an analogue to the description of the Squire is found in an anonymous Art of Poetry from St Omer), the 'beautiful woman' (parodied in the Miller's description of Alisoun), and the 'ugly human being' (where the Summoner's affliction is identified from Latin rhetorical sources as scabies), Specht goes on to illustrate how the common equation between moral and physical beauty is breached in cases where ugliness is equated with low social status.

The revaluation of the title of Howard Schless's study of the influence of Dante upon Chaucer, *Chaucer and Dante: A Revaluation*[10], is directed fundamentally at the findings of a sixty-year-old Harvard thesis, but it offers a challenge too to recent scholarship, in which much attention is currently being paid to possible Italian influences upon Chaucer. Schless's study will serve as a necessary sheet anchor to some of the more arbitrary claims for Dantesque influence, offering as it does a reasoned methodology, and using verbal parallelism and context in relation to one another in order to assess the probability of influence. The author works through the Chaucer canon, considering each alleged parallel in comparison with its supposed source, and, although his verdict is often negative, much of interest arises from his discussion of alternative sources and influences. Yet the major conclusions are by no means entirely negative. The book commences with an essay investigating the circumstances and chronology of Chaucer's earliest contacts with Italian poetry, and an impression of gradual mastery emerges: Schless insists that there was no 'immediate and profound change in Chaucer' as the result of sudden exposure to the poetry of Dante. At first he seems to have appreciated the rhetorical power of Dante and employed images and schemata from the opening and closing cantos of the three *cantiche*, and from the *Inferno* especially. Later, he used the *Convivio*, Tractate 4, as a source of ideas on *gentillesse*, and the *Paradiso* for the lyric expression of religious experience; but, whether borrowing narrative incident (the Ugelino episode of the *Monk's Tale*, for example), lyrical expression, or philosophical reflection, he modified the originals to his own purposes. Dante remained a quarry for materials rather than an overwhelming poetic experience. Of course, the nature of this investigation precludes speculation about the less specific, but perhaps more pervasive, aspects of influence, but Schless does venture the opinion that Chaucer might have found in Dante some encouragement to turn from

10. *Chaucer and Dante: A Revaluation*, by Howard Schless. Pilgrim. pp. xiv + 268. $42.95.

allegorical abstraction to a poetry of the world of human affairs. Overall, this is a cautious and methodical study, which may not find universal approval; but it is precisely for that reason that it is especially valuable.

Two books which will prove useful to Chaucerians in a more peripheral way are *Literature and Law in the Middle Ages*[11], by John A. Alford and Dennis P. Seniff, and *An Anthology of Chancery English*[12], by John H. Fisher and his collaborators. The first is a bibliography covering a wide range of writings of a literary nature which allude to, or benefit from, their authors' familiarity with the law. Primary sources on medieval law are omitted, but modern scholarly commentary upon them is included. The compilers spread their net widely both in terms of the languages covered and in terms of the liberality of their interpretation of what constitutes legal reference. Chaucer receives special treatment, but the book will be as useful for its coverage of related medieval languages. The second book has a slightly misleading title, since more than specifically Chancery English is included. It is a collection of documents – many previously unpublished – dating between 1417 and 1455 and drawn from the Signet letters of Henry V, Signet and Privy Seal papers, and the proceedings of Parliament and Chancery. As such, it complements the collection by Chambers and Daunt. Its importance to Chaucerians lies in its presentation of part of the linguistic environment in which many Chaucer manuscripts were written, and its extended index of forms – a kind of concordance – furnishes useful data for semantic and stylistic work on a language not utterly removed from that of the poet.

A. J. Minnis's book on *Medieval Theory of Authorship*[13] (reviewed by N. F. Blake, *ES* 66.1; Helen Cooper, *TLS* 4240.759; and Warren Ginsberg, *N&Q* 32.2) also approaches Chaucer somewhat obliquely, since its primary concern is with the Latin tradition of the *accessus* which occupies the first part of the book. In the final chapter Minnis demonstrates the Latin inheritance in some vernacular writers including Chaucer. The latter is shown to use some technical vocabulary which coincides with that of the *accessus* tradition: 'entente' (*intentio auctoris*); 'matere' (*materia libri*); 'manere' (*modus agendi*). His use of the verb 'rehersen', which is claimed rather than proved to be equivalent to Latin *recitatio* or *reportatio* (in contrast with *assertio*), is used to suggest that Chaucer consciously hid behind the defence of representing himself as a humble *compilator* (not a *scriptor* or *commentator*), and could therefore deny ultimate responsibility for his compilations. The equations between Latin rhetorical theory and modern critical perceptions of Chaucer may not always be entirely persuasive, but this book is a welcome attempt to place Chaucer's poetics into a truly medieval context.

In 'Lydgate's Canterbury Tale: *The Siege of Thebes* and Fifteenth-Century Chaucerianism'[14] A. C. Spearing makes the significant claim that Chaucer was

11. *Literature and Law in the Middle Ages: A Bibliography of Scholarship*, by John A. Alford and Dennis P. Seniff. Garland Reference Library of the Humanities 378. Garland. pp. xiv + 292. $44.

12. *An Anthology of Chancery English*, ed. by John H. Fisher, Malcolm Richardson, Jane L. Fisher. UTenn. pp. xvi + 416. $49.50.

13. *Medieval Theory of Authorship*, by A. J. Minnis. Scolar. pp. xvii + 323. £35.

14. In *Fifteenth-Century Studies: Recent Essays*, ed. by Robert F. Yeager. Archon. pp. ix + 364. $39.50.

'the father of English literary history' and, by considering those Chaucerian features perceived or misperceived by Lydgate in his *Siege of Thebes*, attempts to establish the problems that faced Chaucer's literary heirs as they sought to occupy the place of their powerful but unassertive 'father'. Spearing's intelligent examination of the Chaucer-inspired eloquence in the poem, and of its misjudged morality, sheds interesting light on Chaucer's influence and Lydgate's achievements. Among Lydgate's moralistic shortcomings are his inability to perceive a classical culture in its wholeness, and his lack of the mediating force of Boethian material. In 'Literary Theory at the Close of the Middle Ages: William Caxton and William Thynne' (*SAC*) R. F. Yeager argues that both Caxton and Thynne employed selective criteria in their publications of Chaucer's works and believed that all they published were by Chaucer. Focusing upon the apocryphal works, Yeager suggests the controlling images held by each publisher. Caxton's Chaucer was a marketable moral poet whose utilitarian message was more important than his versifying skills; but Thynne joined to this figure the love-poet epitomized in the narrator of *The Legend of Good Women* and also affirms Chaucer as an Englishman of views congenial to the historical circumstances of the early sixteenth century. R. F. Yeager has also examined 'British Library Additional MS. 5141: an unnoticed Chaucer *Vita*' (*JMRS*). He analyses the sources and traditions underlying the *vita* and demonstrates it to be the unique compilation of an educated man in the late sixteenth–early seventeenth century from written and perhaps oral sources, seeking to create an appropriate image of the poet. Donald W. Rude has discovered 'Two Unreported Renaissance Allusions to Chaucer' (*AN&Q*) in the work of John Jones, a sixteenth-century medical author, who refers to the treatment of vices in *The Parson's Tale*. William McColly uses statistical procedures in his discussion of '*The Book of Cupid* as an Imitation of Chaucer: A Stylo-Statistical View' (*ChauR*) in order to demonstrate the close association of *The Book of Cupid* with *The Parliament of Fowls*, but argues that more traditional stylistic criteria suggest that the closeness is due to imitation rather than to common authorship. Robert M. Schuler looks at the six independently circulating extracts of the *Canon's Yeoman's Tale* ll. 1428–81, other testimonies to Chaucer's alchemical knowledge, and the Chaucer alchemical pseudepigraphs as testimonies to the reputation of 'The Renaissance Chaucer as Alchemist' (*Viator*). David Aers considers 'Representations of the "Third Estate". Social Conflict and Its Milieu around 1381' (*SoRA*, 1983). Concentrating on the *Parliament of Fowls* and the *Shipman's Tale* among Chaucer's works, he suggests that his 'work represents society as a composite of inevitably competing groups motivated by individualistic forms of material self-interest'. Chaucer accepted the inevitability of a competitive and divided society.

2. Canterbury Tales

Arguably the outstanding event under this heading this year was the appearance of V. A. Kolve's richly illustrated *Chaucer and the Imagery of Narrative*[15] (reviewed by B. A. Windeatt, *Encounter*, July/Aug. 84; Derek Pearsall, *ES* 66.1; Alastair Minnis, *TLS* 4244.865; J. A. Burrow, *EIC* 35.1; and Paula

15. *Chaucer and the Imagery of Narrative. The First Five Canterbury Tales*, by V. A. Kolve. Arnold. pp. xiv + 551 + 175 half-tones. £35.

Neuss, *English* 33.147). That it has been long in preparation is apparent from the wealth of references presented (130 pages of notes) and its extensive bibliography, but best of all, perhaps, from the quiet air of authority with which its insights are proffered. One feels that mature reflection has quelled any temptation brashly to trumpet conclusive critical solutions; and there can be no better way to capture the benevolence of the reader. But this book does not lack controversial assertions, as, for example, the author's belief that the secularity of the tales of Fragment A suffers a kind of retraction in the *Man of Law's Prologue* and *Tale*, which are structurally continuous with them. However this may be, the essence of the book lies in its reconciliation between contemporary art and literature. This it achieves by iconographic means, concentrating on what the author calls 'narrative images'. These latter, like the picture of Custance at sea in a rudderless boat, are those scenes and images in a poem which catch and hold the attention, and which, by the hinterland of associations which they can be shown to have acquired in art and literature, can contribute to the meaning of the tale at a variety of levels. Although it may be that too great an emphasis has occasionally been given to a particular image, and consequently the iconographical exegesis may threaten to become divorced from the text, the subtlety of Kolve's critical reading and the persuasiveness of his writing nearly always recoup the situation. This is a good book, and should prove an important one.

N. F. Blake reviews 'Editorial Assumptions and Problems in *The Canterbury Tales*' (*Poetica*), beginning with the Host stanza at the end of the *Clerk's Tale*, whose omission is traced back to Tyrwhitt. A process is suggested by which the Merchant's Prologue (E.1213–44) was composed to solve the problem of linking *Clerk's Tale* to *Merchant's Tale* in Harley 7334's tale–link–tale structure. The Host stanza is considered to be original, whereas the Merchant's Prologue is spurious. The Adam stanza (B^2 3197–3204) is considered spurious, and the middle placing of the 'Modern Instances' is traced to an error of the Corpus scribe, who is seen as second in copying order after Hengwrt.

In 'Chaucer and Character' (Bald–Weinstock[6]) Stanley S. Hussey expresses his scepticism about applying modern concepts of characterization to the stock figures required in the genres that Chaucer inherited, despite the unusual complexity which Chaucer on occasion gives to such figures. But, drawing upon the Host, January, and Dorigen particularly, he exemplifies Chaucer's experiments with techniques more akin to modern characterization. By contrast, Robert S. Sturges, in 'The Canterbury Tales' Women Narrators: Three Traditions of Female Authority' (*MLS*, 1983), presumes an essentially modern concern in Chaucer's characters. Wife of Bath, Second Nun, and Prioress share an interest in specifically feminine traditions of authority, evoking the example of powerful women of the past. The Wife is shown as belonging to a social network of women, the Prioress as inspired by the Virgin as mother, and the Second Nun appeals to the Virgin as muse. It is quite persuasively argued that these tales reveal a conception of female solidarity where men are shown to benefit from power vested in women. In 'The Rhetoric of Chaucerian Comedy: The Aristotelian Legacy' (*Comparatist*) James R. Andreas claims that Chaucer works within a literary tradition deriving ultimately from Aristotle's comic theory. He examines selected characters, themes, and rhetorical devices in the *Tales* – overall, a series of debates and arguments in the comic mode – in the light of this theory, and emphasizes physical deformities and animal allusions as part of a comic nexus rather than as moral comments. James Dean proposes that 'Chaucer uses degrees or shades rather than levels of spiritual allegory as part of his narrative style'. His discussion of 'Spiritual Allegory and Chaucer's Narrative Style: Three Test Cases' (*ChauR*) examines the yeoman–devil of the *Friar's Tale*, the oak-tree of the *Pardoner's Tale*, and the false Canon of the *Canon's Yeoman's Tale*.

Mary Flowers Braswell's study of *The Medieval Sinner*[16] (reviewed by Cecily Clark *ES* 65.6) ends with 'Penitential Irony: A Look at Chaucer's Prologues'. She finds a penitential imagery associated with Harry Bailey that establishes him as Host-Priest who hears a variety of confessions from his pilgrims. Those developed in the prologues of the Canon's Yeoman, the Pardoner, and the Wife of Bath are examined in the light of penitential forms and formulae, suggesting respectively and paradoxically the circumstances of penance, its motives, and the relationship of priest and penitent. Chaucer's 'Retraction' is presented as a continuation of the pattern and is not to be taken seriously – especially since spoken by his *persona* and echoic of the ending of *Melibee*. Chaucer's achievement in handling the penitential tradition lies in his creation of 'a psychologically plausible context for sin to exist in'.

Derek Pearsall finds, and is unhappy with, 'Epidemic Irony in Modern Approaches to Chaucer's *Canterbury Tales*' (Boitani–Torti[8]). He stresses that unambiguous irony demands a belief shared by author and reader, whereas much modern 'ironic revelation' serves the ideological beliefs of the critic.

The ostensible temporal inconsistencies in the references to Aries and Libra that frame the *Tales* are, according to Charlotte Thompson's account of 'Cosmic Allegory and Cosmic Error in the Frame of *The Canterbury Tales*' (*PCP*, 1983), instances of the devices of conflation and anachronism characteristic of the Church's view of time. Applying this interpretative approach she sees the pilgrimage as moving between Creation (Aries) and Doomsday (Libra) and explicates the reference to Libra as the 'moones exaltacioun' (I.10) as 'the consummation of the age and the assumption of the Church into glory.' Drawing upon Matthew 7.1–5 (cited by the Reeve at 3919–20 at the start of a wrathful exchange) and its interpretations, Judith Shaw emphasizes the element of spiritual homicide in 'Wrath in the Canterbury Pilgrims' (*ELN*).

Responding to Terry Jones's claim that the lack of a coat of arms is evidence for the Knight's mercenary status (*YW* 61.107), William McColly draws upon the Scrope–Grosvenor case of 1385–91 to explain 'Why Chaucer's Knight has no Coat of Arms' (*ELN*), since it suggests the dangers of duplicating existing coats of arms. If, as William Urban claims, *Ruce* (*Prologue*, A.53) 'is probably only Rosenia, a district of Samogithia visited by most of the English crusading expeditions', then the answer to the question 'When Was Chaucer's Knight in "Ruce"?' (*ChauR*) is probably '1390–91'. The allusion may be a flattering reference to Henry Derby, but would certainly not impair the image of the Knight as an ideal Christian warrior. Malcolm Andrew regards *inspired* in l. 6 of 'Chaucer's *General Prologue* to the *Canterbury Tales*' (*Expl*) as a thematically relevant echo of *inspiravit* in Genesis 2.7. In 'Chaucer's *armee*: Its French Ancestors and Its English Posterity' (Bald–Weinstock[6]) Sherman M. Kuhn

16. *The Medieval Sinner: Characterization and Confession in the Literature of the English Middle Ages*, by Mary Flowers Braswell. AUP (1983). pp. 160. £15.75.

addresses the arguments, specifically of Manfred Görlach (*YW* 54.114), in support of *aryve* in the *Prologue*, l. 60. He demonstrates the solid manuscript evidence for *armee* and suggests *aryve* as a transmitted error from the contaminated *ariue* of BL Harley Ms. 7334. He further challenges Görlach's claim that *armee* was a French neologism first introduced into written English by Chaucer by offering numerous examples of its earlier use and subsequent popularity in both languages. C. David Benson, discussing the references in the *Prologue* at A.414–18, finds significant links between 'The Astrological Medicine of Chaucer's Physician and Nicholas of Lynn's *Kalendarium*' (*AN&Q*), indicating that the Physician's grounding in astrology is in accordance with contemporary medical opinion.

In 'Chaucer's *Knight's Tale* and the Three Ages of Man' (Boitani–Torti[8]) John Burrow evaluates the three parallel generations of gods and of men in the light of the traditional triad of youth, middle age, and old age. At the level of youth he finds no essential distinction between Palamon and Arcite, who represent the youthful conjunction of *armes* and *paramours*. And, whereas among men the middle-aged Theseus commands in statesmanlike fashion beside the ineffectual aged Egeus, among the gods it is the aged Saturn rather than his son Jupiter who resolves the conflict of interests. An explanation for these imbalances and asymmetries is sought in the figure of the Knight, whose concept of a governor's role presupposes a universe of hostile circumstances. This essay also appears in the same author's *Essays on Medieval Literature*[17] (reviewed by Dieter Mehl, *N&Q* 32.2 and Derek Pearsall, *ES* 66.1). In contrast, Judith C. Perryman finds that 'The "False Arcite" of Chaucer's Knight's Tale' (*Neophil*) twice breaks his oath and is a creature of Fortune, whereas Palamon is faithful and more spiritual, a difference perhaps alluding to the opposition of body and soul. In '"Tears for Passing Things": The Temple of Diana in the Knight's Tale' (*PQ*) Joseph Harrison finds an emphasis on mutability in the description of Diana's temple. In the contradiction between Emelye's urgency and the actual presence of Diana on the one hand and the goddess's inability to help on the other, mutability is reflected in the person of the goddess herself and the widening gulf between earth and heaven which the Knight addresses through the Boethian framework is underlined.

Ambivalence in attitudes to sexuality between the beautiful and the disgusting are noted by Tracey Jordan in 'Fairy Tale and Fabliau: Chaucer's *The Miller's Tale*' (*SSF*), where she finds parallels with fairy tale, and in particular those of the 'frog king' type. D. Thomas Hanks Jr discusses the phrase '"Goddes Pryvetee" and Chaucer's Miller's Tale' (*C&L*) as a starting point for extended *double entendre* which is one aspect of a general conjunction of the sacred and profane in the tale. He lists other examples of such a conjunction and combats the view that the tale may be somehow covertly moral or religious. Margaret Jennings, C.S.J. confronts the difficulties of explaining the significance of the 'twenty manere' (A.3328) of dances mastered by the 'Ironic Dancing Absolon in the *Miller's Tale*' (*Florilegium*, 1983), and suggests that he was an adept of Cotswold Morris dancing. One particular dance (trunkles) is claimed to have twenty steps. However this may be, the article contains much interesting detail about medieval dances and dancing.

17. *Essays on Medieval Literature*, by John A. Burrow. Clarendon. pp. vi + 218. £19.50.

Joseph E. Grennen examines the academic nuances with which the Reeve invests his tale and which would be clear to an audience accustomed to schematizing about human character and motivation. In his entertainingly allusive account of 'The Calculating Reeve and his *Camera Obscura*' (*JMRS*), Grennen looks at the potential resonances of Symkyn's *camus* nose – from appearance, through simian characterization, to its illustrative function in scholastic commentary, suggesting an opposition of clerkly 'art' and simian 'nature'. He finally links the tale's concluding optical illusion with Witelo's *Opticae*, whose account of the *camera obscura* may have influenced Chaucer. Among a series of notes on the tale, Carl T. Berkhout, in 'A Sixteenth-Century Allusion to Chaucer's "Soler Halle"' (*AN&Q*), records a reference in Matthew Parker's *De Antiquitate Britannicae Ecclesiae* (1572) identifying Clare Hall, Cambridge, as 'Soller Hall, or Schollers Hall'; Charles Lionel Regan, in 'Chaucer's Reeve's Tale, I, 4096 and 4127: More Word Play' (*AN&Q*), sees the appeal to St Cutberd as echoing the phrase 'to make someone's beard', and explores its further resonances; and Edward Vasta, in 'The Devil in Chaucer's Reeve' (*AN&Q*), draws a number of parallels between the Reeve and medieval stereotypes of the Devil. In his Tale, some of these re-appear in the northern students.

Apart from the rather different reading in Kolve's book, V. J. Scattergood's 'Perkyn Revelour and the Cook's Tale' (*ChauR*) is the only discussion of this fragmentary tale this year. Perkin is set in a contemporary historical context of apprentices and the literary satire of medieval 'gallants'. Such satire commonly criticizes contemporary mores and attacks those who seek to adopt a life-style beyond their means. A parallel is drawn between Perkin and the *riotoures* of the *Pardoner's Tale*.

Michael Murphy's anecdotal 'Chaucer's Devil Among the Irish' (*Eire–Ireland*) cites as belated analogues of the *Friar's Tale* two Irish ballads of the encounter between the Devil and one Bailiff McGlynn.

Chaucer's use of charges levelled against the friars, both by opponents like William St Amour, Richard FitzRalph, and Jean de Meun, and among themselves in the dispute between conventuals and spirituals, forms the basis of John V. Fleming's article 'Anticlerical Satire as Theological Essay: Chaucer's *Summoner's Tale*' (*Thalia*, 1983). In passing he notes a source in a spurious fourteenth-century chapter of the *Roman de la Rose*, for a passage about the power of absolution being restricted to priests, and goes on to illustrate the Tale's theme of wrath counterpointed by a consideration of penance and grace.

With some exceptions, the year's work on the *Wife of Bath's Prologue* and *Tale* is of two kinds: those articles which are concerned with Alisoun as a personality, and those concerned with the genre of her *Tale*. Into the first category falls Ann B. Murphy's 'The Process of Personality in Chaucer's *Wife of Bath's* Tale' (*CentR*), where it is proposed that the Wife progresses from 'comic misquotations to ironic antifeminist parody, to a more fully felt and rendered discussion of her last two marriages'. The *Prologue* gives an account of a woman striving for the reconciliation which her *Tale* enacts. *Gentillesse* through Christ knits up the disparate threads – patristic tradition, misogyny, middle-class materialism, sexual and emotional conflict – which had been teased out in the earlier part of her performance. Discussing the misuse of the story of Midas in an article entitled 'The Wife of Bath and Midas' (*SAC*),

D. W. Robertson Jr argues that the Wife's own career parallels Midas's progress from wealth into pleasure, in contrast to the 'pleasure to wealth' progress of her kindred spirit, La Vieille; unwittingly she projects herself also on to all the figures of the *Tale* except the raped maiden, all of whom are devotees of the sensual music of Pan. The knight is restored unenlightened to his original sensual condition, though the hag's long speech has offered him a clear choice between Apollo and Pan – a choice amusingly underlined by her *non-sequitur* at ll. 1217–18. In '"Of a fire in the dark": Public and Private Feminism in the *Wife of Bath's Tale*' (*WS*) H. Marshall Leicester Jr distinguishes the Wife's public, polemicist, feminist stance manifested in her Tale from her private, human, humane attitude which rejects the simplifications of that public feminism. Through her idiosyncratic emphases on Midas, on the quest, and on the figure of the hag, and her *gentillesse* speech, the Wife reveals experiential interests that stand in tension with her public role, signalling her rejection of a stereotype that is interested only in courtly love and marriage. Rather, she favours her own independence and personality, with its concerns of old age, ugliness, and death. That marriage in this tale is constrained to an extent not found in the analogues is claimed by Marc Glasser in 'He Nedes Moste Hire Wedde: The Forced Marriage in the "Wife of Bath's Tale"' (*NM*) to be especially appropriate to the characterization of the Wife, who sees marriage as a struggle for dominion. Douglas Wurtele, in 'The Predicament of Chaucer's Wife of Bath: St. Jerome on Virginity' (*Florilegium*, 1983), looks in detail at the context in Jerome of the borrowings used by Jankyn in the Wife's Prologue, noting (and arguing that Chaucer also noted and protested against) Jerome's celibate distaste for sexuality – *dicta* which aggravated the Wife's 'anxieties about her spiritual state' and outraged her sense of temporal justice. Two articles fall into the second category. Esther C. Quinn, in 'Chaucer's Arthurian Romance' (*ChauR*), believes that Chaucer wrote the Wife's Tale as an ironic Arthurian romance before adapting it to its teller. Chaucer juxtaposes the motifs and traditions of the genre with the perceptions of a contemporary middle-class woman, which results in a combination mocking the pretensions of the knightly class which were the traditional matter of such romances. Robert J. Meyer would disagree with at least the first part of the foregoing because he holds that the Tale was written to accommodate the Wife's mixture of cynicism and innocence, and her ambivalence about love and marriage. He proposes, in 'Chaucer's Tandem Romances: A Generic Approach to the *Wife of Bath's Tale* as Palinode' (*ChauR*), that the Tale has a dual romance structure to which the knight is central, undertaking two quests, the first of an active (seeking the answer to the question), the second of a passive (education by the sermon on *gentillesse*) nature. Somewhat outside the division made above stands Glending Olson's 'The Terrain of Chaucer's Sittingbourne' (*SAC*), in which he supports Greenfield's claim (*YW* 34.62) that the allusion to Sittingbourne by the Wife (D.841–53) is not to a geographically close location; rather, it forms part of the argument between the Friar and the Summoner, may well have topical significance, and is quite distinct from the unspecific allusion *at towne* (D.2294), which is idiomatic in its meaning. Similarities of characterization, event, and theme, together with verbal echoes, exist between the Wife's Tale and *Persuasion*, according to Jocelyn Harris in 'Anne Elliot, the Wife of Bath, and Other Friends' (*W&L*, 1983).

In 'The *Clerk's Tale* of Man Tempting God' (*Criticism*) Edward I. Condren argues that Chaucer changes his Petrarchan source for the Tale in order to make Griselda a figure of Christ, reflecting the incarnate mixture of divinity and humanity. By this reading, Walter's marriage reflects the failure of the 'Man–God' relationship, with its imbalance of torment against love and of temporal domination against patient service. Griselda's behaviour towards her husband also has an analogue in the Clerk's behaviour towards the Host. Though primarily an assessment of the connection between Matthew Prior's *Henry and Emma* and Richardson's *Clarissa*, the first section of Veronica Bassil's article, 'The Faces of Griselda: Chaucer, Prior, and Richardson' (*TSLL*) traces the similarities of diction and organization between the *Clerk's Tale* and *The Not-Browne Mayd*, the literary ballad underlying Prior's poem. Thomas H. Bestul's 'True and False *Cheere* in Chaucer's *Clerk's Tale*' (*JEGP*) deals with Chaucer's representation of facial expression. He notes the idea found in patristic authors, physiognomies, and Cistercian writers that the face reveals the personality. Chaucer exploits the idea that the face may mask as well as reveal, and the concentration in the *Tale* upon the face is a Chaucerian device which increases humanity and pathos. We should not be too eager to dispense with these in the pursuit of symbolic readings.

In 'Antinomic Cluster Analysis and the Boethian Verbal Structure of Chaucer's *Merchant's Tale*' (*Lang&S*) Leigh A. Arrathoon identifies a cluster of characteristically Boethian words – *joie, blisse, sorwe* – and after pointing out verbal parallels between Metre I and the description of Januarie, argues that, in the light of Boethian definitions, an antinomic pattern is used ironically in the *Merchant's Tale*.

The Franklin tells a story centred upon Dorigen, claims Anne Thompson Lee in '"A Woman True and Fair": Chaucer's Portrayal of Dorigen in the *Franklin's Tale*' (*ChauR*), but is too preoccupied with abstractions to be aware of the human realities of Dorigen's position and to answer the generosity question as it should have been answered – in her favour. The phrase 'twenty pound worth lond' (F.683) used by the Franklin in praising the virtues of the Squire is found by Melvin Storm in 'Chaucer's Franklin and Distraint of Knighthood' (*ChauR*) to be significant as the traditional sum in the thirteenth century for distraint of knighthood. In preferring *discrecioun* to such a sum, the Franklin repudiates the proprietorial qualifications for knighthood to emphasize the spiritual ones. Wolfgang E. H. Rudat considers '*Gentillesse* and the Marriage Debate in the *Franklin's Tale*: Chaucer's Squires and the Question of Nobility' (*NM*). Arveragus and Dorigen emerge as subtle manipulators of the constraints of behaviour in the ideal of gentillesse, and the Franklin as a severe critic of the pretensions to that virtue among young squires.

Joerg O. Fichte's title, 'Incident–History–Exemplum–Novella: The Transformation of History in Chaucer's *Physician's Tale*' (*Florilegium*, 1983), indicates the chronological series of generic treatments of the Virginia-story which he traces, concluding in Chaucer's version. Chaucer's complex image of the world, his verisimilar characterization, his functionally variable style, and his intention to reveal a problematic narrative to his reader, all set his version apart from the exemplum and suggest that Chaucer has independently created a new narrative form in English – the novella. In 'The *Physician's Tale*: The Doctor of Physic's Diplomatic "Cure"' (*ChauR*) Daniel Kempton finds a significant link in the Physician's treatment of physical and social ills. Limited to an outlook in which theoretical cure offered no actual remedy for disease, the Physician recognizes his inability to protect the ideal, innocent Virginia against the attacks of the real world and therefore seeks instead to justify and exonerate himself by a rhetorical withdrawal into a conventional *legendum*. His manner of story-telling – his concern to please the literary tastes of his audience and to calm their fears of mortality – accords with the 'public relations' aspect of his lucrative profession, but fails to convince the Host.

The 'Aspects of Gluttony in Chaucer and Gower' (*SP*) considered by R. F. Yeager are, in Chaucer's case, the Pardoner's conjunction of eating, drinking, swearing, and devil-worship (C.468–71), a conjunction for which a well-established tradition existed. In '"Ubi Peccaverant, Ibi Punirentur": The Oak Tree and the *Pardoner's Tale*' (*ChauR*) Carolyn P. Collette explicates the oak tree of the Tale in terms of its associations with idolatry, choice, and death in the Old Testament, and claims that such allusiveness additionally indicates the allegorical nature of the Pardoner's exemplum. Philippa Tristram, in '"Olde Stories Long Tyme Agoon": Death and the Audience of Chaucer's Pardoner'[18], considers three important scenes – the tavern decision to do battle with death; the encounter with the Old Man; and the discovery of the gold and consequent murder – and argues that Chaucer deliberately avoids the material and charnel aspects of death as traditionally represented because 'obsession with mortality ... impeded a true perception of temporal life' and fascination with material details detracted from things of the spirit and salvation. James F. Rhodes looks at the senses of 'veronica' in 'The Pardoner's *Vernycle* and his *Vera Icon*' (*MLS*, 1983) and concludes that it may signify a spiritual receptivity which the wearer had forgotten or denied.

Robert Adams explains the thematic centrality of 'The Concept of Debt in *The Shipman's Tale*' (*SAC*), arguing that the primitive moral justice which he finds characteristic of *fabliaux* inheres in this tale in the suppression of the familiar sense of sin and necessity for penance that was part of the semantic field of ME *dette*. The reader is thereby alerted to the ironic misconceptions of the merchant and his wife to be free from debt, and recognizes the compensatory force of the Parson's treatment of penance, which might in fact have been introduced at this point in the story-game.

John Archer examines 'The Structure of Anti-Semitism in the *Prioress's Tale*' (*ChauR*) in terms of antisemitic traditions and the categories of imagery that they generate in the tale. The latter he identifies as murder–sacrifice, economy, and law, with perhaps more distantly 'the imagery of God the Father ... as an evil or demonic power' responsible for the Mosaic law and the death of his "son", Christ'.

Demanding that we account 'not only for the humor in [the pilgrim-Chaucer's] failure to delight but also for the humor in his failure to instruct' in his Tale, Alan T. Gaylord draws generic parallels between romance marvels and saintly miracles and contrasts *Sir Thopas* with the romances it names or evokes. 'The "Miracle" of *Sir Thopas*' (*SAC*), judging from Chaucer's other 'marvels', would be instructive – counter to the tale of mirth he was to tell but in which also he seems set to fail. The Tale is designed to provide a meaningful critique of the affirmative power of miracle against the exploratory power of poetry. Resemblances between 'Chaucer's *Sir Thopas* and *La Prise de*

---

18. In *Death in the Middle Ages*, ed. Herman Braet and Werner Verbeke. Medievalia Lovanensia Series I, Studia IX. LeuvenU (1983), pp. viii + 285 + 7 half-tones. Bfr 1530.

Nuevile[19] (*YES*) are particular refutations for J. A. Burrow of the claim that Chaucer's burlesque is without precedent, though Chaucer's literary burlesque has a different thrust from the mockery of the *chanson de geste* genre and of the Flemings in *La Prise*. A second note by Burrow, 'The Title "Sir"', contains the discovery that this form of address when preceding a proper noun is to be numbered among 'those non-U expressions which Chaucer confines to burlesque contexts'. Sir Thopas emerges as a 'Flemish knight' of bourgeois origins. E. S. Kooper has examined more than twenty lapidaries to discover possible significances of the name Thopas (topaz). In 'Inverted Images in Chaucer's *Tale of Sir Thopas*' (*SN*) the dominant associations are revealed to be chastity, superlative value and brightness, and the property of reflecting an inverted image. After reviewing the possible literary functions of the first two, he points out a number of literary inversions in *Thopas* and suggests that the *Melibee* may be an inverted reflection of *Thopas*, but ends his piece with a tag from Alanus de Insulis counselling prudence.

In 'Chaucer's "Tale of Melibee": A Reassessment' (*ESC*) Laurel J. Brinton sees a contrast between the other-worldliness of the *Parson's Tale* and the worldly focus of *Melibee*'s Christian ordering of its world, a contrast signalled by the fact that both tales are in prose. *Melibee*, moreover, picks up themes from other Canterbury Tales and contributes to an ongoing dispute between *sentence* and *solas* in the work.

In 'Zenobia's *Vitremite*, or The Case of the Unidentified Headdress' (*Poetica*) Heiner Gillmeister etymologizes *vitremite* (Monk's Tale, B.3562) as 'hermit oyster'.

Derek Pearsall's edition for the Variorum Chaucer of the *Nun's Priest's Tale*[20] (reviewed by Siegfried Wenzel, *N&Q* 32.1) has appeared: one of two in the series this year (see below). The general outline of the edition follows the established pattern with descriptions of manuscripts, printed editions, textual essay, and accounts of sources and analogues, but the individual characteristic of this edition is the editor's decision to treat the Survey of Criticism analytically rather than simply chronologically. This results in a full and lively account of critical attitudes, more informative than the standard format, and a worthwhile departure in cases which, as here, are amenable to such treatment. Professor Pearsall thus presents a valuable bibliographical guide which turns into a review essay, and does not shrink from assessing the worth of critical contributions discussed, expressing those judgements in a more forthright way than is customary. The editor seems to have aimed for maximum inclusiveness in the text, which contains the End-link although it is accepted that Chaucer probably cancelled it, and the Long Form of the Monk–Nun's Priest link appears in full, although part of it is in square brackets. In 'The Modernity of the "Nun's Priest's Tale": Narrator, Theme and Ending' (*Lore&L*) J. F. Galván-Reula discusses the characteristically 'modern' difficulties of establishing the identity of the immediate narrator, the diversity of thematic possibilities, and the range of interpretations available to the reader at the Tale's

---

19. This article also appears in *English Satire and the Satiric Tradition*, ed. by Claude Rawson. Blackwell, pp. xiii + 289. $34.96.

20. *A Variorum Edition of the Works of Geoffrey Chaucer*. Vol. 2: *The Canterbury Tales*. Part 9: *The Nun's Priest's Tale*, ed. by Derek Pearsall. UOkla. pp. xxviii + 284 and colour frontispiece. $42.50.

conclusion. Sheila Delany's '"Mulier est hominis confusio": Chaucer's Anti-popular *Nun's Priest's Tale*' (*Mosaic*) compares Chaucer's tale with its analogues in the *Roman de Renart* and *Reinhart Fuchs*, which are considered to represent a feminist, popular, and materialistic telling of the story in which the hen is vindicated. Chaucer has altered a populist tale of peasant radicalism to substitute 'a vindication of authority over experience, clerical-intellectual tradition over popular tradition, idealism over materialism, as well as husband over wife'. Richard F. Kennedy finds 'Another Chaucerian Allusion' (*N&Q*) in the reference to the fox-chase of the *Nun's Priest's Tale* in Sir Richard Barckley's *Discourse of the Felicitie of Man*, of 1598.

Anne Eggebroten emphasizes the appropriate laughter to be directed at Valerian, Tiburce, and Almachius in her article 'Laughter in the *Second Nun's Tale*: A Redefinition of the Genre' (*ChauR*), stressing that such *hilaritas* is characteristic of the genre of saint's life. Marilyn Malina seeks a link between 'Chaucer's *The Second Nun's Prologue* and *Tale*' (*Expl*) in wordplay on *ydelnesse* in Prologue and *ydoles* in the Tale.

Critical attention to the *Manciple's Tale* seems to be lacking this year, but the tale has been well served by the new Variorum edition by Donald C. Baker[21]. This edition was designed to serve as a model for other Variorum editors, so naturally avoids too many individualistic developments; nevertheless the Survey of Criticism effectively reveals how a previously despised tale has gained in esteem in the last thirty years, and how under the influence of structuralist concerns, a tendency has developed in the 1970s to regard it as a tale about language. The editor makes the interesting observation in passing that the dominantly dramatic form of the tale ranks it with the performances of the Wife of Bath and the Pardoner and almost guarantees that it was purposely written for the Canterbury collection, when viewed in the dramatic perspective of the frame story. Despite reservations arising from textual evidence, the editor believes that Prologue and Tale were written to form a unit and at about the same time.

Unknown until the late 1960s, the *Summa Virtutum De Remediis Anime*[22] is now edited for the first time, by Siegfried Wenzel for The Chaucer Library. Wenzel demonstrates from parallel passages that the work is the major source for the *remedia* section of the *Parson's Tale*; he also comments on the possible sources or origins of 'non-*Summa*' material in the Tale. The edition offers a critical text based upon Einsiedeln Stiftsbibliotek Ms. 275, with full textual apparatus including the asterisking of variants closer to Chaucer's English; there is a facing translation. Endnotes identify the sources of quotations in the text, and the introduction to this important edition includes descriptions of background, authorship and dates, and the various manuscripts. In contrast to the Host, who views language playfully, the Parson sees it as mediating between human consciousness and an objective Truth with its categories. But, argues Laurie A. Finke in '"To Knytte Up Al This Feeste": The Parson's Rhetoric and the Ending of the *Canterbury Tales*' (*LSE*), the Parson is not the

21. *A Variorum Edition of the Works of Geoffrey Chaucer*. Vol. 2: *The Canterbury Tales*. Part 10: *The Manciple's Tale*, ed. by Donald C. Baker. UOkla. pp. xvii + 146 and colour frontispiece. $28.50.·
22. *Summa Virtutum De Remediis Anime*, ed. by Siegfried Wenzel. The Chaucer Library. UGeo. pp. ix + 373. $35.

voice of Chaucer, for, in both his themes and his rhetoric, he suggests that
conformity to external standards can substitute for spiritual struggle and crisis
as the way to salvation. His failure to synthesize his ethical frame with the
aesthetic values of the other tales suggests a more complex issue that is still
unresolved at the end of the work.

3. Troilus and Criseyde

The facsimile of the St John's College manuscript[23] (reviewed by E. G.
Stanley, *N&Q* 32.3) makes more generally available an important early witness to the text of *Troilus and Criseyde*, which played a significant role in
Root's conception of the authorial revision of the poem. The brief but adequate introduction which precedes the plates gives a bibliographical description and a history of the manuscript, and the textual history contained in it
foreshadows the new edition by Windeatt in its implicit views on the development of the work. The quality of the facsimile plates is excellent – the best in
this series so far – but, in the interests of practical utility, line references might
have supplemented the folio numbers at the foot of the page. A useful table of
correspondences between folios, stanza numbers, and line numbers is supplied
by E. G. Stanley in the review mentioned above. The avowed aim of B. A.
Windeatt's major new edition of *Troilus*[24] (reviewed by Bernard
O'Donoghue, *TLS* 4280.416 and J. D. Burnley, *ES* 66.3) is 'to set Chaucer's
poem in the context of the processes both of its creation and of its near
contemporary reception'. To this end, the text of Chaucer's poem is presented
in a conservative editing of Ms. Corpus Christi College Cambridge 61 in
parallel with the Italian text of Boccaccio's *Il Filostrato* which is printed
complete (including sections omitted by Chaucer) to facilitate comparison.
The techniques of Chaucer's translation are described in the opening sections
of the introduction, including an account of 'non-Boccaccean' material and a
refutation of influence from the *Roman de Troilus*. On the page facing the
texts appears the commentary and 'a comprehensive corpus of Readings . . .
and all substantive variants', while the introductory discussion of the text
denies the older thesis that the manuscript groupings preserve earlier, unrevised or 'less revised' versions of the poem in the manner of *Piers Plowman*,
though at isolated points in individual manuscripts particular readings may
reflect local revision. The manuscripts also attest the scribes' attitudes to
Chaucer's innovatory usages. Dr Windeatt also finds evidence that Chaucer
intended to produce a five-stress regular decasyllabic line, determined more
by the Italian than by the French model. The manuscripts are briefly described
at the end of the introduction and there is a select bibliography.

Chauncey Wood's *The Elements of Chaucer's 'Troilus'*[25] claims that in *Il
Filostrato* Boccaccio takes a detached and disapproving look at illicit passion

23. *St. John's College, Cambridge, MS L.1: a Facsimile*, intro. by Richard Beadle and
J. J. Griffiths. The Facsimile Series of the Works of Geoffrey Chaucer 3. Pilgrim/B&B
(1983). pp. xxxii + 274 pls and colour frontispiece. £105.
24. *Geoffrey Chaucer: 'Troilus and Criseyde'*, ed. by B. A. Windeatt. Longman.
pp. xii + 584. £40.
25. *The Elements of Chaucer's 'Troilus'*, by Chauncey Wood. DukeU. pp. xii + 204.
$35.

from behind the persona of an ostensibly engaged and encouraging Narrator. Chaucer, influenced by Gower in his adaptation, made the moral more explicit and the reader more conscious of Troilus's princely status. Finding irony below the surface directness, Wood argues that Troilus submits wilfully to Venus and Cupid, for love is not an irresistible force, does not have ennobling potential, and does not effect a moral improvement in the hero. A close analysis of invocations to Venus in Book III suggests that the proem there should alert the reader to the diverse significations of Venus to stress her carnality in the poem, and detailed examination of the consummation scene suggests the pervasiveness and ironic misapplication of the quasi-religious imagery. The three characters are considered in turn – Criseyde fearful, lacking in *fortitudo* and prudence, characterized by pride; Pandarus the Evil Counsellor, a self-serving realist and corruptor, bullying and sarcastic at times; and Troilus, aligned with Cupid and Fortune in an imagery of 'blindness' climaxing in the Oedipus-allusion and yielding to the true vision of his postmortem ascent. Wood finally defends his morally focused reading against charges of reductiveness.

Reviewing the traditional presentations of Troilus in 'A Separate Peace: Chaucer and the Troilus of Tradition' (*JEGP*), William H. Brown Jr shows how Chaucer's consciousness of other traditions affects his treatment of Boccaccio's narrative of a princely lover impelled primarily by love, who loves a false woman. Though in the action of Chaucer's poem Troilus acts from love, 'the presence of the warrior of tradition balances the weakness and self-indulgence of the character Chaucer draws from Boccaccio's model'. Under the shadow of his elder brother, Troilus exemplifies youthful experience, but attains a dignity through suffering; simultaneously, Criseyde engages our sympathy as victim, but with glimpses of feminine perfection which make her credibly lovable. Though theirs is a human love, different from Christian truths, Troilus – never unqualifiedly admirable or unadmirable – can in the end be granted a separate peace.

Attacking the strained 'erotic' readings of Eugene Vance (*YW* 60.115), Robert apRoberts examines the effect produced by Chaucer's transposition and reshaping of Criseyde's first sight of Troilus in the *Filostrato* on our perception of 'The Growth of Criseyde's Love' (Bald–Weinstock[6]). Chaucer conceals the intense sexual passion apparent in Boccaccio's heroine to concentrate upon realizing through suspense the slow, mysterious growth of love in Criseyde, a process that heightens the reader's awareness of the value Criseyde places on her honour. Chapter 3 of John M. Ganim's *Style and Consciousness in Middle English Narrative*[26] discusses 'Consciousness and Time in *Troilus and Criseyde*'. The reader must experience the love-story as a continuous narrative, refracted through a series of false perspectives (here discussed book by book, showing how each forces a reconsideration of what has preceded). It is only by this reading process, mimetic of the mutability that serves as theme and plot-promoter, that the reader can perceive the empyrean vision which replaces narrative at the poem's end, the point outside time.

In his discussion of *Troilus* as 'both a great exposition of the relations between human and divine love and a major statement on the relationship between Christian vernacular poetry and the pagan classical tradition',

26. *Style and Consciousness in Middle English Narrative*, by John M. Ganim. Princeton (1983). pp. ix + 177. $23.

Winthrop Wetherbee examines Statius's narratorial attitude in the Thebaid and Dante's transformation of Statius into a Christian poet in the *Commedia* as thematic correspondences with Chaucer's poem. His essay, '"*Per te poeta fui, per te cristiano*": Dante, Statius, and the Narrator of Chaucer's *Troilus*' (*Ebin*[9]), first stresses the pessimism and the spiritual doubts of Statius, focusing upon the figures of Menoeceus and Parthenopaeus, then indicates how Dante achieves the transformation of Statius into the embodiment of a spiritually enlightened poetic. Similarly, the Chaucer–Narrator recognizes Troilus's innocent religion of love and his potential for spiritual enlightenment and, in the Epilogue, he becomes aware – like Dante – of the spiritual implications of his work and of its relationship to the work of earlier poets. This transition from 'maker' to 'poet' in which the Narrator distances his work from its pagan context is not absolute and demands no rejection of either the world or poetry. A much expanded version of the arguments presented in the above article is to be found in Winthrop Wetherbee's book, *Chaucer and the Poets*[27] (reviewed by Bernard O' Donoghue, *TLS* 4280.416 and Derek Pearsall, *THES* 647.21), where, in interesting, not to say startling, contrast to Schless's study of the influence of Dante upon Chaucer, the Italian poet is presented as 'an informing and sustaining' presence in *Troilus*. Troilus himself is viewed as in some ways the 'pagan counterpart' to the lover-pilgrim of the *Commedia*, winning his way through to a parallel enlightenment. This analogy is one of a large number upon which the critical methodology of the book is built, in which it is a fundamental assumption that Chaucer (and presumably his audience) were as learned in the classics as Dante himself. Alleged allusions to the *Aeneid*, Ovid, Statius, and Dante's conception of Statius are considered to presuppose a coherent reading of the works alluded to, so that a series of readings emerge significant through their parallelism. The improbability of some of these premises, and the unlikeliness of many of the supposed echoes seriously flaw the argument of the book, but, disregarding its excessive claims, there remain enough good critical insights into Chaucer's poem and its chief protagonists to justify a judicious reading.

Chaucer's awareness and thematic use of the differences between Statius's epic *Thebaid* and the innovatory twelfth-century romance-interpretation of it, the *Roman de Thebes*, is at the centre of Paul M. Clogan's discussion of 'The Theban Scenes in Chaucer's *Troilus*' (*M&H*).

In '"O Moral Gower": Chaucer's Dedication of *Troilus and Criseyde*' (*ChauR*) R. F. Yeager believes that Chaucer, concerned with his audience's possible misunderstanding of the pagan deities and of the opposition of worldly *vanite* and heavenly *felicite*, asks Strode and Gower to correct any resultant errors of response – a request set between concern for the poem's reception and invocation of the omniscient God. Those features of Gower's pre-*Confessio* writings that qualify him for the innovatory epithet *moral* are also discussed.

Stéphen Manning's interesting article, '*Troilus*, Book V: Invention and the Poem as Process' (*ChauR*), traces the development of the Narrator from the second-rate craftsman who, in accord with Geoffrey of Vinsauf's precepts, seeks the right words to translate the unalterable work of another, to the true

27. *Chaucer and the Poets: An Essay on Troilus and Criseyde*, by Winthrop Wetherbee. CornU. pp. 249. $22.50.

poet, indistinguishable from the poet-Chaucer, who relies upon imagination for knowledge and who comes finally to discover the true thematic potential of his material. Relating these ideas to different concepts of the poet's function and of the nature of *inventio*, Manning concludes with a close discussion of the Epilogue, 'constructed around the psychology of the Narrator', in which the Narrator's quest for a suitable conclusion leads to his merging with the Poet and to a differentiation of poetic truth from philosophical truth, suggesting, through love, a telling analogy between the Poet and God.

In 'The Origin and Original Object of *Troilus and Criseyde*' (*ChauR*) Varda Fish finds the Chaucer-narrator a vehicle of a veiled critique of love-poetry of the kind represented by his source in Boccaccio; the poem is a veiled literary autobiography, in contrast to the lover's autobiography of *Filostrato*. The 'tempestuous sea' image in both poems and the invocations to Tisiphone by Chaucer and to his lady by Boccaccio support the argument, which suggests that the final rejection of the poetics and philosophy of love-poetry is unconsciously anticipated at the start of *Troilus*. Anne Falke establishes 'The Comic Function of the Narrator in *Troilus and Criseyde*' (*Neophil*), claiming that the proem to Book I retrospectively is seen to adumbrate the Epilogue. Particularly in Book V, the Narrator serves as a distancing device to hold us from condemning Criseyde and to help us accept Troilus's sufferings and also his comic viewpoint of a divine order beyond Fortune.

The intertwined patterns of white and black, with their associated qualities of love and death, are traced by Gail Turley Houston in '"White by Black": Chaucer's "Effect Contraire" in *Troilus and Criseyde*' (*Comitatus*), culminating in the vision of harmony and radiance that follows the final darkness of Troilus's death, which validates his love. S. L. Clark and Julian N. Wasserman find a coherent pattern in the poem in the conventional image of exchanging hearts in 'The Heart in *Troilus and Criseyde*: The Eye of the Breast, the Mirror of the Mind, the Jewel in its Setting' (*ChauR*), drawing additionally upon the 'ruby in the ring' motif. The earthly exchange of hearts is placed finally when Troilus set his heart on God rather than on sensual love.

David Wallace, in 'Chaucer's "Ambages"' (*AN&Q*), illustrates Chaucer's verbal dependence upon Boccaccio in *Troilus and Criseyde*, seeing it as a conscious attempt at lexical expansion in which Chaucer does not acknowledge his Italian source because he wishes to be thought to have had a Latin one. Jimmie E. Thomas finds a sexual pun in *my pees* at Book III, l. 1309 of 'Chaucer's *Troilus and Criseyde*' (*Expl*). Henrik Specht discusses 'Some Aspects of the Art of Portraiture in Medieval Literature: With Special Reference to the Use of *Ethopoeia* or *Adlocutio*'[28], taking as his main example Criseyde's monologue in Book V, ll. 1054–85. Martin Puhvel suggests that the scepticism of folk-lore marvels may underlie the use of *haselwode* in 'Chaucer's *Troilus and Criseyde*: III.890; V.505; V.1174–5 (*Expl*). In 'Hardyng's *Chronicle* and *Troilus and Criseyde*' (*N&Q*) A. S. G. Edwards finds Troilus III.617 copied by Hardyng.

---

28. In *Proceedings from the Second Nordic Conference for English Studies*, ed. by Hakan Ringbom and Matti Rissanen. PRIAA. Abo. pp. vii + 611.

4. Other Works

Starting from a conception of the poem as a 'literary sampler', Diane M. Ross traces 'The Play of Genres in the *Book of the Duchess*' (*ChauR*). 'Chaucer explores the capacity of certain literary forms to convey information or express truth', finding that since the lyric cannot capture experience but only emotion, Blanche is to be described adequately only by the use of a dual technique of narrative *proces*, that is step-by-step narrative, and biblical lyricism. The poem closes when the Man in Black supplements his *proces* with sacred lyricism (the Song of Songs). Judith Perryman concentrates, in 'How They Talk. Speech and Meaning in "The Book of the Duchess"' (*NM*), on the functional grammar of the speeches in the poem and what they tell us about the psychological states of the speakers. By this means, the feelings and language of the Ceyx and Alcione story are related to those of the main protagonists, and their progress towards *mesure* in confronting love and death is traced. In a second article on the language of the poem, 'From Sentence to "Sentence" in a Medieval Poem' (*EiP*), Gregory Roscow considers consecutive constructions, which he suggests function emphatically along with negatives as part of the rhetorical hyperbole in the work. After examining in detail the function of some examples of such syntactic structures, he closes by comparing the plot and thematic structures of the poem with these syntactic ones. Studies of the role of the Fool form the background to Rose A. Zimbardo's article 'The *Book of the Duchess* and the Dream of Folly' (*ChauR*), in which she claims that 'Chaucer deliberately assumes the identity of the fool and offers his lord (John of Gaunt) folly's redemption from soul-destroying grief'.

Piero Boitani's book, *Chaucer and the Imaginary World of Fame*[29] (reviewed by S. S. Hussey, *THES* 614.16) offers contexts for the ideas, images, and import of Chaucer's *House of Fame*. Much of it is devoted to the place of the poem in European culture. The development of the theme of Fame is traced from Greek, Roman, and Judaeo-Christian legacies to the thirteenth century and thence in more detail through the Italian modifications from Dante to Boccaccio and Petrarch, drawing contrasts with the French and English developments. It is within the Italian tradition that Boitani locates Chaucer, and, before approaching the specific poem, he looks generally at the treatment of Fame in Chaucer's works, concluding with the Clerk's account of Petrarch. The discussion of *The House of Fame* is brief. Its content of wonders and its attitude of wonderment are emphasized and, building on Delany's description of the dream as phantasm, the elements of *fantasye* and secrecy in the work are isolated. Finally, Boitani offers forward and backward readings of the poem to illustrate Chaucer's adaptation of his literary heritage as a fourteenth-century Englishman and also his personal and highly original approach to the contemporary issue of the relationship between literature, language, truth, and reality. The Janus-like status of the poet and the awareness of sources from and means by which a narrative is generated are seen as key elements in Chaucer's poetic development.

In 'Chaucer and Chalcidius: The Platonic Origins of the Hous of Fame' (*Viator*) Joseph E. Grennen illustrates the poem's generic debts to philosophical epic, mystical ascent, and celestial vision and its allusions to Platonic,

---

29. *Chaucer and the Imaginary World of Fame*, by Piero Boitani. Chaucer Studies 10. Brewer. pp. xi + 252. £27.50.

Pauline, and Augustinian traditions. But he persuasively urges, with abundant and stimulating parallels, the direct indebtedness of the work to Plato's *Timaeus* in the translation and commentary of Chalcidius. Chaucer's finely structured design is an obscured transformation of Plato's work – 'a version deliberately substituting a cosmos of unpredictable and jarring confusion for the arithmetical harmonies of the Platonic cosmos'. The discussion ranges over general structural parallels, specific debts (e.g. the Eagle's discourse), the problems of translating objects of intelligence into terms of sense-perception, and Chaucer's interpretation of Plato's *silva* in the House of Rumour. Perhaps in the relation of Chalcidius to Plato Chaucer saw the potential relation of his Narrator to a Man of Great Authority, while Chalcidius's observations on obscure discourse offer a suggestive comment on Chaucer's obtuse Narrator. Chaucer's probable acquaintance with the magnificent Palais de Justice during his 1377 visit to Paris may well have suggested details of the houses of Fame and Rumour and of the Eagle journey, claims Laura Kendrick in 'Chaucer's *House of Fame* and the French Palais de Justice' (*SAC*).

Taking Ambrose as a model, David C. Fowler sees a connection at a deep structural level between Dream, Temple, and Bird-debate in its garden setting in 'Chaucer's *Parliament of Fowls* and the Hexameral Tradition'[30] in its discussion of days two, three, and five. The *Parliament* is both a Valentine poem and a Creation poem, treating of human and divine love. In '*The Parliament of Fowls.* Chaucer's Mirror up to Nature' (*RES*) Victoria Rothschild notes that number symbolism is important to Spenser and in other later epithalamia, and suggests that a parallel interest, with an astrological dimension, is discernible in the *Parliament*. The stanzas of the poem represent the first hundred days of the year, so that the bird song at the end falls appropriately on 10 April. The structural divisions of the poem, which are tonal rather than narrative, coincide with dates when the sun passes from one zodiacal sign into another. Numerous astrological puns and allusions are invoked to identify Venus's temple with that of Mercury, creating a symbol of the night sky on St Valentine's Day. A date of 1384 is suggested for the poem's composition.

James W. Spisak cannot accept praise of Thisbe as a serious act of penance by the Chaucer-narrator and, stressing the changes in frame, narrative, and characterization from Ovid in 'Chaucer's Pyramus and Thisbe' (*ChauR*), he claims that the humour is intensified and the reader distanced from the pathos of the situation. The story shows that women can match men in fidelity to their vows of love as long as they match men in the stupidity of those vows. J. M. Cowen demonstrates the derivation of 'Chaucer's *Legend of Good Women*, lines 2501–3' (*N&Q*) from the Italian translation of Ovid's *Heroides* proposed by Meech as an intermediary/supplementary source (*YW* 11.78), and clarifies the apparent obscurity in the lines.

Distinguishing initially between new adoptions from French and Latin and new derivations on contemporary English patterns, Morton Donner usefully investigates the effect upon Chaucer's language of his role as translator of *Boece*. His study, 'Derived Words in Chaucer's *Boece*: The Translator as Wordsmith' (*ChauR*), looks particularly at Chaucer's new gerunds, his parti-

30. In *The Bible in Middle English Literature*, by David C. Fowler. UWash. pp. xiii + 314. $25.

cipial adjectives as prenominal modifiers, and the formations with the prefix *un-* in illustration of the way in which Chaucer's quest for close translation led him to new formations for the purpose of fine semantic and structural distinctions – a desire for accuracy and precision characteristic of Chaucer's general concern for such matters. Tim William Machan's note, '*Forlynen*: A Ghost Word Rematerialises' (*N&Q*), gives reasons for rejecting the exceptional use of *forlyven* by Chaucer in *Boece*, Book 3, Prose 6, as recorded by Robinson and *MED*, in favour of *forlynen*, from OF *forlignier*, which, as recorded by *OED*, is a ghost-word.

The relationship between music and poetry envisaged by Guillaume de Machaut, and the traditionality of Eustache Deschamps's *L'Art de Dictier* form the context for the assessment of Chaucer's debt to the fourteenth-century French lyric by John Stevens in 'The "Music" of the Lyric: Machaut, Deschamps, Chaucer' (Boitani–Torti[8]). Tentatively, Stevens proposes that Chaucer's 'lines may . . . be designed as *freely grouped* speech-units within a basic ten-syllable line', a possibility he illustrates from *Rosemounde* and *Womanly Noblesse*.

Jay Rudd stresses the ambiguity of the ending to 'Chaucer's *Fortune*' (*Expl*), pointing to the fact that true friendship lies outside Fortune's gift and that the speaker is Fortune herself.

Caroline D. Eckhardt finds fidelity to the French source at the base of 'The Art of Translation in *The Romaunt of the Rose*' (*SAC*), but traces the cumulative features – first-person narrator, sharpening of image, expansions for tonal informality, colloquial tendencies – that tend to impart a new narrative voice to what still remains an English translation of a French poem.

The Sixteenth Century: Excluding Drama after 1550

R. E. PRITCHARD and CHARLES WALTERS WHITWORTH

The chapter has two sections: 1. The Earlier Sixteenth Century; 2. The Later Sixteenth Century. Section 1, by R. E. Pritchard, has two parts: (a) Prose; (b) Verse and Drama. Section 2 is by C. W. Whitworth, except (c) which is by R. E. Pritchard. Its five parts are: (a) General; (b) Sidney; (c) Spenser; (d) Poetry; (e) Prose.

1. The Earlier Sixteenth Century

(a) Prose

Sir Thomas More's probably most popular work in English, his *Life of Richard III*, is one of the works studied by Judith H. Anderson in her clearly written and interesting discussion of English Renaissance biography or 'life-writing'[1]. She provides perceptive analyses of Cavendish's *Wolsey*, Roper's *More*, and Walton's *Donne*, together with the more elaborated *Richard III* by More, Shakespeare's *Richard III* and *Henry VIII*, and Bacon's *Henry VII*, to demonstrate their authors' skilful manipulation of material, whether by selection, ordering, stylistic presentation, or even invention, in order to bring out the essential significance of the subject. For these writers, truth and fiction are by no means opposites: 'fiction and history, creative invention and objective truth, are presumed to be complementary and even inseparable, rather than opposed'; these artfully 'made-up' biographies reflect a sense of the 'made-up' or fictive in the concept of the self, self-hood, and subjectivity (though Anderson is no mere follower in the footsteps of Stephen Greenblatt, being more interested in artistic self-consciousness than in power-relationships).

Another sophisticated and subtle reading of More is provided by Dale B. Billingsley, in his account of the *Dialogue Concerning Heresies* (*SEL*): More's elaborate indirections in his fictional chronology and characterization draw the reader into a serious game of interpretation, in which testing and doubt are both the problem and the answer. There is a movement from Babel's confusion through Pentecost's gift of tongues to the silence at the opening of the seventh seal: until then, there must be doubt and testing. As Mayster Chauncellour is to the Messenger, so is More to his reader, guiding him to a technique of doubting that will secure faith. William Tyndale's response, however, dismounted More from his position of control, raising the reader from pupil to judge. The difference between More and Tyndale as prose stylists is also considered by James Andrew Clark (*Moreana*), comparing two 'tall tales',

---

1. *Biographical Truth: The Representation of Historical Persons in Tudor-Stuart Writing*, by Judith H. Anderson. Yale. pp. ix + 243. £23.

from More's *Dialogue of Comfort* and Tyndale's *The Practice of Prelates*: More, by indirections finds directions out, while Tyndale has a blunt vigour and determinate meaning. Also in *Moreana*, J. A. Guy, in considering why Henry VIII's attitude to More changed between 1532 and 1534, points to the importance of the 1533 controversy between More and Christopher St German; even though St German was writing anonymously, Henry regarded More's writings as an attack upon his policy, and a fatal breach of trust. A pedigree for St German and his relations is provided by R. J. Schoeck (*N&Q*). Walter M. Gordon (*JWCI*) traces More's reference in the *Dialogue of Comfort* to the idea of children's games of funerals or fighting being ominous of death or war to its source in Plutarch's *Moralia*.

Elsewhere in *Moreana*, Yoshinori Suzuki rather mechanically relates More's early writings – principally the poems and *Richard III* – to *Utopia*, to outline the social ideas of the younger More, and their coherence with the later work; Richard G. Maber discusses and reprints the account of Margaret Roper by the French Jesuit Pierre le Moyne in *La Gallerie des femmes fortes* (1647), as part of the French feminist movement of the time; Richard F. Kennedy lists hitherto unrecorded allusions to More by Renaissance English writers, including Owen Felltham and Thomas Fuller; Donald W. Rude traces the influence of More upon *The Arte and Science of Preseruing Bodie and Soule in Healthe* (1579), by John Jones, a Tudor physician and apparently the first English writer to treat More as an authority on matters of science and philosophy; and G. Harold Metz reviews discussion of the sources and authorship of the play of *Sir Thomas More*, suggesting that Anthony Munday was only the copyist, and Shakespeare the main or even sole author. Albert J. Gueritz reports on Morean discussions at the Nineteenth Congress on Medieval Studies at Kalamazoo: Katherine M. Wilson discusses the tradition of the Utopians' nudist technique of spouse-selection, Amos Lee Laine reviews John Rastell's unsuccessful career, and Clare M. Murphy discusses the 'Paris News Letter' account of More's execution, attributing it to the French ambassador Antoine de Castelnau; apparently, More's last words were not, as usually claimed, 'the king's good servant *but* God's first', but '*and* God's first'.

Other works ranging more widely, but including discussion of More, may be noted here. Surprisingly, while More is frequently regarded as the master of the Renaissance English dialogue, he receives only one essay in M. T. Jones-Davies's collection *Le Dialogue au temps de la Renaissance*[2], by Germain Marc'hadour, who begins by relating More's use of the dialogue form to his love of conversation; concentrating on More's directness, he notes More's simple speech-indications in *Utopia* and the *Dialogue Concerning Heresies*, and the quasi-dramatic script presentation of the speakers in the *Dialogue of Comfort*. Elsewhere in the volume, P. Mack considers the use of the dialogue form in sixteenth-century English education; J. Proust discusses William Bullein's medical treatises written in dialogue form, employed as a form accessible to a lay readership and evoking the doctor–patient relationship; E. Cuvelier analyses dialogues of love in Elizabethan prose romances, from interior dialogues to proposals and formal debates, in all of which, she suggests, the writers' main concern is with aesthetic patterning; the editor herself

2. *Le Dialogue au temps de la Renaissance*, ed. by M. T. Jones-Davies. Touzot. pp. 260. Ffr 180.

(remembering her Bakhtin) traces a shift from the fixed objectives and single meanings of the literary dialogue, for example, Thomas Wilson's *Discourse Upon Usury*, to the ambiguities and multiple meanings of dialogues in play form, as represented by Thomas Lodge's *A Looking Glass for London and England* and Shylock and Antonio in *The Merchant of Venice*; while J. R. Mulryne relates the concluding dialogue-song of *Love's Labour's Lost* to a tradition of avian dialogues. The volume also contains discussions of non-English dialogists, such as Cicero, Marsilio Ficino, Ulrich von Hutten, Alonso de Valdés, and Erasmus.

Erasmus is the hero of Joanna Martindale's anthology, *English Humanism: Wyatt to Cowley*[3], that is part of a series designed to provide literature students with access to background and context material. Despite the volume's title and subtitle, neither Wyatt nor Cowley is represented, there is hardly anything from the seventeenth century, and fully one-third of the volume is devoted to translations of Erasmus 'as the main mediator of humanist ideas *to* England' (my emphasis). Certainly this access to Erasmus is welcome, but the volume seems disproportioned: Castiglione and Machiavelli appear briefly, but no Platonists or Montaigne; Jonson (not hard of access) overwhelms the English representation, when the sceptical Bacon, or even Hobbes, might have provided a useful indication of how things developed. Obviously, there are limits on space, and no anthologist can please every reviewer, but she seems to have worked from a rather narrow sense of the humanist spirit and tradition, which has limited the range and usefulness of the volume.

Janel M. Mueller traces developments in English prose style from 1380 to 1580[4], arguing for the presence of a mainstream, native, even 'naive' English style, together with a more mannered and élite style, indebted to classical rhetoric. Mueller's wide-ranging analysis demonstrates the expressive powers of the 'naive' prose of the late fourteenth and fifteenth centuries; while acknowledging the influence of classical rhetoric on English prose, he also proposes the Bible as a significant force: as has frequently been remarked, Hebraic sense-parallelism has many affinities with English prose structure. The vernacular translation of the Bible was crucial in the development of English prose, as Gerald Hammond has noted (*YW* 63.112). With a much narrower focus, Mary C. Erler (*Lib*) analyses the history of Robert Copland's popular translation from the French, *The Maner to Lyue Well*, a layman's primer, noting the role of the printer-publisher in both creating and responding to social change. The first German translation[5] of Roger Ascham's 'Toxophilus', a work concerned with the theory and practice of archery, is undertaken by Harald Schröter. The translation is preceded by three sections setting the text in a broader context. In the first section Schröter discusses the position and eventual disappearance of the bow and arrow as a weapon and, in the second, its subsequent emergence as a popular sport. The third section goes beyond the main history of sport framework, outlining the social and political

3. *English Humanism: Wyatt to Cowley*, ed. by Joanna Martindale. W&W. CH. pp. 292. hb £17.95, pb £9.95.

4. *The Native Tongue and the Word: Developments in English Prose Style 1380–1580*, by Janel M. Mueller. UChic. pp. x + 429. $27.50.

5. *Roger Ascham, Toxophilus. The Schole of Schootinge. London, 1545*, trans. and intro. by Harald Schröter. Richarz (1983). pp. 186. pb DM 39.50.

background of the times and briefly assessing some of the literary qualities of the text. There is a quite extensive bibliography. [M.H.]

Over the last decade there have been several studies of the sociopolitical intentions, implications, and contexts of sixteenth-century writing, with a view to changing the traditional conservative readings to readings more open and sympathetic to 'left' critical attitudes. The latest is David Norbrook's interesting discussion of authors from More to Milton, *Poetry and Politics in the English Renaissance*[6], that is concerned, in Walter Benjamin's phrase, 'to politicise aesthetics', while showing how many Renaissance and modern writers have attempted to 'aestheticise politics' (or viewed matters differently). Discussing *Utopia*, Norbrook rejects 'the narrowly literary approach' less concerned with political ideas than with literary subtleties and ironies, which consequently largely escape him. He is useful in reminding us of the humanists' rhetoricism, and how humanism provided an ideological rationale for economic individualism. Rather disappointed in More, he is happier with the Edwardian political and religious radicals, such as Bale and Luke Shepherd; he is useful in relating style to social and political values. His discussion of *The Shepheardes Calender* is effectively limited to the May eclogue and the presbyterian-episcopal struggle, and the April eclogue in the context of the French marriage feared by the puritan Leicester faction: overall, pastoral oscillates between the activist-reformative and the passive-contemplative modes. The view of Sidney's 'Old' *Arcadia* is persuasive enough, but he gives himself insufficient room to deal adequately with *The Faerie Queene*, concentrating on Book V as a defence of the Leicester–Essex foreign policy, and Book VI's doubts about courtly values. Norbrook is interesting and illuminating in analysing the political issues involved in his chosen texts; it is probably fair to say that the book is better on political history than literary analysis, and better on the less complex, sophisticated works.

(b) Verse and Drama

Three essays on Skelton may be noted. N. F. Budgey (*CP*) argues that Skelton's style, while innovative in southern England, had its antecedents in the alliterative, accentual tradition of northern verse (still being advocated by James VI in 1585), which might help to confirm his descent from the Skeltons of Northumberland. F. W. Brownlow (*ELN*) uses astrological analysis to fix the time of the opening stanza of *The Bowge of Courte* as August 1482, which would suggest Skelton's involvement with the court at that time; his Yorkist sympathies then seem confirmed, and the claim of 'A lamentable of Kyng Edward the IIII' (not included in John Scattergood's edition (*YW* 64.164)), to be by him is strengthened. David A. Loewenstein (*Neophil*), remarking that *The Garland of Laurel* has received less consideration and praise than Skelton's other major works, goes through the poem rather unexcitingly, pointing out how the poet's 'Chaucerian scepticism' is overshadowed by 'Renaissance pride'.

Joost Daalder (*English*) argues that the discontents and unhappinesses in Wyatt's poems derive not from external circumstance but from the speaker's own psychological inadequacies, an incapacity for happiness or a sense of

6. *Poetry and Politics in the English Renaissance*, by David Norbrook. RKP. pp. x + 345. £15.95.

insecurity. Barbara L. Estrin (*ELH*), in a piece somewhat encumbered by contemporary theoretical style, attempts analyses of Wyatt's better-known love poems, to argue that the 'I' of the poems frequently identifies itself (or himself) with the object addressed (the woman, love, etc.); the essay is not wholly persuasive. With a different emphasis, Joe Glaser (*CollL*) insists that the difference in tone and attitude of Wyatt's versions of Petrarch's sonnets from their originals does not derive from technical incompetence, incomprehension of Petrarch's values, or the coarseness of early Tudor culture; rather, they are deliberate and systematic 'aggressive acts of deconstruction', consciously forcing a confrontation between an early Renaissance world of ideal promise, and the dark Machiavellian reality of his time. Other relationships are traced elsewhere: Dennis Kay (*HLQ*) puts 'They Flee from Me . . .' into a Chaucerian context, showing how Chaucer, especially in *Troilus and Criseyde*, had previously used many of the phrases in Wyatt's poem, and arguing that Wyatt is deliberately evoking a specifically Chaucerian imaginative world (though he does not acknowledge that many of Wyatt's phrases are to be found in non-Chaucerian courtly verse, by Charles d'Orleans among others). Martin Buzacott (*N&Q*) suggests that the first two stanzas of 'Who list his Wealth . . .' are a conflation of Seneca's *Phaedra*, ll. 1128 ff., and Boethius's *De consolatione philosophiae*, Book 2, Metre 4 (though the similarities of the Boethius to the Wyatt do not seem very striking). H. A. Mason (*ELH*) demonstrates that the strambotto 'Vulcan begat me . . .' is translated from an epigram by the belle-lettrist humanist Pandolfo Collenuccio of Pesaro in 1497: the epigram has an Aesopian fable that provides the key to the poem's riddle. Mason relates Wyatt's poem to its cultural context, indicates its humanist theme, suggests the metrical principle that Ronald A. Rebholz could not establish in his edition, and relates it to the strambotto derived from Serafino, 'The furious gun . . .'; undoubtedly the most impressive essay of the bunch. John Simons's printing (*ELN*) of an early-sixteenth-century lyric found in the manuscript holdings of the National Library of Wales should also be recorded.

The Malone Society has reproduced the first texts of John Heywood's *The Pardoner and the Friar* and *The Four Ps*[7], reduced in size from the original small folio, with bibliographical notes for each play. In *N&Q* Mark Eccles points out that the 'half a yard of rede sea' recorded as bought for the Coventry Mystery Plays was not necessarily for the Red Sea, but may have been merely a variant spelling of 'red say', or serge, and Marie Collins finds in Richard Whitford's early-sixteenth-century *A Dayly Exercyse and Experyence of Dethe* a reference to an unsophisticated audience's inability to recognize stage devils as artifice; Gordon Kipling argues that the transcribed cartel of 'The Queen of May's Joust at Kennington' indeed refers to a tournament in Henry VII's time, and not, as appears and as Richard Firth Green concluded, in 1441. The Lancastrian names included in the transcription are probably taken from the record of another event, while the poem *The Justes of the Moneths of May and June* refers to this very tournament, dating it as May 1507. The cartel and the poem together suggest how important this tournament was in the development towards Tudor court drama. Such matters are grist to Ian Lancashire's mighty mill, that, in producing *Dramatic Texts and Records of Britain: A Chronologi-*

---

7. *The Pardoner and the Friar, 1533. The Four Ps, ?1544*, by John Heywood. Malone Society Reprints. OUP. pp. ix + unnumbered pages. By sub.

cal Topography to 1558[8], is responsible for a truly monumental achievement. He lists the records of dramatic activity for about four hundred places in Great Britain (and Ireland), from Roman to Elizabeth I's times; his records are of almost every type – church, civic and royal court minutes, Chancery, Parliamentary and Exchequer records, wills and court rolls, jest books, poems, sermons, pictures, as well as archaeological remains and artefacts – and deal with Romano-British theatre, medieval drama, Tudor court revels, and university plays. There are four maps and many illustrations; the organization is topographical, with items listed according to their geographical siting, which, as Lancashire acknowledges, produces some difficulties, for example, for those interested in tracing dramatic subjects, or in a chronological account; nevertheless, this is a remarkable and invaluable volume.

2. The Later Sixteenth Century

(a) General

Perhaps the most important book to appear in the field of English Renaissance literary studies in 1984 was David Norbrook's *Poetry and Politics in the English Renaissance*[6]. The subject is formidable, the author is up to it, the book is outstanding. Norbrook sets out to reconsider the rigid separation of poetry and politics perpetuated by transcendental critics of the post-Romantic era: 'the issue is not so much why one should politicise poetry as why critics have for so long been trying to depoliticise it'. The ball is deftly returned to the opponent's court. Norbrook's period stretches from More to Milton. Some of the recently discovered 'innovative currents of political and religious thought' are his theme, or more particularly, what contribution major writers made to those currents. 'Feigning commonwealths' was their way of questioning political orthodoxy. The introduction is, among other things, modest, and a model of informed, even-handed caution against the excesses of formalist and hence 'depoliticizing' trends in modern criticism. The chapters on less well-known material, like the prophetic poetry of the Reformation, Fulke Greville, and the Spenserians of the first two decades of the seventeenth century, are in some ways the most interesting, whereas the analyses of Sidney's 'political pastoral', *The Faerie Queene*'s visionary politics, or Milton's prophetic voice are no longer novel. This will become a standard work, whether or not its readings of particular works gain undisputed acceptance. There are, unfortunately, some misprints. It is a pity that Routledge too has adopted the photographed-typescript method of printing: right-hand margins are not justified, and the notes confusingly place book titles in inverted commas and do not set off article titles at all, thus deviating from common practice.

French R. Fogle and Louis A. Knafla deal with politics at another level in *Patronage in Late Renaissance England*[9]. Their two papers, first read at a Clark Library seminar in 1977, are on, respectively, the Dowager Countess of Derby and Sir Thomas Egerton, Baron Ellesmere, husband and wife from

---

8. *Dramatic Texts and Records of Britain: A Chronological Topography to 1558*, by Ian Lancashire. UTor/CUP. pp. lxxi + unnumbered pages + 633. £39.50.

9. *Patronage in Late Renaissance England*, by French R. Fogle and Louis A. Knafla. CML (1983). pp. iii + 115. By sub.

1600 until his death in 1617. Both were active patrons and their reputations and influence were enormous, as was the number of writers who sought and received patronage from one or both of them. Samuel Daniel was one such, and John Pitcher (*HLQ*) produces proof that a letter to Egerton, long known in print and thought to be from Daniel, is indeed so. Elizabethan letters and letter-books are A. R. Braunmuller's subject in 'Editing Elizabethan Letters' in the first volume of the impressive new annual, *Text: Transactions of the Society for Textual Scholarship*[10]. (The journal was slow off the mark, Volume I, for 1981, appearing in 1984.) Braunmuller's question 'What is a letter?' isn't as obvious as it may seem, and he canvasses such specimens as Harvey's and Spenser's *Three Proper, and Wittie Familiar Letters*. He warns the prospective editor of Elizabethan letter-books, commonplace books, or miscellanies of several pitfalls, to which he gives such Bunyanesque names as the Fallacy of Certitude, the Crux of Copies, and the Sorrow of Sources. Braunmuller's enthusiasm is infectious, the Lure of Letters clearly irresistible for him.

Two men and several women to conclude this section: Karl Josef Höltgen introduces the life and writings of 'Sir Robert Dallington (1561–1637): Author, Traveler, and Pioneer of Taste' (*HLQ*). Dallington was counsellor to princes Henry and Charles, and is best known for his guidebooks on France and Tuscany, written just after the turn of the century. His main literary production though falls within my period: *Hypnerotomachia: The Strife of Loue in a Dreame* (1592), a part-translation of Francesco Colonna's *Hypnerotomachia Poliphili* of 1499. The translation seems to have influenced a number of English poets at the time. Michael Brennan provides a very useful survey of the career of 'William Ponsonby: Elizabethan Stationer' (*AEB*, 1983), appending a list of works published by him. Greene, Sidney, Spenser, Fraunce, Ralegh, the Countess of Pembroke, Watson, Chapman, Percy, and many others figure among Ponsonby's authors. Brennan lists some seventy items published between 1579 and 1604. This kind of material is of great value for the study of Elizabethan literary production. John Day's *Service Book* of 1560–5 is subjected to microscopic bibliographical scrutiny by the late Howard M. Nixon (*BLJ*). More properly known as *Certaine Notes, Set Forth in Foure and Three Parts*, the work is shown to have been only partly printed in 1560, then laid aside by Day until 1565 when he finished it. *Grove's Dictionary of Music* and other works have referred to two distinct editions from the two years. It is not mentioned, I find, in the *New Grove*, which cites only Day's more famous musical publication, the Sternhold–Hopkins psalter. Despite Day's prominent portrait device on the title-page and a STC entry under his name (plus three other separate entries – a record?), the book was only printed, and not compiled or published, by Day. Betty Travitsky's bulkily titled 'The Lady Doth Protest: Protest in the Popular Writings of Renaissance Englishwomen' (*ELR*) ranges beyond my period at both ends. The two works examined in some detail which appeared in the latter half of the sixteenth century are Isabella Whitney's *The Copy of a Letter . . . by a Yonge Gentilwomen* [*sic*] (1567) and Jane Anger's *Protection for Women* (1589). Anger (it may not be a pseudonym) is 'apparently the first woman in England to have written a feminist pamphlet'. Travitsky covers some of the same ground as

10. *Text: Transactions of the Society for Textual Scholarship*, ed. by D. C. Greetham and W. Speed Hill. AMSP. £33.75.

Linda Woodbridge in her *Women and the English Renaissance* (see Chapter IX below). She makes only modest claims for these modest works, while pointing, rightly, to their original contributions to the tradition of antimisogynistic writing. That tradition is of course a trickle beside the torrent of the anti-feminist one.

(b) Sidney

The steady stream of publications on Sidney and his circle threatens to become another torrent as the four-hundredth anniversary of his death, 1986, approaches. I have twenty items to deal with, including several on the Circle (mainly his brother Robert), and Sidney figures here and there in other works not treated here (for example, in David Norbrook's book discussed above). My two major book-length items on Sidney himself are an excellent edition and translation of William Temple's *Analysis* of the *Apology* and a collection of essays. John Webster (not the Jacobean playwright) renders all Sidney scholars a notable service with his edition and translation of Temple's *Analysis*[11]. Temple, Sidney's secretary, wrote his Ramist *Analysis* well before the *Apology* was published in 1595, and it appears to be addressed to Sidney personally, so must have been composed between 1584, when the two met for the first time, and 1586, when Sidney died, in Temple's arms according to legend. Webster's admirable introduction discusses logic in Tudor England and its relation to rhetoric, Ramism, Temple's reading of Sidney, and Temple's life and career. The Latin text is printed in a format as near as possible to that of the unique manuscript, which is partly in Temple's own hand. On the facing page is Webster's translation, with passages from the *Apology* sometimes interpolated to make clear what Temple is talking about. A very helpful feature is the seven-page glossary of Renaissance logical and rhetorical terminology. This is a fine piece of scholarship, of which its and the series editors may be proud.

Sir Philip Sidney and the Interpretation of Renaissance Culture[12] is a collection of ten essays, divided into two parts, five essays each, labelled 'The Poet in his Time' and '. . . And in ours'; or, old fogies in Part I, trendies in Part II. The essays do not, however, bear out such clumsy classification. All ten of the critics live in 'our time' and of necessity read Sidney from this end of the four hundred years that separate him and us. Two essays on *Astrophil and Stella* in Part I, by Robert L. Montgomery and Charles S. Levy, re-emphasize, respectively, the ironic disjunction between Sidney and Astrophil, and the 'ethical irony' of the work; this emphasis is modern, is it not? (Both authors cite with approval essays by Alan Sinfield, who contributes to Part II of the present volume.) And in Part II Gary F. Waller and Marion Campbell write on Sidney's 'rewriting' and 'reinvention' of Petrarch. What is that but 'sources and influences' or 'what Sidney did to Petrarch' in new guises? Germaine Warkentin considers the relation of the mid-century poetical collections to Sidney's practice in *Certain Sonnets* and, briefly, *Astrophil and Stella* (she too mentions its irony). Had she talked of Sidney's 're-writing' or 're-reading' or

11. *William Temple's 'Analysis' of Sir Philip Sidney's 'Apology for Poetry'*, ed. and trans. by John Webster. MRTS 32. CMERS. pp. 186. $16.
12. *Sir Philip Sidney and the Interpretation of Renaissance Culture: The Poet in his Time and ours: A Collection of Critical and Scholarly Essays*, ed. by Gary F. Waller and Michael D. Moore. CH/B&W. pp. xii + 147. £14.95.

'appropriating' of Turbervile *et al.*, would her essay have been put in Part II?
Waller drops names hectically in his jargon-ridden essay: Althusser, Bakhtin,
Barthes, Descartes, Hegel, Kristeva, Lacan, Macherey, Marx, Nietzsche,
Raymond Williams, even Alain Resnais; some slip in in adjectival guise (e.g.,
'that old Burckhardtian commonplace', 'a Durkheimian or Weberian determinism'). These droppings are usually gratuitous, occurring in such phrases as
'as Macherey puts it', 'what Lacan terms', 'what Barthes calls', 'in Foucault's
words'. The upshot of it all is the assertion that 'in the late twentieth century, in
our history, Sidney's works occupy an especially interesting place'. So say we
all, to be sure, but why the uptight emphasis on *our*? And after the barrage,
'especially interesting' is a damp squib; even old fogies can manage better than
that. Alan Sinfield's essay, 'The Cultural Politics of the *Defence of Poetry*' is
itself rather more defensive than some of his other writings on Sidney have
been. Overpoliticizing can be as distorting as depoliticizing, but Sinfield is
often thoughtful and thought-provoking, always learned and articulate. Other
contributions include, in Part I, S. K. Heninger Jr on poetry and painting in
Sidney and Maurice Evans on the *New Arcadia*, and, in Part II, Jacqueline
T. Miller on the language of *Astrophil and Stella* and Jon A. Quitslund on
'Sidney's Presence in Lyric Verse of the Later English Renaissance'.

Longest and least substantial of the Sidney studies is Shelley Thrasher-
Smith's *The Luminous Globe: Methods of Characterization in Sidney's 'New
Arcadia'*[13], another in the unquenchable stream of American theses published
by Salzburg. 'I began this study in anger' declares the author irrelevantly, in a
preface which is itself not angry but merely puerile, and she ends, two-
hundred-plus pages later, in banality, concluding that 'Sidney effectively
creates strong female characters in the *New Arcadia*'. But, she adds, we need
'an examination of his methods of characterizing his male characters' (Oh
spare us!), to be compared with the present study 'to understand fully Sidney's
estimation of women'. Sidney's 'methods of characterization' turn out to be
structure, style, and content. This work reads, I am afraid, like an extended
undergraduate catalogue-essay on the female characters in *Arcadia*. The two
Arcadias more or less share the honours where articles and essays are concerned, with four and three, respectively. Peter Lindenbaum explores 'The
Geography of Sidney's *Arcadia*' (*PQ*) and the changes Sidney made from *Old*
to *New*, his use of new maps together with Strabo making for a more detailed
and generally more accurate geography in the revision. Most notable is the
removal of Arcadia's seacoast. William Craft examines 'The Shaping Picture
of Love' in the *New Arcadia* (*SP*). The pictorial qualities of Sidney's *exempla*
and his own views about 'speaking pictures' have been much rehearsed; Craft's
point is that in the stories of various lovers known to the principal characters
'Sidney presents an ongoing pageant of the possibilities to which love can
lead'. The article itself goes on a bit (twenty-four pages) and contains too much
summary and paraphrase. A broader perspective upon visual art in the *New
Arcadia* is taken by Norman K. Farmer Jr in the first chapter of his book *Poets
and the Visual Arts in Renaissance England*[14]. He first documents Sidney's

13. *The Luminous Globe: Methods of Characterization in Sidney's 'New Arcadia'*, by
Shelley Thrasher-Smith. SSELER 94. USalz (1982). pp. ii + 233. $25.50.
14. *Poets and the Visual Arts in Renaissance England*, by Norman K. Farmer Jr.
UTex. pp. xiii + 122. $19.95.

serious interest in the techniques of painting and limning and then looks closely at *Arcadia*, especially the descriptions of Kalander's house, gardens, gallery, paintings, and statuary. References to Renaissance artistic theory and Sidney's own views about pictorial poetry in the *Apology*, and nine illustrations, of emblems, engravings, and paintings (Giorgione, Titian, Tintoretto) enrich Farmer's discussion. He also makes the revealing observation that 'there is a conscious order in the progression from landscape to portraiture to emblem and impresa in the three existing books of the *New Arcadia*'. His conclusions are that 'Sidney's use of visual art in the *New Arcadia* is neither impressionistic nor intellectually loose', and that the *Arcadia* was ahead of its time in its sophisticated use of visual art as commentary upon verbal art.

Sukanta Chaudhuri marshalls evidence from the text of the *New Arcadia* in an attempt to deduce Sidney's plans for the arrangement of the Eclogues (*RES*); the only extant manuscript does not contain any Eclogues. Beginning from the 'unquestionable premiss' that the 1590 text draws upon a source which must be a late authorial revision, Chaudhuri concludes, with due caution, that that text, and not that of 1593, despite the latter's editors' derision of its unauthorized predecessor, will be the more authoritative text for students of the Eclogues. No 'final authorial sanction' is – or can be – claimed for 1590, 'but with judicious analysis, it may give us a good idea of what Sidney intended to do with the Eclogues in the *New Arcadia*'. This is hard scholarship at the coalface, closely argued, meticulously substantiated.

Turning to the *Old Arcadia*, we are informed by P. J. Croft[15] that, contrary to the generally accepted view that Sir John Harington's manuscript of Sidney's work has long since been lost, it is in fact none other than the 'Phillipps manuscript', one of the nine examined by all recent Sidney editors, who have not realized what they were looking at. Croft goes on to comment provocatively on Harington's deliberate alterations of Sidney's text in his manuscript. 'Sidney's Didactic Method in the *Old Arcadia*' is not as obvious as many critics would have us think, argues Ann W. Astell (*SEL*). Sidney, following his own precepts about the poet's 'medecine of cherries', administers his lessons by making the reader consume them unknowingly and internalize them. No foregrounding in Arcadia. In 'The Perils of Fancy: Poetry and Self-Love in *The Old Arcadia*' (*TSLL*) Robert E. Stillman argues that Sidney shows himself to be well aware of the limitations of fiction, despite the 'aggressively optimistic poetics' of the *Apology*. Poetry can produce harm, as when it constructs solipsistic visions out of uncontrolled passions, 'the worst kinds of fictions'. The focus on Sidney as pastoralist is instructive. Finally, in the briefest of notes, Michael Cameron Andrews cites another instance of possible influence of *Arcadia* upon *King Lear* (*N&Q*).

While *Arcadia* (especially *Old*) stock continues to rise (wouldn't Eliot be astonished?), the other works are getting a fair share of attention too: *Astrophil and Stella*, of course, *The Lady of May*, the *Psalms*, the *Letter to Queen Elizabeth*. Surprisingly, the year saw no articles primarily devoted to the *Apology* outside the Waller–Moore collection reviewed above. In 'The Politics of *Astrophil and Stella*' (*SEL*) Ann Rosalind Jones and Peter Stallybrass trace the interplay of 'courtship' and 'courtiership' through the

15. In *Literary Autographs*, by Stephen Parks and P. J. Croft. CML (1983). pp. iv + 77. By sub.

sequence, then 'examine the ways in which such poetry could function as a complex displacement of the ideological pressures of the court'. That it is complex there is no doubt, but the assumption that Sidney wanted to or was trying to 'displace ideological pressures of the court' (whatever that may mean exactly) begs too many questions. There is much here of 'strategies' and 'discourses', but I do not think that it adds up to a more genuinely political or politicized sequence than was already available to us. Daniel Traister, eschewing trends, offers close readings of particular sonnets, in two pieces: sonnets 29 and 9 in ' "To Portrait That Which In This World Is Best": Stella in Perspective' (*SP*), and sonnet 89, the 'night'/'day' sonnet (*Expl*). All three have been unjustly disparaged or neglected by critics, says Traister, and sets out to right the wrong; his conclusions are unexciting but unexceptionable.

Robert E. Stillman extends his study of Sidney's concern with language and its limits in 'Justice and the "Good Word" in Sidney's *The Lady of May*' (*SEL*). Sidney's preoccupation with *res et verba* (or signified and signifier) is seen to be an aspect of his larger concern with justice, the 'chief of virtues', and it is justice that is demanded of the queen by the countrywoman at the beginning of the entertainment. (A footnote erroneously implies that Elizabeth found in favour of Therion rather than Espilus.) H. R. Woudhuysen resolves 'A Crux in the Text of Sidney's *A Letter to Queen Elizabeth*' (*N&Q*) by ignoring the contradictory evidence of three dozen manuscripts and referring to a passage in the *Old Arcadia*.

Michael G. Brennan (*N&Q*) finds an inscription on one of the two Trinity College, Cambridge, manuscripts of Sidney's and his sister Mary's versions of the Psalms which indicates that they were licensed for the press sometime in the 1640s, although no complete edition seems to have been published before 1823. A more recent edition of the Countess of Pembroke's *Psalms*, by G. F. Waller (*YW* 58.181–2), is scrutinized by Noel J. Kinnamon, who emends a number of Waller's readings (*AN&Q*); they are mainly misreadings of the illegible hand of one of the manuscripts, but some errors are due to misunderstanding what was clearly written.

Introduction of the Countess of Pembroke broadens my scope from Sir Philip Sidney himself to the Sidney Circle. Mary Ellen Lamb examines 'Three Unpublished Holograph Poems in the Bright Manuscript' (*RES*) and asks if they could be by a new poet in the Circle. She transcribes and edits the poems and discusses their metre, imagery, and other elements. The first poem is in the mid-century mould, while the second is a fine, Golden, Sidneyan piece, 'especially exciting in unpublished material'; the third partakes of both styles. All three poems seem to be written in a young woman's hand.

The daughters of Robert Sidney, Philip's younger brother, are among the candidates for authorship of the Bright poems. Robert Sidney himself emerged into full view in 1984 in a fine edition of his poems and a new biography. *The Poems of Robert Sidney*, edited by P. J. Croft[16], will allow the younger brother to occupy a place of his own among Elizabethan poets. And an honourable place it will prove to be, judging from the contents of his autograph notebook, edited here complete for the first time. The place had been usurped for over a century, due to booksellers' carelessness, by a pre-

16. *The Poems of Robert Sidney: Edited from the Poet's Autograph Notebook*, ed. by P. J. Croft. Clarendon. pp. xviii + 354. £35.

vious, more famous, Earl of Leicester, Robert Dudley. It was Croft who, in 1973, re-assigned the notebook to Sidney. Each poem is transcribed exactly and accompanied by a modernized text *en face*. The editor provides a full critical introduction, a chronological table, commentary, and appendixes, which include evidence for literary relations between Robert Sidney and (besides his brother) Drayton, Daniel, Greville, Shakespeare, and Robert's daughter, Mary Wroth, who echoed her father in a number of the poems in her prose romance *Urania*. The poems form an interlocking double sequence, one of thirty-five sonnets (all of them in the Italian octave-sestet form favoured by Philip Sidney), the other of twenty-four songs, pastorals, and an elegy, each in a different verse form. A table of verse forms, modelled on that in W. A. Ringler's edition of Philip Sidney's poems, facilitates comparison of the brothers' practices. The total of sixty-eight poems makes the notebook the largest surviving body of autograph poetry by any Elizabethan writer. Croft's outstanding edition is complemented by Millicent V. Hay's *Life of Robert Sidney*[17]. She concentrates on his active career as soldier, courtier, and diplomat in the reigns of Elizabeth and James. The book is rather dry, full of dates and embassies, skirmishes, and intrigues. The notes are bleak lists of letter citations (e.g. 'Sidney to Lady Sidney, Greenwich, 2 March 1594/95, etc.'). The narrative style is matter of fact, paragraphs are short. There seem to be a lot of 'probablies' and 'possiblies' in Hay's account, despite the abundance of documentary evidence for Sidney's life and career. A brief chapter, 'Poet and Patron', refers to the notebook and the poems. Between them, Croft and Hay have given us Robert Sidney, his life and works, and in his edition Croft has left a fine monument to himself.

(c) Spenser

Arma virumque canet Michael Leslie, discussing martial and chivalric symbolism in *The Faerie Queene*[18]. Arguing that 'the knight is the basic building block' of the poem, and that 'his characteristic garb, armour, is not left as mere decoration, but is central to the presentation of Spenser's intensely human moral allegory', Leslie first provides careful analyses of the sources and meanings of the knights' armour, shields, and weapons, and their various battles; in the latter part of the book he discusses the chivalric festivals of Books IV and V in the context of the Elizabethan chivalric revival, culminating in a discussion of the relevance of the Order of the Garter. Without providing a fundamentally new or transforming view of the poem, this study usefully illuminates many passages – of arms, as well as of words. Anthea Hume's concise and crisply written study of *Edmund Spenser: Protestant Poet*[19] is concerned to explain the language, imagery, and meaning of Spenser's poetry by Protestant, and in particular, Puritan theologians and writers, such as those connected with the Leicester circle. She provides persuasive readings of *The Shepheardes Calender*, and disputes, on religious principles, A. S. P. Woodhouse's grace/nature separation of Book I of *The Faerie Queene* from the rest (*YW* 30.144); the account of the first book is more successful, though

17. *The Life of Robert Sidney, Earl of Leicester (1563–1626)*, by Millicent V. Hay. Folger/AUP. pp. 260. $36.50.

18. *Spenser's 'Fierce Warres and Faithfull Loves': Martial and Chivalric Symbolism in 'The Faerie Queene'*, by Michael Leslie. Brewer/B&N. pp. viii + 215. £22.50.

19. *Edmund Spenser: Protestant Poet*, by Anthea Hume. CUP. pp. vi + 202. £18.50.

generally the approach is somewhat limiting; a chapter on the Britons and the Elves, while interesting, does not really belong here. William L. Sipple and Bernard J. Vondersmith have produced a bibliography of early-twentieth-century Spenser studies[20], designed to be compatible with the survey of the 1937–72 period compiled by Waldo F. McNeir and Foster Provost (*YW* 57.156).

Among the articles on Spenser, Books I and VI of *The Faerie Queene* have received most attention. John M. Crossett and Donald V. Stump (*JMRS*) analyse the procession of the Seven Deadly Sins in Book I as a Protestant adaptation of medieval Catholic tradition, in accordance with the Aristotelean tradition of contrary extremes and the mean. Spenser varies the usual Infernal Triad: for him, Idleness and Gluttony pair as sins of the flesh, Avarice and Lechery as sins of the world, Envy and Wrath as sins of the Devil; Idleness, Avarice, and Envy are 'froward' sins of deficiency, Gluttony, Lechery, and Wrath 'forward' sins of excess; all meet and culminate in Pride and Lucifera. J. D. Pheifer, in John Scattergood's collection of essays[21], sees Spenser's Error as combining the Echidna of Hesiod's *Theogony* with Herodotus's viper and the traditional application of Herodotus to *Matthew* 3.7; his image probably particularly reflects Theodore Beza's *Icones* of 1580. Kathryn Walls (*N&Q*) argues that Kirkrapine figures not merely corruption in the English Church but also, *pace* Mother Mary Robert Falls (*YW* 34.179), corruption in the Roman Church, as described in Foxe's *Actes and Monuments*. Richard J. DuRocher (*MP*) claims that Arthur's gift to Red Crosse is not just the Eucharist, but Magnificence: Spenser knew Aristotle through Aquinas's commentaries, where magnificence is explicitly connected with holiness. Holiness is R. D. Jordan's theme also (*N&Q*): while Aristotle did not treat holiness as a virtue, Spenser's contemporaries Christianized Aristotle, translating *eudaemonia*, 'happiness', as 'beatitude'. Aristotle's happiness achieved through the pursuit of virtue is what Spenser means by holiness; Aristotle's gifts of the gods parallel the role of grace, and contemplation is supreme happiness for Aristotle and for Spenser's hermit. From Hungary comes a discussion of the iconography of the House of Alma in Book II, by György E. Szõnyi[22], suggesting that Spenser's account is less a didactic metaphor than a 'revelative word-emblem ... under the influence of the hermetic way of thinking', and providing many illustrations of iconographic parallels. Marie H. Buncombe (*CLAJ*) tries to link Spenser's Florimell with Castiglione's account in *Il Corte-giano* of the ideal court lady-in-waiting, chaste, sweet, shamefast, and con-stant. Ronald B. Bond (*Ren&R*) moves from the presentation of Envy in Book I to concentrate on Book VI, claiming that Spenser dramatizes the etymology of 'envy' – *invidia, in-videre*, 'to look maliciously against' – to create telling poetic effects: Book VI stresses the association of envy and jealousy with voyeurism and greed of the eye; Calidore and the cannibals are both guilty; a prayer for spiritual vision concludes *The Mutabilitie Cantoes*. Patrick Cheney

20. *Edmund Spenser 1900–1936: A Reference Guide*, by William L. Sipple with Bernard J. Vondersmith. Hall. pp. xxxviii + 244. $37.50.

21. *Literature and Learning in Medieval and Renaissance England: Essays Presented to Fitzroy Pyle*, ed. by John Scattergood. IAP. pp. 240. £17.50.

22. In *Acta Universitatis Szegedensis de Attila József Nominate: Papers in English and American Studies*, Vol. III, ed. by B. Rozsuyai. USzeged.

has two pieces on Spenser's Dance of the Graces and hundred nymphs: in the first (*ELN*) he argues for Tasso's dance of the sylvan nymphs in *Gerusalemme liberata* as a source; in the second, with P. J. Klemp (*SN*), he sees Spenser's dance as a schematic model of the Ptolemaic universe, whose circling spheres were often likened to a dance. Here the central damsel is the earth, the graces the planets, the outer ring the *primum mobile* or the fixed stars, and Colin is outside it all, like God: Pythagorean art is a creative and ordering magical power, akin to God's. Stanley Stewart (*SEL*) declines to see Book VI as concerned with closure; Calidore's interruption of the dance is not an initiatory moment, but as discourteous and disastrous as his intrusion into Pastorella's world. The book does not end with their union, and pairs less with Book I than with Book V; its primary organizing feature is necessarily disjunction and incompletion. In notes in *Expl*, Murdo William McRae points out that the Brigants who carry off Pastorella live in caves faintly illuminated by candlelight, 'which delt A doubtfull sense of things', and suggests that they are versions of the ignorant inhabitants of Plato's cave, and J. C. Eade provides an astrological explanation of Mutabilitie's criticism of Saturn's 'many turning cranks . . . so many crookes'. A. Bartlett Giamatti (*YR*) concludes this paragraph: he reviews Spenser's whole career in relation to Elizabeth's, whose true education he sees as having been at court, in power and its effects, producing her desire for stability and unity. Spenser was concerned with the power of the poet and of language, and his poem is concerned with restoration and healing; it also shows Spenser's loss of faith in the power of language to present virtue, and concludes with the unitive and transcendent figure of Dame Nature.

The essays in the fourth volume of *Spenser Studies*[23] range widely, if not very excitingly. Elizabeth Bieman mines the generally unremarked vein of bawdy wit in the *Amoretti*: the disguised attribution of sexuality to the lady makes her more like Britomart than the conventional sonnet-lady. Donald Cheney considers Spenser's poem on his fortieth birthday as part of a series of biographical fictions, exploring the conditions of poetic identity and personal survival: where other poet-lovers (such as Sidney and Ralegh) were wrecked, Spenser survives by withdrawing to a private life. For Mary I. Oates, the *Fowre Hymnes* form a narrative of the erotic and religious development of a lover, and are also unified by numerological symbolism. T. P. Roche Jr considers the curious interrelationship in I.ix of Arthur's story of his visitation by the Faerie queen, Trevisan's narrative of Terwin's succumbing to Despair, and Red Crosse's encounter with Despair. Hugh MacLachlan, remarking how Guyon is treated as dead when he is known to have merely fainted, relates this to the Elizabethan *Book of Homilies*, which discusses the man of good deeds who is spiritually dead: a dead faith is grounded in self-confidence, but true lively faith is grounded in confidence in God's support, which Guyon then receives through Arthur. Returning to the relation between Spenser's acquaintance and his characters, James P. Bednarz discusses the treatment of Ralegh's career in Elizabeth's service, in the story of Timias and Belphoebe, while William A. Oram remarks how Spenser uses his contemporaries' situations to analyse the psychological problems they present, fragmenting the historical personages into several different fictional characters and thus permitting a

23. *Spenser Studies: A Renaissance Poetry Annual*, Vol. IV, ed. by Patrick Cullen and Thomas P. Roche Jr. AMSP. pp. viii + 169. $32.50.

portrayal from different perspectives. Russell J. Meyer uses astronomy to illuminate the lunar eclipse of the *Mutabilitie Cantoes*, the date of which must be after April 1595.

The other main collection of discussions of Spenser, *Spenser at Kalamazoo 1984*[24], makes somewhat more lively reading, perhaps because it includes responses to the papers delivered at the Congress on Medieval Studies at WMU. Harold L. Weatherby argues that the details of Una's betrothal to Red Crosse derive, not from Roman marriage practice, as John Upton and others suggested, but from Catholic Easter Vigil ritual as indicated in the Sarum manual, but John Mulryan thinks this unlikely, as Spenser could have drawn on other sources. Elizabeth Jane Bellamy argues that Spenser as dynastic prophet cannot escape, like Aeneas, from the limitations of the past in the attempt to found a new order; the figure of Aesculapius (I.v) embodies the poem's problems regarding the restoration of wholeness to the corrupted; John V. Bernard finds her paper a reflection of contemporary loss of confidence in the possibility of cultural restoration and re-integration. William A. Sessions, while exploiting the insights of Lacan, Derrida, and Jonathan Goldberg, criticizes deconstructionist approaches to Spenser, in considering the possibility and nature of closure, particularly in the story of Amoret and Scudamour; he is firmly put in his humanist place by David L. Miller. Lauren Silberman considers Book II as 'a thoroughgoing and ironic critique of Temperance', while Theresa M. Krier qualifies this, citing Belphoebe and the angel in particular as transcendental numinous images. Richard Helgerson relates the argument between the proponents of quantitative verse and of stress-rhyme verse to alternative Elizabethan concepts of self-fashioning, that operated in other cultural areas, while Humphrey Tonkin discusses the Elizabethans' concept of alternative pasts providing different guidance for the future. William A. Oram provides a lengthy contribution to the debate on the vexatious problem of character in *The Faerie Queene*, considering the different types of character, their relation with each other and with allegory, the quest and the comic mode. Linda M. Vecchi argues that Spenser's *Complaints* is a coherent volume, belonging to the tradition and convention of the complaint. Robin Headlam Wells would have found this a sympathetic approach, as, discussing the *Amoretti* (*CahiersE*), he reminds us that convention is a more reliable guide than biography to the meaning of Renaissance lyric poetry: the *Amoretti* are poetry of praise, epideictic, addressed not just to Elizabeth Boyle, but to the fair beloved tyrant Elizabeth, of whom some conventional phrases were literally true, for whom the high style was appropriate, and whose identity is further indicated by Elizabethan iconography. The nature of Spenser's attitude to Elizabeth is considered also by Barbara J. Bono in her book *Literary Transvaluation: From Vergilian Epic to Shakespearean Tragicomedy*[25], an examination of the uses of the Dido and Aeneas story from Virgil to Renaissance drama, culminating in *Antony and Cleopatra*, as examinations of the relationship between personal, particularly sexual, satisfactions and public responsibilities. In discussing *The Shepheardes Calender* she

24. *Spenser at Kalamazoo 1984*, ed. by Francis G. Greco. ClarionU. pp. iv + 143. $3.75.

25. *Literary Transvaluation: From Vergilian Epic to Shakespearean Tragicomedy*, by Barbara J. Bono. UCal. pp. xi + 264. £27.25.

concentrates on the role of the poet in relation to the woman ruler, and, in *The Faerie Queene*, on Britomart's epic quest to reconcile eros and civilization in a dynastic marriage, and the individual, chaste love theme of Belphoebe as set against the theme of social concord in the marriage story of Amoret. *N&Q* includes three notes on Spenser's reception and influence: John Manning comments on the notes and marginalia in Bishop Percy's copy of the 1611 edition of Spenser; Martin Coyle suggests that Gloucester's Dover 'cliff fall' in *King Lear* echoes Malbecco's suicide bid (*Faerie Queene* III.x) in the characters' situations, and also verbally; and D. C. Kay notes that the name Claribel, in *The Tempest*, was used three times in *The Faerie Queene* (II.iv, IV.ix, and VI.xii).

Ranging more widely and readably are Andrew V. Ettin and A. Bartlett Giamatti. Ettin has written a lively if unorthodox book on the pastoral[26], emphasizing the mode rather than the genre, and irony and ambiguity in particular, ranging so widely that he is in a position to discuss, interestingly enough, not only Virgil and Spenser but Leconte de Lisle and Billie Holiday. Giamatti reprints[27] a selection of his elegant and learned essays dating back to 1962, originally intended as a study of the impact of the Italian upon the English Renaissance, focusing particularly upon themes of mutability, and of a sense of exile from the classical world. He works through representative myths and images – the restored Hippolytus imaging the Renaissance desire to restore the classical world; the restrained stallion as an image of art's resolution of the conflict between control and release; Proteus manifesting civilization's complex involvement in change – and includes two interesting pieces on Spenser, one on the revelation produced by the raising of a visor, the other on the interplay between the foundling child and the salvage man, again on the great theme of primitivism and civility. Last of all is a handsome volume of essays on *The Apocalypse in English Renaissance Thought and Literature*[28]. While the volume ranges from early and medieval apocalyptic to eighteenth- and nineteenth-century writing, the emphasis is on the Renaissance. There are three essays on Renaissance literature, including one on Spenser: Florence Sandler, apart from a last section on *The Mutabilitie Cantoes*, naturally concentrates her discussion on Book I of *The Faerie Queene*, providing in effect a competent summary of recent work on the book, which she sets in a context, first, of Erasmus's *Enchiridion* and paraphrases of the New Testament, and then of Bale's *Image of Both Churches* and Foxe's *Actes and Monuments*, and John Dixon's first-edition annotations.

(d) Poetry

Three editions, a Casebook, and fourteen articles and notes are reviewed here, while work on Robert Sidney appears in section 2(*b*) above. Thomas Tusser is a featherweight poet but an utterly winning character, and OUP is to be commended for reprinting his Tudor bestseller, *Five Hundred Points of Good Husbandry*, with a fond, fanciful introduction by the late Geoffrey

26. *Literature and the Pastoral*, by Andrew V. Ettin. Yale. pp. xii + 199. £22.50.
27. *Exile and Change in Renaissance Literature*, by A. Bartlett Giamatti. Yale. pp. 172. £10.
28. *The Apocalypse in English Renaissance Thought and Literature: Patterns, Antecedents and Repercussions*, ed. by C. A. Patrides and Joseph Wittreich. ManU. pp. x + 452. £37.50.

Grigson[29]. The pathetic Tusser, a failure at farming and unable or unwilling to turn his apparent musical skills to professional use, nevertheless wrote and rewrote, constantly expanding his *Points* from a hundred in Richard Tottel's edition of 1557 to five hundred in 1573. Six editions appeared between then and 1580, the year Tusser died in debtors' prison, pathetic to the end. The Tregaskis edition of 1931 is reprinted, and Sir Walter Scott's introduction to an earlier edition, a glossary, copious notes, and an index are provided. It is easy to share Grigson's 'unexpected pleasure' in reading this 'generous writer . . . forcing himself to wrestle with the intractability of language'.

A class or two up the poetical scale, though no more earnest than Tusser, is Sir Walter Ralegh. He is well served in a selected edition by Gerald Hammond in Carcanet's Fyfield series[30]. I hesitated before following Hammond's lead in considering Ralegh as a poet first, and thus including him here rather than with the prose writers. Of the 255 pages of text, there are only thirty-seven of verse; the remainder is prose. Yet it is as a poet that Ralegh the author is mainly remembered. Hammond includes all of his known poems and most of the contested ones, following the order of Agnes Latham's Muses' Library edition (1951), but rejecting a dozen or so that she included. The prose is generously represented by the famous report of the last fight of the *Revenge*, most of the *Discovery of Guiana* and extracts (150 pages) from *The History of the World*. The editor admits that to choose extracts from that massive work is to misrepresent it. However, few are likely to read all of it today, and there is enough here to allow a reader to judge whether or not it really 'deserves to be set near *King Lear* as one of the English Renaissance's powerfully negative visions of the state of man on "this stage-play world" '. A cheaper, paperback edition of this volume might encourage lecturers to restore Ralegh to courses on Elizabethan literature.

Like Ralegh, George Chapman (as a non-dramatic poet) has been relatively out of favour of late: only one article on each of them was reviewed in this section last year. Both made minor comebacks in 1984. Richard Corballis edits *George Chapman's Minor Translations*[31] in the Salzburg series. In a short introduction, the editor reveals that he has transcribed from microfilm a single copy of each work, due to the inaccessibility of many copies. In the reduced photographic print of the typescript, the texts of the poems have come out very small indeed; incongruously, Chapman's annotations to Hesiod are writ larger than the poem itself. The editing is extremely conservative. What is the point? Scholars and serious students will not be satisfied with what is virtually a transcription, occasionally emended and thus not identical with the original, of a single copy (even when a single copy is all that exists, as for the Musaeus). Readers of poetry would have been better served by a modernized, regularized text. The number of misprints in the introduction (poor Chapman is 'Goerged' on the very first page) must cast doubt on the accuracy of the transcribed texts as well. Corballis elsewhere interprets 'Some Variations on a

29. *Five Hundred Points of Good Husbandry*, by Thomas Tusser, intro. by Geoffrey Grigson. OUP. pp. xxi + 344. pb £3.50.
30. *Sir Walter Ralegh: Selected Writings*, ed. by Gerald Hammond. Fyfield. Carcanet. pp. 296. £14.95.
31. *George Chapman's Minor Translations: A Critical Edition of his Renderings of Musaeus, Hesiod and Juvenal*, ed. by Richard Corballis. SSELJDS 98. USalz. pp. xii + 115. $25.50.

Theme in Chapman's Homer' (*CahiersE*) to suggest that *Bussy D'Ambois* was written before the *Seaven Bookes of the Iliades* (1598). As he expresses it though, it looks as if his main aim was to vindicate some views enunciated a quarter of a century ago by Elias Schwartz (*MP*, 1959; *JEGP*, 1957). 'Ovid's Banquet of Sense' is subjected to numerological analysis by Janet Levarie Smarr in 'The Pyramid and the Circle' (*PQ*). The poem-pyramid seems to be so skilfully stuffed with Neoplatonic, emblematic, and hieroglyphic signs that its sense and Ovid's banquet may lie entombed for ages to come. Marion Campbell argues at great length in ' "Desunt Nonulla": The Construction of Marlowe's *Hero and Leander* as an Unfinished Poem' (*ELH*) that Marlowe's poem has lain entombed for ages in Chapman's construction of it, a con perpetrated by him to justify his finishing it in his own fashion, a con swallowed by most critics, many of whom Campbell lines up and shoots at. There is an air of desperation in her search for internal evidence, and many people do succeed in reading Marlowe's poem in its own right, her insistence that we have all been conned by Chapman to the contrary notwithstanding. The main point though, if worth making, would have been made more effectively if made more economically.

In a Casebook on *Elizabethan Poetry: Lyrical and Narrative*[32], edited by Gerald Hammond, eighteen pre-twentieth-century critics and eighteen twentieth-century ones are represented, but parity ends there. The first eighteen are allotted forty-three pages, the last eighteen, 150 pages. The heart sinks at those guilty ellipses setting off the snippets. Do we need two-and-a-half pages from Sidney's *Apology*, most of it not on Elizabethan poetry at all? Tottel, Gascoigne, Puttenham, Harington, Campion, Daniel each get the briefest of words. Likewise Jonson (half a page), Addison (one page), Warton (two), Hazlitt (one), Swinburne (three), etc. In the longer modern section, many of the expected names are there, mostly in snippets: T. S. Eliot, William Empson, Yvor Winters, Donald Davie, Rosemond Tuve, I. A. Richards, Hallett Smith (but no C. S. Lewis or Douglas Bush, John Buxton or D. L. Peterson). Occasionally a piece is printed whole; it is useful, for instance, to have Leonard Nathan's short essay on structures in the Tudor lyric. The editor errs in trying to include too many critics. A dozen carefully chosen complete essays or chapters with a broad purview and reflecting diverse approaches might have been more valuable than nineteen extracts; likewise a few longer passages from the earlier literary critics and historians – Warton, Coleridge, Hazlitt, Swinburne, Saintsbury – rather than the bits of 'contemporary comment' which is rarely, in fact, comment on the poets and poems. A fuller reading list would fill more lacunae, and the systematic omission from it of items referred to in the notes scattered in clusters through the volume is most unhelpful. There are odd emphases: for example, there are two extracts on Campion, plus one by him, and he has the longest index entry of any poet mentioned. Tusser doesn't rate a mention; nor, in the index, does *The Phoenix Nest*, the Sidney memorial collection published in 1593 to which Lodge was the chief contributor (it is mentioned on p. 129). Breton, Peele, and one 'Richard Barfield' are named only in a list of minor poets in the introduction; Richard

---

32. *Elizabethan Poetry: Lyrical and Narrative*, ed. by Gerald Hammond. Casebook. Macmillan. pp. 227. hb £20, pb £6.95.

Barnfield doesn't appear. Nevertheless, the book does have its uses, not least as a compendious reminder of some of the ways we have been reading Elizabethan poetry for four hundred years.

Of the eleven articles remaining, all but two deal with a single author or his work. In the first of the exceptions, O. B. Hardison Jr surveys 'Blank Verse before Milton' (*SP*). He takes up a hitherto ignored challenge issued in 1937 by George K. Smart (*Anglia*), who criticized historians of literature and prosody for treating dramatic and non-dramatic blank verse as one. It is startling to be reminded that, except for one or two very minor pieces, blank verse was used for heroic poetry only by Surrey in his *Aeneid* and Marlowe in his *Pharsalia* – both of them translations – before Milton's *Paradise Lost*. Hardison's discussion includes drama too, but he has a most helpful section on the context within which blank verse appeared, and observes that Surrey's and Sackville and Norton's uses of it were equally unprecedented. Despite Surrey's innovation, Elizabethan translators of classical heroic verse – Phaer, Stanyhurst, Chapman, *et al.* – went right on using hexameters, fourteeners, and heroic couplets or experimenting with quantitative verse. Another verse form, the sonnet, is Kurt Schlüter's subject in 'The Influence of the Greek Prayer Hymn on the English Renaissance Sonnet' (*Anglia*). Schlüter observes that the sonnet is usually treated as a genre rather than as a verse form, that is, as being of the order of the ballad and the elegy rather than of rhyme royal and the Spenserian stanza. As a non-classical form, the sonnet played an important role in loosening the ties between genres and metrical forms. The sonnet should thus be studied, the author urges, 'from its various generic points of view', and the ancient hymn as it was imitated by poets in the Renaissance is a good starting point. Sonnets by Daniel, Drummond, Sidney, Donne, and Bartholomew Griffin are examined for their hymnic elements before the author moves on to post-Renaissance sonneteers such as Keats, Poe, and Clare; the last few pages seem ill-fitted to an essay on Renaissance poetry. One finishes the article not quite sure what has just been proven.

The poets dealt with in the remaining articles range chronologically from Googe to Daniel and Drayton and alphabetically from Churchyard to Tofte. J. D. Alsop argues for his subject's independence from his model in 'The Sixth Eclogue of Baptista Mantuan and the Elizabethan Poet Barnabe Googe' (*CahiersE*); surely he was never 'Baptista Mantuan', but Baptista Spagnuoli, called 'the Mantuan'. Googe and his contemporaries have always been patronized (except by Yvor Winters) and it is nice to see someone making even modest claims for his modest talents. Another rehabilitation job is done by D. E. L. Crane, on Stanyhurst's notorious translation of Virgil[33]. In a lively piece of close analysis, Crane demonstrates that the maligned Stanyhurst is often nearer to 'the heart of Vergil's meaning' than many other translators. Douglas and Surrey are omitted without comment, but from Phaer onwards, they have sometimes captured Virgil's urbanity (too frequently rendering it anodyne), but missed his local intensities. Stanyhurst went for those at all cost, producing in the process 'some of the strangest poetry in the language'. Phrases like 'the fissiparous quality [of the hexameter] in English' and 'the full-bellied pleasure

---

33. In *Studies in Seventeenth-Century Literature, History and Bibliography: Festschrift for Professor T. A. Birrell on the Occasion of his Sixtieth Birthday*, ed. by G. A. M. Janssens and F. G. A. M. Aarts. Costerus N.S. 46. Rodopi. pp. vii + 268. Fl60.

in emphatic sound' and 'an exploration of what natively the English language might be made to do' hint that Stanyhurstitis may be contagious. But why not? It is certainly infectious, and Crane most engagingly charts the pleasures of the disease, as well as documenting Stanyhurst's knowledgeable and careful approach to his task. In a longish piece, 'Two into One: The Unity of George Gascoigne's Companion Poems' (*SP*), Roy T. Eriksen demonstrates how the poems, 'Gascoignes Good Morrow' and 'Gascoignes Good Nyghte', 'imitate God's plan of regeneration through structural analogies'. They are thus an early contribution to a kind of religious lyric which was to be developed later by poets like Herbert and Vaughan.

Another of those endearing mid-Elizabethans, Thomas Churchyard, did not p blish his first collection of verse until he was over fifty. *Churchyardes Chippes* (1575) contains, among other things, three 'tragedies'. William M. Schutte shows, in 'Thomas Churchyard's "Dollfull Discourse" and the Death of Lady Katherine Grey' (*SCJ*), not only that the piece is a memorial to that important and pathetic lady, but that it is based upon a manuscript account of the Countess's death. As granddaughter of Henry VIII's sister Mary, she had a very strong claim to the succession, and her secret marriage in 1561 displeased Elizabeth, who had it annulled; she lived under house arrest until her death in 1568. Schutte helpfully prints the text of the manuscript and appends passages from Churchyard's poem which illustrate his methods of adaptation. Churchyard's connections with Lady Katherine's husband, Edward Seymour, Earl of Hertford, son of the Protector Somerset, account for his knowledge of the manuscript. An amazing story about that same Earl of Hertford and another poet's place in it is told by John Pitcher in 'Samuel Daniel, the Hertfords, and a Question of Love' (*RES*). The old Earl seems to have been a generous patron to Daniel. Was he so to old Churchyard who, still around in 1602, dedicated a work to Hertford that year?

In ' "Sacred Bards" and "wise Druides" ': Drayton and his Archetype of the Poet' (*ELH*) Geoffrey G. Hiller observes that Drayton was virtually alone among English poets before the eighteenth century, not just in admiring the Druids and bards (which he carefully distinguished) and seeing them as archetypes, but in even referring to them. Druids are not mentioned in *The Faerie Queene*, for example. Vincent F. Petronella examines the notion of 'Double Ecstasy in Drayton's *Endimion and Phoebe*' (*SEL*), with a mass of learned allusion to Neoplatonism, especially Marsilio Ficino's works. It is heavy going, but Drayton was clearly into all that, and so must we be too, I fear, if we are to read him aright. Petronella, however, is fearless in the presence of the four frenzies and the Three Graces, so a mere double ecstasy is workaday stuff.

Finally, two titbits. In a curious volume, half in English, half in Italian, *The Renaissance in Ferrara and its European Horizons*[34], Glyn Pursglove reveals that minor sonneteer Robert Tofte translated the first three cantos of Matteo Boiardo's *Orlando Innamorato*. The translation appeared in 1598, bearing the initials 'R.T.' on the title-page. Tofte's career is sketched and his interest in literary things Italian noted. T. G. Holt publishes a letter in which passing

34. *The Renaissance in Ferrara and its European Horizons/Il Rinascimento a Ferrara e i suoi orizzonti europei*, ed. by J. Salmons and W. Moretti. UWales/Girasole. pp. xxxii + 332. £14.95.

reference is made to 'Southey on Southwell' (*N&Q*). The letter-writer quotes the poet laureate recommending Southwell's 'beautiful productions'.

(e) Prose

Sidney apart, 1984 was not a vintage year for later-sixteenth-century prose (1985 promises better), but it was not a bad one either. Lyly, Lodge, and Nashe among the prose-fiction writers are represented, and minor stalwarts like Harvey and Puttenham make an appearance. The only edition I have is a rarity indeed: Ulpian Fulwell's *Ars Adulandi; or, The Art of Flattery*[35] of 1576, edited by Roberta Buchanan. This good, scholarly edition of a neglected satirical dialogue shows what Salzburg can come up with, and could come up with more often if they were more discriminating. This edition originated in a Ph.D. thesis, like so many others, but the author has pruned it of details about the text and printing, and streamlined the biographical introduction to give us a sensible, *readable* book. The text of the dialogue is in modern spelling, generously spaced; a brisk introduction provides a summary biography, the context of the work (conflict between burghers and bishop in Wells, Fulwell's birthplace), a critical essay. (A charming misprint (p. xxii) has the Queen granting the townspeople a 'character' rather than a charter.) The text is followed by a hundred pages of commentary. This volume deserves wider exposure than it is likely to get in the expensive, inaccessible series in which it appears. I am glad to have been introduced to Fulwell's 'eighth liberal science' in such pleasant fashion.

Apart from the two following articles on prose fiction generally, the items that remain, including two books, are on single authors. R. S. White undertakes a 'geological examination of the development of romantic comedy from its immediate literary precursors in the "golden world" of Elizabethan romance' in 'Metamorphosis by Love' (*RES*). It is therefore only the first section of his article that concerns us here; the rest is on plays of Lyly, Greene, and Shakespeare. This is a long article, but justifiably so, as it covers a lot of ground, clearly and usefully. The 'metamorphosis by love' motif, common to so much romance and the drama that derived in part from it, is anchored in Ovid and then traced in verse and prose works by Sidney, Spenser, Greene, Lodge, and Marston. A. C. Hamilton also takes a broad view in 'Elizabethan Prose Fiction and Some Trends in Recent Criticism' (*RenQ*). Beginning with observations on prose romance's extensiveness in time and place, Elizabethan prose fiction's neglect by successive critical schools, and its misfortune in being succeeded by the novel, Hamilton argues that the poverty is in literary criticism, not Elizabethan fiction. *Pace* many critics, the latter was only succeeded, not superseded, by the novel. Hamilton here backs away from his earlier belief that reader-response criticism might be able to account for the genre's defining characteristics. All methodologies are too 'academic', too given to 'relentless rationalizing' to be capable of responding to the directness, simplicity, and unlearnedness of romance. But there may be hope in such trends as the 'depriviieging' of certain 'literary' works and the extension of 'literature' to include popular fiction, the move 'beyond genre', and the 'assassination of the author'. I think that Hamilton rather dilutes his argument at the end by looking

---

35. *Ars Adulandi; or, The Art of Flattery*, by *Ulpian Fulwell*, ed. by Roberta Buchanan. SSELER 109. USalz. lxxxii + 247. $25.50.

hopefully in too many new directions at once, but his essay is a reminder of that large, neglected body of immensely popular Elizabethan writing, ripe for rereading.

Thomas Lodge at long last gets his due, in a substantial French *thèse d'état* by Eliane Cuvelier[36]. The author's approach is not quite the simple, old, exhaustive *l'homme et l'oeuvre* survey. She sees Lodge as '*témoin de son temps*'. Her interest is thus much the same as that of Lodge's earlier biographers, N. B. Paradise, E. A. Tenney, C. J. Sisson, and Alice Walker, who produced a spatter of monographs some fifty years ago, but her study is far more detailed than theirs were. Lodge's career occupies the first third of the book, then his writings are discussed. Almost equal space is given to the 'literary' works – plays, prose fiction, poetry – and to the non-fiction – pamphlets, medical treatises, devotional tracts, translations. Lodge emerges, in this study, as much a minor moralist and philosopher as a minor poet, dramatist, and romancer. The 'literary' works suffer somewhat by this equal treatment, and sententious tracts of little interest then or now are given disproportionate attention. Nevertheless, this is the first – and perhaps only, forever – major comprehensive study of Lodge's works, and would be dubbed 'standard' if ever it were to be translated and thus made more accessible. Only if it were, and Lodge were to be properly edited, even selectively, might 'the author of *Rosalynde*' ever stand clear of the Elizabethan undergrowth and the Shakespearean shadow, in his own write, for fair appraisal. John L. Selzer valiantly urges 'The Achievement of Lodge's *Robin the Devil*' (*TSLL*), opening with A. C. Hamilton's just claim that Elizabethan fiction is neglected. Selzer is too eager, if well meaning, and Lodge's curious tale can't stand the heat. Nor can this article: Robert of Normandy does not murder his tutor by poison, it is the tutor's son who is so disposed of; the tutor has his throat cut. The date of *Rosalynde* is 1590, not 1591. The legend does not 'derive from' the story of Sir Gowther which, as Karl Breul showed a century ago, belongs to a different branch, with a Breton *lai* behind it. *Robin the Devil* is, we are told, both 'interesting and effective' (p. 20) and 'effective and interesting' (p. 31). 'Lodge's Protestant tale' (p. 24) is an odd description for one written by a Catholic and deriving ultimately from a medieval saint's legend and immediately from the *Croniques de Normandie*, from which Lodge must have got some of his details and which he must have known in a sixteenth-century French edition; Selzer doesn't mention it. The final agony is the attempt to insinuate a likeness between Lodge's homiletic potboiler and *The Faerie Queene* and *Arcadia*.

A full-scale literary biography is an event any time. Charles Nicholl's *A Cup of News: The Life of Thomas Nashe*[37] is such a work and is gratefully received. Here, in 340-plus pages are all our Nashes. The author hypothesizes, fantasizes, speculates, but this is a serious, carefully researched, well-written book. Much of it is familiar, and as dubious as ever: the School of Night business, for instance. Faint-hearts are bowled over: 'the character of Moth in *Loves Labors Lost* is an unmistakable portrait of [Nashe]' (p. 203). Or, 'Nashe may

36. *Thomas Lodge: Témoin de son temps (c. 1558–1625)*, by Eliane Cuvelier. Collection Etudes Anglaises 85. Didier. pp. 574. Ffr 370.

37. *A Cup of News: The Life of Thomas Nashe*, by Charles Nicholl. RKP. pp. xiv + 342. £14.95.

be said to have made the 1590s his own' (p. 1). Well, yes, but so may a few others be said to have done. Nicholl has written a highly readable book, scholarly enough to lay claim to being *the* book on Nashe, entertaining enough to be read for its own sake by those who don't know Robert Greene from Gabriel Harvey, Great Yarmouth from Saffron Walden, Jack Wilton from a red herring. Illustrations, documents, extensive notes, and a bibliography lend weight, Nashe himself the levity, Nicholl a judicious mix. One will still want to have G. R. Hibbard's standard critical study (*YW* 43.159–60) at hand though when assessing Nashe's literary achievement. Too grave (and too long) is Mihoko Suzuki's ' "Signiorie ouer the Pages": The Crisis of Authority in Nashe's *The Unfortunate Traveller*' (*SP*). Maybe it is true that 'the omnipresent crisis of authority that engenders chaos and violence in *The Unfortunate Traveller* arises precisely from Nashe's preoccupation with man's fallen state of exile, a state caused by a primal act of filial disobedience'. Maybe. I wonder how many readers of Nashe's extravaganza have suspected any such thing. Shorter and much more modest is J. J. M. Tobin's 'Nashe and *Othello*' (*N&Q*) in which further possible echoes of the former are found in the latter.

Richard A. McCabe joins the fashionable ranks of the Lewis-bashers at the outset of a long, summarizing piece on 'Wit, Eloquence, and Wisdom in *Euphues: The Anatomy of Wit*' (*SP*). Poor old C. S. Lewis, how he is patronized nowadays! His impact is measurable by the number of times critics feel obliged to put him down as an opening gambit. To be fair, McCabe's point is that eloquence and wit, dissociated from wisdom in the character of Euphues, are re-united with it in him at the end, in a realization of the humanist ideal. Implicitly, and rightly, McCabe is arguing too for the necessity of reading the appended letters, omitted in some modern editions and ignored in many discussions; they are integral to the *Anatomy*, it is unfinished without them.

'A Reference to the *Facetiae* of Poggio Bracciolini in Gabriel Harvey's *An Advertisement for Papp-Hatchett, and Martin Mar-prelate*' shows, argues Joseph S. Salemi (*N&Q*), that Harvey not only knew Poggio's collection well, but probably had his own copy of it at hand as he wrote. Frank Whigham finds 'A Lacuna in Puttenham's *Arte of English Poesie*' (*ELN*), in which a paragraph, at least, introducing the rhetorical figure *paragon* seems to be missing. George Buchanan may well have had in mind Robert Henryson's version of the fable of 'The Lion and the Mouse' when he alluded to the fable in his satirical vernacular prose piece, *Chameleon*, of about 1570, suggests Sally Mapstone (*N&Q*); the dates of several prints of Henryson's *Fables* (1569/70, 1571) lend strong support. Buchanan is not known primarily as a vernacular prose author, but having mentioned him, I should note the short survey of recent work on him by Alasdair A. MacDonald (*ES*). R. J. Fehrenbach introduces and edits '*A Letter Sent by Maydens of London* (1567)' (*ELR*), a spirited if traditional reply to Edward Hake's criticism of city female servants in *The Mery Meeting of Maydens in London*, now lost. The pamphlet's detailed legal knowledge suggests, however, that its author was a man; it makes an interesting companion-piece to Isabella Whitney's *Letter* published the same year, discussed by Betty Travitsky in her article in the same journal (see above). Naseeb Shaheen corrects some 'Misconceptions about the Geneva Bible' (*SB*), such as that it was immediately popular from its first publication in 1560, that most editions were printed in roman type rather than black-letter for the reader's ease, and that it was principally a Puritan's Bible. The last point is especially significant: many Anglican divines used the Geneva, including Authorized Version translator Lancelot Andrewes – even *after* 1611. Even Laud used it. Finally, Bennett A. Brockman (*ELN*) shows that the otherwise unrecorded 'tonsword' in Robert Laneham's letter about Captain Cox and the Earl of Leicester's 1575 Kenilworth entertainment is Laneham's phonological contraction of 'two-hand sword'; that prodigious weapon fits the swashbuckling Cox. And that is my final swash.

Shakespeare

R. V. HOLDSWORTH, RUSSELL JACKSON, DAVID DANIELL and PAUL DEAN

This chapter has the following sections: 1. Editions; 2. Textual Matters; 3. Biography and Background; 4. Shakespeare in the Theatre; 5. General Criticism; 6. Individual Plays. Sections 1 and 2 are by R. V. Holdsworth, Section 4 is by Russell Jackson, Sections 3, 5, and 6 are by David Daniell. Paul Dean contributes reviews of material on the history plays in Sections 5 and 6.

1. Editions

This year's main event has been the launch of the NCaS under the general editorship of Philip Brockbank. Five titles have appeared, each prepared by an established scholar, cheaply priced, and issued simultaneously in hardback and paper[1]. CUP's aim of replacing its antiquated New Shakespeare series, which goes back to 1921 and took forty years to finish, looks like being excellently fulfilled. Each text is freshly edited and its foundations re-examined. A brief 'Note on the Text' indicates the choice of copy-text and the basic policies of normalizing and collation; this is supplemented by a fuller 'Textual Analysis' placed at the back. The foot-of-page collations and commentaries are generally economical and informative, omitting the unhelpful detailing of orthographic variants and rejected emendations, and avoiding the digressive fussing to which the Arden Shakespeares are sometimes prone. The introductions, though shorter than those of the later Ardens (they average some fifty pages), find space not only for careful critical analyses and full discussions of questions of sources and dating, but for detailed attention to the history and the challenges of the play in performance. Illustrations, including sketches by C. Walter Hodges reconstructing the possible contemporary staging of certain scenes, are liberally provided, and two-page reading lists, in some cases with evaluative comments, appear at the end. As these lists will rapidly date, editors will presumably be able to overhaul them at each re-issue.

On the negative side, it is a shame not to have an index of glossed words, a valuable feature of the OS and Revels series, and it must be said that not all of the illustrations are equally called for. Whole pages, for example, are taken up by Holman Hunt's painting of Bianca, a 1597 engraving of Richard II, and a playbill for Garrick's *Romeo*, none of which earns its place. More seriously,

1. All NCaS. CUP. *The Taming of the Shrew*, ed. by Ann Thompson. pp. xiii + 190. hb £15, pb £3.50. *King Richard II*, ed. by Andrew Gurr. pp. xiv + 226. hb £15, pb £2.95. *Romeo and Juliet*, ed. by G. Blakemore Evans. pp. xiv + 249. hb £15, pb £2.95. *A Midsummer Night's Dream*, ed. by R. A. Foakes. pp. xii + 148. hb £15, pb £2.95. *Othello*, ed. by Norman Sanders. pp. xiii + 209. hb £15, pb £2.95.

the decision in a modern-spelling edition to conserve 'forms that appear to be expressive and characteristically Shakespearean' (General Editor's preface) not only produces a scattering of off-putting archaic spellings but is inconsistently applied. Thus, in the *Romeo* volume, 'aleven' and 'cur'sy' are retained, and then have to be glossed, while 'lanthorne' and 'murther' are modernized; in *Richard II* 'Bullingbrook' and 'Bristow' are kept but 'Callice' becomes 'Calais'; and in the *Shrew* 'Petruchio' and 'Litio' (actually more often 'Lisio' in F) are so spelled, although these forms are merely Elizabethan transliterations of what in modern Italian would be 'Petruccio' and 'Licio'. The more radical programme of modernizing advocated by Stanley Wells in *Modernizing Shakespeare's Spelling* (1979) and *Re-editing Shakespeare*, reviewed below, is preferable to such arbitrary concessions to tradition.

Ann Thompson in the *Shrew* had the daunting job of following close upon H. J. Oliver's good Oxford edition (1982) and Brian Morris's excellent Arden (1981), but her own stands up well. She favours a date of 'in or about 1590' but wisely does not press the meagre external evidence, opting instead to explore the resemblances and contrasts which link her play to *The Comedy of Errors* and *The Two Gentlemen*. She writes cogently on Shakespeare's dovetailing of literary sources and folk-lore, provides a commentary which is often critically as well as semantically illuminating, adds helpful appendixes on the music and the staging of the Induction's second scene, and offers a notably thorough analysis of the text, endorsing the view that the copy for F was a transcript embodying a cut version of the play, and deciding that '*A Shrew* derives from a version of *The Shrew* which was not quite the same as the one we now have'. Only her evaluative sections disappoint. The strategy of summarizing other critics' judgements keeps the critical discussion at some distance from the play (Brian Morris is closer and sharper), and attention to the *Shrew* on the stage is limited to interpretations of the central relationship, predictably describing various attempts to soften or play up its unpalatable aspects, and oddly ignoring Jonathan Miller's brilliant 1980 production for the BBC.

Andrew Gurr's *Richard II* is also outstanding. He argues convincingly for a date of 1595, despite an overconfident belief that Sir Edward Hoby's letter of that year refers either to the right Richard or to a play, and he is illuminating on the sources, giving lengthy excerpts in appendixes, and showing that Shakespeare's use of them 'depended more on dramatic form and the principle of balance than on any political predisposition'. The sections on the original and subsequent staging are particularly valuable (John Barton's 1973 RSC production alone gets three detailed pages) and the critical discussion usefully corrects Walter Pater's influential notion of Richard as tragic actor-poet. Gurr's textual policy may prove more controversial. He prefers Q1 against F on the grounds that F 'shows playhouse influences', but such influences are not necessarily non-authorial, and the introduction of eighteen emendations solely to smooth out metre looks back alarmingly to Pope, from whom some of them derive. There is a mistake on p. 6 where the abortive Essex coup is dated 8 September 1601 rather than 8 February.

In his *Romeo and Juliet* G. Blakemore Evans scores heavily over Brian Gibbons's Arden (1980), where stage history is ignored, by devoting nearly half his introduction to this topic. He offers a scene-by-scene analysis of problems of staging, examines post-Restoration adaptations (not just cuts and additions, but scenery and costuming), and charts the slow return of

Shakespeare's play, stopping at 1960 with Franco Zeffirelli's production at the Old Vic. He is also very thorough on the date, advancing new evidence for the second half of 1596, and on the sources, giving extracts from Arthur Brooke's *Romeus* in a thirty-page appendix, and showing how in Shakespeare's compressed time-scheme the lovers become 'swept along by the apparently overwhelming rush and pressure of events'. Q2, the copy-text, is held to be set directly from foul papers, not an annotated copy of Q1, though Q1 despite its 'badness' is reasonably allowed to donate several stage directions as well as three and a half lines of dialogue and eighteen substantive readings. The weakness of this edition is the notes. These are full of mechanical paralleling, reductive paraphrases (it would be better to be told nothing at all than that 'Ancient damnation' means 'Cursed old woman'), and redundant glosses: 'wedded' (married) and 'fearful' (timorous) are explained, as are 'long sword', 'on pain of torture', and, astonishingly, 'doth'. Not surprisingly, Evans requires a hefty 'Supplementary Notes' at the back.

R. A. Foakes's *A Midsummer Night's Dream* is perhaps the slightest edition of the batch, and is inevitably overshadowed by Harold Brooks's monumental Arden of 1979, but it is compact, elegant, and unfailingly sensible, cautious if not sceptical about the play's composition for an aristocratic occasion, illuminating on fairy-lore, and tactfully poised 'between extreme interpretations of the play in terms of sadomasochism as against simple innocence and charm, or in terms of the release of imagination as against the controls of reason'. The Arden's silence on staging is remedied in a survey which takes in the operatic and balletic expansions of previous centuries (Charles Kean's 1856 production had ninety fairies) as well as the revolutionary back-to-the-text interpretations of Harley Granville-Barker and Peter Brook.

Norman Sanders' *Othello* is altogether less satisfactory, which is doubly unfortunate in view of the weaknesses of M. R. Ridley's Arden. The introduction is adequate though dull, offering familiar information on sources and date (Stanley Wells, *TLS*, 20 July 1984, has since established a *terminus a quo* of September 1603), and a routine survey of critical disagreement. The section on stage history scampers through too many productions, or rather character-performances, without pausing to look at any in depth, and there are some errors and oversights in the notes. 'Atone' (reconcile) at IV.i.221, for example, needs glossing, and for 'squire' at IV.ii.144 the context surely demands the sense 'pimp, pander', as often at this date, rather than the pale (and poorly attested) sense 'fellow'. All this is footling, however, compared with Sanders' treatment of the text. He believes that F was set from a manuscript, not from Q1 (a view confirmed in *SQ* (1983) by Gary Taylor), and that the two texts embody 'two Shakespearean versions ... Shakespeare's first version of the play (behind Q1) and his own transcription of it (behind F)'. Incomprehensibly, the editorial corollary of this hypothesis, the ceding of priority to F in all cases of indifferent variation, is swept aside in Sanders' own editorial procedure. He puts together a text which is 'eclectic ... arrived at by treating each pair of variants as a separate entity'. The result is chaos come again, a play which by Sanders' own reckoning Shakespeare never wrote. At I.iii.134 Sanders prefers F's 'Accidents by Flood and Field' to Q1's 'accident of flood and field' (the first of the two variants is not collated); four lines later he prefers Q1's 'with it all my trauells Historie' to F's 'portance in my Trauellours historie'. At I.iii.278 Q1's 'With such things else of quality or respect' and F's

'And such things else of qualitie and respect' become 'With such things else of quality and respect'. At IV.i.130 from Q1's 'this bauble, by this hand she fals thus' and F's 'the Bauble, and falls me thus' he concocts 'this bauble and, by this hand, falls me thus'. Hundreds of similar cases of haphazard conflation could be cited. Sanders observes that 'It is impossible in the present state of knowledge to be dogmatic' about *Othello*'s textual transmission, but that does not exempt an editor from the need to stick to the logic of his own theory.

The Oxford Shakespeare, launched in 1982 but dormant last year, has resumed with *Titus Andronicus* and *Julius Caesar*[2], and the original three plays now join them in paperback[3]. Two of the Oxfords, *Julius Caesar* and *Henry V*, provide fuller editorial material than any of the Cambridge editions, though in the case of the one play the two series at present share, the *Shrew*, Cambridge has the edge. The Oxfords are a little cheaper, but in paperback they are less well produced: the paper is slightly inferior, there is less white space to the page, illustrations threaten to disappear into the spine, and they will not stay open without violence to the binding. Both series are equally at pains to reflect current critical interest in 'the play in performance'.

Eugene M. Waith's *Titus* has some excellent features: a concise but thorough commentary; appendixes which give complete modernized texts of the prose *History of Titus Andronicus* and the ballad 'Titus Andronicus' Complaint'; a notably full discussion of sources which establishes that the order of composition of the three contemporary versions of the story was probably *History* – Shakespeare's play – ballad, weighs the debts to Ovid, Virgil, Seneca, Kyd, and Marlowe, yet preserves a sense of Shakespeare's independence; seven closely argued pages on the Henry Peacham drawing and its problems of authenticity and interpretation; and a discussion of staging which examines Restoration and later adaptation as well as modern productions (not only Peter Brook's of 1955 but Gerald Freedman's of 1967), and interestingly calculates that as many as twenty-seven actors are required to act the original text. Other features are less impressive. The critical discussion is surprisingly brief and unadventurous, and the even briefer account of the text too readily invokes a prompter, acting without Shakespeare's authority, as a reason for rejecting F's divergences from Q1. (In *Re-editing Shakespeare* Stanley Wells is more searching and more cautious.) The weakest section is on the play's authorship, which understates the claim of Peele, whether as reviser, revisee, or co-author, by glancing distantly at only a small sampling of the evidence which favours him, dispersing it through the discussion, and prejudicially referring to the advocates of multiple authorship (who include Dover Wilson, T. W. Baldwin, and J. C. Maxwell, as well as J. M. Robertson) as 'the doubters' who play 'the dangerous game of parallel passages'. In fact the case for the presence of Peele, especially in Act I, has never been adequately controverted, possibly because it is right. There are, too, some arresting links with Nashe, though Waith removes the two which he acknowledges to his

2. Both OS. OUP. *Titus Andronicus*, ed. by Eugene M. Waith. pp. ix + 226. hb £12.95, pb £2.95. *Julius Caesar*, ed. by Arthur Humphreys. pp. ix + 253. hb £12.95, pb £2.50.

3. All OS. OUP. *The Taming of the Shrew*, ed. by H. J. Oliver. pp. 248. pb £2.50. *Henry V*, ed. by Gary Taylor. pp. ix + 330. pb £2.50. *Troilus and Cressida*, ed. by Kenneth Muir. pp. vii + 204. pb £2.95.

section on date. At any event the authorship status of *Titus* will have to be re-examined in the near future after Gary Taylor publishes his study of *1 Henry VI*, in which Nashe and at least one other dramatist besides Shakespeare are given substantial shares.

Arthur Humphreys's *Julius Caesar* is the best Shakespeare edition of the year. The commentary and ninety-page introduction are densely though lucidly detailed, and constantly turn to critical account what less-enterprising editors might have left as mere information. Even the discussion of date, besides assembling and adding to the evidence for 1599, explores how the play is stylistically and thematically as well as chronologically positioned between the histories and the tragedies, just as the section on sources explains how 'Shakespeare vividly filled out what Plutarch drew'. Humphreys compellingly praises the play's 'deeply-felt and responsible realism', placing it 'in the Hegelian tragic category where good struggles not with evil but with incompatible good'. In keeping with such a struggle 'the play bases itself on ambiguities . . . At one pole it shows the Roman ideal of self-mastery, at the other, the vitalities which that mastery cannot repress'. Hence the play's tolerance of seemingly contradictory interpretations, not only by critics but directors: and Humphreys devotes fully twenty-five pages to showing how astonishingly varied the theatrical tradition has been, Brutus, for example, ranging from the 'majestic philosophical stoic' of Thomas Betterton, to 'the perennial liberal' of Orson Welles, 'precipitating calamities even worse than those he seeks to avert', to Trevor Nunn's 'theorizing precursor of Hamlet'. Humphreys also finds room for a painstaking analysis of the Folio text, concluding that the copy was 'a clean scribal transcript of Shakespeare's working papers' which contained theatrical annotation either from, or as a stage towards, the prompt-book, and perhaps some Shakespearean revisions – though he is aware of and accepts the argument of John Jowett noticed below. It is hard to imagine a better edition of *Julius Caesar* appearing, or being needed, for many years to come.

The many other editions of 1984 deserve only the briefest mention. The Macmillan Shakespeare gains *Antony and Cleopatra*[4]. The editors' introduction, though sound, is marred by a pretentious sprinkling of quotations from Yeats and some irritable sniping at A. C. Bradley and Emrys Jones (who is told off for sexism). Their text is out of touch with recent scholarship, printing, for example, F's nonsensical 'ribaudred' at III.x.10 rather than the emendation 'ribald red'. The terrifying William T. Betken and his Other Shakespeare (see *YW* 63.180) have appeared again with *Romeo and Juliet*, ecstatically trumpeted by the blurb as 'the largest . . . most conservative . . . most researched . . . most innovative edition ever published'[5]. It must also be the silliest. Small bits of text are interspersed with notes that are garrulous, jargon-ridden, and sometimes spectacularly wrongheaded, along with a modern paraphrase of brutal ineptitude. 'Hang thee young baggage, disobedient wretch' becomes 'Go hang, young garbage, disobedient bitch'. Bawdy obsesses Betken, who finds it in many undreamt-of places, though not in some obvious ones (e.g.

4. *Antony and Cleopatra*, ed. by Jan McKeith and Richard Adams. MSh. Macmillan. pp. 289. pb £1.95.

5. *Romeo and Juliet*, ed. by William T. Betken. OthS. Bardavon. pp. iv + 531. hb $29.95, pb $12.95.

III.iii.84–90), and has to compile an extra list of it in what he inelegantly but not unaptly calls 'the book's back matter'. It is *Macbeth* s turn next.

An even more irresponsible venture is A. L. Rowse's Contemporary Shakespeare[6], which aims to make 'conventional academic editions . . . unnecessary' by presenting texts 'freed of superfluous difficulties'. These difficulties are 'the rebarbative olde Englishe spelling' of the originals, and their archaic grammar and vocabulary, all of which Rowse will modernize, though 'conservatively'. What one actually gets is a sentimental, anecdotal, self-advertising introduction of two or three pages, no notes or other editorial matter of any kind (even to explain the textual sources), and a text with just enough grammatical tinkering to wreck the metre of the verse, plus a thin and utterly arbitrary scattering of verbal substitutions, some of them more puzzling than the words they replace. An infinitely preferable new series with similar anxieties about intelligibility is Alan Durband's Shakespeare Made Easy[7], 'intended for readers approaching the plays for the first time', which offers a modern-spelling original text (though with no indication of editorial principles or procedure) with a competently idiomatic paraphrase, normally in prose, on the facing page. The introduction gives a brief summary of Shakespeare's life and theatre, followed by a few factual paragraphs on the play; a lively series of quizzes comes at the back. Unfortunately, the paraphrase is strewn with readily avoidable misrenderings ('I cry . . . mercy' in the *Dream* becomes 'Greetings', 'Help me hence' in *Macbeth* 'Help me, please'), the primary text is marred by misprints, and the introductions cannot be trusted (Middleton's *The Witch* 'was published in 1612').

Finally, A. L. Rowse republishes his edition of the Sonnets[8] little changed from the 1964 original, apart from a dedication to Ronald Reagan, a shortened introduction (though it remains long on self-promotional bluster), and the claim, pronounced a certainty, that the Dark Lady was Emilia Lanier. Sonnet readers would be better off with the bare facsimile of the 1609 quarto, published by Nottingham Court Press[9].

2. Textual Matters

Pride of place must go to *Re-Editing Shakespeare for the Modern Reader* by Stanley Wells[10], a crisp, lively, bracingly independent account of some of the problems of Shakespearean editing which Wells has felt impelled to confront afresh in his work as general editor of the Oxford Shakespeare. The book examines three topics: old and modern spelling, emendation, and the editor's

6. All ContS, ed. by A. L. Rowse. UPA. £3.50 each. *King Richard II*. pp. 127. *Romeo and Juliet*. pp. 139. *A Midsummer Night's Dream*. pp. 91. *The Merchant of Venice*. pp. 118. *Julius Caesar*. pp. 122. *As You Like It*. pp. 107. *Hamlet*. pp. 153. *Twelfth Night*. pp. 112. *King Lear*. pp. 151. *Coriolanus*. pp. 157. *The Tempest*. pp. 101.

7. All ShME, ed. by Alan Durband. Hutchinson Educational. £2.25 each. *A Midsummer Night's Dream*. pp. 217. *Henry IV Part One*. pp. 282. *Twelfth Night*. pp. 248. *Macbeth*. pp. 223. *The Tempest*. pp. 220.

8. *Shakespeare's Sonnets: A Modern Edition, with Prose Versions, Introduction and Notes*, ed. by A. L. Rowse. Macmillan. pp. xxv + 311. hb £25, pb £7.95.

9. *Shake-speares Sonnets*. Nottingham Court Press/International Shakespeare Globe Centre. pp. iv + no pagination. £12.50.

10. *Re-Editing Shakespeare for the Modern Reader*, by Stanley Wells. OSS. Clarendon. pp. vii + 131. £15.

responsiveness to his text as one for performance; discussion of each is directed by the author's belief that 'a timorous conservatism', inducing 'a feeble-minded acquiescence in standard practice' and 'an undue subservience to the editorial tradition', has marred many past editors' efforts, and continues to do so. Dealing first with spelling, Wells affirms the value of old-spelling editions, but rebuts in detail the case for their innate superiority over modernized texts put forward by Philip Gaskell, Fredson Bowers, and W. W. Greg. An Elizabethan text's original spelling and punctuation can, Wells shows, limit or obscure its expressiveness quite as damagingly as a modernized version, and stand equally in need of annotation pointing to rhymes, puns, and ambiguities which its accidentals disguise. Wells is particularly critical of modern-spelling editors who, like G. Blakemore Evans, elect 'to preserve a selection of Elizabethan spelling forms that reflect, or may reflect, a distinctive contemporary pronunciation' (*Riverside Shakespeare*, p. 39).

Turning to substantive matters, Wells shows how premature Bowers was in 1954 when he said of Shakespeare's text that 'Just about every emendation has been proposed that is likely to be adopted'. In fact many known cruxes have been inadequately scrutinized and others have not been spotted. This part of Wells's book is full of new solutions to local difficulties, all of them persuasive and some of them brilliant. Two of the most deft and satisfying are 'persuant' for 'perttaunt' in *Love's Labour's Lost* V.ii.67, and, replacing a reading never questioned before, 'figure' for 'vigour' in *Titus Andronicus* IV.ii.108, this being a modernization rather than an emendation. (Waith in the new Oxford edition takes this half-heartedly on board by retaining 'vigour' but glossing 'probably figure'.)

The book's last two chapters concern 'The Editor and the Theatre'. In the first Wells asserts the editor's responsibility 'to make the staging intelligible' to the reader, and explores a succession of cases where editors have been unduly cautious in adding clarifying directions. Wells is particularly engaged by cases where Shakespeare has left it (and may himself have been) unclear as to how certain details of his plays were to be managed in performance, as in failures to mark entries and exits or provide attendants (often too liberally added by editors, none the less), or in stage-direction references to characters who remain without parts, like Innogen in *Much Ado*. Problems of this sort lead to the book's final subject: what to do with those plays, such as *Titus* and *A Midsummer Night's Dream*, where a quarto foul-papers text, with its attendant silences and haziness about staging, is joined by a second in the Folio which has been influenced by actual performance, where the choice is 'not between good and bad, but between one kind of authority and another'. Editors must here ask the hard question: 'Do we prefer the play a little undercooked, perhaps even half-baked, or do we like it in a more finished form, even if a hand other than the author's may have added some of the icing?' A meticulous study of Act I of *Titus*, which J. C. Maxwell in the Arden, siding very much with Q1, viewed as 'not a play with a complicated staging', illustrates how complicated the job of establishing a theatrically realizable text can be, and underpins Wells's contention (which 'may not appeal to everyone') that wherever an editor is faced with variant texts of this kind 'the basic editorial procedure to be followed in a fully edited version for the general reader should be to accept the evidence offered by the Folio that supplements or substantially replaces that offered by the quarto'. An appendix illuminatingly reconstructs the original form of the first act of *Titus*, since even the Q1 version can be shown to contain changes of mind and piecemeal revisions. Everyone interested in Shakespeare will profit from this book. It is much more than an *hors d'oeuvre* to the *Complete Oxford*, though it certainly whets the appetite that way too.

A more unequal achievement is *Play-Texts in Old Spelling*[11], a shockingly overpriced collection of twelve of the papers delivered at a conference on the theory and practice of old-spelling editions of the Renaissance dramatists held at Glendon College, Toronto, as long ago as April 1978. Many of the papers suffer by being severed from the discussions they aimed to launch, and some pay a further penalty because of their delayed arrival into an area of debate which has been transformed in the interval by Stanley Wells's stimulating studies, *Modernizing Shakespeare's Spelling* (1979) and the book reviewed above. Not that the contributors, who are billed as 'committed old-spelling editors', pay much attention to the conference's official subject. The more substantial pieces pursue topics, general and specific, which any editor of a Renaissance play, whatever his or her orthographic intentions, would need to explore, and when old-spelling comes up the reaction is not always delight. The preface, for example, records Stanley Wells as asking 'Who wants to read old-spelling editions except old-spelling editors?', as well as Philip Edwards' confession that 'If it were to do again, I would never do an old-spelling *Massinger*. I would never do an old-spelling edition ... I lost my faith.'

The book nevertheless contains important work. In 'The Editorial Usefulness of Printing House and Compositor Studies' Paul Werstine shows that the three compositors who set William White's 'Newly corrected and augmented' quarto of *Love's Labour's Lost* differed in their spelling preferences according to whether they were setting from manuscript or from print, and that on these grounds the copy for Q is more likely to have been a lost edition than foul papers. Werstine expands his evidence in a lengthy 'Afterword', rebutting in the process the contrary claims of George R. Price (*PBSA*, 1978) and Manfred Draudt (*Lib*, 1981), and ending with the conjecture that 'this first printing may have provided a better, not a worse, text of the play'. His arguments should be read in conjunction with Draudt's subsequent article and the lively exchanges it provoked between Draudt and Stanley Wells and John Kerrigan (*Lib*, 1982–3). In 'Spellbound' Randall McLeod offers a fascinating and disquieting study of 'type-exigent' spellings, such as those dictated by the use of ligatures and kerned letters, which the typography of modern editions, whether in old spelling or not, renders undetectable. Not only may single words be affected (McLeod's examples include variant spellings of 'Cressida' in Q *Troilus* and of the name of Shakespeare himself), but words on either side of them, and even words in adjacent lines. In 'Accidental Evils' Robert Kean Turner is largely concerned with 'illogical, inconsistent, or unnecessary' changes of accidentals in the edition of Massinger by Philip Edwards and Colin Gibson (*YW* 57.146), but his recommended editorial procedure of reconstructing 'how the compositors progressed' also enables him to establish the origin of the Folio's problematic '*Enter Violenta*' in *Twelfth Night* I.v. Richard Morton has a useful

11. *Play-Texts in Old Spelling: Papers from the Glendon Conference*, ed. by G. B. Shand with Raymond C. Shady. AMS Studies in the Renaissance 6. AMSP. pp. ix + 161. £34.95.

discussion of 'Archaic Spellings and the Modern Annotator', in which examples from *King Lear* illustrate the point that the dividing line between substantive and orthographic variants may be hard to fix. Other aspects of the editor's task are treated less successfully. Examining 'Editorial Indications of Stage Business' David Bevington notes many instances of inconsistency and inattentiveness in modern Shakespeare editions, as well as failures to help with insoluble cases, such as where the Second Gravedigger leaves the grave, and then the stage, in *Hamlet* V.i (the Arden editor may now be counted among the defaulters). But some of his proposed additions of directions, for example to indicate the action which accompanies Armado's 'There is remuneration' in *Love's Labour's Lost* III.i.131, and which follows Shallow's 'Will you sit?' in *2 Henry IV* III.ii.94, seem superfluous, and his general position that 'One should not change the *nature* of the copy-text by adding uncharacteristic stage directions' seems inconsistent with such liberality, as well as unduly conservative in itself. In 'The Function of Commentary' Philip Edwards argues that 'editions without commentaries . . . are not imperfect editions; they are not editions at all', and goes on to warn that 'The vices of over-annotation are as bad as the vices of under-annotation', while giving examples of both. He goes astray, however, in urging 'restraint in pointing out sexual innuendoes . . . when so many real difficulties pass by unobserved'. Obscure bits of bawdy, if they are really there, are 'real' difficulties which editors must explain, even if the bawdy seems to them gratuitous, or threatens to turn some commentaries into the 'positive stud-farms' to which Edwards compares them. S. P. Zitner also cautions against 'Excessive Annotation', diagnosing severe symptoms in the Arden *Othello*. However, his use of Glendower's speech about his three victories over Henry in *1 Henry IV* III.i, in order to illustrate the pitfall of importing misleading information from a play's sources, is unconvincing. Zitner reproves the Arden editor for reminding us that Holinshed and John Hardyng attribute Glendower's victories to his 'art magike' and thus implying that the play does too – but it surely does: the speech follows Glendower's claim that he 'can command the devil' and is clearly meant as a boastful proof of this power, as Hotspur assumes when he jeeringly responds by asking how Henry 'scapes . . . agues, in the devil's name'. Annotation is therefore not an indulgence but a duty.

Of more tangential interest is Martin Page's *Britain's Unknown Genius*[12], a short biography of the disintegrator J. M. Robertson. 'Genius' is pitching it a bit high: no one who thought that *A Midsummer Night's Dream* is the canon's single purely Shakespearean text, and that *The Comedy of Errors* is not only not by Shakespeare but by, of all people, Marlowe, seems worthy of the title. Page does remind us, though, that Robertson's dozen books and scores of articles on Shakespeare – incredibly just a fraction of his polymathic labours – did include valuable non-distintegrationist work: *Montaigne and Shakspere* (1897), for example, drew attention to an important and neglected influence, *The Baconian Heresy* (1913) helped to kill the fantasy that Shakespeare was Bacon, and *The Problem of 'Hamlet'* (1919) shaped T. S. Eliot's famous strictures on the play in his essay 'Hamlet and his Problems', which was originally a review of Robertson's book. And quite apart from that, one or two

12. *Britain's Unknown Genius: An Introduction to the Life-Work of John Mackinnon Robertson*, by Martin Page. South Place Ethical Society. pp. 112. pb £2.25.

of Robertson's disintegrative hunches look like being justified. D. J. Lake and M. P. Jackson have recently revived the idea of dual authorship in *Timon of Athens*; Jackson has claimed two strata of composition in *Titus*; and Gary Taylor argues in a forthcoming book for multiple authorship in *1 Henry VI* and against the complete authenticity of the extant text of *Measure for Measure*. Robertson is the star buffoon, 'the prince of disintegrators', in Samuel Schoenbaum's maliciously jocular book *Internal Evidence and Elizabethan Dramatic Authorship* (1966). This verdict may soon appear a little unfair, a symptom of the intemperate reaction against the use of internal evidence in authorship matters that the follies of Robertson and his followers contrived to provoke.

SQ has seven relevant articles and notes. The most important is Sidney Thomas's brief but hard-hitting assault on the new multiple-text theory of *Lear*, in which he concedes that 'there are variants which must be the result of Folio revision', but finds 'no incontrovertible evidence, either internal or external, that Shakespeare at any time after his initial creation of *Lear* deliberately set out to reshape it into a new play'. For future Shakespeares to print both versions separately, as the Oxford editors propose, is a disastrous strategy. This essay raises some awkward objections to the two-text theory to which its adherents will need to respond. Discussing the anti-Shakespeare jibe 'an upstart Crow, beautified with our feathers' Peter Berek supports that view that Robert Greene is sneering at Shakespeare as a plagiarist, and perhaps reviser, of other dramatists' work, rather than as an actor, by quoting Thomas Newton's preface to R. Smythe's posthumous *Strange, Lamentable, and Tragical Histories* (1577), where Newton insists that Smythe should receive full credit for his work; Newton has no wish to be 'lyke Esopes Crow to vsurpe and iette abroade, deckte with the Feathers of other bewtifuller Byrds'. Newton's use of the image should, Berek believes, encourage re-examination of the authorship of the early plays. William Rossky argues, obviously rightly, that Enobarbus's 'Hush, here comes Antony' (*Antony and Cleopatra* I.ii.79), following the entrance of Cleopatra, is neither a 'nonsensical' error in F (M. R. Ridley, Arden), nor an actual mistake by Enobarbus because the lovers have donned each other's clothes as proposed by Gordon P. Jones (*SQ*, 1983), but a typical Enobarbian barb aimed at Antony's unmanly subjection. Rossky might have added that the joke may turn on a Jacobean fad for referring to wives by their husbands' names satirized by Jonson in *Epicoene* IV.iii and *The Devil Is an Ass* IV.ii. Karl P. Wentersdorf persuasively cites a favourite Shakespearean image-cluster, of no less than seventeen components, to argue that F's 'panyn' in *Twelfth Night* V.i.201, almost always emended to 'pavin' or 'pavan', is either an error for or a spelling of 'paynim', a solution first adopted by Alexander Pope but discarded in this century. By contrast Judith Rosenheim's interpretation of F's 'Some run from brakes of Ice, and answer none' (*Measure for Measure* II.i.39) is heavy-handed and sometimes silly (she reads 'none' as a pun on 'nun'); nevertheless she contrives to strengthen the case for understanding 'brakes' as 'breaks' and to stave off emendation (such as 'vice' for 'Ice'). René Graziani finds sporadic numerological patterning in the Sonnets which vindicates their order in the 1609 Quarto. He airs some tortuously recherché notions, but some of his points, such as Sonnet 12 opening with the counting of a clock, and Sonnet 60 with an allusion to minutes, seem beyond coincidence. Michael Warren defends the Folio version of *King Lear*

IV.vi.83–4, 'No, they cannot touch me for crying. / I am the King himself', where instead of 'crying' Q, followed by all modern editors, has 'coyning'. Fortified by the two-text theory and Lear's tendency to weep, he sees 'crying' as a Shakespearean revision which brings into play the idea of touching for the king's evil. Warren counters the objection that 'coyning' fits more smoothly into the context by pointing out that Lear's ensuing speeches contain 'matter and impertinency mixed'. A problem of this kind of defence is that any gibberish could be so justified; and Warren rather plays down the appropriateness of 'touch' to coining, since to touch metal was to test its quality. Presumably we are to view the fact that both words begin with the same letter and share four others in the same order as what suggested the replacement rather than as coincidence, but misreading still seems the more likely explanation.

In 'Ligature Shortage and Speech-Prefix Variation in *Julius Caesar*' (*Lib*) John Jowett ingeniously disproves the idea that the Folio compositors' temporary switchings from '*Cassi.*' to '*Cass.*' or '*Cas.*' in the speech-prefixes for Cassius indicate the presence of passages inserted during a revision. The changes were, he shows, due to shortages of *ssi* ligatures by which both compositors were periodically hampered. Jowett's discovery has immediate critical relevance, for it throws light on the notorious problem in Act IV, where Brutus first announces Portia's death to Cassius (a '*Cass.*' or '*Cas.*' passage) and later claims ignorance of it ('*Cassi.*'). The evidence that the first of these passages was textually distinct in the compositors' copy, and thus intended to replace the second (which was inadvertently left uncancelled), therefore disappears, and the better course may be to accept the contradiction as deliberate, and make sense of F as it stands. R. F. Fleissner (*ShakS*, 1983) rakes over the arguments in favour of retaining F's 'a Table of greene fields' in *Henry V*, reminding us that Hippocrates cited a green face as a death-sign, and that 'table' could mean 'picture'. He adds nothing of substance, and he sidesteps the question of F's improbably squashed syntax and the fact that the Hostess is talking about a nose not a face. The case looks dismal when set beside that for emendation on Theobaldian lines (a babbl'd, a tattl'd, or a talk'd) made by F. W. Bateson in *The Scholar-Critic* (1972), a discussion which Fleissner ignores. In *ShStud* Mariko Ichikawa extends the work of E. A. J. Honigmann (*YW* 57.110) on the relative positioning of entry directions and entry speeches ('Here comes X', etc.) in Shakespeare by tabulating all the examples of their co-occurrence and dividing them into types. She concludes that Shakespeare 'had unconsciously made vague rules' to determine whether speech or direction should come first, and, less novelly, that book-keepers 'moved up many entry directions when they prepared prompt-books'. In a two-part essay in *ShN* M. W. A. Smith demonstrates the inadequacy of A. Q. Morton's stylometric case for the textual integrity of *Pericles*.

In *N&Q* R. W. F. Martin is unable to make sense of Petruchio's 'a sleeve . . . carv'd like an apple Tart? / Heers snip, and nip, and cut, and slish and slash, / Like to a Censor in a barbers shoppe' (*The Taming of the Shrew* IV.iii.88–91), and wishes to change 'Censor' to 'scissor', in the belief that Shakespeare wrote 'Cizor', where all editors (including Ann Thompson in NCaS) have understood 'censer'. Graphically implausible, and requiring a singular form which would be unique in the canon and is very rare outside it (*OED* gives just two examples), this also makes a dull and somewhat confused reading, since scissors would self-evidently perform the snipping of the sleeve, and in the pseudo-parallelism of 'like an apple-tart ... Like to a scissor' object and instrument become jumbled. More compellingly, Thomas Clayton and Malcolm Pittock (*N&Q*) independently urge the reinstatement of 'to' in 'Edmund the base / Shall to th' legitimate' (*King Lear* I.ii.20–1), the reading of both Q and F, in preference to the standard emendation 'top'. Both find 'greater aptness and point' in the unemended version, Clayton usefully adding that

> In a passage edited and enlarged in the Folio there is nothing to suggest that the Quarto's 'too' was *not* intelligible and correct, and the Folio's 'to'th'Legitimate' may therefore be taken to confirm the authority (as far as it went) of the Quarto's 'tooth'legitimate' and to clarify it.

Examining the influence of Shakespeare's close knowledge of Thomas Nashe on *Othello*, J. J. M. Tobin (*N&Q*) argues that the passage in *Pierce Pennilesse* concerning 'the Indians, that have store of gold & pretious stones ... yet are ignorant of their value' is the source of the corresponding lines in the play, which all but confirms Q's 'Indian' against F's 'Iudean' in the well-known crux. Also in *N&Q* R. V. Holdsworth notes that a parallel in Middleton's *More Dissemblers besides Women* to Touchstone's 'It is the right butter-women's rank to market' (*As You Like It* III.ii.98) helps to defend F's 'ranke' against at least one of the emendations which are sometimes proposed.

Several reviews of earlier work make important contributions in their own right. Gary Taylor (*RES*) details a host of ways in which Mark Eccles's New Variorum *Measure for Measure* (1980) is 'both fallible and selective'; in particular he illuminates doubts about the play's date and the authenticity of the Boy's song to Mariana which the edition suppresses. Taylor subjects Antony Hammond's Arden *Richard III* (1981) to equally sharp-eyed inspection in the same journal. He exposes serious shortcomings in the introduction, corrects and supplements the commentary at several points, and demonstrates that Hammond accepts Q readings 'without the guidance of any discernible principle'. G. Blakemore Evans (*MLR*) prints substantial lists of errata for the Arden (1982) and Oxford (1982) editions of *Troilus and Cressida*; in *SQ* he notes errors and inconsistencies in the Oxford *Shrew* (1982). Paul Werstine records detailed disagreements with Stanley Wells and Gary Taylor's *Modernizing Shakespeare's Spelling with Three Studies in the Text of 'Henry V'* (1979) in *ShakS* (1983), and with Eleanor Prosser's *Shakespeare's Anonymous Editors: Scribe and Compositor in the Folio Text of '2 Henry IV'* (1981) in *MP*. Antony Hammond (*Lib*) notes errors in Peter W. M. Blayney's identification of damaged types in his *The Texts of 'King Lear' and their Origins* (1982), sufficient in his view to raise 'grave doubt about the detail of the reconstruction' of the setting of Q1.

Finally, a handy caution against emendatory zeal is supplied by Eric Rasmussen (*HamSt*). Dissatisfied with either 'Polacks' or 'pole-axe' as the meaning of Qq 'pollax' and F 'Pollax' in 'He smot the sleaded pollax on the ice' (*Hamlet* I.i.66, Q2), he proposes a misreading of 'Pollux', Castor's twin. Emboldened by this notion, and finding that it leaves 'sleaded' and 'ice' somewhat marooned, he goes on to muse whether the line should really read 'He smote the dreaded Pollux on the eyes'. While using the edition for references, he does not mention Harold Jenkins's masterly discussion of the crux in the Arden *Hamlet*, and no wonder.

3. Biography and Background

One or two sane items this year, before lunacy strikes. Indeed, I start with a most beautiful, and inexpensive, book. Appropriately produced by Kestrel Books, Peter Goodfellow's *Shakespeare's Birds*[13] is nearly a hundred pages of purest delight, in the text certainly, which is full of information and refers to everything in the canon except *King John* and *Pericles*, with *A Midsummer Night's Dream* holding the record for mentions: but even more in the wonderful illustrations by Peter Hayman. A book for a Shakespearean's birthday.

Carol Chillington proposed, in an article in *ELR* in 1980 (*YW* 61.156) from a reading of Henslowe's 'so-called Diary', that Shakespeare did not collaborate on *Sir Thomas More*. Now in her new book[14] she gives a 'documentary life', 'a collection of manuscripts selected and arranged to chronicle the day-to-day operation of one Elizabethan playhouse, the Rose, over the fifteen years of its existence'. She aims, among other things, to 'present these lively documents in such a way as to release the original energy again, to recreate the push and shove of the Elizabethan playhouse'; this objective is well fulfilled, but she gives as well a vivid account of life in London during much of Shakespeare's life. Shakespeare is not, of course, central: but the book is now essential background – for the Burbages, for example, or the *Henry VI* plays, or Will Kemp. Recommended.

In *SQ* two Public Record Office scholars, D. L. Thomas and N. E. Evans, open up, importantly, the startling and unexplained decline of John Shakespeare after 1576, in 'John Shakespeare in The Exchequer'. In *SJH* Gunter Quarg briefly opens up the Droeshout engraving controversy in 'Gab es eine plastische Vorlage zum Shakespeare-Portrait in der First Folio-Ausgabe?'.

From here it is downhill. I have not, mercifully, seen the revised edition of George Elliott Sweet's book, with a foreword by Erle Stanley Gardner, which, entitled unmissably *Shake-speare: The Mystery* (Vantage), proves apparently that Queen Elizabeth I wrote the plays. But I have seen the book to which the gentle Mr Honey gave eighteen years of his life[15]. It is a big book, 17 cm × 15 cm, beautifully, though privately, produced, and very, very long at 1414 pages. It weighs nearly five pounds. This is only Volume One. Unfortunately, at the mere sight of it my heart sinks and a drowsy numbness pains my sense: the title on the spine reads *The Life, Loves and Achievements of Christopher Marlowe alias Shakespeare*. Calvin Coolidge, the other one who thinks Marlowe wrote Shakespeare, proposed I recall, to excavate in the middle of the River Wye and wondered – this was during the Second World War – why he got so little co-operation from the British. He is now excavating the tomb of Sir Thomas Walsingham. Mr Honey is not a nutter. He is clearly a delightful person, and he is erudite about the last decades of Elizabeth and the first of James, the literature and the happenings, and the views of modern scholars. He is alert to the thousand natural coincidences the flesh is heir to. His main

13. *Shakespeare's Birds*, by Peter Goodfellow, illus. by Peter Hayman. Kestrel (1983). pp. 96. £8.95.

14. *Documents of the Rose Playhouse*, ed. by Carol Chillington Rutter. RevelsCL. ManU. pp. ix + 246. £27.50.

15. *The Life, Loves and Achievements of Christopher Marlowe alias Shakespeare*, by William Honey. MarloweB (1982). pp. xxvi + 1414. £25.

thesis is that Shakespeare, not Marlowe, was killed in the Deptford brawl, and that ... well, the rest is obvious. The book is a marsh of muddled detail, all beautifully indexed. That index, however, does not contain the name Schoenbaum. Here, purest speculation magically transforms into fact. It is all rather sad.

Not sad at all, but arrogant as ever is A. L. Rowse on the Sonnets again in *ContempR*. The piece is entitled 'Shakespeare as Autobiographer', and fans will be delighted to welcome the old chums like Emilia Lanier. My last item does, intentionally, move us into fiction. Telephoned by a television researcher preparing for yet another projected life of Shakespeare, I found myself recommending Anthony Burgess's *Nothing Like the Sun* (1964) for atmosphere. Now this polymath, whose books on Joyce are so exhilarating, whose three symphonies are performed, whose novels have a world-wide following, and whose fiftieth book this is, brings his hero-poet Enderby to life again in *Enderby's Dark Lady*[16], writing the libretto for a musical about Shakespeare in Indiana – but not until after some surprising episodes in the life of William Shakespeare have been recounted, including his famous alteration to the forty-sixth Psalm (in his forty-sixth year) to include his own name forty-six lines from the beginning and forty-six lines from the end. As long as it is firmly understood that this is pure fiction, and that nothing in this line can touch the incomparable Caryl Brahms and S. J. Simon's *No Bed for Bacon* (1941), now coming back into print, this novel is enriching.

4. Shakespeare in the Theatre

(a) Elizabethan and Jacobean performance

The lighting of Shakespeare's stages has occasioned much lively debate. In *EIC* Keith Brown takes up arms against the 'fortress of Received Opinion', challenges notions of evidence, and proposes that open-air theatres made use of artificial lighting – not only in the fifth act of plays performed in the winter season but throughout other plays at other times. He suggests that *Hamlet* (for example) uses three lighting states, 'Dark, Quiet, and Full Blaze'. A subsequent issue of the same journal brings responses by Andrew Gurr and John Orrell, and Brown replies to both his colleagues. Gurr rejects Brown's conclusions on practice and intention in theatre building and on the supposition that some plays make coherent artistic use of natural darkness and light. Orrell supports the notion that artificial light was necessary at the end of outdoor performances in winter and gives evidence for the kind of lighting used in indoor theatres. Brown's reply complains that Gurr has missed his point and accepts Orrell's qualified support. Less controversially inclined is R. B. Graves, whose 'Stage Lighting at the Elizabethan and Early Stuart Courts' (*TN*) concludes that accounts for candles and other lighting expenses offer no information as to the candlepower available for the performances; allowances for candles used in rehearsal and setting-up are not distinguished by the bookkeepers. Little can be said confidently about the brilliance with which

16. *Enderby's Dark Lady, or No End to Enderby*, by Anthony Burgess. Hutchinson. pp. 160. £7.95.

these shows were attended, but a good deal of evidence is collected and an important warning is given:

> Even could we reconstruct the King's Men's performance of *Macbeth* in the Hall at Hampton Court in 1606 . . . this might better be served by hanging ordinary incandescent bulbs unobtrusively above the Hall, because the aura of quaintness and antiquarianism we associate with candles could go far towards destroying any insight that had been gained into the ambience of the original production.

Lightness and darkness are among the topics of Alan C. Dessen's *Elizabethan Stage Conventions and Modern Interpreters*[17]. This is not a comprehensive survey of conventional practices, but a series of arguments about cases, with some consideration of modern productions and editing. Valuable emphasis is laid on the possibility that seemingly anomalous stage effects may have a significant strangeness that ought not to be resolved into makeshift realism. Dessen is interested in the 'logic of stage violence', an area usually claimed as one of relative realism but arguably the source of symbolic rather than mimetic meanings. Less concerned with practice but similarly alive to the metaphorical uses of staging conventions (or attitudes to them) is Andrew Gurr's 'Hearers and Beholders in Shakespearean Drama' (*EiT*), which examines the terms used to describe the audiences of (and in) plays and ponders their implications. In 'Economy and Recognition: Thirteen Shakespearean Puzzles' (*SQ*) John C. Meagher tackles problems by looking at doubling and the audience's realization of it. Peter Holland's subtle and suggestive article on '*Hamlet* and the Art of *Acting*' (*TD*) begins with Thomas Heywood and ends with Erving Goffman, opening out the discussion of theatrical self-reflexivity into the broader topic of 'action' and reminding his readers that 'an act hath three branches'. Although it is not, strictly speaking, an essay in theatrical history Holland's article moves usefully into the area where expediency and poetry meet. Like the discussions of theatre lighting, it raises questions of the distinction between inevitable circumstances and sought-for effects. John Orrell's article on the orientation of the Globe (*TN*) is firmly anchored in the need (for a potential reconstruction on Bankside) of achieving some certainty but cannot discount aesthetic possibilities and problems. Does lengthening shadow 'mean' anything? Are the faces of boy actors softened by the light into something more readily construed as 'feminine'? (It all depends what you mean by . . .) Reporting on 'The Globe Reborn: Tool or Toy' on the other side of the Atlantic, Jay Halio recounts the proceedings of the conference held at Evanston, Illinois, in June 1984 to consider the proper uses for such a building (*SQ*).

Evidence for a different kind of performance is reconsidered by Margaret Knapp and Michael Kabialka in 'Shakespeare and the Prince of Purpoole' (*ThHS*). They suggest a revision of current thinking on the staging of plays in Great Halls, taking as example the 1594 performance of *The Comedy of Errors* at Gray's Inn. They wish to relocate the action on a stage directly 'in front of the dais, in the space between the dais and the fireplace', and forsake the hall screen that has been assumed to serve as background for the show. The

---

17. *Elizabethan Stage Conventions and Modern Interpreters*, by Alan C. Dessen. CUP. pp. xii + 190. £17.50.

platform would, on their reckoning, be 9 ft deep and 34 ft 8 in wide. The implications for this in terms of the dynamics of performance and its relations with the spectators are yet to be pondered.

Omitted from *YW* (1983) but too important to be passed over is Peter Thomson's *Shakespeare's Theatre*[18]. Thomson offers a lively and scholarly account of the theatre business, situating theatrical aesthetics in the realm of audiences, administration, and patronage. He is concise and enterprising simultaneously, able to dart off into useful analogies with other, later, performance styles and working conditions, and assumes that theatre came from somewhere and was supposed to do something. His accounts of *Hamlet*, *Twelfth Night*, and *Macbeth* from a series of theatrical perspectives are stimulating and informative. This is an admirable book that has since been issued in paperback and should show students (or remind scholars) that theatrical history, like the theatre, is useful.

(b) Productions since 1660

No full-length stage-histories of individual plays appeared during 1984, but there have been several brief, selective studies drawing on a selection of major performances. A new series, Shakespeare in Performance, has been inaugurated with J. L. Styan's volume on *All's Well*[19]. Styan gives a sense of the play's stage-life and uses detailed references to productions in a scene-by-scene demonstration of the range of possible interpretations. Not content (as are many stage-historians) to spread out data like curiosities in a flea-market, Styan uses performance points to serve a thesis, proposing that 'the challenge of style in *All's Well* cannot be met by giving it over to tragedy any more than it can be played merely for comedy: the cutting edge comes from whetting the one against the other'. The relative paucity of *All's Well* productions makes it more amenable than, say, *Hamlet*, to such treatment in so elegantly short a book, but Styan sets a high standard for the new series and challenges those whose labours appear under other imprints with similar aims.

The Macmillan Text and Performance series[20] has added four new titles in 1984 to its Shakespearean list: Lois Potter on *Twelfth Night*, David L. Hirst on *The Tempest*, Gāmini Salgādo on *King Lear*, and Gordon Williams on *Macbeth*. Hirst's is the most absorbing, approaching the play from a more rigorously 'theatre studies' angle than the rest and including accounts of Derek Jarman's film and Giorgio Strehler's Milan stage production, together with the London productions of Jonathan Miller and Peter Hall. In some of the volumes in this series there is a gap between the sophistication of the writer's commentary and the naivety of the reader implied in the format: synopses of the play and pages for the reader's own notes are surely too elementary a provision. The division of each book into a 'critical' account followed by a section dealing with performances might engender the kind of split between study and stage that the series hopes to prevent. The sense that performance

18. *Shakespeare's Theatre*, by Peter Thomson. Theatre Production Studies. RKP (1983). pp. xiv + 190. hb £8.95, pb £6.95.
19. *All's Well That Ends Well*, by J. L. Styan. Shakespeare in Performance. ManU. pp. viii + 126. £9.50.
20. All Text and Performance. Macmillan. *Twelfth Night*, by Lois Potter. pp. 80. £3.95. *The Tempest*, by David L. Hirst. pp. 74. £3.95. *King Lear*, by Gāmini Salgādo. pp. 85. £2.95. *Macbeth*, by Gordon Williams. pp. 80. £3.95.

can be evaluated as more or less responsive to 'themes' apprehended through another (implicitly, 'higher') form of critical inquiry is hard to avoid. All the volumes under review have insights and information to offer, and Lois Potter, like Hirst, 'reads' the play in her first section in a theatrically informed way; but the wished-for fusion does not always take place.

Less ambitious, envisaging an audience less experienced than either of these two series, is David A. Male's project in the studies issued by CUP under the title Shakespare on Stage[21]. Each booklet examines a handful of productions of one play (*Antony and Cleopatra*, *The Winter's Tale*, and *Macbeth* have appeared this year). There are well-chosen photographs of parallel scenes from the productions. Although he limits himself to recent RSC productions and to a few selected points of interpretation, Male gives a good sense of the works' responsiveness to performance and the general quality and thrust of the particular interpretations. Many more pretentious publications have given less, and the accounts of the shows are likely to be useful for students of theatrical history. If only Male had been active in Shakespeare's Globe or Irving's Lyceum!

Theatre historians continue to attempt to supply that want, with varying degrees of conviction and success. Jocelyn Powell's *Restoration Theatre Production*[22] includes an analysis of the 'entertainment both intimate and extravagant' afforded by *The Tempest; or, The Enchanted Island*. To his succinct account of the staging methods employed in this spectacle, Powell brings a willingness to consider the kinship between this and Jacobean work, in the face of the Restoration's energetic attempts to 'improve' on what went before. He stresses the theatrical self-consciousness of the adaptation, the sense of a dialogue between actors and audience over the characters' heads, and the musical (as distinct from literary) dramaturgy. He evokes the 'detached excitement of Restoration audiences' and looks on the new *Tempest* and *The Fairy Queen* as successful shows rather than inartistic betrayals of their respective originals. Curtis A. Price's *Henry Purcell and the London Stage*[23] attempts to study the context of Restoration theatre music – usually heard apart from the texts for which it was written. The correspondences between dramatic moment and musical expression are not always straightforward, and it has been suggested that Price is not always correct in his accounts of the plays themselves, but he offers illuminating commentary on the relationship between textual adaptation and musical settings and suggests that the relationship between the two can often be ironic.

Two articles in *SQ* bear on eighteenth-century Shakespearean performance. In 'The Genesis of David Garrick's *Romeo and Juliet*' George C. Branam summarizes the circumstances of the 1748 and 1750 versions and their relationship with earlier productions (notably Theophilus Cibber's of 1744). In 'Elocution and Shakespeare: An Episode in the History of Literary Taste' Paul C. Edwards makes some reference to the influence of contemporary acting on the precepts of elocution teachers and their choice of examples.

21. All Shakespeare on Stage, by David A. Male. CUP. £1.50 each. *Antony and Cleopatra*. pp. 36. *The Winter's Tale*. pp. 32. *Macbeth*. pp. 35.
22. *Restoration Theatre Production*, by Jocelyn Powell. Theatre Production Studies. RKP. pp. xiv + 226. £19.95.
23. *Henry Purcell and the London Stage*, by Curtis A. Price. CUP. pp. xiv + 380. £30. (Rev'd by H. N. Davies, *M&L*, 1985.)

Three publications in the UMIRes series of 'Theater and Dramatic Studies' deal with aspects of nineteenth-century Shakespeare production in Britain and abroad. Rinda F. Lundstrom[24] investigates William Poel's successive *Hamlets* and seeks to show the development of Poel's theoretical and practical work. She describes in detail the 1881 production of Q1, the 1900 staging of a conflated Q1 and F text, the 1914 Q2, and the 1924 *Fratricide Punished*. Poel consistently presented Hamlet as an avenger, in opposition to the Victorian-Romantic prince-philosopher, and Lundstrom defends him against accusations of being an archaist whose work had gone wrong. In *The Art of the Actor-Manager: Wilson Barrett and the Victorian Theater*[25] James Thomas provides serviceable descriptions of this actor's unusual productions of *Hamlet* (1884) and *Othello* (1894) and examines the financial and administrative background to this work. Joyce Vining Morgan, in *Stanislavski's Encounter with Shakespeare*[26], makes important Russian material available and traces the significance of the great director's contribution to (and experience of) European and Russian Shakespeare performance. All these UMI publications are based on graduate theses, and some are more like 'real books' than others: a thesis is not necessarily a 'user-friendly' work. In all of them the illustrations are poorly reproduced and the standard of presentation is contemptuous of the institutions that are obliged to come up with some £40 for each volume. The series editors have not always elicited grace and readability from their authors. It is a relief to encounter Ann Marie Koller's *The Theater Duke: Georg II of Saxe-Meiningen and the German Stage*[27], on which Stanford University Press has lavished the attention that is appropriate to work which aims to attract its readers rather than simply cash in on the fears that one's library will be incomplete without the one recent book on Barrett, Poel, or whoever. Koller seeks to refine the received understanding of this massively influential theatre company. She gives a fascinating account of the artistic, political, and biographical context of the company's work and its relation to theatre in nineteenth-century Germany. The introductory chapter alone introduces to anglophone readers such phenomena as Franz Dingelstedt's 1862 Weimar history cycle (from *Richard II* to *Richard III*) and Eduard Devrient's twenty Karlsruhe productions of Shakespeare (beginning in 1852). The influences of Wagner, Charles Kean, and Samuel Phelps are traced, and the Meiningers' own influence on other theatre workers is discussed. There are evocative sketches, designs, and photographs, and thorough documentation: this is an excellent work of theatre scholarship and a beautifully produced book.

A number of essays on twentieth-century productions are to be found in *ThHS*; Larry D. Clark's account of 'John Barrymore's *Richard III*', a survey by G. Harold Metz of the recent stage-history of *The Two Noble Kinsmen* (whose ten productions in the U.S.A. and U.K. since 1928 are naively alleged to show a 'sudden return to stage popularity' of this play), and a discussion by

24. *William Poel's Hamlets: The Director as Critic*, by Rinda F. Lundstrom. Theater and Dramatic Studies 20. UMIRes. pp. x + 194. $39.95.
25. *The Art of the Actor-Manager: Wilson Barrett and the Victorian Theater*, by James Thomas. Theater and Dramatic Studies 15. UMIRes. pp. xii + 216. $39.95.
26. *Stanislavski's Encounter with Shakespeare: The Evolution of a Method*, by Joyce Vining Morgan. Theater and Dramatic Studies 14. UMIRes. pp. xxiv + 162. $39.95.
27. *The Theater Duke: Georg II of Saxe-Meiningen and the German Stage*, by Ann Marie Koller. Stanford. pp. xiv + 257. $30.

Erroll G. Hill of the playing of Ariel and Caliban in some U.S. *Tempests*. Barrymore's *Richard III* is also touched on in Arthur Feinsod's 'Stage Designs of a Single Gesture: The Early Work of Robert Edmond Jones' (*DRev*). Interesting visual material on Sir Laurence Olivier's performances is included in Melvyn Bragg's picture-book on the actor[28], and John Gielgud's work, Shakespearean and otherwise, is recalled and celebrated by the contributors to a volume of reminiscences in his honour[29] and by Gyles Brandreth in his richly illustrated book[30]. The most rewarding 'trade' book on the theatre for many years is Simon Callow's *Being an Actor*[31], which offers the Shakespearean scholar an actor's insight on specific plays in performance (notably *Titus Andronicus* and *As You Like It*), details of the author's experience in reading the *Sonnets* to audiences in John Padel's ordering, and a frank and penetrating view of the various directors and companies Callow has worked for. Callow's plea for a theatre in which the director is employed by the actors expresses sentiments shared by many of his colleagues, and suggests another way of 'freeing Shakespeare' from the less desirable results of the power-game played in directors' theatre.

Scholarly journals continue to include notices of productions in their review pages, sometimes giving them the status of 'review articles' (*CQ* has printed a number of these in past years), sometimes subsuming them into general accounts of the year's Shakespearean achievements. *SQ*'s reports of far-flung productions include an *As You Like It* in Bergen, in which 'the pastoral idyll was gently mocked by the presence of toy sheep on wheels, a herd of them at one time' (so much for Beerbohm Tree and the rabbits) and in which Hymen's appearance was cut out to demonstrate that this was 'a festive comedy turning into a dark comedy'. At another extreme is the U.S. Naval Academy's *Kings*, a conflation of *Henry IV, Parts One and Two, Richard II*, and *Henry V*, with massed forces of two faculty members and sixty-five midshipmen. The battle scenes would have satisfied a Drury Lane gallery of the nineteenth century. From the pampered stalls of Stratford and London, such reviews can seem a catalogue of amusing eccentricities, doubly inauthentic because of their overseas origin, but there *is* a world elsewhere. *SQ* offers a range of vicarious theatrical experience that includes genuine innovation as well as modish novelty and conservative plodding. Zdeněk Stříbrný writes on 'Recent *Hamlets* in Prague'. Mary Judith Dunbar describes productions of *Merry Wives* and *Macbeth* at Santa Cruz which were part of a fully developed academic project, with faculty as observers and dramaturgs and a conference to round it all off. With its complementary acting classes and workshops, this seems an enviable enterprise. The diversity of plays calling themselves Shakespeare's – especially on European stages – makes British productions look anything but avantgarde. A trawl through the Shakespeare productions given by British repertory theatres at the kindly behest of the O- and A-level examiners would produce more gloom than all the toy sheep in Bergen. A vivid sense of the earnestness and opulence (but not always success) of German Shakespeare is

28. *Laurence Olivier*, by Melvyn Bragg. Hutchinson. pp. 144. £12.50.

29. *The Ages of Gielgud: An Actor at Eighty*, ed. by Ronald Harwood. H&S. pp. x + 182. £9.95.

30. *John Gielgud: A Celebration*, by Gyles Brandreth. Pavilion/Joseph. pp. 186. £12.95.

31. *Being an Actor*, by Simon Callow. Methuen. pp. x + 190. £7.95.

afforded by the surveys in the respective East and West German *Jahrbücher*. *SJH* includes an article by the dramaturg and director responsible for translating and staging plays at Darmstadt, Eike Gramss and Frank Günther. The two activities are usefully brought together in their title, 'Shakespeare übersetzen – Shakespeare inszenieren'. They propose that love is a stronger and more important relationship between the theatre and Shakespeare than respect, have harsh words for the earlier BBC/*Time Life* productions, and claim that great works possess an ability to survive even our misguided notions of 'das Werktreue'. In the same issue Christian Jauslin interviews Gustav Rudolf Sellner and discusses his *Merchant*, *Tempest*, and *King Lear* (also reviewed in the *Bühnenbericht* section). Jill Levenson contributes an account of 'Shakespeare in Canada: The Stratford Festival and a National Theatre' in which she examines the cultural significance of the Canadian Stratford: similar questions of cultural identity are raised by Werner Habicht's essay in *ShS* 'How German is Shakespeare in Germany?'

In *SJW* Armin-Gerd Kuckhoff's review of Shakespeare productions in the DDR during 1982 proposes some distinctions between true and false 'discovery' in a theatre whose work on the classics is increasingly presented in terms of the newly found. His examples range from a meretricious Leipzig *Othello*, in which crude references to racial and sexual stereotypes seemed to reinforce rather than problematize the attitudes under attack, to a Meiningen *Merchant of Venice* in which the dialogue between text and direction was subtler: Shylock was a good, genial man made evil by his treatment at the Christians' hands and Portia made it clear that it was she who chose Bassanio by producing the right key from her bosom in the casket scene. Kuckhoff insists that true discoveries derive from finding points in the action of the play or its imagery and seeing them with new eyes, so that they are made more comprehensible, meaningful, and interesting for us: 'mit neuen Augen sehen, das heisst, mit unseren Erfahrungen das Werk betrachten'.

The most penetrating review of British Shakespearean production is Nick Shrimpton's (*ShS*). The 1982–3 RSC season is proposed as an illustration of the current uncertainty as to how the comedies might be interpreted. John Caird's *Twelfth Night* is (H. B.) Charltonian, Barry Kyle's *Shrew* is (C. L.) Barberian, and Adrian Noble's *Comedy of Errors* is poststructuralist and defamiliarized. 'Meanings of any kind were steadily resisted [by Noble] and in their place we had what Barthes might call the play of signifiers.' Meanwhile, the National Theatre toured a *Dream* that did not 'fit into the neat map of changing production styles' provided by the RSC. Although he limits himself for the most part to work in Stratford and London, Shrimpton's review has a breadth of reference and an ability to mediate between theatrical and other kinds of criticism to arrive at a grasp of cultural meanings that few other academic accounts of performances offer. Like Roger Warren's notes on British Shakespeare in *SQ*, Shrimpton's article embraces the European and historical context of what he has seen and heard. In *CahiersE* the accounts of productions are often vivid and sometimes give authoritative descriptions of productions not accessible to most readers. The 1984 issues include a review of *Titus Andronicus* staged by Théâtre Présent 'in one of the preserved historical buildings of the former Paris slaughterhouse complex' and of the Footsbarn company's *King Lear* as performed in Arles. There are also notices of a richly stylized *Winter's Tale* in Morocco, a *Venus and Adonis* at La Rochelle (no

Adonis, two Venuses!), and *King Lear* in Marseille, as well as reviews of productions in London, Sheffield, and the British and Canadian Stratfords.

Interest in film and TV Shakespeare grows apace. The 1984 issues of *Shakespeare on Film Newsletter* (*ShFN*) include some interesting comment and scholarship, alongside matter based openly on studio publicity (notably an account of Olivier's performance in the Granada TV *King Lear*). One article, on Eric Rohmer's *Perceval*, has no discernible connection with Shakespeare. As well as reviews of currently available and recently released film and TV productions, *ShFN* prints an article by Virginia M. Vaughan on 'The Forgotten Television *Tempest*' – a 1960 production for Hallmark Hall of Fame in which Maurice Evans played Prospero, Roddy McDowall Ariel, Lee Remick Miranda, and (with 'fins, puppy-dog ears, and huge, primordial nose') Richard Burton Caliban. In *SJH* Robert F. Willson Jr writes on 'Fated *Macbeths*: The Film Director as God', arguing that Orson Welles, Akira Kurosawa, and Roman Polanski 'reduce the tragedy to a formalist melodrama lacking the ambiguity and dimension of freewill of the original' and asking 'how far can a film version go in experimenting with the elements of a Shakespearean drama before it deserves to have a different title?'. Graham Holderness (*L&H*) points to E. M. W. Tillyard's reading of the Histories and Olivier's film of *Henry V* as 'establishing an image of "Shakespeare's England" which would serve as an ideological power of social cohesion in Churchill's Britain'. Martin Banham's 1980 essay, 'BBC Television's Dull Shakespeares', is reprinted in an anthology of articles from *CQ*[32]. In 'The BBC Shakespeare and "House Style"' (*SQ*) James C. Bulman is able to take a longer view of the series, suggesting that Jonathan Miller's productions 'seemed to be aimed at an educated and privileged audience, just as [Cedric] Messina's were aimed at an ignorant multitude'. He backs up this assertion with reference to the programmes themselves and to the various statements made by those responsible for them. Mediating between TV and stage performance – not always happily but often to stimulating effect – was the London Weekend Television series *Playing Shakespeare*. In these carefully staged workshop sessions John Barton demonstrated the kind of work that he does with actors: a number of RSC actors took part in the programmes and their comments, together with those of Barton, are transcribed in *Playing Shakespeare*[33]. Although the quality of the performed examples cannot be conveyed in the book, the discussions are often interesting as examples of the actor's and director's approach and (in the case of David Suchet and Patrick Stewart on Shylock) as light cast on past performances.

5. General Criticism

(a) General

The International Shakespeare Association met for its Second Congress in Stratford-upon-Avon in 1981. *Shakespeare, Man of the Theater*[34] claims to be

32. *Shakespeare's Wide and Universal Stage*, ed. by C. B. Cox and D. J. Palmer. ManU. pp. vi + 233. £19.50.

33. *Playing Shakespeare*, by John Barton. Methuen. pp. x + 211. £9.95.

34. *Shakespeare, Man of the Theater: Proceedings of the Second Congress of the International Shakespeare Association, 1981*, ed. by Kenneth Muir, Jay L. Halio, and D. J. Palmer. UDel/AUP. pp. 265. £21.50.

the 'Proceedings'; only a fraction (just over half) of the main lectures are
printed, and only three of the 250 seminar papers, though room was found for
Moelwyn Merchant's feeble 'Sermon'. The book opens with John Mortimer's
enchanting Inaugural Lecture, alone worth the price of the book.

> From an early age I began to act the tragedies . . . for the benefit of my
> mother and father, at the end of the dining room. Unfortunately I was an
> only child and so had to act all the parts. . . . I must be one of the few
> speakers here who has dueled with himself, played a bedroom scene
> with himself as his own mother, and forced himself to drink his own
> poisoned chalice. . . . When I was a child my father took me each year to
> see the plays in this theater, and he was able to help out the actors by
> reciting most of their lines quite loudly and a couple of beats before they
> did.

As a child in the Shakespeare Hotel, terrified in the bedroom called 'Macbeth'
by a supposed apparition, he was brought to his senses 'by a horrendous
matrimonial quarrel going on in "Romeo and Juliet" next door'. To have such
an excellent playwright as Mortimer on the playwright Shakespeare is worth
whole libraries full of the dried butterflies and tomes of casuistry called
academic criticism. He is excellent on Shakespeare thinking 'what you want
him to think. But with some exceptions. He will not be mean and he will not be
pompous, or pretentious, or falsely sentimental, and he will not be a hypocrite.' He is even better on Shakespeare's stagecraft in words – darkness on a
sunny stage, for example: modern technicalities create darkness 'and the
absence of light, as everyone knows, makes words inaudible'. Stephen Orgel's
paper, 'Shakespeare Imagines a Theater', starts from Sebastiano Serlio in 1545
(and incidentally the church in the Comic Scene is not 'partly decayed': Orgel
has clearly never been to Lucca in Tuscany) and goes on to the frontispiece of
Jonson's *Works* in 1616 and a discussion of the qualities of audience via the
Dover Cliff scene in *King Lear*. Bernard Beckerman writes on the shift from
iconic to historic time in late Tudor drama. In a long essay Inga-Stina Ewbank
is suggestive and wise on the relation of words to theatrical event, by way of a
useful comparison between passages from *Pericles* and *A Doll's House*, with
some fine wider insights. There is only slight reference to Shakespeare in M. T.
Jones-Davies's piece on Renaissance metadrama: but Emrys Jones's 'The
Sense of Occasion' is an essay of importance on Shakespeare's presentation
of night, particularly kinds of night, and some all-night sequences. Harriett
Hawkins's subject is ' "Conjectures and Refutations": The Positive Uses of
Negative Feedback in Criticism and Performance'; she attacks scornfully a
number of critics whom she meanly does not name (except in footnotes,
presumably not spoken at the conference): Bertrand Evans for one (*YW*
60.148–50) deserved better. Her clever piece argues for 'the method whereby
one presents the evidence against one's own best arguments, as well as those of
others . . . the method most commonly employed by Shakespeare himself' as
'perhaps the best way to tackle the common problems of influence, fashion,
over-reaction, dogma, and taboo . . .'. G. R. Hibbard, in 'Between a Sob and a
Giggle', says that Shakespeare, as he wrote, 'heard every word he gives his
characters to speak resounding, in its proper accent, tone, pitch, and emphasis, within his own head', and discusses, very well, the richness of possibility
of some Shakespearean statements. A. R. Braunmuller's long essay on 'Char-

acterization through Language in the Early Plays of Shakespeare and His Contemporaries' concludes that Peele never learned to develop the double capacity of making 'character and action define one another reciprocally'. Philip Edwards begins his 'Shakespeare and Kyd' with 'The purpose of this paper is to ask what the significance may be of the absence of the Ghost at the conclusion of *Hamlet*. I think that Kyd may be able to help in this inquiry.' He works by means of the parallels between *Hamlet* and *Julius Caesar*, both 'studies in political failure', and he is very illuminating indeed. Anne Barton reproduces work in print elsewhere in her 'Shakespeare and Jonson'. H. Neville Davies considers imitations of *Hamlet* in Beaumont and Fletcher's *The Maid's Tragedy*. Robert Weimann approaches Shakespeare 'from the point of view of the role of society in the Elizabethan theater and the role of theater in society', emphasizing 'the crisis in the social foundations of the Tudor concept of authority'. Among the seminar papers is a spirited and illuminating piece by Jeanne Addison Roberts about Shakespearean comedy and eighteenth-century actresses; Hannah Pritchard, Kitty Clive, Peg Woffington, and Susanna Maria Cibber.

CQ has for a quarter of a century kept up a high standard of Shakespeare criticism with reference to production of all kinds. C. B. Cox and D. J. Palmer have edited a collection of sixteen Shakespearean essays in *CQ* from 1963, J. R. Brown on 'Mr Beckett's Shakespeare', to W. Hutchings's 1982 'Beast or God: The *Coriolanus* Controversy'. The volume is called *Shakespeare's Wide and Universal Stage*[32]. The other pieces are A. D. Nuttall's 'The Argument about Shakespeare's Characters'; John Edmunds on 'Shakespeare Breaks the Illusion'; Martin Banham on 'BBC Television's Dull Shakespeares'; John Wain's 'The Shakespearean Lie-detector: Thoughts on *Much Ado About Nothing*'; Terence Eagleton on 'Language and Reality in *Twelfth Night*'; R. L. Smallwood (not R. J. as they have it) on '*All's Well That Ends Well* at the Royal Shakespeare Theatre'; Nicholas Brooke's 'Reflecting Gems and Dead Bones: Tragedy versus History in *Richard III*'; Barbara Everett on 'Romeo and Juliet: The Nurse's Story'; A. W. Bellringer's '*Julius Caesar*: Room Enough'; Peter Mercer on '*Othello* and the Form of Heroic Tragedy'; and two each by David Pirie, '*Hamlet* without the Prince' and 'Lear as King'; and D. J. Palmer, 'Casting off the Old Man: History and St Paul in *Henry IV*' and '*As You Like It* and the Idea of Play'. It is a pity that the dust-jacket contains two horrible errors: the theatre it shows is the Beargarden, not the Globe; and the *All's Well* which Robert Smallwood reviews was at the RST not the National.

Muriel Bradbrook on Shakespeare[35] collects a dozen essays over thirty years, from the essay on the structure of *All's Well* of 1950 to 'Shakespeare's Debt to Marlowe' of 1980. The other ten, all good to have collected and in handsome print, are, in chronological order of Shakespeare's works: 'Shakespeare's Primitive Art', 'Shakespeare and the Use of Disguise in Elizabethan Drama', 'Beasts and Gods: The Social Purpose of *Venus and Adonis*', 'Dramatic Role as Social Image: A Study of *The Taming of the Shrew*', '*King Henry IV*', 'What Shakespeare Did to Chaucer's *Troilus and Criseyde*', 'An Interpretation of *Hamlet*', 'The Balance and the Sword in

35. *Muriel Bradbrook on Shakespeare*. Harvester/B&N. pp. viii + 167. hb. £14.95, pb £4.95.

Measure for Measure', 'Othello, Webster and the Tragedy of Violence', and 'The Origins of *Macbeth*'.

The late G. Wilson Knight's thirty books and unforgettable stage presence have affected critics and playgoers ever since the early 1930s. In *Shakespearian Dimensions*[36] are reprinted twelve essays, one, 'Soul and Body in Shakespeare' being new; and there is a newly written introduction, or apologia: in both of these, the note of faintly querulous self-reference is a little hard to take. The centre of the volume is his useful work on *Timon* with which, or whom, Wilson Knight felt increasingly associated towards the end of his very active life. The other items are: 'Society and the Cosmos', 'Folklore and Spiritual Healing', 'Gloucester's Leap', 'Visual Art in Kyd and Shakespeare', 'Caliban as a Red Man', 'Vergil, Shakespeare and the Seraphic'; and pieces on Lyly, Webster, and Ford.

Harriett Hawkins, again, in ' "Players and Scorecards"': Some Principles of Exposition in English Drama', her contribution to *From Renaissance to Restoration: Metamorphoses of the Drama*[37] goes some way to an American position in which the titling is longer than the essay: I exaggerate, of course; but these fifteen small pages about dramatic exposition are more lightweight than the heavy labels suggest, mercifully: she writes lucidly and suggestively. Both matters cause regret that I have not seen her twelve-page piece, 'Critical Counter-Interpretation of Shakespearean Drama: Some Variants of the Dialectical Process' in *Reconciliations: Studies in Honor of Richard Harter Fogle*, edited by Mary Lynn Johnson and Seraphia D. Leyda (USalz, 1983): though, of course, I did note above (p. 205) her thirteen-word title in the *Shakespeare, Man of the Theater* volume.

So from here it is an easy leap to the first eight items in *SJW*, of great interest in the current rapidly growing understanding that Shakespeare, whatever the special pleaders like Peter Milward or Ernst Honigmann may affirm, lived in an assertively Protestant nation. They are: Robert Weimann, 'Shakespeare und Luther. Von neuzeitlicher Autorität und Autor-Funktion'; Adolf Laube, 'Martin Luther und der Beginn einer Epoche revolutionärer Umwälzungen'; Martin Lehnert, 'Shakespeares und Luthers Verdienst um die Herausbildung der englischen und deutschen Nationalsprache'; Walter Cohen, 'The Reformation and Elizabethan Drama'; Margot Heinemann, 'Shakespeare als Dramatiker nachreformatorischer Zeit'; Karl-Heinz Magister, 'Reformation und Autorität im geschichtlichen Wandel des englischen Renaissance-Dramas'; Rolf Soellner, 'Reformation und Deformation in Shakespeares *Heinrich VIII*'; and Günther Klotz, 'Shakespeare und Milton in dem geschichtlichen Prozess von der Reformation zur Revolution'.

Seventeen of the items in *Mirror up to Nature: Essays in Honour of G. R. Hibbard*[38] are about Shakespeare. Kenneth Muir opens the volume with an interesting, and suitably astringent, account of 'T. S. Eliot's Criticism of Elizabethan Drama'. The late Geoffrey Bullough contributed a full and very

36. *Shakespearian Dimensions*, by G. Wilson Knight. Harvester/B&N. pp. xxi + 232. £18.

37. *From Renaissance to Restoration: Metamorphoses of the Drama*, ed. by Robert Markley and Laurie Finke. Bellflower. pp. 206. $16.

38. *Mirror up to Nature: Essays in Honour of G. R. Hibbard*, ed. by J. C. Gray. UTor. pp. x + 315. $35.

useful account of 'Theobald on Shakespeare's Sources', showing the detailed work, sometimes necessarily haphazard and closely involving William Warburton, which the good classical scholar Lewis Theobald put into his source work for his edition of Shakespeare, so entangled with Pope: he is 'the first great editor of Shakespeare'. Neil Carson, in 'Shakespeare and the Dramatic Image', argues elegantly and briefly for the force of a certain scene-painting, visionary quality, for example in the tricking of Sly by the Lord in the *Shrew*, and found too in Hamlet and Prospero. T. W. Craik, in ' "You that Way; We this Way": Shakespeare's Endings' says that to study the endings of a tragedy or history is to see how Shakespeare tragically reinforces the tragic fact, the death of the protagonist. F. D. Hoeniger offers a helpful essay on 'Musical Cures of Melancholy and Mania in Shakespeare'. He opens with examples of the contrary effects of music in Shakespeare – therapy, and goad to madness – and then gives a clear history-of-ideas account of the classical origins, and medieval and Renaissance developments, of the notions as they would come to Shakespeare. There are two pieces on fools: J. A. B. Somerset's 'Shakespeare's Great Stage of Fools 1599–1607' attempts to de-molish the structure of received wisdom which makes Robert Armin's arrival the cause of the development of Shakespeare's fools between those dates – the change from Dogberry to Touchstone. He traces the history of the idea, revealing expected prejudices against comedy, and he looks firmly at Armin's talents. He sees Shakespeare's development as paramount, 'culminating in his unique inclusion of the fool in tragedy'. The actor 'should be celebrated for his astonishing range and variety, not for his "comic line" '. James Black in 'Shakespeare's Mystery of Fooling', looking at the plays from *As You Like It* to *King Lear*, attempts 'a sort of job description for Shakespeare's fools in their working-day world'. He notes the dissipating holiday atmosphere in each court, and the function of Lavache and others to bring life to a bleak commun-ity by suggesting generative warmth which is, with variation, true of the others: he goes on to exposit other characteristics of this 'profession for the very wise'. This is a fine analysis of the major fools – the best thing in the book – and the concluding job description should be pinned above the desk of every critic. Incidentally, the book, though well produced, has alarming inconsistencies of punctuation-convention, and is, dismayingly, without an index.

John Bligh, in *ShS*, following Brian Vickers (*YW* 62.183–4), opens further the subject of the study of character 'not as a literary genre, but as one of the principal divisions of dramatic criticism, corresponding to the second of the six parts, elements, or constituents, of drama distinguished by Aristotle'; he works from 1664, and subjects the material to rigorous classifying, ending with a somewhat Polonius-like list. Also in *ShS* Werner Habicht asks 'How German is Shakespeare in Germany? Recent Trends in Criticism and Performance in West Germany'. His richly documented essay concludes that in spite of every-one in sight examining everything everywhere in the minutest detail before reconstructing, the result is not particularly a German Shakespeare. Kenneth Muir, in the revised and expanded second volume, *The Age of Shakespeare*, in the *New Pelican Guide to English Literature*[39], writes a twenty-page account of 'Changing Interpretations of Shakespeare', from the beginning until the late

---

39. *The New Pelican Guide to English Literature*. Vol. 2: *The Age of Shakespeare*, ed. by Boris Ford. Penguin (1982). pp. 576. pb £2.95.

1970s. He shows clearly that though modern critics have the advantages of better knowledge of the conditions of Shakespeare's age, and marginally better texts, 'the proliferation of criticism makes it more and more difficult to say anything which is both new and true'. He might have added that 'proliferation' means more than five hundred items a year.

All credit then to the Gale Research Company for their ambitious project to print in a series of massive volumes 'Excerpts from the Criticism of William Shakespeare's Plays and Poetry, from the First Published Appraisals to Current Evaluations'. The first volume has arrived[40], and contains 'criticism on (*sic*) one major tragedy (*Hamlet*), one minor tragedy (*Timon of Athens*), one major comedy (*Twelfth Night*), one minor comedy (*Comedy of Errors*), and two histories (*Henry IV, Part I*, and *Henry IV, Part II*) . . .'. Each volume will deal with six or seven plays; 'performance criticism will be treated in a separate special volume', and other specials will cover Shakespeare's poetry, the authorship controversy and the apocrypha, and costume and set design. The volumes are aimed at 'high school and college English classes' in America, which led them to fix the *Riverside Shakespeare* as their basis, and to try to assist a creature not only unknown in Europe, but alarming to contemplate, 'the researcher newly acquainted with the works of Shakespeare'. The *Comedy of Errors* section covers material from 1594 to 1975 over fifty-seven large double-column pages. The entries are heavily dominated by twentieth-century North Americans (R. A. Foakes deserves more than his brief mention), but it is encouraging to see Harold Brooks given the longest chunk. *Hamlet* has 210 pages, material from Jeremy Collier in 1698 to Inga-Stina Ewbank in 1977, and happily this most European of artefacts has noticeably less North American attention recorded. Indeed, I have to say that I found the selection not at all bad, and the six pages of annotated 'Additional Bibliography' unexpectedly lively – whoever wrote this knew what he or she was doing. Of course, it cannot take the place of C. C. H. Williamson's monumental *Readings in the Character of Hamlet 1661–1947* (*YW* 32.133), though that is properly only concerned with character, and one at that. The *Henry IV* plays get 165 pages; *Timon*, after a rather good introduction, eighty-five, from R. Gould in 1685 on; and *Twelfth Night* 130. The extracts throughout are taken from a wide range of locations, with some pleasing surprises. The enterprise is off to a good start.

R. Chris Hassel Jr is a Christianizer. His book on drama and the Christian year, *Renaissance Drama and the English Church Year*[41], attempted 'a systematic study of possible thematic, narrative, or imagistic correlations' between masques and plays 'and their liturgical occasions'. But observation of synchronicity far, far too readily turned into supposed hard 'fact'. That book was Touchstone-scholarship, finding far too much virtue in 'if', and making, for example, unwarranted Christian assumptions about *Measure for Measure*. In the end it was simply a reproduction of the cataloguing work of E. K. Chambers with knobs on – and unwarranted 'Christian' knobs at that. Hassel's more recent book, *Faith and Folly in Shakespeare's Romantic Comedies*[42],

40. *Shakespearean Criticism*, Vol. 1, ed. by Laurie Lanzen Harris and Mark W. Scott. Gale. pp. 683. $70.
41. *Renaissance Drama and the English Church Year*, by R. Chris Hassel Jr. UNeb (1979). pp. xi + 215. $16.95.
42. *Faith and Folly in Shakespeare's Romantic Comedies*, by R. Chris Hassel Jr. UGeo (1980). pp. xvi + 255. $23.

collects and expands work since 1970 on *Love's Labour's Lost, Much Ado*, and *The Merchant of Venice*, and offers new thinking on *A Midsummer Night's Dream, As You Like It,* and *Twelfth Night.* He begins with the missionary intention of correcting the 'glaring oversight' of the lack of Christian readings of these plays. That position is hard to credit (we are only four lines into the book) when so much American criticism has imported Christ into Shakespeare, a movement at best absurd and at worst hideous, with Falstaff, no less, as approaching that nonsense 'a Christ figure' (*YW* 56.161–2; 58.161–2). He starts this book with another gigantic speculation: a sound remark about 'Pauline and Erasmian paradoxes concerning the reversals of folly and wisdom' leads to 'These allusions *would surely* have led his audience to understand and enjoy their pertinence to Shakespeare's unique comic vision' (my italics). The book is altogether odd: to find the middle-aged and vigorous Frank Kermode – I was talking with him yesterday – listed with Tillyard and, incredibly, Richmond Noble (whose work was in the early 1930s) to make a trio called 'earlier Shakespeareans', inspires little confidence. He works, as he himself says, by 'close analogy', without apparently seeing the quicksand. He is right about the vitality of doctrinal debate in the period, but wrong about almost everything else. Of course to understand Erasmus and folly is important for the student of the period: but that is all one can say. Hassel's case is non-existent. In his book subtlety is everywhere and only he can see it, which makes his work an exact parallel with those American bawdy-Shakespeare buffs (*YW* 62.189–90; 60.141; 63.180). Hassel, by repeating the words 'faith and folly' many times, tries to suggest developing argument. There is none. All is analogy. The *Book of Common Prayer* speaks of sin, and grace: the comedies end in joyous festivity: Q.E.D. 'All of them end with marriage, hence communion': my argument against the first appearance of his *Love's Labour's Lost* chapter still stands (*YW* 58.161–2).

It is a relief to turn to pure scholarship and a truer Shakespeare. Marvin Carlson's *Theories of the Theatre: A Historical and Critical Survey, from the Greeks to the Present*[43] is a major book, and of importance, 'the first detailed and comprehensive survey of Western dramatic theory, from Aristotle to the post-structuralists'. He approaches the period of Shakespeare through the Renaissance in Italy, Spain, France, and the Netherlands. He shows in high relief that what theory there was, until the 1590s, was grains of Aristotle. From the moment when Burbage opened the first public theatre in 1576, the sustained attack on the theatre began, and the rest followed. Though the book, in this central chapter, 'The Renaissance in England and the Netherlands', appears to have only one sentence relevant to Shakespeare, it is a pregnant one: 'Only scattered and fragmentary observations may be gleaned from Marlowe, Kyd, and Shakespeare, though Shakespeare's practice unquestionably provided a source of incalculable influence on later theorists.' The rest of the book demonstrates just that, as a glance at the index shows, with at least eighty entries for Shakespeare. His influence is clear right up to the point where the book ends, approaching the 1980s. It is altogether good to have the Bard set in such a context: over four hundred pages follow his main entry.

43. *Theories of the Theatre: A Historical and Critical Survey, from the Greeks to the Present*, by Marvin Carlson. CornU. pp. 529. $45.

William B. Worthen's *The Idea of the Actor*[44] has some excellent pages on *Hamlet* and *Twelfth Night*, amid discussion of *Volpone* and *The Duchess of Malfi*, in the first chapter. His general argument, which stretches from Renaissance theories of acting to the time of Garrick, and then to internationalism and Samuel Beckett in three large leaps, is that each age has tackled the ethics of acting, and dramatized that very problem. Was the Elizabethan actor a Satanic deceiver, or did he, as Philip Sidney said of the poet, affirm the divine power of human creativity? Hamlet's question, 'Is it not monstrous?', sets the tone. 'Although playing is necessary in *Hamlet*, playing is neither as easy to control as the humanists imagine, nor as easy to identify and discriminate from other activities as the Puritans claim.' The dozen pages on *Twelfth Night* begin by noting that, 'a much gentler play than *Volpone*' it 'also offers a surprisingly "puritanical" vision of the actor's performance, and persistently evaluates acting in terms of madness, sexual confusion, and demonic deception'. He concludes,

> For although Shakespeare finally returns us to the world of wind and rain, he also censures Malvolio's 'precisian' vision of a world lacking in cakes and ale, a world that cannot permit, within the proper limits of the theater, the threatening exuberance of the actor's play.

Alan C. Dessen's book, *Elizabethan Stage Conventions and Modern Interpreters*[17] is aimed at a simpler audience. Vividly written, though with a faintly bullying tone, the book sets out to re-interpret the original stage conventions and to show also how out of key 'we' may be. The most interesting chapter is the penultimate one, 'Theatrical Metaphor: Seeing and Not-seeing'. A vigorous book, it is not open enough to the possibility of other ways of seeing and doing things than Dessen's, particularly as found in modern Europe.

Ronald Paulson wrote two distinguished books of art history in the 1970s. Now in *Book and Painting: Shakespeare, Milton and the Bible: Literary Texts and the Emergence of English Painting*[45] he gives a too-brief thirty pages on Shakespeare, starting with John Boydell in the late 1780s and his collection of paintings and engravings. Paulson shows that 'the impact of Shakespeare on English art consisted of a general feeling, some assumptions, and a frame of mind rather than specifically visual structures – or verbal for that matter'. Extended sections on Hogarth's Falstaff and *Tempest*, and a reference to his portrait of David Garrick as Richard III, enclose elaborate discussion of the painterly approach to the oppositions in Shakespeare ('good and evil, light and dark, male and female, left and right'). The book ends with John Zoffany and Henry Fuseli, 'the Miltonic Shakespeare', and Turner and 'Shakespearean/Miltonic Landscape'. Among the ninety-eight illustrations are Shakespearean scenes by Benjamin West, James Northcote, Joseph Wright of Derby, Francis Hayman, and John Runciman, as well as Hogarth, Zoffany, Fuseli, and Turner. The effect on English painting of Shakespeare's felt copiousness and moral and psychological complexity is dominant throughout the book, and much more strongly felt than that of either the Bible or Milton.

44. *The Idea of the Actor: Drama and the Ethics of Performance*, by William B. Worthen. Princeton, pp. iv + 269. £20.90.
45. *Book and Painting: Shakespeare, Milton and the Bible: Literary Texts and the Emergence of English Painting*, by Ronald Paulson. UTenn (1982). pp. xi + 236. $19.95.

Iconography of a more traditional kind is the subject of *Shakespeare and the Emblem: Studies in Renaissance Iconography and Iconology*[46] from Hungary. To begin at the back of this book, an unusual but useful feature is the long section (seventy pages) of reviews of the major book-length items in English on iconographic material, from golden oldies like Henry Green (1870) to David Scott Kastan (1982) (*YW* 63.155–6). There is an air of thoroughness which is attractive, and makes up for a slight inadequacy in production values, with a typewritten text and rather messily reproduced pictures. Tibor Fabiny's opening essay quite admirably summarizes the present state of play in emblem studies, something which is curiously intermittent in the U.K. József Pál follows, on 'Some Iconological Aspects of the Poetic Sign in the Renaissance', exploring the streams of influence. The body of the book is given to studies by Peter M. Daly of McGill University, Clifford Davidson of Western Michigan, Fabiny himself, and others. Daly writes 'Shakespeare and the Emblem: The Use of Evidence and Analogy in Establishing Iconographic and Emblematic Effects' in the plays, a long essay interestingly cautious about both information and its application. Davidson looks hard at 'The Iconography of Wisdom and Folly in *King Lear*', particularly related to the world upside-down. Fabiny has two pieces, '*Veritas Filia Temporis*: The Iconography of Time and Truth and Shakespeare', and '*Theatrum Mundi* and the Ages of Man', both well written and particularly thorough, the first being especially illuminating about Shakespeare's Romances and the second about *Richard III*. Finally, Z. Szilassy writes briefly on 'Emblems, Stage, Dramaturgy' and Gy. E. Szöny on Alma's House in Spenser's *The Faerie Queen*.

Joseph Wittreich's long chapter, ' "Image of that Horror": The Apocalypse in *King Lear*' needs putting into context here – an important book on the Apocalypse[47]. The book is a significant study of apocalyptic thought in general, from its earliest appearance in Old Testament times, in particular its importance for the English Renaissance, and apocalyptic material in England and America during the eighteenth and nineteenth centuries. Wittreich begins with an account of the interest that the *Apocalypse* clearly had for Shakespeare. He observes the de-Christianizing work Shakespeare did on the old *Leir* play, and sees *King Lear* as 'the reversal of all histories'. This chapter grew into its own book, which will be discussed under *King Lear* below.

The American obsession with social class can have some unhappy results. *Blood Will Tell in Shakespeare's Plays*[48] is a peculiar and objectionable book from Oklahoma State University in which the author, David Shelley Berkeley, studies, the book says, 'various manifestations of Shakespeare's class bias seen in the poet's division of all human beings in the plays into two genetic classes, gentle and base', which is a lie. Illustration of this perverse thesis comes, for example, from a perverted reading of Lady Macbeth's cry 'Who would have thought the old man to have had so much blood in him?', and from some very nasty writing indeed by Dr Berkeley, in which he relishes both Richard II's

46. *Shakespeare and the Emblem: Studies in Renaissance Iconography and Iconology*, ed. by Tibor Fabiny. USzeged. pp. 480.

47. *The Apocalypse in English Renaissance Thought and Literature: Patterns, Antecedents and Repercussions*, ed. by C. A. Patrides and Joseph Wittreich. ManU. pp. ix + 452. £37.50.

48. *Blood Will Tell in Shakespeare's Plays*, by David Shelley Berkeley. TTP. pp. 107. hb $35, pb $20.

imagined homosexual experiences and some fantasized sexual perversions in Tudor and Stuart courts, and much else, all in the steady pull of something not too far removed from the racial theories of the Nazis. Such appalling rubbish is appropriately in a book of most unpleasant appearance. Another one for the dustbin.

Dr Sarup Singh's *Family Relationships in Shakespeare and the Restoration Comedy of Manners*[49] after that 'like some ore / Among a mineral of metals base / Shows itself pure'. It is a modest and attractive monograph. Dr Singh is a member of the Upper House of the Indian Parliament and Emeritus Professor of English at Delhi University. He begins with a useful account of the patriarchal doctrine of the family in the sixteenth century, and a longer account of its undermining after the Restoration, with special interest in the relations of men and women. The following chapters look rather simply at parents and children, age and youth, and husbands and wives in Shakespeare and after the Restoration. 'A Note on the "Mothers" in Shakespeare' closes this learned and pleasantly low-key book.

Linda Woodbridge's first book is called *Women and the English Renaissance: Literature and the Nature of Womankind, 1540–1620*[50], a large enough topic: she cuts it down soon enough – 'I propose that some kinds of Renaissance writings about women are fairer game for social and intellectual history than others'; that is, she is selecting her evidence. She understands that 'Renaissance attacks on women are more congenial to modern feminism than are Renaissance defences of women'. She admits, at the close of her 'Exordium', 'It is hard to know quite where to begin, when confronting the strange paradoxical dragon that is Women and the English Renaissance.' Sensibly, she lumps all the manifold writings about women into her own formulation, '. . . one genre, which I shall call the formal controversy about women'. She holds fairly firmly, in all her early chapters, to the *literary* delight participants in the controversies show, whatever the serious intention, if any. She is aware of the possibility of much greater independence among Elizabethan and Jacobean women than theory allowed. Her treatment of cross-dressing produces at least one surprising remark: 'During the 1590s, Shakespeare frequently used transvestite disguise in his plots.' Do Julia, Portia, Rosalind, and Viola make up 'frequent'? Imogen, she says, is 'his last remaining transvestite' – a funny word if it is supposed to unite her with the very different Portia-as-Balthasar and Rosalind-as-Ganymede. Ms Woodbridge has read very widely, but she can sweep everything in sight together to make a point which can then be meaningless in its largeness: '. . . the unisex tendencies of Renaissance life, so often feared and contemned, but occasionally welcomed'. She cheerfully examines evidence from literature, much of it from Shakespeare, to suggest that 'late medieval and Renaissance males felt their dominant position in society threatened' and then she kicks Shakespeare, in a long note on feminist criticism of the *Shrew*, with the patronizing and inexcusably bland remark '. . . it is, perhaps, both presumptious and fruitless to try to reform the opinions of an author so immeasurably great and so irretrievably dead: it would be more

49. *Family Relationships in Shakespeare and the Restoration Comedy of Manners*, by Sarup Singh. OUP (India) (1983). pp. x + 233. £10.50.

50. *Women and the English Renaissance: Literature and the Nature of Womankind, 1540–1620*, by Linda Woodbridge. Harvester. pp. viii + 364. £28.50.

respectful and less exhausting to forgive him'. Always readably stimulating, this book has unexpected material, drawn from identifiable texts. Sweeping generalization is too often a substitute for careful examination, and Renaissance women come out looking a little too like American women of the 1980s for comfort.

Marilyn French (see *YW* 63.150–1) writes in *ShN* that 'Shakespeare associated tragedy with masculine principle and comedy with the feminine principle'. Also in *ShN* Alexander Leggatt writes a useful little piece about 'Shakespeare and the Actor's Body' and John H. Astington some words on 'Eye and Hand on Shakespeare's Stage'. In *JMRS* George Walton Williams writes on 'Shakespeare's Metaphors of Health: Food, Sport and Life-preserving Rest', a pleasant account of Shakespeare's recipe for health, with illustrations from the plays, contemporary medical contexts, and a final section on *King Lear*. Mats Rydén, in *SN*, examines 'The Contextual Significance of Shakespeare's Plant Names', a study of fourteen plant names showing how Shakespeare 'exploits their phonetic and semantic potentialities – contextually and pragmatically'.

In the generally good Methuen Critical Idiom series, David L. Hirst contributes a volume on *Tragicomedy*[51], with a particularly valuable six-page 'Select Bibliography', in all of which Shakespeare appears largely; just over half the plays mentioned, in fact. Hirst's attention is on Shakespeare's interest in mixing genres as his career developed. Most space is given to *The Tempest*, where humanity as 'poor bare forked animal' is invested with nobility and hope. It is valuable to be shown Shakespeare not only impelled forward from sixteenth-century plays, but himself impelling so much into the seventeenth century and 'classical' concerns, and far forward to the twentieth century. David Lindley's collection of essays on *The Court Masque* will be considered below under *The Tempest*, but needs a commendatory mention here.

Arriving garlanded with superlatives on the dust-jacket (David Bevington's excitement on the front, Joel Altman's gasping on the flap), Jonathan Dollimore's *Radical Tragedy: Religion, Ideology and Power in the Drama of Shakespeare and his Contemporaries*[52] suggests that in place of the accepted Christian and humanist readings of Renaissance playwrights, we should substitute views of Jacobean tragedy as radical and subversive. Dollimore sees a drama of radical social and political realism: the plays 'decentre' man, subverting religious orthodoxy, and offering 'a searching critique' of 'dominant ideologies, of state power and the political process'. Does his thesis work? After a few pages on the disjunctions in *Troilus and Cressida*, he later turns to *King Lear*, where he rightly sees off the Christianizers, but becomes possibly too involuted in trying to rid the play of humanist taints: 'Edmund embodies the process whereby, because of the contradictory conditions of its inception, a revolutionary (emergent) insight is folded back into a dominant ideology'; so at the end closure is refused. This is not quite so new as Dollimore makes out. Much recent *Lear* criticism has made the same point, rather better: his models are a little shop-worn. Again, on *Antony and Cleopatra* and *Coriolanus*,

51. *Tragicomedy*, by David L. Hirst. CI 43. Methuen. pp. xiv + 141. hb £7.50, pb £2.95.

52. *Radical Tragedy: Religion, Ideology and Power in the Drama of Shakespeare and his Contemporaries*, by Jonathan Dollimore. Harvester. pp. viii + 312. £19.95.

Dollimore is brief and moderately suggestive, but what is new seems to me to be more the rocky impenetrability of his paragraphs. These three tragedies have been, in better hands, presented as subversive of everything in sight. I do not think they fit his thesis very well.

I once spent most of a night in a New York eating-house discussing with a distinguished American teacher of Shakespeare just what was involved in our shared discipline. As the hours went by it became increasingly clear that what we did had less and less connection: though we used some of the same words, 'lecture', 'seminar', 'classroom', 'course', we came to see that they meant such different things that dialogue virtually ceased. I mention this to introduce *SQ*'s special number on Teaching Shakespeare, which, with three curt bows to the world outside the United States, is wholly engaged with the problem inside that energetic country. Readers of *YW* who live and work outside will perforce find the articles fairly meaningless (indeed bafflingly so in the contribution about 'The Spectogram' from Brigham Young University) or acutely irritating. Charles R. Forker writes in *RMR* on 'Symbolic Staging in Shakespeare and its Importance to the Classroom'.

Putting together thirty-six years of teaching-notes does not necessarily make a good book, even with, as the author explains, generous and repeated leave of absence in which to write them up, and funding from four wealthy sources; and not even with the help of the in-group of 'names' which it is customary to drop at the front of American books. Joseph H. Summers's *Dreams of Love and Power*[53], a peculiarly American theme, too, reprints one essay on the ending of *King Lear* from the Helen Gardner *Festschrift* (*YW* 63.168) but is otherwise offering material not seen in print before. The opening essay, 'Dreams of Love and Power: *A Midsummer Night's Dream*', is a confection of appreciative comments on the play, offering nothing that is not better found by reading Shakespeare's play. The second essay does just the same for *The Winter's Tale*, with much talk of laughter (a continual 'laff-track' seems to have been added to Summers's performances) and a cosy conclusion which seems some miles from Shakespeare: 'At the end ... as in our happiest dreams, we are no longer anxious about either power or time because we have imaginatively experienced their destructive possibilities and we have truly come to know our loves and to understand their languages.' That is highly debatable. In the 1980s it is hard to sentimentalize *Hamlet*, but Summers achieves it. On *Measure for Measure*, with words like 'rapture' about, as well as 'bafflement', and notes on how he got the last two seats at a Saturday matinee in 1957, he is equally benign, finding 'within the play an oddly earthy and comic reflection of a dream of another happiness in another world'. That is even more debatable. The process is then applied to *Antony and Cleopatra* and *The Tempest*, taking us gently through the action of the plays. It is strange to think of this soppy book coming from the Clarendon Press.

I have at last caught Jürgen Schäfer's important *Documentation in the O.E.D.: Shakespeare and Nashe as Test Cases*[54]. At the very start of the *OED* enterprise (*A–Ant* was published exactly a hundred years ago, as Schäfer

53. *Dreams of Love and Power: On Shakespeare's Plays*, by Joseph H. Summers. Clarendon. pp. xii + 161. £15.
54. *Documentation in the O.E.D.: Shakespeare and Nashe as Test Cases*, by Jürgen Schäfer. Clarendon (1980). pp. x + 176. £19.50.

might have reminded us) James Murray set a half-century as a realistic toler-ance for dates of first usage. Jürgen Schäfer's book gives us the first scholarly testing of such statistics, and his book is a landmark. Using Malory and Wyatt as controls, he makes a close philological and statistical examination of the vocabularies of Shakespeare and Nashe. Partly because of the increasing flow of the material as the dictionary proceeded, antedatings vary according to the letter of the alphabet: but Schäfer's statistical evidence is that *OED*'s first citations even in Shakespeare, who is overrepresented, are out in several ways. This is a book which pleasantly combines work and play: it is of the utmost importance to have hard cases so rigorously examined; and the tables and graphs of this scholarly resource are also attractively absorbing.

A fine and important book closes this section: Jane Donawerth's *Shakespeare and the Sixteenth-Century Study of Language*[55]. The recently increasing work on this subject has been valuable. Professor Donawerth refers to *All's Well* with the remark that 'A mature Shakespeare, somewhere in his thirties, wrote this celebration of the power of eloquence that increases as a man loses his youthful capacity for action', and it is with such wisdom that she approaches the matter. Though, as she says, 'no history of Elizabethan linguis-tics and philosophy of language has yet appeared', a few devoted scholars – most of them, strikingly, women – have brought us a long way since Sister Miriam Joseph's pioneering study, *Shakespeare's Use of the Arts of Language* in 1947, especially Madeleine Doran (*YW* 35.87,105) and Marion Trousdale (*YW* 63.158). This book, itself clearly inspired by Madeleine Doran, is good, with the author's heart as well as considerable mind in the right place: 'The excitement of studying language in the Renaissance lay in discovering the supreme importance of humankind', she says. She carries her learning with grace, and like a true scholar tends to conceal the range and depth of it. Three opening chapters are concerned with basic ideas about the nature, history, and powers of language; with ideas related to passion psychology and the body's language; and with Elizabethan attitudes towards language. These things take us exactly half-way through. A following chapter on *Love's Labour's Lost* is excellent, and gets off to a flying start with noting

> the relative frequency of seventeen key words concerning language – speak(s), speech(es), language(s), word(s), name(s), voice(s), tongue(s), mouth(s), throat(s), ear(s), breath, air, airy, pen, paper(s), ink, and parchment

and going on from there. Similarly on *King John*, fourth of Shakespeare's plays 'in frequency of key terms concerning language', though that is rarely noticed. Fine chapters on *The Merchant of Venice* and *All's Well That Ends Well* (especially) lead to *Hamlet* and magnificence.

(b) Comedies

It is good to find modern semioticists holding hands with the neorhetoricians as mentioned above, and such touch is the principal value of Keir Elam's book

---

55. *Shakespeare and the Sixteenth-Century Study of Language*, by Jane Donawerth. UIll. pp. xiv + 279. £18.75.

Shakespeare's Universe of Discourse: Language-Games in the Comedies[56].
This book is a study, he says

> of the self-consciousness of Shakespeare's language. Or more specifi-
> cally, of Shakespeare's discourse. The term 'discourse', now fashionable
> again in literary studies, is Shakespeare's own favourite linguistic word
> in the comedies . . . the general Shakespearean word for language in *use*.

Quoting Ernst Cassirer in 1932, saying that the main motive force of the
comedies as the 'game of the pure self-activity of the word', Elam finds that

> in an age that elects language as both primary channel and primary
> target for its enthusiasms, for its suspicions, and even for its wars, the
> dramatic and theatrical potential of verbal events in themselves be-
> comes virtually limitless.

How, he asks, do the 'modes and instruments of contemporary linguistic
enquiry' explain 'such linguistically formidable texts as Shakespeare's comedies'? The result is a dense and difficult book, plunging straight into both
Wittgenstein and Renaissance rhetorical figures, making no concession to the
mere reader in its craggy sentences as it explores 'language-games' in all their
possible relationships – with the physical stage, the meaning of words, the very
business of speaking. Linguistics, semiotics, the philosophy of language and
sociology: sixteenth-century theories of meaning, language-use, conversational decorum, and rhetoric all crowd round an endeavour to open out *Love's
Labour's Lost* primarily, but the other comedies as well. Though the book has
an eight-page glossary of terms, it has no index of Shakespeare references,
which I find indicative of a lack of focus. Elam, though learned and brilliant,
has set the camera too hastily and moved it, too, so that language is not
properly related to the other 'universes of discourse' in a play. The accumulation of grainy fragments does not give a clear picture. Moreover, it is occasionally fogged with now-discounted occultism. His account of Bottom naming
the fairies – indeed a proportion of what would usually be called 'Chapter
Three' but is here 'Three Signs' – is nearly ridiculous in a late Frances Yates
way, with supposed light from Hermetists. Yet I shall come back to this book,
and treasure it as an early work. Elam's next book, I fancy, will be both clear
and important.

Edward Berry, in *Shakespeare's Comic Rites*[57], finds 'a remarkable affinity
between the structure of Shakespeare's romantic comedies and that of rites of
passage'. He follows closely Arnold van Gennep's three phases; separation,
transition, and incorporation. He discusses the romantic comedies from *The
Comedy of Errors* to *Twelfth Night*, inexplicably and inexcusably omitting *The
Merry Wives of Windsor*, a play which would illuminate his case. His introduction tries to show examples 'of the way in which initiatory, comic, and biological structures converge'. The chapter is hardly about Shakespeare, and he
gives no hint that, to put it mildly, not everyone agrees with Lawrence Stone.
The chapter on separations and mental journeys has some good things –

---

56. *Shakespeare's Universe of Discourse: Language-Games in the Comedies*, by Keir
Elam. CUP. pp. xii + 339. hb £25, pb £8.95.
57. *Shakespeare's Comic Rites*, by Edward Berry. CUP. pp. x + 221. £18.50.

'Shipwrecks are less unsettling than love' – but the level is not remarkable (Petruchio breaks Kate's dependence on social convention). Unlike Marjorie Garber (*YW* 62.187), to whose more valuable study of the same subject Berry refers only in a dismissive four-line note at the back of the book, he claims he sees the experiences of rites of passage in dramatic structure rather than characterization. Both critics depend heavily on van Gennep: Berry is more uncritically in the shadow of Northrop Frye and C. L. Barber; he is also less organized than Garber, and far less alert to *literary* convention. Further chapters repeat the slopping-together of modern anthropology and criticism, and roughly contemporary material (if reports of behaviour in 1641 and 1644 can be properly considered relevant to Shakespeare: Berry does not question this, but it casts doubt on his historical sense). This is an oddly formed book in which parts are bigger than the whole. Marjorie Garber's book, for all its faults, was much more illuminating about Shakespeare.

The Ungar series Literature and Life has a volume, *Shakespeare's Comedies* by Jack A. Vaughn[58], intended for teachers in America, and covering seventeen plays. On the whole the book has value in its close reference to productions; but it is sad to see *The Comedy of Errors* and *The Taming of the Shrew* offered in the current American fashion of stage mayhem; and the touchstone of popularity given as the American musical versions of these two plays.

Three items in *ShS*, whose main theme this year is Shakespeare's earlier comedies: R. S. White's opening essay, 'Criticism of the Comedies up to *The Merchant of Venice*: 1953–82' is a usefully thorough survey of what has been importantly said about the comedies from *The Comedy of Errors* to *Merry Wives*, judiciously and often wittily described by White: on the early plays, he says 'Supporters trembled in anticipation as C. L. Barber brought the tablets down from the cloudy mountain inhabited by Northrop Frye. Their plays had come out!'. At a time when it is thought clever to attack Frye, White's summary is good:

> Although one might now feel impatient with the sweeping range of his generalizations, Frye remains seminal because he established two basic positions: comedy, romance, and tragedy all have intimate formal and visionary links with each other, and comedy can be every bit as serious as tragedy. Without somebody saying these things, the study of Shakespearian comedy could have remained these thirty years the domain of charming, weightless *belles-lettres*.

White's eleven dense pages are too full for summary here. I hail the long passage rescuing *The Merry Wives of Windsor* from its unwarranted neglect. Next in *ShS* K. Tetzeli von Rosador discusses the 'art of precipitation, of prefiguring within the *protasis* both the play's middle and its end' in his 'Plotting the Early Comedies'. He finds in *The Comedy of Errors* oscillation between 'the building up of danger and its sudden, easy evasion, the tripartite scene-division with its regular alternation between turbulence and calm'. *Love's Labour's Lost*, virtually plotless, gives him a problem: he helpfully

---

58. *Shakespeare's Comedies*, by Jack A. Vaughn. Literature and Life. Ungar (1980). pp. v + 249. $15.50.

explores the opening speeches. *Two Gentlemen of Verona* fails 'in the relationship of plot, theme and structure'. And again in *ShS* William W. E. Slights, on 'Nature's Originals: Value in Shakespearian Pastoral', notes how Shakespeare's pastorals, which include *King Lear*, 'a hard pastoral', and *Tempest*, remain lively and thought-provoking by variously presenting myths of human regeneration, finding 'the liberation of self that is instigated when one is prepared either to trace his or her life back to its origins in human kindness or to imagine a fresh version of genesis consonant with pastoral peace and natural piety'.

R. S. White, again, writes finely in *RES* on 'Metamorphosis by Love in Elizabethan Romance, Romantic Comedy, and Shakespeare's Early Comedies'. 'Where, precisely, the plays of Lyly, Greene, and the young Shakespeare came from in any literary tradition is one of the unsolved problems of literary history.' After eight pages on the Romances, with particular reference to *Arcadia* and *The Faerie Queene*, in which Lyly and Greene are well seen, the bulk of the article is given to Shakespeare's romantic comedies with interesting reference out, for example, to *Richard III*. He deals very well indeed with love-change in *Two Gentlemen of Verona* and *Love's Labour's Lost*, and he is fine on the apparently spectacular change in Katherina in *The Taming of the Shrew*; not only the liberation of her many-sided personality, but 'an expansion of character by discovering a true bias, rather than as a negation and reversal'. The whole is summed up after longer treatment of *A Midsummer Night's Dream*, which 'brings to maturity one attitude towards the convention of love-change, the idea that it is essentially a fact of literature and only fitfully a fact of life'.

In *SQ* Dolora G. Cunningham writes on 'Wonder and Love in the Romantic Comedies', also on the possibility of change in the characters, from 'excessive, unstable feeling' to 'something of great constancy'. *SJW* contains Juliet Dusinberre (in German) on 'Shakespeares Frauen: Protestantisches Konzept und dramatische Bildwelt in *Ende gut, Alles gut* und im *Wintermärchen*'. In *SJH* Stephen Hannaford writes '"My Money Is my Daughter": Sexual and Financial Possession in English Renaissance Comedy', in which he draws on *The Merchant of Venice* and *Two Gentlemen of Verona*, among other plays.

(c) Histories

First two books which escaped the net in previous issues of *YW*. In *Shakespeare's Histories*[59] George J. Becker has written an introductory guide which is unpretentious and compact, including an outline of Shakespeare's biography and of the development of the history-play *genre*, plus genealogical tables, a breathless chapter on productions (with some well-reproduced photographs), and comments on the factual background. Some of his critical points come a little too pat – the Tudor myth is trotted out without qualification – and his treatments of the plays tend towards paraphrase. He tries to strike a balance between critical and theatrical comment, occasionally coming unstuck, e.g. his comparison of Hotspur to Tartuffe. It is sad to see the first trilogy written off, in outdated fashion, and he dismisses *Henry VIII* in a

59. *Shakespeare's Histories*, by George J. Becker. Ungar (1977). pp. xii + 196. hb $13.95, pb $6.95.

similarly cavalier way. However, he neither underrates *King John* nor adulates *Henry V*, and he rarely notes Shakespeare's deviations from historical fact without adducing their artistic justification. My main reservation about this sort of book is that it can so easily end up being read instead of the plays.

H. R. Coursen's book on the second tetralogy[60] interprets the plays as dramatizing a process of national decline only temporarily arrested by the personality cult of Henry V. Gaunt's prophetic vision is the yardstick for the subsequent reduction of the sacred to the secular. Richard II violates the sacramental nature of kingship, which he sees as 'personal possession rather than godly stewardship' (Coursen is especially informative about this distinction), and he opens the way for the pragmatic Bolingbroke with his commercial, contractual view of monarchy. In the political and comic scenes of the *Henry IV* plays Coursen identifies a similar profit-motivated world, with Falstaff's predatory and acquisitive instincts in the ascendant in *Part Two* (Coursen is refreshingly unsentimental about Falstaff). This book is independent minded and densely argued, while avoiding all needless obfuscation: it is the product of a genuine involvement with the texts, and should promote the same in its readers.

Robert Rentoul Reed Jr proceeds from the flat assertion that 'Shakespeare looked upon the Wars of the Roses as an instrument of God', and his book, *Crime and God's Judgment in Shakespeare*[61], attempts to restate the case for reading the histories and some of the tragedies as demonstrations of Divine retribution. He puts up an able defence despite his subscription to the fashionable but, in my view, mistaken and dangerous belief that the two tetralogies constitute 'a single prolonged stage play', a 'kind of epic' with 'organic form'; the critic's search for common factors may gloss over the plays' unique characteristics, encouraging him to treat them as though they were all written at one sitting. Reed, for example, accepts Henry IV's explanation in *Part Two* that 'necessity' compelled him to depose Richard II: but is this a legitimate piece of evidence for the interpretation of *Richard II*? A further difficulty of Reed's position is implied in his insistence that, up to Act V of *Richard II*, 'God is the prime mover of events [. . .] although the events appear to be moved by men'. This implies that what is shown in the play is not really true, and that what is really true is not shown in the play – which effectively cripples the critic.

However, Reed's detailed discussions are less hidebound than his opening chapter suggests. His most interesting general chapter traces the development from Anglo-Saxon laws of vendetta, in which Providence played no part, to the Norman institution of trial by combat as a means of determining guilt: both are set against biblical concepts of God's justice (surprisingly Reed confines himself to the Old Testament). The analyses of individual plays follow through the concepts of inherited guilt, man as God's minister or scourge, and conscience as a channel for Divine judgement. Reed ingeniously presents *Richard II* as a revenge play with Bolingbroke avenging Woodstock's murder, although

60. *The Leasing Out of England: Shakespeare's Second Henriad*, by H. R. Coursen. UPA (1982). pp. vii + 223. hb $25.25, pb $12.25.

61. *Crime and God's Judgment in Shakespeare*, by Robert Rentoul Reed Jr. UKen. pp. 225. £24.25.

Bolingbroke's notorious silences drive Reed to put motives in his mouth. Those who believe the Providentialist interpretations have had their day will be compelled at least to meet Reed's detailed arguments.

An interesting volume comes from the Société Française Shakespeare, always a source of good things. Their *Actes du Congrès 1983* is entitled *Mythe et histoire*[62], and it opens with a prefatory piece by H. Suhamy, 'Shakespeare historien: Propagateur de mythes, ou recenseur sceptique?', finding that 'Les mythes deviennent des valeurs, ou plutôt les valeurs ne sont plus des mythes'. M.-M. Martinet follows with 'Les Mythes historiques chez Shakespeare: Rumeur ou Silence?'; then D. Goy-Blanquet, 'Des Histoires tristes'; P. Sahel, '*Henri VI*: Le mythe contre l'histoire'; Y. Peyre, 'Mythes de Renaissance' which includes both meanings. Two lectures in English follow: J. P. Brockbank on 'Myth and History in Shakespeare's Rome', and W. Habicht on 'Hamlet's Prophetic Soul: An Obscured Myth?', about how the old myth of the prophet-hero, though devalued and obscured, has a function in revealing the truth of the past, which is alloted to the actors. J. Chauchaix spoke on Marston, and J. Dubu on 'L'Ambassade de Sully à Londres en 1603' on the death of Elizabeth. The last lecture was by Oliver Ford-Davies of the Royal Shakespeare Company on 'The Roman Plays: An Actor's View', a talk of exceptional interest. The volume ends with records of discussions between 'Universitaires et Gens de Théâtre', that is, with Marcel Marechal about his *Le Roi Lear*, and three recent French *Hamlet*s; and a 'Table Ronde sur Mythe et Histoire'. Altogether, a volume of good value. [D.D.]

I turn now to general essays. A. A. Ansari's 'Political Man in Shakespeare's English History Plays' (*AJES*) is disfigured by misprints, misquotations, infelicitous phrasing, whole sentences of no discernible meaning, and misinterpretations due to careless reading and misunderstanding of the historical context. He writes of one character as 'caricatured with superb and dense brushwork', of another as a 'combustible politician'; he tells us that Henry V is 'one in whom the molecules of being do not attain to the orchestration of the Dionysiac rhythm', that Buckingham is heedless of conscience and the moral law, that Falconbridge is a cynic, and so on. In 'Shakespeare and the Chronicles Reassessed' (*L&H*) Michael Tomlinson tells us little new about Shakespeare's relationship to the chronicles, stressing his superior immediacy, construction, and political sophistication. In a general study of the second tetralogy in *SQ*, entitled 'Uneasy Lies', Ronald R. MacDonald explores the relationship between language and history in a wordy fashion. By contrast, Harry Morris (*PLL*) provides an incisive and illuminating study of 'The Dance of Death Motif in Shakespeare' in the second tetralogy and elsewhere. He begins by expressing surprise that no one has examined the link between Shakespeare and Holbein: then he adds, 'unless, of course, no link exists'. A man who can question his own idea like that in cold print deserves our respect. In fact he shows clearly that there is such a link, and his essay is excellently illustrated. Ruth Morse (*SJH*, 1983) studies Shakespeare's use of images of unnatural food in the first tetralogy and other plays in her article 'Unfit for Human Consumption'.

62. *Mythe et histoire: Société Française Shakespeare; Actes du congrès 1983*, ed. by M. T. Jones-Davies. Touzot. pp. 198. Ffr 160.

(d) Tragedies

A new SUAS volume is welcome. *Shakespearian Tragedy*[63] opens with a long piece by M. J. B. Allen, 'Toys, Prologues and the Great Amiss: Shakespeare's Tragic Openings', in which he tackles the problem of where to begin a tragedy. He himself starts with *Macbeth*, which has a beginning 'so dense, so fraught with fore-echoes and premonitions, so chock-full of ironies and palterings, that it constitutes a premature climax'. This he contrasts with *Titus Andronicus*, itself contrasted again with *Timon of Athens*, where 'the end in this instance ruined the beginning in the beginning'. *Romeo and Juliet* is Shakespeare's first success with the double opening, which leads to doubleness in so many ways, and then on to the complex double openings of *Hamlet* and *Macbeth*. The Roman plays open with 'what we might call the future rhetoric', and '*Othello* and *King Lear* present us with beginnings of a very different kind', with information withheld; *Hamlet* has an opening 'prophetic of the play's larger concern with indecision'. 'Some conclusions' punningly close this very fine essay. In the same volume Ann Thompson asks 'Who Sees Double in the Double Plot?', exploring 'Shakespeare's use of the kind of double plot that could be described as a "doubling" or "mirror" effect . . . most spectacularly deployed in *King Lear*'. She works from a look at doubling devices both in the plays (*Twelfth Night*) and outside (Plutarch's *Parallel Lives*). Though she deals with *Timon of Athens*, *Coriolanus*, and *The Tempest*, her main concentration is on *King Lear*: 'Thus by the end these two apparently similar plots have reached conclusions which feel very different indeed.' This is followed by Rosalind King on 'Black Vesper's Pageants: Emblems of Tragic Stagecraft in Shakespeare', usefully relating the emblem tradition in Shakespeare's working life to *Timon of Athens*, to *Hamlet*, and, finely, to *Othello*. Next in the volume is A. R. Braunmuller's chapter, 'Early Shakespearian Tragedy and Its Contemporary Context: Cause and Emotion in *Titus Andronicus*, *Richard III*, and *The Rape of Lucrece*'. Starting from the revealing changes in Robert Wilmot's play *Tancred and Gismund* between manuscript of 1567 and printed text of 1591, Braunmuller suggests that 'Shakespeare himself had to learn the lessons Wilmot apparently learned . . . from the same teachers, the working dramatists of the popular theatre in the late 1580s and early 1590s'. He goes on to expound what such lessons might have been, with special reference to *Titus Andronicus*, the *Henry VI* plays, *Richard III*, and, unexpectedly and valuably, *The Rape of Lucrece*. One of the editors, D. J. Palmer, follows, in a chapter called 'The Self-Awareness of the Tragic Hero', a very long and dense analysis of self-awareness, from Arthur Golding's Narcissus and some sonnets to *Macbeth*, via *Richard III*, *Julius Caesar*, and *Othello*, showing the complexity of the matter. The last chapter, 'Romans and Barbarians: The Structure of Irony in Shakespeare's Roman Tragedies', by Jacqueline Pearson, is rather repetitive; she clears away critical undergrowth to show the four plays standing together, and then suggests that *Julius Caesar* is ironic within itself, but takes on 'an additional dimension of irony if we read the play in the light of Plutarch'. *Coriolanus* presents 'problems of evaluation in even more extreme form'. She

63. *Shakespearian Tragedy*, ed. by Malcolm Bradbury and David Palmer. SUAS 20. Arnold. pp. vi + 185. pb £6.95.

studies *Titus Andronicus* and *Antony and Cleopatra*, summing up the Roman tragedies (and the book):

> To express this unconsoling view of history, the four plays use similar devices to structure their ambiguities, ironic juxtaposition, polarity, parallelism and repetition, ironic circularity, deflation and undercutting, and a tendency to begin with a hostile version of the central characters and to end with deliberate anticlimax.

SJW has Alexander Tichonowitsch Parfjonow, 'Shakespeares und Ben Jonsons Tragödien als historische Metaphern'; and *SJH* Dieter Mehl on 'Chaucerian Comedy and Shakespearean Tragedy'. Finally, Phyllis Rackin has an excellent little volume in Frederick Ungar's World Dramatists series, as it was, which earlier slipped the net and is now re-issued in paperback: *Shakespeare's Tragedies*[64], which is intended as a teaching aid. It is exceptionally good value, giving accounts of the ten plays which are both sound and sense.

6. Individual Plays

All's Well That Ends Well
In *ShS* R. B. Parker writes on 'War and Sex in *All's Well That Ends Well*'. Through Renaissance attempts to accommodate Mars and Venus (and a slight misreading of Edgar Wind on Veronese, it must be said), Parker suggests that 'the conflict of the play is resolved by having each ideal – war and love – modify the other'. So the conclusion takes the form of 'a wry accommodation between them' in which 'the purity of both ideals has had to be abandoned'. So Bertram 'must be educated from war to accept first sexuality, then its responsibilities', and Helena 'must learn to abandon the false religion of self-abnegation in sexual love and bring it to fruition by increasingly deliberate aggression'. This brings both characters into clearer view and reinforces the value of Shakespeare's originality in using the older generation as a viewpoint. His detailed reading certainly helps with Bertram. Helena is seen in relation to the earlier, comic, Helena in *A Midsummer Night's Dream*, with echoes of *Troilus and Cressida*. *SJW* has two essays: one by Juliet Dusinberre noticed above (p. 219) and one by Susan Bassnett-McGuire: 'An Ill Marriage in an Ill Government: Patterns of Unresolved Conflict in *All's Well That Ends Well*'. In the volume *Shakespeare, Man of the Theater*[34] is a wise piece by Roger Warren, 'Some Approaches to *All's Well That Ends Well* in Performance', in which he suggests ways that stagings of this play, 'including controversial ones', have contributed to his understanding of some important aspects of Helena, Bertram, 'and especially of the king and his court'.

Antony and Cleopatra
In *SJH* Russell Jackson writes interestingly about 'The Triumphs of *Antony and Cleopatra*'; in *N&Q* Michael Cameron Andrews on 'Cleopatra's "Salad Days"' finds salads associated with virginity and the reduction of sexual appetite. In *ShStud* (1981–2) Teruhira Kimura writes simply 'Observations upon Some Textual and Annotatory Problems in *Antony and Cleopatra*'.

64. *Shakespeare's Tragedies*, by Phyllis Rackin. Ungar (1983). pp. 184. pb $6.95.

As You Like It

Helen M. Whall in *HLQ* discusses '*As You Like It*: The Play of Analogy'. 'As you liken it . . . so it shall be . . . Shakespeare will ask us not so much to call into question the answers we have arrived at by pressing analogies, but rather to recognize the fact that we have been using analogies, not directly receiving infallible doctrines.' She is interesting on 'liking and likening', especially the latter. In *Expl* Martin Orkin briefly discusses a use of proverbs and puns, and David-Everett Blythe writes about II.iv.55–6.

Coriolanus

In the Hibbard *Festschrift*[38] are three articles. R. W. Ingram works on how sounds, on-stage and off, affect what we see on stage and the effect of dramatic poetry (with reference too to *Titus Andronicus*). James C. Bulman in '*Coriolanus* and the Matter of Troy' examines most suggestively Shakespeare's complex use of the heroic tradition in his allusion to Troy. He starts from the *topos* of Hector, and sees *Troilus and Cressida* feeding in to *Coriolanus*, with usefully seen resonances between legend and history in the sounding of heroic tragedy. Less satisfactory is R. B. Parker's '*Coriolanus* and "th' Interpretation of the Time"' in which he aims, by historical speculation, to give us *Coriolanus* when new. He sees 'two main political issues', and sees those as class conflict and patriotism. He is, I feel, insufficiently secure on the British culture of the time, and at the same time he is able to be dogmatic about the state of British society under James. He is also prone to the deadly infection of 'salmons in both' as, for example, when dealing with the supposed effect of rural riots on the writing of the play. There is not one scrap of evidence for that. He argues for a Rome where *pietas* has been sacrificed to *virtus*.

Cymbeline

Judiana Lawrence defends the last act in 'Natural Bonds and Artistic Coherence in the Ending of *Cymbeline*' (*SQ*): it 'fosters both assent to the aims of ethical romance and a critical analysis of its means'.

Hamlet

What was the Elizabethan style of acting? Was it formal or 'natural'? The issues are especially important for this play, and critics have long drawn up battle-lines. One of the many good things about Peter Holland's '*Hamlet* and the Art of Acting' (*TD*) is that he says 'my solution to the problem is a simple one: I believe that both sides are right'. This is the most important *Hamlet* item this year, an essay which is neither long nor tedious, and beautifully opens up both the whole matter of what was seen at the Globe, and this particular play, 'obsessed with its own status as a play'. *SR* picks up a rarity: L. C. Knights on '*Hamlet* and the Perplexed Critics' in which he suggests that the 'conflated Q2/F text given by modern editors . . . offers limits to a complete subjectivism, with each reader or spectator creating, so to speak, his own play from a glorified Rorschach blot'. He is examining *Hamlet*'s 'obvious and inescapable openness to interpretation'. In *SQ* James L. Calderwood finds '*Hamlet*'s Readiness' a term for outward clothing and/or inward arming, which leads him to some woolly clothing-links to language. Also in *SQ* Donald K. Hedrick writes windily and pretentiously, apparently about satire and heroism, under the objectionable title ' "It Is No Novelty for a Prince to be a Prince": An Enantiomorphous Hamlet'. Again in *SQ* Eric Rasmussen discusses very briefly indeed 'Fathers and Sons in *Hamlet*', finding new things to say about Brutus as failed revenger, and finally in the same journal E. Kerr Borthwick finds a pun on 'calf', III.ii.105. In *N&Q* Kate G. Frost finds 'An Unreported *Hamlet* Allusion' in the 1614 edition of 'The Philosophers' Banquet'; Dalton Gross and Mary Jean Gross dismiss the idea that Shakespeare knew Bartolommeo Eustachio on poison in ears; Donald K. Anderson Jr and Robert F. G. Spier suggest 'hawk' as 'mortarboard'. In *SJW* Anselm Schlösser writes 'Über das Herangehen an *Hamlet*' ('On the Approach to *Hamlet*').

In the SUAS *Tragedy* volume[63] W. T. Jewkes, in ' "To Tell My Story": The Function of Framed Narrative and Drama in *Hamlet*', begins with telling points about perspective and the relation of *Hamlet* to *Troilus and Cressida* before going quickly to the centre of the early action, the play-within-the-play, discussing the way the play is full of structural explorations of these ironies of revenge as a wild kind of justice, which are then brilliantly demonstrated, so that sets of relationships, 'by a slight twist of the prism reveal another configuration', both inside and outside the play. In the closing section 'Shakespeare begins to open more casements, framing vistas which stretch even further toward infinity than any so far revealed by his frames within frames – all the way back to the creation of the world'. But at the centre is what Joyce called 'the French triangle', embodying every important issue and relationship: 'royalty, familial love and betrayal, poison, usurpation, dissembling, mutability and death . . .'. This is an exhilarating chapter. By contrast, J. A. Bryant Jr's 'Hamlet as Christian Malgré Lui' (*SR*) is wholly ridiculous. Hamlet as Christ, forsooth, with duty put on by a 'ghostly' father . . . That Ghost comes from heaven . . . What nonsense.

In bulk, by a long way the largest item this year is Roland Mushat Frye's *The Renaissance Hamlet: Issues and Responses in 1600*[65], an important book in the revivifying discipline of iconography. It is a learned book, with much that is interesting to say. Big in both page size and length, it summarizes the present position on a number of issues, and gives the evidence which casts some new light on how these might be judged, for example, from the various parts of the story of Mary Queen of Scots. The chapters are 'Problems, Challenges, and Ambiguities'; 'The Court and the Prince'; 'Choosing Sides'; 'The Deliberate Prince'; 'The Prince amid the Tombs'; and 'Finale': thus, as can be seen, he works steadily through the play. Appendixes study Mirrors, Claudius, and Ophelia's Funeral. Notes in small type, bibliography, and index run to almost a quarter of the book, and are deeply impressive. It is a mine of material for the study of *Hamlet* in its original context, and should be on every Shakespearean's shelf. I learned much about tyrannicide, for example, and incest, and funerals ('The Prince amid the Tombs' is particularly fine). Yet I admit some disappointment. His illustrations from modern staging seem to be taken from sentimental American productions – I have seen many *Hamlet*s, and I have never seen anywhere in Europe a Ghost, 'heartbroken because Gertrude could not see it', which he says is 'the modern stage practice'. He can be boring

65. *The Renaissance Hamlet: Issues and Responses in 1600*, by Roland Mushat Frye. Princeton. pp. xvi + 398. £26.50.

and repetitive. While there is much that is illuminating, nothing gripped with a sense of intellectual adventure, which this play demands; for me, there were no moments of sudden illumination of a line or a word. And Princeton University Press should certainly have tried harder, and not issued the book with those, for the most part, smudgy and wholly inadequate reproductions of the ninety illustrations.

Henry IV

Harold Toliver ('Workable Fictions in the *Henry IV* Plays', *UTQ*, 1983) discusses the relationship between truth, fantasy, and propaganda in the plays, with observations on the various ideas about history they examine by these categories. Along similar lines, but less ambitiously, Joseph Candido (*TSLL*) studies the various names and titles applied to Hal, by himself and others, showing how they reflect his task of integrating his private nature and his public role. In the best essay on the plays this year, Sherman Hawkins (*SQ*) writes on 'Teaching the Theatre of Imagination: The Example of *1 Henry IV*'. He makes acute and reasonable criticisms of the fad for seeing the plays in general as theatre-scripts rather than as literary texts, insists on the primacy of the 'theatre of the imagination' and studies 'the interplay of theatrical problems of intonation, gesture and motivation with scholarly problems of theme, symbolism and structural form'. But how he can say that A. C. Bradley's is 'still the finest single essay' on the play, I just don't know. Jack R. Sublette (*AJES*, 1983) studies images of Time in *Part One* in a wholly unexceptionable and predictable fashion. Giles R. Mitchell and Eugene P. Wright (*SCB*, 1983) explain 'Hotspur's Poor Memory' as instances of parapraxis, i.e. unconsciously motivated forgetting. III.i of *Part One* is laboriously studied by S. P. Zitner in 'Staging the Occult . . .', a contribution to the G. R. Hibbard *Festschrift*[38]. He concludes that Glendower is meant to provide music by magic and that in production this would come from under the stage. In the same volume C. E. McGee interprets the ending of *Part Two* in terms of Tudor royal entries, showing that Falstaff's disarray and pretended zeal have pageant precedents and that Hal has no choice but to exercise the authority expected on such ceremonial occasions. This is a helpful perspective on a puzzling scene. Martin R. Orkin (*ES*) analyses 'Sir John Falstaff's Taste for Proverbs', sometimes failing to distinguish between direct quotation or allusion, and exploitation of proverb idiom. He has associated notes in *Expl* and *N&Q*. John W. Sider in 'Falstaff's Broken Voice' (*ShS*) argues that Falstaff, especially in *Part Two*, should speak in an aged high-pitched voice rather than the rich bass we all mentally hear. To complete a series of somewhat tired efforts to say something new about these plays, Harry Berger Jr (*KR*) writes with intolerable pretentiousness and jargon ('generativity', '*écriture*', 'metanarrative', 'rhizomatic', 'detextualization') on the dramatic and thematic function of Rumour, who he suggests may have been androgynous, or even female!

Henry V

Joseph Candido and Charles R. Forker are the compilers of the Garland Shakespeare Bibliographies volume on this play[66]. It has sections on criticism, text, sources, adaptation, editions, stage history, translation, and versions in

66. *'Henry V': An Annotated Bibliography*, ed. by Joseph Candido and Charles R. Forker. GSB 4. Garland (1983). pp. xxiv + 815. $65.

other media. There are 2103 items covering mostly the period 1940–79, and every glancing reference to the play, even in books about other plays, is documented. The comments are summaries with no attempt at evaluation. Entries are chronological within each section. Such a book makes life easy for the researcher – perhaps too easy, since half the charm of research is the discovery of articles more interesting than the one you are looking for – but its authoritativeness is beyond question.

In 'Hazlitt on *Henry V*, and the Appropriation of Shakespeare' (*SQ*) Richard Levin attacks those who claim Hazlitt as an anticipator of the ironic view of Henry's character, shows that they have misread Hazlitt, and then enlists Hazlitt in support of Levin's own, un-ironic reading. Graham Holderness (*L&H*) writes with excruciating prolixity and fussiness about the propagandist use of the play by G. Wilson Knight, Sir Laurence Olivier, and E. M. W. Tillyard in 'Agincourt 1944 . . .'. His Neostructuralist Critspeak is painful to read.

Henry VI

The Garland annotated bibliography, compiled by Judith Hinchcliffe[67], is similar in layout to that on *Henry V*, but runs to only 921 items.

Roger Warren (*ShS*) discusses the juxtaposition of contraries and the reversal of audience expectations as aspects of the dramatic technique of the trilogy. Joseph Candido (*SQ*) calls attention to the frequency of capture and escape as sources of plot and imagery in 'Getting Loose in the *Henry VI* Plays', concentrating on the Suffolk/Margaret relationship, the development of the character of York, and links between Henry and Edward IV. This essay suggests fruitful reflections about the treatment of political power in the plays, but more notable still in that respect is an essay by Donald R. Wineke (*ClioI* 1983) on Machiavellian elements in *Part One*, especially in its treatment of monarchy and militarism. Wineke does not claim Machiavelli as a source, but he suggests enough convincing similarity to make further investigation desirable.

I should like to make a plea to all future critics of these plays to stop calling them the 'Henriad', a word devoid of both euphony and sense.

Henry VIII

Rolf Soellner (*SJW*) writes on 'Reformation und Deformation' in the play. H. R. Woudhuysen (*N&Q*) adds to the evidence that its subtitle was *All Is True* by quoting from a contemporary manuscript diary.

Julius Caesar

A teaching-aid with a difference comes from Germany (in English): many miles away from the ubiquitous and mind-shutting 'model-answer' booklets of 'Notes', Ernst Häublein and Edelbert Weinig's *Julius Caesar: A Teacher's Guide*[68] makes very strenuous demands indeed on the whole classroom – pupils, teachers, blackboard; with a host of scholars and critics singing in the background. Once the non-German reader has become acclimatized to the

---

67. '*King Henry VI, Parts 1, 2 and 3': An Annotated Bibliography*, comp. by Judith Hinchcliffe. GSB 5. Garland. pp. xix + 368. $53.

68. *Shakespeare's 'Julius Caesar': A Teacher's Guide*, by Ernst Häublein and Edelbert Weinig. CVK. pp. 157. DM 19.80.

too-frequent imperative verb (it would be nice to go one's own way from time to time) he or she will learn a vast amount about the play, as well as about an extraordinarily thorough method of teaching.

In *SQ* A. Jonathan Bate finds a wholly unnecessary ribald pun on 'awl' at I.i.21–4; in *Expl* Alan R. Smith says of III.ii.190 'Antony arouses both pity and veneration for Caesar'; in *N&Q* Gary Taylor expands on Dover Wilson in 1949 to find parallels between Samuel Daniel's *Musophilus* and this play, and Martin R. Orkin sees a cluster of proverb allusions at I.ii.266–74; and in *SQ* again Carol Marks Sicherman defends deliberate short lines and metrical pauses. In *CR* Ann Molan's '*Julius Caesar*: The General Good and the Singular Case' tackles unevenness: 'what goes wrong . . . is that the later stretches of the play lose touch with what the earlier acts had grasped firmly as central questions . . . It often happens in the play that largeness of assertion is substituted for complexity of imagining.' Caesar's singularity is a danger. In being extraordinary, singular, he is 'not reducible to, not alignable with, the ordinary, regular and acceptable patterns or orderings of experience, and therefore not predictable or controllable'.

King John

Dean R. Baldwin (*Lang&S*, 1983) on 'Style in *King John*' distinguishes rhetorical from serious style in the play, as embodied, respectively, in Falconbridge and Constance, other characters occupying a middle ground. The distinction, derived from Richard Lanham, is even more tendentious than Baldwin admits in its implication that rhetoric is frivolous.

In a chapter on the play, subtitled 'Mutable Speech' in her book on language[55], Jane Donawerth argues that in *King John* Shakespeare successfully embodies 'in his style the defects in language that the characters perceive in their world', but still admits to thinking the play a failure. Her relentless catalogue of its linguistic images and rhetorical devices leaves her reader as cold as the play leaves her. Virginia M. Vaughan (*SQ*) sees *John* as a bridge between the presentational technique of the first tetralogy and the representational technique of the second, discussing the consequent shifts from set speeches and emblematic staging towards a more exploratory analysis of the effects of political power. Her general level of argument is high, and the essay is a welcome treatment of the poor relation in the canon.

King Lear

In *SJH* E. A. J. Honigmann writes at some length on 'The Uniqueness of *King Lear*: Genre and Production Problems' and in *ShStud* (1981–2) Masahiko Sunohara discusses '*King Lear* as a Tragedy of Love – with Special Regard to Passive Love'. Just how perverse criticism can be is illustrated by Barbara C. Millard in *ShN*, ' "No Blown Ambition": Cordelia and the Problem of the Virago in Shakespeare's Tragedies', which is high-flown nonsense.

The play comes off well this year in relation to iconography. In the volume *Shakespeare and the Emblem*[46] Clifford Davidson writes finely on 'The Iconography of Wisdom and Folly in *King Lear*', a thorough and scholarly coverage. Rolf Soellner in *SQ* studies '*King Lear* and the Magic of the Wheel', with images of the Wheel of Fortune. More remarkable than either is the piece in *HLQ* by Guy Butler, 'Shakespeare's Cliff at Dover and an Emblem Illustration': he presents an illustration accompanying Embleme XX in Guillaume de la Perrière's *The Theatre of Fine Devices* translated by Thomas Combe, which may date from an edition of the 1590s. Here a blindfold man, stooping and with a walking staff, is led by a figure on an eminence overlooking the sea. The figure leading is young and naked and also blindfold. The picture suggests the angel of death leading aged misery to liberty; but the text suggests blindfold Fortune leading the blind. The translator, incidentally, might be the same Thomas Combe of Stratford to whose son Shakespeare left his sword in his will.

Joseph Wittreich's fine book, *'Image of that Horror': History, Prophecy, and Apocalypse in 'King Lear'*[69], grew out of his chapter in the book noticed above (p. 212) on the Apocalypse[47], every part of which section being now expanded, to make a volume of considerable value. The opening chapter now more fully relates the Apocalypse, politics under James, and Shakespeare's play. The second develops the Folio-only Fool's prophecy in III.ii in the Merlin tradition, and illuminates modern critical disarray on the subject, before showing it as epitomizing 'the upside-down world of the Lear universe and all of its confusion' – and essentially apocalyptic. A following chapter studies genre, again with reference to the Apocalypse. He then enriches understanding of the exchange between Kent and Edgar, 'Is this the promis'd end? / Or image of that horror?', in a long and excellent chapter on apocalyptic in the play. His last chapters, on the play and Christianity, and its hypothetical connection with the Anglican liturgy, do right what R. Chris Hassel Jr (see above, pp. 209–10) does less well. In the growing interest of scholars and critics in apocalyptic in Shakespeare, Wittreich has an honourable and valuable place.

In *N&Q* Martin Coyle relates the play and *The Faerie Queene*, and Michael Cameron Andrews finds descriptions of Cordelia taken from *Arcadia*. In *ELN* C. Herbert Gilliland proposes a reading of the Fool's 'Codpiece' song at III.ii.25–26 to solve all problems; and also in *ELN* A. D. Barnes, in a well-argued case, supports a biblical allusion behind Kent's 'Holy Cords' at II.ii.74–6.

Adele Seeff, in the volume *Shakespeare, Man of the Theater*[34], opens up 'Charles Kean's *King Lear* and the Pageant of History'.

A Lover's Complaint

We must wait for John Kerrigan's Penguin *Sonnets* volume for more on this poem: but meanwhile here is a most useful book from Salzburg, *Shakespeare on Love: The Poems and the Plays. Prolegomena to a Variorum Edition of 'A Lover's Complaint'*[70], which compasses a lot in its two hundred small pages. Richard Allan Underwood prints the text, and then gives a long chapter to 'The Form of the Complaint and Laments by Women', followed by general discussion of the poem. He then presents analyses of the poem's style, and another long section on the problematic relationships between the poem, the *Sonnets*, and *All's Well That Ends Well*. An appendix includes an account of a modern

---

69. *'Image of that Horror': History, Prophecy, and Apocalypse in 'King Lear'*, by Joseph Wittreich. Huntington. pp. xiv + 185. $22.

70. *Shakespeare on Love: The Poems and the Plays. Prolegomena to a Variorum Edition of 'A Lover's Complaint'*, by Richard Allan Underwood. SSELER. USalz. pp. xv + 189. DM 40.

American stage production of the poem. There is a five-page bibliography.

Love's Labour's Lost

In *N&Q* Michael Cameron Andrews writes on 'The Owl's "Merry Note"';
in *E&S* Richard Proudfoot finds that 'the play's themes and its techniques both
relate it to its age', in *'Love's Labour's Lost*: Sweet Understanding and the
Five Worthies'. Via Sidney's *Defence of Poesie*, he stresses the importance of
debate as opposed to action, making good use of Ben Jonson's *'Language* most
shewes a man: speake that I may see thee'.

Macbeth

A new series of study-aids for younger British students is worth mentioning:
the Penguin 'Passnotes' volume on this play[71] has a solid old-fashioned
thoroughness – a good nine-page synopsis, distinct from analysis, which CSE
and O-level candidates will be grateful for. In *N&Q* Michael Cameron Andrews
wonders who has no children at IV.iii.215. In *SQ* Howard Jacobson finds
Seneca's *Thyestes*, not *Hercules Furens*, at I.vii.7–10; and King-Kok Cheung,
also in *SQ*, finds *Angst* as the driving force in Macbeth's actions – he is
increasingly fascinated and attracted by the deed (murder): his piece is called
'Shakespeare and Kierkegaard: "Dread" in *Macbeth*'. Arthur Kirsch writes on
'Macbeth's Suicide' in *ELH*; using Renaissance material, Freud, and
Montaigne, he finds that Macbeth's 'deepest wish is to annihilate the very
self he asserts'. Anne Lancashire's piece on emblematic castles in the Hibbard
Festschrift[38] has oblique reference to *Macbeth*. In the same volume the late
James M. Nosworthy relates '*Macbeth*, *Dr Faustus*, and the Juggling Fiends';
Macbeth is a play about damnation and *Dr Faustus* 'the great seminal play
upon that theme'. Looking at Satanism in many aspects, including a study of
the number three, he concludes that Macbeth's downfall

> is rendered the more disturbing because at no point is he offered that
> grace which is available to Faustus and which he constantly rejects. . . . If
> a man of heroic character is to be destroyed both body and soul through
> a venial fault, an astute piece of timing, a cheap trick, and an unchal-
> lenged program of malevolence, life is indeed a tale told by an idiot
> signifying something worse than nothing.

Finally, in the same volume Alexander Leggatt proposes in '*Macbeth* and the
Last Plays' that it might appear as a parody of the last plays. He is very
suggestive about the unnatural links, the returns from the dead, and sleep: 'In
short, motifs that will be used in the final romances to produce a sense of order
and reassurance are used in *Macbeth* for an atmosphere of violation and fear.'
He finds the story of *Macbeth* is 'like an arc cut from a full circle' and
sometimes we get a glimpse of the rest. Theatrical means which belong to the
tradition of Shakespeare's last plays tell a simple tale of a villain punished and a
suffering kingdom restored to order. But this tradition is introduced only to be
broken, parodied, and perverted to make way for another kind of drama – 'the
trip inside the mind of the character who is technically the villain of the story
but cannot be reduced to that alone'.

71. *William Shakespeare: 'Macbeth'*, ed. by S. H. Coote. Penguin Passnotes.
Penguin. pp. 96. pb £0.95.

Measure for Measure
What *ShN* prints quite often defies belief (see above on *King Lear*). Here Carolyn Asp in a piece called 'Desire, the Gaze and the Woman in *Measure for Measure*' relates voyeurism and a desire to avoid gaze – 'the gazer seeks to see castration. . . . By choosing chastity rather than desire, Isabella symbolically denies castration, i.e. the inferior female position.' Less loony, but still over-biased, Marcia Riefer in *SQ*, in ' "Instruments of Some More Mightier Member": The Constriction of Female Power in *Measure for Measure*', finds that Isabella's 'sense of self is undermined and finally destroyed through her encounters with patriarchal authority'. In *N&Q* R. Renehan finds A. E. Housman echoing III.ii.70–1. R. L. P. Jackson's essay, 'Necessary Ambiguity: The Last Act of *Measure For Measure*' in *CR*, begins with L. C. Knights, and Leavis, and James Smith, and remains firmly Cambridge and obscure. After all this it is a relief to turn to Liverpool for sense: N. W. Bawcutt's thoughtful and helpful piece in *ShS*, ' "He Who the Sword of Heaven Will Bear": The Duke versus Angelo in *Measure for Measure*', where he examines Law and Mercy, by way of the much-maligned couplets at the end of Act III, especially in the intense dramatic relationship between the Duke and Angelo, and most particularly the shift in the second half, after those couplets, from 'almost tragic intensity' to 'intrigue and manipulation'.

The Merchant of Venice
Mamoru Saito in *ShStud* (1981–2) finds Lorenzo 'a mysterious youth' and writes sweetly about him. In *ShN* Thomas Moisan rehearses again the incongruities which open Act V, to what point is not clear. Henry Saunders in *N&Q* finds the Staple Courts (Equity) of importance. The Penguin 'Passnotes' volume[72] is like the *Macbeth* noticed above, but surprisingly a little shorter. In *ShS* is a major essay, Keith Geary's 'The Nature of Portia's Victory: Turning to Men in *The Merchant of Venice*', in which he examines the way ambivalence throughout the play is embodied in the double self of Portia and Balthazar, the lady and the lawyer, and how different her 'disguise' is in its completeness from those of Julia, Rosalind, and Viola. He sees the opening scene as 'tense with the loosening of ties' between Antonio and Bassanio, and notes the relationship between the financial and romantic aspects of marriage, before showing Portia entering Venice to recover her husband from the masculine world.

The Merry Wives of Windsor
SJW notes a new translation by Eva Walch. In *SQ* David-Everett Blythe finds 'sea-coal' to mean both sea-freightage and superior quality. In *N&Q* W. L. Godshalk tries to link a real litigation to the first 197 lines, though it took place in August 1600.

A Midsummer Night's Dream
In *SJH* Wolfgang Riehle sees how Benjamin Britten's opera looks today, and in *N&Q* Michael Cameron Andrews writes on enforced chastity and III.i.190–4.

72. *William Shakespeare: 'The Merchant of Venice'*, ed. Peter Millson. Penguin Passnotes. Penguin. pp. 89. pb £0.95.

Much Ado About Nothing

In *SQ* Anne Parten's note on II.i.25–7 gives examples of contemporary accounts of *females* acquiring a cuckold's horns. In *RenP* Mary C. Williams in 'Much Ado about Chastity in *Much Ado About Nothing*' writes clearly and usefully about the 'omnipresent contradictoriness' so that 'chastity is everything, yet nothing'.

Othello

In *ShS* Michael Neill's 'Changing Places in *Othello*' considers the play as 'a tragedy of displacement', its movement 'as remorselessly one-way as the current of that Pontic sea . . .'. He studies at length Venice, and social 'place', above all Iago's obsession with displacement, in all its suggestiveness, and Othello's 'insecurity of placelessness'. In *ShN* Estelle W. Taylor in 'The Masking in *Othello* and Unmasking the Criticism of *Othello*', in spite of a clumsy title, refutes the growing trend to diminish Othello's tragic nobility. Stanford S. Apseloff in *Expl* discusses 'paddle' at II.i.253–8 and *The Winter's Tale* I.ii. In *N&Q* T. Olivier supports A. P. Rossiter's description of the play as 'the last Problem Play' in 'Equivocal Rhetoric in *Othello*'; and Richard Levin identifies the Arabian Trees. *SQ* has notes from T. Sipahigil on 'unbonneted' as a nautical metaphor and Balz Engler on the cod's head and salmon tail of II.i.155.

Pericles

Mary Judith Dunbar is useful in *Shakespeare, Man of the Theater*[34] on iconography and theatre in ' "To the Judgement of Your Eye": Iconography and the Theatrical Art of *Pericles*'.

The Rape of Lucrece

R. C. Horne notes two unrecorded contemporary references to Shakespeare in *N&Q*, and in *ShN* Heather Dubrow offers 'The Rape of Clio: Gender and Genre in Shakespeare's *Lucrece*', which is fashionableness without substance. The best this year is in A. R. Braunmuller's chapter in SUAS[63] noted above under *Tragedies* (p. 222).

Richard II

The critical section of Andrew Gurr's introduction to his New Cambridge edition[1] is excellent on the symmetrical structure of the play and its observance of equilibrium in both characterization and mode, and on the uses of elemental imagery; however, his treatment of the wider functions of language in the play is sketchy.

Scott McMillin (*SQ*) discusses 'Shakespeare's *Richard II*: Eyes of Sorrow, Eyes of Desire' – not as trivial as it sounds, since he develops it into an essay on the educative experiences of grief undergone by various characters, but still the piece is too long and some of its verbal points merely adventitious.

Richard III

In 'Richard III: Shakespeare's First Great Mimetic Fool' Bernard J. Paris (*AJES*, 1983) espouses the psychological theories of Karen Horney. These, when boiled down, say that people either like, dislike, or are indifferent to, other people: hardly headline news. When applied to Richard the theories reveal a man 'treated unfairly because of an accident of birth', who really wants to be loved and whose soliloquies express the pain which is the source of his villainy. Thus the moral framework of the play is brushed aside, and the many non-realistic facets of its characterization forgotten. Paris finally proposes that Shakespeare is trying, through Richard, to work out his own psychological conflicts – a suggestion the reader has seen coming a mile off, but one which still raises a groan.

Hugh M. Richmond's 'Richard III and the Reformation' (JEGP) detects conflicts, characteristic of the Reformation, between grace and damnation in the play, but offers dubious arguments and relies on the kind of word-frequency lists that have long since been discredited. To say Richard III uses 'grace' eighty-five times, 'death' 147, etc., tells us nothing: it is context that matters. Richmond informs us that 'Amen' is used seven times in Richard III but eight in Troilus and Cressida: does this make the latter a slightly more Christian play?

Ralph Berry in the Hibbard Festschrift[38] studies Richard's relationship to the audience in a lacklustre fashion. Wolfgang G. Müller (Anglia) sees Richard as the villain-rhetorician, the antithesis of the Humanist ideal of the orator-statesman; he analyses uses of various rhetorical devices. Another study of rhetoric by R. Chris Hassel Jr, 'Military Oratory in Richard III' (SQ), deploys evidence from Tudor handbooks on oratory to support the view that Richmond is meant to be seen as a superior speaker to Richard, however flat he may seem to be to us. Hassel argues modestly on an initially unattractive topic, and we end his essay (a) in possession of definite information and (b) knowing precisely what he thinks – both rather rare virtues this year.

The Sonnets

Ruth Frfr. v. Ledebur discusses 'Einzelgedicht und Zyklus: Shakespeares Sonette' in SJH. Gordon Cyr has two dotty pieces in ShN (nothing is by Shakespeare). In ELN Carol M. Sicherman continues the debate about Sonnet 94 and the parable of the Dishonest Steward, using Renaissance Bible commentaries. In SQ Priscilla Bawcutt considers the familiarity of the last line of 38; and Brian Vickers pursues the identity of 'W' again: this is SQ surely over the furthest edge of relevance.

The Taming of the Shrew

David Daniell writes in ShS on 'The Good Marriage of Katherine and Petruchio', discussing the play in its theatrical consciousness, particularly in the way the Katherine and Petruchio matter is inset deeply. The play is linked with the early histories to illuminate Katherine's last speech, in which she is saying something private to Petruchio. 'Together, Katherine and Petruchio have filled-in many more areas of the capability of theatre than seemed possible at the beginning . . . they have, like Beatrice and Benedick after them, created an open world for each other: they are themselves, only more so being now together.' Peter Saccio, also in ShS, suggests in 'Shrewd and Kindly Farce' that farce has meant something negative since Dryden: but the Shrew is not rigid. Saccio contrasts views of the play, and how recent critics turn each other's ideas inside-out. Contrary to H. J. Oliver, he argues that characterization and farce are not incompatible. He finds a rhythmic pattern 'of a leisurely opening followed by gathering farce leading to an unusually late climax and a richly toned conclusion, [which] makes possible the blending of farce and romantic development of character': he stresses the importance, and frequency, of the word 'kindly' with its cognates. Richard A. Burt writes in *Criticism* on 'Charisma, Coercion, and Comic Form in *The Taming of the Shrew*', finding 'more enduring forms of domination – discipline and coercion'. Love and power, he says, are deeply connected in Petruchio (why not in Katherine? one wonders): Katherine is 'allowed' to 'improvise her own speech in defense of patriarchy'. Ann Thompson in *N&Q* finds useful dating parallels with *The Spanish Tragedy*; in *Expl* George Cheatham discusses 'best put finger in the eye'.

The Tempest

Rosemary Wright's fine and unusual piece in *ShS*, 'Prospero's Lime Tree and the Pursuit of *Vanitas*', uncovers intriguingly 'one of the odder . . . anticlimaxes' at IV.i. She finds the image descended from emblems of the tree of knowledge, with elements of temptation, and mocking imitation, and of the 'late Gothic device of the pedlar and the apes'. She finds many kinds of overlap, by working through medieval and Renaissance lore of the ape (that 'grotesque parody of the human' which later became in emblem a synonym for the fool) and the tradition of pictures of 'The Pedlar Robbed by Apes'. There are, she finds, rich associations in the play with apes and the sleeping pedlar. In *N&Q* D. C. Kay finds a Spenserian source for Claribel. In *SQ* Gail Kern Paster finds Montaigne behind Dido, and Dennis C. Kay examines Gonzalo's 'lasting pillars' at V.i.208.

David Lindley's chapter, 'Music, Masque and Meaning in *The Tempest*' in *The Court Masque*[73] (a useful volume, edited by him), points out that the play 'employs more music than any other Shakespeare play', and 'most insistently echoes the manner of the masque'. This is a fine, rich assessment, concluding

> The symbolic view of music is comprehensible as an attempt to validate morally the experiential truth of music's power. *The Tempest*, by unpicking without ever quite denying that analogy does not merely reflect a historical moment, the time of 'the untuning of the sky', but forces us as an audience to go beyond a simple criticism of the fragility of the world of the stage. The Platonic theories that sustain a Sidneyan belief in art's golden world are crumbling, but we are left 'wishing it might be so'.

Timon of Athens

Agostino Lombardo writes in *SJW* on 'The Two Utopias of *Timon of Athens*', and in *SQ* William O. Scott discusses interestingly how Timon's words rebound on him in 'The Paradox of Timon's Self-Cursing'.

Titus Andronicus

There are three major essays this year. In *RenP* J. A. Bryant Jr writes on 'Aaron and the Pattern of Shakespeare's Villains'. He finds that 'the treatment of Aaron is one of the uniquely Shakespearean things' about the play. He examines Aaron as an outsider, considering other villains and outsiders in

---

73. *The Court Masque*, ed. by David Lindley. RevelsCL. ManU. pp. viii + 196. £22.50.

Shakespeare, and what makes them so. In the Hibbard *Festschrift*[38] two of the principal critics of this play return valuably to it. Eugene M. Waith (*YW* 38.138) now shows the play as a 'show', a series of spectacular stage ceremonies linked to the 'related images of pictorial poetry' to make 'simultaneously two contrary views of the hero, his family and his enemies'; and G. K. Hunter (*YW* 55.228), also now from Yale, examines the notion that Shakespeare, as I might put it, was the slave of a cultural context and can be let off the charge of barbarism. So R. M. Sargent with his chapbook arrived 'as a kind of Messiah, the answer to a mythic need', only to be rightly pulverized by M. M. Mincoff. In a learned and closely worked article Hunter examines again the issue of 'sources' and offers the conjecture that two classical writers, Herodian (behind Holinshed) and Livy, may have suggested to Shakespeare conflicts of Roman history, especially the relationship of primitive and decadent, to an achievement 'entirely worthy of Shakespeare's inventive powers'. In *N&Q* J. J. M. Tobin discusses 'Nomenclature and the Dating of *Titus Andronicus*', comparing similarities between Shakespeare's play and Nashe's *Christ's Tears over Jerusalem*, entered in the Stationers' Register in 1593.

Troilus and Cressida

In *PQ* Stephen J. Lynch explores Cressida's wit in 'Shakespeare's Cressida: "A Woman of Quick Sense"'. David-Everett Blythe looks at the 'compass'd window' (*N&Q*) and in *ShStud* (1981–2) Yasunari Takada considers cultural debris in the odd, and more oddly titled, 'How to Do Things with "Fall-Out" Systems in *Troilus and Cressida*'.

Twelfth Night

William C. McAvoy, who is engaged on the New Variorum of the play for MLA, has published a valuable Supplementary Bibliography[74] covering everything of value between 1901 and 1981, complete with index: a most useful booklet. The Penguin 'Passnotes'[75] is very similar to those noticed above for *Macbeth* and *Merchant*. In *ShN* Cynthia Lewis finds Christ in Illyria, Heaven help us.

In *SoRA* Linda Woodbridge writes ' "Fire in Your Heart and Brimstone in Your Liver": Towards an Unsaturnalian *Twelfth Night*' (which seems to be a speciality of *SoRA*: see *YW* 57.144). She argues that *Twelfth Night* seems 'closer to being a corrective comedy than a festive comedy', more interested in curbing excess 'to achieve a happy life of moderation'; she makes good use of *The Faerie Queene* Book II.

Two Gentlemen of Verona

Horst Breuer writes in *SJH* 'Liebe und Intimität: Psychohistorische Bemerkungen zu *The Two Gentlemen of Verona* und einigen anderen Komödien Shakespeares'.

74. *Twelfth Night, or, What You Will: A Bibliography to Supplement the New Variorum Edition of 1901*, comp. by William C. McAvoy. MLA. pp. vi + 57. pb $9.
75. *William Shakespeare: 'Twelfth Night'*, ed. by S. H. Coote. Penguin Passnotes. Penguin. pp. 89. pb £0.95.

The Winter's Tale

In the volume *Shakespeare, Man of the Theater*[34] Jörg Hasler has an interesting paper 'Romance in the Theater: The Stagecraft of the "Statue Scene" in *The Winter's Tale*'; and in *N&Q* are pieces by François Laroque, with a different Ovidian source for that scene, and John W. Mahon on Proserpina and Ovid.

Renaissance Drama: Excluding Shakespeare

MICHAEL SMITH

This chapter has five sections: 1. Editions, and Related Scholarship; 2. Reference Works; 3. Theatre History; 4. Criticism, (*a*) General; (*b*) Marlowe; (*c*) Jonson; (*d*) Middleton; (*e*) Other Playwrights, and Plays; 5. Masque and Pageant. A selective review of books may be found in the spring number of *SEL*.

The year 1984 sees the launch of a new annual, *Medieval and Renaissance Drama in England* (*MRDE*)[1], and a new series, The Revels Plays Companion Library. *MRDE* seems to exclude Shakespeare, judging from the first volume, though there is no editorial statement to that effect. There is a short review section, and the editors also commission longer review-articles. Essays in the first volume cover a wide range of plays and playwrights, both familiar and not so familiar. They are reviewed individually later in the chapter. The RevelsCL is designed to supplement its parent series. The general editors promise that the Companion Library will include small collections of plays by single authors, or concerned with single themes; editions of masques, pageants, and dramatists' non-dramatic work; collections of documentary evidence on Elizabethan theatrical conditions, and on the history of performance; and collections of critical essays. Two volumes have so far appeared, a collection of documents relating to the Rose Theatre, and a collection of essays on the court masque: they are reviewed in sections 3 and 5, respectively.

1. Editions, and Related Scholarship

Opening a conference at Glendon College in 1978[2] on the editing of old-spelling play-texts, Samuel Schoenbaum surveyed in inimitable fashion 'The State of the Art', concentrating on progress in the great collected editions. Given the magnitude of most of these undertakings, it is not surprising that, despite the six years between delivery and publication, Schoenbaum's introductory address needs little updating. Cyrus Hoy's Dekker commentary, and two more volumes of Fredson Bowers' Beaumont and Fletcher have

1. *Medieval and Renaissance Drama in England: An Annual Gathering of Research, Criticism, and Reviews*, Vol. I, ed. by J. Leeds Barroll III, asst. ed. Paul Werstine. AMSP. pp. xii + 289. $42.50.
2. *Play-Texts in Old Spelling: Papers from the Glendon Conference*, ed. by G. B. Shand with Raymond C. Shady. AMS Studies in the Renaissance 6. AMSP. pp. ix + 161. £34.95.

appeared. Herford and Simpson has disappeared (from bookshops, anyway). Greene, Heywood, Lyly, Marston, Middleton – are you still there waiting in the wings?

Things have changed since the heady days when these projects were first mooted. Where is it now, the glory and the dream? Consumed in the bibliographer's refining fire? Several contributors to the Glendon volume are a little anxious on this score. Barry Gaines, in the course of a brief, helpful talk on the preparation of textual apparatus, wonders heretically whether it is necessary to weigh one's text down with lists of emended accidentals which even graduate students don't read. Philip Edwards, playing Luddite, flatly states that the 'bewildering technology' of analytical bibliography has diverted editors from their main task: producing editions. Elsewhere in the volume that technology is most conspicuous in papers from Robert Kean Turner, Paul Werstine, and Randall McLeod. Are they the true custodians of the dream, or are they merely fiddling with minutiae while Rome burns?

Certainly, none of them makes the editor's task any easier. Turner is confident that the identity of compositors and the sequence of composition can now be determined by techniques which an editor must master, since following the workmen through their stints line by line is the best way to get a 'feel' for the way they handled accidentals, a necessary preliminary to a 'reasoned consistency' in one's own handling. McLeod makes it more complicated to identify compositors, demonstrating in a fascinating and well-illustrated essay (previously published in Ren&R, 1979) that their spelling habits were often not determined by the abstract 'spelling preference' beloved of bibliographers but by highly practical considerations of typesetting, such as the need to prevent fouling of kerned letters. Werstine's paper (much strengthened since its initial appearance in AEB, 1978, and with revised conclusions) impressively advocates 'the editorial usefulness of printing house ... studies', and further complicates the identification of compositors, showing that the spelling preferences of William White's compositors in 1598–1600 were often overridden by copy spellings when they set from printed copy. Werstine's particular point is that Love's Labour's Lost Q1 bears every sign of having been set from an earlier, lost quarto, which must, since it was followed closely, have been 'good' rather than 'bad'.

Faced with the intricate demands of such analysis, editors have to undertake commentary as well. Is it any wonder that 'the hungry sheep look up and are not fed. The editions do not appear' (Philip Edwards)? One solution is to divide responsibilities for text and commentary, but this Edwards in his wise remarks on 'the function of commentary' forcefully argues against, the Bowers Dekker notwithstanding. Another problem is what to include in the commentary: there are no rules, says Edwards, but there is an ideal shape and moral character – 'chaste, beautiful, and slim'. Then many an old host I know is damned. Yet Sheldon Zitner backs Edwards up, querying the necessity of most of the annotation on a sample page of the New Arden Othello. Readers, it seems, no longer have faith in the road of excess. They do, however, expect help with questions of staging, and David Bevington argues that this should be provided in the commentary as well as in stage directions. More contentiously, Reavley Gair would include in his footnotes detailed speculations about a play's presumed topical reference. I have dwelt at disproportionate length on this slim volume, but in raising questions which infrequently get asked in print the book is valuable, besides being a record of what must have been a memorable occasion, and also containing much helpful, practical advice, as Jon Stallworthy's publisher's-eye view of 'The State of the Business' which closes the proceedings reminds me to stress.

If progress with the collected editions is slow, there is no shortage of single-play editions and student anthologies to report on: eighteen in all, indeed. The sheep will not quite starve this winter! Heading the list are four new accessions to the resurgent Revels series: Jonson's *Volpone* and *New Inn*, Beaumont's *Knight of the Burning Pestle*, and a play of uncertain authorship, *The Insatiate Countess*[3]. The general editors' preface still – and justly – proclaims that the series is 'equally useful for teachers and students, theatre directors and actors'. But no class or cast will be able to afford any of the four presently under review. Let us hope paperbacks are on the way.

Sparest of the four in terms of commentary, as one would expect given the editor's zest for pruning the Arden undergrowth, is Sheldon P. Zitner's *Knight of the Burning Pestle*. This play could give rise to a veritable South Sea of annotator's discoveries, but Zitner has resisted the temptation to set sail (and his decision is surely in keeping: *The Knight* wears its allusiveness lightly). Instead, essential glosses and information are presented with a minimum of fuss, and the play's 'seamless flow' (prized by Zitner) is not disrupted. Possibly, the discussion of theatrical antecedents in the introduction might benefit from being a little less brisk, but this is a minor cavil. Zitner deals succinctly with matters of text, printing history, date, auspices, and authorship, on which he has nothing major to add (he favours the current ascription to Beaumont alone, but admits to 'the dram of a scruple of a reservation'). The bulk of his introduction is taken up with an elegant critical essay which sees *The Knight* as more celebration than satire, as a triumph of the superior vividness and strength of popular festivity over the tame shows of the professional theatre, albeit a triumph tempered by the 'nonchalant' and 'distant' nature of the observing dramatist's sympathies. Four appendixes contain, respectively, an anonymous prologue for a Restoration revival of the play, the droll based on Rafe's combat with the barber, a justification of the editor's treatment of the citizen interludes, and the music for the songs. They conclude a fine edition.

R. B. Parker takes a rather different approach to *Volpone* – his commentary is much fuller, both in density of reference and in interpretative guidance, than Zitner's – but, again, this responds to something in the play itself. Indeed, it is a main point of Parker's critical introduction that 'the aesthetic excitement' deriving from 'an awareness of [*Volpone*'s] brilliant matching of patterns' has the effect, in the theatre as well as the study, of

> moving it away from too exhaustive a concentration on moral indignation towards a more anarchic 'play' level, and substituting for the classical sense of formal inevitability a more open sense of spontaneity – of farcical improvisation and repetition . . . rather than causality.

3. All Revels Plays. ManU. *The Knight of the Burning Pestle*, by Francis Beaumont, ed. by Sheldon P. Zitner. pp. x + 190. £25. *Volpone, or The Fox*, by Ben Jonson, ed. by R. B. Parker. (1983). pp. xviii + 378 + 4 pls. £27.50. *The New Inn*, by Ben Jonson, ed. by Michael Hattaway. pp. xii + 244 + 4 pls. £27.50. *The Insatiate Countess*, by John Marston *et al.*, ed. by Giorgio Melchiori. pp. xvi + 205. £27.50.

This is excellently said. Parker writes illuminatingly about the play's relation to classical satire, estates moralities, the *commedia dell'arte*, and, especially, the beast epic of *Reynard the Fox* (see further his article in *RenD*, 1976). His critical appreciation of the play is throughout infused with his sense of its stage history, and he is interesting, for instance, about both Volpone's own psychology (his need for thespian display, his susceptibility to boredom, his perverse self-destructive urge) and the psychology of his relations with the audience (the saturnalian cruelty appeals to the audience on a premoral level, and functions to 'catharsise' their aggression). There is much more that I have no space to mention. Parker's text is based on an extremely thorough collation of surviving copies of Q and F1, and his introduction on an impressive, purposeful command of the huge body of criticism that has grown up around the play. In an appendix John P. Cutts discusses the music used in the play, and reprints Alfonso Ferrabosco's setting of 'Come, my Celia'. Other appendixes contain (translated) extracts from sources and analogues, a list of modern productions and adaptations, and another of Q and F1 press-variants.

Volpone has a long stage history; *The New Inn* has none at all, and this is a great handicap to any critic, since it renders insoluble except in theory what is surely one of the key questions about the play: is it stageworthy? Michael Hattaway, in his introduction to the Revels *New Inn*, sometimes seems a little unsure of how to proceed to vindication. He relates the play to Jonson's alienation from the prevailing trends of Caroline theatre, stresses the *mixture* of satire and celebration in it, and brings out Jonson's sympathy for Lovel and Lady Frampul, mature lovers 'who do not have youth on their side to prevent their uncertainties from appearing as insincerities'. The suspicion remains that he is praising an excellent closet comedy. An experimental production is badly needed. Unfortunately, Hattaway's text is not up to Jonsonian standards (or, anyway, not in the copy I was sent). Serious mistakes have crept in in the printing: to mention a couple, II.i.12 is misplaced between the two halves of II.i.28, and multiple error has created a ghost line at IV.iv.192 and made nonsense of 193.

Remaining to be considered is Giorgio Melchiori's *Insatiate Countess*. This is a somewhat odd choice for inclusion in the Revels series, since interest in the play is often focused on its disputed authorship, study of which would surely be more facilitated by an old-spelling edition. Largely on the basis of an analysis of inconsistencies in speech prefixes (presented in tabular form in an appendix), Melchiori deduces that the text as we have it

> is a fairly early 'treatment', by William Barksted, Lewis Machin and perhaps other hack-writers in the pay of the short-lived company of the Children of the King's Revels, of a very incomplete draft of the play left by John Marston when, in June 1608, he abandoned the theatrical profession.

This explanation is certainly plausible, but is presented by Melchiori with a confidence which seems in excess of the facts as they appear.

Going downmarket of the Revels, we soon happen on Charles Walters Whitworth's New Mermaid edition of *Three Sixteenth-Century Comedies*[4],

---

4. *Three Sixteenth-Century Comedies: Gammer Gurton's Needle, Roister Doister, The Old Wife's Tale*, ed. by Charles Walters Whitworth. NMer. Benn/Norton (now Black). pp. lxii + 272. pb £4.95.

which it is natural to compare with William Tydeman's *Four Tudor Comedies* for the Penguin English Library[5]. Both collections include *Roister Doister* and *Gammer Gurton's Needle*. Tydeman makes up four with *Jack Juggler* and John Lyly's *Mother Bombie* (neither otherwise inexpensively available, though there has been a good recent edition of *Jack Juggler* by Marie Axton in the Tudor Interludes series, evidently too recent for Tydeman to benefit from, since he does not mention it). Whitworth's third is George Peele's *Old Wife's Tale*, also welcome, since the 1980 Revels edition by Patricia Binnie (*YW* 61.168–9) has attracted a good deal of adverse criticism (e.g. this year, from Paul Werstine in *MRDE*, and from R. V. Holdsworth in *N&Q*). A major difference between the two collections is that Tydeman's is old spelling, while Whitworth's is not. Whitworth's, admittedly, is the more scholarly, being based on an original scrutiny of the early editions, while Tydeman's is textually second-hand. But for an undergraduate reader this will not matter overmuch; and, in my own experience, old spelling helps a student understand the movement of mid-century dramatic verse more than modern spelling clears up the meaning. Other reasons for preferring Tydeman are his more extensive bibliography and his helpful glossary. The two editors' annotations are closely comparable, and the introductions also find them in substantial agreement, even as to how Gammer's needle gets into a pair of breeches where, at first sight, it has no right to be. They differ interestingly about staging, though, Whitworth favouring more scenes and machines than Tydeman. Whitworth is also much fuller in his account of the controversy over the authorship of *Gammer Gurton*, resolving it very tentatively in favour of Dr John Bridges. In the end, choice between two thoroughly competent editions will perhaps depend on the coupling. Here would seem to be a strong argument for Whitworth: Tydeman gives the student rather a lot of much the same, while Whitworth's inclusion of Peele's artful little romance is a pleasant and educational change. I seem to have fought it to an honourable draw.

Before moving on, however, I must say a little more about the New Mermaid *Old Wife's Tale*, outside the framework of comparison with Tydeman. Whitworth's text meets most, if not all, of the detailed criticisms levelled at Binnie's Revels edition by R. V. Holdsworth in *N&Q*, and, although the Mermaid is not perhaps to be preferred outright to its senior rival, it is certainly in close competition. However, Whitworth is hard put to it to account for the nature of printer's copy, postulating finally a touring version of the play cut by the author himself. This, while possible, seems unlikely. If we accept Paul Werstine's evidence in his long review of Binnie (*MRDE*) that 'authorial' stage directions often persisted in prompt-books, we can give the honour of cutting back to the company, where it more probably belongs.

There are two more (very fat) Mermaids to report on, which must rank among the most unpleasant examples of book design I have ever come across, but which will undoubtedly be a boon to course-planners and a bargain to students. The New Mermaid texts of six comedies and six tragedies, complete

5. *Four Tudor Comedies: Jacke Jugeler, Roister Doister, Gammer Gurton's Needle, Mother Bombie*, ed. by William Tydeman. Penguin English Library. Penguin. pp. 440. pb £3.95.

with footnotes, have been assembled to make two anthologies[6]. Individual introductions and bibliographies are replaced in each anthology by a pithy, challenging overview of the plays from the general editor of the New Mermaids, Brian Gibbons, and a sketchy basic booklist. Although it would have been agreeable to hear the editors singing each to each in full consort, the publishers obviously had to keep something back as an incentive to prospective purchasers of the original single-play editions. The plays have been thoughtfully chosen to suggest comparisons with Shakespeare, and as jumping-off points for a more wide-ranging investigation into the drama of the period. They are: comedies – *The Old Wife's Tale, The Shoemakers' Holiday, Eastward Ho!, Bartholomew Fair, The Malcontent,* and *A Trick to Catch the Old One*; tragedies – *The Spanish Tragedy, Doctor Faustus, Sejanus, Women Beware Women, The White Devil,* and *'Tis Pity She's a Whore.*

While on the subject of editions intended for students, I should also mention briefly the latest addition to the Nottingham Drama Texts series and one of the first volumes in a new series, Longman Study Texts. The Longman editions are aimed at sixth-formers; there is not much to say about Linda Cookson's efficient *Doctor Faustus*[7] except that the assimilation (at the end of a fairly well-judged introduction) of Faustus in his desperate final moments to Macbeth's brand of manly fortitude shows how difficult it is to avoid stereotypes at this level. Jan Kott in his 'personal essay' does not even try. The Nottingham series, for those not familiar with it, aims to provide trustworthy texts of otherwise inaccessible plays at prices the most impecunious student can afford. Henry Chettle's *Hoffman*[8] seems a suitable choice for the latest volume, being often enough referred to in books on the revenge-play tradition so arouse students' curiosity, but hitherto only available in Harold Jenkins's MSR. The editor, J. D. Jowett, has steered a sensible line through the shoals of a highly corrupt text, and annotates helpfully. Perhaps in his short introduction he exaggerates the moral coherence of Chettle's splendid farrago.

All eight remaining editions are addressed to a more specialized audience. Of widest interest is likely to be MacDonald P. Jackson's facsimile reprint of the 1607/8 quarto of *The Revenger's Tragedy*[9] – a play perhaps irrevocably known to cataloguers as the work of Cyril Tourneur, but increasingly accepted by scholars as an early play of Thomas Middleton. Jackson's facsimile is designed to promote this acceptance by making possible the independent checking of those 'bibliographical, linguistic, and orthographical details' on which the Middletonian case depends. It is unfortunate that the reproduction is of such indifferent quality. Nevertheless, Jackson's energetic outline survey of the authorship controversy (supported by a full bibliography in the footnotes) is convincingly put together, and the reasonableness of his contention

6. Both NMer Anthologies. Benn (now Black). *Elizabethan and Jacobean Comedies*, intro. by Brian Gibbons. pp. xxii + 686. pb £5.95. *Elizabethan and Jacobean Tragedies*, intro. by Brian Gibbons. pp. xx + 734. pb £5.95.

7. *Doctor Faustus*, by Christopher Marlowe, ed. by Linda Cookson, with a personal essay by Jan Kott. Longman Study Texts. Longman. pp. xxviii + 148. pb £1.60.

8. *The Tragedy of Hoffman, or A Revenge for a Father*, by Henry Chettle, ed. by J. D. Jowett. NDT (1983). pp. vi + 75. pb £2.50.

9. *The Revenger's Tragedy, Attributed to Thomas Middleton: A Facsimile of the 1607/8 Quarto*, intro. by MacDonald P. Jackson. FDU/AUP (1983). pp. 114. £14.50.

that, in this special case, the assembled internal evidence for Middleton's hand is stronger than the shaky external evidence for Tourneur's is apparent. It may be jumping the gun, but one cannot hesitate forever: discussion of an article on *The Revenger's Tragedy* will be found under 'Middleton' later in this chapter. A new Brome (a complete works, that is) is sorely needed; meanwhile, we have reason to be grateful to Sara Jayne Steen for editing the Lichfield manuscript of Richard Brome's *The English Moor*, and to her publishers for printing it so handsomely[10]. Steen includes a full collation of the manuscript with the first printed edition (*Five New Plays*, 1659). A rapid comparison of the two suggests that the manuscript (a presentation copy, possibly holograph) represents an early draft of the play, and the printed text a later, theatrical version, with additions and omissions skilfully designed to render the intrigue more articulate and more plausible. Steen, however, would prefer to date the manuscript some six years after the play's first performance. That is not inconsistent with its being based on an early draft, since the final version would presumably have become the property of the company. But would a noble patron have been flattered by the presentation of old work, even if still unpublished? If so, why? It is an interesting problem. Although for the most part an evidently inferior version of *The English Moor*, the manuscript does clear up several corruptions in the printed text; and comparison of the two versions may yield insight into either Brome's or the company's working methods. The editor's critical introduction is somewhat overmoralistic in points of detail, though in the right general area when it stresses Brome's preservation of a gently mocking balance between the competing extremes of cynical city comedy and romantic revenge heroics.

Three years after the publication of *Five New Plays*, in 1662, the printer Roger Daniel brought out an anthology of three oddly assorted old plays, *Thorney Abbey* (a Red-Bullish tragicomedy), *The Marriage Broker* (a university city comedy), and the more well-known *Grim, the Collier of Croydon*. These have now been edited by William M. Baillie in another nicely printed volume, this time from MRTS[11]. One would like to know more than Baillie has been able to deduce about why Daniel thought these particular plays would sell (though perhaps there is nothing much to know). Baillie overstates the case in calling *Thorney Abbey* 'the earliest known adaptation of a Shakespearean tragedy' – its relationship to *Macbeth* is surely more tenuous, even fortuitous, than the word 'adaptation' implies. His ascription of that robust farce, *Grim, the Collier*, to William Haughton, author of *Englishmen for my Money*, is, however, highly plausible. *Grim* is the best play of the three, and elicits the best and most substantial introduction, though it is stretching a point to praise the dramatist's architecture by claiming that 'in each plot the climactic scene focuses upon an interrupted feast'. Happily, the play's effectiveness does not depend on such academic symmetries. The annotation is pitched curiously low for an edition which no undergraduate is likely to use.

Four volumes in Garland's mushrooming Renaissance Imagination series

10. *The English Moore; or, The Mock-Mariage*, by Richard Brome, ed. by Sara Jayne Steen. UMiss (1983). pp. x + 164. £22.
11. *A Choice Ternary of English Plays. Gratiae Theatrales (1662)*, ed. by William M. Baillie. MRTS 26. CMERS. pp. 321. $18.

are devoted to editions of minor plays of the period[12]. Best of the four (editions, rather than plays) is probably Alan J. Berman's *Greene's Tu Quoque*, a straightforward, scrupulous doctoral dissertation, with a carefully prepared old-spelling text and textual apparatus, a competent commentary, and an introduction which, if it misses the chance to be enlightening about the clown Thomas Greene's performance style, does make some interesting comparisons between the play and Lording Barry's *Ram Alley*, a parallel scene from which is reprinted in an appendix.

Also originating in a doctoral dissertation is Jonathan Rittenhouse's edition of *1 Sir John Oldcastle* (by Munday, Drayton, Wilson, and Hathaway). Rittenhouse's introduction is very comprehensive in scope, but there is sometimes an air of going through the motions about it. Any doubling pattern for this play must be based on pure guesswork, but, even so, there is no need to guess that the actor playing King Harry would also have played Davy, Club, and First Justice, a speculation which surely flies in the face of common sense, and of what little we can infer about the inner hierarchy of Elizabethan acting companies. Rittenhouse piles up a list of the collaborators' 'steals' from Shakespeare's history plays (perhaps an unnecessarily limiting way of looking at the matter); does his best to fulfil the nightmare obligation of sharing out the play among the four co-authors (on the evidence of inconsistencies in action and speech prefixes, and certain anomalous spellings); and his text is carefully established. Unfortunately, since it is in modern spelling, the evidence on which the discussion of authorship is based is partly suppressed. Extracts from the play's narrative sources (Holinshed and Foxe) are reprinted in an appendix.

The other two Garland volumes are less satisfactory. The accuracy of Linda V. Itzoe's transcription of the holograph manuscript of Arthur Wilson's play, *The Swisser*, I have had no opportunity to check, but the critical introduction, though not inaccurate, can be remarkably banal ('Wilson focuses on the theme that good and bad together comprise the world'). Itzoe makes no reference to Margot Heinemann's discussion of Wilson in *Puritanism and Theatre* (*YW* 61.178), and the political implications of the play are not discussed, a surprising omission, since they would seem to be the most interesting thing about it. Leonard Tennenhouse's text of the mid-sixteenth-century interlude, *Impatient Poverty*, I *have* checked (at least, against R. B. McKerrow's 1911 diplomatic reprint of the original). Lines 439–54 appear twice, once in their proper place and once between lines 488 and 489. There are quite a few minor typos. But in essence the modern-spelling text appears to be accurate, and both it and *Nice Wanton* come with the full trappings of historical collation and glossarial commentary. The critical introduction thoughtfully teases out *Nice Wanton*'s ideological tensions (oddly enough, Tennenhouse does not spend so much time on *Impatient Poverty*, where the tensions seem more obvious but also deeper), and relates both interludes to the pervasive sixteenth-century crisis of authority. The plays get a bit dwarfed by this grandly conceived context, but it

---

12. All The Renaissance Imagination. Vols. 7, 8, 9, 10. Garland. *The Swisser*, by Arthur Wilson, ed. by Linda V. Itzoe. pp. viii + 155. $30. *Greene's Tu Quoque or, The Cittie Gallant*, by J. Cooke, ed. by Alan J. Berman. pp. xxvi + 168. $30. *A Critical Edition of '1 Sir John Oldcastle'*, ed. by Jonathan Rittenhouse. pp. xii + 284. $44. *The Tudor Interludes 'Nice Wanton' and 'Impatient Poverty'*, ed. by Leonard Tennenhouse. pp. x + 217. $32.50.

is an interesting perspective all the same. Where, then, is the cause for dissatisfaction? Well, in what does *not* get said: there is discussion of neither staging, auspices, nor versification (and not very much of dramatic traditions). It is difficult to feel that an editor of interludes who provides no guidance on these matters has fully discharged his responsibilities.

Last among the editions, and I am afraid least useful, is David Rush Miller's old-spelling text of John Fletcher's *A Wife for a Month*[13]. My doubts about usefulness have nothing to do with the quality of Miller's work, but concern only the impending appearance of this play in the Bowers collected edition, which will surely have greater textual authority. Miller's critical introduction concentrates on the themes of absolute monarchy, melancholy, and honour (about all of which he understands the play to make 'a powerful and essentially consistent statement'), and on Fletcher's tragicomic mastery of suspense and surprise.

There are two articles on textual matters, both from Paul Mulholland. One, 'Notes on Several Derivatives of Crane's Manuscript of Middleton's *The Witch*' (*PBSA*), I have not seen. The other, '*The Roaring Girl*: New Readings and Further Notes' (*SB*), reports on some significant but hitherto unrecorded press-variants (involving the repositioning of speech prefixes in a short section of II.i) which Mulholland has discovered in a Princeton copy of the 1611 quarto. He further claims that there are numerous instances in the quarto of speech prefixes transferred entire from one forme to another; analysis of their recurrence leads him to the conclusion that the quarto was set by formes.

It seems appropriate to end this section with a gathering of scholarly notes, these being in the nature of editorial commentary. Sven Bäckman's 'Devil *and* Jewel: A Note on a Possible Pun in *The White Devil*' (*MSpr*) is devoted to proving that the two words *could* be pronounced nearly enough alike in the early seventeenth century for a thematically appropriate pun to be heard. Supriya Chaudhuri, in 'Jason's Fleece: The Source of Sir Epicure Mammon's Allegory' (*RES*) identifies the preface by Chrysogonus Polydorus to a collection of alchemical treatises published at Nuremberg in the 1540s as the source of some arcane lore in Jonson's *Alchemist*.

The remaining items all come from *N&Q*. *The Witch of Edmonton* attracts three rather speculative notes, one from Philip Dust, who thinks Old Carter's 'Whom tolls the bell for?' might be an incongruous source for John Donne's *Seventeenth Meditation*; the other two from David Atkinson, who suggests that the relation between the bigamy plot and the witchcraft plot is that both bigamy and entering into compacts with evil spirits were made capital felonies in 1604, and seeks – not entirely successfully – to clarify an ambiguity at II.ii.126–7. Lyly's *Endimion* is the subject of two notes from Donald Edge, who points to the derivation of aspects of the main plot from Ovid's *Metamorphoses* and *Heroides*, and comments in detail on Sir Tophas's poem, reported by Epiton the page in IV.ii, as a Lylyan parody of quantitative verse. And John Ford's *The Broken Heart* also gets two notes – from David Atkinson again, finding a 'precise irony' in Ford's use of the apparently tautologous phrase 'married wives', and from Shanti Padhi, who discerns a source for kings marrying corpses in *The Second Maiden's Tragedy*. Padhi also claims to have

---

13. *A Wife for a Moneth*, by John Fletcher, ed. by David Rush Miller. Costerus 36. Rodopi (1983). pp. viii + 286. pb.

discovered Middleton's source for his character Allwit (in *A Chaste Maid in Cheapside*) in the picaresque novel *Guzman de Alfarache* by Mateo Aleman.

Significant notes come from Ann Thompson, arguing for a late 1580s date for *The Spanish Tragedy* as a consequence of her assignment of *The Taming of the Shrew* to *c.* 1591; and from R. V. Holdsworth, who offers a list of thirteen words that may need glossing as sexual puns in the plays of Middleton, Chapman, and Dekker. Charles Clay Doyle explicates an allusion of Turf's in III.iii of Jonson's *A Tale of a Tub* by reference to a widely disseminated fable that crops up, for instance, in *Pasquils Jests* (1604). Finally, Paul Dean contends that a scene in the anonymous *Tragedy of Tiberius* is modelled on Richard of Gloucester's wooing of the Lady Anne in Shakespeare's play; while Peter Ridgway Jordan identifies a couple of allusions in John Mason's *The Turk* and the anonymous *The Telltale*.

2. Reference Works

Ronald W. Vince's *Renaissance Theatre: A Historiographical Handbook*[14] sets out to point budding theatre historians in the direction of their basic sources, and to survey the methodology of their subject as it has developed over the last century or so. It is very ambitious in scope, with chapters on Italian, Spanish, and French theatre, the *commedia dell'arte*, and festival and pageantry, as well as on Elizabethan theatre. Inevitably, errors creep in, while compression from time to time induces unclearness. A beginner might well be confused, for instance, by Vince's discussion of prompt-books and foul papers. And it is incorrect to say, again for instance, that we possess no information about the 1635 contract between Richard Brome and the Salisbury Court management except for C. W. Wallace's brief commentary in *The Century Magazine* (see Ann Haaker's article in *RenD*, 1968; *YW* 49.174). The book is useful, undoubtedly, but by no means entirely reliable. Infallibility over this vast area could not reasonably be expected of one author, but might be hoped for from a 'handbook'.

My gentle dippings have not turned up errors in D. Heyward Brock's *Ben Jonson Companion*[15], but nor have they been very deep. I did find some entries which struck me as absurd, such as

> **Page (to Paulo).** A boy in *The Case Is Altered*, who fetches Angelo for Paulo, brings him the news that his father is looking for him, and delivers the message to his father that he is coming presently.

A good companion ought to know when he is not needed. Still, the misjudgement is well-intentioned – Brock wants to be complete – and in more important matters he is always at hand with a stream of facts. Always, that is, except where actors and directors are concerned. The decision to omit them is again, it would seem, a consequence of the encyclopaedist's approach: because he could not be sure of naming them all, the compiler prefers to name none (apart from Garrick). This is a pity. Entries for Donald Wolfit and Tyrone Guthrie,

14. *Renaissance Theatre: A Historiographical Handbook*, by Ronald W. Vince. Greenwood. pp. xii + 204. $39.50.

15. *A Ben Jonson Companion*, by D. Heyward Brock. IndU/Harvester (1983). pp. xii + 307. £30.

say, would surely have been more useful than the record of A. C. Swinburne's poetic output and assessment of its worth to which Brock evidently feels he is committed by Swinburne's book and poem on Jonson. A mine of information, much of it necessary, the *Companion* is a tribute to its compiler's unflagging patience, devotion, and energy.

The third work of reference to come my way this year was a concordance to Dekker's plays[16], computer-generated and keyed to Bowers' edition. Non-dramatic works, entertainments, and collaborations (except for *Sir Thomas More*, *Westward Ho!*, and *Northward Ho!*) are excluded. Line references are given for each occurrence of a word, but not the lines themselves. Variant spellings of the same word are not cross-referenced, sometimes an inconvenience (the concordance is of course old spelling). The line references do not always square exactly with those given in the *Dramatic Works*, since the computer has on occasion caught even Bowers out in his counting! It goes without saying that this is a useful addition to the shelves, though it is not recommended for anyone with weak eyesight.

Das ältere englische Schauspiel[17] is the second of three volumes devoted to early English drama and covers work from John Lyly to Shakespeare. It is divided into three: the first section looks at the position of dramatists and actors, and the various acting groups of the period together with a consideration of the principal forms of theatre, public theatre, private theatre, and the court theatre; the second presents the lives and works of the 'University Wits', Lyly, Kyd, Greene, Peele, and Marlowe, while the final and longest part is given over to Shakespeare. The author discusses in detail sources and productions and offers specific analyses of five comedies, the histories, and six tragedies. The volume is complemented by substantial bibliographies and an index. [M.H.]

Still to be noticed in this section are two bibliographies in the *ELR* Recent Studies series. John B. Brooks deals with work on Middleton (1971–81), Josephine A. Roberts with studies of Mary Sidney, Countess of Pembroke.

3. Theatre History

First, books and articles on players; then, material relating to playhouse, Revels Office, and college records; thirdly, studies of staging practice, of the auditorium, and of the audience it contained; in conclusion, two substantial reviews of recent productions: that is the shape of this section.

Undoubtedly the most important book in it, and one of the most significant of the year, is Gerald Eades Bentley's authoritative *The Profession of Player in Shakespeare's Time*[18], a companion volume to his earlier study of the profession of dramatist (*YW* 53.165). Nobody is better qualified than Professor Bentley to sort out from the mass of evidence (some of it newly assembled) the usual conduct and practices of the Elizabethan, Jacobean, and Caroline acting companies – the basic rules and customs of the craft guild, as it were – and this

16. *A Concordance to the Dramatic Works of Thomas Dekker*, by V. A. Small, R. P. Corballis, and J. M. Harding. 5 Vols. SSELJDS 82. USalz. pp. iv + 890. pb DM 200.

17. *Das ältere englische Schauspiel*. Vol. II: *John Lyly bis Shakespeare*, by Robert Frickler. Francke (1983). pp. 368.

18. *The Profession of Player in Shakespeare's Time 1590–1642*, by Gerald Eades Bentley. Princeton. pp. xiv + 315. £20.90.

is the service he here lucidly and concisely performs. Chapters are devoted in turn to the general relations between player and company; the particular responsibilities and rewards of sharers, hired men, and apprentices; the activities of playhouse managers; touring; and casting. In an important appendix, Bentley reprints all cast lists for professional productions of the period extant in printed quartos and play manuscripts, and subjoins to each his own invaluable commentary. Judicious and thoroughly readable, the book immediately becomes the definitive study of its subject.

Sandra Billington, as the indefinite article in her title[19] modestly indicates, does not pretend to Bentley's kind of authority. Even so, her book on the fool disappoints. The two chapters dealing with the Renaissance are rather focusless, heavily dependent on Enid Welsford and one or two later writers, and left me puzzled as to their rationale. The unfortunate impression given is that Will Somers, Richard Tarlton, and company fill the pit between the medieval period and the eighteenth century as well as better, although I am sure this is not what the author intends. It is only fair to add that the book has had a more favourable reception from reviewers not confined to the Renaissance chapters.

The emergence of the fool-type Pickleherring interests Willem Schrickx, whose scholarly article '"Pickleherring" and English Actors in Germany' (ShS, 1983) traces the name to John Green's continental touring troupe in the period 1608–25, that is, before it was joined by Robert Reynolds, with whom Schrickx says Pickleherring is traditionally associated by theatre historians. It is easy to get lost in the complicated wanderings and personnel changes of these travelling players as Schrickx relates them, but the article adds valuably to our knowledge of the troupe's composition and itinerary, and interestingly stresses the importance to them of Queen Anne's patronage and continental connections.

Clowns such as Kemp and Tarlton, half-musicians, half-players, are often said to be heirs of the medieval and early Tudor minstrels. Now William Ingram offers evidence, culled from parish registers, that minstrelsy proper survived the advent of the professional stage, or, at least, that over a hundred men whose profession is given as 'minstrel' died, married, and had children in London between 1550 and 1600. What shades of meaning 'minstrel' carries in these records, and why most minstrels congregated in just two or three parishes, Ingram is not sure. He transcribes all the relevant entries, and asks 'Minstrels in Elizabethan London: Who Were They, What Did They Do?' (ELR). I must not spoil Ingram's best joke by revealing the name of the Puritan lutanist. Another of Ingram's investigations into parish records seems of less immediate interest ('The Globe Playhouse and its Neighbors in 1600' (EiT)). He has established that several quite well-off citizens lived in close proximity to the Globe, which was perhaps not considered such an undesirable neighbour as the Mayor and his aldermen might lead us to think. A second delver in record offices is S. P. Cerasano, who in 'Anthony Jeffes, Player and Brewer' (N&Q) takes us into the marginal area of Jeffes's career after he gave up acting.

Pulling us back to the centre is Scott McMillin's important article, 'The

19. *A Social History of the Fool*, by Sandra Billington. Harvester/St Martin's. pp. x + 150. £18.95.

Queen's Men in 1594: A Study of "Good" and "Bad" Quartos' (*ELR*). Careful analysis of three play quartos published in 1594 with the Queen's Men named on their title-pages (*The True Tragedy of Richard III*, *Selimus*, and Robert Greene's *Friar Bacon and Friar Bungay*) leads McMillin to the conclusion that, although they contain at least thirty-five roles apiece (and one as many as sixty-eight), all three could easily have been performed, with doubling, by a cast of fourteen, a similarity he considers too extraordinary for coincidence. Fourteen, then, would be the Queen's touring strength; and McMillin further contends that the quartos enable us to specify among those fourteen how many were 'leading men', how many 'very capable men', and so on. His forceful case awaits sceptical testing. One of its implications is that none of these three texts is a 'good' quarto, if by 'good' is meant non- or pretheatrical. McMillin would call into question, indeed, the whole antithesis of 'good' and 'bad'.

Moving now from players to theatres, we come to Carol Chillington Rutter's *Documents of the Rose Playhouse*[20], one of the first titles in the new Revels Plays Companion Library. It seeks to introduce students to the 'push and shove of the Elizabethan playhouse' and to 'the possibilities and methods of documentary research'. After an introductory essay has cleared Philip Henslowe from the opprobrium heaped on him by F. G. Fleay and followers, extracts from *Henslowe's Diary*, Privy Council minutes, letters of protest from the Lord Mayor, and other documents are woven together by means of a lively running commentary into a calendar and informal history of the Rose. The intention is to create the illusion of 'Elizabethan theatre in the present tense', and it is partly to this end that spelling is paradoxically not modernized (in defiance of normal Revels practice), while glossary and interpretative footnotes are also eschewed. A certain controlled untidiness is actively sought, the better to re-enact the productive confusion of the playhouse itself, and to prepare students for the realities of archival research. I am not quite sure what kind of students are envisaged as this book's readership; beginning graduates and the keener undergraduates, presumably. The former will soon want to go direct to W. W. Greg, E. K. Chambers, R. A. Foakes and R. T. Rickert; the latter might deserve more help in understanding unfamiliar words and spellings. On the other hand, those who enjoy solving puzzles may well be hooked. It will be interesting to see how this energetic, informative, rather unorthodox book fares with its readers.

The interpretation of some entries in *Henslowe's Diary* concerns Roslyn L. Knutson, who in 'Play Identifications' (*HLQ*) suggests that Henslowe's *Longshanks* and *The Wise Man of West Chester* should not automatically be glossed '*Edward I*' and '*John a Kent*'; they may be rival plays on similar subjects. Knutson's conjecture is no more substantial than the time-honoured one, as she herself admits, but it does remind us not to accept the latter uncritically as fact just because of the great names attached to it.

Other research into dramatic records includes articles by N. W. Bawcutt on the lost office-book of Sir Henry Herbert, Master of the Revels, and by David W. Blewitt on references to plays and players in the account-books of Winchester and Eton. Bawcutt's articles appear in *ELR* ('Craven Ord Transcripts

---

20. *Documents of the Rose Playhouse*, ed. by Carol Chillington Rutter. RevelsCL. ManU. pp. x + 246. £15.

of Sir Henry Herbert's Office-Book in the Folger Shakespeare Library') and *RES* ('New Revels Documents of Sir George Buc and Sir Henry Herbert, 1619–1662'). He traces the extraordinarily complicated history of the lost office-book and of the copies made of it, and identifies and transcribes some hitherto unpublished fragments. Blewitt's 'Records of Drama at Winchester and Eton, 1397–1576' appears in two instalments in *TN*. It would seem from the references he has collected that, although there was a strong tradition of drama at both colleges, the boys themselves took part more often and from an earlier date at Eton, whereas Winchester relied more on visiting professionals.

A book on staging practices comes from Alan C. Dessen: *Elizabethan Stage Conventions and Modern Interpreters*[21]. A primary aim of this study is to use precise Elizabethan stage directions to help understand indefinite ones. Thus it helps with '*Enter Bellafront mad*' to know that there is a large *group* of stage directions of the '*Enter Cassandra with her hair about her ears*' type; or that characters entering '*in haste*' are often booted; or that night is frequently signified by night-gowns. In these sections of his book Dessen's wide knowledge of the drama of the period is put to excellent use. Although, as my examples suggest, his revelations are not, by and large, very startling, when he is on this tack he is working valuably towards a basic phrasebook of Elizabethan stage conventions, firmly grounded in a thorough survey of the extant texts. A persistent theme is the metonymic economy of means enjoined on dramatists by the bare stage, an economy often much more suggestive than modern naturalistic profusion of detail: 'let them see the wood', he in effect urges directors and designers. So far, so good. But it is Dessen's very sensitivity to the symbolic language of stage directions which also gives rise to the more questionable parts of his argument: those interpretations of the contributions made by stage directions to a play's 'logic of imagery or analogy' in which the vice of allegory takes over from the ousted vice of naturalism. For instance, Gertrude's mysterious inability to see her husband's ghost in *Hamlet* III.iv has for Dessen little to do with her own weaknesses and blindnesses (his scepticism here may well be justified); rather, it is a 'signal' to the audience to notice the *issue* of not seeing, and to realize that Hamlet, although he sees the Ghost, is actually the prime not-seer. I do not see this at all. However, supersubtleties apart, the book is a lively and welcome introduction to that often slighted language, 'SD'.

The social worth of the Bankside Globe project may have been questioned; but it is certainly stimulating scholars to think about the physical conditions of the Elizabethan theatre in great detail, and to devise ingenious practical tests of their hypotheses. Having deduced the orientation of the Globe, John Orrell (with the aid of a spotlight, a draughtsman's table, and a model of the theatre) has now simulated 'Sunlight at the Globe' (*TN*). Photographs of the experiment accompanying the text show that the stage would at all times have been in shadow, and the sun usually in the eyes of some of the audience. This arrangement is much more sensible than it may at first sound: even, muted light would have been easier for the players to handle than the uneven direct sun of a changeable London day, and, Orrell speculates, may also have contributed to 'a certain kind of illusionism', for instance softening boys' faces into women's.

21. *Elizabethan Stage Conventions and Modern Interpreters*, by Alan C. Dessen. CUP. pp. xii + 190. £17.50.

Keith Brown, crying for 'More Light, More Light' (*EIC*), is sure that the back-to-the-sun orientation of the stage would have encouraged – and, indeed, in the fifth act necessitated – the use of artificial light, which would have shown up in the gloom. As proof, Brown offers an exasperated common sense (*obviously* no documentation of such an everyday phenomenon would have survived) and readings of *Hamlet* and *Henry V* which purport to show Shakespeare's sensitivity to the exigencies of lighting. There are rejoinders in a later issue of *EIC* from John Orrell, who thinks that artificial lighting might well have been used in the darkest months, but points out very reasonably that this seasonal need would hardly have affected the structure of plays designed to be played year-round; and from Andrew Gurr, who thinks that, if lighting had been used, it *would* have shown up in the documents. Anyway, the stage would not have been all that dark. This may be so, but Gurr's supporting analogy ('Football matches finish these days at 4.40 p.m. (5.40 G.M.T) without the need of stadium lights') seems wrong about both football and G.M.T. Meanwhile, R. B. Graves has assembled a good deal of documentary evidence about 'Stage Lighting at the Elizabethan and Early Stuart Courts' (*TN*). Graves is sceptical of the idea that lighting effects were gained by the laborious extinguishing and relighting of candles or torches (an idea that attracts Brown); the illumination at both court and private theatres would have been of 'an overall, evenly distributed type', stage and audience lit equally, brighter than normal lighting but not essentially different in kind.

Brown is stalking bigger game than lighting in his *EIC* article, however: his quarries, ultimately, are what, to adapt D. F. McKenzie's famous title, one might call 'Players of the Mind'. The resolutely factual air of theatrical and bibliographical scholarship alike can certainly decoy us into forgetting that we half-create what we perceive – and that what we are looking at is only a fragmentary record in the first place. John H. Astington, in his interesting consideration of the mechanics of 'Gallows Scenes on the Elizabethan Stage' (*TN*, 1983), does, nevertheless, fall through this trap when he argues that, because the illusion of a hanging in a court performance of the lost play *Herpetulus the Blue Knight* in 1574 was apparently managed by means of a basketwork truss, this was the way it was always done on the Elizabethan stage. There are comic consequences for the bower scene in *The Spanish Tragedy*, the stiffness of the wooing being accounted for by the creaky contraption Horatio is wearing under his doublet. Astington is aware of the improbable look of this hypothesis, but believes that, in the absence of other evidence, it is one 'we have to take seriously'. Brown, I imagine, would not agree.

There are further contributions from both John Orrell and Andrew Gurr, Orrell on the shape of 'The Private Theatre Auditorium' (*ThR*) and Gurr on how the activity of play-going was described ('Hearers and Beholders in Shakespearean Drama' (*EiT*)). Principally on the basis of references, in plays written for private theatres, to the auditorium as 'round', 'orb', 'sphere', or 'circle', Orrell argues that the seating was arranged in a semicircular (Phoenix) or polygonal (Blackfriars) rather than a rectangular shape: a thesis which, if accepted, puts the private theatres in a continuous line of development stretching from Sebastiano Serlio to the Restoration playhouses. Gurr has collected and analysed a host of contemporary references to the sixteenth- and seventeenth-century audience ('audience' itself not becoming the regular descriptive word until the Restoration). The evidence is somewhat contradictory, but a general pattern can be discerned in which an 'auditory' that 'hears' a play in the sixteenth century gives way to 'spectators' who 'behold' one in the seventeenth. Tied up with this shift of usage is the larger issue of the relative status of the senses of sight and hearing. The article shows that dramatists of the period used the words 'auditors' and 'spectators' with some care as to shades of meaning, and provides an interesting broader context for Jonson's quarrel with Inigo Jones.

I have only three reviews of recent productions to report on, but this is probably because I have not spread my net widely enough in these waters. Tony Howard compiles a 'Census of Renaissance Drama Productions (1984)' in *RORD*. Elizabeth Maslen gives some interesting details of the historic Michael Bogdanov production of *The Spanish Tragedy* in her National Theatre platform lecture on 'The Dynamics of Kyd's *Spanish Tragedy*', reprinted in *English*, 1983. And H. Neville Davies, in '*A New Way to Pay Old Debts*: Massinger and the RSC' (*CritQ*), plays Hamlet to Adrian Noble's clown, warning the director of the RSC's acclaimed revival of Massinger's comedy to cut out the funny business:

> Locally effective stage business that subverts the larger endeavour, and forced delivery of lines to raise a laugh by drawing attention to meanings unforeseen by the writer are sure signs that the play and the production are pulling in different directions.

And shows a most pitiful ambition in the fool that uses it. This one will run and run.

4. Criticism

(a) General

Two books assign to the drama a key role in the creation of the intellectual conditions necessary for the English Revolution, but they adopt very different strategies to substantiate this claim. Jonathan Dollimore, in *Radical Tragedy*[22], takes a grand sweep through Renaissance scepticism from Machiavelli to Hobbes in order to establish the existence of a climate of thought which could have nourished a radical drama. By 'radical' he means that Jacobean tragedies can be seen to mount a persistent onslaught on 'providentialism' and on the 'centrality of the human subject', an onslaught which has profound political implications, since these two beliefs were, in Dollimore's analysis, the supporting pillars of the 'establishment' ideology of church and court. The protagonists are familiar – the Tillyardian world picture and Hobbesian materialism – though here found in a new guise for nowadays, with the latter no longer the villain. Dollimore seems to be indebted to J. W. Lever's characterization of Jacobean tragedy as 'a drama of adversity and stance, not of character and destiny' (*The Tragedy of State*; *YW* 52.202); in his denial that the tragic heroes maintain a transcendent integrity of self, whether through action, suffering, or stoic withdrawal (and, indeed, of the possibility of such transcendence), he ranges himself against a wide array of recent interpretations, notably Richard S. Ide's *Possessed with Greatness* (*YW* 61.141–2, 172 for two very different estimates of this book).

22. *Radical Tragedy: Religion, Ideology and Power in the Drama of Shakespeare and his Contemporaries*, by Jonathan Dollimore. Harvester. pp. viii + 312. £19.95.

Dollimore's protest against the 'teleological' bias of modern academic criticism is timely (although much too sweeping): it is worth pointing out that the search for moral and formal 'unity' can draw these plays' Brechtian teeth. But the limitations of his view of historical context are also apparent: we hear a lot about his chosen plays in relation to great currents of thought, but not much about their more particular entanglements with politics, audiences, theatres, or other plays (it does not even register in the analysis that Fulke Greville's *Mustapha* was not written for performance). This deficiency takes on greater importance because the plays discussed are such a mixed bag (besides *Mustapha*, Dollimore's 'first eleven' is made up of *Doctor Faustus*, Marston's *Antonio's Revenge*, Chapman's *Bussy d'Ambois*, Jonson's *Sejanus*, *The Revenger's Tragedy*, *The White Devil*, and four Shakespeares), and their grouping together begs many questions. Thickets in the middle distance are razed to unclutter the great vistas: the resulting views are indeed majestic, but there remains something artificial about them. A Faustian weakness for tendentiously curtailed quotations (he has Chapman's Monsieur saying firmly that Bussy will 'Do anything') is quite often apparent in Dollimore's analysis. His book is important in that it brings to fuller articulacy certain recent developments in critical thinking about Jacobean tragedy; how lasting that importance will be I am not sure.

It is convenient to interpolate here that Walter Cohen, in 'The Reformation and Elizabethan Drama' (*SJW*), substantially agrees with Dollimore's account of drama in history, and with his interpretation of Faustus as 'located on the axes of [cultural] contradictions which cripple and finally destroy him'. A brutally graphic reading!

If the presiding genius of Dollimore's version of seventeenth-century history is unequivocally Christopher Hill, Martin Butler, in *Theatre and Crisis*[23], seems to have learnt from both Hill and Conrad Russell. Butler's focus is much closer than Dollimore's – on the single decade immediately preceding the outbreak of the Civil War. He cautions against reading back the 1640s opposition between Cavaliers and Roundheads into the much less clearcut 1630s, a historical simplification which he thinks has contributed to the dismissal of Caroline drama as decadent. Nobody at the time knew the Civil War was going to happen; the issues were in suspension; allegiances confused. Take this view of the decade, and the drama, instead of being shouldered aside by the irrevocable march of history, springs into life as a kind of fictional forum (a kind of ideal parliament) in which the period's tensions could be – and were – most fully articulated and explored. There are resemblances here to Dollimore's view of the Jacobean drama, but there are also deep underlying differences, which may be gestured towards by saying that Butler seems to have much more faith in parliaments.

Methodologically, the two books are chalk and cheese. Butler could not be accused of neglecting local context; indeed, a great indigestible slab of it takes up much of a central chapter of the book, as the author indefatigably traces the endlessly ramifying family connections of some members of the Caroline gentry. But it is difficult to see how else this information could have been presented (family trees assist the exposition), and Butler is doing something excitingly novel with it: trying to get behind the generalizations to come at a

23. *Theatre and Crisis 1632–1642*, by Martin Butler. CUP. pp. xii + 340. £25.

specific sense of the social and political complexion of the regular private theatre audience. He builds up a picture of a closely knit, experienced group of playgoers, with strong Puritan and 'country' affiliations (to use labels that Butler has space to resist), a self-sustaining society distinct from the court, more open and outward-looking, and one in which the theatre played a key role. It was for this responsible, politically aware audience that Shirley and Brome wrote their complex, ironic, often sharply critical plays. Butler's argument is convincingly presented, and should lay to rest the old derogatory stereotype of the jaded Caroline audience. If a tinge of scepticism remains, it is only because of the convenient resemblance of Butler's historical audience to the ideal audience he, as defender of Brome's and Shirley's plays, would anyway want to invoke.

Brome also drew, Butler argues, on the easily overlooked but still flourishing traditions of the popular theatres whose repertoire of sturdy old crowd-pleasers provided a direct – and potentially inflammatory – link with that Elizabethan golden age to the memory of which dissatisfied Caroline subjects increasingly turned. Butler's chapter on the public theatres is one of his most impressive; and in a welcome appendix he ably defends their right to be termed 'popular' against the revisionist arguments for 'privileged play-goers' advanced by Ann Jennalie Cook (*YW* 62.202). In short, the theatres were closed down in 1642 not because they were Royalist but because of their subversive potential in a time of national unrest; and, if we wish to appreciate the full quality of the Caroline drama, we must turn our attention away from the court. *Theatre and Crisis* is a fine book. True, there is some special pleading on behalf of some of the plays. But it is not as if committed advocates of the Caroline drama are exactly thick on the ground.

Three articles of Butler's develop further some aspects of his overall case: these are 'Entertaining the Palatine Prince: Plays on Foreign Affairs, 1635–1637' (*ELR*, 1983); 'Royal Slaves? The Stuart Court and the Theatres' (supplement to *RDN*); and 'Two Playgoers, and the Closing of the London Theatres, 1642' (*ThR*).

If Dollimore and Butler are literary critics first and historians second, then Laura Caroline Stevenson is of the other persuasion: a historian interested in literature as evidence of social attitudes. Her useful book, *Praise and Paradox*[24], takes a sceptical look, fifty years on, at the middle-class culture of Elizabethan England analysed in Louis B. Wright's classic study. There simply *wasn't* a coherent bourgeois system of values in the sixteenth century, she argues. Although the old prejudiced stereotypes of the grasping usurer and the clownish cobbler die out in the 1590s as the social position of merchants and craftsmen improves, popular writers can still only praise their 'middle-class' heroes by having recourse to incongruous aristocratic values such as military prowess, devil-may-care magnificence, or pastoral content (this is the 'paradox' of her title). In an age when diligence and thrift were enjoined on all classes of reader by all classes of writer, Stevenson exposes as anachronistic the assumption that there existed a bourgeois 'Protestant work ethic' with those qualities as its class-badges. Plays by dramatists such as Heywood and Dekker figure quite prominently in the carefully defined canon of 'popular literature'

24. *Praise and Paradox: Merchants and Craftsmen in Elizabethan Popular Literature*, by Laura Caroline Stevenson. Past and Present Publications. CUP. pp. xiv + 252. £22.50.

upon which her argument is based (a full index of authors and their individual social backgrounds makes up a useful appendix), although it is about Thomas Deloney's fiction that she writes most illuminatingly. She can see only 'prejudice' and 'implied criticism of craftsmen' in Elizabethan clowns.

'And Elizabethan tragedy' or 'in Renaissance drama' are phrases which can conveniently take a multiplicity of antecedents. This year, books on Fortune, magicians, and masques make up the in-and-in medley.

Frederick Kiefer's *Fortune and Elizabethan Tragedy*[25] knowledgeably traces the history of the concept and iconography of Fortune during the sixteenth century. At the outset of the period a goddess to be feared and distrusted, especially when bearing gifts, she has become by its end Occasion, whose forelock is to be seized, a development Kiefer thinks re-enacted in miniature in the plot of *Hamlet*. In like vein, *Richard II* is interpreted as a contest between Fortuna (Richard) and Virtus (Bolingbroke). *Sejanus* and *King Lear* express the bewildered despair of a humanity governed by Fortune (rather than Providence), but denied Occasion. If these critical insights seem somewhat schematic, that is because Fortune rather than Elizabethan tragedy is the dominant partner in Kiefer's argument. He writes in earlier chapters about the tensions between fortune and providence, chance and design, sympathy and judgement, in the *Mirror for Magistrates* and the Elizabethan translations of Seneca, moving on to Shakespeare by way of Lodge, Marlowe, and Kyd. Fortune's importance to sixteenth-century writers was as a focus for 'the profound doubts and fears of a culture whose faith in providential design was at times precarious'. Although their critical languages are unlike, there is a certain continuity between Kiefer's concerns and those of Jonathan Dollimore in *Radical Tragedy*.

Barbara Howard Traister's *Heavenly Necromancers*[26] begins by outlining two traditional views of the magician: the sage of Neoplatonist philosophy, and the showman of medieval romance. She puts this duality to good use in her analysis of the interplay between comic and serious scenes in *Doctor Faustus*. But as we progress through *Friar Bacon and Friar Bungay* (which deals with 'the proper place of magic within a stable social order'), *Bussy d'Ambois* (Behemoth, inconclusively), and *The Tempest* (an unproblematic view of Prospero as ideal magician) to the court masque, the argument never quite takes wing. The book is more a study of some plays with magicians in them than a solution to the mystery of the 'abrupt rise and fall of the stage magician' which set the author off on her investigations.

Sarah P. Sutherland's *Masques in Jacobean Tragedy*[27] is likewise a study of some plays with masques in them; but, in this case, it is the author's avowed aim to eschew all grander theorizing about 'the masque', which she believes can only mislead. Forthright, and refreshing; but it makes for a very uneven book. Renouncing a thesis, Sutherland is left overdependent on the stimulus of earlier critics' mistakes and confusions. The obverse of the scepticism she directs at her predecessors in the field is an impatience with ambiguity in the

25. *Fortune and Elizabethan Tragedy*, by Frederick Kiefer. Huntington (1983). pp. xx + 354. $22.50.

26. *Heavenly Necromancers: The Magician in English Renaissance Drama*, by Barbara Howard Traister. UMiss. pp. xii + 196. £23.25.

27. *Masques in Jacobean Tragedy*, by Sarah P. Sutherland. AMS Studies in the Renaissance 9. AMSP (1983). pp. xvi + 148. $24.50.

plays, an urge to resolve greys into blacks and whites. Underlying the argument is a very plain division of the characters of revenge tragedy into 'just revengers' and villains who are trapped in their own work. Vindice is one of the former. Chapters are devoted to Marston's *Antonio's Revenge, The Revenger's Tragedy*, Beaumont and Fletcher's *The Maid's Tragedy*, Webster's *The Duchess of Malfi*, Middleton's *Women Beware Women*, and Middleton and Rowley's *The Changeling*. It is naughty of the publishers to claim that the book establishes 'new heights' in the study of Jacobean plays.

We come now to three collections of essays, one a symposium and two by individual critics. Four papers from the Second Congress of the International Shakespeare Association[28] are comparisons of Shakespeare with one of his contemporaries. Anne Barton's fine essay, 'Shakespeare and Jonson', is the pick of these; its arguments are repeated and expanded in her book on Jonson, reviewed in section 4(c) below. Philip Edwards sees Shakespeare in *Hamlet* refining upon the supernatural scheme of *The Spanish Tragedy* by leaving open the possibility that Old Hamlet's ghost is not a hellish emissary. *Hamlet* in its turn is refined upon by Beaumont and Fletcher in *The Maid's Tragedy*, ingeniously argues H. Neville Davies: aspects of Shakespeare's play appear ironically fractured, distorted, and subverted in the two collaborators' 'aggressive emulation' of an overshadowing earlier masterpiece. Finally, A. R. Braunmuller contrasts Peele's formal handling of the rhetorical set speech with the more flexible approach of the young Shakespeare.

Among the essays which comprise the third volume of Muriel Bradbrook's *Collected Papers*[29] are her familiar 'Fate and Chance in *The Duchess of Malfi*' (*YW* 28.156); distinctively packed and suggestive accounts of Peele's *Old Wife's Tale*, and of Beaumont and Fletcher (the latter the introduction to the Everyman *Selected Plays*); a revised version of a section on character-types from her early book *Themes and Conventions of Elizabethan Tragedy*, now entitled 'Bogeymen, Machiavels, and Stoics', and including some fine pages on Chapman's *The Revenge of Bussy d'Ambois*; and the full version of a review of Thomas Heywood's career first published in *EiT*, 1982, and missed by *YW* 63. Professor Bradbrook stresses the practical theatricality of Heywood's plays, and suggests that, with the current interest in performance texts, the time is ripe for further detailed study of a dramatist who openly acknowledged, on the publication of his plays, that 'it was never any great ambition in me, to be in this kind voluminously read'. This is an excellent collection, and welcome.

I cannot warm so much towards Jackson I. Cope's collection, *Dramaturgy of the Daemonic*[30], however, gathering as it does his recent article on *The Old Wife's Tale* (*YW* 63.193); earlier essays on Marlowe's *Dido* (*YW* 55.233) and Jonson's *Bartholomew Fair* (bizarrely arguing in the latter that Adam Overdo is a figure of Jehovah); and a somewhat revised but still rather flimsy ascription of *Common Conditions* and *Clyomon and Clamydes* to Richard Edwardes.

28. *Shakespeare, Man of the Theater. Proceedings of the Second Congress of the International Shakespeare Association, 1981*, ed. by Kenneth Muir, Jay L. Halio, and D. J. Palmer. UDel/AUP (1983). pp. 265. £21.50.

29. *Collected Papers of Muriel Bradbrook*. Vol. III: *Aspects of Dramatic Form in the English and Irish Renaissance*. Harvester/B&N (1983). pp. xvi + 187. £19.95.

30. *Dramaturgy of the Daemonic: Studies in Antigeneric Theater from Ruzante to Grimaldi*, by Jackson I. Cope. JHU. pp. xiv + 166. £19.20.

Articles on George Farquhar and Carlo Goldoni, and previously unpublished work on Ruzante, Joseph Grimaldi, and the figure of Harlequin round out a heterogeneous volume.

There are several short studies of genres to notice. P. K. Ayers, in 'The Protestant Morality Play and Problems of Dramatic Structure' (*EiT*), declares that in such late moralities as William Wager's *The Longer Thou Livest, the More Fool Thou Art*, influenced by Calvinist theories of election and reprobation in its portrayal of an ineducable protagonist, the form itself has reached a dead end – a dead end postponed until 1642 for the theatre at large only through dramatists' conscious or unconscious evasion of the 'implications of religious orthodoxy'. The larger claims of this essay seem predicated on the questionable assumption that it was Puritanism which closed the theatres, and its evolutionary account of a unified 'morality' genre may also be challenged. Paula Neuss, for instance, sees Wager's plays as examples of a distinct sub-genre, 'The Sixteenth-Century English "Proverb" Play' (*CompD*), of which Shakespeare's *All's Well That Ends Well* and *Measure for Measure* are later adaptations. Their common structural principle is the rhetorical amplification of a chosen proverbial theme, a procedure Neuss analyses thoroughly in Wager's *Enough Is as Good as a Feast* (itself selected as a proverb suitable for amplification in Thomas Wilson's *Art of Rhetoric*).

Two articles deal with comedy. The 'motif' of 'Metamorphosis by Love in Elizabethan Romance, Romantic Comedy, and Shakespeare's Early Comedies' is R. S. White's subject in *RES*. His definition of metamorphosis is rather too elastic really to constitute it as a generic motif, but he writes with insight about Shakespeare's comedies in relation to, for instance, Ovid and *The Faerie Queene*, and includes discussion of Lyly's *Gallathea* and *Love's Metamorphosis*, praising the dramatist for the 'Jamesian discriminations and compromises made by his characters'. Stephen Hannaford, in '"My Money Is My Daughter": Sexual and Financial Possession in English Renaissance Comedy' (*SJH*), offers, by contrast, two triads which, in their various interrelations, define the genre: Senex + Woman + Lover; Treasure + Closed Space + Key. This is claimed as an anatomical improvement on Northrop Frye.

Tragicomedy is a very slippery term indeed, since its meanings shade imperceptibly from the precise (*Il Pastor Fido*) to the extremely vague (any comedy with unhappiness in it, any tragedy that makes you laugh). Given the unenviable task of writing a brief introduction to tragicomedy for students[31], David L. Hirst bravely tackles this ambiguity head on by distinguishing between two kinds within the genre: the Guarinian, which seeks to synthesize tragedy and comedy, and the mongrel English, which sets them to buffets, personified in the vice Ambidexter in *Cambises*. But it is another vice, Subtle Shift, who insinuates himself into Hirst's argument, for it is difficult to make this distinction hold. Shakespeare's *The Tempest*, for instance, is adduced as an example of the synthesizing kind, but Shakespeare is also praised as a great breeder of mongrels. When *The Tempest* is finally summed up as 'a consummate achievement in the field of English tragicomedy', it has become unclear whether 'English' here means 'English Italian' or 'English English', Fido or Crab. Although Fido is so much smaller than Crab, Hirst does not always spring to

31. *Tragicomedy*, by David L. Hirst. CI 43. Methuen. pp. xiv + 141. hb £7.50, pb £2.95.

his defence, scarcely having a kind word to throw in the direction of Beaumont and Fletcher; about Crab he writes more appreciatively, though not everyone will agree with all of his *ex cathedra* pronouncements, for instance that *The Revenger's Tragedy* is 'essentially frivolous'. In general, there is rather more personal thesis and rather less weighing of others' theses than one would ideally like in a book that sets out to guide students in 'the critical idiom'. A discussion of Corneille's tragicomedies rounds off the seventeenth-century section of the book; the second part interestingly considers some modern derivatives and extensions of the form.

On revenge tragedy there is a stimulating essay from Michael Neill, who argues that the revenger is typically a 'remembrancer', a representative of an older order which is being swept aside by 'new men', and that in the violent fantasies of the revenge plays resistance to the painful but unstoppable social transformations of the sixteenth and seventeenth centuries found expression. Increasing revenge tragedy's deep popular appeal was that

> the revenger's preoccupation with a suppressed and violated past answered to a more specific psychological need . . . the genre provided a way of imaginatively confronting the repressed guilts and anxieties created by the crises of the Reformation and Counter-Reformation, and even the questionable legitimacy of the usurping Tudor dynasty itself.

Revenge drama covertly expressed ways of feeling about the past which its audience could not ordinarily allow themselves to articulate, offering release to pent-up guilts and resentments through apocalyptic fantasies of violent destruction of 'the ruthless world which had replaced the lost paradise'. Here is the useful 'fictional forum' idea again, as in Butler's *Theatre and Crisis*, although now the forum is a site for bloody murders rather than rational debate. Neill's essay is to be found in the Canberra collection, *Jonson and Shakespeare*[32], other contributions to which are reviewed in section 4(c) below.

An oddly assorted miscellany of articles brings this section to a close. *Gorboduc* has probably been compared to many things in its long career, but never before, I think it is safe to say, has the fifth act been claimed to resemble the 'fantastic rooftop architecture' of Longleat House. Alan T. Bradford's point in drawing this novel parallel, in 'Drama and Architecture under Elizabeth I: The "Regular" Phase' (*ELR*), is that both *Gorboduc* and Longleat finally break free from the severe formal discipline of classicism, and should therefore be regarded as carriers of the 'native Gothic tradition' through the 'regular' phases of English tragedy and English architecture, instead of as alien obstacles in that tradition's path. John Loftis, usefully reviewing the claims that have been made for Spanish influence on seventeenth-century English drama, can find no strong tradition of 'English Renaissance Plays from the Spanish *Comoedia*' (*ELR*). Only four plays, he concludes, are based directly on Spanish originals: Massinger's *The Renegado*, Shirley's *The Young Admiral* and *The Opportunity*, and Fletcher and Massinger's *Love's Cure*.

Anne Parten's 'Masculine Adultery and Feminine Rejoinders in

---

32. *Jonson and Shakespeare*, ed. by Ian Donaldson. Macmillan (1983). pp. xiv + 221. £15.

Shakespeare, Dekker and Sharpham' (*Mosaic*) explores the operation of the sexual double standard in several comedies, and finds that Shakespeare, although sympathetic to his wronged heroines, is more conservative in his attitude to wifely self-sacrifice than either Dekker or Sharpham. Suzanne Gossett prefers the Elizabethan dramatists' insistence that rape victims must die to their Jacobean successors' readiness to let them marry their assailants, because the earlier attitude, though seemingly harsh and prejudiced, actually shows more true respect for women than the later casualness towards rape ('"Best Men are Molded out of Faults": Marrying the Rapist in Jacobean Drama' (*ELR*)).

Finally, in *CahiersE* R. P. Corballis contends, with some straining of the evidence, that 'The Name Antonio in English Renaissance Drama' was usually given to characters virtuous to the point of folly; while Caroline di Miceli, also in *CahiersE*, piles up a very lengthy list of references to 'Sickness and Physic in Some Plays by Middleton and Webster', to what end I know not.

(b) Marlowe

The Jew of Malta seems temporarily out of favour, but all Marlowe's other plays received critical attention, with *Doctor Faustus* predictably attracting the most. Defensive or apologetic stances are quite frequently adopted; there is evidently an expectation that many readers and audiences will still find Marlowe beyond the pale.

Only two articles deal with more than one play, Richard F. Hardin's 'Marlowe and the Fruits of Scholarism' (*PQ*) and Ronald Huebert's 'Tobacco and Boys and Marlowe' (*SR*). Both use biography as a key to the understanding of the plays, and both draw parallels with modern life, but there the resemblances end: the fruits of scholarism are not to be identified with tobacco and boys! Hardin explores Marlowe's divided response to the scholarly life, variously embodied in the straightforwardly heroic Ramus of *The Massacre at Paris*; in the 'minor tragedy' of the needy scholar Baldock, finding, with his master Edward II, momentary consolation for the collapse of worldly fortunes in a nostalgic return to the cloister; and, of course, in the brilliant, disputatious, slothful, quintessentially doctoral Faustus, innovatively placed by Marlowe within a supportive, if complacent, collegiate community. Huebert's Faustus is driven by an addictive desire to defy authority; Marlowe's admiration for all such acts of defiance is claimed to be ultimately bound up with his own homosexuality. Since we can be sure about the university but not about the homosexuality, it is Hardin who is on the firmer ground. Huebert compensates by energetic presentation.

Concerned solely with *Doctor Faustus* are a short book by William Tydeman in the Macmillan Text and Performance series[33], and an article by Malcolm Pittock on Faustus's last soliloquy. Patrick Cheney considers the relationship between Faustian and Spenserian magic, while Ailene S. Goodman, writing briefly on 'Alchemistic Diabolism in the *Faust* of Marlowe and Goethe' (*JEP*), is more concerned with the historical sources for the legend.

Tydeman's book, following the standard format of its series, deals in its first part with critical interpretations of the play, and in its second with several

---

33. *Doctor Faustus: Text and Performance*, by William Tydeman. Macmillan. pp. 87 + 4 pls. pb £2.95.

representative productions. Despite Tydeman's appreciative and detailed accounts of the performances, the impression finally given is of their failure to realize fully an ideal interpretation arrived at in the study: 'a totally satisfying rendition of the part of Faustus continues to elude even our most enterprising actors'; 'no single production of *Doctor Faustus* in recent times can be deemed truly satisfactory'. From one point of view, this is undeniable (and, as an academic playgoer, them's my sentiments too); but it is a point of view I am slightly surprised to find governing a study of this sort. However, if the tension between text and performance resolves itself rather too easily in favour of the former, the book is still one that students will find very useful, containing as it does lucid and sensible reviews of the various solutions that have been offered to major problems, such as Marlowe's moral standpoint, Faustus's character, and the comic scenes. Tydeman's own preference (too neat?) is for a Faustus with whose mortal failings we sympathize, while deploring his false sense of values.

Tydeman devotes a couple of pages to an appreciation of Faustus's last soliloquy in his section on the play's language. Malcolm Pittock has space for a more detailed commentary in 'God's Mercy Is Infinite: Faustus's Last Soliloquy' (*ES*), where he argues that Faustus is damned not before, but during the speech (at 'O spare me, Lucifer!' to be precise), and showing how, to the end, Faustus takes refuge from absolute truth in his own fatal, speculative philosopher's ability 'to make play with a variety of perspectives and possibilities'. Patrick Cheney, in 'Love and Magic in *Doctor Faustus*: Marlowe's Indictment of Spenserian Idealism' (*Mosaic*), effectively contrasts Spenser's Neoplatonic ideal of the beloved as an incarnation of 'heavenly beauty' with Marlowe's ironic presentation of Helen of Troy, but does not quite establish that the latter constitutes an 'indictment' of the former.

Two articles on *Tamburlaine*, in their different ways, oppose modern ironic or moralized readings. In 'The Contemporary Perception of Marlowe's Tamburlaine' (*MRDE*) Richard Levin usefully collects a host of early comments on the plays, not one of which suggests to him that its original audiences thought Marlowe meant the hero to be anything but admired and wondered at. Modern commentators who do not agree, says Levin, are guilty of 'critical narcissism', fathering upon the dramatist their own moral disapproval. Johannes H. Birringer, writing under the title 'Marlowe's Violent Stage: "Mirrors" of Honor in *Tamburlaine*' (*ELH*), rather worriedly concurs. Transgressing the 'fixed moral boundaries' of the 'prevailing mode of tragedy', the play imposes on its audience 'a turbulent dramatization of extravagant human claims and engages them in violent fantasies of unconditional power'. In the course of his article, Birringer makes some interesting observations about the contrast between other playwrights' morally emblematic use of spectacle, and Marlowe's 'distinctly confusing' use of it in *1 Tamburlaine* IV.iv.

Finally, three rescue operations. In 'Repetition, Contrariety, and Individualization in *Edward II*' (*SEL*) John F. McElroy is warm in the defence of *Edward II*, a play he praises as Beckettian in the grimness of its outlook and the repeating patterns of its language and action. What Wilbur Sanders, for instance, takes as evidence of flagging inspiration and moral confusion, McElroy interprets as 'self-imposed limitation' of style and calm 'objectivity'. It is difficult to see how this debate will ever be resolved, particularly while the two sides continue to overstate their cases. McElroy's worst enemy is his own partisanship, which will not let him miss any local chance of imputing design to Marlowe, even if it weakens his overall argument. But there are many good points mixed in; and, as the more generous to Marlowe, McElroy's would certainly seem to be the better side to take. A similar argument is advanced by Julia Briggs *vis-à-vis The Massacre at Paris*, which she subjects to 'A Reconsideration' (*RES*, 1983). What we know of Marlowe's other work ought to make us think twice before dismissing this play as 'a piece of crude Protestant propaganda'. Re-examination of Marlowe's sources for the second half of the play shows that Paul Kocher's findings (*PMLA*, 1941; *MLQ*, 1947; etc.) need revision: Marlowe followed Catholic League rather than Huguenot accounts of the Guise's murder, and his version of the events is more historically accurate, less coloured by an extreme viewpoint, than Kocher made out. Although chary of the text's corruptions, and often hedging her interpretative bets, Briggs finally comes down in favour of an ironic reading of the play, with the dying Henry III horribly urging Navarre to a replay of St Bartholomew with colours reversed. There are a suggestive few pages on the resemblance of Marlowe's portrayal of the massacre to the historical 'rites of violence' in sixteenth-century France described by Natalie Zemon Davis. This is an important re-assessment, passed over last year. Somewhat less edifying is W. Craig Turner's 'Love and the Queen of Carthage: A Look at Marlowe's *Dido*' (*ELWIU*), which does little for the play by identifying its central theme as the perverseness and destructiveness of sensual passion, but may do more by its suggestion (not fully pursued) that Aeneas's passion for building the new Troy is seen by Marlowe as equally perverse and destructive.

(c) Jonson

Pride of place must be granted to Anne Barton's splendid book, *Ben Jonson, Dramatist*[34]. The Jonson here presented is a playwright complexly entangled in a love–hate relationship with the Elizabethan theatre, and a man of powerful feelings which often ran counter to his strenuously cherished ideals. In her book's first chapter, Barton makes a strong case for Jonson's authorship of the 1602 additions to *The Spanish Tragedy*, on characteristic grounds – their 'most Jonsonian concern' with fatherhood, and with 'the difficulty of coming to terms with the death of a child'. With one part of his mind, it is argued, Jonson had understood, loved, and could subdue himself to the mode of Kyd's play, a work he would later mercilessly scorn, and a work representative of a dramatic tradition from which he was simultaneously and uncompromisingly (in the early satires) labouring to set himself free. Towards the end of his dramatic career, in an expansion of sympathies first presaged in his portrayal of the relationship between Wittipol and Mrs Fitzdottrel in *The Devil Is an Ass* (the subject of a very fine chapter), Jonson returns to his Elizabethan origins, forging in *The New Inn* and *A Tale of a Tub* (restored appreciatively to what is surely its rightful place in the chronology) his own distinctive, nostalgic version of Shakespearean festive romance. Parts of this case are already familiar from the author's articles on *The New Inn* (*ELR*, 1979; *YW* 60.176–7), and on Jonson and Caroline nostalgia (*ELH*, 1981; *YW* 62.212); the appetite whetted by those first instalments can now be fully satisfied.

34. *Ben Jonson, Dramatist*, by Anne Barton. CUP. pp. xiv + 370. hb £30, pb £9.95.

It is in the opening and closing sections of the book that the really original thrust of the argument resides; but this is not to imply that Anne Barton has nothing of value to say about the greatest period of Jonson's career. Indeed, each of the plays is given its head in a substantial chapter, or part-chapter, and it is only rarely that the author's writing loses its edge and zest. She is particularly good at searching out what might be called the distinctive unconformities of plays, commenting insightfully, for instance, on the role of Tucca in *Poetaster*, Truewit's disquisition on face-painting in *Epicoene*, or the unusual 'density of reminiscence' that 'enwraps' the characters of *Bartholomew Fair*. It is a very personal portrait of Jonson we are ultimately offered, of a great moralist also 'oppressed with fantasie', as Drummond recorded, and with unsuspected reserves of sentiment. Nobody will agree entirely with it. To me, for example, although Barton's summing-up of the positives of *Bartholomew Fair* could hardly be bettered in its kind (who else would perceive Whit's perceptiveness?), Jonson's tone is nevertheless here lost in Another's: she refers us to

> those instances of generosity and understanding which can be found in the most unexpected places at Smithfield: in the ragged but genuine loyalty which the Fair people are capable of giving each other, the homely affection of Haggis and neighbour Bristle, in what is truly compassionate and honest in Overdo's nature, or in the perceptiveness of Whit, the roaring bawd, when he gently restrains Knock-hum from persecuting Cokes at the puppet-play.

In fact, in

> ... that best portion of a good man's life,
> His little, nameless, unremembered, acts
> Of kindness and of love.

But it is a book which consistently sets you thinking, and makes you see Jonson afresh; and than that can any higher praise be offered?

Spare a thought, though, for Richard Dutton, whose *Ben Jonson: To the First Folio*[35] must be in danger of being overshadowed by its illustrious successor from the same press. The two books actually take almost diametrically opposed views of Jonson, and a selection of parallel extracts from them might well set a lively seminar discussion going. Dutton's focus is on the Jonson First Folio as a great act of literary self-definition. The question-begging exception is the inclusion of *Bartholomew Fair* – which could indeed hardly be left out of a book intended primarily as a students' introduction to Jonson, but which, of course, did not get into the Folio. Dutton takes the line that it was omitted simply through lack of space. Keeping the Folio at the centre of the picture means that Dutton's emphasis is firmly on the public image, on the way Jonson *wanted* himself to be understood. And this, on Dutton's showing, is as a sage and serious poet squarely in the line from Spenser to Milton. Throughout, Dutton recurs to Jonson's mercilessness 'on our penchant for simple answers and pleasures'; the plays challenge their audiences to difficult moral judgements, urge right

35. *Ben Jonson: To the First Folio*, by Richard Dutton. British and Irish Authors: Introductory Critical Studies. CUP (1983). pp. xii + 188. hb £15, pb £4.95.

thinking and action by the satirical presentation of negative examples. The book offers a useful guide to Jonson's moral thinking, presents necessary information about his life, the court masque, and so forth, lucidly and compactly, and is well calculated to give the student the sense of making progress (*Every Man in his Humour* sets four 'problems' for comical satire which we gradually see Jonson resolving).

But Dutton's unremitting stress on Jonson the moralist ultimately narrows the reader's understanding – of both Jonson and, paradoxically, moral judgement itself. Dutton just will not be gulled, whether by the gracefulness of 'Come, my Celia' (Jonson is making his 'best efforts' here 'to remind us always to check the small print of life's choices') or by the exposure of the would-be reformers in *Bartholomew Fair* ('the audience's responsibility to judge and understand is, if anything, increased by the failure of these characters to do the job properly'). Still, if the book presents a rather one-sided view of Jonson, it is a view that the playwright himself did something to encourage, and that students should encounter.

Neither Barton nor Dutton contemplate the possibility that Jonson in a strange way *enjoyed*, and wanted the audience to enjoy, the crude brawling of the puppet-play in *Bartholomew Fair*. This is one of the several perspectives opened up, however, by Ian Donaldson's excellent article, 'Jonson and Anger' (*YES*), a discussion of the importance of anger to Jonson as a major source of moral and creative energy throughout his work. A 'guarantee of moral integrity' in the Roman tragedies (though also confronted as amoral Bacchic frenzy when the mob tears Sejanus to pieces), it is the 'great informing idea' of *Bartholomew Fair* (in which it is seen as ridiculous and dangerous, though also – in that strange way – sociable), but creates awkwardnesses of tone in the verse-satires and is later, with good reason, avoided by Dryden. Donaldson remarks on Jonson's frequently aggressive attitude towards his audience; the quarrelsomeness was, however, a way of negotiating a peace treaty, suggests George E. Rowe Jr, a way of creating fit hearers who would respect the author's intentions (and try patiently to unravel them) rather than tyrannizing over plays by extracting whatever scandalous meanings took their fancy. In 'Ben Jonson's Quarrel with Audience and its Renaissance Context' (*SP*) Rowe links this battle between playwright and audience to the larger Renaissance shift from allegorical to historical methods of reading, and considers it as embodied (obviously) in the Choruses of *The Magnetic Lady* and (not so obviously) in the action of *Sejanus*.

A conference was convened in Canberra in 1979 with the objective of brushing the dust off that venerable piece of critical furniture, the comparison between Jonson and Shakespeare. Papers from the conference have now been published[32]. In a helpful introduction Ian Donaldson outlines the history of the gambit; the essays which follow introduce no startling new variations. Of course, the cruder prejudices do not rear their heads: Shakespeare is allowed art and Jonson not denied all nature. But the volume's overall effect is confirmatory, rather than critical of the received tradition. Thus D. H. Craig, comparing *Pyramus and Thisbe* to Proctor Littlewit's puppet-play, evokes in the reader a reassuring feeling of familiarity when he finds that Shakespeare's audience is asked to co-operate in creating the magic of illusion, while Jonson expects from his a more rational detachment; as does F. H. Mares, carefully arguing that Shakespeare trusts in the imagination and presents characters capable of change, while Jonson is a voluntarist and his characters fixed. Ann Blake, writing about the two dramatists' portrayal of duping is substantially in agreement with Mares: Shakespeare shows compassion for the victims of 'sportful malice'; Jonson sometimes wants 'eart. Anthony Miller adds the political dimension: *Julius Caesar* is fundamentally monarchist in its outlook, *Sejanus* republican, though Jonson follows Tacitus in accepting that monarchy must be lived with. Other contributions come from Alvin Kernan, contrasting the two playwrights' attitude to their audiences in a more extensive way than Craig, and from Francis Berry, on points of staging in *Sejanus* and *Coriolanus*.

There is much good sense in these six essays. None of them can compete, though, with Anne Barton's excellent 'Shakespeare and Jonson' (see section 4(*a*) above). Also clamouring for a mention at this point is Lawrence Danson's 'Jonsonian Comedy and the Discovery of the Social Self' (*PMLA*), which effectively contrasts the endings of Shakespeare's comedies (in which renewal is promised through characters' discovery of their deeper selves) and those of Jonson's (in which selfhood is revealed as radically and dismayingly contingent, an entirely social construct). Sir Politick Would-Be's shame is emblematic:

> his 'uncasing' reveals unaccommodated man to be no more than such a creeping set of legs, garters, gloves, and the jumbled notes for a million incomprehensible social projects ... like Sir Pol, all the play's characters 'would-be'. They would be rich or powerful or sexually gratified, but at bottom, underneath the insufficiently protective shell, each would, simply, *be*.

Not all the essays in the Canberra collection are devoted to comparisons of Jonson and Shakespeare. There are, besides, three essays on Shakespeare *solus*, one by Michael Neill on revenge tragedy (already reviewed in section 4(*a*)), and three purely on Jonson: some vigorous remarks from Peter Barnes about adapting Jonson for the modern stage, a warning from Peter Walls about the difficulties inherent in reconstructing the music for Jonsonian masques, and J. B. Bamborough's good essay on Jonson's conservative 'rusticity', his interest in country life and rural customs as 'a repository of elements in the national life which were under threat, and which needed to be preserved' – a concern most fully displayed in the two late works, *A Tale of a Tub* and *The Sad Shepherd*.

Of the articles on Jonson that remain to be reviewed, one deals with *Every Man out of his Humour*, two with *Epicoene*, and three with *Bartholomew Fair*. Terrance Dunford's declaration that 'change is the hallmark of the Jonsonian humours character' is not perhaps the howler it at first appears to be (he has his eye on the obsessive imitativeness of the characters in *Every Man out*), but it *is* a sample of the difficulties he puts in the reader's way. 'Consumption of the world because one is identical to it', is, he asserts, 'the unifying theme' of the play ('Consumption of the World: Reading, Eating, and Imitation in *Every Man out of his Humour*' (*ELR*)).

The dominant analogy of *Epicoene*, claims Michael Flachmann, is of Morose's experience with that of the sinner trapped in the noisy torments of hell. He backs this up with many supportive quotations, although – instructively reflecting an ambivalence in the play? – never actually settles whether it is hell or purgatory to which he thinks Morose is consigned ('*Epicoene*: A Comic Hell for a Comic Sinner' (*MRDE*)). Barbara C. Millard, in '"An Acceptable Violence"': Sexual Contest in Jonson's *Epicoene*' (*MRDE*), is more interested in the wits and the collegiate ladies, who share similar motives and failings, and whose sexual conflict Jonson does not depict from an exclusively male standpoint, suggesting wider senses in which the world of the play is 'epicene'.

Easily the most substantial of the three articles on *Bartholomew Fair* is Jonathan Haynes's 'Festivity and the Dramatic Economy of Jonson's *Bartholomew Fair*' (*ELH*). Haynes argues that Jonson and his audience were unable to accept uncritically the older communal traditions of carnivalesque celebration, and that the play, in consequence, depicts a fairground not to be identified with Mikhail Bakhtin's utopian 'festive marketplace', but one commercially and criminally debased. Winwife and Grace in their 'detachment and condescension and even scorn', Quarlous in his perception of the Fair as a chance 'to get ahead in the rough scramble' exhibit 'post-festive' attitudes, attitudes that Jonson, with his high value for an 'austere independence of judgement' and a 'personal autonomy that the traditional society could not support' was concerned to recommend to, at least, the more socially privileged sections of his audience. Haynes valuably elucidates social tensions which the play embodies, but in arguing that Jonson is seeking to intervene in those tensions on the side of Winwife and Quarlous perhaps underestimates the effect on an audience of Ursula's description of the former as 'snotty-nose'.

Other contributions on *Bartholomew Fair* come from Mary W. Bledsoe, in 'The Function of Linguistic Enormity in Ben Jonson's *Bartholomew Fair*' (*Lang&S*), who dissects neatly each character's particular enormity of style, without adding a great deal to Jonas Barish's classic treatment of this subject in *Ben Jonson and the Language of Prose Comedy* (*YW* 41.128); and from Michael W. Bugeja ('Rosalind's Rival: Ursula as the Fallen Eve' (*ReAL*)), who compares *As You Like It* to *Bartholomew Fair* on the grounds that there are Adams in both, but an Eve only in the latter – 'Ursula . . . grown fat not on apples but on the equally evil fare of pork'. Finally, to restore some sobriety, I should mention that Geoffrey Hill's essay on the dramatic poetry of *Sejanus* and *Catiline* (*YW* 41.125–6) has been reprinted in his collection, *The Lords of Limit*[36].

(d) Middleton

Five out of eight articles on Middleton this year are devoted to *The Changeling*, a concentration which, great play though it is, seems a little unhealthy. A more even light is cast on the canon, as is proper, by the belated quatercentenary volume, '*Accompaninge the Players*'[37],

36. *The Lords of Limit: Essays on Literature and Ideas*, by Geoffrey Hill. Deutsch. pp. xii + 203. £12.95.

37. '*Accompaninge the Players*': *Essays Celebrating Thomas Middleton, 1580–1980*, ed. by Kenneth Friedenreich. AMS Studies in the Renaissance 8. AMSP (1983). pp. xiv + 248 + 8 pls. $34.50.

though here too *The Changeling* is prominent, eliciting the liveliest contribution.

It seems perverse of the collection's editor, Kenneth Friedenreich, to choose the virtually inaccessible *The Widow* as his sample play in an introduction aimed at teaching novices 'How to Read Middleton'; luckily, Roma Gill is soon at hand to provide a quick tour of Middleton's world. Four subsequent essays on the city comedies are largely uninspiring. David Richman describes the experience of directing what comes across as a spectacularly crude production of *A Chaste Maid in Cheapside*. David M. Bergeron develops the obvious contrast between *Chaste Maid* as a fictional representation of civic vice and Middleton's pageant, *The Triumphs of Truth*, as an allegorical representation of civic virtue. W. Nicholas Knight goes through *Michaelmas Term* providing glosses on the legal references: useful, but the 'take-them-as-they-come' approach makes his larger argument about the articulation of central themes difficult to grasp. And Joseph Messina worries away at the grotesque incongruity of the Dampit scenes in *A Trick to Catch the Old One*, and at whether the play has a 'moral design'. Also included in the first half of the book are a paper from Norman A. Brittin on Middleton's adjectives, and a short essay by G. B. Shand identifying the political and religious bias of Middleton's early work, *The Wisdom of Solomon Paraphrased*.

The pace begins to pick up as we move into the second half of the volume, and the tragedies hove into view. Kenneth Muir expertly drums up readers for two neglected plays, *More Dissemblers Besides Women* and *No Wit, No Help Like a Woman's*. Anne Lancashire reconstructs the topical context of *The Witch*; unfortunately, her argument that it reflects the Essex divorce scandal, written in 1979, had been 'anticipated' in print by both A. A. Bromham and Margot Heinemann (*YW* 61.178,179) by the time it was published four years later. Still, the late Lancashire *Witch* usefully supplements these other accounts. And, having negotiated these comparatively little-known passages, the reader emerges onto familiar tragic ground in the company of Stephen Wigler, Michael McCanles, and Peter Morrison.

Psychoanalysis is in the air. Wigler observes that it is not only the relationship between Isabella and Hippolito in *Women Beware Women* that is incestuous: Bianca may not be the Duke's daughter but she has a 'secure filial trust' in him; while Livia's revengefulness after Leantio's death 'is like that of a she-bear who has lost her cub'. Wigler goes on to speculate about the roots of this pattern in Middleton's personal psychology. Wild, but free, and with some good insights into the play. McCanles promptly brings the spirits plummeting down by writing out a string of mathematical formulae to express the 'moral dialectic' of *Women Beware Women*, but proceeds to a more enlivening appreciation of the 'mimetic power' with which Middleton 'renders this dialectic as a fissure in the minds of Bianca and Leantio'. And, finally, there is Morrison's passionate sympathy for Beatrice in *The Changeling*, whom he sees as a 'sad inheritress of a social structure predicated on a smug, masculine, thorough-going but thoroughly impotent dualism', a woman who has no way to reconcile her deep desires with her superficial socially given sense of self. Critics who avoid the madhouse by absorbing themselves in the analysis of formal patterns of 'changes' in the play, believes Morrison, are just as guilty as the 'zombie' Alsemero of trying to rationalize away the play's 'profoundly disturbing reminder' of the 'essential and irreducible reality of human kind'. At the very least he makes you want to argue.

Despite Morrison's scorn for the theme of 'change' and the questions 'who/what is the Changeling?', enthusiasm for these strategies continues unabated. Dale B. J. Randall begins 'Some Observations on the Theme of Chastity in *The Changeling*' (*ELR*) by noting that 'changeling' is defined as 'lamia' in a 1640 dictionary, and wonders whether Beatrice-Joanna's double name points to her lamian duality. He goes on to adduce evidence that the virginity test would not have seemed comical to the play's original audience. Charles W. Crupi, who writes on 'The Transformation of De Flores in *The Changeling*' (*Neophil*), is a staunch supporter of De Flores for chief changeling: it is not his wickedness that turns Beatrice from angel to whore, it is her lying hypocrisy that turns him from reasonable man to blind beast. Crupi intends merely to redress what he sees as a critical bias towards Beatrice, but he ends up by replacing one bias with another. Lois E. Bueler redirects attention from the characters to 'The Rhetoric of Change in *The Changeling*' (*ELR*). Three recurrent rhetorical patterns, she claims, keep the audience aware of the theme of change – the catechism with riddling answers, the syllogism, and the figure of antonomasia. But a more inclusive rhetorical approach is that of Ann Pasternak Slater, who sees the play's governing figure as hypallage (defined by George Puttenham as 'the Changeling'), at least if the significance of the term is metaphorically extended to cover the crossover of antithetical moral qualities as well as merely the exchange of words ('Hypallage, Barley-Break, and *The Changeling*' (*RES*, 1983)). Central to the game of barley-break, twice referred to at crucial moments in the action, is the change of partners; and the game provides a key to the shifting patterns of relationships in the play. Some of this schematizing does not seem very convincing – nor really necessary – but the article certainly has several sharp insights into the play's moral confusions and reversals, particularly as embodied in stage action. An advantage Slater claims for her interpretation is that it keeps all ambiguities open – in Beatrice's case, indeed, down to her last wordless cries of pain and/or sexual ecstasy, trapped finally with her partner De Flores in the Hell of the barley-break game. A last article on *The Changeling* is Christiane Gallenca's 'Baroque Sensibility in *The Changeling*' (*CahiersE*), mainly devoted to tracing connections between mythological references in the mad-speech of the subplot and their distorted reflections in the main plot.

As far as the rest of the Middleton canon is concerned, there are only articles on *Women Beware Women*, *The Old Law*, and *The Revenger's Tragedy* to report, all of which appeared in *SEL* (an article on *The Roaring Girl*, by Middleton and Dekker, is reviewed in section 4(*e*) below). Neil Taylor and Bryan Loughrey consider the significance of the chess game in *Women Beware Women* II.ii, and deduce from it a surprising number of the play's leading problems and ironies ('Middleton's Chess Strategies in *Women Beware Women*'). A. A. Bromham's discussion of 'The Contemporary Significance of *The Old Law*' lends support to those who view Middleton as an 'opposition' dramatist: the play is found to be critical of the Duke of Buckingham, on the side of Sir Edward Coke and the common lawyers against the encroaching powers of Chancery and Star Chamber, and puritan in its stance on the Oath of Allegiance controversy. Thirdly, and on my part tendentiously, there is Scott McMillin's fine article on *The Revenger's Tragedy* ('Acting and Violence: *The*

Revenger's Tragedy and its Departures from *Hamlet*'). McMillin develops a contrast between *Hamlet*, in which revenge is intimately associated with remembrance, with an exploration of the processes of the past, and *The Revenger's Tragedy*, which 'shifts the burden of clarity forward to the present' and 'reduces all social and temporal processes to a point of revenge'. This 'drive for compactness and finish' is intensely present in both the play's language and its stage imagery, but there is also an opposing principle at work: the proliferation of identities incident to the actor's craft, of which Vindice becomes such a master. McMillin's exploration of these drives and tensions is suggestive and densely wrought.

(e) Other Playwrights, and Plays

The ordering of items within this section is roughly chronological, but only roughly. Inevitably it is something of a gallimaufry. There are three essays on the theatre of the 1580s and 1590s; most, however, deal with the Jacobean period. Tragic tones predominate over comic.

To begin with the Elizabethans. It seems reasonable to assume that Elizabethan audiences would have recognized allusions to bull- and bear-baiting, but would their knowledge have stretched to the customs of the Spanish bullfight? Frank R. Ardolino thinks so, and in '*Corrida* of Blood in *The Spanish Tragedy*: Kyd's Use of Revenge as National Destiny' (*MRDE*) elaborates a fancied resemblance between Hieronimo and the *alguacil* of the bull-ring into a larger account of the play's political significance. A rather slight study of Robert Wilmot's revision of the twenty-five-year-old Inns of Court play *Gismond of Salerne* into *Tancred and Gismund* is contributed by Robert Seufert under the title '"The Decorum of these Daies": Robert Wilmot and the Idea of the Theater' (*ISJR*). More substantial is Alexander Leggatt's excellent essay on *Arden of Faversham* (*ShS*, 1983). Leggatt praises *Arden* for its 'hard tough appraisal of things as they are, and . . . resistance to conventional formulae', a resistance tactfully rather than toughly embodied in his own essay, too. The play stands up well to Leggatt's exact close scrutiny, which brings to light its cunning ironies of structure, its tightly woven network of allusions to bargains made and broken, and the compact precision to which its verbal art can rise. Historically important in that it 'opens a vein of realism in Elizabethan drama', *Arden* is nevertheless quite unlike any other play of the period, and Leggatt's account of it does full justice to its uniqueness.

Two articles on a later domestic tragedy, Thomas Heywood's *A Woman Killed with Kindness*, are less meaty. Rick Bowers, in '*A Woman Killed with Kindness*: Plausibility on a Smaller Scale' (*SEL*), argues for the play's unheroic authenticity to common experience, the 'closely packed detail' of its 'subtle psychological portrayals', but as he unpacks the detail shows himself to be rather uncomfortable with the non-naturalistic conventions that Heywood employs, feeling it necessary to justify an aside by Wendoll, for instance, by supposing that his previous line (an ordinary civility) has thrown Anne into 'speechless puzzlement'. What Bowers is here trying to do is find a credible motivation in the text for Anne's adultery. In 'Anne Frankford's Fall: A Complementary Perspective' (*AUMLA*) Harry Garlick, frankly stumped by the text, tries accounts of John Dexter's 1971 National Theatre production to see if they throw any light on the matter, but meets only with blankness from director and reviewers alike.

Turning to the intellectuals now, I find three articles on Marston and two on Chapman. Robert Beale Bennett's article on *The Malcontent*, 'The Royal Ruse: Malcontentedness in John Marston's *The Malcontent*' (*MRDE*), takes such a blandly approving view of Altofront's Malevolence as 'a disguise which does not violate right reason or the nature of the wearer' as to beggar belief, and, more seriously, remove most of the play's dramatic tension. The bias of his argument is well indicated by an aside on *The Tempest*: 'During the play Prospero remains awake while nearly everyone else *is allowed* at some point to sleep' (my italics). Scott Colley offers a more satisfying account of *The Malcontent* in his suggestive essay on 'Marston, Calvinism, and Satire', also in *MRDE*. He sees the paradoxes of Calvinist doctrine as a determining influence on Marston's satire, with its unstable mixture of vehement cleansing rage and doubt of its own ultimate efficacy. The only true judgement is the Last Judgement; mere human judgements are necessarily imperfect; and 'the real conclusion of *The Malcontent* seems postponed to a time when the term "conclusion" might have some meaning'. 'Because life was to him a jumble of intermittent grandeur and inevitable confusion, Marston came to interpret human experience as a dream or as a kind of glittery theatrical experience.' Besides being an excellent answer to Bennett, Colley's essay is also a valuable reminder that, despite Jonathan Dollimore's claim that in 'radical tragedy' an attack on the 'centrality of the human subject' was indissolubly associated with an attack on 'providentialism' (see section 4(*a*) above), scepticism about that 'centrality' in the early seventeenth century was often the result of a very firm faith in Providence indeed (admittedly, not a Providence which constantly intervened in human affairs). The third Marston item is Carol W. Pollard's 'Immoral Morality: Combinations of Morality Types in *All's Well that Ends Well* and *The Dutch Courtesan*' (*CahiersE*), which, as the title perhaps indicates, runs into some difficulty in interpreting Shakespeare's and Marston's comedies as complex adaptations of simple morality-play patterns.

Chapman's philosophy is respected by Richard S. Ide, and his control of tone and structure by Alexander Leggatt. Ide makes a strong case against 'easy ironic readings' of *The Revenge of Bussy d'Ambois* in 'Exploiting the Tradition: The Elizabethan Revenger as Chapman's "Complete Man"' (*MRDE*). Clermont is Chapman's version of the 'complete man', and, if there is a failure, it is the play's (and the genre's), unequal to the 'moral and philosophical freight' it has to bear, rather than the hero's. Leggatt's closely observed account of 'Tone and Structure in Chapman's *Byron*' (*SEL*) leads him to propose that the two *Byron* plays offer contrasting perspectives (the first comic, the second tragic) on essentially the same configuration of events.

Of the other dramatists, it is on Beaumont and Fletcher, and, to a lesser extent, Dekker, that interest is chiefly focused. Both Robert Y. Turner, writing about 'Heroic Passion in the Early Tragicomedies of Beaumont and Fletcher' (*MRDE*), and Eugene M. Waith, in his discussion of Fletcher's *The Mad Lover*, 'Mad Lovers, Vainglorious Soldiers' (*RORD*), lay stress on the 'flexibility of response' the two playwrights demand of their audience. In the early tragicomedies, argues Turner, heroic passion is acknowledged as an exception to the rule of temperance, a rare and dangerous force which may be ruinous, but which may also, as in *A King and No King*, 'drive a character beyond all calculations of prudence and the accepted laws of reason to ultimately beneficial results'. The dramatists' understanding of the dual nature of heroic passion derives from Sidney's *Arcadia* and Spenser's *Faerie Queene*. Waith's less weighty essay focuses on the ambiguous presentation of General Memnon in *The Mad Lover* as object of both satire and admiration, and on Fletcher's 'constant confounding of game and earnest' in the play. A more wide-ranging view of 'Fletcherian Romantic Comedy' is provided by Cyrus Hoy (*RORD*), who observes that, whereas in the Shakespearean variety heroines dominate, in Fletcher's comedies it is the young men who are the centre of interest (Jonson's *Epicoene* being a major influence). This makes for an 'air of aggressive sexuality', but an air tempered by Fletcher at his best with 'carefully timed accessions of male gentleness or embarrassment'. As Fletcher's settings in his later comedies become more exotic, so his heroes dwindle from recklessly improvident London sophisticates into more conventionally romantic types.

Dekker as a social commentator (in collaboration with Middleton) figures in an article by Mary Beth Rose, and as an old theatrical pro (in collaboration with the tyro Massinger) in one by Larry S. Champion. In 'Women in Men's Clothing: Apparel and Social Stability in *The Roaring Girl*' (*ELR*) Rose relates *The Roaring Girl* to the *Hic Mulier/Haec Vir* pamphlet controversy, and to the wider uneasiness about sexual roles of which it formed part. The play exposes prejudices against the transvestite Moll as narrow-minded, but nevertheless she remains a social anomaly, and cannot be included in the comic resolution of marriage: the dramatists' treatment of her reflects, as do the pamphlets, a 'simultaneous search for and rejection of greater flexibility in sexual values' characteristic of Jacobean England. Champion's '"Disaster with my So Many Joys": Structure and Perspective in Massinger and Dekker's *The Virgin Martyr*' (*MRDE*) deals with a very different kind of play, aiming to show how the two collaborators made an unpromising saint's life into one of 'the most innovative and challenging' tragedies of the Jacobean period(?) by skilful transfusion of dramatic stereotypes into an unusual setting.

Resistance to gallimaufry is no longer feasible: this final paragraph has to gather together five articles with little in common. 'Machiavelli, Policy, and *The Devil's Charter*' is Jacqueline E. M. Latham's subject (*MRDE*). She takes us through Barnabe Barnes's sensational play, pointing out that there are true Machiavellians, credibly amoral politicians, as well as grotesque stage Machiavels to be seen in it. Rupin W. Desai offers 'A Phenomenological Reading of Webster's *The White Devil*' (*MRDE*), arguing that Webster here performs 'the Reduction' of tragedy to its 'essence' – which is, seemingly, the sense-experience of dying as put into words by Flamineo. A metatheatrical reading of *The Second Maiden's Tragedy* is proposed by David M. Bergeron ('Art within *The Second Maiden's Tragedy*' (*MRDE*)), who analyses in great detail what he sees as the play's many self-conscious references to its own conventions, and finds that the two plots are 'unified' by a shared theatricality. The 'two books of God' of Bruce Boehrer's title, '"Nice Philosophy": '*Tis Pity She's a Whore* and the Two Books of God' (*SEL*), are Nature and Scripture. Giovanni sets one book against the other by claiming that Nature legitimizes his love for his sister, and Boehrer discusses the consequences of this challenge to religious orthodoxy. And lastly, in his interesting article 'The Globe Bewitched and *El Hombre Fiel*' (*MRDE*), Herbert Berry prints the text of a previously unpublished eye-witness report of a performance of Heywood and Brome's *The Late Lancashire Witches*, shows how it helps us to understand some of the play's stage business, and goes on to a consideration of the circumstances of the play's composition.

5. Masque and Pageant

Another instalment of C. E. McGee's and John C. Meagher's very useful 'Preliminary Checklist of Tudor–Stuart Entertainments' appears in *RORD*: it covers the years 1603–13. Middle Temple accounts relating to Chapman's *The Memorable Masque* and Shirley's *The Triumph of Peace* are transcribed by Tucker Orbison in the twelfth volume of the Malone Society's *Collections*[38]. They show how the huge sums of money needed to pay for these two princely magnificences were collected, and help to sort out which members of the Inn were responsible for which aspects of the masques' preparation. Orbison's introductions explain the documents' nature and context, and all names mentioned in them are glossed in sets of biographical notes. The volume also includes the text of an eccentric academic morality play, transcribed from a manuscript at the English College in Rome by Suzanne Gossett. In *RenQ* John R. Elliott Jr prints, and discusses, the text of '*Mr Moore's Revels*: A "Lost" Oxford Masque'. Hitherto incorrectly known to scholars as *Moore's Mask*, or *The Moor's Mask*, this curious piece may lampoon the lavish entertainments recently bestowed upon Charles I at Christ Church and St John's. A much earlier curiosity concerns Bennett A. Brockman, who in *ELN* supports F. J. Furnivall's conjecture that the 'tonsword' carried by Captain Cox at Kenilworth was a two-handed sword, a large weapon, possession of which would have associated him with the romance heroes whose exploits filled the books in his library ('O. E. D. "Tonsword", Robert Laneham's Letter, and the Character of Captain Cox').

A significant re-issue from Boydell is Sir Roy Strong's introductory history of Renaissance court festivals, originally known as *Splendour at Court* (*YW* 54.149–50), and now retitled *Art and Power*[39]. After a general survey of the intellectual, political, and artistic context of Renaissance festivals come particular studies of the royal entries of Charles V, the court festivals of Catherine de'Medici, the Florentine *intermezzi*, and the Caroline masque. Although the chapters on the French and Florentine festivals have been somewhat revised to take account of scholarship that has appeared in the eleven years since the book's first publication, this second edition is more accurately described as an 'augmented' one, since almost all the original text appears word for word, neatly spliced with new insertions which much extend the range and depth of the discussion. Augmented, that is, but for the pictures, a great splendour of *Splendour at Court*, now diminished in number and size, and tucked away in black and white at the back of the book, a stark dualism replacing, presumably for economic reasons, the generous inter-inanimation of soul and body which made the first edition such a delightful read. However, it would not be fair to go on grumbling: *Art and Power* is still a very handsomely produced book. Its

38. *Collections*, Vol. XII. (*The Middle Temple Documents Relating to George Chapman's 'The Memorable Masque': The Middle Temple Documents Relating to James Shirley's 'The Triumph of Peace'*, both ed. by Tucker Orbison; *Blame Not Our Author*, ed. by Suzanne Gossett.) MSR. Malone Society (1983). pp. 132. By subscription.

39. *Art and Power: Renaissance Festivals 1450–1650*, by Roy Strong. Boydell. pp. xiv + 230 + 104 pls. £19.50.

usefulness as a scholarly introduction to the subject is considerably increased by the guide to sources provided by the newly included (and often very full) footnotes – though it would have been even better if the information contained in these could have been presented in the form of a fully annotated bibliography.

It is striking that, of the ten essays gathered in a new collection devoted to the court masque[40], only one, Sara Pearl's discussion of the political context of the masques of 1620–5, takes Jonson as its subject. Indeed, several of the contributors are concerned with explicit challenges to the Jonsonian tradition. John Pitcher finds Samuel Daniel, in *Tethys' Festival*, taking a principled stand against imperialist policies, and also, therefore, against what he would have seen as Jonson's 'preposterous' claims for the masque's transforming power: Daniel's art is firmly grounded in a sense of its own limitations. David Lindley interprets *The Tempest*, with its recurrent pattern of disrupted shows and its uneasy ending, as Shakespeare's sceptical interrogation of masque's efficacy in working changes in an audience – a raising of doubts that the masque itself 'resolutely sidestepped and contained'. A wider perspective is offered by David Norbrook's survey of Stuart masquing, which makes the valuable point that the political exclusiveness of the masque form can be exaggerated: 'there was no inherent incompatibility between Puritan sympathies and an interest in masques'. And detailed proof is immediately at hand in fine studies of *Comus* by John Creaser and Helen Cooper, Creaser appreciative of the tact and ingenuity with which Milton 'inserts human limitation' into masque idealism without disrupting the decorum of an important royalist occasion, Cooper suggesting that Milton's deep sympathy for more 'open' Elizabethan traditions of entertainment 'gives the piece an undertone of tough moral realism such as the fantasy associated with the masque form rarely achieves'.

These five essays strike me as the heart of the volume, but that is not to dismiss as negligible the interesting contributions from Elizabeth Cook on Nashe's *Summer's Last Will and Testament*; Jennifer Chibnall, refining on Stephen Orgel and Roy Strong's definition of the Caroline masque form by means of an extended analysis of Aurelian Townshend's *Tempe Restored* and Thomas Carew's *Coelum Britannicum*; John Peacock on the French element in Inigo Jones's masque designs; and Paul Hammond on the decay of the masque form as exemplified in Dryden's *Albion and Albanius*. Lucidly introduced by the editor, David Lindley, the volume concludes with an excellent bibliography. The essays maintain a high standard, and there is material here that will interest both the specialist and the more general scholarly reader. The Revels Plays Companion Library has got off to a flying start.

There is one other book dealing with masques, and hard going it is, too: Joseph Loewenstein's idiosyncratic *Responsive Readings*[41]. I do not quite know what to make of this clever study. Its subject is Echo as a mythological personage and as a poetic device in classical literature, *Il Pastor Fido*, Gascoigne's *Princely Pleasures at Kenilworth*, Milton's *Comus*, and, most importantly, Jonson's *Cynthia's Revels* and several of his masques (especi-

40. *The Court Masque*, ed. by David Lindley. RevelsCL. ManU. pp. viii + 196 + 12 pls. £22.50.

41. *Responsive Readings: Versions of Echo in Pastoral, Epic, and the Jonsonian Masque*, by Joseph Loewenstein. YSE 192. Yale. pp. xii + 191. pb £17.50.

ally the *Masques of Blackness and Beauty*, and the *Masque of Queens*). Loewenstein extracts a remarkable amount of significance from scenes which most readers, unaided, would probably pass over without a second thought. He finds that, in the Renaissance, Echo is particularly associated with the 'patronage of liminal functions' and the 'metalepsis of genre'. A recurrent theme of the book is the struggle of masque-writers to assert their poetic autonomy from the constraints of occasion and of specific political contexts: Gascoigne strikes the first blow in this battle by publishing the text of the *Princely Pleasures*, and is said to accomplish thereby 'a very sober calculus of vulgarization'. This should be enough to give a taste of the book's flavour. Its readings of masques are certainly subtly responsive, but often have the feel of a private dialogue between the author and his chosen texts.

I have a last article to mention: Anne Lake Prescott's 'The Stuart Masque and Pantagruel's Dreams' (*ELH*). Prescott demonstrates the influence of *Les Songes drolatiques de Pantagruel* (a sixteenth-century collection of grotesque figures) on Inigo Jones's designs for the antimasque of Davenant's *Salmacida Spolia*, and argues that the *Songes* may also be drawn on in Shirley's *The Triumph of Peace*, and in Jonson's *The Vision of Delight*. Rabelaisian images also crop up in *Pleasure Reconcil'd to Virtue* and *Neptune's Triumph*. Pantagruel's dreams cannot simply be dismissed as disordered gothic delusions, adds Prescott, for they are the raw stuff of the creative imagination, the source 'when rightly ruled, of the feigning that can become the truest poetry'. Jonson understands this, which lends a special richness to his treatment of the antimasque.

The Earlier Seventeenth Century: Excluding Drama

HELEN WILCOX

Material in this chapter is discussed under three headings: 1. General; 2. Poetry; 3. Prose.

1. General

What were the constraints on English writers and readers in the early seventeenth century? The debate continues, in a healthy variety of guises, over the extent to which men and women of the period were free to indulge their cultural pursuits. The threat to popular customs and balladry from the holy war against the 'devil's dance' has recently been reconsidered by Jeremy Goring[1], and the repression of more courtly culture by institutionalized censorship is the subject of Annabel Patterson's latest book[2]. This commanding and impressive study argues that censorship impinged on all the literature of the period – not just a few celebrated cases – and is therefore central to our definition of what constitutes 'literature', and to the act of interpretation both then and now. Censorship, in her treatment, can take many forms, from the refusal of permission to perform or publish, to a general climate in which caution and self-censorship were the norm. Among her examples are a brilliant contextual analysis of Jonson's lyrics in *Underwood*, a discussion of the functional obscurity of Cowley's Pindaric odes, and a chapter on the familiar letter, demonstrating both the convention of secrecy and the expectation of official interception. Patterson's book is given refreshing immediacy by her sense of the parallels between the subject of her academic endeavour and the reality of cultural and political life now in many parts of the world, both 'free' and not-so-free. The publication of this important book coincidentally gives added significance to two slightly overlapping articles by N. W. Bawcutt (*RES*, *ELR*) on transcriptions of the records of Sir Henry Herbert, Master of the Revels – and particularly to Herbert's claim that he controlled 'all and every playes, Players and Playmakers . . . in all places' throughout the kingdom.

One of the problems raised by Patterson's work is that textual ambiguity (here shown to be tactically necessary for seventeenth-century authors) is once again enshrined by criticism. Is this, one fears, yet another evasion of the

1. *Godly Exercises or the Devil's Dance?: Puritanism and Popular Culture in Pre-Civil War England*, by Jeremy Goring. DWL (1983). pp. 28. £1.
2. *Censorship and Interpretation: The Conditions of Writing and Reading in Early Modern England*, by Annabel Patterson. UWisc. pp. ix + 283. $27.50.

business of determining meaning? Perhaps Jonathan Goldberg (*SEL*) is right to warn us that 'criticism cannot' (and should not attempt to) 'stabilize texts', which 'resist our attempts to fix them' in any kind of stable meaning. Certainly a good deal of assumption about the meaning of early-seventeenth-century literature and its relation to political history has been 'unfixed' by Patterson, and by David Norbrook's excellent book[3] on poetry, power, and subversion in the English Renaissance. He argues that critical and historical interpreters have failed to understand the common ground between poetry and the discourse of politics; borrowing a phrase from Walter Benjamin, he asserts that critics must learn to 'politicise aesthetics'. The result in his case is the discovery of three phases of English Renaissance poetry: the generation of the radical prophets (Sidney and Spenser), the Jonsonian reaction, and the attempt by Milton to challenge the ideology of Jonson and his tribe. The argument and evidence are impeccable throughout, but there are particularly strong chapters on Greville – in whose work the critical subtexts of the Sidney tradition became dangerously explicit – and the Jacobean Spenserian poets who adapted the pastoral convention into a commodity for poetic opposition. It is a shame that so significant a book should be shoddily presented on rough paper in Routledge's now customary photographed typescript (in which last-minute corrections may be spotted by the change of typeface or even misalignment). On the other hand, perhaps such a format is ironically appropriate for a work which radically calls into question some traditional attitudes to texts, truth, and the 'real world'.

The seventeenth century was, of course, itself a time when almost everything traditional was thrown into doubt. T. B. Tomlinson (*L&H*) turns to the pamphlets of John Lilburne, William Walwyn, and their contemporaries to examine the growth of secularism in the 1640s and 1650s, particularly the increasing reliance placed upon an energetic political intelligence as opposed to acceptance of providence. Francis Barker[4] examines a parallel but altogether more novel transition during the century, from public to private sensibility, as revealed in attitudes towards the human body. His intriguing sequence of readings demonstrates the shift from the spectacular – the stage, the scaffold – to the private body of bourgeois subjectivity, hidden or even 'incarcerated' within the text. His evidence comes from, among other sources, revenge tragedy, Milton, Descartes, Marvell, Rembrandt, and Pepys, informed and directed by poststructuralist approaches. The work is clearly intended to be controversial and thought-provoking; it succeeds magnificently.

A book which one might have expected to be controversial but proves to be less so, is Linda Woodbridge's study[5] of Renaissance attitudes to women. This is a clear-sighted and thorough (even, long-winded) introduction to the formal genre of 'controversy' within which the nature of woman was debated, from Thomas Elyot's *Defence of Good Women* (1540) to Joseph Swetnam's *Araignment of Lewde, Idle, Froward, and Unconstant Women* (1615). Woodbridge

3. *Poetry and Politics in the English Renaissance*, by David Norbrook. RKP. pp. x + 345. £15.95.

4. *The Tremulous Private Body: Essays on Subjection*, by Francis Barker. Methuen. pp. xi + 116. hb £8.95, pb £4.50.

5. *Women and the English Renaissance: Literature and the Nature of Womankind, 1540–1620*, by Linda Woodbridge. Harvester. pp. viii + 364. £28.50.

argues that, interesting (and enraging) though these texts are, they must be regarded as a literary game; to get closer to genuine contemporary views, she then examines generically mixed controversies and literary conventions such as the stage misogynist and the sonneteer's marble mistress. Especially fascinating is her account of two essays of 1620, *Hic Mulier* and *Haec Vir*, which fought out the debate between the female transvestite and the foppish male. Her conclusions are a series of paradoxes: for example, it was verbal *defenses* of women which led to equivalent attacks (and not vice versa); these violently opposed positions both served to uphold the same norm of godly womanhood; the misogynist in drama was a tool for the defense of women, while the romance and sonnet traditions glorified women only to enslave them. These ideas arise from the survey of a wealth of literary and historical material, and the book as a whole must be welcomed, despite the occasionally simplistic links made between textual and historical women. As Woodbridge herself is only too well aware, 'the relationship between literature and life is a very slippery subject', and nowhere more slippery than in the history of 'Worthy Women of the World'.

Margaret J. M. Ezell (*SCN*) confronts this very problem in attempting to correct the common view of Sir Robert Filmer, friend of Jonson and George Herbert and author of *Patriarcha*. Far from being a tyrannous patriarch, Ezell claims, Filmer was fairly moderate in seventeenth-century terms, and his manuscript essay 'In Praise of the Virtuous Wife' proposes a role of considerable importance for the good wife. The opinions of one famous seventeenth-century wife, Margaret Cavendish, are scrutinized by Lisa T. Sarasohn (*HLQ*) and shown to represent a double threat to traditional authority, combining feminism and the new science – an unusual intellectual subversion appropriate to one who aimed to be as 'singular' as she could.

In a special edition of *ELR* devoted to the subject of Women in the Renaissance, Sylvia Bowerbank gives extended consideration to Margaret Cavendish's singular imagination, noting that the feminine aesthetic principle for Cavendish was precisely that triumph of fancy over reason, the subjective spider over the Neoclassical bee, which to Swift was a definition of decline and madness. Though she analyses Cavendish's antirational stance in refreshing detail, Bowerbank ultimately warns of the dangers of equating the 'female' imagination with chaotic artlessness. This issue also contains the text of one of the earliest known literary critical essays by an English woman: a short defense of poetry – which can 'never enough bee admired' – by Lady Anne Southwell, written in 1627 in the form of a letter to a friend who seemed to prefer prose. The mixed prose and poetry of Lady Mary Wroth's romance, *Urania*, published six years earlier, comes under scrutiny in Carolyn Ruth Swift's article on feminine identity in Wroth's work. Swift claims that the subject of *Urania* is 'the alienation of women from men', and demonstrates this at length by observation of Wroth's strong heroines and contrast with Sidney's *Arcadia*. The article synthesizes history, biography, and genre study to reveal in *Urania* 'a feminine consciousness in conflict with societal values'. An article by Betty Travitsky, entitled 'The Lady Doth Protest', discusses six works of protest by Renaissance middle-class English women, each written for a popular audience and often under pseudonyms such as 'Joane hit-him-home'. The earliest of these works – by Isabella Whitney and Jane Anger – fall outside our period, but the article as a whole importantly studies the range of written protest and voices created for women by women in the English Renaissance. In response to Joseph Swetnam the 'woman-hater' (see Woodbridge, above), for example, Rachel Speght composed a tract on women's nobility, 'Ester Sowernam' wrote the first mock-trial of Swetnam and his views, and 'Constantia Munda' responded to the *Araignment of . . . Women* with a polemical dramatic monologue. Interestingly, Swetnam's misogynist tract had gone through ten editions by 1640, whereas none of the replies was given a second printing.

In a discussion of notions of the 'ideal' ladies of seventeenth-century England – those women whose 'bashfull silence' was 'an ornament to their Sexe' – Jan de Bruyn (*Mosaic*) observes that, simultaneously, the mid seventeenth century saw a rise in feminist writing. Though the arguments of Mary Astell later in the century are better known (and also discussed by de Bruyn), the article also notes earlier writers who claimed, for example, that if women had 'the Mens Education, they'd, perhaps, exceed them'. Among the most significant and pioneering of such works was *The Learned Maid; or, Whether a Maid May be a Scholar* by Anna Maria van Schurman, published in English in 1659.

The interrelation of natural science, religion, history, law, and literature between 1630 and 1690 is the ambitious subject of Barbara J. Shapiro's study[6] of the seventeenth-century approach to truth and certainty. She contends that the divisions between knowledge and opinion, fact and appearance, logic and rhetoric, were breaking down into a continuum in this period, resulting in the development of a 'probabilist approach' with a 'distinct intellectual style', admitting imperfect knowledge but still seeking moral certainty. The thesis is profound and promising, but the treatment of it in the rest of the book is disappointingly superficial, separating the discussion into individual chapters on religion, law, history (and so on) which then spend half their pages pointing out how each overlaps with the others. The chapter on literature suggests that the 'probabilist' mood resulted in the desire for closer links between words and things, and the development of a literature of exploration which eventually led to the novel.

Sir Robert Dallington, best known as the author of two guidebooks for the English gentleman traveller in the early seventeenth century, is the subject of a substantial article by Karl Josef Höltgen (*HLQ*) which gives long overdue consideration to the life and works of this interesting figure in Jacobean culture. Among Dallington's contributions to the 'Jacobean revival of art and taste' were three works which encouraged links between England and Italy, especially the world of Italian 'art, love and visual beauty'. His translations of treatises on art and architecture revealed the weakness of English vocabulary for visual experience; he frequently had to resort to phrases such as 'past my skill to report'. Such difficulties do not seem to have prevented the 1604 translation into German of James I's *Basilicon Doron*, noted by Alisdair M. Stewart (*ScLJ*). Woodbridge (above) mentions that Swetnam's woman-hating pamphlet was soon translated into Dutch, and contemporary translations of Browne and Hobbes into Dutch are discussed by Cornelis W. Schoneveld in

6. *Probability and Certainty in Seventeenth-Century England: A Study of the Relationships between Natural Science, Religion, History, Law, and Literature*, by Barbara J. Shapiro. Princeton (1983). pp. x + 347. $35.

Inter-traffic of the Mind: Studies in Seventeenth-Century Anglo-Dutch Transla-tion, 1600–1700 (Publications of the Sir Thomas Browne Institute, N.S. 3, Brill, 1983) which was not seen by the reviewer.

International cultural relations – travel, translation, influence – are indeed the focus of much current interest. Daniel L. Heiple (*CompL*) examines the use of the concept 'metaphysical' by Lope de Vega in 1634 – the only writer contemporary with the English metaphysicals to use the term with reference to poetry. He finds that, despite some obvious cultural differences, the term carries meanings of contrived subtlety or falsely displayed learning very similar to the implications later given to the word by Dryden and Johnson. Joshua Sylvester's translation of Du Bartas is shown by John Louis Lepage (*ELH*) to use antithesis not only in its subject matter (the combining of science and poetry) but in its stylistic 'marriage of opposites' – what Lepage calls 'meta-physical androgyny' – which considerably influenced seventeenth-century English poets. Several of the essays in a *Festschrift* for Prof. T. A. Birrell[7] also address the subject of international literary borrowings. A. F. Allison traces the influence of treatises by François de Sales and Jean Puget de la Serre on *Manchester al mondo*, the contemplative work of Henry Montagu, first Earl of Manchester. F. J. M. Blom further illustrates the effect of continental Roman Catholic writers on English non-Catholic devotional practice, with the case of the popular German Jesuit writer, Jeremias Drexelius. One of those whose translations made such influence possible, as David Rogers demonstrates, was the Benedictine Antony Blatt. One of the vital tools for translation, a work revealing *The Marrow of the French Tongue*, prepared by the personable soldier John Wodroephe in his 'Spared Houres', is described by Anna E. C. Simoni. Crashaw's 'neglected' early poem, 'Sospetto d'Herode', is considered by D. R .M. Wilkinson both as a translation of Giambattista Marino and in its own right.

A second major interest of T. A. Birrell is reflected in the number of essays concerned with bibliography and the spread of learning through the building-up of libraries. F. J. M. Blom looks at the contacts between English writers or book collectors and Lucas Holstenius, custodian of the Vatican in the early seventeenth century. The history of the library of Sir Thomas Tempest, many volumes of which came originally from Durham Cathedral, is recounted by A. I. Doyle; Mirjam M. Foot examines the range of bindings for Charles I's library. In one of a series of articles on 'Unfamiliar Libraries', Mary Hobbs (*BC*) discovers that Bishop Henry King's own collection must have been used to refound Chichester Cathedral Library after its destruction during the Civil War. King's books also included Donne's, of whose will King was an executor; however, less than one-third of the books are now at Chichester, and many were sold as recently as 1949. For those unable to purchase seventeenth-century books or even gain access to ancient libraries, the publication of reliable facsimiles is an enormous boon. There has been a cluster of facsimile publications in the last two years, including the Bodleian manuscript of Herbert's *Temple*[8] (see below), William Prynne's prose work

    7. *Studies in Seventeenth-Century English Literature, History and Bibliography: Festschrift for Professor T. A. Birrell on the Occasion of his Sixtieth Birthday*, ed. by G. A. M. Janssens and F. G. A. M. Aarts. Costerus N.S. 46. Rodopi. pp. viii + 268. Fl 60.
    8. *The Bodleian Manuscript of George Herbert's Poems: A Facsimile of Tanner 307*, intro. by Amy M. Charles and Mario A. Di Cesare. SF&R. pp. xli + no pagination. $100.

Mount-Orgueil[9], and (not seen) the manuscript of Thomas Gainsford's *Vox Spiritus; or, Sir Walter Rawleigh's Ghost* (The Rota, 1983). Most importantly, Thomas Jenner's *Emblem Books*[10] have been published in their original form, making possible that particularly seventeenth-century reading which involves visual as well as mental contemplation.

Norman K. Farmer Jr has produced a book of essays[11] on English Renaissance poetry and its interaction with the visual arts which concludes with a fascinating chapter on Lady Anne Drury's oratory at Hawstead Hall, a room whose walls were decorated with emblems, presumably to stimulate private meditation. Earlier chapters treat individual authors from Sidney to Waller, including, for instance, a comparison of Crashaw's own paintings with his sensitivity to colour, texture, and pattern in the poems. Studies of Donne, Carew, Edward Herbert, and Lovelace reveal extensive use of specialized art-historical knowledge in their writings. The book is, as one might expect, pleasingly presented and well illustrated with black-and-white photographs. Farmer ultimately argues that Herrick's *Hesperides* might be considered to exemplify Horace's 'ut pictura poesis'; Jay A. Gertzman (*StHum*, 1983) looks at the fruits of such a view in the work of Herrick's Victorian illustrator, Edwin Abbey. In an elegant account of the influence of an artistic movement – mannerism – on European Renaissance poetry, James V. Mirollo[12] surveys the controversy over the nature of mannerism from Giorgio Vasari to the present day, and then focuses on two details, the veiled face and the gloved hand, to demonstrate both visual and verbal mannerism. Most of Mirollo's examples are from other literatures, but English poems such as Lovelace's 'Ellinda's Glove' are given a vivid context as Mirollo explores the literary mannerism of imitative Petrarchism (*sic*). The book is scholarly, perhaps itself a little too mannered, but the argument is well sustained. He does not claim a 'style' for mannerism, rather a mode of inner design, as perceived in, for example, Donne's 'The Bait' but not in the Marlowe and Ralegh pastorals which preceded it. Elsewhere Martin Elsky (*MLS*, 1983) demonstrates affinities in spatiality and temporality between Donne's *La Corona* and specific mannerist painters.

Returning from the intensity of continental art to the needs of today's English students, two general books deserve recommendation. Julia Briggs[13] offers a survey of English Renaissance literature and its 'background' which takes as exempla the views of Sir Thomas Browne, who 'perfectly formulated the characteristic dilemmas of the age'. The work is informed and historically alert without being cluttered by footnotes; the literary landscape is sensitively depicted in a readable style. Briggs is acutely aware of the temptation to create the period in our own image, finding complexities and doubt in the same texts

9. *William Prynne: Mount-Orgueil (1641)*, intro. by Edmund Miller. SF&R. pp. xiii + no pagination. $40.

10. *The Emblem Books of Thomas Jenner*, intro. by S. Gottlieb. SF&R (1983). pp. xxvi + no pagination. $45.

11. *Poets and the Visual Arts in Renaissance England*, by Norman K. Farmer Jr. UTex. pp. xiii + 122. $19.95.

12. *Mannerism and Renaissance Poetry: Concept, Mode, Inner Design*, by James V. Mirollo. Yale. pp. xv + 225. £30.

13. *This Stage-Play World: English Literature and its Background, 1580–1625*, by Julia Briggs. An Opus Book. OUP (1983). pp. viii + 225. hb £9.95, pb £3.95.

which spoke to our predecessors of confidence and serenity. But this very admission should be an important signal to newcomers to the business of reading and interpreting the 'divided and distinguished worlds' in which Elizabethan and Jacobean writers found themselves. The Renaissance volume of the Great Writers Student Library[14] will also be helpful to new readers, offering as it does for each writer included a brief biography, very select bibliography (often somewhat cautious about recent interpretations), and a short critical essay. Despite its drab appearance and small print, this guide should be a useful tool if treated only as a *starting-point* for study; there is an uncomfortable sense of 'fixing' authors in the brief though authoritative essays. If readers find the time to read Elizabeth Story Donno's introductory essay, they will be taken on an alarmingly brisk romp through the historical and literary events of the Renaissance, though, given the circumstances, this account is written with considerable poise. In particular she gives a creditable amount of attention to the multiple 'kinds' of literature in the period, from epyllion and emblem to character and sermon. The large number of 'great' (and almost-great) writers covered by the book is itself testimony to the 'multiple and diverse strands' of English Renaissance literature.

Our understanding of one of these genres – the lyric – has been greatly enhanced this year by Louise Schleiner's account of 'The Living Lyre' in seventeenth-century verse[15]. Examining the changes in lyric style from Herbert to Cowley, Schleiner interprets the verbal evidence in the light of its musical context. Though well supplied with musical extracts and musicological insight, the book is clearly designed for literary, if not general, readers, and its observations are accessible and constructive. It begins with a definition of three lyric modes found in the seventeenth century: verbal song, simulated conversation, and declamation. The categories are not new but they are, for the first time, systematically defined, and form the basis for the analyses of individual writers. The subsequent chapters are perhaps a little too separate (some of them originally appeared independently as articles), though the concluding chapter gathers together impressions of a general trend during the century away from strophic patterns towards an increased dramatization of lyric and song. Of the particular writers within our period discussed by Schleiner, Herbert is shown to be influenced by lute song in his prosody and stanza forms, yet his speech-mode poems were those most often set to music. Herrick, whom Swinburne regarded as the greatest English songwriter, moved towards the speech-mode lyric in revising *Hesperides*, while Crashaw used musical allusion, in the structural form of song refrains or declamatory looseness, for moments of particular effect. In all her analyses, Schleiner demonstrates the truth of her own belief that a knowledge of song features helps us towards 'responsive reading'.

2. Poetry

As Elizabeth Story Donno (see above) points out, the ten-year-old Drayton begged his tutor, 'Make me a poet'. Drayton himself later made one original

14. *The Renaissance, Excluding Drama*, intro. by Elizabeth Story Donno. Great Writers Student Library 2. Macmillan (1983). pp. vii + 194. hb £15, pb £5.95.

15. *The Living Lyre in English Verse from Elizabeth through the Restoration*, by Louise Schleiner. UMiss. pp. viii + 218. £23.

contribution to the Renaissance view of the poet, according to Geoffrey G. Hiller (*ELH*): he discovered, and used increasingly during his career, the poet-archetype of the 'sacred bards' and 'wise Druides' of old Britain. Something of the holy didacticism of such an archetype crept into Drayton's *England's Heroicall Epistles*, which are the subject of two articles by Barbara C. Ewell (*JEGP* 1983; *MLQ*). She shows that Drayton's development of the epistolary form, and loosening of his stiff style into a more dramatic mode, provided him with a means of using history to explore 'the Chaos in the Mind'. Vincent F. Petronella (*SEL*) examines the Neoplatonic background to the double ecstasy of *Endimion and Phoebe*.

Two discoveries this year have added to our understanding of the social context for Samuel Daniels' work. John Pitcher (*RES*) considers the implications of the single sheet inserted into one copy of Daniel's 1601 *Works*, containing a poem celebrating the incongruous love-match between the Earl of Hertford and Frances Pranell, widow of a London wine-seller. The arrangement of the inserted leaves suggests some link between Lady Frances and *Delia*; the poem's tone implies that Daniel's intimacy with the family began earlier than had previously been assumed. Meanwhile Pitcher (*HLQ*) has also discovered, among the papers of the Duke of Sutherland, the missing original of Daniel's letter to Sir Thomas Egerton – a rather special find since fewer than ten of Daniel's letters are extant.

This year is an important one for Jonson studies: the work of Patterson and Norbrook (above) will stimulate newly controversial discussion of Jonson's verse. This will surely dislodge the opinion, as identified by Richard Dutton in his introduction to a new edition of *Epigrams* and *The Forest*[16], that Jonson's poetry is 'known, understood, weighed up'. One of Dutton's ambitions for this edition is that it should 'break through that complacency and offer something of Jonson as he was to his contemporaries: an urgent and challenging figure'. Dutton's introduction will certainly help here, bringing out Jonson's energies and passionate concerns (as well as his fallibility); physically, the texts are clear and accessible (as always with Carcanet editions). What makes this text especially welcome, however, is the selection of two complete sequences rather than a random anthology; as Dutton demonstrates in his introduction, these poems are part of larger structures (which he finds analogous to Herbert's *Temple*) and reading them in context must enhance their force and pleasure.

The context offered by Don E. Wayne[17] for an understanding of 'To Penshurst' is none other than the place itself: he juxtaposes the way that the Sidney house has been 'written' in and by history with the way that the poem has been 'read'. The name 'Penshurst' connotes two different sign systems – place and poem – which Wayne compares and connects, delighting in the aesthetic and psychological tension which he sees as 'grounded in ideological conflict'. The idea is ingenious but should have formed the basis of a bulky article rather than a (slim) book; the argument gives the often tedious impression of being pressed too far and stretched too thin.

16. *Ben Jonson: Epigrams and The Forest*, ed. by Richard Dutton. Carcanet. pp. 121. pb £3.95.

17. *Penshurst: The Semiotics of Place and the Poetics of History*, by Don E. Wayne. Methuen. pp. xv + 228. £20.

Several studies dealing primarily with Jonson the dramatist have interesting things to say about the poet in passing. Katherine Eisaman Maus[18] explores Jonson's Roman inheritance, showing that his reading in the classics can help to explain why issues such as authority and self-control should have been crucial to his work. In reading the restrained lament for Jonson's 'first Son', for example, Maus points out that Seneca and Cicero regarded with awe those who could take the death of a child with philosophical calm. Ian Donaldson (YES[19]) focuses more on Jonson's anger than his restraint, arguing that satiric anger was a vitally creative, even if at times unnerving, force within his work. Again concentrating mainly on the drama, George E. Rowe Jr (SP) looks at Jonson's quarrel with his audience, and analyses his attempt to win both authorial power and a responsive audience. Part of the solution he found, as shown in the poems, was to make his own audience: 'Rare poemes aske rare friends.'

The friends of Louis Martz recently gathered together a volume of short essays[20] in his honour, and among them is an investigation by Alastair Fowler of the *silva* tradition – a collection of rough works in a range of genres – in relation to Jonson's *Forrest* (and his other 'woody' titles). Fowler perhaps becomes too fanciful when he goes on to argue that the symbolic numbers of poems in *The Forrest* make them into a ladder of love, a meditative *scala*, leading out of the entangling forest of error into a clearer Christian vision. In a more down-to-earth article Paulette S. Goll (SCN) looks at the ironic discrepancies between biographical fact and literary fiction in the *Epigrams*. Sir Thomas Egerton, for instance, is praised by Jonson for his 'conscience', yet as Viscount Brackley he was commonly known as 'Break-law'. She concludes that while weaknesses are deliberately shown up in Jonson's unnamed characters, named individuals are consciously moulded into virtuous models for the reader. Three short articles clarify details of Jonson's skill. William W. E. Slights (*Expl*) notes the presence of an angling image in *Epigram LXXXII*, whereby 'cast' means superficially that Surly will 'cast off' his whore but might also imply 'casting' his hook to catch her once again. Using a holograph in Dulwich College Library, Anthony Miller (*ELN*, 1983) establishes the punctuation, and therefore interpretation, of the closing lines in Jonson's translation of Martial's epigram X.xlvii. In a swift analysis of 'To Edward Allen', Robert C. Evans (*Expl*) shows that Jonson's reference to Cicero – used to justify praising the actor – actually re-asserts the social priority of the poet.

A recent anthology of Donne's poems[21], though a positive move to win him a wider audience, need not detain us long here. Announced on the cover as 'containing Donne's most passionate, lyrical and erotic verses', it simply offers modernized texts (no source cited) of the *Songs and Sonnets* and the *Elegies*, and describes itself as 'the perfect gift for lovers everywhere'. The introduction fills in details of Donne's life (and loves, of course) and suggests that the poems

18. *Ben Jonson and the Roman Frame of Mind*, by Katherine Eisaman Maus. Princeton. pp. ix + 212. £30.30.

19. *YES* (1984) was also issued in book form: *English Satire and the Satiric Tradition*, ed. by Claude Rawson. Blackwell. pp. xiii + 289. hb £22.50, pb £7.50.

20. *Poetic Traditions of the English Renaissance*, ed. by Maynard Mack and George deF. Lord. Yale (1982). pp. xiii + 319. $24. (Hereafter Martz.)

21. *The Love Poems of John Donne*, ed. and intro. by Charles Fowkes. Macmillan (1983). pp. xi + 100. pb £2.95.

are autobiographical; critics who disagree with this 'obvious truth' are those who 'weave simplicity into complexity as Rumplestiltskin wove straw into gold because it is the only currency they understand'. That Donne himself wove complex poems does not seem to trouble the editor; he offers his 'lovers' no guidance there.

A great deal of guidance through the circles of Donne's mind and reading is provided this year by Terry G. Sherwood[22], who sees the same principles of thought at work throughout Donne's writing career. Is there a danger here of misleadingly imprinting later ideas on Donne's earlier work? Sherwood thinks not, and demonstrates that serious fascination with theological and meta-physical argument can be perceived in Donne's earliest writing, with the same epistemological and psychological system underlying, for example, the *Songs and Sonnets* and the sermons. The key points in this invigorating reading of Donne 'whole' are his preoccupation with time and creation, the mediating language of the flesh, the power of reason, and fulfilment through suffering. Sherwood's introductory section outlining these themes becomes a little dry in places, but the applied scholarship in the reading of texts such as 'A Valedic-tion: of Weeping', 'Good Friday.1613', and the *Devotions* is of a very high standard. Anne Ferry's study[23] of the sonnets of Wyatt, Sidney, Shakespeare, and Donne suffers from the opposite problem. Her introductory exploration of the development of English vocabulary for the 'inward' self in the sixteenth and seventeenth centuries is the best part of the book; when she proceeds to demonstrate this inner language at work in the sonnets – culminating in the 'white sincerity' of Donne's *La Corona* and *Holy Sonnets* – the readings are disappointingly repetitive and unadventurous.

JDJ, still in its early days, continues its strangely symbiotic relationship with the Variorum edition currently in preparation. John T. Shawcross looks at the textual background of the *Anniversaries* (including 'A Funeral Elegy') and promises that the Variorum text will be 'different in some way from any other text there has been'. Ted-Larry Pebworth criticizes the anachronistic assump-tions of Donne's editors, highlighting the difference between Jonson's 'mod-ern' attitude towards printing and Donne's manuscript tradition; Pebworth, too, claims that the Variorum will be the 'definitive text', bringing us closer to 'what Donne actually wrote'. These are grand promises, indeed. James S. Baumlin modestly notes further evidence, in a hitherto unrecorded copy of Donne's 1649 *Poems*, of the closeness of the 1649 and 1650 editions.

It is something of a relief to come across a couple of articles urging us to find Donne funny. Maria Cornelia (*ArielE*) insists that 'far too much of Donne's poetry has been taken too seriously for too long', and demonstrates that Donne used many of the rhetorical devices found in Thomas Wilson's *Arte of Rhetoricke* under the heading of 'rousing mirth'. In the end these all turn out to be rather obvious features of the poems – dramatization, exaggeration, intro-ducing 'an unknowne matter and weightie affaire' in connection with 'a trifle', and so on – but the article's intention is good. Alison R. Rieke (*JEGP*) brings forward an impressive array of evidence to prove the importance of riddles in

22. *Fulfilling the Circle: A Study of John Donne's Thought*, by Terry G. Sherwood. UTor. pp. 231. £19.50.
23. *The 'Inward' Language: Sonnets of Wyatt, Sidney, Shakespeare, Donne*, by Anne Ferry. UChic (1983). pp. xii + 285. £23.

Donne's work, regarding many of his cryptic poems as riddling questions demanding an answer from the reader. Donne owned and annotated a copy of Nicholas Reusner's *Aenigmatographia*, and who would have thought there were so many types of 'enigmatic subgenres'? The riddle turns out to encompass number games, logographs, licentious teasing, impossible questions, and paradoxes – all of which are fully displayed in the *Songs and Sonnets* and *Epigrams*.

Two of the *Songs and Sonnets* have been re-interpreted in the light of traditional or 'folk' beliefs. Greg Bentley (*Expl*) argues that the speaker in 'Witchcraft by a Picture' may well be bewitching his mistress, and not vice versa as is usually assumed. The evidence lies not only in the syntax but also in the tradition that a witch should not be able to weep – hence the weeping mistress must be innocent. Richard F. Kennedy (*Expl*, 1983) notes that those two antipathetical birds, the eagle and the dove in the third stanza of 'The Canonization', were believed to 'consume of themselves' if their feathers were combined after death. This reinforces Donne's antithesis and leads to the phoenix image later in the stanza. Edward le Comte (*SCN*, 1983) supplies contemporary references to confirm that 'spring' in l. 13 of 'The Canonization' refers primarily to the season rather than water. Stanton J. Linden (*JDJ*) brings forward pictorial evidence to confirm the connection between compasses (as used in 'A Valediction: Forbidding Mourning') and dividers which measured distances on Renaissance maps. He clearly demonstrates the utilitarian and aesthetic function of these compasses – but has the link really never been made before? Helen Gardner's contribution to Martz[20] also takes up an apparently old idea – the connection between the 'Nocturnal upon St. Lucy's Day' and the death of Donne's wife – and examines it in the light of manuscript datings, patronage, and the relations between poet, subject, and reader.

Donne's response to contemporary events is variously considered in recent articles. John T. Shawcross (*ELN*, 1983) identifies the source of Donne's 'Fall of a Wall' epigram, not in personal experience of the Lisbon expedition, but in a contemporary prose account attributed to Anthony Wingfield. In an analysis of the development of Donne's *Satires*, Frank Kerins (*TSLL*) shows the poet gradually outgrowing the traditional anger or vulnerability of the satirist, and establishing an integrated persona, morally sensitive but wise enough to confront the world. Arnold Stein (*YES*[19]) explores Donne's use of the satirist persona – in particular, satirical voices – not only in the *Satires* but the *Elegies* and his religious prose. He sensibly observes the 'related separatenesses' of persona, narrator, and author. In a discussion of the *Anniversaries*, Thomas Willard (*JDJ*) looks at the implications of their titles: 'anatomy' carries medical as well as structural meaning for Donne's examination of his world, while 'progress' is both a royal journey and the spiritual advancement of the soul. Exploring Paracelsian doctrine – a risky but fruitful exercise – Willard links the two poems by identifying the dead Elizabeth Drury with the 'anima mundi' or world soul.

The problems of closure in devotional poetry are considered by Susan E. Linville (*PLL*), who discovers the potential for the unexpected in a sudden final 'disclosure' of human weakness or the introduction of a triumphant extra-poetic truth. Donne's closing strategies – in fact, his formal brilliance – are highlighted, as are parallels with the Huguenot poet Jean Ogier de Gombauld. Elsewhere Linville (*Style*) continues to press her point that

Donne's 'rough carelessness' in the *Holy Sonnets* is only superficial and disguises metrical and formal control, particularly in relation to enjambment and end-stopping. Julia J. Smith (*MLR*) is more concerned with Donne's 'intense' imaginative response to the crucifixion, meeting-point of human death (his obsession) and divine redemption (his hope). She notes the shift from the early formality of the *Paradoxes* to the drama of the *Holy Sonnets*, and finally to the compassionate treatment and central importance of the crucifixion in his sermons. As always, we have the statutory note on *Holy Sonnet* XIV: this year Tunis Romein (*Expl*) claims that God is depicted not as a metalworker but a glassblower.

Three articles concern themselves with Donne's verse epistles – perhaps a promising sign that criticism is beginning to broaden its outlook on Donne's poetic significance. Ted-Larry Pebworth and Claude J. Summers (*MP*) recover the contexts – biographical, textual, and political – for the exchange of verse letters between Donne and Henry Wotton, showing them to be much more than exercises on abstract issues. Barbara L. DeStefano (*SP*) examines their 'emphatic high style', a mixture of classical panegyric and Christian praise, and claims that the epistles embody 'a radical vision of virtue as contemporary to this life'. A detailed study of the biblical symbols in Donne's Latin verse epistle to George Herbert convinces Raymond-Jean Frontain (*MP*) of the poem's integrity. In particular he points out that the serpent, uplifted in the Old Testament as a type of Christ on the cross, thus prefigures man's salvation even as the crawling serpent signifies the Fall; typically, Donne makes poetical capital out of such 'contraries meeting in one'.

The publication of a facsimile of the Bodleian manuscript of George Herbert's poems[8] was heralded last year by the inclusion of the introductory essays by Amy M. Charles and Mario A. Di Cesare in *GHJ* (*YW* 64.245). Now the large, handsomely bound volume has itself appeared, displaying the splendid Little Gidding presentation manuscript but also, as the collated Table of Contents indicates (showing page or folio numbers for the Dr Williams Library manuscript, the Bodleian facsimile, the first edition, and F. E. Hutchinson's Oxford edition), intended for scholarly use as well as admiration. Di Cesare states that the availability of the facsimile should 'reopen the discussion of Herbert's text', and this it will surely achieve, despite considerable problems encountered through the sometimes pale reproduction of the manuscript.

Diana Benet[24] has written a study of Herbert's calling to be God's 'secretary of praise', claiming that an understanding of the concepts of grace and charity – the very basis of his vocation – is essential to a reading of *The Temple*. Though she observes a proper sense of the separation of poet and speaker in Herbert's lyrics, the book's overall premise asserts the importance of the poet's biography in an interpretation of the poems. In many ways, therefore, this is a very conservative reading of Herbert, though distinguished by the detailed accounts of her chosen poems on the theme of 'employment' which are consistently enlightening. The reliability and openness of Benet's critical manner will recommend her book to students discovering Herbert's poetry. At the other extreme of criticism, the self-conscious scholarship of Bart

24. *Secretary of Praise: The Poetic Vocation of George Herbert*, by Diana Benet. UMiss. pp. vii + 207. £21.25.

Westerweel's study[25] of four poems from *The Temple* claims a more special-ized readership. Begun as an assessment of the tradition of pattern poems (it surveys Herbert's heritage helpfully and examines 'Easter-wings' and 'The Altar'), it proceeds to argue that these hieroglyphs are part of the emblematic aspect of Herbert's poems. In the second half of the book Westerweel analyses 'The Pilgrimage', which he regards as a complex work for an erudite audience, a poem which 'does not yield its riches easily', and finally 'Love' III – a poem which he sees as centring round the imagery of the senses and man's newfound ability to 'look on God'. One might argue that the choice of poems (here the emblems are taken to be 'a starting-point for the exploration of mysteries') is fairly arbitrary, and the style of the work rather laboured; but it would be churlish to dwell on these aspects at the expense of the considerable learning displayed on the way. Robert W. Halli Jr (*PQ*) points out that 'Easter-wings' is in fact a double hieroglyph, showing wings from one angle but hour-glasses from another; the triumph of 'flight' in the poem shows time transcended by eternity. Looking at the larger shape of *The Temple*, Anne Williams (*MP*) asserts that 'Love' III, seen in the context of Herbert's theology as well as the poetic sequence, renders 'The Church' satisfyingly complete, offering 'a parable that allows us to participate before we may know'. Grant Garber (*Comitatus*, 1983) takes on the more difficult task of integrating 'The Church Militant', suggesting (with some force) that this awkward prophetic poem may be seen as a New Testament equivalent of the 'holy of holies' in the tripartite structure of *The Temple*.

Harold Toliver (*SEL*) takes a rather inconclusive look at the 'places', both temporary and final, in which Herbert finds and addresses God's presence, while Karen L. Wadman (*Lang&S*, 1983) uses sociolinguistic models of 'politeness strategies' to examine what Herbert says once he has found God. It is novel to find Herbert's poems discussed in terms of 'face-threatening acts' (known as FTAs) but the idea is pursued with relentless monotony. Frank L. Huntley (*GHJ*) surveys the images of 'violent containment' in *The Temple*, from the familiar boxes and cabinets to the less obvious tear-drops and, even, the frown of Christ upon the cross. Huntley asserts that Herbert's metaphors are not charming miniatures but tense epitomes which cram 'so much in so small a space as to induce in the reader the kinaesthetic sensation of strain'. Another strand of metaphor in Herbert's work – gambling imagery – is investigated by Michael Clifton (*GHJ*), who, in addition to supplying a lot of useful information about 'primero' and other tavern games, manages to create a lively discussion of the parallels between poetry, worship, and the surrender to rules and fate involved in gambling.

The liturgical patterns of Anglican worship and their influence on *The Temple* are considered in a posthumous article by Brewster S. Ford (*SoAR*). The twofold liturgies of time and space are perceived in Herbert's closeness to both the Prayer Book Calendar and the idea of the 'church-space' as the enclosing context for the Christian seeker. Stanley Stewart (*Cithara*) looks at the evidence of the Little Gidding *Harmonies of the Gospels* as a means of establishing Herbert's context; the members of the Little Gidding community, after all, formed Herbert's immediate audience. Stewart finds that, contrary to

25. *Patterns and Patterning: A Study of Four Poems by George Herbert*, by Bart Westerweel. Rodopi. pp. x + 273. Fl 80.

the Rosemond Tuve tradition, Herbert and his friends did not inhabit a 'medieval' world but a topical and lively context. The *Harmonies* represent a 'Biblical tradition . . . not uniquely Protestant, surely not Puritan, and might even be described as Catholic'. Within this context, one chief feature that persists in *The Temple*, according to Sibyl Lutz Severance (*HSL*) is the continuing self – paradoxical, pressed by contraries, but always active with the processes of remembering, understanding, and willing. She examines 'Artillerie' as a complex and illuminating example of Herbert's tussle between 'minde', 'mine', and 'thine' in the personae of *The Temple*.

In addition to Louise Schleiner's study of Herbert's lyrics[15] (see above), the presence of musical references in Herbert's lyrics is noted in three articles this year. David Lindley (*N&Q*) discerns a specific allusion to Dowland in 'Grief', and points out that the poem in general also parodies the self-indulgence of Dowland's lute songs, which had 'cornered the market in lacrimose lyrics'. Robert Boenig (*Ren&R*) looks at Herbert's poems as lute songs themselves, but unfortunately indulges in facile conjecture as to what Herbert's lute accompaniments might have been like, and how they would have affected our interpretation of the poems. In a more helpful article Boenig (*N&Q*) identifies what Herbert was really referring to with the phrase 'broken consort' in 'Doomsday'.

How far do Herbert's poems actually 'refer to' contemporary political and theological controversy? Claude J. Summers and Ted-Larry Pebworth (*GHJ*) demonstrate convincingly that critics have been wrong to see 'The Familie' as a purely personal lyric; they argue that it is (also) political, seriously concerned with dissent within the 'family' of the Church of England. Summers and Pebworth insist that one can regard Herbert as both Calvinist and simultaneously anti-Puritan; Daniel W. Doerksen (*Ren&R*) also takes on these issues in trying to rechart Herbert's 'via media' in comparison with that of Spenser. Martin Elsky (*JEGP*) interestingly suggests that *The Temple* is framed by a Protestant view of the Eucharist, beginning with Christ's sacrifice but dwelling at length on the necessity of personal response, and ending with the sequence of poems on the 'Last Things'. In Protestant typology, he states, the individual is required in the present to complete the providential pattern of history. Ilona Bell (*JDJ*) sees a progression in Herbert's poetry from a Laudian to a Calvinist position, exemplified in a close reading of 'Affliction' I. She hints, too, at similarities between Reformation Protestantism and modern literary theory (such as rebellion, and constantly redefined meanings) which might explain why Herbert's poems have suddenly become so alluring.

The attraction of *The Temple* is not, of course, simply a recent phenomenon. In a collection of papers from the first National (British) Conference of Literature and Religion[26], Helen Wilcox puts forward evidence that Herbert's seventeenth-century readers (of whom there were many) treated the poems with a reverence and practicality remarkably similar to the approach recommended by Herbert himself for the Bible, 'Heaven's Lidger here'. In Martz[20] Frank Manley postulates that Herbert's plain style is not so much a biblical feature as an apt reflection of the poet's complex mind – honest but difficult. The complexities of 'The Collar' in particular continue to exercise the critics. Raymond A. Anselment (*NM*, 1983) studies emblems of cages and collars

26. *Images of Belief in Literature*, ed. by David Jasper. Macmillan. pp. ix + 195. £20.

to demonstrate the proverbial background to Herbert's angriest poem. Dale B. J. Randall (*SP*) castigates editorial side-stepping of the multiple meanings of the title, and adds four new ideas, including the discovery that iron rings were kept in seventeenth-century churches for the punishment of parishioners.

In a note on the paradoxes of Herbert's 'Anagram of the Virgin Marie', Lee Passarella (*ELN*, 1983) considers the significance of the 'tent' as a temporary tabernacle, with implications of a nomadic existence, aptly signifying Christ's temporary lodgings in the 'wilderness' of this world. Noel J. Kinnamon (*GHJ*) gives details of the Old Testament (Psalmic) and classical sources of 'Constancie', in comparison with Henry Vaughan's 'Righteousness'. He asserts a measure of independence from Herbert for Vaughan, and particularly notes the influence of the Psalms on the composition of Vaughan's religious verse.

After many years of critical effort to establish Vaughan's debt to Herbert, the trend now seems to be to reveal Vaughan's poetic strengths in his own right. Ironically, this is particularly true of the essays published in a special double issue of *GHJ* devoted to Vaughan studies. As the guest editor, Jonathan F. S. Post, implies, there is also a tendency to talk about Vaughan's wider achievement than 'his visions of paradise and light' (perpetually impressive though these are). It is appropriate, therefore, that the number should open with a discussion by Cedric C. Brown of 'Daphnis' as a prophetic poem with a strongly felt sense of the past; in this calling, both private and public, the elegy is compared to Milton's 'Lycidas'. Mary Jane Doherty then offers a welcome study of *Flores Solitudinis* as a series of choices between the godly and ungodly ways, expressed in terms of Vaughan's sequence of texts. His ordering of material – culminating in the example of Paulinus – is seen as a flight of steps leading, not to *The Temple* (as Crashaw's title claimed) but to the devotional mood of Vaughan's own *Silex Scintillans*, poems which occupy several critics. The case of the humbly private Paulinus is invoked by Janet E. Halley in her study of privacy, revealing the ironic tensions between private and social lyric personae, especially in the 1655 edition. The desire for retreat, particularly into childhood as a political and/or spiritual escape, is analysed as Vaughan's psychological need – ultimately a passing phase – by Boyd M. Berry. Susanne Woods scrutinizes Vaughan's versification in *Silex Scintillans*, seeing it as reflective of his dynamic participation in a period of great change in English style. And the last two studies in the special issue address more specific topics: Jeff S. Johnson offers a reading of 'The Night' and its images of Christ perceived as a unifying feature, and Richard F. Kennedy documents Vaughan's sustained interest in, and borrowings from, Owen Felltham.

In a thoroughly detailed consideration of Vaughan's wordplay, Gerald Hammond (*MLR*) looks at the poet's method of allowing words to meet in almost random association, resulting in subtle patterns of strangely interlinked meanings. Armand Himy (*CahiersE*) examines images of petrification in *Silex Scintillans*, representing a spiritual state of being ('mort-vivant'). Also in French, Marie-Madeleine Martinet (*EA*) looks at *Silex Scintillans* as a collection of poetic sequences, each beginning with a poem on the 'Last Things' – thus opening up an interplay of ends and beginnings which underlies spiritual matters throughout the volume. In a study of 'The Rain-bow' and 'Midnight', Gertrude Hamilton (*Cithara*) focuses on Vaughan's light imagery and contrasts its sources in the Bible and Neoplatonic or Hermetic thought. Michael

Bird (*English*) echoes the current trend in his dislike of Vaughan as the 'Wordsworthianised minor-Herbert of critical tradition', but offers a vaguely intangible replacement – a poet of withdrawal, in whose work 'whiteness' is 'everything and nothing', a writer who 'incites the nothing sayable'. There is nothing more to be said about this article.

Belated recognition must be given here to the usefulness of R. V. Young's learned work[27] drawing together Crashaw and the Spanish devotional and poetic traditions of the Golden Age. Unlike those critics who lamely attempt to integrate Crashaw into the line of English metaphysical verse, Young demonstrates that Crashaw's taste was profoundly foreign and, what is more, thoroughly good. He maintains that the Spanish tradition – known in England, as, for example, the Spanish motto on the 1635 edition of Donne's *Poems* indicates – reveals the 'essential nature' and 'intrinsic value' of Crashaw's work. The book is not easy to read, demanding much of the reader in terms of knowledge and integration of the two cultures which Young explores; but its scholarship and its placing of Crashaw are both of significance.

Meanwhile, Crashaw forms the centrepiece of the argument in Anthony Raspa's book[28] on Jesuit poetics in the English Renaissance. Far from being simply a repeat of Louis Martz's pioneering work, or merely a refutation of Barbara Lewalski's *Protestant Poetics* (*YW* 60.196), Raspa's contribution examines the aesthetic outcome of Jesuit influence on English poetry. He shows that Donne, Robert Southwell, and William Alabaster treated the poem as an 'emotive image', and he studies the role of the affective aesthetic in the use of epigrams, metaphors, and the idea of imitation. He also gives consideration to the little known but interesting poet Eldred Revett, but the main focus is on Crashaw, the 'flowering of the Ignatian tradition' in England. But perhaps most helpful of all, especially to students of Crashaw, is the splendid introduction on the Baroque world view and its moral assumptions. Carroll Viera (*Expl*) offers a further detail for the interpretation of tears in 'St Mary Magdalene; or, The Weeper', drawing attention to the practical and biblical tradition of weeping while sowing seed – thus anticipating, even in sorrow, the joyful harvest. As noted above, the 'Birrell Collection'[7] (as one is tempted to call his *Festschrift*) includes an essay by D. R. M. Wilkinson discussing Crashaw's 'Sospetto d'Herode'.

A bibliography of the 'lesser' metaphysical poets[29] (which, oddly, includes Vaughan, along with Carew, Cleveland, Cowley, Lord Herbert, Henry King, Katherine Philips, and Traherne, though not Crashaw) gathers together books, articles, and dissertations – the latter forming one-sixth of the entries – from the 1960s and 1970s. Traherne turns out to have attracted the most attention in the period, followed closely by Vaughan. This counting game is about the only interesting by-product of the bibliography, which offers little by way of explanatory comment on its entries and is, unfortunately, not always accurate. Readers of Herrick, however, have been better served by Elizabeth

27. *Richard Crashaw and the Spanish Golden Age*, by R. V. Young. Yale (1982). pp. x + 204. $21.50.

28. *The Emotive Image: Jesuit Poetics in the English Renaissance*, by Anthony Raspa. TCUP (1983). pp. xii + 173. $19.50.

29. *Lesser Metaphysical Poets: A Bibliography, 1961–1980*, ed. by William McCarron and Robert Shenk. TrinityU (1983). pp. xii + 52. $8.50.

H. Hageman whose modestly titled *Reference Guide*[30] is an annotated bibliography covering Herrick criticism since 1625. Her comments on the items are full and helpful, the entries are consistently accurate, and there are three indexes to enable the reader to make the most of the information given. One item too recent to have been included is Dale B. J. Randall's discovery (*ELN*) of a likely source for Herrick's 'Upon Julia's Clothes' in Martial's epigrams, confirming – among other things – Randall's impression that the Julia of the poem is clothed rather than naked. Alan Fischler (*MLS*, 1983) considers the relationship between the imagery of flowers and harvests and the divinity of what he calls Herrick's 'holy Hedonism'.

Eleven poems by Sir John Harington which were omitted by Norman McClure in his 1930 edition (*YW* 11.210) have been transcribed by R. H. Miller (*ELR*). Miller suggests that the bawdiness of the epigrams probably caused them to be left out – Harington 'had a cultivated taste for the crude joke' – and the other (religious) verses were omitted because they had been cancelled, though fortunately not obliterated, in the manuscript. The reinstatement of all the poems, though a fine scholarly contribution, substantiates rather than alters the received view of Harington as one who could move between the bawdy and the devotional with ease. Lee Piepho (*Ren&R*) supplies the texts of manuscript translations by Thomas Lord Fairfax of poems by Mantuan and other Italian neo-Latin writers. Fairfax's interest in the texts may well have been polemical rather than literary, since it seems he first came across them in collections of anti-Papal writings. A more humdrum purpose is discerned by Peter Davidson (*N&Q*) in the notebook of the second Sir Henry Rainsford (1599–1641). Among the miscellaneous items in the manuscript are two poems probably written by Sir Henry for his son, later Colonel Henry Rainsford, at the time of the boy's going up to Oxford. One of these, a warning against extravagance, strikes Davidson as 'exactly the sort of thing which a wise father might wish an undergraduate son to have by him'.

The extant verse of William Austin – comprising nine poems from *Devotionis Augustinianae Flamma* (1635) – has just been republished[31] for the first time in nearly 350 years, in a beautiful handset collectors' edition (with a price to match). Though few will be able to own a copy, it is to be hoped that such a publication will win a place for one or two of Austin's restrained metaphysical carols, meditations, and funeral odes in future anthologies. This is more than could be wished for the 'lumpish' verse of Samuel Sheppard's *Faerie King*, an epic poem 'Fashioning Love and Honour in an Heroicall Heliconian Dress', published for the first time[32]. Sheppard's modern editor, P. J. Klemp, does not try to disguise the frequent weakness of the verse; instead he points out the significance of the poem, not so much as an extension of Spenser's epic (Ralph Knevet's *Supplement* to the *Faerie Queene* is much closer to Spenser) but as poetic evidence of the uncertain mood of Royalists in the late 1640s. Stylistically, Klemp locates *The Faerie King* in the romance epic tradition; Sheppard's choice of *ottava rima* hints at the influence of Daniel's

30. *Robert Herrick: A Reference Guide*, ed. by Elizabeth H. Hageman. Hall (1983). pp. xix + 245. $34.

31. *The Poems of William Austin*, ed. by Anne Ridler. Perpetua. pp. 32. £45.

32. *Samuel Sheppard: The Faerie King (c. 1650)*, ed. by P. J. Klemp. SSELER. USalz. pp. xliii + 355. DM 40.

Civil Wars. In tracing other lines of poetic connection, Michael Cordner (*N&Q*) links Richard Fanshawe with Dryden in building up a tradition of praise in seventeenth-century English verse which showed some independence from their common classical sources.

The edition of Marvell's poems by George deF. Lord, first published in America in 1968, has been re-issued[33], available now in England in a cheap paperback format perhaps intended to rival the popular Penguin English Library edition by Elizabeth Story Donno (*YW* 53.233). Lord used the Bodleian manuscript and arranged the poems into groups – 'lyrics', 'Cromwell era', 'Poets and Heroes', and so on – with thin annotation at the foot of the occasional page. (Even when they appear, the footnotes are not overhelpful: for example, for 'chordage' in 'A Dialogue, between the Resolved Soul, and Created Pleasure', simply 'Note the pun'). The only change made to the original 1968 edition involves the bibliography; the editor explains that, because a great deal has been written on Marvell in the intervening sixteen years, the section of the bibliography on Marvell studies has been omitted. (The logic of this is perplexing.) The decision to leave the introduction, arrangement, and annotation of the poems equally untouched by recent scholarship must surely have been unwise.

Among the new contributions to Marvell criticism is John Klause's inquiry[34] into what he calls 'Marvell's allegiances'. While other critics see Marvell as detached, a strategist, even a player of games, Klause regards him as grappling with 'large question of justice' and, above all, the problem of evil. The poet who to Gerard Manley Hopkins was 'most rich and nervous' had indeed, according to Klause, the 'nervousness of a skeptic at the mercy of his doubts'. Consequently Klause does not look for consistent viewpoints in the poems, but tries to establish the 'lingering preoccupations' which lay behind them. Any conclusions he arrives at are, of course, only tentative probes into Marvell's famous 'silent judgment', and there is a worrying sense that Klause may be more preoccupied with the 'metaphysical labyrinth' than the poems themselves. However, this serious interest in the context of Marvell's thought is what is notably lacking from Michael Long's bland juxtaposition of Marvell and Nabokov[35]. 'No doubt my book is idiosyncratic', he confesses, but no one objects to an individual approach if it is enlightening. The problem here is that the vague thematic links add very little to our understanding of either author, and few parallels are actually pursued as we leap from one brief encounter with a text to the next. The 'Nymph' of Marvell's poem is, for example, said to have 'many Nabokovian relatives, exiled from Arcadia and left with nothing but bewilderment and sentiment dominating their imaginations ever afterwards'. The parallel between this situation and the experience of reading Long's book is uncomfortably close.

In his collection of essays exploring the language of poetry, Christopher Ricks[36] reprints his 1978 piece, looking at what he calls the 'self-inwoven

33. *Andrew Marvell. Complete Poetry*, ed. by George deF. Lord. Everyman's Library, 358. Dent. pp. xl + 275. hb £9.95, pb £2.95.

34. *The Unfortunate Fall: Theodicy and the Moral Imagination of Andrew Marvell*, by John Klause. Archon (1983). pp. x + 208. £26.

35. *Marvell, Nabokov: Childhood and Arcadia*, by Michael Long. Clarendon. pp. xvi + 270. £19.50.

36. *The Force of Poetry*, by Christopher Ricks. Clarendon. pp. xvi + 447. £19.50.

simile' in Marvell's poetry, the inturning image by which Marvell's mind is 'its own resemblance'. This is a feature which Ricks now finds flourishing again in the poets of contemporary Ulster. Clearly the appropriate analogues for Marvell – at least in this year's criticism – are to be found in the twentieth century: Nabokov, Seamus Heaney, and, according to Charles O. Hartman (*Ironw*), W. H. Auden. Even when Robert Cummings (*HLQ*) examines the forest sequence in 'Upon Appleton House' and sees the poet as a priest of Diana in the temple of the wood, he finds it necessary to look into 'Celtic and American analogs' for the cult of Diana. Katharine Sheldahl Thomason (*Genre*, 1983) is slightly more restrained when she suggests that the structure of 'Appleton House' resembles a hexagonal 'bee-like cell'.

Pauline Burdon (*N&Q*) sheds more light on Marvell and his kindred; in the first instalment of a long article, she looks at his stepmother's family, the Alureds of Charterhouse. Meanwhile Phoebe S. Spinrad (*PLL*) applauds Marvell's ability to stand back and laugh in the midst of chaos, welcoming (as, she suggests, the reader should) the excitement of multiple interpretations and contradictions. As an example she suggests that 'The Garden' can be a place of contemplation, or a biblical type, but also the 'Land of Cockayne' where people 'trip over melons'. Appropriately, she herself writes casually and only loosely advances the theory that Marvell is in tune with a 'mystic laughter'. Cleanth Brooks[20] speculates on how the same person could write 'The Garden' and 'To His Coy Mistress'; Allan Pritchard (*SEL*, 1983) cites evidence to show that 'The Garden' might well be a Restoration poem, and therefore suggests that Marvell may have worked on his lyrics right through to his death.

3. Prose

Edmund Bolton has, according to Daniel Woolf (*BLR*, 1983), been 'a prisoner of the footnote for three centuries'. Woolf's article releases him at last, showing him to be an innovative historiographer and early literary critic in his *Hypercritica*. Using the evidence of a reference to Francis Bacon as Viscount St Albans, Woolf also demonstrates that *Hypercritica* cannot have been completed before 1621, and not in 1618 as previously thought. Woolf (*N&Q*) has also discovered an unpublished letter from John Selden to Bacon which indicates that Selden and Sir John Borough were Bacon's sources for the material used in his *History of Henry VII*. D. Weiser (*N&Q*) notes that Bacon's *Essays* and *Advancement* were echoed later in the century by Sir John Denham. In an important article on Bacon's attitude to language, Martin Elsky (*PQ*) asserts that Bacon's role lay in separating language and reality, not in uniting them as is often claimed. For Bacon, language was not part of the world which it represents; instead of an allegorical reading of the universe, Bacon encouraged the study of individual phenomena according to their own natural history, and it was from there that a (separately defined) vocabulary would develop.

Lancelot Andrewes' four versions of a 'prayer before sermon', two in manuscript and two printed with the *Private Devotions*, are offered in a parallel text by P. J. Klemp (*BLR*). This arrangement highlights the fact that, though they are all distinct prayers written at different times in Andrewes's life, they all follow a common formal pattern, almost a liturgy in miniature which allowed local varieties specific to a particular occasion.

Donne's *Biathanatos* has been republished this year in a fine edition[37] whose thoroughness matches Donne's own incredible industry in arguing the case for suicide. The text chosen is the Bodleian manuscript presented to Edward Herbert, though all other major variants are noted; Donne's sources are fully annotated, and there is a useful index to the critical apparatus. In his introduction Ernest W. Sullivan II argues that the treatise is not autobiographical (except perhaps in its initial idea) but casuistical – an immensely learned case of conscience. He also asserts that, contrary to the view of Rosalie Colie and others, it was not intended as a paradox; he demonstrates this with reference to Donne's prose style and the reaction of seventeenth-century readers. Bravely but probably correctly, Sullivan ranks *Biathanatos* among the great Renaissance humanist documents.

Donne features prominently in Horton Davies's analysis of the characteristics of 'English Metaphysical Preaching' in a collection of essays honouring the ecclesiastical historian Robert S. Paul[38]. The features identified by Davies range from patristic learning and allegorical exegesis through style and organization (the 'crumbling' of the text, as George Herbert called it) to the linking of doctrinal and devotional preaching with the liturgical calendar. The detailed preparation of Donne's sermon on Guy Fawkes' Day, 1622, taking into account political as well as theological concerns, is well traced by John N. Wall Jr and Terry Bunce Burgin (*SoAR*). Their article, which supplies the immediate political context but also spots a significant echo of the 1547 *Book of Homilies*, sharpens and invigorates one's reading of the sermon. Donne's sermons are treated to semantic analysis by Winifred Crombie (*Lang&S*) in order to demonstrate that his apparently 'loose' sentences are tightly structured – and that this is the basis of descriptions of Donne's prose style as 'Baroque'. Julia J. Smith (*N&Q*) contends that there are parallels between Donne's writing on the name of Jesus, and Carolus Stengelius's *Sacrosancti nominis Iesu cultus et miracula* (Augsburg, 1613), of which there was a copy in Donne's library. Jeanne Shami (*UTQ*) looks more generally at Donne's authoritative use of dramatic individual examples to rouse his audiences to conversion, in the sermons and the *Anniversaries*. Philip Dust (*N&Q*) finds a source for Donne's famous tolling bell of the *Devotions* in *The Witch of Edmonton*.

Delayed notice is offered here to a collection of essays on Sir Thomas Browne[39], united only in that they 'address themselves' to the subject of Browne; there is no editorial plan or structure, nor even an index to unite them in common reference or usefulness. Inevitably, however, certain interconnecting themes emerge as one reads the varied essays. Several, for example, consider Browne in relation to 'ethics' – of knowledge (Leonard Nathanson), of truth (John R. Knott Jr), of critical responses to Browne (Frank J. Warnke refuting Stanley Fish). Others set Browne in a comparative context – with the familiar (Balachandra Rajan on Browne and Milton) or the unusual (Philip

37. *John Donne: Biathanatos*, ed. by Ernest W. Sullivan II. UDel. pp. lxxi + 280. $38.50.

38. *Studies of the Church in History*, ed. by Horton Davies. Pickwick (1983). pp. x + 276. $19.95.

39. *Approaches to Sir Thomas Browne: The Ann Arbor Tercentenary Lectures and Essays*, ed. by C. A. Patrides. UMiss (1982). pp. x + 187. £11.90.

Brockbank on Browne and Paul Nash). Not surprisingly, many essays cluster around Browne's major texts: J. R. Mulryne examines the function of Browne's persona in *Religio Medici* and sees the work approaching the 'condition of theatre'; the interplay of scepticism and faith in this 'doubting Thomas' is considered by Murray Roston; Raymond B. Waddington justifies the bipartite structure of *Religio Medici* by reference to the 'Two Tables' of duty to God and charity to one's neighbour. In the most original of the contributions on *Religio Medici*, Michael Wilding sets the work in its revolutionary historical context and argues that Browne's spiritual meanings are not reduced by the suggestion that they might also have been put to political uses. D. W. Jefferson touches on the interplay between Browne's theology, vocabulary, and science; Robin Robbins, fresh from the experience of editing *Pseudodoxia Epidemica* (*YW* 62.230), argues convincingly that it is more than an encyclopaedia – it is an imaginative evocation in the metonymic mode, the display of one man's world by means of the fascinated accumulation of detail. Ted-Larry Pebworth suggests that *Pseudodoxia Epidemica* is in the tradition of personal essays; Frank L. Huntley examines the *Garden of Cyrus* as a form of prophetic writing. Browne's 'grave Humour', his method of looking 'asquint' on his subject, forms the basis of an essay by C. A. Patrides; finally, Marie Boas Hall adds a brief contribution on Browne's status as a pure natural historian. Brian Foley (*MP*) considers the impact of Browne's writings on Herman Melville: the nineteenth-century American regarded the seventeenth-century English doctor as a 'crack'd Archangel' who 'heartily hugged . . . all mysteries'. Foley demonstrates stylistic affinities between the two authors, but notes the tensions between the desire to seek truth and the will to believe – between science and metaphysical speculation – which inform the work of both. Browne's Oxford tutor, Dr Thomas Lushington, is the subject of Frank L. Huntley's investigations (*MP*, 1983). He reveals that Lushington deserves independent recognition as a wit, a fine scholar, and preacher, and one who was unjustly accused by his contemporaries of heretical writing.

The Book of Revelation, regarded by D. H. Lawrence as the scriptural book which had the deepest influence on Western culture, is the focus of a new collection of essays, discussing apocalyptic thought in the English Renaissance[40]. In fact, the 'Renaissance' is interpreted rather loosely – stretching back to the early medieval period and forwards to the *Communist Manifesto* – and the only essay of direct relevance to this chapter is Michael Murrin's discussion of two seventeenth-century commentators on Revelation, David Pareus and Joseph Mede. Pareus took an aesthetic approach, seeing the Book of Revelation as a tragedy, whereas Mede based his exegesis on philology, perceiving synchronic patterns in the scripture. These commentators are shown to be of interest, not just because of their connections with Henry More and Milton, but also as their work raises issues of literary structure and methods of interpretation.

Thomas Vaughan has at last been rescued from his unhappy reputation as a messy purveyor of strange Hermetic ideas, and an influence on his poet brother, Henry: his complete *Works* have now been published in a modern

40. *The Apocalypse in English Renaissance Thought and Literature*, ed. by C. A. Patrides and Joseph Wittreich. ManU. pp. ix + 452. £37.50.

edition[41]. All Thomas Vaughan's published works are here, plus a splendidly personal manuscript notebook in which he recorded, among other memoranda, details of his dreams. This gathering of Vaughan's works reminds the reader of the enormity of the tasks which he set himself – 'it is my onely intention in this place to handle *Exterior Actions*, or the Processe of the *Trinity* from the *Center* to the *Circumference*'. We are also shown the visionary colour and energy, as well as the rational demonstration, in his writing – the air is 'no Element, but a certain miraculous *Hermaphrodit*'; the 'divine *Beauty*' in *Lumen de Lumine* has eyes which are '*quick, fresh,* and *Celestiall*'. Alan Rudrum's introduction places Thomas Vaughan's work and supplies a newly thorough biography, revealing in particular Vaughan's tendency to intemperateness and his involvement in several lawsuits; as Vaughan confessed of his need for opposition, 'I would *advance* the *Truth*, because they (his Adversaries) would *suppresse* it'. Rudrum's annotation shows the sources for Vaughan's truth – biblical, classical, alchemical – and resists the temptation to gloss with too many parallels from Henry Vaughan's poetry. In the ironic opening to his preface to *Anima Magica Abscondita*, Thomas Vaughan exclaimed, 'Now God defend! What will become of me?' Thanks to this edition, Vaughan's chances of a more just reputation have considerably increased.

Henry Vaughan's *Man in Darkness* (the second part of *The Mount of Olives*) is shown by Oliver Johnson (*N&Q*) to be indebted to Robert Bolton's *Last and Learned Worke of the Foure Last Things* (1632). J. S. Gill (*N&Q*) establishes that Fairfax's Hermetic manuscript (currently in the British Library) must have been written after about 1650, since it is derived in part from Dr John Everard's *The Divine Pymander of Hermes Mercurius Trismegistus* (1649 or 1650).

Geoffrey M. Ridden (*N&Q*) shows that Gerard Winstanley echoed Milton's *Eikonoklastes* in his *Law of Freedom*. Perhaps more striking is that the independent Antinomian preacher, Henry Pinnell, echoed George Herbert's words, in the pamphlet *Nil Novi* (1654); Nigel Smith (*N&Q*) uses this fact to help demonstrate the resources of the radical imagination. N. H. Keeble (*English*) examines the biblical patterns in Puritan narratives of the seventeenth century, showing convincingly that Old Testament texts offered the Puritan mind not only the key to interpreting contemporary history, but also a complex narrative model of decision, journey, testing, and covenant. Keeble (*JEH*) has also documented Richard Baxter's sermons and offers a checklist of those which were published. In his discussion of Baxter's preaching style, Keeble points out that the ultimate purpose of all Baxter's publishing was in fact pastoral, and notes that the five extra galleries built at his church in Kidderminster in the 1650s are an indicator of Baxter's success as a preacher.

In a volume of essays in honour of the historian R. H. Hilton[42], Joan Thirsk looks at the work of seventeenth-century agricultural writers, those who wielded both pen and plough to the improvement of English husbandry. In particular she considers the contribution of Gervase Markham, whose works were trusted by the first settlers in Virginia as well as by farmers nearer home,

41. *The Works of Thomas Vaughan*, ed. by Alan Rudrum, with Jennifer Drake-Brockman. Clarendon. pp. xiii + 761. £50.
42. *Social Relations and Ideas: Essays in Honour of R. H. Hilton*, ed. by T. H. Aston, P. R. Cross, Christopher Dyer, and Joan Thirsk. CUP (1983). pp. xiii + 337. £25.

and the writings of Walter Blith, a Parliamentarian whose books published during the Interregnum were deliberately cast in a 'country language'. Thirsk notes that agrarian writing combined practical knowledge with 'a philosophical conviction that was idyllic in expression, but was as much political as religious in inspiration'.

Dirk Passmann (*N&Q*) contends that the early-seventeenth-century travel book *Purchas his Pilgrimes*, with its accounts of talking horses and eagles which carry men, clearly influenced *Gulliver's Travels*; Swift is known to have owned the 1625 edition of Samuel Purchas's work. John Taylor 'the Water-Poet', contrary to the impression given by his nickname, 'discovered his metier in travel writing', according to Warren W. Wooden (*PSt*, 1983). In a lively article, Wooden describes the strange mixture of patriotism, history, mirth, and morality in Taylor's prolific output of travel books, which boasted such colourful titles as *News from Hell, Hull and Hallifax* (1639). Wooden claims that these works are worth studying if only for their picture of the practical difficulties of seventeenth-century travel, down to the detail of the 'Ethiopian Army of Fleas' encountered at one inn. It was Taylor who described Sir Thomas Parsons, subject of a short article by Roy J. Booth (*N&Q*), as the 'heire apparent to the invisible kingdom of the Fairies'. Parsons was also cited in Herrick's 'The Fairie Temple' and was the subject of Robert Anton's burlesque pamphlet, *Moriomachia* (1613), the first English imitation of *Don Quixote*. Booth establishes that the pamphlet was based on a real incident: in a challenge to the King's Jester, Parsons appeared as the Fairy Knight. As Henry Wotton pointed out, this was therefore a tilt between a fool by profession and a 'fool by necessity'.

Milton

GORDON CAMPBELL

This chapter has the following sections: 1. General; 2. Comus; 3. Lycidas; 4. Latin Poetry; 5. Minor Poems; 6. Prose; 7. Paradise Lost; 8. Paradise Regain'd and Samson Agonistes; 9. Influence.

1. General

In the closing pages of his monumental *Milton: A Biography* (*YW* 49.209), W. R. Parker commented that

> a thorough, full-scale bibliography of Milton for the years 1628–1800 continues to be a striking gap and a great desideratum of literary scholarship. It is no undertaking for a neophyte, but some truly extraordinary collections await the trained bibliographer with patience and imagination enough for the attempt.

John Shawcross, the best all-round Miltonist in America, has these requisite skills and qualities, and his *Milton: A Bibliography for the Years 1624–1700*[1] constitutes an immensely valuable contribution to Milton studies. The adjustment of Parker's *terminus ad quem* may seem to reflect the limits of human endurance, but in fact it only marks the limit of the first volume; the second will stretch to 1800. The first half of the book is a primary bibliography; this is followed by a secondary bibliography which catalogues allusions, quotations, and imitations. In a work of this scale slips inevitably occur, but the standard of accuracy seems satisfactorily high. The only descriptive error which I noticed is the assertion that the letters from Henry Lawes and Sir Henry Wotton which preface *Comus* are said to be reprinted in the 1673 *Poems*; they are not, and the absence of the Lawes letter is highly significant. And at least one location is wrong: the very early manuscript containing two Latin poems and a Latin prose essay is no longer at Netherby Hall (nor, for that matter, is Netherby Hall still in Cumberland). The scholarship is remarkably up to date: the Bodleian manuscript of 'On Time' which was overlooked by the Variorum editors to their cost, for example, is here noted with a date which was only established in 1983. The canon of the state papers is not yet stable, but Professor Shawcross's entries reflect the current state of research, both published and unpublished. My only reservation is that useful information is

---

1. *Milton: A Bibliography for the Years 1624–1700*, by John T. Shawcross. MRTS 30. CMERS. pp. xiv + 452. $22.

sometimes missing. Number 137, for example, is an alleged reprint of *Pro Populo Anglicano* of which no copy has been located; surely we should have been told who did the alledging (Günter Berghaus in *MiltonQ*, 1983). Similarly, the statement that the Bodleian manuscript of *Ad Joannem Rousium* is written in the hand of Milton's nephew John Phillips is not supported by reference to Professor Shawcross's essay (*JEGP*, 1959) which advances this controversial identification. At the end of the volume there are no fewer than eight indexes. Professor Shawcross has enjoyed rare fortune in his choice of publisher; not only is the book attractive and well printed, but it is also extremely cheap. No serious Miltonist can afford not to buy it.

In *Milton and the English Revolution* (1977) Christopher Hill mocked the American Milton industry; the organ of that industry, *MiltonQ*, memorably cautioned its readers not 'to mutter "Arrogant son of a bitch" at this point and shut the book'. In his latest book, *The Experience of Defeat: Milton and Some Contemporaries*[2], Dr Hill regularly commends the work of American scholars. This unlikely reconciliation between the radical historian and the conservative Milton establishment is based on a common interest in ideas. Dr Hill believes in 'the importance of ideas in motivating political action'; American Miltonists (abetted by the Yale *Prose Works*) tend to believe that Milton had 'ideas' which are manifested in his works. In recent years revisionist historians have undermined the concept of an English revolution and deprecated the importance of ideas. This book is Dr Hill's response. At its best it provides a historical context for aspects of Milton's life and works. The discussion of the idea of apostasy, for example, with its consequent denial of the legitimacy of the church on earth, might be considered (though Dr Hill does not do so) as a gloss on John Toland's remark that in later life Milton did not attend church. Similarly, Dr Hill's fine exposition of 'God on trial' destroys the usual assumption that for Milton's fellow believers the ways of God did not stand in need of justification. Dr Hill's contention that Milton's 'last three great poems deal with intensely topical problems set by the defeat of God's cause' deserves a loud cheer from every serious student of Milton.

Charles R. Geisst attempts to reconstruct *The Political Thought of John Milton*[3]. Mr Geisst deprecates traditional literary and historical approaches to Milton's political thought on the grounds that 'both methods have sought to topically dissect Milton's writings and assemble the results so as to critically evaluate his portent as a thinker. The result in a political context can often be . . . a logical hypallage'; the term might equally be applied to the split infinitives. Mr Geisst proposes instead to examine Milton's political thought in the context of his 'ethical orientation'. One wonders when this book was actually written. Although Dr Hill's *Milton and the English Revolution* appears in the bibliography, it seems to have made no mark on the text, and Mr Geisst cites no other secondary material (other than his own articles) published since 1970; he seems blissfully unaware of important studies of his subject by scholars such as Mary Ann Radzinowicz and Austin Woolrych. Mr Geisst's exposition of his chosen theme is flat and uninteresting, and his prose is primitive: when he says,

    2. *The Experience of Defeat: Milton and Some Contemporaries*, by Christopher Hill. Faber. pp. 342. £12.50.
    3. *The Political Thought of John Milton*, by Charles R. Geisst. Macmillan. pp. 127. £25.

for example, that 'this type of "pre-dogmatic" allegiance was not necessarily espousing heresy to Milton since the concept of the trinity was not affirmed in retaliation to Arius until the Council of Nicea, called by Constantine in 325', the monotone is relieved only by the misprint. I am astonished that Macmillan should have chosen to publish an old thesis which has not even been reheated.

The complex problem of Milton's attitude to war regularly produces scholarship which mirrors the attitudes of the scholar more clearly than it elucidates Milton's shifting position. Books such as James Freeman's excellent *Milton and the Martial Muse* (*YW* 61.214), for example, reflect the disenchantment of American scholars who have lived through the horrors of Vietnam and seen in Milton a reflection of their own conviction of the futility of war and the ignominy of the soldier's task. Now Robert Thomas Fallon, who served for more than twenty years as a soldier in the U.S. Army before turning to academic life, has produced an elegant antidote to Professor Freeman and the pacificists, a study of Milton's military imagery in which soldiering is honoured rather than despised. *Captain or Colonel: The Soldier in Milton's Life and Art*[4] is, as its subtitle suggests, concerned both with biography and with literary criticism. Professor Fallon's introduction is a spirited defence of biographical criticism. The high quality of this chapter sets the standard for the rest of the book, in which Professor Fallon deploys his formidable knowledge of military literature and the 'units' active in Milton's time to elucidate the experiences of the poet and the images of his poems. He misses very little, but seems to be unaware of Gervase Markham's *Soldier's Grammar* (1627), which has already been used (*N&Q*, 1978) to explicate Milton's 'hollow cube'. Professor Fallon knows the history of the period and the minutiae of Milton's life; his command of English prose is also a powerful weapon. The argument is generally convincing, but sometimes is pressed too militantly. It is not necessary, for example, for Professor Fallon to be so patronizing about the possibility of literary influences on Milton's depiction of war: the 'obscure European epics' which he dismisses contain a tradition stretching from the *Thebais* of Statius to Luigi Pulci's *Morgante Maggiore* in which hyperbole borders on parody, and a sympathetic consideration of such works would have strengthened the argument. But these are small reservations about a fine book. Professor Fallon is to be congratulated for having produced the best critical book of the year, one which I shall heartily commend to my undergraduates.

Walter Schindler's book is a study of *Invocation in Milton's Poetry*[5]. Professor Schindler pursues his chosen theme through Milton's poetry with considerable skill, and his prose style is admirably clear. But although he provides a survey of the history of the invocation in his introductory chapter, and later acknowledges Castelvetro's censure of invocations, he seems to be largely unaware of the controversy surrounding poetic invocations in Milton's time. Consider Hobbes, for example:

why a Christian should think it an ornament to his poem either to profane the true God or invoke a false one, I can imagine no cause but a

---

4. *Captain or Colonel: The Soldier in Milton's Life and Art*, by Robert Thomas Fallon. UMiss. pp. x + 272. £32.

5. *Voice and Crisis: Invocation in Milton's Poetry*, by Walter Schindler. Archon. pp. x + 130. £13.95.

reasonless imitation of custom, of a foolish custom, by which a man, enabled to speak wisely from the principles of nature and his own meditation, loves rather to be thought to speak by inspiration, like a bagpipe.

Many agreed with Hobbes that the practice of poetic invocation was blasphemous, and surely Professor Schindler could have done more than assert that Milton flies in the face of 'this peevish tradition of Castelvetro'. A long and interesting final chapter considers Milton's debt to the Psalms, but the observations are vitiated by a failure to consider the Psalms in the languages in which Milton read them.

Milton and Scriptural Tradition: The Bible into Poetry[6] contains nine new essays, all by well-known Miltonists. Leland Ryken's nicely written introductory essay seeks to establish a theoretical framework suitable for describing the relationship between Milton's poetry and the Bible. The notion of the Bible as a source is merely the starting-point of a discussion which formulates more sophisticated models in the light of recent developments in critical theory. Professor Ryken is soaked in the phraseology of the Authorized Version (A.V.), and readily recognizes biblical echoes in Milton's phrases. The danger inherent in this ability is twofold. First, it associates Milton with a version of the Bible which he would not have read in later life, a point to which I shall return. Second, it lumps rather than splits. One example must suffice to illustrate the point: 'thy mansion wants thee' (*Paradise Lost* VIII.296) is set in the context of the 'many mansions' which Jesus describes (John 14.2). Thus Milton draws on the A.V.; but this is wrong. The A.V. phrase is lifted from Tyndale, whose choice of 'mansions' was doubtless influenced by *mansiones* in the Vulgate. The English word in Tyndale and the A.V. probably refers to an apartment in a large house. Milton's 'mansion' draws on the legal sense of *mansio*, meaning the manor house of a lord: it is Adam's 'seat'. In short, Milton's 'mansion' should be sharply distinguished from the A.V.'s 'mansions', not lumped together with it. Michael Lieb's essay explores the phrases 'once more' and 'no more' in *Lycidas*. I have long considered Professor Lieb's earlier article on the same subject (*MiltonQ*, 1978) to be the definitive explication, but here he returns to the theme and brings his daunting learning to bear on a discussion of these phrases as scriptural formulas. This short but brilliant essay is the best study of individual phrases in Milton to have appeared in recent years. Professor Ryken's second essay, on *Paradise Lost* and its biblical epic models, identifies various epic and anti-epic strains in the Bible as models which Milton imitated in *Paradise Lost*. This improbable thesis is argued with vigour and intelligence, and in the end I was convinced of its solid merits. The late Sister M. Christopher Pecheux argues that the council scenes in *Paradise Lost* derive in part from the tradition of the divine council in the Old Testament. I suspect that in this instance the biblical tradition is more important than the Bible: the divine council in the Ludus Coventriae *Parliament of Heaven*, for example, seems closer to Milton's councils than does any Old Testament source. Harold Fisch is the doyen of the distinguished community of Miltonists in Israel. In his essay on *Paradise Lost* and the Book of Job,

6. *Milton and Scriptural Tradition: The Bible into Poetry*, ed. by James H. Sims and Leland Ryken. UMiss. pp. x + 212. £21.50.

Professor Fisch draws lightly on his immense knowledge of Old Testament scholarship to sketch the tradition (unknown to me) of Job as a great Creation-poem and demonstrate the complexity of Milton's debt to the patterns of imagery in Job. Michael Fixler, another good student of both the Bible and Milton, begins his essay on the name of God in the Bible and *Paradise Lost* with a discussion of the word 'all' in Milton's poem which makes Empson's discussion of the same subject (in *The Structure of Complex Words*) look distinctly thin. Professor Fixler's discussion demonstrates conclusively the centrality of the name of God for Milton's poem. A study of the Gospel of John and *Paradise Regain'd* may seem perverse, as John's is the only gospel not to contain an account of the temptations which Milton's poem describes. None the less, the redoubtable Stella Revard manages to extract blood from the stone by showing how Milton drew on John's characterization of Jesus and his account of other biblical scenes. In recent years Professor Revard has produced distinguished work on the classical side of Milton studies, and in this essay she shows herself equally capable of working with Christian sources. John Shawcross has turned his attention to Milton and covenant theology. This is a notoriously difficult problem, but Professor Shawcross has unravelled it successfully, and his exposition may be tentatively regarded as definitive. One important by-way of this article concerns the method by which Milton's theology must be explored. Translations of Milton's *De Doctrina Christiana* (like translations of the Bible) are often treated as canonical by those who are too lazy to learn the appropriate languages. In the introduction to his translation of *De Doctrina Christiana*, John Carey noted that 'scholars who wish to argue closely about Milton's beliefs will always, in any event, have to rest their case on the original Latin'. Professor Shawcross's observations on the inexactitudes of the two translations of Milton's treatise demonstrate the truth of Professor Carey's injunction. The volume concludes with a useful 'afterword' by James Sims on the relationship of the Miltonic narrator and the scriptural tradition.

The one weakness in the volume is an unstated assumption in some of the essays which is made explicit in a related essay (in *MiltonS* XX) by Philip J. Gallagher, who has written a vast and detailed comparison of the accounts of creation in Genesis and *Paradise Lost*. Professor Gallagher argues that 'although Milton read Hebrew and Greek and had access to other versions, *Paradise Lost* VII echoes chiefly the A.V.', and proclaims his conviction that 'verbal parallels demonstrate to a moral certainty that Milton's source for the creation is the Bible in the Authorized Version'. This conviction is a shamefully immoral excuse for not reading Genesis in the languages (and through the commentaries) in which Milton read it, and reveals a woeful ignorance of the history of the A.V. in the seventeenth century. The bill enabling revision of the A.V. which came before the Long Parliament in 1653 spoke of its inaccuracies and its 'prelatical language', and a man of Milton's convictions would hardly have read the A.V. after the 1640s. Milton's working Bible was of course the Latin version favoured by Protestants, Junius-Tremellius. He owned and used a Hebrew Bible all his life, and after he was blind had it read to him. There are many passages in *Paradise Lost* which suggest regular reading in the Septuagint. And Milton thought the Syriac New Testament sufficiently important to teach the language to his nephews. Tendentiousness in Milton scholarship often serves political or religious convictions, but Miltonists who insist that

Milton used this Anglican Bible are guilty of a tendentiousness which has sunk to the service of sloth and scholarly complacency.

The final volume of *A Milton Encyclopedia*[7] consists largely of bibliographies and indexes, but there are four new entries. William B. Hunter Jr contributes a note on Milton's Egyptology. Joan Bennett offers a judicious outline of Milton's antinomianism, an important subject which Professor Bennett has pioneered. Jun Harada chronicles the history of Milton studies in Japan. The central essay is Valentine Boss's magisterial survey of Milton in Russia. Professor Boss introduces much valuable new material, and he sustains a good scholarly standard. The only scholarly lapse seems to be the account of Pushkin, which fails to represent accurately the subject of Pushkin's important essay and to give its publication details (*Sovremennik*, 1837). There is, however, a major critical lapse: Soviet criticism is presented harshly and unsympathetically. It seems that godless communists have tried to turn Milton into a revolutionary, whereas in fact his religion places him firmly in the tradition of the free world.

David Norbrook's *Poetry and Politics in the English Renaissance*[8] concludes with a masterful essay on the politics of Milton's early poetry. This is a lucid and well-informed study, filled with penetrating observations, but there are several slips. Joseph Mede was not 'the head of Milton's Cambridge College'. The Henry King of *Jonsonus Virbius* is not the man of the same name whose poems appear in *Justa Edouardo King*. The only poet to publish poems in both collections was not this composite King, but John Cleveland. The unpublished commemorative poem by Clement Paman which Dr Norbrook notes is followed in the manuscript by another much longer poem by the same author. The casual remark about Georg Rudolf Weckherlin's politics might have been more powerful had Dr Norbrook been aware of Weckherlin's letter to Hermann Mylius in praise of Milton. And the 'steep' of *Lycidas* l. 52 is not Anglesey/Mona but Bardsey: the mistake is in a sense Milton's rather than Dr Norbrook's, for Milton had botched his geography by relying on William Camden's English translator, who mistranslated Camden's *proxima hinc Mona* (meaning 'I shall deal next with Mona') as 'Next unto [Bardsey] lieth Mona'. These errors should be corrected in any reprinting of what is likely to become a classic essay.

The best thematic essay of the year is undoubtedly 'Apocalyptic Configurations in Milton' by C. A. Patrides[9]. Professor Patrides commands two weapons which are the envy of every Miltonist: a magnificent elevated prose style, and unmatched reading in the deadly theological works of the period. He begins this essay with an authoritative survey of the Apocalypse in Renaissance thought, and proceeds to a wide-ranging exposition of this theme in Milton's works. There is a particularly fine section on the convention of *diabolus simius Dei*. The one small slip echoes Dr Norbrook's: Joseph Mede was not 'Milton's tutor at Cambridge'.

7. *A Milton Encyclopedia*, gen. ed. William B. Hunter Jr. Vol. 9: *Bibliographies and Indexes*. BuckU/AUP (1983). pp. 170. $30.

8. *Poetry and Politics in the English Renaissance*, by David Norbrook. RKP. pp. x + 345. £15.95.

9. *The Apocalypse in English Renaissance Thought and Literature: Patterns, Antecedents and Repercussions*, ed. by C. A. Patrides and Joseph Wittreich. ManU. pp. x + 452. £37.50.

Geoffrey Ridden has published three notes on Milton (*N&Q*). He exhumes a passage in Henry Burton's *For God, and the King* (1636) which echoes the St Peter passage in *Lycidas*. Burton lost his ears in 1637, and Mr Ridden suggests that the phrase about ear-clipping in 'On the New Forcers of Conscience' may allude to Burton rather than William Prynne. I am sceptical, because the draft version of the line in the Trinity manuscript is 'Crop ye as close as marginal P– – –'s ears', which seems to allude to Prynne. In his second note Mr Ridden detects a slur on *Lycidas* in *The Dippers Dipt*: Daniel Featley's injunction to 'hearken not to a single oaten-pipe, or the harsh sound of Rams hornes' is taken to refer to *Lycidas* ('the "oaten-pipe" is Milton's *persona* in the poem, and the "Rams horne" a punning reference to the false teaching and the libertinism of the divorce tracts'); perhaps. In his third note Mr Ridden finds an allusion to Milton in Gerard Winstanley, and again I remain sceptical.

Ann Ashworth (*N&Q*) attempts to elucidate the words 'mutation' (and its cognates) and 'change' in Milton and Spenser, but her argument lacks supporting lexicographical evidence. She also argues that the image of the two suns in *Paradise Lost* VI.305 echoes a passage in Spenser; as the parhelion is hardly a rarity in Renaissance literature (e.g. Sir Philip Sidney's 'When two suns do appear'), a debt to Spenser seems unlikely.

Archie Burnett (*ELN*) continues his task of placing the study of Milton's style on a solid footing with an analysis of noun phrases in which a noun is placed between two adjectives (e.g. 'vast profundity obscure'). Critics have endeavoured to show that this 'foreign' construction derives from other languages which they happen to know. Dr Burnett exposes this argument as nonsensical, demonstrates that the construction is firmly embedded in English, and concludes with a series of acute critical observations on Milton's use of the construction. This article constitutes stylistic analysis of the highest order, and could usefully serve as a model for such studies in the future.

Paul Stevens (*MiltonS* XX) studies 'Milton and the Icastic Imagination'. Professor Stevens defines this impressive word by reference to Sidney, who is alleged to have said that poetry 'should be *eikastike*, which some learned have defined, "figuring forth good things" '. Professor Stevens is able to describe this example of *eikastike* as 'the best-known instance of the term in English', because he is unaware that the modernized edition of Sidney which he uses transliterates the word, which Sidney prints in Greek; the *OED* records no example in English before 1664. I do not know the identity of the learned ones whose names Sidney has forgotten (presumably Renaissance commentators on Plato's *Sophist*), but the definition is of course nonsensical, and Professor Stevens's attempt to justify it with reference to Italian theorists whom he has read in translation does not assuage one's unease about Sidney's use of the word 'good'. After this unpromising beginning the article unexpectedly improves, and Professor Stevens provides a useful discussion of the icastic imagination in prophecy, and a careful examination of the concept in Milton's poetry.

John Peter Rumrich (*MiltonS* XX) examines the meaning of 'glory' in Milton. He considers what he describes as 'the etymology of glory' in Hebrew (*kabod*) and New Testament Greek (*doxa*). This seems an odd approach, as the English word 'glory' is indebted to neither language. Professor Rumrich should have looked at the antecedents of the English word in Latin and Italian, and a good starting point would have been Russell Price's history of the term in his examination of Machiavelli's theme of *gloria* (*RenQ*, 1977).

Leo Miller is the best Hebraist ever to have examined Milton's Hebrew. In 'Some Inferences from Milton's Hebrew' (*MiltonQ*) Mr Miller examines the three errors in Milton's transliteration of Hebrew words printed in the margins of his translations of the Psalms. He then scrutinizes Milton's attack on the misprinting of a Hebrew word by Claudius Salmasius. Finally, he examines the Hebrew of *De Doctrina Christiana*; his conclusion that Milton never heard the Daniel Skinner transcription read back to him supports the view (which I share) that the transcription was undertaken after Milton's death. Mr Miller is justly censorious of those who misprint Milton's Hebrew, but he does not name the sorry author of a paper in which the Hebrew word for 'create' is misprinted five out of six times; the present reviewer has reason to be grateful for this kindness.

Arthur Sherbo's strange essay on Milton's rustication (*MiltonQ*) exhumes several late-eighteenth-century letters to the *Gentleman's Magazine* in which the issue of Milton's rustication was debated; these essays add nothing to our knowledge. Professor Sherbo's assertion that April 1626 is the generally accepted date of *Elegia Prima* is contested by the editor of *MiltonQ* in a footnote which refers the reader to Leo Miller's powerful argument for 1627 (*MiltonQ*, 1980). One wonders why the editor printed an article which did not at least contend with Mr Miller's argument. Mr Miller himself continues the task of correcting traditional errors with a re-examination of the date of Christoph Arnold's famous letter (*N&Q*), arguing that 7 August 1651 was a printer's misreading for 7 October. He is surely right (as he always is), and this new date reveals that our understanding of Milton in 1651 has been obscured by garbled chronology.

Gordon Campbell (*JWCI*) argues that many of Milton's autobiographical statements derive from ancient sources, especially the ancient lives of Virgil. Campbell fails to confront the central question which this material raises: was it Milton's life or Milton's account of his life which was shaped by reference to these exemplary lives of the ancients?

In the second half of his article on editorial principles (*RES*) which I praised last year (*YW* 64.257), John Creaser turns his attention to Milton's punctuation. The principle championed in the edition of *The Poems* by John Carey and Alastair Fowler (1968) of modernizing Milton's spelling while preserving the original punctuation is placed under critical scrutiny, and is found wanting. Professor Creaser argues convincingly for an eclectic approach to punctuation, on the grounds that an editor should be willing to subordinate the minor virtue of consistency to the ideal of the best possible text. The proof of this particular pudding will be Professor Creaser's eagerly awaited Yale/Penguin edition of Milton's poetry. The issue of Milton's spelling which Professor Creaser raised in the first part of his article is explored in one particular by Alan Ward[10], who concentrates on Milton's use of −'n and −en; his conclusions constitute a qualified endorsement of Helen Darbishire's views. Masahiko Agari (*ELN*) examines occurrences of the letter 'a' with a diagonal downstroke over it in the

10. In *Five Hundred Years of Words and Sounds: A Festschrift for Eric Dobson*, ed. by E. G. Stanley and Douglas Gray. Brewer (1983). pp. 177. £29.50.

Trinity manuscript; he argues that between 1634 and 1636 Milton's habit of writing with a downstroke gradually disappeared. If this is correct (I have not checked the manuscript), it has important implications for the dating of certain passages in the manuscript.

Eid Dahiyat (*MiltonQ*) discusses writing on Milton in Arabic. The horrifying distortions which he describes make one wonder if a similarly demented view of Arabic literature is proclaimed by the English Arabists. A former professor of English at Cairo argues that Milton's opinions, such as his assertion of the superiority of man to woman, lead one to the conclusion 'that Milton was not a Christian, but rather a pious Moslem'. A professor at the University of Lebanon notes the influence of the Quran on the portrait of Satan in *Paradise Lost*. And most Arabic critics believe that Milton was indebted to Abū al-Alá al Ma'arrí's *Risálat al-ghufrán*; the argument falls a little short of absolute proof. Safá Khūlusí, who is described as 'professor of Arabic at Oxford University', considers Satan to be Milton himself, noting that Milton became a Prince of Darkness after he went blind; one would fear for the study of Arabic at Oxford, but for the fact that no such person appears in the list of faculty at that university.

It comes as a relief to move to Japan, and note that Japanese Miltonists have had another productive year. Noboru Watanabe has published a book on Milton and the Bible (*Milton to Seisho*)[11] and Minori Matsuda has published *Milton Kenkyu: Milton to Kako no Shisei oyobi Dento*[12], a collection of studies of Milton and his predecessors. In a *Festschrift* on Shakespeare dedicated to Dr Isao Mikami[13], Yutaka Akagawa writes on Milton's 'On Shakespeare' (*John Milton no Kenshi*). *MCJNews* VII records the various activities of the Milton Center of Japan. Abstracts of papers read at the fifteenth and sixteenth colloquia of the Center are printed, and there is a detailed account of the papers read at the ninth annual conference of the Center, which was devoted to the theme of 'Milton and the English Revolution'. Papers by the four reporters considered various aspects of Christopher Hill's book of the same title. Other papers explored Milton and the tradition of love poetry, Milton's view of Ireland, the first edition of *Comus*, and the metaphysics of love in *Paradise Lost*. The volume ends with a bibliography of more than twenty studies of Milton published in Japan in 1982. One hopes that this thriving community of Miltonists will soon see fit to host the International Milton Symposium, as such a gathering would clearly be mutually beneficial.

There seems to be growing Chinese interest in Milton. This year two essays on *Paradise Lost* have appeared in the Chinese language journal *Foreign Literature Studies* published in Beijing. Shaolong Qiu discusses images of Satan in *Paradise Lost*, and Yisan Liang describes the nature and themes of *Paradise Lost*, and discusses the poem's reflections of Milton's ideological tendencies. The authors have somehow overcome the formidable problems of securing foreign books in China: Yisan Liang, for example, cites critics from

11. *Milton to Seisho*, by Noboru Watanabe. Kaibunsha. pp. x + 228. Y 2400.

12. *Milton Kenkyu: Milton to Kako no Shisei oyobi Dento*, by Minori Matsuda. Yamaguchi. pp. viii + 374. Y 3800.

13. *Shakespeare no Shiki*, ed by Hisashi Shigeo and others. Shinozaki. pp. x + 618. Y 3600.

Walter Bagehot to Christopher Hill and Andrew Milner. One hopes that these articles will be translated in one of China's English-language journals, as many Miltonists would be interested to learn about Chinese perspectives on this revolutionary author.

2. Comus

The unsettling title of Maryann Cale McGuire's book on *Comus* is *Milton's Puritan Masque*[14]. She sets *Comus* in the context of the rift between Puritans and Royalists. This is an outrageously anachronistic distinction, as there was no such thing as a Royalist in 1634. Similarly, the notion of Puritan opposition to the theatres in the 1630s has been discredited: William Prynne's *Histrio-Mastix* is an isolated attack, not the expression of Puritan convictions. In short, the historical framework through which Professor McGuire reads *Comus* is out of date. The revisionist historians have shattered the myth of rival political ideologies warring in the 1630s. Recent books on the theatre of the period such as Margot Heinemann's *Puritanism and Theatre (YW* 61.178) and Martin Butler's *Theatre and Crisis 1632–1642* have benefited from recent historical work which does not seem to have touched Professor McGuire's book. I suspect that this study was written many years ago: the prefatory 'note on texts' for example, refers to the Yale Milton as a four-volume work published in 1966, since which date four more volumes have been published.

The four essays which John Creaser has published this year consolidate his reputation as England's most versatile student of Milton. Two of the essays are devoted to *Comus*, and both are very important. The trial and execution of the Earl of Castlehaven has in recent years dominated critical readings of *Comus*. Now Professor Creaser has published a closely argued essay *(N&Q)* on 'The Irrelevance of the Castlehaven Scandal'. He demolishes the three central hypotheses: that the scandal delayed Bridgewater's assumption of the office of President of the Council of Wales, that it determined both the theme of *Comus* and some of the treatment of that theme (notably the Sabrina episode), and that its presence is suggested by the nature of the cuts in the performance text. I have no room to summarize the arguments here. Suffice it to say that I am convinced, and that I shall miss the opportunity to introduce a measure of lively prurience into my undergraduate lectures on *Comus*. Professor Creaser's other essay on *Comus*, in David Lindley's collection of essays on *The Court Masque*[15], is a long-overdue antidote to the view that Milton's masque, in the words of W. R. Parker, is 'essentially a children's party'. Professor Creaser argues 'that *Comus* was commissioned for a state event of some significance'. His essay introduces a considerable body of new material on the Bridgewater family, clarifying their politics and thus providing a clearer context for an understanding of *Comus*. The quality of the reading of *Comus* which emerges from this new perspective should quickly establish this paper as the standard essay on *Comus*; it is arguably the best essay ever devoted to Milton's masque. None of the other essays in *The Court Masque* is substan-

14. *Milton's Puritan Masque*, by Maryann Cale McGuire. UGeo (1983). pp. xii + 208. £22.15.
15. *The Court Masque*, ed. by David Lindley. RevelsCL. ManU. pp. 196. £22.50.

tially devoted to Milton, but three essayists conclude their essays with a consideration of *Comus*. Jennifer Chibnall argues that Caroline masques contrive to celebrate harmony in society, whereas *Comus* champions individual virtue, 'requiring that society be changed to match the highest ideal of that individual's conception'; this is a shrewd argument with important implications for Milton's masque. David Norbrook teases the Protestant strains from *Comus* with great skill. And Helen Cooper makes some characteristically perceptive remarks about the significance of the landscape descriptions in *Comus*, the fullness and vividness of which are associated 'more with the bare Elizabethan stage, where setting could only be created verbally, than with masque spectacle'. Viewed as contextual studies of *Comus* (which none of these essays was intended to be), these three essays contribute very considerably to our understanding of Milton's masque.

Anthony Mortimer (*ES*) shares Professor Creaser's doubt about the importance of the Castlehaven affair for *Comus*. He wrests an alternative context out of the fact that *Comus* was performed 'on Michaelmas Night'. He argues that Milton draws on the liturgy for Michaelmas (not a new point) and on popular traditions associated with Michael and Michaelmas. I cannot see the Attendant Spirit as a disguised angel, but I welcome the information about the social conventions of Michaelmas, to which Milton clearly responded in his masque.

James Andrew Clark (*MiltonS* XX) tries to bring the distinction between *natura naturans* and *natura naturatus* to bear on *Comus*. Unfortunately he has not done his homework. He introduces Spinoza's identification of *natura naturans* with God, and deals with the uncomfortable fact that Spinoza was still in nappies in 1634 by adducing Sir John Denham's lyric 'Natura Naturata' (1650) as evidence which 'suggests the currency of those terms before Spinoza'. Such statements make one weep at the current state of Milton studies. Even in English drama, 'nature naturate' was distinguished from 'nature naturynge' as early as *The Nature of the Four Elements* (*c.* 1520). And any discussion of the manifestation of this distinction in Renaissance literature (or Spinoza, for that matter) must of course contend with Giordano Bruno, an obscure Italian philosopher who seems to have escaped the notice of Professor Clark.

William Oram (*SEL*) surveys the functions of Sabrina in *Comus*; he is particularly illuminating on the notion of Cotytto as an antitype of Sabrina.

3. Lycidas

Barbara A. Johnson (*MiltonQ*) sees the motif of the search for the body in *Lycidas* as an adumbration of Milton's later espousal of mortalism. She also argues that Milton's 'sleeps't by the fable' may have been suggested by Aristotle's 'fabled to have slept' (W. D. Ross's translation of a phrase in *Physica*). She concedes that the verbal echo does not exist in the Greek text, but if the passage in *Physica* really does lie behind the phrase in *Lycidas* (which I doubt), it would presumably be reflected in the phrasing of Renaissance Latin editions of Aristotle, which Professor Johnson seems not to have checked. Charlotte F. Otten (*N&Q*) discourses learnedly on 'primrose' and 'pink' in *Lycidas*. Mythographers and poets have failed to produce material enabling scholars to elucidate these flowers. Professor Otten has uncovered immensely useful accounts of myths associated with these flowers in an early-eighteenth-century horticultural manual, and she is surely right to assume that these accounts derive from traditions on which Milton drew. Robert E. Jungman (*Expl*, 1983) thinks that 'for their bellie;' sake' (*Lycidas* l. 144) derives from Philippians 3.18–19; he may be right. Joyce Stith (*MiltonQ*) advances 'a personal interpretation' of the two-handed engine, which she identifies as St Peter. She describes her explication as 'almost absurdly simple and obvious'; one agrees in part.

Gordon Campbell's note on the contributors to *Justa Edouardo King* (*MiltonQ*, 1983), about which I found it difficult to be charitable last year, is this year trounced in several particulars by Edward Le Comte and Jeremy Maule (*MiltonQ*). Professor Le Comte points out that Campbell has confused Old Style and New Style in dating Ralph Widdrington's elevation, and notes that Sir John Hayward could only have written the poem attributed to him by Campbell from the grave. Mr Maule establishes that the abbreviation P.M.S. was hardly obscure, as Campbell would have it, and offers evidence to show that it means either *Piis Manibus Sacrum* or *Piae Memoriae Sacrum*.

4. Latin Poetry

There were two volumes of *Milton Studies* this year; Volume XIX is a special issue devoted to Milton's Latin poetry, and Volume XX is the annual miscellany. The special issue contains thirteen essays and an eighty-page annotated bibliography of Milton's Latin and Greek verse; in some respects John Dillon's elegant and wry bibliography is the most useful item in the collection. John Demaray has written a book describing *Paradise Lost* as a theatrical epic (*YW* 61.213–14); here he has written an article on 'In Quintum Novembris' as a theatrical poem. His allusion to Giambattista Marino's 'Latin poem *La Strage degl'Innocenti*' is disconcerting, but it is arguably an improvement over the usual 'famous Marini' (W. R. Parker, translating Milton's *fama Marini*, following Watson Kirkconnell, David Masson, etc.). Anthony Low begins his essay with a witty account of various attempts to squeeze autobiographical titbits out of 'Elegia Septima', and goes on to subject the poem to what is probably its first serious critical examination; Professor Low's thought-provoking account has convinced me that the poem is much more than youthful froth. Christopher Collins attempts to sketch the poetical cosmos of the early Milton, which he sees as a series of 'contiguous and permeable durational zones'. He then turns to Milton's use of the fall of Mulciber; this account would have been more useful had Professor Collins consulted Renaissance mythographers as well as classical accounts. William Sessions thinks that 'Naturam Non Pati Senium' is an oration, and explicates each of the sections which he discerns in terms of classical rhetoric. Professor Sessions's hopeful assumption that 'Naturam' is the lost Commencement poem which Milton sent to Alexander Gil in 1628 leads him to imagine a 'Cambridge audience of 1628'; it reminds me of the quest for *Love's Labour's Won*. William Kennedy detects four audiences in 'Ad Patrem': Milton's father, the lover of ancient treasures of ll. 93–4, the abstractions of ll. 105–9, and his own poems (ll. 115–20). This may seem an unpromising framework through which to explicate the poem, but one very interesting point emerges: Professor Kennedy discerns a sustained allusion to Ovid's account of Apollo and Phaëthon, with Milton casting himself as Phaëthon and his father as Apollo. I remain sceptical about some details of the argument, but am happy to accept the general point as a useful indication of the tone of the poem. James Freeman begins his essay with a whistle-stop tour of the Italian academies, and then proceeds to a very fine analysis of 'Ad Salsillum'. Professor Freeman has had the bright idea of consulting Salzilli's poems with a view to considering the interplay between his poems and Milton's. This proves to be a very fruitful approach; I wish that I had thought of it. I would quibble with only one point in this remarkable essay: it is hardly necessary to cite *Paradise Lost* I.708–9 to show 'that Milton had at some time observed an organ carefully'. Milton's childhood home contained an organ, and he owned and played an organ in his own house in Jewin Street. Professor Low's second essay in the volume is an excellent exposition of 'Mansus'. In discussing Giovanni-Baptista Manso's distich to Milton he notes the obvious *Anglus-Angelus* pun which derives from Pope Gregory, but fails to note that the terminology of Manso's criticism of Milton's Protestantism is also adumbrated by Gregory. In Bede's account (*Historia Ecclesiastica* II.i) Gregory laments that the bright faces of the boys are controlled by the author of darkness, and that such graceful features conceal minds devoid of grace (' "Heu, pro dolor!", inquit, "quod tam lucidi vultus homines tenebrarum auctor possidet, tantaque gratia frontispicii mentem ab interna gratia vacuam gestat!" '); the sting in Manso's distich surely derives from this passage. Diane Kelsey McColley discusses the first of Milton's three epigrams to Leonora Baroni in the context of angelic love. She wrestles valiantly with the notoriously obscure *mens tertia*, but the match must be declared a draw. Professor McColley's statement that 'Milton believed in creation *de Deo* rather than *ex nihilo*' is wrong: Milton never uses *de Deo* of the creation, always preferring *ex Deo* or *a Deo*. As Augustine clearly explains in *De natura boni*, ' "from Him" [*ex ipso*] does not mean the same thing as "of Him" [*de ipso*]'. There are three essays on 'Epitaphium Damonis' in this volume. Gordon Campbell's essay on imitation in the 'Epitaphium' was described by one anonymous press reader as 'critically puerile, vague, unimportant'; this seems a reasonable judgement. Janet Leslie Knedlik attempts to remove 'Epitaphium Damonis' from the shadow of *Lycidas* to its own place in the sun by distinguishing the Latin poem as a purer form of pastoral. Her discussion of the refrain is vitiated by the conviction that *domino jam non vacat* means 'your master does not care about you'. In a fine essay Albert Labriola rises far above the usual practice of rifling Milton's 'Epitaphium' for autobiographical information, instead exploring it as a stage in Milton's intellectual autobiography. He relates the poem to some of Milton's other autobiographical statements, and is particularly illuminating on the letter to Leonard Philaras of 1652; there is also an excellent discussion of the importance of the *rota Virgilii* for the poem. Thomas Corns offers a suggestive and highly intelligent overview of the 1645 *Poemata*, considering the collection in the context of Milton's standing as a radical polemicist in 1645. Dr Corns demonstrates that 'the discrepancies between the ideological position of many poems and his own known position in 1645 are marked and bewildering'. 'Haec ego mente' is said to document the transformation of Milton's outlook, aspirations, and ideological position. But what is being retracted in that poem? Does *nequitia* mean 'worthlessness' (as Dr Corns translates it) or 'wantonness'? The line clearly imitates Ovid's 'ille ego nequitiae Naso poeta meae', where *nequitia* surely means 'wantonness' – Augustan poets did not proclaim their worthlessness. In short, I do not think that the reference of 'Haec ego mente' can be extended beyond the erotic elements in Elegies I, V, and VII. Stella Revard's essay examines 'Ad Joannem Rousium', the metrics and tone of which have never satisfied critics whose standard of correctness is the pedantic Latinity of Victorian public schools. Professor Revard provides a very fine analysis of the tone of the poem, and authoritatively sorts out its relationship to Pindar.

Elsewhere, Edward Le Comte (*ELR*) offers a dazzling display of verbal parallels between Elegy VII and Milton's other poems, in the course of which he offers a new textual emendation for the perplexing form *surdeat* in Elegy VII.90. John Carey (*Poems of John Milton*, 1968) noted that there is no such verb as *surdeo*; Douglas Bush (*Variorum*, 1970) speculated correctly that it must be a Renaissance coinage, and John B. Dillon (*HumLov*, 1978) found *surdeo* in Stephanus's *Thesaurus Linguae Latinae*. Now Professor Le Comte proposes that *surdeat* may be an erroneous conflation of *surda eat*. As this reading is consonant with the classical bias of Milton's Latin, and manages to preserve the present subjunctive without violating the metre (if it is elided), it must be a serious possibility about which future editors will agonize.

5. Minor Poems

Judith Scherer Herz (*MiltonS* XX) studies the epigrammatic elements in Milton's sonnets. This is a sensible idea, as sonnets were regularly described as vernacular epigrams. It is not clear, however, why Professor Herz has chosen to argue her thesis with special reference to Ben Jonson (her subtitle is 'Milton in the Manner of Jonson'), as most of the points of comparison which she adduces could as easily have been drawn from Latin epigrammists such as the Welshman John Owen. J. E. Adams (*MiltonQ*), alarmed at the lack of commentary on 'Cyriack, this three years day', attempts to fill the gap by exploring the sonnet's themes of grandeur and fortitude, arguing that it is 'subtle, supple, and centrally Miltonic in its concerns'. Kay Stanton (*HSL*) joins the ranks of those who see groupings within the sonnets by connecting Sonnet I ('O Nightingale') with the Italian sonnets. She argues that pagan and Christian deities link the sonnets thematically, and that the use of these two deities explains Milton's use of two different languages; I am not convinced. William L. Stull (*HSL*) discerns a steady development in the religious sonnet from Wyatt to Milton; this is not a surprising conclusion. In an excellent note on Milton's phrase 'my light is spent' (*MiltonQ*) Joel F. Wilcox proposes a source in Achilles' opaque image of 'a light to friends' (*Iliad* XVIII.102) and buttresses his argument with an astute consideration of George Chapman's translation. Edward Le Comte (*MiltonQ*) brings together scattered material on Milton's Emilia (and Shakespeare's) and makes several useful suggestions for further research.

Professor Le Comte (*MiltonQ*) also brings his customary erudition to bear on the question of whether Milton's phrase 'to the stern God of Sea' is a mistranslation of the last line of Horace's 'Ad Pyrrham', and declares him not necessarily guilty, or at least guilty in good and multitudinous company. Margaret M. Byard (*Expl*, 1983) thinks that the verse patterns and rhythms of 'On Time' and 'At a Solemn Musick' extend beyond the poems themselves to create a parallel between the sounds of the poems being recited and the thematic sense which the sound reflects. John Creaser (*N&Q*) replies to

Archie Burnett's reply (*N&Q*, 1982) to Professor Creaser's article (*N&Q*, 1982) on the text of Milton's minor poems. The battle now centres on 'L'Allegro' l. 104: 'by the' (1673) or 'he by' (1645); I change sides with every instalment. Thomas M. Greene, who recently published a brilliant book on imitation in Renaissance poetry, turns his attention to 'L'Allegro' and 'Il Penseroso' (*ELR*). He argues that the true subject of each poem is the 'meeting soul' of 'L'Allegro' l. 138; a subtle and highly intelligent reading of the poems emerges from this central contention. In an equally good piece Christopher Grose (*JEGP*) focuses on the much-debated phrase 'Lydian airs' ('L'Allegro' l. 136), and uses his scholarly explication of that phrase as an occasion for a perceptive critical reading of the twin poems.

Pietro Bongo, that touchstone of numerological terrorism, is invoked by John Gouws (*N&Q*) to gloss the number twenty-three (which Bongo associates with retribution for sin) in 'How Soon Hath Time' ('my three and twentieth year') and 'Epitaph on the Marchioness of Winchester' ('Summers three times eight save one').

6. Prose

Gladys J. Willis argues in her book[16] on Milton and divorce that the 'rule of charity' which Milton describes in *The Doctrine and Discipline of Divorce* derives from Augustine's *De Doctrina Christiana*. Professor Willis acknowledges that there is no hard evidence to show that Milton had read *De Doctrina Christiana*, but offers 'the fact that Milton gave one of his works the very same title as that of St Augustine's work – *De Doctrina Christiana* – and wrote it in Latin'. I am not confident that this is a 'fact', as it is not unlikely that Milton's treatise was given its final title by Daniel Skinner, in whose handwriting it appears. And the suggestion that Milton wrote his treatise in Latin as a gesture towards Augustine points to a certain lack of intimacy with the Latin theological tradition, as does the fact that the Latin name of Augustine is given as 'Sancti Aurelii Augustini'. Indeed, the cultural framework of Professor Willis's book is not the Latin tradition but modern America. Thus a distinction in Augustine is glossed by analogy 'to the predicament of a man headed to California by plane, but [who] becomes engrossed in the metroliner, forgets his destination and climbs aboard the metroliner which is bound for Alabama'. As Comus would say, 'it is for homely features to keep home; they had their name hence'. This book was doubtless an exemplary Ph.D. thesis, but it is not a satisfactory scholarly study. Professor Willis is completely out of her depth with Augustine; similarly, observations such as 'Milton was indeed sincere' or 'it is from Milton's divorce tracts that one learns what the ingredients of a happy marriage are' point to a naive partisanship with Milton that is inimical to detached scholarship.

R. Kenneth Kirby (*MiltonQ*) examines Milton's 'Biblical Hermeneutics' in *The Doctrine and Discipline of Divorce*, and contrives to convince his readers that Milton's self-confident and resolute flaunting of his own hermeneutical principles in the interests of buttressing his own interpretation constitutes 'one

16. *The Penalty of Eve: John Milton and Divorce*, by Gladys J. Willis. Lang. pp. 156. $21.60.

of the marks of creative genius'; on that assessment many a tendentious Milton scholar may now be praised for creative genius. Stanley Stewart (*MiltonS* XX) examines the ideological and stylistic significance of Milton's revisions of *The Readie and Easie Way*. Geoffrey M. Ridden (*MiltonQ*) prints a sharp note on the disguise of Bishop Longchamp to which Milton refers in *An Apology*; this is yet another instance of the inadequacy of the commentary in the Yale Milton. In a lively article Thomas Corns (*PSt*) assesses this execrable edition which should have been strangled at birth, for its existence has queered the pitch for a scholarly edition of Milton's prose works. Howard Jacobson (*N&Q*) devotes a taut note to a demonstration that the introduction to Milton's *Second Defence* is indebted to the prefatory material in Sallust's *Catilinae coniuratio*. Thomas Kranidas (*ELR*) offers a very fine essay on *Areopagitica*, examining a series of polarities – public and private, Greek and Latin, etc. – and commenting with characteristic acuity on the structures of Milton's tract. Gordon Campbell (*JWCI*) speculates fussily on the meaning of the word 'Areopagitica'; he may be right.

7. Paradise Lost

J. M. Evans, a good scholar with a fine critical intelligence, explicates the *triple entendre* on the word 'secure' in the separation scene, and reads the scene in the context of contemporary ideas about the need for Christian watchfulness (*MiltonS* XX). Christopher Fitter's maiden address to the community of Miltonists (*MiltonS* XX) is an insightful study of the relevance of the topos of exile consolation to the notice of eviction which Michael serves on Adam and Eve; his application of Plutarch's epistolary essay 'On Exile' to *Paradise Lost* illuminates Milton's use of an important convention. In an exemplary study in the history of an idea Eugene R. Cunnar (*ELN*) returns to the scales which he discussed last year (*MiltonQ*) to trace the traditions which underlie God's 'golden scales' in *Paradise Lost* Book IV. Malabika Sarkar has already (*N&Q*, 1979) written illuminatingly on Satan's astronomical journey in *Paradise Lost* Book IX, and this year she returns to the poem (*MiltonQ*) to explore its astronomical images of space and time. She argues that the images of space establish the concept of infinite space even within the Ptolemaic cosmos, and that the astronomical images of time 'project the simultaneous presence of the temporal in the midst of eternity'. In a characteristically laboured essay Gordon Campbell (*MiltonQ*) attempts to unscramble Milton's catalogue of the winds (*Paradise Lost* X.695–706) by reference to the anemology of antiquity. F. Peczenik (*Mosaic*) argues that the prelapsarian marriage of Adam and Eve is devoid of hierarchy, and that readers who insist that their relationship is hierarchical (I plead guilty) have attributed fallen values to the state of innocence. Kay Gilliland Stevenson (*RenP*), who is always worth reading, examines *Paradise Lost* Book IX as a tragedy within the frame 'no more . . . no end'. This essay is filled with useful observations, but I remain uneasy about its contention that Book IX can, with the aid of Sir William Davenant's preface to *Gondibert*, be read as a tragedy in five acts. Harinder Marjara (*MiltonQ*) provides a context in Renaissance art theory for the relationship between 'beauty' and 'grace' in *Paradise Lost*. He demonstrates that these qualities were traditionally seen as contraries, and argues that 'the opposition between beauty and grace is recurrent in *Paradise Lost*'. This is an excellent paper, but its accidental attribution of *Delle perfette proporzioni* to Dante rather than Vincenzio Danti may lead gullible Miltonists astray. William B. Hunter Jr (*MiltonQ*) muses on the alienating effects of Milton's epic catalogues for the modern reader, and concludes despairingly that Milton's intended 'fit audience, though few' are today 'even fewer'. Mary Nyquist (*ELR*) offers a sound reading of the fall in *Paradise Lost* centred on what she terrifyingly calls 'the discontinuity of modal heterogeneity in *Paradise Lost*', by which she seems to refer to the transition from epic to tragedy ('I now must change / Those notes to tragic'). In a demanding but rewarding analysis she argues that this shift is reflected in Milton's use of distinct kinds of dialogue. R. D. Bedford conducts a useful word-study of 'field' in *Paradise Lost* (*ELN*). Richard S. Ide (*SEL*) relates the perplexing account of the begetting of the Son in *Paradise Lost* to three distinct traditions of commentary on Psalms 2.7; this method does not produce unassailable conclusions, but it clarifies important aspects of the problem. In a dense and highly philosophical essay (*MP*) Marshall Grossman inquires into the nature of narrative in *Paradise Lost* with a view to elucidating Milton's 'dialectical visions'; readers who persevere with this difficult essay will be rewarded with some good critical observations. Osamu Nakayama (*English*) submits the disjunctive similes in *Paradise Lost* to intelligent critical scrutiny, and demonstrates the ways in which they reflect both their immediate contexts and the larger concerns of the poem. Kathleen M. Swaim (*PQ*) examines 'the structural deployments of light' within Book III of *Paradise Lost*, and relates Milton's treatment of light to the 'mimesis of accommodation' in that book. Christine Froula's provocative feminist article on *Paradise Lost* in *Critical Inquiry* (1983) has sparked a lively exchange in the current issue of that journal. Edward Pechter mounts a witty rearguard attack on the claims of feminist criticism, concluding that 'new feminist is but old priest writ large'; Professor Froula provides a spirited but good-natured reply in defence of feminist perspectives on *Paradise Lost*.

Jean Pironon, who in 1979 published a massive two-volume assessment of *La Critique de la poésie Miltonienne 1942–1978*, has this year returned to the arena with a monograph entitled *Le Temps figé et l'inexprimable distance*[17] (I trust that everyone recognizes both phrases). The subtitle suggests that this is a straightforward study of 'les images de la fixité et du mouvement dans le *Paradis Perdu*'; however, these images of stability and motion are not only explored for their own sake, but also act as a springboard for assaults on much larger issues. Study of these images leads Dr Pironon to an affirmation of the ambiguity of the poetic and moral universe of the poem. The implications of this ambiguity extend to the reader's perception of Milton's characters and his assessment of Milton's politics. Dr Pironon relates his chosen images to the succession of cosmological systems from the Renaissance to the present. He moves confidently through areas of scholarly inquiry not familiar to most Miltonists, but those who make the effort to keep up will undergo an experience at once rewarding and intellectually unsettling.

This year our knowledge of Milton's sources has increased incrementally. Potential readers of a paper entitled 'Pretexts and Subtexts in "That Fair Field

---

17. *Le Temps figé et l'inexprimable distance: Les Images de la fixité et du mouvement dans le 'Paradis Perdu' de John Milton*, by Jean Pironon. Adosa. pp. 96. Ffr 80.

of Enna"' (*MiltonS* XX) emanating from Yale should not be deterred by the title (such titles may be obligatory at Yale), which does not introduce a display of theoretical exhibitionism but rather a learned and exceedingly competent source study. George deForest Lord proposes as a source the pseudo-Homeric *Hymn to Demeter*, which underlies the more familiar later accounts. Professor Lord worries unduly about the fact that the only surviving text of the *Hymn* first appeared in Moscow in 1777. We know, for example, that Milton was familiar with the traditions embodied in the Ethiopic Book of Enoch, which was discovered in 1773 and was not accessible in a language which Milton could read (Greek) until 1890, but none the less can be shown to have shaped several passages in *Paradise Lost*. Stephen M. Fallon (*MiltonQ*) examines the Homeric and Virgilian passages which underlie Satan's return to Pandemonium (*Paradise Lost* X.441–50). Until I read this article I did not believe that the allusion (first noted by Thomas Newton) existed, but I am now convinced that I was wrong. Ann Ashworth (*MiltonQ*) detects echoes of the myth of Psyche in *Paradise Lost*. But Milton's Psyche was neither the goddess of antiquity nor the reconstruction of twentieth-century scholarship, but rather the Psyche of the Renaissance mythographers, whom Professor Ashworth knows only at second hand; this could have been a useful paper had Professor Ashworth taken the trouble to consult encyclopaedists such as Lilio Gregorio Giraldi, Vincenzo Cartari, and Natale Conti. I. S. MacLaren (*N&Q*) attempts to relate Milton's description of the 'frozen continent' to contemporary journals of Arctic exploration. The general contention is probably correct, but Professor MacLaren comes to grief when he tries to make specific connections: Thomas James records that his crew feared that they would 'starve upon a piece of ice' and Professor MacLaren points hopefully to Milton's 'starve in Ice'. But in both cases 'starve' refers not to hunger, but to the now obsolete sense of 'suffering from extreme cold', a not unlikely concomitant of living in ice. John Simons (*N&Q*) thinks that the source of 'no fear lest dinner cool' (*Paradise Lost* V.396) may be Timon's injunction to 'make not a city feast of it, to let the meat cool ere we can agree upon the first place' (III.vi.67–8). I find it hard to believe that Shakespeare's anachronistic joke about London ('city' should, I think, be printed 'City') lies behind Milton's line. Merrill H. Goldwyn (*ELN*) thinks that several phrases in *Paradise Lost* have their source in the second part of Marlowe's *Tamburlaine*. Certainly there are similarities in phrasing, but they remind me of the analogous phrases from Elizabethan playwrights which one finds in the notes of older editions of Shakespeare; such phrases can help to elucidate meaning, but they are not necessarily sources.

8. Paradise Regain'd and Samson Agonistes

Alastair Fowler[18], Britain's most learned student of Renaissance literature, confronts the 'problems of style' in *Paradise Regain'd*. The connection between *Paradise Regain'd* and Virgil's *Georgics*, which was first suggested by Louis Martz and last year developed in a fine essay by Anthony Low (*YW* 64.267), is, in Professor Fowler's essay, explored at the level of stylistics. The

18. *Medieval and Pseudo-Medieval Literature: The J. A. W. Bennett Memorial Lectures, Perugia 1982–1983*, ed. by Piero Boitani and Anna Torti. Brewer/Narr. pp. viii + 198. £17.50.

MILTON 315

best part of this excellent study is the consideration of the many alternatives in Milton's descriptions (e.g. 'beasts of chase, or foul of game, / In pastry built, or from the spit or boiled'). This practice is convincingly shown to be a mimetic reflection of the element of choice which is at the heart of temptation. Lawrence W. Hyman (*MiltonQ*) re-examines the conclusion of *Paradise Regain'd*, and wrestles energetically with the disjunction between the admirable Christ of the conclusion and the repugnant Christ of the rest of the poem. Readers who share Professor Hyman's concern to promote the religious power of the poem will perhaps cheer more loudly than can I. Mary Ann Radzinowicz (*HSL*) brings her formidable intelligence to the analysis of *Paradise Regain'd* as a 'hermeneutic combat' centred on the messianic Psalms. Lady Radzinowicz is particularly illuminating on the slippery phrase 'Son of God'.

Kathleen M. Swaim (*MiltonS* XX) examines various forms of doubleness in *Samson Agonistes*, focusing particularly on the second semichorus (ll. 1687–1707). She argues that 'in this climactic instance of choral bifurcation into balanced semichoruses, the Chorus duplicate the psychic alteration the off-stage hero has undergone and mediate that change for the poetic audience'. One might feel happier about this judgement if some consideration had been given to the way in which the semichorus is used in ancient and Neoclassical drama; a useful starting point would be Joseph Lammers's *Die Doppel- und Halb-Chöre in der antiken Tragödie* (1931), which commentators on Milton's semichoruses have ignored. *Studi di letteratura e di linguistica*[19] from the Universitá degli Studi di Salerno is mostly devoted to English literature; it includes a wide-ranging essay on *Samson Agonistes* by Antonella Piazza Coppola. Steven Blakemore (*Expl*) relates *Samson Agonistes* ll. 80–2 to Deuteronomy 28–9. Leo Miller (*MiltonQ*) attacks the article on the baseness of Samson (*YW* 64.268) about which I was so censorious last year, demonstrating that its arguments are 'utterly without foundation'; in a later issue David S. Berkeley and Salwa Khoddam, the authors of the offending article, offer a rejoinder. The wounds will not heal quickly.

9. Influence

Richard Bentley's edition of *Paradise Lost* is often belittled for its editorial perversions, but Bentley thought more carefully about Milton's text than do many of those who mock him. John K. Hale (*MiltonQ*) offers an excellent account of the background of Bentley's edition; Mr Hale's refreshingly un-dogmatic approach to the evidence yields useful results. In another study (*PQ*) Mr Hale discusses the significance of early translations of *Paradise Lost* into Latin, German, French, and Italian, and comments briefly on versions in Dutch and Greek. This is a superb essay on an important subject, filled with useful comparisons of the translations within each language. As a comparison of translations of Milton's Latin poems in modern editions shows, translators work with earlier translations on their desks; Mr Hale shows that this practice has existed from the beginning.

19. *Studi di letteratura e di linguistica*, Quaderno 3, by various authors. Pubblicazioni dell'Universitá degli Studi di Salerno, Sezione di studi filologici, letterari, e artistici, 7. ESI. pp. 140.

Miltonists may be familiar with the translations of *Paradise Regain'd* and *Samson Agonistes* into German prose executed by Simon Grynäus of Basle in 1752, but they may not be aware (as I was not) that Grynäus also translated at least seven books of *Paradise Lost*, and that the manuscript of Book I survives. J. H. Tisch has recently produced a critical assessment[20] (in German) of this translation. This year Professor Tisch returns to Milton with a brief study[21] (again in German) of *Samson Agonistes* in the context of worldly and religious immorality in seventeenth-century literature.

Deborah H. Lockwood (*ELN*) surveys eighteenth-century responses to the last two books of *Paradise Lost*; this is a competent study in an area which tends not to attract good scholarship. James Gray (*MiltonQ*) explores Alexander Pope's 'reluctant debt' to Milton in his translation of the *Odyssey*, arguing that several of Milton's stylistic mannerisms appear in Pope's translations. Many of the examples which Professor Gray adduces lend spectacular support to his contention, and his study should send students of Pope scurrying to re-annotate their texts. Malabika Sarkar[22] paints in broad brush-strokes a picture of Milton and the Romantics, contrasting the absorption of *Paradise Lost* with the rejection of *Paradise Regain'd*. Mary D. Ravenhall (*MiltonS* XX) examines Francis Hayman's illustrations to Thomas Newton's edition of *Paradise Lost* (1749). This fine essay raises the standard of studies of Milton's illustrators, for Professor Ravenhall looks carefully at the relationship between design and text, and cautiously sets the illustrations in the context of contemporary critical attitudes to *Paradise Lost*. Leo Miller (*MiltonQ*) cites the remark of Henry Pomer (*Milton and Melville*, 1957) that 'Melville's copy of Milton either does not exist or exists unknown . . . it is almost unbelievable that for many decades there did not stand on Melville's shelves an edition of . . . Milton's poetry, marked, annotated and well worn'. That edition has now been found, and Mr Miller (who is not given to overstatement) claims that Melville's annotations may rank in significance with Blake's comments.

20. *Paradise Lost 'In der vollen Pracht des Deutschen Hexameters': Ein kritische Würdigung der Milton-Übersetzung von Simon Grynäus*, by J. H. Tisch. UTas (1980). pp. 13.

21. *Samson Agonistes*, by J. H. Tisch. UTas. pp. 4.

22. *The Romantic Tradition*, ed. by Visvanath Chatterjee. JadavpurU Essays and Studies 4. JadavpurU. Rs 24, £3.

The Later Seventeenth Century

JAMES OGDEN and STUART SILLARS

This chapter has its usual four sections – 1. General; 2. Dryden; 3. Other Authors; 4. Background – but philosophy and the history of ideas have this year been relegated to section 4. The treatment of background studies is highly selective, depending partly on what was sent for review, and the supply of review copies may have affected the balance of other sections. Stuart Sillars has written sections 1(*b*) and 3(*b*) and part of section 4(*a*). The rest is by James Ogden.

1. General

As usual comprehensive annotated lists of current publications appeared promptly in *Restoration*. They were compiled this year by Martha Regalis and Marie E. Devine, and I am especially grateful to Dr Devine for mentioning items I might well have missed. In '*Restoration* and the Revival of Later Seventeenth-Century Studies: Comments and a Booklist' (*EdN*) J. M. Armistead describes the foundation and policy of the journal, and lists over a hundred books published from 1976 to 1984 which are either wholly or partly concerned with Restoration culture. 'We have come a long way in Restoration studies since 1975', he concludes, 'but we need more research before we can confidently begin 'experimentation with critical approaches'. In 'Recent Studies in the Restoration and Eighteenth Century' (*SEL*) Morris R. Brownell briefly but fairly reviews about a dozen Restoration books. A number of books and articles were reviewed and characterized in *Scriblerian* and *SCN*: very pungently in the former, quite blandly in the latter. The latest volume of *The Eighteenth Century: A Current Bibliography*[1] records work published in or before 1980. Like its predecessors it lists and usually reviews or evaluates the major books and articles on life, literature, and the arts from about 1660 to 1800. Reviewing earlier volumes (*MLR*, 1985) Paula R. Backscheider calls the bibliography 'a worthwhile but somewhat eccentric endeavour' and regrets that the price now makes it too expensive for individual scholars; which is unfortunate, because it is 'in many ways, more suitable for browsing than for reference'. What I said some years ago remains true: readers of this chapter of *YW* should consult *ECCB* for specialist book reviews and fuller treatment of bibliography, philosophy, and background studies; readers of *ECCB* should

---

1. *The Eighteenth Century: A Current Bibliography*, N.S. 6 (for 1980), ed. by Jim Springer Borck. AMSP. pp. xii + 643. $67.50. (Rev'd by the editors, *Scriblerian*, 1985.)

consult this chapter for fuller and more current coverage of work on Restoration literature, especially articles.

Ideas of the Restoration in English Literature, 1660–71[2], by Nicholas Jose, is a study of the 'royalist propaganda' and 'radical literature' of the decade – a distinction made rather casually (p. 54). Understandably doubtful whether the Restoration would give the desired stability, Dryden and other purveyors of royalist panegyric sought to convince themselves and their audience that it was providential. More of a poet, Abraham Cowley acknowledged the problems of such mythologizing and achieved a degree of integrity. The disastrous second Dutch War produced 'a heroic but wishful apology' in Dryden's *Annus Mirabilis*, and a harsh but powerful satire in Marvell's 'Last Instructions'. Meanwhile, in the theatre the royalist position was bolstered by plays showing how wicked usurpers are deposed and virtuous monarchs restored. In this context Milton's *Samson Agonistes* is the masterpiece, turning the myths upside down to imply that the nation really needed spiritual restoration. In all this political literature we are to feel 'the pressure of a time which denied the consolations of providence and forced men into the flux of history'. It must be said, of course, that the book is subtler than summary can show; and should be added perhaps that it is more tiresome. There are many signs of its origin in a thesis, as Jose displays extensive knowledge of sources and avoids frivolous elegance of style. The best chapter is that on Cowley, whose difficulties in 'saying what he had to say', though 'in the end he managed', evoke sympathy, perhaps through their curious analogies with those of thesis writers. Essays which might be read in conjunction with this book are Michael Ketcham's on Dryden and Marvell (section 1(*a*) below) and Carolyn Edie's on 'News from Abroad' (section 4).

Other general studies include H. A. Mason's series of essays on 'The Founding of Modern European Literary Criticism' (*YW* 63.225), which continued with 'A Bundle of Letters' and 'Rapin's Critical Reflections on Modern Poetry' (*CQ*, 1983–4). These are anthologies of extracts from René Rapin's correspondence with Roger Rabutin and *Reflexions sur la poétique*, with English translations and commentary. Mason argues that modern criticism was founded on the application to modern literature and culture of the classical ideals 'd'écrire simplement sans paroître bas et d'être naturel sans être plat'; and that Rapin's greatness as a critic depended on his ability to appreciate both the strengths and the weaknesses of Racine and Molière. Rapin's influence on Pope and Addison is emphasized, but presumably another essay will be needed to make good the claim that the *Essay on Criticism* is a classic formulation of ideas derived from the seventeenth-century French critics. An apparently similar theme is developed in an extraordinarily different manner in Colin J. Horne's 'The Classical Temper in Britain: Origins and Components'[3]. Horne claims that English Protestantism, mercantilism, and science invoked classical authority for their justification, and that 'a contemporary national hero, Sir Isaac Newton' was 'the representative figure for the

2. *Ideas of the Restoration in English Literature, 1660–71*, by Nicholas Jose. Harvard/ Macmillan. pp. xvi + 205. $15, £20. (Rev'd by Cedric D. Reverand II, *Scriblerian*, 1985.)

3. In *The Classical Temper in Western Europe: Papers from the Annual Symposium of the Australian Academy of the Humanities*, ed. by John Hardy and Andrew McCredie. OUPM (1983). pp. vi + 120. £19.

classical temper in Britain'. In 'Commerce Approved, 1650–1700', a chapter in his book[4] on attitudes to capitalism in English literature, John McVeagh maintains that those who approved of commerce – Denham, Waller, Evelyn, Pepys, Thomas Sprat – may at times sound simple-minded, but those who disapproved – Wycherley, Butler, Oldham, Bunyan – often look old-fashioned. Dryden's attitude was ambivalent, but he tended to become more and more suspicious of commerce, as the comparison of *Annus Mirabilis* and *Don Sebastian* shows; in this late play Dryden condemns what Coleridge later saw as the great evil of commerce, the treating of persons as things. This book might be dismissed as a mere survey, but should be recommended as a comparative study.

(a) Poetry

The second part of Pierre Danchin's *Prologues and Epilogues of the Restoration* came out this year[5]. I have already described the work's general character (*YW* 64.272–3): it is a collection of some 1200 of these fugitive pieces, arranged in chronological order, and as a rule printed from the earliest sources. The second part has a valuable introduction covering developments from 1677 to 1690. By that time prologues and epilogues were essentially addresses to theatre audiences written for well-known actors and actresses; often they attack 'the Criticks' and wheedle 'the Ladies'. After the Popish Plot many were primed and loaded with political satire, and fired off separately as broadsides. The satire was usually against the Whigs, but there is evidence that audiences remained politically and socially mixed. The turmoil of the times was often blamed for the problems and poverty of the theatres themselves. Because these pieces are more allusive than those of the earlier period, fuller notes are needed, but broadly the plan of this second part resembles that of the first. Once again Professor Danchin can be congratulated: for finding some pieces which were previously unknown, for bringing together many which were practically inaccessible, and for providing the appropriate critical apparatus. Danchin's 'Prologues et epilogues du théâtre anglais de la Restauration (1660–1700): À propos d'une edition'[6] is based on a conference paper given in 1979 and is largely superseded by the edition itself; but it offers comments on the potential value of the work, and revelations about the difficulties of carrying it out and getting it published in English in France. For many years to come scholars will be indebted both to the tireless energy of Professor Danchin, and to the enlightened attitude of the Presses Universitaires de Nancy. Anthony Kaufman's essay on satirical epilogues is noted in section 1(*b*).

In *The Brink of All We Hate*[7] Felicity A. Nussbaum offers 'a significant

4. *Tradefull Merchants: The Portrayal of the Capitalist in Literature*, by John McVeagh. RKP (1981). pp. xvi + 221. £11.95. (Rev'd, severely, by J. A. Downie, *MLR*; sympathetically, by the editors, *Scriblerian*.)

5. *The Prologues and Epilogues of the Restoration, 1660–1700*. Part II: *1677–1690*, ed. by Pierre Danchin. 2 vols. UNancy. pp. xxxvi + 858; 11 illus. pb. Ffr 355.14.

6. In *Arts du spectacle et histoire des idées: Recueil offert en hommage à Jean Jacquot*. CESR. pp. 325. Ffr 99.

7. *The Brink of All We Hate: English Satires on Women, 1660–1750*, by Felicity A. Nussbaum. UKen. pp. viii + 192. $20. (Rev'd by Douglas Brooks-Davies, *TLS*; by Margaret J. M. Ezell, *SCN*; by Katharine M. Rogers, *JEGP*, 1985.)

sampling' of the 'myths' developed in Restoration and eighteenth-century verse satires on women. These myths – stereotypes seems a better word – include the angel, the learned lady, the irrational creature, the coquette, the whore, and the Amazon. The English tradition of antifeminist satire draws on classical and French sources, especially Ovid, Juvenal, and Boileau; its representatives in our period include Butler, Rochester, and Dryden among major figures, and Oldham, Robert Gould, and Richard Adams among minor ones. The book has some of the uses and limitations of a descriptive survey, but the chapters on Butler and Rochester do support Professor Nussbaum's thesis that an awareness of their literary context helps us to read these poets in a more informed way. They both partly avoid the stereotypes, create credible female figures, and explore real human problems.

In 'Myth and Anti-Myth and the Poetics of Political Events in Two Restoration Poems'[8] Michael G. Ketcham considers Dryden's *Annus Mirabilis* and Marvell's 'Last Instructions to a Painter'. His main argument seems to be that the Virgilian myth-making of *Annus Mirabilis* tries to put the Court party's conduct of the second Dutch War beyond criticism, while the parody of such rhetoric in 'Last Instructions' brings politics back to the realm of rational debate. The essay sustains interest, but perhaps overemphasizes Dryden's propagandist purpose. Ketcham admits that '*Annus Mirabilis* is often an awkward poem', but quotes the line where Charles II 'Out-weeps an Hermit, and out-prays a Saint' without noting a mock-heroic effect at odds with the apparent intention of identifying Charles with Christ.

(b) Drama

The progressive broadening of our view of the Restoration stage has continued this year with the appearance of two major volumes which consider the relation between theatre and the other arts. What is especially heartening is that both present this relationship not as an aspect of background studies but as integral to our grasp of the theatre in general and our understanding of individual plays.

Henry Purcell and the London Stage[9], by Curtis A. Price, rehabilitates Purcell from the accepted view that he was a composer who failed to establish a European tradition of opera in England, instead showing how his music is an essential part of the structure and movement of every play in which it appears. Price is well aware of the problems of writing for both a musical and a dramatic audience, but solves them with an ease that sometimes serves to conceal the range and depth of research which has gone into the book, which rests on sure footings in musicology, theatre history, and dramatic criticism. Purcell's use of key symbolism and the melodic re-creation of verbal images is sensibly defined in the opening chapter, and shown throughout the book to be of great subtlety in underlining dramatic ideas. For example, in 'I look'd and saw within the book of Fate' from Dryden's *The Indian Emperour*, the sudden shift from G minor – associated with death by Purcell – to B flat hints at Montezuma's

---

8. In *Studies in Eighteenth-Century Culture*, Vol. 13, ed. by O. M. Brack Jr. UWisc. pp. xii + 287. $25.

9. *Henry Purcell and the London Stage*, by Curtis A. Price. CUP. pp. xiv + 380; frontis. and 7 pls. £30.

reprieve and thus makes a genuine contribution to the play's growth. In discussing Dryden's *Tyrannick Love*, Price suggests that the duet 'Hark my Damilcar' was first composed for a text in Buckingham's parody *The Rehearsal*. In consequence, Purcell is undercutting the apparently serious meaning of the lyric, supporting the view that the 'rant and bombast' of the play is not meant to be taken seriously. We may well disagree with this, but no matter: Purcell's music is being shown as a vital dimension in the play's tone and movement. Insights of this sort continue throughout the book, through sections on 'Serious Dramas', 'Tragic Extravaganzas', 'Comedies', and the full-scale operas. The music for *The Indian Queen* is shown as integral to the characterization of Zempoalla instead of being 'simply grafted-on entertainment'; that in Southerne's *Sir Anthony Love* shows the eponymous heroine as a 'strong-willed, clever, and somewhat rapacious female rake' – a view shared by Harold Weber in an essay noted in section 3(*b*). Sometimes Purcell's music can solve problems of meaning: the setting of Mrs Lovely's words of apparent contrition near the end of Crowne's *The Married Beau* makes the situation clear, and will 'speak far more distinctly across the centuries than any modern dissertation on Restoration attitudes about marriage'.

Price is equally incisive about the operas. By seeing *Dido and Aeneas* as a monarchist allegory which is 'an affront rather than a compliment to the new monarchs', he solves the theatrical problem of how Dido dies. She does not die, since this would be 'the epitome of bad taste'. Perhaps most important, he sees *The Fairy Queen* as containing Purcell's finest theatre music, although the first act masque should, he argues, be omitted as it was not part of the original conception of the work and 'badly disfigures the drama'. The separation of Purcell's music from Shakespeare's text is not a failure, but the essence of the opera's success, since it allowed the composer to 'build upon the lyricism of the drama without having to stand forever in Shakespeare's shadow'. This is a vibrant and suggestive book which all engaged in Restoration theatre studies should read. Not least of its pleasures are the illustrations which punctuate the text, and the copious music examples which support it.

Similar in both subject and importance is *British Theatre and the Other Arts*[10], a symposium edited by Shirley Strum Kenny. In the opening essay, 'Theatre, Related Arts, and the Profit Motive: An Overview', Kenny chronicles the growth of theatrical painting, music engraving, and the more ephemeral forms of 'theatrical memorabilia', as well as discussing music and spectacle in the theatre, and the links between drama and the novel. It is a valuable and wide-ranging introduction. Judith Milhous's 'The Multimedia Spectacular on the Restoration Stage', which comes next, considers Betterton's 'Dorset Garden spectaculars', comparing them in cast size, rehearsal time, complexity of staging, and musical resources with contemporary plays, to ask why, when they involved vast cost and physical difficulties, they were produced. The answer is reassuring: simply because their richness was a vital stimulus for the company.

The same collection contains two pieces on visual art. 'Looking upon His Like Again: Garrick and the Artist', by Kalman A. Burnim, reproduces and

10. *British Theatre and the Other Arts, 1660–1800*, ed. by Shirley Strum Kenny. Folger/AUP. pp. 311; frontis. and 45 pls. $35.

discusses two paintings by Johann Zoffany of Garrick in Vanbrugh revivals. Robert Halsband's 'Stage Drama as a Source for Pictorial and Plastic Arts' covers a wider range and is useful as a very broad introduction to the subject. There is also a fine article by Arthur H. Scouten, 'The Anti-Evolutionary Development of the London Theatres'. This repudiates the idea of 'an evolutionary progress in the development of English playhouses' which, Scouten argues, arose from a desire to assert the scientific validity of theatre history by adopting a Darwinist approach. It is an incisive, witty, and beautifully controlled essay in which assumptions of earlier historians are demolished and a simpler model of theatre history created on the foundations of architectural realism and the demands of the actors themselves. Other essays from the collection are discussed elsewhere in this chapter and the next. Overall, despite some unevenness, it is a major milestone in the journey towards a properly inclusive awareness of Restoration theatre and, like Price's book on Purcell, should become required reading for students.

Carolyn Kephart sheds 'New Light on the Theatre from *Wit and Mirth: or, Pills to Purge Melancholy*' (*TN*). The article claims to resolve 'many mysteries regarding the dating and placement of the songs, prologues, and epilogues in *Pills* I and II' with regard to seven such pieces, giving details of dates and actors not recorded elsewhere.

A group of separate but related articles discusses aspects of revels, processions, and popular manifestations of theatre. N. W. Bawcutt reports the discovery of 'New Revels Documents of Sir George Buc and Sir Henry Herbert, 1619–1662' (*RES*). These are collections of extracts from the office books of the Master of the Revels, concerning the licensing of freak shows, displays of animals (including 'a strange Ratt'), and exhibitions of 'daunceing on the Roapes, Tumbling, Vaulting and other such like ffeates'. It provides further valuable evidence of the pervasive control of the Revels Office over entertainment of every kind during the Commonwealth. Barry Russell's 'The Case of the Recusant Acrobat' (*TN*) quotes a statement made by the lawyer of Towstan le Young, a strolling player, on the absconding of a man hired by him at Abingdon Hiring Fair in 1668. This reveals the wide range of skills expected of such entertainers: rope-dancing, performance on a number of musical instruments, and acting in 'drolleries and farces' were essential for any aspiring player. Martin N. Walsh, in 'Killigrew's Cap and Bells' (*TN*), examines the suggestions in Pepys and elsewhere that Killigrew held the office of 'King's Foole or Jester' in literal as well as metaphorical terms. He concludes that the dramatist was indeed granted the position by warrant, but that it was an 'empty title' which he accepted for financial reasons, possibly as compensation for the delay in taking up the office of Master of the Revels. The article also has interesting things to say about Archie Armstrong, the last official court fool, and the decadence of the domestic fool both on and off the stage in the 1670s and 1680s. In 'Fabulous Wild Men: American Indians in European Pageants, 1493–1700 (*ThS*) August W. Staub and Robert L. Pinson describe the characterization of 'wild men' in popular pageants, and show how Amerindians in Europe were dressed and presented according to this popular iconography rather than as they really were. This prevented the European onlookers from seeing the Amerindian as 'a fellow human with problems not unlike their own': a disturbing thought, which deserves deeper examination than the article provides, especially in the light of plays such as Southerne's *Oroonoko*.

Robert Poole's 'Lancashire Wakes Week' (*HT*) is a general but finely illustrated history of the annual pageant. Not unrelated to such topics is Harold Weber's 'Rakes, Rogues, and the Empire of Misrule' (*HLQ*), since it is concerned mainly with the rogue in picaresque fiction. Rakes and rogues both 'make related but distinct challenges' to bourgeois society, by showing a subversive desire for freedom as well as – by the way they are regarded – asserting the need for order. Although the main focus is on fiction, the article has useful things to say about the rake's function of revealing 'the desires, frustrations, and fears of the audience'.

Robert D. Hume discusses 'The Origins of the Actor Benefit in London' (*ThR*). After listing the various practices from which the actor benefit might have evolved, he suggests that they began in 1696 at Drury Lane after the model of the 'third night benefit' for actors. This explains the proliferation of the 'actor's play' (twenty-six in the last decade of the century): when the Patent Company was unable to pay them, the actors simply took to writing or arranging plays and claiming the third night's takings as 'dramatist's benefit'. Actors at Lincoln's Inn Fields soon followed suit – 'probably no later than 1699'. The article usefully extends our awareness of theatre finances and the relation between actors and management at this period. Theatre history of a more tangible kind is the subject of R. Jordan's 'Observations on the Backstage Area in the Restoration Theatre' (*TN*). This takes as its starting point some depositions concerning the death of one Captain Goring after a brawl over who was to escort Elizabeth Barry to her dressing room after a performance in 1685. Jordan argues lucidly that these show 'the existence of dressing rooms set one above the other', probably in tiers along both sides of the stage, and linked by backstage passages. That the brawl was heard by other actors suggests that the rooms were flimsily constructed; that the rival suitors were able to reach the backstage area suggests that passages connected the auditorium and stage.

J. Douglas Canfield's 'The Ideology of Restoration Tragicomedy' (*ELH*) represents a continuation of the generic school of criticism. It challenges the view that tragicomedies elevate form to the detriment of meaning, by examining the growth of the genre. Central to it, in Canfield's view, is the idea of sexual fidelity as a reinforcement of aristocratic power. This is present in both the 'unified' and the 'divided' tragicomedies, all of which have an 'ideological coherence' and re-affirm aristocratic values strongly. Dryden's *Marriage à-la-Mode* is 'the jewel of the genre', its themes 'coherent and profound'. The essay is perhaps overargued, but it is a useful counter to the poor regard in which tragicomedy is often held. *Domestic Tragedy in English: Brief Survey*[11], by Ada Lou Carson and Herbert L. Carson, has little of value or interest to say about the Restoration, being mainly concerned with a derivative and reductive discussion of the shift to bourgeois sentimental comedy. In 'The Smiler with the Knife: Covert Aggression in Some Restoration Epilogues' (*SLitI*) Anthony Kaufman makes some general observations on epilogues, and considers those to *The Country Wife*, *Amphitryon*, and Southerne's *The Wives' Excuse* as 'subtle extensions of the plays' satiric themes'.

---

11. *Domestic Tragedy in English: Brief Survey*, by Ada Lou Carson and Herbert L. Carson. SSPDPT 67. 2 vols in one. USalz (1982). pp. 465. pb. Sch 245.

2. Dryden

James M. Hall's *John Dryden: A Reference Guide*[12] is an annotated bibliography of some 2600 editions, books, dissertations, and shorter writings from 1668 to 1981. The arrangement is chronological, but there is an excellent index of authors, titles, and subjects. In a brief introduction Hall discerns four phases of Dryden's reputation: to his death in 1700; to Johnson's *Life* in 1779; to Van Doren's book in 1920; and to the present. For the first three phases 'much remains to be done', especially on the periodical literature of the eighteenth and nineteenth centuries; 'what appears here should be taken as only representative of what might have been listed'. But Hall is probably safe in saying that Dryden's reputation declined in the third phase and revived in the fourth. As about two-thirds of the items listed belong to the fourth phase, perhaps a fifth should be distinguished: that of the Dryden industry. This went into full production soon after World War II, but has now perhaps gone into recession. In 1961 the annual production exceeded fifty items for the first time; in 1972 it reached one hundred; in 1979 it fell below fifty again. Many theses remain unpublished. The reference books Hall recommends for those interested in recent criticism and research do not include *YW*, so I had better point out that during the years 1973–80 I mentioned over thirty items he omits. These include some interesting articles, such as those by Derek Attridge (*YW* 60.228), Eric Havelock (*YW* 55.304), and Willard Spiegelman (*YW* 55.305); some useful editions, such as those by Philip Roberts (*YW* 55.302–3) and N. J. Andrew (*YW* 56.229); and the personal selection by W. H. Auden (*YW* 54.259). Some of these omissions may be owing to the policy – mistaken I think – of not including 'school texts'. A more important comparison is with D. J. Latt and S. H. Monk's bibliography (*YW* 57.190–1), which is fuller for the years they survey, 1895–1974, but of course does not include the items, some 650 in all, from the earlier and later years. And it is not annotated; Hall's notes are often quite detailed. Altogether this is an intelligent and approachable guide, which should be available in university libraries.

Several short articles will be of interest to Dryden's future biographers. Alan Roper's 'Bringing Home the Bacon in a New Dryden Letter' (*ClarkN*, 1983) reports an additional letter from Dryden to his kinswoman Mrs Elizabeth Steward, in which he thanks her for a chine of bacon. Roper gives a transcript of the letter, suggests that there is more to be said about parallels between the Steward correspondence and the *Fables*, and includes for good measure a family tree based on the one signed by John Driden of Chesterton in 1684. Paul Hammond's 'Dryden's Library' (*N&Q*) describes a copy of Daniel Heinsius's edition of Virgil, with corrections in Dryden's hand, and argues that James Osborne was mistaken in thinking that Dryden owned either the British Library copy of Josua Poole's *English Parnassus* or Ms. Harley 3253. David Hopkins's 'An Unrecorded Epigram on Dryden' (ibid.) records a verse inscribed in his copy of Dryden's *Poems* (1701), which refers to the attacks on Dryden by Sir Richard Blackmore and Jeremy Collier.

Dryden's future biographers will inevitably make use of two major sources: Dryden's own work, and Johnson's *Life*. Thomas H. Fujimura's ' "Autobiography" in Dryden's Later Work' (*Restoration*) finds that the later work

---

12. *John Dryden: A Reference Guide*, by James M. Hall. Hall. pp. xx + 424. $50.

expresses his 'perplexity and anguish' after the Revolution of 1688. *Don Sebastian*, *Amphitryon*, *Eleonora*, *Cleomenes*, and the translation of Juvenal's third satire 'repeat the same insistent pattern – of a man of integrity who is deposed, exiled, rejected, or even driven to suicide, but who rises superior to his foes and his times, often in the face of an inscrutable universe'. Here Fujimura is himself insistent on ideas he has put forward before, notably in 'The Personal Element in Dryden's Poetry' (*PMLA*, 1974; *YW* 55.303). Fujimura's Dryden is a romantic, not to say Conradian, figure. Maximillian E. Novak's 'Johnson, Dryden, and the Wild Vicissitudes of Taste'[13] praises both the biographical and the critical parts of Johnson's *Life*, and maintains that Johnson, especially when compared with some modern scholars, had a thorough knowledge of Restoration history and a profound understanding of Dryden. Sir William Empson's biographical and critical studies of Dryden, 'Dryden's Apparent Scepticism' and 'A Deist Tract' (*YW* 51.245; 56.230) have been reprinted in his *Using Biography* (see section 3(*a*) below).

(a) Poetry
There are proposals to add one poem to the Dryden canon, to take one away, and to distinguish two versions of another. John Barnard and Paul Hammond's 'Dryden and a Poem for Lewis Maidwell' (*TLS*) proposes the addition. A Brotherton Library manuscript consists of a Latin grammar by Maidwell prefaced by two poems, one by Nahum Tate, and one signed 'J. Drydon'. The text of the latter is given in full. Maidwell was a friend of both Tate and Dryden, who were themselves closely associated at the time the manuscript was probably written, 1677–1684. The poem suggests that J. Drydon and Maidwell had the same 'Reverend Master', and both Dryden and Maidwell had been educated at Westminster under Dr Richard Busby. While the poem as a whole is not very good, it has some lines which are worthy of Dryden and some words and phrases which are characteristic. There is some correspondence about the poem in the *TLS*. Alan Roper argues that it was almost certainly written in 1684, but should not be attributed to Dryden, because the circumstantial evidence is not good enough, and the poem itself is too bad. David Yonge explains and justifies its metaphor of refining coins. Barnard and Hammond accept Roper's revised dating, but consider the evidence and the poem better than he allows, and maintain that it is Dryden's. Hammond's 'Did Dryden Write the *Prologue to "Julius Caesar"*?' (*ES*) casts doubt on the authenticity of this poem, which has been attributed to Dryden by James Kinsley and other authorities. Its presence in *Covent Garden Drollery* (1672) alongside poems which are certainly Dryden's does not prove that it is too. It lacks his characteristic shaping of lines and paragraphs, and its argument about Shakespeare and Jonson is at odds with Dryden's comparisons of them elsewhere. Hammond concludes that it must be 'the work of one who has caught up some of the current commonplaces of critical debate and presented them in a slapdash form', though he is open to persuasion otherwise before deciding to omit it from the forthcoming Longman Annotated Poets edition. In 'Dryden's Revision of *To the Lady Castlemain*' (*PBSA*) Hammond collates

13. In *The Unknown Samuel Johnson*, ed. by John J. Burke Jr and Donald Kay. UWisc (1983). pp. xi + 182. $30.

the two early printed and four manuscript versions. The poem that Dryden intended Lady Castlemaine to read in the 1660s can be reconstructed; the poem that he authorized for publication appeared in the 1693 *Examen Poeticum*. A modern editor may print either, but should not conflate them, as the Oxford and California editors do. In 'A Crux in *Mac Flecknoe*' (*Scriblerian*) Pat Rogers suggests that 'A— Hall' may be 'Arm'rers Hall', which is 'metrically viable, topographically plausible, and poetically inoffensive'. In a letter to *Scriblerian* David M. Vieth rejects this idea, pointing out that twelve early manuscripts read *'Aston-Hall'* or *'Ashton-hall'*, with variants in accidentals. He still believes there is an allusion to Thomas Shadwell's friend Edmund Ashton.

General studies of Dryden as a poet included two broadly favourable estimates, and one broadly unfavourable. Ian Jack's 'Dryden: Servant to the King'[14] shows how Dryden's 'instinct to serve as the official poet of his age' assured him of an increasing readership throughout his career, 'and even helped him to make the transition to the new order of things after 1688'. The essay includes some interesting speculation and information: on the cause of Dryden's attack on Shadwell, and on the subscribers to his edition of Virgil. As a whole it makes a good introduction to Dryden. Harold Love's 'Dryden's Rationale of Paradox' (*ELH*) defines 'paradoxes of explanation': they are a more serious and structural type of paradox than the 'Dalilahs of the theatre' Love illustrated in an earlier essay (*ECS*, 1978; *YW* 59.223). He contends that the poet sought to understand life through a variety of explanations rather than a system of thought, and disputes Laura Brown's view (*PMLA*, 1982; *YW* 63.231–2) that Dryden's inconsistencies betray a confused sense of the discord between conservative theory and historical fact. He concludes that for Dryden,

> as for all good poets, the test of what is known is that it has been lived, and the test of the living that the world has been experienced in all its complexity and in the fullness of its contradictions and discontinuities.

To take the argument a little further: the good poet is not vexed when contraries meet in one, and avoids irritable reaching after fact and reason. But Nicholas Jose's 'Dryden and Other Selves' (*CR*, 1983) argues that Dryden cannot 'sustain his best poetry for more than a few lines at a time'. Mainly on the evidence of the 'Character of a Good Parson', the epistles to John Driden, Kneller, and Congreve, and the Oldham elegy, Jose suggests that Dryden often so merges his identity with that of his subject that we lack a clear idea of either; his 'poetic self' tends to be a parasite on other selves. When this parasitism is somehow checked, as in the Anne Killigrew ode and the Zimri portrait, the other person is imagined better, and the poetry is more interesting. And yet Jose's Dryden blest with 'fluidity of selfhood' much resembles Dryden's Zimri, 'every thing by starts, and nothing long'.

Now for studies of specific poems, in roughly chronological order. James A. Winn's 'The Promise of Dryden's Elegy for Hastings' (*MLR*) persuasively relates this early essay in versification to Dryden's later achievements in panegyric and satire. The elegy exhibits not only technical awkwardness but also organizational skill, and expresses not only extravagant grief at the death

14. In *The Poet and his Audience*, by Ian Jack. CUP. pp. viii + 193. pb £6.95.

of Hastings but also genuine nostalgia for the passing of the court of Charles I. Dryden's sense of having been born too late and longing for an irrecoverable past are already detectable. Michael Cordner's 'Dryden's "Astraea Redux" and Fanshawe's "Ode"' (*N&Q*) shows how Dryden's poem both recalls the language of panegyric used by Sir Richard Fanshawe and others about Charles I, and seeks to purge it of any associations with Cromwell possibly acquired during the interregnum.

An Italian view of *Absalom and Achitophel* was a not unwelcome novelty this year. In 'The Augustan Ideal of Order as Form and Content in *Absalom and Achitophel*'[15] Antonella Piazza Coppola 'tries to penetrate the unifying imaginative organization running through the structure of the poem, which is divided into four parts according to the balancing alternation of satirical and epic modes'. The first and third parts (ll. 1–149 and 490–932) are satirical, and the second and fourth are epic. The poem as a whole is an epic or at least a 'witty heroic poem', rather than a satire, and 'probably the most effective section' is the second, the temptation scene. The essay is unfortunately seasoned with jargon. In 'Dryden's History: The Case of Slingsby Bethel' (*HLQ*) Robert W. McHenry Jr compares the historical Bethel with the poetical Shimei, and argues that we need to know more about the character of the one to appreciate the artistry of the other. In ' "The Sons of Belial" in *Absalom and Achitophel*' (*ELN*) McHenry discerns in this phrase an allusion to the story of the false witnesses against Naboth in 1 Kings 21.10 and in John Caryll's *Naboth's Vineyard* (1679), an attack on the corrupt trials following the Popish Plot. Dryden's object was to associate Bethel and the exclusionists with Titus Oates and the other disreputable witnesses. I would suggest that a possible source for Dryden's phrase 'sheds his Venome' (l. 229) and Caryll's 'pour'd his Venom in her Ear' (l. 177) is Milton's description of Satan 'close at the ear of Eve ... inspiring venom' (*Paradise Lost*, IV.800–4).

Dryden's attempts at explaining his religion prompted some diverse commentaries. In 'Reading and/as Swerving' G. Douglas Atkins considers 'The Quest(ion) of Interpretive Authority in Dryden's *Religio Laici*'[16]. Atkins has published his views on this poem twice already, but has since been converted to deconstruction, so new readings or misreadings are required, though his old ones are not invalidated. He now believes that Dryden's use of figurative language inevitably makes him 'swerve' from his declared purpose. The poem asserts that man both can and cannot comprehend God; hence it is 'heterogeneous, dialogical, bifurcated, different from "itself"', for what the text describes differs from, indeed wars with, what it declares'; and hence it is 'unreadable in the sense that no complete understanding, no fully present comprehension, is possible'. Atkins relies heavily on supposed ambiguities (not a word he uses, incidentally) in ll. 39–41. But are these lines ambiguous? I think they simply suggest that man cannot fathom God. And even if they are, does new deconstructive philosophy call the whole poem in doubt? Everyone

---

15. In *Studi di letteratura e di linguistica*, Quaderno 3, by various authors. Pubblicazioni dell'Università degli Studi di Salerno, Sezione di studi filologici letterari e artistici, 7. ESI. pp. 140.

16. In *Reading Deconstruction: Deconstructive Reading*, by G. Douglas Atkins. UKen (1983). pp. x + 158. $18. (Rev'd by Chris Norris, *TLS*; by Elias F. Mengel, *Scriblerian*, 1985.)

knows that complete understanding of complex poems is impossible, but it does not follow that they are all muddled. In '*Religio Laici* and the Principle of Legal Continuity' (*PLL*) Anne Barbeau Gardiner offers a detailed commentary on the ideas in the poem. Dryden maintains that divine law is like English common law in that it must be interpreted according to precedent. In their various ways the deists, Catholics, and sectarians offend against the principle of legal continuity and threaten the '*Common quiet*' in church and state. When he becomes a Catholic apologist in *The Hind and the Panther* Dryden does not offend against this principle, but urges that infallibility is part of the ancient constitution of the church. Incidentally Professor Gardiner's argument that 'the *Deist*' is associated with Shaftesbury could be supported by noting that both their deities will 'wink at Crimes' (*The Medall*, l. 282; *Religio Laici*, l. 100). An approach differing widely from Gardiner's and more subtly from Atkins's informs the next essay. In 'The Poetry of *The Hind and the Panther*' (*MLR*) D. W. Jefferson maintains that neither this poem nor *Religio Laici* should be treated as if they were works of apologetics written in prose. A theological position may be deduced from *The Hind and the Panther*, but its poetry conveys Dryden's imaginative response to religion, which for Jefferson is more individual, and more inspired than his 'thought'. There are confessional passages, but the 'complex artifice' of the beast fable 'more truly represents his genius':

> There never was a beast fable with such a daring range of treatment. . . .
> The main fable, that of the two beasts, is on a sufficiently huge scale, but
> it contains within itself the two bird fables, each developed with con-
> siderable fullness and piquancy. This is a massive conception . . .

Jefferson relies a good deal on quotation and enthusiastic commentary, and sometimes calls to mind Bayes ('Gadsookers, what a conceipt is there!') but as always he praises Dryden eloquently; few critics have done more than Jefferson for Dryden as a poet (*YW* 63.233–4; 46.216; 35.146–7).

Articles on Dryden's later poetry included Donald R. Benson's 'Space, Time, and the Language of Transcendence in Dryden's Later Poetry' (*Restoration*). Benson interprets the Anne Killigrew ode and *Eleonora* as solutions to the problem of affirming moral and spiritual transcendence on the assumptions of Newtonian ontology. It strikes me that, faced with such a problem, Dryden's Muse could have been forgiven for deserting him entirely. Douglas Murray's 'Dryden's Inversion to Disorder in *Alexander's Feast*' (*Scriblerian*) notes that in the sources Timotheus first enrages and then calms Alexander. Dryden inverts the sequence of events, thus denigrating both of them and emphasizing the power of music to bring about disorder.

Some of Dryden's translations figure prominently in Charles Tomlinson's Clark Lectures[17] on the translation of Ovid and other poets. Tomlinson emphasizes Dryden's contributions to 'that neglected classic', Sir Samuel Garth's composite edition of the *Metamorphoses* in English, and sees him as 'the Poundian figure of his age'. The epithet is meant to be honorific but may be thought unhappy; it honours Dryden's inspiration and correction of the

---

17. *Poetry and Metamorphosis*, by Charles Tomlinson. CUP (1983). pp. xii + 97. £9.95.

work of other poets, but not his patriotic motives. Tomlinson writes enthusiastically about the stories of Ceyx and Alcyone, Baucis and Philemon, and Deucalion and Pyrrha, believing that if they were better known they would enable us to see Ovid 'translated to a higher plane', where Dryden is 'the poet of the tenderness and pathos of married love'. Janice Haney-Peritz also praises Dryden as a translator in 'Dryden's Ethical Experiment: A Reading of "Horace. Ode 29. Book 3."' (*JEGP*), claiming that this fine poem 'has evoked little interpretive commentary' but not mentioning H. A. Mason's (*CQ*, 1981; *YW* 62.247). In a lively, complex, and perhaps overingenious essay she associates Dryden's metrical, ethical, and political concerns. To summarize: the harmonies of Horace, Pindar, and Dryden himself represent both the ethics of pleasure, power, and strength, and the political postures of feeble retirement, military force, and magnanimous resolution. Dryden's ideal is represented by the ninth stanza; the harmonies and ethics of Pindar and Horace return in the tenth and last, but we feel that something is missing.

(b) Plays

Two essays on Dryden's adaptations aroused my interest. George R. Guffey's 'Politics, Weather, and the Contemporary Reception of the Dryden–Davenant *Tempest*' (*Restoration*) points out apparent allusions to foreign politics and the severe gales of early 1667. Dryden and Davenant altered Shakespeare's play so that it could refer to the relationships between Savoy, Milan, and Mantua in the later seventeenth century, and perhaps to those between France, Spain, and England. This essay explains why the adaptation was enjoyed more by Restoration audiences than it is by modern critics. Melissa Cowansage's 'The Libertine–Libertarian Dichotomy in Dryden's *The State of Innocence*' (*ELN*) contends that this version of *Paradise Lost* is a drama about 'the receptiveness of innocence to determinism'; Dryden's Adam is so innocent that he tragically fails to take free will into account. The argument is well worth developing but seems debatable in its present form. In 'Milton's Ideal of Innocence' (*CritQ*, 1982) I have suggested that Dryden tried to obviate Johnson's criticism of *Paradise Lost*: 'it comprises neither human actions nor human manners'. Dryden makes Adam and Eve not more innocent than Milton's but more recognizably human; their fall may therefore seem less catastrophic.

As usual *All for Love* received disproportionate attention. Charles H. Hinnant's '*All for Love* and the Heroic Ideal' (*Genre*, 1983) answers critics who think the play sentimental. The lovers, Ventidius, Octavia, and 'even Charmion and Iras' achieve the heroic ideal of self-transcendence; Dolabella, Serapion, Caesar, and Alexas exhibit the Hobbesian preoccupation with self-preservation. The former triumph over their 'creaturely limitations', but the latter descend to mawkish pathos and cold rationalism. Harry M. Solomon's 'Tragic Reconciliation: An Hegelian Analysis of *All for Love*' (*SP*) agrees with Hinnant at least in finding previous criticism unsatisfactory. Solomon believes that the Hegelian approach enables us to see in Dryden's tragedy 'the vital working of a necessity which, itself self-reposing, resolves every conflict and contradiction'. Aubrey Williams's 'The Decking of Ruins: Dryden's *All for Love*' (*SoAR*) follows Hinnant and Solomon in noting the discrepancy between the play itself and Dryden's preface: the play seems to exalt 'unlawful love', and the preface seems to moralize about it. Williams explains his own ambivalent response in a detailed analysis of the imagery, which suggests that Antony is at once decked by Cleopatra's fruitful vines, and ruined by her wanton ivy.

(c) Prose

In 'Dryden's *Discourse* and "Bi-partite Structure" in the Design of Formal Verse Satire' (*ELN*) Peter J. Schakel disputes some arguments of Mary Claire Randolph's 'The Structural Design of the Formal Verse Satire' (*PQ*, 1942). She was mistaken in thinking, or in thinking that Dryden thought, that bi-partite structure was a characteristic feature of Roman verse satire. The *Discourse concerning Satire* shows that what he actually thought was that a balance of praise and blame ought to be characteristic of all satire. Professor Randolph's essay is not just an Aunt Sally; having been reprinted in Bernard N. Schilling's *Essential Articles for the Study of English Augustan Backgrounds* (1961) it has been influential, at least in America.

3. Other Authors

(a) Poets

The last words of Sir William Empson on Marvell, a first edition of the poems of Dudley, fourth Lord North, a new edition of Rochester, and a book on John Oldham, were the chief contributions.

Three essays mainly about Marvell as a Restoration figure are included in Empson's *Using Biography*[18]: 'Natural Magic and Populism in Marvell's Poetry' has been published before (*YW* 60.229); 'Other People's Views' praises J. P. Kenyon's Hull tercentenary lecture on Marvell (*YW* 60.205,229) and condemns most of the York tercentenary lectures except those by Christopher Ricks and John Carey (*YW* 59.199,227); 'The Marriage of Marvell', a new fifty-page essay, seeks to 'explode Tupper' (the American authority on the subject) and to prove that Mary Palmer was not lying when she claimed she and Marvell were secretly married. Broadly, Empson's argument is that literary criticism and biographical speculation are more nearly allied than American New Criticism ever allowed; that New Criticism was mainly an excuse for 'neo-Christian' interpretations; and that such interpretations of Marvell and Dryden are untenable in view of the paganism of the one and the deism of the other. What about the populism? What about the populism indeed: it accounts for Marvell's early poem praising mowers, his marriage to Mrs Palmer, and his later poems attacking courtiers. Empson believes Marvell felt his sexual potency was threatened by ladies, but found it was restored by his landlady. The essay on Marvell's marriage reads like a good historical novel, and only left me wondering what advice Marvell had from Milton.

The writings of Dudley, fourth Lord North, are nowadays unknown, ignored, or confused with those of his father: a moderately regrettable state of

18. *Using Biography*, by William Empson. C&W. pp. viii + 259. £12.95. (Rev'd by Christopher Ricks, *LRB*; by Jonathan Culler, *TLS*.)

affairs which should be illuminated by Dale B. J. Randall's *Gentle Flame*[19]. This includes a biography, an edition of North's poems, a bibliography of printed and manuscript sources, and an invaluable genealogical chart. North emerges as a representative figure of his times: instinctively loyal to the monarchy, reluctantly involved with the parliamentarians, purged by Colonel Pride, pardoned by Charles II. In his retirement he wrote a book on how to run a great house on a small income. His verse was written at intervals throughout his life in a variety of genres, but more often than not in iambic pentameter couplets, 'tending towards the sententious and the commonsensical . . . hovering only slightly above prose'; indeed demanding the epithet Neoclassical. His son John, who became Professor of Greek at Cambridge, thought the verse 'to bee such as may pass under the most critical eye & censorious Judgement', but it was not meant for publication. It has survived in manuscript and has now been edited with a full account of the text, a critical discussion, and extensive notes. This is a wholly scholarly work and a nicely produced volume.

Rochester Studies, 1925–1982: An Annotated Bibliography by David M. Vieth (Garland) was not available for review. The new edition of Rochester's *Poems*, by Keith Walker[20], seeks to improve on Vieth's, which was published in 1968 and described as 'likely to remain definitive for a long time to come' (*YW* 49.229–30). On the canon of the poems Walker differs only slightly. In his introduction he mentions having eliminated one poem ('Trust not that thing called woman', known to be by Ben Jonson) and restored two ('Why do'st thou shade thy lovely face' and 'The Heaven drinks each Day a Cup'). He adds these and 'I Rise at Eleven' to Vieth's section of 'Poems Possibly by Rochester', and subtracts from it five others, which he elevates to the poems probably or certainly by the poet. He also differs from Vieth in thinking that 'A Session of the Poets' could be by Rochester, and includes it in an appendix. These procedures might have been better explained. On the chronology, Walker considers Vieth's attempt to arrange the poems in a chronological sequence was a failure, so he re-arranges them in sections determined mainly by genre, though within the sections the order remains 'a conjectural chronological one'. On the very difficult problem of the choice of copy-texts, Walker has done much independent research but has in the main reached the same conclusions as Vieth. However, Vieth thought there was no basis for an old-spelling text and modernized almost everything, including the punctuation; Walker aims at presenting the poems as they were read in Rochester's lifetime, and is at pains to reproduce the peculiarities of the texts and manuscripts. Most of his departures from copy are recorded in the textual notes, which are fuller than Vieth's. Walker's explanatory notes make good use of the critical and scholarly work of the last fifteen years, especially Jeremy Treglown's, and answer most questions about authorship, date, publication, obscurities, and allusions. One blurb-claim, that these poems have 'only been available in poor, unsatisfactory editions', seems a gratuitous insult to Vieth and other editors; but another, that in this edition 'they have been printed to

19. *Gentle Flame: The Life and Verse of Dudley, Fourth Lord North (1602–1677)*, by Dale B. J. Randall. DukeU (1983). pp. xviii + 254; 3 pls. $40. (Rev'd by Margaret J. M. Ezell, *SCN*, 1985.)

20. *The Poems of John Wilmot, Earl of Rochester*, ed. by Keith Walker. Blackwell. pp. xx + 319. £35. (Rev'd by Conrad Russell, *LRB*; by Claude Rawson, *TLS*, 1985.)

be read and enjoyed' is largely justified. The book is nicely printed and highly readable, but – in hardback at least – very expensive.

Critical studies of Rochester continue to arouse interest and to prompt reply. Paul Hammond's 'Was Rochester an Artist?' (*CQ*, 1983) is a review-article on the recent symposium *Spirit of Wit* (*YW* 63.235–6). Hammond notes that the poet's text is more unsettled than his critics sometimes realize, and argues that his work is less artistic than they generally assume. The lyrics are very variable; the satires historically important and momentarily brilliant, but sadly ill-considered. So for Hammond, 'Rochester's poetry describes a world in which values are dissolving, and it not only depicts this state but is itself part of it'. Rochester's modern critics should be in similar difficulties, but Ken Robinson's 'The Art of Violence in Rochester's Satire' (*YES*[21]) struck me as an acute and forceful account of satiric cruelty in the invectives, lampoons, epigrams, and impromptus. It has become a commonplace of academic criticism that Augustan satire serves positive and affirmative ends; but Robinson shows that in these poems at least Rochester's violence may be susceptible of artistic control, but it is not compatible with moral affirmation. Tom Brown was not far from the truth when he said of Rochester that 'reforming the Age was none of his Province'.

One of the most puzzling satires inspired two further essays. Isabelle White's ' "So Great a Disproportion": Paradox and Structure in Rochester's *A Satyr against Reason and Mankind*' (*Restoration*) has been published before (*KPAB*, 1976) and is reprinted without much alteration, though in a footnote Professor White explains how her essay differs from James E. Gill's 'Mind against Itself' (*TSLL*, 1981; *YW* 62.250). She believes that in this poem the paradoxes leave 'the speaker . . . divided against himself in a world of moral disorder'; its tensions 'cannot be resolved into a satisfying logical and unified pattern', though they 'can at least be understood'. This speaker does not seem sharply distinguished from Rochester himself, who is 'skeptical of fulfillment' but 'still yearns for it'. A. D. Cousins's 'The Context, Design, and Argument of Rochester's *A Satyr against Reason and Mankind*' (*SEL*) seemed to me a better essay, having the merits of clarity and concision, though perhaps leaving Rochester excessively cut and dried. Cousins relates the satire to the other poems, and suggests that it is distinguishable as 'Rochester's attempt to locate, within the world of Charles's failed rule, a basis for a genuine restoration of order to the individual and society'. The broad features of its design are the two deliberative orations and the paradoxical epilogue; the main conclusions of its argument are that while man cannot be changed, right reason can order human behaviour; hence a good man is a theoretical if unlikely possibility.

Oldham's critics are a comparatively small and overworked band, troubled by the feeling that their poet has few readers. In *John Oldham*[22] James Zigerell gives a preliminary biographical sketch, a critical discussion of the 'Satire against Virtue' and other early poems which may have impressed Rochester and 'the wits', a long chapter on the *Satires upon the Jesuits*, a rather short one

---

21. *YES* (1984) was also issued in book form: *English Satire and the Satiric Tradition*, ed. by Claude Rawson. Blackwell. pp. xiii + 289. hb £22.50, pb £7.50.

22. *John Oldham*, by James Zigerell. TEAS 372. Twayne (1983). pp. xii + 145; frontis. $16.95.

on the imitations, and a very short one on the poet's reputation. The book is clearly written, quotes Oldham quite often, and achieves its aim of providing an introduction or 'overview'. But on important critical questions Zigerell seems confused. The *Satires upon the Jesuits* are seen as Oldham's 'major work' and almost half the book is devoted to them and their background. Then we are told:

> It is unfortunate that most students of the period seldom get beyond the more loudly abusive works of Oldham like the *Satires Upon the Jesuits*, for it is in his imitations of Horace and Juvenal and a writer of his own century, Boileau, that he can be most readable.

Likewise we are first told that 'Oldham's real talent was for invective and the direct attack', but later that 'unfortunately, as is too often the case with him, Oldham is least effective when he goes on the direct attack'. Zigerell's views should surely have made him give more space to the imitations, which he rightly considers historically important and comparatively readable. He would probably have reached clearer conclusions if he had read some of the criticism of Earl Miner, Ken Robinson, Raman Selden, or Paul Hammond, but his bibliography lists nothing more recent than 1972. It is headed 'Selective Bibliography', and the same adjective might have been applied to the index. In 'Oldham, Pope, and Restoration Satire' (*YES*[21]) Raman Selden argues simultaneously that 'any rehabilitation of Oldham requires a thorough reconsideration of his place in the tradition of Augustan satire', and that his poetry is 'distinctive, not merely derivative or anticipatory'. Dr Selden tries to do too much in one essay, though he succeeds in suggesting that Oldham's range was considerable; it includes 'Rochesterian intensity of feeling, metaphysical hyperbole, Ovidian passion, pastoral pathos, Elizabethan–Juvenalian vehemence, heroic rant, and poetry of irony and comic reversal'. There is evidence that Pope read him carefully and assimilated aspects of his work. In 'An Echo of Oldham in Johnson' (*N&Q*) James A. Means compares a couplet from 'Loyola's Will' with one from *The Vanity of Human Wishes*.

In 'The Rediscovery of Thomas Traherne' (*TLS*) Hilton Kelliher gives a brief but not perfectly clear history of the recovery of the Traherne manuscripts, and draws attention to the British Library's purchase of the 'Commentaries of Heaven'. In 'Traherne's Apostasy' (*DUJ*) Michael J. Ponsford maintains that Traherne's thought was deeply influenced by the philosophers of the Neoplatonic revival, especially Marsilio Ficino, Niccolò de Cusa, and Pico della Mirandola; and that his work is generally consistent with the theology of Pelagius, so it belongs essentially to the Restoration. Traherne tends to deny the doctrine of original sin, to see the fall (or 'apostacie') as a loss of 'the first Light which shined in my Infancy in its Primitive and Innocent Clarity', and to believe that this vision can be recovered through an effort of will; such ideas are wholly at odds with the Augustinian theology which still predominated in the earlier seventeenth century. Ponsford does not mention Barbara Kiefer Lewalski's *Protestant Poetics and the Seventeeth-Century Religious Lyric*, now reprinted in paperback[23], but his impression of Traherne as thinker and poet is

---

23. *Protestant Poetics and the Seventeenth-Century Religious Lyric*, by Barbara Kiefer Lewalski. Princeton. pp. xiv + 536; 25 illus. pb £12.20. (Rev'd at length by Louis Martz, *MP*, 1982.)

not readily compatible with hers. She is not unaware of Neoplatonic influences which 'appear to set him apart' from the other religious poets, but the aim of her book is to emphasize Protestant and English sources rather than Catholic and continental ones, so she argues that 'the fundamental elements of the Protestant poetics shape Traherne's poetry'.

In 'The Derby MS Book of Cotton's Poems and "Contentation" Reconsidered' (*SB*) Alvin I. Dust corrects and expands his earlier work (*Lib*, 1975; *YW* 56.231). He now thinks that 'Contentation' could have been written as early as 1666, and that 'An Elegie' ('How was I blest') could be an early poem addressed to Mary Cromwell FitzHerbert. Dust's attitude to Stephen Parks (a rival authority) is more conciliatory, and though he does not note Parks's recent essay on the Derby manuscript (*YW* 64.283) he agrees with him in thinking that the Yale manuscript was originally part of it. The binding of the Derby one has so deteriorated that a more accurate bibliographical description is possible; but if it is now rebound 'possibilities of further studies of this type – I hope not necessary – will be diminished'.

(b) Dramatists

Two short articles discuss early Restoration plays. 'Iago at Lincoln's Inn Fields: Thomas Porter's *The Villain* on the Early Restoration Stage' (*SEL*), by J. P. Vander Motten, examines Porter's debt to *Othello* and tries to explain the play's success when performed just after a revival of *The Duchess of Malfi* in 1662. There are clear similarities in the jealousy of Porter's Malignii, Charlotte's 'willow song', and the brawl between Boutefou and Beaupres, as well as in larger areas of 'construction and effect'. The play is the 'earliest dramatic commentary on Iago in the Restoration period', and is important in showing that imitations, as well as revivals and adaptations of Shakespeare, were significant in meeting 'the repertorial needs of the moment'. John Horden's 'Sir William Killigrew's *Four New Plays* (1666) with his *Imperial Tragedy* (1669): A Second Annotated Copy' (*Lib*) records a new copy of the plays, extensively annotated by Killigrew, now in the Brotherton Library at Leeds. Killigrew's authorship of *The Imperial Tragedy* was confirmed by Joseph S. Johnston Jr in 1977 on the discovery of a revised copy of *Four New Plays* in the Rosenbach Library (*YW* 57.198), and Killigrew's revisions of *The Seege of Urbin* in that volume were recorded by Johnston and J. P. Vander Motten (*YW* 64.284). This new copy offers further evidence of authorial revision, and the proposed parallel text of both copies will be of value in showing the working methods of a practising dramatist in the early Restoration. Martin N. Walsh's 'Killigrew's Cap and Bells' (*TN*) is noted in section 1(*b*).

Wycherley continues to attract much critical attention. James Thompson's *Language in Wycherley's Plays: Seventeenth-Century Language Theory and Drama*[24] argues that, in spite of being seen as 'dark' or subversive, the comedies assert the primacy of established aristocratic social structure through their use of language. This is possible because, despite the satiric and ironic functions of language, the contemporary ideology of words as instruments of moral and political rectitude ultimately triumphs. Restoration ethics stressed propriety of language and consequently mistrusted metaphor: irony and satire

24. *Language in Wycherley's Plays: Seventeenth-Century Language Theory and Drama*, by James Thompson. UAla. pp. ix + 151. $17.75.

thus arise in the plays because of the characters' imperfections, and are ultimately displaced by more fitting diction. The workings of language in each of the plays are examined in successive chapters, and Thompson concludes that 'underlying truths come to light whether characters will or no, most often in the fulfillment of ironically true words'. There are unanswered questions here about the degree of control each character has over his or her language, over which many will disagree: but the book is a valuable attempt to bring together linguistic theory and dramatic practice, which offers some lucid insights into particular exchanges, and deserves serious attention if not wholehearted acceptance. A different explanation of the complexities of *The Plain Dealer* is advanced by Ronald Berman in 'Wycherley's Unheroic Society' (*ELH*). The play demonstrates the rejection of Restoration standards, and Restoration style, as Wycherley, like Rochester and Swift in their last works, is overwhelmed by 'the extent of depravity, and the degree to which he shares it'. Manly uses 'the language of feeling' instead of the polished epigram or argument of Wycherley's earlier heroes, raging against reason as well as mankind, and cursing all, including himself. The dedication to Mother Bennett, the London procuress who represents the prostitution of both life and art, is a burlesque of patronage; the decay of the court is summed up in its laughter at those with wooden legs, whom Olivia likens to 'a pair of Compasses'. Berman sees this image as being as representative of 'this cultural moment' as was Donne's compass image – in 'A Valediction Forbidding Mourning' – of his. It is an appealing index of social and psychological change, and a provocative conclusion to an essay which is very perceptive about Wycherley's stance in his final play, and also about the darker states of Restoration satire.

Two articles approach Wycherley in a less concentrated fashion. Jack Yashinsky, in 'Voltaire's *Le Prude*: Influences, Philosophy, Dramaturgy' (*SVEC* 217, 1983), claims that Voltaire's use of *The Plain Dealer* as a source for *Le Prude* involved 'a reassessment of his own former comic creations' which led to 'the more successful elements' of his play. In a short but worthwhile essay, David D. Mann defines 'The Function of the Quack in *The Country Wife*' (*Restoration*, 1983). He is 'a disseminator, observer, commentator, and savior of Horner's subterfuge'. Because he is also the representative of the audience on stage, he both directs our responses and makes us 'accomplices' in the fraud, so that Wycherley's satire recoils on us – 'we are the dupes at last'.

Audience involvement is also the concern of John Barnard, in 'Point of View in *The Man of Mode*' (*EIC*). The presentation of Molly, through her note at the end of Act I and her quotation from a song from Shadwell's *Tempest*, is managed so that we share Dorimant's view of her – one of youthful, aristocratic disdain. The Prologue and Epilogue similarly direct our sympathy to Dorimant by channelling our resistance against Fopling. This is a significant essay not only for what it tells us about Etherege's skilful audience manipulation, but also because it extends our awareness of the role of the audience in Restoration comedy, following Harold Love's recent article on 'The Theatrical Geography of *The Country Wife*' (*YW* 64.285). Less satisfying is C. Harry Bruder's 'Women in the Comedies of Sir George Etherege' (*PAPA*). This rests on assumptions that are more than questionable, first that it is possible to separate 'women' from the texture of the plays (an essay on 'Men in Etherege' seems equally unlikely); and, secondly, that each successive woman character evolves from her predecessors in the Etherege canon. An essay examining the dramatist's ideas of the sex roles would be worth while, but as it stands the article lacks the breadth of vision fully to tackle such issues.

Aphra Behn's *The Lucky Chance* has been issued by Methuen in an edition by Fidelis Morgan[25]. The text is a reproduction of that in *The Female Wits* (*YW* 62.243–4), with a new introduction to accompany the 1982 production by the Women's Playhouse Trust. The latter is rather breathless, but has some useful quotations from early critics and Behn's vindication of her right to produce plays. Despite the lack of textual and critical apparatus, its appearance in a cheap, convenient format can only be welcomed. Another of Behn's plays is the subject of a note by Jeff Shulman: 'An Ovidian Echo in Behn's *The Rover*' (*N&Q*). This shows that, like her contemporaries, Behn turned to the *magister amoris* to present 'the bemusing perplexities of the game of love', in a passage in IV.ii. In a similar note D. E. L. Crane, in 'Burton and Buckingham' (*N&Q*), refers to his own edition of *The Rehearsal* (*YW* 57.196) in which he heard in 'Experto crede Roberto' (II.i.126) an echo of Virgil. He now records the phrase's appearance in Robert Burton's *The Anatomy of Melancholy*. Jessica Munns offers a more detailed study of textual influence and originality in 'Thomas Otway's *Titus and Berenice* and Racine's *Bérénice*' (*Restoration*, 1983). She concludes that Otway's version 'works towards dismantling the basis for an admiration of the heroic, as Titus's struggle to accommodate his nature to the harsh choices before him results in a perversion of his nature'. The play is also seen as pivotal in Otway's output, since after it he became concerned with the relation between personal failure and public disorder.

J. M. Armistead's 'Thomas Southerne: Three Centuries of Criticism' (*BB*) provides an excellent and comprehensive annotated bibliography, in chronological order, of writings about Southerne, with a short introductory overview of the changing course of the dramatist's reputation. It charts the movement from the view of Southerne's first critics that the plays ranked with Otway's – 'just below Shakespeare's' – through the Victorian reverence for his craftsmanship, and early-twentieth-century mistrust of his verse as lacking 'bone' and 'thought'. Armistead sees recent evaluations as centring on his sensitivity to domestic psychology, perception of female anxieties in marriage, and facility for 'hard' satire. The bibliography extends to 1982: Julia Rich's 'Heroic Tragedy in Southerne's *Oroonoko*' (*YW* 64.287) is an important later addition to the catalogue, which is an exemplary and indispensable first research tool. Leo Hughes and A. H. Scouten consider 'The Troublesome Play: A Promptbook of *Oroonoko*' (*TN*). The prompt-book is a 1696 quarto with marginal notes by William Chetwood, dating from a period 'impossible to fix' in the earlier eighteenth century, and with further annotations by Richard Cross made in 1747. Entries, sets, and cuts in the text are considered in detail, and the whole is supported by four plates showing pages from the quarto. There are uncertainties in attribution – hence the article's title – but this is a valuable contribution to our awareness of changing styles of performance of Restoration drama, forming an essential pendant to Edward A. Langhans's *Restora-*

25. *The Lucky Chance*, by Aphra Behn, ed. by Fidelis Morgan. Royal Court Writers. Methuen. pp. 69. pb £1.95.

tion Promptbooks (*YW* 63.228). Harold Weber discusses 'The Female Libertine in Southerne's *Sir Anthony Love* and *The Wives' Excuse*' (*EiT*). Sir Anthony is both within and without the 'breeches role' tradition, but her male disguise comes to dominate her nature so that she relishes the freedom of the part instead of reverting to submissiveness as the tradition demands, causing an isolation which reveals the isolation of all rakes, whatever their gender. In both plays, the female lead was taken by Mrs Susannah Mountfort, with her off-stage husband in the complementary roles, and Weber contends that this added further significance to her isolation by creating expectations which are not fulfilled. This is an intriguing and suggestive essay, not least in the parallels it suggests between Wittwoud and Malvolio, as well as in the use it makes of actors' off-stage relationships to stress the growing darkness of the presentation of the female rake.

D. F. McKenzie furnishes 'Six Readings in a Recent Edition of Congreve's Comedies' (*N&Q*). The edition is that of Anthony G. Henderson, about which an earlier notice expressed reservations (*YW* 63.239). McKenzie gives a rapid summary of the printing history of the plays, to point out that changes in the first four quartos were not corruptions but authorial corrections. Congreve compiled the 1710 edition from Q6, a direct reprint of Q5, which relied not on the 'corrected' Q4 but on the inaccurate Q1; Henderson used only the 1710 text for his edition; *ergo* it is corrupt. The six readings are masterly fusions of bibliography, textual criticism, and sensitivity to performance. For example, in V.i.41 of *The Old Bachelor*, Lucy's 'O Lord' should be 'O Lurrd', the phonetic spelling giving 'a wondrously lengthened and so more expressive response to Bellmour's kiss'. McKenzie concludes by stressing 'the need for an editor to observe a few simple routine bibliographical procedures if a claim to sound textual (and therefore critical) scholarship is to be sustained'. An incisive, inclusive article which gains much from its brevity – a model of its kind. C. A. Gibson's 'Floundermen and Pea-Sellers in Congreve's *Way of the World*' (*N&Q*) offers a lexicon of literary uses of the phrase 'flat as a flounder' and cognate constructions to show its bawdy significance when used by Mrs Marwood. The play is also the subject of an article in *MP* by James E. Neufeld, 'The Indigestion of Widdow-hood: Blood, Jonson, and *The Way of the World*'. Starting from passages in the correspondence between Congreve and John Dennis, Neufeld claims that Congreve regarded the corrective role of comedy in a serious, Jonsonian fashion, and examines the way in which characters showing affectation – those deliberately assuming some eccentricity – and those of humours – whose eccentricities are not assumed, and therefore cannot be remedied – are used for this purpose. In *The Way of the World*, he contends, Lady Wishfort is the humours character, representing 'blood' in her desire for marriage, which he regards as a symptom of a larger longing to recapture her youth. The 'affected' character of Millamant, who retains the capacity for change, is the main instrument of instructive comedy. This has its value, but it does at times read like an exercise in codification rather than an exploration of the valid notion of Jonsonian method in Congreve. Stoddard Lincoln considers a rather different area of the dramatist's output in 'The Librettos and Lyrics of William Congreve'[10]. Starting from the songs in the comedies, which he finds too complex for proper setting, Lincoln charts the growth of a style more fitting to musical treatment in rhythm and structure in the works with music by Henry Eccles. He concludes that 'together they had brought the English tradition to a state of perfection in *The Judgement of Paris* and had created a synthesis of Italian and English styles in *Semele*'.

B. J. McMullin has produced a fine edition of *The Comedies of John Crowne*[26]. There is a thorough introduction detailing editorial attitude and procedure, and each play has a separate introduction covering sources, stage and publication history, and critical reputation, as well as a list of textual exemplars consulted and an account of the copy-text and record of variants. Possibly a little more by way of critical introduction would be helpful since, despite the assertion that 'the emphasis is mainly literary rather than bibliographical or typographical', there is little on Crowne's place and reputation within the growth of Restoration comedy, although there is sensible and informed writing on seventeenth-century printing practice. Crowne's five comedies, together with the songs from *Justice Buisy*, are presented in a photographically reduced, unjustified typescript which, though certainly clear enough, is not easy on the eye. This is a small price to pay for having all the comedies together in a single text, though – the first since James Maidment and W. H. Logan's Edinburgh edition of 1874. The editor's notes compare well with those of the other scholarly versions – J. H. Wilson's *City Politiques* in the Regents series (*YW* 48.241) and Charlotte Hughes's *Sir Courtly Nice* (*YW* 47.219). Where Wilson gives simply 'fiery dangers' for 'firedrakes' (II.i), for example, McMullin gives a far fuller gloss covering both a ship full of explosives cast adrift among an enemy fleet and an angry whore, which adds much to the usage in its context. He is also sensible and clear on Stephen College, Titus Oates, and the Popish Plot. In all, this is an important new standard edition.

Interest continues in both the life and works of Vanbrugh. Frank McCormick's 'Vanbrugh and the Duke of Newcastle: The Genesis of the Loverule Plot in *A Journey to London*' (*BRH*, 1983) offers significant new information. It dates the 'frequently brilliant three and a half acts' at 1715–17, when Vanbrugh was engaged in negotiating a marriage between the Duke of Newcastle and the Duchess of Marlborough's granddaughter Harriet Godolphin, by showing how Sir Charles's advice to Loverule on the qualities needed in a wife (II.i) echoes Vanbrugh's advice to Newcastle in a letter of 1716. The play was not completed, McCormick claims, because to reveal such events would have exposed Newcastle to ridicule, and further endangered Vanbrugh's already insecure relationship with the Duchess of Marlborough, which he wished to protect as he was still negotiating the development of Claremont House – a venture 'vastly more remunerative than the proceeds from any play'. McCormick also considers 'The Unity of Vanbrugh's *A Journey to London*' (*DUJ*). He claims that the play has a firm structure in 'a body of recurrent images and motifs', most of which stem from the fertile opening scene, and in the balance of Sir Charles's marital aspirations against Loverule's marital trials. Vanbrugh is coming to terms with the change in married life seen by recent historians, from an authoritarian relationship to one rooted in companionship. The lack of an ending is perhaps due to the difficulty of finding a satisfactory conclusion in the portrayal of such a relationship. Michael

26. *The Comedies of John Crowne*, ed. by B. J. McMullin. The Renaissance Imagination. Garland. pp. xxxiii + 776. $90.

Cordner's 'Time, the Churches and Vanbrugh's Lord Foppington' (*DUJ*) explores the way in which the play subverts and ridicules 'the attitudes characteristic of conventional piety'. The influence of works in the tradition of moral denunciation is shown in its linguistic forms, but these are used ironically, as Vanbrugh's use of 'the commonplaces of sermon rhetoric' lacks 'the preacher's note of excoriation and admonition'. Thus the play takes advantage of its audience's knowledge of the language of piety to ridicule it in a way which made it one of the targets of the antistage campaign of the 1690s. This is a thoughtful insight into the relationship between dramatist and audience, a theme which is becoming another facet of our increasing awareness of the Restoration stage, as other articles noted in this section testify. Frank M. Patterson's 'Lord Foppington and *Le Bourgeois gentilhomme*' (*N&Q*) claims that the scene in *The Relapse* in which Foppington quarrels with his shoemaker is a 'direct borrowing' from Molière's scene where M. Jourdain quarrels with his tailor on the same subject. European theatre of a more arcane nature is the subject of 'Andreas Gryphius and Jesuit Theatre' (*Daphnis*) by James A. Parente Jr. Its major interest may be in its discussion of Joseph Simons, an English dramatist who wrote five tragedies while rhetoric instructor at St Omer, and whose *Leo Armenus*, produced in Rome in 1645, may have been known to Gryphius.

Bruce Podewell offers some 'Notes on Thomas Betterton's Merchant Venture' (*Restoration*, 1983). He records the failure of a venture of Sir Francis Watson's in which Betterton had invested heavily, and its repercussions in Betterton's bankruptcy and the return of Mary Betterton to the stage in 1691–2. That he was able to invest so heavily, Podewell claims, enhances our awareness of the 'enviable financial situation' of leading Restoration actors. John McVeagh's 'George Farquhar and Commercial England' (*SVEC* 217, 1983) claims that Farquhar introduces 'a more analytical approach to economic matters and a closer reflection of the commercial character of English national life'. *Love and a Bottle* discusses seriously the tensions arising from the lack of money; the later plays show how those suddenly bereft of income face both 'an anxiety about the loss of caste' and a genuine hunger and need. Conversely, Sir Harry Wildair reflects modern attitudes in placing money above honour and chivalry. The culmination of this new, serious concern is in *The Beaux Stratagem*, where the search for income through marriage and other sources shows the blurring of the division between pleasure and business in the commercial ethics of the day. Shirley Strum Kenny has discovered three 'Songs in *Love and a Bottle*' (*Scriblerian*) in the Folger Shakespeare Library. Kenny concludes that the songs – usefully reproduced in facsimile – were included in the first performance in December 1698 and suggests that, since they were issued in a collection of songs and not in the printed play text, 'collections of published songs should be considered an important research tool for the editor of dramatic texts'.

In 'Power and Conversion in Cibber's *The Careless Husband*' (*Restoration*, 1983) John A. Vance asserts that the play shows Cibber's interest in 'the innate desire for power' which lies beneath human relations. This is shown not only in Lady Betty Modish, but also in Lady Easy. The latter is not the 'eighteenth-century "Patient Griselda"' as which she has traditionally been seen, but instead conceals an astute control beneath an apparently complaisant exterior. This does much to lift the play above the current 'sentimental vogue', and the article also contains striking support for its thesis from contemporary writings on women, marriage, and 'Sovereignty'.

(c) Prose Writers

Bunyan studies made a pretty good shift to wag along and will be further encouraged by James F. Forrest and Richard Lee Greaves's *John Bunyan: A Reference Guide*[27]. This is an annotated bibliography of some 2200 writings about Bunyan from 1656 to 1980. While 'rigorous principles of selection' have been devised, this bibliography seems more comprehensive than the Dryden one in the same series (section 2, above), as it includes all writings deemed significant in themselves, relevant to Bunyan's reputation, or useful to future scholars. The arrangement is chronological, with an index mainly of authors and titles. From the introductory survey of Bunyan's reputation broad ironies emerge: when his influence as a practical theologian dwindled, his popularity as an imaginative writer rose; when his popularity as an imaginative writer fell, his importance as a research field grew. Since 1960 the weight of studies has made ours 'an era unparalleled in Bunyan criticism'; in fact about one-quarter of the items in the bibliography belong to the years 1960–80. Compared with the Dryden consortium, Bunyan studies look like a cottage industry but seem less vulnerable to cuts in research funding. The *Guide* has some omissions, errors, and imperfections. It omits some studies which have been mentioned in *YW*, notably four articles in *ZAA* in 1979. Sometimes the date of first publication of important studies is not given: F. R. Leavis's 'Bunyan through Modern Eyes' first appeared in a more expansive form in *Scrutiny* in 1938; Wolfgang Iser's *Der implizite Leser* first appeared in Germany in 1972 (*YW* 53.268–9). Sometimes the date is given, but a later source is cited; Isaac D'Israeli's periphrasis for Bunyan is given under 1818, but cited from a later American edition, rather than from *The Literary Character*, London, John Murray, p. 58. The names of Vaughan Williams and Basil Willey are misspelt. The index is not much use for finding out what has been written on specific books and subjects. But such shortcomings may be excused in a pioneering work; at present this guide is unrivalled, and it will help future scholars for many years.

The Pilgrim's Progress was edited by N. H. Keeble for The World's Classics[28]. The text is that established by Roger Sharrock, and the book has an introduction, a descriptive bibliography, explanatory notes, a glossary, and an index. In his introduction Keeble disputes Coleridge's view that 'the Bunyan of Parnassus had the better of the Bunyan of the Conventicle', and concludes that 'it was the Conventicle that enabled him to scale Parnassus'. Theology, experience, and genius combine, for example when Bunyan shows that 'no human personality is ever wholly subsumed into a particular virtue or vice'. Together the introduction, bibliography, and notes admirably assimilate much recent scholarly and critical work, making this an excellent edition for students. The only respect in which the rival Penguin English Library edition has a distinct advantage is in the clarity of its typeface.

Bunyan's critics have tended to think that his artistry is at odds with his didacticism and perhaps even unconscious. In *John Bunyan: Allegory and*

27. *John Bunyan: A Reference Guide*, by James F. Forrest and Richard Lee Greaves. Hall. pp. xx + 478. $50. (Rev'd by Jacques B. H. Alblas, *ES*.)
28. *The Pilgrim's Progress*, ed. by N. H. Keeble. WC. OUP. pp. xxxii + 301. pb £1.95.

Imagination[29] E. Beatrice Batson argues that on the contrary he belongs to a tradition of religious writing in which it was felt that 'things are perceived more readily through similitudes', as St Augustine put it, and hence that the way to spiritual understanding is through literary language. His prefaces suggest that he was not unconscious of this tradition. Professor Batson covers some of the same ground as Charles Baird in his book on Bunyan's narrative technique (*YW* 58.228), but she goes beyond him in discussing the *Divine Emblems* and sermons as well as the major works, and falls short of him in having no clearer end in view than 'to call attention to literary qualities'. Her lists of such qualities – narrative structure, allegorical devices, dialogue, anecdote, metaphors and similes, riddles, and so forth – do not fully substantiate her conclusion that nearly all Bunyan's works have artistic unity. Her style is better than Baird's but could be improved in places: 'The seventeenth century provides a literal gold mine for thought on the relation of literal language to spiritual understanding' is a strangely ill-considered sentence in a work dealing with allegory, though it exemplifies her characteristic enthusiasm and straightforwardness. The book makes a good short introduction to Bunyan as a literary figure.

Two substantial Bunyan essays appeared in learned journals. In 'Bunyan: Language, Convention, Authority' (*ELH*) Peter J. Carlton notes that in *Grace Abounding* Bunyan often says heavenly voices darted into his soul or biblical texts entered his spirit. Such 'disclaiming locutions' are meant to transform the individual's thoughts into God's authoritative utterances, and hence to compensate for the absence of such an authority as that provided for Catholics by the church. In Puritanism an utterance could only be judged inspired if it sounded like other inspired utterances, so narratives tended to conform to established conventions. A similar blend of inspiration and convention can be seen in the modern Charismatic movement. In 'The Way and the Ways of Puritan Story: Biblical Patterns in Bunyan and his Contemporaries' (*English*) N. H. Keeble shows that to the Puritan both personal and national history were comprehensible only in relation to the history of Israel. Puritan narratives were shaped by quite a small number of biblical episodes, whose significance Keeble very fully if rather laboriously explains. *Pilgrim's Progress* in particular is about not only Christian and Bunyan, but also Old Testament experience, the state of England, and the New Testament resolution of both Israel's earlier and England's later history.

The origins of the novel were examined from several angles. In *A Being More Intense*[30] Paula R. Backscheider is especially concerned with the treatment of character in the fictional works of Bunyan, Defoe, and Swift (and not with all their prose works, as her subtitle suggests). By displaying the inner lives and the social settings of their protagonists, these writers 'created characters which were more gripping, more familiar, more real than any created in English literature before'. No reference is made to Chaucer or Shakespeare, so perhaps for 'literature' we should read 'prose fiction'.

29. *John Bunyan: Allegory and Imagination*, by E. Beatrice Batson. CH/B&N. pp. vii + 157. £14.95.
30. *A Being More Intense: A Study of the Prose Works of Bunyan, Swift, and Defoe*, by Paula R. Backscheider. Studies in the Eighteenth Century 7. AMSP. pp. xxii + 222; frontis. $29.50.

Professor Backscheider does not claim that Bunyan, Defoe, and Swift are novelists, but assesses their contribution to the birth of the genre. The two parts of *Pilgrim's Progress* are discussed frequently, *The Holy War* and *Mr Badman* intermittently. Possibly this book should be judged by what it says of Defoe and Swift; but I was glad I did not feel obliged to read any more, as it is written for a highly specialized audience. In 'The Earliest American Novel: Aphra Behn's *Oroonoko*' (*NCF*) William C. Spengemann sees the novel as the offspring of Romance and the Brief True Relation, and the American novel as essentially a response to American experience. In *Oroonoko* the reader expects a happy ending to the romantic conflict when the lovers are re-united in America, but their entanglement in colonial politics leads to horror and misery; and this mixture of romance and history gives rise to effects which can only be called novelistic. Incidentally, I feel less certain than Spengemann that Aphra Behn was 'an avowed Catholic', but more certain that 'one Dr Burnet' was Bishop Gilbert Burnet. In 'Congreve, Fielding, and the Rise of Some Novels'[10] Brian Corman shows that Congreve anticipates Fielding, in both his general idea of the novel and his narrative techniques in *Incognita*.

Recent work on Pepys and Evelyn will have to be rather briefly reported. Robert Latham, the general editor of Pepys's *Diary*, gave the Aldred Memorial Lecture on 'Pepys and his Editors' (*JRSA*), about the achievements of earlier editors, and the work of those engaged on the recent definitive edition. He recalls the delights and difficulties of gathering information, suggests that the annotator should emulate Wodehouse's Jeeves rather than Beachcomber's Prodnose, and advises against the use of computers for indexing. Having written a note to explain that 'Heaven' was a tavern Pepys visited, when the name recurred Latham had difficulty in resisting the temptation to write 'For Heaven, see above'. Anyone who undertakes scholarly work in any field will find this lecture both entertaining and helpful. Latham is also general editor of the *Catalogue of the Pepys Library*[31], which now includes, as well as the catalogue of printed books already noticed (*YW* 59.232), catalogues of prints and drawings, postmedieval manuscripts, and bindings. Edward M. Wilson and Don W. Cruickshank's *Samuel Pepys's Spanish Plays*[32] is a bibliographical study of the volume Pepys 1553. This contains twenty-six *comedias sueltas*, including five by Calderon and four by Lope de Vega, and two pamphlets. Wilson and Cruickshank give full bibliographical accounts of each play, and a short history of the *comedia suelta*. Sarah Tyacke's 'Samuel Pepys as Map Collector'[33] is an authoritative account. C. A. Rivington's 'Samuel Pepys and the Oxford University Press' (*N&Q*) is about Pepys's correspondence with Dr John Wallis and Dr Arthur Chaslett, but has less to do with Pepys than with the Press. Finally, two studies of John Evelyn, one appreciative and one learned.

31. *Catalogue of the Pepys Library at Magdalene College, Cambridge*, ed. by Robert Latham. B&B. Vol. III.i: *Prints and Drawings (General)*, ed. by A. Aspital. (1980.) pp. xxiv + 357; 8 illus. £45. Vol. V.ii: *Modern Manuscripts*, ed. by Charles Knighton. (1981.) pp. xxvi + 275. £75. Vol. VI: *Bindings*, ed. by Howard Nixon. pp. 160; 64 illus. £60.

32. *Samuel Pepys's Spanish Plays*, by Edward M. Wilson and Don W. Cruickshank. BibS (1980.) pp. viii + 196. £20.

33. In *Maps and Prints: Aspects of the English Booktrade*, ed. by Robin Myers and Michael Harris. OPP. pp. xiii + 124. pb £6.25.

Marvin Mudrick's 'The Public Servant' (*HudR*) emphasizes not only Evelyn's loyalty to the Crown but also his unconventional ideas. 'He could almost be called a pacifist if such a term or notion had then existed', and was perhaps 'the first conscious and aggressive environmentalist'. Evelyn was undoubtedly ahead of his time; and ours; in some ways. Albert B. Cook III's 'John Evelyn's *English Grammer*' (*LeedsSE*) offers a carefully edited text of this British Library manuscript, with an introduction and notes. It is essentially an abridgement of Ben Jonson's *English Grammar*; Evelyn adds some examples of his own, but has scarcely anything original to say about seventeenth-century English, and sometimes seriously misunderstands Jonson. This not self-evidently useful piece of editing was supported by a research grant from the University of Kansas.

Now for the historians, Clarendon and Burnet. Clarendon's dialogues 'Of the Want of Respect due to Age' and 'Concerning Education' are reprinted in facsimile[34], from the second edition of the *Miscellaneous Works* (1651). In a succinct introduction Martine Watson Brownley remarks that 'Clarendon had learned from bitter experience that the court of Charles II was no country for old men', and the first dialogue is amazingly generous towards the young. The second helps to explain the staying-power of traditional education. Clarendon knew the arguments for experimental science, but defends the usefulness of logic and Latin 'in the serious Part of human life'; it is ironical that his name is associated, *inter alia*, with a laboratory. The dialogue includes debates on the educational value of wet-nurses, travel, and the theatre, to which the conclusions are that the mother's milk is the most natural, and wet-nurses should be selected carefully; that travel is good for those who want it, but not for those who do not; and that theatres 'are amongst the best and most innocent of Divertissements', though the playing of women's parts by women 'possibly too much exposes the Modesty of that Sex'. In discussing this last point Professor Brownley might have mentioned James F. Forrest's 'Clarendon on the Stage' (*MLR*, 1974; *YW* 55.317). Raymond A. Anselment's 'Clarendon and the Caroline Myth of Peace' (*JBS*) proposes that Clarendon's argument in the *History of the Rebellion*, that the Civil War was caused by a surfeit of peace, may not be as fanciful as modern historians think. It is based on contemporary tradition, which Clarendon followed not merely to praise a halcyon moment, but rather to disclose a poignant irony: Englishmen failed to value their own happiness. John E. Drabble's 'Gilbert Burnet and the History of the English Reformation: The Historian and his Milieu' (*JRH*) shows how the first two volumes of Burnet's *History of the Reformation of the Church of England* (1679–81) originated in the anti-Catholic mania of the time. The work was encouraged by important people in both church and state, and presented very much the Anglican view; but being convinced that the facts spoke for themselves Burnet printed many sources, and his work retained value as a collection of records for some two hundred years. One of his assistants was his friend Edward Stillingfleet, who was himself compiling his *Antiquities of the British Church*. According to Irène Simon, Stillingfleet 'was a thinker of a high order who could apply his learning to problems of his time'. Professor Simon's

---

34. *Two Dialogues: 'Of the Want of Respect due to Age' and 'Concerning Education'*, by Edward Hyde, Earl of Clarendon, intro. by Martine Watson Brownley. ARS 227–8. CML. pp. xii + (iv) + 285–348. By subscription.

'Stillingfleet's Sermon Preached before the King on the Anniversary of the Execution of Charles I (30 January 1688/9)'[35] shows how the preacher dealt with the revolt of Corah (Numbers 16) as a type of the Puritan rebellion. Although the occasion lent itself to a eulogy of Charles the Martyr and an attack on the 'Sons of Violence', Stillingfleet carefully avoided support for absolutism or condemnation of Presbyterianism.

Finally some miscellaneous items. Janet Todd's 'Marketing the Self: Mary Carleton, Miss F and Susannah Gunning' (*SVEC* 217, 1983) suggests that the autobiographical 'vindications' of these three women show how 'taste in women veered from wit to sensibility, and from ingenuity to ingenuousness'. The most ingenious was the Restoration adventuress Mary Carleton, whose *The Case of Madam Mary Carleton* (1663) offers a mixture of 'wit and pathos, girlish innocence and risqué sophistication'. But whatever the literary merits of her various pamphlets, they neither made her rich nor saved her from the gallows. R. A. Beddard's 'Two Letters from the Tower, 1688' (*N&Q*) outlines the career of Sir Edward Sherburne and publishes two letters from him to Anthony Wood. Robert H. Ray's 'John Dunton and the Origin of "A Penny Saved Is a Penny Got" ' (ibid.) gives Dunton the credit for the most familiar phrasing of the proverb.

4. Background

As usual *The Locke Newsletter* includes a list of recent publications, articles on Locke's philosophy, and substantial reviews. John J. Jenkins reviews *Reason and Experience: Locke* by Ian Tipton[36] and Ian Tipton reviews *Understanding Locke* by John J. Jenkins[37]. In 'John Locke's Images of Childhood' (*ECS*) Margaret J. M. Ezell considers possible sources of Locke's ideas in John Earle, Joseph Glanvill, and other seventeenth-century writers, but concentrates on responses to *Some Thoughts concerning Education* in the eighteenth century. Locke differed sharply from most of his predecessors in recognizing children as individuals and rational creatures; he opposed swaddling, corporal punishment, and excessive discipline, and favoured letting children play and express their 'natural gaiety'. In 'The Noble Primitive as Bourgeois Subject' (*L&H*) Peter J. Weston covers some of the same ground. He ranges widely in the literature of three centuries to show that the notion of the noble primitive helped to undermine traditional values and is closely connected with what he would call 'the bourgeois revolution' of 1688. The 'noble savage' is a 'paradigm' of the 'bourgeois subject' or free individual; Dryden supplied the name, Aphra Behn's *Oroonoko* exemplified the idea, and Locke's philosophy incorporated it into the 'founding myth of bourgeois society'. A late variant is Thomas Day's *Sandford and Merton*, a children's book which was warmly praised by the radical Leigh Hunt. Margaret Ezell relates it to Locke's *Con-*

35. In *Studies in Seventeenth-Century English Literature, History and Bibliography: Festschrift for Professor T. A. Birrell on the Occasion of his Sixtieth Birthday*, ed. by G. A. M. Janssens and F. G. A. M. Aarts. Costerus N.S. 46. Rodopi. pp. viii + 268 + (v); 3 illus. pb Fl 60.

36. *Reason and Experience: Locke*, by Ian Tipton. Arts: A Third Level Course A311, Block 3. OpenU (1983). pp. 109.

37. *Understanding Locke*, by John J. Jenkins. EdinU (1983). pp. xviii + 256. hb £15, pb £7.50.

cerning Education, and I would add that Day also wrote the popular *History of Little Jack*, the story of a wild boy suckled by goats. But Weston's stimulating essay is already somewhat overloaded.

'Science in 17th-Century England' by Michael Hunter (*HT*) is a useful survey of recent books, which have a tendency to relate experimental science and culture as a whole. For instance, Mordechai Feingold[38] has suggested that the universities, though – then as now – often attacked as obscurantist, played a major role in the development of science throughout the century. In 'A Science Turned Upside Down: Feminism and the Natural Philosophy of Margaret Cavendish' (*HLQ*) Lisa T. Sarasohn argues that Lady Cavendish used the sceptical methodology of the new science as a weapon in her battle for the recognition of women as the intellectual equals of men, though it became 'a two-edged sword, both damning and justifying female subservience'. In 'English Socinianism around Newton and Whiston' (*SVEC* 216, 1983) E. R Briggs contends that William Whiston's ideas offended both sceptical scientists and orthodox clergymen; he remains a 'grossly neglected' figure. In 'Robert Midgeley and *A New Treatise of Natural Philosophy*: A Wrong Attribution' (*N&Q*) Sabina Fleitmann shows that this popular work was not Midgeley's but a translation of G. B. de Saint-Romain's *La Science naturelle* (1679).

A number of articles on Restoration history and personalities attracted my attention. Carolyn A. Edie's 'News from Abroad: Advice to the People of England on the Eve of the Stuart Restoration' (*BJRL*) describes broadsides and pamphlets purporting to be messages from abroad, mostly Royalist in tendency, and including some bogus royal proclamations. These revived or kept alive the idea of a restoration, and gave some idea of the exiled king's character and policies. Amos C. Miller's 'A Man of "Unquiet Spirit": Mordaunt Webster' (*RH*) gives a biographical sketch of this High Anglican priest who was converted to Rome late in the reign of Charles II. I noted that Webster was born at Aldwinckle St Peter, Northants, in 1637; so there are parallels between him and Dryden, but apparently no direct link. R. A. Beddard's 'Bishop Cartwright's Death-Bed' (*BLR*) shows that Thomas Cartwright, Bishop of Chester in the reign of James II, was neither a secret Catholic nor a death-bed convert. Some contemporaries thought Cartwright had been or would be secretly converted, but Gilbert Burnet soberly pointed out that the Bishop was a married man. He was also an extreme Royalist, who followed James into exile, accompanied him on his Irish expedition, and died in Dublin in 1689. A letter from the Anglican priest who attended Cartwright on his death-bed shows that he remained loyal to the Church of England. There was even a baseless rumour that he had been 'poysoned by the popish clergy'.

(a) Music

There is much to enlighten students of our period in James Anderson Winn's history of the relations between poetry and music, *Unsuspected Eloquence* (*YW* 62.156), and the paperback edition is well worth the outlay[39]. In his

---

38. *The Mathematicians' Apprenticeship: Science, Universities and Society in England, 1560–1640*, by Mordechai Feingold. CUP. pp. viii + 248. £22.50.

39. *Unsuspected Eloquence: A History of the Relations between Poetry and Music*, by James Anderson Winn. Yale. pp. xiv + 381. pb £10.95.

chapter on 'Imitations' and the origins of Romanticism, Winn argues that while writers sought to free themselves from 'the rules', musicians tried to discover rules; these musical rules were eventually codified in J. J. Fux's *Gradus ad Parnassum* (1725), the influence of which is still felt today; and ironically, music gained prestige at the expense of poetry, as a way of expressing thoughts too deep for words. But in conservative England literary men attacked music as foreign and effeminate. Although Dryden obviously respected Purcell, and in the *Song for St Cecilia's Day* achieved 'a maximum application to poetry of a technique far better suited to music, the expansion of locally imitative ideas into structural principles', perhaps his strongest feelings come out in the preface to *Albion and Albanius*, where 'we hear the irritated voice of the poet threatened by music'. As a whole, this book seems to me extraordinarily original, disciplined, and eloquent. [J.O.]

Pierre Danchin's 'The Foundation of the Royal Academy of Music in 1674 and Pierre Perrin's *Ariane*' (*ThS*) discusses the evidence for the foundation of an academy on French lines in England. It is concerned with circumstances surrounding the performance of Sébastien Brémond's *Ballet et musique pour le divertissement du Roi* and Perrin's *Ariane* in 1674, and attempts by the composer Robert Cambert to produce his works on the London stage. The membership of the academy remains uncertain, but Danchin recounts Brémond's imprisonment for killing a musician in a duel, and a brawl on the attempted seizure from prison of the leader of the French actors. It is these events, Danchin asserts, that we have to thank for the failure of the academy, which thus 'left the field open for Purcell'. Few Restoration brawls can have had so positive an outcome.

Lucyle Hook's 'Motteux and the Classical Masque'[10] chronicles the efforts of Peter Motteux to establish opera of the full, Italian kind in England, both in his propagandist articles in the *Gentleman's Journal* and his librettos for *The Mad Lover* and *Acis and Galatea*. It is good to have a clear account of this figure, which nicely complements Hook's recent edition of *Acis* and *The Rape of Europa by Jupiter* (*YW* 63.240). By contrast, Robert D. Hume's 'Opera in London, 1695–1705'[10] concentrates on the native tradition of masque and semi-opera, refuting the idea that there was a hiatus in English opera between the death of Purcell and the establishment of the Italian tradition by Handel in 1705. Hume discusses three strands of operatic production during his ten-year period: the masques of Betterton at Lincoln's Inn Fields, the spectaculars mounted in their wake by Christopher Rich, and the lesser-known works dating from the struggle between Rich and Vanbrugh. As well as providing valuable stage history, this is another step in establishing English opera as a tradition and genre as strong and as valid as the Italian form. Judith Milhous covers similar ground in 'Opera Finances in London, 1674–1738' (*JAMS*). Much of the article is concerned with eighteenth-century productions, but its opening section is a forceful reminder of the vast cost of early English opera. Spending between £1200 and £1500 in the 1670s on a production lasting less than a fortnight was, as Milhous says, 'a tremendous gamble', especially from an annual budget of £5000, when £50 was a good year's earnings for a 'third-rank actor'. Costs increased in the 1690s: *The Fairy Queen* was rumoured to have cost £3000 for a twelve-day run. Even in those days, it seems, opera was subsidized – by profits from straight plays instead of institutional philanthropy. Milhous concludes that such ventures were never feasible, and, to balance against the idea of artistic stimulus she advances in the Kenny symposium[10], suggests another reason why they were still undertaken: 'snob appeal . . . gave opera its cachet'. By implication, people went to the opera simply because it was expensive as well as spectacular. *Plus ça change . . .*

A revised edition of Franklin B. Zimmerman's comprehensive biographical and critical study of Purcell[40] can be welcomed with reservations, though it grieves me to say anything against such an enthusiast for such a composer. Zimmerman clarifies neither the nature nor the extent of his revisions, but the blurb promises 'the reworking of the Purcell family genealogy; a complete Purcell iconography; and new findings on many significant aspects of his personal, religious, and musical life'. The iconography is a substantial addition, and includes twenty-four illustrations, mostly paintings, drawings, and engravings of Purcell. Indeed, the book as a whole is lavishly illustrated. But the appendix on 'Henry Purcell's Origins' does not seem to have been revised much; for instance, a statement made in 1967, 'when I may travel to England again, I hope to follow promising lines of investigation', still stands. The main text has been revised to add information, modify opinion, and improve the style; but more changes seem called for. Having noted when reviewing Zimmerman's contribution to a volume of the California *Dryden* that he 'now thinks more highly of Grabu than he did when he wrote his book on Purcell' (*YW* 57.193), I was surprised to find unaltered references to Louis Grabu's 'musical ineptitude'. And in a part that has been altered I was still more surprised to find a play called *Pyrrhus, King of Epirus* attributed to Congreve. To conclude: libraries should have both editions; libraries and individuals who did not acquire the first should get the second; individuals who did acquire the first could content themselves with consulting the second in libraries. [J.O.]

Essays on Purcell included Richard Luckett's ' "Or rather our musical Shakespeare": Charles Burney's Purcell'[41], an examination of the composer's reputation in the eighteenth century. Luckett concludes that apathy in literary quarters, where 'sympathy' might have been expected, 'retarded Purcell's fame'. Margaret Laurie's 'Purcell's Extended Solo Songs' (*MT*) looks at the thirty or so longer songs in the British Library and the Guildhall Library, and finds in them 'an extraordinary capacity for encapsulating the emotional content of a wide variety of texts' in a rich and flexible declamatory style. This essay makes an important extension to the view of the theatre music offered by Curtis Price's *Henry Purcell and the London Stage* (see section 1(*b*) above). Robert Ford's 'A Sacred Song Not by Purcell' (*MT*) shows that 'Full of Wrath', a mediocre setting of words by Jeremy Taylor, 'may be removed from the Purcell canon'; it is by Humphry Brailsford, who, as it happens, was an ill-tempered minor canon of Canterbury.

In 'Blow's Court Odes: A New Discovery' (*MT*) David R. Evans discusses fragmentary manuscripts of Blow's New Year's Day odes for 1693 and 1694, which were settings of 'The Happy, Happy Year is Born' by Nahum Tate, and

40. *Henry Purcell, 1659–1695: His Life and Times*, by Franklin B. Zimmerman. Second, rev. ed. UPenn (1983). pp. xxxvi + 473; 67 illus. hb £37.58, pb £19.95. (Rev'd by Curtis A. Price. *M&L*; by Nigel Fortune, *MT*.)

41. *Music in Eighteenth-Century England: Essays in Memory of Charles Cudworth*, ed. by Christopher Hogwood and Richard Luckett. CUP (1983). pp. xviii + 265; frontis. and 10 pls. £25.

'Sound, Sound the Trumpet', by Peter Motteux. These and other music manuscripts belong to the George Powell collection, now in the library of the University College of Wales, Aberystwyth. In 'The Publication and Dating of an Early Eighteenth-Century English Song Book' (*BLR*) David Hunter explains the practices of collecting and publishing song books, using 'A Collection of the Choicest Songs and Dialogues Composed by the Most Eminent Masters of the Age', published by John Walsh in, Hunter asserts, 1703. This essay offers a useful view of the music trade at the turn of the century.

The Eighteenth Century

ELIZABETH DUTHIE and ALAN BOWER

This chapter is arranged as follows: 1. General, by Elizabeth Duthie; 2. Poetry, by Alan Bower; 3. Drama, by Elizabeth Duthie; 4. Prose, by Elizabeth Duthie; 5. The Novel, by Alan Bower.

1. General

The year 1984 saw the publication of the 1980 volume of *The Eighteenth Century: A Current Bibliography*[1] as well as the more up-to-date listings and reviews in *The Scriblerian* and *SEL* (by Morris R. Brownell). *ECent* ran a special issue on British approaches to the eighteenth century, in which G. S. Rousseau describes his experience of Marxism, ideology, and scholarship in Cambridge (England). In *Annals of Scholarship* Rousseau, Paul Alkon, and D. J. Roorda debate the declining enthusiasm of undergraduates for the eighteenth century. Waldo Sumner Glock's admittedly imperfect bibliography of twenty-four authors[2] (3701 items) omits most biographical, textual, and bibliographical material. It may offer 'an overview of the main criticism' for its selected authors, but will not satisfy the specialist. Robert A. Smith's historical bibliography[3] for the period 1760–1837 is also for the non-specialist. Its 2500 entries are subdivided into constitutional, diplomatic, social, and economic history, and so on. Strictly literary history is excluded, but the section on intellectual history has some odd inclusions, given the selectivity of the work.

Virginia C. Kenny's discussion of the linked themes of personal retreat and national expansion, the 'country-house ethos', falls into three sections[4]. From 1688 to 1714 the older attitudes prevail – among the 'heterogeneous collection of poems and prose fragments' discussed are *The Spectator*, Mandeville, Pomfret, and Lady Winchilsea. From 1715 to 1730 the aristocratic country-house ethos is modified in the work of Defoe, Swift (a very short discussion), and Thomson, with the exploration of the individual's dilemma in searching

1. *The Eighteenth Century: A Current Bibliography*, gen. ed., Jim Springer Borck. AMSP. pp. xii + 643. $57.50.
2. *Eighteenth-Century English Literary Studies: A Bibliography*, by Waldo Sumner Glock. Scarecrow. pp. xviii + 865. $52.50.
3. *Late Georgian and Regency England, 1760–1837*, by Robert A. Smith. Conference on British Studies Bibliographical Handbooks. CUP. pp. ix + 114. £15.
4. *The Country-House Ethos in English Literature 1688–1750: Themes of personal retreat and national expansion*, by Virginia C. Kenny. Harvester/St Martin's. pp. xi + 236. £28.50.

for a role. From 1731 to 1750 the emphasis on the proper use of wealth for the individual becomes absorbed into the 'larger problem of the nature of social institutions'. Here Kenny discusses Pope, Thomson's dramas and *Liberty*, and later editions of *The Seasons*, with references to Lillo, Glover, and Fielding. There is sensible comment on texts (although Defoe is not well served), but the links between 'images and fantasies of the retired life and descriptions and allusions from the world beyond Europe' are not convincingly analysed. Vincent Carretta's[5] discussion of verbal and visual satire from Pope to Churchill concentrates on Pope – *Windsor Forest, Bathurst*, the *Imitations of Horace*, and *The Dunciad* – and also offers a cogent and erudite account of the shared satiric vocabulary and iconography. He gives a convincing account of the decline of satire after Walpole's fall, citing the diversity of targets, the artistic trend away from emblem towards caricature, and the historiographical changes which made historical allusion less possible. The conclusion exemplifies these changes in the work of Churchill. Jerry C. Beasley's sketch (*SECC* 13) of three types of 'political character' needs amplification.

In *Literature and Insubstantiality in Later Eighteenth-Century England*[6] Fredric V. Bogel, like Carretta, sees the mid century as a literary watershed. The later writers are concerned rather with being than with knowing, and 'to a surprising degree, united by a perception of the impoverishment or insubstantiality of their experience and by their effort both to register and to resist that insubstantiality'. In that effort, a wide range of writers – poets, biographers and autobiographers, Burke in aesthetics and Sterne in the novel, with Samuel Johnson as a special instance of the general condition – 'constructed from their impoverishment a defense of common experience', by appealing to the past and to a newly scrutinized present, achieving both 'a reclamation of the nontranscendant' and a 'complex, inventive, often reluctant' re-adjustment to the transcendant. Bogel's is an interesting and fruitful discussion, which helps to define the common features of the wayward 'Age of Sensibility'.

Less slippery writers like John Nichols, 'the last of the learned printers', are discussed by Martin Maner (*ES*) and Arthur Sherbo (*SB*). Sherbo also lists (*SB*) Isaac Reed's contributions to the *European Magazine*, and John Feather (*SB*) gives an account of the career of John Clay, stationer of Daventry.

One of the central topics in science, philosophy, and religion, the nature of thought and of matter, and the connection between them, is very thoroughly surveyed by John W. Yolton[7]. His discussion illuminates major writers – Locke, Hume, Priestley – as well as summarizing many little-known works. 'Behind much of the controversy over thinking matter lurked the fear of materializing man': Yolton provides an expert guide to this crucial debate. Richard E. Brantley's thesis[8] is initially more limited – that Locke's theory

5. *The Snarling Muse: Verbal and Visual Political Satire from Pope to Churchill*, by Vincent Carretta. UPenn (1983). pp. xxi + 290. $25.

6. *Literature and Insubstantiality in Later Eighteenth-Century England*, by Fredric V. Bogel. Princeton. pp. xi + 226. $29.50.

7. *Thinking Matter: Materialism in eighteenth-century England*, by John W. Yolton. Blackwell. pp. xiv + 238. £19.50.

8. *Locke, Wesley, and the Method of English Romanticism*, by Richard E. Brantley. UFlor. pp. xi + 300. $30.

of knowledge 'grounds the intellectual method of Wesley's Methodism'. Brantley then advances a more ambitious claim, that Wesley's 'progress from empiricism through quasi-empirical apprehension to faith', is an important factor in Romanticism: 'Romantic tension in England at least is both partially reconcilable and fully understandable along clear lines of Wesley's philosophical theology.' This 'single vision' is unlikely to convince either intellectual historians or students of particular Romantic authors, although there may be some suggestive points in the rather perfunctory discussion of the major figures. Clarke Garrett's account (*JHI*) of Swedenborg's influence confines itself to little-known devotees.

Important historical works included John Cannon's impressive account[9] of the eighteenth-century peerage, which concludes that 'a comparatively small number of peers controlled to a great extent the commanding heights of political and social life', using as one of its most potent weapons of defence 'a powerful affirmation of the liberal and open nature of English society' – an affirmation in many respects mythical. Cannon's argument that aristocratic influence grew stronger as the century progressed is not much taken up by Ian R. Christie in his 'reflections on the British avoidance of revolution'[10], which concentrates on the 1780s and 1790s, discussing religion, social mobility, intellectual conservatism, the poor law and philanthropy, and finally (in contradiction of his title), the Englishness of England. Thomas Turner's diary[11], in the middle years of the century, provides 'one of the few intimate pictures of life at parish level in eighteenth-century England'. This selection, about a third of the whole, is much fuller than any previously available, and has useful annotation, although the list of Turner's reading is rather slapdash in its citations. The life of George Grenville[12], not previously told, is very much an account of political dealings. I have not seen the second volume of John Ehrman's acclaimed biography, *The Younger Pitt* (Stanford).

W. A. Speck's *Society and Literature in England 1700–60*[13], 'an attempt to reclaim creative writing for the historian', is unlikely to be greatly praised either by historians or by literary critics, although it has some good discussions – on politics and literature at the beginning of the century, for instance. But the narrative seldom rises to any very provoking analysis, and there is little discussion of language or (except in basic terms) ideology. The introduction to Stephen Copley's selection of extracts[14] does provide a useful framework in which to see the perception of social change. Copley distinguishes three

9. *Aristocratic Century: The peerage of eighteenth-century England*, by John Cannon. CUP. pp. x + 193. £19.50.

10. *Stress and Stability in late eighteenth-century Britain: Reflections on the British Avoidance of Revolution*, by Ian R. Christie. The Ford lectures. Clarendon. pp. 226. £19.50.

11. *The Diary of Thomas Turner 1754–1765*, ed. by David Vaisey. OUP. pp. xxxix + 386. £17.50.

12. *George Grenville: A Political Life*, by Philip Lawson. Clarendon. pp. x + 309. £19.50.

13. *Society and Literature in England 1700–60*, by W. A. Speck. G&M/Humanities (1983). pp. x + 228. £20.

14. *Literature and the Social Order in Eighteenth-Century England*, ed. by Stephen Copley. World and Word. CH. pp. 202. hb £17.95, pb £8.95.

discourses – civic humanism, Mandevillian economic analysis, and an embryonic political economy. He provides a wide range of extracts, which the specialist will find as flawed as such undertakings generally are, on the social establishment, commerce and industry, the economy and the social order, the poor, and crime.

Bridget Hill's anthology, *Eighteenth-Century Women*[15], has some very short extracts, in thirteen sections, each subdivided. The introduction is sensible, and the extracts, although not always from the best editions, are well chosen. Two articles suggest defects in Lawrence Stone's 'rise of the affective family' theory. Eileen Spring (*Albion*) bases her comments on legal history, and Mary Joe Hughes (*SECC* 13) on the letters of the Collier family of Hastings. Patricia M. Spacks considers women's gossip in conduct books and in the novel[16]. Conversation manuals are discussed by Leland E. Warren (*ECLife*, 1983).

Peter Wagner (*ECLife*, 1983) reviews eighteenth-century erotica, one example of which, Nicholas Venette's *Tableau de l'Amour Conjugal*, is discussed by Roy Porter (*JES*). John Mullan's article (*ECent*) on hypochondria and hysteria usefully comments both on medical and literary history. The interactions between the language of science and that of literature are also considered by Serge Soupel[17]. Smollett is one of the sources for Roger A. Hambridge's account of quackery, which tries to analyse the conditions for its success[17]. Barbara Brandon Schnorrenberg's 'Medical Men of Bath' (*SECC* 13) is more of a narrative.

The reader begins Geoffrey Summerfield's history of children's literature[18] with interest in his antithesis of fantasy and reason, but concludes it with some exasperation at what becomes a disabling opposition, licensing Summerfield to make superior comments on the authors surveyed. The book is short on spadework – the nature of Locke's influence, for instance, or the details of what children were actually reading – but it has some interesting comments on the childhood reading of certain Romantic authors and some lesser-known writers. The discussion, avowedly 'ruthlessly selective', includes Blake and Wordsworth's *Prelude*, as well as Newbery's children's books, Mrs Trimmer, R. L. and Maria Edgeworth, Thomas Day, and Mrs Barbauld. Summerfield complains of the 'philistine and grubbily commercial influence' of the Godwins, who published them, on Charles and Mary Lamb's work for children. A more practical response was the foundation, by the Rev David Williams, of the Royal Literary Fund, whose archives from 1790 to 1918 have been published on microfilm, with an index and introduction in book form[19].

15. *Eighteenth-Century Women: An Anthology*, ed. by Bridget Hill. A&U. pp. ix + 271. £18.

16. In *Women and Society in the Eighteenth Century*, ed. by Ian P. H. Duffy. Bethlehem, Pa.: Lawrence Henry Gipson Institute (1983). pp. vii + 38. np.

17. *Literature and Science and Medicine*, by Serge Soupel and Roger A. Hambridge. Papers read at the Clark Library Summer Seminar 1981. CML (1982). pp. viii + 102. np.

18. *Fantasy and Reason: Children's Literature in the eighteenth century*, by Geoffrey Summerfield. Methuen. pp. xvii + 315. £20.

19. *The Royal Literary Fund 1790–1918. An introduction to the Fund's history and archives with an index of applicants*, by Nigel Cross, with a foreword by Janet Adam Smith. WMP. pp. 72. £15. Microfilms, 145 reels, £3000.

Charles Camic's sociological study[20], based on secondary sources, advances the hypothesis that 'the independence and universalism of the Scottish Enlightenment first emerged out of the social experiences of the five intellectuals who comprise' it. The five are Hume, Smith, Ferguson, Millar, and Robertson, only the first two of whom are discussed in the more solid essays of *Philosophers of the Scottish Enlightenment*[21]. This volume also includes contributions on Thomas Reid, Gershom Carmichael, Dugald Stewart, and James Hutton. Peter Jones's thorough account of the Ciceronian and French contexts of Hume's thought is for philosophers rather than literary scholars[22]. In *N&Q* Richard H. Popkin prints a Hume letter of 1746, and in *JHI* Donald T. Siebert discusses Hume's views on idolatry and incarnation, Steven Wallech considers social status in the *Treatise*, and James E. Force argues that Hume's scepticism 'can be read in the light of' the efforts of members of the Royal Society 'to balance naturalism and supernaturalism'.

The Liberty Classics reprints of the Glasgow Edition of Adam Smith now include the *Essays on Philosophical Subjects*, the *Lectures on Jurisprudence*, and the *Wealth of Nations*[23]. Ian Ross (*SECC* 13) considers Smith's view of education as 'an integral part of his civic humanism'. David Marshall argues (*CI*) that the *Theory of Moral Sentiments* explores the nature of sympathy in 'a world that is structured and governed by theatrical relations', 'where people face each other as spectators and spectacles'. Two manuscripts with Thomas Reid's consideration of Smith's moral philosophy are reprinted by J. C. Stewart-Robertson and David Fate Norton (*JHI*). Joseph Priestley's utilitarianism and the compatibility of Richard Price's politics and ethics are discussed respectively by Margaret Canovan (*JHI*) and Susan Rae Peterson (*JHI*). Gregory Hollingshead (*ScLJ*) argues that Bishop Berkeley was an influence on Blackwell's views of Homer.

James Gibbs's building career is very fully documented in Terry Friedman's study[24]. His most famous church, St Martin-in-the-Fields, was 'the most significant ecclesiastical building in the English-speaking world of the eighteenth century'; his country houses demonstrated 'how such apparently irreconcilable stylistic attitudes as Baroque and Classical might be combined into a workable architectural design'. Friedman also discusses Gibbs's garden buildings and the *Book of Architecture*, and lists his documented works and the books he bequeathed to the Radcliffe. The life of William Kent, a less

20. *Experience and Enlightenment: Socialization for Cultural Change in eighteenth-century Scotland*, by Charles Camic. EdinU/UChic (1983). pp. xii + 301. £20.

21. *Philosophers of the Scottish Enlightenment*, ed. by V. Hope. EdinU. pp. xii + 261. £17.50.

22. *Hume's Sentiments: Their Ciceronian and French Context*, by Peter Jones. EdinU (1982). pp. viii + 230. £17.50.

23. All Liberty Classics. *Essays on Philosophical Subjects*, ed. by W. P. D. Wightman. Liberty (1982). pp. ix + 358. pb $5.50. *Lectures on Jurisprudence*, ed. by R. L. Meek, D. D. Raphael, and P. G. Stein. Liberty (1982). pp. viii + 610. pb $5.50. *An Inquiry into the Nature and Causes of the Wealth of Nations*, ed. by R. H. Campbell and A. S. Skinner, textual ed. W. B. Todd. Liberty. 2 vols. pp. viii + 544; pp. vii + 545–1080. $11.

24. *James Gibbs*, by Terry Friedman. Yale for the Paul Mellon Centre for Studies in British Art. pp. viii + 362. £40.

significant artist (except as a designer of furniture), is more interesting than that of Gibbs, partly because the range of his talents brought him into contact with many of the important men of arts and letters of his time. Michael I. Wilson's biography[25] gives a broad survey of the work 'against the background' of a narrative of his life, with a separate chapter on the landscape gardens. The plan of Pope's garden made by John Serle, his factotum as well as his gardener, is reprinted with an introduction by Morris R. Brownell[26]. The illustrated catalogue of an exhibition at Yale, *The Early Georgian Landscape Garden*[27], has a short introduction to each of the ten gardens – Hagley and The Leasowes, and Claremont and Esher, are discussed together, with the others ranging more or less chronologically from Chiswick to Stourhead.

Jonathan Richardson's 'rational and specifically Lockean empirical method' in *Two Discourses* is discussed by Carol Gibson-Wood (*AH*), who argues that the work 'represents one of the most remarkable and programmatic texts on connoisseurship within the entire literature of art'. Richard Wendorf (*NLH*) finds that a comparison of Richardson's graphic and literary work reveals how 'his conventional practice as a painter of faces is dramatically at odds with his intensely personal and emotionally charged biography of Milton, and with the visual images associated with it'.

Robert L. S. Cowley's very detailed analysis[28] of the six 'Marriage a-la-mode' paintings leads him to praise Hogarth's 'mastery over a wide range of forms of art' and his varied erudition: 'The intellectual and artistic achievement lay in making unity out of this medley of encyclopaedic reach.' Ronald Paulson (*YES*) teases the political allusions (to the Broad Bottoms) out of the 'Country Inn Yard at Election Time', and Peter de Bolla (*ECent*) considers the *Analysis* in terms of Hogarth's attempts to 'construct and project the consequences for a synecdoche-based rhetoric'.

Two of Reynolds's theatrical portraits, 'Garrick Between Tragedy and Comedy', and 'Mrs. Abington as "Miss Prue"', are discussed by David Mannings (*ECS*) and Joseph F. Musser Jr (*SAQ*), respectively. Irène Simon (*ES*) argues that Reynolds was less of a 'staunch supporter of prejudice' than is often thought. James Barry's *Inquiry into the Real and Imaginary Obstructions to the Acquisition of the Arts in England* (1775) is the centre of John Barrell's interesting consideration (*ECent*) of the lack of history-painting celebrating Britain's rise to power in the later eighteenth century. Marcia Pointon (*AH*) gives much solid information on how material conditions affected the style of portrait-painting in the 1780s. The problems of ethnic portraiture for the artists on Cook's voyages are discussed by Bernard Smith (*AH*).

25. *William Kent: Architect, Designer, Painter, Gardener, 1685–1748*, by Michael I. Wilson. RKP. pp. x + 276. £30.

26. *A Plan of Mr. Pope's Garden*, by John Serle, intro. by Morris R. Brownell. ARS 211. CML (1982). pp. xvi + 29. np.

27. *The Early Georgian Landscape Garden*, by Kimerly Rorschach. Yale Center for British Art (1983). pp. xii + 107. np.

28. *Marriage a-la-mode: a re-view of Hogarth's narrative art*, by Robert L. S. Cowley. ManU (1983). pp. xi + 177. £27.50.

The theme of Barbara Maria Stafford's *Voyage into Substance*[29] is the portrayal not of human beings but of the earth itself, of the explorers' 'unblunted appetite for natural phenomena', and the 'strong alliance' between art and science that brought about 'the widespread apprehension of a universe filled with both enduring robust substances and intermittent or fleeting apparitions and natural powers'. The range of Stafford's theme, geographically, stylistically, and in citation of travellers' accounts from England, France, Germany, Spain, Sweden, and Russia, can only be noted here. The book is lavishly produced and illustrated, and the discussion expansive and stimulating.

2. Poetry

Roger Lonsdale's *New Oxford Book of Eighteenth Century Verse*[30] reaches into all corners of its period, explores every latent tract and giddy height. Though Swift and Burns sing their distinctively substantial major parts at either end of the poetic concert, hundreds of minor talents swell a packed chorus. The editor's introduction sets its sights squarely on those obfuscating nineteenth-century pieties which continue to tempt into despair all teachers of eighteenth-century literature; and if his polemical contention that 'The "Peace of the Augustans" has come increasingly to seem a dangerous delusion' is familiar to the *YW* faithful, it may do some good to be repeated in an anthology which one hopes will reach many more readers than have the specialist analyses of enthusiasts. Not that Lonsdale can be accused of lacking enthusiasm, far from it, but he is an unusually well-read enthusiast and one who backs up his claims with the sheer weight and variety of the new material he adds to the secure curriculum of David Nichol Smith's earlier selection. Lonsdale also points out that canonical choices which determined the very concept of 'eighteenth-century poetry' were established long before Nichol Smith, by the collections of Robert Anderson and Alexander Chalmers in the nervous years after the French Revolution. One dangerously subversive sort of poetry thus specifically excluded was that written by women; and given the substantial contribution of women's studies to recent research on the eighteenth century, it is entirely appropriate that contemporary female poetic complaint should also sound through this new anthology, from Sarah Fyge Egerton in 1703, through Mary Leapor in 1751, to Mary Alcock (on Irish 'bigotry and all its guile') in 1799. A third Mary, Mary Scott, is found no corner of representative space by Lonsdale, though her *Female Advocate* (1774) appears under the imprint of the Augustan Reprint Society this year[31]. Introducing it, Gae Holladay explores the tactics of eighteenth-century feminism but says virtually nothing about the poetry. It is a wise choice of emphasis in this case. When Scott asks,

29. *Voyage into Substance: Art, Science, Nature, and the Illustrated Travel Account, 1760–1840*, by Barbara Maria Stafford. MITP. pp. xxiii + 645. $39.95.

30. *The New Oxford Book of Eighteenth Century Verse*, chosen and ed. by Roger Lonsdale. OUP. pp. xlii + 870. £25.

31. *The Female Advocate; a Poem. Occasioned by Reading Mr. Duncombe's Feminiad*, by Mary Scott, intro. by Gae Holladay. ARS. CML. pp. xiv + 50. pb $5.

What theme demands the tributary strain,
Whilst LORDLY MAN asserts his right divine,
Alone to bow at wisdom's sacred shrine;
With tyrant sway would keep the female mind
In error's cheerless dark abyss confin'd?
Tell what bright daughters BRITAIN once could boast,
What daughters now adorn HER happy coast.

the sentiment is righteous, the verse no more than verse. Compare Mary Leapor's uncompromising directness in the masculine couplet:

Since, whether sunk in avarice or pride,
A wanton virgin or a starving bride;
Or wond'ring crowds attend her charming tongue,
Or, deemed an idiot, ever speaks the wrong...
Yet, with ten thousand follies to her charge
Unhappy woman's but a slave at large.

The mere two pages of Anne Finch in Lonsdale is no answer to Denys Thompson's critical-biographical cameo (*PNR*, 1982) which complained about the lack of texts. Still, Thompson's conclusion might serve as a neat epigraph to so much in the *New Oxford* anthology, and not only the occasional female poet: 'when she has something to say and is moved to write in the traditions of her time, Anne Finch is at least as much worth reading as any of the minor poets'. Anne Williams's *Prophetic Strain: the Greater Lyric in the Eighteenth Century* (UChic) was unavailable for review, and there are times when one almost wishes the same was true of the more expansive theorizing in Fredric V. Bogel's *Literature and Insubstantiality in Later Eighteenth-Century English Literature*[32] which posits the old distinction between true Augustan grit and a withdrawing Age of Sensibility in a style which becomes progressively more opaque and then finally reduces to lists and diagrams in the closing chapters. Fredric Bogel can and does write impressively well on poets and poems: he is much less convincing when he pushes into generality. So it was when he wrote on Augustan poetics and 'Dulness Unbound' (*PMLA*, 1982; *YW* 63.259).

There is certainly no theoretical cohesiveness about the assorted papers on poets of the early decades this year, but the very variety seems to support Roger Lonsdale's eclectic thesis well enough. Norman Gillespie (*RES*) not only fleshes out the remarkable popularity of Henry Carey's *Ballad of Sally in Our Alley* – a reflexively anthologized piece which finds its inevitable niche in the *New Oxford* anthology – he also fixes its date as two years later than the tentative 1715 offered by Lonsdale, at the end of the 1716–17 Drury Lane season; and, for good measure, he reprints a wickedly parodic version from 1728 which contains fascinating glimpses into the contemporary literary scene. Hans Östman's claim (*MSpr*, 1983) that Defoe's *Caledonia* is 'a landmark in bourgeois literature' pre-dates both Lonsdale's and Gillespie's championing of half-forgotten poems, but delayed notice at least brings into a sympathetic

---

32. *Literature and Insubstantiality in Later Eighteenth-Century England*, by Fredric V. Bogel. Princeton. pp. xi + 226. £22.30.

context this essay on Defoe's characteristic combination of 'all-pervading utilitarianism' with passionate support for the indigent poor. Östman protests too stridently and is over-indulgent to Defoe's poetic gaffes; nevertheless, sturdy defence of Defoe as an occasional poet worth the reading is certainly timely. The immediate stimulus to *Caledonia* was Defoe's employment by Harley. Matthew Prior, new Tory chalk to Defoe's old Whig cheese, was also employed by the supple Prime Minister on a clandestine mission which J. D. Alsop (*BJECS*) re-investigates in a piece of historical detection which will please all readers of poetry who also have a taste for Le Carré. Indeed, Veronica Bassil (*TSLL*) is the only scholar interested primarily in Prior's literary ventures this year and even she is more concerned with *Henry and Emma* as the 'missing link' between Chaucer's *Clerk's Tale* and *Clarissa* than with the poem itself. The strain tells: because Prior wrote fluid narrative couplets 'his organizational unit seems to approximate not so much [to] the poetic stanza as the prose paragraph'. Much more soundly based are Samuel J. Rogal's 'Thoughts on Prior' (*ELWIU*), though here again there is only tangential reference to the poetry as Rogal pursues proof that the 'ingenious writer' taken to task by John Wesley in *Thoughts on the Character and Writings of Mr. Prior* is Johnson, in the *Life of Prior*. Here Prior is once more the mere focus for cagey manoeuvring by more powerful men – as he was in the power struggle between Harley and Bolingbroke. Poor Matt's fate thus dogs him down the centuries.

Another of Prior's friends, Jonathan Swift, has been treated more kindly in the last few decades. This year Angus Ross and David Woolley edit a hefty selection of the works which excludes *Gulliver's Travels* but includes a generous sampling of the poems[33] (these interleave the chronological progression of his other writings); and David M. Veith's choice of *Essential Articles* on the poetry[34] – all, of course, previously noted in *YW* – is another indication that Swift's verse now enjoys almost equal status with his prose satire. Quite new to these pages, though a piece of lively scholarship which should have been noted before, is the demolition by Pat Rogers of Samuel Macey's argument that *Bounce to Fop* could be the work of Henry Carey (*BRH*, 1982). Here Rogers has the elbow-room for a full statement of the case briefly summarized in his massive edition of the *Poems*, published and reviewed last year. Quite new in every respect are two papers on other individual poems. John M. Aden (*ELN*) shows how the art of sinking in astrology informs the *Elegy on Mr. Partridge* with its 'structural parody of the ascending and descending signs of the zodiac' (and with wickedly mischievous intent); and Leland D. Peterson (*MP*) makes his second contribution to the question of the disputed relationship between *On the Day of Judgement* and a Scriblerian prose-squib first printed in 'the third volume' of the Pope–Swift *Miscellanies*. Peterson insists that the squib was probably Swift's, that it served as a catalyst for the poem (when Swift's fears about Dissent's insidious influence were particularly urgent), and that it thus helps confirm the poem's composition in 1732 or 1733. Rogers agreed, more economically and also more cautiously, last year.

33. *Jonathan Swift*, ed. by Angus Ross and David Woolley. Oxford Authors. OUP. pp. xxxv + 724. pb £6.95.

34. *Essential Articles for the Study of Jonathan Swift's Poetry*, ed. by David M. Veith. Archon. pp. xii + 345. $35.

Pope had an impressive 1984 even by the crude estimate which measures the volume of publication. Pride of place is demanded by Maynard Mack with *The Last and Greatest Art*[35], a handsome 'volume of manuscripts and transcripts [which] represents the attainable and certainly the most useful part of what was once intended to be a collection of the entire canon of Pope's surviving manuscripts apart from the translation of Homer'. Here are manuscripts with facing (and blessedly large-format) transcriptions from the *Pastorals*, through the younger Jonathan Richardson's collations of early *Dunciad* drafts, the Epistles, *Burlington* and *Fortescue*, and the *Essay on Man*, to *Arbuthnot*. Since each of these has an 'Introduction' worthy of such a gifted scholar-critic there are penetrating insights and clear-eyed shrewdnesses aplenty. The recreation of *Arbuthnot*'s genesis is particularly fine: but it is perhaps more justly representative to quote a few lines from the 'General Introduction' on what 'a leaf from Pope's work-table' reveals:

> Always there is the stately processional of perceived intent coursing in a firm column down one side of the page. Always nearby there are the dance and play of new perceptions spinning off, developing their own fields of force, some wandering afield to die upon the margins or possibly to be revived in later contexts, others colliding, warring, at last fusing with the original column, altering its direction, sometimes causing it to disintegrate altogether.

If David Fairer thus has tough competition among potential readers restricted to only one purchase on Pope this year, at least he has Mack's implicit blessing for the thrust of a book which asserts the primacy of *Pope's Imagination*[36]. Fairer's main thesis is that Pope was a syncretic humanist to whom inconsistencies may all be true when applied to man. Imagination was literally and figuratively a vital concern. Byron was therefore right about Pope's genius, Wordsworth quite wrong. Like the imagination itself, Belinda is 'brilliant, unstable, alluring and independent of morality', Fairer asserts in an allegorical reading of the *Rape* which is firmly developed from his theoretical basis in the tradition of Renaissance faculty psychology. No mention here of ethical or social concerns, let alone the transformed nymph at her toilette as the gravitational centre for all the energies of a trading, bourgeois Britain; but few teachers of eighteenth-century literature will fail to find some sympathy with the special pleading – even, one suspects, the more cautious historians of ideas such as N. M. Goldsmith (*PSt*) who also tracks backwards to the Renaissance and then forwards to the first-generation Romantics as he puts Pope's 'Concept of the Mind' in a larger context. Fairer warns us against Coleridge's theory of the imagination where N. M. Goldsmith finds both poets in accord against the variant forms of mechanistic philosophy current in their times. Indeed, to Goldsmith, 'Pope's ideas about the ... poetic mind ... resembled fundamentally those of Coleridge'. Yet the apparent divide between the critics is not so great as it seems. Fairer's own version of the bi-partite imaginative faculty and his combative defence of 'the power which an *un*synthesised view

35. *The Last and Greatest Art: Some Unpublished Poetical Manuscripts of Alexander Pope*, transcribed and ed. by Maynard Mack. UDel. pp. 454. £36.
36. *Pope's Imagination*, by David Fairer. ManU. pp. 189. £24.50.

... could have for a creative artist' is not so different from Goldsmith's measured distinction between Pope's 'working assumptions' and the Coleridgean synthesis of theoretical developments which had developed slowly but surely from 1600. After all this stress upon the creative imagination it is the more unfortunate that David B. Morris's book *Alexander Pope: the Genius of Sense* (Harvard) was unavailable for review. Its title promised the inevitable counterstress.

The influence of Maynard Mack's years of work is again obvious – and recognized – in Peter Martin's *Pursuing Innocent Pleasures: the Gardening World of Alexander Pope*[37]. In *The Garden and the City* Mack analysed the symbolic and literary import of Pope's lifelong fascination with gardening. Here Martin concentrates on the physical application of his landscape theory to design, not only at Twickenham but also in the gardens of his friends. This Pope is the one who retired to gardening so that wounds might heal and spiritual batteries be restored as he created in miniature organisms the sweeps of his theoretical vision. There is much that is illuminating in this survey – for example in the analysis of the Peterboroughs' Bevis Mount as 'a genuine retreat, a *hortus conclusus*, where ... he responded profoundly to the reign of Spirit personified by the Lady, the dramatic beauty of the setting, its remoteness from high society, and the eccentricities of its owner, as if they were all part of a comprehensive allegory' – but Martin's grasp of gardening history (complemented by his eighty-four plates) is more secure than either the occasional biographical 'innocence' or his confidence that Pope's physical creativity celebrated only 'a past age of simple and honest tastes'. 'Innocence' can be a semantic trap. No less than Twickenham, *Windsor Forest* was a celebration which wove together past and present; but it was neither 'simple' nor 'honest' in these terms. Landscape gardening with more palpably ideological intent also provides the starting point for an expansively belletristic essay by John N. Morris (*SR*, 1983) on the poet as maker, always aware of his limitations and the irreducible gap between experience and art. Morris writes particularly well about Pope's ponderings on the shield of Achilles; so too does Robert W. Williams (*SSEng*, 1983–4) as he explores, with singularity and determination, the older, more casual observation that Pope followed the doctrine of *ut pictura poesis*. If the limitations of all monist concentrations are obvious enough here (as they are in David Fairer's insistence on a different sort of Renaissance influence), Williams's concluding paragraph on Pope as landscape gardener in a letter to Robert Digby (where the prose is a 'perfectly composed landscape painting on Claudian principles ... [and] also the *enactment* of a painting') reminds us of the harmonious relationships between the sister arts very persuasively.

Patricia Meyer Spacks (*SAQ*) gives the perspective glass a vigorous shake as she writes on Pope's literary flirtation with Lady Mary Wortley Montagu, a traffic in which the poet manipulated all the male advantages of romance to mould the lady in his own fanciful image while she retorted with 'antiromantic, antitender self-presentation of refusal' in her struggle to escape the creeping advance of epistolary amber. This essay has something in common with those on *Epistle to a Lady* noted below; but papers on *Eloisa to Abelard* deserve

37. *Pursuing Innocent Pleasures: the Gardening World of Alexander Pope*, by Peter Martin. Archon. pp. xxiv + 309. £31.75.

prior mention among the items on individual works if only because the chronological propriety of this choice from Pope's early poems may make part
amends for the chronological impropriety of belated recognitions. Gillian
Beer's eloquent essay on 'The Heroic Epistle, Pope and Women's Gothic'
(*YES*, 1982) was a particularly culpable omission from review of its year for,
with considerable critical and historical tact, this sets *Eloisa* in a continuum
(from Ovid, through Drayton and Daniel, to Dryden) which offered Pope 'a
language of sensation, an iconography, a grandeur of scale, an emphasis on
sequestration, and an acceptance of women's extreme emotion which was
[subsequently] central to the Gothic novelists'. By complete contrast, Nancy
McNeal's paper, in the *Journal of Evolutionary Psychology* (1980) was an
understandable oversight and one hardly worth the correcting. This naively
romantic version of psychosexual possibilities in the 'imagestic' (*sic*?) fabric of
the poem takes off from Murray Krieger's reading of the Church scene as
literally orgasmic via the iron constraints of the couplet to a soaringly secular
affirmation of 'the inadequacy of societal and institutional solutions'. Robert
James Merrett (*WascanaR*, 1983) also cites Murray Krieger but ploughs a
more sober and, it must be said, a less colourful middle way between, on the
one hand, Krieger's reading of an *Eloisa* in which the inconsistencies between
secular and divine were found to be beyond Pope's control and, on the other,
Dr Johnson's opinion that the poles are reconciled. Merrett's Pope is a conscious ironist who dramatizes Eloisa's bogus theologizing to make doctrinal
and even liturgical points. At least we're now back in familiar critical territory,
if not quite yet up to date, for mention must also be made of Colin N.
Manlove's fresh look at an older view of 'change and metamorphosis [which]
define [the] essential character' of the *Rape* (*DUJ*, 1983): since judgement,
which requires distancing, and sympathy, which presupposes intimacy, are the
simultaneous demands of the poem, truth is never singular, and Clarissa's
speech becomes a matrix for the whole work's shifting attitudes which belie the
surface monovocality. Howard Erskine-Hill digs deeper into the implications
of another well-established facet of the *Rape* (*YES*[38]). Wordsworth no less
than Pope was alive to the mock-heroic potential in the political 'Game at
Cards', but Pope wrung more out of it in a highly allusive structure not yet fully
exhausted, the commentator admits, by even someone so steeped in Popeiana
and its possibilities as himself. Wolfgang E. H. Rudat (*DUJ*) wants to pursue
allusion to its absolute extremes – if it has any – in his latest attempt to expand
Earl Wasserman's 'allusive context'. On this occasion he finds echoes of the
Aeneid at the opening of Canto IV of the *Rape* (mediated through Pope's
earlier parodic use of the same Virgilian resonance in *January and May*)
powering the sexual undertow in the work of a poet green in judgement and
thus tempted to mock the epic. It is an ingenious but necessarily very contingent argument.

Two other monographs not mentioned thus far also concentrate on single
poems: Steven Shankman on *Pope's 'Iliad'*[39], and A. D. Nuttall on *Pope's*

38. *English Satire and the Satiric Tradition*, ed. by Claude Rawson. Blackwell. pp. xiii
+ 289. hb £34.95, pb £12.95. This is a re-issue in hardcover of the *YES* special number on
Satire.
39. *Pope's 'Iliad': Homer in the Age of Passion*, by Steven Shankman. Princeton
(1983). pp. xviii + 194. £21.30.

'*Essay on Man*'[40]. The first part of Shankman's book is a thorough re-examination of Pope's Achilles which uses Chapman's 1611 translation as a sounding-board. Only a classicist could judge with confidence the arguments Shankman presents about the validity of either version *vis à vis* the original, but he does seem to make his case for Pope's passionate Achilles as a more faithful rendering. Whether or not one can then make the jump into agreement with Shankman that Pope's poem is the product of an 'Age of Passion' is another matter. If Chapman's hero is an enviably controlled Renaissance prince, and Cowper's an angry force, Pope's Achilles seems to fall betwixt and between in more than just chronological terms. The remainder of this study concerns itself with less contentious and more useful matters such as the influence of Longinus on Pope's choice of diction and the 'translation' of Homer into couplets. Nuttall's book is another, and welcome, close analysis of a poem which has proved stubbornly problematic for the student readership which the Unwin Critical Library addresses. This audience naturally prescribes the scope of Nuttall's ambition, but anyone will profit from following his persistent, progressive exploration of that finished plastic intricacy also made available (in its development) by Maynard Mack in the volume of manuscripts noted above. Nuttall, though, dissents from Mack's argument (in the Twickenham *Essay on Man*) on important matters such as influence and intellectual coherence; for example, he writes with direct conviction on the *Essay* as engaging poetry precisely *because* it represents inconsistent philosophy:

> It is *the* philosophical poem of the age in that it assembles, in a sort of brilliant display, the fractured systems of the age. . . . Its virtual exclusion of Revelation and its running tone of urbane compromise and balance (all savage in-fighting of sects transcended by polite reason) stamps it very plainly with the character of a specific period.

There's the rub. The poem has been so misrepresented to and by students as a statement of bland 'Augustan' smugness that one can understand why Nuttall was first persuaded to face the old categories head on and why he then felt the need to justify his decision: 'The frequency with which I have been forced in this study to use words proper to a later period, such as "Romanticism", is a mark of Pope's vital power as a thinker and a poet.' Lonsdale faced the same problem, but he rejected conventional terms such as 'Augustanism'. Nuttall's insistent attempts to qualify them *in use* may, one fears, deflect his student readers and annoy many others. Even Thomas Warton, that prophet of Romantic hostility to Pope, excepted the 'Poor Indian' passage in the first epistle of the *Essay* from his strictures about Pope's 'having written eclogues without invention', as Edward J. Reilly notes (*N&Q*).

Among the Moral Essays, *To a Lady* receives the most starkly varied attentions. Robert W. Williams (*SSEng*, 1984–5) continues his explorations of *ut pictura poesis* with an almost forensic eye to the poem's foundation 'upon the continued device of sketches in a poet-painter's studio'; but Ellen M. Pollak (*SEL*) sweeps all such ideologically ignorant niceties aside as she

40. *Pope's 'Essay on Man'*, by A. D. Nuttall. Unwin Critical Library. A&U. pp. 250. £15.

excoriates both the poet's and his critics' contentment with the socially-sanctioned, bourgeois myths of femininity. The hectoring polemic tone has been heard before, so Pollak's critical liveliness (which even allows her the odd witticism) is the more welcome: Martha Blount, for example, the supposed contrast within the poem as a *chaste* representation of sexually experienced yet dutiful perfection 'is no more an id/entity . . . no more unmixed or less impure than Pope's adulterous and vicious scattered women'. Aubrey L. Williams (*ELH*) is quite as ideologically convinced – if from a very different basis – that *Burlington* should be regarded as a companion-piece to *Bathurst*: 'Offences in the use of riches in both poems are to be seen as refusals of proper stewardship of wealth.' The 'apparatus of information' on Christian theology which prefaces this argument is rather laboured even if one concedes his repeated claim that such a construct will be either unavailable or distasteful to modern sensibilities. Niall Rudd (*YES*) strikes fewer sparks and will antagonize fewer readers (of either gender) as he makes his patient comparisons between the Latin original and Pope's *Epistle* II(ii).

Competing 'keys' to understanding dominate papers on *The Dunciad* this year. Indeed, Gregory Hollingshead (*ESC*) first argues on internal evidence (for the external, see his piece in *DUJ*, 1982) that George Berkeley's *Alciphron: or, the Minute Philosopher*, in particular its delight in analogue, is the 'true key' proposed as the transforming agent in the 1743 edition and which thus explains 'how it is that the dunces and their shadowy world, however mean and insignificant *in themselves*, function *in the text* as signs of the larger compass of folly, ignorance, and spiritual decay that constitutes the full effect of Dulness upon a civilized world'. Then (in *ScLJ*) Hollingshead finds the same source an equally 'key' influence on Thomas Blackwell's 'revolutionary conception of Homer as the perfect product of a perfect environment for poetry'. 'Revolutionary'? These essays are not exceptions to the rule that prospectors for influence are prone to exaggerate the exclusivity and extent of the claims they stake out. Roger D. Lund (*PLL*) almost admits as much, after he has elaborated on William King's *Rufinus* as a rival, compelling source for *The Dunciad*: the 'evidence of Pope's borrowings is circumstantial but nonetheless convincing', writes Lund, to which the respective replies must be 'true' and 'possibly'. From the mass of evidence supplied by Douglas Brooks-Davies (*SML*, 1983) in defence of an equally partial claim that 'Pope's . . . mock-epic and mock-Georgic . . . should be read as an alchemical poem', this scholar too would have his reservations about *Rufinus* as a source, but none about the relevance of other state poems (which used the image of the king's redeeming alchemy) as an influence on Pope who simply (or complicatedly) reversed the panegyric parallel in *The Dunciad*'s demolition of a quack Laureate who doubled for the Hanoverian King. After all the novelties of these contending keys, it is reassuring to plod through the inductive linguistic analysis of Marina Tarlinskaja's formulae, tables, and graphs (*Style*) to the grave conclusion that 'English iambic meter makes use of the general tendencies of the English language, but exaggerates them to form a specific convention' in Pope's couplets. Well, yes. There is more to catch the attention in the Augustan Reprint Society's *Satires Written by Mr. Whitehead*[41], with a useful introduc-

41. *Satires Written by Mr. Whitehead*, by Paul Whitehead, intro. by Vincent Carretta. ARS. CML. pp. xiv + 52. pb $5.

tion by Vincent Carretta which assesses the relationship between Pope and this less-gifted, more genial fellow satirist.

Non-satiric and couplet-eschewing poets of the early and middle decades have their followers too, of course. Dustin Griffin (*SEL*) beats the drum for 'John Philips and Miltonic Imitation' – rather than for the poet's venture into truly martial verse, the unfortunate *Blenheim* – in a protest against the 'anxiety of influence' as perceived by Harold Bloom and Walter Jackson Bate. Griffin makes his point about Philips's affectionate, confident adaptation of Miltonic prosody. Still, fine as the *Splendid Shilling* is in its genre, it does represent a flimsy test-case for Griffin's larger claims, and even those are preferable to the assertions of Mitsuo Kamio (*SELit*) who would turn the literary critical clock decades backwards in the name of an Edward Young 'helpful to bridge the rift between neoclassicism and romanticism'. David R. Anderson offers a more tangible service in his introduction to Young's sermon *A Vindication of Providence* (1728)[42] as a gloss on *Night Thoughts*. Single contributions on other poets or poems, all in *N&Q*, are equally modest: D. C. Kay finds both Donne and Thomson contributing to the pejorative connotations of 'ant-hill' available to Wordsworth; Mark Box identifies a quotation 'taken, with some liberties' from Francis Hutcheson by Mark Akenside; and John G. Radcliffe finds further evidence to confirm David Foxon's attribution of *A New Canto of Spenser's Fairy Queen* (1746–7) to John Upton. By comparison, Gray and Collins receive more muscular attention. The *Elegy*, in particular, is well served this year. The first paper is another brief note by T. P. Foley (*N&Q*) on a possible source of 'mute inglorious' resonance in George Stubbes's *Dialogue on Beauty in the Manner of Plato*. More substantial in every sense is the proposal by R. J. Dingley (*AUMLA*) that the *Elegy*'s 'Epitaph' was an unmistakable signal, warning its contemporary readers that the poem's private meditation had shifted into a public mode (a thoughtful argument made to seem unnecessarily knotty by the printing of transposed but consecutively numbered pages in the copy I read). A second essay on the *Elegy*, by W. Hutchings (*SP*), not only takes a different view, it also takes its place among the best articles I have seen on any topic this year. Starting from the explorations of earlier generations (Latinists to New Critics), Hutchings moves smoothly into his own elaboration of both fine detail and wide context; for example, Gray's manipulation of Latinate syntax so that objects and actions melt consistently and meaningfully together in a truly poetic 'argument' for death as oblivion. Here the *Elegy*'s linguistic logic and emotional integrity is unquestionable, and the 'Epitaph' an irresistibly necessary conclusion rather than a shift of mode.

Collins too is the subject of lively dispute. John Barrell's chapter on the *Ode to Evening* in *Teaching the Text*[43] reconstructs what must have been an enviably responsive extempore class. He analyses variant literal 'readings' (plus another of his own) to draw out ambivalencies of syntax which – in contradis-

---

42. *A Vindication of Providence: Or, a True Estimate of Human Life*, by Edward Young, intro. by David R. Anderson. ARS. CML. pp. xi + 104. pb $7.

43. *Teaching the Text*, ed. by Susanne Kappeler and Norman Bryson. RKP (1983). pp. viii + 219. pb £5.95.

tinction to Hutchings's version of Gray – represent an *indeterminate* mediation between the public, allegorical address and personal, contemplative impulses encoded in the descriptions. Gerald A. Kirk (*SCeR*) is a theoretician with different, mythological concerns who divines a sustained (and strained) progression in the *Ode on the Poetical Character* to the 'tortured cry of a man in the throes of unrequited love ... deserted by his loved one', a decidedly sexy Muse. Meanwhile, Patricia Meyer Spacks (*MLQ*, 1983) fights back against the critics who have offered or stimulate such readings, such as Harold Bloom, Geoffrey Hartman, and Thomas Weiskel (the latter is quoted with approval by Kirk):

> The criticism that glorifies [Collins's poetry] for its intimations of a new sensibility – minimizing its incoherence and constantly deflected purpose, or attributing them to the bad influence of eighteenth-century rationality – ignores Collins's occasional, true, modest achievement: a verse of quiet, faintly melancholy compromise.

Patricia Spacks chooses her ground well. Some modern critics of Collins have indeed made the clarities he did not find; but William Forbes (*N&Q*) and Nigel Wood (*DUJ*) return comment to the relative quiet of historical annotation. Forbes observes that *An Indian Pastoral Eclogue*, ascribed to Joseph Harris by Foxon, was a precursor of the *Persian Eclogues*, while Wood traces 'the retreat' of the Shepherd pastoral into the same oriental mode – and a dead end. If it was not such a gross pun, one might have used the same phrase to describe the utter disagreement on Chatterton. Brian E. Mayne, in the improbable context of the *MTJ* (1983), waxes lyrical about 'The brief life of the greatest prodigy in the history of English literature' and berates those desiccated grammarians who displayed such sterility of spirit when they rumbled the marvellous boy: 'One wonders what conclusion Skeat might have drawn had he been familiar with present-day research into multiple personalities – or what speculations he might have made had he been a believer in reincarnation.' What indeed! Undeterred, Ian Haywood fossicks on (*N&Q*) to show that in one of the most celebrated 'antiquarian' pieces, *The Rolle of Seynte Bartlemeweis Priorie* (1769), Chatterton added to his repertoire as the complete forger by plagiarizing Goldsmith's *Bee*.

By a convoluted irony, Goldsmith's own poetry is also the subject of two thoroughly opposed evaluations in two chapters from Andrew Swarbrick's collection, *The Art of Oliver Goldsmith*[44]. John Montague first presents Goldsmith's credentials as an Irish poet-critic prepared to reject the appropriation of Auburn to an exclusively Irish meaning only to return home with a vengeance, 'For although the idea of an Irish literature in English was outside his experience, *The Deserted Village* rehearses one of the most Irish themes of all, a forecast of the downfall of Britain through imperial greed'. This special pleading is the more seductive because it declares itself in every aspect of its rhetoric. Elsewhere in the same volume, J. A. Downie writes on the satires as a very English dissenter who (at least implicitly) rejects all the claims to 'universal application' on which Montague builds his case. The nub of Downie's

44. *The Art of Oliver Goldsmith*, ed. by Andrew Swarbrick. Vision Critical Studies. Vision/B&N. pp. 200. £13.95.

complaint is that Goldsmith had insufficient fire in his belly, or, to be more precise, 'The "refinement" of Goldsmith's irony is the tasteful elegance of the new era of sensibility . . . not the purifying fire of the Augustans'. Although that conclusion is persuasive, as a verdict on the early satires at least, the old terminology is less than helpful. 'Sentiment', another code-word which is applied with some justification (and flexibility) by both Montague and Downie, is coincidentally the central issue of a stanza-by-stanza plod through Johnson's *Ode on the Death of Dr. Robert Levet (PLL)*. John A. Vance rejects the opinions of all who have disputed the degree and type of grief expressed by the poem: 'We find, instead of a grieving poet, a jubilant moralist informing his readers that they need not despair.' 'Jubilant'? Such a startling claim might have demanded more consideration had its proponent's own method been more consistently applied. It is, for example, simply not true that after the fifth stanza 'Johnson . . . takes the reader from the cavern into the sunlight': witness the first verses of the seventh stanza, 'His virtues walked their narrow *round, / Nor made a pause, nor left a void'*. Readers can now check such textual claims in yet another inexpensive edition, the Oxford Authors *Samuel Johnson*[45] with its substantial selection assembled (in opposition to the principle which governs the companion-volume on Swift) in a discrete body of 'Poetry'. Like Vance, two of the commentators on *The Vanity of Human Wishes* begin by taking issue with most of their predecessors, but they then pursue their arguments, based upon Johnson's sources, more rigorously. First Chester Chapin (*ECS*) objects to dismissals of its 'weak' or 'contradictory' conclusion as ignorant of Juvenal imitated since the allusive context of classical stoicism provides an instructive subtext; then Thomas Jemielity (*ELWIU*) allies himself with Howard Weinbrot on the *Vanity* as 'true satire' against Walter Jackson Bate's 'satire manqué'. Jemielity points shrewdly to the fact that Juvenal offered Johnson philosophical alternatives to the chilling panorama of humanity – Heraclitus (to weep over it) and Democritus (to laugh derisively) – but that Johnson invokes only the latter and supports his choice with a mass of pejorative theatrical metaphors. James A. Means (*PQ*) also supports the *Vanity* as 'true satire', at least by association, when he finds a correspondence between the couplet on Marlborough and Swift (a venemously enforced cohabitation I have always thought) and a swing at Loyola in Oldham's third *Satyr upon the Jesuits*. Mention of Oldham and a more obviously raw-boned type of satire brings to mind (and relevance) Peter M. Briggs's attempt to modify received wisdoms about Charles Churchill's 'crude talent' (*MLS*). Briggs offers instead an uncertain satirist who might have found his true, consistent voice had he lived to sort out his epistemological dilemma over the status of objective as against subjective authority. This is a well-made if also charitable apology for Churchill's unevenness, in which the high jinks at High Wycombe become escapes from agonizing rather than the cause of a thick head and a careless pen. Certainly *The Crab*, a previously unpublished poem by Churchill (written 1762–4 and possibly intended as a ribald entertainment for the Medmenham brotherhood), which is reproduced and glossed by Lance Bertelsen (*PQ*), shows all the characteristics of the erratic Churchill well documented elsewhere; but there is no sign of epistemological uncertainty in

45. *Samuel Johnson*, ed. by Donald Greene. Oxford Authors. OUP. pp. xxxii + 840. pb £6.95.

this bawdy parody of the Moral Fable, not that one would reasonably expect to find such *angst* if Bertelsen's surmise about the occasion for it is accurate.

Yet among the later-eighteenth-century poets considered oddly peripheral until well into our age, 1984 is the year of Christopher Smart rather than any satirist. Lonsdale's anthology allows him twenty-two pages, far more than any other contemporary (indeed, more than Gray and Collins); but more importantly, Marcus Walsh and Karina Williamson give us the second volume of their *Poetical Works of Christopher Smart: Religious Poetry, 1763–1771*[46] which contains – in order of appearance – *Hymns and Spiritual Songs* (1765), *A Song to David* (1763), two oratorios, *Hannah* (1764) and *Abimelech* (1768), *The Parables of Our Lord and Saviour* (1768), and *Hymns for the Amusement of Children* (1771) in an edition which maintains the enviable reputation of the Oxford English Texts and with full introductions to each section plus a commentary which runs to almost one hundred pages of meticulous annotation. It would be tautologous to heap more praise on this, the second of five promised volumes, than it has already received in, for example, Claude Rawson's exceptionally full review for *TLS* (9 November); and it will be interesting to see if the completed venture does for Smart what the James King and Charles Ryskamp edition of the *Letters* has done for Cowper studies. As if to prime this pump too, James King (*ES*) supports his fellow Oxford editors with an economical paper on the psychological and structural relationship between *Jubilate Agno* and *A Song to David*: the first, written during mental turmoil, is a mimesis in which a David/Smart struggles desperately for redemption, the second, bathed in the light of grace, is a joyously *structured* poem glorifying in its own articulateness. Other, more established champions of Smart keep their shoulders to the scholarly plough, and this year Betty Rizzo (*N&Q*) identifies Smart as the author of a popular burlesque cantata, *The Dust Cart* (first performed in 1753), though she makes no inflated claims for its merit. She also (in *RES*) deftly puts together the text of a letter to Charles Burney with a secular version of *Hymn XXXII*, published in the *London Chronicle*, 16 June 1770, to fill out more of our physical and some of our psychological knowledge of Smart's last year – in King's Bench prison. Harriet Guest (*ECent*) tackles wider scholarly perspectives in her survey of Smart's views about the relationship between religion and natural science. As she develops her thesis, she takes discriminating issue with Karina Williamson's '*fundamentally* unscientific' Smart and with other oversimplifications of the debate between pro- and anti-Newtonians: 'the habit of mind that informs *Jubilate Agno* is perhaps more representative of the eighteenth-century concern to place science in a role and context crucial to and wholly interrelated with man's understanding of his relation to history and society, to faith, and to creation'. Smart emerges as not unique, or even very eccentric, in his insistence that interpretation of the natural world must involve an *interpretative* act (though he was certainly more conscious than many of mankind's capacity for error consequent on the Fall): 'in a Newtonian world-view ... the nature of this act is disguised by the assumption of the purity and rightness of man's reasoning power and by the partly rhetorical device of ostensibly rejecting hypotheses'. Guest does not

46. *The Poetical Works of Christopher Smart*. Vol. II: *Religious Poetry, 1763–1771*, ed. by Marcus Walsh and Karina Williamson. OET. Clarendon. pp. xix + 472. £35.

indulge herself in broad literary comparisons, but this review can afford to be less tactful, and it is an intriguing thought that in this one crucial area of conviction there is little difference between Smart and Swift. Little by little, year by year, the divide between 'Augustan' and 'neo-Romantic' also seems more a creation of 'the assumption of the purity and rightness of [and views of] man's reasoning power'.

'Adieu Dear Sir, whom in those days I call'd Dear Friend, with feelings that justified the appellation' is the last sentence of Cowper's last extant letter, to John Newton on Thursday, 11 April 1799. This final flicker of an earlier, gracious, genial poet, in remembrance of times past, is perhaps more melancholy than all the melancholic brooding and enervating sickness which fills his correspondence in the fourth volume of his *Letters and Prose Writings* (1792–9)[47]. The editing of James King and Charles Ryskamp remains unobtrusive and precise but there are many contextual reasons why even Cowper devotees may not pause too long over the last letters and look forward instead to the concluding volume of this long and splendid project, a collection of miscellaneous prose. Meanwhile, Thomas Dilworth (*Expl*) works busily with the complex paradoxes given harrowing tactility in the *Lines Written during a Period of Insanity*; Arthur Sherbo (*BRH*, 1982) ranges far and wide, hunting 'stricken deer' in poem after poem to conclude that 'Cowper took a much used image' rather than a specific usage for his emblem; and Joan Owen Digby (also *BRH*, 1982) replies that those thus accused of blinkered source-identification are in fact more concerned with the power evident *in* the emblematic tradition – whether in poetry or the other arts – to block real observation of real deer by the otherwise most observant of poets.

Two items on Burns demand notice this year, although the most substantial, a monograph by Mary Ellen Brown, *Burns and Tradition* (UIll) was not available for review. More's the pity, since it would have provided an appropriate coda to the review essay of G. Ross Roy (*SSL*) in which he works his partial, astute way through works on Burns between 1968 and 1982. Commenting on a 1969 monograph, he writes that it was one of those 'Books on Burns [which] fall into the category of publications on which a house can confidently expect to make money. In this respect they are like cookbooks [for] although nothing new appears . . . the public is willing to purchase . . . the same old menu.' It will be interesting to hear his opinion of Brown's *table d'hôte*. Everard B. King seems to have been pleading his case for Beattie's *Minstrel* as a seminal, all-pervading influence on the major Romantics for longer than the span covered by Ross Roy's review. In fact he began – in print anyway – no earlier than 1977. This year (in *ScLJ*) it is the French Romantics who owe the *Minstrel* a great debt, particularly de Chateaubriand (it seems that culinary associations are inescapable on Scots poets in 1984) and, via his *René*, the Byronic hero. Yet it is Robert Fergusson who elicits the most appetizing re-assessments this year. Allan T. McKenzie (also *ScLJ*) serves up a crisp textual analysis and background context for *To the Principal and Professors of the University of St. Andrews, on Their Superb Treat to Dr. Samuel Johnson*, published in the *Weekly Magazine*, 1 September 1773. This is an

---

47. *The Letters and Prose Writings of William Cowper*. Vol. IV: *1792–1799*, ed. by James King and Charles Ryskamp. Clarendon. pp. xxxiv + 498. £48.

enjoyable taste of a Scots humanist so like the Great Cham in some aspects but so unlike him (and indignantly, wittily nationalistic) in others. F. W. Freeman's study, *Robert Fergusson and the Scots Humanist Compromise*[48] is more ponderous on occasion ('we have argued that', 'It is now time to examine', and so forth) but his committed analysis of dilemmas and solutions is a welcome contribution to the growing body of serious work on an unduly neglected poet. Both Freeman's method and his concerns are confidently old-fashioned; for example, his introductory chapter owes more to Kathleen Williams's 'Age of Compromise' than the later attempts to unite criticism with the history of ideas, and his steady progress through categorized poems which slot into their discrete places during the following chapters (each on a facet of the Scottish Enlightenment) is overly schematic. Nevertheless, the sheer information collected here would have been of value even without the extensive quotation – sometimes whole pages of it – from texts which remain difficult to find, and the Fergusson who emerges is quite as clearly a poet of creative contradiction as he is an example of Scots 'compromise'. The comparison with Burns is, of course, irresistible, and Jerry O'Brien (*SSL*) duly offers Fergusson as Burns's model for the decision about which language to use for verse. He is less convincing when he argues that 'Fergusson is [also] Burns's source for the satiric application of classical imagery [which] represents in miniature the greater tension that both felt' in choosing between English and dialectal Scots. There are other candidates, in both languages, and even O'Brien has to admit that the Neoclassical could be harmonized (and 'humanized') for purposes other than satiric contrast. Moreover, his conclusion – that 'Fergusson's rejection of the neoclassical mode taught [Burns] a lesson that only a mortal muse could provide: to look into his heart and write' – implicitly takes us back to the old assumptions about 'Augustan' and 'neo-Romantic' tackled by Roger Lonsdale and mentioned at the outset of this review of writing on eighteenth-century poetry in 1984. The rage for and against order continues.

3. Drama

This year, 1984, was a rather more fruitful year than usual for books on the drama, but not for your reviewer, who was unable to find copies of three of the most promising. The latest two volumes of the *Biographical Dictionary*[49] – Kickill to Machin and M'Intosh to Nash – can rest on the virtues of the preceding eight volumes of this indispensable reference work. *British Theatre and Other Arts, 1660–1800* (Folger) edited by S. S. Kenny contains essays on promising topics like drama as a source for the pictorial and plastic arts, theatre and the art of caricature, and the relationship between the theatre and the novel (by Robert Halsband, Leo Hughes, and J. Paul Hunter). *The Licensing Act of 1737*, by Vincent J. Liesenfeld (UWisc), should, one hopes, illuminate that crucial parliamentary intervention in dramatic history.

48. *Robert Fergusson and the Scots Humanist Compromise*, by F. W. Freeman. EdinU. pp. viii + 249. £15.

49. *A Biographical Dictionary of Actors, Actresses, Musicians, Dancers, Managers, and other stage Personnel in London, 1660–1800*, by Philip H. Highfill Jr, Kalman A. Burnim, and Edward A. Langhans. SIU. $40 each.

Robert D. Hume (*ThR*) supplements the *London Stage*'s account of the origins of the actor benefit, arguing for the 'actors' plays' of the 1690s as the key link between group and individual benefits. A prologue from the Portland manuscripts, possibly used at the New Theatre, Lincoln's Inn Fields, in 1714, is printed by Graham Barlow (*TN*). Norman Gillespie (*ES*) discusses an operatic version of Gay's *Dione*, and Charles C. Mish a prose version of *The Tempest* (in Kenny). Jeannette Massy-Westropp's consideration (*ThR*) of the technique of acting the villain is mostly based upon French sources.

Sybil Rosenfeld's history of the theatre in Richmond, Yorkshire[50], unique among provincial theatres in the preservation of its records, includes much quotation from the diaries and letters of the actor-managing family under whom the theatre flourished from the mid eighteenth to the early ...neteenth century. An appendix lists plays otherwise unknown, from the almost complete set of playbills. Garrick's portraits are discussed by Kalman A. Burnim (in Kenny), and a little-known pamphlet, *Common Prayer as Read by the Late Mr. Garrick* (1797) by Derek Forbes (*TN*). A new series for schools, the Longman Study Texts, includes *The School for Scandal*[51], with not very impressive introductory matter. I have not seen Robert Hogan's and Jerry C. Beasley's edition of Frances Sheridan's plays (UDel/AUP).

Gerald Kahan discusses George Alexander Stevens's great theatrical success, the 'Lecture on Heads', as a 'work perfectly suited to its time and place', and prints a text as well as details of the paraphernalia and stage business[52]. There is a bibliography of Stevens and a production history – comprehensive but not complete – of the 'Lecture'. In his edition of plays by Samuel Foote and Arthur Murphy, George Taylor compares their 'workmanlike efficiency' with contemporary TV drama[53]. Biographical records and lists of their published plays are given for both men. The plays reprinted are Foote's *The Minor* and *The Nabob*, and Murphy's *The Citizen*, *Three Weeks After Marriage*, and *Know Your Own Mind*.

4. Prose

After the completion of Ehrenpreis's biography last year, 1984 brought another good crop of works on Swift. Richard H. Rodino's annotated bibliography, *Swift Studies, 1965–1980*[54], updates Tobin and Landa and Stathis, with nearly 1200 entries for fifteen years, where Stathis had 659 for twenty years. The lists and annotation are very good, although it would have been

50. *The Georgian Theatre of Richmond, Yorkshire and its circuit: Beverley, Harrogate, Kendal, Northallerton, Ulverston and Whitby*, by Sybil Rosenfeld. STR in association with William Sessions, Ltd, York. pp. vi + 114. np.

51. *The School for Scandal*, by Richard Brinsley Sheridan, ed. by Ray Heath, with a personal essay by Michael Billington. Longman Study Texts. Longman. pp. 1 + 105. pb £1.50.

52. *George Alexander Stevens and The Lecture on Heads*, by Gerald Kahan. UGeo. pp. ix + 222. £22.95.

53. *Plays by Samuel Foote and Arthur Murphy*, ed. with an intro. and notes by George Taylor. CUP. pp. xi + 233. hb £24, pb £8.95.

54. *Swift Studies, 1965–1980. An Annotated Bibliography*, by Richard H. Rodino. Garland. pp. xl + 299. $46.

better to abandon the cross-references (where consistency breaks down) in favour of more thorough indexing. The introduction discusses five representative controversies – the persona in *A Tale of a Tub*, the 'fool among knaves', the hard and soft interpretations of *Gulliver's Travels*, and the elements of travesty or seriousness in the *Project for the Advancement of Religion* and in 'The Lady's Dressing Room'. The Oxford Authors Swift, edited by Angus Ross and David Woolley[55], sensibly excludes *Gulliver's Travels*, but has everything else the non-specialist would want, except perhaps an ode or two, in texts carefully established for this selection. The contents are chronologically arranged, so that poems (thirty or so), prose works, periodical papers, letters (eighteen), and sermons gain by being read in context with each other. There are ninety pages of notes, indexes, and a useful introduction.

Ross and Woolley's briefer analysis – 'so much may be said of the political and religious complexity of Swift's position, not to "explain" his writing, but to suggest the centres of potential disturbance in it' – has thematic similarities with J. A. Downie's, in his *Jonathan Swift Political Writer*[56]. Downie aims to present the facts of Swift's life, with the emphasis on the political rather than the personal, and to give some commentary on the major works for a possible 'general reader'. For that reason, Swift is more simply explained for Downie than he is for Ross and Woolley. Compare, for instance, Downie's verdict that for Swift man is 'merely an animal capable of reason but dominated, more often than not, by his passions' with their expression of Swift's 'passionate wish for order, a clear and steady awareness not only of how far human beings fell short of their potential, but also of that "treasury of vileness and baseness . . . in the heart of man"'. On his political theme, Downie argues for the consistency of Swift's 'Country' or 'Old Whig' views, from the beginning of Anne's reign (when Swift did not realize his political differences from the Whig party) to his Irish pamphlets, maintaining that 'it is crucial to grasp the extent to which his Irish pamphlets were simply an extension of his English ones' (in opposition, for example, to Fabricant's *Swift's Landscape, YW* 64.313). If Ehrenpreis's Swift was a man freed from 'sibylline frenzy', Downie's is yet more orderly and consistent.

Much of Ehrenpreis's masterful range of detail on Swift's everyday life came from his research into nine extant annual account books, which have been transcribed by Paul V. and Dorothy Jay Thompson, along with two other financial notebooks[57]. Their long introduction gives a very thorough and interesting review of what can be gleaned from these notebooks about Swift's friendships, travels, health, and routine activities, including his dogs and horses, as well as his private and ecclesiastical finances. There is an index of proper names and a concordance. Finally, Rex Whistler's illustrated *Gulliver's Travels*[58] of 1930 (the 1735 text) has been reprinted, in a smaller size, with an

55. *Jonathan Swift*, ed. by Angus Ross and David Woolley. Oxford Authors. OUP. pp. xxxv + 722. hb £15, pb £6.95.

56. *Jonathan Swift Political Writer*, by J. A. Downie. RKP. pp. xv + 391. £25.

57. *The Account Books of Jonathan Swift*, transcribed and intro. by Paul V. Thompson and Dorothy Jay Thompson. UDel/Scolar. pp. cxxxvi + 350. £30.

58. *Gulliver's Travels*, illustrated by Rex Whistler, with a foreword by Laurence Whistler. London: Herbert Press. pp. 256. £12.50.

introduction by Laurence Whistler on the original edition and the artist's methods.

Everett Zimmerman's purpose in *Swift's Narrative Satires*[59] is to 'explore the strategic position of Swift's satires' in relation to developments in intellectual history – biblical hermeneutics, the epistemology of empiricism and the new science – and the political conflicts of the seventeenth century. Swift transmutes inherited literary forms, and both *A Tale of a Tub* and *Gulliver's Travels* 'make the oppositions of the literal and the allegoric, and of narrative and satire, into both formal and thematic concerns'. The argument is interesting and sophisticated, using the intellectual context as an analytical tool, with a wide range of well-digested reference. The book might have been shorter, and it is sometimes difficult to disentangle the 'epistemology' and 'language' themes of the argument, but it provides good insights into the two main works, and into Swift's relationship with the intellectual trends of his time. A somewhat similar argument is advanced in Timothy J. Reiss's *The Discourse of Modernism*[60], in which fictions of a Utopian nature (including *Robinson Crusoe*) are considered to demonstrate 'the creation and development of the various elements fundamental to analytico-referential discourse'. Reiss's discussion concentrates on Book IV of *Gulliver's Travels*, where the behaviour of the Houyhnhnms 'follows the discourse of experimentalism'.

Herman J. Real and Heinz J. Vienken's study in German of *Gulliver's Travels*[61] offers an extensive introduction to Swift's text starting with a synopsis of the changing critical response since the first publication of *Gulliver's Travels* in 1726 and including reference to the implications of the discovery of the Armagh edition, Swift's own first edition with seventy-five annotations in his hand, in 1976. Separate chapters treat the inception, publication and initial reception of the text, its objectives, satirical intention and Swift's anthropological philosophy, the etymology and semantics of the proper names, the function of the hero and the structure of the narrative. The main chapter gives the authors' interpretations of the four voyages. The text is complemented by a tabular biography of Swift and a comprehensive bibliography including many items in English.

Gulliver's Travels is, as usual, the theme of many of the Swift articles. John Traugott (*YES*) argues that the 'big and little' offers satiric emphasis through the perspectives of childhood: in the political rope-dancing, for instance, 'by the aesthetic trick of miniaturization made charming and "cute", the picture of political man is devastating and without relief'. In *SEL* Robert R. Fitzgerald and E. E. Sullivan discuss the Struldbruggs, and the inconsistency of all parties in Book IV, respectively. Many of the other contributions consider sources and influence, at greater or less length. William S. Anderson (*YES*) argues that Swift used the 'satiric strategy and ironic vision' of Horace together with

59. *Swift's Narrative Satires: Author and Authority*, by Everett Zimmerman. CornU (1983) (*recte* 1984). pp. 183. $19.50.

60. *The Discourse of Modernism*, by Timothy J. Reiss. CornU (1982). pp. 410. $28.50.

61. *Jonathan Swift: 'Gulliver's Travels'*, by Herman J. Real and Heinz J. Vienken. Fink. pp. 187. pb.

theological input to create in Book IV 'a false or parodic paradise that is well lost'. Other influences considered are Sir Isaac Newton (Bruce Olsen, *EAS*), Dr Derham (Eric Rothstein, *EA*), Xenophon (Leon Guilhamet, *ELN*), the Rosicrucians (Marie Roberts, *N&Q*), and *Purchas* (Dirk Passman, *N&Q*). William Kupersmith (*MP*) gives patristic sources for the Aeolists in *A Tale of a Tub* and Richard N. Ramsey (*PLL*) sources in Sir William Temple for *The Battle of the Books*. In *N&Q* Simon C. Pugh notes a variant second edition of *The Conduct of the Allies*, and Frank H. Ellis announces that Teerink's variant, 45A(1), is a ghost. I have not seen W. B. Carnochan's article on Swift and Stella in *Mothering the Mind: Twelve Studies of Writers and Their Silent Partners* (H&M), edited by R. Perry and M. Watson Brownley.

Laura A. Curtis's study[62] of the 'elusive' Defoe constructs two Defoes, a plain dealer and a sophisticated trickster, from *The Review*, to help us understand Defoe as a personality drawn on the one hand to 'an ideal world of order and rational conduct', and on the other 'to a real world of disorder and impulse'. She discusses vocabulary, imagery, and syntax in *The Review* and in *Robinson Crusoe, Moll Flanders, Roxana*, and *Plague Year*, with many parallels from lesser-known pamphlets in an argument that offers many insights even if the basic dichotomy it propounds fails to convince. There is little else on Defoe's prose works except the discussion by W. R. Owens and P. N. Furbank (*PBSA*) of the attribution of *A Vindication of the Press* (1718). One of Addison's supposititious works, and his daughter, are discussed by Arthur Sherbo (*MP*). I have not seen *Educating the Audience* (CML), which contains a paper on Addison by Edward A. Bloom and Lillian D. Bloom, and one on Steele by Edmund Leites.

In *Henry Fielding: Political Writer*[63] Thomas R. Cleary examines the political works, at great length, in support of his thesis that before 1735 Fielding's political writings followed no consistent allegiance unless 'his natural attitude of neutral contempt for contemporary party politics', briefly interrupted by pro- or anti-Walpole sallies. In the second half of 1735, suddenly, Fielding gave his allegiance to the Broad Bottoms, and supported them until his death: 'the same attachments that had made him an opposition firebrand in the later 1730s and earlier 1740s and a strong anti-opposition voice in the later 1740s made him a most cautious political commentator in his last years'. Cleary's argument overwhelms the reader with detailed discussion of the plays, periodicals, and pamphlets (there is little on the novels). Arguing that McCrea's study of Fielding's politics (*YW* 62.272) is too brief and simplistic, Cleary goes to the other extreme in a study which marshals detail rather than argument. Thomas Lockwood (*RES*) argues that a four-issue periodical, *The History of Our Times* (1741), contains essays by Fielding. Simon Varey, who edited Bolingbroke's contributions to the *Craftsman* (*YW* 63.263), has produced a TEAS volume on Bolingbroke (Twayne). I have seen neither it nor Robert Voitle's biography of Shaftesbury (LSU).

The bicentenary of Samuel Johnson's death, 1984, brought a number of

---

62. *The Elusive Daniel Defoe*, by Laura A. Curtis. Vision Critical Studies. Vision/B&N. pp. 216. £14.95.
63. *Henry Fielding: Political Writer*, by Thomas R. Cleary. WLU. pp. xviii + 347. $27.95.

good studies, if not, alas, much in the way of texts. The reprint of R. W. Chapman's edition of the *Letters*[64] misses the chance of adding those letters brought to light since 1952. Donald Greene's selection[65] for the Oxford Authors does, however, seize the chance to add to an 'adequate representation' of Johnson's best-known writings a 'fairly large sampling' on 'matters historical, scientific, bibliographical, legal, theological, political', to introduce Johnson's 'wide-ranging curiosity ... intense concern ... and penetrating insight', and the 'verbal artistry' with which he made 'his observations and reflections on the human condition'. The arrangement is in sections – poetry, early prose, periodical essays, and so on down to diaries and letters – and there are a few pages of facsimiles of the *Dictionary* and the Shakespeare.

The Arts Council bicentenary exhibition focused on Johnson's writing career and on the portraits, well illustrated in the catalogue[66], which also contains an essay by W. W. Robson on the poetry, and good brief accounts by David Fleeman of the *Dictionary* and by John Wain of 'reason, bias and faith'. In Yale, an exhibition catalogued by Herman W. Liebert (*YULG*) focused on Johnson's books – their original condition and the materials for their bibliographical study. J. D. Fleeman's annotated list of books associated with Johnson provides fascinating reading[67] – Milton's 12/6d copy of Euripides lent by Johnson to Joseph Cradock, and the Gaelic translation of Baxter's *A Call to the Unconverted*, kindly presented by Johnson to the Bodleian. Listed are 285 books, with notes of inscriptions, annotations, provenance, and location. A book owned by Johnson is noted by Arthur Sherbo (*N&Q*).

John A. Vance's study of Johnson's sense of history[68] suffers from the difficulties of following any one interest through a writer's works, and picking up sometimes isolated references. Vance marshals his material well, however, to discuss Johnson's knowledge of and response to history, his attitude towards antiquarianism, his use of history in writings on other topics, and his own historical thought. T. F. Wharton's thesis[69] also has its concomitant problems: he sees the master-theme of Johnson's works as 'fantasy, vain hope, and the power of imagination [which] actively shape his creative work, frequently focussing on the imaginative act itself'. The obvious parallel is with Paul Fussell's 'vanity' theme. Wharton discusses the major works carefully enough, arguing that after the 'creative decade' ending with *Rasselas*, Johnson's 'retreat from the imagination, in his criticism, coincid[ed] with his own Imlac-like

---

64. *The Letters of Samuel Johnson with Mrs Thrale's genuine letters to him*, coll. and ed. by R. W. Chapman. Clarendon. Vol. I: *1719–1774*, pp. xxxviii + 452; Vol. II: *1775–1782*, pp. viii + 531; Vol. III: *1783–1784*, pp. viii + 477. £19.50 each.

65. *Samuel Johnson*, ed. by Donald Greene. Oxford Authors. OUP. pp. xxxii + 840. hb £15, pb £6.95.

66. *Samuel Johnson 1709–84*, by Kai Kin Yung, with essays by John Wain, W. W. Robson, and David Fleeman. London: Herbert Press. pp. 144. £9.95.

67. *A Preliminary Handlist of Copies of Books associated with Dr. Samuel Johnson*, by J. D. Fleeman. OBS. pp. vii + 101. £5.

68. *Samuel Johnson and the Sense of History*, by John A. Vance. UGeo. pp. xi + 206. $22.50.

69. *Samuel Johnson and the theme of hope*, by T. F. Wharton. Macmillan. pp. ix + 190. £25.

retreat from the life of writing'. In the *Lives* he defines imagination in terms of the intelligence.

The bicentenary brought two collections of essays, one of which I have not been able to read. Edited by James Engell, *Johnson and His Age* (Harvard) contains, *inter alia*, essays by Gwin J. Kolb on *The Vision of Theodore*, Bertrand H. Bronson on the *Journey* and Boswell's *Journal*, John D. Boyd on the literary criticism, Martine Watson Brownley on the *Lives*, W. H. Bond on Johnson, Thomas Hollis and the Society for Promoting Arts, Manufactures, and Commerce, John H. Middendorf on Johnson's relationship with George Steevens, and Lawrence Lipking on 'Johnson and the Meaning of Life'. The essays collected by Isobel Grundy[70] offer aspects of Johnson 'which have been least well recognized and which have strongest contemporary interest'. There are surveys of his use of maxims (Isobel Grundy), his range of interests (Robert Folkenflik), his scholarly endeavours (Paul J. Korshin), his parliamentary reports (Robert Giddings), his occasional commemorative pieces (Mary Lascelles), and Menippean satire in *Rasselas* (James F. Woodruff). Mark Kinkead-Weekes argues that Johnson's work on Shakespeare gave him a 'new "Shakespearean" sense of the inward complexity of characterization' which led him to prefer Richardson's novels to Fielding's. Johnson's political character is summed up by Howard Erskine-Hill as that of a non-juror with strong Jacobite inclinations. Erskine-Hill includes some discussion of *London* and *The Vanity of Human Wishes*. J. S. Cunningham, finally, gives a very interesting account of the discussions of 'our present state' and of the passions in the essays of the 1750s.

Johnson's use of Locke in promoting the 'moral discipline of the mind' is considered by Claudia L. Johnson (*SEL*). Her essay on Johnson and Jane Austen (*MLQ*, 1983) concentrates on the latter. Isobel Grundy argues (*MLR*) that in his presentation of death Johnson stands at a watershed between ancient and modern – death as a moral confirmation of life or as a confusing, ambiguous, even farcical ending. Eithne Henson (*PSt*) discusses the *Journey* in terms of Johnson's desire, on the one hand, for the 'stability of truth', and on the other, 'his enthusiastic participation in the idea of feudal Scotland'.

Johnson's role in Robert James's *Medicinal Dictionary* is considered by O. M. Barck and Thomas Kaminski (*MP*), and his relationship with Zachariah Williams and the search for longitude by Albert J. Kuhn (*MP*). An account of the sermon he wrote for Dodd is given by James Gray (*DR*, 1983). G. N. Leech (*PSt*) applies discourse analysis to the letter to Chesterfield, whose own letters are annotated and added to by Pat Rogers (*N&Q*). Another notable victim, Soame Jenyns, is fixed in the amber of a TEAS volume[71].

One of the bicentenary reprints, rather confusingly titled, gives the *Thraliana* version of the anecdotes about Johnson[72]. There is an introduction, notes, and eleven illustrations. The relationship between Johnson and Mrs Thrale is discussed by John Riely in *Johnson and His Age* (Harvard) edited by

70. *Samuel Johnson: New Critical Essays*, ed. by Isobel Grundy. Vision/B&N. pp. 208. £14.95.

71. *Soame Jenyns*, by Ronald Rompkey. TEAS 391. Twayne. pp. 184. np.

72. *Dr Johnson by Mrs Thrale. The 'Anecdotes' of Mrs Piozzi in their original form*, ed. and intro. by Richard Ingrams. C&W/Hogarth. pp. xvii + 137. £10.95.

J. Engell and by Martine Watson Brownley in *Mothering the Mind* (H&M). Frank Brady's biography of Boswell's later years[73] is leisurely and expansive, giving a full account of all the facets of the life, and of the societies in which Boswell moved. Brady is sensitive and charitable on Boswell's failings, and on his relationship with Johnson. On the *Life*, he discusses biographical theory and practice, the composition, the presentation of Johnson, Boswell as author and character, and contemporary and modern critical opinion. In *PQ* Bruce Redford describes Boswell's correspondence with John Wilkes and with the tenth Earl of Pembroke.

That Oliver Goldsmith needs rescuing 'from our own baffled affection for his charming naivety' is the proclaimed thesis of the essays collected by Andrew Swarbrick[74]. His argument that in Goldsmith we have 'a sometimes perfect arrangement . . . the voice of a language at a particular phase of its development', is not well taken up by some contributors. The best essays are D. W. Jefferson's reconsideration of Goldsmith's prose, and Seamus Deane's account of *The Citizen of the World*. Other contributors on Goldsmith's view of created nature, his classicism, his politics, his place in the theatre, and in Anglo-Irish literature are, respectively, Graham Parry, John Buxton, Donald Davie, Bernard Harris, and W. J. McCormack. In *SP* Oliver W. Ferguson argues against the view that Goldsmith is primarily an ironist.

Kerry S. Grant's study of Dr Charles Burney as musicologist[75] uses the private papers to reveal how 'Burney's extraordinary intelligence, wit, and unerring social instincts enabled him' to discuss controversial subjects without giving offence, balancing 'veracity and concern for the taste of his readers'. Grant defends Burney at all points, giving a very thorough account of the *History*, Burney's continental tours, comparisons with Hawkins's work, and so on.

The bibliography of secondary studies on Burke by Clara I. Gandy and Peter J. Stanlis[76] has a comprehensive aim, including works with significant although incidental material on Burke, and works important for understanding his age. Alphabetically (not chronologically) listed are 1614 items, in thirteen sections. There are author and subject indexes, and some annotation. I have not seen G. Fasel's TEAS volume on Burke (Twayne). Steven Blakemore argues (*ECS*) that in his writings on the French Revolution Burke sees both how civilization is ordered by language and 'how language can be used to assault civilization'. Burke seeks in his own writings to re-establish the 'sense of circumscribed order' being destroyed in the external world. The essays by George Watson (*CQ*) and F. E. L. Priestley (*DR*, 1983) are general accounts of Burke.

73. *James Boswell: The Later Years 1769–1795*, by Frank Brady. Heinemann. pp. xviii + 609. £20.

74. *The Art of Oliver Goldsmith*, ed. by Andrew Swarbrick. Vision Critical Studies. Vision/B&N. pp. 200. £13.95.

75. *Dr. Burney as Critic and Historian of Music*, by Kerry S. Grant. Studies in Musicology 62. UMIRes/Bowker (1983). pp. xiv + 381. £53.50.

76. *Edmund Burke: A Bibliography of Secondary Sources to 1982*, by Clara I. Gandy and Peter J. Stanlis, with a foreword by William B. Todd. Garland (1983). pp. xxxi + 357. $49.

Jack Fruchtman Jr (*SECC* 13) argues that Tom Paine had a limited belief in millenialism. In his biography of Godwin, Peter H. Marshall[77] emphasizes the importance of the dissenting tradition, specifically the Sandemanian branch, in the formation of Godwin's philosophical views. Marshall also considers that the 'spirit and outline of his system' was developed well before the publication of *Political Justice*, and that it remained fundamentally unchanged. Godwin's influence on his contemporaries and on nineteenth-century thought has been underestimated. The account of his life and writings is thorough, sometimes excessively so, and always readable, even if it fails wholly to convince us that Godwin was 'an authentic human being, a truly creative writer, and one of the great humanists in the Western tradition'.

5. The Novel

Discursive studies are thin on the ground in 1984; but one of them, from Terry Castle on 'The Carnivalization of Eighteenth-Century English Narrative' (*PMLA*), is that critic at her best. Attracted by 'the ways in which the masquerade, the emblem of universal transformation, is linked to the pleasurable process of narrative transformation', she applies Bakhtin's theory of carnivalization to novels in which fascination with the masquerade cuts across overt moral righteousness. *Pamela* and *Amelia* are merely the best known exempla of novels which establish the total impropriety of the masquerade-gathering, then promptly wrench narrative plausibility to accommodate a visit and thus signal 'eighteenth-century England's ... ambivalent escape from consistency, transparency, and the claims of an otherwise passive decorum'. The same novels are again used in evidence during Castle's second bite at the cherry (*ECS*), but here the narrative focus is John Cleland's *Fanny Hill* and subtextual homo-eroticism. Robert Markley (*PQ*), on the same novel, is illuminating and quirkily speculative by turn as he subverts other subversive and feminist deconstructions. He is most convincing about Cleland's linguistic stratagems, self-conscious manipulation of Fanny, and the novel's chinese-box voyeurism. It therefore defies belief that Markley was innocent in his extension of societal eroticism one stage further by extensive quotation from Cleland's public couplings.

If Cleland thus claimed unusually vigorous attention, Defoe scholars seemed to be taking a breather after their exertions of the early 1980s. The only book-length studies were John A. Stoler's *Annotated Bibliography* for Garland (not available for review) and a monograph by Laura Curtis[78], who, hot in pursuit of *The Elusive Daniel Defoe*, searches the novels for evidence of their author's psychic tangles from the less cluttered base-camp in non-fictional prose, notably *The Review*. Persona thus combines uneasily with psychoanalytic criticism to find a novelist already defined and circumscribed by prior assumptions. Indeed, he becomes a type of Fielding, forced into fiction when his preferred medium is closed to him (though in Defoe's case the

77. *William Godwin*, by Peter H. Marshall. Yale. pp. x + 497. £14.95.
78. *The Elusive Daniel Defoe*, by Laura A. Curtis. Vision Critical Studies. Vision/B&N. pp. 216. £14.95.

shift is from ineffective ideological pamphleteering rather than from drama too successful for a government's comfort), and Curtis leaves us struggling with the dilemma which has been the cause of contention since the first backlash against Ian Watt. Where and when is Defoe a manipulative ironist as opposed to a blinkered ideologue driven by an 'unconscious desire to have things two ways at once'? David McNeil (*SoRA*, 1983) follows an analogous lure in 'Defoe and Claustrophobia', seemingly unconcerned that his fixation with Dissenting paranoia reduces the novels to studies in 'physical and circumstantial entrapment [which] are really symbols of spiritual crisis' and for which all the hard evidence comes from the *Journal of the Plague Year*. It would, wouldn't it? An article in the same journal two years ago by Michael White (*YW* 63.270), on nineteenth-century 're-writings' of *Crusoe*, provides a more useful and stimulating context for Anthony Purdy's comparison (*CRCL*) of the original with Michel Tournier's *Vendredi ou les Limbes du Pacifique*, published in 1967, which shifts the story forward a century to 'extend and transform' the economic analysis. James H. Maddox Jr returns us fruitfully to an unmediated but troubled Defoe in two papers. The first (*ELH*) explores Crusoe's attempts to impose a moral clarity on his history through his *Life and Adventures* into the *Farther Adventures* (after 'the triumph of the first novel, the second dramatizes Crusoe's diminishing ability to master by interpretation'); the second (also *ELH*) finds a similar but more marked degeneration as the facility of Moll Flanders for rationalizing or sentimentalizing away her responsibility gives way to 'Roxana's self-torment [which] constantly brands the consciousness of her guilt deeper into her brain'. Hints that these companion-pieces may represent the exploratory drafts for a promising monograph are confirmed by the conclusion to the second paper which mentions applications of the pattern thus established to Richardson, Diderot, and Sterne. Two other critics explore the strategies of *Roxana* in isolation. Albert J. Rivero (*ELWIU*), a critic in the mould of J. Paul Hunter or George A. Starr, seizes upon the Satanic craftiness of the 'kind landlord' who walks in the garden with the unfallen Roxana and who then returns 'on the third day' for payment. Certainly this narrative passage is pivotal in the plot, but if Defoe intended the deformed *imitatio Christi* as the crux that Rivero insists it is, he buried his single talent rather too well. David Blewett (*SECC*) likewise pounds an allusive argument into friability after he adds to Rodney M. Baines's list of Georgian settings another skein of references from and to the Restoration. One can accept that *Roxana* is 'possessed of a double time-scheme for the excellent reason that Defoe wants us to see the moral parallel between the luxurious time of Charles II and the equally dissolute reign of George I', but the delight in discovery which leads Blewett to claim an *absolute* parallel scheme pushes him and the argument too far.

Items on Fielding's *Joseph Andrews* insist primarily on its Christian probity. In 'Social Change and Religious Faith' (*SNNTS*) Brian McCrea speculates plausibly that the seriousness of the threat posed by Pamela's upward mobility precluded full treatment in parody; only a classical, romantic comic plot provided the adequate response to dramatize Fielding's anti-democratic (or at least anti-subversive) latitudinarianism. Not so, says James E. Evans (*ArielE*): the novel's comedy and its theology unite in the matrix of 1 Corinthians 3.18–19 and both are witnessed in that Pauline 'wise fool', Parson Adams. No doubt the *Concordance and Word-Lists to Henry Fielding's 'Joseph*

Andrews'[79] will enable subsequent commentators to extend or disprove many such theses with crushing linguistic calculation. The first essay on *Tom Jones* this year needs no such advantage to unite Fielding's classicism with his Christianity: Laura F. Hodges (*PQ*) explains the embarrassments and un-easinesses of Tom's progress as a model for the history of Western civilization or, to be precise, Aristotelean ethics (yet again) slowly refined by *Christian prudence*. If this essay is hardly improved by its repetitiveness, neither is that of James E. Evans (*SAQ*) – in his second contribution on Fielding – by the weight of diffuse and familiar comment on 'comedy' and 'tragedy' attached to his rather modest proposal that the varied allusions to famous tragedies and the tragic potential in the plot of *Tom Jones* are 'reminders to the reader of the tragic alternative to the comic fantasy and of the [more] complete truth of comedy'. Morris Golden's paper on the same novel (*PLL*) is a deal more substantial: a long, packed dissection of the tapestry which combines projection of Fielding's autobiographical persona with political allusion (ranging from the providential sweep of Hanoverian triumph to the trivia of newspaper reports on student debauchery). The approach is hardly novel – scholars such as Martin C. Battestin have been weaving these patchworks for years – but Golden spins his threads into a pleasing artefact. Martin C. Battestin himself puts a quarter-century of work on Fielding to admirable effect in his *Amelia* for the Wesleyan edition[80]. Perhaps only he and Fredson Bowers (on textual matters) could together offer that range of experience and scholarship necessary to attempt a fully annotated, full-dress edition of what Battestin admits (in the first sentence of the introduction) is 'Henry Fielding's last and most problematic novel'. The result is an established text (at last), an introduction which sets that text in its political and autobiographical context, and annotation which elucidates the editor's view of 'the first novel of social protest and reform in English'. Mona Scheuermann (*FMLS*) is indeed fortunate that coincidence of publication gives such support to her '*Amelia* as a Novel of Social Criticism'. Thus far I have noted three items on *Joseph Andrews*, three on *Tom Jones* and two on *Amelia*, with a third to come. Three times three, the ultimate trinity. The omens could hardly be more propitious for Carla Mulford's 'Booth's Progress' (*SNNTS*), and for her contribution to the work on theological structurings which has dominated criticism of Fielding's major novels in 1984. Martin Battestin adds an appendix on the double time-scheme of his text but does not assay a defence of Booth's conversion; Mona Scheuermann agrees with the established wisdom on this 'unconvincing' conclusion, yet cites its failure in proof of 'the truthfulness' of a fiction which anatomizes the corruptions of its time so urgently that no other sort of resolution is possible; but Carla Mulford protests that Booth's revelation is a totally satisfying end to a very Christian narrative: 'The novel . . . structurally demonstrates a kind of secular pilgrim's progress as it tells Booth's story as exemplary history' through his various erratic commitments to forms of stoicism, benevolent theory, and rationalist philosophy. The key problem, as Mulford herself recognizes, is *Amelia*'s unusual (for Fielding) stress on character rather than

---

79. *A Concordance and Word-Lists to Henry Fielding's 'Joseph Andrews'*, ed. by Michael G. Farringdon. Ariel. pp. viii + 117 + 2820 microfiches. £38.

80. *Henry Fielding: Amelia*, ed. by Martin C. Battestin with textual intro. by Fredson Bowers. Wesleyan Fielding. Clarendon. pp. lxxx + 613. £45.

plot. She analyses 'Booth's progress' well enough, but she fails to show how or why any reader should identify or empathize with him on his journey towards latitudinarian salvation. As Battestin notes charitably, Lady Mary Wortley Montagu inscribed on her copy of *Amelia* what 'may be the truest verdict: "inferior to himselfe, superior to most others"'.

There is a coincidental advantage, for my purpose, in belated mention of a paper by Ivor Indyk (*SoRA*, 1983) on a Richardsonian topic which is in fact as concerned with academic rivalries about texts as it is with a text. So many writers have been so obsessed with in-fighting that there is wry semiotic honesty about the word-order and punctuation of Indyk's title, 'Interpretative Relevance, and Richardson's *Pamela*' and about his briskly overt use of the novel as a test case for competing theorists. His conclusion, that there is nothing absolutely new under the critical sun, is confirmed from an improbable direction by Samuel Pickering Jr (*JNT*) in a study of the *Pamela* story for children, under other titles and by different hands, during the later eighteenth century. Where Indyk finds *Pamela* a prism reflecting back theoretical preferences, Pickering proves that even in its own time it 'served as a touchstone for contemporary beliefs about reading and education'. *Plus ça change*. Only indirectly 'relevant' as these two papers may be, they profess a deal more critical wit than the stodgy, mechanical offering by Barbara Belyea (*ESC*) who almost literally weighs *Pamela*'s narrative structure, characterization, and point of view (which she claims are those of a romance) against 'certain realistic and moralistic aspects of the story' to find that, on balance, this is a 'novel treatment of romance' rather than a novel proper. As usual, though, it is only when the critics turn to *Clarissa* that they sharpen their knives for the really dirty house-to-house (or school-to-school) combat. They also write more.

The Paradox of Privacy: Epistolary Form in 'Clarissa' by Christina Marsden Gillis[81] is one of the two book-length studies this year. She accepts that Clarissa's is an enclosed world but she also attempts to square the circle (or perhaps, in this case, to circle the Palladian square),

> in looking at form as a spatial construct and examining the tension between private and public in spatial terms. Spaces literally open up in *Clarissa*; closed rooms are transformed into stage space. I will not be the first to point out that the dramatizing tendency in Richardson counters the privatizing. My purpose, however, is to align rooms [from the Palladian model] and rhetorical modes in letter writing, in order to contrast writing and acting ... spaces and to indicate how the tension between the closed and the open, private and public, is also one between writing for the self and creating an instructive 'story' for the audience.

The first part of this study duly explores 'Spaces' as models for letters, then such spaces opened to the public in 'Letters'. This is an ingenious thesis which literally connects eighteenth-century life and letters in a stimulating way. Of course it also has the weaknesses of a precisely targeted thesis too, and as if to

---

81. *The Paradox of Privacy: Epistolary Form in 'Clarissa'*, by Christina Marsden Gillis. UFlor Monographs, Humanities 54. UFlor. pp. 173. pb $12.

undercut the Palladian paradigm as a perfect (let alone the sole) 'space' for
Clarissa, Janet Butler (*ECS*) begins her essay on 'Clarissa's Complicity' by
allusion to the bourgeois-Dutchified modishness of the garden at Harlowe
Place. Butler's purpose is also at odds with Gillis in other, more important
ways, of course, as she explores the paths by which the garden as space and
image – suitably extended by biblical archetypes – permitted Richardson 'to
participate in Clarissa's erotic excitement [and] allowed him to assent to her
sexual complicity at the same time that, on the public level, he was insisting on
the rectitude of will'. Restricted to *this* space, her conclusion, that Richardson
is 'the classic example of a man not altogether sure of what he is doing but who
insists on doing it nonetheless', is plausible. Rita Goldberg's spaces are very
expansive indeed, for her book, *Sex and Enlightenment*[82], is 'proposed as a
case study' of the 'feminization of culture' in the second half of the eighteenth
century through England and France, represented here by Richardson and his
improbable admirer, the highly sophisticated, anticlerical Diderot. From Puritan conduct books *Clarissa* emerges as (another sort of) model

> for sexualization of religion; and the story of the heroine's fall and rise,
> as it were, is the mythic narrative of that process. There is a distinct shift
> of sexual responsibility in this novel. Men become the evil sexual force in
> culture and women become suffering servants, guardians and emblems
> of a property-centred and individualistic moral universe. The profane
> and secular have become, in a word, sacred.

This too is an absorbing book despite occasional lapses into feminist-
psychoanalytic ruthlessness. For example, Goldberg's interpretation of the
serpent emblem on Clarissa's coffin is needlessly prescriptive: 'Serpents have
always been associated with goddesses, with the feminine, material and
destructive principle, rather than with the masculine, spiritual and creative
principle embodied in the Cross', she writes. True, but not the whole truth. The
'deeply sexual', serpentine female has also been associated with teeming
fecundity; and as for Clarissa's choice of the serpent device for her coffin, 'an
effective iconographic containment of the evil of sexual feeling', one recalls
the words of someone who brought a real snake to the 'serpent of Old Nile' as
Cleopatra prepared the iconographic tableau for *her* death, 'a very honest
woman, but something given to lie, as a woman should not do but in the way of
honesty'. A shorter piece which also rests ultimately on the sexuality of
Clarissa has already been mentioned in section 2 of this chapter, Veronica
Bassil (*TSLL*) on Prior's *Henry and Emma* as the missing link between
medieval 'Faces of Griselda' and Richardson. Prior's poem 'facilitated [the]
movement from . . . piety and militarism . . . to [*Clarissa*'s] sadomasochistic
pornography' is a typical judgement: equally typical is the opinion that what
really discomforted Richardson was Prior's notion, personified in Emma, that
a female hero could combine love with sexuality. Bassil and Goldberg make
lively reading, for very different reasons.
    More directly sociological matters exercise John A. Dussinger's 'Love and
Consanguinity in Richardson's Novels' (*SEL*), which applies Lawrence

    82. *Sex and Enlightenment: Women in Richardson and Diderot*, by Rita Goldberg.
CUP. pp. xi + 239. £22.50.

Stone's analyses to a Richardson who is a pioneer of the nuclear family and the bourgeois eroticizing of wealth and power. Here the myth of *Clarissa* is secularized with a vengeance: indeed, 'the bourgeois prototype in Richardson's myth actually creates new forms of subordination and clientage while replacing the old', feudal ones. Terry Castle returns us quite as firmly to narrative matters in 'Lovelace's Dream' (*SECC*) after the rape. As usual in this critic's work, minor polemic detail irritates (Clarissa does show experienced suspicion after her violation, she is never remotely 'streetwise, savvy'), but Castle's sinuously reversed and reversing explications of the waking dream – as a matrix in which contradictory and self-contradictory readings co-exist – ultimately build both logical and also near-mimetic defences for her contention that it represents 'a new allegory for plot itself . . . [not] Aristotle's extended piece of thread, with its single central twist, but an endlessly turning, endlessly twisting loop'. Other papers can be noted more economically. T. C. Duncan Eaves and Ben D. Kimpel (*PQ*) make more readily available the original letter, in the form of an eleven-page pamphlet, written by Richardson to defend the fire scene but never published until Johannes Sinstra printed a version in his Dutch translation of *Clarissa*; and E. B. Moon (*NQ*) finds the irony of Lady Grandison's didactic tale (of heroic wilfulness in love turned shrewdly against her) a possible source for Sheridan's *The Rivals*. But three further items plunge back into the battle of interpreters. W. A. Trotter (*English*) anatomizes Romantic distortions of *Clarissa* into its eclipse behind 'the contradictory moral sensibility of the Victorian age' (Leslie Stephen is the most ferocious mangler, George Eliot the honourable exception), while William Beatty Warner (*Diac*, 1983) and Janet E. Aikins (*UTQ*) castigate more recent 'misreaders' in very long review-articles on the recent books by Terry Castle and Terry Eagleton (*YW* 63.272). Aikins damns with faint, and late, praise; Warner parades his ethical *bona fides* and protests his horror at sexual violence but stubbornly maintains his reading of Clarissa's rape as a *textual* experience against the equally determined accusations of sexism by the two Terrys. Thus the polemics about *Clarissa*'s (and Clarissa's) probity continue to overshadow not only Richardson studies but also much else in the landscape of novel criticism. Another simple measure of Richardson's looming presence is that he accounts for almost half the annual *SEL* issue which spans 'The Restoration and Eighteenth Century'. To the papers from this issue already mentioned above must now be added Mary V. Yates on 'The Christian Rake in *Sir Charles Grandison*'. Here the tone of critical dispute moderates as Yates takes gently to task all those readers who have agonized over the hero. They missed the point, as did so many contemporary readers of *Clarissa*, says Yates, hence Richardson's last model of a Christian Hero, 'for *Grandison* is a document of enlightenment pedagogical method, as well as an extended commentary on *Clarissa*, written for an audience that knew and loved the earlier novel perhaps too well'. She argues her case lucidly, but that will hardly satisfy antagonists for whom Richardson's impeccable overt aims and moral defences are almost literally beside the point.

Apart from the generic *tour de force* by Alan Liu which compares *Vathek* with *Rasselas* (reviewed below), the only other substantial piece on Johnson's prose fiction I have seen this year attaches it even more firmly to another and very different work, for it appears as part of the 'Coda' to A. D. Nuttall's

Pope's 'Essay on Man'[83]. Nuttall's summation, 'In writing *Rasselas* [Johnson] built the tomb of eighteenth-century theodicy', is justified in context, but the preceding argument puzzles. Nuttall is too perceptive a critic to ignore 'deliciously funny' ironies: he also asserts that 'The style . . . except for a very few passages [is] unironic and grave'. Yet the reflexiveness of the one substantial quotation he chooses in evidence – as Rasselas leaves the sorrowing teacher 'convinced of . . . the inefficacy of polished periods and studied sentences' illustrates only Johnson's 'crushingly monochrome style' as 'The words seem to die on the page'. Nothing here about the wry engagement of the reader with a teacher of morality mocking his own vocation.

Irony is also an issue in two of the essays on *The Vicar of Wakefield* which will, however, satisfy partisans behind neither the holistic nor the satiric barricades. D. W. Jefferson modifies but essentially re-affirms his view of Goldsmith as a Christian comedian, comfortably aware of his stylistic and narrative lapses[84]. Oliver W. Ferguson comes to a similar conclusion in his unobjectionable (if laboured) account of Goldsmith the occasional ironist in the first of two items on the *Vicar* in *SP*. The second, by Thomas R. Preston, is a business-like assault on modern versions of Goldsmith's hero as 'a pious fraud who is really a money-conscious, fortune-hunting materialist' and an extension of the case for the novel as a tropological 'tale exemplifying the Christian's "progress of the soul"'. John Irwin Fischer (*SCRev*) extends it further still in an important contribution to the recent debate on the *Vicar* which offers a full anatomy of that debate as prelude to his ranging over the story of Job as an allegorical basis, the influence of the Whiston controversy, and analyses of the text's complex tones, to its ultimate affirmation of human love as a type of the divine. Fischer's *Vicar* is a scriptural triumph for many reasons, then, finally, in part because 'its fiction engaged [Goldsmith] at deeper levels than conscious opinion' and projected an intense vision 'which he himself may never have fully embraced'. That, whether by accident or design, leaves a chink of daylight for proponents of the satiric Goldsmith. I doubt they will need more. Meanwhile, Fanny Burney, his contemporary in the Johnson orbit, is confirmed in the propriety of her place by Coral Ann Howells (*BJECS*). If 'is it moral?', then 'will it work?', are the twin tests applied by Imlac, so *Camilla* is the novel of a woman sympathetically qualifying with practicalities the righteousness of Mary Wollstonecraft: 'Fanny Burney writes like a feminist who is also a lady, with all the necessary subterfuges and doubts that go with the combination.' The second item of note on Burney, Tara Wallace's edition of *A Busy Day* (Rutgers) was unavailable for review, and only single items appear on her other contemporaries or near-contemporaries. Laurie Langbauer (*Novel*) subtly transforms *The Female Quixote* from ostensible mockery of (female) romance in the guise of a (patriarchal) novel to a discourse which 'needs romance to set itself up as a novel but, when prodded, romance deconstructs and merges into the novel'. The prodding is clearly that of Langbauer rather than Charlotte Lennox. Elsewhere, Pamela Lloyd (*N&Q*) offers 'Some New Information on Jane West';

83. *Pope's 'Essay on Man'*, by A. D. Nuttall. Unwin Critical Library. A&U. pp. 250. £15.

84. *The Art of Oliver Goldsmith*, ed. by Andrew Swarbrick. Vision Critical Studies. Vision/B&N. pp. 200. £13.95.

Madeleine Blondel (also *N&Q*) reports tracing an apparently unique copy of *The Life and Adventures of a Reformed Magdalen* (1763) to the Bibliothèque Nationale but claims nothing for it beyond a footnote in publishing history; and Jerry C. Beasley writes on 'Smollett's Novels: *Ferdinand Count Fathom* for the Defense' (*PLL*). The most persuasive aspect of this last essay is Beasley's elucidation of Smollett's theory of fiction sketched in the *Preface* to *Ferdinand* (if analogues between the novel, painting, and drama can be termed 'a theory'). When illustrating Smollett's application of the analogues, Beasley writes as an editor-apologist, and it sometimes shows.

Sadly, Melvyn New's *Notes* to the Florida edition of *Tristram Shandy* was yet another substantial publication unavailable for review this year. At least I saw New's contribution to the collection on *Lawrence Sterne: Riddles and Mysteries*[85]. He writes entertainingly here on annotating the novel's sexual jokes. The 'end is nowhere in sight, and properly so', he concludes. The *end*, in sight, *properly*? Surely this is mimetic Shandyan innuendo; yet that suspicion may be provoked by a combination of Sterne and the cumulative persuasiveness of the other contributors to the first grouping in this collection: Jacques Berthoud, Alan B. Howes, then Edward and Lillian D. Bloom also write well on 'Sex, Laughter and Death'. Is that – sirs and madam – because you prove Sex and Death are synonymous in *Shandy*, alpha and omega simultaneously linked and separated only by Laughter – or because Sex and procreation is an obsession, while nervous Laughter fills the brief time between homunculus and that other inevitability, Death – or because you could die laughing at sex? Enough of that. In the next section W. G. Day, Roy Porter, and Valerie Grosvenor Myer, the overall editor, compose themselves for worthy but earnest perspectives on 'The Intellectual Background' (Locke again, medical matters, and 'animal spirits', respectively). The volume then rather subsides into 'Interpretation' – Bruce Stovel on the novel as sustained gossip, Mark Loveridge on analogues for its digressive progressiveness, K. G. Simpson on Sterne the Modernist – picks up again – with an 'Afterword' from Park Honan on the lessons Whiggish Sterne taught the young Tory talent of Jane Austen – then settles into scholarly listings with W. G. Day's second contribution, an annotated bibliography, 1977–83. In *Model as Motif*[86] Fritz Gysin calls useful attention to the physical stuff of *Tristram Shandy*, particularly 'four central motifs: miniature life [the Homunculus], the hobbyhorse, warfare on the bowling-green, and the journey'. All these qualify as 'models' in a specific definition:

> A model is usually three-dimensional in space; metaphorically speaking, we can also recognize three dimensions of its function: first, it is used to replace an argument in order to simplify and speed up the clarification of a difficult question, secondly, it actually complicates matters . . . and thirdly . . . it nevertheless suggests significant structural relationship.

85. *Lawrence Sterne: Riddles and Mysteries*, ed. by Valerie Grosvenor Myer. Vision Critical Studies. Vision/B&N. pp. 184. £12.95.
86. *Model as Motif in 'Tristram Shandy'*, by Fritz Gysin. Cooper Monographs 31. Francke (1983). pp. 176. Sfr 38.

Some of this is not quite as original as Gysin seems to think, and the 'total interpretation' to which he aspires inevitably escapes his 'moderate formalism' – as it has escaped every other 'ism' and as he himself half anticipates in the last sentences of his introduction. Nevertheless, his tolerant sort of formalism works well, particularly well on that 'model' *of* a model, the bowling-green. Promptly, back comes the retort, from Homer Obed Brown (*MLN*), on *Shandy* as a 'Canonic Text' which glories in its self-conscious intertextuality as a discourse dependent on an endless chain of prior displaced texts. Brown's essay pays more than conceptual homage to methodology here, for it too is a text displaced from a prior and broader context. Perhaps that is mere coincidence: his essay lacks any sense of Shandyan *delight* in endless play, something to which Jeffrey Smitten (*N&Q*) is responsive as he identifies Peter Browne, Bishop of Cork and Ross from 1710 to his death in 1735 as 'the great Metheglingius' of II, 19. Kunimori Kimijima (*SELit*) is clearly repelled by all such flippant treatments of 'grave yet eccentric' worthies: this is a bizarre, indignant complaint about Sterne's malformed personality as witnessed in his sadomasochistic treatment of his readers. After that, Robert M. Ryley (*N&Q*), who identifies John 'Estimate' Brown rather than Sterne as the intended reference in a paranoid letter by William Warburton, and B. A. B. Pasta (*N&Q* again), on 'the Name Eliza in the *Sentimental Journey*', seem souls of sanity; but further reflection gives one pause over Eliza as an allusion both to Elizabeth Draper (after Swift's Esther) and to the Anglican Church wherever she is a presence in passages which trace 'a meaning consistent with a churchman's journey through life'. Such disproportion seems a bit much even for the teller of Slawkenbergius's tale. Also on the *Sentimental Journey*, Eve Kosofsky Sedgwick (*CritI*) gives due warning of a book on ' "male homosocial desire" – the whole spectrum of bonds between men ... within which the various forms of traffic in women take place'. 'Madam, peace with your similitudes', said one of Congreve's falsewits; but when a critic can claim that Wycherley's Horner and Sterne's sentimental traveller are virtually indistinguishable in their burgeoning, class-ridden sexism (nothing else seems remotely relevant), what springs readily to mind is Pope's 'Tell me if Congreve's Fools be Fools indeed'.

Ronald D. Spector's *The English Gothic: a Bibliographic Guide*[87] is a timely gathering of materials, from the earliest reviews to the recent explosion of commentaries. It is also an achievement which belies its modest claims with substantial essays on the genre followed by others on paired Gothicists, Horace Walpole and Clara Reeve ('The Beginnings'), Charlotte Smith and Anne Radcliffe ('Sentimental Gothicism'), Matthew Gregory Lewis and William Beckford ('Schauer-Romantik'), and Charles Robert Maturin with Mary Shelley ('The Inheritors'). Spector's packed lists at the end of each chapter are catholic in range and reach 1983. They are therefore already out of date by some dozen items, though some of these, admittedly, represent no great loss. French critics of the last decade have been notably curious about English Gothicism. It is therefore no surprise that a whole issue of *Europe* should be given over to '*Le Roman Gothique*'; but it is unfortunate that Maurice Lévy should give Anglo-Saxon xenophobes the ammunition of his claim that the

87. *The English Gothic: a Bibliographic Guide to Writers from Horace Walpole to Mary Shelley*, by Ronald D. Spector. Greenwood. pp. xiii + 269. £33.95.

genre 'est anglais dans son essence' basically because England failed to have a Revolution, particularly as this claim introduces a collection of essays in which *French* Gothicists – presumably those who evaded Robespierre (or their progeny) – also figure very prominently. Still, Liliane Absenour and Chantal Tatu do their best to restore the *entente cordiale* in their surveys of the English Gothic's influence in France. Both mention 'Monk' Lewis, among others, but reserve most attention for Anne Radcliffe, a proportion which is repeated among Anglo-Saxon commentators too. Even *The Female Gothic*[88], a collection of essays which ranges from the eighteenth-century pioneers to Margaret Atwood, has two contributions on Radcliffe. Cynthia Griffin Wolff is a grudging polemicist who admits Radcliffe's influence on women's writing only as preface to her plea for the invention of 'other, less mutilating conventions for the rendering of feminine sexual desire'. (Shouldn't that read *female* desire?) Nina da Vinci Nichols clearly sympathizes with Wolff but does see some value in Radcliffe as opposed to the 'pornography, defined as a consuming interest in sexuality at the service of power' in Lewis. Elsewhere, Charles C. Murrah (*UWR*) urges that writers in the renaissance of Radcliffe studies 'should include a careful analysis of [her] descriptions of landscape', apparently unaware that they have been doing little else in the 1980s; and Elizabeth Nollen (*ELN*) offers *A Sicilian Romance* as a source for *Sense and Sensibility* in a list of correspondences which one could duplicate from quite other novels of this formulaic genre. Randall Craig uses such formulas for adventure in 'Beckford's Inversion of Romance in *Vathek*' (*OL*) as he traces a reciprocal archetype of romance designed to frustrate the would-be escapist. The argument is ingenious and logical but *Vathek* is consistently neither, and it defies plain sense to describe this apparent 'feast of the Orient' as an artful coating for 'a bitter pill of reality'. Yet even that starts to seem a humbly reasonable proposition after a few pages of Alan Liu's extraordinary mini-thesis on *Vathek* and *Rasselas* (*TSLL*). Liu's pyrotechnics leave one gasping behind, and the clearest statement of his faith is shunted into a footnote:

> structuralism shading into deconstruction – has a mimetic function premised on a similarity between eighteenth-century and current intellectual climates. The tension between neo-classicism and skepticism (a tension marrying, and yet divorcing, the two) is most closely reproduced in our own habits of thinking as a tension between Saussureian structuralism and deconstruction.

Sterne would have savoured such a virtuoso performance. Everyone will find something to argue with in it, if they can keep their footing in the torrent of idiolectal usage.

William Godwin, the last of the novelists in the parameters of this chapter, is more than usually well represented in the journals which, as if to confirm this, print papers on novels other than *Caleb Williams* too. It is true that Gary Kelly's interest (*KSJ*) in 'the Shandean play of *Damon and Delia* . . . the much greater seriousness of *Italian Letters* . . . [or] the rhetorical play found in *Imogen*' looks backwards from the later novel; nevertheless, this tracing of Godwin's mimicry in the fictive modes used by his ideological antagonists is

---

88. *The Female Gothic*, ed. by Juliann Fleenor. Eden (1983). pp. 311. pb £14.

something to argue with in it, if they can keep their footing in the torrent of idiolectal usage.

William Godwin, the last of the novelists in the parameters of this chapter, is more than usually well represented in the journals which, as if to confirm this, print papers on novels other than *Caleb Williams* too. It is true that Gary Kelly's interest (*KSJ*) in 'the Shandean play of *Damon and Delia* . . . the much greater seriousness of *Italian Letters* . . . [or] the rhetorical play found in *Imogen*' looks backwards from the later novel; nevertheless, this tracing of Godwin's mimicry in the fictive modes used by his ideological antagonists is instructive in its own right. Two other essays, both in *PLL*, contribute intelligently to a growing body of criticism on Godwin's central novel: Kenneth W. Graham artfully melds the bifurcation of variant drafts (*Things as They Are/Caleb Williams*) in the approved version's 'creative grasp of the psychological Gothic'; and Michael DePorte complements his journal-colleague as he picks up webs of 'entrapment' – the theme of many recent *PLL* essays – spun out of many levels and types of 'Mystery in *Caleb Williams*'. These, he claims, rather subvert than dramatize much of *Political Justice*; and that is fighting talk which makes his concluding quotation – from Godwin looking back on his diaries for the forty previous years – the more startlingly apposite: 'All this at present is mere abstraction, symbols, not realities. Nothing is actually seen: the whole is cyphers, conventional marks, imaginary boundaries of unimagined things.' Either unaware of or unimpressed by this apparent recantation, Thomas Balfour Elder (*ArielE*, 1983) re-asserted – but added little to – the current established wisdom about the close relationship between Godwin's political and fictional writing. To Elder, the key which unlocks Godwin's novels from *Caleb Williams*, through *St. Leon*, *Fleetwood*, and *Mandeville* is the combination of passion with intellect also tangible in *Political Justice*. This rather contradicts Mona Scheuermann (also *ArielE*, 1983) on the novels as progressively intense studies in alienation. The argument is intelligent but some of her supporting statements are unworthily dismissive. Take only one: 'for the most part, eighteenth-century novelists are describing social rather than psychological situations'. 'Cyphers, conventional marks, imaginary boundaries of unimagined things' again?

The Nineteenth Century: Romantic Period

VINCENT NEWEY, BRYAN BURNS, and JAMES MICHIE

The chapter has three sections: 1. Verse and Drama, by Vincent Newey;
2. Prose Fiction, by Bryan Burns; 3. Prose, by James Michie.

1. Verse and Drama

Aside from *ABELL* and the *MLAIB* the main general aid for the period is
the critical *Bibliography of the Romantic Movement*, edited by David V.
Erdman (Garland), which deserves all its reputation as a salient contribution
to the ongoing Romantic re-assessment. I have found the comprehensive
review number of *WC* an invaluable source of information during my years as
compiler of this section of *YWES*. The selective reviews in *SIR* are sometimes
workmanlike and sometimes full-scale interpretative articles: only reasons of
space and format have prevented me from including many of the latter kind
among the best of the essays on Romanticism and Romantic poetry. Important
specialist reviews, surveys, or checklists also appear in *BIQ*, *KSJ*, *KSMB*,
SEL, and *NCTR*.

M. H. Abrams is a presence at once massive, subtle, and peculiarly un-
assuming in the landscape of Romantic studies. As the title may suggest, *The
Correspondent Breeze*[1] is a selection of his previously published essays. 'The
Correspondent Breeze' itself and 'Structure and Style in the Greater Romantic
Lyric' are two of the most influential statements in the history of the discipline
Abrams has done so much to foster and extend; and to this twin foundation are
added pieces, some better known than others, on the revolutionary spirit of
Romanticism, apocalypticism, the linguistic theories and 'modernity' of
Wordsworth and Coleridge, and the philosophic background to Coleridge's
thinking. Jack Stillinger's mildly combative foreword emphasizes Abrams's
pre-eminence in the so-called 'humanist' tradition and thus his status as an
exemplar of that which abides amid the ebb and flow of fashionable 'theoretical innovations'. But Abrams's is also a potently independent mind which,
though never veering from the standard of useful accessible practice, has left
its mark deeply, if often in hidden or assimilated form, across a range of
approaches, including the recent oppositional stance towards his transcenden-
talist – 'natural supernatural' – readings.

I commented in an earlier volume of *YWES* (63.298) on Christopher Ricks's
piquant revaluation of the 'very distinctly odd and very oddly distinct' Thomas

1. *The Correspondent Breeze: Essays on English Romanticism*, by M. H. Abrams.
Norton. pp. xii + 296. £19.95.

Lovell Beddoes and his minor masterpiece, *Death's Jest-Book*. This is one of the essays reprinted in Ricks's *The Force of Poetry*[2], a commanding and incisive – and, as with Abrams, always accessible – collection of criticism taking us from John Gower to Geoffrey Hill. Also included are the two classic analyses of neglected aspects of the eventfulness of language and verse structure in Wordsworth: 'A Sinking Inward', which above all unlocks the force of Wordsworth's prepositions and conjunctions, and 'A Pure Organic Pleasure from the Lines', where the same is done for line-endings and the 'white space' immediately beyond. The whole volume is a model, but not easily imitable, performance in the readerly skills and excitement involved in acts of close encounter with the words and shapes on the page.

Like Ricks's method, the work represented in *Romanticism and Language*[3] calls to mind Wordsworth's underscoring, in his note to 'The Thorn', of 'the interest which the mind attaches to words, not only as symbols of the passion, but as *things*, active and efficient, which are of themselves part of the passion'. To all intents and purposes, however, the similarity ends there: *Romanticism and Language* inhabits a domain of linguistic and literary theory which Ricks studiously avoids. The contributors are Timothy Bahti, Leslie Brisman, Cynthia Chase, Jerome Christensen, Frances Ferguson, Mary Jacobus, Richard Macksey, Reeve Parker, Susan Wolfson, and Arden Reed himself. Of the Romantics, Wordsworth, Coleridge, Shelley, and Keats loom largest; among the concerns, one is struck by the recurrent foregrounding of the relations between mimesis and rhetoric, the literal and the figural, and voice and text, with some rather more straightforward categories like politics and the genre of autobiography. I shall respect Arden Reed's poststructuralist position and not attempt here the summarizing overview and apportioning of essays (texts) which he refuses to undertake in his introduction because it would mean sustaining that very concept of the harmonizing imagination which makes the authors of *Romanticism and Language* uneasy. Suffice it to say that his remarks do provide evidence of common ground, not all of it subterranean: the volume offers, in Geoffrey Hartman's phrase, 'a hermeneutics of indeterminacy', insisting as it does on the irresolvable dissonances and differences of Romantic literature; it elevates rhetorical, as opposed to referential, perspectives, celebrating linguistic play as that which resists reduction to a single meaning; it views its materials intertextually rather than as autonomous entities (out with the persistent ghosts of New Criticism); and it resists the hegemony (already seriously weakened) of the inherited construct of 'the sacramental vision' (no Abrams here). Several of the writings in this drama of re-interpretation fix upon the metaphor of theft, the self's appropriation of or appropriation by language; and they all, though composed in different styles, centre on the alertness of Romantic literature to its own status as language. None of this of course is really unfamiliar nowadays, when even the radical voice of the pure deconstructionist is well on the way to being naturalized within the field of our critical discourse. But the standard of the varied examples in *Romanticism and Language* is consistently very high indeed. It is a book to please veterans and enlist advanced beginners.

2. *The Force of Poetry*, by Christopher Ricks. Clarendon. pp. xvi + 447. £19.50.
3. *Romanticism and Language*, ed. by Arden Reed. CornU/Methuen. pp. 327. pb £9.95.

Readers may get a distinct impression of the obvious being laboured in the early pages of Paul A. Cantor's *Creature and Creator: Myth-Making and English Romanticism*[4]. Do we really need to be told, for example, that the Romantics discovered 'nobility' in 'revolutionary figures', or that their battles with Miltonic accounts of the Creation were not merely a literary issue but an ideological one involving 'new conceptions of man'? Yet this is all in all a well-argued and interesting book, rooted in the desire to reclaim Harold Bloom the quondam myth-maker from his subsequent apostasy in the realms of misreading and the arcane (so that Bloom becomes in fact the strong father who is contradicted but ultimately relied upon). Cantor's most original idea is to take as his starting point the undermining of orthodox religious or teleological views in Rousseau's *Second Discourse*, where Rousseau makes man both creature and creator by portraying his development as a concatenation of material forces and his own actions. If this approach perhaps overprivileges a single text, when Rousseau actually reflects a broad groundswell of Enlightenment thinking, it does have the advantage of bringing into sharp focus certain oppositions, such as nature versus civilization and reason versus passion, which the Romantics aimed to reconcile in their conception of human creativity but which Rousseau left as antimonies. The main direction of the study is then to explore in Blake, the Shelleys, Byron, and Keats the Romantic myth-makers' dreams of man remaking the creature into something divine, yet also their experiences in the darker reaches of imaginative life and endeavour where they meet the pressures of isolation, suffering, and the urge to annihilation.

The principal strength of Peter L. Thorslev Jr's *Romantic Contraries: Freedom Versus Destiny*[5] is the ease with which it interconnects literary criticism and the history of ideas. Ranging widely in territory similar to that of which Cantor makes trial, Thorslev first negotiates the conceptual problem of 'free will' and 'determinism' as it emerged in a newly secularized form in the late-Enlightenment and Romantic periods, not least within the sphere of scientific necessitarianism espoused by Hartley and Godwin and felt by the Romantic poets to deprive man of freedom and destiny alike. In the second half of the book we are taken into three hypothetical universes – the 'organic', the Gothic, and the 'open-ironic' – which serve as contexts for interpreting works by Wordsworth, Coleridge, and Byron. Its lively and informed inquiry makes *Romantic Contraries* a worthy addition to the recent crop of studies that have stimulated fresh attention to the contemporary relations between philosophy and aesthetic, especially poetic, form. Also relevant in this regard are two anthologies in the Cambridge three-volume series devoted to German aesthetics and criticism – Kathleen Wheeler's selection from the Romantic Ironists and Goethe[6] and David Simpson's from Kant, Fichte, Schelling, Schopenhauer, and Hegel[7]. The editors (both of whom have written on

4. *Creature and Creator: Myth-Making and English Romanticism*, by Paul A. Cantor. CUP. pp. xxii + 223. £19.50.

5. *Romantic Contraries: Freedom Versus Destiny*, by Peter L. Thorslev Jr. Yale. pp. x + 225. £21.50.

6. *The Romantic Ironists and Goethe*, ed. by Kathleen Wheeler. CUP. pp. x + 259. hb £25, pb £7.95.

7. *Kant, Fichte, Schelling, Schopenhauer, Hegel*, ed. by David Simpson. CUP. pp. x + 294. hb £25, pb £7.95.

Romantic poetry itself) display a vigorous expertise not only in the choice of texts, which is very substantial, but also in the more difficult procedures of introduction and annotation, where they keep both the seasoned scholar and the student successfully in view. In *SIR* the customary weight of Michael G. Cooke's learning, insight, and intellectual honesty is brought to bear on the Romantic phenomenon of 'the poising of the individual yearningly between annihilation and omnipotence' – the 'paradox of wholeness', seen in Blake's Thel, Goethe's Faust, Martha Ray of 'The Thorn', or Wordsworth on Snowdon, where the desire for participation in a great universal totality is shadowed by the inevitable claims of self-knowledge and self-situating.

The aim of Carlos Baker's *The Echoing Green: Romanticism, Modernism, and the Phenomena of Transference in Poetry*[8] is to examine the work of six modern poets against the seminal background of English Romanticism as represented by the major Romantic poets. It is in two parts: firstly, chapters accurately described by Baker as giving 'a normative view of the romantic achievement as it looks to an objective but sympathetic observer in the late twentieth century'; secondly, an assessment of the several ways in which Yeats, Frost, Pound, Stevens, Eliot, and Auden responded to the relevant ancestral voices. The advantage lies, necessarily, all with Part II. Here *The Echoing Green* is more than a straightforward 'influence' study but never quite a deep study of intertextual relations. Harkening to Northrop Frye's remark that 'Poetry can only be made out of other poems', Baker identifies the works that most engaged the interest of the moderns, summarizes the latter's varied attitudes to the past historical epoch, considers their use of aesthetic and ethical ideas derived from the verse and prose of that epoch, and shows where, when, and how they borrowed images and echoed phrases. The result is an impressive combination of generalized discussion and precise documentation; but readers seeking a rigorous analysis of the operations of 'transference' (by which Baker understands something much simpler than the modern theorist) will, I fear, be disappointed.

BIQ was, unfortunately, not available for consultation this year. In *TLS* Geoffrey Keynes prints an unpublished poem by Blake addressed to the wife of his friend, Thomas Butts, and entitled 'The Phoenix to Mrs. Butts'. In Keynes's view, this reveals that the poet was in practice 'a moral man' since it offers a gentle rebuke, in symbolic terms, on the subject of emotional and sexual involvement. There are two articles relating to the figure of Los: a snappy piece by John Adlard (*N&Q*) connecting the relay of Los's messages, as referred to in Plates 35 and 42 of *Milton*, with the siting of a telegraph station at Wimbledon in 1795–6, and Rodney M. Baine's thorough explication (*PQ*) of the twelve 'generated' sons of Los (the sons also of Jacob) in the light of their tribal roles, the biblical commentaries of Jacob Boehme and Emmanuel Swedenborg, and traditional representations in art. In 'The Sign of Blake' (*Criticism*) David Punter writes stylishly and at length on Blake as the author who resists structuralist and poststructuralist de-authorization because his discourses are *about* the fashioning of the self. The idea yields complex configurations of meaning based on Blake's meanings in the areas of revolution, the feminine, the finite and the infinite, and sex.

8. *The Echoing Green: Romanticism, Modernism, and the Phenomena of Transference in Poetry*, by Carlos Baker. Princeton. pp. xiv + 378. £32.30.

Greg Crossan (*SIR*) tabulates the errors and misprints in twelve books, published between 1968 and 1983, which transcribe or include transcriptions of Clare's texts. His seventeen pages constitute a warning, but he is able on the whole to celebrate the good work done. I doubt if there will be much for him to argue with in the two-volume OET edition of *The Later Poems*, prepared, with annotation and full apparatus, by Eric Robinson and David Powell[9]. These poems, covering the period from Clare's admission to the High Beach asylum in 1837 to his death in 1864, present fewer textual problems than earlier parts of the corpus, and it is perhaps for this reason that they are the first to appear in the planned collected *Poetical Works*. The difficulties of decipherment and manuscript dispersal are formidable nevertheless, and Robinson and Powell are to be congratulated for their impeccable scholarship, which extends with manifest rigour even into such concerns as the preservation of authentic accidentals.

Though there are some favourites among the later poems ('Now is past', for example), their critical status remains uncertain in comparison with other groupings in the Clare canon. Clearly, any revaluation will turn to a large extent on the question of Clare's technical virtuosity in relation to traditions of popular lyricism and song-making, his continuing yet less intimate observation of nature, and his uncanny obsession with love and sexuality (this being the period of his delusion that he was Byron, and the consequent production of a *Don Juan* and a *Child Harold*). We now have the full material to judge from, in the first fruits of a major venture of which the best is still to come (hopefully in chronological order). That 'best' is heralded in the same editors' selection of Clare's verse and prose in the excellent OA series[10].

It is good to see Wordsworth getting the lion's share of attention in 1984, decidedly turning the tables on his recent rivals, Blake and Coleridge. There are, to begin with, significant additions to the justly acclaimed Cornell Wordsworth, which, in common with previous volumes, combine reading texts, exhaustive presentation of variants, transcriptions of manuscripts (with photographs), and scholarly introductions. Eric Birdsall's edition of *Descriptive Sketches* (done with Paul M. Zall)[11] usefully prints the 1793 text and the extensively revised version of 1836 on facing pages. The introduction is mostly historical but there is an appendix containing new insights into Coleridge's appropriation of Wordsworthian materials. James Averill's treatment of *An Evening Walk*[12] establishes a complete textual history of Wordsworth's earliest long poem. Studied in its eventual gestation over five decades, the work provides minute evidence of the poet's changing artistic principles. Jared Curtis's quarry is the 1807 *Poems*, together with the printer's copy from which items were deleted before publication and all the remaining lyrics and shorter narrative poems (forty-four in all) composed between 1800 and 1807 but

9. *The Later Poems of John Clare, 1837–1864*. Vol. I and II, ed. by Eric Robinson and David Powell. OET. Clarendon. pp. xxiv + 1165. £85 (two vols).

10. *John Clare*, ed. by Eric Robinson and David Powell. OA. OUP. pp. xxx + 530. pb £4.95.

11. *William Wordsworth: Descriptive Sketches*, ed. by Eric Birdsall, with Paul M. Zall. The Cornell Wordsworth. CornU. pp. xiv + 301. $48.50.

12. *William Wordsworth: An Evening Walk*, ed. by James Averill. The Cornell Wordsworth. CornU. pp. xii + 306. $38.50.

published later or not at all[13]. This is a clear advance on other editorial accounts of this phase of Wordsworth's career because it is the first to make thorough use of the printer's copy and earlier associated manuscripts.

In his OA selection of Wordsworth's poetry and prose[14] Stephen Gill adopts the unusual policy of arranging the poems in the order in which they were written (rather than as Wordsworth categorized them) and of preferring versions as near as possible to the earliest 'completed' states. This may prompt debate, but the outcome is for general purposes a first-rate working text. Alan G. Hill's selection from his Oxford edition of the *Letters*[15] has many attractive features – not least the fact that it can be read as a continuous narrative, with the minimum of editorial intrusion. And there is an equally handsome companion volume of letters by Dorothy Wordsworth[16].

The autumn issue of *WC* is given over in its entirety to a first publication of the letters of Dora Wordsworth to her friend, Maria Kinnaird, edited by John O. Hayden. Stretching from 1826 to 1843, the correspondence brings a fascinating inside glimpse of Rydal Mount during much of its heyday. David McCracken's *Wordsworth and the Lake District*[17] sets out the connections between Wordsworth's poetry and its origins in Lake District places, drawing on the Fenwick notes, Wordsworth's *Guide to the Lakes*, and other sources. Although some connections are made for the first time, this is in tone and character a book chiefly for general readers – and indeed, in Part II, for travellers, armchair or otherwise, who will surely find themselves leaving the detailed maps and walking guides well thumbed. It is in all respects an immensely pleasurable volume, executed with skill and patient enthusiasm.

The squeamish need not be alarmed by the title of David Ellis's *Wordsworth, Freud and the Spots of Time*[18], which is very much the work of an intelligent scholar-critic writing out of normative assumptions about reading and poetic creation, rather than that of the dedicated expert in or aficionado of psychoanalytical theory. Ellis emerges indeed in the role of honest doubter, confidently sensitive to the problems of how much or how little to let in biography, the uses and misuse of Freud, and the value and dangers of hermeneutic methodologies in general. His own procedure in dealing with the 'spots of time' is to stalk around the poetry at a steady pace, making energetic probes to the interior so as to uncover some new dimension or addition to our understanding of the episode, as in his grasp of the less obvious workings of the oedipus complex in various places or (a different sort of example which gives an idea of Ellis's range) his insistence on the 'self-satisfied and relieved' ending of the meeting with the discharged soldier. In the final analysis, his study does not stand as a rival to or extension of the Freudian analyses of R. J. Onorato

13. *William Wordsworth: Poems, in Two Volumes, and Other Poems, 1800–1807*, ed. by Jared Curtis. The Cornell Wordsworth. CornU (1983). pp. xxxvi + 731. $99.50.

14. *William Wordsworth*, ed. by Stephen Gill. OA. OUP. pp. xxxii + 752. pb £5.95.

15. *Letters of William Wordsworth*, ed. by Alan G. Hill. Clarendon. pp. xxx + 330. £17.50.

16. *Letters of Dorothy Wordsworth*, ed. by Alan G. Hill. Clarendon. pp. xxii + 200. £9.95.

17. *Wordsworth and the Lake District: a Guide to the Poems and Their Places*, by David McCracken. OUP. pp. xvii + 300. £12.50.

18. *Wordsworth, Freud and the Spots of Time*, by David Ellis. CUP. pp. viii + 199. £19.50.

and Michael H. Friedman but as a contribution, aided by a knowledge of Freud and his status, to a tradition of more generalized interpretation of the nature and goals of self-presentation in Wordsworth.

Freud features alongside Hegel and Nietzsche, Derrida and de Man, in Paul Jay's *Being in The Text*[19], which has two compelling chapters on *The Prelude* within an ambitious and flexible application of contemporary literary theory to an unravelling of the strategies of self-representation, and the concepts behind them, in a series of texts from the Romantic and modern periods. Wordsworth's poem is crucial because it forges, in the space created by the withdrawal of the stabilizing harmonies of religious belief, an absolute link between the emergence of a problematical subjectivity and the rise of autobiographical art (though a lot remains to be said about the valorization of self and psyche in Puritan spiritual autobiographies like *Grace Abounding*). As this suggests, there is a strong diachronic bent to Jay's overall approach. Yet it is one that allows sharp, often exceptional, insights into what is, psychologically understood, timeless and essential: his best pages are, to my mind, those on Wordsworth's structuring of experience and 'the compulsion to repeat'.

Wordsworth's Language of Men by J. P. Ward[20] reflects a familiarity not only with poststructuralist concepts but also, which is still unusual, with current linguistics. But it is really a very individual – personal – book, as might be expected from one poet writing on another. For Ward, Wordsworth 'let the language flow as he felt', urging it to sway and swell 'as though no known foundation existed for it outside of the writer's subjective experience of language itself'; and in this he broke decisively with 'the rationalist base and the perpetual mythic source', a great innovator who saved poetry in an environment where it was under potentially terminal pressure from materialist philosophy and attitudes, and who in his practice foretold the recognitions of Wittgenstein, J. L. Austin, and John Searle. The argument is boldly conducted, informed, and ultimately persuasive, but for many readers the true riches of this monograph will lie in its attentiveness to those formal aspects of Wordsworth's poetry – vibrancy and motion, metaphor, nominals, the copula, modes of 'speech' – which are the constant, though often unobtrusive, carriers of potent signification. Here especially *Wordsworth's Language of Men* has the sort of concentrated freshness and scope that can make a difference to how an author is ordinarily thought about and responded to.

J. R. Watson's perceptive and discerning essay on Wordsworth[21] makes its welcome appearance in the introductory WTW series. For Watson's important recent work, however, we must go to his study of the sacred and profane in Wordsworth's poetry, *Wordsworth's Vital Soul*[22]. The presiding presences here are such writers as Mircea Eliade, Martin Buber, and Victor Turner – modern thinkers whose philosophic and anthropological concepts, and terminology, are made to illuminate Wordsworth so effectively that one is left, after reading Watson, with a sense not only of something new having been

19. *Being in The Text: Self-Representation from Wordsworth to Roland Barthes*, by Paul Jay. CornU. pp. 189. $25.50.

20. *Wordsworth's Language of Men*, by J. P. Ward. Harvester. pp. xii + 235. £22.50.

21. *Wordsworth*, by J. R. Watson. WTW. Profile. pp. 69. np.

22. *Wordsworth's Vital Soul: The Sacred and Profane in Wordsworth's Poetry*, by J. R. Watson. Macmillan (1982). pp. ix + 259. £20.

done but also something intrinsically apt and fertile. As Watson presents him, through analysis and comparison, Wordsworth remains very much the poet of the mind of man but with that status firmly re-oriented in the direction of 'sacred' poet in the broad meaning of the word: to read Wordsworth is to encounter 'a kind of religious belief which is very close to patterns of religious behaviour in primitive communities'. Although the theme is pursued across the range of its manifestations in Wordsworth's dealings with the individual, nature, and society, I found *Wordsworth's Vital Soul* specially rewarding where it concentrates on *communitas* itself, on the poetry of suffering, and on liminal states or stages of development. In discussing the last of these, for example, Watson discovers in the Wordsworthian motif of the threshold a powerful vehicle for defining a phase of corporate existence, as well as a phase in the subjective life and its maturation, and thus enriches our understanding both of a salient aspect of the poetic structure and the breadth of Wordsworth's human concern. But this twofold yield, the opening of vistas through form onto the content of Wordsworth's humane and humanizing vision, is characteristic of the whole of this admirably judicious and often enlightening book.

Did Wordsworth write his epic, *The Recluse*, after all? Kenneth R. Johnston, in his monumental *Wordsworth and The Recluse*[23], argues that in a sense he did: the poem is no unrealized great idea but an extant work consisting of a coherent, though fragmentary, body of interrelated texts. In Johnston's own words, reading *The Recluse* is 'an archaeological project, uncovering the buried, ruined outlines of an immense but only partly constructed cathedral, and causing the realignment of the bearings of the smaller finished structures still standing around and above it'. While this pre-emptive declaration of interventionist expository tactics may arouse as much as allay scepticism about the method and projected claims of the book, Johnston's revelation and re-assessment of the landscape are in the event highly convincing. One important reason for his success is that he resists the temptation to trace any simply progressive emergence of the 'text' of *The Recluse* but instead keeps faith with the evidences of a pervasive dialectical movement in Wordsworth's career during 1797–1814 between commitment to a public epic of secular redemption and a fascination with personal history and vocation. Thus, we have three major episodes, each of which repeats the same pattern of crisis and provisional resolution. The pattern is itself threefold: an abortive start on *The Recluse*; a recoil, motivated by self-doubt, into autobiographical poetry exemplified above all by *The Prelude*; a return, after restoration, to complete some larger or smaller portion of *The Recluse*. Yet neither is Johnston's procedure as neatly programmatic as this overview might suggest, for at every point the materials – textual, biographical, and critical – are examined with intense care and flexibility. The volume is a remarkable feat of formalist interpretation – an outstanding contribution to Wordsworth scholarship that stretches our attention in new and profitable ways well beyond the bounds of its nominal subject.

In Evan Radcliffe's view (*SIR*), Wordsworth, much preoccupied during late 1797 and early 1798 with fears of being condemned as a mere dreamer, expanded *The Ruined Cottage* to include the biography of the Pedlar in order to define, for himself and others, the special sense in which the Poet is, and is

23. *Wordsworth and The Recluse*, by Kenneth R. Johnston. Yale. pp. xxxii + 397. £30.

not, a dreaming man. The Pedlar's ability to transcend the immediate reality and its pressures is the power through which he maintains a 'just equipoise' that takes account of, but is not overwhelmed by, human suffering. Though the word 'dream' is used rather vaguely, the article does helpfully highlight the relation between inner strength and imaginative idealization in Wordsworth's conception of his own worthier self as it is projected in the figure of Armytage. Also in *SIR* Keith Hinchcliffe looks at certain resonant key words, which appear across several poems and show Wordsworth's search for a pre-dualistic manner of thinking and talking about mind and nature. Hinchcliffe's grasp of the terms, and their complex signification, is exact.

David Sampson's 'Wordsworth and the Deficiencies of Language' (*ELH*) takes up the theme of *Lyrical Ballads* as the 'new poetry'. His general point is that Wordsworth set out deliberately to disturb complacent notions of simplicity among his middle-class readers by evoking the distinctiveness of the life and language of the rural poor. The most interesting remarks are those on tautology in its function, not as an actual model of speech, but as a symbolic goal, a representation of the utterance that is entirely liberated from convention. In *SIR* we find the same critic again insisting on the 'radical originality' of *Lyrical Ballads*: Wordsworth's respect for the poor is a valorization of true 'community' as opposed to the artificial framework of relationships in sophisticated society. Linda Venis (*SEL*) compares the volume with a large sample of broadside ballads from contemporary chapbooks, confirming our sense of Wordsworth's greater penetration of psychological states and subtler uses of 'simple' language but, to my mind, failing to prove that he was everywhere closer to the 'reality' of the historical situation of the lower classes.

There is no more memorable item this year than Christian La Cassagnère's enterprising disclosure of unconscious meanings in the text of 'The Thorn' (*EA*, in French). We learn that the poem has a dual diegesis arising from Wordsworth's subversion of the ballad genre: behind the manifest story is the story of a gaze, relatable to Freud's discourse on the primal phantasy dramatized in the myth of Medusa's petrifying vision. In 'Wordsworth's *Michael* and the Pastoral Tradition' (*UTQ*) Richard Lessa, showing scant knowledge of what 'pastoral' is, reaches the shaky conclusion that Wordsworth's poem reflects a profound change in the genre by attesting its survival only as elegy rather than in the earlier form of celebration. Thomas Dilworth (*Expl*) notes the primacy of olfactory, tactile, and visual sensation in the middle stanza of 'She Dwelt among Untrodden Ways', which he sees as a post-mortem heightening, and complication, of the poet's response to Lucy. Steven Knapp's 'The Sublime, Self-reference, and Wordsworth's "Resolution and Independence"' (*MLN*) offers an absorbing interrogation of the ways in which figures like the Leech-gatherer shrug off, evade, or frustrate whatever narcissistic investment they seem to invite from the poet. The article ends, however, with a somewhat puzzling surprise, or anticlimax: the Leech-gatherer turns out to be nothing other than a 'naturalized deposit' of the Spenserian stanza. Knapp's willingness to chance his arm stands in marked contrast to Bette Charlene Werner's point-to-point comparison of 'The Solitary Reaper' and Constable's picture of *The Gleaners* (*CompL*), where we are told that both poet and painter transform 'outer seeing' into 'inner vision' and 'achieve universality through their development of the particular'.

The Prelude is considered more or less exclusively in its parts this year, rather than in its entirety. Sections of the poem supply the central material, alongside *The Borderers* and 'The Immortality Ode', in Ross Woodman's authoritative review (*SIR*) of the demonic-satanic strain in Wordsworth, especially as it derived from Milton, and of the manner in which it is countered by a fundamentally redemptive project of consciousness. Warren Stevenson (*WC*) uses Roderick McGill's article on 'Anecdote for Fathers' (*ESC*) as a springboard for analysing two other places – the 'death of the father' episode in *The Prelude* and 'Elegiac Stanzas Suggested by a Picture of Peele Castle' – where the motif of satanic impulse is linked to self-directed irony on Wordsworth's part. The 'Dream of the Arab' in Book V continues to raise questions. For Glenn W. Most (*ELN*) the issue is whether evidence can be found to suggest that it was generated by or forms a comment upon anything in Cervantes' *Don Quixote* – a possible source oddly ignored by scholars in spite of Wordsworth's reference to Cervantes at the dream's opening. The mention of 'dromedaries' in both texts leads Most to the discovery of a parallel sense of the frailty of human art, which, though not without interest as a general topic, does nothing in my view to clinch the argument for specific influence or interconnection. In *SIR* Ernest Bernhardt-Kabish places the episode in the context of Wordsworth's absorption in theories of global catastrophe, and provides good background material for appreciating the poet's struggle to elide apocalyptic assumptions through symbolic representation of man's position.

Two substantial essays on Wordsworth and imagination revisit the Simplon Pass. The semiological bias of Douglas Kneale's 'The Rhetoric of Imagination in *The Prelude*' (*ArielE*) yields an autobiographical poem forced repeatedly to meditate on the deficiencies of its translation of a self into language, with de Man's 'allegory of reading' and Derrida's ideas on the usurpation of speech by writing being enlisted to give new interpretations of the crossing of the Alps and the encounter with the signs beneath the gibbet-mast. By re-imagining Wordsworth's 1790 Simplon Pass trip and *The Prelude*'s insertion of Imagination into that trip Alan Liu (*ELH*) lets back 'history' into our thinking about the formation of the self as it takes place in Wordsworth's text; but history, it is argued, is also the mind's antagonist in the poet's efforts to bring self into being. With a certain poignant sense of trespass and elegiac longing for lost faith, Liu lingers over a deconstructionist reading of Geoffrey Hartman's original Wordsworth and banishes nature, the old enemy and guide, to the very periphery of the poem's psychodrama and mental topography. Yet pre-structuralist Hartman is in the final analysis also the ancestor who cannot be cast out: Liu's ultimate logocentric affirmation of the power of mind, as that which 'tours' or 'turns' the world, is in essence a renewal of the consolatory vision of the subjective spirit embodied in *Wordsworth's Poetry*.

These last two are difficult articles which will repay patient attention. Andrzej Warminski's 'Missed Crossing: Wordsworth's Apocalypses' (*MLN*), dealing with 'meaning' and 'not meaning' in language and experience, is altogether harder to decipher. An extended note by Matthew Brennan (*Expl*) on 'A Night Piece', the blank verse poem of 1797–8 associated with the Snowdon episode in *The Prelude*, emphasizes the poet-traveller's recoil from visionary apprehension of the sublime in nature to contemplation of the inner vastness of his own creative depths. In 'Wordsworth, Hartley and the Revisionists' (*SP*) John Hayden convincingly challenges the familiar view that Wordsworth owed a significant debt to the central Associationist philosophic tradition of David Hartley in the early part of his career, arguing instead that the poet's starting point was the reaction against Hartley by Abraham Tucker, Archibald Tucker, and Dugald Stewart, the 'revisionists' who rescued the mind from passivity by ascribing our actions to its agency and performance. The seminal period of the mid 1790s comes to the fore in a different way in Nicholas Roe's return (*WC*) to the events of 1797 when Wordsworth and Coleridge were mistaken for French spies, and especially to the issue of the identity of the government informer, 'Spy Nozy', whom he identifies as James Walsh. Political idealism, metropolitan corruptness, and the moral status of Lake District life in Wordsworth's thinking are among the themes developed in Donald H. Reiman's comprehensive researching (*Criticism*) of the tragic story of Mary Robinson, the 'maiden of Buttermere' of *The Prelude*, Book VII, and its importance to the poet and his circle. D. C. Kay (*N&Q*) detects likely sources for the address to London as 'monstrous ant-hill' (*Prelude*, 1850, XI.149–51) in Thomson's *Castle of Indolence* and in Donne, who was peculiarly fond of this image.

As always, *PMLA* prints one of the very best articles of the year. Here Susan J. Wolfson compares the three versions of the 'Drowned Man of Esthwaite' episode (*Prelude*, 1799, 1805, and 1850), where she discovers the progressive interpolation of a commentary that denies the boy's fear and converts the corpse into a figure of ideal grace but also other changes that suggest Wordsworth's persistent ambivalence about the strategy of gaining argumentative control over the mysteries which haunt his imagination. This opens up the theoretical topic of the nature of revision itself – how each stage revives the originating inquiry, how the process sustains the illusion of mastery yet steadily postpones its achievement.

One result of Marilyn Butler's selection of contemporary prose documents, *Burke, Paine, Godwin, and the Revolution Controversy*[24], is to bring home the extent to which the political writings of the period form a close-knit debate, with works constantly intersecting and depending for their meaning not simply upon the historical situation but upon one another. Wordsworth and Coleridge are both there with the big names and a series of lesser yet trenchant radical voices like Thomas Spence and Joseph Ritson.

The damaged archangel himself continues to get the occasional pounding. This time, in *WC*, Richard Gravil affirms, with good reason, that the critique of Wordsworth's poetry in *Biographia Literaria* is not a soul-brother's privileged revelation of truth but an exercise in misrepresentation and self-exoneration: the handling of *Lyrical Ballads* in particular is the delayed surfacing of a long-suppressed Neoclassical distaste for Wordsworth's revolutionary practice, while overall Coleridge myopically blames his fellow poet for not being the ideal philosopher pictured in his own imagination. I. M. Wylie's learned article in *RES*, arcanely entitled 'How the Natural Philosophers Defeated the Whore of Babylon in the Thought of S. T. Coleridge, 1795–1796', begins with the evidence in the 1796 notebooks of Coleridge's interest in the millenarianism of Thomas Burnet's *Telluris Theoria Sacra* (1689) and also of his desire to modify Burnet's theory by stressing the need for a positively 'progressive', rather than simply 'evolutionary', understanding of nature. This

24. *Burke, Paine, Godwin, and the Revolution Controversy*, ed. by Marilyn Butler, CUP. pp. xii + 260. hb £25, pb £7.95.

then leads, via Joseph Priestley and others, to a consideration of how the philosophical issues at stake, and the metaphors in which they had been familiarly framed, influenced 'Religious Musings' and related texts by Coleridge. *N&Q* includes two items on the prose: Peter Kitson pinpoints the publication date of the lecture known as *The Plot Discovered* which Coleridge gave in support of the 1795 movement for parliamentary reform, and James Flavin finds further proof for the proposition that the first paragraph of *Biographia Literaria* was written after the greater part of the work was finished, so that we see more clearly the retrospective nature of Coleridge's introductory characterization of the unity of the text as deriving from the continuous presence of a distinct authorial personality. In *WC* David Ullrich revalues Coleridge's poetic and intellectual responses to the work of Erasmus Darwin, showing them to have been much more complex than the usual assumption of an ungenerous dislike will allow; and in the same journal Bradford K. Mudge discusses Sara Coleridge's *Quarterly Review* article on Tennyson's *The Princess* with special reference to her reasoned belief (interesting from a literary-historical point of view) that her father occupied a crucial mediating position between a Wordsworthian moral-reflective tradition and a 'Sensation' school embracing Keats, Shelley, and Tennyson himself.

Among the essays on the poetry, pride of place must go to David S. Miall's muscular, inquisitive, semi-psychoanalytical reading of *The Ancient Mariner* (*SEL*), which discloses at the heart of the poem, in the protagonist's encounter with death, the imposition of a mental wound from which recovery can only be partial. This central event sets up within the text an irreducible resistance to closure, highlighted by the inadequacy of the concluding moral and indeed any allegorical interpretation. In *N&Q* Massimo Bacigalupo detects in Homer's description of the departure of Odysseus's ship homewards for Ithaca (XIII.81–5) a source for the simile in ll. 389–92 of *The Ancient Mariner*. Study of the sources of 'Kubla Khan' is still very much in evidence, with Nai-Tung Ting (*SIR*) detailing additional documents and historical background in relation to 'Xanadu' and Michael Bright (*CLS*) establishing the currency – in Coleridge's day, and earlier, in works like Charles Perrault's *Parallèle des Anciens et des Modernes* (1688) – of ideas expressed in the poem about war and the conditions in which art may flourish or wither. Two of the longer articles close in on the elusive figure of Geraldine in *Christabel*. Karen Swann's (*SIR*) is by far the more vigorous and productive assault, energized by intelligent feminist commitment. For Swann, Geraldine translates the story 'Christabel' into a conventional tale of terror – a translation which, though apparently fixing the identity of 'woman', ultimately complicates the issue of feminine identity by implying its entanglement, at the origin, with genre. Rhonda Johnson Ray's Geraldine (*PQ*) is disguised evil usurping the Christ with whom Christabel desires union. The religious symbolism is there of course, but not so neatly or superficially as this translator would appear to believe.

Little has been done in the past to identify Southey's extensive list of contributions to the radical newspaper, the *Morning Post* (in which Wordsworth and Coleridge also published). The situation is now remedied, as far as is possible, by Kenneth Curry's edited collection of the two hundred or more Southey poems that appeared in its columns over the years 1798–9, 1801, and 1803[25], many of which are ascribed for the first time, primarily on the evidence of outlines written down in the poet's *Common-Place Book*. The materials are interesting not only in themselves but as better-than-average examples of the type of verse circulating in periodicals around the turn of the century, at the time of *Lyrical Ballads*. By coincidence, Oskar Wellens (*WC*) makes some new attributions to Southey among pieces printed anonymously in the *Critical Review* during the period 1798–1801.

The well-known Penguin selection of Byron's prose has been reprinted under a different title[26]. Happily, it retains the convenient chronological-thematic arrangement which takes us in sections from 'the formative years', through 'fame and society' and 'marriage and exile', down to 'the poet as hero'. In a notable textual item (*N&Q*) John Spalding Gatton presents an unpublished signed holograph letter written by Byron in 1819 to Richard Belgrave Hoppner, British Consul in Venice, with whom he was involved in a financial matter. Strong claims are made by John Hayden (*KSJ*) for the authenticity of the uncollected three-stanza poem, 'To Barbara', printed as Byron's in the *New Bon Ton Magazine* for November 1819. Dick Hoefnagel's brief biographical outline, in *N&Q*, of Byron's correspondent, Jean Jacques Coulmann, proves that Leslie Marchand was wrong when saying that nothing was known about him except from the poet's letters.

Working tenaciously to fill a gap in Byron criticism by considering *Childe Harold's Pilgrimage* within the context of eighteenth-century precedents for the poem's stanzaic and romance design, Michael Vicario (*KSJ*) is drawn into the lively problem of Byron's quest for a wise and unified grasp of history where history descends only in fragmented and corrupt perceptions. Vicario's conclusion is both valid and shapely: Byron regrets the warpings of actuality by romance but must finally respect romance's capability for bestowing necessary significance on the disordered array of human experience and events. In 'Byron's "Prisoner of Chillon": The Poetry of Being and the Poetry of Belief' (*KSMB*) Vincent Newey analyses the means by which the psychodrama of isolation, confinement, and death-in-life is realized in the text, distinguishes the poem from eighteenth-century and previous Romantic treatments of imprisonment (where there is customarily some explicit or implicit drive towards moral statement), and explores the opposition between Byron's concern with the dark side of inward experience and his apparent commitment to sociopolitical statement when he chooses to preface 'The Prisoner of Chillon' with the 'Sonnet' celebrating liberty. One of Newey's aims is to evaluate the quality of Byron's 'dynamic pessimism' – which, he hopes, may help to challenge a serious underestimation of the poem by a recent critic (see *YW* 63.292). The task Dennis Dahl sets himself (*Criticism*) is to decide what it signifies that Poe's 'The Assignation' evades making direct reference to Byron though Byron is so clearly present in the story. The answer, it is alleged, lies in recognizing that this text poses the question, relevant to all biography, of how far language dissolves the essential being of the self it represents. Byron's role as the fiction into which Poe reads himself must also be taken into account.

25. *The Contributions of Robert Southey to The Morning Post*, ed. by Kenneth Curry. UAla. pp. 224. $19.75.
26. *Byron: Selected Letters and Journals*, ed. by Peter Gunn. Penguin. pp. 432. pb £4.95.

A neglected but (when one thinks of it) obvious side of Keats is ably brought to life in Donald C. Goellnicht's study of the influence of his medical training and knowledge on his poems and letters – *The Poet-Physician: Keats and Medical Science*[27]. An outline of the chief biographical facts and the state of medical education at the time is followed by chapters centring on each of the branches of the science that Keats would have learned about, which are chemistry, botany, anatomy and physiology, and pathology. Though perhaps in parts too readily betraying the book's origin as a doctoral thesis, Goellnicht's measured and conscientious documenting of the relevant ideas, perspectives, details, and images, as they emerge throughout and in all corners of the poetry and prose, serves useful and sometimes innovative ends. We are made to see general Keatsian themes like organicism and the health–disease dichotomy against a new background but the volume's most effective contribution may well lie, in the long run, in its identification of specific, 'hard' sources of influence such as brain anatomy (which has bearing on the 'Chamber of Maiden-thought' letter) or chemical process (which helped to shape Keats's statements about creativity). Future annotators will have much to thank Goellnicht for.

Ulrich Hoffmann's study[28] of Keats's letters and some of his poems addresses the problem of the ambivalent nature of personal identity as an artist and poetic identity as the author of a work of art in Keats's writing. The first chapter is devoted to the letters, discussing their form and unity and the recurrent themes of the relationship of the individual to his world and the poet to his poetry. In the next three chapters 'Ode to May', the two *Hyperion* poems and 'To Autumn' are analysed fully with respect to the central problem, and Hoffmann concludes that Keats attained no more than an 'imaginary identity'. The text contains an extensive bibliography and a short summary in English. [M.H.]

The accepted status of the first edition as copy text for *Endymion* comes under pressure from Margaret Ketchum Powell's scrutiny (*Lib*) of the printer's holograph fair copy, biographical information, and letters from the period, for these together suggest that Keats was more interested in detail and less happy with press alterations than is normally assumed. The same poem supplies Beth Lau (*PQ*) with an embryonic example of the humanitarian goddess, or Muse, which reached fully fledged form in bountiful Autumn and the figure of Moneta in *Hyperion*, mature deities that function as guides not lovers and reconcile the values of Keats's early visionary idealism with those of his later scepticism about the pleasures of art. In Bruce Clarke's sophisticated reading (*SIR*), which will please some and just as surely alarm others, *Lamia* is a poem that demonstrates how 'the forms of poetic exchanges and transferences underwrite all other human economies', dealing as it does in the placings and displacings involved in the negotiations by which consciences are constructed, and the furtive relations holding between the sexual and the spiritual for the shaping of gender identities. Joseph Sitterson Jr (*JEGP*) goes back to Plato, via Keats's reference to 'Platonic shades', to give a canny twist to the

27. *The Poet-Physician: Keats and Medical Science*, by Donald C. Goellnicht. UPitt. pp. xii + 291. $26.95.
28. *Die erdichtete Identität, Subjekt des Autors und auktoriales subjekt in den Briefen und einigen Gedichten von John Keats*, by Ulrich Hoffmann. Niemeyer. pp. viii + 247. pb DM 74.

obvious point that *Lamia* is about the 'real' and the 'apparent' by stressing the
poet's familiarity with a philosophy which presented these concepts as inter-
changeable rather than as true oppositions and would have led him, in the
poem, to assert that *everything* in our experience is shadowy, dreamlike,
enigmatic, 'unreal'.

By 'The Sub-Text of Keats's "Ode to a Nightingale"' (*KSJ*) Karl P.
Wentersdorf means the series of images located in Keats's allusions to the
experiences of those who in ancient times have known the ecstasy of mortal
love, through which is expressed his own deep yearning for that rapture. Also
in *KSJ* we find Philip Fisher juggling, in somewhat giddy fashion, with the
much more intriguing idea of the 'museum' or 'anthology' containing one
object, of which 'Ode on a Grecian Urn', is a leading instance: the work of art,
the urn, is not only preserved by but also survives as mute culture to generate
the work of art, Keats's poem. *Keats's Major Odes: An Annotated Bibliography of the Criticism*[29], by Jack Wright Rhodes, takes in the whole period from
1820 to 1980. Scholars will be grateful for this coverage, as for the astute
commentaries and indexing. The introduction is a good source of information
about the shifts in critical attitudes to Keats over the decades, but the author's
own perspectives are pretty basic, sometimes even bizarre in their drift into
such academic backwaters as the statistics for completed Ph.D.s in English in
1977 (1094 in fact) and the total expenditure of institutions of higher learning
in the United States in 1960. (One senses here that there is another kind of
project, wholly desirable, struggling to get out, and it must be admitted that it
is fascinating to know that in 1954 *ELH* had only 574 registered readers and
KSJ only 193.) I should perhaps point out that A. C. Bradley can hardly be
listed among 'recent scholars', despite his origination of some modern critical
trends.

Angela Leighton gives us, in *Shelley and the Sublime*[30], a first-rate critical
book distinguished by a tough sparkle, a combination of hard thinking and
lightness of touch, an aliveness in all things – style, ideas, practical engagement
with the text. On one level it opposes, or rather counterbalances, some recent
studies of Shelley by presenting his politics and philosophy, not in isolation,
but as inseparable from questions of poetic utterance. Despite a strong chapter
on the 'politics of creativity' in *Prometheus Unbound*, however, the main
thrust of the book is carried by its expository grasp of Shelley's aesthetic itself
and the tensions embodied and unfolding within it: for Leighton, Shelley's
poetry is above all about the struggles and triumphs of making. Shelley's poetic
theory is first related to the eighteenth-century sublime, with some excellent
remarks on the rejection of empiricism in the course of that tradition, a
progressive internalization of the eye linked to a switch from object to subject.
While he consistently keeps faith with the celebration of prelinguistic inspiration, he also denies the religious basis of the sublime as it had come to be
habitually understood by his predecessors; and it is this strain between scepticism and a positive or purist stance *vis-à-vis* the act of creation that underlies
and orders the language and vision of his major poetry, reaching its severest
form in *The Triumph of Life*. 'Hymn to Intellectual Beauty', 'Mont Blanc',

29. *Keats's Major Odes: An Annotated Bibliography of the Criticism*, by Jack Wright
Rhodes. Greenwood, pp. 224. £33.95.
30. *Shelley and the Sublime*, by Angela Leighton. CUP. pp. x + 195. hb £17.50,
pb £6.50.

'Ode to the West Wind', 'To a Skylark', and *Adonais* are the other fore-grounded texts, each a version of the fundamental Shelleyan 'complex' of doubt and transcendent aspiration, the double acknowledgement of both the inadequacy and sufficiency of rhetorical questing.

Anthony D. Knerr's critical edition of *Adonais*[31], the first such undertaking since W. M. Rossetti's volume of 1891, constitutes the perfect apparatus for appreciating the process of shaping and refinement that led to what Shelley called 'the least imperfect of my compositions' – text, manuscript drafts, associated fragments, background and circumstances of writing, sources, reception, criticism. The special Shelley number of *SIR* opens and closes with articles on *Adonais*. James A. W. Heffernan explains how, in a response to the fiction that Keats's death was hastened by damning reviews of *Endymion*, Shelley 'consumes' as well as re-creates the identity of Keats within the elegy and at the very end envisions the survival of that identity, in a state beyond the reach of detractors, as a way of foreseeing the survival of his own. Peter Sacks's equally well-argued interpretation of the poem has some fulgent remarks on the 'mourning imagination' which, in its climax, draws Shelley on to what all mourners need most to avoid – their own drive beyond life and beyond the language whose saving distances keep them alive. *Prometheus Unbound* holds the central position in Tilottama Rajan's specialist incursion into 'Deconstruction and Reconstruction', the subject of how far the fracturing of significance in the romantic text denies, or does not deny, readings that affirm synthesis or unity; and in Jean Hall's contribution *Prometheus* is the lyric drama of the human imagination set over against *The Cenci*, a tragedy of social actuality and 'sad reality', in an opposition created by Shelley to declare, not exclusive possibilities, but continuities that turn upon the urge to promote the idea of making ourselves anew through the redemptive potential of poetic idealism. While Hall is content to labour a commonplace thesis, Edward Duffey, in a fruitfully adventurous (if sometimes overly vatic) essay, appropriates 'Ode to the West Wind' as proof-text for an argument that vivifies Shelley as 'poet *antagonistes*', a user of language locked in a strenuous dialogue with the semantic and semiotic codes of his civilization, a writer whose personal strivings for authority symbolize humanity's everlasting struggle with the place and power of the word in collective experience.

It rates as common knowledge that the 1816 *Alastor* volume is unified by Shelley's obsession with the problem of becoming and remaining a poet in the contemporary world, but no one before Neil Fraistat (*KSJ*) has, I think, realized the full extent to which its components are interrelated in imagery and theme, with the first six and last six poems forming a counterpoise structure wherein solipsism contends with self-sacrifice, private cares with public commitments, and despair with hope. For Edward Strickland, writing in the same journal, the title poem divulges, not just the destructive seduction of imagination, but the 'secular martyrdom' of the whole poetic process itself, an event involving alienation and narcissism and inviting the application of Freud, Jung, and existential philosophy.

In an exemplary scholarly exposition, no less insightful than precise in the handling of materials, Timothy Webb (*KSMB*) builds a firmer, and also more

---

31. *Shelley's Adonais: a Critical Edition*, ed. by Anthony D. Knerr. ColU. pp. xii + 292. $32.50.

expansive, understanding of Shelley's concept of atheism as expressed in prose writings and *Prometheus Unbound*. The article includes the first full publication of a prose passage, from the Bodleian Shelley papers, on the subject of the 'Defence of Atheism', which Webb explicates in relation to a draft, written on the same folded manuscript sheet, of elements of Asia's speech on the Creation and the origins of the material world (*Prometheus Unbound*, II.iii.28–42). In *Expl* Fred L. Milne elucidates the Spirit of the Hour's reference to the delayed sunrise (II.v.10–11).

No one who reads Neil Dorman's 'Sadism, Masochism, and Simbiosis in Shelley's *Cenci*' (*L&P*, xxxi.4 – no date) will fall into the easy trap of seeing the relationship between Count Cenci and Beatrice as simply that of oppressor and victim. As well as needing to be dominated and humiliated, the masochist identifies with the sadist; and thus the daughter takes on the attitudes and practices of her sadistic father, ultimately internalizing the values of the patriarchal family and the Renaissance Italian religious and political system, until she is destroyed by them. A clear-sighted, concise essay, this – getting to grips with something that matters and altering our perception of the drama. The two remaining articles are also well worth consulting, making it a rather good year for Shelley in the periodicals. Anne Janowitz, in *PQ*, diagnoses the effects through which 'Ozymandias' pushes the reader to intuit a judgement on the vanity of worldly glory *and* the vitality of art in the face of time's ravages. In thus inscribing a message to be gradually deciphered Shelley departs from the explicitness of the eighteenth-century ruin poem: he 'de-monumentalizes' moralization. 'To a Skylark' is in William A. Ulmer's view (*SIR*) a far less unreflecting poem than may be apparent and in fact communicates, in its antiphonal structure, the impossibility of either gratifying or renouncing infinite desire.

2. Prose Fiction

This year has produced interesting material on the Gothic novel from the French periodical *Europe*. In its best article, Maurice Lévy argues that the Gothic novel occurred first in England because it was there alone that feudalism and tyranny could be handled with the fascination that comes from security. Liliane Abensour, commenting on the richly influential career of Lewis's *The Monk*, ascribes the book's continuing appeal to the dynamism which keeps it constantly in motion and suggestively open to re-interpretation and re-use. Following similar lines, Chantal Tutu traces the fertile, varied fortunes of Ann Radcliffe's *The Mysteries of Udolpho* in France, and finds that the novel was so well received because of its great symbolic resourcefulness. In his more conventional comparative study, Alain Faure notes the many similarities of incident between *The Monk* and E. T. A. Hoffmann's *The Devil's Elixirs*, but comes in the end to prefer the lavish phantasmagoria of Hoffmann to Lewis's simpler world. A final essay by Jacqueline Chénieux-Gendron points interestingly to the strong but often indirect influence of the English Gothic novel, above all of *The Monk*, on the French surrealists.

The period since about 1980 has seen a renaissance of scholarly concern with Scott's novels, but Jane Millgate's sophisticated critical account[32] is outstand-

32. *Walter Scott: The Making of the Novelist*, by Jane Millgate. EdinU. pp. xii + 223. £17.50.

ing for its subtle tracing of the complex designs of the Waverley novels and its acute observation of the ingenuity and variety of Scott's techniques. Millgate begins with a sound account of the *Minstrelsy* and of Scott's poetry, in whose annotations and frequent use of frames and distancing devices she detects signs of an underlying unease with the naked function of the imagination. This leads into an excellent chapter on *Waverley*, interpreted with much astute noticing of stratagems of placing and mediating as a dramatization of the ways in which the power of the imagination may find a youthful outlet in romance, but can also, in maturity, lead towards a fuller sense of the world outside the self. The study of *Guy Mannering* pays illuminating attention to the book's 'analogical structure', particularly in its use of parallelism and its Shakespearean allusions, and treats the work itself as a poignant analysis of conditions of exile and isolation. *The Antiquary* Millgate praises for the power of its narrative impetus, and interprets rather conventionally as a depiction of the qualities of a genuine relationship between a man and a woman. Millgate notes the separateness of *The Black Dwarf* and *Old Mortality* from the first three novels discussed, and comments on the less definite conclusions Scott has devised for them. There follows a fresh account of the often neglected *Rob Roy*, seen as a work in which Scott makes elegant phenomenological play with problems of meaning and interpretation and which therefore leaves the reader with a 'bleak' sense that frankness alone may be insufficient, and narration alone prove a feeble guide to the truth. Millgate's treatment of *The Heart of Midlothian*, described as a 'puritan fable' in which Scott is seeking to restrain the power of the imagination which he had earlier elevated, is slighter, though entirely sensible. A concluding chapter on *The Bride of Lammermoor* and *A Legend of Montrose* brings sharply into focus one of the underlying topics of Millgate's study, the combination in Scott of the conventions and patterns appropriate both to romance and to history, and shows its triumphant success.

By its nature, this year's second book on Scott, the publication of most of the papers of the Aberdeen Scott Conference of 1982[33], could hardly equal the crispness and exhilaration of the first; nevertheless, it seems fair to be dismayed by the too frequently pedestrian and old-fashioned nature of its contents. The book is not subdivided, but consists of a number of essays on Scott and on themes from his novels and poetry, followed by a larger number of less lively comparative pieces, some of which are more ingenious than convincing. In the first papers, Richard Waswo makes a case for the continued relevance of Scott's work, Gary Kelly reports on the proposal to carry out a critical edition of the Waverley novels at the University of Alberta, and William Ruddick evokes Scott's affection for Northumberland. J. H. Alexander next neatly points out the ways in which a visit to the sites of Scott's poems may enrich one's appreciation of them, above all in the quality of their 'resonance'. Nancy M. Goslee indicates the care with which Scott shapes his sense of the culture clash, both past and present, in *Rokeby*. A clever comparison between the poetry of Scott and that of Wordsworth lies behind Kathryn Sutherland's revelation of how, in both writers, an understanding of the processes of history grows into an analogue for the development of the individual imagination. Interpreting Scott's narrative verse as a dramatization of his rationalist under-

33. *Scott and his Influence*, ed. by J. H. Alexander and David Hewitt. Association for Scottish Literary Studies (1983). pp. 517. np.

standing of the past, C. I. Rothery then explains the writer's movement towards fiction as a move towards a form more congenial to this understanding. In the following three pieces, Ruth Eller has a rather heavy description of the many artistically self-conscious and 'poetic' stratagems in Scott's novels, Alexander M. Ross gives a straightforward account of the effective picturesqueness of *Waverley*, and Barton Thurber notes Scott's employment of sublimity to localize the abstract historical notions at the centre of his work. Jane Millgate's explanation of the fractured chronology of *Guy Mannering* in terms of the novel's need to bring together past and present is elegant and convincing. The same book is thoughtfully interpreted as a treatment of 'the pursuit of knowledge' by Jana Davis. J. Derrick McLure, describing the use of language as a characterizing device in *Rob Roy*, Mark A. Weinstein, detailing the quizzical attitude towards the law in *Redgauntlet*, and Philip Hobsbaum, mounting a brief defence of the later novels, are less substantial. Patricia Harkin makes the interesting suggestion that the historical novel in Scott in fact derives from a mixture of the generic conventions that we now associate primarily with the *Bildungsroman*. Scott's debt to Scottish folk-narrative is again and incontestably considered by W. F. H. Nicolaisen. But of greater critical value is Douglas Gifford's acute account of *Waverley*, *Old Mortality*, and *The Heart of Midlothian*, which he describes as offering extended metaphoric expression, richly felt and understood, to Scott's deepest feelings about Scotland.

In succeeding essays, Jill Rubinstein gives a lucid view of Scott as a literary biographer, William Baker makes a plea for the fuller consideration of the late *Tales of a Grandfather – France. Second Series*, and P. H. Scott presents a firm picture of the Enlightenment origins of Scott's conservative political views. Peter Garside gives a characteristically dense and allusive consideration of the attitude of Scott towards the Scottish Regalia, which he saw, and was much impressed by, in 1818. In his essay on Scott's religion, Henry R. Sefton finds that the writer's Christianity is not in doubt, though his exact sectarian allegiance may be. Donald Sultana has a detailed and interesting study of the letters of Sir William Gell, a leading English topographer and expert on Pompeii, which mention Scott's residence in Naples and Rome in 1832, and also of Gell's retrospective account of Scott's stay in Italy, much reduced for publication in Lockhart's *Life of Scott*.

From this point, many of the papers concentrate on Scott's influence: some, such as those which deal with the similarities between *Waverley* and Maria Edgeworth's *Ormond*, or the works of Scott and J. G. Farrell, or the echoes of *Old Mortality* in Dickens and Katherine Anne Porter, or Scott's impact on nineteenth-century Canadian historical writing, are rather tenuous. But Robert C. Gordon has good things to say about the influence upon Scott of French drama of the seventeenth century and the boost that the Waverley novels gave to the ideals of honour and chivalric behaviour of the nineteenth century. Frederick Burwick argues that Scott found in Dryden's plays a rich quarrying-ground for narrative strategies he could later use in his own fiction. Frank Jordan considers Scott in the company of Byron and Chatterton, and finds that all three writers make use of masks to free themselves for tasks and perceptions that were not directly available to them. Of the three pieces centring on Galt, R. H. Carnie's is a staid exposition of the novelist's use of names as an element of characterization, Erik Frykman's suggests that Galt's less abstract view of society and use of the first-person narrative separate him from Scott, and H. B. de Groot's argues that although the handling of history in *Old Mortality* is complex and aware, there are also advantages to Galt's narrowness and intensity in *Ringan Gilhaize*. Robin W. MacLachlan shows that while Scott had a considerable personal influence upon Hogg, the literary relationship between the two figures was slight. Scott's determining influence upon his followers is well documented by Graham Tulloch, who shows that just as Scott tended to employ Scots in his dialogue but little in his narrative, so too did the Scottish novelists who came after him. The sharpest critical study in this part of the book is Robin Gilmour's crisp discrimination of the two types of historical novel that were encouraged by Scott's example, the historical romance and the provincial novel, and analysis of Scott's shadow upon *Wuthering Heights*, though there given a highly individual and psychological new bearing. David Hewitt evaluates *Rob Roy* as a novel in which, in the guise of a fictional autobiography, the narrator both presents his own experiences and also judges them, and shows how this may well have influenced the Dickens of *Great Expectations* and *David Copperfield*. Ina Ferris praises Scott's transformation of the rather disparaged private sphere of the novel as he found it into the more notable public sphere of his historical fiction, and the paving of the way, therefore, for the later successes of George Eliot and Thackeray. Harry E. Shaw points acutely to ways in which her reading of Scott may have encouraged George Eliot in a symbolic representation of great historical moments, and suggests how different this is from the lower-key handling of such moments by Scott himself. Peter F. Morgan documents Ruskin's interest in Scott, whom the Victorian writer evidently found a most 'benign' moral teacher. Discussing mainly their short stories, Susan Manning argues that Scott and Hawthorne used their common Puritan background as a means of transcending the constrictions of the provinciality that threatened them both. The wider dimension of Scott's work interests Marinell Ash, who presents a case for the vigour of the novelist's impact upon the sciences of archaeology and anthropology and also Elizabeth Waterston, who suggests that *The Lady of the Lake* gave impetus to the notion of a Scottish poetry based in the memorials of the past and bolstering a national consciousness. The last papers consider Scott's popularity in Denmark and Norway, some nineteenth-century adaptations of *The Bridal of Triermain* and Scott in the theatre, and give a list of operas made from his works. The only noteworthy piece is Mary Ambrose's fascinating account of the influence of Scott on Michele Amari, Italian translator of *Marmion*, who liberated to Sicilians the romance and national pride of Scott at just the moment when these qualities had most meaning for them.

In *ELN* Margaret Movshin Criscuola has a study of Scott's handling of his Porteous Mob scenes in *The Heart of Midlothian* in which she finds that Scott has adapted historical fact in the interests of presenting a celebratory view of the national character. Considering the same novel in *ScLJ*, Thomas Dale attempts too tidily to explain away Jeanie Deans's falsehoods as elements of the convincing, human imperfection of her character. Peter Garside's suggestive study of 'unions' in *The Bride of Lammermoor* (*SSL*) parallels the alliances of characters in the story with the increased political closeness of England and Scotland around 1707, and demonstrates how far the later version of the book is from any crassly nationalistic feelings. Brian Hollingworth's full and sensible account of the novel, also in *SSL*, covers most of its aspects, especially its use of chance and the supernatural, and concentrates on its qualities as a tragedy. In her rather forced study of *The Monastery*, Patricia Harkin (*SSL*) interprets the book as a generic experiment with the *Bildungsroman* and the fantastic, the two linked together by Scott for the purposes of an examination of the power of the imagination. In *WC* Daniel Whitmore has a crisp account of some of the ways in which, above all in the figure of Bois-Guilbert, *Ivanhoe* seems influenced by the more passionate dramas of Goethe and Schiller. Less interesting is Kenneth M. Sroka's elucidation in *ELWIU* (1983) of the two-part structure of *Old Mortality* which, he suggests, dramatizes Scott's twin love for fiction and history, and his responsiveness alike to their closeness and to the tension between them.

Mary Poovey has one of the most intelligent studies of the problems of women as writers that has appeared[34], and offers both superb accounts of, in particular, *Frankenstein* and the novels of Jane Austen, and also an acute reading of the role of women in the society of the Romantic period. Poovey's rich and thoughtful introduction analyses the oppressive pattern of sublimation and indirection to which the women, and especially the women writers, of her chosen period seemed condemned: their sexual desire tied to the family unit, their expectations of love firmly attached to property and their self-image limited to the narrow ideal of a lady-like propriety. In the works of Mary Wollstonecraft, Poovey then traces the persistent internalization of this notion of the 'proper lady', and suggests ways in which, in spite of her questioning attitude towards her world, Wollstonecraft is unable to dissociate herself from the male structures of control that hem her in. Poovey passes on to discuss the greater freedom achieved by Mary Wollstonecraft's daughter, Mary Shelley. Largely through a brilliant account of *Frankenstein*, Poovey demonstrates how, at this later date, it was possible for the career of writing to give Mary Shelley some fuller means of self-definition. Poovey finds in *Frankenstein* a separation between the liberating expression of the imagination and the more egotistical act of public self-assertion; she interprets the book in terms of this opposition and sees it as a subtle accommodation of Mary Shelley's difficult urge both to express and to efface herself. In her study of Mary Shelley's later work, Poovey discovers signs of guilt at this radical questioning, above all that embodied in *Frankenstein*. Poovey's last two chapters offer the sharpest and most convincing analysis of Jane Austen, from a judiciously feminist perspective, that I have ever read. Poovey considers the role of 'female energy' in Jane Austen's early works, in which she perceives the novelist finely bringing individual desire into conflict with society in order both to discipline 'anarchic passion' and to enlarge the boundaries of the socially permissible; this chapter ends with an account of *Pride and Prejudice* in which Poovey shows how the reader is bought off with aesthetic pleasure to make up for the absence of practical solutions to the vigorously individual aspirations of Elizabeth. The second Austen chapter, which includes a definitive study of *Mansfield Park*, continues Poovey's investigation of the novelist's ambiguous feelings about individualism, and points to some of the means by which she attempts to make it 'moral'. 'Austen's goal is to make propriety and romantic desire absolutely congruent', writes Poovey, but she also argues that the novelist can in the end

34. *The Proper Lady and the Woman Writer*, by Mary Poovey. UChic. pp. xxii + 287. £17.

achieve this goal only by *assertion*. In her conclusion, Poovey points out authoritatively 'the discrepancy between the promises of bourgeois ideology and the satisfactions that life in bourgeois society actually yields'; a discrepancy which is acutely and observantly handled in her own book.

John Halperin's[35] is the fullest modern biography of Jane Austen, and a work which gives an ambitious, comprehensive account both of the novelist's personality and of her books. It is the securest source of factual material concerning Jane Austen, and also offers a refreshingly revisionist, unsentimental view of a writer whose letters at least reveal a sharper and more acerbic figure than the genteel miniaturist of convention. Halperin covers the life in considerable but lucid detail, and includes much interesting material concerning the genesis and publication of the novels as well as a very well-supported interpretation of the novelist herself. His book is framed by accounts of Jane Austen's death, between which are thoroughly researched studies of her life, extensive analyses of the two trilogies into which her fiction may be divided and a comprehensive presentation of her family and the background to her career. Jane Austen is plausibly defined as a clever, rather private and intensely discriminating woman, not at all inclined to suffer fools gladly, and more enthusiastic in witty disapprobation than in warm-hearted understanding. This definition is fully borne out by the correspondence, such as it is, but Halperin also makes a case for the novels as works of a more personally involved and acidulous observer than has often been done in the past. He certainly puts paid for good to the unthinkingly susceptible 'Janeite' position that has survived earlier re-interpretations. Apart from this valuable task of demystification, Halperin has much else to offer: an extremely clear and useful detailing of the publication history of the novels, for instance, an excellent elucidation of the surprising extent of the Austen family (with a helpful table), and the best account I know of the rich, occasionally claustrophobic, but ultimately fulfilling family life of the novelist. This is a cool, lucid and above all modern study of Jane Austen, well written and very ably presenting both the appropriate facts concerning her life and works and a salutary rereading of her personality as well.

Robert K. Wallace's book[36] is stylishly and authoritatively written and beautifully produced. It shows signs of a rare, sympathetic response to both the novelist (Jane Austen) and the composer (Mozart) whose interrelationship forms its subject. In its own terms it is delightfully done, then; the only question is, should it have been done at all? Wallace subtitles his book, 'Classical Equilibrium in Fiction and Music', and he begins by lucidly apportioning the qualities of this equilibrium in each of his chosen arts, and employing larger categories of terminology, theme, and 'tendency' to assist him in this large endeavour. Parts of this selection of Wallace's work are most suggestive, and he gives a good account, for instance, of the struggles with genre which are characteristic of periods of unease or of rapid transition like Jane Austen's. His underlying theme, which he handles with elegance, points to the undeniably similar stresses to which works of art of the same time, though in different areas of expression, are subject. If Wallace had stopped here, he would have produced a nice, old-fashioned study to which few could

35. *The Life of Jane Austen*, by John Halperin. Harvester. pp. xiii + 399. £25.
36. *Jane Austen and Mozart*, by Robert K. Wallace. UGeo. pp. 295. $25.

have taken exception. But he continues amazingly further. He takes three Jane Austen novels, *Pride and Prejudice*, *Emma*, and *Persuasion*, identified as her mature masterpieces, and then compares them minutely with supposedly cognate works by Mozart: respectively, Piano Concerto No. 9, Piano Concerto No. 25, and Piano Concerto No. 27. Comparisons between Jane Austen and Mozart are hardly new, but they have a certain imaginative appositeness: there seem to be some 'classical' qualities at least which unarguably link the novelist with the composer. But what is entirely arguable is whether or not it is useful or even possible to attempt the sort of exact paralleling of tone, structure, and 'theme' with which Wallace struggles here. His whole Alexandrian enterprise, in fact, proves doomed, and all that he can do is to descend to resolutely separate accounts, unconvincingly twinned, of his chosen novels and concertos. Thus he gives sensitive, metaphorically rather apt analyses of the music and warm, underquestioning studies of the novels from which nice perception is not at all missing (in his comments on the elaborate structural symmetries of *Persuasion*, for example, or the aura of the word 'home' in the same book). Wallace is not incompetent, therefore; it is only, infuriatingly, that his topic is an impossible one.

This has been a rich year for periodical accounts of Jane Austen's novels. In *NCF* Zelda Boyd has a sophisticated study of the important and uneasy role of hypothesis in Jane Austen's work, and especially of the linguistic (in particular, the modal) reflections of this unease. Joyce Quiring Erickson's lucid but unsearching essay in *MQ* concentrates on defining the values appropriate both to public and to private life finally achieved by Jane Austen's heroines, and mainly embodied in marriage. In *Persuasions* Donald Greene points interestingly to the remarkably wide ramifications of Jane Austen's family. Park Honan (*ContempR*) gives a brief, sympathetic account of Jane Austen's short engagement to the young Harris Bigg-Wither in 1802, together with some comments on her views of the importance of marriage in general. The same author has an excellent study of Jane Austen's comedy[37], which he sees as deriving in part from the influence of that other 'realistic, unsaccharine sentimentalist', Sterne, especially in terms of technique and the handling of language. In *N&Q* David Hopkinson has a short account of the popular novelist, Mrs Hubback, eighth child of Jane Austen's brother Francis and a prolific author of works on women's issues. Claudia L. Johnson's rich essay in *MLQ* (1983) makes a good case for Dr Johnson's influence upon Jane Austen in terms mainly of ideas, and especially ideas of the operation and moral impulse of the mind, rather than of style. In *PSt* Deborah Kaplan takes three early, influential biographies of the novelist, and makes somewhat too much of the fact that the images these give of Jane Austen, though diverse, are all caricaturally of a 'non-laboring person'. Deirdre Le Faye (*N&Q*) considers the famous 'nephew who missed Jane Austen' from the Austen–Leigh *Memoir*, and puts forward a well-supported case for his being not James Edward, author of the *Memoir*, but rather Henry, third son of Jane Austen's brother, Edward Knight. In *Persuasions* (1983) Mary Poovey has a characteristically acute study of the ways in which the ambiguous problems of love and marriage raised by the subplots of Jane Austen's novels are not straightforwardly

37. In *Laurence Sterne: Riddles and Mysteries*, ed. by Valerie Grosvenor Myer. Vision. pp. 184. £12.95.

resolved. Clifford Siskin (*CentR*, 1984/5) gives a good summary of modern scholarship and its various, contradictory attempts at 'placing' the elusive Jane Austen, and himself defines her art in Romantic terms of 'developmental lyricism', a definition thoughtfully sustained by comparison with *The Prelude*.

In *PQ* Walter E. Anderson shows how Jane Austen blends the apparently contradictory elements of *Northanger Abbey* by using Catherine as a heroine who comes to realize that feelings founded in reality are superior to those insecurely based in fantasy. Kenneth L. Moler (*Persuasions*) looks briefly but usefully at the subtly satirized disingenuousness of much of General Tilney's speech. In *ELN* Elizabeth Nollen points to the numerous similarities of detail between *Sense and Sensibility* and Ann Radcliffe's *A Sicilian Romance*, and suggests that both novelists are aiming at a balance between the real and the imaginative in their works. A. Walton Litz (*Persuasions*, 1979) argues that Gilpin's *Observations* lies behind Jane Austen's affectionate and humorous attitude towards the picturesque in *Pride and Prejudice* and that the novelist was attracted to Gilpin because of her warm, pre-Romantic sense of the natural world. In *SNNTS* Joseph Wiesenfarth gives a rather formal account of the same novel in which he argues that Jane Austen dramatizes the growth of individuals to freedom but also of society from a static to a more liberal state. In *Persuasions* (1983) Wayne C. Booth has a thoughtful study of the ending of *Emma*, which he finds wholehearted and unironic, yet at the same time at least partly to be experienced 'as we experience fairy-tales or fantasies'. In *ELH* Adena Rosmarin gives a similarly sophisticated account of the novel, which she treats as a work of 'suspense, not surprise', and which she comes finally to interpret as resistant to a merely mimetic reading, and perhaps best to be seen as a complex tease to our understanding, a novel which constantly puts obstacles in the way of a simplistic approach. Nina Auerbach (*Persuasions*, 1980) writes powerfully and freshly about *Mansfield Park*'s Fanny Price, a character whose uneasy strength seems to her to come from Fanny's opposition to the patterns of romantic comedy and whose role also appears to be ambiguously both pro- and anti-Romantic. In *SNNTS* (1983) Margaret Lenta has an interesting account of *Mansfield Park* as a work in which a single, dominant, male authority (Sir Thomas's) is displaced in favour of a more equal sharing of power. Jane McDonnell (*Novel*) studies the book as an epigone of later female *Bildungsromane* and shows how Fanny, although largely by negative means, does uphold her female rights and does preserve her integrity. In *DUJ* Trevor Davison has an admirable study of the new and modern 'feeling of selfhood' in *Persuasion* and of the wider linguistic and technical usages that the presentation of this complex state makes necessary. David Groves (*Persuasions*) nicely traces the glancing but acute social satire in the novel, though conceding that in the end Jane Austen remains in favour of acquiescence in the status quo. In the same periodical Alice Hufstader briefly notes Jane Austen's apparently cool feelings about the standard family pattern and her avoidance of this pattern in *Persuasion*. Gene Koppel (*Persuasions*) gives a sensitive analysis of the way in which in this novel the reader is both permitted a commonsensical view of the self and also encouraged to see a more mysterious and indefinable area beyond. In the same periodical, Gene W. Ruoff praises a new richness in the characterization of Anne Elliot, which he traces in part to her embodiment of a fresh equivalence of value as between men and women, and K. K. Smith studies the use of Mrs Smith as a tester of prejudices in

Persuasion, and as an agent in its questioning of the possibilities of objective judgement.

Writing on Mary Shelley has been sparse, especially by contrast with the boom of recent years. In *BuR* (1983) Burton Hatlen has a thoughtful if overstretched account of *Frankenstein* as a kind of parody of *Paradise Lost*, concerned to subvert the poem's patriarchal conservatism in the interests of a new liberty and egalitarianism. Joyce Carol Oates (*CritI*) gives a fresh, wide-ranging study of the enduring emotional appeal of *Frankenstein*, which she describes as 'a remarkably acute diagnosis of the lethal nature of *denial*'. In *SFS* (1982) John Reider traces the use of the figure of the alien from *Frankenstein* to *Star Wars*, and discovers that the *process* of alienation which is so emphasized in Mary Shelley's book plays little part in later versions. Anca Vlasopolos (*SFS*, 1983) has a rather overdone explication of the subtext of *Frankenstein*, which she treats in terms of class ascendancy.

In *SSL* John Bligh argues that Hogg's *Justified Sinner* is really an attack on Antinomianism, and that the book's experimental narrative technique is organized so that the reader will hate Antinomianism but will merely pity its adherents. In the year's single contribution to Peacock studies, Anthony Harris (*N&Q*) tentatively identifies Lord Littlebrain in *Headlong Hall* with the 'improving' Lord Lyttelton of Hagley Hall in Worcestershire.

3. Prose

Romantic autobiography is attracting increasing critical attention, and there seems to be a growing tendency to think of autobiography as a peculiarly Romantic genre. The life represented is seen not as something established but as a process. The narrative may be considered as a journey of discovery. John C. Whale[38] demonstrates how an imaginative talent, typical to some extent of the isolated Romantic artist, was forced to comply with a pressing need for social sanction. He analyses what he considers a basic problem facing De Quincey as autobiographer: to find an audience and win its sympathy as well as being true to a vision of himself. He assesses the environment in which he wrote, examining the autobiographical writings in relation to De Quincey's situation as a journalist, and outlining the significant relationships which take place within that context. The writer–reader relationship in particular is subjected to close scrutiny, the *Confessions* being seen not simply as a presentation of experience but as a more enterprising and flexible structure involving a creative interaction with the reader. Gaining the reader's sympathy seems inevitably to create a split between the autobiographer and his past experiences. Whale demonstrates, too, how the recalcitrant nature of language, its resistance to an autobiographical concern for correspondence to past experience, leads to certain difficulties in the task of translating private experience into public statement.

Though there is still a whiff of the original thesis throughout this study, the author makes a commendable effort to keep his mind open to experience. He refrains fastidiously from facile generalizations and rigid preconceptions of Romanticism. His approach is flexibly and rewardingly inclusive, not least in

38. *Thomas De Quincey's Reluctant Autobiography*, by John C. Whale. CH/B&N. pp. 245. £16.95.

showing how De Quincey achieves a vision of Romantic unity by a method of apparent fragmentation. The discontinuity between process and assessment creates, rather than swamps, meaning. The autobiographical texts are shown to be structured around a gap between dramatic enactment and analytical evaluation. From the friction in the relationship of experience and analysis, writer and reader, experience and language is generated the creative vitality of De Quincey's writing.

De Quincey is also one of the writers examined in an important essay by Mary Jacobus on 'The Art of Managing Books: Romantic Prose and the Writing of the Past'[39]. She explores the hidden contradictions in what three major prose writers of the Romantic period have to say about language – De Quincey's essays on style and rhetoric, Hazlitt's 'On Familiar Style', and Lamb's 'Genteel Style in Writing'. Each of these writers develops questions which she introduces by way of *The Prelude*, questions which are bound up with the writing of Romantic autobiography. Her concern is not with prose style as such but with the part played by previous writing in constituting it; not with any simple view of literary influence but with the relation between the language of books and what she calls 'the inscribing of temporality'. Paul de Man's essay 'The Rhetoric of Temporality' (in *Interpretation: Theory and Practice*, 1969) is a shaping influence, and so too is Jacques Ehrmann's 'The Death of Literature' (*NLH*, 1971).

In his memorable image of the poet bending over the surface of past time, 'As one who hangs down-bending from the side / Of a slow moving boat' (*The Prelude* IV), Wordsworth highlights the perplexity of trying to disentangle past from present, depths from surface reflections. Mary Jacobus maintains that although Romantic autobiographers seek to re-integrate past and present selves – or, like Wordsworth, to replace self-mirroring with a natural fusion of image and reflection – the closing of the gap would swamp autobiography altogether. Her thesis is that in attempting to 'overbridge' the 'two consciousnesses' of past and present ('. . . conscious of myself / And of some other Being' – *The Prelude* II), 'writing simultaneously brings that "other Being" into alien half-existence and makes the split manageable'. Wordsworth had been perplexed by his inability to 'part / The shadow from the substance'. Jacobus argues that, in seeking to do so, writing becomes the language of temporality, a means of structuring the self in time. 'Inscribing both temporal alterity and an origin that is always lost', writing is thus seen as at once 'a form of archaeology' and 'a means of ordering the past'. The past cannot swamp the present, nor the present the past. 'What is salvaged' is also, in the terminology of the title, 'managed'.

Marilyn Butler's expedition into the field of Romantic autobiography may be seen as part of her general strategy against arterio-sclerotic notions of Romanticism. In 'Satire and the Images of Self in the Romantic Period: The Long Tradition of Hazlitt's *Liber Amoris*' (*YES*), she is a lively opponent of what looks at times like a critical conspiracy to exclude satire as too frisky and overintellectual a mode to be accepted unreservedly within the hallowed precincts. Hazlitt's work is not simply autobiography. It is 'a tale of character', a satirical novel. This is not a new idea, in fact, but it is here explored and

39. In *Romanticism and Language*, ed. by Arden Reed. CornU. Methuen. pp. 327. pb £9.95.

developed with vigour and freshness. *Liber Amoris* is considered as a critical, not simply an apologetic, portrait of the artist, a counter-example to challenge De Quincey's *Confessions*, a book which had adapted to his own purposes the exalted conception of the artist and his imagination which he found in the works of Wordsworth and Coleridge. After discussing and illustrating the theme of satire and images of the self in the poetry of Wordsworth, Shelley, and Byron, Marilyn Butler feels that there is enough evidence to suggest that we underestimate the element of scepticism present in Romantic portraiture of the poets. Some readers may feel that she is slightly more persuasive in citing novels like Godwin's *Fleetwood* and *Mandeville* as precedents for a novel which is apparently autobiographical but in spirit critical. At least she shows a healthy disposition to ask questions rather than make easy assumptions. Is the hero Hazlitt? Or is he an emanation of Hazlitt's persona as a writer, subjected to criticism and mockery? Or is he an even more detached figure, a composite of other characters in life and in books? On balance she is inclined to the view that fictionalizing the story is Hazlitt's device for objectifying it, setting up a certain distance – and therefore control – between the author and H, who is to be seen as a character and not Hazlitt himself. The very divergence of possible answers, she thinks, makes the work a classic instance of the period's sceptical and divided approach to the self.

While Hazlitt was resident in Scotland in 1822, waiting for a divorce in the hope of marrying Sarah Walker, he wrote an essay 'On the Fear of Death', the subject of a scholarly analysis by W. P. Albrecht entitled 'Hazlitt's "On the Fear of Death"': Reason Versus Imagination' (*WC*). Imprisoned in his infatuation with a girl half his age, Hazlitt was never more painfully aware than he was during this period of the unbridgeable gap between the deceptive simplifications of reason, operating in terms of general truths, and the reality encompassed by the imagination kindled by vivid particulars. Among the realities encompassed by his imagination was his frustrated passion for Sarah. Albrecht interestingly traces the developing dialectic of reason and imagination through the four parts of Hazlitt's essay, but he does not make the point that a dialectical reading of the essay has an illuminating relevance to the final paragraph of *Liber Amoris*, where Hazlitt says, 'I am afraid she will soon grow common to my imagination, as well as worthless in herself.' Where reason operates coldly and abstractly in reconciling us to death, realistically reducing the worth of what we have to lose, imagination can vividly project the claims of life in less abstract terms, so that death seems more to be feared. In such a context the analyst (in both senses) of Hazlitt might profitably consider the possible significances of 'I am afraid . . .'.

Interest in Hazlitt's aesthetics grows. Joel Haefner, in ' "The Soul Speaking in the Face": Hazlitt's Concept of Character' (*SEL*), makes a useful minor contribution to this field of scholarship. His essay is based on the belief that Hazlitt's efforts to move his readers, to make them see anew, has been 'overlooked'. (*Underestimated* would perhaps be a more appropriate word.) From the flagship Fish he turns his glass on the affective dimensions of Hazlitt's criticism. The message is that we must restore the reader to the literary act, and that for Hazlitt such a restoration should begin with his idea of character. Haefner thereupon takes soundings of Hazlitt's theoretical comments on character and imagination, on art, on writing, and finally his use of character in his dramatic criticism, particularly his reviews of Edmund Kean. It is all very shipshape.

Jon Klancher, in 'Reading the Social Text: Power, Signs, and Audience in Early Nineteenth Century Prose' (*SIR*), shows an intelligent, discriminating (not to say highly selective) interest in how nineteenth-century writers used the periodical journal to define, individuate, and expand audiences 'whose interpretations of the world seemed more and more to conflict'. His specific aim is to consider how writers used prose to transform the interpretative strategies and cultural identity of a middle-class readership increasingly forced to become aware of its own powers. He examines, judiciously and comparatively, the organs used for 'this ideological and semiotic task', particularly *Blackwood's*, the *New Monthly*, *Fraser's*, and the *Edinburgh Review*.

In '*Blackwood's*: Magazine as Romantic Form' (*WC*) J. H. Alexander takes as his starting point the *Preface* to the nineteenth volume of *Blackwood's Edinburgh Magazine* (January–June 1826), marking the end of its first phase under the joint editorship of John Wilson and Lockhart. He believes that a close reading of this *Preface* indicates that the preceding volumes should be regarded as a unique, daring, and fascinating experiment in Romantic criticism. His cool, balanced, well-informed approach helps, within the limits allowed to develop his argument, to substantiate a claim that requires, however, to be trimmed. He also usefully reminds us that *Maga* may be linked with what he rightly refers to as 'the often underestimated wealth of humour, wit, and irony (frequently wild and quasi-anarchic) which runs through all the great writers of the period . . .'.

Charles Lamb is one of those writers of the period whose qualities defy easy classification. The pathos, sensibility, and preoccupation with dreams and children have been aligned of course with stock ideas of Romanticism, while his wit, humour, and irony have been left like outcast orphans in the *Sturm und Drang*. Lamb has also suffered somewhat from the extremists. On the one hand, the worshippers have bequeathed a legacy of either panegyric pap (like Lionel Johnson's 'Gentle *Saint Charles*! I turn to thee') or exquisitely mannered exercises in involuted narcissism (with Pater it is hard sometimes to say where Walter ends and Charles begins). At the other end of the critical spectrum are the demolition experts, the hard men, like Denys Thomson, who saw him as a droll, sentimental, remote writer with a regressive mind which shrinks from full consciousness. Graham Greene saw in his work a head (calculating pathos) but not a heart, a self-dramatization that had nothing to do with truth. It is fifty years since these unsympathetic critics made their indictments, and in that time remarkably few champions have rushed effectively to Lamb's defence. There is still a case to answer.

That case is not fully answered by William Flesch in ' "Friendly and Judicious" Reading: Affect and Irony in the Works of Charles Lamb' (*SIR*). He rightly observes how Lamb usually generates affect by juxtaposing the fanciful and the literal, ironically undercutting the former with the latter. The affective power is generated, as he says, by 'distancing the tentative desires of the dream-world from a realistic estimation of the possibilities of the waking world'. This is, in many respects, a sensitive, nicely discriminating analysis, not prone to either embarrassing adulation or callous butchery. Unfortunately it ends rather limply. There is a reference to Lamb's 'destruction of literality in the form of a distortion'; there is an admission of 'a distorted picture' of the essayist's own making, 'one he has control over'; there is an acknowledgement of '*ingenuous* disingenuousness'. A little blood has been let, to good therapeutic purpose, one hopes. Alas, the sight of the surgeon's knife sticking out of Lamb's back is more than Flesch can bear. Unwilling to go further, he ruefully decides to 'defer undoing the real power and the pathos of so subtle a writer', and he is last seen retreating down the middle of the road. The balanced outlook, it seems, has its own peculiar pains and perils.

The Nineteenth Century: Victorian Period

STEPHEN REGAN, LYN PYKETT, LAUREL BRAKE, and JAMES FOWLER

This chapter is arranged as follows: 1. Verse, by Stephen Regan; 2. The Novel, by Lyn Pykett; 3. Prose, by Laurel Brake; 4. Drama, by James Fowler.

1. Verse

Victorian poetry still provides a rich field of inquiry for those critics in search of the roots of modernism. Carol T. Christ's *Victorian and Modern Poetics*[1] examines a number of areas in which two generations of poets tried to establish a more objective context for poetic discourse than they felt was available to them in the Romantic tradition. Close attention is given to shared ideas of mask and persona, theories of image and symbol, and constructs of myth and history. The development of the dramatic monologue is central to this thesis because it embodies the dilemma of poetic self-expression and suggests a compelling relationship between the psychological concerns of Browning and those of Eliot and Pound. A more sustained and extensive account of this relationship can be found in Carol Christ's article, 'Self-Concealment and Self-Expression in Eliot's and Pound's Dramatic Monologues' (*VP*). It might be argued that there are certain aspects of twentieth-century poetry on which Victorian poets made less of an impact: to explain the emergence of free verse (misnomer as it is) one would have to look to the example of Jules Laforgue and perhaps claim Arthur Hugh Clough as a near relation. But a more substantial argument against this view of literary history is that it doesn't fully explain the 'dilemma' of Romantic subjectivism, mainly because it tends to regard questions of epistemology in isolation from the broader social currents of the nineteenth century.

In contrast, Isobel Armstrong's *Language as Living Form in Nineteenth Century Poetry*[2] is deeply embedded in the ideological conflicts of the period and rigorously questions those concepts which define the nature and scope of Romantic idealism. Adopting Blake's notion of 'living form' as that which 'makes' rather than 'copies', Professor Armstrong gives scrupulous consideration to the difficulties inherent in those structures of language which seek to express the transforming powers of the individual mind. What lends conviction to this study is its insistence that questions of epistemology and language have

1. *Victorian and Modern Poetics*, by Carol T. Christ. UChic. pp. x + 178. £16.75.

2. *Language as Living Form in Nineteenth Century Poetry*, by Isobel Armstrong. Harvester (1982). pp. xiv + 220. hb £25, pb £7.95.

disturbing political and cultural implications, and that 'paradigms of relationship and action' must be considered in both a linguistic and an extra-linguistic sense. This is not an easy thesis to grasp, but its importance is established in the crucial opening chapter, 'Hopkins, Hegel, Marx and the Language of Nineteenth-Century Poetry'. While the Jesuit priest might at first sight appear to have little in common with the father of revolutionary socialism, it is clear that both were deeply concerned with the cultural and ideological implications of a Romantic philosophy and language (typified by Hegel) which failed to construct the external world as 'substantial'. Hopkins in his *Notes of 1868* (considered here as 'the beginnings of a recognisably modern account of poetry') demonstrated an essentially conservative reaction against Romantic notions of instability and flux, while Marx in his 1840 critique of Hegel feared the implications of an idealist philosophy in which the relationship between self and world dissolved into solipsism. For different ideological reasons both Hopkins and Marx were concerned to re-establish a concrete referential world in terms of human relationships and actions. The dilemma of Romantic idealism, as becomes apparent here in the study of Wordsworth, Blake, and Shelley, is that the writer is left with a poetry that can only take the mind as its content and is therefore caught in its own reflexiveness. Into this context Professor Armstrong introduces the poetry of Browning and Tennyson, offering a particularly astute reading of *Sordello* as a poem that registers both the political and the psychological significance of Sordello's isolation from the world of action. Similarly, *In Memoriam* has a compelling relevance within the terms of this discussion; as a poem of bereavement it already envisages a world without relationships and a self without an object. What makes it a poem of great intelligence for Professor Armstrong is that it recognizes acutely the problems of dissolution and fragmentation in Romantic idealist language and yet struggles within its framework to find articulation and expression.

Pauline Fletcher's argument in *Gardens and Grim Ravines: The Language of Landscape in Victorian Poetry*[3] takes as its starting point the fundamental conflict between an inherited Romantic subjectivism and an increasing urge to confront the disrupted social environment of the later nineteenth century. 'Language' here refers to the changing conceptions of landscape in a period when the landed aristocracy was being supplanted by a rising industrial middle class. While admitting that it is difficult to generalize about a typically Victorian landscape, Pauline Fletcher recognizes a steady decline in the cult of the picturesque and the corresponding emergence of two distinct poetic responses to landscape: the social and the antisocial. These dominant patterns of engagement and withdrawal are given careful discrimination in individual chapters on the poetry of Tennyson, Arnold, Browning, Rossetti, Morris, Swinburne, and Hardy. The approach is avowedly eclectic and pluralist, though its psychological insights are often ill at ease with what is drawn from the sociological and political criticism of Raymond Williams and John Barrell. The friction sometimes leads to an unnecessary and complicating diffuseness. The assertion that there are more positive aspects to Swinburne than his rebelliousness and iconoclasm gives rise to the peculiarly disjunctive remark that 'his love of wild

3. *Gardens and Grim Ravines: The Language of Landscape in Victorian Poetry*, by Pauline Fletcher. Princeton (1983). pp. xii + 277. £23.90.

and solitary settings springs not merely from his rejection of society, but from the most profound and passionate depths of his nature'. Swinburne is admired for 'throwing open the Victorian drawing room and exposing its inmates to the elemental clash of wind and waves', as if this were not in itself a positive symptom of his rebelliousness. Other weaknesses stem from simplification (the unquestioning acceptance of J. D. Rosenberg's idea that Ruskin turned 'from mountains to men, from art to society') and from generalization (as with 'the social concerns of the Victorians, and their essential human compassion'). But this book nevertheless bears out its claims to be the first systematic study of the development of nineteenth-century ideas of landscape in English poetry.

The interaction of feminist and psychoanalytic criticism has been much in evidence recently, enhancing the reputations of Christina Rossetti, Elizabeth Barrett Browning, and other nineteenth-century women poets. Kathleen Blake's *Love and the Woman Question in Victorian Literature: The Art of Self-Postponement*[4] is something of an exception in that its critical method is committed to 'historical sympathy' and shows a wariness of post-Freudian doctrine, especially ideas of eroticism in recent feminist criticism. The essential argument is that 'literature may find its material and even its creative basis in love's deferral as well as in its consummation'. The title of the study is drawn from William Michael Rossetti's remark that his sister's life was 'replete with the spirit of self-postponement'. Christina Rossetti's writings, including prose pieces such as *Maude: A Tale for Girls*, are seen in the context of feminine waiting, while Elizabeth Barrett Browning's poetry, especially *Aurora Leigh*, is upheld as a 'striking testimony to the deep embeddedness of ambivalence toward love in the woman artist's thinking about herself in the nineteenth century'. The placing of George Eliot's work as novelist and poet within the discussion of 'Self-Postponement and the Woman Artist' gives further identification to the conflict between love and authorship. More recently, a closely related approach has been adopted by Bonnie J. Lisle in 'Art and Egoism in George Eliot's Poetry' (*VP*). The question of why George Eliot's heroines never become artists finds an answer in the poems, with their revelation of a persistent tension between art as selfless duty and art as selfish indulgence.

Kathleen Hickok's *Representations of Women: Nineteenth Century British Women's Poetry*[5] is concerned to establish an appropriate context in which to view conventional images of women and discuss the literary responses which they engendered. An initial chapter on womanhood is followed by chapters on daughters, wives, mothers, fallen women, spinsters, working women, and 'New Women'. This organization of prominent images lends itself particularly well to a sociocultural analysis of women's changing status and provides a means of assessing the representation of women by nineteenth-century writers. Part of Kathleen Hickok's intention is to re-evaluate women's literary history by considering the work of thirty or more women poets who were significant writers in their day but who are now virtually forgotten. Included here are Felicia Hemans, Letitia Landon, Dora Greenwell, 'Michael Field', and Mary Elizabeth Coleridge. Her selection appears to be English rather than

4. *Love and the Woman Question in Victorian Literature: The Art of Self-Postponement*, by Kathleen Blake. Harvester (1983). pp. xvii + 254. £28.50.
5. *Representations of Women: Nineteenth Century British Women's Poetry*, by Kathleen Hickok. Greenwood. pp. viii + 277. £28.95.

British; she doesn't include, for instance, the Scots dialect poet Janet Hamilton (1795–1873), whose *Selected Works*[6] appeared recently in a slim pamphlet. Individual chapters are devoted to Elizabeth Barrett Browning and Christina Rossetti as 'the twin stars of nineteenth-century English women's poetry', though Kathleen Hickok agrees with Kathleen Blake that E.B.B. is 'the more directly feminist of the two'. What Kathleen Hickok claims for her women poets as a group is that under a dominant male culture they were able to devise the continuing means for women's self-expression and solidarity. The exemplified method is habitually clandestine and oblique, an ironic and subversive twist within an apparently conformist or conservative structure of thought and feeling. Elaine Showalter's notion of 'covert solidarity' in nineteenth-century novels is detected in the poetry of the period, with *Aurora Leigh* seen as the most overtly feminist example of a technique which aims at presenting radical ideas within a familiar context. Admirable care is taken with the book's approach to class structure and class consciousness, especially with its indication that a passive and delicate feminine ideal was of little relevance to the majority of working-class women, just as the debilitating tasks of that class had little in common with the leisured mode of a female aristocracy. There is nevertheless some hesitation in facing the proposition that a commitment to the advanced status of women does not in itself make for egalitarianism, and as a result the sometimes clashing priorities of gender and class are left unclarified. The main achievement of this study is in its task of 'reclamation' and in its sharp rebuttal of Robert Southey's notorious suggestion to Charlotte Brontë that 'literature cannot be the business of a woman's life and it ought not to be'.

Mothering the Mind: Twelve Studies of Writers and Their Silent Partners[7] is a different kind of study, consisting of biographical essays with a shared interest in feminist and psychoanalytic criticism. Ruth Perry's introduction is concerned with the fostering of creativity through personal relationships and entertains the possibility of a 'caretaking' or 'mothering' relationship which protects the space available for another's play and exploration. In this sense she works against 'the mythology of the individual genius toiling alone to realize his solitary vision' and reinstates the value of 'connectedness'. Among the literary partnerships in this volume are Jonathan Swift and Stella, Samuel Johnson and Hester Thrale, and George Eliot and George Henry Lewes. Dorothy Mermin's essay, 'The Domestic Economy of Art: Elizabeth Barrett and Robert Browning', draws on the letters of both poets to create an intimate picture of their domestic circumstances abroad and to suggest the effect of their marriage on what they wrote. The relationship is described as one of 'mutual nurturing' and shared influence. In Elizabeth Barrett's 'The Runaway Slave at Pilgrim's Point' and Robert Browning's 'The Guardian Angel: A Picture at Fano' – both poems about mothering – voice and identity appear to be exchanged. Marriage freed Elizabeth Barrett from a restrictive environment, allowing her to write on contemporary public themes, while it encouraged her partner's transition from the poetry of psychological aberration to that of ordinary human love. In the same collection John O. Jordan's essay,

6. *Selected Works*, by Janet Hamilton. Monklands Library Services Dept. pp. 16 (unpaginated). pb £0.85.

7. *Mothering the Mind: Twelve Studies of Writers and Their Silent Partners*, ed. by Ruth Perry and Martine Watson Brownley. H&M. pp. 261. hb £28, pb £14.75.

'Closer than a Brother: Swinburne and Watts-Dunton', takes issue with the familiar picture of life at No. 2 The Pines in which Swinburne is tamed and reformed at the cost of his poetic energy and talent. Jordan argues that far from being a passive and helpless recipient of his partner's good will, Swinburne drew Watts into his life and established a relationship that fostered and sustained his creative work. Two pieces of evidence lend support to this claim: a sonnet of 1882 written to accompany *Tristram of Lyonesse*, in which Watts is referred to as being 'closer than a brother', and the mythic narrative 'Thalassius', in which Cymothoe anticipates the role of Watts as a soothing and supportive maternal figure and effectively counterbalances that other 'great sweet mother', the sea.

A much more extensive form of biographical research is underway with the Dictionary of Literary Biography. Volume 32, *Victorian Poets Before 1850*[8], is now available and Volume 35, *Victorian Poets After 1850*, will be reviewed here next year. This sort of enterprise is always open to criticisms of classification and categorization, and inevitably there are anomalies of one kind or another, particularly where writers such as Thomas Hardy evade any simple classification either by genre or by chronology. In this instance 1850 is chosen as a convenient boundary marking the death of Wordsworth and the publication of *The Prelude* as well as the appointment of Tennyson as poet laureate and the publication of *In Memoriam*. *Victorian Poets Before 1850* consists of forty-one entries and includes Matthew Arnold, William Barnes, Emily Brontë, Elizabeth Barrett Browning, Robert Browning, Arthur Hugh Clough, Edward Lear, John Henry Newman, and Alfred Tennyson. Various groupings are established around the Spasmodic School of Poetry or the Tractarian Movement, but this in no way diminishes the striking individualism of relatively unknown poets like William James Linton, biographer of Thomas Paine. The format of each entry makes these volumes a pleasing and accessible source of reference. Entries are prefaced by a chronological table and list of publications and supplemented by a short secondary bibliography with information on major holdings of manuscript items. Each volume is lavishly illustrated with facsimile title and text pages, manuscript letters and drafts, drawings, paintings, and photographs. Entries are generally well balanced in critical and biographical information and adequately documented, though perhaps by design they tend to be uncontentious and restrained. The insistence on assigning relative positions of greatness to major and minor poets seems unnecessary: Browning, with Tennyson, is considered to be 'one of the two major poets of the Victorian age', while Clough is 'one of the most interesting, most significant, and most enjoyable of Victorian poets below the first rank'. Two minor criticisms remain: the pace of research overtakes some entries very quickly so that new information on Arnold and Marguerite (*YW* 62.308) goes unrecorded; secondly, it is not clear who is responsible for the Tennyson entry. The appendix to this volume is a valuable collection of essays by Victorian scholars, including Arthur Hallam's 'On Some of the Characteristics of Modern Poetry' and Robert Browning's 'Essay on Chatterton'.

One of the curious anomalies of DLB 32 is that only one of the Brontës (Emily) appears to gain recognition as a poet. It is pleasing, then, to find new

8. *Victorian Poets Before 1850*, ed. by William E. Fredeman and Ira B. Nadel. DLB 32. Gale. pp. xvi + 417. $82.

critical editions of the poems by Branwell and Charlotte Brontë[9]. What we have, in effect, are two newly annotated and enlarged volumes to replace the notoriously unreliable Shakespeare Head edition of the *Poems of Charlotte and Patrick Branwell Brontë* (1934). The black sheep who emerges here is not Branwell but the editor T. J. Wise, who along with J. A. Symington unscrupulously obtained Brontë manuscripts, inaccurately copied them, and then made their retrieval extremely difficult for future scholars. In his edition of Branwell's poems Tom Winnifrith restores important omissions, makes extensive corrections based on manuscript sources, and records known variants. The arrangement of poems is not entirely satisfactory, partly for reasons of economy: the Shakespeare Head edition of the poems is conveniently reproduced with corrections and variations confined to the notes at the end. Two further sections include poems from Branwell's 1837 *Notebook* and a number of other poems which the Shakespeare Head edition overlooked. An appendix lists several poems not included in the new edition and some which remain unpublished. A few of the poems are short on annotation; there is no suggestion, for instance, that the lyric 'Drink to me only with thine eyes, / And I will pledge in wine!' is a burlesque of Ben Jonson's 'Song, to Celia'. While Tom Winnifrith admits that there is further work to be done on the manuscripts of these poems, his efforts in establishing a competent text are to be applauded. Charlotte Brontë's poems present a different set of editorial problems from those of her brother. Since a reliable copy-text exists in the Aylott and Jones edition of 1846, the task is largely one of recording variants and adding poems which were published posthumously. As with Branwell's work, however, it becomes difficult to make a firm distinction between those poems which should remain as part of the Angrian cycle and those which might be printed independently. Those poems by Charlotte Brontë which do not appear in this new volume are listed in the appendix and will be published in the forthcoming edition of the juvenilia by Christine Alexander.

There is not a great deal of work on the poetry of Arnold and Clough to report this year, but some compensation is to be found in David J. DeLaura's outstanding and exemplary essay, 'Arnold and Goethe: The One on the Intellectual Throne', which is part of the impressive *Victorian Literature and Society* volume dedicated to Richard D. Altick[10]. DeLaura's main contention is that Goethe was central to the formation of Arnold's doctrine and method of criticism, especially up to 1865, but that he was not regarded uncritically and was not adopted as a model in Arnold's later cultural and religious writings. The real crux of the argument, though, turns on ll. 182–91 of 'The Scholar-Gipsy' which, according to DeLaura, are functionally and intentionally anonymous but point unmistakably to Goethe. An important source for the poem is Arnold's reading of Goethe's *Dichtung und Wahrheit*, especially those passages on the *Sturm und Drang* movement and the related suicidal weariness of life. What DeLaura identifies as the *Werther* pattern of suffering and despair finds a similar context of cultural malaise in Arnold's 'strange disease of modern life'. Ironically, the poem shows Goethe's way to be unattainable in

9. *The Poems of Patrick Branwell Brontë*, ed. by Tom Winnifrith. Blackwell. pp. xxxviii + 339. £25. *The Poems of Charlotte Brontë*, ed. by Tom Winnifrith. Blackwell. pp. xxxiv + 429. £19.50.

10. *Victorian Literature and Society: Essays Presented to Richard D. Altick*, ed. by James R. Kincaid and Albert J. Kuhn. OSU. pp. viii + 374. $25.

the very act of extolling his achievements and casts 'a thoroughly Arnoldian jibe at the very notion of a "modern" and specifically "Goethean" wisdom'. For this reason, DeLaura sees the poem as being 'grimly reactionary under its mellifluous Keatsian surfaces'; it embodies 'a universal bafflement in which all representative positions are undermined', and leads to a deadlock in which 'the actual is intolerable and the ideal unattainable or barely imaginable'. The Gipsy's 'one aim' remains incompatible with a life of participation in society and his 'one business' devoid of human actions and relationships.

In 'The Human Seasons: Arnold, Keats, and "The Scholar-Gipsy"' (*VP*) William A. Ulmer's interesting thesis about 'the problematic availability of Keats' loses some of its impact through an overinsistent suggestion that 'Arnold kills off the scholar-gipsy as John Keats so as to resurrect him as Matthew Arnold'. In a companion piece in *The Arnoldian*, '"Thyrsis" and the Consolation of Natural Magic', Ulmer interprets Arnold's elegy to Clough as an autobiographical reminiscence which makes revaluative use of both classical pastoralism and Romantic landscape description in its imaginative quest for creative life. Also in *The Arnoldian*, R. Peter Burnham's ' "Empedocles on Etna" and Matthew Arnold's Argument with History' views Arnold's early poem as an expression of his search for the equilibrium that would deliver him from the flux and uncertainty of history. Accordingly, Empedocles might be seen as the suffering part of Arnold and Callicles as an embodiment of his cultural ideals. Marvel Shmiefsky writes impressively about *Tristram and Iseult* in 'Arnold's Attempt to Tame a Shrew Called Passion' (*VP*) and asks why Arnold diagnosed passionate love as part of the 'strange disease of modern life'. John Tyree Fain offers a brief note on the structural relations of sight and sound in 'Dover Beach' (*Expl*). There are two good essays on Arnold and Browning in *MLR*: John Coates contributes 'Two Versions of the Problem of the Modern Intellectual: "Empedocles on Etna" and "Cleon"', while Jane A. McCusker in ' "Aristophanes' Apology" and Matthew Arnold' sees Browning's poem as a complex contemporary debate with Arnold about what constitutes the best poetry for the age.

The major event in Browning scholarship this year is the appearance of *The Browning Collections: A Reconstruction with Other Memorabilia*[11]. The history of this volume goes back to the Sotheby's sale of May 1913 which led to the dispersal of Browning books, documents, and personal effects and, in the words of John Maynard, condemned Browning students 'to wander eternally from library to library like moaning restless shades'. But this is not simply a facsimile catalogue as the frontispiece might suggest; the compilers have committed themselves to the enormous task of listing and describing all relevant additional items, supplying locations, appendixes, and a full index. Their original checklist of the Brownings' library, for instance, was expanded to include 'any article which might have influenced Robert or Elizabeth Barrett Browning; any work which they created, possessed or presented; and items which indicated the breadth of their influence on others'. The great achievement is that reference tools are now available for tracing all known primary source materials relating to the two poets. Even without autograph

---

11. *The Browning Collections: A Reconstruction with Other Memorabilia*, comp. by Philip Kelley and Betty A. Coley. Wedgestone/ABL/BI/Mansell. pp. lviii + 708. £65, $85.

letters – previously listed in *The Brownings' Correspondence: A Checklist* (1978) – there are some 7000 items recorded. Inevitably, additional items will surface (Robert Browning's manuscript alterations to *Paracelsus* have since been located), but the compilers have invited correspondence on the collections to be sent to the Armstrong Browning Library of Baylor University in Texas and have agreed to publish a periodical list of corrections and editions in *SBHC*. As the introduction to the volume points out, the material possessions of the Brownings were few when they departed from London in 1846, but after Robert Browning's death in 1889 the estate was valued at over £16,000. It is not easy to convey an impression of the rich diversity of *The Browning Collections*, but a brief glance at the twelve sections of individual lots reveals a library of 2519 items, including such gems as an autographed presentation copy of Wilde's Newdigate Prize Poem *Ravenna*; 15 surviving copies of *The Battle of Marathon* and 23 copies of *Pauline*; 642 presentation volumes, including Robert's gifts to Swinburne and Tennyson and Elizabeth's to Rossetti and Ruskin; over 2000 manuscript items from the works of the two poets, and a vast array of associated documents and volumes.

Elizabeth Barrett's early letters occupy the first two volumes of *The Brownings' Correspondence*[12]. While the letters between the two lovers are seen to represent 'one of the most important of all Victorian literary correspondences', there are four major series of letters prior to their meeting: those between Elizabeth Barrett and Hugh Stuart Boyd, R. H. Horne, Julia Martin, and Mary Russell Mitford. Although parts of the Brownings' correspondence have been published already – *The Letters of Elizabeth Barrett Browning to Mary Russell Mitford*[13] appeared last year – there are still fewer than a third of all known letters in print. The rationale behind a separate edition of five hundred letters to Mary Russell Mitford is that it represents the best of Elizabeth Barrett's correspondence, written in the crucial decades of her life (1836–54) to a woman with whom she shared a professional relationship and an enduring friendship. The editors argue that the letters exhibit a range of intellectual and emotional concerns which even the correspondence with Robert Browning does not equal and claim that there is an important advantage in seeing Elizabeth Barrett in a steady flow of consciousness, 'without the kaleidoscopic effect produced by juxtaposing letters to different correspondents'.

On the other hand, the editors of *The Brownings' Correspondence* insist that there can be no substitute for a conventionally published edition of the collected correspondence. Their aims are simple and direct: to provide a complete and accurate transcription of all known letters written by and to Robert and Elizabeth Barrett Browning and to complement them with adequate annotations. Even so, the scale of the project is such that it is likely to run to 12,000 letters in forty volumes, making funding problematical. Volume 1 has a valuable introduction with details of the poets' early lives and of the development of their general and joint correspondence. The letters are arranged

12. *The Brownings' Correspondence*, ed. by Philip Kelley and Ronald Hudson. Wedgestone. Vol. 1, pp. xlviii + 383; Vol. 2, xiv + 413. $47.50 each.
13. *The Letters of Elizabeth Barrett Browning to Mary Russell Mitford*, ed. by Meredith B. Raymond and Mary Rose Sullivan. ABL/BI/Wedgestone (1983). Vol. 1, pp. xliv + 432; Vol. 2, xii + 464; Vol. 3, xii + 496. $160 the set.

chronologically and numbered, and careful annotation is given to places, events, and quotations. Both volumes are attractively illustrated with paintings of Hope End and portraits of the Moulton-Barrett family. We discover Elizabeth Barrett at the tender age of ten, writing letters in French and composing birthday odes for relatives. There is a fascinating group of her brother Edward's letters from Charterhouse and a brief exchange with Uvedale Price which leads to more extensive correspondence in Volume 2. There are clear signs of her feminist independence in the sympathy which she declares for Queen Caroline during the investigation and trial of 1820; the same sentiments are evident in one of the five autobiographical essays which form Appendix Three of the first volume: 'At this period when the base and servile aristocracy of my beloved country overwhelm with insults our magnanimous and unfortunate Queen I cannot restrain my indignation.' She firmly believed that justice would be found in the hearts of the people if not in the hands of the government, and this democratic fervour bursts through the insularity and solitariness of her correspondence.

The letters in Volume 2 make note of rick-burning by agricultural workers in 1830 and comment on Les Trois Glorieuses in Paris in July of the same year. In June 1831 Elizabeth Barrett chastises Hugh Stuart Boyd for his lukewarm attitude to reform – 'is not the "cry of the people" a cry to be attended to?' – and when parliament is later prorogued during the difficult passage of the Reform Bill, she expresses satisfaction that the antireformers are made to feel 'almost as uncomfortable as if they were in the neighbourhood of rope & lamp post, & out of sight of the police!'. Her passion for freedom emerges from the dismal history of her family's involvement in slavery, a subject which appears to be suppressed. She tells Boyd in 1827: 'I am sorry not to be able to answer your questions respecting our West Indian connections, but I know hardly anything on the subject.' Given the extensive supporting documents supplied by Philip Kelley and Ronald Hudson, it would seem that Elizabeth Barrett knew more than she was prepared to admit. It is in such crucial areas of inquiry that these volumes of correspondence assert their immense importance and lasting value.

One of the most significant developments in recent Browning research has been the discovery of Elizabeth Barrett's early 'Fragment of an "Essay on Woman"', of which a full transcription and facsimile extract are given in SBHC with a note by Eleanor Hoag. The fragment appears to have been written around 1822 when Elizabeth Barrett was sixteen years old; it is housed in the Charles Patterson Van Pelt Library of the University of Pennsylvania in Philadelphia. In an accompanying article, 'Elizabeth Barrett's Youthful Feminism: Fragment of an "Essay on Woman"', Kay Moser offers a lucid commentary on what she sees as an early feminist poem written under the influence of Mary Wollstonecraft's A Vindication of the Rights of Woman. The fragment appears to be a rebuttal of Pope's Essay on Man and of the common notion of poetry as an exclusively male domain. Traditional female roles and responses are dismissed with the assertion that woman 'stands the equal of her Master Man'. As Kay Moser concludes, there is strong evidence here that despite the social and domestic repression of her early youth, Elizabeth Barrett wasn't afraid to assert her independence and individuality.

In 'Elizabeth Barrett's Poems (1844)', also in SBHC, J. Don Vann considers the reception of the two-volume Poems published by Moxon, basing the article on seven unrecorded notices in contemporary London newspapers. Sandra M. Gilbert's far-reaching article 'From Patria to Matria: Elizabeth Barrett Browning's Risorgimento' (*PMLA*) develops the assertion that Elizabeth Barrett's version of a re-unified Italy had more to do with her feminism and femaleness than is usually supposed. She argues cogently and impressively that just as Ruskin and Byron had seen Italy as a fallen woman, such writers as Elizabeth Barrett and Christina Rossetti 'wistfully set the natural emotiveness of this mother country against the icy artifice of the Victorian culture in which they had been brought up'. Italy becomes a female aesthetic utopia and its speech an appropriate mother tongue.

The second volume of *The Poetical Works of Robert Browning*, containing *Strafford* and *Sordello*, is now available.[14] Like its predecessor, this volume strives to establish a critical and accurate text with informative and intelligible footnotes. A lengthy introduction accompanies each work, giving careful attention to questions of composition and emendation. With *Strafford*, Ian Jack borrows from *The Diaries of William Charles Macready* to give a vivid account of Browning's meeting with the actor-manager and his subsequent initiation into theatre. Similarly, he makes good use of Browning's correspondence with Emily Hickey, editor of the 1884 *Strafford*. Rather than attempting to establish a variorum text along the lines of the current Ohio edition, Ian Jack and Margaret Smith have tried to incorporate as many significant variant readings as possible into clearly organized textual notes and annotations. In this they succeed admirably. The appendixes, too, are a valuable source of scholarly information: Appendix A gives the 'Dramatis Personae' for the first performance of *Strafford* and Browning's preface to the first edition, while Appendix B offers a meticulously detailed account of revisions in the important Berg copy of *Strafford* in the New York Public Library. It is now apparent, however, that significant editorial decisions had to be made without a complete record of the textual history of the play. Assuming that no manuscript survived, the editors directed their attention to the printed edition of 1837 and its successors, choosing the 1888 edition as their copy-text. But as Anneliese Meidl explains in *BIS*, there is an extant manuscript in the Lord Chamberlain's Office Records in the British Library which was submitted for licensing four days before the first performance of *Strafford* on 1 May 1837. It is catalogued in *The Browning Collections* under E450. The importance of this manuscript for textual criticism is that a collation with the first edition shows significant variations in over two hundred places, as well as many minor differences of a metrical and semantic kind. Anneliese Meidl offers a careful and informed commentary on the manuscript, explaining certain cuts or omissions as the result of a conflict of aims between Browning's dramatization of a difficult subject and Macready's desire for an adaptation with theatricality and clarity.

As their copy-text for *Sordello*, Jack and Smith once again choose the 1888 edition but restore the 'running commentary' which Browning devised for the 1863 *Poetical Works*. They have also incorporated in their textual and explanatory notes the intended revisions and marginal comments which appear in three important copies of the 1840 first edition: a proof copy in the Boston

---

14. *The Poetical Works of Robert Browning*, Vol. 2, ed. by Ian Jack and Margaret Smith. Clarendon. pp. 531. £48.

Public Library, containing corrections in Browning's hand and other unidentified comments; a copy in Syracuse University, N.Y., with extensive annotations by Browning, and the Ashley copy in the British Library, containing comments by its recipient Alfred Domett. Many readers must have since agreed with Domett's criticism in his diary that 'the poem is undoubtedly somewhat obscure', but the editors of the Clarendon edition go a long way towards elucidating its textual difficulties. The annotations are clear and precise, and the introduction provides a learned account of the poem's composition with a full translation of the article on Sordello in *Biographie Universelle*. Appendix C gives what is sure to be a welcome summary of each book and Appendix D lists a number of quotations, mainly in Latin and Greek, which are believed to be cryptic references used by Browning in his preparation of *Sordello*. Jack and Smith certainly fulfil their modest intention of rendering the poem 'a little more intelligible'.

An admirably clear and concise critical study is to be found in *Robert Browning: His Poetry and His Audiences*[15]. Lee Erickson claims that Browning's work is best understood not as the expression of an assured perspective but as the drama of self-development. He sees the relationship between speakers and their audiences as grounded in the poet's own search for an audience and an appropriate form. An essential aspect of Erickson's thesis is that in turning from a public to a private sense of audience, Browning abandons the explicitly political poetry of his early years. His opening chapter on *Pauline*, *Paracelsus*, *Strafford*, and *Sordello* is soundly argued and identifies a fundamental tension in Browning's liberal individualism. *Sordello*, presented here as 'a poem that is more important to the history of English poetry than has been acknowledged or recognized', is placed in the context of the 1832 Reform Bill and rising Chartist agitation. Erickson gives more than usual attention to questions of social class, emphasizing Browning's tendency to moralize and spiritualize class conflict. What *Sordello*'s predicament reveals is the tension of a bourgeois class caught between liberal sentiments and political alliance with the aristocracy. Similarly, in Chapter Two, Erickson interprets the plays as tragedies of liberal sentiment in which domestic and religious love are called upon to settle complex social and political problems. Chapter Three considers the audience which Browning found and lost in Elizabeth Barrett, but moves beyond this to ask 'Why didn't his love for Elizabeth allow him to overcome his reserve and embrace the confessional mode for himself instead of doing the police in different voices?' The reason given is that the relationship between self and others finds its ultimate model in an awareness of God or what Hegel calls 'Absolute Spirit'. Browning's speakers are seen to achieve only a limited self-consciousness which readers must 'fill out for themselves'; their incomplete relationships must be worked out dramatically and symbolically as they are within *Men and Women*. Accordingly, Erickson moves the discussion of the monologues away from ideas of solipsism towards an understanding of the ways in which the audience shapes the speaker. It is because so much of the poetry seems to turn upon the conception of audience that this study constitutes such an essential critical guide.

On a much smaller and less ambitious scale, Mary Montaut's *Robert*

15. *Robert Browning: His Poetry and His Audiences*, by Lee Erickson. CornU. pp. 287. $27.50.

Browning: Men and Women[16] offers a brief introduction to the monologues for the non-specialist reader. As part of the York Notes series, it is designed as a useful and inexpensive study-aid and follows a format which includes a biographical introduction, a summary of the text, a critical commentary, specimen questions and answers, and suggestions for further reading. Mary Montaut pitches her study at the optimum level and elucidates the poems of *Men and Women* in a thoughtful and accessible way.

For Clyde De L. Ryals in *Becoming Browning: The Poems and Plays of Robert Browning, 1833–46*[17] a belief in the principle of restlessness or 'non-teleological becoming' distinguishes the work of Browning from that of Shelley and other Romantics and marks him as a philosophical ironist in the tradition of Schlegel. The nature of this irony is evident in Browning's awareness that his speakers can never attain full consciousness or an infinite sense of self but must exist in a dialectic of order and change, love and power, the conditioned and the free. Ryals is most convincing when demonstrating the ironic mode at work in individual poems, especially in the dramatic monologues, but he occasionally drifts into an abstract mystification of 'art', with 'the artist seeking a progressive enfranchisement of his soul from limiting embodiments'.

Samuel L. Chell agrees with Ryals that Browning's poetry discloses a world of ceaseless becoming, though his principal interest is in Browning's concept of time as the creative medium in which individuals discover themselves. *The Dynamic Self: Browning's Poetry of Duration*[18] begins with the Romantic quest for identity but looks forward to Henri Bergson's notion of an intuitive understanding of the self in flux. Chell's identification of 'intuitive moments' in Browning's poetry is illuminating, though understandably there is a special sort of pleading in the claim that 'Childe Roland', for example, is 'principally about time'. Chell is on firmer ground in arguing that particular views of life in the monologues are indicated by respective attitudes towards time and that time functions as a test of selfhood. His classification of the monologues according to the subjects of religion, love, and art is useful, and there is some attempt here to define what Browning himself meant by 'art'.

Italian culture certainly had an impact on Browning's understanding of art, as Jacob Korg illustrates in *Browning and Italy*[19]. Surprisingly, this would appear to be the first extensive study of Browning's often contradictory relationship with a country that looms so large in his work. Korg presents a fascinating web of details about Italian places and people, dealing successively with the image of Italy in the English mind, Italian social conditions and political developments, Browning's acquaintances abroad, and Browning's travels and other preoccupations in Italy. In Korg's vivid terms, Italy was 'more than a bath of sensation and perception for Browning'. On the other hand, it is difficult to estimate the extent to which the country 'enlarged his conception of human nature and deepened his sense of moral life'. The least

16. *Robert Browning: Men and Women*, by Mary Montaut. YNS. Longman. pp. 104. pb £0.99.

17. *Becoming Browning: The Poems and Plays of Robert Browning, 1833–46*, by Clyde De L. Ryals. OSU (1983). pp. x + 292. $25.

18. *The Dynamic Self: Browning's Poetry of Duration*, by Samuel L. Chell. ELS 32. UVict. pp. 135. pb $6.

19. *Browning and Italy*, by Jacob Korg. OhioU (1983). pp. ix + 246. £22.95.

effective part of Korg's study is his rather strained attempt to demonstrate that Browning's perceptions of Italy shaped his career and determined the kind of poetry he wrote. While the biographical and historical elements of the study are well balanced, the critical commentary is occasionally weak. In his discussion of what must be a key poem, 'The Englishman in Italy', Korg disappointingly evades its complex shifts in consciousness by interpreting the closing reference to the Corn Laws as 'an obvious offering to spurious relevance, and probably an afterthought added on impulse'.

A more vigorous and discerning response to Browning's Italian poem is offered by Daniel Karlin in 'The Sources of "The Englishman in Italy"' (*BSNotes*). Karlin argues that the poem was composed polemically in response to a translation of *The Improvisatore* by Hans Christian Andersen and to the related exchange of letters in which Elizabeth Barrett challenged Browning's provocative remark that 'Italy is stuff for the use of the north'. Korg discusses this remark in Chapter Four of his book but doesn't relate it to the poem. Karlin's claim is that a scrutiny of the sources reveals in the poem 'a clearer and more satisfying motive than a vague nostalgic wish to verify sightseeing memories'. He demonstrates that the poem is more complex and serious than is usually considered but seems to evade the full implications of the ending which Elizabeth Barrett thought gave 'unity to the whole'. It is left to Robert Viscusi to discuss the poem comprehensively and thoroughly in a special edition of *BIS* devoted to *Italy and the Victorian Imagination*. In a compelling article, ' "The Englishman in Italy": Free Trade as a Principle of Aesthetics', Viscusi explores Browning's liberal ideology and discovers behind his desire to see Italy 'free' the vestiges of racism and mercantile colonialism. Italy is the land of appetite, to be possessed through the power of wealth. Abolishing the Corn Laws is a matter of elementary justice, but it also provides the opportunity for obtaining a delicious and seductive European produce inexpensively. *BIS* also includes an article on Browning's acquaintance with Ronsard, ' "The Glove" and the Poets' by Richard A. Katz, and 'Robert and Elizabeth Barrett Browning: An Annotated Bibliography for 1982' by Adrienne Auslander Munich.

BSNotes has a special issue on *Browning and the Sublime* (No. 1). Ian Beck makes some introductory remarks on Browning's sublime mode in 'The Body's Purpose: Browning, and so to Beddoes', while Elizabeth Bolton's 'Browning and the Sublime' looks at the grouping of the 1863 *Poetical Works* and concludes disappointingly, though perhaps inevitably, that Browning's sublime is 'of necessity undefinable'. Jeremy Black contributes 'King Victor and King Charles: The Historical Background'. In a later issue of *BSNotes* John Woolford's 'The Philosophy and Poetics of Power in Browning's Early Works' contains some stimulating remarks on Browning's liberal humanism. Woolford claims that while Browning shared Shelley's sympathy with the oppressed, his essentially Christian principles of liberty and equality led him to repudiate any belief that politics as such might be the instrument of human improvement. Browning's uneasy response to the revolutionary impulse of Romantic poetry is also the subject of David E. Latane's ' "See You?": Browning, Byron, and the Revolutionary Deluge in *Sordello*, Book 1' (*VP*).

As usual, a good deal of research has focused on Browning's dramatic monologues, though that generic description is used very cautiously these days. Ralph W. Rader opens a special issue of *VP* (No. 2) on this subject with his instructive 'Notes on Some Structural Varieties and Variations in Dramatic "I" Poems and Their Theoretical Implications'. 'Porphyria's Lover', *In Memoriam*, and 'Leda and the Swan' are presented as poems that in different significant ways do not fit Rader's own previously developed categories of dramatic monologue, dramatic lyric, mask lyric, and expressive lyric. In a timely way, Mary Ellis Gibson's 'One More Word on Browning's "One Word More"' (*SBHC*) calls attention to a dramatic lyric that shares characteristics with what Rader identifies as the expressive lyric, and insists that the placement of the speaker in such poems continues to be a matter of critical debate.

U. C. Knoepflmacher contributes a powerfully sustained piece of criticism to *VP*'s special issue with 'Projection and the Female Other: Romanticism, Browning, and the Victorian Dramatic Monologue'. Placing Browning in a problematic relationship to the Romantic search for a female epipsyche, Knoepflmacher claims that Porphyria and the Duchess are imprisoned by male rhetoric but permitted to plead for liberation by the reader. The dramatic monologue is able to function as a mode which is both ironic and idealistic; as a response to 'The Eve of St. Agnes', 'Porphyria's Lover' is both a parody of the Romantic quest for an epipsyche and an attempt to restore a voice to the Female Other. A closely related thesis is proposed by Martin Bidney in 'The Exploration of Keatsian Aesthetic Problems in Browning's "Madhouse Cells"' (*SEL*). Bidney claims that 'Porphyria's Lover' and 'Johannes Agricola in Meditation' are not merely studies of sexual pathology and religious fanaticism but highly innovative explorations of the psychology of imagination, revealing the disturbing implications of aesthetic contemplation.

Myra Armstead sees the freeing of the anima or undeveloped feminine component of the male personality as a familiar preoccupation in Browning's work. In ' "Childe Roland" and Two Other Poems by Browning' (*VN*) she discusses the unifying function of the female image in 'Women and Roses' and 'Love Among the Ruins', and establishes a link between the symbols of Browning's famous 'quest' poem and the texts of Jungian psychology. Mike Tierce in ' "Childe Roland": A Poetic Version of Browning's "Perfection in Imperfection" Doctrine' (*AN&Q*) agrees that there is an element of the rebirth archetype in the poem but prefers to see this in terms of Browning's attempt to regenerate his own poetic energies. Frederick Glaysher's 'At the Dark Tower' (*SBHC*) openly rejects the Jungian approach and asserts that 'Childe Roland' is really about 'the struggle of the soul to reach God', a struggle which he thinks is noticeably absent in postmodern poetry.

'Caliban upon Setebos' has long been a source of critical conflict, but there are several attempts this year to settle the differences. John Hunter Lammers in ' "Caliban upon Setebos": Browning's Divine Comedy' (*SBHC*) argues that the poem is a synthesis of comic satire and serious religious purpose which attempts to 'redefine' Milton's version of the Bible. In 'Browning's "Caliban upon Setebos"' (*Expl*) James Harrison accepts that there is an element of religious satire in the poem but stresses that Caliban is portrayed sympathetically. Terrell L. Tebbetts presents a similar but more expansive argument in 'The Question of Satire in "Caliban upon Setebos"' (*VP*). The claim here is that Browning is offering the intuitive revelation of Caliban the 'maker/mock-poet' as an alternative to the dominant rationality of contemporary theology, but in a gently critical rather than satirical manner. Also in *VP*, Carla Graham explains in 'Gigadib's Bible Lesson' why the concluding lines of 'Bishop

Blougram's Apology' ought to be read in the context of John 21. Another gospel story – that of Lazarus – is the subject of an article by Michael J. Berens, 'Browning's Karshish: An Unwitting Gospeller' (*SBHC*), in which certain linguistic tensions are interpreted as evidence of a struggle between faith and empiricism. Two further articles on the monologues are concerned with art and artists. Susie Campbell's 'Painting in Browning's *Men and Women*' (*BSNotes*) claims that the ambiguities and difficulties of pictorial art are used by Browning in certain poems to engage the reader's interest and participation. David Healy's '"Fra Lippo Lippi" and "Andrea Del Sarto" as Complementary Poems' (*SBHC*) encourages a related reading of the painter poems, though the notion of a resulting 'overpoem' is not entirely convincing.

A comparison of the dramatic monologues within *The Ring and the Book* leads William Walker in 'Pompilia and Pompilia' (*VP*) to raise new questions about perspective and relativism in Browning's later work. A feminist reading of *The Ring and the Book* by Nina Auerbach also generates important questions about Pompilia's role. 'Robert Browning's Last Word' (*VP*) contends that the poet recast his wife's thought and speech into his own epic but drained them of authority, so that 'a woman speaks with purity only by dying unheard'. Patricia Stephens in 'Browning's "A Woman's Last Word"' (*Expl*) believes that the woman's offer of total self-surrender is to be regarded not as an act of weakness and passivity but as one of insight and efficacy.

A new Browning poem from the later years of his career appears in *TLS* (27 April) with a commentary by Michael Mason. 'Duty' was first published in April 1886 in *The Present Day*, edited by George Jacob Holyoake. Mason tells the remarkable story of Browning's contacts with Holyoake, involving the printing of the first American edition of *Poetical Works* in the monthly timetables of a railroad company. In 'Ripeness Is All: Historical Perspective in Browning's "Apollo and the Fates"' (*VP*) Blair Ross offers a new reading of Browning's late poem and attempts to resolve its apparent inconsistencies by accepting it as a dramatization of a cosmic power struggle and not simply as a clash between optimistic and pessimistic views of the human condition. Along with Ronald E. Freeman's welcome 'Checklist of Publications for 1983', there are several interesting articles on Browning's later work to be found in *SBHC*. Arnold Cheskin insists that the ironic dimension of 'Jochanan Hakkadosh' is only fully appreciated by an understanding of the poem's key Hebrew word 'tsaddik', meaning just or righteous. The critical reception of Browning's later poetry is discussed by Ashby Bland Crowder in 'Browning's Contemporaries and *The Inn Album*'. William Baker and Stephen Glass contribute some helpful remarks on Browning's classicism in 'Robert Browning's *Iliad*: An Unnoted Copy', and Charles Flint Thomas offers 'Real Sources for the Bishop's Tomb in the Church of St. Praxed'. Suzanne Edwards claims that 'James Lee's Wife' is 'Browning's Tennysonian Poem' in that it exceeds his normally restrictive use of setting and allows for a more sustained evocation of mood and atmosphere.

F. B. Pinion has added *A Tennyson Companion*[20] to his Macmillan series of handbooks. Part One of his study is largely biographical, but Pinion tells the familiar Tennyson story in a lively and entertaining way. Part Two concentrates on Tennyson's writings, organizing individual chapters around specific

20. *A Tennyson Companion*, by F. B. Pinion. Macmillan. pp. ix + 267. £22.50.

poems, thematic concerns, and poetic forms. There are sixteen pages of illustrations, including sketches and photographs of Farringford and Aldworth, and a useful glossary as part of the appendixes. The notes are surprisingly slight and the reader looks in vain for the supporting documentation to W. J. Fox's 1831 review of *Poems, Chiefly Lyrical*, twice mentioned by Pinion. These Companion volumes tend to be descriptive rather than critical, but even so there are comments here which require or deserve amplification, as with the suggested link between the *paysage interieur* of 'Mariana' and the development of French Symbolist poetry. Pinion deals tactfully with Tennyson's assurances about the rightness of British imperialism and reserves his greatest criticism for the blind irrationality which leads the poet to conceive of life in itself as 'but a murmur of gnats in the gloom'. The scientific and philosophic context of Tennyson's work is made accessible without the commentary becoming reductive, and the question of Tennyson's belief is approached through what is seen as the Platonic bias in his religious outlook. The final emphasis of this study is far from uncritical, though Pinion in his epilogue tends to attribute Tennyson's shortcomings to temperamental deficiencies and to speculate in a curiously hypothetical way on what the poet might have achieved had he been gifted with greater originality. One suspects that he can't quite suppress his feelings of disappointment that Tennyson's cultivation of traditional styles and classical models was too conservative to revitalize English poetry.

Thomas J. Assad, on the other hand, argues that Tennyson's use of the lyric was 'consistently brilliant', and that the irrational was only one of the psychic functions in his work. *Tennysonian Lyric*[21] is a meticulously detailed reading of ten early lyrics, including those which Tennyson himself called 'songs of the deeper kind', followed by a sustained examination of the individual lyrics which constitute *In Memoriam*. Assad's study is Jungian in its approach, in that it classifies the lyrics according to the four modes of sensation, thinking, intuition, and feeling, and considers a sequence of this kind as a principal structural component in Tennyson's work. By arranging the lyrics in chronological order from 1827 to 1889, Assad is able to trace a development from poetry as statement to poetry as the objectification of a dynamic psychical event, and from poetry as a mirror of organic life to poetry as an intuitive perception of what lies beyond that life. There is an appealing frankness and clarity in Assad's procedure, even if his Jungian concepts are sometimes too rigorously adapted to Tennyson's prosody and imagery. The overall effect of this study is expansive and suggestive rather than reductive; it offers an unusual revisionary approach to well-known lyrics like 'Break, Break, Break' and 'Tears, Idle Tears', and it arranges the lyrics of *In Memoriam* so as to reveal 'the way of the poem'.

Idylls of the King continues to receive extensive critical attention and has recently appeared in a useful single edition, available in hardback and paperback[22]. J. M. Gray is reticent about his editorial procedure, simply stating that the text is based on the Eversley edition and supplemented by the Christopher Ricks edition of Tennyson's poems. There is a brief

21. *Tennysonian Lyric: 'Songs of the Deeper Kind' and 'In Memoriam'*, by Thomas J. Assad. TSE 24. TulaneU. pp. 323. $28.

22. *Alfred Lord Tennyson: 'Idylls of the King'*, ed. by J. M. Gray. Yale/Penguin (1983). pp. 371. hb £16, pb £6.95.

introduction and a selection of notes incorporating those of Tennyson and Hallam Tennyson.

Whereas F. B. Pinion sees the *Idylls* as 'agglomerative and disproportionate', William E. Buckler makes enormous claims for the work as 'a poetic document in ultimate literary relevance' and develops this judgement into a full-length study, *Man and His Myths: Tennyson's 'Idylls of the King' in Critical Context*[23]. He begins by positioning the reader into what he believes to be the appropriate critical stance; he then offers a reading of the *Idylls*, giving careful attention to Tennyson's process of composition. In Section Three he presents a critical profile of the work based on studies of Tennyson since 1953, organizing abstracts and quotations firstly around ideas of allegory, epic, and tragedy, and secondly around the separate idylls. Section Four consists of five essays in 'redirection' in which Buckler deftly waves swords with modern critics of Tennyson and offers some discriminating remarks on the critical problems associated with allegory, symbolism, and ambiguity. Like Churton Collins, he believes in submitting Tennyson to 'the ordeal of the minutest critical investigation', and there is no doubt that he knows the text thoroughly and genuinely subscribes to the notion of 'universal literary experience'. But it is precisely this belief in something called 'the Tennysonian poetic experience' which makes one question the entire approach and view its 'critical context' with less than equanimity. From the outset, Buckler insists that his study is non-polemical, non-contentious, and that his aim is to suspend the reader in 'a locus of imaginative apprehensiveness'. It is not just the inflated diction which is objectionable here; what results is an oppressive set of reader relations under the apparently innocent assumption that the poem provides 'a universal reading act' and testifies to the truth that 'the good life is both knowable and available'. While expressing an uncompromising view of Tennyson's 'nondoctrinaire aesthetic dispositions and tendencies', Buckler wishes to believe that the myth 'will somehow obliquely but organically affect our "ways with men"'. Perhaps it will, but Buckler is short of convincing explanations. Instead, his insistence that the 'meaning' of the poem is implicit in its 'manner' becomes a strategy for playing down the ideological significance of the *Idylls*. Buckler has a dismally inhibitive view of what constitutes ideology; it appears to be a pathological complaint from which great poets, like great critics, are singularly immune. It is hardly surprising, then, that the only reference to Tennyson's concern for the British Empire occurs in an extract from Valerie Pitt's *Tennyson Laureate* (1962). The result is symptomatic of what Jerome Buckley in 'Looking Backward: Victorian Poetry and Prose' (*VN*) perceives as 'the bloodless formalism of an ahistorical critical analysis'. A radically different kind of critical context is evident, for instance, in Victor Kiernan's contribution to *Culture, Ideology and Politics*[24], 'Tennyson, King Arthur and Imperialism'. Kiernan reminds us that the first group of *Idylls* belonged to the years of the Crimean War and the Indian Mutiny and that comparisons between Camelot and the Empire cannot be overlooked. In Kiernan's view, the poem constitutes an appeal for imperial solidarity, with a 'paternalist Arthur creating an aristocracy of merit'.

23. *Man and His Myths: Tennyson's 'Idylls of the King' in Critical Context*, by William E. Buckler. NYU. pp. xiii + 360. $55.

24. *Culture, Ideology and Politics*, ed. by Raphael Samuel and Gareth Stedman Jones. HWS. RKP (1982). pp. x + 368. £7.95.

While William Buckler writes in defence of King Arthur, David Staines in *Tennyson's Camelot: The 'Idylls of the King' and its Medieval Sources*[25] makes the provocative claim that 'the central character on whom Tennyson structured his Arthurian world is not Arthur, the embodiment of Camelot's ideal values and the ultimate focus of the entire work, but his Queen Guinevere'. Staines believes that Tennyson's growing independence from Malory and other medieval accounts of King Arthur is paralleled by the increasing stature of Guinevere, and that the Guinevere idyll is the most original in the series. His impressive analysis of Tennyson's evolving conception of the poem and his changing attitude to his sources is given enlarged perspective through a rich collection of appendixes, including the prose drafts of the *Idylls*. The epilogue is a brief but useful chapter on Tennyson and Victorian Arthuriana. Despite this wealth of research, the overall conclusion that Tennyson reshaped his medieval sources into an idealistic philosophy for the late nineteenth century is hardly new, even with a final, overwrought attempt to bring Guinevere into the foreground: 'Like the young Guinevere, Victorian society seemed unwilling or unable to look beyond the base desires of its struggling humanity.' Unlike Buckler, Staines gives explicit recognition to the doctrinal nature of the poem in teaching a generation 'the need of the Ideal' (including the ideal of an empire). It is a shame that Staines doesn't feel the need to question the adequacy of that ideal. In view of Tennyson's paternal attitude to Canada in his epilogue 'To the Queen', it is surprising to find a Canadian critic who reads those lines simply as 'a tribute to the poet's affection and respect for Queen Victoria and a commentary on his poem'.

In 1859 Tennyson received a gift of Thomas Wright's new edition of *Morte d'Arthur* from Julia Margaret Cameron, which was to initiate an important collaboration between poet and photographer. The creative nature of their relationship is described by Mike Weaver in the splendid catalogue, *Julia Margaret Cameron 1815–1879*[26], produced by the John Hansard Gallery to accompany its 1984 exhibition. In 1874 Cameron was working on photographic illustrations for the Cabinet edition of Tennyson's works and she later designed her own edition of *Idylls of the King and Other Poems*. The catalogue reproduces 'Lancelot and Elaine', 'The Parting of Sir Lancelot and Queen Guinevere', 'Sir Galahad and the Pale Nun', 'The Little Novice and the Queen', and 'King Arthur', but also includes a study for *Maud*, an illustration for 'The May Queen', and the memorable portraits of Tennyson himself from the 1860s. Weaver's commentary is particularly astute in its attention to Christian iconography and to the shapes and attitudes which the photographs share with the Moxon Tennyson. The catalogue includes two poems by Julia Margaret Cameron: 'On Receiving a Copy of Arthur Clough's Poems at Fresh Water Bay' (1862) and 'On a Portrait' (1876).

After leaving the Isle of Wight and during the progress of the *Idylls* Tennyson met another neighbour, whose recorded conversations with the poet form the basis of *Tennyson at Aldworth: The Diary of James Henry Mangles*[27].

25. *Tennyson's Camelot: The 'Idylls of the King' and its Medieval Sources*, by David Staines. WLU (1982). pp. xviii + 218. £15.

26. *Julia Margaret Cameron 1815–1879*, comp. by Mike Weaver. John Hansard Gallery, USouthampton. pp. 160. pb £5.50.

27. *Tennyson at Aldworth: The Diary of James Henry Mangles*, ed. by Earl A. Knies. OhioU. pp. xviii + 155. £24.95.

The diary was discovered in 1961 in the former laundry room of the Mangles estate and consists of seventeen entries from August 1870 to October 1872. Earl A. Knies has provided a light-hearted but well-documented introduction to Tennyson's life at Aldworth and has edited the diary with scrupulous care and extensive annotation. He is modest in his claims for the diary, but sees it as more than a collection of the poet's opinions and anecdotes. Its importance is that it presents a candid and unselective view of Tennyson and captures a private sense of his personality and his conversation. The entries range from Tennyson's interest in mole-tracks and worm-casts to his concern about the enclosure of the New Forest. Some of the entries are unintentionally comic, as with Tennyson's story of Carlyle's report to Queen Victoria that England was in a state of decadence: 'the Queen, when he left, said he was a very strange person'. Occasionally, Mangles creates what seem like vignettes from the early poems, with Tennyson finding 'a bit of ivy half-broken by the wind from the wall'.

Tennyson's sense of place continues to preoccupy biographers and critics alike. Philip Collins views the title of his lecture, *Tennyson, Poet of Lincolnshire*[28], rather uneasily, noting of the poetry that 'although its predominant setting is rural and natural and often recognisably Lincolnshire in its origins, it is never explicitly so'. Tennyson appears to have taken little interest in the social or economic life of Lincolnshire or other rural parts and to have been in sympathy with the conservatism of his native county. But the dialect poems written in later years release a rich store of memories of Lincolnshire ways and accents. There is no doubt that Lincolnshire continues to remember Tennyson: the County Library Department has published an attractive chronology[29] with a selection of photographs and drawings and a simplified Tennyson pedigree. This is a useful compendium of facts and figures, recording Tennyson's major works, including the plays, and giving a brief account of his family, friends, and publishers.

As usual, there is a wide-ranging and critically diverse selection of Tennyson articles to note. Matthew Rowlinson constructs an unusual thesis in 'The Skipping Muse: Repetition and Difference in Two Early Poems of Tennyson' (*VP*), claiming that 'The Skipping-Rope' and 'The Hesperides' are poems in which 'writing is figured by narcissistic or auto-erotic activity in women'. One poem is a playful response to the rhyming dictionary in which it was written, while the other suppresses its own 'precursor text', Keats's 'To Autumn'. In *TRB* Roger Simpson offers a reading of Louisa Stuart Costello's poem 'The Funeral Boat' (the first nineteenth-century version of the Elaine legend?) as an analogue of 'The Lady of Shalott'. There is no evidence to suggest that Tennyson ever read 'The Funeral Boat', but Costello's poem confirms the contemporary availability of the Italian source of the legend, the *Cento Novelle Antiche*, and provides a distinctively feminine viewpoint. In an article on *The Princess* (*ELH*) Eileen Tess Johnston examines Tennyson's claim that the poem is 'only a medley' and concludes that despite this apparent disclaimer the poem's vitality and originality arise because it *is* a medley. Philip Cohen

28. *Tennyson, Poet of Lincolnshire*, by Philip Collins. Tennyson Society Occasional Paper: Number Six. pp. 20. pb.

29. *Alfred Lord Tennyson: A Chronology*. Lincolnshire Recreational Services, County Library Dept. pp. 15. £0.50.

adds a note on Tennyson's revisions to *The Princess* in *AN&Q*, suggesting that the 'weird seizures' attributed to the Prince in the fourth edition of 1851 create more problems of characterization than they solve. 'From Monomania to Monologue: "St. Simeon Stylites" and the Rise of the Victorian Dramatic Monologue' is the formidable contribution of Herbert F. Tucker Jr to the special monologue issue of *VP*. The importance of Tucker's article is that it goes a long way to explaining why the early monologues of Tennyson and Browning have a lyrical tendency and seem to be preoccupied with extremes of psychopathic aberration. 'St. Simeon Stylites' is considered along with Browning's 'Madhouse Cells' as a prototype of its genre which analyses the 'Romantic' or 'lyrical' self.

'Did Tennyson have intellectual insights to offer us concerning man's place in nature, as many Victorians thought, or was he simply a subjective lyricist, anxious to maintain the claims of theology at the expense of the empirical findings of the physical sciences?' This is the complex question raised by Howard W. Fulweiler in 'Tennyson's *In Memoriam* and the Scientific Imagination' (*Thought*). Fulweiler concludes that there is no evidence to support familiar claims (including Eliot's notion of dissociated sensibility) that Tennyson intended to emphasize emotion over reason or to replace scientific inquiry by subjective mysticism. He defines Tennyson's philosophical position as that of objective idealism, embracing both religious faith and scientific imagination. George Ford is equally concerned to defend Tennyson's intellectual status in his curiously titled article ' "A Great Poetical Boa-Constrictor," Alfred Tennyson: An Educated Victorian Mind', one of the valuable essays presented to Richard D. Altick in *Victorian Literature and Society*[10]. Against Auden's notorious remark that Tennyson was 'the stupidest of poets', he places Thackeray's report of Tennyson's eager consumption of knowledge and goes on to view the poet's interest in astronomy, geology, biology and theology as evidence of his 'admirable supplemindedness'. Timothy Peltason's 'Tennyson's Philosophy: Some Lyric Examples' is also part of a collective enterprise[30]. Peltason takes his cue from Heidegger in claiming the conception of mood as a necessary philosophical category. Challenging the opinion of Leavis that the emotional quality in lyrics like 'Tears, Idle Tears' crowds out the thought entirely, he points to the 'strenuous thoughtfulness' behind Tennyson's evocations of mood. Another carefully discriminating article by Peltason, 'Tennyson, Nature, and Romantic Nature Poetry' (*PQ*), is concerned both with Tennyson's scrupulous fidelity to natural appearances and with the ways in which his lyrics differ from earlier Romantic poems. 'Tennyson's "Flower in the Crannied Wall" ' by J. E. Sait (*Expl*) considers Goethe's ideas of morphological transformation as a possible source and places the lyric in a familiar context in which scientific empiricism is weighed against metaphysical uncertainty.

Maud receives individual attention in 'The Sounds and Silence of Madness: Language as Theme in Tennyson's *Maud*' (*VP*). Robert E. Lougy sees the poem as 'perhaps the most haunting and frightening attempt to explore . . . the language of madness'. His claim that *Maud*, like many of Tennyson's poems, is about poetry and the poet is not likely, at first sight, to impress the hardened

30. *Philosophical Approaches to Literature: New Essays on Nineteenth and Twentieth Century Texts*, ed. by William E. Cain. AUP. pp. 257. £21.50.

Tennyson scholar, but the development of this idea with the help of Michel Foucault's *Madness and Civilization* leads to the powerful suggestion that *Maud* considers 'the necessity of its own destruction'. Lougy insists that the 'public myth of resolution' which concludes the poem is belied by all that the reader has seen and heard, and that images of madness and fear remain. There are three articles which deal with *Idylls of the King*. In 'Beast of Eden: Tennyson's "Lancelot and Elaine" ' (*CLAJ*) Dennis Grimes argues against the standard conception of Elaine as 'a sweet and lovely maid' by proposing that like Guinevere she seeks to appropriate and possess Lancelot. Accordingly, Lancelot's rejection of Elaine marks a positive step towards his disengagement from the Queen. Paul Zietlow in 'Psychological Exploration in *Idylls of the King*: The Case of Geraint and Enid' (*SEL*) argues that there is a general progression in the *Idylls* from an idealistic desire for moral certainty and spiritual transcendence to increasing psychological complexity and darkness. The transcendent meanings and realms of myth, symbol, and allegory are increasingly countered by a demand for the most concentrated powers of perception, judgement, and self-knowledge. In a brief article in *THSR* Diana Basham considers the *Idylls* as a possible source for Hardy's *Jude the Obscure* and makes some illuminating comparisons between Camelot and Christminster. 'The Ancient Sage' is the poem which Joseph Carroll chooses to demonstrate some elements of continuity between Victorian and modern poetry. In 'The Ancient and the Modern Sage: Tennyson and Stevens' (*VP*) he comments upon the relationship of the two poets and remarks that Tennyson's dialogue between a mystic seer and a hedonistic sceptic corresponds with the main tendencies in the mind of Wallace Stevens.

TRB contains some important and interesting items, including an amusing extract from Sir William Empson's contribution to the 1972 BBC programme 'Tennyson: Eighty Years On', in which the critic in his inimitable fashion identifies the 'mouldy wedding cake' effect in certain Tennyson lines. Christopher Ricks provides a transcript of Spedding's annotations of the Trinity manuscript of *In Memoriam*, which were still under interdiction when Susan Shatto and Marion Shaw edited the poem in 1982, and Christopher Sturman comments upon the annotations by Tennyson in a newly discovered copy of *Poems, Chiefly Lyrical*. Rowland L. Collins adds a note on the Tennyson manuscripts at the University of Rochester, N.Y., and emphasizes the importance of that collection in his article on the texts of 'The Vicar of Shiplake'. *N&Q* includes an item by Richard Bates, linking 'Ulysses' with a famous passage in Marlowe's *Tamburlaine*. In 'Recollections of Tennyson by Sir George Prothero in the Tennyson Research Centre' (*VN*) Richard Collins comments upon the record of the poet's interests and activities left by Sir George Walter Prothero (1848–1922). A conversation between the two men in December 1885 reveals something of Tennyson's view of the Brownings and their work: *Aurora Leigh* was thought to be a great creation but 'not a poem' and *The Ring and the Book* was considered to be esoteric, morbid, and unlikely to impress the public. Next year's review will give comprehensive coverage to *Tennyson: A Bibliography, 1827–1982*[31] by Kirk H. Beetz, which appeared too late to be included in the current year's work.

---

31. *Tennyson: A Bibliography, 1827–1982*, ed. by Kirk H. Beetz. Scarecrow Author Bibliographies 68. Scarecrow. pp. 528. $35.

In the absence of any recent full-length study of Swinburne, it is pleasing to record a new issue of C. K. Hyder's *Swinburne's Literary Career and Fame*[32], first published in 1933 and still very much a classic. Hyder launches into a vigorous discussion of Swinburne's relations with the Victorian reading and writing public by observing that, like Blake, 'he was born into the church of rebels'. We find Swinburne rallying to the support of Meredith after an adverse review of *Modern Love*, and Meredith later reporting 'low mutterings from the lion of British prudery' and pleading with Swinburne to 'play savagely with a knife among the proofs'. Hyder has an eye for memorable quotations like the *Saturday Review*'s striking estimation of what had happened to poetic diction: 'Before Mr Swinburne we almost doubt whether girls were called "white", or necks and other portions of the human frame "warm": certainly kisses did not "sting", nor were things in general apt to be so "wet".' The discussion of Swinburne's critical reception in America with the capable assistance of Edmund Clarence Stedman and the chapter on Swinburne in parody and fiction make compulsive reading. The book is a feast of curious anecdotes and opinions, of which Ruskin's assessment of Swinburne cannot go unquoted: 'Whether ever he will be clothed and in his right mind, heaven only knows. His foam at the mouth is fine, meantime.' Hyder provides a splendid evocation not only of Victorian decadence but of literary criticism in the 1930s, and he appears as something of a latter-day aesthete himself, believing as he does that 'beauty transcends all creeds and critical doctrines'.

According to William Wilson, writing in *VP*, Swinburne's aestheticism is 'based on an awareness that the meaning of objective experience . . . lies finally behind a veil, forbidden to man, absent from his consciousness'. He analyses 'Before the Mirror' as an 'iconic' poem which explores the nature of subjective imagination in Whistler's *The Little White Girl* and is best understood, like 'The Lady of Shalott', within the contemporary debate about the relationship of art and life. But Wilson is further tempted to see Swinburne as a prototypical semiotician or poststructuralist. For Thaïs E. Morgan, also writing in *VP*, such an approach tends to overlook the obvious polemical nature of much of Swinburne's work. In 'Swinburne's Dramatic Monologues: Sex and Ideology' she claims that the classical and medieval speakers of *Poems and Ballads, First Series* are essentially ironic masks with a subversive intent. Her vigorous readings of 'Anactoria', 'Laus Veneris', and 'Hymn to Proserpine' draw attention to the mingling of pornography and religious iconography through which Swinburne exposes the contradictions in Victorian moral and religious values. Ideology is also the dominant concern of an outstanding essay by Richard Sieburth: 'Poetry and Obscenity: Baudelaire and Swinburne' (*CL*). Sieburth draws impressively on the writings of Michel Foucault and Roland Barthes to explore the ideological implications of censorship, particularly 'those strategies by which the production of discourse is limited'. The prosecution against *Les Fleurs du Mal* in 1857 and the critical reception of *Poems and Ballads* in 1866 reveal that while both poets insist on the sacred nature of *l'art pour l'art*, their critics have frequent recourse to metaphors of filth and pollution. Sieburth's explanation is that both *poesie pure* and obscenity 'stand outside accepted norms and codes of representation . . . and both are therefore

32. *Swinburne's Literary Career and Fame*, by C. K. Hyder. AMSP. pp. xii + 388. $34.50.

relegated to marginal social and aesthetic spaces'. He leaves us with the compelling suggestion that those poems singled out for indictment were chosen not because they were pornographic but because they exploited paradox and ambiguity in ways which subverted contemporary ideologies of representation and signification. In a less imposing essay, '"Time and Fruitful Hour": Pre-Raphaelite Sincerity in *Atalanta in Calydon*' (*JPRS*), Ann Marie Prendergast views the boar hunt as a metaphor for the search for meaning in mortal life, generated by a foreknowledge of death. Leslie Brisman contributes 'Of Lips Divine and Calm: Swinburne and the Language of Shelleyan Love' to an impressive array of essays in *Romanticism and Language*[33], but his application of Ruskin's concepts of imagination to Swinburne's poetry tends towards obfuscation rather than enlightenment.

Carcanet Press has been expanding its Victorian poetry list recently, and to its selected editions of Swinburne (*YW* 63.318), Meredith, and Elizabeth Barrett Browning (*YW* 64.354,363) it now adds *Christina Rossetti: Selected Poems*[34]. C. H. Sisson introduces this edition by remarking that Ford Madox Ford's estimation of Christina Rossetti as 'the most valuable poet that the Victorian age produced' is 'hardly questionable in the 1980s'. He regards Christina Rossetti as 'the spearhead of the new poetry of the final third of the century', and claims that *Goblin Market* was the first Pre-Raphaelite writing to catch the public attention. His enthusiasm is dampened only in his tired closing remark that he is too old to understand the approach of those who acknowledge 'that special thing, a Woman Poet'. Sisson's selection is broad and generous, almost doubling the number of poems in the Faber edition and including in full the early prose work *Maude, A Story for Girls*. While individual volumes are discussed in the introduction, they are not indicated in the list of contents, nor is there any other chronological guide to the publication of the poems. A simple dating device would have enhanced this selection, as would an index and a few textual notes.

Goblin Market is now available in the glossy Harrap paperback series in an attractive format with quality paper and large, clear print[35]. Arthur Rackham's wonderful illustrations capture the poem's unnerving sense of the enchanting and the sinister and are complemented throughout the text by a series of devilish line drawings. Also from Harrap is a lavishly produced edition of Edward Fitzgerald's *Rubaiyat of Omar Khayyam*[36], magically illustrated by Willy Pogány.

In 'Christina Rossetti: poet' (*CritQ*) Joan Rees launches an attack on recent feminist and poststructuralist readings, which she regards as an act of disrespect to a woman who was a skilful and distinctive poet. She objects, for instance, to those readings of *Goblin Market* which detect a subversive view of Victorian social and sexual relations, though she doesn't explain why such interpretations should be considered 'pernicious and reductive'. As a contribution to 'a

33. *Romanticism and Language*, ed. by Arden Reed. CornU/Methuen. pp. 327. pb $9.95.

34. *Christina Rossetti: Selected Poems*, ed. by C. H. Sisson. Carcanet. pp. 161. pb £3.95.

35. *Goblin Market*, by Christina Rossetti, illus. by Arthur Rackham. Harrap. pp. 47. pb £2.95.

36. *Rubaiyat of Omar Khayyam*, by Edward Fitzgerald, illus. by Willy Pogány. Harrap. pp. 95 (unpaginated). pb £3.95.

juster and fuller appreciation' she offers a 'traditional' approach to 'The Prince's Progress' as a moral and spiritual poem of pilgrimage. Her reading of the poem, however, offers little that is new or inspiring.

Jeanie Watson's '"Men Sell Not Such in any Town": Christina Rossetti's Goblin Fruit of Fairy Tale' (*ChildL*) seems calculated to confound the traditional ideals of Joan Rees. Giving special attention to the themes and forms of children's literature rather than to the usual questions of Christian allegory, she argues impressively that 'it is the interplay between moral tale and fairy tale that allows *Goblin Market*'s thematic statement to be utterly subversive and yet ultimately moral'. The overt text of the moral tale with its acceptable wisdom is quietly undermined by the subtext of the fairy tale which affirms the truth of imagination and knowledge over conventional moral conduct.

Similarly, Steven Connor's excellent short article, '"Speaking Likenesses": Language and Repetition in Christina Rossetti's *Goblin Market*' (*VP*), insists on the capacity of the poem to unsettle the reader in a variety of ways. At the same time the article demonstrates the fruitful application of poststructuralist critical theory. Connor makes an invigorating reading of *Goblin Market*, progressing from the attractive form of the nursery rhyme to the ultimate indeterminacy of genre and meaning, while giving a skilful analysis throughout of the conception of language as play. In Connor's estimation the poem compacts a happy ending with the disturbing inconclusiveness of language as process.

There are two articles on Christina Rossetti in *JPRS*. Eugene Zasadinski looks at ideas of self-reliance and its limitations in 'A Better Resurrection' and 'Up-Hill' and comments on the development of heterodox ideas within apparently safe, conventional contexts. Of particular interest here is the suggestion of how an Anglican reading of the poems might differ from a Roman Catholic approach. In 'Muse from Nowhere: Christina Rossetti's Fantasy World in "Speaking Likenesses"' Wendy R. Katz considers Christina Rossetti's preoccupations as a short-story writer.

The poetry of Dante Gabriel Rossetti is viewed from an interesting variety of critical perspectives this year. In 'Rossetti's *intellegenza nova*: Perception, Poetry and Vision in "Dante at Verona"' (*VN*) Thomas L. Cooksey suggests that Rossetti re-interprets Dante in terms of his own 'autopsychology', presenting him to the nineteenth century not simply as an archetype of the poet but as a Romantic visionary who stands in opposition to the world that alienates him. Cooksey sees the formal tension between epic and dramatic ballad in 'Dante at Verona' as underlining the tension of Dante's torment between the demands of the world and the aspirations of the spirit. This essay should be read alongside a very instructive account of the development and revision of ideas about Dante since the Romantic period in *Dante and English Poetry*[37] by Steve Ellis. Also in *VN* is 'Rossetti's Use of the "Great Mother" Mythos in "A Last Confession"', in which Nathan Cervo argues that the women of Rossetti's poems exist mainly as images of his own psychic projection and contemplation. The myth of the 'Great Mother' provides 'a kind of womblike shelter to which a regressive Rossetti can safely retreat and retain ... his masculinity'. A different view of Rossetti's sexual ideology is presented

37. *Dante and English Poetry*, by Steve Ellis. CUP (1983). pp. viii + 280. £22.50.

by Daniel A. Harris in 'D. G. Rossetti's "Jenny": Sex, Money, and the Interior Monologue' (*VP*). Harris sees 'Jenny' as both the first 'interior monologue' in English poetry and a crucial indictment of prostitution and the dominant male culture under which it is perpetrated. Rossetti's achievement is to convert the dramatic monologue into a silent discourse which mimics the dehumanizing systems of sexual and economic exchange. In 'The Critique of the Mirror in Rossetti's *The House of Life*' (*JPRS*) John Granger submits the sonnet sequence to a formidable and sometimes baffling exercise in deconstruction. Rossetti's search for 'the ideal of the ideal' is located in a swirling linguistic matrix in which words are 'signs of signs, unattached, free from relation and reference', while the interplay of tautology and contradiction is seen to be reflected in Rossetti's persistent use of mirror imagery. In a later number of *JPRS* Christopher S. Nassaar argues that Rossetti's poem 'The Card-Dealer' is only rightly understood in a context of religious devotion which includes 'The Ancient Mariner' and the Book of Job. *JPRS* has two articles of general interest to devotees of the PRB. Sushma Kapoor comments on the poems of John L. Tupper, one of the lesser known members of the Brotherhood, and Jack T. Harris declares 'I Have Never Seen a Naked Lady of Shalott' in response to last year's illustrated article by Shelah Horvitz (*YW* 64.368). Also of Pre-Raphaelite appeal is Elisabeth G. Gitter's article 'The Power of Women's Hair in the Victorian Imagination' (*PMLA*).

The poetry of William Morris is given detailed attention by Florence S. Boos this year. In 'Sources for Morris' "Wanderers' Prologue" ' (*AN&Q*) she comments upon Morris's complex and ramified interest in accounts of Utopian exploration and discovery, and in 'The Evolution of "The Wanderers' Prologue" ' (*PLL*) she claims that the narrative ballad with which Morris prefaced the first volume of *The Earthly Paradise* contains important revisions which reflect his developing political outlook. The Victorian response to *The Earthly Paradise* is the subject of a third article by Florence Boos in *JWMS*. She argues that Victorian readers generally concentrated on the separate tales rather than on the overall structure of the poem and that Walter Pater was one of the few critics to empathize with its unusual amalgam of cultures and attitudes. David G. Riede's 'Morris, Modernism, and Romance' (*ELH*) is a stimulating article which claims that Morris's modernity is evident not in his choice of subject and setting but in the self-reflexive stance which many of the poems adopt towards the form and meaning of romance in the nineteenth century.

Meredith's poetry receives very little attention this year. Stephen Watt in 'Neurotic Responses to a Failed Marriage: George Meredith's *Modern Love*' (*Mosaic*) believes that most critical studies of *Modern Love* fail to explain how the narration relates to the inner conflicts of the central character. He proposes that the narrator's disturbances are caused by the opposing aims of three powerful 'neurotic trends' which battle for control of his response to the dissolving marriage. These three 'trends' or 'strategies' are drawn from Karen Horney's study of neurosis and are identified as helplessness, hostility, and isolation. In 'George Meredith and Alice Meynell: A Spurious Attribution' (*N&Q*) A. D. Burnett reveals that 'Mr Meredith's odes to France', a review which appeared in *The Bookman* in December 1898, was in fact written by Anne Macdonell.

The Complete Poetical Works of Thomas Hardy has reached its second splendid volume[38], incorporating the three collections of poems which Hardy published between 1914 and 1922. Hardy's industrious methods of revision were unabated during the war years, but even so he never established a final amended text and left his future editors the awesome task of constructing an authoritative version of his collected poems. Samuel Hynes estimates that there is at least one extant manuscript for each poem, as well as copies containing Hardy's own corrections in magazines, individual volumes, collected editions, page proofs, diaries, notebooks, and letters. As with Volume I, Hynes takes as his copy-text the first editions of Hardy's poems and meticulously records all substantive variants occurring in manuscript and printed text. The most important variant accidentals such as punctuation and capitalized personification (of which Hardy was fond) are also listed in the textual notes. Hynes is alert to the difficulties of producing the 'ideal text', of having to distinguish between tentative changes and firm decisions or of having to record words that Hardy cancelled and subsequently restored, but he carries out his decisions with admirable tact and sensitivity. What makes this a particularly pleasing edition to use, apart from the high-quality print and spacious design of the Clarendon Press, is that all variants are listed in their chronological order of transcription and/or publication, together with their sources. In 'Poems of 1912–13' a holograph version of 'The Voice' begins 'O Woman weird' and pictures her not in 'the original air-blue gown' but in the much more prosaic 'hat and gown'. In the first edition of *Satires of Circumstance* she was 'consigned to existlessness', but Hardy later preferred to see her 'dissolved to wan wistlessness'. In 'After a Journey' we find Hardy initially setting out like a journalist from the *Dorset County Chronicle* to 'interview a ghost'. In both poems Hardy's revisions appear to be directed towards greater intensity of perception and feeling. The explanatory notes to each volume throw further light on the process of composition and production. Hynes takes a sympathetic view of Hardy's uneasiness about placing 'Poems of 1912–13' in *Satires of Circumstance* and follows his revised order. In the notes to *Moments of Vision* he reminds us that three of the war poems, 'Men Who March Away', 'In Time of "the Breaking of Nations"', and 'A Call to National Service', were first published without any claim to copyright, the evident intention being to increase their circulation as a contribution to the war effort. Hynes also reprints Hardy's longest critical defence of his own poetry: his 'Apology' to *Late Lyrics and Earlier*.

An ample and reasonably priced selection from *The Complete Poetical Works* is available in the OA series, without textual notes but containing a separate introduction[39]. Hynes returns to the troubled ground of Hardy anthologists, raising questions about the transition from novelist to full-time poet and about the classification and distinctive merits of Hardy's verse, but his own views are quietly insistent. He sees Hardy as a poet who aligns himself with 'the old poets of the old, tragic world', whose characteristic form of expression is lyrical and personal, and whose poetry is essentially that of normative experience: 'plain, low-pitched, physical, and abiding'. He places Hardy in what he sees as 'the principal tradition in English verse', stretching back to

38. *The Complete Poetical Works of Thomas Hardy*, Vol. II, ed. by Samuel Hynes. Clarendon. pp. x + 543. £35.
39. *Thomas Hardy*, ed. by Samuel Hynes. OA. OUP. pp. xxxvi + 547. pb £4.95.

Wordsworth and Clare and forward to Edward Thomas and Philip Larkin. None of this may seem exceptional, but what makes this anthology better than most is that it offers a generous and carefully edited selection of the poems – over half of Hardy's total output – arranged chronologically by volume from *Wessex Poems* to *Winter Words* (including all of 'Poems of 1912–13' and 'Satires of Circumstance'), with an additional selection of uncollected poems and extracts from *The Dynasts*. A short prose section provides notes from Hardy's journals, his 1908 preface to *Select Poems of William Barnes*, the 'General Preface to the Novels and Poems', and letters to Alfred Noyes. There is a useful glossary based on the shared interests of Hardy and Barnes in the Dorset dialect and an equally useful combined index of first lines and titles.

Thomas Hardy: An Autobiography in Verse[40] contains only eighty of Hardy's nine hundred or so poems but affords a special pleasure on every page. Eliane Wilson has selected those poems which she believes to be most illustrative of Hardy's life, and they range in feeling from the childhood reminiscences of 'The Self-Unseeing' to the elegiac mood of 'Afterwards'. Her design is supported by Howard Shaw's restrained but incisive biographical introduction. But the real genius of this shared endeavour comes from the pen of Frederick Marns. Each poem is delicately transcribed in a fine calligraphy which seems to lend a curious intimacy to Hardy's words, while the Wessex scenes of poems like 'Neutral Tones' are sensitively evoked in a series of exquisite and minutely detailed pencil drawings.

There are two notable articles on Hardy's poetry among this year's offering in *THA*. In 'Hardy's Narrative Muse and the Ballad Connection' Norman Arkans discusses the appeal of poems like 'The Bride-Night Fire', 'The Rash Bride', and 'Burning the Holly'. He identifies the ballad impulse in Hardy's poetry, relating this to traditional themes and subjects, but also gives consideration to Hardy's distinctive emphasis on the narrator's experience. Peter J. Casagrande claims that the fourteenth line of 'In Tenebris, II' ('if way to the Better there be, it exacts a full look at the worst') has too often been removed from context and that the result has been a narrowly focused reading of the poem and a narrow assessment of Hardy's outlook. In a short article in *THSR* Mary Bevan suggests that Hardy's 'Poems of 1912–13' represent 'his most sustained attempt to defeat the seemingly irreversible onrush of time' and reveal the capacity of the human mind to assert the present reality of the past. In a letter to *TLS* (6 January) Desmond Hawkins comments upon 'An Expostulation' and reveals that the subject of Hardy's poem is Gertrude Bugler. He reads 'our artless masquings here' as a reference to the amateur dramatic productions of the Hardy players in Dorchester. The circumstance behind the poem appears to be the probable departure of Gertrude Bugler for the London Production of *Tess of the d'Urbervilles* in 1925.

Gerard Manley Hopkins[41] by Graham Storey succeeds the earlier monograph by Geoffrey Grigson in the popular WTW series. As an editor of the poetry and prose of Hopkins, Storey is a well-qualified guide whose pleasing balance of biographical and textual details provides an excellent introductory

---

40. *Thomas Hardy: An Autobiography in Verse*, ed. by Eliane Wilson, with intro. by Howard Shaw and calligraphy and illus. by Frederick Marns. S-W. pp. 160. £9.95.
41. *Gerard Manley Hopkins*, by Graham Storey. WTW. Profile. pp. 59. pb £1.95.

study. Large tracts of well-trodden ground have to be covered – the early clash of Keatsian sensuousness with Christian asceticism, the origins of inscape and instress, the nature of sprung rhythm, the relationship between the journal and the poems – but Storey does the job in an admirably concise and critically perceptive way. In addition he elucidates many of the difficulties of reading Hopkins and provides a brief but up-to-date bibliography.

Gerard Manley Hopkins: A Tribute[42] by W. A. M. Peters S.J. is not so much a scholarly introduction for the general reader as a personal record of a long and intimate 'friendship' between the poet and the author. Father Peters gives an unusual insight into Hopkins scholarship in the 1930s and describes his first acquaintance with the work of Hopkins (and with W. H. Gardner) at Manresa House. Hopkins spent two years there after leaving Oxford and the changing circumstances of his life as a young Jesuit are portrayed by Father Peters with a profound sympathy. The critical direction of the book is to make the poetry accessible by stressing how much of it (including the sonnets of 1885) is narrative. For this author what is most striking is not the difficulty or obliquity but 'the simple childlike straightforwardness of Hopkins'.

In *Mined with a Motion: The Poetry of Gerard Manley Hopkins*[43] Marylou Motto presents us with a much more complex thesis by asking us to consider a poet who 'enacts a decidedly post-Romantic ontology'. In other words, Hopkins rejects the Romantic concept of imagination as an instrument of transformation and moves much closer to Auden's dictum that 'poetry makes nothing happen'. This is not quite the case since this study is principally concerned with the ways in which Hopkins's poetry reaches out to affirm an externally determined world. The struggle for belief is discerned in two interacting patterns or 'motions' of language: motions of assent or 'ways in which Hopkins' voice moves to celebrate the revealed world', and motions of recurrence or 'ways in which his voice moves to discover meaning by sighting connections between events in time'. The problem here is that those rather vague and slippery concepts of motion and voice are not always as readily discernible in the poetry as Marylou Motto implies and tend to shift their meanings and relationships in unexpected ways. It is difficult to apprehend, for instance, a turning from 'motions of densely figured sensual language' to 'motions of consciously chosen meaning'. In Chapters Two and Three, however, these motions become much more pronounced as the methods by which Hopkins directs his lyrical impulse towards argument and design, and there is a close examination of those structures of speech such as imperative, exclamation, interjection, and question through which Hopkins 'bids' a response from the reader. Chapter Four includes a skilful and extensive reading of 'Spring and Fall' and Chapter Five considers *The Wreck of the Deutschland* as a poem intensely concerned with the right reading of signs and the decoding of the world. The acute sensitivity to language and form in this study opens up new ways of reading and interpreting Hopkins, though Father Peters and other members of an older Hopkins tradition of scholarship might be perplexed by its portrait of the artist as a young structuralist.

42. *Gerard Manley Hopkins: A Tribute*, by W. A. M. Peters S.J. Loyola. pp. xiv + 99. pb $5.95.

43. *Mined with a Motion: The Poetry of Gerard Manley Hopkins*, by Marylou Motto. Rutgers. pp. xvi + 203. $22.50.

Vital Candle: Victorian and Modern Bearings in Gerard Manley Hopkins[44] is a small but significant beacon in the history of Hopkins criticism, illuminating the growing vistas of interest in the poet's life and work. There are nine contributions to the volume: four essays provide specifically nineteenth-century contexts for Hopkins's poetry, two consider his reception and influence in the twentieth century, and three give particular emphasis to the nature and structure of Hopkins's language. Joaquin Kuhn begins with 'Hopkins in his Time out of Time', placing his subject within the epistemological dilemmas of the age but arguing that the Jesuit tradition provided Hopkins with a scholastic philosophy that eventually took precedence over the influence of Kant and Hegel. The result was 'a quality of perception that is made possible by faith', a way of seeing that did not turn nature into symbol. Norman H. MacKenzie has a way of investing his writing on Hopkins with the excitement of impending revelation. In 'Hopkins and St. Dorothea: Lines for whose Picture?' he looks at possible sources for the interest of Hopkins, Swinburne, Morris, Burne-Jones, and Christina Rossetti in the life of the saint. He concludes that Hopkins's 'Lines for a picture of St. Dorothea' was based on a picture that never reached canvas, by Hopkins himself. Sheelagh Russell-Brown explores a shared sense of Catholic mystery in 'Gerard Manley Hopkins and Francis Thompson: Poets of the "Incomprehensible Certainty"', and Alison G. Sulloway discusses the moral pragmatism of Victorian humanism, though her essay 'The Nature of Art, Nature, and Human Nature in Hopkins's Poetry' sometimes lacks the 'specificity' which she lauds in her subject. Lionel Adey offers a discerning study in literary psychology with 'The Inscapes of Insomnia in Hopkins, Thompson and Lowell', and Peter Hinchcliffe looks at the nature of literary influence in 'Hopkins and Some Poets of the Thirties'. Hinchcliffe concludes that Hopkins was perhaps less of an influence on W. H. Auden and Dylan Thomas than an authority who would justify their own experiments. In 'Hopkins's Revolt Against Parnassian: The Poet as Critic' John Ferns quotes from a letter in which Hopkins confesses: 'Do you know, a horrible thing has happened to me. I have begun to doubt Tennyson.' The 'poetry of inspiration' with which Hopkins opposed the Parnassian procedures of the elder poet is viewed here as a vital and lasting creative principle. Michael Ballin's 'Overthought and Underthought in Some Poems by Gerard Manley Hopkins' argues that Hopkins's modernity lies in the way in which he 'equates the mental contemplation of the object in aesthetic experience with the operations of language'. The principles of active reasoning and deeper contemplation (overthought and underthought) are applied to *The Wreck of the Deutschland* to create an impressive typological and linguistic study which makes this one of the most searching and revealing pieces of criticism in the volume. Also of outstanding merit is James Milroy's closing essay 'Hopkins the Purist(?): Some Comments on the Sources and Applications of Hopkins's Principles of Poetic Diction'. Milroy argues boldly that Hopkins was the only Victorian poet to have broken away from the 'Standard Model' of poetic diction and that his

44. *Vital Candle: Victorian and Modern Bearings in Gerard Manley Hopkins. Proceedings of the International Conference, March 1981, 'Gerard Manley Hopkins: The Poet in His Age', organized jointly by the University of Waterloo and Wilfrid Laurier University*, ed. by John S. North and Michael D. Moore. Waterloo. pp. viii + 155. $(Can.)19.95.

critical theory anticipates the basic principles of twentieth-century structural linguistics.

It is pleasing to find the same degree of critical diversity on Hopkins in this year's selection of periodical articles, though British libraries have experienced some delay in obtaining a full issue of *HQ* from Canada. Fuller coverage will be given to *HQ* next year. Jerome Bump's 'Influence and Intertextuality: Hopkins and the School of Dante' (*JEGP*) considers Hopkins's rivalry with Swinburne and the Rossettis. The main contention is that Hopkins was drawn to Pre-Raphaelitism as the school of Dante rather than of Keats, and that he tried to be more 'radical' than the other members in effectively tapping the 'root' of their movement in the Middle Ages. Charles Lock emphasizes a later aesthetic context in his provocative article 'Hopkins as a Decadent Poet' (*EIC*). Lock makes a crucial departure from critical orthodoxy by insisting that Robert Bridges was not necessarily mistaken in his judgements of Hopkins's poetry, but that his remarks are only fully comprehensible in the context of late-nineteenth-century Decadence. Furthermore, Lock readily concedes that there are dubious and subversive elements in Hopkins's work, such as its voyeurism and vicarious sensuality, but he identifies these as characteristically Decadent traits and raises them to a new level of ideological significance. As well as demonstrating the appeal of Catholicism for writers of a Decadent sensibility, the article calls for a more fundamental appreciation of the disruptive vitality of language with which Hopkins defied the conventions of English Protestantism.

Familiar assumptions about Hopkins's spiritual and aesthetic development are questioned by Rachel Salmon in 'Prayers of Praise and Prayers of Petition: Simultaneity in the Sonnet World of Gerard Manley Hopkins' (*VP*). Rather than reading the 'nature sonnets' and the 'terrible sonnets' in chronological sequence or as generic counterparts, she offers a synchronic reading which views the two types of sonnets as complementary, simultaneous forms of meditative poetry. To adopt the Ignatian model, the songs of the elective will do not replace those of the affective will but work to renew them. In ' "The Windhover" as Carmen Figuratum' (*HQ*) William A. Quinn examines Hopkins's patterning devices in the tradition of George Herbert and emblematic composition. His diagrams have an air of contrivance about them, but there is a persuasive coherence to his argument that as well as giving visual significance to typographical design Hopkins exploits the aural patterns of syntax, rhyme, and metre. Robert F. Fleissner makes a brief assertion in 'Hopkins' "The Windhover" ' (*Expl*) that the phrase 'my dear' is addressed neither to Christ nor to an imagined listener but to the bird as God's creation.

According to John S. Tanner, Hopkins's enthusiasm for heroes is one of the characteristic traits of his late Victorian sensibility. 'When God Is Hero: Worshipping God as Hero in Carlyle and Hopkins' (*HQ*) compares Hopkins's sermon on Christ as hero with Carlyle's lecture 'The Hero as Divinity', making the important distinction that while hero-worship forms a sort of secular religion for Carlyle, it represents only an aspect of Hopkins's complex religious devotion. *The Wreck of the Deutschland* is placed within this framework as the first of Hopkins's poems to nominate Christ as hero. Norman H. MacKenzie comes up with yet another piece of impressive detective work in 'Gerard Manley Hopkins – An Unrecognized Translation: "Not Kind! To Freeze Me With Forecast" ' (*CML*). The enigmatic title alludes to poem number 134 in the Oxford fourth edition of *The Poems of Gerard Manley Hopkins*, probably written at Newman's Oratory in Edgbaston, Birmingham, and previously thought to be of biographical import. It now appears that the untitled quatrain is a 'spirited rendering' from Horace, *Ode* 2.17. Jeffrey B. Loomis writes on Hopkins's 'To R. B.' (*Expl*) with the suggestion that while the poem to Bridges is elaborately designed, its final theme is that union with God demands the silencing of poetry.

Hopkins scholars will be among the first to welcome *The Selected Letters of Robert Bridges*[45] edited in two magnificent volumes by Donald E. Stanford. Over a thousand letters are included, most of them unpublished, dating from Bridges's undergraduate days at Oxford in the 1860s to his death at Boar's Hill in 1930. Among the correspondents are George Santayana, W. B. Yeats, Sir Henry Newbolt, George Bernard Shaw, and G. K. Chesterton. Both sides of the correspondence between Bridges and Lionel Muirhead are included, with some memorable glances at Muirhead's travels in the Near East. Volume 1 contains the letters from 1865 to 1908 with a chronology of Bridges's life and a knowledgeable introduction to his literary career; Volume 2 carries the letters from 1908 to 1930 with textual and biographical notes, appendixes, and indexes. Of special interest are those letters which discuss the essay on Keats and those which provide a background to *The Testament of Beauty*. There are some cutting remarks by Bridges on his contemporaries, as with Rossetti's sonnets ('sensuality affected to dulness') and the Wilde trial ('the collapse of the traducer of idealism'), but his letter to Richard Watson Dixon on the death of Hopkins is written out of profound distress. Only three of his letters to Hopkins survive, but a series of letters to the poet's mother and sister give Bridges's reasons for delaying publication of his friend's poems. Stanford judiciously defends this decision and argues that it was not an act of professional jealousy and Protestant bias but essentially a move to forestall any further adverse criticism and ridicule by readers unfamiliar with Hopkins's unusual prosody, imagery, and diction. It seems to be a burst of poignant humour rather than maliciousness which prompts the letter to Kate Hopkins in March 1918: 'That terrible "Deutschland" looks and reads much better in type – you will be glad to hear. But I wish those nuns had stayed at home.'

In May 1918 Bridges wrote to A. E. Housman asking for three or four lines of Latin as a dedication to Hopkins's mother in his forthcoming edition of *Poems of Gerard Manley Hopkins*. These lines appear incorrectly as a dedication to Bridges's mother in item 43 of *A. E. Housman: A Bibliography*[46]. Although Housman himself thought of bibliophiles as 'an idiotic class', there is still much to be gained from a work that was originally published in *Lib* in 1940 and subsequently in book form in 1952 as *A. E. Housman: An Annotated Hand-List*. It is now available in a handsome green and gold volume with illustrations of title pages, manuscript extracts, and variant labels. William White has updated, revised, and enlarged the list from 49 entries to 140, including all of Housman's major writings and all of the materials in other books and magazines, except for classical periodical articles and book reviews.

45. *The Selected Letters of Robert Bridges*, ed. by Donald E. Stanford. 2 vols. AUP. pp. 1039. £42.95 each.

46. *A. E. Housman: A Bibliography*, ed. by John Carter and John Sparrow, revised by William White. Second edn. StPB (1982). pp. xviii + 94. £16.

This compilation is not intended to be a definitive bibliography and certain omissions and errata have recently been reported by Archie Burnett in *HSJ*. Housman bibliographers should also take note of P. G. Naiditch's 'Dating Errors in the Classical Papers of A. E. Housman' (*AN&Q*). Naiditch makes several contributions to *HSJ*, including a chronological analysis of Housman's *Notebook A* and a commentary on a letter about Housman by the classical scholar J. D. Duff. John Gates writes informatively about Housman's rhymes and brings a knowledge of nineteenth-century versification to bear on the anonymous poem 'Are you going for a soldier . . .?', published in the *Pall Mall Gazette* in November 1875 and in some ways reminiscent of Housman. In 'These Bones Will Rise Again: Housman's "The Immortal Part"' L. M. Thompson surveys the numerous and often conflicting sources which determine the irony of lyric 43 in *A Shropshire Lad*. Benjamin Franklin Fisher offers 'An Excursus on Clemence Housman', which should help to encourage research on the neglected work of the poet's sister. In 'A. E. Housman's Two Strategies: *A Shropshire Lad* and *Last Poems*' (*VN*) Robert K. Martin develops the thesis that these volumes represent different forms of homosexual discourse, one being preoccupied with survival and the other with revolt. His reading of *A Shropshire Lad* as a series of dramatic monologues depicting a fallen pastoral is based very astutely on the idea that Housman's stoic elegy is an ironic reversal of the Christian re-assurance found in 'Lycidas'. The Shakespearean echoes of *A Shropshire Lad* are briefly documented by R. Renehan (*N&Q*).

There is a rich hoard of decadent pleasures from the 1890s, especially with the arrival of the monumental twenty-nine-volume facsimile series, *Degeneration and Regeneration: Texts of the Premodern Era*[47], edited by Ian Fletcher and John Stokes. The black and silver bindings of these volumes revive the preciousness of the 1890s and recover it from further degeneration on acid-free, 250-year-life paper. Aesthetes and Decadents can indulge themselves anew on the delicate nuances of Theodore Wratislaw's *Orchids* and *Caprices* or on the plangent lyricism of Count Stenbock's *Studies of Death*. Long overdue for re-issue are those works by the anti-imperialist George Ives and the socialist poet John Barlas ('Evelyn Douglas'). Arthur Symons is well represented, particularly by *Amoris Victima* and *Amoris Victimia* (*sic*), the 1897 volume of poems from Leonard Smithers bound with its 1940 privately printed counterpart. *Amoris Victima* has an intense biographical interest in that it celebrates Symons's involvement with Lydia, a ballet dancer at the Empire Theatre; it is full of those sultry moods and curious sensations that make Symons such a compelling study in psychology. As Ian Fletcher reminds us in a crisp introduction, the early Symons lyrics resemble the love lyrics of Yeats, being written in those years when the two poets were in close intellectual sympathy. Bruce Morris comments briefly upon the later years of this literary friendship in 'Symons, Yeats, and *The Knave of Hearts*' (*N&Q*).

Charles Sayle's *Musa Consolatrix*, also part of the *Degeneration* series, records his attraction to Rome in Easter 1892: 'There would I lay my head at the end of day', and includes a sonnet of 1889 to Ernest Dowson. By a

47. *Degeneration and Regeneration: Texts of the Premodern Era. A Twenty-Nine-Volume Facsimile Series Representing the Highly Varied Cultural Themes of the 1890s in Prose and Poetry*, ed. by Ian Fletcher and John Stokes. Garland. Pagination and price vary with each volume.

timely coincidence, twenty letters from Dowson to Sayle have just appeared in a beautifully produced volume[48]. Four of these precede the earliest letter available to Desmond Flower and Henry Maas when they prepared their excellent edition of *The Letters of Ernest Dowson* in 1967. As Desmond Flower explains in his biographical introduction, these new letters provide valuable information about Dowson's conversion to Catholicism. Dowson reports a visit to a Servite church with Lionel Johnson in August 1890, but the nature of his worship is sometimes overwhelmingly aesthetic: 'I kiss the feet of a man who can write such prose.' Flower's annotations are painstakingly precise and he reviews the circumstances of Dowson's life with scrupulous honesty; but while he is concerned to erase the Dowson legend created by Arthur Symons and others, the Dowson we are likely to remember from these letters is the poet with his burgundy and cigars, wearily proclaiming that 'the world is a bankrupt concern and life a play that ought to have been damned the first night'.

Dowson's peregrinations are recorded in *A Friendship of the Nineties: Letters Between John Gray and Pierre Louÿs*[49], along with important references to Oscar Wilde and Robert Sherard. The production of a reading text of these letters in translation and chronological arrangement from June 1892 to July 1899 represents an important contribution to our slowly developing picture of the period. Scholars with an interest in the 1890s should also consult Isobel Murray's cogent review article, 'John Gray: the Person and the Work in Question' (*DUJ*) and Peter J. Vernon's transcript from the manuscript of Gray's dramatic rendering of the Pierrot story in 'John Gray's Adaptation of *Le Baiser*' (*JENS*). Also in *JENS*, Lawrence Schrieber's ' "Helas!" and an Early Love of Oscar Wilde' is a splendid piece of literary investigation which surpasses even Richard Ellman's reading of the poem in its ingenuity. Schrieber argues convincingly that 'Helas!' is an artistic working-out of the moral problems Wilde confronted after an early homosexual affair with Rennell Rodd.

Investigative work of a different kind provides John S. Anson with material for 'W. E. Henley's "Hospital Outlines": Rejections and Revisions' (*VP*). The article records the discovery in California of two sets of proofs, including five rejected poems and two rejected versions of the poems Henley selected for publication in the *Cornhill Magazine* in July 1875. Anson gives a valuable commentary on the overall conception and arrangement of Henley's hospital sequence. Also in *VP*, William Sharpe's 'Learning to Read *The City*' provides an enlightening critical approach to Thomson's celebrated long poem. Sharpe argues that *The City of Dreadful Night* is exceptional among Victorian poems of urban life in that it offers a way of overcoming fear and despair. Contrary to familiar views of the poem as a nightmarish monument to Victorian pessimism, this interpretation sees the poem as a map or thread, turning strangers into readers and guiding them to a shared sense of stoicism. James Thomson is one of the principal subjects in Simone Lavabre's 'Les Plaisirs De La Melancholie Dans La Poesie Victorienne' (*CVE*). Lavabre believes that the quality of suffering in nineteenth-century poetry gives rise to curious forms of satisfac-

48. *New Letters From Ernest Dowson*, ed. by Desmond Flower. Whittington. pp. x + 29. £15.

49. *A Friendship of the Nineties: Letters Between John Gray and Pierre Louÿs*, ed. by Allan Walter Campbell, trans. by Suzanne Robinson. Tragara. pp. 37. £12.

tion, and he cites three main areas of compensatory pleasure: the refuge and repose of nature, the capacity of dream and imagination, and the narcissistic savouring of emotion. But as with *The City of Dreadful Night*, there are those extreme cases where melancholy prevails and pleasure cannot prevent damnation; the drug that eases suffering and exalts the imagination leads to the torture of dependence and suicide.

To end on a lighter note, it is worth remembering that nonsense, comedy, and parody were also the stuff of Victorian poetry. Edward Lear, for one, hoped that the Queen might honour him as 'Lord High Bosh and Nonsense Producer'. A splendid edition of *The Nonsense Verse of Edward Lear*[50] is now available with an instructive essay and dozens of marvellously suggestive illustrations by John Vernon Lord. This collection of 236 limericks is probably the most extensive to date and includes some entirely new lyrics from a group of seventy-nine recently discovered among the Duncan papers in Naughton House, Fife. A further delightful offering from the laureate of nonsense is *The Quangle Wangle's Hat*[51], a children's book with colourfully exuberant pictures by Helen Oxenbury. Another Victorian limerick spinner was Harry Graham, whose first book of *Ruthless Rhymes* was prepared in 1899 and illustrated by G.H. Two collections of calamitous verse from this rhyming 'chronicler of misfortune' can now be obtained in a single volume[52].

It seems, however, that even the most comic forms of Victorian poetry were informed by a characteristic earnestness. Such is the claim of Terry Caesar in his lively and engaging article ' "I Quite Forget What – Say a Daffodilly": Victorian Parody' (*ELH*). He explains the important status of parody in the late nineteenth century by suggesting that it represented a special way of reading which permitted intimate acquaintance and yet maintained sufficient detachment. Parody was at once an act of homage and an act of exposure: it preserved the conventions within which poetry was written and at the same time overturned them. We are left with a sobering equation: 'If the nineteenth century was the great age of nonsense because it was the great age of sense, it was similarly the great age of parody because it articulated itself as the great age of poetry.'

2. The Novel

(a) General

No doubt students of the Victorian novel suffer from many anxieties, but on the evidence of this year's crop of books and articles they do not suffer from the anxiety of indolence. As always there is a solid core of scholars who labour to uncover T. S. Eliot's cherished 'fact even of the lowest order' about a particular work. However, the greater part of this year's work is of a more speculative nature and, as we shall see, re-examines the novels and novelists of the period from a variety of approaches grounded in history, historiography,

50. *The Nonsense Verse of Edward Lear*, ed. and illus. by John Vernon Lord. Cape. pp. xviii + 234. £9.95.

51. *The Quangle Wangle's Hat*, by Edward Lear, illus. by Helen Oxenbury. Heinemann. pp. 30 (unpaginated). £6.95.

52. *Ruthless Rhymes*, by Harry Graham, illus. by G.H. and Ridgewell. Arnold. pp. 64. pb £2.95.

psychoanalysis, literary theory, philosophy, history of science, feminism, and so on. Some of these perspectives (in some hands) result in radical new insights; others merely call old things by new names, but even this sometimes produces a revitalized reading. Louis James provides some guidance through this minefield in his brief review of recent trends in 'Fiction and Context in Recent Victorian Criticism' (*DSA*). His title is perhaps misleading, for we can no longer speak of 'context' as unproblematic and unitary, as the studies discussed below will reveal.

James, quite properly, cites Kathleen Tillotson's *Novels of the Eighteen Forties* as a milestone in the process of rediscovering the Victorian novel through the recovery of its context. In their study of *The Victorian Novel Before Victoria*[53] Elliot Engel and Margaret F. King attempt both to follow Tillotson's example and to rescue the novels of the 1830s from the over-shadowing which resulted (they argue) from her 'dazzling illumination' of the fiction of the 1840s. They scrutinize the fiction of the reign of William IV in an effort to demonstrate that this was not a fallow period of postromantic exhaustion, as Richard Altick, Walter Allen, and others have argued, but that it was 'the seed bed for the great flowering of Victorian fiction' that began with the publication of *Pickwick Papers* in 1837. Unfortunately the authors do not fully succeed in their aims and the book is more potted history than the act of literary historical recovery that Tillotson performed. Although it is useful to see Marryat, Bulwer Lytton, and Disraeli restored to their historical milieu and their work related to other fictional subgenres of the period, the treatment of the central authors remains perfunctory. Marryat is compared favourably with Smollett and is presented as saving the stagnating British sea-novel by 'infusing it with realism and heroic pride'; the Bulwer of the 1830s is seen as transforming his earlier romantic aliens into Carlylean heroes who transform their transcendent vision into practical social action; and Disraeli's novels of this period are viewed as interesting failures, flawed by his inability to 'create a realistic structure onto which his Romanticism could be effectively grafted'. Despite its many shortcomings, this book is a reasonably readable introduction to the period and its discussion of the historical novel supplements Andrew Sanders's study (*YW* 59.311–12) which begins at 1840.

The perspectives of Sanders and Avrom Fleishman (*YW* 52.329) are considerably widened in Stephen Bann's *The Clothing of Clio*[54], which examines the wide variety of representational forms used in nineteenth-century Britain and France to express a new and changing sense of the past. Following the example of Hayden White's *Metahistory* (JHU, 1973), Bann uses the techniques of rhetorical analysis to discover a 'historical poetics' in this 'forcing period for historical mindedness'. This is a scholarly, complex, and densely argued book which attempts to understand an important moment in European cultural history. Students of the Victorian novel will be particularly interested in Chapter Seven, in which Bann uses Roland Barthes' notion of the end of the classic text to analyse the postromantic historical novel. He shows how Thackeray, Charles Reade, and George Eliot used the set of distinctive devices they inherited from Scott to 'create abrupt reversals and fascinating

53. *The Victorian Novel Before Victoria: British Fiction During the Reign of William IV*, by Elliot Engel and Margaret F. King. Macmillan. pp. x + 156. £22.50.

54. *The Clothing of Clio: a study of the representation of history in nineteenth-century Britain and France*, by Stephen Bann. CUP. pp. xii + 196; illus. £19.50.

contradictions' within the genre, and he examines their novels as responses to 'a crisis in the notion of historical reconstruction and period authenticity'. He offers an interesting reading of *Henry Esmond* as a systematic violation of the prescriptive realism of the genre, which problematizes 'the relation of words to things in the historical milieu'. *Romola* is also seen as an attempted mutilation of the genre's 'simple-minded and amoral assumptions about human behaviour'.

Bann's concern with the question of what happened to historical narrative and the historical novel after Scott also preoccupies Peter Smith in *Public and Private Value*[55]. While Bann cites Thackeray, George Eliot, and Reade as evidence that the historical novel remained at the centre of imaginative writing, only slipping into 'the *demi-monde* of literary production' by the 1870s, Smith thinks that there is a widely held view that the death of the historical novel occurred somewhat earlier. He now seeks to challenge the supposed orthodoxy that history disappeared from the novel with this early demise of the historical novel and argues that Scott's preoccupation with historical change continued as a subterranean force in the six European novels he examines: *Little Dorrit*, *L'Éducation Sentimentale*, *Bouvard et Pécuchet*, *The Princess Casamassima*, *The Ambassadors*, and *Nostromo*. Smith shares Bann's concern to relate literary texts to the experience of historical change and political transformation, but unlike Bann, who is concerned with a wide variety of representational forms, Smith seeks to privilege the literary and in particular the novel: 'only the novel possessed at once the amplitude and minute precision to articulate the sense of dislocated public life simultaneously with the private quandary of those who tried to evaluate it'. It is perhaps not surprising that Smith should value *Little Dorrit* (which he reads as a reworking of the dialectic between 'gentility and reality' first encountered in Pickwick and Sam Weller) for its transcendence of politics.

The complex relation of fiction to history and the problematic nature of the historical novel also arise in J. M. Rignall's examination of the historical double in *Waverley*, *Sylvia's Lovers*, and *The Trumpet Major* (*EIC*). This is a very interesting essay which views the double, not in the traditional psychological or psychoanalytic terms, but as a formal device which produces narrative fissures through which may be glimpsed the 'problematic doubleness in the very term "history"' . . . which can refer both to what men make and to what they write'.

The inextricable relationship between the history that we make and the history that we write underlies Gertrude Himmelfarb's chapters on 'The Fictional Poor' in the first volume of *The Idea of Poverty*[56]. Himmelfarb uses fiction as a historical source full of the 'hum and buzz' of cultural implication. Some of her judgements are surprising – she believes that only social historians read *Mary Barton* and *North and South* with any interest – but she writes interestingly on the critical debate about the perils of glamorizing the dangerous classes in the Newgate Novel, and on the politics of G. M. W. Reynolds's 'gothicizing' of poverty in the *Mysteries of London*. She also revisits the

---

55. *Public and Private Value: Studies in the 19th Century Novel*, by Peter Smith. CUP. pp. ix + 244. £22.50.

56. *The Idea of Poverty: England in the Early Industrial Age*, by Gertrude Himmelfarb. Faber. pp. x + 595; illus. hb £20, pb £11.50.

familiar territory of the 'Two Nations', the Dickensian poor and the industrial poor.

Himmelfarb's approach insists on seeing 'high' and 'low' culture as equally important as historical evidence. Grahame Smith will have none of this in *The Novel and Society*[57] which argues uncompromisingly that the relation of 'lesser works' to society is a matter merely of 'unconscious assimilation'. His chapters on Thackeray, Dickens, and George Eliot seek to further his view that the depiction of society is central to the aesthetic success of the novel as a genre, and that the 'classic English novel' is largely experimental and innovatory. Smith attempts to ground his account of the Victorian novelists in a discussion of nineteenth-century melodrama, but his rather second-hand and lacklustre approach fails to bear fruit.

Victorian literature and society, and sometimes the relations between the two, are also the subject of a collection of essays presented to Richard D. Altick[58]: R. A. Colby surveys attitudes to fiction in the period and examines some of the pressures that moulded the novel into a form of 'Rational Amusement'; Arthur Adrian writes on Dickens as a father, and George J. Worth attempts to rescue *Tom Brown's Schooldays* from abuse or neglect by re-examining the muscular Christianity and the concept of 'manliness' which lie at its centre. I will reserve a number of other essays on individual novels for the next section.

Another collection worth noting is Don Richard Cox's gathering of essays on *Sexuality and Victorian Literature*[59] in which Jenni Calder writes on the differing treatment of sexuality in the novels of George Meredith, Robert Louis Stevenson, and Henry James; Loralee McPike examines childbirth as a metaphor for female sexuality; Ellen Miller Casey examines the tension between Victorian propriety and a 'counterworld of feminine rebellion' in the sensation novels of Mary Elizabeth Braddon, and John Maynard provides a useful bibliographical guide to work on Victorian sexuality (an early version of the introduction to his book on Charlotte Brontë discussed below). There are also a number of other essays on individual novels or novelists which I will mention in the next section.

The textual and social contexts of the novel are also the subject of two essays in *VPR*. Barbara Quinn Schmidt provides a straightforwardly informative piece on fiction in the middle-class magazines in the 1860s and 1870s. She gives an account of the house styles and preferred formats of the main publications and describes the relationships between particular authors and the periodicals which published them. She argues that the proliferation of the magazines as a form of middle-class self-validation was ultimately a self-defeating process, since the rigidity of the magazines' oft-repeated formulas produced the aesthetic rebellion of the 1890s. In a more complex essay on 'Novels, Writers and Readers in 1850', Michael Lund employs the reader-oriented criticism of Wolfgang Iser and engages with the problems raised by this approach. He documents contemporary responses to *Pendennis* and *David Copperfield*, in

57. *The Novel and Society: Defoe to George Eliot*, by Grahame Smith. Batsford. pp. 240. pb £7.95.
58. *Victorian Literature and Society: Essays Presented to Richard D. Altick*, ed. by James R. Kincaid and Albert J. Kuhn. OSU. pp. viii + 374. $25.
59. *Sexuality and Victorian Literature*, ed. by Don Richard Cox. TSL 27. UTenn. pp. x + 268. hb £21.95, pb £10.95.

an attempt to construct an 'actual historical reader' and thus to avoid what he sees as the overtheoretical and subjective tendencies of reader-response criticism. Lund charts the interplay between Thackeray and those of his readers who were also critics in the periodical press, and examines the influence which the resulting debate on the role of the writer had on both the later numbers of *Pendennis* and on *David Copperfield*, which was appearing at the same time. Lund provides an intriguing view of literary production.

Anthea Trodd also makes extensive use of material from the periodicals in 'The Policeman and the Lady' (*VS*) in which she argues that the 'spectre of criminality lurking in every home' and anxieties about new, sophisticated methods of policing extended beyond the boundaries of the sensation novel into the fiction of, *inter alia*, Gaskell, Dickens, and Trollope. In a fascinating and well-documented examination of some significant encounters between policemen and ladies, Trodd traces subtle changes in the concept of the lady and perceives an anxiety that threatened the domestic epic of the Victorian novel. Class-anxieties and the fragility of the domestic epic also emerge from John R. Reed's 'A Friend to Mammon' (*VS*) which investigates changing attitudes to English economic life by focusing, once more, on the theme of speculation in a variety of novels before and after the financial crisis of 1873. Reed's essay is useful for its chronological breadth and for its treatment of such lesser-known works as J. H. Riddell's *The Race for Wealth* (1866) and such little-discussed works as Ouida's *The Massarenes* (1897), in which 'a venal and needy aristocracy' exploits the vanity of a 'venal and wealthy commercial class'.

In recent years there has been a significant body of work which has aimed to demonstrate the centrality of scientific ideas to Victorian literature, particularly the novel. Books by Tess Cosslett (*YW* 63.339), Gillian Beer (*YW* 64.388–9), and Roger Ebbatson (*YW* 63.322) have added a great deal to our knowledge and stimulated interest in various aspects of this subject. In *The Vital Science*[60] Peter Morton concentrates on the science of biology and seeks to show that in late-Victorian Britain 'a group of novelists and essayists ... *thoroughly searched* among the data of the life sciences and found there material peculiarly susceptible to imaginative transformation' (my emphasis). Although the literary evidence he produces is less mechanistic than this quotation would suggest, Morton does tend to see the traffic between 'biology and the literary imagination' as being rather one way. He traces changing attitudes to Darwinism and evolutionism and shows how they were fused into such 'warily optimistic speculative fictions' as W. H. Hudson's *A Crystal Age*; he investigates the link between retrogressionist biology and Wells's tales of the future, and considers Grant Allen in relation to late-Victorian eugenics; finally, he examines the differing responses of Samuel Butler and Thomas Hardy to the controversies on heredity, in an analysis of *The Way of All Flesh* and *Tess of the d'Urbervilles*. Like Gillian Beer in *Darwin's Plots*, Morton stresses that he is concerned more with the cultural than the technical history of his chosen science, but despite this his approach is less illuminating than Gillian Beer's exploration of science as cultural production.

Susan Peck MacDonald (*Mosaic*) also investigates the connections between

60. *The Vital Science: Biology and the Literary Imagination 1860–1900*, by Peter Morton. A&U. pp. x + 297. £18.

scientific and fictional paradigms. She suggests that the shift from 'typological' to 'population' thinking that accompanied the Darwinian revolution in biology was paralleled by some of the major developments of nineteenth-century realism such as complex plot-structures, a greater interest in individual variation, and the tendency to 'place more of the burden of interpretation and evaluation on the reader'. The novels of Dickens, Wilkie Collins, George Eliot, and Trollope provide her with illustrations for her refining of a fairly familiar argument.

In *Eros and Psyche*[61] Karen Chase is also interested in the way the Victorian novelists quarried scientific ideas for literary conceits and the way in which new psychological theories 'engendered figures for the psyche'. Interestingly, Chase sees her chosen novelists as prescientific, as identifying the experience 'that any science must explain'. Chase's central concern is to identify and investigate the 'expressive structure' of novels by Charlotte Brontë, Dickens, and George Eliot in an attempt to discover how Victorian fiction represents personality, how it imagines the mind, and how it expresses emotion. This lively if somewhat verbose study begins with chapters on Brontë's Angrian Tales and *Pickwick Papers* as examples of nascent Victorian novels, still bearing the birth-marks of romance but beginning to find expressive alternatives to the undifferentiated energies of Brontë's Byronic heroes, or Dickens's Mr Jingle. The author then proceeds, through close study of *Jane Eyre, Bleak House*, and *Middlemarch* to trace the path of the novel's development through 'the activity of *constructing* personality – drawing new connections, precipitating new emotions' and contemplating limitations on desire. The book is saved from the developmental fallacy by its author's insistence on diversity, failure, and fragmentation in the works studied. The story of the novel, as Chase tells it, is a story of uneasy and shifting negotiation between romance and realism, and she offers some interesting redefinitions of this latter term.

Finally, in a book which surveys the whole century, Merryn Williams[62] studies the prevailing images of women in fiction and analyses novelists' attitudes to women's changing role. Williams's coverage is fairly comprehensive; she includes general chapters on women in the novel and society, ideology and the novel, and the male image of women. She devotes a chapter to each of the major female novelists and considers a number of best sellers, both feminists and antifeminists. However, this is a disappointing book: too general to be of much use to those who already have an informed interest in the subject, too summary and too bland to stimulate the interest of the uninitiated.

(b) Individual Novelists

The novelists of the 1830s, in particular Bulwer Lytton, Disraeli, and Marryat, are re-assessed in *The Victorian Novel Before Victoria*, which I have already mentioned (p. 450). Elsewhere two of Bulwer's later novels receive a closer historical and generic scrutiny: John Coates (*DUJ*) finds the late-Gothic quality of *Zanoni* (1842) less interesting than its 'social and political bias', which he relates to its author's conversion from Benthamite reform to the conservative mystical tendency of the 1840s. Darko Suvin's apparently inex-

61. *Eros and Psyche: The Representation of Personality in Charlotte Brontë, Dickens and George Eliot*, by Karen Chase. Methuen. pp. 213. hb £12.95, pb £5.95.

62. *Women in The English Novel, 1800–1900*, by Merryn Williams. Macmillan. pp. xiv + 201. £20.

haustible interest in late-nineteenth-century science fiction has led him to *The Coming Race* (1871) (*L&H*). He undertakes an ideological analysis of Bulwer's mixing of the 'old sub-genre' of the 'Extraordinary Voyage' and the 'new sub-genres' of the 'Future War' and 'Alternative History'.

Thackeray seems, at least temporarily, to be out of fashion. Apart from Stephen Bann's interesting treatment of him in *The Clothing of Clio*[54] and Dieter Hamblock's study of *Henry Esmond* as a historical novel (*A&E*), which I have not seen, Thackeray has only attracted attention of the 'Notes and Queries' variety: Natalie Maynor (*ELN*) discusses the role of the compositors in producing the style of *Vanity Fair*, and Gerald Sorensen (*RES*) examines Thackeray's use of historical material in *The Virginians*, in order to demonstrate the author's carefully acquired historical knowledge. *The Memoirs of Barry Lyndon Esq*[63] has been added to the World's Classics list and Andrew Sanders has provided a useful new introduction to George Saintsbury's 1908 text.

OUP have also re-issued George Borrow's *The Romany Rye*[64], evidence perhaps of a growing interest in this author in recent years. Michael Collie and Angus Fraser's new bibliographical study[65] now provides a wealth of material for continuing the re-assessment of Borrow's oeuvre undertaken in biographies by David Williams and Michael Collie in 1982 (*YW* 63.342–3). The authors of this new study pay particular attention to how Borrow's works came to be written, how they were published, and how they developed into the form in which we know them. They give detailed listings of manuscript materials and their locations, and full bibliographical treatment of Borrow's translations, works edited by him, his letters, work for the periodicals, and his posthumous publications. The authors combine detailed bibliographical analysis with a critical and biographical narrative to produce a book which serves as a critical introduction to Borrow, as well as replacing T. J. Wise's unreliable bibliography of 1914.

Wilkie Collins is another author who has received increasing attention in recent years, as Kirk Beetz testifies in his review of Collins studies for 1972–83 (*DSA*). Developing interests in popular fiction, the form of the detective novel, the discourses of sexuality, and feminist approaches have led numerous critics, especially in the U.S.A., to look again at this author. Mark Hennelly Jr embraces a number of these issues in his investigation of the special role of gemology in *The Moonstone* (*NCF*). For Hennelly this novel constitutes 'that crucial moment in literary history when the nascent form of detective fiction confronts the established form of Victorian fiction for the first time'. Hennelly's prose is opaque and his argument weaves almost as mysteriously as the novel, but he makes some interesting points about the way in which the diamond, with its rich 'mineralogical and mythological pedigree' co-ordinates themes and devices common to both detective and mainstream fiction. Patricia Miller Frick (*PQ*) traces the significance of the moonstone back to Collins's grandfather's 'Memoirs of a Picture', a combination of biography and picar-

63. *The Memoirs of Barry Lyndon Esq*, by William Thackeray, ed. by Andrew Sanders. WC. OUP. pp. xxxii + 349. pb £2.50.

64. *The Romany Rye*, by George Borrow, ed. by Peter Quennell. OUP. pp. xiv + 309. pb £3.95.

65. *George Borrow: A Bibliographical Study*, by Michael Collie and Angus Fraser. StPB. pp. 231; illus. £22.50.

esque novel which uses the mystery of a stolen and counterfeited painting to attack the hypocrisy of the eighteenth-century art world in the same way that the younger Collins uses the mystery of the jewel in his criticism of genteel life in the nineteenth century.

The mills of the Dickens industry grind on apace. Reviewing recent Dickens studies in *DSA*, Robert L. Patten notes that 'there were probably upward of 500 publications' on Dickens in 1982. I have a great deal of sympathy with his disarming confession that his review 'is the result less of enterprise than of accident'. However, serendipity has served him well, and he has produced a full and knowledgeable survey of what he judges to be 'a great year in Dickens studies'. The year 1984 is not quite such a bumper year but Dickens continues to receive considerably more attention than any other Victorian novelist. Hapless students just entering the maze of Dickens studies and overburdened professionals who have long since lost their way may turn with relief to Norman Page's new *Dickens Companion*[66] which is a handy compendium of information on Dickens's life and writings. The main part of the *Companion* is a chronological guide to the composition, publication (in both serial and volume form), and reception of the novels. Page reviews the best available editions, indicates some of the main lines of interpretation, and suggests further reading. There are also sections on Dickens's illustrators and the topography of his fiction, as well as a bibliography, filmography, and list of early dramatizations.

The beginner or general reader might also usefully turn to Allan Grant's sensible introduction in the Longman's Preface Series[67]. Grant gives biographical details, examines Dickens's connections with journalism, the theatre, and public life and briefly relates the London of Dickens's fiction to the tradition of the city in literature. His second section takes the form of a critical commentary and there is also a reference section. Arthur A. Adrian's *Dickens and the Parent–Child Relationship*[68], on the other hand, proclaims itself to be the first full-length treatment of the subject. Unfortunately it contains few surprises; his discussions of the novels recycle familiar material and the biographical sections are marred by a rather naïve psychology. For a more sophisticated and succinct account of Dickens's fictional children we may turn to Mark Spilka's essay in *Sexuality and Victorian Literature*[59].

The most suggestive of this year's books on Dickens is undoubtedly Michael Hollington's *Dickens and the Grotesque*[69] which seeks to add depth and detail to this important aspect of Dickens's art. Hollington relates Dickens's use of the grotesque to visual satire and to the grotesque tradition of popular theatre, *commedia dell'arte*, pantomime, and the puppet theatre. Most importantly he sees Dickens as part of a European tradition of 'fantastic' or 'romantic' realism, of which the major theorizers were Schlegel and Novalis. His opening chapter, which explores current theories and definitions of the grotesque, is rather overburdened with a scholarship which has not been fully assimilated

66. *A Dickens Companion*, by Norman Page. Literary Companions. Macmillan. pp. xv + 369; illus. £20.

67. *A Preface to Dickens*, by Allan Grant. Preface Series. Longman. pp. xii + 193; illus. hb £7.95, pb £5.25.

68. *Dickens and the Parent–Child Relationship*, by Arthur A. Adrian. OhioU. pp. xii + 169; illus. £22.95.

69. *Dickens and the Grotesque*, by Michael Hollington. CH. pp. 261. £15.95.

but is worth quarrying. Hollington is best when he gets down to cases. A series of studies of (usually) pairs of novels demonstrates how Dickens developed a 'rhetoric of the grotesque', an ironic mode of perception which was used to satirize a society which, on the whole, disapproved of the grotesque. Hollington questions Ruskin's view of Dickens as a crude progressivist of the 'steam and whistle party' and argues that Dickens's ironic, contrastive view of history tends to undermine complacent progressivist fantasies.

Hollington's thesis takes the debate about Dickens's aesthetic firmly outside the confines of classic realism, as does Chris Brookes in *Signs for the Times*[70]. Dickens forms the literary component of Brookes's exploration of 'symbolic realism' in the literature, painting, and architecture of the mid-Victorian period. Brookes sees Dickens's 'symbolic realism' as a specifically Carlylean inheritance and he examines the rhetorical processes by which the novels of the 1840s and 1850s present a world which is simultaneously 'real' and 'phantasmagoric'. In particular Brookes seeks to explain Dickens's 'symbolic realism' in terms of a Christian theology, and while it is clear that we need to find an adequate critical vocabulary for discussing Dickens's Christian fables and his fictions of transcendence I do not think that this rather impenetrable book will be very helpful.

Dickens's transformations of the real also preoccupy several other critics. For K. J. Fielding (*DSA*) the nature of Dickens's realism is best explained in terms of its links with oral culture and the folk-tale. Fielding grounds his argument in an interesting re-assessment of 'The Spirit of Fiction' which he now attributes (on internal and circumstantial evidence) to Henry Morley. A number of other writers in *DSA* approach the Dickensian phantasmagoria by way of 'the uncanny'. Glancing at Freud and Tzvetan Todorov, H. M. Daleski attempts to show that Dickens uses the uncanny as a structural device, 'as a means of disclosure, functioning to hint at what is hidden and only later fully revealed'. Dianne Sadoff agrees that Dickens's moments of the uncanny 'advertise mystery', but her main purpose is to 'produce' a series of Dickensian texts as examples of 'castration-writing'. Hers is a virtuoso piece of infinite textual regression which left this reader behind.

When we turn to studies of individual novels we find a great (although not bewildering) variety of approaches and interests. Kathryn Chittick (*NCF*) makes a worth-while attempt to relocate the early fiction in its cultural context of a postreform act periodical press in which literary interest had begun to re-emerge after the political furore of the prereform years. She re-examines the *Sun* review of *Pickwick Papers*, noting that it appeared in the column reserved for monthly magazine reviews and encourages us to see the novel as 'a periodical with only one article' which was transformed into a novel by Dickens's introduction of 'pathetic elements' into the 'comic strip progress' of his characters. N. N. Feltes (*L&H*), on the other hand, sees the gradual transformation of the first five numbers of *Pickwick* as 'an effect of the ideological structuration of the commodity text'. Feltes's materialist analysis, which follows the theories of Pierre Macherey and Terry Eagleton, seems plausible enough; however, it might have gained in force had it been expressed in a more widely accessible language. Max Vega-Ritter (*CVE*) traces the

70. *Signs for the Times: Symbolic Realism in the Mid-Victorian World*, by Chris Brookes. A&U. pp. xvii + 202; illus. £18.

education of the quixotic child Pickwick, following Stephen Marcus and Angus Wilson's view that he is simultaneously an idealization of John Dickens and an expression of Dickens's ambivalence towards his father.

Oliver Twist is a neglected orphan this year: David Paroissien offers some speculations about Fagin in *The Dickensian*, and Thê Hung Nguyen takes a Marxist approach to Nancy (*ZAA*) which I have not seen. Wilfred Dvorak's examination of Shakespearean echoes in *The Old Curiosity Shop* in *SNNTS* relates Quilp's death scene to the knocking at the gate episode in *Macbeth* (as performed by Macready).

Dickens's use of dreams and visions interests a number of writers this year, as we have already seen. In addition, Juliet MacMaster (*DSA*) investigates the dreams, hauntings, and disordered mental states of *Barnaby Rudge* which she sees as expressing simultaneously the dark forces of the unconscious and the power of the human imagination to mediate between 'authority and impulse', while Marilyn Kurata's reading of *The Chimes* (*DSA*) insists on the 'elemental relation of dream vision and vision' in the only Christmas book to reflect Dickens's increasingly realistic assessment of social problems. On a slightly different tack, Jerome Meckier (*MLR*) charts the overturning of Rousseau-istic dreams by a nightmare reality in *Martin Chuzzlewit* and *American Notes*, which he sees as works of self-discovery in which Dickens defines and confronts his changing conceptions of 'civilization' and 'civility'. In a sprightly, opportunistic essay[58] James R. Kincaid returns to his earlier reading of *Martin Chuzzlewit* (*Dickens and The Rhetoric of Laughter* [Clarendon, 1971]), in which he suggested that the anarchic force of Sairey Gamp and Young Bailey subverts the novel's moralistic centre so as to suggest 'not righteous reconciliation but joyous carnival', and now 'plays' with other 'subversive' readings in a demonstration of the novel's virtually unlimited openness to interpretation.

The supposed collapse of realism into romance and melodrama in *Dombey and Son* is seen in a new light in Robert Clark's 'Riddling the Family Firm' (*ELH*) which undertakes a Foucaultian analysis of the 'sexual economy' of Dickens's 'textual weave'. In his very lively and polemical essay Clarke suggests that the riddle of 'why Dombey and son makes sense whilst Dombey and daughter makes non-sense' lies at the centre of the patterns of 'money power, patriarchy, exchange and history' which structure the novel.

David Copperfield appears in the guise of a 'Masterpiece of World Literature' in Richard Dunn's collection of essays on *Approaches to Teaching Dickens*[71]. Dunn himself provides a selective and evaluative discussion of paperback editions, background reading, and aids to teaching, and a number of teachers discuss their classroom use of the novel in literature classes of various kinds. Other essays demonstrate specific teaching approaches based in, for example, reader-response theory or 'psychoanalytic, post-structuralist, feminist theory'. This is a frankly self-conscious and introspective account of teaching the text in the North American context. Elsewhere Philip Collins (*CVE*) supplements Nina Burgis's attempts, in the Clarendon Edition, to tease out the facts of the relationship of Dickens's Autobiographical Fragment to his most autobiographical novel. Collins offers the evidence for his confident assertion that Forster had more of the fragment in his possession than he published; that it continued beyond the blacking-warehouse episode; and that what Forster had before him in 1870–2 was less extensive than the material Dickens worked from in 1849. The debate goes on. Jerome Buckley[58], on the other hand, concentrates on the novel as David's autobiography in a sensitive and succinct essay which takes issue with some of the absurder psychological interpretations. He suggests that David's vocation of novelist should be compared with the vocation of the poet in *In Memoriam* which, like *David Copperfield*, charts a process of establishing identity through the disciplined self-knowledge that accompanies the successful integration of past and present. In *CVE* Joseph Dobrinsky's examination of Traddles as a Dickensian hero in the Carlylean mould of industrious endeavour has some interesting asides on the way in which Dickens tempered his criticism of 'a highly unfair and unequal society'. I have not seen Robert M. de Graaf's essay on the novel's 'self-articulating' characters (*JNT*).

Bleak House has given rise to some of the most interesting as well as the most tedious of the Dickens essays. Christopher Herbert's outstanding piece on 'The Occult in *Bleak House*' (*Novel*) embraces Hollington's 'rhetoric of the grotesque', Brookes's 'symbolic realism', and the uncanny of the *DSA* essayists. Herbert defends Dickens's conception of gothic, which he differentiates from the 'invidious' theory of gothic romance shared by Wordsworth and Ruskin. Rather than affording 'pleasurably exciting escape from the supposed "torpor" . . . of contemporary life', the gothic of *Bleak House*, Herbert suggests, exposes a 'feeling of latent panic' beneath the surface of the nineteenth-century world. The 'epidemic of neuroses' and 'strange evaporations of selfhood' which the novel reveals are treated as 'cognate manifestations of some underlying principle that itself remains enigmatic' and which eludes transcription by the techniques of ordinary realism. Whereas Herbert links the novel's 'intimations of occult mystery' to ghost fiction, Janet Larson looks to biblical tradition in an extremely well-documented and suggestive essay on its 'Joban Subtext' (*DSA*). Larson discusses some Victorian readings of Job and examines Joban allusions in Chapters 1 and 32, but most importantly she tries to show how the 'equivocal challenge to traditional authority' which is embodied in the literary strategies of the Book of Job is paralleled by the narrative and rhetorical disjunctions of *Bleak House*: Dickens's mixing of modes in his own parable of loss and gain is seen as an echo of Job's fusion of biblical fairy-tale in prose with poetic chapters of perplexity and suffering. This is an important addition to the current re-examination of Dickens and religion by Dennis Walder and others (*YW* 62.321). Another interesting essay is John J. Fenstermaker's[58] detailed analysis of the first instalment of the novel, designed to show how Dickens consistently focuses on the failure of both written and spoken language to express truth and communicate fellow-feeling. Fenstermaker demonstrates how the 'abuse of language' pervades each of the four public institutions Dickens indicts, as it does the private institution of the family.

In *DQu* Marc Beckwith offers a reasonably plausible case for seeing Bucket as a kind of Sybil who secures Snagsby's safe conduct through the underworld of criminality and slums; Michael Kearns analyses the 'discourse component' of Esther's narrative; George Worth examines the significance of what Guppy knows and when he knows it; Irene Woods compares the Jarndyce and

Jarndyce case with the labyrinth of German Romanticism, and Angus Easson reviews paperback editions of the novel. *CVE* contains a number of fairly routine essays on the novel: Jean Louis Chevalier writes on Esther's role as 'the best wife man ever had'; Claude Fierobe looks at Dickens's use of lists; Jean-Marie Baissus sees the novel's spatial discourse as 'the modern equivalent of the Aristotelian square'.

In the only study of *Hard Times* I have seen this year, Stephen Spector (*ELH*) interestingly converts to praise George Eliot's condemnation of Dickens's failure to do more than 'render the external traits of our town population'; he sees the lifelessness of Dickens's individual workers as evidence of a humanity which caused him to abandon the metonymy of realism and its assumption that an invisible quality like character could be identified by a visible exterior.

Two essays in *DQu* confront the question of whether *Little Dorrit* is Dickens's darkest novel. Janet Larson reads the novel as 'skeptical Apocalyptic' and employs the perspectives of Frank Kermode's *The Sense of an Ending* (OUP, 1967) in her examination of the linguistic and rhetorical features that correspond to 'the narrative's rhythm of expectation and disconfirmation'. Dvora Zelicovici steers a steady course between the view of the novel as a circular structure of irreversible futility and the overoptimistic linear reading. J. M. Rignall (*ELH*), on the other hand, sees the 'rigorously linear, end-determined narrative' of *A Tale of Two Cities* as subverted by the novel's flirtation with the view of history as a chain of violence. Rignall certainly makes the novel come alive but, like a number of the other essayists, he seems to be trying to 'save the text', to recover a text authored by a 'best self', rather than by the author's 'ordinary everyday self' which usually contrived to retain the upper hand.

In *DSA* David Gervais offers a very elegant appreciation of the poetry and prose of *Great Expectations*, and Michael Ginsburg makes an interesting attempt to answer the question of why it was '*necessary* for Pip to misinterpret the signs which pointed toward Magwitch as pointing toward Miss Havisham'. Ginsburg interprets the substitution as repression; a displacement of guilt to desire which 'opens up a space where a story can be told'. Ginsburg's interest in 'repression' and 'repetition' is shared by Peter Brooks who includes an essay on *Great Expectations* in his *Reading for the Plot*[72]. Brooks sees the characteristic nineteenth-century plot as involving a state of deviance or error, and he suggests that Dickens's novel enacts a cure from this condition. Brooks's contention that the novel ends with the sense of a 'life that has outlived plot', a left-over life, is echoed by Douglas Thomson's rather strained rereading of the novel's revised ending (*DQu*). Gail Finney looks again at Wemmick's castle in a study of the garden image in the nineteenth-century European novel (*CompL*) and in *The Dickensian* Paul Davis reads Pip's characterization in the light of Hogarth's 'Industry and Idleness', while Richard Witt re-examines the death of Miss Havisham. I have not seen Michael Haig's 'The Allegory of *Great Expectations*' (*SSEng*).

Dickens's attitudes to money and financial speculation in the 1860s are explored by Wilfred Dvorak and Michael Cotsell. Dvorak (*The Dickensian*)

---

72. *Reading for the Plot: Design and Intention in Narrative*, by Peter Brooks. Clarendon. pp. xviii + 363. £17.50.

examines the ambivalence of Dickens's social attitudes through an examination of *The Uncommercial Traveller* and articles in *All the Year Round*, and in particular those by M. L. Meason on the evils of speculative abuses. Cotsell (*DSA*) suggests how Dickens's treatment of speculation in *Our Mutual Friend* might have been influenced by Meason's articles. Cotsell also considers Dickens's contradictory perceptions of the character of John Harmon (*DQu*) and in *The Dickensian* he celebrates the artistic success of the late grafting of Mr Venus onto the novel.

And so, finally, to *The Mystery of Edwin Drood*. John Beer attempts to tease out the mysteries of Dickens's unfinished novel in a fascinating essay in *DSA*. Beer finds the 'mystery' of the novel in Jasper's 'apartness', a 'daemonism, like that of the novelist himself' which acts independently as a prefigurative force; Kathleen Wales (*Lang&S*) is also interested in Dickens's treatment of mental processes which she approaches through a linguistic analysis of his interior monologues. In *The Dickensian* Charles Forsyte considers the significance of the novel's numerous allusions to Jack the Giant-killer.

Sexuality and textuality are major preoccupations in this year's interpretations of the novels of the Brontë sisters. Jan B. Gordon (*ELH*) sets the tone in her discussion of the narrative of *The Tenant of Wildfell Hall* as a 'proliferating world of texts', which analyses the way in which the novel structures its competing discourses of gossip, letters, and diary. She is also quite interesting on the novel's intertextuality and sees its indebtedness to *Wuthering Heights* as a form of 'structural belatedness' which parallels the historical belatedness of its epistolary form. Gordon is best when close-reading the text, less clear when engaging with poststructuralist theories of Gothic.

The anxiety of critical influence also mars Elizabeth Napier's examination of the 'Problem of Boundaries' in *Wuthering Heights* (*PQ*) which sees the destabilizing narrative method as collapsing categories and dissolving the limits between characters, thus rendering impossible the novel's central moral imperative of choice. Selection, rather than choice, provides the key to interpretation for Barbara Munson Goff (*VS*). Goff approaches *Wuthering Heights* from the context of Victorian natural science and suggests that Emily Brontë shared Darwin's early project of subverting the social and psychological complacency sanctioned by natural theology. She sees the novel as a 'hypothetical experiment' in human development constructed to show the enfeebling of the breed by civilization, and she presents Heathcliff as a God-like creature who operates as ruthlessly as Darwin's mechanism of selection. The article is not convincing in all its details but it offers a challenging view, and Goff's suggestion that the 'romantic, symbolic, mystical readings' of Brontë's early critics were more able to come to terms with the novel than modern approaches gives food for further thought.

Sexual passion is the central subject of John Maynard's new study of Charlotte Brontë[73] which argues that her novels not only create 'a full discourse of sexuality' but that they also offer the most sophisticated and fullest treatment of sexual issues of any Victorian writer before Hardy. Maynard offers a brief introduction to 'The Worlds of Victorian Sexuality' and provides a useful bibliographical essay in his first footnote. He shows how the early tales treat of a 'world below' of adultery, seduction, promiscuity, and incest, and traces how

73. *Charlotte Brontë and Sexuality*, by John Maynard. CUP. pp. x + 262. £19.50.

these themes were incorporated into the published work in which the most important sexual theme is the process of sexual awakening. This is a revisionist work which attempts to counteract the supposedly distorting perspectives of those critics who see Charlotte Brontë either as a sick woman lashing out at men', or as 'an irregular, unconscious warrior in the battle against patriarchal society and literature'. However, Maynard does not entirely escape the biographical and interpretative fallacies of which he accuses his opponents; his biographical excursions are often very speculative, and his insistence that Brontë's treatment of sexuality is fully conscious leads to some overinterpretation. Moreover, his revisionist project sometimes results in an infelicitous tendentiousness of tone, and his impatience with the feminists leads to some crudity of judgement. Ruth Gounelas (*AUMLA*) gives a different perspective on the limitations of the female author and the strengths of 'writing as a woman' in her competent survey of critical attitudes to the 'female qualities' in Charlotte Brontë's writings in the last 150 years.

Elsewhere attention is fairly evenly divided between *Jane Eyre* and *Villette*. In an interesting essay which refers widely to other early Victorian novels, Jerome Beaty[58] re-examines the early chapters of *Jane Eyre* in order to focus more closely on the way in which the novel not only conflates the themes and conventions of the 'high Romantic' Byronic tradition with those of the 'lower' domestic or Wordsworthian tradition, but also uses contemporary fiction to provide 'precautionary signals' to the reader. Mark M. Hennelly Jr, in a detailed and interesting piece in *ELH*, uses reader-response theories to examine some of the main reading experiences in *Jane Eyre*. Where Hennelly sees the novel as a 'reading lesson', Janet H. Freeman (*SEL*) sees it as a speaking lesson, the story of Jane's discovery of the power of speech and of speech as power. Like Hennelly, Freeman re-examines the relationship between the speaker/writer and the implied listener/reader of Jane's narrative, a relationship which she sees as a dialectic of speech and silence. Freeman provides a reasonably interesting case, despite her tendency to state the obvious with a rhetorical flourish. Alan Bacon (*N&Q*) has an interesting note on the Miltonic references in Jane's paintings and suggests that we should read them as a sequence representing temptation, sin, and death.

This year sees the publication of the Clarendon *Villette*[74]. Herbert Rosengarten and Margaret Smith have based their text on the first edition collated with the manuscript and they have also referred to some recently discovered early proofs, and early drafts for an alternative chapter, as well as to the author's corrections to the Nicholl's copy. Smith gives a lucid account of the state of the text and of the editorial procedures, and Rosengarten carefully examines the circumstances of the novel's composition.

Christina Crosby (*SEL*) shares John Maynard's impatience with feminist readings of *Villette*, but does so on the grounds that such readings have accepted too uncritically the apparently 'natural' oppositions of 'illusion and reality, false and true consciousness'. Crosby argues, on the contrary, that the novel challenges these distinctions. She borrows Jacques Lacan's concept of 'the imaginary' to show how the ghostly nun 'images' Lucy, and suggests how Lucy and de Hamal are 'implicated in each other' through a series of doublings

74. *Villette*, by Charlotte Brontë, ed. by Herbert Rosengarten and Margaret Smith. The Clarendon Edition of the Novels of the Brontës. Clarendon. pp. lv + 768. £48.

and displacements which disrupt the 'presumably fixed terms of sexual antithesis'. The unfixing of the terms of sexual antithesis is taken a stage further in Sara Putzell-Korab's examination of the novel's treatment of 'passion between women'[59]. Lucy's spirited wooing of Ginevra Fanshawe is discussed in detail and the argument is given added substance by reference to attitudes towards sexual feeling between women in other Victorian texts.

If, like Tom Winnifrith, you believe 'that as the author of two great novels ... anything she wrote must be of interest' you may be interested in his new edition of Charlotte Brontë's poems[75]. You may even like them, despite the editor's bluff contention that 'Charlotte was probably the worst poet in the family after her father'. Winnifrith has attempted to date the poems and provides explanatory notes to those which have Angrian contexts; a number of specifically Angrian poems have been left for Christine Alexander's forthcoming edition of the juvenilia.

Two of the most interesting essays on Elizabeth Gaskell approach her work from a feminist perspective. Barbara Weiss (*SNNTS*) attempts to combat the marginalization that has accompanied the customary use of the adjective 'charming' to describe Elizabeth Gaskell's love of plot-making and appreciation of anecdote, and suggests that Gaskell's use of interpolated tales is an example of a specifically female response to patriarchal culture, an attempt to give a feminine shape to reality by allowing women to tell their own tales. Rowena Fowler (*SEL*) celebrates *Cranford* as a female utopia in which 'women's language and values are the accepted currency', in an article which attempts to revise Martin Dodsworth's influential 'Women without men at Cranford' (*EIC*, 1963). Thomas E. Recchio (*SELit*) re-examines the generic division of *Mary Barton* and sees its narrative order as 'essentially mythic'; this is hardly a novel view and his argument is greatly indebted to John Lucas's *The Literature of Change* (*YW* 58.302) but he provides a careful illustration of his case for reading the novel as Utopian myth. Barbara Brill's portrait of William Gaskell[76] enables us to see Elizabeth Gaskell's life from the perspective of her role as wife and companion to a busy teacher, preacher, and social reformer.

The growing interest in the relationships between Victorian literature and science evident in the work of Peter Morton and Susan Peck MacDonald (p. 453) also informs one of this year's most readable books on George Eliot. Like a number of George Eliot's earliest readers, Sally Shuttleworth[77] is struck by the author's unparalleled breadth of knowledge of contemporary social and scientific theory, and she attempts to show how scientific ideas and methods affected both the social vision and narrative structure of the novels. There is no doubt that Shuttleworth's readings are limited by her exclusive concentration on organic theory, and her contention that all the novels draw their moral framework from the premise of organicism *is* contentious, but this is an incisive account. An introductory chapter discusses the social, psychological, and political ramifications of organic theory in European thought, while subsequent chapters treat each novel individually, focusing each time on a separate

75. *The Poems of Charlotte Brontë*, ed. by Tom Winnifrith. Blackwell. pp. xxxiv + 429. £19.50.

76. *William Gaskell, 1805–84: A Portrait*, by Barbara Brill. MLPP. pp. xii + 148. £7.95.

77. *George Eliot and Nineteenth-Century Science: The Make-Believe of a Beginning*, by Sally Shuttleworth. CUP. pp. xiv + 257. £20.

issue: natural history as social vision in *Adam Bede*; the internal narrative conflict between theories of organic social and psychological development and the catastrophic structure of *The Mill on the Floss*; the competing models of history in the 'divided Eden' of *Silas Marner*; the exploration of the social limitations of Comtean theory in *Romola*; the social and sexual politics of *Felix Holt*; the complex model of organic life in *Middlemarch*, and the development of alternative experimental hypotheses in the divided structure of *Daniel Deronda*. If the narrowness of Shuttleworth's hypothesis is sometimes limiting, the intensity of her microscope summons an attentiveness which may stimulate a fresh examination of what is left out of her account.

Sally Shuttleworth's interest in organic social theory overlaps with Suzanne Graver's attempt to locate George Eliot's novels in a 'tradition of social thought . . . pre-occupied with the rediscovery of community'[78]. Graver draws heavily on Ferdinand Tonnies' *Gemeinschaft und Gesellschaft*, as well as the theories of Strauss, Feuerbach, Comte, Spencer, J. S. Mill, and G. H. Lewes. The study is organized in a series of pairs of chapters of which the first is devoted to theoretical issues and its partner to an analysis of George Eliot's incorporation of these issues into the form of her fiction; the concluding pair explores the concept of a 'community of readers' through an examination of the narrator's interaction with its implied readers and a consideration of the author's interaction with her actual readers. The inclusion of Strauss and Feuerbach, in particular, means that this is a different tradition from that constructed by Shuttleworth, and Graver's treatment of her social theorists is generally more detailed and varied than Shuttleworth's; these are important advantages, but this book would have benefited from some of Shuttleworth's incisiveness, and for all the wealth of detail the George Eliot who emerges from these pages is a very familiar figure.

William Myers[79] also attempts to relate George Eliot to an intellectual tradition, but his project is more frankly intentionalist than either Shuttleworth's or Graver's. He sees George Eliot's writings as a consistent, deliberate, and systematic attempt 'to synthesize in fiction an elaborate and coherent theoretical analysis of the human situation'. Myers outlines the author's Associationist philosophy, her Feuerbachian concept of religion, her Comtean ethic of submission, and her sense that positivism can be transcended in art and vision, and then subjects them in turn to a Marxist, Nietzchean, and Freudian critique. After the thesis and antithesis comes the synthesis of Part Three, a detailed study of 'what George Eliot consciously chose to teach' in the later novels. Myers's project is not merely 'unfashionable' (as he freely admits in a deferential nod towards Derrida), it is also fraught with difficulties, and the author's anxieties on this matter result in a rather embattled tone and a good deal of shadow-boxing with opponents. However, despite some wrenching of the novels to fit his thesis Myers enriches our sense of George Eliot's intellectual milieu and produces some interesting readings of individual novels.

There is a marked lack of interest in the very early work this year, with the exception of Carroll Viera's examination of the origins of 'The Lifted Veil' in George Eliot's uneasy romanticism of the 1840s and 1850s (*SEL*). Elsewhere

78. *George Eliot and Community: A Study in Social Theory and Fictional Form*, by Suzanne Graver. UCal. pp. xi + 340. £29.50.

79. *The Teaching of George Eliot*, by William Myers. ULeics. pp. 264. £16.95.

we return to familiar preoccupations. The ending of *The Mill on the Floss* continues to be a challenge to interpreters, and John P. Bushnell performs in spirited fashion for the 'think positive' school (*SNNTS*), with his suggestion that we should see Maggie's end not as a drift towards death but as a confirmation of her 'stored up force'. Thus read, the novel is an anti-*Bildungsroman*, the story of a girl who refuses to grow up into an adult world whose values she finds inadequate: not drowning but waving? For U. C. Knoepflmacher, however, the ending of this novel is a Wordsworthian moment of romantic realism, a mythic vision of 'a childhood paradise of undifferentiated gender'[58]. *The Mill on the Floss* is the central text in a thought-provoking essay on 'Genre and the Integration of Gender' from Wordsworth to George Eliot and Virginia Woolf, in which Knoepflmacher reconsiders his own earlier views of George Eliot's realism. He now sees the novels in terms of George Eliot's persistent effort to integrate history and romance, which he relates to her commitment to a mythic memory which, unlike Wordsworth, she continued to endow with female properties. Unfortunately I have not seen Elizabeth Gemmette's comparison of the novel with *Jude the Obscure* (*Expl*), Lisa Gerard's feminist view of Maggie as romantic heroine (*IJWS*), nor Carol Martin's examination of pastoral and romance (*CLAJ*). Nor have I succeeded in tracking down Catherine Gallagher's essay on 'the politics of culture' in *Felix Holt* (*Representations*).

Kerry McSweeney's study of *Middlemarch* in the Unwin Critical Library[80] more than adequately fulfils the aim of the series' editor to provide 'reliable and stimulating works of reference and guidance, embodying the present state of knowledge and opinion in a conveniently accessible form'. McSweeney locates the novel in its broad literary and historical context as well as relating it to its author's intellectual, religious, and aesthetic concerns. He pays close attention to the nature and function of the narrator and its role in the novel's 'humanistic economy of salvation'; he devotes a chapter to outlining and displacing the Jamesian objections to the novel's form; and concludes with a critical history of the novel. This lively and intelligent study not only outlines the critical problems raised by the novel and the debates it has generated, it also makes an interesting contribution of its own. McSweeney's chapter on Dorothea provides ample evidence of the 'uneasiness about the exact nature of Dorothea, and therefore of *Middlemarch* itself', which concerns Harriet Farwell Adams in her re-examination of George Eliot's fusion of 'Miss Brooke' with her abandoned novel *Middlemarch* (*NCF*). Adams relates the author's changing conception of Dorothea to her evolution of a new conception of tragedy, and to her developing views on the nature and importance of religious feeling. T. R. Wright also considers the religious dimension in a volume of essays on *Images of Belief in Literature*[81].

In *E&S* James R. Bennett uncovers the novel's 'scenic structure of judgement' in an analysis of key scenes; Selma Brody (*ELN*) locates the origins of the pier-glass image in the optics of John Tyndall; Vince Newey (*N&Q*), noting Dorothea's echoing of Christian's 'What shall I do?', argues that George Eliot evokes *Pilgrim's Progress* only to modify or reject its religious ontology; and Mildred Greene adds a Feuerbachian footnote to Dorothea's

80. *Middlemarch*, by Kerry McSweeney. Unwin Critical Library. A&U. pp. 167. hb £15, pb £5.95.

81. *Images of Belief in Literature*, ed. by D. Jasper. Macmillan. pp. 195. £20.

marriages (*GEFR*) and examines the novel's treatment of love, marriage, and emotional repression (*Expl*).

The intense critical interest in *Daniel Deronda* in recent years will be augmented by the appearance of Graham Handley's Clarendon edition[82], based on the part-issue edition of 1876 and incorporating superior readings from the manuscript and corrections in editions published in the author's lifetime. The introduction gives details of interpolations, contractions, and changes of sequence. Like the other volumes in the series, this provides an uncluttered text with useful, if sparing, annotation.

Among the interpreters, Mary Wilson Carpenter (*PMLA*) follows Cynthia Chase's example (*PMLA*, 1978) and takes another deconstructive turn with the novel in relating George Eliot's 'Book of Daniel' to its Old Testament precursor. Carpenter sees the novel as a 'Book of Origins' which deconstructs conventions of history that separate past from present; it is a lively piece, despite a tendency to become carried away with its own deconstructive brilliance. Where Carpenter sees the novel's apocalyptic symbolism as uniting the divided narrative into a universal history of humanity in exile, Joseph Allen Boone, who approaches the novel with an interest in 'closure and the Victorian marriage ideal' (*Mosaic*), argues that the gaps between the two narratives grow ever wider as the novel articulates the 'diverging possibilities of selfhood' available to men and women in Victorian society. M. D. Kubitschek also writes on marriage (and politics) in the novel in *CLAJ*, which I have not seen, and there are essays by J. M. Chard and H. S. Kakar in *GEFR* on the quest for identity and vocation, and the growth of Gwendolen's conscience, respectively. Eugene Hollahan's 'Therapist or The Rapist? George Eliot's *Daniel Deronda* as a Pre-Freudian Example of Psychoanalysis in Literature' (*JEGP*) sounds intriguing but regrettably I have not seen it.

Finally, William Baker provides more material for future scholars with his latest volume of the George Eliot notebooks in the Pforzheimer Library[83]. The present notebook contains miscellaneous quotations, unadorned by authorial comment. Baker records everything, even deletions, and attributes as many of the quotations as he can.

Trollope studies seem to have gone into a decline this year: R. H. Super attempts to unravel the early publishing history of *The Way We Live Now* (*NCF*), Sarah Gilead discusses the imagery of *Orley Farm* and Trollope's treatment of sexuality (*Expl*), and Laura Hake examines the lady as criminal in the same novel (*VN*).

Sexuality and mathematics provide the points of departure for the only two noteworthy essays on Lewis Carroll: Morton Cohen[59] surveys Carroll's voluminous journals and correspondence for details of his sexuality, and concludes that despite contemporary tongue-wagging about his child-friendships, he was more Catcher in the Rye than Humbert Humbert; while Helen Pycior's examination of the state of nineteenth-century mathematics (*VS*) relates the Alice books to their author's misgivings about symbolical algebra, which stressed the predominance of structure over meaning.

82. *Daniel Deronda*, by George Eliot, ed. by Graham Handley. The Clarendon Edition of the Novels of George Eliot. Clarendon. pp. xxxvi + 755; illus. £48.

83. *Some George Eliot Notebooks: An Edition of the Carl H. Pforzheimer Library's George Eliot Holograph Notebooks*. Vol. 2: *Ms. 708*, ed. by William Baker. SSAA. USalz. pp. viii + 203.

Thomas Hardy, that 'most elusive of literary figures', has been brought into slightly sharper focus by Michael Millgate's continued efforts. The Hardy of the latest volume of the collected letters[84] is very much the sixty-year-old unsmiling public man, and we learn little about his writing practices or conceptions of art apart from the occasional aside. This volume, which maintains the high editorial standards of its predecessors, covers the period of Hardy's preparation of the collected edition of his novels and the death of his first wife; a fascinating subtext is suggested by the appallingly businesslike tone of Hardy's letters to his wife and the constant discreet references to trips to his friend Clodd in the company of Miss Dugdale.

Hardy's ultimate self-defensive act, the life and works published under the name of Florence Emily Hardy, is now published 'as nearly as . . . possible' as it stood at the time of Hardy's death, before the intervention of his widow and Sir James Barrie. Michael Millgate's introduction to *The Life and Works of Thomas Hardy*[85] gives a summary of its growth and development with a detailed discussion of some of the posthumous additions and deletions. Millgate does not underestimate the difficulties involved in attempting to recover the text 'intended' by Hardy, but his clear explanation of editorial procedures and his inclusion (in appendixes) of some of the deleted material will enable readers to make informed judgements. Millgate is surely correct in his view that Hardy emerges from the new edition as a less attractive character than the softened-up version offered by his widow, but the newly revealed Hardy is also, perhaps, more vulnerable. Ian Gregor and Michael Irwin, in *THA*, share Millgate's view of the 'autobiography' as 'a pre-emptive strike'; however, they convert its apparent deficiencies into virtues, suggesting that we should see its 'scrap-book, spatch-cocked' structure as a 'series of seemings' which display the workings of Hardy's imagination.

The other essays in this year's *THA* cover a wide range of topics: Simon Gattrell attempts to flesh out our knowledge of Hardy's working practices in an essay on the early stages of his fiction; Lawrence Jones examines a plot outline (dated 1871) for what he takes to be a second sensation novel; Norman Arkans relates Hardy's narrative voice to ballad conventions; Lloyd Siemens surveys Hardy's annotations to scrapbooks of reviews and critical appreciations, and finds him more sensitive to criticism of his poetry than his prose; Annie Escuret reports on Hardy's reputation in France, and Richard H. Taylor reviews recent Hardy studies and provides a bibliography for 1981–2. Also in *THA*, J. T. Laird compares *Tess of the d'Urbervilles* with *The Portrait of A Lady* in an attempt to throw fresh light on the relative merits of the fictional theories of Hardy and Henry James, and comes down firmly on the side of Hardy the 'seer' in preference to the 'tighter, intrinsically more prosaic' formulas of James the 'watcher'. Arlene Jackson, on the other hand, sees elements of the watcher in Hardy's photographic technique; as well as looking again at Hardy's presentation of scene, she examines photographs in *Jude the Obscure* as part of a wider iconographic pattern.

'How pervasive . . . is self-destruction in Hardy's novels? Through what artistic means does he embody his conviction that renunciation and suicide are

84. *The Collected Letters of Thomas Hardy*. Vol. 4: *1909–1913*, ed. by R. L. Purdy and Michael Millgate. Clarendon. pp. ix + 337. £25.

85. *The Life and Works of Thomas Hardy by Thomas Hardy*, ed. by Michael Millgate. Macmillan. pp. xxxvii + 604; illus. £30.

preferable to the endurance of life's irremediable evils . . .? What personal and broadly cultural and intellectual factors account for self-destruction in his works?' These are the central, perhaps question-begging, questions that Frank R. Giordano Jr seeks to answer in his study of Hardy's self-destructive characters[86]. Giordano examines the roots of Hardy's melancholy and outlines changing views on suicide from Wertherism to the *fin de siècle*, and then considers the novels within the framework of Durkheim's typology of egoistic (Eustacia and Henchard), anomic (Boldwood and Jude) and altruistic suicides (Giles Winterbourne and Tess). The result is a series of readings of the stories of particular characters which tends to lose sight of more complex structural and thematic patterns.

Donald D. Stone and Michael Benson discuss what they consider to be significant absences from Hardy's work. Stone (*NCF*) notes the absence of 'home and all that the word means to other Victorian novelists', but his conclusion that Hardy has a closer affinity with the alienated vision of Victorian poetry than with the comic vision of the novelists seems to be based on a radically oversimplified view of both the fiction and poetry. Michael Benson, rather quirkily, connects Hardy's comparative lack of interest in portraying bodily movement to the techniques of Samuel Beckett (*EIC*).

The most interesting of the essays on the early works is Ian Ousby's study of Hardy's inversion of the usual class attitudes of the sensation novel in *Desperate Remedies* (*DUJ*). Timothy Hands provides a footnote to *Under the Greenwood Tree* in a biographical examination of Arthur Shirley, Vicar of Stinsford (*THA*), and Susan Beegel[59] examines male sexuality in *Far from the Madding Crowd* only to discover a phallic Gabriel Oak who rescues Bathsheba by the restorative power of his 'miraculous rod'. Frank Giordano's altruistic suicide makes another appearance in his discussion of the meaning of martyrdom in *The Woodlanders* (*THA*), while Glen Irvine (*THA*) analyses the tone and structure of that novel to reveal 'a carefully constructed but subdued story that demonstrates the power of comedy to absorb and contain tragedy'; it is hardly a novel view, but it is sensibly argued.

The new Everyman Classics edition of *Tess of the d'Urbervilles*[87] has the considerable advantage of being extremely cheap; the text is the 1920 reprint of the Wessex edition, and the introduction gives details of the serial version of the novel. Kaja Silverman's essay on 'History, Figuration and Female Subjectivity' in *Tess of the d'Urbervilles* (*Novel*) combines obfuscation and illumination in almost equal proportions, but is one of this year's most interesting and challenging essays on Hardy. Silverman's starting point is the narrator's point of view which has long preoccupied Hardy critics; and she argues that in this novel 'the gaze never innocently alights on its object . . . it *constructs* its object through a process of colonization, delimitation, configuration and inscription'. Her concerns overlap with those of Penny Boumelha in *Thomas Hardy and Women* (*YW* 63.334) but Silverman pursues her argument in more detail and takes it further. She is particularly interested in the way in which Tess is articulated 'as figure' and in the narrator's attraction to Tess as figure. She uses Erich Auerbach's figural view of history to discuss the view of history proposed

86. *'I'd Have My Life Unbe'*: *Thomas Hardy's Self-destructive Characters*, by Frank R. Giordano Jr. UAla. pp. xix + 211. £18.75.

87. *Tess of the d'Urbervilles*, by Thomas Hardy, intro. by James Gibson. Dent. pp. xxviii + 419. pb £1.

by this novel and employs a Lacanian analysis to produce two readings of the novel: one as a 'nightmarish view of the symbolic order', the second (and specifically female reading) as offering different subjective possibilities in a different symbolic order. The essay is, perhaps, rather self-referential and its conclusions extremely debatable, but it provides some stimulating rereadings. She is particularly interesting on the rape/seduction scene.

Whereas Silverman deconstructs Tess's sexuality, Richard McGhee[59] celebrates it in his comparison of the battles of Hardy and Swinburne with prevailing Victorian views of sexuality. McGhee also examines the differing responses of Jude and Sue to the pleasures and pains of sexuality in 'the artificial system of things, under which the normal sex-impulses are turned into devilish domestic gins and springes'. Jude's 'gins and springes' also figure in Alexander Fischler's essay in *SNNTS* which sees *Jude the Obscure* as a bitter reversal of 'The Revolt of Islam'. Fischler argues that the novel punningly confuses spiritual and spirituous intoxication; it presents the 'Modern Spirit' as 'gin' (both trap and alcohol), and charts the entrapment of its protagonists by romantic as well as by Victorian 'self-congratulatory' spirituality.

George Meredith's *The Ordeal of Richard Feverel* appears in a new paperback edition[88] introduced by John Halperin. The text is a reproduction of Volume Two of the Memorial Edition and thus follows the 1878 revised version rather than the 1859 original. Gillian Beer and Margaret Harris have diligently edited the Meredith notebooks in the Beinecke Rare Books Collection[89]. These notebooks span virtually the whole of Meredith's writing career and contain, among other things, a draft outline which eventually became part of *The Adventures of Harry Richmond*. Meredith's ironic vision is deconstructed in Gary Handwerk's essay on linguistic blindness in *The Egoist* (*NCF*), while Roslyn Belkin (in an essay which I have not seen) looks at that novel's treatment of 'Older Women' (*IJWS*). Susan Morgan examines the 'Lost Harmonies' of Meredith's later fiction (*HLQ*).

Harvester continues its commitment to re-issuing the novels of George Gissing with *A Life's Morning*[90]. Pierre Coustillas's introduction charts the novel's genesis and its publishing history (a notable example of Victorian conflict between author and publisher) and tells the story of the changed ending. John Halperin (*SAQ*) examines Gissing's reading of Dickens in an effort to throw fresh light on both authors, and in particular on their similarities. He makes the obvious comparisons between, for example, their attitudes to women and class, but his rather surprising view that they shared a 'hatred of the modern and veneration of the past' surely fails to make important distinctions between their respective attitudes to past and present.

GissingN has several interesting essays. David Grylls writes on Gissing's view of Samuel Johnson and Old Grub Street; T. R. Wright examines the influence on Gissing of Positivism; David Dowling looks at the treatment of German Socialism, Positivism, and realism in six of Gissing's essays; and Andre Guillaume attempts to demonstrate the Jamesian pattern in *New Grub*

88. *The Ordeal of Richard Feverel*, by George Meredith, ed. by John Halperin. WC. OUP. pp. xxv + 561. pb £3.95.

89. *The Notebooks of George Meredith*, ed. by Gillian Beer and Margaret Harris. SSELR 73:2. USalz (1983). pp. xiii + 216.

90. *A Life's Morning*, by George Gissing, ed. by Pierre Coustillas. Harvester. pp. liii + 348. £12.95.

Street by means of comparison of that novel with *Washington Square* and *The Portrait of a Lady*.

Charles Swann's interesting essay on *Born in Exile* (*L&H*) directs us towards the Nietzschean Gissing, with its suggestion that Peake's attempts to become assimilated into a social system which he simultaneously envies and despises raise questions about the self which echo Nietzsche's articulation of the problems of alienation and deracination. Swann bases his approach to the problem of identity in the novel on Lionel Trilling's concepts of 'sincerity' and 'authenticity'. He treats the novel as cultural symptom and sees it as seeking (and significantly failing to find) a vocabulary with which to negotiate the gap between the two value-systems implied by Trilling's terms. Swann sets Gissing in a European context in an essay which also provides a useful pointer to how we might read other late-nineteenth-century novels.

It is hardly surprising that the latest flowering of feminist criticism should have redirected our attention towards *The Odd Women*. Karen Chase (*Criticism*) sees no point in either claiming Gissing as a protofeminist or castigating him as a misogynist, and instead she focuses on the 'new rhetorical possibilities' offered by Gissing's social, historical, and economic location. She is particularly interested in the new rhetorical possibilities in the rise of the female clerk, and suggests that the struggle between Rhoda Nunn and Everard Barfoot might be seen as a rhetorical conflict between her female clerk's literalism and his masculine irony. This is an interestingly speculative essay, but Chase's argument might have been assisted by a more detailed sense of the novel's sociohistoric context. Wendy Lesser (*HudR*) would presumably see Chase's historical shortcomings as typical of feminist critics, from whose clutches she seeks to rescue Gissing. She compares *The Odd Women* with James's *The Bostonians* in order to demonstrate that Gissing's 'fairmindedness' produced 'one of the best portrayals of the women's movement, old or new'; perhaps she will persuade the 'fairminded'. Deirdre David also joins the fray in 'Ideologies of Patriarchy; Feminism and Fiction in *The Odd Women*' (*FS*) which I have not seen.

Beate Kasper's study of Margaret Harkness and *A City Girl*[91] is divided into three sections: an extensive bibliography of Harkness's work including much previously unavailable material, an analysis of the novel *A City Girl* (1887), covering plot, characterization, theme, narrative perspective and structure of the text, and a broad discussion of its social and literary-historical context. The author refers to Friedrich Engels's much-quoted *Letter to Miss Harkness* of April 1888 which set out many of the basic principles of the Marxist theory of literature. Her own interpretation, however, seeks to argue that this novel, with its precise picture of the social setting and the problems and conflicts among the lower classes of London's East End, and the intended shock effect of its neutral, objective narration, demonstrates that there was in this period an independent naturalist movement in Britain. The text includes three appendixes (including Harkness's reply to Engels), a bibliography, and a short summary in English. [M.H.]

The prose fictions of William Morris offer a very different view of the late

91. *Margaret Harkness, 'A City Girl', Eine literaturwissenschaftliche Untersuchung zum naturalistischen Roman des spätviktorianismus*, by Beate Kasper. Niemeyer. pp. vii + 111. pb DM 39.

nineteenth century and of the nature of history from that found in Gissing's novels. Michael Holzman (*ELH*) returns *News from Nowhere* to its original context in the pages of *Commonweal* and reads it as an intervention in a specific debate about anarchism and the nature of socialism which was being conducted in that paper. Florence Boos (*VS*) shows how, in his German Romances, Morris sought to construct an alternative socialist history which would serve as a prototype for social revolution.

The fiftieth anniversary of the death of George Moore, in 1983, was marked by a collection of essays edited by Janet Egelson Dunleavy[92]. In her introductory reappraisal of Moore, the editor outlines some of the major problems that now confront serious students of Moore's work: the difficulties of separating the author's persona from the author; the problems caused by Moore's extensive, successive revisions; and the problem of tracing what she calls his 'aesthetic journey'. Unfortunately the essays she has gathered do not, on the whole, address these problems, and anecdote prevails over appraisal. The only contributor to engage seriously with Moore's writing is Robert S. Becker, who uses the letters to examine the public and private Moore. Edwin Gilcher discusses collecting Moore editions and supplements his own bibliography of the author. Other essays discuss Moore's knowledge of medieval literature; contrast the Paris of the 1870s with the London and Dublin to which Moore returned in the 1880s; describe Dublin in the period 1901–11, and explore the links between Moore and Joyce, and Moore and Beckett. *ELT* translates Raffaella Uslenghi's 1964 essay on Moore's works, which surveys the whole of his writings and traces his conversion from naturalism to aestheticism back to his early work.

The newer critical theories have produced a number of interesting rereadings of popular fiction of late. Kirby Farrell (*SNNTS*) undertakes a symptomatic reading of the treatment of imperialism and class in Conan Doyle's *The Sign of Four* and concludes that both Holmes's detection and the criminal striving of his opponents may be seen as expressing a 'dread of death and nullity'. Geoffrey Wall (*L&H*) offers a Foucaultian analysis of *Dracula* which he also reads symptomatically 'against the grain' of its manifest argument for sexual repression' in an effort to recover its 'discourses on the family, sexuality, race and empire'. In a more detailed and empirical discussion Allan P. Johnson[59] relates the novel's presentation of the 'dual life' of Lucy and Minna to the concept of the New Woman, and suggests that *Dracula* presents a sympathetic analysis of the female lot in the late nineteenth century.

Finally, a 'new' Victorian novella. According to Barry Menikoff[93], Robert Louis Stevenson's *The Beach of Falesa* so offended the political, religious, and sexual convictions of his Victorian publishers that it never appeared in the form in which he wrote it. Menikoff has transcribed the story from the original manuscript and provides a detailed, if embattled, analysis of how the text was systematically corrupted, as its author was relegated to the role of 'source of production with little control over the final product'. It is an interesting piece of textual detective work, although not quite the act of restoration which the editor claims, as an 'unexpurgated' version of the story has long been available in Jenni Calder's Penguin English Library edition.

92. *George Moore in Perspective*, ed. by Janet Egelson Dunleavy. Irish Literary Studies 16. Smythe (1983). pp. 174; illus. £10.50.

93. *Robert Louis Stevenson and 'The Beach of Falesa': A study in Victorian Publishing with the original text*, by Barry Menikoff. EdinU. pp. 199. £17.50.

3. Prose

(a) Bibliography and General Works

A second edition of the famous *An Enquiry into the Nature of Certain Nineteenth Century Pamphlets* (1934) in which John Carter and Graham Pollard revealed in an absorbing narrative the forgery of rare editions of works by Arnold, the Brownings, Dickens, Morris, Rossetti, Ruskin, Stevenson, Swinburne, Tennyson, Thackeray, Wordsworth, and Edmund Yates, has appeared, with an epilogue which the original authors had prepared for a second edition and some annotation by Nicolas Barker and John Collins[94]. In a second volume, *A Sequel to An Enquiry*, Barker and Collins integrate the subsequent work of Carter and Pollard (who both died in the mid-1970s) with their own research to show Buxton Forman's equal degree of responsibility with T. J. Wise in perpetrating the fraud. In documentation, they make full use of the new material which emerged in 1972 when Forman's collection was sold, and of typographic analysis of a new kind. *A Sequel* contains four parts – the first provides parallel biographies of Wise and Forman, the second the new material arising out of typographical inquiry, the third a new version of the course of the crime, and the fourth the dossiers that have accrued from the knowledge of Forman's participation. The new volume is every bit as informative and meticulous as the original, and affords an example of bibliography which is both technical and compelling. The insights in these pages into nineteenth-century publishing, authorship, and the book trade are considerable.

Excerpts from criticism of the works of Balzac, Elizabeth Gaskell, Laforgue, Lermontov, Sainte-Beuve, Robert Louis Stevenson, Thackeray, and John Wilson (Christopher North), each prefaced by a biographical and critical introduction, appear in Volume 5 of *Nineteenth-Century Literature Criticism*[95]. This collection of very fragmented excerpts is perhaps suitable for rapid reference, but students may well opt for the Critical Heritage volume where one exists, and scholars for the originals.

James G. Nelson looks into the publication of poetry in the 1890s in *PBSA*, where he describes a project inspired by Lawrence Binyon in 'Elkin Matthews' Shilling Garland Series', ten booklets of poetry written by seven young poets and Robert Bridges, published at a cheap price between December 1895 and December 1898. The article includes a detailed account of puffing in the 1890s which resulted in six printings of a book of poems, *Christ in Hades* by Stephen Phillips. In a lively study of Victorian critics' reviews of the *Earthly Paradise* narratives (*JWMS*) Florence Boos comments interestingly on the effect on reviewing of the 'considerable evolution' of the poem which occurred during its serial publication in three volumes, and the reluctance of critics to assess the work as a whole. Other pieces on serial publication are Uta Schumacher

94. *An Enquiry into the Nature of Certain Nineteenth Century Pamphlets*, by John Carter and Graham Pollard, ed. by Nicolas Barker and John Collins. Second edn. Scolar (1983). pp. 400 + 41; *A Sequel to 'An Enquiry into the Nature of Certain Nineteenth Century Pamphlets by John Carter and Graham Pollard': The Book Forgeries of H. Buxton Forman and T. J. Wise Re-examined* by Nicolas Barker and John Collins. Scolar (1983). pp. 394. £65 the set.

95. *Nineteenth-Century Literature Criticism*, Vol. 5, ed. by Laurie Harris, Sheila Fitzgerald, and Emily Barrett. Gale. pp. 604. $85.

Voelker's 'The Success of Mrs Beeton', in *ABMR*, which contains bibliographical description of the first serial publication of *Household Management* and of successive series and editions, and a general piece on *DNB* in *E&S* by Pat Rogers.

News concerning manuscripts from the period appears in *BLR* and *N&Q*: *BLR* reports that among the papers of the bookseller, editor, and poet Bertram Dobell in the Bodleian are Dobell's journals for 1868–9 and 1881–1914, papers relating to James Thomson, two volumes of manuscript reviews of plays seen by Dobell between 1866 and 1869, and literary papers relating to his life as editor. In 'The Album of a Minor Nineteenth-century Friend of the Arts' (*N&Q*) Roger Ellis reports in detail on the discovery of albums kept by Thomas Pickering of Royston, a friend of Charles and Mary Cowden Clarke and the Novello family. Their contents are fullest for the years 1830–5 and 1870–5.

I end this section with reference to some periodicals which carry bibliographical information. Nina Auerbach's stint as author of 'Recent Studies in the Nineteenth Century' (*SEL*) is welcome as she begins with 'I enjoyed reading the one hundred and fifty-odd scholarly books on this list', but its voice is also distinctive and lively, rather than bland, and its reviews detailed, not general. In *Arnoldian* Fraser Neiman contributes 'A Note on Arnold Scholarship', a review-essay to which is appended an annotated checklist of scholarship between spring 1983 and spring 1984. The quarterly *VSB* circulates valuable information about scholarly activities in America, Britain, and Canada. Calls for papers, courses, periodicals, lectures, and conferences are announced and then reported on in considerable detail.

Richard D. Altick, author of the seminal *The English Common Reader* (1957), has been honoured by a *Festschrift*, *Victorian Literature and Society*[96], which contains a high proportion of good essays, some of which range generally. Wendell V. Harris attempts to rethink the problems of the term 'aestheticism' (rejected as vague by Ruth Temple in 1974) and the existence of an aesthetic movement (also rejected by Temple): 'But of course there *was* something called an aesthetic movement', insists Harris, and to support his contention he suggests six unexceptionable tendencies from which the various submovements are blended – the medievalizing, the botanical, the ornamental, the omnibeautiful, the dreamily melancholic, and the demand for art for the artist's sake. What is of interest is Harris's use in his article of an edition of forty-eight late-nineteenth-century volumes edited by Peter Stansky and Rodney Shewan and reprinted in a series, *The Aesthetic Movement and the Arts and Crafts Movement* (1977–9), and his contemplation of the link, such as it was, between the two movements. A comparatively miniature anthology, Derek Stanford's one-volume selection of *Pre-Raphaelite Writing*[97], is re-issued ten years after it first appeared, without any updating – even of its bibliographies. Attempting to show the breadth and history of the movement, it is organized by topic (such as 'The Founding of the Brotherhood') and contains polemic, criticism (literary and art), poetry, and parodies. Its price is

96. *Victorian Literature and Society: Essays Presented to Richard D. Altick*, ed. by James R. Kincaid and Albert J. Kuhn. OSU. pp. viii + 374. $25.

97. *Pre-Raphaelite Writing*, ed. by Derek Stanford. Dent (1973). pp. xxxvii + 207. hb £6.95, pb £2.95.

unbeatable, but its value as a reliable guide to the subject is seriously reduced by its outdated booklists.

Manfred Pfister and Bernd Schulte-Middelich collect eighteen articles[98] on various aspects of literature and art in the late Victorian period, specified in the subtitle as 'Turn of the century England between decadence and social critique'. The range of the contributions is broad, covering Victorian consciousness and the sense of new beginnings, foreign influences on English culture, social and sexual mores, and the emergence and response to new political movements. Most space, however, is devoted to literary themes with essays on Hardy, Wilde, and Shaw, on the English short story and on the novel of development, and on the lyric and theatre of the 1890s. There is also a piece on Sherlock Holmes and one on the English Music Hall; the final chapter on the art and design of the period is complemented by fifteen reproductions, in the main of Beardsley's work. [M.H.]

Despite its forthright title, *The Image of the Middle Ages in Romantic and Victorian Literature*[99] by Kevin L. Morris is written in tortuous prose; extraneous quotation and detail, suggestive of an unrevised dissertation, are exacerbated by the typescript format which readers must hope publishers will abandon now as 'unfriendly' and typographically gross: one line here begins with a colon! Morris's interest is in religious medievalism in the main, from which he distinguishes English literary religious medievalism which is predominantly Protestant, particularly in the Romantic period. His book and thought are constructed along a Catholic versus Protestant axis, with chapters on 'Religious Medievalism: 1750–1825' and 'Anti-Medievalism: 1750–1900'; and the chapter on Ruskin and medieval art posits a Protestant, an anti-Catholic, and a Catholic Ruskin. Among the Victorians, Newman, Kingsley, and Chesterton also figure extensively but pride of place goes to Kenelm Henry Digby (1796/7–1880), 'the chief British religious medievalist of the nineteenth century' whose book on chivalry, *Broad Stone of Honour* (1822), was a 'crucial formative influence' on Young England and English Catholics.

Digby does not appear in *Nineteenth-Century English Literature*[100], Margaret Stonyk's volume in the Macmillan History of Literature, which is nevertheless inclusive and not unintelligent. However, it is still wedded to the author-centred notion of the history of literature so that the table of contents is essentially a list of authors' surnames, and the text has a standard form of biography and brief précis of and commentary on main works of successive authors; unevenness in treatment results in unexpected if welcome expansiveness and regrettable crowding: Romantic prose writers are featured, while their Victorian counterparts are scattered, with two pages on Pater in a section called 'Pater and the poets of the 1890s'. Strains of this survey genre also appear in odd diction (are *Biographia Literaria*, *Sartor Resartus*, and *Praeterita* in any sense 'sequels' to *The Prelude*?) and odder contentions such as the claim in the book's last sentence that 31 December 1900, the day on which Hardy

98. *Die 'Nineties, Das englische Fin de Siècle zwischen Dekadenz und Sozialkritik*, ed. by Manfred Pfister and Bernd Schulte-Middelich. Francke (1983). pp. 422. pb DM 29.80.

99. *The Image of the Middle Ages in Romantic and Victorian Literature*, by Kevin L. Morris. CH. pp. 259. £18.95.

100. *Nineteenth-Century English Literature*, by Margaret Stonyk. Macmillan History of Literature. Macmillan. pp. xiv + 307. hb £15, pb £3.95.

wrote 'The Darkling Thrush', is 'the last day of the nineteenth century'. A chronology of the works and events of the century, and a list of further reading are included in this volume which at its best can be lively.

The same cannot be said for another survey from Macmillan's, Harold Orel's *Victorian Literary Critics*[101], which concerns an area that Stonyk ignores. Orel wishes to create a context for Arnold, and his seven critics are George Henry Lewes, Walter Bagehot, Richard Holt Hutton, Leslie Stephen, Andrew Lang, George Saintsbury, and Edmund Gosse. The book consists of seven discrete belle-lettrist essays with little comparison among these critics or with others, and no conscious theoretical, historical, or even structural framework, the scrappiest of introductions, and no conclusion. The essays are uneven, with that on Lewes inadequate and the one on Hutton far better. It appears to be a rushed book on a subject that requires more research, familiarity with the periodicals, and thought than is in evidence here.

A more finished and fully conceived book is A. O. J. Cockshut's *The Art of Autobiography*[102] in which Ruskin's *Praeterita* and Gosse's *Father and Son* receive glancing critical attention, in a section which links them mainly through its title, 'The Dedicated Child'. Cockshut's scholarship is absorbed to the point of invisibility (there are very few notes), the prose stylish, and the criticism belle-lettrist, but without pretensions to be otherwise. In his disarming and sensible introduction Cockshut writes interestingly of his view of autobiography, and of the shape of his own book, over a quarter of which he devotes to childhood because of 'the enormous space' it occupies in autobiography which 'with respect to Dickens and a few others ... is the only literary form which shows its full importance'.

In a substantial essay in *PSt* Brian Maidment considers a mode of Victorian biography, an author, and publishing history in 'Popular Exemplary Biography in the Nineteenth Century: Edwin Paxton Hood and His Books'. Hood, who combined the ministry with a career of prolific publication for the masses, as a biographer, editor, and writer of didactic prose, is another Victorian purveyor of mass culture brought to our attention by Maidment who attempts, perhaps unnecessarily, to distinguish Hood by his interest in genre 'from the many other fluent popular Victorian moral writers'. Maidment fastens on a clutch of books, authors, and phenomena overlooked on the whole by mainstream criticism, and the piece should not be missed.

Alexander Welsh's thoughtful piece in Altick[96], 'Writing and Copying in the Age of Steam', is a meditation on copying in the Victorian period which quotes interesting material from Bentham and Charles Babbage (who as a Victorian originator of modern information technology figures in *VS*'s history of science issue), as well as Dickens's fable on writing and copying involving Mr Dick's initiation into copying legal documents.

Examples from Dickens, and many other familiar and unfamiliar Victorian authors of novels, grammars, and books on etiquette appear in K. C. Phillipps's eye-opening *Language and Class in Victorian England*[103]. Chapters on the upper classes, the lower orders, pronunciation, and modes of address

101. *Victorian Literary Critics*, by Harold Orel. Macmillan. pp. ix + 243. £22.50.

102. *The Art of Autobiography in 19th and 20th Century England*, by A. O. J. Cockshut. Yale. pp. x + 222. £10.95.

103. *Language and Class in Victorian England*, by K. C. Phillipps. The Language Library. Blackwell. pp. x + 190. £19.50.

range widely through usage, and alert present-day readers to unsuspected nuances and distinctions in the written language of the period. While the author avows that his bias is towards upper-class usage, there is a useful index of words which directs us to 'trade', 'walk together' and 'ain't' among many others.

In ' "Bureau and Barrack": Early Victorian Attitudes Towards the Continent' (VS) Bernard Porter attempts to determine whether early Victorians *were* xenophobic as is commonly alleged; he decides tentatively that 'for most of the attitudes the early Victorians took towards the Continent, they had convincing reasons . . . based upon fairly good observation rather than on pure antiforeign prejudice'. The same subject is tackled very successfully (and with more conviction) by Robert O. Preyer in *BIS*. In 'Breaking Out: The English Assimilation of Continental Thought in Nineteenth-Century Rome' the author reviews some first reactions to Rome by fictional and historical Victorians, and goes on to specify a network, originating with the Hare-Naylor family and taking in B. G. Niebuhr and his *Roman History*, Thomas Arnold, and Christian Bunsen (a key figure), by which the Roman experience was mediated for Clough, Arthur Hallam, Charles Eastlake, and William Dyce among others. Philip Collins divagates agreeably and informatively on Victorians abroad, on the American Lecture Circuit, in ' "Agglomerating Dollars with Prodigious Rapidity" ' in Altick[96]; looking at the American agents, the conditions, the pay, and the varied responses to the New World by lecturers including Dickens and Wilde, the article treats the institution rather than individuals.

Karl Kroeber's 'The Evolution of Literary Study, 1883–1983' (*PMLA*) contains little about the nineteenth century (and that primarily in footnotes), but even the account of twentieth-century study, and the resulting spectrum, as indicated by his aphorism 'in 1883 no modern literature was studied, while today only modern literature is studied' is hardly recognizable in Britain. Phyllis Franklin, in the same journal, who writes on 'English Studies: The World of Scholarship in 1883', treats the life and work of George Marsh, an American scholar.

Two general articles involving aspects of the visual imagination appear: 'The Power of Women's Hair in the Victorian Imagination' is illustrated by Elizabeth G. Gitter's detailed survey (*PMLA*) of a rich array of specific paintings, novels, and poems. Because Dickens and Ruskin are the two prose writers in the nineteenth century 'who see the physical world most clearly and who attempt in the greatest detail to elicit and understand its meaning', Brian Rosenberg briefly compares description in two roughly contemporaneous works, *Hard Times* and *The Stones of Venice*, in 'Reading the World: Visual Imagination in Dickens and Ruskin' (*Arnoldian*).

In *PSt* Valerie Purton examines 'The Two Voices' dualism in the prose of Ruskin, Carlyle, Macaulay, and Thackeray in order to contextualize the 'critical commonplace' of Dickens's 'divided style'. Considering specific passages from these writers, she finds a tendency 'to polarise reason and imagination by antithesis in order to repress the disruptive power of imaginative truth'. This is a closely argued and interesting essay which brings welcome breadth and fresh specificity to her expected conclusion: 'stylistic dualism is inevitable in an age in which public certainties conflicted with the increasingly insistent demands of the individual imagination'.

Terry Caesar looks at Victorian parody in '"I Quite Forget What – Say a Daffodilly"' (*ELH*) and, mining Walter Hamilton's anthology, *Parodies of the Works of English and American Authors* (1884–9) and considering individual authors and works, speculates about possible explanations for it.

The first number of *VS* this year comprises articles on the history of science. Robert Yeo's well-written reception study, 'Science and Intellectual Authority in Mid-nineteenth-century Britain' treats Robert Chambers' controversial and anonymous *Vestiges of the Natural History of Creation*. It reviews the reviews such as those by Adam Sedgwick, and usefully analyses aspects of their response, as well as Chambers' responses to their criticism in his *Explanations* (1845) and successive editions of the book, while charting the tensions between the popularizers and the specialists. Dorothy K. Stein's 'Lady Lovelace's Notes: Technical Text and Cultural Context' explores the social and cultural context of Ada (Byron) Lovelace's extensively annotated translation of L. F. Menabrea's report on the Analytical Engine of Charles Babbage, the Victorian originator of computer technology, using unpublished correspondence from the Lovelace–Byron papers. In the same journal Harvey W. Becker analyses the social origins and postgraduate careers of the ten highest wranglers from Cambridge for each of the years from 1830 to 1860. Margaret Schabas examines 'The Worldly Philosophy of William Stanley Jevons', the person who first proposed that economics must be treated mathematically, and David K. van Keuren offers 'Museums and Ideology', which relates Augustus Pitt-Rivers, and the local history and anthropological museums he founded, to social change in later Victorian Britain.

Religious matters occupy two critics: David B. Wilson describes 'A Physicist's Alternative to Materialism' (*VS*) by studying the religious thoughts of George Gabriel Stokes, who advocated what he called 'directionism' which combined ideas from evangelical Christianity, William Paley, and certain critics of Paley. In '"So Careful of the Type?"' (*E&S*) G. B. Tennyson tellingly questions the received view of Victorian typology by removing it from the confines of evangelical sectarianism and observing its wider dispersal in the age, through the Oxford Movement particularly – with its doctrines of Reserve and Analogy – and the poetry of Isaac Williams which embodies them. Tennyson seeks to demonstrate that the Tractarian forms of typology antedate its alleged evangelical forms attributed to Holman Hunt, and to Ruskin whom he shows to have been in contact as an undergraduate with Isaac Williams in the Oxford Society for Promoting the Study of Gothic Architecture. This is an important intervention in current debate on Victorian typology.

(b) Individual Authors

Michael Collie and Angus Fraser's bibliography of George Borrow[104] is the first since T. J. Wise's in 1914, and it aims to provide 'an account of Borrow's entire writing and publishing career', and an emphasis on 'the genesis and evolution' of his works. So, besides including orthodox bibliographical description, entries for each work are prefaced by informative notes, which taken together, constitute an inviting and absorbing narrative about Borrow and the publishing world. Appendixes concern the evolution of Borrow's handwriting,

---

104. *George Borrow. A Bibliographical Study*, ed. by Michael Collie and Angus Fraser. StPB. pp. viii + 233. £22.50.

a tabulation of Murray printings of Borrow's works, and Borrow's income from works published by Murray. The volume is beautifully produced and printed, with pertinent and functional illustrations.

While Fred Kaplan's scholarly biography of Carlyle[105] is dramatically conceived and wears its considerable documentation lightly, it nevertheless makes a successful bid to sit beside Froude's first-hand, if controversial, account of Carlyle, the authority of which has only been realistically diminished by recent evidence (e.g. *YW* 63.345). Kaplan's narrative benefits from its author's distance from its subject and his period; its presentation of the marriage, and the psychology of work and friendships is balanced, unstinting, and astute. It is a biography which exemplifies some of the most characteristic insights and strategies afforded by the late twentieth century; tolerance, with all its problems, is pre-eminent among them.

G. B. Tennyson's *A Carlyle Reader*[106] is ambitious in its inclusiveness and breadth, offering the whole of *Sartor Resartus*, the two essays on history, and *Signs of the Times*, and selections from the letters and, barring 'Chartism', *Cromwell*, and the *Life of John Sterling*, most of the other major works. Unlike the briefer selection from Carlyle's work in Penguin, these are not annotated, but the editor's lively introductory essay, an intelligent selected bibliography, and a helpful chronology aid understanding of what follows.

Carlyle's notion of history interests a number of critics this year. Lowell T. Frye comments briefly on the two early essays on history in 1830 and 1833 and finds 'Chaos and Cosmos' (*VN*) while, in 'History *Writing* in Carlyle's *Past and Present*' (*PSt*), Gordon Hirsch decides that Carlyle recognizes that the order, meaning, and image of self that he strove for in writing narrative 'are fictions not found in one's experience of the flux of events'. History is history *writing*. 'Carlyle as Epic Historian' (Altick[96]) occupies John Clubbe who argues convincingly that Carlyle began to write history prodigiously in 1834, stimulated by his reading of the *Iliad* which influenced significantly all his subsequent historical writing: *The French Revolution* and *Frederick the Great* were written as modern epics and *Past and Present* and *Latter Day Pamphlets* as attempts to redefine the nature of epic. Clubbe himself writes critical discourse imaginatively, and is always a pleasure to read. An article on history involving Carlyle and others appears in *VN*: Linda Dowling's 'Nero and the Aesthetics of Torture' posits a shift in Victorian theories of history from the literary and providentialist history of Carlyle and Arnold to the empirical and antiteleological notions of Theodor Mommsen, E. A. Freeman, and J. B. Bury, by studying Lionel Johnson's essay 'On the Character of Nero' in the midst of the controversy in which Nero's misdeeds are portrayed as a kind of playful aestheticism. De Quincey, Swinburne, and Pater's *Marius* figure in detail as the tradition on which Johnson draws and from which he diverges.

CarlyleN, rather than being primarily a vehicle for news of events and scholarly notes like *RuskinN* or *PaterN*, affords another opportunity for scholars to publish short pieces on Carlyle. Much of this material is an outgrowth of the Duke–Edinburgh edition of the Carlyles' letters. K. J. Fielding provides insight into the 'finds' of an editor in 'Carlyle and Esais Tegner: An

105. *Thomas Carlyle: A Biography*, by Fred Kaplan. CUP. pp. 614. £25.
106. *A Carlyle Reader*, ed. by G. B. Tennyson. CUP. pp. xvi + 497. hb £25, pb £5.95.

Unpublished MS.' in which he prints a summary by Carlyle of Frithiof's saga found among notes and drafts for *Cromwell*. Other unpublished material appears in the newsletter: Owen Dudley Edwards reports on the manuscript of a lecture on Carlyle in 1886 in 'Conan Doyle on Carlyle: A New Edinburgh Manuscript', a lecture which reveals an unlooked-for enthusiasm, and serves to remind us of the high quality of Doyle's criticism of which the lecture on Carlyle is an early example. D. J. Trela publishes a fragmentary 'enconium on aristocratic rule' from the 1850s in 'Carlyle and the Beautiful People'. Fred Kaplan has a wry but interesting piece on 'Carlyle's Marginalia' in novels by George Henry Lewes which were presented to Jane by the author. They show Carlyle reading novels, and his use of marginalia not as art, but as expletive. Two biographical articles by Virginia Surtees and Ian Campbell treat, respectively, Carlyle's visit to Louisa Ashburton's villa in Mentone in 1867 and an unpublished record by John Aitken, Carlyle's nephew, of Carlyle's last visits to Scotland. And in *SSL* Erik Frykman reports on 'Carlyle's Reception and Influence in Sweden' from the late 1880s to the present.

H. Montgomery Hyde's long-standing interest in Wilde bears fruit in his latest biography, of Lord Alfred Douglas[107], whose life after the Wilde trials continued to involve scandal, acrimony, license, litigation, and passion much as it did before 1896. Hyde makes well-documented use of unpublished material in presenting his prickly protagonist's chaotic progress which involves many well-known literary people such as Olive Custance, Robert Ross, and Arthur Ransome, Douglas's interesting stint as editor of *The Academy*, and a succession of legal actions. I can find little evidence to support the author's concluding contention that Douglas's 'conversion to the Roman Catholic faith ... gave his life a stability and a spiritual substance which it had previously lacked'. Unlike Kaplan's study of Carlyle, Hyde's *Life* seems engaged, with lingering traces of enthusiasm which are manifest in this interested final gloss. Hyde knew Douglas; that is one source of difference.

The third biography this year is Ann Thwaite's *Edmund Gosse: A Literary Landscape*[108], a volume which is particularly welcome in the absence of any modern predecessor. Much of what Thwaite unfolds is drawn from unpublished or disparate published sources, and she tackles patiently some of the known cruxes of his life which have emerged from the biographies or affairs of others, such as the question of his role in the T. J. Wise forgeries, his homosexuality, his professional integrity, and the unreliability of his scholarship detailed by John Churton Collins and eventually the entire 1880s press. But such is the amount of material that the author makes an early announcement of her self-imposed limitations: 'I have concentrated on the characters in Gosse's story in whom there is most interest' (lest the text run to more than one volume), and there follow names of close friends of Gosse who are omitted. But what is not said is that even those friendships mentioned are not always treated in satisfying detail, commensurate with their significance in Gosse's life. One of the great achievements of this biography is that it has brought together widely scattered material and perspectives, but its undeniable value is

107. *Lord Alfred Douglas: A Biography*, by H. Montgomery Hyde. Methuen. pp. xvi + 366. £14.95.

108. *Edmund Gosse: A Literary Landscape 1849–1928*, by Ann Thwaite. S&W. pp. viii + 567; illus. £15.

somewhat mitigated by the amount it has by necessity excluded. To do the job fully its successor will have to be two volumes.

One of the men to whom Gosse confessed his sympathy and past familiarity with homosexual love was John Addington Symonds whose memoirs (which mainly concern that subject) Phyllis Grosskurth edits and introduces[109]. Also faced by too much material, she has cut 'roughly one-fifth of the text . . . mainly . . . Symonds's execrable poetry and . . . self-conscious nature descriptions quoted from his own letters', a decision students of autobiography will regret. Nevertheless, Symonds's obsession and fascination with his own sexuality, as a child and adult, in Bristol, at Harrow and Oxford, in London, and on the Continent emerge clearly in one of the relatively few Victorian documents on this subject, a fact that in part motivated Symonds to persevere with it. Symonds writes well, and the narrative is compelling and informative about the man, the educational institutions he attended, Victorian sexuality and homosexuality, and the human condition. It is a rich companion to the myriad Victorian texts and lives whose silence on these matters shouts out.

One of the areas of Gosse's life which Ann Thwaite only briefly covers is the *DNB* and his dealings with its editor, Sidney Lee. Carolyn W. White details the ramifications of Lee's biographies of Edward VII for the *DNB* and for a full-length book in 'The Biographer and Edward VII' (*VS*); she shows that Arthur Davidson's dissatisfaction with the *DNB* Life required the mediation of Arthur Balfour and John Morley and threatened Lee's reputation and that of the *DNB*; and Lee's careful research for the book proved similarly fraught with tensions between professional and official considerations, the same problems Gosse had encountered in his contributions to *DNB* and about which he wrote in his various articles on biography.

The first volume of *The Collected Letters of William Morris*[110], edited by Norman Kelvin and handsomely published by Princeton, has appeared, including letters written between 1848 and 1880. That more than half of the 2400 documents to comprise the edition have not been published before indicates the importance of the project to scholars. Morris writes fluently and openly, and the reader is aided by annotation following each letter which never overwhelms the text. The period covered by Volume 1 takes in Morris's youth, his time at school and Oxford, his poetry and painting, marriage with and estrangement from Jane, the early days of the Firm, his journeys to Iceland, and political activity, but it appears that the editor's full introduction here is the general introduction to the edition. A Morris chronology, a generous subject index, and an index of correspondents complete the volume.

News from Nowhere is considered from contrasting perspectives by two critics: in '*News from Nowhere*: Utopia, Arcadia, or Elysium?' (*JPRS*) Roger Lewis considers the genre of the work and concludes that it is an idyll, while in *ELH*'s 'Anarchism and Utopia' Michael Holzman considers its political aspects by examining its serialization in *Commonweal*, the Socialist newspaper, and relating it usefully to a concurrent debate on anarchism appearing there. Three versions of 'Art and Labour' and press reports are studied by

109. *The Memoirs of John Addington Symonds*, by J. A. Symonds, ed. by Phyllis Grosskurth. Hutchinson. pp. 319. £14.95.
110. *The Collected Letters of William Morris*. Vol. I: *1848–1880*, ed. by Norman Kelvin. Princeton. pp. lxiv + 626. $55.

Alan Bacon in *YULG* to determine the character of the different audience for each version of the lecture.

Some sixteen texts from Morris's socialist prose are collected and edited by A. L. Morton for a new edition of *Political Writings of William Morris* (1973)[111] which has been expanded to include reviews of More's *Utopia* and Edward Bellamy's *Looking Backward* alongside lectures such as 'The Lesser Arts', 'Art Under Plutocracy', 'London in a State of Siege', and 'Art and Socialism'. A Headnote which is both bibliographical and polemical precedes each lecture.

JWMS continues to publish scholarly and memorial articles, and information of such diversity, reflecting Morris's activity and achievement, that it touches on many aspects of the period – architecture, poetry, design, prose romance, politics, and journalism. Carolyn P. Collette informatively compares Morris's ideas with those of Young England forty years before, with attention to *Sybil* and John Manners's *A Plea for National Holydays* (1843). Despite an off-putting title – 'Wallpaper and propaganda' – Teresa Newman comments critically, in a lively article, on the ICA exhibition 'William Morris Today' which she created, and the Pre-Raphaelite show at the Tate Gallery. *The Journal* also publishes posthumously a widely ranging, if short, article on Morris's writing by Geoffrey Tillotson which is characteristically both precise and general. Peter Faulkner edited it and brought it to light.

Hiroko Hagiwara's *Walter Pater and his Circle*[112] is written in Japanese; a detailed review of its contents appears in *PaterN* (No. 15) which also publishes three notes, as well as annotated bibliography and news; in 'A Pater Concordance' Ian Small explains some of the implications for Paterians of work he has been doing on *Marius* with the Kurzweil Data Entry Machine; in 'Walter Pater and the Fine Art of Murder' Paul Barolsky identifies an allusion to Pater's description of Mona Lisa in Raymond Chandler's *The High Window*, and Richard Dellamora reports on work-in-progress on Pater, sexual politics, and tradition.

Four hitherto unknown letters from Pater included in Hagiwara's book are annotated by Hagiwara in an article in English in *Daito Bunka Review 1983*: 'Walter Pater and Mark-André Raffalovich' also includes a biography of Raffalovich and an assessment of Pater's view of him.

Ian Small's computer work on literary texts noted in *PaterN* is explained in full in *PSt*. In 'Computational Stylistics and the Construction of Literary Readings: Work in Progress' Small illustrates the use of computer-aided stylistic analysis in a comparison of two accounts of Pater's (alleged) vocabulary by two critics with the evidence derived from the computer. He concludes that the critical practice of identifying an author's personal vocabulary or 'restricted lexis' is 'frequently a projection onto a text of a set of prior critical presuppositions or values' or worse.

The second number of *ELT* comprises work on *Marius the Epicurean*. In 'Stopping the Press in *Marius*' Bernard Richards launches a robust, if wry attack on the novel as a novel and as 'a caricature of the standard historical novel'. Richards's generic criteria for the novel and (his distaste for) the

---

111. *Political Writings of William Morris*, ed. by A. L. Morton. L&W. pp. 259. £7.50.
112. *Walter Pater and his Circle*, by Hiroko Hagiwara. Yushodo, Tokyo. pp. vii + 313; illus. Y 3200. (In Japanese, with manuscript material in English.)

historical novel are self-avowedly those of Henry James. Altogether more appreciative is Ian Small's argument in 'The "Fictional" and the "Real" in *Marius*' that Pater's fiction is peculiar to Pater, and only 'partly Victorian and partly modernist', containing as it does both fictive and serious utterances, and combinations of both sorts of statement. Intent on this, it only touches on Pater's techniques of realism attaching to depiction of the historical characters which are alleged 'simple notions of representation found in the novels of his contemporaries'.

Billie Inman writes on 'The Emergence of Pater's *Marius* Mentality'. In a detailed argument she shows that *Marius* represents Pater's thinking at a time before he wrote it; Pater's 'crucial self-appraisal' took place in 1874–5, prompted by his reading of Merimée, and of Stendhal who influenced his notion of epicureanism, and by his experience of censure by the clergy for the 'anti-Christian' ideas in *The Renaissance*. Essays written in 1875, 'The Myth of Demeter and Persephone', 'A Study of Dionysus', and his review of J. A. Symonds's *Age of the Despots* are shown to express 'the *Marius* mentality'.

Franklin Court examines and catalogues reviews of *Marius* in American and British periodicals in 'The Critical Reception of Pater's *Marius*', and attributes the diversity of the reviews to the 'personal motives' of their authors, though he ends by arguing that the reviews provide us with an opportunity to view the novel 'within the "living" world of late nineteenth-century literary production'. Two short special collections reports complete the number, with Bernard Richards commenting on those in Oxford, and Elizabeth Ann Falsy on library holdings at Harvard.

Critics have articles on Pater's sources and influences, and his epistemology. In *N&Q* Warwick Gould locates in Flaubert's *La Tentation de Saint Antoine* an important stylistic source which has been overlooked by editors for Pater's well-known description of the Mona Lisa in 'Lionardo' and Wilde's parody of it in *The Picture of Dorian Gray*, and in 'Pater, Moore and the Fatal Book' (*PSt*) Linda Dowling examines the influence of George Moore's *Confessions of a Young Man* (March 1888) on 'Style' (December 1888). Dowling argues that in 'Style' Pater rewrote the version of Pater and *Marius* presented in the *Confessions*: Pater 'transforms Moore's notion of "sense-judgment" or "sensualism" in literature into the idea of "soul in style"' and 'makes Marius's aggressive appropriation of religious language . . . yield up its antinomian heat and become a mild invocation of "theological interests"'. At the end of this interesting article, the author contemplates 'what exactly is sexual about literary style' and the sexual element of Pater's style, its linguistic anxiety, its sense of 'illicit textual pleasure'. In *Criticism*'s ' "Definite History and Dogmatic Interpretation" ' Gerald Monsman writes on the 'White-nights' chapter of *Marius* and shows that 'Pater's originality is constituted by his realization that meaning always eludes any final form', that the dream text is interpreted by Pater by offering other dreams as explanation. I have not seen Paul Barolsky's 'Walter Pater and Bernard Berenson' in *New Criterion* or Mary R. Anderson's 'Walter Pater and the Self' in *Art in a Desacralized World* (UPA).

J. L. Bradley introduces, selects, and annotates nineteenth-century reviews of Ruskin's work in *Ruskin: The Critical Heritage*[113]. As is common

113. *Ruskin: The Critical Heritage*, by J. L. Bradley. RKP. pp. 319. £18.95.

by now, the editor's long introduction is a reception study, but Bradley's is distinguished by a welcome recognition that research tools such as the *Wellesley Index* signal a relatively new ingredient in reception study – the periodicals in which reviews appeared – and his essay charts both editorial practices and points of view of the periodical press. His selections pertain to individual works up to *Lectures on Art* (1870) and to more general articles on the place of Ruskin and his work from 1872 to 1900. Bradley's volume is valuable for readers of Ruskin and the Victorian periodicals.

Bradley's complaint about the low number of editions of Ruskin's 'enduring works' in print is echoed by Kristine Ottesen Garrigan who has an intelligent review-article in *VS*; in 'Approaching the Maze: Recent Writings on John Ruskin' she appends a wistful observation that the number of critical books in print *on* Ruskin is accompanied by a serious dearth of books *by* Ruskin.

P. D. Anthony studies Ruskin's social criticism and theory in *John Ruskin's Labour*[114], a book in which it is argued that Ruskin's social criticism and work on art and architecture are closely related, and that Morris's critique of capitalism is rooted not in Marx but 'almost entirely' in Ruskin. The author's interest in Ruskin includes the use of Ruskin's 'alternative to our present social relationships' to 'measure our performance within a social and economic structure which has become . . . an iron cage', and throughout the polemic he strives to rescue Ruskin from alleged impurities and detractors, and to claim him for a tradition of spiritual regeneration to which the thought of such disparate figures such as Morris, G. K. Chesterton and Hilaire Belloc, and G. D. H. Cole and guild socialism belongs.

James Dearden has two articles in journals published by libraries: in *HLB* he publishes six uncollected letters written by Ruskin to Bernard Quaritch between 1873 and 1884 on the subject of manuscripts, books, and drawings sold by Quaritch, and in 'John Ruskin and Illuminated Addresses' (*BJR*) he brings to our attention an 1899 laudatory illuminated 'National Address' from the joint Ruskin Societies to Ruskin, and elaborates on the tradition of addresses in general. The creator of the elaborate decoration was Albert Pilley of Sheffield, and the designer William White, then curator of Sheffield's Ruskin Museum, whose troubled history the author supplies.

RuskinN 1983 (which appeared late in 1984), edited by James Dearden, contains news of Ruskin research scholarships, the opening of a Ruskin Gallery in Sheffield and of a Ruskin library in Tokyo, reviews of art exhibitions, a record of Ruskin in the sale rooms, a list of recent books and articles, a number of book reviews, and various other short but interesting notes and news items.

Jeffrey L. Spear, in 'Ruskin's Italy' (*BIS*), explores to good purpose the approaches to Italy suggested by Ruskin's tutors and in particular the importance of the illustrated editions of Samuel Rogers's *Italy* (1830), which contained many Turner vignettes, and *Poems*. Spear's placing of Ruskin's interest in Italy in context is a welcome adjunct to other biographical accounts, by Jeanne Clegg for example (*YW* 62.339).

114. *John Ruskin's Labour. A Study of Ruskin's Social Theory*, by P. D. Anthony. CUP. pp. viii + 220. £20.

Robert Secor offers an interesting perspective on Ruskin's biography, his experience and view of children. In 'John Ruskin and the Summer of 1873', an article in two parts in *JPRS*, Secor includes unpublished correspondence between Ruskin and Alfred and Margaret Hunt whose daughters, Venice (Ruskin's godchild) and Violet, were viewed in part as compensatory for Rose la Touche's absence, coldness, and eventually, death.

Unusually, Leslie Stephen preoccupies two critics this year. In a suggestive piece on 'Elegy in *To the Lighthouse*' in *EIC*, Gillian Beer compares Stephen's evaluation of David Hume, as expressed in *History of English Thought in the Eighteenth Century*, with the presence of Hume and ideas associated with him in *To the Lighthouse*, and W. A. Trotter's 'Richardson and the "new lights": "Clarissa" among Victorians' (*English*) has at its heart a comparison of Leslie Stephen's comments and essay on Richardson in the 1870s with the views of Hazlitt and Anna Barbauld, editor of Richardson's correspondence in 1804, critics whose moral orientation he reflects; these are distinguished from George Eliot who, according to Trotter, 'grounded her estimation of Richardson in central artistic concerns'.

Work on Wilde includes two biographical articles and one on *De Profundis*. In *Criticism* Regina Gagnier offers a convincing materialist reading of Wilde's autobiography in '*De Profundis* as *Epistola: in Carcere et Vinculis*'; she views the letter as prison writing – an 'imaginative act of resistance against insanity and prison space and time' – rather than as fiction or the construct of a poseur. 'Oscar at Oxford' is a fluent and lively critical biography in miniature by Richard Ellmann which appears in *NYRB* (29 March), and George Sims is informative on aspects of Wilde's biography and literary remains in a piece on Vyvyan Holland, 'Son of Oscar Wilde' in *ABMR*.

Single essays on individual authors include Martha S. Vogeler's full and informed review-article in *VPR* on 'Frederic Harrison and the Higher Journalism', John Walker's 'Cunninghame Graham and the Critics: A Reappraisal' in *SSL* which refers to twentieth-century commentary, and an intelligent and wide-ranging review-article by Isobel Murray on 'John Gray: The Person and the Work in Question' in *DUJ*. D. J. Trela publishes two letters of 1844 in *N&Q*, one from Edward Fitzgerald to Carlyle, giving a lead to some Cromwell autograph letters, and Carlyle's reply, both of which do not appear in the recent edition of Fitzgerald's *Letters* (*YW* 61.327), and in 'Hutton Visits Arnold's Monastery of the Grande Chartreuse' (*Arnoldian*) Robert H. Tener reprints and annotates a travel letter by Hutton published in the *Spectator* in 1868 which indicates the extent to which Hutton's memory was saturated with Arnold's verse. In *Lib* Mark Greenberg reveals how in 1851 William Michael and Dante Gabriel Rossetti contributed to a Blake revival by inviting William Bell Scott to illustrate Blake's poems from a notebook of Blake's they had purchased, and how they constructed their own Victorian Blake by copying out extracts from the poems and emending them. Lastly, Eneas Sweetland Dallas's *The Gay Science* is rediscovered by Jenny Taylor in '*The Gay Science*: The "Hidden Soul" of Victorian Criticism' (*L&H*). Noting that the book is outside the mainstream of literary criticism, Taylor surveys its repression, its emphasis on pleasure in art, and its explanation of the role of the unconscious which Dallas calls 'the hidden soul', and relates Dallas's notions to those of some contemporaries such as

Freud, Lewes, Blair, Spencer, Morris, and Ruskin. She concludes that *The Gay Science* is a 'crucial text' for cultural historians.

(c) Periodicals and the History of Publishing
   British Literary Magazines: The Victorian and Edwardian Age, 1837–1913[115] is the third of a four-part reference guide to literary magazines from 1698 to 1984. This volume covers ninety titles, with an essay, a list of information-sources, and a publication history for each. A host of scholars have contributed entries. There are three appendixes with brief paragraphs about journals in categories not normally included in Sullivan's definition of literary magazines – foreign reviews, comic journals, and religious magazines with literary contents, although a few of the journals listed here are included in the main entries of this volume or the others. These lists are useful in themselves and enhance the number of journals covered by the volume; they also indicate what the main entries omit. Two problems stand out: What constitutes a literary magazine among Victorian periodicals when not one confined itself to the specialized notion of 'literary' prevalent today? What are the principles of selection from among a total number which is prohibitive? The latter question is addressed in a brief, mainly technical preface by the editor who explains, with a number of qualifications, how the selection of 'representative' periodicals was made. The former question is never consciously put, although the assumptions behind such a definition seriously affect how the content is treated by scholars. In his more leisured introduction, which is mainly a descriptive survey, Christopher Kent raises the question immediately if limply: 'The greater proportion of these [Victorian periodicals] would not be judged literary by most definitions, but one is still left with an astonishing number that carried at least some reviews, reflective prose, poetry, or fiction.' Then it is dropped. But there is no question that this volume is welcome, for it brings together basic information about a far greater number of periodicals than *Wellesley* covers, gives some guidelines on information sources (including some undetailed locations), and is bound to introduce even the experienced reader of Victorian periodicals to unfamiliar journals, or facts about them.
   Two books concern periodical journalism without taking it as a principal subject. Charles Reid's *The Music Monster*[116] is the biography of a music critic of *The Times* by a former music critic of the *Observer*, though the periodicals and newspapers where James William Davison published his influential and often vituperative criticism (some of it is excerpted here) do not substantially figure in Reid's book, which is organized around musical matters such as Davison's reviews of a Wagner season. Still, there is quite a lot here for the devotee of Victorian periodicals, not least the combination of power and whimsicality in a Victorian critic. J. Kimberley Roberts's *Ernest Rhys*[117] includes a section on Rhys's editorial activities, and his involvement with *The Hampstead Annual* between 1897 and 1906.

115. *British Literary Magazines: The Victorian and Edwardian Age, 1837–1913*, ed. by Alvin Sullivan. Historical Guides to the World's Periodicals and Newspapers. Greenwood/Westport. pp. xxvi + 560. £72.50.
   116. *The Music Monster: A Biography of James William Davison, Music Critic of 'The Times' of London, 1846–78, With Excerpts from his Critical Writings*, by Charles Reid. Quartet. pp. 243. £11.95.
   117. *Ernest Rhys*, by J. Kimberley Roberts. UWales (1983). pp. 84. pb £6.25.

In *VPR* Diana Dixon provides a bibliography of 'The Provincial Press: A Decade of Writings, 1972–1981' and in an introduction a short survey of recent developments in the field; in the same journal Jerold J. Savory introduces and lists the holdings in 'An Uncommon Comic Collection: Humorous [British and American] Victorian Periodicals in the Newberry Library'. Jean H. Slingerland, reporting on the future of the *Wellesley Index* (*VPR*), expects to see Volumes IV and V in print by the late 1980s.

Two critics stress the effect of context on content. In the course of an absorbing article in *VN* on Elizabeth Sewell and 'the genrification of Victorian published opinion', Patrick Scott tellingly shows that the particular periodical context of various articles by Sewell 'probably dictated the openness or dogmatism' of the discussions within them; Monica Correa Fryckstedt's 'New Sources on Geraldine Jewsbury and the Women Question' (*RS*) redirects the limelight from Jewsbury's popular mid-century fiction to twenty-one reviews of feminist books in the *Athenaeum*, which Fryckstedt specifies at the end of the article. That some feminist books and criticism did appear is established, and Fryckstedt shows that significant differences in position exist between the unconventional heroines in Jewsbury's novels and the more historically harmonious and vacillating notions found in the anonymous reviews, which comment on the demographic preponderance of men in the period, education of women, women's right to work, and the legal status of women. While the material is interesting, the commentary is raw.

Several items in *VPR* pertain to religion or sectarian periodicals. Thomas Costa briefly surveys the career of a spiritualist clergyman in 'Charles M. Davies [1828–1910]: The Broad Churchman as Journalist', Maurice Milne writes conclusively on the vexed question of J. G. Lockhart's motives in assigning the *Quarterly Review* response to the Catholic question to Robert Southey, 'a firm anti-Catholic'; that Lockhart shared Southey's opinion is confirmed by a new reading of correspondence which removes discrepancies between it and Lockhart's anti-Catholic article on Blanco White in *Blackwood's* in 1825 by referring them to another review by Lockhart. Thus Lockhart's authorship of the Blanco White article is confirmed, and the query in *Wellesley* III removed. Josef L. Altholz has located a marked file of *The Church Quarterly Review* in the Institute of Historical Research and by combining it with other sources offers a list of attributions for articles appearing between 1875 and 1900 which 'reads like a virtual Who's Who of the late Victorian High Church'. The same critic is also informative about the origins of *Crockford's Clerical Directory* which he describes as 'the fourth-generation descendant of a series of unrelated periodicals, an incidental by-product of the publishing empire of the greatest entrepreneur of "class" journalism, Edward William Cox' (see *YW* 63.353).

The activities of Edward Lloyd, author in 1837 of a plagiarism of *Pickwick Papers* called *The Penny Pickwick* which launched his diverse career in publishing popular fiction (including other plagiarisms), periodicals, and newspapers, are P. R. Hoggart's subject in 'The Father of the Cheap Press' in *The Dickensian*. *Lloyd's Weekly Newspaper*, 1842–1902 (which became such an institution among the working class that it is thought to have been the inspiration for Marie Lloyd taking her particular stage name), Douglas Jerrold who edited it from 1852, and Lloyd's *Daily Chronicle* figure in this short pithy article which is squarely about Lloyd rather than any direct Dickens connection.

In 'James Greenwood's London: A Precursor of Charles Booth' (*VPR*) B. I. Diamond and J. O. Baylen examine the background to research into the state of London in 1866 and after, which appeared in *The Pall Mall Gazette* and *The Daily Telegraph*. In 'Henry Mayhew and the Undiscovered Country of the Poor' (*SR*) George Woodcock traces Mayhew's career, which began with the founding of a satirical illustrated weekly called *Figaro in London* and then *Punch*, and included stints as a dramatist and amateur actor, a comic novelist, and a bankrupt before he wrote the *Illustrated London News* piece on Jacob's Island and *London Labour and the London Poor*. He compares Mayhew's project and discourse with Orwell's, and with Turgenev's use of detail and revelation in his description of serfs in *A Sportsman's Sketches*.

Two authors in *JWMS* discuss Morris and the socialist press. In 'William Morris and the contemporary socialist press' Helen Irving examines the references to Morris by socialist journalists – 'the manner in which Morris was seen and represented' – in order to further understanding of the reception and evolution of his socialism. The references by the press are revealing. Adam Buick treats Morris's early revolutionary socialism when he belonged to the Socialist League (1884–90), opposed parliamentary activity, and wrote for *Commonweal*. The piece is unexceptionable but for some reason does not engage with Meier (*YW* 59.305).

A note on the circumstances of *The Day* by Robert H. Tener (*VPR*) attempts to dissociate Richard Holt Hutton from this short-lived newspaper of 1867, but while he finds that the proprietor was James rather than Richard Hutton he does not satisfactorily explain where two able critics such as Alan Lee and Stephen Koss found their evidence which mentions specific figures and distributors associated with the venture.

Both of the weighty pieces in *VPR* this year treat periodicals for the mass audience. Utilizing content analysis, Scott Bennett contributes a lucid and provocative estimate of 'The Editorial Character and Readership of *The Penny Magazine*' (1832–45), the first mass-market periodical published in Britain. In 'Magazines of Popular Progress and the Artisans', a substantial article, Brian E. Maidment describes and analyses a genre of periodicals typified by *Howitt's Journal of Literature and Popular Progress* and *The People's Journal*, which flourished in the period of the late 1840s and early 1850s. Maidment is briefly concerned with the theoretical problem of defining genres of periodicals, but he goes on to a description of this genre as an ideological construct characterized by the possibility of cultural negotiation between social and economic groups, a quality evident in the middle- and working-class origins of the contributors and readers. Maidment is openly exploratory and tentative, and raises a number of very interesting problems.

In *ABMR* William Baker's piece on *Chamber's London Journal* (1841–3), 'Reynolds Vs. Dickens', bristles with facts or quotations in every sentence of the introduction before it reaches its subject, an ostensibly anonymous and vitriolic attack on the initial number of *Martin Chuzzlewit*. Baker attributes the review to G. W. M. Reynolds who edited the journal from January to October 1843. A checklist of Reynolds's seventy-three contributions to the journal is appended. Two pieces in *ABMR* were overlooked last year: George Sims writes generally in two instalments on 'Leonard Smithers. A Publisher of the 1890s', and John Turner interestingly describes some of the fine books printed on 'The Daniel Press of Oxford'. In the same journal's 'Harriet Martineau of the Daily News' Gaby Weiner writes generally about Martineau, despite the article's title.

Joel S. Schwartz offers a curious and unfocused piece in *VPR* which treats Alfred Russel Wallace's ill-informed attribution of a poem published in the *Fortnightly* in February 1904 to Poe; quoting extensively from correspondence between Wallace and Ernest Marriott, a Manchester librarian, Schwartz shows that Wallace persisted in his attribution even after he was informed in the British press of the true author of 'Leonainie', James Whitcomb Riley, a fact long known in America. Schwartz's article is more engaged in plot than analysis, and lacks any serious contemplation of the periodicals it mentions although there is ample scope here for commentary on the vital and ineradicable life of literary hoaxes, and the odd lack of communication between American and British critics (is this found elsewhere in the period?) as well as on the press.

In 'Theatre Critics in Late Victorian and Edwardian Periodicals' (*VPR*) Tracy C. Davis provides a supplementary list to Christopher Kent's 'Preliminary List' (1980).

(d) Visual Arts

Bernard Denvir's *The Early Nineteenth Century: Art, Design and Society, 1789–1852*[118] is Volume 3 of Longman's series, A Documentary History of Taste. It is a 'reader', that is an anthology of short excerpts annotated and selected so as to survey a field which is here divided into sections on the picturesque and the past; improving public taste; the world of the artist; patronage, public and private; and art, design and the machine. An index consisting of short biographies of the authors of the excerpts is included, but the emphasis here is not on the authors but on their commentary. Denvir has assembled a lot of revealing contemporary material, on art student life, for example, and on the prices of pigments, the problems of public statuary, and colour in architecture. It is ripe for dipping into, as well as for study.

Jeremy Maas's book which documents *The Victorian Art World in Photographs*[119] derives from the author's collection of photographic *cartes-de-visite* and early portrait photographs of nearly all the celebrated people of Victorian art. Each photograph is accompanied by a short biography of the subject, a description of the photographic process and the photograph, and a paragraph or two from a contemporary source about the sitter. The artists are grouped into chapters by the kind of art they practised, such as landscape and narrative painters, the Pre-Raphaelites, models, illustrators, patrons, dealers, sculptors, engravers, literary associates *et al.*, and each section has a generous explanatory headnote. This book, which is full of memorable quotations and images (settings as well as faces and figures), is something of a feast of

118. *The Early Nineteenth Century: Art, Design and Society 1789–1852*, ed. by Bernard Denvir. Longman. pp. xi + 316. pb £6.95.
119. *The Victorian Art World in Photographs*, by Jeremy Maas. B&J. pp. 224. £20.

Victoriana, and Maas prefaces his material with an informal, informative, and enthusiastic introduction.

The visual dimension of the Pre-Raphaelite movement is documented and celebrated by the catalogue[120] for the Tate Gallery's exhibition of Pre-Raphaelite art which is written by various experts and edited by Leslie Parris. It is divided into chronological sections, with a last part for drawings and watercolours; generous narratives attach to each work, all of which are illustrated, some with colour plates. Preceding the chronological sections are biographical notes for the twenty-nine artists exhibited, and an introduction by Alan Bowness. This catalogue brings together a great range of information about Pre-Raphaelitism and constitutes a standard reference source already, alongside William Fredeman's.

JPRS publishes a number of pieces associated with Pre-Raphaelite art. In 'A Pagoda in Knightsbridge' Elizabeth Phillips has gathered information about the Chinese Gallery (1842–55) in Knightsbridge where the first Pre-Raphaelite painting was exhibited in London. Adeline R. Tintner shows that Henry James's story, 'The Birthplace' (1903), is informed by two paintings of Abraham Solomon, brother of the Pre-Raphaelite painter, Simeon, whose treatment of themes of the Romantic poets is annotated by Steven Kolsteren. It is Jenny R. Elkan's contention that Ford Madox Brown's documentation of his own picture, *Chaucer at the Court of Edward III*, tells only half the story and she attempts to highlight its symbolism, typological and personal, which remains alongside its acclaimed realism. Two other Pre-Raphaelite painters, Rossetti and Burne-Jones, figure in Barbara Munson Goff's thoughtful piece on the influence of Dante's *La Vita Nuova* on the Beatrices (the women) in their paintings. Edward Lear's association with the PRB is limned by Ann C. Colley in 'Edward Lear and Thomas Seddon: The Paradox of Inquiry', which looks at the moment of Seddon's death and its effect on the Brotherhood, an unfamiliar subject which involves unpublished material.

Before turning to his announced subject of images of Rome in Victorian painting, George P. Landow in *BIS* runs through exempla of 'Victorianized Romans' in Bulwer, George Eliot, Robert Browning, Swinburne, and Macaulay; he settles on Alma-Tadema whose realism and detail, like that of Poynter and Millais, tended to 'produce singularly unheroic views of ancient greatness' but finally turns to Swinburne's preoccupation with the spiritual problems, ennui, and despair of Roman decadence. Cumulatively, Landow's survey is suggestive and useful, if mistitled.

(e) Social History

Michael Bentley's *Politics Without Democracy: 1815–1914*[121] is a well-researched, knowledgeable, and well-written political history of the period, with full documentation, and a thorough and meticulous bibliography. In lively and informal prose, the narrative is divided into sections, pressure from without and pressure from within, and the personal stamp of the author's style and notion of history is apparent.

120. *The Pre-Raphaelites*, ed. by Leslie Parris. Tate Gallery/Penguin. pp. 312. hb £25, pb £10.95.

121. *Politics Without Democracy, 1815–1914*, by Michael Bentley. The Fontana History of England, ed. by G. R. Elton. Fontana. pp. 446. pb £4.50.

Town, City, and Nation: England 1850–1914[122] by P. J. Waller is the work of an urban historian, and contains chapters on London, the manufacturing towns, country towns, and central, local, and municipal government. It is drier, more ponderous, and less experienced and provocative than Bentley's book, but provides a useful overview of a subject which Dyos and Wolff's *The Victorian City* (1973) treats more evocatively if unevenly.

Two volumes address themselves to aspects of class. Paul Adelman's *Victorian Radicalism*[123] looks at the middle-class experience between 1830 and 1914. Aimed at student readers, it treats radicals such as James Mill, Richard Cobden, John Bright, Henry Ashworth, John Morley, and Chamberlain. In a chapter on 'Intellectual Radicals and Democracy' about J. S. Mill, there is an extended and interesting discussion of *Essays in Reform* (1867), a collection directed against Robert Lowe's antireform and antidemocratic position. Takao Matsumura designates his labour artisans as 'the Labour aristocracy' (a concept debated by historians) in a book[124] about the Victorian flint glass makers, 1850–80, which originates in the rediscovery of a run of the *Flint Glass Makers Magazine* (1851–97). This monograph gives a full picture of an industry ('in particular the relay system prevented the glass maker from getting a full night's sleep'), but three out of the five sections may interest readers of Victorian literature particularly, those on the work situation, the development of their union, and the strike and lockout in 1858–9.

In *HW* Mick Reed seeks to establish 'The Peasantry of Nineteenth Century England – a Neglected Class', arguing that small farmers were more common than historians usually believe, and that they played an important social and economic role. Although the article draws on evidence from the south-east of England, it may interest readers of Hardy.

In Cambridge English Prose Texts, volumes devoted to substantial selections from non-fictional prose, CUP have devised a valuable series for teaching purposes – provided that the price of the paperbacks remains within reach of students. Two volumes of nineteenth-century material have appeared, *Science and Religion in the Nineteenth Century*[125] edited by Tess Cosslett, and *The Evangelical and Oxford Movements*[126] edited by Elisabeth Jay. Cosslett's selection includes nine excerpts (each of which *is* substantial) from William Paley, Robert Chambers, Darwin, Leonard Huxley, John Tyndall, Hugh Miller (a geologist), Charles Goodwin (a contributor to *Essays and Reviews*), and Frederick Temple; each has an explanatory headnote and annotation, and the developments and myriad controversies are clearly and intelligently delineated in the introduction. Jay's volume contains thirteen extracts from eight authors, among them Francis Close, Isaac Williams,

122. *Town, City, and Nation: England 1850–1914*, by P. J. Waller. OUP. pp. xii + 339. hb £12.50, pb £4.95.

123. *Victorian Radicalism: The Middle-class Experience*, by Paul Adelman. Longman. pp. vii + 172. pb £4.95.

124. *The Labour Aristocracy Revisited: The Victorian Flint Glass Makers 1850–80*, by Takao Matsumura. ManU. pp. x + 196. £15.

125. *Science and Religion in the Nineteenth Century*, ed. by Tess Cosslett. Cambridge English Prose Texts. CUP. pp. vi + 249. hb £22.50, pb £7.95.

126. *The Evangelical and Oxford Movements*, ed. by Elisabeth Jay. Cambridge English Prose Texts. CUP. pp. x + 219. hb £18.50, pb £6.95.

Keble, Pusey, and Newman; the introductory essay attempts to probe the implications of Evangelicism and Tractarianism as well as to describe them. Both of these volumes provide good places to start understanding the period.

Nicolaas A. Rupke's *The Great Chain of History*[127] concerns William Buckland, the Anglican cleric who wrote a Bridgewater Treatise on Geology and Mineralogy in 1836, and the English school of geology in the 1820s and 1830s. In addition to providing a history of the school, Rupke discusses the geology of the school as an institutionalized subject, which both took its character from Oxbridge and instigated reform in the teaching of science. Rupke's monograph successfully combines technical material with cultural history.

Two authors have written social histories of education. One, A. J. Engel's *From Clergyman to Don*[128] treats reform at Oxford from the perspective of the rise of the academic profession in the nineteenth century, and the other, John Chandos's *Boys Together: English Public Schools 1800–1864*[129], examines the unreformed English public schools. Chandos provides a superb view of the public-school world and experience of many well-known male Victorians, a world valued by its inmates at the time and cherished afterwards, with its hideous rule and practices sedulously kept from public view. Among the many unpublished sources he draws on concerning school life at Eton, Harrow, Rugby, Westminster, Winchester, Shrewsbury, and Charterhouse, is material that has recently surfaced: J. A. Symonds's autobiography, concerning the forced resignation of Charles Vaughan, the brilliant Master of Harrow, and A. C. Benson's diary, also recently reviewed here. Anyone involved in study of the literature and the history of the period will find that *Boys Together* offers an excellent and well-written account of primal formative experience for a few thousand of the upper and middle classes.

From Clergyman to Don focuses on transformation of the Oxford don from clerical gentleman to a secular profession between 1850 and 1914, although statistics from the earlier period and an introductory section are used to reveal the degree of later change. Engel draws on a prodigious range of manuscript, pamphlet, and periodical material for a competent account of the rise of the tutors, the three government commissions on university reform, the ambivalence about research, and the emergence of an academic profession. In a chapter entitled 'The Agricultural Depression' there is an abbreviated explanation of the establishment of English as part of the debate concerning the desirability of specialisms. Engel's narrative keeps entirely to Oxford and, with the exception of the introduction, references to parallel developments at Cambridge (as described in Sheldon Rothblatt's *Revolution of the Dons* and elsewhere) are few. That aside, Engel's account is welcome, valuable, and well-documented.

127. *The Great Chain of History: William Buckland and the English School of Geology 1814–1849*, by Nicolaas A. Rupke. OUP. pp. xii + 322. £22.50.

128. *From Clergyman to Don. The Rise of the Academic Profession in Nineteenth-Century Oxford*, by A. J. Engel. OUP. pp. 302. £22.50.

129. *Boys Together: English Public Schools 1800–1864*, by John Chandos. Hutchinson. pp. 412. £15.

4. Drama

Dion Boucicault's *London Assurance*, produced in 1841 when he was only twenty-one, now appears in a fully annotated edition – its first ever – prepared by James L. Smith for the New Mermaids[130]. After outlining the dramatist's life and work, he disentangles the complex evolution of *London Assurance* before critically assessing it, its stage history, and text in a succinct, informative style which also characterizes the notes underneath the text. Pertinent extracts from the dramatist's own writings and newspaper reviews of the day round off a handy and inexpensive volume. Those keen to explore Boucicault's dramas further will welcome Peter Thomson's rich offering of five more in the British and American Playwrights series, *Plays by Dion Boucicault: 'Used Up', 'Old Heads and Young Hearts', 'Jessie Brown', 'The Octoroon', 'The Shaughraun'*[131]. This illustrates his mastery of both comic and melodramatic forms through a mixture of familiar with less accessible titles such as *Used Up* and *Jessie Brown*, here reprinted for the first time this century. In addition to a biographical record, list of author's works, and other useful appendixes standard to the series, Thomson provides a highly readable account of Boucicault's life and output. Full of insight and stimulating judgements, it whets the appetite for the plays that follow, in the best editorial tradition. In contrast to his general editor's essentially critical approach, Jim Davis adopts a scholarly line in his introduction to *Plays by H. J. Byron: 'The Babes in the Wood', 'The Lancashire Lass', 'Our Boys', 'The Gaiety Gulliver'*[132]. This contains much useful information which sets H. J. Byron's talents for melodrama, sentimental comedy, and burlesque in the context of his times, albeit sometimes at the expense of readability. In the same series, *Plays by Augustin Daly: 'A Flash of Lightning', 'Horizon', 'Love on Crutches'* also receives scholarly treatment from Don B. Wilmeth and Rosemary Cullen[133]. They present a nicely rounded account of Daly's activities as manager, *régisseur*, trainer of actors, adapter, and dramatist. Although their critical appreciation of his plays seems overreliant upon the pronouncements of others, this does not seriously detract from the value of their survey as a whole.

G.B.S. gains attention at last from his analyst Richard F. Dietrich, who sees in 'Shavian Psychology' (*ABSS*) the notions of Realist, Idealist, and Philistine as primarily psychological categories that predate those of Freud and Jung. He explores the principles at work in Shaw's studies of Ibsen, Wagner, *The Sanity of Art*, and also in plays such as *Mrs Warren's Profession*, which hinges on Vivie's inner conflict as she exchanges her Idealist self for a Realist self.

130. *London Assurance*, by Dion Boucicault, ed. by James L. Smith. NMer. Black. pp. xlviii + 137; 3 illus. pb £3.95.

131. *Plays by Dion Boucicault: 'Used Up', 'Old Heads and Young Hearts', 'Jessie Brown', 'The Octoroon', 'The Shaughraun'*, ed. by Peter Thomson. BAP. CUP. pp. xii + 238; 6 illus. hb £24, pb £8.95.

132. *Plays by H. J. Byron: 'The Babes in the Wood', 'The Lancashire Lass', 'Our Boys', 'The Gaiety Gulliver'*, ed. by Jim Davis. BAP. CUP. pp. xii + 222; 6 illus. hb £22.50, pb £7.95.

133. *Plays by Augustin Daly: 'A Flash of Lightning', 'Horizon', 'Love on Crutches'*, ed. by Don B. Wilmeth and Rosemary Cullen. BAP. CUP. pp. xii + 208; 8 illus. hb £24, pb £8.95.

Dietrich's aim is not to deny Shaw's sociological and political thinking that idealist critics delight in, but to recommend his psychological thought as an extra, and perhaps more fundamental, dimension. In 'Shaw's Dramatic Criticism in "Our Corner", 1885–1886' (*ABSS*) Stanley Weintraub introduces and reprints in full for the first time nine theatrical reviews G.B.S. wrote for Annie Besant's socialist publication. Productions include Pinero's *Mayfair*, Shelley's *The Cenci*, Wills's *Faust*, and a student performance of *Love's Labour's Lost* which elicited one of Shaw's earliest critiques of Shakespeare on stage, nine years before he was to leave no turn unstoned in *The Saturday Review*. Also in *ABSS*, John R. Pfeiffer updates his meticulous annual bibliography in 'A Continuing Checklist of Shaviana'.

Laurence Senelick supplements Graham Good's account of the impact of Wilde's *Salome* on Europe and the U.S.A. (*YW* 64.409) with further evidence of Russian attempts to stage the play in '*Salome* in Russia' (*NCTR*). He cites a St Petersburg production of 1908 that had to be scrapped on the grounds of blasphemy even though Wilde enjoyed a cult following among Russian symbolists and decadents from the turn of the century. The problem of doing justice to Wilde's radicalism in the theatre today concerns Russell Jackson in 'A classic without danger: the National Theatre's *Importance of Being Earnest*' (*CritQ*, 1983). Considering first the classic status Wilde's comedy has acquired over the years, he finds that Peter Hall's recent revival on the South Bank placed too much emphasis upon the play's formal qualities at the expense of its innate farcical energy. Ann Saddlemyer rounds off her definitive edition of *The Collected Letters of John Millington Synge*[134] with a second and final volume covering his last twenty-one months as a director of plays and manager of the Abbey Theatre. Exhaustively annotated and indexed, the correspondence is completed with an epilogue that recounts his final weeks and the reactions of Lady Gregory and W. B. Yeats to the loss of their codirector.

Interest in Victorian spectacle presented to mass audiences outside the confines of orthodox theatres gains a fillip from David Mayer's illuminating account of a famous 'pyrodrama' and its revivals in 'Romans in Britain 1886–1910: Pain's *The Last Days of Pompeii*' (*Thph*). While centring upon pyrotechnic effect, such shows also involved professional actors and musicians; had their scripts submitted to the Lord Chamberlain; and were regularly reviewed in the press. *The Last Days of Pompeii* is typical of the genre. It was performed outdoors at the Alexandra Palace on a stage of standard specifications measuring 350 feet by 75 feet and featured scenery ingeniously designed by Joseph Harker to accommodate stunning firework effects. Mayer analyses the financing, production, and popularity of such dramas – each 'a living lesson in ancient or contemporary history' – that were terminated – if not upstaged – by the First World War. In a study of *Propaganda and Empire: The Manipulation of British Public Opinion, 1880–1960*[135], John M. MacKenzie devotes a chapter to the impact of imperial concerns and events upon the stage of the day. He

134. *The Collected Letters of John Millington Synge*. Vol. Two: *1907–1909*, ed. by Ann Saddlemyer. Clarendon. pp. xviii + 270; 2 illus. £25.

135. *Propaganda and Empire: The Manipulation of British Public Opinion, 1880–1960*, by John M. MacKenzie. ManU. pp. viii + 277. £25.

shows how colonial subject matter supplied ample opportunity for spectacle and melodrama in a surprising number of plays, and how the expression of jingoism in music-hall songs varied from hall to hall. The survey is wide ranging and draws heavily upon many useful references.

How great nineteenth-century actors managed to produce great performances on what we would regard as minimal preparation is a question Frederick J. Marker fruitfully raises in 'An Actor Prepares: The Prenaturalistic Alternative' in *EiT* (1983), a new journal of theatre and drama launched in 1982 from the University of Guelph. Despite Macready's attempts to prolong rehearsal time during the 1840s, old habits died hard: Joseph Jefferson still held in 1890 that 'very numerous rehearsals are not always necessary to attain perfection'. Marker shows how in the old stock system much individual preparation occurred outside rehearsals in an era when actors specialized in a particular role-type and directed themselves to a great extent. Victorian performers from the provinces and the West End steal much of the limelight this year. A legendary stroller of the north-east receives a fitting salute from Joe Ging in ' "The Morn's the Fair": a bi-centennial tribute to Billy Purvis (1784–1853)' (*Thph*). This nicely illustrated account of Purvis's life and career shows how he responded to the growing urbanization of the early years of Victoria's reign by concentrating his efforts on the industrial areas of Tyne, Wear and Tees, and by building a permanent booth for his company's use in Newcastle. His popularity, though considerable, remained confined to the north-east and Scotland on account of his dialect. Kathleen Barker continues her pioneering studies of provincial theatre with the illuminating life-story of 'Harvey Teasdale, Clown of Theatre, Circus and Music Hall' (*NCTR*). Sheffield-born in 1817, he spent most of his thirty-year stage career in various northern venues, at one stage appearing in a monkey skin with an African Bushman troupe. Besides providing valuable information about travelling booths and pub shows of the 1830s, his life 'illustrates well the interrelationship between the various genres of entertainment' in the early Victorian period. Unlike Teasdale who was not a great success in London in the 1850s, George Leybourne worked only for a short time in the Midlands and the north before taking the capital by storm in 1864–5. In a well-illustrated account, 'Leybourne! "Lion Comique of the Halls" ' (*Thph*), Peter Honri describes how Leybourne adopted the 'swell' type and rivalled the Great Vance in it. He cultivated a uniquely 'casual air' through his manner and dress which was immortalized by the publication of almost two hundred illustrated music sheets of his songs.

The obscurity that surrounded Charles Wyndham's involvement in the American Civil War is dispelled at last in George Rowell's 'An Acting Assistant Surgeon' (*NCTR*). Drawing on fresh evidence, he shows how the future actor-manager moved in and out of military service as he oscillated between medicine, and acting on the American stage from 1862 to 1864. The latter year marks the professional debut of the eighteen-year-old Wilson Barrett. Quickly gaining recognition as an actor and manager in the provinces, he pioneered the combination touring company complete with its own repertory in 1870. The need for a full account of his illustrious career is now remedied by James Thomas's *The Art of the Actor-Manager: Wilson Barrett and the Victorian*

Theatre[136], which should help restore the reputation of one whose management Clement Scott rated as second only to Henry Irving's. Thoroughly researched and documented, it ably describes the nature and background of Barrett's achievements as performer, producer, and playwright. It also analyses his leaning towards popular and traditional taste, as well as his promotion of contemporary plays by English writers. In 'Beerbohm Tree as Director: Three Shakespearean Productions' (*EiT*, 1983) Ralph Berry explores the production concepts underlying Tree's *Macbeth* (1911), *Much Ado About Nothing* (1905), and *Antony and Cleopatra* (1906). He argues that the resourcefulness and imagination Tree shows in applying his concepts to the stage stems from his weakness as an actor, which is 'the obverse of his strength, a capacity to see the production as something other than a vehicle for himself'. Many of Tree's contemporaries praised his productions for their vitality, and it is time that we at least learnt to appreciate why they did so. In the opposite camp to Tree, William Poel gains a fine in-depth study of four versions of *Hamlet* he produced over forty years, in Rinda F. Lundstrom's *William Poel's Hamlets: The Director as Critic*[137]. By selecting key scenes she details Poel's changing production techniques and shows how they interact with his critical views of the play over the years. Her analysis reveals a complex figure who cannot be oversimplified as an archaist or textual purist. Well considered and documented with a 'selected' bibliography running to seven pages, this is a valuable contribution to Poel studies.

Mrs Patrick Campbell is the subject of a major biography by Margot Peters[138] who portrays the first Paula Tanqueray and Eliza Doolittle in lavish detail, often devoting a chapter to a single year in her life. The wealth of comment and stories included – some notorious, others less well known – conjures up as near-rounded a picture as one could hope for of such a contradictory personality. Her frequently stormy relationships with fellow-actors such as George Alexander are qualified by her playful sparring with Bernhardt with whom she developed a good understanding both on and off the stage. Though not supplied with footnotes, each chapter has extensive notes on sources, one of which demands immediate correction. The Enthoven Collection is *not* in the Museum of London but part of the Theatre Museum, V&A, and will move to the new Covent Garden premises in 1987. Margot Peters tells how Eleonora Duse borrowed Mrs Pat's *Tanqueray* scenery for her London production of *La Seconda Moglie* in 1905 and then had the gall to charge her for a box and make her throw down a bouquet at her feet during the performance. Such a revealing incident escapes William Weaver's *Duse: A Biography*[139]. Though illuminating when it draws on unpublished material, it gives rather a patchy account of Duse's London visits. This makes it hard to glean what roles she played here, or what English critics thought of her (apart from Shaw whose 1895 reviews of her are considered at length). John Stoke's

---

136. *The Art of the Actor-Manager: Wilson Barrett and the Victorian Theatre*, by James Thomas. Theater and Dramatic Studies 15. UMIRes. pp. xii + 204; 14 illus. £35.50.

137. *William Poel's Hamlets: The Director as Critic*, by Rinda F. Lundstrom. Theater and Dramatic Studies 20. UMIRes. pp. x + 194; 15 illus. £33.50.

138. *Mrs Pat: The Life of Mrs Patrick Campbell*, by Margot Peters. Bodley. pp. x + 534; 75 illus. (incl. 4 in colour). £15.

139. *Duse: A Biography*, by William Weaver. T&H. pp. 383; 53 illus. £12.50.

'A kind of beauty, Rejane in London' in *Drama and the Actor: Themes in Drama 6*[140] presents a more satisfactory analysis of the French star whose comic acting delighted London audiences from 1894. He assesses her art and roles through contemporary observation and illustrations and shows how English reviewers preferred her intimate technique and repertory to the formal qualities of French theatre embodied by Rachel.

In effervescent style, J. C. Trewin surveys the impact of 'Bernhardt on the London Stage' on her numerous visits to this country during 1879–1921 in *Bernhardt and the Theatre of her Time* edited by Eric Salmon[141]. The simple fact of being French earned Bernhardt a licence of expression on stage unavailable to respectable English actresses of her day, as Richard Findlater observes in 'Bernhardt and the British Player Queens: A Venture into Comparative Theatrical Mythology' in the same volume. But the same writer's quest for an exact female counterpart in British stage history demonstrates little except the poverty of this kind of comparative method. Elsewhere, the collection contains some good observations of Bernhardt as performer and manager, notably in the first-hand accounts of her carefully analysed by Robert Horville in 'The Stage Techniques of Sarah Bernhardt'. But too many contributors use Bernhardt as a springboard to study other performers such as Coquelin, Hortense Rhea, Ristori, and John Martin-Harvey. The reason for this becomes apparent when one realizes that the papers on which the book is based were given at a 1977 conference called 'The International Stage in the Bernhardt Era' which is surely a more accurate description of the contents here. In a thoughtful essay concluding the volume, S. Beynon John considers 'Actors as Puppets: Variations on a Nineteenth-Century Theatrical Idea' that surfaces frequently in the 1890s at the very time when stars such as Irving and Bernhardt dominated the stage. He analyses how the idea assumes various forms in the work of Maeterlinck, Jarry, Gordon Craig, and Yeats, and reflected their disaffection with the acting of their time.

The influence of groups such as the Independent Stage Society (1891) and Stage Society (1899) dedicated to presenting Ibsen on the drama is well known, but what of their influence upon acting? Jan McDonald usefully confronts the question in 'New Actors for the New Drama' in *TD 6*[140]. She shows how the Societies' one-performance policy and lack of outstanding directors tended to inhibit the development of a special acting style in the 1890s. The social prose dramas of Ibsen, however, enabled actors to experiment with earlier naturalistic techniques fostered by T. W. Robertson and to combine this with a more rhetorical technique well suited to Greek tragedy and Shavian comedy produced by Granville Barker at the Royal Court from 1904 to 1908. The new acting style of the Barker-Vedrenne seasons was actually a synthesis of existing traditions destined to influence twentieth-century acting in London and the provincial reps. Laurence Senelick manfully assays another underresearched area in 'The Evolution of the Male Impersonator on the Nineteenth-Century Popular Stage' (*EiT*, 1982). He identifies

140. *Drama and the Actor: TD 6*, ed. by James Redmond. CUP. pp. 264. hb £21 (institutions), £13 (individuals).

141. *Bernhardt and the Theatre of her Time*, ed. by Eric Salmon. Contributions in Drama and Theatre Studies 6. Greenwood. pp. xii + 289; 15 illus. £27.95.

Annie Hindle, music-hall star of the 1860s, as the first true example of impersonation of a 'real' man. The development of the phenomenon is traced through to Vesta Tilley, whose boyishness still managed to cause offence before such acts died out with the First World War. Senelick plausibly concludes that male impersonation, seriously intended, is subversive of patriarchal right, which is why feminists of late have re-adopted it as a potent shock tactic.

Robin Wilson and Frederic Lloyd's official picture history of *Gilbert and Sullivan: The D'Oyly Carte Years*[142] is a valuable source of illustration with over 450 well-captioned photographs of performers, production material, theatres, and press pictures of the day. It spans the whole D'Oyly Carte involvement with G&S from 1875 to 1982 – the first two chapters documenting productions up to the end of the second D'Oyly Carte repertory season of 1908–9. Both informative and attractively presented, it represents very good value at £12.95. In 'Whose "Zoo"; Or, When did the "Trial" Begin?' (*NCTR*) George C. McElroy speculates as to the identity of a two-act Sullivan opera announced early in 1875, usually taken to be *Trial by Jury*. He argues that the mysterious work was condensed by Sullivan into a one-acter, *The Zoo*, produced at St James's Theatre in June of the same year. Six life-size figure portraits, actually pieces of theatrical scenery painted on canvas that exist at Normansfield Entertainments Hall, are discussed by Terence Rees in '*Ruddigore* Rediscovered' (*Thph*). With careful reference to other evidence, he assesses the likelihood of their being survivals from the first Savoy production of *Ruddigore* of 1887, whose scenery was auctioned off four years later. Arthur Jacobs's definitive biography of Sullivan[143], the fruit of many years' research, makes a welcome entry. Refreshingly, it allows one to view the twenty-five-year partnership with Gilbert in terms of the composer's career as a whole, and to appreciate other theatre music he wrote – particularly for productions of Shakespeare. Judicious quotation from diaries and correspondence evokes a vital sense of the man both in public and in the private life he concealed so carefully from his contemporaries. Numbered footnotes are avoided for the sake of readability but the account is highly documented with a full list of works, bibliography, and index. It is a volume unlikely to be superseded for many years to come. Although G&S never used the term 'operetta' formally to describe any of their joint works, their output rightly earns a full chapter to itself in Richard Traubner's comprehensive survey of *Operetta, A Theatrical History*[144]. He examines definitions and antecedents of the form before discussing major examples from Europe and the U.S.A. by composer. This gives a truly international perspective to the study so necessary to a proper understanding of the subject. It is both readable and a good work of reference with details of premieres and major revivals liberally provided along with a seven-page bibliography.

142. *Gilbert and Sullivan: The D'Oyly Carte Years: The Official Picture History*, by Robin Wilson and Frederic Lloyd, intro. by Lord Wilson, forewords by Dame Bridget D'Oyly Carte and John Reed. W&N. pp. 216; 450 + illus. (incl. 35 in colour). £12.95.
143. *Arthur Sullivan: A Victorian Musician*, by Arthur Jacobs. OUP. pp. xviii + 470; 25 illus. £17.50.
144. *Operetta, A Theatrical History*, by Richard Traubner. Gollancz. pp. xviii + 461. £12.95.

On the subject of theatre personnel, Hilary Norris offers a highly useful biographical 'Directory of Victorian Scene Painters' (*Thph*) which is full of production details and sources consulted, and prefaced with a general introduction by Sean McCarthy. The career of 'Henry Isherwood: Early American Scene Painter', one of the first native-born American stage artists of distinction, is ably recounted by W. Joseph Stell in *NCTR*. Robert Thorne surveys 'Thomas Grieve's Scene-Painting Workshop' (*Thph*) built in 1850–1 and still standing today despite recent depredation. Dennis Castle's biography of Sensation Smith of Drury Lane (Skilton) was unavailable for inspection. John Franks reproduces with fresh annotation caricatures of West End managers that appeared from 1868 to 1914 in '*Vanity Fair* and the Theatre: The Managers' (*Thph*), together with an account of their publication. Studies of theatre buildings include John Earl's account of 'J. G. Buckle: a note on the Theatre Royal, Stratford East' (*Thph*), an elusive Victorian architect whose only surviving complete theatre still functions in Stratford East. The subject of theatre safety – actively supported by Buckle in the 1880s – emerges in a chapter on 'Fires in Theatres' in the first full biography of the London Fire Brigade chief who championed the safety cause, Ronald Cox's *Oh, Captain Shaw*[145]. This is useful in so far as it traces Shaw's involvement with the safety movement but more background detail on the subject would have been welcome or at least a bibliography. Victorian venues destroyed by design not accident in the 1950s are nicely illustrated and annotated by Colin Sorensen in 'Losing London Theatres: a portfolio of photographs' (*Thph*). Concerning 'Forgotten Theatre Machinery: The Corsican Effect or Ghost Glide' (*Thph*), David Anderson discusses the unique effect created for Charles Kean's production of *The Corsican Brothers* (1852) through examination of surviving evidence and model reconstructions. *Thph* also provides a cluster of studies of seaside entertainment complexes that includes Christopher Brereton and Bill Slinn's account of 'The Winter Gardens, Blackpool' founded in 1875 and here illustrated with photographs and building plans.

Finally, two important studies that apply a socio-economic approach to two very different Victorian venues. In 'A Wet Bank Holiday at the Ally Pally' (*NCTR*) David Mayer ably analyses how Londoners spent a bank holiday at one of the two major recreational centres, the Alexandra Palace, on 6 June 1881. He describes performances ranging from a clown cricket match to an appearance by J. L. Toole's company in relation to the management's policy of providing popular attractions. Also investigated are refreshment and other facilities, admission charges, class composition of the audience, and their means of travel. Jeremy Crump focuses on the fortunes of a provincial theatre not in one day but over half a century in 'Patronage, Pleasure and Profit: A Study of the Theatre Royal, Leicester 1847–1900' (*TN*). He shows how the theatre functioned as a company with shareholders; the relations between proprietors and managers; the economic pressures the latter were subject to, and the audiences they tried to attract. The study qualifies Michael Booth's assertion that 'by 1880 the middle-class conquest of

---

145. *Oh, Captain Shaw: The Life Story of the First and Most Famous Chief of The London Fire Brigade*, by Ronald Cox. Victor Green Publications Ltd. pp. 191; 38 illus. £13.50.

the theatre auditorium and consequently of the drama itself was complete'. Crump endorses this so far as ownership, management, and policy are concerned but not in terms of the audience. Working-class patrons were not totally siphoned off by the music halls though they were coerced into better behaviour by 1880.

The Twentieth Century

JUDIE NEWMAN, JOHN SAUNDERS, JOHN CHALKER, and
TREVOR R. GRIFFITHS

This chapter has the following sections: 1. The Novel, by Judie Newman and John Saunders; 2. Poetry, by John Chalker; 3. Drama, by Trevor R. Griffiths.

1. The Novel
    This section has three categories: (a) General Studies, by Judie Newman; (b) Individual Authors: 1900–45, by John Saunders; (c) Individual Authors: Post-1945, by Judie Newman. The attribution [J.S.] denotes isolate reviews by John Saunders.

(a) General Studies
    The relevant volumes of *BHI* and *BNB* provide useful bibliographical aid. *MFS* contains helpful lists of books received and of books reviewed. The annual bibliography of scholarship on modern literature published by *JML* is invaluable, while *Current Contents* lists the contents of periodicals as they appear.
    Worth-while studies of the fiction of the period have appeared this year on a variety of topics, with a particularly rich critical harvest in the field of popular fiction.
    It is perhaps not too late to draw attention to Jefferson Hunter's *Edwardian Fiction*[1], the fullest discussion of the subject in recent years, differing from John Batchelor's *The Edwardian Novelists* (*YW* 63.365–6) in going beyond the major figures to their 'unambitious and ephemeral' contemporaries. Questioning the cliché of an endless country-house afternoon, he sees the period as 'less ignorant and more critical', constrained by the conventions of the Victorian age but struggling to get out. His first section, 'The Sense of a Period', looks at continuities of form and examples of personal influence, unexamined assumptions and attempts to counteract them, and the various subgenres of the time: whimsy, historical romance, ghost stories, and silver-fork novels. The frame-tale, often exploited by the Edwardians, allowed them to be simple and sophisticated at the same time, but the real best sellers tended to engage with issues less seriously than their predecessors, though with H. G. Wells there are signs of an expansion into new subject matter. Part II, 'Adventures Abroad', looks at parables of escape and the search for a lost Eden and the bitterly controversial question of imperialism. Novels as dissimilar as *Green*

1. *Edwardian Fiction*, by Jefferson Hunter. Harvard (1982). pp. xi + 280. £15.95.

Mansions and *The First Men in the Moon* have it as their covert subject, though the disillusioned Conrad of *Nostromo* is the main focus, with intelligent if unsurprising analysis of *Lord Jim* and *Heart of Darkness*. 'Coming Home', Part III, examines the withdrawal symptoms, with Kipling turning to the past in *Rewards and Fairies*, James moving out to Rye, the predilection for landscape and folk-song, the autumnal shades of Forster and Galsworthy, though again Wells, emerging more clearly as the hero of the piece, goes for inclusion rather than exclusion, *Tono Bungay* reaching out where *Howards End* narrows. If, as Hunter concludes, the Edwardian novel is a relative failure, the individual incomplete attempts, like his own book, are full of interest. [J.S.]

Hunter's cut-off point, 1910, marks the start of Anne Wright's *Literature of Crisis*[2]. Prompted by the 'extraordinary similarities' between four acknowledged masterpieces, all of which shift from realism to a non-naturalistic mode in order to achieve resolution, she concentrates on the 'final configurations' of her chosen texts with the help of Frank Kermode's fertile suggestions. *Howards End* is a condition-of-England novel whose ending gave Forster a good deal of trouble, raising questions more far-reaching than can be answered by the narrative alone, as the unremitting irony appears to recognize. 'Who is the real enemy?' asks *Heartbreak House*, without giving any clear answer, in spite of Shaw's later simply positive ending. Dunn emerges as the Parsifal of the story, and Boss Mangan its Gerald Crich, but this is Armageddon rather than healing quest. For *Women in Love*, too, Wright has gone to the manuscripts in search of alternative endings, in one of which Ursula does not appear, while another leaves us with the birth of Gerald's child to Gudrun. Imbalance and uncertainty characterize the novel's crisis. Any hope of a 'single unironic conclusion is to be despaired of in *The Wasteland*, that paradigm of modernist poetry' where crisis is presented as a continuous present. This attempt to 'reproblematise' the works in question involves much sensitive detail (the way in which the war provides a language for Lawrence's novels, for instance, or the use of lexical groupings in delineating Eliot's 'landscape of anxiety') but one cannot pretend that her thesis – and in a postscript she extends it to the other works of the period – really brings the texts into a new focus or answers any deeply felt need. [J.S.]

Michael H. Levenson's *A Genealogy of Modernism*[3], in following certain concepts from 1908 to 1922, has illuminating things to say about Conrad and Ford. The preface to *The Nigger of the 'Narcissus'* reflects the tensions within early Modernism, balancing the value of consciousness against unselfconscious immersion in practical activity, while the period's concern for order and personal experience can be traced back to Arnold and Pater. Ford's 'acute sensibility to the movements of the age' earns him a chapter here, as the representative of impressionism and yet a critic of the modern inability to see life steadily and whole, politically sceptical and yet alert to the new possibilities for the artist in contemporary disintegration. Though not entirely proof against the centrifugal tendencies of his subject, Levenson writes clearly and well, at home both with Conrad's narrative techniques and the more abstract

2. *Literature of Crisis, 1910–22*, by Anne Wright. Macmillan. pp. vii + 236. £20.
3. *A Genealogy of Modernism: A Study of English Literary Doctrine 1908–1922*, by Michael H. Levenson. CUP. pp. xiii + 250. £22.50.

aspects of the movement, which he sees as acceding to cultural legitimacy with the founding of Eliot's *Criterion*. [J.S.]

The Divided Heroine[4] examines 'a recurrent pattern in six English novels', half of which fall within our period. The pattern, whether understood in Plato's figure of the charioteer and horses or the Pauline tension between flesh and spirit, in fiction is generally encountered in love triangles where the woman is attracted to two opposing men. *Wuthering Heights*, *The Mill on the Floss*, and *Tess of the d'Urbervilles* are obvious examples, and in *The White Peacock* Lettie is the firm centre assailed by the competing claims of blood-consciousness (George) and mental consciousness (Leslie). Though Daleski omitted this novel from his earlier book on Lawrence what he has to say here involves predictable dualisms, though a little less reductively than summary suggests. *Mrs Dalloway* externalizes the heroine's inner conflict through her choice between Peter and Richard, while the juxtaposition of Clarissa and Septimus is relevant too. Again, what Daleski says is sensible enough, but he is more engaging in his final chapter on *The End of the Affair*, where he judges Greene's sense of duality as strikingly like Hardy's, and Sarah as driven to destroy herself by her various lovers, including the Divine one. [J.S.]

The preface to *The British Working-Class Novel in the Twentieth Century*[5], a collection of essays by various hands, draws attention to the contradictions the term involves, but the problematic relationship between realism and working-class writing is more rigorously explored in a piece by Tony Davies later in the volume. Starting from a letter of Engels to Margaret Harkness, proceeding to its misreading by Lukács in the service of 'a kind of cultural version of the Popular Front', he goes on to find Brecht's view of realism as a 'productivity' of meanings, rather than mimetic transcription, more adequate. Seen this way, as 'the scene of an unfinished argument', realism remains a worth-while ideal for a class still seeking to articulate its collective awareness. This highly theoretical exposition is balanced by an entertaining interview with Sid Chaplin on his commitment to 'sensible writing about things that count'. The transition from bourgeois to proletarian fiction in the development of the mining novel is the subject of a valuable essay by Graham Holderness, moving from Zola to Barry Hines by way of Lawrence and Lewis Jones. The recovery of works once downgraded as formally unexciting, whatever their political trenchancy, is continued in Roger Webster's account of *Love on the Dole*, quoting Pierre Macherey in support of his argument for a naturalism which foregrounds the conventions of bourgeois realism in a way that brings out the contradictions of the ideology behind them. Exploring the 'mode of existence' of *The Ragged Trousered Philanthropists*, Peter Miles sees Tressell's book as 'a self-contained kit for the dissemination of ideas', kept alive not by the academics but the readers whose response enacts a solidarity with the value it embodies. Though the editor regrets that no female writers are considered here, Deirdre Burton offers a feminist reading of *A Scots Quair*, focusing on Chris rather than her son Ewan, and praising Gibbon's sense of 'the massive centrality of the dilemma of contradictory subject positions in female experience'. Ruth Sherry

4. *The Divided Heroine: A Recurrent Pattern in Six English Novels*, by H. M. Daleski. H&M. pp. xi + 164. £23.50.

5. *The British Working-Class Novel in the Twentieth Century*, ed. by Jeremy Hawthorn. SUAS. Arnold. pp. x + 162. pb £6.95.

too, in an essay on Irish working-class fiction which necessarily involves a good deal of summary of unfamiliar works, discovers a surprising understanding of the position of women among her male authors, who include Patrick MacGill, Michael McLaverty, and James Stephens. Graham Martin is on more familiar ground with his discussion of the three versions of *Lady Chatterley's Lover*, though he leads off by proposing Lawrence's 1926 visit to Eastwood as more influential than the mythical, apocalyptic thinking noticed by Kermode and others. One of Lawrence's successors, Alan Sillitoe, also writes best out of the conflicting feelings dating back to his Nottinghamshire childhood, and is least successful when he moves outside his class. Such is David Craig's view, and he goes on to describe Sillitoe as almost unique in giving us working-class characters at ease with themselves and their environment, even when in the factory. The thread running through a discussion of Jack Common's autobiographical fiction by Michael Pickering and Kevin Robins is the author's resentment of the movement from the timeless world of childhood into the time-bound adult working-class world. Yet in his fiction, at least, Common kept the imagination and a sense of play alive. This is an interesting collection, both in its particular readings and as an opportunity to see modern critical practice engaging with authors who could not have made head or tail of it. [J.S.]

Patrick Swinden's *The English Novel of History and Society, 1940–80*[6] purports to argue that the postwar English novel is neither parochial nor excessively experimental, but has developed historical reportage and social comedy to a fine art. An initial chapter condemning 'provincial' writers (Pym, Bowen, Taylor) and solipsistic experimentalists (Beckett and others) is followed by chapters on Hughes, Powell, Green, Kingsley Amis, Angus Wilson and V. S. Naipaul, each of which supposedly offers a comprehensive description and evaluation of the writer. In fact, however, Swinden does not marshall his arguments or evidence in any very clear-cut manner, preferring simply to tell the reader what he likes about each writer, and to dismiss others briskly. There is no conclusion, no bibliography, and a very scant apparatus of notes. The chapter on Wilson, however, is genuinely illuminating, particularly in the analysis of the relation between Wilson's satire and his preoccupation with the family. Swinden also has interesting things to say about snobbery in Powell, Green's prose style, and Amis's comedy. The chapter on Hughes is a detailed and useful analysis of a somewhat neglected writer, though Swinden's arbitrary cut-off date deprives the reader of any discussion of *A High Wind in Jamaica*.

The Theory of Reading[7], edited by Frank Gloversmith, is not a theory of reading, still less *the* theory of reading, but rather a collection of critical essays, in many of which theoretical issues are the prime focus, with particular texts functioning as examples. As far as the essays which consider the modern novel are concerned, the quality of insight varies. Valentine Cunningham's contention that language is primary in the works of Joyce is unlikely to provoke dissent, though Cunningham's own language certainly does ('Joyce begins realist-wise with Ibsen'). Alistair Davies's argument that *The Rainbow* and

6. *The English Novel of History and Society, 1940–80*, by Patrick Swinden. Macmillan. pp. xii + 255. £20.

7. *The Theory of Reading*, ed. by Frank Gloversmith. Harvester. pp. xvii + 246. hb £18.95, pb £6.95.

Women in Love should be read in terms of a European context comes close to an old-fashioned influence study, the influence in question being Romain Rolland's *Jean-Christophe*. The editor himself, however, draws usefully on the theories of Roger Fry and Ortega Y Gasset to explore Woolf's critical writing and to illuminate the intense concern with form in her fiction. The best essay, 'Making and Breaking the Novel Tradition', comes from Stuart Laing who discusses the ways in which the literary canon is constructed, using postwar English novels and criticism as his major examples. This is an admirably clear and interesting essay which deserves a wide readership.

Holger Klein's *The Second World War in Fiction*[8] contains chapters on France, Germany, the Soviet Union, America, and Japan, with one chapter on British fiction. Inevitably a rather brisk overview of a very large field, the chapter is essentially a series of extremely well-annotated lists, though Evelyn Waugh comes in for slightly fuller treatment. On the whole, too much attention is paid to tripe, not enough to more serious writers. (One misses Olivia Manning, for example.)

Metafiction, both British and American, is the subject of a short but pithy volume by Patricia Waugh[9], which draws on Russian Formalist theories of literary evolution. While to some extent introductory in style, the book covers such subjects as the relation between self-reflexive fiction and parody, play, frame-analysis, postmodernism, and popular forms. Occasionally Waugh covers her ground too rapidly (there are lists of writers and techniques which make for slow reading) but on the whole she handles complex material with a light touch, and communicates a great deal of information with clarity and grace. Linda Hutcheon's study of the same topic[10] (originally published in 1980 by WLU) has been issued by Methuen in paperback. While ranging widely over British, American, and other writers, the volume includes an excellent discussion of *The French Lieutenant's Woman* which occupies one entire chapter. Another book of a general nature is Shlomith Rimmon-Kenan's *Narrative Fiction*[11] (see also *YW* 64.597) which applies insights drawn from a host of different literary theories (from New Criticism to the Tel-Aviv School of Poetics) to various elements of fiction (plot, time, character, and others). Though no single text is examined in detail the volume is a useful handbook to the variety of approaches currently available to the critic.

The year has seen some good general essays. In *ELH* Marianne Dekoven argues that literary modernism is often discussed as if there were an absence of explicit historical reference, whereas in fact, in modernist fiction, there is more often a suppressed and veiled representation of the historical event. Using *To The Lighthouse* among others as a primary instance, Dekoven argues that the simultaneous muffling and assertion of history grants it considerable power. This is an exceptionally important essay which argues a convincing case. Another good general essay, in *PQ*, investigates the relationship between

8. *The Second World War in Fiction*, ed. by Holger Klein. Macmillan. pp. ix + 249. £25.

9. *Metafiction: The Theory and Practice of Self-Conscious Fiction*, by Patricia Waugh. New Accents. Methuen. pp. ix + 176. hb £8.95, pb £3.95.

10. *Narcissistic Narrative: The Metafictional Paradox*, by Linda Hutcheon. Methuen. pp. xix + 168. pb £4.50.

11. *Narrative Fiction: Contemporary Poetics*, by Shlomith Rimmon-Kenan. New Accents. Methuen (1983). pp. xi + 173. pb £3.50.

fictional structures and characterization in the novel, drawing on Woolf, Joyce, and Conrad among other modern writers. The author, William J. Scheick, finds that a positive correspondence seems to exist between the novelist's emphasis on structure and an interest in the ethos of the human community. *CritQ* publishes a strongly argued essay from Peter Widdowson establishing similarities between the writings of Malcolm Bradbury and David Lodge, claiming that despite the 'progressive' surface of their novels, their work contains ideological implications of considerable reactionary force. Both are seen as representing Arnoldian and Leavisite culturalism, which seems to be the equivalent of thoughtcrime in Widdowson's view. All Bradbury's novels and Lodge's most recent three are analysed, in an essay which is often interesting, if rather overtly designed to provoke.

Isobel Murray and Bob Tait have chosen ten of the best Scottish novels written in the last fifty years, and have written an essay on each[12]. The selection is designed to highlight the cultural diversity and variety of literary technique within Scotland, while at the same time illustrating certain common themes – Calvinism, the sense of history, the idea of community. Most of the essays are somewhat introductory in nature, tending to sum up plot and themes, then moving through a detailed analysis of the novel in question. In the essays on Alasdair Gray, Robin Jenkins, and William McIlvanney this spelling-out process is probably necessary, though the chapters on Spark and Gordon Williams seem more pedestrian. The authors avoid patriotic excess, recognizing the weaknesses in George Mackay Brown's fiction, and the extent to which the polemical impulse damages Fionn Mac Colla. The chapters on James Kennaway, Gibbon, and Neil Gunn are the best. *A Scots Quair* is rightly approached as one novel, and the essay emphasizes a social and personal interpretation, indicating the limitations of symbolic and allegorical readings. The ironies of *Tunes of Glory* are skilfully developed and the authors bring out the full subtlety of *The Silver Darlings*. On the whole this is a useful collection though the non-Scottish reader would have benefited from more background information and the authors themselves from a good map. (Their description of Dunbeath as flat will surprise its inhabitants.)

The 1984 volume of *Ecosse* collects conference papers on Scottish subjects, including essays (in French) on modern novelists. Bernard Sallin offers a preliminary assessment of Robin Jenkins, with a detailed analysis of *Fergus Lamont*, emphasizing its humour. Keith Dixon discusses the underlying ideology of Gibbon and MacDiarmid's *Scottish Scene*, and matters political are also to the fore in Pierre Morere's essay on *The Green Isle of the Great Deep*, which analyses the relationship between Celtic myth and an antitotalitarian vision in the novel. This is clearly a very useful journal for students and critics of Scottish fiction.

James M. Cahalan[13] has found an important topic which has been unjustly neglected. His is the first study of the Irish historical novel and deserves to be widely known. After a preliminary assessment of the influence of Scott, Cahalan proceeds to discuss examples from the nineteenth and twentieth

12. *Ten Modern Scottish Novels*, by Isobel Murray and Bob Tait. AberdeenU. pp. vii + 243. hb £11.90, pb £6.90.

13. *Great Hatred, Little Room: The Irish Historical Novel*, by James M. Cahalan. Syracuse (1983). pp. xiv + 240. £25.

centuries, with the emphasis on novels written in the last fifty years. An outline of Irish history and potted biographies of the writers precede analyses of representative novels, which indicate the extent to which Irish writers draw upon popular versions of history, and explore opposing political forces in history, in order to understand the polarities still at work in their own day (in contradistinction to Scott's peaceful syntheses). Writers include Iris Murdoch, Seán Ó Faoláin, Liam O'Flaherty, and James Plunkett, though given that Cahalan also discusses American writers, it is odd that he completely neglects J. G. Farrell, whose *Troubles* is a glaring omission in an otherwise comprehensive book.

Maureen Waters's study of different types of comic Irishmen is a more modest achievement, though not without interest[14]. After tracing the evolution of various comic figures (clown, rogue, stage Irishman) in nineteenth-century drama and fiction, Waters moves on to discuss twentieth-century writers who have exploited or challenged the stereotype. A nicely balanced account of Somerville and Ross's 'Irish R.M.' stories acknowledges their contribution to stereotyping, while later chapters concentrate on satire, Menippean in the case of Beckett's *Murphy*, satire on Irish myth-making in Joyce, satire on Joyce in the works of Flann O'Brien.

Irish questions are also to the forefront in *Ireland and the English Crisis*[15], a collection of some thirty reviews and lectures written by Tom Paulin in the last five years, all but three of them previously published. In his introduction Paulin compares what he thinks is a crisis in English literature with the wrecked state of Northern Ireland, drawing an analogy between the abandonment of the classic canon of English literature and the British attitude to Northern Ireland. Politics aside, however, the volume generates fresh insights on a wide variety of topics. Readings of Joyce emphasize the social vision developed in a stagnant, colonial society. Angela Carter's postimperial sensibility, Lawrence's un-English celebration of lawlessness, and a fascinating assessment of le Carré as myth-maker, all make excellent short essays. Paulin interestingly highlights the oddly dated atmosphere of William Trevor's stories, laments Brian Moore's descent into *ersatz* Irishness, and briskly demolishes Kingsley Amis. ('More of Amis's prose emphatically means worse.') While the volume is sometimes gratuitously provocative, it is also genuinely thought-provoking.

Where Paulin is at his best on imperialist or colonialist topics, other writers approach similar questions with varying degrees of intelligence. Martin Green's *The English Novel in the Twentieth Century [The Doom of Empire]*[16] is devoted to the idea that major twentieth-century novelists (Lawrence, Joyce, Waugh, Kingsley Amis, Doris Lessing) were primarily reacting against the influence of Kipling. This entirely risible proposition is repeatedly asserted, with Kipling's influence seen in the most unlikely quarters, and no proper argument constructed to support Green's hilarious generalizations. One wonders why he did not choose Baden-Powell and *Scouting for Boys* as

14. *The Comic Irishman*, by Maureen Waters. SUNY. pp. 204. hb $28.50, pb $8.95.
15. *Ireland and the English Crisis*, by Tom Paulin. Bloodaxe. pp. 222. hb £12.95, pb £5.95.
16. *The English Novel in the Twentieth Century [The Doom of Empire]*, by Martin Green. RKP. pp. xix + 236. hb £12.95, pb £5.95.

his *éminence grise*; the case seems just as likely. Even worse, in his actual discussions of the writers concerned, Green comes badly unstuck. Dickens appears as a mere 'preliminary' to Kipling's work, Conrad is seen as glorifying imperialism, Greene's protagonists are 'genuine Kipling heroes', and a monumental disservice is done to Twain, whose anti-imperialism is surely well known. The schoolboy essay on British immigration is lamentable, and the discussion of Waugh's view of Churchill is erroneous. In addition Green distorts Kipling's literary reputation, asserting that it is in eclipse, when, if anything, the reverse is true. Green has previously written excellent books (on literary dandyism and imperial adventure) but here he is the victim of an *ideé fixe*.

'Selective history' is the focus of an essay in *Encounter*, in which Maria Couto argues that both Forster and Paul Scott (among others) perpetuate racist and colonial stereotypes in their novels about India. While the case against Forster has at least the merit of familiarity, that against Scott is vitiated by naive and selective reading. Couto neglects the ironic effects of Scott's narrative structure, underemphasizes the degree of change in the characters, and chooses to consider only *The Raj Quartet*. In *DQR* David Seed handles a similar topic with much more subtlety, comparing Kipling, Orwell, and Forster's attitudes to the empire. Seed argues that *Kim* does play down racial issues in order to present an idyllic view of India, but he does not underestimate the complexity of the tale. Forster's scepticism about racial contact (*Passage to India*) is underlined, and a strong case made for basing Orwell's failure in *Burmese Days* on the author's overinvolvement with his protagonist. Among other things this interesting essay also includes a comparison of the attitudes of Conrad and Twain to colonialism in the Belgian Congo.

Several volumes deal with literary periods. Penguin have re-issued Julian Maclaren-Ross's *Memoirs of the Forties*[17], originally published in 1965, with an introduction by Alan Ross. Essentially an informal account of Bohemian Soho in wartime, the book is rich in anecdotes, consistently readable, and pleasantly rounded out with a memoir of Alun Lewis, and half a dozen of Maclaren-Ross's better stories. The description of the author's meeting with Graham Greene in 1938 is of special interest. Paul Webster and Nicholas Powell[18] have written an engaging account of French postwar culture, centring on the literary group of Saint-Germain-des-Prés. While the primary focus is inevitably French writers, the volume discusses Beckett's relation to the group, while in the Resistance and after the Liberation, a relation which appears to have been beset by disaster. (Notably, when Beckett sent only half of the manuscript of a story to *Les Temps Modernes*, Simone de Beauvoir failed to detect the error and published it as received.) Koestler's quarrel with Sartre, which seems to have been as much the result of his sexual attitudes as his position on Communism, is also touched upon. The 1950s is the focus of a collection of interviews with 'Angry Young Men', conducted by Dale Salwak[19]. In fact, none of the writers concerned (Amis, Braine, Wain, Bill Hopkins, Colin Wilson) is either

17. *Memoirs of the Forties*, by Julian Maclaren-Ross. Penguin. pp. xiv + 348. £4.95.
18. *Saint-Germain-des-Prés*, by Paul Webster and Nicholas Powell. Constable. pp. 265. £9.95.
19. *Interviews with Britain's Angry Young Men*, conducted by Dale Salwak. The Milford Series: Popular Writers of Today. Borgo. pp. 96. hb $9.95, pb $3.95.

young or particularly angry, or among the 'popular writers of today', the series title. All rebut the label 'Angry Young Men' as a media coinage. As Braine points out, the only factor common to the group appears to be their political stance (non-leftwing). What emerges from these interviews, however, is a strong sense of what it means to be a working novelist.

The working writer is the focus of two volumes. Victor Bonham-Carter[20] has now written the second volume of his history of authorship, covering the period 1911–81, and investigating such issues as writers' contracts and earnings, changes in legislation, libel and copyright, taxation, censorship, and public patronage of the arts. Though more than a third of the book is concerned with writing for performance, many novelists also appear in the volume, which covers a lot of ground rapidly, lucidly, and without loss of interest. Bonham-Carter has a knack of communicating hard facts without dryness, and also without becoming excessively anecdotal. This is really the only history of the business of writing in modern Britain, and is full of information. In connection with *Authors by Profession*, the report of the Registrar of Public Lending Right[21] makes fascinating reading. A factual summary describes the build-up to the scheme and the first year's operation, explaining how the system works. Three salient points emerge. The concentration of payments among fiction writers is high, particularly in romantic fiction, with war, western, and science fiction trailing behind. Serious novelists of high literary standing do not figure in the maximum category, but are none the less benefiting from the scheme. The mixture of authors and titles at the top of library borrowing is significantly different from best sellers in paperback. The author provides a list of the one hundred most issued titles (twenty-seven by Catherine Cookson). Clearly this information is going to be of major significance to students of popular fiction and of the economics of the book trade.

Christopher Pawling has edited a fine collection of essays on popular fiction[22]. Criticism of popular literature is no longer as untheorized and eclectic as in previous years, as the editor points out in his introduction, which usefully surveys various theoretical approaches to the topic. The essays which follow, on women's romance, science fiction, thrillers, fantasy and working-class novels, are of uniformly high quality, clearly written and persuasive. Adrian Mellor's overview of the relation between science fiction and its readership is complemented by Martin Jordin's analysis of the 1950s science-fiction novel as actively challenging ideological assumptions about the role of science in society. Jerry Palmer argues that the type of suspense specific to the conventional thriller demands that the reader adopt the perspective of the hero, who is distinguished by professionalism and success, and by solving a crime which threatens social order. This pattern effectively combines the competitive self-seeking urge with the social order, and is therefore particularly satisfying to the reader. Two writers discuss women's romance fiction. Bridget Fowler explores the plot structures and images of society in the fiction of low-priced magazines for women in the 1930s, concluding that they rely on

20. *Authors by Profession*. Vol. 2: *1911–1981*, by Victor Bonham-Carter. Bodley/SoA. pp. 336. £12.50.

21. *Setting Up Public Lending Right: A Report to the Advisory Committee*, by John Sumsion. Registrar of Public Lending Right. pp. 36. pb £2.95.

22. *Popular Fiction and Social Change*, ed. by Christopher Pawling. Macmillan. pp. vii + 246. hb £14, pb £4.95.

bourgeois norms, while Rosalind Brunt argues that Cartland's awareness of women's involvement in a patriarchal commodity market contradicts the apparent idealism of her romances. The last three essays highlight the relationship between popular fiction and social change. Stuart Laing accounts for the success of *Room at the Top* in terms of its appeal to latent anxieties about the morality of affluence in the 1950s, David Glover considers the cult of fantasy (Tolkien, Burroughs, Moorcock) in the counterculture of the 1960s, and the editor himself closes the volume with a chapter on *Watership Down* which emphasizes the return to conservative values in the fantasy of the 1970s. There is also an excellent annotated bibliography of recent criticism of popular fiction, and of classic studies, a category to which the volume under discussion clearly belongs.

Three recent books consider British spy thrillers. John Atkins's *The British Spy Novel: Styles in Treachery*[23] is impressively comprehensive in its coverage, discussing practically every writer of spy novels from Childers onwards. Atkins's drily humorous style is a delight. Indeed his book is considerably more readable than many of the works he discusses. One of his strengths is his ability to identify features of the genre from undistinguished examples. He is forthright in his evaluation of the demerits of Buchan ('This is bosh'), and in his discussion of political and social questions makes interesting connections between fiction and life. While subchapters on torture, anarchism, and sex are inevitably brief, they are none the less sharp and suggestive. He is particularly perceptive on the question of ethics, and on the 'Great Game' metaphor, with chapters on Greene and le Carré which deserve special attention. Lars Ole Sauerberg's book[24] is a more heavyweight literary study, concentrating on three authors (Fleming, Deighton, le Carré) and expending more effort on definition of generic formulae and on the relation between thriller and romance. Sauerberg identifies five main features in the literary formula of the spy story, and makes a fair case for his hypothesis in detailed studies of his chosen three authors. Inevitably, perhaps, the book tells the reader more about genre than about the spy story in all its variety. Mention should also be made of J. Kenneth Van Dover's *Murder in the Millions*[25], which is mostly concerned with the popularity in America of Mickey Spillane, Erle Stanley Gardner, and Ian Fleming. The Fleming chapter gives an extended analysis of *Casino Royale*, then proceeds chronologically through the novels, observing ways in which they strike variations on the initial formula. Crisply written, the book brings out the fairy-tale elements of the action, its conservative and chauvinistic qualities, and also provides biographical information.

Ernest Mandel's social history of the crime story[26] rests on the thesis that crime literature mirrors capitalism because bourgeois society is criminal in its essence. The author, a prominent Marxist political economist, traces the evolution of the genre from the tradition of social protest in bandit stories to

23. *The British Spy Novel: Styles in Treachery*, by John Atkins. Calder. pp. 287. £14.95.

24. *Secret Agents in Fiction: Ian Fleming, John le Carré and Len Deighton*, by Lars Ole Sauerberg. Macmillan. pp. xvi + 260. £22.50.

25. *Murder in the Millions*, by J. Kenneth Van Dover. Ungar. pp. xi + 235. hb $12.95, pb $7.95.

26. *Delightful Murder: A Social History of the Crime Story*, by Ernest Mandel. Pluto. pp. viii + 152. pb £3.95.

the classic detective story which legitimizes the values of bourgeois society, and thence via the transitional spy thriller, to its present form, in which the state has once more become ambiguous in character and the hero a tragic rebel. Examples are drawn from a wide range of writers (including a short but perceptive study of Greene) making the book a very useful introduction to the topic. In *Genre* (1983) Rick A. Eden considers the problem of classifying detective fiction generically, reviewing other classifications and making a strong case for detective fiction as satire. In his view, what engages the reader is the sordid nature of the meretricious society in which murder occurs. Acceptance of this argument changes the way in which we understand the relation between detective and 'hard-boiled' fiction, which may now be seen less as a radical shift than as an evolution from Horatian to Juvenalian satire.

Ann Swinfen[27] has written a wide-ranging account of British and American fantasy fiction since 1945. The approach is thematic, rather than by individual author, with chapters on animal fantasy, fantasies of parallel worlds, symbolism and allegory, and the purposes of fantasy, whether religious, philosophical, or social. Writers extensively discussed elsewhere (Tolkien, Peake) are omitted, though proper attention is paid to their influence and to the relationship of modern fantasy to earlier literature. C. S. Lewis, T. H. White, and Richard Adams receive detailed attention, though at times the author moves rather too briskly through a host of different examples. On the whole, however, Swinfen substantiates her claim that fantasy is not escapism but a method of approaching and evaluating the real world, and thus is a serious form of the modern novel. Kathryn Hume also argues against the marginalization of fantasy in *Fantasy and Mimesis: Responses to Reality in Western Literature*[28], claiming that fantasy and mimesis are twin impulses behind literary creation. Where Swinfen's work is relatively untheorized, Hume pays close attention to definitions of genre, concepts of reality in literary history, and the relationship between fantasy and philosophy. The discussion includes continental, British, and American examples from the sagas and classical writings to the present. It therefore leans towards the overview, but a valuable one nevertheless.

What George Eliot called 'Silly Novels by Lady Novelists' have found their defenders this year. Janice A. Radway's study[29] of popular romantic fiction and its readers is quite the best book to date. Drawing on reader-response criticism, feminist psychology, anthropology, and in-depth interviews with romance readers, Radway challenges the normal interpretation of popular romantic fiction as conservative, ideologically repressive, and formulaic. An initial chapter on the mechanics of publishing and distribution establishes a firm basis for the study which goes on to analyse reading habits, the relation of romance to patriarchal culture, and the language and conventions of romance narrative. While the book will be of primary value to critics of popular culture, it is also of exceptional interest, in its attention to reader-response, to criticism of the novel. The flexibility of the romance formula is also emphasized in Kay Mussell's *Fantasy and Reconciliation: Contemporary Formulas of Women's*

27. *In Defence of Fantasy: A Study of the Genre in English and American Literature since 1945*, by Ann Swinfen. RKP. pp. x + 253. pb £6.95.

28. *Fantasy and Mimesis: Responses to Reality in Western Literature*, by Kathryn Hume. Methuen. pp. xvi + 213. hb £16, pb £6.95.

29. *Reading the Romance: Women, Patriarchy and Popular Literature*, by Janice A. Radway. UNC. pp. x + 274. hb £25, pb £7.95.

Romance Fiction[30], though the genre is seen in more conservative terms. Mussell's study is more of a general overview of varieties of romance, including many British examples, and with valuable insights into historical romance in particular. While Mussell is less concerned with reader-response and with the mechanics of publishing, the interested reader would do well to read these two works in tandem, as they complement each other extremely well. The essential precursor of both studies, Tania Modleski's *Loving with a Vengeance: Mass-Produced Fantasies for Women*[31], first published in 1982, has now been brought out in paperback by Methuen. Using largely American examples, Modleski sets out to determine what constitutes narrative pleasure for women, analysing romances, popular Gothics, and soap operas. While her analysis suggests that such common elements as the transformation of brutal men into tender lovers and the insistent denial of male hostility towards women, point to ideological conflicts in romance fiction, she none the less argues that each type of narrative also contains elements of resistance to the female subservient role.

The specifically female aspects of the urban experience are the focus of a collection of essays edited by Susan Merrill Squier[32], which explore the literary treatment of the city in the work of continental, British, and American women writers. In general, British writers appear to produce a less negative vision of the city than their foreign counterparts. With the exception of an essay on George Eliot's response to Florence, the emphasis falls on modern novelists. Louise A. De Salvo explores the city as a symbol of male domination in the work of Vita Sackville-West; Jane Marcus argues that the novels of Rebecca West and Sylvia Townsend Warner are versions of pastoral, in which the feminist imagination grapples with women's marginal place in the city; and Sydney Janet Kaplan studies Katherine Mansfield's attitude to London. Christine W. Sizemore's essay on Doris Lessing's *The Four-Gated City* establishes the nature of urban experience as palimpsestic, in the sense that the city itself is seen as a layered text built up over time, and connected with the way in which women's novels hide the 'real' story about women beneath a surface textual layer. Most interestingly, the author discusses ways in which Woolf's *Night and Day* draws upon the conventions of the classic city novel, while challenging its values, in associating the city with work and virtue. These are all workmanlike essays, using a variety of methodologies to good effect.

While essentially a work of feminist literary history, Joanna Russ's *How to Suppress Women's Writing*[33] deserves a brief mention, drawing as it does on a wealth of examples of writing by and about women writers. Honest, entertaining, free from jargon, the book explicates patterns in the suppression of women's writing, outlining the most common strategies of dismissal. Woolf figures fairly prominently, with Russ emphasizing her political activities, and attention is also drawn to women writers of science fiction and detective stories.

30. *Fantasy and Reconciliation: Contemporary Formulas of Women's Romance Fiction*, by Kay Mussell. Greenwood. pp. xix + 217. £26.95.

31. *Loving with a Vengeance: Mass-Produced Fantasies for Women*, by Tania Modleski. Methuen. pp. 140. pb £4.95.

32. *Women Writers and the City: Essays in Feminist Literary Criticism*, ed. by Susan Merrill Squier. UTenn. pp. 306. hb $22.95, pb $9.95.

33. *How to Suppress Women's Writing*, by Joanna Russ. WP. pp. 160. pb £3.50.

As Clare Hanson remarks in *Short Stories and Short Fictions, 1880–1980*[34] the short story has made something of a comeback in England of late, with larger publishing opportunities and a feeling in the air that the short form is *the* form for innovation. Hanson traces the genesis of the various forms of the short story in the British 1890s, distinguishing two major trends – the well-plotted traditional tale (Maugham, Kipling, O'Connor, O'Faoláin, T. F. Powys) and the plotless psychological sketch adapted by the modernists (Woolf, Joyce, Mansfield), the postmodernists (Beckett), and such recent writers as Clive Sinclair, Ian McEwan, and Adam Mars-Jones. Although this binary model makes for clarity and ease of generalization, writers whose work is more responsive to social pressures fit awkwardly into the generic outline. Hanson christens this type of writing 'free story', exemplified in the works of Bowen, Pritchett, and Sansom. While Hanson offers many extremely perceptive analyses of individual stories, writes gracefully, and is able to link disparate writers in interesting ways, some questions are begged. The title should really be 'British Short Stories'. Comparatively little attention is paid to the possibility that American or French writers may have been crucial influences before the 1890s, and although Hanson discusses Stein, Borges, and Hemingway, Commonwealth writers do not appear.

The second number of *Les Cahiers de la Nouvelle* consists of the proceedings of a 'Round Table' on the forms and evolution of the short story, held in 1983 in Angers, together with essays on various short-story writers. Contributors include Anthony Burgess and John Wain. Burgess describes his experiments with the form and his reactions to Joyce, Maugham, and Kipling. John Wain makes a spirited case for the short story as a modern form with its own laws and logic. Barry Menikoff surveys the various ways in which the form has been defined, and in addition Alain Blayac re-assesses 'After the Race', arguing, from a very close reading of the text, that it is epiphanic of the history of Ireland, and central to the message of *Dubliners*. On a humbler level, Longman have produced two anthologies of short stories, aimed at students. *Short Stories for Today*[35] includes work by Mary Lavin, Susan Hill, Angus Wilson, V. S. Pritchett, Alan Sillitoe, and Stan Barstow, among others, with brief biographies and notes. *Meetings and Partings*[36] includes Greene, Sillitoe, Sid Chaplin, Walter Macken, John Wain, Liam O'Flaherty, and Angela Huth. Both collections draw attention to Irish and Commonwealth writers.

Charles E. May's essay on the short story in *SSF* is of exceptional interest. In essence, May argues that there are basic differences in the ontology and epistemology of the novel and the short story. Drawing on philosophical and theoretical writers, May suggests that where the long fiction establishes the primacy of 'experience', conceptually created, the short story concentrates on 'an experience' directly created and encountered, and tends towards the lyrical, mythic, spiritual, and intuitive. The reality which the short story presents to us is that of those subuniverses of the supernatural and the fable which exist within the world of sense-perception and conceptual abstraction.

34. *Short Stories and Short Fictions, 1880–1980*, by Clare Hanson. Macmillan. pp. viii + 189. £20.
35. *Short Stories for Today*, ed. by Michael Marland. Longman. pp. xx + 218. pb £1.50.
36. *Meetings and Partings*, ed. by Michael Marland. Longman. pp. xx + 160. pb £1.95.

Interest is growing in the relationship between autobiography and other imaginative writing. A. O. J. Cockshut's study[37] begins from the premise that the autobiographer is concerned to construct a self as much as to express one, and he illustrates his analysis of the underlying features of the genre from both the well known (Wells, Bertrand and Dora Russell, Beatrice Webb, John Cowper Powys, C. S. Lewis) and the completely obscure. Special emphasis falls upon childhood, religious conversion, and rebellion against parental norms, but the book is not narrowly thematic and is distinguished by some splendid close readings of the texts under consideration. Fictive selves are also the focus of H. Porter Abbott's *Diary Fiction: Writing as Action*[38] which treats a variety of writers who have employed the literary strategy of the diary. General chapters consider the special functions of the form in relation to time, realism, and reflexivity, and Abbott emphasizes the different aesthetic effects created by the diary. For English readers the chapters on Beckett and Lessing are of particular interest. Abbott argues persuasively that both writers use the diary form in order to bring into focus not just a type of writing, but writing itself, Lessing in *The Golden Notebook* by combining notebooks with a contrasting 'traditional novel', Beckett in *Malone Dies* by reducing the genre of diary novel to its skeletal parts. The book includes a very full bibliography, and will be indispensable to further study of the genre.

Gale have published an annotated bibliographical guide[39] to non-fictional prose in modern British literature. Part One (twenty-three pages) covers studies of essay and prose style, travel-writing, biography, autobiography, literary criticism, and also bibliographies and literary histories. By any standards the coverage is extremely slim. The bulk of the volume is taken up by entries for thirty-seven novelists, playwrights, and poets, each entry listing the author's non-fictional prose, his or her works edited by others, biographies, bibliographies, and criticism. The annotations, both descriptive and evaluative, are sometimes useful, but most of the information is readily available elsewhere. Two volumes of the series *Contemporary Literary Criticism*[40] appeared in 1984. Each volume contains excerpts from criticism of some sixty writers, together with a brief biographical and critical essay on each, and a photograph. Authors include song-writers, film directors, playwrights, and poets, as well as novelists. Volume 29 treats Beckett, Brigid Brophy, David Caute, Elizabeth Jane Howard, and Elizabeth Taylor, among others. Volume 30 is particularly concerned with writing for 'young adults' but includes T. H. White and Ian Fleming. While one is sceptical about the editors' claims to have fulfilled 'an essential need' in producing 'an ongoing digest of current literary opinion', the critical excerpts are judiciously chosen, and not always easily obtainable elsewhere. The major strength of the series lies in the inclusion of little-known writers and in the variety of nationalities covered.

37. *The Art of Autobiography in 19th and 20th Century England*, by A. O. J. Cockshut. Yale. pp. x + 222. £10.95.

38. *Diary Fiction: Writing as Action*, by H. Porter Abbott. CornU. pp. 228. $22.50.

39. *English Prose and Criticism, 1900–1950: A Guide to Information Sources*, ed. by Christopher C. Brown and William B. Thesing. Gale (1983). pp. xxii + 553. $44.

40. *Contemporary Literary Criticism: Excerpts from Criticism of the Works of Today's Novelists, Poets, Playwrights, Short Story Writers, Filmmakers, Scriptwriters, and Other Creative Writers*. Vol. 29, ed. by Jean C. Stine and Daniel G. Marowski. Gale. pp. 642. $82. Vol. 30, ed. by Jean C. Stine and Daniel G. Marowski. Gale. pp. 664. $82.

Volume 15 of the Dictionary of Literary Biography[41] is devoted to British novelists who flourished between 1930 and 1959, covering fifty-nine writers, and with five special essays on such topics as the literary effects of World War II, sex, class and politics, literary prizes, and 'Angry Young Men'. Two appendixes offer a checklist of further reading and a list of films based on the novelists' works, the latter illustrated with stills. The editor's foreword is embarrassingly fulsome, invoking Britain's 'finest hour', praising the novelists for continuing to write in Churchillian times, and perpetuating the myth that British fiction of the period is not innovatory. But the individual essays are excellent. Each provides brief biographical details, a bibliography and a longish critical essay, handsomely illustrated in most cases with photographs of the author, dust-jackets, and pages of manuscript. Many contributors are acknowledged experts on their subjects (e.g. Deirdre Bair on Beckett) but there is no lack of sophistication and freshness in any of the essays. (Richard Hauer Costa's essay on Greene deserves to be singled out as particularly sparkling.) Commendably, British really means British here, with Scots, Welsh, and Irish writers well represented.

Less interesting is Gale's *Twentieth Century Author Biographies Master Index*[42], a new 'research tool' with 171,000 citations of articles, essays and sketches of a biographical character, many of them in Gale's own Contemporary Authors series and in other places where common sense might soon lead one to look. Since it is not restricted to English Language authors, many will be of people one has never heard of, and may never miss. [J.S.]

(b) Individual Authors: 1900–45

'The century's most textualized year', as one of many essays on *Nineteen Eighty-Four* inelegantly styled it, dawned with a flurry of attention to George Orwell, if not a great deal of lasting interest. But 1984 did bring a splendid edition of *Ulysses*, edited in Munich, a newly discovered novel by D. H. Lawrence, and the final volume of Virginia Woolf's *Diaries*.

'Silken tents without poles', Virginia Woolf called the novels of George Moore, but Raffaella Maiguashca Uslenghi (*ELT*) writes at length to chart the growing coherence of his work after 1900, when, though still faithful to the 1890s ideal of beauty, Moore discovered his true subject in the theme of 'recall' at all levels. While the central thesis is not compelling, there is useful discussion of the technical devices Moore employed.

The unifying structural pattern in Conrad's fiction, according to Stephen K. Land[43], can be expressed as the law whereby 'the hero's compromised exertion of will brings about its own negation', hence the paradox of his title, that purposive action is self-nullifying. The pattern undergoes modification as the career develops, the paradox located more firmly within the central characters, and becoming more centrally the subject of the novel. In a mature work like *Nostromo* the paradox is not merely psychological but universal. The 'bipolar symmetries' increase in complexity, with the women's roles emerging

41. *British Novelists, 1930–1959*, ed. by Bernard Oldsey. DLB 15. Gale (1983). pp. xx + 713. $148.

42. *Twentieth Century Author Biographies Master Index*, ed. by Barbara McNeil. Gale. pp. xx + 519. hb $60, pb $25.

43. *Conrad and the Paradox of Plot*, by Stephen K. Land. Macmillan. pp. vii + 311. £25.

more strongly, and the late novels providing a continuation of what has gone before, rather than the falling-off frequently discerned there. Land's pattern-making can seem a little forced, even obsessive (there are no footnotes or references to other critics), but he offers a pragmatic defence to the charge of reductivism, and there are gains in his even-handed chronological approach, not least in giving the less familiar work a fair crack of the whip.

Cedric Watts[44] starts from a similar interest in paradox and contradiction, born of a distrust of the 'organic unity' fashionable in the criticism of his youth, though aware of temptations to the 'binary fallacy'. The approach is often playful, and students of Conrad will be familiar with the ideas on 'janiformity' in fiction which Watts has advanced before. 'Covert plots' are to be distinguished from subplots in being a series of alternative possibilities which once recognized cause us to see the surface plot in a new light; Golding's *Pincher Martin* is a clear example of the kind of thing he has in mind, and the final section surveys a whole range from *Tristram Shandy* to *The Wild Duck*. The body of the book, though, is concerned with Conrad, and related ideas, like those of 'transtextual narrators', and the device Ian Watt defined as 'delayed decoding'. Watts is attracted to the notion of plot, seeing it as active and diachronic, where theme is passive and synchronic, but his use of the term is pretty elastic. Sometimes it is a 'symbolic glow or resonance', produced by the evocation of supernatural or metaphysical habits of imagination, sometimes an effect of defamiliarization when the result is presented but the cause withheld. But methodological purity is not Watts's aim, and there are stimulating readings of many of the novels and tales.

Less playful is Benita Parry[45], though for her too *Heart of Darkness* is a 'facing-both-ways' fiction and Conrad a highly ambivalent artist. She reads the oppositions in his work in terms of politics and culture, rather than metaphysics or transhistorical values. While sabotaging the mystique of empire, Conrad does not come out with a clear-cut denunciation of imperialism; like Marlow he mythologizes what he sees in line with colonial assumptions. What really shocks the latter is not the savage customs, but that Kurtz, a white man, should have succumbed to them. In *Lord Jim*, too, the redeeming idea has racial overtones, and even *Nostromo* is 'a radical political fiction mediated by a deeply conservative consciousness'. There are subtle and challenging chapters on both these novels, and on *The Rescue*, a bleak political allegory in Parry's reading, and *The Nigger of the 'Narcissus'*. Her conclusion is surprisingly positive, with Conrad's vatic impulse finally judged as not an escape from history but a route towards its making. Nostromo survives in the minds of the poor, a beacon to a better future.

Conrad's analysis of the colonial experience, this time viewed in terms of Freud's ideas on narcissism and fetishism, occupies the concluding chapters of David Simpson's inquiry[46] into 'the ethics of perception and representation in certain important nineteenth-century writers'. Dickens and Melville are his other examples, but as colonialism advances, enslavement by mere images becomes more complete, with the silver of the mine an obvious instance.

44. *The Deceptive Text: An Introduction to Covert Plots*, by Cedric Watts. Harvester. pp. xiv + 203. £25.

45. *Conrad and Imperialism*, by Benita Parry. Macmillan (1983). pp. vii + 162. £25.

46. *Fetishism and Imagination: Dickens, Melville, Conrad*, by David Simpson. JHU (1982). pp. xviii + 141. £11.95.

'Treasure', as Nostromo says, 'fastens upon a man's mind', and Simpson pursues his fetishes freely among Conrad's fiction, to gloomy conclusions. All heroic energies 'seem to be dying for want of air' in Conrad's world, all 'signifying activity' hopelessly alienated, in this highly selective reading.

Conrad's hunger for permanence attracted him to the world of nineteenth-century physics, a universe of static qualities where biological man-time is irrelevant. Such is the contention of Redmond O'Hanlon's *Joseph Conrad and Charles Darwin*[47], which examines the influence of contemporary science, biology in particular, on the writer's changing conception of sex, chance, and nature. Believing the ideological substructure more clearly visible in something less than an absolute masterpiece, he focuses on *Lord Jim*, with its hero less capable of action than his instinctive forefathers, more subject to assaults from the primitive primaeval past. Theories of evolution robbed the world of certainty without endowing it with hopes of human progress. There is some overlap with Allan Hunter's book on *Joseph Conrad and the Ethics of Darwinism*, published last year (*YW* 64.427–8), but O'Hanlon's account is much more sophisticated, though intriguing lines of thought are almost swamped by a wealth of scientific detail.

The central ideas in Wit Tarnawski's 'essay in psychological biography'[48], are clear enough, though this book is really a collection of essays, published in an earlier form in Poland back in 1972. Tarnawski was himself already thirty when Conrad died, and he brings a fellow countryman's eye to the fiction, noting for example the indebtedness of the rhythms of his prose to Polish poetry, the connection between his story-telling and the *gavenda*, or 'rambling narrative' of his native land, and the lifelong sense of guilt he felt at leaving it. Conrad's 'Polish complex', the key to his fiction, most visible in 'the Lord Jim theme', is open to objection, and indeed Tarnawski prints a letter from Eloise Hay making some of the obvious points, but he sticks to his guns. The dreamily romantic Jim is spiritually a Pole, the whole book a subconscious reply to Eliza Orzeszkowa's charge of desertion. The theme of the late *The Rover* reflects Conrad's desire to return home, and a more hopeful phase which Tarnawski connects with Poland's defeat of Communist Russia. He looks at some of the lesser works like 'Karain' and 'The Return' for Conrad's 'impassioned criticism of the materialist civilisation of the West', and there are chapters comparing him with Sartre and Dostoevski. Critically the book is old-fashioned, detailed summary leading on to analysis, but the result is more impressive than much academic modishness, and the closing comments on the ageing Conrad, made from the perspective of Tarnawski's own dying years, genuinely moving.

The 'influence of repudiation' in Conrad's reading of Dostoevski receives further attention from L. R. Lewitter (*MLR*), though he modestly offers it as 'no more than a paragraph in the painful history of Russo-Polish relations'. The expected parallels between *Crime and Punishment* and *Under Western Eyes* are supplemented with echoes of *The Devils* and verbal reminiscences of *The Brothers Karamazov*. *Under Western Eyes* figures again in a valuable essay by Martin Price (*YES*), investigating the novel's uneasy mixture of satire

47. *Joseph Conrad and Charles Darwin: The influence of scientific thought on Conrad's fiction*, by Redmond O'Hanlon. Salamander. pp. 189. £17.50.

48. *Conrad the Man, the Writer, the Pole*, by Wit Tarnawski, trans. by Rosamund Batchelor. Polish Cultural Foundation. pp. 198.

and fiction, where it is seen as an advance on *The Secret Agent* and stories like 'The Return' and 'An Outpost of Progress'. In the earlier pieces the narrator's animus against the characters denies them any consciousness of their own though raising larger questions about the distinction between satire and fully achieved fiction. The plot of *The Secret Agent* engages Paul Dolan (*Conradiana*), who argues that the key to its interlocking structures lies in the analogy between Winnie and the Professor, he with his concealed bomb, she with the family savings under her bodice. Money and dynamite are part of a series of analogies which give the book its political dimension, or so this overfanciful reading would seek to persuade us. A variety of approaches are employed by the other contributors of *Conradiana*. The psychology of the same novel is more fruitfully investigated by Martin Ray, who proposes Max Nordau's *Degeneration* as an important source: a 'silly book' but useful to Conrad in providing stereotypes for him to satirize. Cedric Watts has noticed something similar, and Redmond O'Hanlon examines the influence of Nordau on Stein in his book on Conrad and Darwin, reviewed above. More tendentious is Merrill Harvey Goldwyn's case for precedents for *Heart of Darkness* in Hawthorne's fiction. Stretching a point, one might see the connection between Dimmesdale and Kurtz, but the suggested verbal links hardly add up to the 'direct influence' Goldwyn claims. Much more plausibly, G. Peter Winnington finds a new source for *Heart of Darkness* in the boys' stories of Charles Cutcliffe Hyne. Hyne's hero, Captain Kettle, like his creator, travelled to the Congo, and the illustrations in *Pearson's Magazine* even bear a resemblance to Conrad himself. Conrad's inexhaustible novella receives attention from Thomas R. Cleary and Terry G. Sherwood, the symbolic journey suggesting ironic parallels with the *Aeneid* and the *Divine Comedy*. Kurtz becomes 'a failed Aeneas' and Marlow 'a hapless Dante'. Conrad may make the connection with Roman imperialism, but can we really see Kurtz's African mistress as another Dido? Unlikely as it may seem, there is a better case for seeing Kurtz as 'a narcissistically cathected primary ego-ideal', with the mirrors and doubles in Conrad's writing raising questions of identity and desublimation. Marshall W. Alcorn Jr's Freudian reading makes a distinction between Kurtz, a pathological case, and Marlow, who 'works through' his own narcissistic aspirations to a true morality. A number of scholars raise epistemological questions. Martin Bock writes on the connection between sensation and knowledge in the early fiction, taking his terms from the preface to *The Nigger of the 'Narcissus'* and arguing that Conrad is no mere impressionist but structures his scenes and events around a three-stage model of sensation, thought, and image. Martin Ray ranges more widely in an absorbing discussion of the ambiguities of Conrad's feelings about language, embracing both the functional self-effacement of sea-speech and the depraved eloquence of Kurtz and Donkin. Barton Thurber finds in the traditional rhetorical category of the sublime a model for the indeterminacy so characteristic of Conrad's prose, with all rules called into question, as Kant was among the first to recognize. In the same issue Charles I. Schuster proposes a 'telling analogy' between *Typhoon*'s Captain MacWhirr and Pooh Bear, the improbability perhaps excused by his view of the tale as a comic fiction mocking the improbability of its own telling. Problems of narrative are the subject of a somewhat overtechnical analysis of *The Nigger of the 'Narcissus'* by Jakob Lothe, detailing seven distinct narrative situations, while Robert Siegle compares the serial and book versions of *Chance*, showing how 'destabilizing' of the verities pursued by characters and narrators is much more striking in the serialization. Steve Ressler contributes an intelligent reading of 'The Secret Sharer' as the romantic counterpart to *Under Western Eyes*, with Leggatt succeeding where Razumov fails. More surprising though, is Susan Lundvall Brodie's discovery of a feminine perspective in Conrad's fiction, with love offered as a positive emotion and women providing the affirmation and solidarity in much of his output from *Almayer's Folly* onward.

Turning to *The Conradian*, we find John F. Lewis defending the final chapter of *Victory* by arguing that all along we are meant to identify Mr Jones with Davy Jones, he of the locker, and so a figure of death appropriately returning to the sea on the last page. Martin Ray unearths a lost review of *The Nigger of the 'Narcissus'* by H. G. Wells, while Jan Verleun continues his article on books by Jacques Darras and Cedric Watts, 'The Changing Face of Charlie Marlow'. Verleun finds it difficult to recognize Conrad's story-teller in Darras's version, but much to admire in Watts's picture. Owen Knowles, the new editor of *The Conradian*, offers a note on the naming of Archbold in 'The Secret Sharer' and a masterly survey of work on Conrad in the 1983 periodicals. The second issue publishes a selection of papers from the 1984 London Conrad Conference. Jean Szczypien examines Conrad's use of his Uncle Tadeusz's *Memoirs* for his own *A Personal Record*, and Yves Hervouet considers the whole question of Conrad's borrowing, giving various justifications, his weak sense of identity and personal worth and the need to meet deadlines among them. Another Polish contribution comes from Stefan Zabierowski, who discusses a *vie romancée* of the young Conrad by one of his younger compatriots, but the most entertaining paper comes from Sylvère Monod on the difficulties of translating Conrad into French.

In *MFS* Peter Lindenbaum brings much nautical ingenuity to a consideration of the narrative frame of *Heart of Darkness*, showing how the position of the *Nellie* at her moorings is relevant to an understanding of the story. In the same journal David L. Higdon prints and discusses the newly discovered reader's report on *Romance*, recording the 'irritation and tediousness' which led Macmillan to reject the novel. In *Mosaic* (1982), belatedly to hand, T. McAlindon notes that *Nostromo* has been called 'a novel obsessed with history', and in an enterprising article argues that the history is of a Carlylean organicist stamp. Through historical allusion and iconographic language Conrad deploys the ideas on belief, heroes, and hero worship set out in *Sartor Resartus*, though his own scepticism produces an imaginative critique as well as an exploration. Though admitting to possible overingenuity, McAlindon sustains his case that Conrad should be considered, along with Joyce and Eliot, as a master of the 'mythico-historical pun'.

Conrad's Endings, by Arnold E. Davidson, and *Theories of Action in Conrad*, by Francis A. Hubbard, both from UMIRes, will be reviewed in the next volume of *YWES*.

Though Eden Phillpotts was a prolific writer, one hesitates to agree with James Y. Dayanada that the selection of letters he has edited[49] presents 'a unique picture of the Victorian world in microcosm'. Yet his introduction is

49. *Eden Phillpotts: Selected Letters (1862–1960)*, ed. with intro. by James Y. Dayanada. UPA. pp. xii + 319. hb £28.35, pb £17.05.

generally restrained in its claims: only four of Phillpotts' 225 books deserve to survive, his constant preoccupation was money, and, we might add, if the 293 letters here are a fair sample of the other 6000 or so, they are enough to make the point. Dayanada divides the letters into six categories – letters to Americans, letters to editors and writers, and so on. The most surprising are those to his daughter, Adelaide, the object of his incestuous attention, as Dayanada established with the aid of a bizarre questionnaire ('At what age did you experience physical intimacies with your father?', etc.). There are touches of humour from Phillpotts ('To chop the heart out of my old friend [Thomas Hardy] appeared to me a gross indignity, but sentimentalism will go to any lengths if you give a Scot [James Barrie] his head'), but he is scarcely an attractive character, though Dayanada has edited these letters modestly and well, with useful biographies of Phillpotts and his daughter.

Kipling's psychological make-up is the subject of an extended essay by Zohreh T. Sullivan (*MFS*), who takes 'The Brushwood Boy' as a paradigm for the fiction and even the personal myth of the autobiography. The protagonist's descent into the unconscious is given the full Freudian treatment, but the defences he evolves bring no real insight into the nature of his hidden fears, and Kipling himself cannot reconcile in his art his deeply divided consciousness. An earlier tale, 'The Man Who Would Be King', occupies Manfred Draudt (*ES*), who sees the strongly characterized narrator as a foil to the two protagonists, and demonstrates in convincing detail the way the frame-tale's technique informs the meaning.

A 'lonely and neglected child's' animus against his mother informs Anthony West's biography of his father[50]. With a nice irony she is listed among the acknowledgements as 'helpful in a rather different way', and he begins with the determination to be involved with Wells, 'and monumentally so', which led Rebecca West to give birth to himself. Wells is only occasionally present to the young boy, as an 'endlessly fascinating' visitor, and it is not until Chapter VIII that we get back to Wells's own birth, and the days at Bromley and Uppas Park. And so round again to Rebecca, 'doggedly playing her loser's hand' and fabricating evidence against the man who neglected to marry her, while he travels the world, hob-nobbing with the great and good. In his role of righter of wrongs West has hard things to say about Henry James's patronizing of Wells; he 'did not know what seriousness was', and was probably senile anyway. Shaw, who jeered at *The Outline of History*, was 'a coldly cruel man by nature', and the Webbs are taken to task for their 'organized social persecution' of the struggling author. As his title suggests, West's approach is selective, concentrating on relationships which illustrate certain aspects of his father's life, and there are detailed pages on Gissing, Dorothy Richardson, and the Fabians. The familiar stories are vigorously told, but one has the feeling that Wells could look after himself well enough.

Another of Wells's sons has edited a collection of his writings[51] to coincide with the fiftieth anniversary of *Experiment in Autobiography*. It includes the introduction to *The Book of Catherine Wells*, with its contrast between the active 'Jane' known in daily life ('a very tough cookie indeed', is Anthony

50. *H. G. Wells: Aspects of a Life*, by Anthony West. Hutchinson. pp. 405. £12.95.
51. *H. G. Wells in Love: Postscript to an Experiment in Autobiography*, ed. by G. P. Wells. Faber. pp. 253 + 30 illus. £8.95.

West's phrase) and the 'wistful melancholy' revealed in her writings. Readers might reflect that she had much to be melancholy about, even before the onset of the cancer that killed her, but Wells remembers the gaiety and courage. The most substantial of the new material is the much revised 'On Loves and the Lover-Shadow', purporting to treat the side of his personality omitted from his autobiography, those reveries of sensuous delights which the 'more complex mammals' seek to embody in some actual lover. After a certain amount of quasi-scientific theorizing, Wells settles down to tell the tale of the women in his life, only three of whom he actually loved. Usually 'two libertines met', though the other party was not always prepared to treat love as 'an incidental refreshment in life'. Rebecca West has a chapter, a 'splendid *disturbed* brain' he recalls, while admitting that he got much the best out of the relationship; Amber Reeve, Elizabeth Von Arnim, Odette Keun, and Moura Budberg all receive honourable mentions, the last of them one of his great loves. It would be easy to see Wells as fatuously self-regarding, but difficult not to warm to the energy and even the fair-mindedness on display here. The final part of the volume consists of a loose-leaf diary which he kept from 1935 to his death, a death reported, as he prophesied, by his son. No hidden depths are revealed but it is a readable collection, and published, as Wells insisted, with a new edition of *Experiment in Autobiography*[52], where we can renew acquaintance with 'the Discoveries and Conclusions of a Very Ordinary Brain'. Other Wells re-issues include *Kipps*[53], again strongly autobiographical in flavour, with a readable and scholarly introduction by Benny Green, noting the deletions from the manuscript version, and *The Wheels of Chance*[54], edited by Bernard Bergonzi, another product of Wells's early phase with a draper's assistant for hero. A *Reader's Guide to H. G. Wells*, edited by Roger C. Schobin (Starmont House), was not available for review, but Patrick Parrinder (*RMS*) contributed a piece on Wells and the fiction of catastrophe to a collection of 'Visions of Dystopia', setting him in a tradition of such writing going back to Mary Shelley's *The Last Man* and defending Wells's own later work, already foreshadowed in *The War of the Worlds*. More interesting is his discussion of some of the rhetorical features of catastrophe writing: the extraterrestrial point of view, the maintenance of reader passivity, and the re-assuring figure of post-disaster Utopia.

Ian Small (*ELT*) records the fate of the Galsworthy Collection at Birmingham, the 2000 items dispersed, though most are now in New York. In the same issue, Brian J. Hudson looks at the influence of Arnold Bennett's interest in geology, identifying sources and noticing the effect even on his figures of speech. More substantially, again in *ELT*, Andrew Lincoln argues that *Clayhanger* is the product not of artless realism but a thoroughgoing sociological thesis, seen in the organization of Bennett's book around a series of parallels to show consciousness slowly winning out over habit and instinct. Other critics have recognized something of this, but Lincoln persuasively modifies points made by N. J. Hall and James Hepburn. Olga R. Broomfield's *Arnold Bennett* (Twayne) was not seen.

52. *Experiment in Autobiography*, by H. G. Wells. 2 vols. Faber. pp. 838 + 59 illus. £8.95 each.

53. *Kipps*, by H. G. Wells, intro. by Benny Green. OUP. pp. 330. pb £3.95.

54. *The Wheels of Chance*, by H. G. Wells, ed. and intro. by Bernard Bergonzi. Dent. pp. xii + 197. pb £2.50.

A. N. Wilson is well qualified to write a life of Hilaire Belloc[55], bringing a more sympathetic attitude to his subject's religion and politics than is fashionable today. Cardinal Manning, instrumental in the conversion of Belloc's mother to Catholicism, is really the hero of the opening chapter, and her son continued to prefer him to Newman, his teacher at the Oratory. His faith, Wilson opines, was a matter of will rather than emotion, with none of 'this union with God business', though he was lucky in not having to withstand the 'scarcely superable test' of Vatican II. Belloc's account of modern society as 'an increasingly cumbrous collectivist state, shackled . . . to big business' awakens an echo in Wilson's breast, and many of his political judgements, he claims, rather unspecifically, we can now see to have been right. He deals clearly and well with Belloc's part in the Liberal landslide of 1906, and his subsequent disillusionment, and also the protracted courtship of Elodie and his life as a rural gentleman at his uncomfortable Sussex home. As an author, Belloc was 'best over a short distance', but at that best 'one of the finest prose-writers of the century', and there are judicious comments on his voluminous output. His later years were somewhat dispiriting, though his natural belligerence was unabated, and there were good things, like *The Battleground* and his book on Milton. Decrepit old age brought 'an unquestionable growth in holiness' at the end of a long life which perhaps falls short of the 'greatness and genius' Wilson asks us to see there.

The fourth issue of *ELT* is devoted to 'Articles on Max', N. J. Hall leading off with a consideration of a minor genre, the caricatures Beerbohm used to decorate the title pages of books in his library. Since they are not readily accessible, Hall reproduces a number of them, and quotes from his 'The Spirit of Caricature' (1901) to show that Max did not always practise the non-hostile satire he preached. Roger Lewis is less impressed by the drawings, though conceding his success with Henry James and James Barrie. Like Barrie's Peter Pan, Beerbohm was reluctant to grow up, and 'earned the reputation for being major because he stubbornly remained minor'. It is refreshing to meet a dissenting voice, but in contrast Robert Viscusi contributes a rather frothy piece on Max's relations with others, with large claims for his 'biograms' as opening up more far-reaching questions of biography and literary history. The association between Beerbohm and Lytton Strachey is explored by Ira B. Nadel, drawing attention to stylistic affinities, their irony, and the importance both men attached to style itself. Finally John Burgass reports on the Beerbohm collection at Merton College, Oxford.

Ann Barr Snitow combines historical and generic approaches in her valuable study of Ford Madox Ford[56], tracing the development of his characteristic voice (a voice that was to become 'the common property of all twentieth-century writers') from the Pre-Raphaelite beginnings through to *Parade's End*. Tentative, ironic, subjective, the voice was formed in counterpoint to more confident tones, and much of the book goes to distinguishing it from the manner of Conrad, James, Wells, and others. Many of Ford's works reconstruct some period when a form of moral certainty was being undermined by a more modern pluralism. Two chapters go to the collaboration with Conrad,

55. *Hilaire Belloc*, by A. N. Wilson. HH. pp. x + 398 + 26 illus. £12.95.
56. *Ford Madox Ford and the Voice of Uncertainty*, by Ann Barr Snitow. LSU. pp. xiii + 242. £22.55.

for whom irony was saying one thing and meaning another, while for Ford it was saying one thing and not being sure of what other meanings lurked beneath. From Conrad he learnt 'a large arsenal of distancing devices', yet while she recognizes that in underlining Ford's ambivalences she may be simplifying Conrad, Snitow comes close to seeing the older man as a drag on Ford's development. After intelligent discussion of Ford's Jamesian novels, *The Benefactor* and *An English Girl*, she moves on to the new phase marked by his association with *The English Review*, and the novel where the unstable mix of tones begins to gel. In *The Good Soldier*, moral ambivalence is raised to a structural principle, and appropriately we are offered alternative readings of the ending. The retreat from irony to romance can be seen as weakness, or as expressive of the times. The war was a breeding ground for escapist romance, and in *Parade's End* the ironies are 'mythic and celebratory', though the cacophony of voices is still 'wonderfully suggestive'. Believing that for understanding his cultural dilemma 'no date is important after 1914', she declines to follow Ford into his final phase, but her case has already been strongly presented.

Two essays on *The Good Soldier* illustrate their argument from Ford's aesthetics. Michael Levenson (*TCL*) looks at conflicting concepts of character, stemming from Ford's belief that passion challenges the rules which allow us to understand human behaviour as intelligible. The novel mixes traditional accretive character-building with an impressionism which is not as simply complementary as the author hoped, but the result is far from negative: 'we see radical innocence perpetually rediscovering the world'. Miriam Bailin (*MFS*) pursues the relationship between character and author in the person of Dowell. Ford's narrator repeatedly employs aesthetic principles to control and order the descriptive nature of his experience; his consideration of how to make the story seem 'real' in fact distances him further from the reality of the situation, the search being a retreat. And in all this he is like Ford, who finds not a new stability of values, but only a stabilizing aesthetic. The argument is a little tortuous in places, but persuasively documented. Cornelia Cook (*English*) in a review of the recently re-issued *The Rash Act* gives an unusually penetrating study of the novel and its companion piece *Henry for Hugh*. History is no longer a source of values, but of fictions, as Ford goes beyond modernism and his own earlier impressionism, killing off not only a character but an idea of character. Ford's historical trilogy, *The Fifth Queen*[57], is one of the most useful re-issues so far in Oxford Twentieth-century Classics, and comes with a well-informed introduction by A. S. Byatt, demonstrating that the characters are more subtly understood than Ford's conservatism might promise, recognizably the product of the author of *The Good Soldier* and *Parade's End*. Sondra M. Stang's *Ford Madox Ford Reader* (Carcanet) was not available for review, nor was Timothy Weiss's *Fairy Tale and Romance in Ford Madox Ford* (UPA).

John D. Coates has put together a stimulating book on G. K. Chesterton[58], attempting to dispel the 'appallingly inaccurate' stock image of the man and to

57. *The Fifth Queen*, by Ford Madox Ford, intro. by A. S. Byatt. OUP. pp. xiv + 592. pb £4.95.

58. *Chesterton and the Edwardian Cultural Crisis*, by John D. Coates. UHull. pp. xii + 266. pb £8.95.

put him in the context of the age. The 'cultural crisis' of his title involves the seductive movement towards monotheist ideologies, deriving from the prewar myth of creative evolution in the work of Spencer, Shaw, Ernst Haeckel, and others. Chesterton stands out for sanity in a troubled world, his journalistic experience keeping him in touch with ordinary people, but works like *The Flying Inn* aspiring to the status of art. Coates devotes a chapter to the systematic symbolism of the 1914 novel, a deliberate probing of Nietzchean-ism, and there are chapters on the grotesque, the Don Quixote theme in his work, and his rejection of impressionism. The book betrays its origin in a variety of essays adopting different approaches, several of which have been published before, but is more challenging than a conventional life-and-works. Coates has to concede that Chesterton was less effective than T. S. Eliot, for one, in promulgating his artistic and social theories, but he believes he was also less tendentious, a 'loveable and courageous man' who deserves to be more read than he is today. Contributors to *CRev* would no doubt concur, though there is not a great deal of substance in the two issues I have seen this year. One is devoted to Father Brown, prefaced by Chesterton's own 'How to Write a Detective Story', while Jane Donahue Eberwein speculates on the character's appeal to poets, a little inconclusively, and Melvin Cherno on his relevance for historians. Father Brown's intuitive methods are more fruitful, it seems, than modern positivism, and for Gertrude M. White he is 'an artist of the moral life', the stories a mirror of the author's philosophical world, especially the best of them in *The Innocence of Father Brown*. Best of the essays is Barbara Reynolds's extended comparison of Chesterton and Dorothy Sayers, both sharing an 'unashamed vulgarity', a love of craftsmanship, and an interest in the serious possibilities of the detective story. In the August issue Barry Druker has a topical piece on the political art of Chesterton and George Orwell, seeing *The Napoleon of Notting Hill* as a forerunner of the latter's most famous novel (it opens in 1984), and looks at broad parallels in the political thinking of the two men. Nicholas Paxton examines the links between Chesterton's 'The Pagans' and Francis Thompson's 'The Kingdom of God', both treating the theme of redemption. Father Brown appears again: Walter Reindorf rather repetitively defends his intuition as more comprehensive than materialist reasoning, but Douglas G. Greene is on firmer ground with his comparison of Chesterton and John Dickson Carr. As the latter admitted, his detective, Dr Gideon Fell, was modelled on Chesterton.

After the recent memoir of his son, John Buchan's own autobiography is re-issued with an elegant introduction by David Daniell[59]. Though Buchan described his reminiscences as 'brazenly egotistic' there is a marked reluctance to give intimate details, and as Daniell says, it resembles a gallery of fine pictures rather than a conventional autobiography. Since it is issued in Oxford's Twentieth-century Classics, Rainer Maria Rilke's largely auto-biographical *The Notebook of Malte Laurids Brigge*[60], might be mentioned here. This portrait of the artist as a young existentialist, as Stephen Spender calls it in his brief preface, reads well, though one has to scour the copyright details for the translator's name.

59. *Memory Hold-the-Door. The Autobiography of John Buchan*, with intro. by David Daniell. Dent. pp. xvii + 327. pb £4.95.

60. *The Notebook of Malte Laurids Brigge*, by Rainer Maria Rilke, trans. by John Linton, with intro. by Stephen Spender. OUP. pp. xix + 243. pb £3.50.

The Longest Journey[61] comes with all the scholarly apparatus we have come to expect from the Abinger edition, including a ninety-page appendix on the manuscripts, enabling us to see which episodes caused Forster trouble; not surprisingly they include the handling of Stephen Wonham and Wiltshire in general. Additional appendixes deal with Forster's Uncle Willie, a model for Mrs Failing, and other writings relevant to the novel, while Elizabeth Heine's introduction has intelligent discussion of the rhythm of the book, its triadic structure, and 'strikingly modern' use of symbolism. The Cambridge background, the effect of Forster's revision of Julia Wedgwood's *The Moral Ideal*, and his knowledge of homosexuality at that date help to fill out the picture, and the textual and general notes are agreeably full, as always.

One critic with a high opinion of *The Longest Journey* is P. J. M. Scott, whose book[62] on Forster is one of the most readable of recent years, with a strong personal flavour. An opening chapter dismisses Forster's shortcomings as 'manques', among them his 'scrappy' essays, 'shallow assumptions', and the 'whole boggy tract' of his attempts at depicting homosexual relations. This out of the way, he moves on to a breezy discussion of the prewar fiction, singling out his treatment of landscape ('the last great Romantic poet in English letters') and his strengths as a social critic in comparison with the overrated D. H. Lawrence. All this is interspersed with asides on AIDS, the punitive local rating system, Idi Amin, and the Chinese character. Believing that the more directly he tackled homosexual themes the less well he wrote, Scott wishes Forster had abandoned *Maurice* and pressed on with the much more promising *Arctic Summer*. And since tragedy is 'entirely an outrageous posture', *Passage to India* might have been a little less gloomy, though Forster remains 'one of the great funny writers'. Scott met the author in 1968, and he records conversations they had, but otherwise there is little here that is new, though the blend of enthusiasm and the ability to see that Forster was in some ways 'wonderfully unappealing', ensures that the book is never dull.

Rukun Advani's study of Forster's criticism[63] is more straightforwardly academic, originating in a Ph.D. thesis. Chapters on Forster's view of human existence, the social order, and religion precede chapters devoted to his aesthetics and literary criticism. Advani has dug out a good deal of unnoticed material, like the 1938 essay 'The Ivory Tower' which expounds Forster's view of the civilized individual as the end of society, and his account of the 'ambivalent sceptical mysticism' which characterized Forster's view of religion is persuasive. What Scott calls 'wishy-washy liberalism' appears more coherent here, though Foster is not a powerful thinker, nor does Advani claim that he is. One problem is that Forster seems sufficiently accessible as an essayist not to require lengthy exposition, but it is perhaps convenient to have his likes and dislikes set out so clearly, and the unpublished 1908 essay on Kipling, judging by Advani's summary, should be available. His summing-up of Forster's position as 'minor but quirky' seems exactly right, and there is a pleasing modesty about Advani's own approach.

61. *The Longest Journey*, by E. M. Forster, ed. and intro. by Elizabeth Heine. Arnold. pp. lxx + 434. £37.50.

62. *E. M. Forster: Our Permanent Contemporary*, by P. J. M. Scott. Vision. pp. 215. £14.95.

63. *E. M. Forster as Critic*, by Rukun Advani. CH. pp. 225. £16.95.

The 1973 Critical Heritage volume on Forster[64] has been re-issued in paper-back, its terminal date covering the publication of *Maurice*, but not the posthumous short fiction. This figures largely in an essay by Jane Perry Levine (*PMLA*) under the heading of 'The Tame in Pursuit of the Savage'. The homosexual fiction is to be understood not only in emotional terms, but politically too, as intending to subvert the prevailing ethos. Edward Carpenter receives attention as a campaigner for the positive value of homoerotic love, extending beyond the merely private realm, and there is good use of the manuscripts of *Maurice* and some of the stories in *The Life to Come* to support her readings. They call for no major revision of our picture of Forster, but he seems a little more of an outsider, a little further removed from Bloomsbury.

It has long been known that the available texts of *Ulysses* are 'replete with errors', over 5000 of them in the first edition and still an average of seven a page in 1961. Now after seven years' labour and all the latest technology the Munich editors offer 'the ideal state of development' of Joyce's masterpiece[65] as it stood in 1922 – in effect the Rosenbach manuscript with Joyce's revisions but free from copying errors. This occupies the right-hand pages of the present edition, while the left-hand page, once one has mastered the bewildering variety of editorial symbols, shows the stages by which Joyce arrived at it. A lengthy afterword discusses these stages in detail, and there are the expected textual and bibliographical notes. Though the intention is 'radically conserva-tive', from the nature of the material – with so much of the text added at the proof stage – editorial decisions have to be made in distinguishing deliberate changes from inadvertent ones; but the experts have generally greeted the new edition with enthusiasm. Hugh Kenner (*TLS*) finds only one editorial decision to deplore, and that an insignificant one, though his valuing of the new price for Bloom's bar of chocolate (one shilling) would not find favour with Denis Donoghue (*LRB*). Richard Ellmann (*NYRB*) is pleased to have his guess at the 'word known to all men' in the 'Circe' episode confirmed (it is 'love') and shows how it sheds light on Stephen's reply to his mother. To the more casual observer the changes seem less than world-shaking, and the cost will no doubt restrict sales to university libraries, but the result of so much scholarship is surprisingly accessible, laid out on eminently sensible principles, and it is good to know that the right-hand pages at least will soon be available at a moderate price.

Joyce's struggle with the censors is commemorated in documents[66] relating to the lawsuit which led Judge John M. Woolsey to find for the American publishers in December 1933. The documents range from office memos to Edmund Wilson's piece in the *NR*, including letters of support from assorted big names and more general press reaction. There is some dissent, with Francis Talbot S.J. inveighing against 'this immoral crusade against decency' but

64. *E. M. Forster: The Critical Heritage*, ed. by Philip Gardner. RKP. pp. xx + 498. pb £8.95.

65. *Ulysses: A Critical and Synoptic Edition*, by James Joyce, prepared by Hans Walter Gabler, Wolfhard Steppe and Claus Melchior. 3 vols. Garland. pp. xiii + 1919. $200.

66. *The United States of America v. One Book entitled 'Ulysses' by James Joyce: Documents and Commentary – A 50-year Retrospective*, ed. by Michael Moscato and Leslie LeBlanc, intro. by Richard Ellmann. UPA. pp. xxvii + 482. $27.50.

history was against him. If some of the more bizarre lines of defence are to be credited it did not much matter, since the 'stream-of-consciousness method' would 'discourage and repel' the average reader. The lawyers were lucky with their judge, possessed of an elegant prose style, first editions of Dr Johnson, and a fund of common sense. Inevitably the present collection is tedious when spread over nearly five hundred pages, and one cannot hope for anything remarkable in the way of literary criticism, but perhaps one of the judge's less elegant pronouncements got it right: 'Parts of it are pretty rough, but other parts are swell.'

The rough and the swell receive attention in UMIRes's simultaneous publication of a number of theses on aspects of *Ulysses*. To begin at the beginning, Rodney Wilson Owen[67] asks 'Why June 16th, 1904?'. The funeral of Martin Cunningham's real-life original, and the date of the new moon in the *Odyssey* are part of the answer, which involves much scholarly persistence and a detailed review of Joyce's work on *Ulysses* over more than ten years. The detective work has its own fascination, and Owen's claim that it shows *Exiles*, *Portrait*, and *Ulysses* to be more 'coterminous' than has been realized, is persuasive. Robert Janusko aims to increase our enjoyment of 'Oxen of the Sun'[68] by showing how Joyce wrote the chapter and giving the specific passages on which he drew for his parodies. Over sixty pages go to the latter, drawing on the 2500 notes which Joyce made for the purpose. Other chapters discuss the narratives and themes, the embryological framework, and the parodies themselves, relying a good deal on Stuart Gilbert, but arguing with A. M. Klein's 1949 article on 'Oxen'. It is hard to care whether Janusko is right or not, though there is something to be said for his point that the general connection between human and artistic conception and growth is more significant than particular correspondences between the authors parodied and the months in which they appear. A more substantial contribution, though overlapping to some extent with the Munich edition, is Richard E. Madtes's treatment of 'Ithaca'[69]. The first three chapters discuss the evolution of the text, with detailed description of the notesheets and plenty of statistics, revealing that a quarter of the questions in this section were added at proof stage and speculating sensibly on reasons for the additions. The next two chapters consider some of the critical issues raised by Joyce's apparent detachment. As Madtes sees it, there are really two texts, the explicit boring one and the 'inconspicuous hinterland' which is humorous and touching. As for the significance of the meeting of Bloom and Stephen, as naturalistic narrative it points to failure, but as symbolic suggestion to something more hopeful. Finally we have a useful page-by-page survey, explaining and commenting on the whole chapter, and the Rosenbach manuscript is an appendix.

The narration of 'Ithaca' also attracts Patrick A. McCarthy (*ELH*), who argues that the air of objectivity is undercut by deliberate inconsistencies casting doubt on the reliability of the narrator and narrative itself through a kind of artistic uncertainty principle. Flaubert had pioneered similar satiric

67. *James Joyce and the Beginnings of Ulysses*, by Rodney Wilson Owen. UMIRes (1983). pp. x + 154. £31.25.

68. *The Sources and Structure of James Joyce's 'Oxen'*, by Robert Janusko. UMIRes (1983). pp. ix + 170. £31.25.

69. *The 'Ithaca' Chapter of Joyce's 'Ulysses'*, by Richard E. Madtes. UMIRes (1983). pp. xiii + 160. £31.25.

techniques in *Madame Bovary*, and the Munich edition makes it easier to confirm the intentional nature of the errors on which it depends.

Though not from UMIRes, *An Anatomy of 'Penelope'*[70] has a similar pattern, with an appendix clearly setting out Joyce's additions to the Rosenbach manuscript. Card's basic point is that the supposed free flow is the result of meticulous organization, as he demonstrates with chapters on the stages of composition, the contradictions and their bearing on what he calls 'the selective fallacy', and the structure of the repetitions, where he elaborates on Diane Tolomeo's numerological pattern. Card is an honest journeyman and master of the card index, but his book has its uses. The patterns in *Ulysses* as a whole and their dependence on coincidence in the interaction of the characters are subtly probed by John Hannay (*ELH*), who like Patrick McCarthy sees parallels in *Madame Bovary* in the way irony is generated though the characters' projection on events of their own psychological structures. Yet a sense of destiny and order survives the irony, amounting to more than random comedy. The logic of the book provokes much ingenuity and erudition from Ralph W. Rader (*CritI*), taking in the 'pervasively autobiographical' nature of Joyce's imaginative return to his own early life, and emphasizing the import of the garrulous old sailor W. B. Murphy as 'linchpin' of the action who, like the ghost of Hamlet's father, helps to link Bloom and Stephen. Rader's own logic is by no means compelling, but he ranges wide and wittily. For Mack Smith (*TCL*) the structural rhythm of the book can best be seen in musical terms, with the reconciliation of father and son and the notion of consubstantiality subjected to innumerable variations. Ezra Pound and Anthony Burgess have gestured in this direction before, but Mack Smith works it out in detail, with the first six chapters as exposition of the theme, and so on through to the ending where although the action of the characters gives only an ambiguous picture of reconciliation, the underlying musical pattern resolves into the tonic. In *Expl* David G. Wright comments on the one-legged sailor in 'Wandering Rocks', adding a few more ironic touches, and Yael Renan, translator of *Ulysses* into Hebrew, corrects a few points in Gifford and Seidman's *Notes for Joyce*.

The Joyce centennial continues to bear fruit, though there are only meagre pickings in *Light Rays: James Joyce and Modernism*[71], a spin-off from the conference at Rutgers University. Richard Ellmann leads with general reflections on Joyce's attitudes to church, state, and women. For all his scepticism, Joyce was not without religious feeling; though never a flag-waving nationalist, the picture of Ireland in his books discloses a 'higher politics'; whatever his relations with the opposite sex in life, in fiction he gave them their due. Hayward Ehrlich introduces the formative idea of the collection: Joyce is at one centre of our century, his sun illuminating knowledge, sexuality, philosophy, and all the arts, and the essays that follow are grouped to show his contribution to these areas. A good many of them have appeared before, like John Cage's account of his settings of parts of the *Wake*, Shari Benstock's discussion of the Matisse illustrations for the 1935 publication of *Ulysses*, and Evan R. Firestone's essay on Joyce's impact on the New York painters of the

70. *An Anatomy of 'Penelope'*, by James Van Dyck Card. AUP. pp. 167. £18.50.
71. *Light Rays: James Joyce and Modernism*, ed. by Heyward Ehrlich, prologue by Richard Ellmann. New Horizon Press. pp. xii + 224. $19.95.

1940s and 1950s for whom he became 'a sort of patron saint'. These pieces along with the reproduction of part of a Pierre Boulez piano sonata, stimulated by Joyce's example, represent 'Avant Garde Music', and 'Abstract Art', while 'Neoteric Psychology' is the heading given to a farcical pastiche of Joycean ideas and methods by Norman O. Brown. 'Contemporary Philosophy' disappointingly comprises only the introduction to Margaret Norris's structuralist analysis of the *Wake*, and a rather general piece by Morton P. Levitt charting the movement from Edwardian to Modernist narration but denying any real break with earlier humanist traditions. Zack Bowen sees Joyce's chief contribution to the age as his re-affirmation of 'the basic proposition that everything is ultimately the same', and demonstrates the working out of processes of amalgamation and synthesis in detailed analysis of two examples from *Ulysses*. The first links Wagner's *Ring* and Music Hall songs in 'Wandering Rocks' and 'Circe', while the second again brings together the comic and sublime in examining the function of W. B. Murphy, already touched on in the essay by Ralph Rader mentioned above. Finally, he turns to *A Portrait of the Artist* and the pattern of *recorso* and recapitulation, characteristic of all Joyce's work, most comprehensively seen in the *Wake* which draws together the total *oeuvre*. Bowen's substantial piece is accompanied under the heading of 'Popular Culture' by an entertaining essay by Leslie Fiedler, dissenting from Judge Woolsey's high-minded pronouncement on *Ulysses* and reclaiming it for the truly popular modes of porn, pop, and parody. As he says, only a hostility to the whole of 'Eng. Lit.' could have prompted the perpetration of the deliberately boring 'Oxen of the Sun'. 'The New Sexuality' is covered by an essay of Morris Beja's reviewed last year in *The Seventh of Joyce* (*YW* 64.436–8), and another by Robert Boyle S.J., building on his earlier *James Joyce's Pauline Vision* (*YW* 60.367–8) to argue that the Third Person of Joyce's Trinity is female, given flesh in Molly and ALP. Some of the best pieces, not surprisingly, come under the heading of Joyce and Experimental Literature. 'All good structuralists,' as Ihab Hassan puts it, 'go to *Finnegans Wake* on their way to heaven.' He then offers seven perspectives on the question he sets himself: how does the work make itself available to the postmodern imagination? His answer and qualifications do more justice to the aim of the collection than most of the other contributions, though he ends with a reservation. May not human destiny be 'larger than this vast, retrograde, and reversible riddle' (the *Wake*) implies? Justified by his contention that 'a Wakean consciousness permits the past to be affected by the future', Fritz Senn heads in the opposite direction, bringing his revivifying scholarship to bear on Joyce's source. On closer inspection, Homer too is self-reflective and full of deceit, when scrutinized through a post-*Ulyssean* lens. Finally, there is a typical display of pyrotechnics from Hugh Kenner to show how identities for Bloom are created in the contexts jointly produced by Joyce's tropes and the reader's imagination. That metempsychosis which puzzles Molly over her morning cup of tea is the premise of the whole book.

Newly translated, mostly from the Parisian journals of the 1970s, are seven essays[72] aimed both at Joyceans and literary theorists. In a well-judged introduction, the editors note how the older criticism has largely assimilated what

---

72. *Post-Structuralist Joyce: Essays from the French*, ed. by Derek Attridge and Daniel Ferrer. CUP. pp. xi + 162. hb £20, pb £6.95.

was so puzzling in 1922, either transcendently (through myth and symbol), empirically (through biography and contemporary reference), or by claiming it for that humane tradition of letters it once seemed to deny. Perhaps we need to go to the French to feel the force of Joyce's revolution, to 'confront the unreadability of the text' anew. Unreadability in a more traditional sense characterizes much of what follows, though Stephen Heath has good things to say on Joyce's 'strategies of hesitation', and the self-reflexive irony pioneered by Flaubert, while Daniel Ferrer is at least comprehensible in his investigation of 'Circe' and the uncanny that lies at the heart of it. André Topia considers intertextuality in *Ulysses* and the status of the quotation, the text becoming a 'configuration within which both orphaned and hypercoded discourses circulate', while Jacques Aubert proposes a reading of the opening word of *Finnegans Wake*, borrowing terminology from mechanics and cybernetics. The editors tell us the various metaphoric models on offer need not be taken too seriously, so perhaps Jean-Michel Rabaté's notion of the *Wake* as a 'perverse semic machine', dislocating the classical relationship between production and information, requires a pinch of salt. Hélène Cixous goes back to the opening of 'The Sisters' and 'a perceptible hesitating on the surface to be inscribed', finally seeing the whole story as a way of saying that saying Dublin equals saying death. Many of the positions in these essays have filtered through to the general consciousness – the text as a multiplicity of possibilities, the reader as producer rather than consumer, and so on – and the particular analyses defy summary. The heavy playfulness is another legacy of the period, though the final piece a 'more or less extempore talk' by Jacques Derrida, was given at the Pompidou Centre as recently as 1982. One hopes the chairs were comfortable. (See also p. 781 for another notice of this collection.)

Best of these collections of essays is *A Companion to Joyce Studies*[73], the attempt to provide a 'complete guide' through the complexities of Joyce's work. The pieces are specially written for the occasion, but there are differences in the way contributors approach their task. Some, like James Carens writing on the *Portrait*, attempt to cover the best that has been thought and said, while others, like Chester Anderson discussing Joyce's verses, or Bernard Benstock on *Exiles*, seem more concerned with an individual reading. Edmund L. Epstein begins with a biographical essay on the Joyce family and its connection with the work, noting sadly that the difficulties with Book II of the *Wake* reflect those at home: his family was not really every family and 'the procession of the generations did not really occur'. Joyce's correspondence is discussed under various headings by Mary T. Reynolds. 'Prolific rather than elegant' it nevertheless adds up to a 'major document in literary history'. Michael Groden copes manfully with the tangled textual and publishing history of Joyce's career, volume by volume. Anderson's analysis of the verse concentrates on 'The Holy Office' and 'I would in that sweet bosom be', with tentative Freudian suggestions and some attention to the literary allusions, and without making inflated claims for it. Florence L. Walzl has nothing very new to say about *Dubliners*, though she has space to consider the revisions, and allows Dante to loom pretty large. *Stephen Hero*, to be read, Thomas E. Connelly advises, only after the more finished work, is summarized and

73. *A Companion to Joyce Studies*, ed. by Zack Bowen and James F. Carens. Greenwood. pp. xiv + 818. £71.95.

treated as a sketch book or diary rather than a novel. Over a hundred pages go
to Carens' pleasingly full account of the novel which emerged from it, stressing
the ironies and ambiguities of the ending in view of the fate of the son of
Stephen's namesake. Joyce's 'Notes by the Author' are heavily utilized in
Benstock's analysis of *Exiles*, with Richard seen as less dominant than in some
interpretations. Vicki Mahaffy makes up for the 'strange neglect' of Joyce's
Trieste sketches, *Giacomo Joyce*, by claiming it is a more 'pivotal phase' in the
movement towards *Ulysses* with its protean lady one of the prototypes for the
many women of the later novels. *Ulysses* itself is seen as the work of a 'comic
virtuoso', the provider not of ultimate myths but of the possibilities for patterns and motifs, in a lengthy chapter-by-chapter survey from Zack Bowen.
Finnegans Wake is covered, if that is the word, by three essays, the first from
Patrick A. McCarthy on the structure and meanings, with chapter-by-chapter
analysis, a preference for the middle ground between interpretive extremes
and a final improbable assertion that the *Wake* is a book 'about ordinary life
for ordinary people'. Michael H. Begnal looks more closely at the language
and the essential plurality of the *Wakean* word, while Barbara DiBernard
examines the way in which it is built up through accumulation and expansion,
taking as an example the motif of 'ashes to ashes, dust to dust' which she
follows for seventy-one pages. She draws on the acknowledged authorities on
the book and concludes by recommending us to revel in its uncertainties.
Joyce's aesthetic theories and critical writings are the subject of a chapter by
Robert Scholes and Marlena G. Corcoran, and Morris Beja defends the idea
of the epiphany – so pervasive in modern criticism though it occurs only in a
few pages of discarded manuscript – against those who have questioned its
utility as a critical term. Finally, Sidney Feshbach and William Herman conduct a comprehensive survey of Joyce criticism and scholarship, now amounting to more than 10,000 items, though mercifully not all are mentioned here.
The preceding essays each have their own bibliographies, and all in all, for
anyone with the patience and the inclination this collection does seem to offer
everything the editors promise.

Companionable on a smaller scale is Patrick Parrinder's new book[74] on
Joyce, a middle-of-the-road introduction, though the road follows a different
route nowadays, with the poststructuralists beckoning seductively from the
other side of the Channel. Parrinder acknowledges them, but hears in *Ulysses*
'an imaginatively congruent pattern of voices' rather than the babble of narra-
tivity. Nor is he convinced by Stuart Gilbert's hushed solemnities, finding
something livelier and more subversive, a work of fiction masquerading as
scripture. On *Dubliners* he is resistant to symbol-hunting and allegory, and
offers a surprisingly unironic reading of the close of 'The Dead'. *Ulysses* and
the *Wake* are at the centre of the study, and a first chapter on 'Joyce and the
Grotesque' aims to make this emphasis clear, though inevitably the succeeding
chapters drop back into more conventional guided tours through familiar
landscape. 'The rewards of reading the *Wake* are immense', Parrinder tells us,
but he has space only to indicate his enthusiasm. In fact a characteristic of the
book is that although the comic Joyce he presents is convincing and appealing,
the discussion floats ideas without trenchantly pursuing them home, excusably
perhaps with so slippery a customer.

74. *James Joyce*, by Patrick Parrinder. CUP. pp. ix + 262. hb £20, pb £6.95.

Feminism was bound to catch up with Joyce eventually, and the recent *Women in Joyce* (*YW* 64.439–40) is followed by Bonnie Kime Scott's single-handed survey[75], which suffers from trying to include everything that could come under the heading. An opening chapter gives supposedly relevant cultural contexts, ranging from Celtic prehistory and Sheela-na-gig to Mariolatry and the suffragists. Other chapters follow on Joyce's early encounters with feminism (in the works of Ibsen mainly and the home of the Skeffington family), and on the women in his own extended family, including the '23 sisters' he joked about and even two of Nora's. The various females who fostered his genius and the critics like Mary Colum and Virginia Woolf who wrote about him all get a mention, though the information is heaped up rather than deployed. The three leading women in the fiction get a chapter each: Emma Clery (this is a version of Scott's contribution to *Women in Joyce*, reviewed last year), Molly Bloom, and Issy of the *Wake*. The approach is to relate them to 'real life': Molly's plans for the future of her daughter, for instance, provide an opportunity to consider 'the options open to young women in 1904'. The result is readable, with plenty of reference to what other critics have said. Indeed, the author's forte seems to be summary rather than analysis, and though she is not, as she fears, off-puttingly feminist, her revision is less than the promised revelation.

Even so, it has more substance than Archie K. Loss's *Joyce's Visible Art*[76], a dissertation on the relationship between Joyce's fiction and what was going on in painting over the same period. Beginning with the persistent *fin de siècle* element in the prose, Loss parallels developments in Joyce's art with cubism, dadaism, surrealism, and so on, all convincing enough in a general sense, but the literary models usually seem much closer and the particular paintings (given in illustration) of only doubtful relevance. There are parallels between cubism and collage and what Joyce does in *Ulysses*, as we know, and connections between impressionism and the stream-of-consciousness, but Loss's study gets little further than modest assertion of the fact.

The literary response to *Hamlet* in the heroic age of modernism is the subject of another thesis[77], which opens with a survey of earlier Shakespeare criticism, singling out figures of special interest to Joyce and Eliot like George Brandes and Jules Laforgue. The chapter on Joyce's *Hamlet* criticism considers the rather scrappy manuscript notes which survive from his 1912 Trieste lectures, concluding that his attitude was 'not radically different' from Stephen's in 'Scylla and Charybdis'. Eliot's famous 1919 essay on Hamlet and his problems is the subject of another chapter, with lengthy summaries of E. E. Stoll and J. M. Robertson. For both Joyce and Eliot the 'archaeological' approach takes precedence over the nineteenth century's more personal involvement, but their own interpretations are dismissed rather unkindly as 'no more than curiosities for the literary historian'. Some of the material under discussion has an intrinsic interest (though the appendixes reproducing Joyce's notebooks are disappointing), but Quillian does not do a great deal with it.

75. *Joyce and Feminism*, by Bonnie Kime Scott. Harvester. pp. x + 242. £25.
76. *Joyce's Visible Art: The Work of Joyce and the Visual Arts, 1904–1922*, by Archie K. Loss. UMIRes. pp. xi + 128 + 40 illus. £35.75.
77. *Hamlet and the New Poetic: James Joyce and T. S. Eliot*, by William H. Quillian. UMIRes (1983). pp. xvi + 171. £31.25.

Likely to prove of more lasting value is Vincent John Cheng's[78] study of the use Joyce made of Shakespeare, listing over 1000 allusions page by page in the middle section and in an appendix giving the Shakespearean sources alluded to, but making good its claim to be more than simply a work of reference. Five chapters consider the allusions in relation to the themes and organization of the *Wake*. 'History and Possibility' are the subject of the first, while the second, 'All the World's a Stage', aims to show how Joyce conceived of his last work as a drama. The 'structural matrix' of the *Wake* is *Hamlet*, and the correspondences between the two get a chapter to themselves, while 'Fathers and Sons' and 'The Strife Between Brothers' are seen to occupy Shakespeare and Joyce alike. Though Vico takes precedence, Cheng shows how Joyce's reading of Ernest Jones's interpretation of *Hamlet* clarifies the family drama as we meet it in the *Wake*, and though he presumes more familiarity with the latter than most of us can claim, he writes clearly and well about it. This is less obviously the case in *PQ* with Shari Benstock's 'reframing' of Joyce's text through Jacques Derrida's *La Carte Postale*, part of her continuing interest in correspondence in Joyce. At any rate, confronted with two such difficult texts, this reader for one fails to get the message.

Turning to the more manageable *Portrait of the Artist*, one is scarcely surprised by B. L. Reid's contention (*SR*) that the novel is highly patterned, though his detailed argument that the first chapter is a 'gnomon' of the whole novel becomes tedious, in spite of his breezy approach. To see the book as 'five individual planes slanting from low to high' cannot add much to our enjoyment. More of a discovery comes with Theoharis C. Theoharis's identification (*SoR*) of a source for Stephen's aesthetics in an *Encyclopaedia Britannica* article by W. T. Watts-Dunton. One can only agree that the verbal similarities are 'too striking to be accidental', and his conclusion that the novel exalts Stephen's genius while ridiculing his aesthetics as 'stagnant Victorian orthodoxy' has much to commend it. For Thérèse Vichy (*EA*) the crisis of modernism can be read in the split between Chapter V and what has gone before, though her study of the rhetoric is both detailed and difficult. A new concept of the hero, inherited from Ibsen, is visible in the *Portrait*, according to Daniel Schenker (*ELH*), but Stephen's ironic aloofness is to be distinguished from the 'profoundly religious' sensibility of his creator. All this is part of an overelaborate argument taking in Flaubert and Kierkegaard, designed to demonstrate 'the failure of modern irony' and the superiority of the comic mode. Similarly overblown is Adrienne Auslander Munich's probing of 'The Dead' (*MP*) for the subtext which exemplifies Joyce's struggle, indicated through allusions to dead authors, past life, and lost languages, to evolve his modernist style. There is some good close analysis, but rich as it is, Joyce's tale is taken for more than its worth. Where Munich sees the ending as 'mock epic but comic', Claire Tarplee (*Proceedings of the Seville International Joyce Centenary*) finds in 'the impersonal snow of eternity' a positive note to replace the satire on Catholicism with which the intention to round off the collection with 'Grace' would have left us. We are conducted briskly through the other stories, but there is nothing really new to add to previous speculation on Joyce's addition to the original *Dubliners*.

78. *Shakespeare and Joyce: A Study of 'Finnegans Wake'*, by Vincent John Cheng. PSU. pp. 271. £19.

There is still more to say about 'The Sisters' argues Brian A. Bremen in the only issue of *JJQ* I have been able to see. Examining the revisions, he follows the movement away from the sisters to the relationship between the boy and the priest, seeing in the 'scrupulousness' of both a way of underlining the coherence of the development. He also notices an interesting parallel between the description of 'Dante' Riordan in Stanislaus's recollections and that of the priest in Joyce's story. Cordell D. K. Yee, also in *JJQ*, comes to the defence of Stephen's aesthetics, backing up her case with the *Summa Theologiae* and arguing for the consistency of Joyce's theories and Thomist principles. Joyce emerges as a devotee of the medieval cult of number and proportion, and although the distance between Stephen and the narrator widens, this does not necessarily signal ironic intent. The mockery is reserved for Lynch, even though he has most of the best lines. Descartes, rather than Aquinas, provides Philip Sicker with a key to Stephen's dream in *Ulysses*. He too dreamt of an oriental bearing a melon, back in 1618, likewise triggered by guilt at rejecting the old wisdom, and both men pass from doubt and terror to love and harmony, though only after much ingenious analysis by Sicker. Writing as a professor of music, Heath Lees subjects the introduction to 'Sirens' to musicological attention, discovering there a double fugue and precise rhythmic parallels with Bach's *The Art of Fugue*. Certainly he takes the often-noticed musical analogy more literally than has been usual and has the notation to prove his point, though it is one that only the specialist could really appreciate. The non-musical notes in this issue include items from Bonnie Kime Scott, exhuming discussion of Giordano Bruno and Ernest Renan from back numbers of the University College *Lyceum*, and Darcy O'Brien discovering a pamphlet on Ibsen by Patrick Pearse, evidence that Joyce was not alone in his enthusiasm for the Norwegian dramatist. Elsewhere, in *Expl*, among the trivia that only Joyce scholarship could accommodate, Kitti Carriker Eastman points out that the 'hacking chestnut' of the *Portrait* belonged to Walsh and not to Stephen, and Jerry Leath Mills finds evidence of the Director's spiritual pride in Joyce's allusion to a speech from *Everyman*, later utilized in 'Oxen of the Sun'. But enough, and already too much, though Marguerite Harknell's the *Aesthetics of Daedalus and Bloom* (AUP) was not available for review.

The last volume of Virginia Woolf's *Diary*[79] opens as she nears her fifty-fourth birthday and closes four days before her death. There are the usual doubts – is *The Years*, she wonders, 'feeble twaddle'? – and fits of depression, when whole months go by unrecorded, but as Anne Olivier Bell says, it is 'by no means a wholly cheerless or dispiriting chronicle'. There are many of the sharp and catty comments that have led some readers to prefer the diary to the fiction. We glimpse Tom Eliot, rapt and enthusiastic over *Ulysses*, Morgan Forster at a party 'with the usual Bugger crew', and Lord David 'like the stalk of a bluebell . . . no juice'. The hunger for experience continues to the end, with observation a method for holding onto the world, though the ordinary can appear threatening, like the conversation overheard in the ladies' loo at the Sussex Grill. 'We pay the penalty for our rung in society by infernal boredom', she complained, but she continues to entertain her readers, and the editors to maintain their exemplary standards. A substantial review of this volume by

79. *The Diary of Virginia Woolf*. Vol. V: *1936–41*, ed. by Anne Olivier Bell, assisted by Andrew McNeillie. Hogarth. pp. xiv + 402. £17.50.

John Bayley (*LRB*) adds some bracing dissent to the general chorus of praise.

Brenda Silver introduces a guide to Virginia Woolf's notebooks[80], all sixty-seven of them, the results of her reading pen in hand, giving us still more material on critic, biographer, novelist, and feminist. The last named looms large in the preface, larger perhaps than is justified by what follows, though notes for *Three Guineas* fill three volumes, providing 'an important contribution to the social history of the Thirties'. Silver has done her job well, but we cannot expect the riches of, say, Coleridge's notebooks, for this is a guide not a transcript. We may be told that 'the entry includes a large number of general notes about Sterne's style and about the poetic novel', for example, but to discover exactly what we must repair to Sussex or the Berg Collection, or remain content with the use Woolf made of the jottings in her published work. A further guide to the essays is provided by Elizabeth Steele's investigation[81] of these same sources, itself an ingenious piece of detective work documenting Woolf's use of her material under four categories: main, supportive, important allusions, and passing allusions. In effect, she provides the footnotes Woolf omitted, and the alphabetical compilation allows us to see at a glance what is used where. There are appendixes on the collections of books from her library, and listings of the ten collections of essays she produced. The use of literary allusions as a rhetorical strategy in *A Room of One's Own* receives detailed attention from Alice Fox (*PQ*). Woolf's argument is that a writer depends on his or her predecessors, hence the difficulties for women who can learn only so much from men, an argument reinforced by ironical allusion to Tennyson, Milton, Gray, and others. Though the Hogarth edition of the *Letters* is now complete, Joanne Trautmann Banks (*MFS*) prints nineteen discovered recently. They 'yield no startling revelation', as she admits, but there are agreeable letters to her nephew, Julian Bell, to Duncan Grant, and to her sister Vanessa. Virginia is not included, but many of her friends and her future husband appear in *Euphrosyne*, a 1905 collection of poems which S. P. Rosenbaum (*TCL*) proposes as 'The First Book of Bloomsbury', discussing the unremarkable contents at length.

'No writer's life can be so fully documented', begins Lyndall Gordon[82] in her book on Virginia Woolf; and she is content to accept Quentin Bell's biography as 'definitive', but her individual contribution is to link the writing with the life. The first section, 'Victorian Models', sees her celebrated modernism as 'in a sense spurious', with Leslie Stephen, 'the most loveable of men', her most enduring intellectual model. In spite of the sickness and the 'twenty dark years' from her mother's death to the publication of *The Voyage Out*, she was tough, like her father. In that first book she 'rewrites the Victorian ideal', though finally the book falls short of its promise. Section Two, 'The Life Composed', considers the bearing of her marriage on the writing, taking a fairly positive view of it and of Leonard, in spite of a certain inflexibility and his reluctance to have the children she wanted. Her letters are performances, revealing the 'flamboyant artist', but in her 'great diary' we see 'her most sustained counter to history'. The relationship with Katherine Mansfield is played up, and her

80. *Virginia Woolf's Reading Notebooks*, ed. by Brenda Silver. Princeton (1983). pp. xv + 384. $27.50.

81. *Virginia Woolf's Literary Sources and Allusions: A Guide to the Essays*, by Elizabeth Steele. Garland (1983). pp. ix + 364. $43.

82. *Virginia Woolf: A Writer's Life*, by Lyndall Gordon. OUP. pp. 341. £12.95.

affair with Vita Sackville-West played down: her flirtation with androgyny was short-lived. There is excellent critical discussion of *The Waves*, for Gordon along with *To the Lighthouse* her greatest work, and illuminating comparisons with Joyce, Eliot, and the romantic poets. Committed to 'the "dark" side of Virginia Woolf', she gives less space to more superficial books, like *The Years*, and concedes only 'a partial truth' to the feminist view of her subject. Some reviews of *A Writer's Life* had complaints about the style, but for me it reads intelligently and well; those who have looked at Gordon's earlier book on T. S. Eliot will know what to expect.

Good again, though in marked contrast, is Madeline Moore's study[83] of the mystical and the political in Woolf's fiction. Woolf emerges not so much as the daughter of Leslie Stephen but as the spiritual sister of Sylvia Plath or Adrienne Rich, fellow practitioners of the 'self-defining confessional mode'. A lesbian, for whom heterosexual love and death seemed inextricably connected after the bereavements of her adolescence, her relationship with her mother was 'like that of an unrequited lover', though it was not until *To the Lighthouse* that the magic centre of the world is stolen from the illusory mother and re-established in the artistic daughter. A chapter on *The Voyage Out* first appeared in *New Feminist Essays* three years ago (see *YW* 62.377–8); but another on *Orlando* is unusual in reading it as 'her most mature treatment of the battle of the sexes', the happy result of her passion for Vita, the 'real woman' she herself could never be. The ideal is female rather than androgynous, and late works like *Between the Acts* and *Anon* present the drama of female recollection, with La Trobe's play a parody of masculine culture. The tone is darker, as it is in *The Waves*, though we meet there the yearning for community which is one of the sources of her radicalism. The space Moore devotes to the seventeenth-century mystic Jane Lead, whom Woolf only may have known about, is scarcely justified, and some of the elaborate use of mythology in accounts of *The Voyage Out* and *Between the Acts* is more ingenious than persuasive, but for the most part she dispels the prejudices she invites.

Some of Moore's emphases Quentin Bell would no doubt count among the fashionable errors he aims to rebut in a piece in *CritI*, though Jane Marcus is the principal target. Examining some of Woolf's 'radiant friendships' with women, he doubts whether she ever read Caroline Emelie Stephen and her real feelings about Margaret Llewelyn Davies and the Woman's Cooperative Guild of which she was secretary were less enthusiastic than the published work suggests. *A Feminist Slant* (UNeb), edited by Jane Marcus was not seen, but Bell provides the foreword to a collection of papers[84] delivered at the 1982 Cambridge conference, a last-minute affair arranged when Woolf's centenary seemed likely to be a 'non-event in Great Britain', compared with the junketings elsewhere. If the picture of Woolf as a neglected author is hard to swallow, the conference was worth recording, with a number of lively contributions, though one of the panel discussions at the end includes an impassioned intervention by Roger Poole, protesting that they are burying rather than praising, with a spirited defence of Woolf as a living presence against the

83. *The Short Season Between Two Silences: The Mystical and the Political in the Novels of Virginia Woolf*, by Madeline Moore. A&U. pp. xiv + 189. £17.50.

84. *Virginia Woolf: A Centenary Perspective*, ed. by Eric Warner, with a foreword by Quentin Bell. Macmillan. pp. xiv + 169. £20.

depredations of the structuralists. In fact most of the criticism on view is traditional enough, though none the worse for that. Hermione Lee looks at images of transparency and reflection in the fiction as metaphors for detailing perception, drawing on the Romantic tradition and M. H. Abrams's *The Mirror and the Lamp*, but noting the moderns' need for the broken mirror to give back a multiform reality. T. C. Apter examines the function of vanity and friendship, the strategies characters adopt for self-knowledge and self-defence, again ranging widely if a shade humourlessly. Allen McLaurin makes useful discriminations among techniques often loosely referred to as 'stream of consciousness' before going on to demonstrate the importance of group consciousness in Woolf's writing, an idea in vogue at the time, convincingly arguing for the influence of Jules Romains and Wilfred Trotter in addition to the generally acknowledged role of William James. As *The Waves* reminds us, the sea rather than the stream is an appropriate image for Woolf's fiction. Lyndall Gordon would probably agree, and her contribution consists of speculations on the 'moments of being' dear to Woolf and Eliot and their place in the work. Like the biographer, they seek 'the fact that suggests and engenders'. The reading process interests Ian Gregor who considers the ways in which it modifies our response, sometimes as a steady unfolding, sometimes as a movement of check and countercheck. There is good close analysis, if perhaps too smooth a synthesis, in the steps which take him to a judgement on *To the Lighthouse* as the novel where Woolf gets the balance exactly right. More mischievously, John Bayley chooses *The Voyage Out* as the 'most interesting' of the novels, because the closest to the Victorian models she struggled to escape. In getting away from sequence she deserted the mainspring of fiction. In leaving the free make-believe of the masculine world for the restrictions of the female domain she approached self-parody, her later books 'the rather forlorn stepchildren of the old doctrine of Naturalism'. Perhaps the best piece here is Gillian Beer's use of 'the most powerful new metaphor for the past 150 years', Darwinian evolutionary theory, to look in particular at Woolf's first and last novels. In the wake of the *Beagle*, Rachel Vinrace attempts a voyage of discovery to the primaeval past, while *Between the Acts* rests on an unsettling, post-Darwinian sense of humankind as no longer central or permanent. Beer's writing is infinitely suggestive, though a clearer overall argument would make summary easier. The transcriptions of the panel discussions which round off the collection allow us to hear from Frank Kermode, Bernard Bergonzi, Iris Murdoch, and others, pondering on Virginia Woolf's standing and influence a hundred years after her birth, without much excitement, until the intervention of Roger Poole mentioned above.

Though Frank Kermode goes for *Between the Acts* as Woolf's 'undoubted masterpiece', the consensus preferred *To the Lighthouse*, an opinion reflected in the periodicals. Gillian Beer (*EIC*) characterizes it as a novel which asks where the line between object and subject can be drawn, a question dear to Leslie Stephen's heart and to his admired Hume. It is also the subject of Mr Ramsay's books and, in a sense, the concern of elegy. Hume's interest in the survival of the object without a perceiver present is discussed in Stephen's study of the philosopher, and the examples he chooses appear again from Mr Ramsay, all blended in Beer's subtle account of the novel as sustaining entity in a kind of writing which eschews permanence.

For Bruce Bassoff the crucial problem is not the relation between subject and object, but between subject and mediator, the goal of desire which nothing material can satisfy. Lily aims not at mimetic transcription, but at harmony. The world is not to be uncovered in some skeletal purity, but seen as clothed by the desires of others. Like many pieces in *SNNTS*, this presents an academic writing for academics, and little temptation to break the charmed circle. Analogies between human and aesthetic problems, and again the question of where to draw the line, this time in Lily's painting, lead Thomas G. Matro (*PMLA*) to look again at Roger Fry's *Vision and Design*, but he sees the novel as casting an ironic light on the notion of unity, with the artist finally no more privileged than the other characters. A basic polarity between fusion and detachment is elaborated on the mythic plane by Anne Golomb Hoffman (*SNNTS*), taking up hints from the manuscript and the finished novel which cast Mrs Ramsay as Demeter and Mr Carmichael as Poseidon, benevolently presiding over the waters of chaos. The Demeter story also lends itself to the kind of questions about identity and the mother–daughter relationship discussed by Nancy Chodorow, but perhaps the best part of this somewhat oversubtle essay is Hoffman's account of the role of reading, both ours and that of the principal characters, as participation in a civilized ritual where the individual self fuses with a larger whole. One welcomes attention to Woolf's humour, but in *Edilia* Claire Margaret Tylee's placing of *To the Lighthouse* in a comic tradition running back to Jonson and even Chaucer, with satire functioning as 'witty transformation' and Mrs Ramsay as some latterday Mrs Bennett, serves only to reinforce a sufficiently conventional reading of the book. Woolf's known fondness for Shelley (Volume V of the *Diary* finds her reading *Mont Blanc*) leads William J. Burling (*ELN*) to *Queen Mab* for a parallel to the meaning of the title: 'Show somewhat stable, somewhat certain still, / A lighthouse o'er the wild of dreary waves.' The novel itself appears in Longman's Study Text[85] series, with intelligent introduction and notes by Kate Flint and is a good cheap text. A revolutionary book, about 'the different ways of perceiving the process of life' and bearing the message that nothing is simply one thing, it survives separating out into digestible 'themes' better here than in some similar reader's guides.

Martine Stemerick's *From Clapham to Bloomsbury: Virginia Woolf* (Harvester) was not available. *The Letters of Vita Sackville-West to Virginia Woolf*, edited by Louise de Salvo and Mitchell A. Leaska (Hutchinson) were likewise unforthcoming, but if the reviewer who found them 'tiresome in the extreme' is to be believed, the loss is not insuperable.

In the diary Virginia Woolf refers to Desmond MacCarthy's latest book as 'small beer', and now it seems not one is in print, but we do have a selection from the writings[86] made by his son-in-law, Lord David Cecil, with a twenty-page introduction which has appeared before, urging his claims as 'one of the most distinguished men of his time'. The Leavises, of course, thought otherwise, but there is little in what follows to explain either the admiration or vituperation. As Arnold Bennett said of Henry James, with less justification, 'he never fairly bites a subject and makes it bleed', but there is pleasant

85. *Virginia Woolf: 'To the Lighthouse'*, ed. by Kate Flint. Longman. pp. xlv + 197. pb £1.60.

86. *Desmond MacCarthy; The Man and His Writings*, intro. by David Cecil. Constable. pp. 313. £9.95.

browsing to be had among subjects ranging from Swinburne to Gertrude Stein and from 'the artistic temperament' to 'Shooting with Wilfred Blunt'.

YES has an article by Hugh Kenner on 'The Satirist as Barbarian', showing how Wyndham Lewis's disparagement of our literary heritage governed his satire, essentially a written genre addressing itself to bookish people. As usual, there is much intellectual display by Kenner, and some valuable commentary on *Mrs Dukes' Million* and *The Apes of God*, but Lewis's star still seems in decline, though Quartet have re-issued *Blast 3*.

Lawrence's *Mr Noon*[87] is presented as 'a new work of major importance' but both adjectives need qualification. The first third is readily available in *Phoenix II*, and recounts the amorous adventures of a 'Woodhouse' school-teacher, based on Lawrence's friend George Henry Neville. With its amusing account of local customs such as 'spooning' and thinly disguised portraits of Lawrence's Eastwood friends, it contradicts those who see the author as lacking a sense of humour. The remainder of the unfinished manuscript, also written during the winter of 1920–1, was left with Thomas Seltzer but dropped from sight for fifty years. It is more 'peppery' than the first part, to use Lawrence's term, since Gilbert Noon is 're-incarnated', waking up in Germany in what is recognizably the family of Lawrence's brother-in-law, Edgar Jaffe, to live out Lawrence's own adventures there. Indeed, the main interest of what follows is biographical, not to say prurient, with details of Johanna's affairs with earlier lovers and her first husband Everard and her infidelity to Gilbert on what is in effect their honeymoon, all clearly relatable to Frieda's goings-on. There is a good deal of narratorial self-display, the freely facetious inventiveness which appears also in *Studies in Classic American Literature* written at the same period, but also something of the freshness and vitality of Lawrence's best work. Fuller discussion of the novel, if not a conventional review, is to be found in an article by Michael Black (*LRB*), one of the Cambridge editors (and so in a position to give a considered opinion of the new work), and an interesting footnote comes from Dieter Mehl (*N&Q*), who investigates the two weeks Lawrence spent in Waldbröl (the Wensdorf of *Mr Noon*) in May 1912 on the way to meet Frieda. One of his connections there, Johanna Krenkow, may have contributed something to the Johanna of the novel.

There are many references to *Mr Noon* in the new volume of the Cambridge *Letters*[88], but the book most on Lawrence's mind was *Women in Love*, completed in 1916 but still unpublished in the spring of 1920. There are 942 letters here, compared with 199 for the same five-year period in Moore's edition, and a good number have not been published before. It opens with him in 'a black fury with the world', and later there are some savage remarks about Middleton Murry, though the famous letter to Katherine Mansfield ('stewing in your consumption') is here only in her reporting of it. We find him enjoying the opera (conducted by Beecham), disliking the Jews (but the bourgeois are the real enemy), worrying about the mosquitoes in Taormina (like 'winged rattle-snakes'), and disparaging Freud ('dangerous for weak-minded people'). The editors in their introduction draw attention to his correspondence with

87. *Mr Noon*, by D. H. Lawrence, ed. by Lindeth Vasey. CUP. pp. xliv + 370. £12.95.

88. *The Letters of D. H. Lawrence*. Vol. III: *1916–21*, ed. by James T. Boulton and Andrew Robertson. CUP. pp. xxv + 762. £25.

Douglas Goldring from July 1919, while admitting that they may be getting the importance to Lawrence of his brand of political radicalism out of proportion. New letters to Robert Mountsier and Marie Hubrecht fill in the picture of Italy and Germany during these years. Running through the whole collection are worries about money, quite moving when one thinks of the quality of the work Lawrence had produced and was finding so difficult to publish.

Lawrence's first novel[89], the one placed in his mother's hands shortly before her death, is published by Cambridge, with appendixes of surviving fragments from earlier drafts. 'Laetitia', 'Tendrils', and 'Nethermere' were among the titles considered, and the scene with the peacock and Annable the gamekeeper was written relatively late. The textual apparatus and notes are characteristically detailed, and the section on critical reception shows that although 'an immense stride forward' in Jessie Chambers's eyes, it was by no means a best seller. The text printed here is based on Lawrence's revised 1910 manuscript.

No details are given of the text of *The Rainbow*[90] used for the new paperback from Macmillan Education, and the introduction, disappointingly mealy-mouthed, smacks of the classroom, but there are notes and even illustrations, at a modest price. *The Rainbow*, along with *Women in Love*, is the evidence presented by M. Labbé (*EA*) in an essay on the Freudian family romance as thematic material common to both Lawrence and Thomas Hardy. In the first chapter of *The Rainbow*, the Lord and Lady of the Manor are named Hardy, and Hardy himself was the spiritual father Lawrence had to kill off. In a general sense it is true that the work of both novelists can be seen as constituting a single myth of intellectual and sexual emancipation, but the particular argument is highly tendentious. Freud is called on again in J. P. Naugrette's discussion of *The Fox*, also in *EA*, centring on an analysis of March's two dreams and finding parallels with Leonardo's dreams of the vulture, but adding little to received opinion on the novella.

While acknowledging that Frank Kermode and L. D. Clark have gone before her in investigating the part played by Apocalypse in Lawrence's thinking, Sarah Urang[91] justifies her claim that there is more to be said about its effect on the *mythos* of his narrative. An introductory chapter on the utility of the 'rhetoric of vision' in enabling Lawrence to express his belief in the interfusion of the spiritual and the temporal leads on to chapters on *The Rainbow* and *Women in Love*. In the former, she writes subtly and well of the novel's development through a 'series of psychic conflagrations and renewals', not simply a matter of symbolism but of 'fluidity of reference in the event between inner and outer'. *Women in Love*, the most obvious candidate for her angle of vision, emerges more affirmatively than in some recent readings, with surprisingly fresh formulations deriving from Lawrence's non-fictional writings, of which Urang makes good use throughout. The fourth chapter, on *The Plumed Serpent*, discovers apocalypse formalized into ritual, and a 'geological fault' in the book when Kate though drawn to Ramón in fact marries Cipriano.

89. *The White Peacock*, by D. H. Lawrence, ed. by Andrew Robertson. CUP (1983). pp. liii + 449. £27.50.

90. *The Rainbow*, by D. H. Lawrence, ed. by James Gibson. Macmillan. pp. xxxv + 453. pb £1.25.

91. *Kindled in the Flame: The Apocalyptic Scene in D. H. Lawrence*, by Sarah Urang. UMIRes (1983). pp. 161. £40.

But the later work shows a more contemplative stance and a chastened tone, seen in the movement through the three versions of *Lady Chatterley's Lover* from saving to healing. Though Urang values the writing of Lawrence's last years, she becomes a little abstract in her treatment of it, and the strongest part of her own study focuses on the middle period.

The novels of Lawrence's so-called 'leadership phase' are at the centre of Judith Ruderman's psychoanalytic study[92]. Her rather off-putting title comes from a phrase Lawrence used about Frieda in a letter, and her general thesis is that the mother–child relationship became still more pronounced after *Sons and Lovers*, coloured by his dependence on his wife and his resentment of it. Consequently the pre-oedipal dilemma, as analysed by Erik Erikson, Joseph Rheingold, and others, is more relevant than any narrowly political perspective, and Lawrence's own 'pollyanalytics' are summarized at length. We can trace a direct path, she argues, from *The Lost Girl*, which depicts the invidious rule of the Magna Mater, to *The Plumed Serpent*, which restores the Pater Magnus to his rightful throne. Both these novels are the subject of separate chapters, in the case of the latter curiously paired with *Movements in European History*, and in addition there are chapters on *The Fox*, *Aaron's Rod*, *Kangaroo*, and *The Boy in the Bush*. It is good to have discussion of Lawrence's rewriting of Mollie Skinner's narrative, and it does rather neatly fit her thesis, but then nearly everything does, or can be made to. Kangaroo, for instance, is a devouring mother in man's clothing, and the more perverse activities of Lawrence's lovers are not 'buggery per se' but 'a generalised pregenital rejection of the mother's enveloping love'. In *The Fox*, Grenfel is also a mother rather than an unequivocal saviour, hence March's resistance, and her own relationship with Banford is once more the pre-oedipal conflict between mother and child. Ruderman's method mingles psychoanalytic theory and detailed biographical investigation, in the case of *The Fox* examining real-life originals for the characters (the volume of *Letters* reviewed above contains much relevant material). She is doubtful whether Lawrence ever left behind the 'leader-cum-follower' idea and went for tenderness; in *Lady Chatterley* Mellors continues to bully, and his patriarchal ideal seems to involve the same abnegation of individual personality as the mother-worship it replaces. Yet, she concludes, Lawrence's analysis is still valuable, and his advocacy of 'good parenting' can be commended, as perhaps can her own book, despite initial reservations.

A throwback to a much earlier view of Lawrence, as 'rotten and rotting others', comes in an essay by Tariq Rahman who connects the novelist's influence and the decay of liberal-humanist values (*LHY*). By debunking rationalism, recommending flagellation, combining 'puritanical sanctimoniousness' with 'sexual latitudinarianism', and generally underwriting his characters' 'indulgence in anti-social behaviour', Lawrence, this 'priest of hate', is the 'positive force for evil' that Russell identified. The evidence for all this, in the essays and novels, is presented in so distorted a fashion that even lukewarm Lawrentians would be moved to protest.

Less contentiously, though scarcely more usefully, Anne Darling Barker (*FMLS*) considers *St Mawr* as an inversion of the Sleeping Beauty story,

---

92. *D. H. Lawrence and the Devouring Mother: The search for a patriarchal ideal of leadership*, by Judith Ruderman. DukeU. pp. xi + 211. $33.75.

discovering other fairy-tale elements, including parallels between St Mawr himself and the talking horse in the tale of the goosegirl, but employing them only to reinforce a perfectly conventional reading of Lawrence's novella. Other sources for Lawrence's fiction appear in *N&Q* and *Expl*: in the former P. T. Whelan and others identify a Rilke sonnet on Apollo with the scene where the gamekeeper in *Lady Chatterley* washes his back, and in the latter Samuel E. Longmire points out that the picture which Miriam admires in *Sons and Lovers* is not Veronese's 'St Catherine', but rather 'St Helen: A Vision of the Cross', acquired by the National Gallery in 1875.

In the one issue of *DHLR* I was able to see, Michael Ross contributes a topical piece on Lawrence and Orwell, putting forward *Nineteen Eighty-Four* and *Lady Chatterley's Lover* as the two novels that have had the most impact on the general public's habits of thinking this century, and noting various parallels, most of them readily apparent, to no very clear end. There is a little more substance in Debra Journet's examination of Lawrence's criticism of modern literature, seeing it as running counter to central modernist theory as expounded by Eliot, Mallarmé, and others, and looking at his disagreements with Clive Bell and Roger Fry over significant form. Marko Modiano unearths an early Swedish production of *The Daughter-in-Law*, in Walter Greenwood's 1936 revision of the play, which helped launch one of the country's leading actors and provides evidence of Lawrence's favourable reception in Scandinavia. A little-known Ibsen play, *Lady Inger of Ostrat*, mentioned by Lawrence in a letter, is a possible source for the character of Ursula's teacher in *The Rainbow*, Earl G. Ingersoll quite plausibly suggests. Kathleen Verduin, a little less persuasively, sees parallels between *Lady Chatterley* and Frances Hodgson Burnett's *The Secret Garden* (1911), drawing attention to the essential innocence of both works rather than any 'deep Freudianism'. *A Strange Sapience: The Creative Imagination of D. H. Lawrence*, by Daniel Dervin (UMass) and *D. H. Lawrence: The Artist as Psychologist* (UKan), by Daniel Schneider arrived too late for inclusion in this volume.

Joyce Cary's Trilogies[93] is really two books in one. Hazard Adams devotes chapters to the Gulley Jimson trilogy and the later novels following the rise and fall of Chester Nimmo, even providing chronologies of the main events, all in a reasonably straightforward literary critical manner, though with special emphasis on Cary's manipulation of the narrative. But since he believes the novels raise questions important for the study of narrative 'in a relatively pure form', these chapters are embedded in a highly theoretical context, culminating in an elaborate categorization of eleven perspectives from which our approach to the fictional work may be organized. These involve a sophistication of insights by Hillis Miller, Wayne Booth, Gérard Genette, and others, and as Adams admits, 'a somewhat barbaric vocabulary', though he always writes clearly and well. Cary's own theoretical writing, in particular *Art and Reality* and his political treatise, *Power in Men*, is utilized in the first three chapters, concerned with the novelist's metaphysics and his theory of symbolism, derived from Blake and Croce, and also with the existing critical debate on Cary. Finally, Adams employs his critical categories, deduced from the fiction, to locate Cary's ethical stance not in the 'content' of the trilogies but in

93. *Joyce Cary's Trilogies: Pursuit of the Particular Real*, by Hazard Adams. UFlor (1983). pp. xvi + 279. $20.

the processes by which we ourselves are constituted in the reading. In short, this is a valuable book for those who think Cary worth this degree of attention, though no doubt its more speculative chapters overlap with the same author's *Philosophy of the Literary Symbolic* (1983).

More modestly, Greg Hill[94] has written a monograph on Llewelyn Wyn Griffith for the Writers of Wales series. Born in Denbighshire, but living mostly in England and author of a history of the British Civil Service, along with poetry, novels, translations, and short stories, Wyn Griffith emerges as a sentimental nationalist, committed to the rural Welsh-speaking Wales of his youth, but as Hill notes with a mixture of asperity and regret, ambivalent about the industrial south. As a writer he preferred to keep the two languages separate, though his second and best novel, *The Way Lies West* (1945) is influenced for the good by the work of Kate Roberts whom he translated.

The long-awaited second volume of Hilary Spurling's life of Ivy Compton-Burnett[95] covers the period of all her important fiction, but more awkwardly for the biographer, in the subject's own view she had no 'real or organic knowledge of life later than 1910'. Julia Strachey comments on meeting Ivy at a christening party, 'her drawbridge, portcullis and visor were all down', and for information about what went on behind the inscrutable front and the unnerving public image, Hilary Spurling is driven to make inferences from the novels. She manages this with a good deal of tact and usually convincingly, and indeed these are more valuable pages than those given over to the social world in which Ivy moved among the wartime London intelligentsia and the more recent friends of the 1950s and 1960s. Her companion for thirty years, Margaret Jourdain, necessarily dominates much of the action, with Ivy content to play second fiddle, though distressing quarrels are also recorded. There were jealousies too, although all agree that any physical relationship between Ivy and Margaret is 'frankly preposterous'. For Joan Evans she was 'poison Ivy', and her spoilt, tyrannical streak was too much indulged, though it seems she blossomed out once the despair after Margaret's death was relieved by the passage of time. All this is fully documented here, though one would welcome a more selective approach to the wealth of detail.

Unlike the vast majority of contemporary critics, Aldous Huxley at least 'knew when to shut up' according to Kirpal Singh (*AUMLA*) in an essay on his literary criticism. The essays may not be given the attention they deserve, and Huxley was generally shrewd in his pronouncements, but this rather uninspired survey is unlikely to win him new admirers. The future of poetry in *Brave New World* prompts a stimulating essay by Jerome Meckier (*RMS*) comparing Huxley with Orwell and Zamyatin. Whereas the others locate individual freedom in love and sexuality, Huxley looks to the independent poetic sensibility to keep man's evolutionary hope alive. One might argue that Meckier is identifying Orwell with Winston too simply, in seeing both Winston and D-503 (Zamyatin's hero) as atavistic while Huxley's Watson evolves, but he makes out a case for his preference for *Brave New World*.

Orwell's novel, surely superior, is celebrated with the publication of a

94. *Llewelyn Wyn Griffith*, by Greg Hill. UWales. pp. 71. pb £2.95.
95. *Secrets of a Woman's Heart: The Later Life of I. Compton-Burnett, 1920–1962*, by Hilary Spurling. H&S. pp. 336. £14.95.

handsome facsimile of the manuscript[96], in effect just under half the familiar version, though in an earlier draft and partly in Orwell's typing. Arranged in narrative order, rather than order of composition, and breaking off at the Chestnut Cafe just before Winston's final meeting with Julia, it includes a couple of scenes not in the published book, though otherwise the changes are not very significant. Siegel's preface rather gloatingly describes his acquisition of the manuscript, but Davison's introduction provides exemplary scholarly details and what he modestly calls 'one or two initial reactions' to his labours. These include the consistency of Orwell's whole conception, perhaps from as early as 1940, his sense of urgency, and the information that 1980 was to have been the ominous year. Peter Davison is also responsible for the text of *Nineteen Eighty-Four* issued by the Clarendon Press[97], introduced copiously (we hear the clocks striking thirteen only on p. 157) by Bernard Crick. As he says, this involves some recycling of material in his earlier *George Orwell: A Life*, but his conclusion is somewhat different. Initially, he saw the totalitarian theme as dominant; now he sees the book as 'Swiftian satire', and one section of his introduction is devoted to the 'Seven Satiric Thrusts' around which it is organized. These include the betrayal of the intellectuals, the mass media as an agent of proletarization, and the theses of James Burnham. The latter's *Managerial Revolution*, famous in its day, is now neglected so some of the satire falls flat, though Goldstein's book is incomprehensible without it, Orwell sharing some of Burnham's concepts while rejecting his conclusions. On the positive side we have the themes of memory, in the decency and loyalty still alive among the proles, and mutual trust, rather than love. Crick is concerned to refute some of the bleaker readings of the book, defending Orwell against the charge of mystifying cruelty, and pointing out that Winston is a very brave man, holding out astonishingly long. The ending he sees as grotesque comedy rather than utter despair. Perhaps he labours his main point – that the novel is satire rather than morbid prophecy – overmuch, but there is lively and detailed discussion of the main issues, and he makes no bones about his own preference for *Animal Farm* and the best of the essays.

Bernard Crick, who had a busy year, appears again as one of the editors of *Orwell Remembered*[98], a collection of reminiscences, many from radio and television interviews broadcast to commemorate *Nineteen Eighty-Four*, or from the Orwell archive at Birkbeck College. We move from the two-year-old Eric Blair, already calling things 'beastly' according to his mother's diary, right through to the *New Statesman* obituary, a 'noble piece of writing' according to Crick's headnote. Malcolm Muggeridge notices that Orwell died on Lenin's birthday and was buried by the Astors, 'which seems to me to cover the full range of his life'. The selection is made by Audrey Coppard, who apparently sees Orwell differently from Crick, but he provides the introduction to this attractive compilation.

About a hundred previously unpublished letters from Orwell to Leonard

96. *Nineteen Eighty-Four: The Facsimile*, ed. by Peter Davison, with a preface by Daniel G. Siegel. S&W. pp. xix + 381. £25.

97. *Nineteen Eighty-Four*, by George Orwell, ed. by Peter Davison, with a critical intro. and annotations by Bernard Crick. OUP. pp. vii + 460. £17.50.

98. *Orwell Remembered*, ed. by Audrey Coppard and Bernard Crick. BBC. pp. 287. pb £3.95.

Moore, his literary agent, clarifying his relationship with Victor Gollancz, are discussed by Michael Shelden (*TLS*). He quotes several, and speculates that if Orwell had persuaded Gollancz to release him sooner, he might have experimented more freely with political fiction.

For Robert Currie (*EIC*) the 'big truth' in *Nineteen Eighty-Four* is not what it is usually taken to be: the subject is madness rather than politics, with Winston a 'text-book schizophrenic'. Whether as a result of social conditioning or the relationship with his mother, he is probably homosexual, hence his attitude to Julia; and the central question, 'who ratted on whom?' involves his mother as much as his lover. All highly ingenious, but probably wrong, as Roger Sharrock argues in a later issue, in seeing the novel too simply in terms of individual psychology. For Sharrock, more interestingly, the central contradiction of the novel is that Winston-Orwell has proved the triumph of social conditioning, while the indignation of the text rejects the idea. The Party, rather than Winston, is responsible for the schizophrenia, but Orwell clings to a radical difference between individual and social organization. Sharrock's stimulating essay takes in Burnham's *The Managerial Revolution* once more, Arthur Koestler's *Arrival and Departure*, and more puzzlingly, a recent French exercise in Marxist-Freudianism, Gilles Deleuze's *Anti-Oedipe*.

The clash and combination of genres in *Nineteen Eighty-Four* worries Carl Freedman (*MFS*) quite fruitfully in an essay on the antinomies in the book. Wellsian naturalism and Swiftian satire engage in a dialectic which animates the book, but produces problems when, as Freedman puts it, the debt to reality borrowed from the naturalistic elements is not paid. O'Brien's justification of power for power's sake remains an 'abstractly posited bogey', as Orwell, unable to conceive of the destruction of individual autonomy, cannot imagine its transcendence either. Not all of the problems Freedman discovers are easy to see, but his conclusions are sufficiently familiar. Familiar, too, is the picture of Orwell that emerges from a well-balanced overview by Alfred Kazin (*NYRB*), one of many pundits called upon in the public prints, with Orwell valued for his capacity to absorb truth in the form of pain and to give it back.

Stewart Justman (*UTQ*) traces Orwell's famous plain style back to the experimental science of the seventeenth century, but also notices its complexities, with the author both observer and actor, turning from experiment to experience. He discusses the bearing of Orwell's liberalism on all this, his commitment to persuasion rather than mystification, skilfully and subtly shuffling through his paradoxes without greatly changing the accepted view of his subject. More far-reaching is another essay on Orwell's language by Graham Good (*PSt*), discovering not the neutral 'window pane' but something embattled, 'dialogic', high-pitched. In the novels the official ideological discourse (imperialism, anglicanism, or whatever) can be submissively repeated, or the hero can produce 'a kind of inner monologue of dissent'. But the protagonist can only try to subvert the dominant forms, negatively rather than creatively, and Winston is doomed to defeat. For Orwell, too, objectivity stems from objection: 'the power of prose to tell the truth is inwoven with its power to lie'.

One of Orwell's favourite boyhood authors, H. G. Wells, and his use of the animal fable are examined by Myrddin Jones (*English*), who traces parallels between *The Island of Dr Moreau* and *Animal Farm*. Yet Orwell's use of the fable is radically different, closer to formal allegory without the mediating narrator, though in *Nineteen Eighty-Four* the disturbing ambivalence is in fact close to Wells's mixture of realism and myth, even if he did not share Wells's confidence in scientific socialism. Timothy Cook (*MFS*) sees Upton Sinclair's *The Jungle* as a more important source for *Animal Farm* than any preceding beast fable, with Jurgis and his wife as prototypes for Boxer and Clover. Orwell was familiar with Sinclair's work, but Cook's parallels are not really convincing.

The need to demythologize Orwell 'the patron saint of current Cold-War doublethink', prompts a collection of new essays[99] of varying quality. Some of these views from the Left are decidely jaundiced. Stephen Sedley, for one, finds *Animal Farm* 'an abdication of imaginative art', deficient in humour and falling short even of Beatrix Potter, let alone *The Wind in the Willows*, while Andy Croft sees *Nineteen Eighty-Four* as overrated, the 'tail-end' of a more original and important literary development in the 1930s. He documents some of the futuristic novels of the period, singling out Murray Constantine's *Swastika Night* as clearly anticipating Orwell's novel though he may not have read it. He proves his point that Orwell falsified the record in dismissing this body of writing, but he doesn't actually say whether any of it is as good as *Nineteen Eighty-Four*. Alaric Jacob judges it 'one of the most disgusting books ever written', and as a fellow old boy of St Cyprian's he is in a position to comment on Orwell's exaggeration, self-pity, and 'quite astonishing' lack of political nous. Jacob, who presents himself as a Salieri to Orwell's Mozart is at least entertaining, but there is not much fun to be had in Deirdre Beddoe's predictable discovery of a 'pervasive anti-feminism' in his writing, not so much a matter of active hostility as that 'conspiracy of silence' which Orwell shared with so many men, including those on the Left. Beatrix Campbell has the same account of Orwell's 'sexual filter' though she is principally concerned with his misrepresentation of the whole working class. Orwell's failure to learn 'the true lesson of Spain' exercises Bill Alexander, himself an officer in the International Brigade who would no doubt dearly have loved to get Orwell under his command. Certainly he would have shot the man with his trousers down whom Orwell spared. Robert Stradling continues the belabouring from a more historical viewpoint, correcting details of *Homage to Catalonia* and even managing a few back-handed compliments along the way. No doubt there is truth in what they both say, but the carping tone has one siding with Orwell. Christopher Norris's contribution is a lively if somewhat unfocused piece on Orwell's relationship with the postwar British Left, part of an empirical tradition in contrast with the continental Marxists. E. P. Thompson's quarrel with the poverty of theory places him in this tradition, like a latter-day Orwell, while contemporary Left-wing thought is still stuck with the divorce between subject and structure analysed by Perry Anderson. For Antony Easthope, Mrs Thatcher's Britain has brought the death of social-democratic England that much closer, so the totalitarian theme has lost none of its relevance, but he prefers to read the book less referentially, or at least an interpretation of the novel's success in 'undermining precisely the liberal assertion it proposes for itself' is only one among a plurality of accounts he offers. It can be seen as science fiction, fantasy, or 'writing' in the sense of that term which occupies Derrida and others. Typically eliptical formulations involve Room 101 ('the

99. *Inside the Myth: Orwell: Views from the Left*, ed. by Christopher Norris. L&W. pp. 287. hb £12.50, pb £4.95.

phallic number with absence at its centre') and Winston's homosexual love for O'Brien, though some of the more strained passages may result from misprints. What does it *mean* to say 'Within Winston's fetishistic imaginary Julia figures as the phallus of his fully present heterosexuality'? More soberly, Stuart Hall probes some of the familiar contradictions, which he argues we should value rather than dismiss and sketches in the 'rich theoretical background' against which Orwell's ideas evolved. The statist quality of socialism is still a problem, and Orwell offers some piercing insights into it. Orwell's contradictions also occupy Malcolm Evans, and again Macherey and Lacan are wheeled out, in '20 things you never knew about George Orwell' (a headline from the *Sun*). Even if one already knew some of them, the presentation is engaging, and there are good things on Orwell's language and 'decency'. Included in Evans's piece are parodies of examination questions on Orwell, and the use, or rather, exploitation, of Orwell in teaching is examined at length in a disturbing investigation by Alan Brown. Disturbing that is, even if one does not share the distrust of the idea of individual autonomy common to many of the contributors to the present collection.

One of the most substantial essays in Norris's book is by Lynette Hunter, taking Orwell's fascination with the tensions between dominator and dominated as instrumental in the evolution of his handling of stance and structure. She is prepared to give Orwell the benefit of the doubt, when reading the early fiction, seeing him as 'fully aware' of the apparent contradictions, a consciously experimental writer in search of a voice. This more generous response to Orwell informs her full-length study[100], the best of the books on the subject to have come my way this year. Orwell's strategy, or more particularly, his 'stance', her term for the combined activity of writer, work, and reader, and necessarily a moral category, develops throughout his career, and she gives chapters to the documentaries and early novels, the essays, letters and broadcasts, and the mature fantasies. As the narrator's stance shifts, so does the basis for the reader's evaluation of his judgement, and Hunter is unusual nowadays in seeing the problems of literary expression more satisfactorily handled in *Animal Farm* and *Nineteen Eighty-Four* than in the contemporary essays. She sees allegorical readings of these works as much richer than merely satirical ones, though the reader is required to participate more actively than is usually the case with fantasy literature. Orwell's last novel is 'an allegory about the negative stance of fantasy' and the reader has to work hard to establish the differences that make the allegory possible. Perhaps she is guilty of oversophistication in writing of the earlier books, and one wishes her style was a little less drab, but hers is a much more fruitful approach to Orwell than the others on view during the past year.

David L. Kubal's *Outside the Whale: Orwell, Art and Politics* (UND) was not seen, nor was *Unwelcome Guerilla: George Orwell and the 'New Statesman' – An Anthology*, edited by Alan George (New Statesman).

Another writer to draw on his experiences during the Spanish Civil War was Laurie Lee, and Longman have issued a selection of his work[101], including prose, poetry, and photographs from the family album. One questions the

---

100. *George Orwell: The Search for a Voice*, by Lynette Hunter. OpenU. pp. vii + 242. hb £18, pb £5.95.
101. *A Laurie Lee Selection*, ed. by Chris Buckton. Longman. pp. 166. pb £1.75.

need, when the texts are readily available, but Lee's work lends itself to this treatment. The editor offers no introduction, but V. S. Pritchett provides one for a re-issue of short stories[102] by H. E. Bates, a writer not unlike Lee. As Pritchett says, in his somewhat skimpy preface (there is considerable variety in the quality of the introductions to these '20th Century Classics'), 'he was always best in the country landscape of his childhood where the hours seemed fuller and longer'.

(c) Individual Authors: Post-1945

This section deals with writers who produced all or part of their work after 1945. Authors have been arranged in chronological order. There has been a very large amount of published work this year, involving a wide variety of critical methodologies. While some authors attract a fairly constant body of material, others fare less equally on the critical roundabout. Inevitably Koestler's death and Greene's eightieth birthday have lent a special impetus to their critics in 1984. Women writers also command considerable attention, with Murdoch, Spark, Drabble, and Lessing figuring prominently. An interest in sexual politics seems to be a prime factor in recent work on Angela Carter, Barbara Pym, D. M. Thomas, and John Fowles. (The Fowles industry grows from year to year, with saturation coverage of *The Ebony Tower* in 1984.) Several critics, however, turned their attention to less fêted writers, with a welcome consideration of J. L. Carr, Richard Hughes, and Richard Vaughan.

PowysR is exceptionally rich in good material this year. In Number 13 three essays are especially worthy of note. Martin Steinmann Jr outlines T. F. Powys's relation to tradition, Elizabeth Barrett discusses romance and naturalism in *A Glastonbury Romance*, and Tony Head examines dualism in the major works of John Cowper Powys, with special attention to the alternation between the sublime and the bathetic. In addition, Ben Jones points to variations in editions of *Wolf Solent*, Tom Copeman Hart describes a correspondence with John Cowper Powys, and Charles Rogers offers recollections of the Powys family. The volume also contains short notes and reviews, and is handsomely illustrated. Number 14 is even more interesting, including reprints of interviews with John Cowper Powys and a story by Llewelyn Powys, and publishing for the first time John Cowper Powys's introduction to Aristophanes' *Acharnians*. Letters from John Cowper Powys to his sister Marian and to Hal and Violet Trovillon appear, together with an essay by A. Thomas Southwick on the relationship between Marian and John, as expressed in their correspondence from 1914 to 1934. Glen Cavaliero describes the work of Phyllis Paul, whose novels John Cowper Powys knew, making a vigorous case for her as a serious novelist. Laurence Coupe argues against the view of T. F. Powys's art as folksy and tragic, and in favour of him as a comic writer, basing his work on pagan fertility myth and romance. Lastly, T. J. Diffey brings his understanding of philosophy to bear on the question of John Cowper Powys's imagination, in an extensive and authoritative essay. The review is extremely good value, and amply deserves its support from the Welsh Arts Council.

John Cowper Powys wrote upwards of 40,000 letters in his life, often as

---

102. *My Uncle Silas*, by H. E. Bates, intro. by V. S. Pritchett, illus. by Edward Ardizzone. 20th Century Classics. OUP. pp. 190. pb £2.95.

many as twenty in one day, and two examples of his correspondence have now appeared in print. Robert Blackmore[103] has edited a collection of fifty letters written to G. R. Wilson Knight between 1937 and 1962, which make interesting, and often indeed startling reading. The influence of Nietzsche on both correspondents emerges strongly, and Powys's belief in onanism is frankly expressed. Gastric details are also to the fore and the volume includes an account of John Cowper Powys's spirit returning to hover over Wilson Knight at a spiritualist church. Inevitably, Cedric Hentschel's edition[104] of Powys's letters to Sven-Erik Täckmark makes somewhat duller reading, though the letters are more literary in content. Each edition includes photographs, useful notes, and appendixes.

In her life of Agatha Christie[105] Janet Morgan has benefited from sole access to family papers, and the resultant biography is solid and well researched. Unfortunately it is also dull, and makes its subject appear even duller. One gets little insight into Christie's personality, nor is very much light shed on her works. The discussion of the 1926 disappearance adds little to previous accounts, though it is, at least, sensibly and carefully investigated. The most interesting parts of the book concern Christie's relations with her publishers and her financial affairs.

C. S. Lewis is the subject of two recent books. Peter J. Schakel[106] examines the place of reason and imagination in Lewis's thought, showing that a shift in emphasis (towards imagination) occurs in the late 1940s. A detailed reading of *Till We Have Faces* occupies about half of the study, with the remainder examining Lewis's other writings. Schakel writes well and treats his subject with a critical detachment rare in Lewis studies. The result is an excellent book, carefully researched and intellectually sophisticated. Dabney Adams Hart's book[107] is less detached, focusing on Lewis as scholar, critic, and teacher and drawing on meetings with and letters from Lewis. While very much the record of a personal and enthusiastic response, by a writer whose early work was the starting point for other writers on Lewis, the volume includes a sharp discussion of Owen Barfield's influence on Lewis's use of language and the theory of history, and makes a fair case for Lewis as a less conservative figure than is often thought. In *Renascence* Robert F. Brown examines the extended temptation scenario at the heart of *Perelandra*, as a fantasy presentation of Christian beliefs about the Fall.

Elizabeth Bowen's wartime short stories are the focus of an essay in *MFS*, in a special issue on war fiction, in which Jeslyn Medoff argues that Bowen concentrates on the psychological effects of war. In a short note in *SSF*, Brad Hooper finds that Bowen deliberately created dual realities in 'The Happy Autumn Fields', not, as has been argued, one reality and a 'saving hallucination'.

103. *The Letters of John Cowper Powys to G. R. Wilson Knight*, ed. by Robert Blackmore. Woolf (1983). pp. 144. £8.50.
104. *The Letters of John Cowper Powys to Sven-Erik Täckmark*, ed. by Cedric Hentschel. Woolf (1983). pp. 112. £8.50.
105. *Agatha Christie*, by Janet Morgan. Collins. pp. xvii + 393. £12.95.
106. *Reason and Imagination in C. S. Lewis: A Study of 'Till We Have Faces'*, by Peter J. Schakel. Eerdmans. pp. xii + 208. $8.95.
107. *Through the Open Door: A New Look at C. S. Lewis*, by Dabney Adams Hart. UAla. pp. x + 164. $15.75.

In *Richard Hughes: Author, Father*[108] Penelope Hughes offers her memories of her father and of her own childhood. Rather too much space is devoted to the latter, particularly when Miss Hughes is mucking about in small boats, though since the war, boarding school, and university seem to have separated father and daughter for appreciable periods, this is not really surprising. The volume, however, contains interesting anecdotes about Koestler, Dylan Thomas, and other literary figures, quotes extensively from Hughes's letters, describes the genesis of several stories, and is attractively illustrated with photographs and drawings. From the literary point of view the most interesting part of the book consists of the account of the development of *The Fox in the Attic*, which includes rejected versions of the novel and source material.

William K. Malcolm's *A Blasphemer and Reformer*[109] is a significant addition to work on Lewis Grassic Gibbon, on whom surprisingly little has been written. Malcolm's study approaches Gibbon in the context of international artistic and intellectual movements, devoting two fascinating chapters to his subject's political and philosophical thought, and then analysing stories and novels in detail. While the contradictions in Gibbon's thinking are somewhat underestimated, and the decision to rest the case for him on thematic rather than technical grounds is arguable, the book is solidly researched, drawing on manuscript material, some of which is reproduced in appendixes. One's only quarrel is with the style of the book, which involves abuse of the first person, a somewhat doctoral tone, too many short paragraphs and subsections, and an intermittent tendency to gush. In *ScLJ* Glenda Norquay produces a very full and interesting essay on *A Scots Quair*. In her view, the narrative of the novel abides only superficially by the conventions of linear time, and is extended beyond its limitations by the use of changing voices (the voice of the individual, the community, the age) in order to create textual density. Gibbon's correspondence is the concern of Ian Campbell in *The Bibliotheck*, in an essay which reviews critical work on Gibbon, lists all letters which have come to light, and describes the manuscript material in the National Library of Scotland.

James Matthews has written a biography of Frank O'Connor[110] which should be approached with caution. There are textual inaccuracies, loose syntax, and many inconsistencies between the volume and O'Connor's own account in *An Only Child* (1961). An extensive review in the autumn issue of *IUR* lists many points of contention.

Donat Gallagher[111] has edited a fat selection of Evelyn Waugh's essays, journalism, reviews, and news reports, arranged chronologically in periods corresponding to phases of Waugh's development – student, 'ultra-modern', traveller, right-wing propagandist, Catholic, and social critic. Each period is preceded by a short introduction and the volume closes with a list of other occasional pieces not reprinted here. While Waugh would no doubt have preferred some of the earlier pieces to remain in decent obscurity, the selection includes everything of any significance and does much to illustrate both

108. *Richard Hughes: Author, Father*, by Penelope Hughes. Sutton. pp. 194. £10.95.

109. *A Blasphemer and Reformer*, by William K. Malcolm. AberdeenU. pp. xv + 212. £12.50.

110. *Voices: A Life of Frank O'Connor*, by James Matthews. G&M (1983). pp. vii + 451. £20.

111. *The Essays, Articles and Reviews of Evelyn Waugh*, ed. by Donat Gallagher. Methuen. pp. xxv + 662. £20.

the creation of the Waugh persona and the diversity of his working career as a prolific writer. In such a large volume there are inevitably minor errors, but only one (p. 298 'popular' for 'unpopular') is a howler. Readers of Waugh will be grateful to both editor and publisher for an excellent collection which is also comparatively inexpensive.

Martin Stannard is the editor of a collection of pieces on Waugh in the now familiar 'Critical Heritage'[112] format. The volume's major aim is to provide a representative sample of contemporary reviews (from 1926 to 1966) together with reviews of later editions, items of bibliographical and biographical interest, and some edited essays. On the whole the selection seems judicious, though the editor's own review of the diaries is one of the longer pieces. In addition, the decision to dismember important essays on Waugh, scattering their remains through the sections on individual novels, should have been resisted. The editor's introduction, however, is both well written and astute, particularly in the treatment of the discrepancy between the writer and his public personality, and on the whole the work is a mine of information on the subject of Waugh's reception. A piece by Martin Stannard in *THES*, describing his discovery of the manuscript of *Vile Bodies* in the library of Jonathan Guinness, prompted a swift reply from Jacqueline McDonnell, also in possession of a copy of the manuscript, from which she is preparing a new annotated edition. A manuscript of the novel was later sold at Christie's to an anonymous bidder.

The year saw several good periodical essays on Waugh. In *PLL* Colman O'Hare demonstrates that the *Sword of Honour* trilogy is filled with deliberately ironic echoes of *Brideshead Revisited*. In his view, careful use of religious allusion in the trilogy extends the liturgical overtones of *Brideshead*, in order to treat seriously issues which were previously treated somewhat sanctimoniously. O'Hare handles a great deal of fresh material economically and effectively here. In *MFS* Claire Hopley argues that *Put Out More Flags* is only superficially lacking in seriousness, and that, as one of the finest works of the early 1940s it deserves more sympathetic attention than it has hitherto received. Interesting links are established to the *Sword of Honour* trilogy and to other novels of the period. In *SSF* Robert Murray Davis discusses 'Period Piece', a short story which anticipates the ending of the dynastic plot in *Sword of Honour*. By comparing the carbon typescript and the printed versions he demonstrates how carefully Waugh considered questions of style, character, and narrative strategy.

Of related interest are several shorter pieces. In *AntigR* Auberon Waugh describes his mother's family background and character, and gives a brief account of her life. In *SR* Walter Sullivan describes the difficulties posed to the reader by Waugh's stubborn conservatism and Catholicism. John Louis Lepage argues, in *Expl*, that 'the pudendal joke is a formidable presence in *The Loved One*', as if one were not already aware of the fact (though perhaps the American reader may need puns on British slang explained). In the same journal Randall Toye rediscovers the origin of the word 'sheepish' in *Vile Bodies*, a point previously revealed by Jessica Mitford in 1960.

EWN continues to provide much of interest, with reviews, brief notes, and

112. *Evelyn Waugh: The Critical Heritage*, ed. by Martin Stannard. RKP. pp. xxii + 537. £18.95.

bibliographical information. In the spring issue, Robert Murray Davis expands his previous discussion of Waugh's reading in aesthetics, preparatory to writing *Rossetti*. Donald Greene discusses the characters of Hooper and Trimmer, and Pamela R. Johnson considers the significance of Tony Last's relation to Thérèse de Vitré. Paul A. Doyle continues the record of the year's work on Waugh. In the autumn issue, Claire Hirshfield points out that Mrs Ryder is modelled on a British feminist, killed by a shell in Serbia in the First World War; K. M. Burke examines dialogue and satire in several novels; Gerhard Wölk adds a supplementary list of criticism; and Paul Doyle publishes references to Evelyn Waugh in Arthur Waugh's diary (continued in the following issue). The winter issue contains an unconvincing essay on Proustian elements in *Brideshead* by Richard G. Hodgson, and James J. Lynch notes an allusion to Dante in *Men At Arms*.

Tony Bianchi's study of Richard Vaughan[113] argues for Vaughan's work as a representative example of a prevailing strain in modern fiction, the pastoral romance, drawing suggestive parallels between Vaughan and other Welsh regionalists, American pastoralists, and European writers. The format of the pamphlet is irritating, however. No Welsh terms are translated, no footnotes are provided, the short bibliography does not include works mentioned in the text, and there is a curious use of italics to indicate quotation, without the source being given. This is a pity, as in other respects Bianchi has provided the reader with a valuable short essay which indicates Vaughan's failings and virtues, is perceptive in its local readings, and succeeds in relating Vaughan both to his immediate social context and to such wider issues as the novelist's relation to history.

It has been a rewarding year for critics of Graham Greene. OUP have re-issued a collection of writers' reminiscences of their schooldays, originally edited by Greene[114] in 1934. Contributors include H. E. Bates, Elizabeth Bowen, Walter Greenwood, L. P. Hartley, Seán O'Faoláin, Anthony Powell, E. Arnot Robertson, and Antonia White. Greene's own contribution seems somewhat guarded but is none the less of interest, particularly when compared with his later, fuller, autobiographical writings. More revealing, however, is Greene's *Getting to Know the General*[115], an account of his visits to Panama, 1976–83, and his friendship with its ruler, Omar Torrijos. Interestingly Greene describes his fascination with Spain and Latin America as of long date, mentioning an early unpublished novel on the subject and ascribing its attraction to his belief that in these countries politics is a matter of life and death. Greene also describes his involvement (with Gabriel García Márquez) as a neutral intermediary in attempts to secure the release of the victims of kidnapping in El Salvador. In addition, the volume also sheds considerable light on Greene's methods of composition, centred here on an unfinished novel, which Greene abandoned when he realized that its characters had emerged from life rather than from his unconscious.

Greene's novels have been translated into film more than those of any other major novelist of the century. Two books examine the cinema of Graham

113. *Richard Vaughan*, by Tony Bianchi. UWales. pp. 89. pb £2.95.

114. *The Old School: Essays by Divers Hands*, ed. by Graham Greene. OUP. pp. viii + 236. pb £3.50.

115. *Getting to Know the General: The Story of an Involvement*, by Graham Greene. Bodley. pp. 224. £8.95.

Greene. Quentin Falk[116] offers a straightforward account of every film based on Greene's fiction, together with other cinematic projects in which Greene was involved, as actor, adaptor, or critic. While film is the major focus, the volume also brings out the losses involved in filming fiction, and makes suggestive comments on the novels. In addition, Falk has an ear for the interesting anecdote and an eye for the right illustrations. Judith Adamson's study[117], similarly well illustrated, goes further in considering the influence of film on the novels, particularly emphasizing the way in which Greene's writing techniques evolved as a result of his activities as a film critic. Adamson argues convincingly that Greene's early interest in melodrama and his commitment to popular art should be seen in the light of his concern to find new directions outside the field of a decaying bourgeois culture. While film is still the primary focus, Adamson quotes from two interviews with Greene and offers perceptive readings of *Brighton Rock* and *Our Man in Havana*, among others. Greene is described as having read the book in manuscript, but it is a pity he was not also its proof-reader. 'Cheval' for 'Chaval' (in *The Tenth Man*) and '*rapportage*' for '*reportage*' are two notable howlers.

Three book-length studies of Greene have appeared. Roger Sharrock[118] concentrates on the novels, adopting a broadly chronological approach, while dividing the work into three phases: prewar thrillers, Catholic novels, and political fiction. Clearly the record of a personal response, the volume suffers a little from an overexpository tone, and a general lack of emphasis on questions of form and structure. Where Sharrock scores, however, particularly in the discussion of thrillers, is in the sense of Greene as a contributor to popular myth-making. The analyses of the political novels (especially *The Quiet American* and *The Honorary Consul*) are among the best to date, and the subsidiary consideration of cinematic and comic techniques is thought-provoking in the best sense. Georg M. A. Gaston's volume[119] offers a more familiar thematic reading of Greene as a writer in pursuit of salvation, though the author acknowledges that Greene's Catholicism is unorthodox, and he also emphasizes the comic novels. *The Quiet American* rightly receives a chapter to itself, and discussions of Greene's criticism and of the later novels (to 1982) are useful. Gaston's style, however, makes for reader irritation, particularly in the misuse of 'it's' and of split infinitives. Richard Kelly's *Graham Greene*[120] has the merit of being comprehensive, concerning itself with most of Greene's published work to 1982. Separate chapters are devoted to the plays and short stories, which usually receive little attention, and the brief analysis of 'Under the Garden' is worth reading. Kelly sees Greene's main strength as residing in his plots (which are summarized at unnecessary length) and his obsessive concern with such themes as innocence, evil, pity, and betrayal. On the whole the volume is introductory, combining low-powered critical analysis with a

116. *Travels in Greeneland: The Cinema of Graham Greene*, by Quentin Falk. Quartet. pp. x + 229. £14.95.
117. *Graham Greene and Cinema*, by Judith Adamson. Pilgrim. pp. xiv + 191. $31.95.
118. *Saints, Sinners and Comedians: The Novels of Graham Greene*, by Roger Sharrock. B&O/UND. pp. 298. hb £15.95, pb £5.95.
119. *The Pursuit of Salvation: A Critical Guide to the Novels of Graham Greene*, by Georg M. A. Gaston. Whitston. pp. vi + 164. $18.50.
120. *Graham Greene*, by Richard Kelly. Ungar. pp. 195. £13.95.

brisk run over familiar ground. The paucity of footnotes, the unattached quotations, and the occasional inaccuracy (e.g. 'Wormwold' for 'Wormold') lessen its usefulness, and the suggestion of similarity between Greene and the character of Henry ('Cheap in August') strikes a jarring note.

Two periodical essays examine Greene's analysis of politics in *The Human Factor*. Gary P. Storhoff (in *ELWIU*) argues that the novel demonstrates the Christian cast of Greene's politics, in which selfless commitment transcends the failure of institutional politics. In my own essay (*DQR*) I suggest that Greene's political vision is informed by psychological insight, and is articulated in the novel through a complex network of allusions to games and play, a concern of Greene's also in *Our Man in Havana*. In *ELN* Lisa Vargo turns to *The Quiet American*, examining different texts of the novel from 1955 to 1973, and demonstrating that Greene continued working on Pyle's American accent, which provoked harsh reviews when the novel first came out. Lastly, in *TSLL*, Ronald G. Walker sets out to remedy the neglect of the formal artistry of Greene's novels with a detailed account of the narrative structure of *The End of the Affair*, concluding that Greene's strategy is essentially designed to expose the sham of reductive fictions. One agrees, but one rather wishes Walker had been less leisurely in his presentation, and had got to the point more swiftly. Tabulation (percentage of whole text devoted to particular sequences, for example) rather eclipses fabulation here.

The last 1983 issue of *TCL* is a special number devoted to Henry Green, and illustrates the variety of critical responses to his work. Carey Wall argues that Green is a traditional writer, operating within the romance tradition, while Joseph Hynes discusses his experience in the classroom teaching the novels of Green on a modernist and metafictional course. Barbara Brothers's essay, the best of the volume, draws on reader-response criticism and deconstructionism to argue that *Blindness* demonstrates that meaning is circular and non-verifiable, beginning and ending in the self. Rod Mengham's discussion of 'The Lull' makes a good companion piece with its similar emphasis on loss of meaning, while John Russell provides an analysis of three stories of the Blitz, drawing parallels with Joyce. Dorothy Lygon and James Lees-Milne offer short biographical sketches, and an interview with John Lehmann also provides biographical information. Richard Heinzkill compiles a checklist of work by and about Green. Two pieces are reprints, Angus Wilson's review of *Blindness*, and V. S. Pritchett's obituary, and as both are easily available elsewhere, the editor might better have employed the space for new writing. But this is a minor cavil.

Memorials to Arthur Koestler continue to appear. Hutchinson have published *Stranger on the Square*[121], a joint autobiography by Arthur and Cynthia Koestler, covering the years 1941 to 1956. The manuscript of the book was found in Koestler's desk after his suicide, and has been edited and re-arranged by Harold Harris to add to its coherence. It is of exceptional interest, in particular in the frankness with which Cynthia discusses her husband. The *Paris Review* also contains reminiscences from Cynthia Koestler, illustrated with photographs, and the last interview Koestler ever gave, to Duncan Fallowell. Koestler is somewhat unforthcoming, though the interview does

121. *Stranger on the Square*, by Cynthia and Arthur Koestler, intro. by Harold Harris. Hutchinson. pp. 242. £9.95.

include an account of his experiences with drugs. George Mikes's *Arthur Koestler*[122] is the story of a friendship extending over some thirty years between fellow Hungarians. While very much a 'warts and all' treatment, Mikes's candour does not prevent the resultant close-up portrait from being both instructive and moving, engaged and ironic.

Only one essay on Anthony Powell has appeared, a general appreciation by William H. Pritchard in *HudR*, and there is a similar lack of work on Fionn Mac Colla, with only *ScLJ*'s publication of an excerpt from one of his unpublished works, and a letter, to report.

No such scarcity is apparent in critical work on Beckett, particularly on his earlier work. Rubin Rabinovitz's study[123] analyses both unpublished and published fiction written between 1929 and the end of the Second World War, before Beckett began to write in French. While Rabinovitz does not underestimate the difficulty in understanding Beckett's innovatory techniques, his analysis is illuminating and does much to make the texts in question more accessible. For most readers the discussion of philosophy in *Watt* and of repetition in *Murphy* will be of most interest. (The latter is supplemented by two substantial appendixes.) Rabinovitz handles his considerable learning gracefully and writes with clarity and perception. Beckett scholars unable to read German will welcome the translation by Joseph P. Dolan of Gottfried Büttner's full-length study of *Watt*[124], first published in 1981 and favourably reviewed. The volume is especially interesting in that it draws on twenty years of friendship with Beckett, with whom the author also corresponded on a number of topics. Lance St John Butler's book[125] is distinctly a work for the specialist and for those interested in the relation between philosophy and literature. Separate chapters discuss Beckett in the light of one major philosophical work by each of Heidegger, Sartre, and Hegel. The major works are the principal focus, with a final chapter which tackles short pieces produced since 1961.

JBeckS contains four essays on fiction. Heath Lees argues that critics have underestimated Beckett's understanding of music, and concentrates his attention on images of tuning and untuning in *Watt*, claiming that, had Watt learned to respond to the non-literal language of music, his mental catastrophe might have been avoided. It seems an excellent idea, though readers without musical awareness (as is the case of the current reviewer) may find it a difficult essay, despite the diagram. Two essays of a comparative nature are of exceptionally good value. Nicholas Zurbrugg considers 'Dream of fair to middling women' as illustrating the differences between Beckett and Proust's respective responses to the limits of language and perception. Linda Ben-Zvi clarifies Beckett's response to the work of Fritz Mauthner, which he read on Joyce's behalf while Joyce was composing *Finnegans Wake*. Again the 'Dream of fair to middling women' figures in the discussion, together with *Company*. Lastly,

122. *Arthur Koestler: The Story of a Friendship*, by George Mikes. Deutsch (1983). pp. 80. £5.95.

123. *The Development of Samuel Beckett's Fiction*, by Rubin Rabinovitz. UIll. pp. x + 231. $17.50.

124. *Samuel Beckett's Novel 'Watt'*, by Gottfried Büttner, trans. by Joseph P. Dolan. UPenn. pp. xv + 174. $20.

125. *Samuel Beckett and the Meaning of Being: A Study in Ontological Parable*, by Lance St John Butler. Macmillan. pp. ix + 213. £25.

Jean Yamasaki analyses *Malone meurt*, arguing, somewhat hermetically, that the novel marks the pivotal point at which three metaphors (philosophic, religious, and aesthetic) merge. The journal also includes reviews of recent work on Beckett.

The spring issue of *IUR* is a special Beckett number, of fairly limited interest, as far as Beckett's fiction is concerned, as the content of the relevant articles indicates. Seamus Deane compares Beckett and Joyce, David Berkman re-assesses the influence of Berkeley on Beckett, and Patrick Wakeling contributes a psychobiographical piece. J. C. Mays welcomes Beckett's reinstatement in the Irish tradition, and explores his attitude to Irish writing of the 1930s, while Roger Little provides a portrait of Professor Thomas Rudmose-Brown, an influence on the writer. Other essayists consider the drama and poetry.

The other periodical essays are a mixed bag. In *EIC* Michael Benson finds that Hardy's method of presenting moving bodies not altogether in control of their limbs seems to be echoed in Beckett's novels, where absurd and problematic movements are common. The essay sheds more light on Hardy than on Beckett. In *IFR* Peter Murphy makes a good case for the existence in the later prose works (specifically the 'Still' trilogy) of a movement towards a regeneration of the Orpheus myth. In the same journal K. J. Phillips reads *Molloy* as a thorough parody of *The Odyssey*. One essay deserves special, if belated, mention. In *Boundary* (1983) Dennis A. Foster argues that the 'I' of *The Unnamable* refers to no unified subject, and that this unsettling of the narrative at its source prompts the reader to mimic the struggle of the speaker of the text to possess the 'I' as his own. While not every reader will welcome Foster's description of the reader's symbolic castration by the text (female readers do not seem to be envisaged) the essay uses Lacan intelligently to challenge most critical readings of Beckett's work.

Beckett appears prominently in two books on more general topics. Alan Singer explores the connections between models of metaphor and narrative structure in his *A Metaphorics of Fiction*[126] which includes a close reading of *How It Is*. Interestingly Singer contests the critical emphasis on the passivity of an absurdist stance, which he sees as belied by the rhetorical density of Beckett's art. The language of the novels is a focus in Zulfikar Ghose's *The Fiction of Reality*[127] which discusses the significance of the various languages in *Watt* and analyses the style of *How It Is*.

J. Howard Woolmer's bibliography of Malcolm Lowry[128] covers books and pamphlets by Lowry, contributions to books and periodicals, letters, song lyrics, translations of Lowry's works and also recordings, films, radio and television programmes concerning Lowry. Attractively illustrated with some fifty photographs it is comprehensive and accurate. As its author points out, its only weakness is the lack of productive information for a number of Lowry's books, the result of lost or inaccessible publishers' records. Ronald Binns[129]

126. *A Metaphorics of Fiction: Discontinuity and Discourse in the Modern Novel*, by Alan Singer. UFlorS. pp. xi + 183. $18.

127. *The Fiction of Reality*, by Zulfikar Ghose. Macmillan (1983). pp. 143. £20.

128. *Malcolm Lowry: A Bibliography*, by J. Howard Woolmer. W/B (1983). pp. xiv + 183. $30.

129. *Malcolm Lowry*, by Ronald Binns. Contemporary Writers Series. Methuen. pp. 96. pb £2.25.

has written a short critical study of Lowry which concentrates on the major works. While emphasizing the expressionist modernism of *Under the Volcano* he also does much to de-mystify Lowry and to make his work more accessible. Binns distinguishes briskly between Lowry's own account of the novel and its actual form, insisting that there is a plot, there are characters, and that the sociopolitical dimension is important. (A short course in Mexican history is provided.) As well as arguing that the later tales anticipate contemporary metafiction, Binns also draws comparisons to Hardy, Melville, and Dante. At times the 'no nonsense' style is irritatingly bold ('Mexico still has one of the highest murder rates in the world'. '*Under the Volcano* is about the aftermath of a divorce'). But on the whole Binns substantiates his claim that what is unique to Lowry is his ability to situate the hero's *Angst* amid the entanglements of politics and history.

Douglas Day's *Malcolm Lowry*[130] is a paperback re-issue of the biography first published in 1973 (*YW* 57.347). While it is regrettable that no attempt has been made to revise, to incorporate fresh material, or even to update the bibliography, the work remains useful. In *CanL* Elizabeth D. Rankin argues that *Under the Volcano* is not a tragic novel and that the later work is in general more comic. She illustrates her point with a close reading of 'Elephant and Colosseum'. In *R&L* in an essay which has points of contact with Rankin's, David Falk argues for a powerful religious vision in Lowry's late fiction, which attempts to transcend the vision of doom in *Under the Volcano*. Falk notes the contradictions in Lowry's position and does not overestimate his success, but again highlights comedy. The *MLNew* includes a discussion of references to the Spanish Civil War in *Under the Volcano* (C. J. Ackerley) together with conference reports, a guide to Lowry's London, and descriptions of manuscript acquisitions. The second volume changes both in format and in name, becoming the *Malcolm Lowry Review*. Apart from reviews, a bibliography, and other news items, the issue is noteworthy for Ackerley's extensive essay on the background of Mexican history in *Under the Volcano*, and Sue Vice's discussion of correspondences between Lowry's work and that of a contemporary Mexican photographer.

Gordon Smith's *Mervyn Peake*[131] does not pretend to be a biography but rather a personal memoir of a long friendship with Peake, extending from schooldays to Peake's death. Half the book is taken up with illustrations, lending it a coffee-table appearance. On the other hand, the emphasis on Peake's younger days and on his poetry is valuable and if the format is anecdotal, they are, at least, highly entertaining anecdotes. *The Drawings of Mervyn Peake*[132], first published in 1974 (see *YW* 56.365–6), has now been re-issued in paperback. Hilary Spurling's introduction interestingly relates the sketches, illustrations, and drawings to the novels and to the author's life. *MPR* continues to appear. The spring issue reprints articles by and on Peake. Dee Berkeley and G. Peter Winnington continue their checklist of Peake's works in print. Winnington also publishes an informative essay on Peake's parents and their years in China, and there are the usual reviews.

130. *Malcolm Lowry: A Biography*, by Douglas Day. OUP. pp. xiii + 483. pb £5.95.
131. *Mervyn Peake: A Personal Memoir*, by Gordon Smith. Gollancz. pp. 128. £10.95.
132. *The Drawings of Mervyn Peake*, intro. by Hilary Spurling. A&B. Unpaginated. pb £5.95.

Critical response to the novels of William Golding has centred on the later novels. Don Crompton died before he could finish his study of Golding[133], which has now been edited and completed by Julia Briggs. The resultant book is essentially dedicated to the proposition that the later novels (from *The Spire* to *The Paper Men*) testify to spiritual truths, though secondary themes linking them include the role of the artist, the sense of history, and the poetic quality of Golding's later style. Careful research pays off in the discussion of the biblical context of *Darkness Visible* and of the significance of 'rites' in *Rites of Passage* and the scapegoat in *The Spire*. Much of the material is fresh and illuminating, especially the section on 'The Scorpion God' which reveals the centrality of Egypt in Golding's imagination, and includes an admirably clear account of the significance of setting and title, the latter illustrated by a drawing of the mace-head on which the scorpion-king appears.

Two re-issues from Faber will be of interest to Golding readers. *The Hot Gates*[134] is a collection of Golding's occasional essays, reviews, and travel pieces first published in 1965, but as attractive as ever. The critical study by Mark Kinkead-Weekes and Ian Gregor[135] was first published in 1967. The writers' original aim, to provide detailed readings of the novels while also describing the evolving nature of Golding's imagination, is ably continued in the revised edition, which contains a new and first-rate chapter on *The Pyramid*, *Rites of Passage*, and *Darkness Visible*.

The periodical essays on Golding are of a very high standard. In *WLT* Peter Bien argues that the award of the Nobel Prize to Golding in 1983 recognizes his value as a latter-day modernist, at a time when modernism is considered passé. In the same issue Roy Arthur Swanson discusses 'alter egoism and oxymoronic dualisms' in *Darkness Visible*, in a genuinely comparative essay on the topic of 'doublethink' in works by Orwell, Golding, and Pynchon. The award of the Nobel Prize also prompts Richard Jones, in *VQR*, to offer a general assessment of Golding, not sparing in brickbats, especially as concerns *The Paper Men*. In *CritQ*, however, *The Paper Men* finds a defender in Philip Redpath, who claims that most reviewers missed the point of the novel, by assuming that Golding was to be identified with Barclay, the fictional novelist. This common view of the novel as semi-confessional autobiography detracts from its complex structure and the questions it raises about the relationship between art and criticism, two issues which Redpath develops in a very carefully structured and consistently impressive essay. Also good is Hetty Clews's piece in *ESC*, which finds *Darkness Visible* a strikingly Manichaean novel, with its roots in apocalyptic tradition. The essay includes a valuable discussion of the relation between the novel and Julian Jaynes's *The Origin of Consciousness in the Breakdown of the Bicameral Mind*.

The earlier novels do not attract the same degree of attention. In *EA* Gerard Klaus employs a wealth of anthropological material to urge that *Lord of the Flies* involves a new ludic structure, based on hunting, ritual dancing, and sacrifice. Where most anthropologists emphasize the opposition between concepts of play and the sacred, Klaus argues that in the novel play leads to an

133. *A View from the Spire: William Golding's Later Novels*, by Don Crompton. Blackwell. pp. vii + 199. £15.

134. *The Hot Gates*, by William Golding. Faber. pp. 175. pb £2.95.

135. *William Golding: A Critical Study*, by Mark Kinkead-Weekes and Ian Gregor. Faber. pp. 292. pb £3.50.

intuitive and collective apprehension of the sacred, in contradistinction to the individual quests of Ralph and Simon. A short note in *Expl*, from Thomas Dilworth, suggests that the title of *The Inheritors* uses a quotation from Orwell. In *English* Philip Redpath examines antitheses of various kinds in *Lord of the Flies* and *The Inheritors*.

LMag features a rare essay on the novels of J. L. Carr. While David Taylor admits that Carr is a marginal figure, his novels largely unobtainable, and bearing little relation to the rest of contemporary fiction, he commends Carr's Englishness, and argues that his novels provide a unique view of provincial society, which is neither patronizing nor rose-tinted.

Throughout her life Barbara Pym kept diaries and working notebooks, and also maintained a lively correspondence. From about half of the extant materials (the rest are in the Bodleian) her sister and a close friend have produced a quasi-autobiography[136] of exceptional interest and value, covering Pym's years at Oxford, the war, and her life as a novelist. Despite Pym's apparent 'failure' in fiction and in love, the book is lively, often hilarious, and consistently fascinating. Two particular points emerge – the influence on Pym's novels of her work for the International African Institute, and above all, the way in which the persona of 'spinsterish Miss Pym' was actively created. One looks forward to full editions of the letters and papers in the future, though preferably without the printer's errors which abound here. Barbara Pym was a close friend of Robert Liddell from 1933 until her death, and he has contributed a memoir of her to *LMag*. Two periodical essays have appeared. In a special issue of *Mosaic* (on 'Attitudes Towards Marriage in Literature') Robert J. Graham surveys the fiction, and focuses on Pym's evaluation of the 'marriage idyll and spinster myth'. Although inevitably thematic, the essay includes a side-glance at changes in society which may account for Pym's renewed popularity, and the coverage of the novels is full and sensible. In *Thought* Diana Benet examines the presentation of the Christian church in Pym's novels, isolating three areas in which the church is seen as failing: a devitalized language, outmoded devotional forms, and a clergy with communication problems. Despite this modestly thematic intention, Benet's essay does much to deepen understanding of Pym's comic techniques and her style.

There is the beginning of a revival of interest in Colin MacInnes as a figure who accurately reflects, in his best writings, the innocence and optimism of the 1950s. Tony Gould has written a good, straightforward biography[137], which does not underemphasize the less attractive aspects of his subject's personality. To put it at its mildest, not everyone remembers MacInnes with affection, and Gould's account of his sexual activities, alcoholism, cruelty, and confused negrophilia amply demonstrates why. Gould makes no great claims for MacInnes as a writer, sensibly conceding that his novels are only intermittently good, while defending his essays. Those who are interested in MacInnes will not find a better consideration of him, though new readers are unlikely to be attracted. (The catalogue of rapes, incest, sodomy, and masochistic acts in *Fancy Free*, for example, discouraged this reader.)

---

136. *A Very Private Eye: The Diaries, Letters and Notebooks of Barbara Pym*, ed. by Hazel Holt and Hilary Pym. Macmillan. pp. xvi + 358. £12.95.

137. *Inside Outsider: The Life and Times of Colin MacInnes*, by Tony Gould. C&W/Hogarth (1983). pp. xvi + 261. £12.50.

In *Chapman* Don W. Nichol compares translations by Robert Garioch and Anthony Burgess (in *Abba Abba*) of Giuseppe Gioachino Belli's sonnets, drawing attention to the differing effects of translation into Scots (Garioch) and English (Burgess).

Muriel Spark is the subject of a collection of essays[138] edited by Alan Bold, in which the emphasis falls squarely on the metaphysical and religious aspects of her fiction. Francis Russell Hart takes issue with other critics' understanding of Spark's supernaturalism; Allan Massie discusses the relation between Catholicism and Calvinism in her work; Jennifer L. Randisi finds in Spark's satiric approach a view of art as demonic. In the best essay, Valerie Shaw draws attention to Spark's antitranscendental stance and to her insistence on empirical reality. Focusing particularly on *Loitering with Intent* Shaw demonstrates the importance in Spark's work of realistic settings which afford glimpses of social history. Other essays analyse Spark's criticism, her short stories, her verse, her duplicitous handling of female characters, and her Scottish context. On the whole, individual essays tend to be somewhat discursive, offering general overviews of the entire opus, but the volume is nevertheless a welcome addition to criticism of Spark.

The difficulty of writing a short study of a novelist who has published twenty-one novels, plus a rich array of philosophical and critical work, should never be underestimated. Even so Richard Todd's study of Iris Murdoch[139] remains at an introductory level, with too many summary descriptions of plot and theme. Todd's assessment of Murdoch's strengths and weaknesses is balanced and objective, but tends to lack punch as a result. None the less, Murdoch's complex conception of realism, her concern with secret fantasy, the influence of Canetti and Queneau, are all well explicated and the author makes useful connections to the non-fiction, especially when discussing the relation between the theme of literacy in *A Word Child* and Murdoch's own contribution to educational debates. In *CritQ* D. W. Jefferson explores the various complex ways in which Murdoch gives structure to character. A large part of the essay is devoted to *The Sea, The Sea*, recognized as a flawed, if interesting, work. Lastly, in a brief essay in *EI*, Colette Charpentier argues that the use of fantasy in *The Unicorn* is designed to express Anglo-Irish tensions.

Barbara Dahlhaus-Beilner's study of Doris Lessing[140] is founded on the contention that the numerous analyses of Lessing's work from either a feminist or a specifically political point of view are only partially adequate. The author's thesis is that from *The Grass is Singing* (1950) on, Lessing progressively develops a particular psychological model which finds its fullest realization in *The Memoirs of a Survivor* (1974). This model is evident in a theory of the unconscious which is presented in the protagonists as varying degrees of irrationality and an ambivalent madness which originates as a destructive force and symbol of alienation and becomes a source of new sensibility, identity,

138. *Muriel Spark: An Odd Capacity for Vision*, ed. by Alan Bold. Vision/B&N. pp. 208. £14.95.
139. *Iris Murdoch*, by Richard Todd. Contemporary Writers Series. Methuen. pp. 112. pb £2.25.
140. *Wahnsinn: Symptom und Befreiung, Funktion und narrative Vermittlung extremen Irrationalismus im Werk Doris Lessings*, by Barbara Dahlhaus-Beilner. Grüner. pp. 261. pb Fl 50.

mysticism, and Utopia. This thesis is rigorously analysed and illustrated in the discussions of five of Lessing's novels. The study includes an extensive bibliography with many titles in English, and an English summary. [M.H.]

In *JCL* Antony Beck demonstrates that the events and observations which feed Lessing's 'African' fiction belong mainly to the decade 1939–49, when Doris Lessing moved from farm to city life in Salisbury, and from apoliticality to the National Executive Committee of the Southern Rhodesia Labour Party. Beck locates Lessing firmly in the traditions of liberal individualism, arguing that her work sidesteps the practical implications of racial equality, and lacks awareness of modes of economic subjugation. While not every reader will agree, the detailed discussion of Rhodesian politics makes this an unusual and interesting essay. In *Foundation* Peter Caracciolo contributes an equally interesting essay on *Canopus in Argus: Archives*, demonstrating the importance of Oriental sacred traditions in Lessing's work. Marleen S. Barr and Nicholas D. Smith[141] have edited a collection of essays on women and Utopia, which includes two on Lessing. Lee Cullen Khanna points out that Utopian novels by women in the contemporary period include substantial consideration of aesthetic pleasure or creativity, so that the high estimation of art in feminine Utopian fiction may be seen as distinguishing it from its predecessors. Song is particularly important in Lessing's *Marriages Between Zones Three, Four and Five*. Thomas I. White argues that the *Canopus in Argos* novels are distinguished by the rejection of the political. Politics is seen here as an emotional enterprise, proceeding especially from pity and pride, which Lessing replaces with aesthetic experience as a contributor to evolutionary growth. Both essays are well worth reading.

The two volumes of *DLessingN* are not particularly distinguished this year. The spring volume is a British issue, paying special attention to the African stories, the *Golden Notebook* phase, and the space fiction, with a strong tendency towards general evaluation. Angela Smith discusses 'The Old Chief Mshlanga' as a record of cultural alienation, Jenny Taylor relates to Lessing as a feminist writer, and Elizabeth Maslen offers a sympathetic overview. The volume is marred, however, by Carol Hayes's piece which generalizes about the British critical response to Lessing by castigating a recent essay by Patrick Parrinder and extolling the work of Jenny Taylor. Parrinder's short reply is sufficient to convince the reader that he has been crudely misrepresented, but even so, this type of personal attack does not deserve a place in a respectable journal. There are, however, two good pieces – a brief note from Peter Caracciolo on nomenclature in the later fiction, and an essay from Jane Mooney on the connections between *Shikasta* and the earlier realist fiction. The latter argues cogently that the novel indicates a return to humanism and an act of faith in literature. The second volume is monopolized almost entirely by accounts of Lessing in America, conference reports, and reviews, but does contain an interesting interview with Lessing, who vigorously disputes the facile equation of space fiction with escapism.

The year 1984 saw a major study of the writings of Brian Aldiss[142], co-

141. *Women and Utopia: Critical Interpretations*, ed. by Marleen S. Barr and Nicholas D. Smith. UPA. pp. 171. hb £29.90, pb £13.45.

142. *Apertures: A Study of the Writings of Brian Aldiss*, by Brian Griffin and David Wingrove. Greenwood. pp. xvi + 261. £27.95.

authored by Brian Griffin and David Wingrove. Aldiss is seen as a representative of the transition between old and new schools of science fiction, and the authors draw engaging comparisons to the early modernists, in terms of stylistic exploration and similarity of aims. The approach is generally, though not slavishly, chronological, and the disparities of viewpoint between the two authors make for a sense of lively debate.

Both essays on John Berger are stimulating and full of insight. In *Crit* A. R. Brás argues that Berger's conviction that art is revolutionary essentially at a perceptual level dictates his emphasis on historical continuity. This is a balanced appraisal of the first four novels, which draws attention to Berger's curious failure to depict the potential on which so much emphasis is placed. In the same issue Raymond A. Mazurek turns his attention to *Pig Earth* to argue that Berger's recent fiction has returned to the realist tradition and to situating events and action in a broad historical frame.

In contrast, John Fowles attracts writers of varying sophistication. H. W. Fawkner's volume[143] on the structure of time and timelessness in Fowles's major novels looked promising, particularly as it includes a foreword by Fowles, who states that he is interested in Fawkner's approach. Fawkner does make some interesting points here and there but this reader, at least, found the book singularly graceless. The author cheerfully says that he has avoided reading critical works on Fowles, but goes on to dissociate his own book from 'journalistic introductions to the Fowlesian landscape', setting his work up as a 'master key' and 'scientific investigation'. The resultant farrago invokes neuropsychology, esotericism, structuralism, chronosophy, and other 'isms' and 'ologies', in a prose style varying from the impenetrable to the brash.

Bruce Woodcock's examination[144] of Fowles in the context of the social construction of masculinity looked unpromisingly 'relevant' at first glance, but turned out to be a convincing and perceptive book. In a detailed reading of the major novels, Woodcock draws out the contradictions in the fiction, arguing that 'Even when he analyses male power most directly he does so in ways which perpetuate some of masculinity's most tenacious myths'. While referring intelligently to recent theorists of sexuality, the book is not narrowly thematic, but includes a fine analysis of the ways in which narrative strategies invite voyeuristic interest from the reader. The account of the drastic regression in *Mantissa* is highly persuasive, and the entire book is admirably clear without any sacrifice of intellectual sophistication, making it a must for both male and female readers of Fowles.

JML publishes an essay by Sherrill Grace which analyses the Bluebeard tale, with some of its prototypes and modern analogues, to argue that, though Fowles maintains the admonitory purpose of the tale (*The Collector*) he alters its significance radically to refuse any affirmation. In *ES* David Leon Higdon studies the typescript of *The French Lieutenant's Woman* (now in the possession of the University of Texas) to examine the various endings discarded by Fowles in the process of revision. The essay sheds light on Fowles, and more generally, presents a very full discussion of problems of closure in the novel. *WHR* prints a lively article by Philip Cohen, demonstrating that *The French*

---

143. *The Timescapes of John Fowles*, by H. W. Fawkner. AUP. pp. 180. £12.95.
144. *Male Mythologies: John Fowles and Masculinity*, by Bruce Woodcock. Harvester. pp. 192. £20.

Lieutenant's Woman depends upon a balanced alternation of two modes – naive realism and antirealism. The resultant 'sophisticated realism' allows the novelist to pursue both existentialist and postmodernist programmes. Finally, Ruth Morse, in *PQ*, explores Fowles's debts to medieval romance, especially to Marie de France, in 'Eliduc', a subject which seems to have an immense fascination for recent essay-writers. Morse extends her analysis to consider the function of allusion in his novels in more general terms, but one does feel that this subject has been sufficiently well covered by now.

In *EI* Rüdiger Imhof and Jürgen Kamm analyse Aidan Higgins's 'Killachter Meadow', drawing parallels between the use of shifting point of view in the story and its theme of paralysis, and underlining its connections with *Dubliners*. The short stories of William Trevor also come in for attention in *EI*, where Mark Mortimer offers a general assessment, emphasizing Trevor's ironic detachment and playful understatement, his comic gifts and lack of sentimentality.

For some reason, Raymond G. McCall has written an essay on the novels of Tom Sharpe (*Crit*). He describes the novels as formulaic, mechanical, predictable, violent, scatological, and, despite their anarchism, fundamentally confirming the values and assumptions of his readers. It seems a rather unrewarding exercise.

ParisR continues to interview contemporary novelists, with J. G. Ballard and Edna O'Brien figuring in 1984. Ballard describes himself as reliant on his obsessions and influenced by surrealism. O'Brien is extremely expansive and says interesting things about her reading, her relation to Ireland, and her sense of herself as a woman writer.

In *CQ* Anita Guiton reviews the novels of David Storey and contrasts them interestingly with his plays. In her view Storey does not use the novel expansively to portray society, but explores the consciousness of a single character.

In *ConL* Mary F. Robertson analyses D. M. Thomas's *The White Hotel* as a test case for whether the late-twentieth-century novelist can handle the relation between fact and fantasy in any authentic manner. While Robertson concludes that Thomas fails to overcome the problem of the cultural representativeness of woman and Holocaust victim, her essay raises good questions and makes intelligent use of psychoanalytic and postmodernist insights.

Auberon Waugh is the subject of an essay in *DUJ* by Anthony G. Dykes, who argues unconvincingly that he is 'an heir of the modern movement'.

As usual there has been a large amount of published work on Margaret Drabble. Mary Hurley Moran's book[145] is intended as a revisionist study, arguing that Drabble's characters are not free, but caught in the structures of family, nature, and fate, and that Drabble is strongly marked by determinism. While certainly challenging the current view of Drabble as a feminist, Moran is rather overthematic, tending to use many similar examples to prove her point. One looks in vain for a sense of the correlation between narrative and thematic structures. In addition, though Moran sees comedy and the visionary impulse as mitigating its miseries, what sticks in the reader's mind are the gloomy lists of crippled children, disfigured women, deaths, and disasters.

ELWIU records an interview with Drabble (by Sharon Whitehill) which

145. *Margaret Drabble: Existing Within Structures*, by Mary Hurley Moran. SIU (1983). pp. ix + 133. $13.95.

brings out Drabble's belief in a spiritual world transcending the material. Two writers look at the influence of Henry James on Drabble. In *CLAJ* Mary M. Lay draws some suggestive parallels between *The Needle's Eye* and *The Ambassadors*, finding that in both novels the strong characters are those who perceive their choices clearly. In *SSF* Charles W. Mayer argues for the existence of parallels between 'A Voyage to Cythera' and James's 'In the Cage'. *JNT* features two essays on *The Middle Ground*. Jane Campbell's is lucid, clearly organized, and convincing. Campbell argues that Drabble's fiction is marked by a tension between the search for elegance and form and the admission that no permanent pattern can be found. The novel may seem shapeless, but is carefully designed to resist classification and to dramatize the impossibility of final statement. Roberta Rubinstein finds that a network of symbols and images holds the novel together, particularly references to illness, mutilation, infection, waste products, and sewage, and tends to get lost in minutiae in her discussion thereof. Nora Foster Stovel's essay on *The Garrick Year* (*Mosaic*) displays a similar inability to see the wood for the trees, with plot summary to boot.

Two essays consider the work of Angela Carter. In *Crit* David Punter proposes to identify a shift of intention in her writing in the 1970s, by a close examination of *The Infernal Desire Machines of Doctor Hoffman* and *The Passion of New Eve*. Although both have to do with sexuality and the unconscious, the latter marks a new attention to issues of gender. In *L&H* Patricia Duncker is less positive about Carter. While her tales supposedly celebrate erotic desire, she finds that in fact they mirror patriarchal realities and envisage women's sexuality as a response to male arousal.

Ian McEwan is the subject of a fine essay in *SoR*, in which David Sampson argues that *The Cement Garden* is a text which deliberately pre-empts the 'close reader' by its transparent idiom. This is an extremely interesting, detailed analysis which draws on Barthes and Lacan profitably.

2. Poetry

The latest volume in the Dictionary of Literary Biography deals with poets of Great Britain and Ireland from 1945 to 1960[146]. The generous format allows for the inclusion of a good range of biographical detail and for useful descriptive accounts of the poets selected. There are bibliographies of primary work and references to secondary sources, and a good selection of photographs, including many of manuscripts. An introduction by Vincent B. Sherry Jr gives a survey of the period.

The most important general study this year is David Trotter's *The Making of the Reader*[147]. This is an important and highly readable, if sometimes undisciplined examination of the relationship between the twentieth-century poet and his audience. It is partly concerned with rhetorical strategies which involve the reader in the process of interpretation and this often leads to minute analysis of verbal features. There are excellent accounts, for example, of

146. *Poets of Great Britain and Ireland, 1945–1960*, ed. by Vincent B. Sherry Jr. DLB 27. Gale. pp. xv + 393. $85.

147. *The Making of the Reader: Language and Subjectivity in Modern American, English and Irish Poetry*, by David Trotter. Macmillan. pp. vii + 272. £20.

different functions of the pronoun 'one' or the kinds of involvement demanded by the demonstratives 'this' and 'that'. But Trotter is not simply a 'lemon-squeezer' critic. He makes effective use of anthropological and psychological models in discussing aspects of poetic ritual and he includes a wide range of historical and sociological knowledge to sustain investigations of reader response. He has important successes here, particularly in relation to *The Waste Land*. A final chapter discusses the achievement of the Carcanet Press in fostering an audience but points to the social and political implications of its stance. Trotter concludes with a plea for 'criticism to sustain a plurality of readerships, if necessary, against the monopoly power of any institution or rhetoric'.

Two books are concerned with the influence of Romantic and Victorian writers. Carlos Baker's *The Echoing Green*[148] examines and interprets some modern poets against the background of English Romanticism as represented by Wordsworth, Coleridge, Byron, Shelley, Keats, and, to a lesser degree, Blake. It begins with a general survey of modern attitudes towards these major Romantics and has separate chapters discussing their influence on Yeats, Eliot, and Auden. Baker assembles a good deal of useful information but he does not push critical discussion on the absorption and transmutation of influence very hard. In a more penetrating study, Carol T. Christ[149] argues that, although Yeats and Eliot both reacted sharply against their Victorian inheritance, they remained in important ways dependent on their immediate past. Like the Modernists, Victorians often found the prominence which they felt Romanticism gave to the poet's subjectivity 'burdensome and restrictive' and sought in reaction to 'objectify the materials of poetry'. This process is studied in sections on 'Dramatic Monologue, Mask and Persona', 'The Picturesque and Modernist Theories of the Image' and 'Myth, History and the Structure of the Long Poem'. Dr Christ concludes that the continuities between nineteenth- and twentieth-century writing are patent and that 'relying upon Modernist interpretations of Victorianism blinds us to the complex affinities in the literature written from 1830–1930'.

Lachlan Mackinnon[150] is concerned with a more specific influence, that of Baudelaire, on Eliot, Auden, and Lowell, and particularly with Baudelaire's conception of the poet and his relationship to the *bourgeoisie*. Mackinnon somewhat confusingly uses the term 'dandyism' to define Baudelaire's attitude, insisting that, divested of its sartorial implications, the word connotes a self-conscious and flaunted pursuit of an ideal. 'Baudelaire is pursuing his ideal, and dandyism signals his pursuit to the world.' With various shifts and reversals, Mackinnon's three poets demonstrate the influence of this idealism. A final chapter considers the political and social significance of their work. There are many stimulating passages here but the overall thesis is strained.

Steve Ellis has written a book on *Dante and English Poetry*[151] of which two chapters deal with twentieth-century writing. 'W. B. Yeats and Dante's Mask'

148. *The Echoing Green: Romanticism, Modernism and the Phenomena of Transference in Poetry*, by Carlos Baker. Princeton. pp. xiii + 377. $32.50.

149. *Victorian and Modern Poetics*, by Carol T. Christ. UChic. pp. ix + 178. £14.70.

150. *Eliot, Auden, Lowell: Aspects of the Baudelairean Inheritance*, by Lachlan Mackinnon. Macmillan (1983). pp. ix + 191. £20.

151. *Dante and English Poetry: Shelley to T. S. Eliot*, by Steve Ellis. CUP (1983). pp. vii + 280. £22.50.

discusses the development of Yeats's interest in Dante and the influence of the *Commedia* on *A Vision*. Despite the evident differences between the two works, Yeats was powerfully affected by the *Commedia*'s 'formal design, its systematisation of images' and its 'imposition of regularity on a world of disordered conflict'. 'T. S. Eliot: the Return to Reality' is a substantial and detailed examination of the influence of Dante, with particular reference to *Four Quartets*.

Some general articles may be grouped here chronologically. In 'Publishing the New Poetry. Harriet Monroe's Anthology' (*JML*) Craig S. Abbott discusses the anthology *The New Poetry*, published in America in 1917, 1923, and 1932, which had considerable influence in diffusing new work. 'The Barrier of a Common Language: British Poetry in the Eighties' (*HudR*) by Dana Gioia is a general survey intended as an introduction to American readers: it pays particular attention to Craig Raine and James Fenton. *PoetryR* (1983) published a supplement of West-Indian–British poetry, including a review article on its themes and achievements by James Berry. In 'Poetry Chronicle. Giants in the Earth: Recent Myths for British Poets' (*ELH*) Avril Fleishman discusses the importance of folk-lore for a number of poets, including David Jones and George Barker.

Turning to writers from the early part of the century, John Masefield's letters to Margaret Bridges have been edited by Donald Stanford[152]. The letters, to the daughter of Robert Bridges, are often purely personal but they also give Masefield's response to his experience of the war in France and later discuss two visits to the United States as well as some matters of general literary interest. There are also a few letters from Margaret Bridges to Masefield, some poems by Masefield, and a previously unpublished poem on the Armistice by Elizabeth Daryush, Margaret Bridges' sister. Donald Stanford has also edited a substantial selection of Masefield's poetry[153], attractively printed and grouped thematically rather than in chronological order, with a brief introduction.

There is one item on De La Mare. John LeVay comments on the appositeness of the title of 'Please to Remember' (*Expl*), with its reference to the Guy Fawkes rhyme.

Although Ernest Rhys will remain best known as the founder of the Everyman Library he was also a minor poet, short-story writer, and novelist. J. Kimberley Roberts's *Ernst Rhys* is a brief, sympathetic, biographical and critical study[154].

There is substantial work this year on Yeats. *The Poems: A New Edition*[155] edited by R. J. Finneran, replaces the second edition of *Collected Poems*, previously the only version generally available. The textual policy has been to present the final versions of the poems authorized by Yeats and the order is that of 'a hypothetical reconstruction' of the contents and order of an

152. *Letters to Margaret Bridges (1915–1919)*, by John Masefield, ed. by Donald Stanford. Carcanet. pp. 123. £6.95.

153. *Selected Poems*, by John Masefield, ed. by Donald Stanford. Carcanet. pp. 341. pb £7.95.

154. *Ernest Rhys*, by J. Kimberley Roberts. Writers of Wales Series. UWales for The Welsh Arts Council (1983). pp. 73. pb £2.95.

155. *The Poems: A New Edition*, by W. B. Yeats, ed. by R. J. Finneran. Macmillan. pp. 768. £16.95.

expanded *Collected Poems*, had Yeats authorized such an edition at the time of his death. That is to say that the body of the work is arranged in the familiar groupings: 'Lyrical' followed by 'Narrative and Dramatic'. A final section prints 'Additional Poems', containing not only those excluded by Yeats from collected editions but others drawn from essays, plays, and stories. Yeats's own notes are reprinted and editorial explanatory notes aim to elucidate all direct allusions in the poems. The volume is handsomely printed and bound and is likely to remain standard for some time. The ordering of the poems has, however, been severely criticized on the grounds that it obscures Yeats's chronological development. A clear statement of the objections and of the reasons for thinking that Yeats himself would have preferred a chronological scheme is given by A. N. Jeffares in the preface to *A New Commentary on the Poems of W. B. Yeats*[156] This revised edition of a standard reference work incorporates much new information and now keys its references both to *Collected Poems* and to *Poems: A New Edition.*

Yeats Annual, No. 2[157], edited by R. J. Finneran contains a number of important articles, some offering biographical and others critical interest. Ronald Schuchard's 'The Minstrel in the Theatre: Arnold, Chaucer and Yeats's New Spiritual Democracy' discusses Yeats's concern for the public recitation of verse, the lecture performances he gave with Florence Farr, and his 'concept of the theatre's role in creating spiritual democracy'. In 'Yeats's Ruskinian Byzantium' Herbert J. Levine contends that 'Yeats's habit of evaluating an historic civilisation through its art stems from his early and lifelong acquaintance with the work of John Ruskin'. He examines *The Stones of Venice* to show that 'if we look carefully at what Ruskin valued in mediaeval Venice, particularly at his cyclical vision of its rise and fall, we will find remarkable similarities to Yeats's presentation of Byzantium in both prose and verse'. Lee Zimmerman's 'Singing Amid Uncertainty: Yeats's Closing Questions' notes that thirty-eight of the *Collected Poems* end with a question mark and argues that these often 'provide a conversational effect and a sharpened sense of immediacy . . . they make us feel the presence of a man thinking and feeling'. But the article also analyses the justification for ending on a question in a number of individual cases. In 'W. B. Yeats and Norreys Connell' Richard F. Petersen and Gary Phillips write on Connell's year as Director of the Abbey Theatre. Carolyn Holdsworth's ' "Shelley Plain": Yeats and Katharine Tynan' is a chronological account of the relationship between Yeats and Tynan which discusses their reviews of each other's work. Finally, George Bornstein contributes a note on 'Yeats's "Those Dancing Days Are Gone" and Pound's "Canto 23" '. There are also reviews and dissertation abstracts.

Unaging Intellect: Essays on W. B. Yeats[158], edited by Kamta C. Srivastava and Ujjal Dutta is a wide-ranging collection, containing both new and re-printed work. Two articles may be particularly mentioned. J. R. Mulryne's 'No Fabulous Symbol: Yeats and the Language of Poetry' is a sensitive account of Yeats's search for a fruitful liaison 'between the world of art and archetype, and the world of fact'. In 'Sons and Fathers: W. B. Yeats and a Problem of

156. *A New Commentary on the Poems of W. B. Yeats*, by A. N. Jeffares. Macmillan. pp. xl + 543. £35.
157. *Yeats Annual, No. 2*, ed. by R. J. Finneran. Macmillan (1983). pp. xi + 158. £20.
158. *Unaging Intellect: Essays on W. B. Yeats*, ed. by Kamta C. Srivastava and Ujjal Dutta. Doaba (1983). pp. 208.

Modernism' W. J. McCormack pursues the idea that literary treatment of relations between father and son may 'reveal the anxious relation of the artist to his world and to his work'. The volume in general suffers from the lack of a unifying theme.

A casebook, *Yeats: Poems, 1919–1935*[159], edited by Elizabeth Cullingford, begins with extracts from Yeats's own discussions of his art and inspiration. It contains a number of early critical studies, including selections from R. P. Blackmur, T. S. Eliot, and Allen Tate; some now classical general work by such critics as Ellmann and Hugh Kenner, and a number of more recent studies of individual poems. Although there may be dispute about particular exclusions, the volume fulfils the editor's purpose 'to illuminate the main issues that Yeats's work has raised in the minds of his critics, and to provide specific detailed commentary on some of his major poems'. The introduction gives a brief history of Yeatsian criticism.

Yeats's fascination with the occult continues to attract attention. Graham Hough's *The Mystery Religion of W. B. Yeats*[160] is the published version of the Northcliffe Lectures in Literature, delivered at University College London in 1983. In the first chapter Hough's aim is to give 'a broad outline of the main tenets of the occultist complex . . . so that we shall know where to situate Yeats on the occultist map'. Hough aims at 'radical simplification' and achieves a remarkable clarity of exposition in this difficult area. He then gives an account of Yeats's acquaintance with occultist beliefs, particularly through Madame Blavatsky's Theosophical Society and the Order of the Golden Dawn. The third chapter introduces *A Vision* and applies occultist ideas to some of the early poetry, and the fourth takes up some specific questions of interpretation raised by *A Vision*. This is a useful guide to complicated territory, intelligible to non-specialists.

In *Yeats and Zen*[161] Shiro Naito attempts not only to show how some specific texts influenced Yeats's later poems (notably Yone Noguchi's *The Spirit of Japanese Art* and Daisetz Suzuki's *Essays in Zen Buddhism*) but also to draw attention to the 'philosophical sympathy' between Yeats and Zen and to trace the development of Yeats's understanding of Zen. This is a well-presented and persuasive argument. There are detailed discussions of 'The Gyres', 'Lapis Lazuli', 'Long-legged Fly', 'The Statues', and 'A Bronze Head'.

Yeats's Heroic Figures[162], by Michael Steinman, is an attractively written account of Yeats's developing attitude towards four men who had a mythical resonance for him as heroes and martyrs. Wilde was the model of the artist, 'a man who glorified the life lived for art's sake' and Parnell the national political hero, paralleled later by Roger Casement. Swift, it is suggested, combined the two, blending the ideas of poet and patriot with those of a heroic thinker and passionate sufferer.

Alan Himber, with the assistance of George Mills Harper, has edited John

159. *Yeats: Poems, 1919–1935*, ed. by Elizabeth Cullingford. Casebook Series. Macmillan. pp. 240. hb £14, pb £5.95.

160. *The Mystery Religion of W. B. Yeats*, by Graham Hough. Harvester. pp. 129. £15.95.

161. *Yeats and Zen: A Study of the Transformation of His Mask*, by Shiro Naito. Yamaguchi. pp. 182. £8.

162. *Yeats's Heroic Figures: Wilde, Parnell, Swift, Casement*, by Michael Steinman. SUNY (1983). pp. 198. hb $34.50, pb $14.95.

Quinn's letters to Yeats[163]. Quinn met Yeats in Ireland in 1902 and their correspondence, which extends from then until shortly before Quinn's death in 1924, is a source of biographical information about both Yeats and his family, particularly his father who spent the last fourteen years of his life in New York, and they clarify the part played by Quinn in making Yeats and the Irish Literary Movement known in America. The letters (191 in all) end with Quinn's enthusiastic response to the award to Yeats of the Nobel Prize.

Geoffrey Thurley's *The Turbulent Dream: Passion and Politics in the Poetry of Yeats* (UQueen) has not yet been available.

In 'Yeats's Quarrel with Modernism' (*SoR*) Delva Journet defines Modernism as involving above all a search for 'formal autonomy' and argues that Yeats's striving for 'conceptual intelligibility' reflects a distrust of this position. A number of articles make minor contributions to the explication of individual poems. 'The Judeo-Christian Background of W. B. Yeats's "Who Goes With Fergus"' (*ArQ*, 1983) finds both Old and New Testament analogues for folk-lore motifs and stylistic aspects of the poem. Nancy D. Hargrove's 'Esthetic Distance in Yeats's "Leda and the Swan"' (*ArQ*, 1983) examines Yeats's use of language, structure, and technical devices to maintain a balance between 'intense involvement with the subject and detachment from it'. T. G. A. Nelson, in 'Yeats's "An Acre of Grass"' (*Expl*), compares the poem with 'The Circus Animals' Desertion' to show the 'active, stirring, restless quality of the later work'. 'Crazy Jane Talks with the Bishop' (*Expl*) by Thomas Ramsey Watson quotes Tertullian to argue that Jane's defence of earthly love against the bishop ironically owes something to incarnational theology, with its stress on the bodily realities of Christ's birth. T. P. Foley finds 'A Source for Yeats's "Terrible Beauty"' (*N&Q*) in a deleted variant in Coleridge's 'The British Stripling's War Song'. Beverly Olson Flanigan's 'Nominal Groups in the Poetry of Yeats and Auden: Notes on the Function of Deixis in Literature' (*Style*) discusses 'Leda and the Swan' and 'Musée des Beaux Arts', calling attention to the way grammatical arrangements of nouns and modifiers may produce a sense of dynamism or stasis.

It has been a very active year amongst critics of T. S. Eliot, with ten books on aspects of his life and work. The refusal of the T. S. Eliot estate to sanction any extended quotation from the poet's unpublished work or correspondence significantly hampers an attempt to write his biography and a final view of the poetic personality will have to wait at least until the publication of the edition of the *Correspondence* now being prepared by Valerie Eliot. Meanwhile, Peter Ackroyd[164] gives a fuller account of the life than any previously available and though the story is often a painful one, particularly in relation to Eliot's first marriage, there is substantial gain, twenty years after Eliot's death, in having a single well-researched account which sets Eliot's work in the context of a life that would have been an industrious and anxious one even without the production of the poetry and plays. Ackroyd cites Eliot's comment to Herbert Read that the best of his poetry 'had cost him dearly in experience' and says that it is his aim to 'elucidate the mystery of that connection'. In the end,

163. *The Letters of John Quinn to William Butler Yeats*, ed. by Alan Himber with the assistance of George Mills Harper. Studies in Modern Literature 28. Bowker (1983). pp. xiii + 302. £35.50.

164. *T. S. Eliot*, by Peter Ackroyd. HH. pp. 400. £12.50.

however, the link remains obstinately elusive and the reader is usefully warned of the dangers of impetuous biographical interpretation. Any temptation, for example, to read the first section of 'A Game of Chess' as a reflection of Eliot's relationship with Vivien breaks down in the light of Ackroyd's account of the state of the marriage at the point when the lines were written. Yet the section does seem more than a simple dramatization even though the connection between life and art continues to tease us out of thought. As far as the evidence is available it is presented here and elsewhere in the volume with sympathy and undogmatic candour.

Ronald Bush's *T. S. Eliot: A Study in Character and Style*[165] considers 'why and how' Eliot's poetry evolved from *The Waste Land* to *Four Quartets*. Bush, like other recent critics, finds a conflict in Eliot between the natural strength of his feelings and the Puritan restraints imposed by his background and upbringing, and he argues that this conflict is echoed in terms of literary influence by the two strands of Romantic thought that Eliot inherited, first a Wordsworthian insistence on fidelity to the expression of the innermost self, and second a symbolist belief in pure and impersonal poetry. Eliot's initial response to this conflict involves a particular consciousness of those 'moments when the heart becomes aware of its own rhetoric', its own self-dramatization and self-deception, a self-awareness seen above all in *Gerontion*. But there is also an underlying sense of nightmarish horror which Bush analyses well in *The Waste Land*. Although the development of Eliot's later discursive style involves a revolutionary change it is seen as one rooted in the oppositions of his early experience. Some of Eliot's experiments 'amplified his suppressed impulses . . . others seem to have been founded not in the amplification but in the evasion of impulse'.

Women in the Poetry of T. S. Eliot[166] by Tony Pinkney takes as its starting point the psychological theories of Melanie Klein and D. W. Winnicott concerning the most primitive phases of a relationship between infant and mother and focuses attention on the importance of representations of the mother and the female body in Eliot's work. To the non-psychologist it is a densely written study and one that sometimes seems forced in its teasing out of psychological influences. But there will be broad assent to the view that 'the fascination of Eliot's poetry is precisely in the fraught *dialectic* of its psychic impulses' and there is no doubt that much of the analysis is extremely suggestive, particularly perhaps of the early poems. The discussion of 'Hysteria' gives that prose-poem a more central place in Eliot's work than it has achieved before.

In *Conflicts in Consciousness*[167] David Spurr 'shares with psychoanalytic approaches to literature the attempt to establish connections between the text and the author's unconscious', but he is aware that 'the multilayered quality of psychological motivation' may make for a similar quality in the text, and it is with the conflicts in Eliot's mind and work that he is concerned in this perceptive study. The approach yields fresh readings of the major poems and a

165. *T. S. Eliot: A Study in Character and Style*, by Ronald Bush. OUP. pp. xiii + 287. £17.50.

166. *Women in the Poetry of T. S. Eliot: A Psychoanalytic Approach*, by Tony Pinkney. Macmillan. pp. xii + 156. £20.

167. *Conflicts in Consciousness: T. S. Eliot's Poetry and Criticism*, by David Spurr. UIll. pp. xx + 136. £12.75.

final chapter showing how the evolution of Eliot's sensibility in his critical writings parallels that of the poems. Throughout Spurr shows himself well aware of the present state of critical debate about Eliot and he is attractively lucid in presenting his own analysis.

T. S. Eliot and the Poetics of Literary History[168] by Gregory S. Jay is a study primarily of Eliot's critical discourse in relation to tradition. Jay, like Spurr, is conscious of conflict and discontinuity in Eliot's writing and attempts to accommodate these elements within a theoretical framework which uses the terms 'figuration' and 'refiguration' to denote 'the way poetic and critical identities take shape in Eliot's work'. He argues that 'the structure of Eliot's thought turns upon an active alteration of previous figures, including that of the poet himself'. The discussion of Eliot's ideas is often illuminating on a local level but the overall argument is frequently obscured by a forbidding rhetorical terminology.

In *The Tempering of T. S. Eliot*[169] John T. Soldo investigates Eliot's relationship with his family and the environment in which he lived for the first twenty-one years of his life. The book contains a useful assemblage of material on Eliot's school and university career and on his early reading and some discussion of the influence on him of Laforgue, Baudelaire, Santayana, Babbitt, and, very briefly, Dante. Appendixes list the 'Books Read and Grades Received at Smith Academy' and note 'Eliot's Markings in His Copy of the *Divina Commedia*'.

Grover Smith's book on *The Waste Land*[170] is a concentrated and helpful study, a distillation of the author's work on the poem which now extends over nearly forty years. Grover Smith is concerned to demonstrate the unity of Eliot's criticism, his aesthetic theory, and his poems so that, although primarily a response to *The Waste Land*, the book also includes a considerable amount of biographical material and important discussions of the early poems and criticism. There are good accounts of the composition of *The Waste Land*, of Eliot's use of sources, of the poem as myth, and of critical responses since its publication. But in addition to the standard aspects there are many fresh observations: for example, on Eliot's use of caricature, a mode in which 'the ridiculous and the sordid are exalted into art', or the suggestion that the poem is, in a sense, 'a compressed novel'. This is a stimulating study both for student and general reader.

T. S. Eliot's Poems in French Translation[171] by Joan Fillmore Hooker is a substantial and original study which offers more of general interest than the title might suggest. It is based on the idea that there is a considerable similarity between the processes of creation, translation, criticism, and reading itself, and that an examination of translations therefore has broad implications. Certainly, the analysis of translations here focuses attention very sharply on

168. *T. S. Eliot and the Poetics of Literary History*, by Gregory S. Jay. LSU (1983). pp. xii + 251. £27.50.

169. *The Tempering of T. S. Eliot*, by John J. Soldo. Studies in Modern Literature 33. UMIRes. pp. xv + 191. £31.25.

170. *The Waste Land*, by Grover Smith. Unwin Critical Library. A&U. pp. xiv + 170. pb £5.50.

171. *T. S. Eliot's Poems in French Translation: Pierre Leyris and Others*, by Joan Fillmore Hooker. Studies in Modern Literature 26. UMIRes. pp. xi + 332. £40.25.

problems of interpretation as well as on the sound and rhythm of the verse and it frequently enforces a new view. The volume also contains a survey of the translations, bibliographical listings, and extensive reprintings of translations that have previously appeared only in periodicals.

Marianne Thormählen distrusts attempts to interpret Eliot's work in terms of mythical and other patterns, believing rightly that such methods lead to distortion and simplification unless very carefully handled. Instead, in *Eliot's Animals*[172], she studies individual images in their context, citing parallels and recurrent motifs where appropriate but also stressing the variety in Eliot's use of apparently similar material. There are chapters on Dogs, Cats, Birds, Small Creatures, Rats, and Fishes. The tone is marred by a rather querulous combativeness but the evidence is usefully arranged and the discussion of individual passages often illuminating.

In *T. S. Eliot and the Myth of Adequation*[173] by Alan Weinblatt, the awkward term 'adequation' refers to attempts to find an appropriate or adequate expression for feeling and emotion. Eliot's treatment of the problem is clearly central to his critical theory and Weinblatt offers an analysis based largely on *Selected Essays*. A final section discusses the search for form with reference to 'Journey of the Magi', 'Coriolan', *Murder in the Cathedral*, and *The Family Reunion*. This is a sound but pedestrian account.

In 'The Case of the Missing Abstraction: Eliot, Frazer and Modernism' (*MR*) Jewel Spears Brooker studies Frazer's inductive scientific method in *The Golden Bough* and suggests that this is analogous to Eliot's poetic method. 'By enabling the artist and his reader to begin with fragments and generate comprehensive abstractions' Frazer offers the poet a way of 'making art possible in the modern world'. Christina C. Stough's 'Pound vs Eliot' (*JML*, 1983) is a detailed examination of an exchange between Pound and Eliot in *The New English Weekly* in 1934 occasioned by the publication of *After Strange Gods* and *The Use of Poetry and the Use of Criticism*. The controversy is particularly interesting on stylistic grounds, Pound 'choosing incendiary words and phrases', Eliot maintaining 'a tone of condescending congeniality'.

'T. S. Eliot's *The Love Song of J. Alfred Prufrock* and Dante's *Divine Comedy*' (*Expl*) by Jay Dougherty argues that the reference to Guido de Montefeltro in the epigraph provides an essential context for our understanding of Prufrock's spiritually empty world.

Several notes concern *The Waste Land*. C. J. Ackerley's 'Eliot's *The Waste Land* and Shackleton's *South*' (*N&Q*) explicates the line 'Who is the third who walks always beside you?' in 'What the Thunder said'. In 'Eliot, Dickens and *The Waste Land*' (*N&Q*) Patrick Diskin convincingly finds echoes of *Dombey and Son* in the opening of 'A Game of Chess'. Peter L. Hays notes, in 'T. S. Eliot's *The Waste Land*' (*Expl*), that Hieronimo is the Spanish for Jerome and suggests that at l. 432 Eliot 'is echoing and recapitulating not just the secular matter of a revenge play but religious concerns as well'. A. N. Dwivedi comments on the two final lines of the poem in 'T. S. Eliot's *The Waste Land*' (*Expl*). 'Dry Bones Can Harm No One: Ezekiel xxxvi in *The Waste Land* V and *Ash Wednesday* II' (*ES*) by Marianne Thormählen shows that, despite a

172. *Eliot's Animals*, by Marianne Thormählen. LSE 70. Gleerup. pp. 197.
173. *T. S. Eliot and the Myth of Adequation*, by Alan Weinblatt. Studies in Modern Literature 29. UMIRes. pp. xx + 184. £31.25.

common debt to Ezekiel's prophecy, the symbolic image of dry bones in a barren place has different functions in the two passages.

Robert F. Fleissner applies Jungian symbolism to 'T. S. Eliot's *The Hollow Men*' (*Expl*). In 'T. S. Eliot's *The Journey of the Magi*' (*Expl*) E. F. Burgess VII comments on 'voices singing in our ears' in l. 19 and 'satisfactory' in l. 31. T. S. Eliot's "Animula": A Source for Boudin' (*N&Q*) by Tom Gibbons suggests that in the phrase 'Boudin, blown to pieces' Eliot, perhaps unconsciously, had in mind Martial Bourdin who was killed in the Greenwich Observatory bomb outrage in 1896. Eliot either misremembered the name or deliberately varied it.

In ' "The Progress of the Intellectual Soul": Eliot, Pascal and *Four Quartets*' (*JML*, 1983) Frank Burch Brown examines Eliot's essay on the *Pensées* of Pascal to show how Pascal's personality and concerns reflect Eliot's own and argues that the structure of spiritual autobiography in the *Quartets* owes a good deal to Eliot's reading of the *Pensées*. Ruth Barton's 'T. S. Eliot's Secret Garden' (*N&Q*) finds significant parallels between the rose-garden imagery of both *Burnt Norton* and *The Family Reunion* and the children's story *The Secret Garden* by Frances Hodgson Burnett. Eleanor Cook in 'The Senses of Eliot's Salvages' (*EIC*) discusses 'the punning and etymological and multilingual life' of the title of the third *Quartet* and argues that the multiple allusions are fully functional. Peter Barry's 'Making Sense of Syntax Perhaps: A Reply Note to Frances Austin's "Ing Forms in *Four Quartets*" ' (*ES*) comments on an article published in 1982 and argues that recent attempts to show that 'syntactical forms have semantic values' are generally fallacious. 'Accentual Forms in Eliot's Poetry from *The Hollow Men* to *Four Quartets*' (*ES*), by J. M. Reibetanz, is a sensitive and precisely detailed account of Eliot's metrical development after *The Waste Land*. Finally, Anne Ridler's 'Working for T. S. Eliot: A Personal Reminiscence' (*PoetryR*, 1983) gives some anecdotes from the author's years as secretary and junior editor in Faber and Faber.

Two articles discuss the poetry of D. H. Lawrence. Roger Poole's 'D. H. Lawrence, Major Poet' (*TSLL*) analyses Lawrence's craftsmanship, especially in terms of metre. He concludes that Lawrence is a major poet 'because he uniquely marries the texture of expression to the texture of the imagination'. Thomas M. Antrim's 'Lawrence's Wild Garden' (*DHLR*) is a discussion of *Pansies* which suggests ways in which each poem draws 'meaning from its connections with the poems that cluster about it and from the interrelationships between its cluster and others'.

Gail Porter Mandell's *The Phoenix Paradox: A Study of Renewal Through Change in the 'Collected Poems' and 'Last Poems' of D. H. Lawrence* (SIU) has not yet been available for review.

Some work on poets of the First World War may be grouped together. Desmond Graham argues in *The Truth of War*[174] that our familiarity with some aspects of the Great War experience predisposes us to interpret war poetry in a somewhat automatic way. He uses close reading to force a fresh view. There are good discussions of Owen's 'testing of language and reappraisal of register, meaning and metaphor' and of his use of literary allusion, though the effect here is rather to reinforce our responses than to provide a completely new

174. *The Truth of War: Owen, Blunden and Rosenberg*, by Desmond Graham. Carcanet. pp. 168. £12.95.

interpretation. But there are sensitive accounts of the 'impress of war on Blunden's mind' and of the transformations of language in his verse, and there is an effective substantiation of the claim that Rosenberg 'charted for us, perhaps more thoroughly than any of the war poets, the main elements of war experience'.

Unfortunately Jon Stallworthy's edition of Wilfred Owen's *Complete Poems* (C&W) has not been available. It is hoped to include a review next year. Hilda D. Spear's 'Not Well Content: Wilfred Owen's Dislocation of the Sonnet' (*DUJ*) shows that in 'The Dead Beat' and 'Dulce et Decorum', Owen frustrates our formal expectations of the sonnet form to foster a sense of unease in the reader and jar his or her sensibilities. Elizabeth Marshland's 'Literature as Interaction: Readers and "Non-Readers" in First World War Propagandist Poetry' (*Poetics*) is an interesting technical analysis both of populist patriotic verse and minority protest poetry. Both have in common a *persona* spokesman (though protest poets usually use 'I', populists 'We') and both show a 'strong sense of animosity towards the enemy, the excluded non-reader'.

'Gurney's "Hobby"' (*EIC*) by Geoffrey Hill is the printed version of the F. W. Bateson Memorial Lecture. It gives an affectionate and incisive appreciation of Gurney's poetry and is concerned in particular with the relationship between spontaneity and craftsmanship and with Gurney's 'magnanimous ironic awareness'.

Two books are concerned with poetry of the 1930s. Lucy McDiarmid's *Saving Civilization: Yeats, Eliot, and Auden Between the Wars*[175] examines the various answers the poets gave to the question of how a 'mere writer' could affect the world of his audience. Although Yeats and Eliot are commonly thought of as reactionaries and Auden as a man of the Left, the social views of these writers are linked by the fact that 'all three sought to save civilization through some form of communal identity based on inherited myths, legends and religious truths'. Drawing on material from letters, diaries, and essays, as well as on the verse, McDiarmid gives chapters to the idea of the civilizing influence of an elite group, the 'myth' of the seventeenth century as a time of crisis, the search for a popular audience, and the notion of a perfect work of art. This is an agreeably written and well-researched book which gives a new view of issues that were of central importance to the poets concerned.

Ronald Carter has edited a casebook on *Thirties Poets: 'The Auden Group'*[176] which is concerned with Auden, Spender, Day Lewis, and MacNeice. It brings together a useful collection of statements by the poets themselves, both on poetry and on each other, and it includes some contemporary discussions, notably by Michael Roberts, of their work. The final section presents 'Modern Views', ranging from Richard Hoggart writing in 1951 to Bernard Bergonzi in 1978. Most of these discussions are already available in book form and this makes the collection less evidently useful than casebooks drawing on relatively inaccessible periodical literature, but it will prove very serviceable for undergraduate use.

175. *Saving Civilization: Yeats, Eliot, and Auden Between the Wars*, by Lucy McDiarmid. CUP. pp. xx + 144. hb £15, pb £7.95.

176. *Thirties Poets: 'The Auden Group'*, ed. by Ronald Carter. Casebook. Macmillan. pp. 211. hb £14, pb £5.95.

Elemental Things. The Poetry of Hugh MacDiarmid[177], by an American scholar and poet, Harvey Oxenhorn, takes full account of the difficulties non-Scottish readers may experience in approaching MacDiarmid's work. In the extensive quotations Scottish words are given marginal glosses on their first appearance and there is a helpful introduction to the background and the main features of the twentieth-century Scottish 'renaissance'. Oxenhorn proceeds always by close analysis, paying particular attention to the poetry of the 1930s. He concludes that, compared with the major poets of English and American modernism, MacDiarmid seeks to balance intellectual modernism with abiding humanism. 'Written in a period of impending holocaust the poems offer something we, in no less difficult times, could use: a sense of hope in what we can't yet know; an impulse to redeem.' This is an unfashionable but refreshing stance. Oxenhorn also contributes 'Water Music: Wordsworth, MacDiarmid, and Frost' (*SoR*). Here he compares the poem 'Water of Life' with *Tintern Abbey* and Frost's 'West Running Brook' to show that MacDiarmid insists that 'the natural world remains larger than human sorrow and folly . . . because of its inherent, infinite capacity for change'.

Whether Austin Clarke deserves a book-length study is perhaps an open question. Gregory A. Schirmer[178] believes that Clarke's work not only 'succeeds, to an extent that the work of no other modern Irish writer succeeds, in expressing accurately the Catholic and Gaelic dimensions of the Irish sensibility and in describing the political, social and religious realities of life in modern Ireland' but that it also has a 'universal dimension'. He argues this vigorous contention with sympathetic analysis and brings out the wide-ranging interest of Austin's work without quite justifying the overall judgement.

Dorothy J. Farnam's *Auden in Love*[179] is an anecdotal account of the poet's relationship with Chester Kallman. It is hoped that Kevin J. McManus's *W. H. Auden: the Poetry of Betrayal* (CornU) will be available for review next year. ' "Or one could weep because another wept": The Counterplot of Auden's *The Shield of Achilles*' (*JEGP*) by Claude J. Summers is a study of the poem's allusions. Summers argues that Auden qualifies the surface pessimism of the work in ways that imply the possibility of Christian heroism and of individual responsibility even in a regimented world. The poem 'discloses its Christian ideology, indirectly through implication and allusion, rather than through overt statement'. Charles H. Long contributes a note on the opening of the last section of 'Auden's *For the Time Being*' (*Expl*) and Nicholas Ruddick comments on the enigmatic narrative of 'Auden's *Lady Weeping at the Crossroads*' (*Expl*).

Rikky Rooksby's 'A Graves Revision' (*MLN*) discusses substantial changes made by Robert Graves to 'In Dedication' which prefaced the first edition of *The White Goddess*. Kiernan Quinlan's 'Donald Davie: The Irish Years' (*SoR*) discusses the effect of Davie's experience as a teacher at Trinity College Dublin before his move to the United States in 1957 and suggests that his

177. *Elemental Things. The Poetry of Hugh MacDiarmid*, by Harvey Oxenhorn. EdinU. pp. x + 215. £15.

178. *The Poetry of Austin Clarke*, by Gregory A. Schirmer. UND/Dolmen. pp. vii + 167. $12.95.

179. *Auden in Love*, by Dorothy J. Farnam. Faber. pp. 253. £9.95.

alienation from English life at that time foreshadowed his greater exile, cultural and intellectual, in America.

In 'Metonymic Ways of Sympathising with the Underdog: Philip Larkin's *Mr Bleaney* and Anthony Thwaite's *Mr Cooper*' (*ES*), Hans Osterwalder presents a subtle analysis which shows how symbolic meaning is made to emerge from the trivia of everyday experience. Somewhat similarly John Bayley's 'Larkin and the Romantic Tradition' (*CQ*) explores, through a comparison with Keats, the relationship between common, even banal, reality and moments of visionary experience. In Larkin the ' "inexpressible" is, ironically, conjured up by the totally unromantic and up-to-date routines of living'. ' "The thought-fox" and the Poetry of Ted Hughes' (*CQ*) by Richard Webster sees an intense conflict between violence and tenderness in Hughes's work and suggests that his poetic powers are fully realized, not when this conflict is resolved but when it is unleashed 'in its most violent form'.

Peter Porter, interviewed by Martin Harrison (*ALS*), discusses his *Collected Poems*, his relation to European and Australian culture, and some technical aspects of his verse. The publication of Porter's *Collected Poems* was marked by a supplement in *PoetryR* (1983).

'Tony Harrison: An Interview' (*PoetryR*) by John Haffenden presents a stimulating discussion dealing with the poet's background and choice of subject matter and with technical aspects of his work as poet and translator. In 'Weeds and White Roses: the Poetry of Tony Harrison' (*CQ*) Alan Young comments on Harrison's success in dramatic translation and emphasizes his role as 'spokesman for the inarticulate, for the mass of people who have been exploited throughout history'. In *PoetryR* Haffenden interviews Peter Levi following his election as Professor of Poetry at Oxford.

Grevel Lindop's 'Myth and Blood: The Poetry of Geoffrey Hill' (*CQ*) is particularly concerned with *The Mystery of the Charity of Charles Péguy* (1983) and with the use of Péguy as an instance of 'the spiritual enigmas Hill has often presented'. He sees a greater expansiveness of form here than in Hill's earlier work but argues that he needs to 'reveal more of himself and turn away from the historical preoccupations and personae, the paradoxes and ambiguities, that have so far refracted his concerns'. In ' "These shifting constancies": time, place and personality in three new collections of verse' in the same journal, Bill Ruddick examines recent work by Jeremy Hooker, Clive Wilmer, and Neill Powell in the light of their concern with the value of the 'private sense of history'.

The Salzburg Peter Russell Seminar 1981/2[180], edited by James Hogg, contains two poems by Peter Russell and eight articles on his work. Further discussion, together with articles on William Oxley and two essays by Anthony L. Johnson are to be found in *A Vitalist Seminar*[181], again edited by James Hogg.

Finally, John Lucas contributes a brief obituary appreciation of William Empson (*PoetryR*).

180. *The Salzburg Peter Russell Seminar 1981/2*, ed. by James Hogg. SSELPDPT 72. USalz. pp. iii + 143.

181. *A Vitalist Seminar: Studies in the Poetry of Peter Russell, Anthony L. Johnson and William Oxley*, ed. by James Hogg. SSELPDPT. USalz. pp. 313.

3. Drama

Books and articles covering individual authors are considered alphabetically in the later part of this essay. *MD* should be consulted for bibliographical information and specialist reviews. The magazines *Plays and Players*, *Plays*, and *Drama* contain theatre reviews and brief interviews which are usually particularly relevant to the study of contemporary theatre. *Theatrephile* is 'a popular theatre history journal', and *London Theatre Record* reprints first-night reviews from the majority of national newspapers. The *British Theatre Directory 1984/5*, *British Alternative Theatre Directory*, and the new *Directory of Playwrights/Directors/Designers 1*[182], together constitute a primary research tool of major importance for many aspects of current repertory, practice, and theatrical organization. Donald Cooper's *Theatre Year*[183] is an annual selective photographic record of (mainly) London productions.

Several major studies this year fill gaps in the history of British twentieth-century theatre. Michael Sanderson's *From Irving to Olivier*[184], an indispensable and authoritative 'social history of the acting profession in England 1880–1983' which complements Michael Baker's *Rise of the Victorian Actor* (*YW* 59.338), deserves to be a standard work and a source of fruitful research. Judicious and imaginative use of primary material illuminates such issues as unionization, training, career patterns, changing class backgrounds of actors, and organizational aspects of acting in electronic media. Some developments in, for example, Equity's internal political battles are taken as far as 1984 but the later chapters are, inevitably, more impressionistic. In *The Repertory Movement*[185] George Rowell and Anthony Jackson provide an equally authoritative introduction to the development of the idea of a repertory theatre during the twentieth century. The authors offer an excellent blend of sociological and aesthetic insights and trace the complex interplay of personalities, politics, and policies with sympathetic discrimination. Ironically, many of the dramatist Steve Gooch's arguments in favour of his ideal of a community theatre, in *All Together Now*[186], parallel those of the repertory movement in the earlier part of the century as he argues for 'a more integral relationship between theatre practitioners and their public'.

In *These Our Actors*[187] Richard Findlater offers an informal kind of social history in his celebration of the stage acting of Peggy Ashcroft, John Gielgud, Laurence Olivier, and Ralph Richardson. The book is a fine evocation of their individual geniuses, presented through the traditional means of accounts of

182. *The British Theatre Directory 1984/5*, ed. by John Offord. Offord. pp. 592. £12.50. *The British Alternative Theatre Directory*, ed. by Catherine Itzin. Offord. pp. 270. pb £6.95. *Directory of Playwrights/Directors/Designers 1*, ed. by Catherine Itzin. Offord. pp. 186. pb £4.

183. *Theatre Year 1984*, by Donald Cooper. IP. Unpaginated. pb £6.95.

184. *From Irving to Olivier: A Social History of the Acting Profession in England 1880–1983*, by Michael Sanderson. Athlone. pp. xii + 375. £14.50.

185. *The Repertory Movement: A History of Regional Theatre in Britain*, by George Rowell and Anthony Jackson. CUP. pp. ix + 230. hb £22.50, pb £7.95.

186. *All Together Now*, by Steve Gooch. Methuen. pp. 87. pb £3.95.

187. *These Our Actors*, by Richard Findlater. Elm Tree/HH (1983). pp. 191. pb £7.50.

performances. *Being an Actor*[188], by a much younger actor, Simon Callow, is part autobiography, part guide to the everyday practice of being an actor, and culminates in an antidirector manifesto which started a journalistic controversy. There are useful insights into productions he has appeared in, particularly of plays by Ayckbourn, Tony Bicât, Bond, Brenton, Edgar, Hampton, Hare, Keeffe, Peter Shaffer, and C. P. Taylor. The working methods of notable British directors, the Joint Stock company, and the Drama Centre also figure. Callow also appears in *Peter Hall's Diaries*[189], his personal account of the 1972–80 period which naturally focuses on the National Theatre. Apart from his own view of arts politics in that period, Hall offers much revealing incidental comment on the day-to-day processes of theatre. The diary format precludes extended comment but even brief references can illuminate the process of working with Ayckbourn, Beckett, Pinter, or Shaffer. Although there is probably more on these authors than other twentieth-century British playwrights, most major writers are mentioned – Hall's favourable comparison of Granville Barker with Shaw is particularly noteworthy. The National Theatre is also the subject of John Elsom's 'A National Cause' and 'Gentlemen's Agreements' in *ContempR*.

The prehistory of the National Theatre figures in James Woodfield's *English Theatre in Transition, 1881–1914*[190] which offers a synoptic account of antiestablishment trends in theatre of the period for the student or general reader. J. T. Grein and the Independent Theatre, Elizabeth Robins, the Stage Society, Shaw, Granville Barker, Poel, Craig, campaigns for Ibsen, against censorship and for a National Theatre are all covered succinctly. Overall the book is a good general introduction though, as in most such works, the specialist will find some judgements a little simplistic. Michael Sidnell's *Dances of Death: The Group Theatre of London in the Thirties*[191] is a thoroughly researched critical history of the influential group led by Rupert Doone which staged plays by Auden and Isherwood, T. S. Eliot, Louis MacNeice and Stephen Spender. Sidnell very effectively conveys the slightly manic, underorganized, emotionally charged atmosphere of the whole project, paying judicious attention to wider social issues and the development of individuals' political positions. There are good critical accounts of plays and productions, including Eliot's attempts at a later Sweeney play, as well as various projects involving Ashley Dukes, Michel Saint-Denis, and Yeats.

Students of Irish theatre will welcome D. E. S. Maxwell's *Critical History of Modern Irish Drama*[192]. Although 250 pages are scarcely long enough to chart the history of Irish drama since 1891, Maxwell has produced a good general introduction to the subject bolstered by production photographs and a useful bibliography. Considerable attention is paid to companies and theatres but the focus is on the dramatists. At times the development of Maxwell's broad thesis, that a convention-expanding realism has been the dominant strand in

188. *Being an Actor*, by Simon Callow. Methuen. pp. ix + 190. £7.95.

189. *Peter Hall's Diaries*, ed. by John Goodwin. HH. pp. xiii + 507. pb £5.95.

190. *English Theatre in Transition, 1881–1914*, by James Woodfield. CH. pp. 213. £15.95.

191. *Dances of Death: The Group Theatre of London in the Thirties*, by Michael Sidnell. Faber. pp. 368. £18.50.

192. *A Critical History of Modern Irish Drama, 1891–1980*, by D. E. S. Maxwell. CUP. pp. xvii + 250. hb £25, pb £8.50.

Irish drama, is subordinated, particularly in the contemporary section, to the desire to provide a comprehensive catalogue of plays and dramatists. Hugh Kenner gives a sprightly account of the *Playboy* riots, aspects of the Abbey's history, and the composition of Synge's plays in *A Colder Eye*[193], which contains much acute criticism as well as some strongly atmospheric descriptive writing.

On a rather different plane *Theatre in Britain*[194], Harold Hobson's highly idiosyncratic account of twentieth-century British theatre, blends persuasively written accounts of performances with specious pseudo-sociological moralizing about the British way of life in an eccentric melange innocent of critical rigour. The book's chief interest lies in its contentious re-arrangement of the orthodox map of British theatrical achievement: the expected names appear in unusual places and forgotten ones are reclaimed.

John Russell Brown has edited *Modern British Dramatists*[195] which reprints mostly familiar essays on Arden, Ayckbourn, Bond, Hampton, Hare, Nichols, Orton, Osborne, Pinter, Shaffer, Stoppard, and contemporary socialist theatre. Brown contributes a wide-ranging but bland introduction and there is a somewhat eccentric select chronology which stops at 1977. In view of the explosion of feminist theatre it is disturbing that there is no essay on a woman dramatist. Fortunately Helene Keyssar's *Feminist Theatre*[196], Susan Todd's *Women and Theatre*[197], and Michelene Wandor's third collection of *Plays by Women*[198] fill the gap. Keyssar offers a useful introduction to her subject, concentrating on the upsurge in feminist theatre in Britain and America since the 1960s. The numerous insights into plays by recent writers, Caryl Churchill, Nell Dunn, Pam Gems, Catherine Hayes, Mary O'Malley, and Michelene Wandor, as well as Shelagh Delaney, Ann Jellicoe, and Joan Littlewood from earlier decades are considered in the light of a feminist strategy of transformation, 'the theatrical manifestation of metamorphosis of contexts, actions and, most crucially, of characters'. The author's grasp of the British sociopolitical and theatrical scenes is slightly haphazard since Steve Gooch, Stephen Lowe, and David Rudkin figure as sympathetic male writers but there is no reference to David Hare, Trevor Griffiths' *Through the Night*, or David Edgar's collaboration with Susan Todd. Todd herself collects a number of challenging first-hand reports by female dramatists, performers, directors, designers, and technicians, some well established like Ann Jellicoe, others better known on the fringe, in which they discuss 'how they represent their sex and its experience in their work'. Michelene Wandor contributes a trenchant introduction to her latest collection of recent plays by women. The plays also have brief informative afterwords by their authors, Pam Gems, Debbie Horsfield, Sharon Pollock, and Lou Wakefield and The Women's Theatre Group.

193. *A Colder Eye: The Modern Irish Writers*, by Hugh Kenner. Penguin. pp. 368. pb £4.95.
194. *Theatre in Britain*, by Harold Hobson. Phaidon. pp. 240. £19.50.
195. *Modern British Dramatists: New Perspectives*, ed. by John Russell Brown. PH. pp. 186. pb $5.95.
196. *Feminist Theatre*, by Helene Keyssar. Macmillan. pp. xvi + 223. hb £15, pb £4.95.
197. *Women and Theatre*, ed. by Susan Todd. Faber. pp. 119. pb £3.95.
198. *Plays by Women*, 3, ed. by Michelene Wandor. Methuen. pp. 162. pb £3.50.

John Bull's *New British Political Dramatists*[199], an excellent introduction to the work of Howard Brenton, David Edgar, Trevor Griffiths, and David Hare, stresses the importance of situationist analyses to their approaches to political dramaturgy and also places the individual writers firmly in the context of approaches to political drama exemplified by John McGrath and John Arden.

Three studies offer insights into theatrical processes from the perspectives of scene painting, an individual theatre, and producing. Dennis Castle's life of his grandfather, *Sensation Smith of Drury Lane*[200], is a rich compilation of anecdote about one of the great exponents of spectacular scenery which casts much light on the theatre before the Second World War. Michael Coren's *Theatre Royal: 100 Years of Stratford East*[201], written without the help of Joan Littlewood, economically charts the fortunes of the theatre from its beginning through the tempestuous glories of Theatre Workshop to the uncertain present. There is little space for in-depth analysis but most productions are mentioned and there are more substantial references to *The Hostage* and *The Quare Fellow, A Taste of Honey, Oh What a Lovely War*, and *Steaming*. Impresario Michael White's *Empty Seats*[202] deals anecdotally with his productions of *Loot, Oh! Calcutta, Sleuth*, and *The Rocky Horror Show*, his relationship with Peter Daubeny, many aspects of commercial production processes and costings, and the abolition of the Lord Chamberlain's powers of censorship.

Lisa Appignanesi has updated her 1975 study of *Cabaret*[203] to cover recent developments in English alternative cabaret at the expense of deleting the original's bibliography.

Two essays look at broad topics referring to a wide range of plays: J. Ditsky tackles 'Child Sacrifice in Modern Drama' (*ArielE*); H. I. Schvey considers 'The Grinning Reaper: Death and Dying in Contemporary British and American Drama' (*DQR*); and, in the first part of an extensive critique of 'The Establishment and the Absurd' (*ZAA*), Klaus Köhler offers a more substantial analysis of 'Trends, Ideologies and Techniques in Non-Realistic Drama from Beckett to Pinter'.

In 'Actors or Gramophones: The Paradox of Granville Barker' (*TJ*) Cary M. Mazer discusses Barker's view that the director is the centre of a dialectic between actor and dramatist in the light of a controversy in the *New Age* over his directing methods. Richard Nickson challenges the supposed denigration of the word in contemporary theatre with reflections from Shaw and Barker on dialogue and speech in 'Using Words on the Stage: Shaw and Granville Barker' (*MD*).

The fullest discussion to date of Howard Barker's plays occurs in a special issue of *Gambit* edited by Tony Dunn. As well as the text of *No Pity in History* it includes an interview with the dramatist by Dunn, who also contributes a critical essay on Barker as 'Socialist Playwright for Our Times'. Ruth Shade

199. *New British Political Dramatists*, by John Bull. Macmillan. pp. xx + 244. hb £15, pb £4.95.

200. *Sensation Smith of Drury Lane*, by Dennis Castle. Skilton. pp. 276. £14.95.

201. *Theatre Royal: 100 Years of Stratford East*, by Michael Coren. Quartet. pp. xii + 112. £12.95.

202. *Empty Seats*, by Michael White. HH. pp. 193. £9.95.

203. *Cabaret*, by Lisa Appignanesi. Methuen. pp. 192. pb £5.95.

discusses 'Sex and Sexual Politics' in Barker's plays, Eric Mottram writes on 'The Vital Language of Our Times', Ian McDiarmid, the actor, contributes 'A Personal View', and the bibliography reveals the dearth of critical interest which the editorial attempts to explain:

> For continuous inventiveness of language and plot, for humour of the grotesque, for above all a scandalous undermining of idyll and reconciliation, Barker is unequalled. And unloved. His plays excoriate not only the fascist but also the liberal. Since socialism doesn't exist, any audience for a Barker play will pass an evening seeing itself flayed alive on stage. He is not the best-loved of his generation and critical attention to him has been minimal compared to his colleagues.

Beckett continues to attract critics who draw on a wide variety of critical and philosophical positions to examine his plays. Lance St John Butler's *Samuel Beckett and the Meaning of Being*[204] is a thorough-going reading of Beckett in the light of Heidegger, Sartre, and Hegel which casts much incidental light on the plays' philosophical contexts without greatly enhancing our understanding of Beckett's dramaturgy. (See also p. 554 for another notice of this volume.) Martin Esslin traces the historical development of the *Doppelgänger* motif in 'From *Doppelgänger* to *Doubles* in Drama' (*SFR*) and discusses its applicability to a number of Beckett plays. An issue of *IUR* devoted to Beckett includes three essays on fairly traditional lines devoted to his drama as well as incidental references in other pieces: Christopher Murray surveys 'Beckett Productions in Ireland', economically charting the fortunes of the plays with extracts from reviews, participants' reminiscences, and Beckett's own interventions; T. P. Dolan exhaustively discusses the 'Dramatic Use of Hiberno-English' in *All That Fall* and *The Old Tune*; Ben Barnes perceptively discusses 'Aspects of Directing Beckett', drawing heavily on his own experience of working with *Godot*. In an unstartling discussion of 'La Crise du Christianisme dans l'Oeuvre de Samuel Barclay Beckett' (*Neohelicon*) S. Ade Ojo's statement that 'les autorités' of the Royal Court censored Roger Blin's production of *Fin de Partie* in 1957 confuses the Lord Chamberlain's office with the management of the theatre. Per Nykrog's 'In the Ruins of the Past: Reading Samuel Beckett Intertextually' (*CompL*) tackles similar issues with greater success: he regards Beckett's earlier plays as an exorcism of specific sections of the cultural tradition which are represented in the plays as 'hideous caricatures of themselves in a state of utter decrepitude'. Although, as the author acknowledges, his approach is by no means new, he does add some new intertexts in a lively and informative essay.

In *JBeckS* Rei Noguchi's 'Style and Strategy in *Endgame*' is a slightly ponderous application of speech-act theory to Hamm and Clov's conversational interaction and Paul Lawley's 'Beckett's Dramatic Counterpoint: A Reading of *Play*' is a comprehensive and detailed analysis of that play. Speech-act theory also influences Manuela Corfariu and Daniela Roventa-Frumuşani in their 'Absurd Dialogue and Speech Acts: Beckett's *En attendant Godot*' (*Poetics*) and Shimon Levy in 'Notions of Audience in Beckett's Plays' (*Assaph*). Gabriele Schwab, writing 'On the Dialectic of Closing and Opening

---

204. *Samuel Beckett and the Meaning of Being: A Study in Ontological Parable*, by Lance St John Butler. Macmillan. pp. ix + 213. £25.

in Samuel Beckett's *Endgame*' (*YFS*), applies aspects of Derrida's theories to demonstrate successfully that closure is central to *Endgame*, both as an implicit theme and as 'a nucleus for the strategies guiding aesthetic response'.

Also of interest are Wanda Avila's attempt to find 'The Poem within the Play in Beckett's *Embers*' (*Lang&S*), Katharine Worth's discovery of possible sources for ... *But the Clouds* ... in 'Yeats and Beckett' (*Gaeliana*), Antoni Libera's examination of 'Samuel Beckett's *Catastrophe*' (*Quadrant*), and Errol Durbach's look at Beckett's (and Sophocles's) influence on Fugard in 'Sophocles in South Africa: Athol Fugard's *The Island*' (*CompD*). Toni O'Brien Johnson compares *Godot* with *The Well of the Saints* in *The Irish Writer and the City*, edited by Maurice Harmon for Smythe. I have not seen the special issue of *Prépub* devoted to *Act Without Words*.

In a lean year, Terry Eagleton's discussion of 'Nature and Violence in the Prefaces of Edward Bond' (*CritQ*) is the most substantial discussion of the work of Edward Bond. Howard Brenton contributes an introduction and director Roland Rees a note on the unusual methods of collaboration between the authors and director of Brenton and Tunde Ikoli's *Sleeping Policemen*[205].

In 'Waiting for Amanda' (*JML*) A. K. Loss sees Noel Coward's *Private Lives* as an example of 'theatre of the absurd thirty years ahead of its time', comparing Amanda and Elyot with Vladimir and Estragon in *Waiting for Godot* as characters drawn together by mutual attraction and repulsion who mix seriousness and flippancy in their dialogue.

The most substantial discussion of T. S. Eliot's plays comes in Sidnell's account of the Group Theatre, but Peter Ackroyd's biography[206] contains some criticism and useful background material on the composition of the plays. Where the accounts overlap Sidnell's is fuller since he was able to use material barred to Ackroyd. Auden's 'The Martyr as Dramatic Hero', an acute discussion of *Murder in the Cathedral* and Charles Williams's *Thomas Cranmer*, is now available in paperback[207]. Barbara Everett considers 'The New Style in *Sweeney Agonistes*' in *YES* and the musical *Cats*, based on Eliot's cat poems, figures in Johannes Hedberg's 'T. S. Eliot, Old Possum and *Cats*' (*MSpr*).

'Choreographed Chaos' (*ThC*), Ronn Smith's account of the Broadway set for Michael Frayn's *Noises Off*, includes comments from Michael Annals who designed both London and Broadway productions.

Brian Friel's work is still less well known outside Ireland than it deserves, but an important and low-priced collection of six plays[208] (all except *Philadelphia Here I Come*, from the last fifteen years) should help to remedy that defect. In a well-judged introduction Seamus Deane discusses Friel's overall development as well as the plays in this volume, rightly emphasizing Friel's preoccupation with the power of language but somewhat undervaluing his theatricality. Klaus Birker considers 'The Relationship between the Stage and the Audience in Brian Friel's *The Freedom of the City*' in *The Irish Writer and the City* (a Smythe publication edited by Maurice Harmon).

205. *Sleeping Policemen*, by Howard Brenton and Tunde Ikoli. Methuen. pp. 46. pb £1.95.

206. *T. S. Eliot*, by Peter Ackroyd. HH. pp. 400. £12.50.

207. *Secondary Worlds*, by W. H. Auden. Faber. pp. 127. pb £2.95.

208. *Selected Plays*, by Brian Friel. Faber. pp. 455. hb £9.95, pb £4.95.

Mary Ann K. Davis notes Christopher Fry's claim that 'Comedy offers its joyous alternative ... through "a narrow escape into faith" '. In a purely literary analysis of 'The Narrow Escape in *The Lady's Not for Burning*' (*MD*) she suggests that its comic escape is more sophisticated and more successful than is usually granted. In *Renascence* Alvin Vos examines 'Christopher Fry's Christian Dialectic in *A Phoenix Too Frequent*'.

Methuen have published *Five Plays* by John Galsworthy and a Student Edition of *Strife*[209]. Benedict Nightingale contributes a lively critical and biographical introduction to the *Five Plays* (*Strife*, *Justice*, *The Eldest Son*, *The Skin Game*, *Loyalties*) and Non Worrall a Galsworthy chronology. Nightingale sees Galsworthy as 'a born peacemaker who, for that very reason, elected to be a war correspondent'. In the Student Edition Worrall adds a commentary and notes aimed at school students and useful photographs of the 1978 National Theatre production to the chronology and text from *Five Plays*. The commentary includes brief character analysis and a sensible estimate of Galsworthy's skills as a dramatist.

Lady Gregory's *Selected Plays*[210] is a very useful edition which should encourage the appreciation of Lady Gregory in her own right, rather than as an adjunct to Yeats and the Abbey. Thirteen plays are included, together with O'Casey's 1962 foreword, a crisp introduction by Mary FitzGerald, a bibliographical checklist by Colin Smythe, and a selection of comments on playwriting by Lady Gregory herself.

Powerplays: Trevor Griffiths in Television[211], the first book-length study of Griffiths' work is an acute analysis which lucidly and economically sketches in the social, institutional, political, and theatrical contexts of his contributions to television and film. The authors are slightly less assured in their dealings with the stage plays and theatrical contexts but the book is a significant contribution to our knowledge and understanding of a major contemporary writer. Complementing *Powerplays* is Clive Merrison's 'Building the Party', an actor's diary of the first production of *The Party* at the National Theatre, which runs in several issues of *Plays and Players*.

For *The History Plays*[212], a new collection which reprints *Knuckle*, *Licking Hitler*, and *Plenty*, David Hare has provided an introduction which outlines the circumstances of composition and offers some critical analysis of the plays and their reception. In *SJS* Bert Cardullo writes on '*Fanshen*; Western Drama and David Hare's *Oeuvre*'. William J. Free's 'Mischief and Frustration in David Hare's *Knuckle*' (*CDCP*) is reprinted in *Legacy of Thespis* (edited by Karelisa V. Hartigan for UPA), which I have not seen.

Anthony Roche considers 'The Fortunate Fall: Two Plays by Thomas Kilroy' in *The Irish Writer and The City* (edited by Maurice Harmon, Smythe).

209. *Five Plays*, by John Galsworthy, with intro. by Benedict Nightingale and chronology by Non Worrall. Methuen. pp. xxi + 277. pb £2.95. *Strife*, by John Galsworthy, with commentary and notes by Non Worrall. Methuen. pp. xxxix + 69. pb £1.95.
210. *Selected Plays*, by Lady Gregory, chosen and intro. by Mary FitzGerald. Smythe. pp. 377. pb £3.95.
211. *Powerplays: Trevor Griffiths in Television*, by Mike Poole and John Wyver. BFI. pp. 203. pb £6.95.
212. *The History Plays*, by David Hare. Faber. pp. 207. pb £3.50.

In *The Improvised Play: The Work of Mike Leigh*[213] Paul Clements offers a frankly partisan account of the methods and achievements of one of the leading British devisers of improvised plays which is the only substantial discussion of his work to date.

Peter Nichols's *Day in the Death of Joe Egg* is apparently the subject of an article by Niels Bugge Hansen, 'Wise Saws and Modern Instances: Observations on the Applicability of Traditional and More Recent Concepts of Comedy to 20th Century Drama', which is found in *Proceedings from the Second Nordic Conference for English Studies* (edited by H. Ringbom and M. Rissanen for Åbo) but which was not available for review.

John O'Riordan's *Guide to O'Casey's Plays*[214], the first comprehensive work to discuss all of O'Casey's plays, does so on fairly traditional lines: each play is provided with a critical introduction, plot outline, character analysis, and brief stage history of significant productions. The comprehensiveness of this much needed work is, in itself, a useful corrective to the usual concentration on the Dublin trilogy and a few other plays. That the professional theatre would benefit if more companies delved deeper into O'Casey's work was amply borne out by the Leicester Haymarket's first British professional production of *Bedtime Story* which I saw in 1985 and which more than confirmed O'Riordan's estimate of it. In the most provocative essay in the *O'Casey Annual No. 3*[215] Horst Höhne sees Brecht and O'Casey as the major playwrights of their time because of their 'vast comprehensiveness of poetic endeavour and theoretical depth, national significance and social commitment, political consciousness and artistic sublimity, topical relevance and historical penetration', comparing *Purple Dust* with *Puntila* and *Red Roses for Me* with *Days of the Commune*. In the same volume, the editor Robert G. Lowery, who has also edited a book on the riots at the first production of *The Plough and the Stars*[216], considers O'Casey's contributions to the *Irish Worker* and provides an index for it; Heinz Kosok discusses Irish translations of O'Casey's plays for An Taibhdhearc, the Galway Irish language theatre; Michael Kenneally considers O'Casey's novelistic treatment of biographical material; David Krause castigates recent Irish and Marxist detractors of O'Casey; Cecilia Zeiss considers 'Liturgy and Epiphany: Religious Experience as Dramatic Form' in *Silver Tassie* and *Red Roses for Me*; and E. H. Mikhail contributes his annual bibliography of Sean O'Casey. *JIL* includes Robert Hogan's interview 'Talking to Sean' (1960).

Maurice Charney's *Joe Orton*[217] is a sound but unexcited account of Orton's work, developing Charney's concept of quotidian farce. The book's uneasiness in dealing with the nuances of the English class system precludes it from fully coming to terms with Orton's strengths and weaknesses. I have not seen Peter Walcot's 'An Acquired Taste: Joe Orton and the Greeks' (*CDCP*) reprinted in *Legacy of Thespis* (UPA, edited by Karelisa V. Hartigan).

213. *The Improvised Play: The Work of Mike Leigh*, by Paul Clements. Methuen. pp. 96. pb £3.50.

214. *A Guide to O'Casey's Plays*, by John O'Riordan. Macmillan. pp. xi + 419. £30.

215. *O'Casey Annual No. 3*, ed. by Robert G. Lowery. Macmillan. pp. vii + 189. £25.

216. *A Whirlwind in Dublin: 'The Plough and the Stars' Riots*, ed. by Robert G. Lowery. Greenwood. pp. xiii + 121. $27.95.

217. *Joe Orton*, by Maurice Charney. Macmillan. pp. xiv + 145. hb £13, pb £3.95.

Hans-Dieter Heitmann's critical study of Pinter's 'Comedies of Menace'[218] concentrates on an area which, according to the author, has been previously substantially neglected, the dramaturgy of place. The first section offers a theoretical structure for such an analysis, discussing the particular dual existence of drama as text and as theatrical performance, but maintaining the written text as the basis for literary criticism and with this suggesting a method for the examination of dramatic place. The plays with which this method is then specifically exemplified are: *The Room*, *The Dumb Waiter*, *The Birthday Party*, and *A Slight Ache*. A separate chapter looks in general terms at Pinter as a practitioner of the theatre, at new directions in drama, and the influences on Pinter, while the final chapter suggests that precisely this dramaturgy of place is the essential feature and quality of 'Pinterism' although Pinter himself departs from its typical application in his later work. The study has a substantial bibliography with many titles in English. [M.H.]

In a varied collection of essays on *Harold Pinter*[219] Alan Bold repeats the increasingly accepted and critically helpful assertion that 'Pinter does not transcribe conversational commonplaces but organises speech artistically to give the theatrical illusion of everyday discourse'. Randall Stevenson argues with examples that 'a genuinely original aspect of Pinter's work is his extension onto the stage of innovations which had previously been almost exclusively the property of fiction'. Stanley Eveling usefully considers Pinter as a writer whose work is distinguished by 'how the image or decayed presence of the plot operates' and by the 'rise of sub-plot people to positions of dramatic power and dominance'. Katherine H. Burkman argues that in *A Slight Ache*, *Old Times*, and *No Man's Land* 'the protagonist's encounters with a double institute an inward journey which brings them face to face both with their mortality and with previously unknown aspects of themselves'; these doubles are 'partially the central characters' mirror images, partially their projections, and partially allegorical figures of good and evil come to save or damn them'. Bernard Dukore argues that *A Kind of Alaska* is less of a radical departure for Pinter than it first appeared. The other essays are also informative and their scope is adequately delineated by their titles: 'Directing Pinter' by Peter Hall (originally in *TQ*); 'Harold Pinter as Screenwriter' by Jennifer L. Randisi; Charles A. Carpenter's revised version of his *MD* article on *The Birthday Party*; 'Names and Naming in the Plays of Harold Pinter' by Ronald Knowles, and '*Family Voices* and the Concept of Family' by Steven Gale. Hersh Zeifman's analysis of *Family Voices* in 'Ghost Trio: Pinter's *Family Voices*' (*MD*) also considers the developing concept of the family in Pinter's canon. In 'Acting on the Cutting Edge: Pinter and the Syntax of Cinema' (*MD*) Gay Gibson Cima suggests, unsurprisingly, that Pinter's plays, particularly *Old Times*, require 'film acting on stage: the ability to undertake a number of different scenes, not necessarily in chronological order, on one evening's "shoot" '.

D. Keith Peacock's 'The Fascination of Fascism: The Plays of Stephen Poliakoff' (*MD*) is an excellent introduction to Poliakoff's work, showing that, in the absence of any analysis of the causes of the characteristic extreme

218. *Dramaturgie des Raumes, eine literarische Analyse an Hand von H. Pinters 'Comedies of Menace'*, by Hans-Dieter Heitmann. Richarz (1982). pp. 320. pb.
219. *Harold Pinter: You Never Heard Such Silence*, ed. by Alan Bold. Vision. pp. 184. £13.95.

emotional instability of Poliakoff's world, energetic characters become fascinating despite their otherwise repulsive characteristics. Peacock pinpoints many features of Poliakoff's concerns and dramaturgy from his persuasive rather than discursive techniques to the predominant linguistic image of monstrous growth and the preponderance of plays about contemporary life.

Dennis Potter contributes a witty and incisive preface on writing for television and an introduction to each of the plays (*Blue Remembered Hills, Joe's Ark, Cream in my Coffee*) in *Waiting for the Boat*[220].

Peter Shaffer's plays continue to attract a surprising amount of attention. The Longman Study Text edition of *Amadeus*[221], which prints the third version of the text, includes notes 'intended to serve the needs of overseas students as well as those of British-born users' and a personal essay and preface by Peter Shaffer. Werner Huber and Hubert Zapf, writing 'On the Structure of Peter Shaffer's *Amadeus*' in *MD*, use the 1981 Penguin edition to read the play's hermeneutic structure to their own satisfaction as

> a multidimensional act of interpretation, continually mediating between past and present, stage and audience, fiction and reality. In this process, many twentieth-century theories and modes of explanation are consulted, representing different possibilities for interpreting the play's theme, and giving it, besides its sophisticated technique, its intellectual density.

In contrast, Frank X. Mikels and James Rurak, who 'felt let down by Salieri's final blessing and vowed to discover why' when they saw the Broadway production, suggest in 'Finishing Salieri: Another Act to *Amadeus*' (*Soundings*) that 'Inherently unfinished, *Amadeus* clears the clatter from everyday living and fills it with the silence which precedes, and is the basis for, all crucial decisions in life ... This paper describes the way *Amadeus* creates this silence and the fundamental option the audience is called upon to exercise.' Barbara Lounsberry looks at 'Peter Shaffer's *Amadeus* and Shrivings: God-Hunting Continued' (*TA*), and Doyle W. Walls's '*Equus*, Shaffer, Nietzsche and the Neuroses of Health' (*MD*) offers a routine approach to *Equus*, arguing that the play's challenge is to see Dysart's madness and using *The Birth of Tragedy* to illustrate Shaffer's and Nietzsche's concern with health. In 'Die Rekonstruktion der Vergangenheit bei Heiner Kipphardt und Peter Shaffer' (*DU*) Martin Brunkhorst compares Shaffer's methods of dealing with the past in *Equus* and *Amadeus* with Kipphardt's in *März*, while Karl Heinz Westarp compares the treatment of 'Myth in Peter Shaffer's *The Royal Hunt of the Sun* and in Arthur Kopit's *Indians*' (*ES*).

Shaw benefits from a paperback re-issue of the volume devoted to him in the Critical Heritage series[222] (*YW* 57.379–80), although its usefulness remains limited by the decision to omit 'lengthy discussions of details of production and acting'. John O'Donovan offers a lively popular life[223], and Penguin print 'the definitive text of *Misalliance* and *The Fascinating Foundling* under the

220. *Waiting for the Boat*, by Dennis Potter. Faber. pp. 189. pb £3.50.

221. *Amadeus*, by Peter Shaffer, ed. by Richard Adams, with a personal essay by Peter Shaffer. Longman. pp. xxxi + 128. pb £1.60.

222. *Shaw: The Critical Heritage*, ed. by T. F. Evans. RKP. pp. xvi + 422. pb £8.95.

223. *G. B. Shaw*, by John O'Donovan. G&M (1983). pp. 155. hb £8.95, pb £3.95.

editorial supervision of Dan H. Laurence'[224]. The Longman Study Text editions of *Arms and the Man*, edited by Geoffrey Parker, and *The Devil's Disciple*, edited by Margery Morgan[225], each offers the usual notes aimed at overseas students and an essay by John Russell Brown aimed at enthusing the student reader. *Arms and the Man* includes the preface to *Plays Pleasant*, while *The Devil's Disciple* has the preface to *Plays for Puritans* (less 'Better than Shakespear?'), Shaw's own notes, and an appendix on *The Devil's Disciple* for the screen. Geoffrey Parker's introduction concentrates on characters and themes and is less theatrically orientated than Margery Morgan's which compresses a wealth of scholarship and critical insight into a brief compass.

The annual *Shaw*[226] includes a reprint of Shaw's drama criticism from *Our Corner* and the first full reprint of an article by William Archer which was, according to Martin Quinn's introduction, 'the proximate cause' of *The Doctor's Dilemma*. The critical articles are sound and scholarly without offering any major new advance in Shaw criticism. Bernard F. Dukore considers *Man and Superman*, *John Bull's Other Island* and *Major Barbara* as a trilogy, Lisë Pedersen compares 'Ducats and Daughters in *The Merchant of Venice* and *Major Barbara*', and Marianne Bosch examines 'Mother, Sister and Wife in *The Millionairess*'. Jean-Claude Amalric writes on 'Shaw, Hamon and Rémy de Gourmont', Richard F. Dietrich looks at 'Shavian Psychology', W. R. Martin considers some similarities between *Too True to be Good* and *Lady Chatterley's Lover*, and Constance Cummings recollects meeting Shaw and 'Playing Joan on Radio and Television'.

Patrick and Stella Mervyn Beech's notes of conversations with Shaw are reprinted in *ISh* which also includes George Levinson's and Jacques Barzun's differing assessments of Shaw as a music critic, Richard Nickson's gathering of Shaw's views on nuclear war, and Katrine Keunemann on 'GBS in New Zealand'.

Other essays elsewhere concentrate on parallels with other writers: H. G. Myer finds 'Dickensian Echoes in Shaw' (*N&Q*) and M. Quinn confirms that finding in 'The Informing Presence of Charles Dickens in Bernard Shaw's *Pygmalion*' (*Dickensian*); N. O. Warner discusses the 'Russian Reputation of Shaw, Tolstoy and Blake' in *BIQ*; Jacques Barzun considers 'Shaw versus Stendhal' as critics of music in *PR*; and Richard Nickson, in 'The Lure of Stalinism: Bernard Shaw and Company' (*MQ*) considers Shaw's championing of communism in the context of the reality of Stalinism.

Tom Stoppard's *Squaring the Circle*[227] has now been published in a single volume with *Every Good Boy Deserves Favour* and *Professional Foul*. Stoppard gives a brief account of the genesis of all three plays in an introduction which subsumes those to the two previously published plays. In a full-

---

224. *Misalliance* and *The Fascinating Foundling*, by Bernard Shaw, ed. by Dan H. Laurence. Penguin. pp. 222. pb £1.95.

225. *Arms and the Man*, by Bernard Shaw, ed. by Geoffrey Parker, with a personal essay by John Russell Brown. Longman. pp. xxxvii + 108. pb £1.50. *The Devil's Disciple*, by Bernard Shaw, ed. by Margery Morgan, with a personal essay by John Russell Brown. Longman. pp. 1 + 124. pb £1.50.

226. *Shaw: The Annual of Bernard Shaw Studies*, ed. by Stanley Weintraub. PSU. pp. 226.

227. *'Squaring the Circle'*, together with *'Every Good Boy Deserves Favour'* and *'Professional Foul'*, by Tom Stoppard. Faber. pp. 179. hb £8.95, pb £3.50.

length study which covers the plays as far as *The Real Thing* Richard Corballis[228] argues that 'in all Stoppard's work an abstract, artificial view of the world . . . is pitted against the flux of reality . . . and the audience is invited to eschew the "clockwork" of the former in favour of the "mystery" of the latter'. The book has a useful bibliography in which revised published versions of the playscripts are differentiated from one another. Keir Elam, in 'After Magritte, After Carroll, After Wittgenstein: What Tom Stoppard's Tortoise Taught Us' (*MD*), examines Stoppard's 'intertextual "afterness" or "posteriority"' in relation to Magritte, Lewis Carroll, and Wittgenstein, 'those figures whose artistic practice or theoretical models are closest to the principles of his theatrical poetics'. He argues that his major success is 'in finding precise and persuasive theatrical co-ordinates for apparently intractable conceptual material'. Wittgenstein emerges as the 'presiding deity of Stoppard's semiologically reflexive poetics'. In 'Stoppard's Adaptations of Shakespeare: *Dogg's Hamlet, Cahoot's Macbeth*' (*CompD*) C. J. Giankaris suggests that 'Stoppard's adapting process represents a critical index for comprehending his dramatic methods'. Evelyn Cobley illuminates the use of 'Catastrophe Theory in Tom Stoppard's *Professional Foul*' (*ConL*) and Bruno von Lutz examines '*Night and Day*: Der politische Tom Stoppard' (*NS*).

The second volume of Ann Saddlemyer's admirable edition of Synge's letters[229] covers the period of his final illness. The majority of the letters are to his fiancée, the actress Molly Allgood, although there are some concerning the business of the Abbey to Yeats and Lady Gregory among others. *Riders to the Sea* generates three articles: D. S. Neff, in 'Synge's Hecuba' (*Éire*), reads the play in the light of Euripides's *Hecuba* which offers 'a paradigm for consolidating the various anecdotes from *The Aran Islands* into a coherent dramatic pattern' concentrating on victimology; in *CJIS* Bert Cardullo offers '*Riders to the Sea*: A New View', and Sidney Poger relates 'Brecht's *Señora Carrar's Rifles* and Synge's *Riders to the Sea*'. Toni O'Brien Johnson discusses '*The Well of the Saints* and *Waiting for Godot*: Stylistic Variations on a Tradition' in *The Irish Writer and The City* (edited by Maurice Harmon, Smythe).

In 'Ben Travers and the Aldwych Farces' (*MD*), after some good opening remarks on farce and farces in general, Leslie Smith examines *Rookery Nook*, *Thark*, and *Plunder* as classic examples of a productive collaboration between a playwright and a team of actors. Evelyne Ginestet's 'Wodehouse Amuseur Edouardien?' (*CVE*) includes references to Wodehouse's activities as a lyricist.

The Methuen Student Edition of Wesker's *The Merchant*[230] prints a revised and re-ordered text of the play, together with Glenda Leeming's thoughtful commentary, a preface by Wesker, and photographs of New York and Danish productions.

In his useful *Reader's Guide to the Plays of W. B. Yeats*[231] Richard Taylor

---

228. *Stoppard: The Mystery and the Clockwork*, by Richard Corballis. AmberL. pp. 204. £11.95.

229. *The Collected Letters of John Millington Synge*. Vol. 2: *1907–1909*, ed. by Ann Saddlemyer. Clarendon. pp. xvii + 270. £25.

230. *The Merchant*, by Arnold Wesker, with commentary and notes by Glenda Leeming. Methuen (1983). pp. lv + 101. pb £1.95.

231. *A Reader's Guide to the Plays of W. B. Yeats*, by Richard Taylor. Macmillan. pp. ix + 197. £20.

discusses each of Yeats's plays individually 'in the belief that help in reading and understanding specific aspects of the text is more important than repeating critical generalities readily available elsewhere' and includes 'observations on the rhythmic structure of each play, and the patterning of images'. In the introduction Taylor concentrates on an exposition of Yeats's aesthetic interests but, although he pays little attention to contemporary theatrical contexts, Taylor never loses sight of the plays as performance texts. Elsewhere Birgit Bramsbäck[232] studies the function of folk-lore elements in *The Countess Cathleen*, *The Land of Heart's Desire*, and *The Shadowy Waters* in scholarly detail and Robert Tracy, in 'Yeats and the Death of Robert Gregory' (*Éire*), sees Robert Gregory as conforming closely to the Cuchulain pattern as Yeats perceived it.

---

232. *Folklore and W. B. Yeats: The Function of Folklore Elements in Three Early Plays*, by Birgit Bramsbäck. SAU 51. Uppsala. pp. xii + 178. pb Skr 115.

American Literature to 1900

ALLAN LLOYD-SMITH and DAVID CORKER

Reviews of literature before 1800 have been contributed by David Corker.

1. General

American Literature in Context. Volume 1: *1620–1830*[1], by Stephen Fender, is designed primarily as an undergraduate textbook and includes short extracts from John Smith, William Bradford, Franklin, Paine, Jefferson, Irving, and Cooper, among others. Each extract is followed by an extended commentary which places it in a wider historical and cultural context. Engagingly written, with a wealth of reference right up to the present day, the absence of religious texts tends to reinforce the author's stress on America as a secular myth, as a growing unity and success story.

Philip F. Gura, in *A Glimpse of Sion's Glory: Puritan Radicalism in New England 1620–1660*[2], attacks Perry Miller's view that there was a monolithic uniformity of belief in New England, arguing that the colonies' stability emerged not in spite of but by virtue of radical challenges and reactions, the 'centrifugal dynamic at the core of Puritan ideology'. The book covers separatists, spiritists, Baptists, millenarians, and Quakers, with separate chapters on Anne Hutchinson, Samuel Gorton, and William Pynchon. Especially convincing are his treatments of Quaker thinking and of 'Anne Hutchinson and the "Antinomians"' among the most significant of the dissenting voices which he asserts went up to make the 'inherent radicalism' of the 'New England Mind'.

In *The Land Before Her: Fantasy and Experience of the American Frontiers, 1630–1860*[3] Annette Kolodny utilizes some diaries and letters but works mainly from narratives intended for publication, to argue that such accounts demonstrate changes in the dominant myth of the frontier, a fantasy moving from the Indian captivity to the pastoral conversion of prairie into garden, and, in the nineteenth century, to a subgenre of domestic fiction with the yeoman wives of the West. While the wide variety of metaphors shows a consistent underlying horror of poverty and a hatred of untamed nature, the author's more tendentious theses of a decline in the status of middle-class women in the

1. *American Literature in Context.* Vol. 1: *1620–1830*, by Stephen Fender. Methuen (1983). pp. vii + 209. £5.50.

2. *A Glimpse of Sion's Glory: Puritan Radicalism in New England 1620–1660*, by Philip F. Gura. Wesleyan. pp. xv + 398. $29.95.

3. *The Land Before Her: Fantasy and Experience of the American Frontiers, 1630–1860*, by Annette Kolodny. UNC. pp. xv + 293. hb. $28, pb $9.95.

nineteenth century and of a sharp opposition between destructive male myths and constructive female ones are not supported by her own evidence.

The following works not seen for review might also be noted: *American Writers Before 1800: A Biographical and Criticial Reference Guide*, edited by James Levernier and Douglas R. Wilmes in three volumes (Greenwood), and *American Puritan Studies: An Annotated Bibliography of Dissertations, 1882– 1981*, edited by Michael S. Montgomery (Greenwood).

Nina Baym challenges the assumption that has determined the course of much criticism of American fiction in her article 'Concepts of the Romance in Hawthorne's America' in *NCF*. By studying reviews of longer fictions that appeared in a variety of major American magazines between 1820 and 1860 she discovers that Hawthorne's distinction between the novel and the romance, which critics have often assumed to echo a consensus (and which was drawn from Scott), was actually not in general acceptance. The reviewers often used 'romance' as synonymous with 'novel', and when they made a distinction between the two forms, the distinction varied. The implication of this finding, of course, is to question some of the most influential studies of the development of American fiction, and especially Richard Chase's work. This article represents part of the argument of Baym's forthcoming book, *Novels, Readers and Reviewers: Responses to Fiction in Antebellum America*.

In *Hawthorne, Melville and the American Character, A Looking-Glass Business*[4] John P. McWilliams attempts to define the American character as it was portrayed in fiction. The intensity of national commitment to the idea of an American identity between 1820 and 1850 is demonstrated by observations of the Republic by both European and American commentators, and the threads of these assumptions are picked up in the fictions. Perhaps it will seem unkind to comment that so broad a theme deserves a wider canvas than this. But if such a book is seriously to challenge Lewis's *American Adam*, for example, it should surely allow attention to more than two writers.

Robert Clark argues in *History, Ideology & Myth in American Fiction, 1823–1850*[5] that the familiar myth of American innocence presented in classic American fictions is a transformation of ideological and historical propositions according to the kind of inversions and condensations Freud identified in the dreamwork. The condensation and displacement of contradictory material and ideological elements results in the representation of figures of innocence in association with the white man's victims, whether red or black. An area of some difficulty lies in the extent to which such writers as Cooper, Hawthorne, and Melville should be seen as proponents of myth or as purveyors of unwelcome social truth: 'Their work is . . . the expression of a more capacious and critical view than contemporary opinion was prepared to admit, and often needs to be read as an attempt to communicate unpalatable perceptions across the censorship imposed by readers.' A strong reading of Cooper suggests how unacknowledged concerns regarding his father's appropriation of lands distorted his account of Indian history in the Leatherstocking series. The brief readings of Hawthorne and Melville are not developed as far as the importance

4. *Hawthorne, Melville and the American Character, A Looking-Glass Business*, by John P. McWilliams. CUP. pp. xi + 261. £19.50.
5. *History, Ideology & Myth in American Fiction, 1823–1850*, by Robert Clark. Studies in American Literature. Macmillan. pp. x + 186. £22.50.

of their implication of these authors in contemporary political contradictions might warrant, and it is not always clear whether the myth addressed is of nature's malignity or beneficence. Nevertheless, this is an important contribution to the Macmillan series of Studies in American Literature.

The Failure of the Word: the Protagonist as Lawyer in Modern Fiction[6], by Richard H. Weisberg has a useful section on law in American fiction – Part 4, 'The Creative Use of Statutes for Subjective Ends: The case of *Billy Budd, Sailor*' – as well as valuable remarks on law in modern literature generally. The Melville chapters systematize what critics have increasingly recognized as Vere's biased reasoning in the law he pretended to apply to Billy's case.

In *NCF* Richard Lehan focuses on the French Connection of American literary naturalism in a detailed account of the 'true social and historical basis of literary naturalism: the willing ability of these writers to examine the cultural matrix in a way that it had not been examined by previous novelists'. His account sees the literary form as inseparable from the historical movement of a feudal and aristocratic world into an urban, commercial, and industrial one, and illustrates this in the panoramas of Zola's Rougon-Macquart novels. Lehan draws attention to the substratum of American novels on similar topics.

The following are relevant but were not seen for review: the fifth edition of the *Bibliographical Guide to the Study of the Literature of the USA* by Clarence Ghodes and Sanford E. Marovitz (DukeU); Barbara Foley, 'From New Criticism to Deconstruction: The Example of Charles Feidelson's *Symbolism in American Literature*' (*AQ*); *Critical Essays on American Humour*, edited by W. B. Clark and W. C. Turner (Hall); *The Origins and Originality of American Culture*, edited by Tibor Frank (AK); and *From Rags to Riches: Le mythe du self-made man*, edited by Serge Ricard (UProvence), which includes essays on James, Clemens, and Dreiser. Kenneth Cameron's *American Writers in Pictures: The Major Nineteenth-Century Writers and Their Backgrounds* (Transcendental) contains photographs relating to Emerson, Thoreau, Hawthorne, and Whitman. Donald Pizer has an article on 'Recent Studies on Nineteenth-Century American Realism and Naturalism' (*ESQ*) and has revised *Realism and Naturalism*. There is also a new survey of American naturalism by John J. Conder entitled *Naturalism in American Fiction: The Classic Phase* (UKen). Joseph Riddel, in 'Reading America / American Readers' (*MLN*), studies the relationship of national identity to reading, with examples from Hawthorne and Adams.

Joel Myerson has edited a collection on *The Transcendentalists: A Review of Research and Criticism* (*MLA*), and another collection on criticism is edited by E. N. Harbert and R. Rees: *Fifteen American Authors Before 1900: Bibliographical Essays on Research and Criticism* (UWisc). Wilma Garcia studies the treatment of gender in *Mothers and Others: Myths of the Female in the Works of Melville, Twain, and Hemingway* (Lang), while Martin Green's book on adventure fiction treats of masculinity and its relationship to nationalism (*The Great American Adventure*, published by Beacon). Joyce W. Warren writes on the treatment of women in *The American Narcissus: Individualism and Women in Nineteenth-Century American Fiction* (Rutgers).

---

6. *The Failure of the Word: the Protagonist as Lawyer in Modern Fiction*, by Richard H. Weisberg. Yale. pp. xvi + 218. £20.

2. Poetry

There is an essay on 'Puritan Poetry: Its Public and Private Strain' by Agnieszka Salska in *EAL*, and Wendy Martin has a book linking three poets: *An American Triptych: Anne Bradstreet, Emily Dickinson, Adrienne Rich* (UNC). Another book on Emily Dickinson is by Christopher E. G. Benfey, *Emily Dickinson and the Problem of Others* (UMass). Paul J. Ferlazzo edits and introduces *Critical Essays on Emily Dickinson* (Hall), and Vivian R. Pollak has considered the question of gender in *Dickinson: The Anxiety of Gender* (CornU).

Dickinson's use of 'indirection' is the focus of an essay by Lynn Keller and Christianne Miller in *NEQ*: 'Emily Dickinson, Elizabeth Bishop, and the Rewards of Indirection'. Their thesis is that indirection characterizes women's writing and speech, and that the effect of this frequently observed propensity in poetry is to cause the subtexts to conflict with direct statements, and thus to reveal a more daring and personal or disruptive involvement. Keller and Miller note the uses of indirect self-portraiture, and multiple ambiguities of reference in Dickinson and Bishop's writing. Douglas Anderson writes on Dickinson in *NEQ*, 'Presence and Place in Emily Dickinson's Poetry'. He argues that Dickinson's modification of the Puritan spiritual geography stresses that the 'other' is *here*: is 'presence', producing an intimate proximity of transcendental experience. Presence yields to 'place', but the aftermath is fullness, not deprivation. He notes that her poetry constantly suggests plots: a funeral, a journey, a death-bed farewell, but refuses closure. In *ESQ* Robert M. Luscher finds 'An Emersonian Context of Dickinson's "The Soul Selects Her Own Society"' in RWE's 'Spiritual Laws'.

A welcome examination of Frederick Tuckerman's British connection is given by Eugene England in 'Tuckerman and Tennyson: "Two Friends . . . On Either Side the Atlantic"' (*NEQ*). England discusses Tuckerman's visit to the monumental poet, in which the American demonstrated his profound knowledge of and admiration for Tennyson's poetry (helped, it seems, by his facility for total recall). Tennyson responded warmly, and England reports that after an initial adoption of a Tennysonian manner Tuckerman was encouraged by this relationship to have confidence to move on into his own independent realm.

Larzer Ziff writes on 'Whitman and the Crowd' in *CritI*, comparing Whitman's usages to Poe's and Emerson's. Two articles by James Perrin Warren are concerned with Whitman's language practice: 'The "Real Grammar": Deverbal Style in "Song of Myself"' in *AL*, and '"The Free Growth of Metrical Laws": Syntactic Parallelism in "Song of Myself"' in *Style*. The 'real grammar' that Whitman aspires to is not a set of laws but a set of possibilities, as he explains in *The Primer of Words* (1856): '. . . a nucleus of the spirit of the laws with liberty to carry out the spirit . . . by violating them if necessary'. The deverbal style in question concerns the production of nouns from verb bases, as in sniff, urge, knit, breed, merge, sluff, and so on. The use of syntactic parallelism substitutes rhythm for metre: Warren offers an alternative framework to Gay Wilson Allen's for understanding Whitman's 'metrical laws' in a taxonomy of his 'catalogues'. This argument seems fairly familiar, as does that of Harold Aspiz in 'Walt Whitman: The Spermatic Imagination' (*AL*). Aspiz discusses the relation of sexual excitement to the urge to speak and write poems, and suggests that the development of a spermatic trope was the inevitable next step. Emerson and other romantics had used this trope, but in a sublimated form. Aspiz digs out fascinating information about nineteenth-century beliefs concerning sperm (as brain fluid, for example), and contrasts conventional ideas of conservation of the precious substance to Whitman's 'unflagging' sexual prowess in the poetry. 'So Long!' and *Children of Adam* provide examples. Essays on Whitman and Dickinson are to be found in H. Butterfield's collection *Modern American Poetry* (Vision) which was not seen in time for detailed review this year.

3. Prose

A bibliography of the colonial period comes from Emory Elliott: *American Colonial Writers* (Gale). In *JAmS* Andrew Delbanco considers the relationship of Puritanism to American Isolationism in 'The Puritan Errand Re-Viewed'. Robert Pincus discusses Benjamin Tompson's use of the 'advice-to-a-painter' theme in *EAL*, where Jeffrey Hammond has an article on *The Day of Doom* and the repudiation of carnal reason. Edward Taylor and the New Astronomy is the subject of a study in *AmerP* by Catherine Rainwater.

By careful textual analysis Patricia Caldwell elicits the features which distinguished American from English conversion narratives in *The Puritan Conversion Narratives: The Beginnings of American Expression*[7]. Her argument is that the biblical references came to be structural rather than illustrative in America, since they were the main source of order and meaning in a strange land, amid trying circumstances and disappointments. The belief that literary expression could test religious sincerity challenges the orthodox view that the Puritans were not interested in style, and feeds into the debate about the boundaries between public and private experience, the relative demands of community and conscience.

American Colonial Prose: John Smith to Thomas Jefferson[8], edited by Mary Ann Radzinowicz, contains longish extracts from historical and personal narratives which tend to focus this collection upon political propaganda and conflict and upon religious creeds. Cotton Mather and Jonathan Edwards are, interestingly, placed alongside John Smith, William Bradford, Franklin, and Jefferson among others. The long introduction is sceptical of myths of Americanness and stresses heterogeneity, provincialism, and successive waves of English influence rather than national consciousness or a homogenous culture.

William B. Willcox *et al.* have edited volume 24 of *The Papers of Benjamin Franklin* (Yale). In *AL* Julie Ellison discusses 'The Sociology of "Holy Indifference": Sarah Edwards' Narrative'. In using his wife's spiritual narrative as the basis for a description of an exemplary Christian, Jonathan Edwards suppressed her name, sex, and the origin of at least some of her crises, in envy, anger, and frustration precipitated by her husband's social alienation. Such disparities are, Ellison argues, symptomatic of the tensions between personal salvation through worldly withdrawal and communal millennialism which entails the regeneration of the social fabric. The argument relies upon the

7. *The Puritan Conversion Narratives: The Beginnings of American Expression*, by Patricia Caldwell. CUP (1983). pp. 210. £17.50.
8. *American Colonial Prose: John Smith to Thomas Jefferson*, ed. by Mary Ann Radzinowicz. CUP. pp. 285. hb £25, pb £7.95.

assumption that religious ecstasy has its origins in personal pain and in social repressiveness.

In *ECS* Christopher Looby argues that Franklin saw in language a metaphor for society and in speech a model for human social action, since language is both socially generated and a law-governed activity. Looby's article, 'Franklin's Alphabet as a Political Design', suggests that the reformed alphabet was conceived as a means of uniting England and the colonies through uniform spelling and punctuation, as a political rather than a linguistic reform.

Teresa Toulouse suggests, in 'Syllabical Idolatry: Benjamin Colman and the Rhetoric of Balance' (*EAL*), that Colman's sermons gave his audience both individual and communal responses to the issues of his day, mediating between religious emotion and rational explanation. Also in *EAL*, 'The Spectral Identity of Sir William Phips' by Daniel Walters suggests that in *Pietas in Patram* Cotton Mather defends Phips by suggesting that political opposition to him was Satanic in origin, thereby establishing a link between political and religious rhetoric.

Irving's *Journals and Notebooks IV: 1826–1829* are edited by Wayne R. Kime and Andrew B. Myers in the Critical Edition (Twayne). John Seelye suggests in *NCF* that whereas Irving is often considered in terms of his eighteenth-century forerunners an English essayist wit he is actually closer to the tradition of American humour that followed. 'Sleepy Hollow' provides Seelye's primary example of how the characteristic theme of sectionalism is in evidence. Rather unjustifiably, I think, Seelye chooses to interpret Ichabod's departure for 'distant' parts as a movement west, an argument for which there seems little textual support. In *SSF* Barbara Tepa Lupack considers the parodic elements in 'The Adventure of the German Student', and in *EAL* Lloyd M. Daigrepont describes 'Ichabod Crane: Inglorious Man of Letters'.

A study of Paulding by Larry J. Reynolds: *James Kirke Paulding* (Twayne) was also published this year.

G. R. Thompson has edited Poe's *Essays and Reviews* (LAm). Poe's curious reluctance to name the cloaked figure of 'The Assignation' as Lord Byron provokes Dennis Pahl to speculation along Derridean lines in 'Recovering Byron: Poe's "The Assignation"' in *Criticism*. The title puns on the covering up of the figure and its identity, and Pahl makes a good deal of the similarities between the Marchesa and her lover. Susan Levine and Stuart Levine develop the range of Poe's influence in 'Poe and Fuentes: The Reader's Prerogatives' in *CL* where they suggest that the frequent and unusual uses to which Fuentes puts Poe's materials is significant for the reading of both authors. This is according to Borges's dictum that the way an author is read is determined as much by his successors as by his predecessors, as Seelye's article on Irving also proves.

Another piece on the significance of North American writers for South American literature is by Renata R. Mautner Wasserman, 'Reinventing the New World: Cooper and Alencar' (*CL*) in which she notes the similarities between the American and Brazilian and shows some illuminating contrasts in their treatment of interracial sexuality, aboriginal 'pre' history, and the radicalism of Alencar's utopian vision.

Lawrence Buell surveys 'The Emerson Industry in the 1980's' in *ESQ*, and Julie Ellison comments on Emerson's irony and 'The Comic' in the same journal. An extended discussion of the authorship of Emerson's late essay 'Immortality' is given by Glen M. Dolan who details in *AL* the provenance of the essays in *Letters and Social Aims* (1875). By then, of course, Emerson's powers had much declined and so the work was extensively edited by James Cabot. The words, however, were entirely Emerson's own.

Thoreau owed something to the language theories of the French Enlightenment, according to Michael West's article in *ELH*. His classical education and his interest in philology led him to appreciate the work of Condillac, Rousseau, de Sivry, De Brosses, and Court de Gebelin. West's study is representative of a larger interest now being taken in the European sources of American romantic thought. On a more domestic level, that of politics, Thoreau shared in the metalanguage of republicanism common to his times, but within this vocabulary practised his own idiolect, as Leonard N. Neufeldt shows in his article on 'Thoreau's Political Economy' in *NEQ*. He combined a sense of American exceptionalism with a withering distaste for those who failed to live up to the ideals of the republic, and thought that action by intellectually and morally independent individuals both within and outside of government was the key to the better state. Another article on Thoreau's theoretics is '"Action From Principle": Thoreau's Transcendental Economics' by William L. Stull in *ELN*.

A view of Thoreau by an admiring friend is reported by Francis B. Dedmond in *AL* who offers revealing notes from the diary of James Walter Spooner (1831–88). Thomas Altherr studies Thoreau's ambivalence towards hunting in 'Chaplain to the Hunters' (also in *AL*) and shows how Thoreau veered between praising it and preaching against it. He believed in an evolution away from primitive impulses of this kind, but felt them himself and, of course, often accepted specimens from hunters. Thoreau's deep interest in the sea, which was so near in New England, provides Haskell S. Springer with a new understanding of *Walden*'s metaphors in 'The Nautical Walden' (*NEQ*). In Thoreau's period there was much interest in pattern books which offered models for domestic architecture: another article in *NEQ*, by Richard and Jean Carwile Masteller, draws attention to Thoreau's parodic recasting of books like Andrew Jackson Downing's, which suggested the moral qualities implied by features like turrets or spiral pillars, porches, and bracketing. Thoreau and the meaning of dreams is the topic of an article by Jeffrey E. Simpson in *MLS*, 'Thoreau Dreaming Awake and Asleep'.

Bruce Michelson attempts to reconcile the apparently conflicting popularly held views of Hawthorne as both moralist and social observer and as self-questioning, self-reflexive writer, using *The House of the Seven Gables* as illustration, in 'Hawthorne's House of Three Stories' (*NEQ*). The proposed reconciliation is chiefly interesting for the notion that Judge Pyncheon and Holgrave are both versions of traditional haunts called 'shape-shifters'.

A close attention to history in *The Marble Faun* distinguishes Arnold Goldman's essay in *JAmS*, 'The Plot of *The Marble Faun*', which establishes how Hawthorne set his novel against a complex field of Italian history, both past and present, and thus should be read as a fiction of surveillance, detection, and intrigue. It is important to Goldman's argument that Miriam and Donatello have agreed to surrender on the condition that Hilda be released by the Roman authorities, but the point is perhaps arguable since it is rather the *mode* of Hilda's release (in the carnival) that is properly described in the narrator's comment that 'the fitful and fantastic imagination of a woman . . . had arranged the incident'. Conrad Shumaker also discusses the role of history in *The Marble Faun* but whereas Goldman draws attention to our neglect of the facts of Italian history in the period of the novel, Shumaker describes *American* history as at issue ('A Daughter of the Puritans: History in Hawthorne's *The Marble Faun*', *NEQ*). He sees Hilda as representative of New World history in her opposition to Miriam and Donatello.

The Blithedale Romance is concerned with the poles of translation and transformation, mime and mimesis in Charles Swann's study of the implications generated by the names of Coverdale (a renowned biblical translator) and Fauntleroy (notorious as a forger) in *JAmS*. Swann adds the model of 'forgery' to the romantic models of the mirror and the lamp, as 'a kind of bastard realism', which claims to be "the real thing"', unlike mimetic art, which only pretends to be 'like' reality. Translation in *The Blithedale Romance* remains only translation, and never becomes 'transformation'.

The peculiarity of Hawthorne's descriptions is examined by John Dolis in 'Hawthorne's Metonymic Gaze: Image and Object' (*AL*), which sets out the terms of Hawthorne's registration of the object as an unfolding of perception through time and as situated in the observer's subjectivity, unlike a photograph's elucidation of an invariable object. Thus the variable constitution of the objects reflects the affective distance between scene and spectator. Dolis seems to be applying techniques developed in film criticism, such as the concept of the 'gaze', to those aspects of displacement and distancing in Hawthorne's writing which have increasingly attracted critical attention, as in Allan Lloyd-Smith's book *Eve Tempted: Writing and Sexuality in Hawthorne's Fiction*[9], which considers Hawthorne in relation to Derrida's reading of Rousseau, and shows that Hawthorne's discourse is a version of the contemporary discourse of sexuality: that his recurrent tropes are determined by the fixations of reference and innuendo of this language.

A more traditional direction is taken by Kenneth Marc Harris in an article on Hawthorne and Puritan hypocrisy theories in *NCF*, which examines Hawthorne's likely knowledge of the theoretical work on hypocrisy in the seventeenth century, when detection of such apparent saints but actual sinners as Judge Pyncheon was a matter of some urgency. Harris's scholarship is impressive but does not affect reading of *The House of the Seven Gables* as much as one might hope. In *Family Themes and Hawthorne's Fiction: The Tenacious Web* (Rutgers), Gloria C. Erlich proposes the applicability of Erik Erikson's and Daniel Levinson's theories, to *Doctor Grimshawe's Secret* in particular. In *ELN* Rosemary F. Franklin assesses the seashore sketches in *Twice Told Tales* and their influence on Melville. Hawthorne and Melville's treatment of society as akin to a prison is reviewed in *MLS* by Robert Shulman in 'The Artist in the Slammer'.

Herman Melville: Reassessments[10] is the title of a collection edited by A. Robert Lee, which proposes to open new avenues into this 'so plural and carefully self-masking' writer's work. Herbie Butterfield discusses the vitality of both dream and nightmare in *Typee* and *Omoo*, and Harold Beaver com-

9. *Eve Tempted: Writing and Sexuality in Hawthorne's Fiction*, by Allan Lloyd-Smith. CH. pp. 182. £15.95.

10. *Herman Melville: Reassessments*, ed. by A. Robert Lee. Vision. pp. 221. £14.95.

ments on the apparent unreadability of *Mardi*: a farrago, a mess, in which splintering of consciousness is the most constant mode, and yet which demonstrates how, for Melville, fiction had to become the source and testing-ground of inconsistencies.

In the same volume, 'Society and Sexuality in the Narrators of 1849' by James H. Justus, compares the narrators of *Redburn* and *Whitejacket*, noting their instinctive self-regard, and also their ambivalent attraction to homoerotic sexuality: the 'sly gusto' of the sexual jokes and the fastidious distaste for homosexual practises on a man-of-war. A. Robert Lee considers *Moby-Dick* as an *anatomy* in his account of the novel's underlying iconoclasm and 'risk-laden curiosity'; and Melville's recognition of the provisionality of all language and codes, the gap between words and things, in this struggle to anatomize the world. In 'Grown in America' Eric Mottram discusses Melville's sense of control, in terms of American Renaissance dramatizations of the desire both to inherit laws and to project the individual on an open road, the routes of law and non-recurring events, and the imbalances of democratic control. Richard Gray stresses the centripetal structure of *Pierre*, its irony and inwardness, its labyrinthine nature, in which the narrator reminds us of both his presence and of the hopelessness of his task. Here rock replaces the whale as the central image of the material world; it is impenetrable and uninterpretable, offering only blank surfaces. But Melville's bitterness at this distinguishes him from postmodernist writers. The short fiction is addressed by William Wasserstrom, who is 'startled to realize how truly acerbic' it is when taken in bulk. Wasserstrom argues that critics in pursuing Melville's exceptionalism, either in the 1950s terms of alienation, or the 1980s plague of signs and symptoms, have overlooked a 'mainstream of American writings whose hallmark is a roughness of grain in the texture and shape of a text'. Melville was animated by the strain 'of contriving mannerist ways to skew a tale' in his eschewing of both ordinary good sense and transcendent wisdom, in the attempt to recognize unsolvable oppositions, the 'split personality' which ruled the life of politics and letters in the United States. Like Richard Gray, Wasserstrom notes that it is to 'signification' that his work is riveted, no matter how fruitful semiotic investigations may be; it is for Melville the world itself towards which all signs tend.

That this may be at least arguable is suggested by *The Confidence Man*, for who after reading the masquerade could be sure that Melville had any 'real' world in mind? A. Robert Lee sees this novel as projecting a view of American history that is both utterly particular, yet also, and even beyond allegory, a 'surrealized, waking-dream Masquerade' calling upon masterly ventriloquism among its several voices. Melville's generally neglected poetry is examined by Andrew Hook, who finds that although Melville is not a great poet he can be usefully paralleled to Thomas Hardy. Hook sees the Civil War and postwar corruption as a crucial determinant of Melville's movement away from prose, for there was no longer an audience for the kind of fiction he needed to write. Finally, H. Bruce Franklin draws attention to Melville's awareness of the late-nineteenth-century world of empire at the time of the composition of *Billy Budd, Sailor*, arguing, like Weisberg, against the distortions that have led some academics to see Vere as admirable, and showing how the British Empire looked to American (and politically radical) eyes in the 1880s and 1890s.

A connection with Dickens is noted by Raymond Benoit in '*Bleak House* and "Bartleby the Scrivener"', and the naming of Vere is documented by S. A. Cowan (both in *SSF*). An important essay on Melville and the doctrine of Manifest Destiny comes from Allan Moore Emery in *NCF*: ' "Benito Cereno" and Manifest Destiny'. Emery challenges the use sometimes made of *Moby-Dick* as central evidence of Melville's political awareness and proposes 'Benito Cereno' as a stronger example. This essay follows up Emery's piece on the political significance of 'I and My Chimney' (*NEQ*, 1982) by showing how Melville may have been concerned more with the arguments for American expansionism than with slavery. Proponents of American intervention in South America stressed the disorderliness, weakness, and despotism of the Spanish, in articles appearing in *Putnam's* and *Harper's* alongside Melville's own work. Emery ingeniously suggests that we see Delano as the real 'inquisitor' of the piece. Barbara J. Baines discusses 'Ritualized Cannibalism in "Benito Cereno"' in *ESQ*.

In 'Nowhere a Stranger: Melville and Cosmopolitanism' (*NCF*) John Bryant asks what this 'type' would have meant to Melville and his audience. Examples go back to Diogenes, and can be found in Johnson, Kant, Voltaire, and Goldsmith, but in America the type was increasingly identified with the mercantile world. Its negative aspects included opportunism, vagrancy, distrust, and shiftiness, and an example is provided in the once notorious Vincent Nolte, whose history appeared in *Putnam's* of 1854. Bryant concludes that 'that shade of difference between the certain and seeming malice in the cosmopolitan's latitudinarianism is the almost Jamesian subject matter on which Melville builds *The Confidence Man*'. In *ESQ* David Sewell pursues the question of 'Mercantile Philosophy and the Dialectics of Confidence'. Another study of the confidence man figure, in *CLS*, compares Melville's paradigm to Rousseau's, finding linguistic and stylistic similarities to *Emile*, and the Discourses *On the Sciences and the Arts*, and *On the Sources of Inequality among Men*. Christopher S. Durer submits that Melville could well have been reading Rousseau while writing his novels, and transferred some thoughts and passages from *Emile*, probably Books I and II, in a modified form, into his text. Although Durer falls victim to 'what Melville intended, most likely, was . . .' temptation, he valuably draws attention to the interest of the American Romantics in their European mentors, which is too often ignored in American scholarship. More on Melville's intertextuality comes in John Samson's 'Profaning the Sacred: Melville's *Omoo* and the Missionary Narratives' (*AL*) which manages to offer some new views beyond T. Walter Herbert's interesting account of such matters in *Marquesan Encounters*. In *ESQ* Gerard Shepherd proposes a psychological approach to *Pierre*; Michael Kearns assesses Melville's view of Idealistic Psychology; and John Samson describes the dynamics of history and fiction in *Typee*. In *ES* is an account of the short stories by Werner Senn: 'Reading Melville's Mazes'.

A book on Louisa May Alcott, edited by Madeleine Stern, *Critical Essays on Louisa May Alcott* (Hall), includes biographical information.

Forrest G. Robinson attempts the redemption of *Tom Sawyer* in *NCF*, following the lead of James M. Cox in seeing it as a novel of social analysis and using the notion of play as a window on the social world of St Petersburg. Tom plays adult games as much as childish ones, and is a 'gamesman' figure. In *ALR* John Earl Bassett suggests that the ending of *Huckleberry Finn* lies in its beginning. The ending restores circularity after the linear river episodes, and answers the question implicitly posed: will Huck become Tom Sawyer – or Pap? Kevin Murphy's article, 'Illiterate's Progress: The Descent into Literacy in *Huckleberry Finn*', which is the only piece from our period to be included in the special 'Later American Fiction' issue of *TSLL*, also addresses the question of the ending, and shows how a 'progressive entanglement in literacy' immures Huck in the social norms that so distress him, for language is the repository of values. Huck's final act is not to light out for the territory but to write the book; the capstone on his literacy ... and his civilizing. Lucinda H. MacKethan observes that 'lighting out' was a good old frontier tradition, especially practised by American slaves ('*Huckleberry Finn* and the Slave Narratives: Lighting Out as Design', *SoR*). Although the influence of such narratives on Twain remains a matter for speculation, he did have several in his library, and seems to have used them in *A Connecticut Yankee* and probably in Huck's and Jim's experiences.

A book on Twain's reception, *The Mythologizing of Mark Twain* edited by Sara deSaussure Davis and Philip D. Beidler (UAla), contains such pieces as 'A Talent for Posturing: The Achievement of Twain's Public Personality' by Louis J. Budd. Processions in Twain's work occasion a piece by Chris Merritt in *ALR*, suggesting a use of such activities as both show and symbol. In *CLS* Bobby J. Chamberlain traces similarities between Twain's frontier humour and that of the Brazilian writer Carvalho. There is no new material on Twain here, and as Chamberlain disarmingly admits, what is to be deduced from his analyses 'is perhaps not altogether clear'. In *ALR* M. E. Cronander suggests that professional rivalry may have prompted Twain's unkind comments on Ambrose Bierce's *Nuggets and Dust*.

Bierce himself is the subject of a book from Cathy N. Davidson, *The Experimental Fictions of Ambrose Bierce: Structuring the Ineffable* (UNeb), which discusses Bierce's narrative technique and which will be reviewed in detail in the next volume.

Characterization in the work of Charles Chesnutt is addressed by Charles Hackenberry in *ALR*, in an article that describes how Chesnutt uses character types to attempt to change racial attitudes. The relation between social theory and fiction in Hamlin Garland's work is explored by Michael Clark, also in *ALR*, in an article concerning the influence of Herbert Spencer on 'Rose of Dutcher's Coolly'.

Harriet Beecher Stowe is beginning to receive more critical attention after the neglect since 1945 which James M. Cox calls 'almost scandalous' in an article in *NCF*. Perhaps it was F. O. Matthiessen's fault for leaving *Uncle Tom's Cabin* out of his *American Renaissance*? Cox sees the celebrated work as revolutionary rather than reformist, because it is *against* the law. Stowe saw the South in terms of melodrama, as the place where evil existed; in her later New England local colour novels 'Puritanism converted into melodrama suddenly becomes Puritanism converted into history'. In a subsequent issue of *NCF* Thomas P. Joswick takes up the question of Mrs Stowe's language, arguing that the religious rhetoric of the novel 'encourages an aesthetic practice blind to its own implication in the moral evil it intends to expose and change'. Gillian Brown considers the interrelations of domesticity, patriarchy, and slavery in ' "Getting in the Kitchen with Dinah": Domestic Politics in *Uncle Tom's Cabin*' (*AQ*). Another New England local colourist, Alice Brown

(1857–1948), receives acknowledgement in a bibliography from Margaret Ann Baker in *ALR*.

Owen Wister's racialist attitudes are exposed by Sanford Marovitz in 'Unseemly Realities in Wister's Western American Myth' in *ALR*. Careful readers will have noted Wister's prejudice in favour of Anglo superiority in *The Virginian*; Marovitz shows the pervasive influence of these southern attitudes in *Lady Baltimore*.

In '*The Awakening* and the Failure of Psyche' (*AL*) Rosemary F. Franklin uses the Psyche myth to examine the progress of Edna Pontelier. The myth illustrates the 'labor towards self of the female hero' and the attempt of that nascent self to resist the lure of the unconscious. She deals capably with the matter of the apparent Creole matriarchy but runs against one substantial problem: there just doesn't seem to be any evidence that Chopin had the Cupid/Psyche myth in mind in the way that Edith Wharton, say, uses legend in 'Pomegranate Seed'. Another account of Chopin's novel, Robert White's 'Inner and Outer Space in *The Awakening*' (*Mosaic*), applies Erik Erikson's idea of gender-determined imagination to Edna and finds that she does not conform to the notional female imagination of 'inner space'. He draws attention to the spatial metaphors of the novel, and sees her last swim as a positive movement towards the 'outer' space.

Henry Adams wrote two novels which told essentially the same story, according to Denis Donoghue's reading of *Democracy* and *Esther* in *NCF*. In each novel a vacancy is felt in life; a change of place provides interest; a powerful person more. The final movement, of self-assertion and rejection, provides a pattern which helps illuminate the whole of Adams's fiction and his work in politics, history, and autobiography. Donoghue sees the pathos of *The Education* as being in Adams's attempt to bring Enlightenment values to bear on a society that had rejected them, arguing that his mind was predominantly ironic and liable to prepattern experience, which for Adams had to be an experience of failure.

Edith Wharton receives a feminist rereading from Judith Fryer in *ALR*: 'Purity and Power in *The Age of Innocence*', which argues that Ellen Olenska's world of cultural and sexual richness is impossible in America, or for Newland Archer.

Stephen Crane's 'Episode of War' is collated by Paul Sorrentino in *SB*. Jack London's biographical legend is questioned in *ALR* by David H. Stanley, who compares him with Norman Mailer, and discusses his difficulty in living down his popular identification with Wolf Larsen. Two articles in *ALR* deal with Dreiser: Joseph Griffith describes an early tale of New York City, and in 'The Feast of Belshazzar and *Sister Carrie*' William J. Beeching discusses the possible significance of the title of Chapter XXXII and draws a parallel between Ames and Daniel. Also in this journal William Dean Howells's development of a popular literary form, the dramatic essay, is examined by George C. Carrington, and an article by John C. Hirsch in *ALR* shows how Harold Frederic probably drew on the McGlynn affair in creating *The Damnation of Theron Ware*. McGlynn, a radical New York priest, received much newspaper attention when he was excommunicated.

A new Critical Series study on Sarah Orne Jewett is edited by Gwen L. Nagel: *Critical Essays on Sarah Orne Jewett* (Hall).

As always, Henry James has attracted much critical attention. In the popular Macmillan Casebook Series is *Washington Square and The Portrait of A Lady*[11], which collects useful contributions from Q. D. Leavis, Mary McCarthy, F. W. Dupee, Richard Poirier, and John Lucas on *Washington Square*; Richard Chase, Leon Edel, Dorothea Krook, Sister Corona Sharp, Tony Tanner, Denis Donoghue, and Nina Baym on *The Portrait of a Lady*. It is perhaps unfortunate that the editor, Alan Shelston, has not discovered anything of significance written since 1976. *The Ambassadors*, a study by Alan W. Bellringer in the Unwin Critical Library (A&U) will be reviewed in the next volume of *YWES*, together with John Carlos Rowe's *The Theoretical Dimensions of Henry James* (Methuen).

The essays collected in Ian Bell's *Henry James: Fiction as History*[12] are intended, as the title suggests, to present James in his historical context, which is so often denied through a focus on his 'technique'. Several of the essays in this volume do in fact achieve a sense of James's engagement in and with history, although one may be sceptical of the claim that a restructuring which recognizes the 'ruptures and difficulties of [the fiction's] historical occasions' is finally produced. Bell's own essay on *Washington Square* proposes that the 'commodification' of Catherine be understood in terms of the hard versus soft currency debates of the 1830s and the 1870s. Townsend, who might be expected to be a representative of the paper-money side, is read as figuring a change that the bourgeois mind refuses to acknowledge. The parallel between paper-money and writing is of much interest.

David Howard discusses a little known story, 'The Papers', and allows himself some outrageous puns, such as that Milly Theale dies of 'conspicuous consumption'. His most useful observation is, I think, that James's intellectuals, like Merton Densher, display a degree of bitterness. Millicent Bell does some important work in rethinking the question of the Governess's state of mind in *The Turn of the Screw*. She observes that the question of hallucination is less significant than the Governess's moral state, which is Manichean and prevents her from any 'mixed' interpretations of behaviour. Nichola Bradbury collects absences and differences in *The Wings*, noticing the 'necessary chaos of the text' and even allowing herself the indulgence of a 'wonderfully' at the end of her essay, '"Nothing that is not there and the nothing that is": The Celebration of Absence in *The Wings of the Dove*'. Her proposition is that structuralism in *The Ambassadors* gives way to deconstruction in *The Wings*; an argument that I think should be made in some sort of historical context: for example the parallels to be drawn between these recent intellectual movements and those of the late romantic period. Maud Ellmann fishes in similarly troubled ahistorical waters in 'The Intimate Difference: Power and Representation in *The Ambassadors*'. The fiction 'shrinks behind the veil of its own representation of itself ... representation is its central theme as well as its cocoon'. Sometimes an oversensitivity to possible implication appears, as when she reads 'members' and 'detachments' as terms for representatives which 'whisper that they mutilate their origins'. But there are very interesting *aperçus*, such as the way that every incident in the text repeats or represents itself.

11. *Washington Square and The Portrait of A Lady*, ed. by Alan Shelston. Casebook Series. Macmillan. pp. 210. hb £14, pb £5.95.

12. *Henry James: Fiction as History*, ed. by Ian Bell. Vision. pp. 188. £13.95.

Stuart Culver works on the question of how the prefaces to the New York edition are related to the works themselves: are they, as Lubbock thought, a platform for articulating a theory of composition, or are they rather, as Gosse assumed, personal reminiscences of the author? Culver compares the Society of Authors with the Society of Civil Engineers to show how professional expertise was theoreticized in James's period and by James himself (who uses the metaphor of construction extensively in the prefaces). The redefinition of the text's value in the Collected Edition provides an understanding of the author's 'managerial' function in relation to his own productions. In 'James as Janus: Opposition and Economy' Ellman Crasnow discusses the subversion of opposites and transgression of realms in James's work. Crasnow sees, like Bell, the relevance of the model of coinage, or the exchange of symbolic tokens of value, and compares this with Freud's notion of psychic economy. The aim is to encompass the fictions and non-fictions in 'a more fundamental economy than that of genre'. The opposition between impression and expression provides a key to the shift from passivity to active response, just as in James's own criticism an active aggression counterpoints its passive guilt. Impression and expression are not exclusive alternatives, 'one can move back and forth through the door that divides them'. An essay by Richard Godden concludes this collection: 'Some Slight Shifts in the Novel of Manners'. Starting from Veblen's ideas of the relation between manners and the economic base of a society Godden looks at the mystifications of economic production and consumption in James and Fitzgerald. The argument centres upon an apparent shift in the disposition of capital from 'accumulation' to 'reproduction' and the consequences of this for fictional heroes, and perhaps more particularly, heroines, like Verena Tarrant in *The Bostonians*, who embodies the potentiality for advertising required by the new economic conditions.

Robert Martin writes in *MLS* on James's ecstatic vision; Elizabeth Allen has a book on James's treatment of women as signs, *A Woman's Place in the Novels of Henry James* (St Martin's); and Carren Kaston a study of *Imagination and Desire in the Novels of Henry James* (Rutgers). Robert Levine discusses 'The Aspern Papers' in *EAS*.

The celebrated ghosts are re-assessed by David S. Miall in an article called 'Designed Horror: James's Vision of Evil in *The Turn of the Screw*' in *NCF*. Miall asks what the ghosts *might* mean if they were intended to be seen as a reality in the manner of Coleridge's argument in the preface to the *Lyrical Ballads*: what would be the emotions accompanying such situations, supposing them real? His answer extends what Martha Banta said in *Henry James and the Occult* some years ago, and is developed through reference to Freud's essay, 'The Uncanny'. The evil specified in *The Turn of the Screw* is of a state, not an act: a kind of paralysis or stasis which is equivalent to the state of death as envisaged by the living in Freud's scheme. There is a familiarity in the Governess's view of Quint, an intimacy beyond speech, which Miall connects with Freud's idea of the death instinct and the repetition compulsion. In 'The Selfish Eye: Strether's Principles of Psychology' (*AL*) Susan M. Griffin discusses Jamesian visual perception, stressing involvement of the seer, not the mere spectator, and James's use of functionalist rather than associationalist psychology. She does not argue that William's psychology finds its way into Henry's fiction, but she does claim that Henry James's perceivers 'confront the problems and enact the solutions central to the psychology of his time'.

Inevitably William James's *Psychology* provides the aptest illustration of that psychology, and his dictum that 'my experience is what I agree to attend to' the best description for James's fictional seers. Jean Gooder's article in *CQ* compares James's savage indictment of English society in *The Awkward Age* with Goya's *Caprices* in which the artist revealed his private scorn for court behaviour. In another piece in the same journal Ms Gooder uses Dante as a guide to the demoralizations of *The Golden Bowl*. Alan Bird draws attention to suspect chronology in *The American* in *N&Q*.

Marcia Ian suggests a continuum of Jamesian criticism placed according to its degree of moral valorization in 'The Elaboration of Privacy in *The Wings of the Dove*' (*ELH*). All the critics agree, she claims, that the novel is a drama of self-definition through negation. Ian suggests key terms such as 'coherence', 'self-hood', and 'discrimination' as openings into the subtleties of Jamesian ontology: concealment of the self by representation and negation is desired but leads to a terror of others breaking in (another clue to the workings of the uncanny in late James). A piece which one might expect to be related, but is not, comes from Stuart Johnson in *Criticism*: 'Prelinguistic Consciousness in James's "Is There a Life After Death?"'. This essay is most useful for its consideration of what light may be thrown by the essay on the stories, especially 'The Altar of the Dead' and 'The Great Good Place'. Johnson argues that memory and desire were much more significant here for James than belief, and that James remained the artist rather than the philosopher.

In *SSF* Adeline Tintner applies the theories of Bergson on time to James's fiction. Hershel Parker concentrates on the later period in 'Henry James "In the Wood": Sequence and Significance of His Literary Labours, 1905–1907'. This essay (in *NCF*) comes from a book on literary authority to be published by Northwestern, which considers such questions as whether slight revisions might ramify into 'new areas of authorial intentionality' which previous critics of these revisions have failed to allow. Rayburn S. Moore discusses James's correspondence with Edmund Gosse in 'A Literary – Gossippy Friendship' (*SoR*). Readers new to James's letter writing may be amused by the charming campness of these examples. The *ArQ* of spring 1984 is a special Henry James issue, edited by George Monteiro, with essays by Barry Maid on *The Ambassadors*, John D. Barbour on *The Princess Casamassima*, James W. Gargano on 'The Patagonia', and Judith Funston on 'The Siege of London'. There is a book on the short stories from Edward Wagenknecht: *The Tales of Henry James* (Ungar).

Another selection from work in progress is part of R. W. B. Lewis's study of the James family, 'The Names of Action: Henry James in the Early 1870's' (*NCF*). The larger work is to be called *The Jameses: A Family Narrative* and promises illumination of the literary and cultural context by examining the relations within the family as a whole. And Leon Edel details the peculiar nexus of friendship between Proust, James, Wharton, and the snobbish diplomat, Walter Berry, for whom Edel feels less sympathy than the writers, calling him a 'self-centered bachelor intent upon being a man of the world' and comparing him to Gilbert Osmond in 'Walter Berry and the Novelists: Proust, James, and Edith Wharton' (*NCF*).

American Literature: The Twentieth Century

DAVID SEED and IAN BELL

This chapter has five sections: 1. General, by David Seed; 2. Poetry, by Ian Bell; 3. Prose Fiction, by David Seed; 4. Non-fictional Prose, by David Seed; and 5. Drama, by Ian Bell.

1. General

Apart from the regular bibliographies which appear in *AL*, *JML*, and *TCL* the number of *AmLS* has now appeared which covers 1982[1]. Although it has changed its personnel slightly for this volume it maintains the annual's generally impeccable standard of thoroughness (in indexing some three hundred periodicals, for instance). Most of its pages are devoted to different areas of modern literature with separate sections on black literature and foreign scholarship.

Several new volumes of the Dictionary of Literary Biography have appeared which deserve mention. John Cech has edited a volume on American writers for children[2], including the creators of such series as Mother West Wind (Thornton Burgess), Black Stallion (Walter Farley), and Raggedy Ann (Johnny Gruelle). The most prolific writer was certainly Howard R. Garis who under the pen-name of Victor Appleton wrote literally hundreds of books. Other figures emerge as surprisingly versatile – L. Frank Baum wrote for the theatre and the graphic artist Wanda Gag illustrated *New Masses* as well as children's books. Although not a writer in the strict sense, few could quarrel with Walt Disney's presence in this volume which is amply justified by his pioneering work on cartoons and comic-books. *American Screenwriters*[3] faced an obvious problem of selection. The editors have chosen to exclude figures like Faulkner and Eric Chandler who did not establish themselves primarily through screenplays. Thus obvious names appear like John Huston, Ben Hecht, and Anita Loos, as well as the 1930s novelist Daniel Fuchs and the dramatist Clifford Odets; the latter's early Broadway successes brought immediate offers from Hollywood. Users of Ann Charters' DLB volumes on

1. *American Literary Scholarship. An Annual, 1982*, ed. by J. Albert Robbins. DukeU. pp. xvii + 551. $37.
2. *American Writers for Children, 1900–1960*, ed. by John Cech. DLB 22. Gale. pp. xiii + 412. $85.
3. *American Screenwriters*, ed. by Robert E. Morsberger, Stephen O. Lesser, and Randall Clark. DLB 26. Gale. pp. xi + 382. $82.

the Beats (see *YW* 64.503) might wish to consult an article by John Osborne and Peter Easy in *Over Here*. They argue that there is a crying need for discrimination between life-style and literary output in examining the Beats. For all its value this is a discrimination which Charters' compilation works against.

Thomas D. Clareson's *Science Fiction in America, 1870s–1930s*[4] concentrates on what he argues were the formative years of this genre for his fully annotated bibliography of texts. In particular he is concerned to show the varied reactions to contemporary science and has interpreted 'Science Fiction' in a flexible and intelligent way. Thus he includes fiction of the occult and also works showing the 'lost race' motif. Of his 838 entries the majority are American but he also lists American editions of foreign works. Clareson is an undoubted expert in this field, having already produced various checklists, and a study of the genre, *Some Kind of Paradise*, which will complement this bibliography, is also due out from the Greenwood Press.

The Origins and Originality of American Culture[5] consists of a collection of papers delivered at the 1980 Budapest International Conference in American Studies. The sheer number of articles (seventy-three) virtually defies summary. They range over a predictably broad span of topics from the call for a national epic, through Southern fiction and mythic themes to the issue of ethnicity. The last two sections present papers on American English analysed from cultural as well as linguistic viewpoints. The contributors to this volume form an international cross-section of Americanists. A. Bartlett Giamatti's *Dante in America*[6] brings together previously published essays from 1813 to 1981 in an anthology designed to show the impact Dante has had on American letters and thought. Naturally enough literary figures are prominent – Longfellow and Lowell from the previous century; Pound, Eliot, and Allen Tate from the twentieth. Following the sensible editorial policy of preferring complete items to excerpts, Pound's little-known review of Lawrence Binyon's *Inferno* has been chosen rather than a passage from *The Spirit of Romance*. Also represented are philosophers (W. T. Harris) and Italian specialists like Charles S. Singleton or Thomas G. Bergin. An interesting recurring theme is the American comments (not always complimentary) on British attempts to mediate Dante to the English-speaking world.

H. L. Gates Jr's *Black Literature and Literary Theory*[7] directs us squarely to theoretical issues inherent in the concept of negritude. The collection falls into two parts. The first concentrates on defining the book's central topic, paying considerable attention to the Trickster myth and the importance of naming. The second section focuses on specific American texts or writers. Story-telling in Frederick Douglass's 'The Heroic Slave' is examined as is voice in Jean Toomer's *Cane* and the Trueblood episode of *Invisible Man* (the latter is described as a subversive historical regression). Other writers dealt with

4. *Science Fiction in America, 1870s–1930s. An Annotated Bibliography of Primary Sources*, comp. by Thomas D. Clareson. Greenwood. pp. xiv + 306. £39.95.

5. *The Origins and Originality of American Culture*, ed. by Tibor Frank. AK. pp. xi + 801. £37.50.

6. *Dante in America. The First Two Centuries*, ed. by A. Bartlett Giamatti. MRTS 23. MRTS. pp. xii + 415. $20.

7. *Black Literature and Literary Theory*, ed. by H. L. Gates Jr. Methuen. pp. 328. hb £15, pb £6.95.

include Zora Hurston, Gwendolyn Brooks, and Toni Morrison. Structuralism is prominent in the theoretical approach of many of these essays. Christopher Brookeman has added another volume to Macmillan's series on the Contemporary United States called *American Culture and Society since the 1930s*[8]. The aim of this volume is to give a history of 'selected developments in literary criticism, cultural theory and artistic practice' in the U.S.A. Brookeman combines a lightly worn Marxism with critical shrewdness to examine theories of culture (Eliot on tradition, Ransom on agrarianism, etc.), indicating the prominence of myth as a stabilizer against historical flux. The later chapters concentrate on the debate over mass culture, devoting substantial sections to Tom Wolfe and the New Journalism, and to Norman Mailer who Brookeman uses as an index to political change in the postwar United States.

Two new general studies of Southern literature have appeared. In *A Gallery of Southerners*[9] Louis D. Rubin Jr, one of the leading scholars in the field, collects together some eleven articles mostly from the 1970s. Rubin argues throughout that being a Southern writer inevitably involves some notion of community, even though that can vary considerably from author to author. He examines Faulkner's sense of vocation and subsequently uses him as a point of reference throughout the volume. Rubin contrasts Thomas Wolfe's rejection of stifling social mores with Carson McCullers' depiction of entrapment. Other essays survey Eudora Welty, *Gone with the Wind*, Flannery O'Connor, and James Agee. Whereas Rubin's essays are general and suggestive, Thomas W. Cutrer's *Parnassus on the Mississippi*[10] is primarily historical and specific. Cutrer narrates in close detail the formation of the *Southern Review* in 1935 and its subsequent career until wartime economies forced its closure in 1942. Founded with money raised by the infamous Huey Long and based at Louisiana State University (Baton Rouge), this review was non-sectional although it did promote Southern writers and had close links with the Agrarians. In its heyday it was, Cutrer argues, one of the leading American journals, publishing new writers like Mary McCarthy and Nelson Algren, as well as more established figures such as T. S. Eliot and Aldous Huxley. Thanks to the editorial skills of Cleanth Brooks and Robert Penn Warren it even rode out the prosecution of LSU President Smith in 1939 and the subsequent purging of the university. *Parnassus on the Mississippi* tells an important chapter of Southern literary history.

2. Poetry

The fiftieth anniversary of The Academy of American Poets is commemorated by a handsome compilation unsurprisingly titled *Fifty Years of American Poetry*[11]. An uncontroversial introduction by Robert Penn Warren is followed by 126 poems, chosen from each of the chancellors, fellows, and

8. *American Culture and Society since the 1930s*, by Christopher Brookeman. Macmillan. pp. xv + 241. hb £15, pb £5.95.

9. *A Gallery of Southerners*, by Louis D. Rubin Jr. LSU. pp. xxi + 233. hb £16.95, pb £8.95.

10. *Parnassus on the Mississippi. The 'Southern Review' and the Baton Rouge Literary Community 1935–1942*, by Thomas W. Cutrer. LSU. pp. 290. £42.90.

11. *Fifty Years of American Poetry*, intro. by Robert Penn Warren. Abrams. pp. 260. $27.50.

award winners since the Academy's founding and ranging from E. A. Robinson to Charles Wright. As a delightful bonus, it includes six wood-engravings by Barry Moser. In a period of mean typography, parsimonious margins, and cheap paper, the volume is a veritable feast. Of less elaborate fare, but very useful in an ever-shrinking market of available texts, all teachers of American poetry will find their task lightened by reprintings of Robert Lowell's *Imitations*[12], William Carlos Williams's *Selected Poems*[13], and Marianne Moore's *Complete Poems*[14]. Particularly welcome is the first paperback edition of the revised version of Moore's poems which will, one hopes, occasion for her a more substantial place in poetry courses.

For *In Praise of What Persists*[15], Stephen Berg has collected reminiscences by contemporary novelists, essayists, and poets which, in a variety of ways, attempt to probe the earliest productive forces behind their work. The volume marks a fascinating excursion into the biography of 'influence' and includes among its poets Hayden Carruth, Raymond Carver, Carolyn Forche, Tess Gallagher, Richard Hugo, Dave Smith, Gerald Stern, C. K. Williams, and Paul Zweig. More widely ranging in scope are two compilations of interviews: L. S. Dembo's *Interviews With Contemporary Writers*[16] and Joe David Bellamy's *American Poetry Observed*[17]. Dembo's second collection of interviews from *ConL* is as various, interesting, and provocative as the first, negotiating an admirable sweep from the largest generalization to the minutest textual detail. Its occasions match impressive knowledge from the interviewers with a sturdy willingness to talk from the interviewees and display admirably the scope of the 'genre' for criticism and scholarship. The American poets selected here include Paul Blackburn, Stanley Kunitz, James Dickey, Edward Dorn, Robert Duncan, A. R. Ammons, and Richard Hugo. Twenty-six poets of stature are represented in Bellamy's important collection. The interviews were conducted, in the main, during the 1970s and although, with the exception of the conversation with Denise Levertov, all have appeared in print previously, their prior publications have suffered from varying degrees of obscurity or difficulty of access. Bellamy has performed a serviceable task in resurrecting these potentially 'lost' moments of contemporary literary history and has chosen those interviews which have something to say about the individual poet's own work, about the craft of writing, and about the condition of American poetry in general. As source material, this volume locates a fertile depository of the thoughts of Ai, John Ashbery, Marvin Bell, Michael Benedikt, Elizabeth Bishop, Robert Bly, James Dickey, Michael S. Harper, Richard Hugo, Donald Justice, Galway Kinnell, Stanley Kunitz, Denise Levertov, W. S. Merwin, Josephine Miles, Adrienne Rich, May Sarton, Charles Simic, W. D. Snodgrass, William Stafford, Mark Strand, James Tate, David Wagoner, Diane Wakoski, Richard Wilbur, and James Wright.

12. *Imitations*, by Robert Lowell. Faber. pp. xiv + 149. pb £2.50.
13. *Selected Poems*, by William Carlos Williams, ed. and intro. by Charles Tomlinson. Penguin (1983). pp. 272. pb £2.95.
14. *Complete Poems*, by Marianne Moore. Faber. pp. xiv + 305. pb £2.95.
15. *In Praise of What Persists*, ed. by Stephen Berg. Harper. pp. xi + 289. pb £7.50.
16. *Interviews With Contemporary Writers: Second Series, 1972–1982*, ed. by L. S. Dembo. UWisc (1983). pp. ix + 381. pb £13.15.
17. *American Poetry Observed: Poets on Their Work*, ed. by Joe David Bellamy. UIll. pp. xi + 313. £18.95.

Harriet Semmes Alexander has produced, in *American and British Poetry: A Guide to the Criticism*[18], a laudable gathering which, sensibly and purposively, has no pretensions towards comprehensiveness. She lists the criticism published between 1925 and 1978 on the works of most of the poets one would want to know about (from Chaucer onwards) which has not been collected elsewhere. Her working criteria operate to include only criticism of poems of a thousand lines or less and only criticism of an entire work, except in cases where little information is available on a given poem or where the criticism is particularly noteworthy. Alexander excludes criticism of less than four sentences and books on specific poets. The main virtue of the volume (apart from its obvious bibliographical function to list items we might easily have missed) is that it enables the reader to determine very easily the degree of attention received by each poem during the period it covers. In addition to attending to the work of the major American poets (John Ashbery, John Berryman, Anne Bradstreet, Hart Crane, e. e. cummings, Emily Dickinson, H.D., T. S. Eliot, Robert Frost, Allen Ginsberg, Henry Wadsworth Longfellow, Robert Lowell, Archibald MacLeish, Marianne Moore, Charles Olson, George Oppen, Ezra Pound, Wallace Stevens, Walt Whitman, William Carlos Williams, and Louis Zukofsky), Alexander includes the poems of several figures who do not customarily appear on the curriculum: Henry Adams, William Cullen Bryant, and Thomas Pynchon, for example.

There remains, one supposes, a kind of need for collections of essays by several hands on standard, general topics, and Herbie Butterfield, in *Modern American Poetry*,[19] has edited a sturdy volume which moves chronologically to those poets who came to prominence after World War Two. Its choice of poets is (with the suggested interruptions of Robinson Jeffers and J. V. Cunningham), roughly, canonical. The reader will find matter here for any college course which follows the volume's title and, while it is slightly disappointing that the selection is not more adventurous (or more up to date), the new readings of established figures are usually profitable. The two opening essays establish nineteenth-century precursors in which Jackie Kay sustains the liberating effects of Walt Whitman's disordering of language and events, and, rather worryingly, Joseph Allard eschews issues of history as 'fruitless' on behalf of a specious argument that Emily Dickinson's poetry is 'amongst the purest in the language' in order to persuade a mystical 'communion' between reader and text whereby our isolation may be breached. Richard Gray inaugurates the volume's entry into the new century by a cleaner attention to a similar problem in which he proposes a 'kinship' (predominantly Romantic – French and American) within Wallace Stevens's characteristic solitariness. Concentrating mainly upon *Paterson*, a lively and persuasive essay by Jim Philip stresses the relationships between form, feeling, and value through William Carlos Williams's debates with his own culture. Eric Mottram, with his customary verve and interest, recharges Ezra Pound's use of the 'Great Bass', while Herbie Butterfield, in an honest and humane reclamation, promotes a correction to the 'neglect' of Robinson Jeffers. Marianne Moore's

18. *American and British Poetry: A Guide to the Criticism, 1925–1978*, by Harriet Semmes Alexander. OSU. pp. xi + 486. $46.
19. *Modern American Poetry*, ed. by R. W. (Herbie) Butterfield. Vision/B&N. pp. 239. £15.95.

concern with perception is yielded a Christian context by Michael Edwards, and Jeremy Reed inquires into Hart Crane's use of the drowned sailor to examine metaphoric and symbolic functions within the 'Cutty Sark' section of *The Bridge*. The two best essays of the volume follow each other. Andrew Crozier negotiates the complex movements between *Discrete Series* and *The Materials* to offer subtle grounds for new understandings of the discourses which constitute George Oppen's early project. Graham Clarke, in an equally exciting and donative piece, presents a sophisticated tracking of Charles Olson's seeking after a recovered creation of history. Jack Hill proposes a 'new' voice for American poetry, a 'Roman' voice of wit, poise, sadness, clarity, and shape he finds in J. V. Cunningham. The stylish and fluent prose of Gabriel Pearson reads *For Lizzie and Harriet* as Robert Lowell's 'domestic apocalypse' of writing, and Clive Meachen approaches Robert Duncan's work through the poles of mutuality and opposition. Finally, Donald Wesling locates Edward Dorn's achievement as an attempt to confront public concerns without surrendering 'the rectitude of a personal witness'.

Two important analyses of contemporary poetics which clash productively have emerged from CUP: Stephen Fredman's *Poet's Prose*[20] and Charles Altieri's *Self and Sensibility in Contemporary American Poetry*[21].

Fredman takes on a genuinely new subject. His term 'Poet's Prose' is explicitly set against 'prose poem' to describe the tendency in American writers of the twentieth century towards composing what they themselves would call 'poetry' in sentences rather than verse. The 'Crisis' of his subtitle points not to any particular moment in literary history, but to the sense that the decision to write an American poem is 'always crucial, always existential' and never merely a matter of settling upon a subject and a form. Within the dual focus of his title, Fredman takes as his *exempla* William Carlos Williams's *Kora in Hell*, Robert Creeley's *Presences*, and John Ashbery's *Three Poems* to demonstrate how Williams's deployment of the sentence as a poetic form created possibilities for the interactions of poetry, philosophy, and criticism in the work of Creeley and Ashbery. A final chapter considers those contemporary poets (David Antin, David Bromige, Ron Silliman, and Michael Davidson) who are engaged in a new mode of literary activity beyond the separation of poetry and prose altogether. This latter tendency is argued as supplying the ground for the present enlargement of epistemological concerns within American poetics and its ultimate display of 'the absolutely constitutive role language plays in the world' as language is revealed in an office that is investigative and exploratory. Fredman has written an exciting book.

Through a leisurely and graceful prose, Charles Altieri, with a subtlety that a brief review cannot begin to encompass, expresses a significant worry about both the state of contemporary poetry and the contexts in which it is appropriated – a worry about poetry's failure to play a formative role in the world and about criticism's allegiance in that failure. Altieri covers a substantial range of recent work and offers important re-assessments of Robert Creeley, John Ashbery, and Adrienne Rich in particular. His main

20. *Poet's Prose: The Crisis in American Verse*, by Stephen Fredman. CUP. pp. x + 173. £17.50.

21. *Self and Sensibility in Contemporary American Poetry*, by Charles Altieri. CUP. pp. viii + 237. £18.50.

intervention, however, is to read the institutions of poetry workshops and fellowship boards (which he takes to be symptomatic of the ways in which poetry is engineered) as analogous to the situation of French painting during the 1850s – a situation where 'skill' and 'craft' commandeered the notions of professionalism which governed both the production of artistry and the judgements upon its effects. Such aesthetic incest is an urgent cause for concern because it instigates a priority of an essentially private technical intelligence at the expense of a serious public discourse that might return literary activities to the responsibilities of non-literary, communal issues. If Fredman places too much trust in language, then Altieri similarly favours ideas. Each needs to read the other, and we need to read both.

Admirable in its own anachronistic way (and of significantly sinuous fluidity), but of an entirely different order as an interrogative event from the forays of Fredman and Altieri, is *The Modern Poetic Sequence*[22], a joint production by M. L. Rosenthal and Sally M. Gall. The authors want to draw attention to what they describe as the 'crucial genre of modern poetic art', the modern poetic sequence which for them is '*the* modern poetic form'. At one level, they trace the history of the form and its innovations. They begin with Walt Whitman and Emily Dickinson, switching to the British interventions of Thomas Hardy and W. B. Yeats, and finding the 'American Flowering' in T. S. Eliot, Ezra Pound, and William Carlos Williams. Rosenthal and Gall then essay into the 'neo-regionalist' sequences, those works of, for example, Hugh MacDiarmid, Basil Bunting, David Jones, Hart Crane, and Charles Olson, which root themselves in specific locales, before examining the 'Meditative Mode' of Wallace Stevens and W. H. Auden, the 'Confessional Mode' of, for example, Robert Lowell, John Berryman, and Sylvia Plath, and, finally, the 'Post Confessional' work of writers such as Ramon Guthrie, Ted Hughes, Galway Kinnell, H.D., and Adrienne Rich. Rosenthal and Gall intend, however, something more than a history of a form (and its subplot of reconstituting the canon). Their main interest is revealed to be in the 'essential process' of the poems, in what turns out to be the poems' 'lyrical structure', an opening-up of the lyrical possibilities of language as a resource for 'equilibrium or balance' against disorder. The call of this study, quite deliberately against virtually all critical discoveries of the past two decades (seen as a series of 'autotelic and self-adoring postures'), is thus for 'a critical method and theory congruent with and reflexive from poetic practice – a poet's poetics'. A 'cultivated empathy', a faith in the 'organic whole' and similar cardinal virtues constitute the rubric for the critic. In the search for the transcendental realizations of the lyric, questions of history and society may not raise their theoretical (and foreign) heads – or, if they do, then the search cannot be sanctified as literary criticism.

Rosenthal and Gall are, however, passionate readers, and such passion is not commonly found these days. It emerges in another form, reminiscent of Yvor Winters, in *American Poets from the Puritans to the Present*,[23] Hyatt H. Waggoner's advertisedly Emersonian account of the line of American poetry

22. *The Modern Poetic Sequence: The Genius of Modern Poetry*, by M. L. Rosenthal and Sally M. Gall. OUP (1983). pp. xiv + 508. £29.

23. *American Poets from the Puritans to the Present*, by Hyatt H. Waggoner. Rev. edn. LSU. pp. xxiv + 735. hb $30, pb $14.95.

which was first published in 1968. This revised edition is welcome, not simply because it brings the line more up to date (with discussions of Galway Kinnell, James Merrill, James Wright, W. S. Merwin, Robert Bly, John Ashbery, A. R. Ammons, and David Wagoner), but because it testifies to the possibilities, within the increasingly and deleteriously professionalized academy, for a voice which simply cares about poetry, which wants to write about poems through the sinewy grit of that care without the paraphernalia of a minutely detailed thesis. Waggoner's provocativeness and his courage in taking things on has a more enlivening effect upon the reader than any number of the scholarly volumes that distractedly clutter our desks.

David Daiches' Gifford lectures for 1983 emerge as *God and the Poets*[24], and examine the ways in which poets have approached the nature of God. His range is from the Book of Job through Milton to a variety of British poets, and includes a carefully discriminating chapter which traces the American experience from Puritanism through post-Puritanism to agnosticism via the works of Edward Taylor, Emily Dickinson, and Wallace Stevens.

As his title, *How to Read a Poem*[25], suggests, Burton Raffel has a suitably modest ambition to write a primer on the basic techniques of reading. He draws his illustrative material from both British and American poetry (including the work of John Berryman, Gregory Corso, Hart Crane, Robert Creeley, e. e. cummings, Emily Dickinson, H.D., T. S. Eliot, Robert Frost, Denise Levertov, Edgar Lee Masters, Marianne Moore, Ogden Nash, George Oppen, Kenneth Patchen, Ezra Pound, Theodore Roethke, Wallace Stevens, Diane Wakoski, William Carlos Williams, and James Wright) and produces a useful guide of sturdy common sense.

Richard Stamelman's sternly clever 'Critical Reflections: Poetry and Art Criticism in Ashbery's "Self-Portrait in a Convex Mirror" ' (*NLH*) places John Ashbery's poem alongside Francesco Parmigianino's sixteenth-century painting of the same title to argue for Ashbery's interest in portraiture as a meditation on 'difference' rather than on 'likeness'. We are then given the familiar deconstructionist posing of 'the very idea of otherness' within an aesthetic of the endlessness of interpretation, representation, and reflection that is guaranteed by the postmodernist canons of the discontinuity of the self, the fragmentariness of knowledge, and the principle of uncertainty. Less severely, in 'The Comic Thrust of Ashbery's Poetry' (*TCL*), Thomas A. Fink presents an intelligent and perceptive account of the dispersive and protean mischief of Ashbery's playfulness.

The spring issue of *TCL* includes two essays on John Berryman. In 'The Li(v)es of the Poet', Kathe Davis takes as her cue Berryman's predilection for Coleridgean 'fusing', the interpenetration of life and art, in order to berate Haffenden's biography for its omission of the second half of the equation. She then charts Berryman's biographical impulses to show how 'art permits an empathy with others that is also a means to move beyond the self'. Sarah Provost's 'Erato's Fool and Bitter Sister: Two Aspects of John Berryman' may be paired usefully with Davis's argument in that, after a persuasive exploration of the ways in which *Homage to Mistress Bradstreet* functions as 'a sublimation, idealization and redemption' of the earlier *Berryman's Sonnets*, Provost

---

24. *God and the Poets*, by David Daiches. OUP. pp. vii + 227. £19.50.
25. *How to Read a Poem*, by Burton Raffel. NAL. pp. xii + 260. pb $7.95.

concludes 'the poem is at once art *and* pure self' since in Anne Bradstreet the poet re-created images of both Lise and himself.

In '*Mont d'Espoir* or *Mount Despair*: The Re-Verses of Elizabeth Bishop' (*ConL*), Mutlu Konuk Blasing presents a supple and subtle examination of the capacity of Bishop's poetry for questioning the priority of nature, of experience over representation, to argue that 'representations counter nature: they "re-verse" the world, turn it around, and right its wrong'.

The great merit of the Columbia Introductions to Twentieth-Century American Poetry series is that its authors seem to have been chosen largely on the criteria of commitment to, and genuine feeling for, their subjects. These criteria do not elide scholarly or critical edge (one of the most useful features of Howard Nelson's *Robert Bly*[26], for instance, is its 'Chronology', compiled with the collaboration of Bly himself), but what makes each volume unfailingly interesting is, quite simply, a sense of personal excitement and energy. Bly, without a trace of sentimentality, views poetry as a 'healing process', and Nelson provides ample testimony to a poetics that values energy over technique.

Tom Chaffin's 'Toward a Poetics of Technology: Hart Crane and the American Sublime' (*SoR*) reads the 'Cape Hatteras' section of *The Bridge* as 'Whitmanian in nature and Modernist in approach', or, in other words, as symptomatic of Crane's willingness to examine the issues of modern civilization within a tradition (deriving from Whitmanian faith) of the sublime. Chaffin claims Crane as 'the poet who pushed nineteenth-century poetics as far into the twentieth century as they would reach' in order to suggest some new and productive reasons for the risks the poem takes and their inevitable 'failure'.

e. e. cummings is currently reaching print in the form of 'The Cummings Typescript Edition' of his published and unpublished writings, based upon the author's typed and autograph manuscripts under the general editorship of George James Firmage. The 166 poems included in *Etcetera*[27] (only forty-six of which have been published already) are arranged chronologically from cummings's Harvard years onward, with the exception of the very earliest verse (taken as terminating in his sophomore year) which is placed in appendixes. The volume's presentation adopts, expressively, the poet's own predilection for 'typewriter language', and the collection as a whole graphs admirably the shape of cummings's design through its new printings. *Hist Whist*[28] is a more modest affair which marks the first public appearance of twenty poems cummings had printed privately in 1962. The inclusion of line-drawings by David Calsada for each poem is a delightful addition to a charming project.

James Dickey's most recent volume, *Night Hurdling*[29], is subtitled 'Poems, Essays, Conversations, Commencements, and Afterwords'. That just about

26. *Robert Bly: An Introduction to the Poetry*, by Howard Nelson. CITAP. ColU. pp. xl + 261. $26.

27. *Etcetera: The Unpublished Poems of E. E. Cummings*, ed. by George James Firmage and Richard S. Kennedy. Liveright (1983). pp. xiii + 188. hb $16.95, pb $7.95.

28. *Hist Whist and Other Poems for Children*, by e. e. cummings, ed. by George James Firmage. Liveright (1983). Unpaginated. £11.95.

29. *Night Hurdling: Poems, Essays, Conversations, Commencements, and Afterwords*, by James Dickey. B Clark (1983). pp. xi + 356. $19.95.

covers its range of some twenty years' variousness in the world of letters, beginning with a view of a Blowgunner in the swamps and ending with a Commencement Address to Pitzer College. Dickey's literary discussions move from the familiar (Ezra Pound, Robert Penn Warren, Scott Fitzgerald (as a poet), Jack London, and Vachel Lindsay) to the less widely read (Thomas Boyd and Joe Simmons), and he has expressive things to say about infrared photography, cars, fishing, and courage. The most substantial parts of the collection are given over to his own views on poetry (interspersed with some fascinating comments on the composition of *Deliverance* and on its filming), and although 'The G.I. Can of Beets, the Fox in the Wave, and the Hammers over Open Ground' presents what is probably his most sustained notion of poetics, it is in the series of interviews which are reprinted here that he reveals his sense of writing most trenchantly.

At last, we have H.D.'s work in the form of a volume of *Collected Poems*[30]. Gathered here are the volumes which have been long out of print (*Collected Poems* of 1925 and *Red Roses for Bronze* of 1931), plus (most usefully of all, and surprising in their extent) her uncollected and unpublished poems (written mainly during the 1930s) and the *Trilogy* of 1944. This collection will instigate widespread serious recognition of the importance of a body of poetry that, customarily, has been considered predominantly only in relation to that of the more familiar modernists. Here is work produced on the 'tight-rope', in a telling phrase from Louis L. Martz's excellent introduction, 'at the seething junction of opposite forces'. The publication of this volume registers a genuinely major event in the history of twentieth-century poetry. Adalaide Morris, in 'The Concept of Projection: H.D.'s Visionary Powers' (*ConL*), energetically reads H.D.'s world as a 'projective universe' of immanence and immediacy.

T. S. Eliot has been well served this year by two attentive monographs. The first substantial biography of the poet, Peter Ackroyd's *T. S. Eliot: A Life*[31], ends its acknowledgements on a familiarly forlorn note: 'I am forbidden by the Eliot estate to quote from Eliot's published work, except for purposes of fair comment in a critical context, or to quote from Eliot's unpublished work or correspondence.' The intellectual (and probably other) parsimony of the Eliot estate is one of the disgraces of contemporary letters, and Ackroyd, given the nature of his project, must suffer from it more than most. It is instructive that Faber and Faber are not the English publishers of the present work. Nevertheless, Ackroyd is a first-rate researcher and his finely written, perceptive biography is a worthy addition to the supportive material we need in order to read his subject. With agility and tact, he negotiates the difficult (particularly so in Eliot's case) entanglement of the poetry and what we know of the man, revealing himself as an alert, sensitive reader and a discriminating historian. Ronald Bush's *T. S. Eliot: A Study in Character and Style*[32] has been antici- pated with eagerness, an eagerness which is amply satisfied by a splendid book. Bush has written a wisely perceptive and richly informative account of Eliot's movement from the charged drama of *The Waste Land* to the deferred

30. *H.D. Collected Poems 1912–1944*, ed. by Louis L. Martz. ND. pp. xxxvi + 629. $35.

31. *T. S. Eliot: A Life*, by Peter Ackroyd. S&S. pp. 400. £12.50.

32. *T. S. Eliot: A Study in Character and Style*, by Ronald Bush. OUP. pp. xiii + 287. £17.50.

immediacy of *Four Quartets*. His strategy is to chart a simultaneous rejection of received form and an urgency of repression: the result is one of the most productive considerations of the shared arena between 'character' and 'style' that we have. Bush's learning is sympathetic and wide-ranging in its project to display how the two poles of his inquiry belong to a relationship not of causality but of contiguity in which each is structured by the other. Such a perspective allows him to recast the infamous red herring of 'impersonality' as a potency not of 'feeling and intellect working hand-in-glove' but of 'powerful emotion held in powerful check'. Bush is a critic who is always rewarding, not only because of his firm mingling of sensitivity and scholarship, but because he creates a persistent sense of wanting to know how a text gets to be as it is and because he is rigorously sceptical (it is especially pleasing to find here, for example, one's distrust of the 'English' Eliot confirmed). The sweep of this book's perception and understanding renders it as one of the few places from which to begin reading Eliot with confidence.

Two essays chart differing modes of appropriating Eliot. Bernard Bergonzi, in 'Leavis and Eliot: the long road to rejection' (*CritQ*), tracks the changing pattern of F. R. Leavis's attitude towards Eliot, while Hyatt H. Waggoner's 'Eliot as Poet' (*SR*) is a reclamation of Eliot without the apparatus of scholarly exegesis in response to Eliot's demotion by the 'new romanticism' of the 1970s. Eleanor Cook's 'The Senses of Eliot's Salvages' (*EIC*) is a delicate tracing of the associative powers to be derived from Eliot's title in order to argue that not only do they 'enrich our sense of different kinds of journeying' but that they are also self-descriptive and persuade us to reflect upon language's denotative force. Of course, the probing of Eliotic sources continues in *N&Q*: Patrick Diskin's 'Eliot, Dickens, and *The Waste Land*' locates the lady's surroundings in 'A Game of Chess' in *Dombey and Son*, while Ruth Barton's 'T. S. Eliot's Secret Garden' proposes Frances Hodgson Burnett's *The Secret Garden* as a context for the rose garden imagery in *Four Quartets* and *The Family Reunion*, and C. J. Ackerley's 'Eliot's *The Waste Land* and Shackleton's *South*' presents a rather thin tracking of implications behind Eliot's borrowing of the hooded figure.

William Faulkner's *Vision in Spring*[33] consists of a sequence of fourteen love poems written in 1921 and is published here for the first time to the accompaniment of a scholarly introduction by Judith L. Sensibar, a list of known versions of the poems in the sequence, and selected photographs and photocopies of surviving fragments in their typescript form. Sensibar offers the sequence as 'the pivotal work in Faulkner's self-apprenticeship' and as 'revolutionary to his own development'. Her scholarship is exemplary, and she provides a firm account of the poem's significance for the fiction, but many may feel that, indispensable as this volume will be for the specialist, the poems themselves are unlikely to have much vitality beyond the footnotes of literary history.

The adjective 'playful', borrowed from Robert Frost himself, usefully and expressively instigates the governing evaluative vocabulary of William H. Pritchard's *Frost: A Literary Life Reconsidered*[34]. When Frost noted that 'I have made a life study of what I can say', he implied, as Pritchard recognizes,

33. *Vision in Spring*, by William Faulkner, intro. by Judith L. Sensibar. UTex. pp. xlvi + 88. $14.95.

34. *Frost: A Literary Life Reconsidered*, by William H. Pritchard. OUP. pp. xix + 286. £14.95.

that most modernist of Emersonian commitments to the 'hieroglyphic' of human thought and action. Frost's own term for this commitment is, perhaps, 'guessing', and it is a term which is established as a premise for Pritchard's fine study. Elegantly and acutely, Pritchard shocks (again a Frostian indicator) biography and poetry into a productive arena that resists the easy matchings which usually deaden such an enterprise, and engenders a convincing picture of a difficult life and a difficult art by agile disharmony. Somewhat less lively is Dorothy Judd Hall's *Robert Frost: Contours of Belief*[35], which tracks, thematically rather than chronologically, an argument for Frost's religiosity in an attempt to rescue the poet from Yvor Winters's charge of 'spiritual drifter' without consigning his spiritual impulses to forms of sectarian narrowness. She finds the core of Frost's religious sensibility in acts of '*converting* experience into poetry', claiming the consciousness of design in the poetry to be 'a synecdochic expression of his faith in the possibility of universal form and meaning'. The strength of Hall's case lies in her stress on design as a *made* form: for Frost, there existed a parallel between God and poet as *makers* wherein poetic metaphors were conceived as performing a 'sacred' activity by their very capacity for manufacture. In 'Water Music: Wordsworth, MacDiarmid, and Frost' (*SoR*) Harvey Oxenhorn focuses mainly upon Hugh MacDiarmid, but reads Frost as belonging to an arena (shared with Wordsworth) formed by a blending of political sympathy and a feeling for nature. As part of a special issue on 'The Interrelation of Interpretation and Creation' in *NLH*, Norman N. Holland's 'The Brain of Robert Frost' argues that 'interpretation' and 'creation' are virtually synonymous since both are acts of 'building' by a personal style. Following the work of the computer scientist William T. Powers, Holland claims the brain which constructs such style is 'a series of feedbacks in hierarchies in which higher loops set standards for lower loops', and on the basis of this way of looking at things, we can think of identity as 'permeating and setting the top level in a hierarchy of feedbacks' and so 'gain a way of imagining the relation between a personal style and the codes or rules or competencies or interpretive communities within which it operates'. Frost is in there, somewhere.

In 'Randall Jarrell: The Paintings in the Poems' (*SoR*) Jeffrey Meyers examines those poems of Jarrell's inspired by specific paintings: 'The Knight, Death, and the Devil' (by Durer's 'Knight, Death and Devil'), 'Jerome' (by Durer's 'St Jerome Penitent in the Wilderness' and 'St Jerome by the Pollard Willow'), and 'The Old and the New Masters' (by La Tour's 'St Sebastian Tended by Irene' and van der Goes' 'Nativity'). The poems are read to illustrate Jarrell's deployment of themes from those two of his major mentors who also shared an interest in the poetic uses of the visual arts, Auden and Rilke, the 'modern' themes of 'the loss of faith, the indifference to suffering, and the transcendent power of art'.

A new series, American Poets in Profile, presents a very useful format for promoting the discussion of less well-known contemporary poets. Michael Waters's editing of a volume on John Logan, *Dissolve to Island*[36], reprints selected poems from *Only the Dreamer Can Change the Dream*, *The Bridge of*

35. *Robert Frost: Contours of Belief*, by Dorothy Judd Hall. OhioU. pp. xxvi + 148. $23.95.
36. *Dissolve to Island: on the Poetry of John Logan*, ed. by Michael Waters. American Poets in Profile. F-B. pp. 151. pb $9.95.

Change, and *Manhattan Movements* alongside two biographical essays by Marvin Bell and Dennis Schmitz, a substantial bibliography of primary and secondary works, a series of expressive photographs, and a number of critical essays in which Peter Makuck discusses the themes of bridging, change, and transformation in Logan's work, Anthony Petrosky argues for his 'continually enlarging brotherhood or community of love and grace', Tama Baldwin examines Logan's sense of language, and David Wojahin reads the poems on literary figures as strategies for the 'personal'. The volume presents a good introduction to Logan, and it is to be hoped that its format will be repeated on behalf of other poets of similar stature.

What punningly fascinates Mark Rudman in *Robert Lowell: An Introduction to the Poetry*[37] is 'how well Lowell could weave his words out of the fibers of the world', and the story he tells is of Lowell's poetic weaving through the relations between childhood, landscape, language, and imagination. Rudman sets out to cover this weaving as a poet rather than as a scholar, and although his prose can veer towards the purple, it produces one of the most stimulating readings we have of Lowell. In the same Columbia series, Judith Moffett's *James Merrill: An Introduction to the Poetry*[38] has a more measured, academic voice, but perhaps the particular difficulties of Merrill are best approached through this form of distance. Most usefully of all, Moffett casts a clear eye upon the notorious sequence of *The Changing Light at Sandover*.

The summer/fall issue of *TCL* is devoted to Marianne Moore under the guest editorship of Andrew J. Kappel. It reprints her review of *Harmonium*, 'Well Moused, Lion' from *The Dial* of January 1924, and publishes a late manuscript version of 'An Octopus'. The editor's carefully discriminating introductory essay, 'The Achievement of M.M.', locates her place among the major Modernists (Eliot, Stevens, Williams, and Pound), establishes her 'greatest theme' as 'the relationship between the imagination and morality', and offers some explanations for her 'relative neglect' within the body of critical judgement which establishes the tradition of modern American and British literature. Bonnie Costello's 'M.M. and Elizabeth Bishop: Friendship and Influence' documents 'one of the most abiding and significant literary friendships in either woman's career', while Arthur Gregor's ' "Omissions are not Accidents": Reminiscences' tracks the beginnings of his own association with Moore in 1966–7. Celeste Goodridge, in 'Private Exchanges and Public Reviews: M.M.'s Criticism of William Carlos Williams', displays the private uneasiness Moore felt about Williams's work, an uneasiness that had been masked by her public reviews. Grace Schulman, in 'M.M. and E. McKnight Kauffer: Two Characteristic Americans', finds the poet united with the painter through 'a kind of American adventurousness and control that brought curiosity to its furthest reaches and most staggering dangers and risks'. An illuminating examination of Moore's return to the syllabically measured stanza during the 1930s as part of her modernist urge to demythologize traditional notions of poetry is provided by Margaret Holley in 'The Model Stanza: The Organic Origin of Moore's Syllabic Verse'. The 'myth' of Taffy Martin's title, 'Portrait

37. *Robert Lowell: An Introduction to the Poetry*, by Mark Rudman. CITAP. ColU (1983). pp. xxvi + 205. $26.50.

38. *James Merrill: An Introduction to the Poetry*, by Judith Moffett. CITAP. ColU. pp. xxiv + 247. $26.

of a Writing Master: Beyond the Myth of M.M.', is the view of Moore as 'a decorative oddity rather than as an active, perhaps even dangerous force' which Martin revises by an extensive use of unpublished letters documenting Moore's preparation for a career as poet and critic. Similarly extensive use of unpublished material from the Rosenbach Library is made by Lisa M. Steinman in 'Modern America, Modernism, and M.M.' in order, energetically and productively, to place Moore within the context of modernism's preoccupations (particularly in their American forms) with science and technology. Ralph Rees's 'The Reality of Imagination in the Poetry of M.M.' is a rather ordinary essay whose substance is adequately glossed by its title. In 'The Road to Paradise: First Notes on M.M.'s "An Octopus"' Patricia C. Willis records Moore's trip to Paradise Park in July 1922, examines the first extant version of 'An Octopus' (which is usefully reproduced at the end of her essay), and analyses its major set of images – Mt Rainier and the references to Greece. Willis's meticulous scholarship through Moore's notebooks renders her account of the poem the most substantial we have. One of the most impressive essays on Moore for some time is John M. Slatin's ' "Advancing Backward in a Circle": M.M. as (Natural) Historian' which reads 'Half Deity', 'Smooth Gnarled Crape Myrtle', 'Virginia Britannia', and 'Bird Witted' within the traditions of the American innocent eye and English Romanticism where, radically, he advances convincing testimony to Moore's historical sense. Vivienne Koch, in 1948, was the last to examine Moore's work through a fabulist tradition, and Bruce Ross's 'Fables of the Golden Age: The Poetry of M.M.' resurrects that tradition to display it as a subsequently neglected and expressive arena for a consideration of her poetry. Along similar lines, but within a more confined perspective, Rosalie Sprout, in 'After *The Fables*: The Translator as Poet', concentrates upon Moore's again rather neglected translations of La Fontaine and stresses the impact this nine years of work had on the later poetry. Finally, Stanley Lourdeaux's 'M.M. and a Psychoanalytic Paradigm for the Dissociated Image' acutely compares an early published poem, 'Peter', with the unpublished 'A Tiger' to show how Moore's speaker 'establishes a distinctly new relation to the animal subject as a significant Other', thereby providing for a shift in the speaker's relation to her readers in which 'both cat and readers may be tolerated as separate, free, and potentially aggressive'.

Ogden Nash's daughters, Linell Smith and Isabel Eberstadt, have selected over four hundred of his poems for *I Wouldn't Have Missed It*[39], the most complete collection to date which also contains an introduction by Anthony Burgess and sixteen of Nash's own previously unpublished line-drawings. The selectors have dealt with the problem of Nash's constant revisions by using the latest published version of each poem, all of which, with a few exceptions, are itemized in the notes at the end of the volume.

Eleanor Berry's 'Language Made Fluid: The Grammetrics of George Oppen's Recent Poetry' (*ConL*) is a clever and careful analysis of Oppen's experiments with syntax, punctuation, lineation, and line-grouping to argue that 'what is objectified in Oppen's recent poetry are the very processes by which language makes and unmakes meaning'.

---

39. *I Wouldn't Have Missed It: Selected Poems of Ogden Nash*, sel. by Linell Smith and Isabel Eberstadt, intro. by Anthony Burgess. Deutsch (1983). pp. xxiv + 407. £9.95.

Adam J. Sorkin's 'An Interview with Robert Pinsky' (*ConL*) is as unremarkable as its title.

The Ezra Pound industry continues to boom, and beyond any question, the most significant event for the year (and, indeed, for several years) is the publication of new letters from Pound's formative period, *Ezra Pound and Dorothy Shakespear: Their Letters*[40] magnificently edited by Omar Pound and A. Walton Litz. Since I have already reviewed the volume elsewhere (*THES*, 15 March 1985), I should like to stress here that its obvious importance for any consideration of Pound's early aesthetics should not overshadow its parallel focus on Dorothy Shakespear herself, whose paintings warrant signally more attention than that which is customarily accorded in footnotes to modernist poetry.

It seems somehow impertinent to 'review' the revised edition of Donald Gallup's marvellous *Ezra Pound: A Bibliography*[41], particularly within the limited space afforded by *YWES*, so let us be content with statistics. The new version lists additionally twenty-six items of books and pamphlets by Pound, fifty-three items of books and pamphlets contributed to or edited by him, ninety-nine contributions to periodicals, seventeen items of leaflets and broadsides, seventeen items of musical settings, and five readings. New categories list one item of a foreign edition of Pound's work (in Chinese) and eleven items of books contracted for but not published. Gallup's intellectual generosity is acknowledged in virtually every critical study of Pound, and for those whose subject falls beyond his ambit, Gallup's scholarship must stand as a model which most can aspire only to envy. His bibliography is a volume that no student of modernism may leave absent from the personal shelf.

In 1906 Pound and William Carlos Williams received their respective degrees from the University of Pennsylvania. In 1981 Daniel Hoffman organized a distinguished conference to celebrate the seventy-fifth anniversary of the event and collected its papers as *Ezra Pound and William Carlos Williams*[42], thereby adding a lively and valuable permanence to that celebration. Papers by Hugh Kenner and by Emily Mitchell Wallace examine the poets' student days. Ronald Bush finds in the *Homage to Sextus Propertius* a 'rejuvenating power of the Orphic imagination'. Papers by Michael Harper and Wendy Stallard Flory approach the problems of Pound's politics: Harper argues that Pound's linguistic commitment was to a language whose function was ultimately to record rather than to create, and that this commitment informs the dogmatism that led to fascism, while Flory poses the complex self-deception of Pound's antisemitism. Denise Levertov gracefully attends to the openness of Williams by reading 'A Morning Imagination of Russia' as a 'parable' of Williams's poetic struggles during the 1920s within the perspective that 'there are many more "ideas" in "things" than he is commonly credited with'. The question of openness also concerns Paul Christensen who sees in it a movement from modernism to postmodernism as Williams, under the impact of World War Two and the European emigrations of the 1930s and 1940s, shifted

40. *Ezra Pound and Dorothy Shakespear: Their Letters: 1909–1914*, ed. by Omar Pound and A. Walton Litz. ND. pp. xv + 399. $37.50.

41. *Ezra Pound: A Bibliography*, by Donald Gallup. Virginia (1983). pp. xiv + 548. $30.

42. *Ezra Pound and William Carlos Williams*, ed. by Daniel Hoffman. PSU (1983). pp. xx + 247. $27.50.

from objectivism to the variable foot. Theodora R. Graham skilfully uses Williams's relationship with Marcia Nardi at the level of friendship rather than 'influence' to examine his conception of *Paterson*, and James Laughlin employs items from the Pound–Williams correspondence to assay the connections and disconnections between the two friends. The volume usefully concludes with Neda M. Westlake's carefully descriptive listing of memorabilia and the letters from both poets to various recipients held by the University of Pennsylvania.

The UMI Research Press series on Pound (and, indeed, on other major modernists) under the alert editorship of George Bornstein is rapidly becoming an important repository of materials and ideas. The best monograph so far is Jo Brantley Berryman's exegesis of *Hugh Selwyn Mauberley* in *Circe's Craft*.[43] Since I have reviewed this book elsewhere (*JAmS*), suffice it to say here that Berryman extends, brilliantly, the issues of the *Mauberley* sequence into Pound's entire London period. This is, quite simply, one of the most detailed and intelligent studies we have of his poetics prior to his final 'farewell' to England. Berryman's scholarship is agile and substantial, and her reading of the sequence as a tactic of rich and complex irony engenders a welcome freshness on its behalf to maintain a productive dissociation of Mauberley and Pound himself. As an added bonus, her study concludes with a printing of the poem's typescript form.

Pound devoted more research to Sigismondo Malatesta than to any comparable figure in the *Cantos*, and Peter D'Epiro's *A Touch of Rhetoric*[44] provides a detailed explication of that research from Pound's voluminous manuscript drafts and notes to produce the most extensive treatment available of the Malatesta sequence. Rigorously, the author documents the historical and historiographical background of the sequence and its complicated, much revised process of composition in order to trace its stylistic and thematic implications on behalf of the rest of Pound's works. The value of this study lies in the scrupulousness and comprehensiveness of its research, revealing D'Epiro as a first-rate textual scholar. Less useful, because less novel, are his general claims for the sequence's importance: its registration of stylistic innovation 'from the epic stateliness of the earlier cantos to a predominantly colloquial diction and tone', and its embodiment of a major 'type' in Pound's poetry, that of the 'outsider'. Nevertheless, D'Epiro has given one of the most comprehensive accounts of Pound's mind in action that I have seen.

Pound's life-long interest in translation as a 'process of transformation or metamorphosis or renewal of self' instigates Ron Thomas's cue for *The Latin Masks of Ezra Pound*[45]. His study focuses upon Pound's struggle to 'be at home with himself in his otherness', and, despite a stylistic predilection for lyrical overkill, Thomas ably recharts Pound's negotiations of Catullus, Propertius, Ovid, and Horace as synecdoches for the progress of his poetic maturity. These figures are also revealed as fields of resistance to Virgil, and most productive in Thomas's thesis is his reworking of the accepted view of the

43. *Circe's Craft: Ezra Pound's 'Hugh Selwyn Mauberley'* by Jo Brantley Berryman. Studies in Modern Literature. UMIRes (1983). pp. xii + 245. £33.50.

44. *A Touch of Rhetoric: Ezra Pound's Malatesta Cantos*, by Peter D'Epiro. Studies in Modern Literature. UMIRes (1983). pp. xxiii + 158. £29.50.

45. *The Latin Masks of Ezra Pound*, by Ron Thomas. Studies in Modern Literature. UMIRes (1983). pp. xvi + 180. £29.50.

Virgilian model in Pound's work to suggest 'the poetic father whom the son could not love freely and fully without first disobeying', a form of antimask whose achievement had to be repressed in order to create space for Pound's own epic.

A work of, predominantly, exegesis such as Guy Davenport's analysis of Pound's first thirty cantos in *Cities on Hills*[46], inevitably carries a danger of imprisonment by the history of its own state of knowledge, especially when it is first published some twenty-two years after its original composition and, apart from a new five-page introduction which only gestures towards the subsequent research of others, refuses to incorporate any of the massive amount of scholarship produced by that research. Nevertheless, Davenport's graceful and humane wisdom proves abundantly that exegesis, properly handled, moves far beyond the anaesthetized comfort of mere sources which so tames the production of literary criticism. Drawing his impulse from the investigations into iconography and comparative form by Ruskin and, later, Panofsky and Frye, Davenport concentrates upon the ideogram as the inventive, exploratory, uncompromising 'new form of the imagination' which organizes the poem's subject-matter (the emergence and decline of civilized states) in terms of what he calls its 'moral crunch', 'the uncaring'. Particularly noteworthy is Davenport's positing of the 'rule' of the *Cantos*: 'In every subject to be treated, choose the matter which most perversely exemplifies it.' The rule is a good one in so far as its violence creates possibilities for the reader's interrogations of the poem's values, and a bad one at those moments when it tyrannizes its manipulator – it is then that perversity ceases to be strategic, and 'much in the poem that rings false can be traced to this simple rule'.

Philip Furia's *Pound's Cantos Declassified*[47] would not have made it into the UMI series. He attends to the so-called 'unpoetic' elements of Pound's epic, those constituted by historical documents which, for Pound himself, had been suppressed and required renewal on behalf of contemporary urgencies. Furia's material is, thus, largely familiar, following a chronology from Malatesta to Sir Edward Coke and Joseph Rock. His story has little that is new to offer either on Pound's historicism or his poetic technique. Furia uncovers no fresh material, nor is he sufficiently familiar with the recent more interrogative trend in Pound criticism whose sophistication might have provided the subtlety of theoretical perspectives his subject needs.

In the realm of the journals, *Paideuma* continues to be the font of specialized work on Pound. Present exigencies of space preclude a complete narrative of the three issues which appear annually, particularly since it is a familiar location, and so the reviewer would like to permit himself the (dangerous) luxury of suggesting the following articles as being among the most noteworthy (in order of publication): James J. Wilhelm, 'On the Trail of the "One" Crawfordsville Incident or, The Poet in Hoosierland'; Colin McDowell, ' "As Towards a Bridge Over Worlds": The Way of the Soul in *The Cantos*'; John Cayley, 'Ch'eng or Sincerity'; Hwa Yol Jung, 'Misreading the Ideogram: From Fenollosa to Derrida and McLuhan'; and Peter Faulkner, 'Pound and the Pre-Raphaelites'. Elsewhere, the paternally benign Donald Davie, in 'The

46. *Cities on Hills: A Study of I–XXX of Ezra Pound's Cantos*, by Guy Davenport. Studies in Modern Literature. UMIRes (1983). pp. xviii + 275. £33.50.

47. *Pound's Cantos Declassified*, by Philip Furia. PSU. pp. x + 153. £16.95.

Critics Who Made Us – Ezra Pound' (*SR*), commenting mainly on the 1918 essay 'The Hard and Soft in French Poetry', sturdily employs Pound to locate a contemporary 'pressing need' for a critic who 'cuts the critic down to size'. Ian F. A. Bell's 'A Marginality of Context: Dobson's Gautier and Pound's Mauberley' (*AN&Q*) renders the marginality of Austin Dobson's mediation of the Gautier Pound used in *Hugh Selwyn Mauberley* as an index to Pound's ironic critique of contemporary letters. M. L. Rosenthal asks 'Is There a Pound–Williams Tradition?' (*SoR*) to suggest overtly that the positing of such a 'tradition' inscribes too parochial a field. Again, however, in line with the argument of the book he recently co-authored with Sally M. Gall, *The Modern Poetic Sequence* (see p. 610), Rosenthal's principal position is to maintain a case for the 'individual voice' and for the 'lyric' as 'the clear tendency of our greatest poetry'.

The winter issue of *SAQ* is devoted to Pound, taking, mainly, a selection of the papers presented to the Ezra Pound Conference held at the University of Sheffield in 1981. In 'Imagism and Irony: The Shaping of the International Style' William Pratt takes his cue from Baudelaire, adding 'Pound the Ironist' to 'Pound the Imagist' to construct 'Pound the Internationalist' and hence 'the Father of Modernism in English Poetry'. Jo Brantley Berryman's 'Mauberley, Logopoeia, and the Language of Modernism' also attends to the question of Pound's irony, but in a much more sophisticated manner, extending it from the untrustworthy critical voices within *Hugh Selwyn Mauberley* to the situation of the reader. This excellent essay, in a slightly different form, is included in her *Circe's Craft* (see p. 619), but it deserves, fully, separate regard. Equally excellent in terms of its range, density of argument, and scrupulousness of scholarship is Richard Sieburth's 'Dada Pound', a real *tour de force* which attends to the relatively little regarded period of Pound's years in Paris during the early 1920s as part of his protracted search for the 'Beginning' of the cantos, a search which is revealingly read within the European issues of Dada. This essay rests easily among the high-points of the year's work on Pound. A worthy addition to the growing attention regarding the 'missing' Cantos LXXII and LXXIII is 'The Poet at War: Ezra Pound's Suppressed Italian Cantos' where Massimo Bacigalupo finds exposed the limitations of Pound's approach as 'aesthetic traveller' and his impermeability to historical consciousness. A. G. Woodward's 'Pound and Santayana' productively compares the poet and philosopher to examine the interaction between contemplative and active ideals of life. In ' "The Fulsomeness of her Prolixity": Reflections on "H.D., Imagiste" ' Brendan Jackson examines H.D.'s reputation for 'ruthless pruning, for a relentless artistic conscience' to suggest that on the evidence of the 'expansive subjectivity' revealed in the less familiar of her works, it is a reputation that warrants re-examination. The concluding essay (which was not presented at Sheffield) by Ben D. Kimpel and T. C. Duncan Eaves, 'The Intentional-Fallacy Fallacy and Related Contemporary Orthodoxies', is an unfortunate sign of the times. It takes to task recent work that, informed by Lacan and Derrida, has the temerity to be sceptical about 'what the poet intended to say'. There is a growing move among a small group of scholarly writings on Pound to develop more rigorous and sophisticated modes of critical debate than those presented by traditional 'lit. crit.', but in the face of the kind of opposition symptomatically graphed by Kimpel and Eaves, their efforts to restore Pound to an available history are falling on wilfully deaf ears.

It is a debilitating paradox that the most radical of poetic innovators should continue to be appropriated by the most anachronistic of critical discourses.

An invaluable archive is being constituted by The Riverside Interviews series, represented here in the handling of *Jerome Rothenberg*[48] by Gavin Selerie and Eric Mottram. The volume contains two extended discussions ('interviews' is too bland a term for their energies and, indeed, for the performative nature of Rothenberg's work as a whole) between the poet and the editors, a transcript of Rothenberg's talk at San Diego in May 1983 on 'Innovation and Disruption as Ritual Modes', a bibliography of primary and secondary materials, and a series of illuminating photographs. After watching the poetry, readers would be well advised to begin here.

In *Wallace Stevens and the Idealist Tradition*[49] Margaret Peterson begins by reading Stevens's prose through the Romantic debates of the nineteenth century where, via Coleridge and Kant, the art–science antithesis is seen as conditional for Stevens's epistemology of the imagination. Croce, Richards, Bergson, Santayana, and, in particular, William James, are then invoked as a continuation of the philosophical tradition which attempts to salvage reality from a despiritualized world. *Harmonium*, *Ideas of Order*, and 'Notes Toward a Supreme Fiction' are taken as illustrations from Stevens's early and late phases in order to argue that the obscurities of the works may best be explicated through the lens of his philosophical interests. Peterson has an impressive understanding of philosophy and aesthetics, and is usefully sceptical of urges to seek forms of resolution through their interaction. Her study presents what is probably the first sustained attempt to read Stevens within an epistemological context, but its value is inevitably reduced by a failure to acknowledge anything that has been written since its composition in 1965.

The aphorism, for Beverly Coyle's clever book *A Thought to be Rehearsed*[50] is the basic unit of Stevens's expression and it is to be understood not so much as a rhetoric of content but as a rhetoric of formulation. Indeed, although Coyle seems unwilling to take on the point fully, Stevens may be seen at his most effective in those tensions between the sense of finality and stability instigated by the centripetal office of formulation (Coyle's main interest) and the sense of uncertainty with regard to the meaning of content. Within Stevens's poetics, the poem stands as what Coyle terms a 'momentary agreement' between a changing reality and a changing imaginative awareness, and it is here that the aphorism finds its role within a range of styles 'for the purpose of finding the most adequate means of embedding ideas in a poetic context'. The shift Coyle plots is from the bravura and riddle-like posture of Stevens's early aphorisms to their predicative, directly assertive role in the later poetry, by which time they serve as a model for the process of thinking itself. Here, aphorisms assume a double function:

> As initiating statements producing an authoritative effect, aphorisms give the reader a sense that the poetic experience begins with thought

48. *Jerome Rothenberg*, ed. by Gavin Selerie and Eric Mottram. The Riverside Interviews 4. Binnacle. pp. 96. pb £3.95.

49. *Wallace Stevens and the Idealist Tradition*, by Margaret Peterson. Studies in Modern Literature. UMIRes. pp. ix + 189. £29.50.

50. *A Thought to be Rehearsed: Aphorism in Wallace Stevens' Poetry*, by Beverly Coyle. Studies in Modern Literature. UMIRes (1983). pp. ix + 120. £29.50.

and retains an anchor in it. As parts of a compendium, taken in context with their respective cantos and in interaction with each other, aphorisms also provide a simulacrum of the process of moving from thought to feeling – from abstraction to pleasure.

In *Wallace Stevens and Company*[51] Glen G. MacLeod, rightly, wants to dispel the myth of Stevens's isolationism. He proceeds via an examination of Stevens's most 'experimental' decade which, he argues, marked the period of Stevens's closest involvement with other writers and artists. MacLeod begins with a consideration of Stevens's association in 1913–15 with what he calls the 'Patagonians' (Donald Evans, Allen and Louise Norton, Carl Van Vechten) and a general account of Stevens's affiliations with the avant-garde in New York from 1914–15 onwards. He then focuses upon Stevens's most productive connections with individual writers until the publication of *Harmonium* (Walter Arensberg, Eugene Emmanuel Lemercier, Evans, and William Carlos Williams). The author would not pretend 'answers' to one of the abiding questions for Stevens scholarship, the extraordinary rapidity of his poetic maturation during the early years of this decade, but his careful and perceptive analysis of Stevens's 'Company' certainly provides a fecund context in which that question may be freshly grounded. MacLeod charts his story with clarity and tact.

Some continuities and discontinuities between Victorian and modern poetry are found in 'The Ancient and the Modern Sage: Tennyson and Stevens' (*VP*) where Joseph Carroll examines the ways in which several of Stevens's later poems draw images and phrases from *In Memoriam*, 'The Ancient Sage', and 'Demeter and Persephone'. James S. Leonard and Christine E. Wharton, in 'Wallace Stevens as Phenomenologist' (*TSLL*), impressively take issue with recent readings of Stevens through Husserl and Heidegger as unable to be accommodated within Stevens's own philosophizing. In a dense and clearly argued essay, they find Cassirer's philosophy of symbolic forms to be better suited for clarifying the relations between the aesthetic and the religious in Stevens's work as part of an argument for locating 'truth' in the image itself: 'In the consciously originated "fiction", man becomes part of the truth, partaking of the symbolic value of the structured image seen, accepted, and understood as image.'

Jefferson Humphries's 'The Cemeteries of Allen Tate and Paul Valéry: The Ghosts of Aeneas and Narcissus' (*SoR*) considers Southern comparisons between the myth of defeat and the story of the fall of Troy through Tate's self-identification with European literary strategies, comparing his 'Ode to the Confederate Dead' and Valéry's 'Le Cimetière Marin'. French connections are also considered on behalf of Richard Wilbur by R. S. Gwynn, in 'Wilbur's Techniques of Translation' (*SR*), who discusses *The Whale*, Wilbur's uncollected translations from the last three decades, and his translations of Molière (*The Misanthrope, The School for Wives, Tartuffe, The Learned Ladies*) and Racine (*Andromache*). Rather unsurprisingly, Gwynn admires Wilbur because 'he has refused to allow his own voice to overwhelm his precursors' voices'.

For some time now, there has been a campaign to reread the major poets of

51. *Wallace Stevens and Company: The Harmonium Years, 1913–1923*, by Glen G. MacLeod. Studies in Modern Literature. UMIRes (1983). pp. xii + 119. £29.25.

the century as Romantics despite their more overt modernity, and it now appears to be William Carlos Williams's turn to come under this revisionary lens in Carl Rapp's *William Carlos Williams and Romantic Idealism*[52]. Rapp is willing to propose that 'Williams more nearly resembles Emerson's idea of a poet than any other poet we have had since Emerson', and it has to be acknowledged that this particular combination has not been exactly to the forefront in previous commentaries. After examining 'The Wanderer' through Keats and Hegel, Rapp advances Williams's version of the Fall (an instrument of criticism for discerning the inadequacies of contemporary culture, their fixity) as a means of access to his 'Emersonian concept of the work of art as a sign of [mental or spiritual] power' (cf. Rapp's 'William Carlos Williams and the Modern Myth of the Fall' (*SoR*) where he opposes arguments that Williams represents a radical departure from tradition by stressing his adherence to this myth, 'that the present time is essentially unsatisfactory by comparison to the remote past and to the future and that it is so because, for the moment, we have lost an original vitality or innocence which we must struggle to regain'). Such power, throughout Williams's commitments to imagism, objectivism, and the 'new measure' of speech rhythms, is revealed for Rapp as the activity of the mind itself in the process of thinking about the world, bringing 'all things into spiritual subjection to himself', and it is this activity (as Rapp titles his final chapter, 'Thinking as Salvation') which most profoundly informs the later poetry.

It is the element of risk we find missing from Rapp's equation for Williams, but that is the element which is well caught in Roy Miki's *The Prepoetics of William Carlos Williams*[53]. In this first extended study of *Kora in Hell: Improvisations*, Miki claims it is here in 'the first modernist text wholly written and produced in America' that we see Williams at the inception of preparing himself for newness. Fruitfully, Miki bases his claim not so much on the text's ideational propositions, but on the process of its production. This process involved translating the crises in Williams's experiential and writing lives into a crisis in language by attempting to break out of the closed forms of perception he felt were imprisoning contemporary writing in general and his own in particular. Williams wrote of the material in *Others*, 'we seek the seclusion of a style, of a technique, we make replicas of the world we live in and we live in them and not in the world'; and it was to the disfiguring of such 'seclusion' that the practice of *Kora* testified as its linguistic play obliged a continual remaking in an avoidance of fixity and an honesty to the riskiness of the text's subtitle. Equally sensitive to such textual riskiness is Tony Baker, in 'The Comedian as the Letter "N": Sight and Sound in the Poetry of William Carlos' (*JAmS*), who offers a lively and alert reading of 'Della Primavera Transportata Al Morale'. Baker manipulates the discrepancies of spelling in its various printings, exposing a series of puns and jokes which he allies with Williams's commitment to the poem as an actual object which is to be regarded visually and his avoidance of fixative patterns in order to argue that the poem's project is instigatory, 'to make a poem–object that will initiate rather than imprison knowledge'.

52. *William Carlos Williams and Romantic Idealism*, by Carl Rapp. UPNE. pp. xi + 163. £17.50.

53. *The Prepoetics of William Carlos Williams: 'Kora in Hell'*, by Roy Miki. Studies in Modern Literature. UMIRes (1983). pp. xii + 207. £33.50.

There has been a growing body of serious interest in Williams's connections with the visual arts since Bram Dijkstra published *Cubism, Stieglitz and the Early Poetry of William Carlos Williams* in 1969. Christopher J. MacGowan's *William Carlos Williams' Early Poetry*[54] and William Marling's *William Carlos Williams and the Painters*[55] both attend to the same period of Williams's career from a similar perspective but with a variance of success. MacGowan has a modest ambition: to document Williams's contacts with the visual arts and to offer those contacts as informative for readings of the poetry. His study thus moves from the 1909 *Poems* and *The Tempers* in a strict chronology through to *Spring and All* via, principally, the Vorticists, Charles Demuth, Marcel Duchamp, Mardsen Hartley, Wassily Kandinsky, the Dadaists, and Juan Gris. If there is an organizing thesis to the book, it is probably that poetry and painting share a common objective by resisting convention and narrative in favour of strategies such as juxtaposition and the new areas of subject and treatment released by a concern with art's own distinctive materiality. MacGowan fulfils his ambition modestly enough, but those scholars who are familiar with the relationships he provides will have to content themselves with an efficient compilation. The visual frame of Williams's mind receives richer and wiser treatment by Marling who replaces the question of 'influences' (constituted by what Williams may, or usually may not, have read) with the question of 'circles' (constituted by friendships, particularly with Charles Sheeler, Duchamp, Demuth, Hartley, and Walter Arensberg, which always had a more enduring role in Williams's imaginative universe) in order to stress that Williams's early poetry had a concern, above all, to operate in visual terms – what Williams himself called 'pre-writing'. Marling's 'circles' render a more gracious reading than do the 'influences' that are rather tightly listed by MacGowan. His first four chapters chronicle the friendships germane to Williams's painterly interests; and, after a chapter whose title ('Sheer Paint, Sheer Poetry') points succinctly the nature of its analysis and, indeed, the central preoccupation of the poet's formative period, Marling examines the poetry of the period within the convincing rubric that 'there is, in fact, no more obvious source for Williams' shift away from the neo-Keatsian, traditionally-oriented poetry that he wrote before 1914 to the lean, rapid poetry he wrote afterward than the Arensberg Circle'.

In an excellent essay on Louis Zukofsky, 'Art And/As Labor: Some Dialectical Patterns in "A"–1 through "A"–10' (*ConL*), Burton Hatlen continues his investigations into what still remains the major issue of modernist poetry: the relationship between social and artistic views and practices. Here, Hatlen examines the conflict between aesthetic experience and political action that plays through the first ten sections of 'A' to present a perceptive, sophisticated, and most welcome display of modernist political poetry by demonstrating the poem's structural and procedural commitment to human agency within history.

A special issue of *ChiR* on 'Poetry and Politics' contains 'Conceptual Space:

54. *William Carlos Williams' Early Poetry: The Visual Arts Background*, by Christopher J. MacGowan. Studies in Modern Literature. UMIRes. pp. xvi + 160. £40.
55. *William Carlos Williams and the Painters, 1909–1923*, by William Marling. OhioU (1982). pp. ix + 224. $21.95.

The Politics of Modernism', a valuable and perceptive essay by Anthony Libby which argues 'to the extent that "spatial" can be distinguished from "temporal" form, it can be seen as supportive of liberal or progressive political visions'. Libby discusses the issue in general terms, but makes specific use of Pound, Stevens, and Williams. Three of the accompanying essays in this issue, although not geared nominatively to *American* poetry, contain important implications for its consideration: Gerald L. Bruns, 'Language and Power'; Hugh Kenner, 'The Making of the Modernist Canon'; and Marjorie Perloff, '"Violence and Precision": The Manifesto as Art Form'.

J. D. McClatchy's 'Letter from America' (*PRev*) presents an uncontroversial complaint about the state of American poetry within the confines of modernism and postmodernism, finding relief in the examples of Charles Wright, Louise Gluck, and Adrienne Rich.

3. Prose Fiction

In some ways the most challenging and startling general work on American fiction is Hershel Parker's *Flawed Texts and Verbal Icons*[56]. Parker draws on his numerous bibliographical essays to demonstrate that the texts of most American fictional classics are corrupt and unreliable. He supports this claim with detailed examinations of *Tender is the Night, The Red Badge of Courage,* and other works. His discussions level a polemic against New Critics and Structuralists alike who assume that the text is fixed and final, whereas Parker demonstrates that it is contingent on the author and vulnerable to editorial interference. Drawing on the theories of John Dewey, he argues that intentionality is built into the very processes of the text. In an examination of Mailer's revisions of *An American Dream* he even argues that the text can be vulnerable to the author and that Mailer coarsened and oversimplified his fiction. Parker's study cannot afford to be ignored.

Two surveys of American fiction have appeared. The first and most ambitious is Frederick R. Karl's *American Fictions 1940–1980*[57]. Although a number of introductory essays locate American fiction within its national literary traditions (he is interesting, for instance, on the persistence of the pastoral dream in contemporary landscapes), his simultaneous claim to be comprehensive, historical, *and* critical is frankly impossible to realize. It is gratifying to see recognition being granted at last to William Gaddis, Edward Wallant, and Rudolph Wurlitzer, but also surprising to see nothing on Paul Bowles. Karl assembles close readings of an impressively large number of novels (and his work will probably be consulted mainly for these), all broadly designed to demonstrate one of his main theses: the persistence of the original modernist impulse into contemporary American fiction. Colin Partridge's *Minor American Fiction 1920–1940*[58] is an altogether more modest undertaking but still a valuable one. Although he argues that the minor fiction of a period gives insight into its history, his survey mainly concentrates on the works themselves and inevitably contains a high proportion of summary. He

56. *Flawed Texts and Verbal Icons*, by Hershel Parker. Northwestern. pp. xix + 249. $19.95.

57. *American Fictions 1940–1980. A Comprehensive History and Critical Evaluation*, by Frederick R. Karl. Harper. pp. xiv + 637. £26.50.

58. *Minor American Fiction 1920–1940*, by Colin Partridge. Rodopi. pp. 98. Fl 25.

divides his study into subject groups which range from rural through black fiction to novels of political protest. This is a useful volume for shedding further light on several novelists currently enjoying a revival such as Zora Hurston and Anzia Yezierska, and also on the general fictional themes of the interwar period.

Two general studies have been centrally preoccupied with gender. Susan Merrill Squier has edited a collection of essays called *Women Writers and the City*[59] which concentrates extensively but not exclusively on America. S. H. Bremer argues that turn-of-the-century American women writers had a much more dominant role to play in Chicago than is generally recognized and that they tend to present the city as a continuous community, unlike their male counterparts' emphasis on alienation. Blanche Gelfant interestingly identifies a certain kind of female character, a 'generic heroine' who, in the fiction of Anzia Yezierska and others, demonstrates independence, ambition, and adventurousness. There are also essays on Ntozake Shange and Adrienne Rich. In contrast with this lively collection Peter Schwenger takes us over well-trodden ground in his *Phallic Critiques*[60]. During a general discussion of masculine styles of writing in modern literature he predictably devotes entire chapters to Hemingway and Mailer. Hemingway, we are told, establishes a 'masculine reserve' through his general distrust of talking, whereas Mailer adopts macho language as part of the psychological battles in his fiction. Schwenger also looks briefly at Philip Roth and James Dickey.

In the area of popular fiction J. Kenneth Van Dover's *Murder in the Millions*[61] examines the best-selling novels of Erle Stanley Gardner, Mickey Spillane, and Ian Fleming. This book is mainly useful for pin-pointing the formulaic nature of the series which each writer produced and which centres on one recurring figure: Gardner's Perry Mason, Spillane's Mike Hammer, and Fleming's James Bond. Character stereotyping and plot permutations are also discussed as essential factors in the success of this fiction. In *Pulp Voices*[62] Jeffrey M. Elliott edits interviews with five science fiction writers such as Jack Williamson and H. L. Gold. And also from the Borgo Press comes a history of the pulp western[63] by John A. Dinan. Dinan surveys the popular western magazine from the dime novels of the 1870s through the pulp magazines of the 1920s to the war period. By then strong competing pressure from radio, cinema, and the new comic-books forced radical changes on the pulp westerns. Dinan gives a compact but well-informed account of the main themes and patterns in this literature as well as the historical changes. In a related survey of the American literature of war (*AQ*) David Lundberg does not propose a thesis but gives a useful account of the criticism in this area from Edmund Wilson's *Patriotic Gore* onwards.

A new volume from the DLB[64] edited by Daniel Walden gives

59. *Women Writers and the City*, ed. by Susan Merrill Squier. UTenn. pp. 306. $22.95.

60. *Phallic Critiques*, by Peter Schwenger. RKP. pp. 172. £12.95.

61. *Murder in the Millions*, by J. Kenneth Van Dover. Ungar. pp. xi + 235. pb $7.95.

62. *Pulp Voices*, ed. by Jeffrey M. Elliott. Borgo (1983). pp. 64. pb $3.95.

63. *The Pulp Western*, by John A. Dinan. Borgo (1983). pp. 128. pb $5.95.

64. *Twentieth-Century American-Jewish Writers*, ed. by Daniel Walden. DLB 28. Gale. pp. xv + 367. $85.

critical/bibliographical essays on fifty-one Jewish-American novelists from such seminal figures as Abraham Cahan through the 1930s (Henry Roth, Michael Gold, etc.) to the 1960s' generation which includes Malamud and Bellow. The volume follows the general DLB pattern of combining criticism with biography and bibliography, and is a valuable and thorough survey. Two rather surprising omissions were Sholem Asch, who was prominent in keeping Yiddish literature alive, and Leo Rosten, whose Hyman Kaplan novels alone deserve mention for their comic treatment of assimilation. In his article 'Conjured Lives' (*DQR*) M. P. Woolf argues that Jewish-American fiction is a fluid and pluralistic category, so much so that Jewishness often has to be invented within the novels themselves. He notes a repeated tension between the pull of the past and the need to engage with contemporary America, and contrasts two broad methods of treating this dilemma: through nostalgia and piety (Yuri Suhl, for example) or as comedy (Philip Roth, Heller, etc.). In the same area Sam B. Girgus's *The New Covenant*[65] applies Sacvan Bercovitch's thesis that the jeremiad is the prime literary form in America, to Jewish-American writing from Louis Brandeis to Mailer and Doctorow. He shows that Jewish immigrants quickly adopted American cultural patterns and argues that contemporary novelists still draw on the jeremiad to criticize the actuality of America which constantly falls short of its stated ideals. Jewish-American writing thus constitutes a sustained challenge to these American myths. Girgus skilfully combines history, literary criticism, and cultural analysis in this account.

Overlapping with Girgus's topic, but applied in a less ethnic direction, Donald Weber focuses on the same jeremiad tradition as it figures in West, Pynchon, and Mailer (*SAQ*). After outlining the Puritan paradigm he argues that *The Day of the Locust* is an antijeremiad because it mocks rather than expresses consensus dreams. By the same token, *The Crying of Lot 49* 'holds both hope and despair in suspension' without affirming any sacred design. *The Armies of the Night* is similarly about the decline in American ideals. Robert A. Hipkiss also discusses Pynchon, this time in the company of Vonnegut and Barth in his *The American Absurd*[66]. Postwar absurdism, he suggests, demonstrates the 'disjunction between man's ideal conceptualizations and his mortal condition'. He notes the anti-institutional animus of Pynchon's works, describing them as absurd quests. In Vonnegut he finds a cycle of evolution and dissolution, whereas in Barth characters' self-consciousness leads directly to their role-playing. In *The Soft Machine*[67] David Porush (himself a practising novelist) investigates how contemporary fiction (mainly American) has responded to the machine and specifically to cybernetics. Examining works by Burroughs, Pynchon, Vonnegut, and others, he demonstrates how technology pervades their fiction, implicating the novelists in the very mechanisms they are resisting.

Turning from thematics to stylistic studies, Jerome Klinkowitz's *The Self-Apparent Word*[68] continues the argument of his earlier studies, *Literary*

65. *The New Covenant. Jewish Writers and the American Idea*, by Sam B. Girgus. UNC. pp. xi + 220. £19.95.

66. *The American Absurd*, by Robert A. Hipkiss. AFP. pp. 135. £17.25.

67. *The Soft Machine: Cybernetic Fiction*, by David Porush. Methuen. pp. xii + 244. hb £10.95, pb £4.95.

68. *The Self-Apparent Word*, by Jerome Klinkowitz. SIU. pp. 153. $14.95.

Disruptions (1975) and *The American 1960's* (1980), that a wave of experimentation over the past two decades had been producing fiction which is antimimetic and non-representational. These texts are characterized by 'self-apparent' words which draw attention to themselves as objects. Making extensive application of the theory of signs, Klinkowitz examines a number of writers who exemplify this trend – notably Donald Barthelme, Ronald Sukenick, Clarence Major, and Stephen Dixon. He simultaneously shows that practitioners of this mode are also some of its most articulate theorists. In 'The Role of Voice in Nonmodernist Fiction' (*ConL*) Douglas Messerli locates a line of non-realistic fiction which belies modernist claims to objectivity. Despite the posture, Wyndham Lewis, Gertrude Stein, and Djuna Barnes (to take only three examples) repeatedly 'intrude' in their fiction to address the reader directly. Messerli thus sets up a context for discussing the work of Gilbert Sorrentino who violates his own objectivism, turning the novel against himself; and of Walter Abish who disrupts his narratives with questions. This kind of fiction tends towards an autobiographical stance. Djuna Barnes also figures in one of the most theoretically ambitious critical works of the year – Alan Singer's *A Metaphorics of Fiction*[69]. Singer suggests that the notion of metaphor is useful for explaining how a text's meaning emerges and he chooses three novels for specific discussion (*Nightwood, Second Skin*, and *How It Is*) because Barnes, Hawkes, and Beckett have abandoned what he ponderously calls the 'hegemony of literal meaning' (here it should be remarked that the technical density of Singer's style is a real obstacle to his many insights emerging clearly). Metaphors shatter contextual limits and open up new associative possibilities (Barnes) or create contradictions which threaten the coherence of the narrative (Hawkes). In both these cases metaphorical experiments question conventional novelistic expectation.

Reprints of Edith Wharton's works have been appearing from the Virago Press, which continues to maintain a high standard in its introductions. Among others should be noted *The Children*[70] (1928) which has been comparatively neglected by the critics, and *The Fruit of the Tree*[71] (1907), both of which Marilyn French introduces. French analyses *The Children*'s main theme – a man's love for a teenage girl – which revolves around a contrast between two moral worlds, that of old New York gentility and the new outspoken freedom of the children, and she notes the prominence of political analysis and the creation of a new kind of female character in Justine Brent, in *The Fruit of the Tree*. Century have also re-issued *In Morocco*[72] (1920) as part of their series of travel reprints. This book describes a tour Edith Wharton made in 1917 with the help of the French military government. It combines travelogue with historical commentary and gives interesting impressions of Morocco on the eve of Europeanization.

Judith Fryer has examined the theme of purity in *The Age of Innocence* (*ALR*), identifying a general pattern of retreats in Edith Wharton's fiction and the repeated act of 'fixing an image of security'. Wharton shows an ambivalence towards the past and likewise towards adultery in this novel. It is argued

69. *A Metaphorics of Fiction: Discontinuity and Discourse in the Modern Novel*, by Alan Singer. UFlor. pp. xi + 183. $18.

70. *The Children*, by Edith Wharton. Virago. pp. xiii + 347. pb £3.95.

71. *The Fruit of the Tree*, by Edith Wharton. Virago. pp. xvi + 633. pb £4.95.

72. *In Morocco*, by Edith Wharton. Century. pp. 223. pb £4.95.

that Newland Archer's role is fated here because his world combines innocence with a controlling shrewdness. Nancy Morrow concentrates on *The
Custom of the Country*, taking the game as an extended metaphor of social
behaviour (*ALR*). Undine Spragg has to learn social rules but her marriages
fail. Wall Street is also presented, but as a 'world of empty and amoral gestures
and forms'. E. P. Dupree (*AL*) uses recently discovered letters to document
the friendship between Edith Wharton and Sinclair Lewis, culminating in her
congratulations on the latter's 1930 Nobel Prize. In spite of their friendship
Lewis's speech of acceptance conspicuously failed to mention Wharton among
the leading novelists of the day.

Robert Bush has written a biography of Grace King[73] (1852–1932) who was
one of the most important New Orleans writers at the turn of the century.
Indignation over George Washington Cable's betrayal (as she saw it) of the
South in *The Grandissimes* (1880) triggered off her writing career. She produced three novels: *Monsieur Motte*, 1886; *The Pleasant Ways of St. Médard*,
1916; and *La Dame de Sainte Hermine*, 1924. These together with her short
stories, essays and historical writings (she was secretary of the Louisiana
Historical Society) investigate the position of women, interracial relations,
and above all the passing of the Old South. Robert Bush, who has also edited a
selection of Grace King's works, has produced an impressively thorough
biography of a novelist who described herself modestly as just a 'Southern
woman of letters'.

Two volumes of Jack London's writings[74] have appeared in the recently
started Library of America. The first, entitled *Novels and Stories*, contains *The
Call of the Wild, White Fang, The Sea-Wolf*, and his Klondike stories. The
second, entitled *Novels and Social Writings*, includes *The People of the Abyss,
The Road, The Iron Heel, Martin Eden, John Barleycorn*, and four of
London's most famous essays. Seafarer Books have issued a photographic
reprint of the 1913 illustrated Mills & Boon edition of *The Cruise of the Snark*
and Press Pacifica have re-issued five stories about Hawaii which were only
published in book form as recently as 1965[75]. The stories date from 1907 when
London was delayed in Hawaii while the Snark underwent repairs, and deal
mainly with the lepers whom London describes sympathetically as social
outcasts. David H. Stanley briefly investigates London's biographical legend
(*ALR*) and demonstrates that London helped to promote it by projecting a
romantic myth of himself in *The Sea-Wolf, Martin Eden*, and *John Barleycorn*.
In spite of using the third person *Martin Eden* demonstrates its autobio-
graphical relevance in its central theme, the artist's role in society; and *John
Barleycorn* could best be seen as a 'self-analytic confessional'. Stanley notes
the divergences in these works from London's actual life. Gorman
Beauchamp[76] has produced an interesting pamphlet on a neglected side of
London's writings for the Starmont Reader's Guides. He examines the non-

73. *Grace King. A Southern Destiny*, by Robert Bush. LSU. pp. xv + 317. £30.
74. *Novels and Stories*, by Jack London, ed. by Donald Pizer. CUP. pp. 1040. £17.50.
Novels and Social Writings, by Jack London, ed. by Donald Pizer. CUP. pp. 1216.
£17.50.
75. *The Cruise of the Snark*, by Jack London. Seafarer. pp. 340. pb £4.50. *Jack
London's Tales of Hawaii*, intro. by Miriam Rappolt. Pacifica. pp. ix + 68. pb $3.95.
76. *Jack London*, by Gorman Beauchamp. Starmont Reader's Guide 15. Starmont.
pp. 96. pb $5.95.

realistic fiction, concentrating on examples of political fantasy ('The Dream of Debs'), anthropological romance (*Before Adam*), biological disaster (*The Scarlet Plague*), anti-utopia (*The Iron Heel*), and finally science fiction in *The Star Rover*. Beauchamp discusses the variety of London's narrative methods, his Darwinian themes, etc. His pamphlet will make a good critical companion to the 1975 anthology, *The Science Fiction of Jack London* (edited by Richard Grid Powers).

The latest in a series of texts by Theodore Dreiser to appear from UPenn is *An Amateur Laborer*[77] which was written in 1904 but left unfinished. It draws on Dreiser's own breakdown and subsequent spell as a railroad labourer. Richard W. Dowell's introduction admirably sets this novel in its biographical context and James L. W. West III has established the text from the one manuscript. The twenty-five chapters of narrative are followed by a series of fragments Dreiser had planned to incorporate into the novel. The standard of editing here is as impeccable as it has been in the series' earlier volumes. Joseph Griffin has given the first really detailed account of one of Dreiser's earliest stories, 'Butcher Rogaum's Door', and shown that it draws on the tradition of the tale (*ALR*). This story from 1899 is based on a triad of characters, and is seen by Griffin as a 'contemporary fairy tale of New York'. William J. Burling (*ALR*) has briefly discussed the original title for Chapter 32 of *Sister Carrie* and has examined the relevance of the biblical story of Belshazzar's feast. More substantially Thomas P. Riggio has given a full historical account of Dreiser's friendship with H. L. Mencken (*AS*). The relationship began in 1908 and lasted until Dreiser's death in 1945 in spite of tensions over their differing attitudes towards religion. The two writers formed a common cause in the 1910s against native pieties and both had serious problems during the First World War because of their ethnic backgrounds. This defensiveness during the 1920s brought their friendship under pressure but it survived none the less.

Gertrude Stein has received considerable attention this year through a number of reprints from Brilliance Books and the Virago Press. The former[78] has issued the first British paperback edition of *Paris France* (1940) with a new introduction by Jean Strauss examining its themes and methods, and has also re-issued *Wars I Have Seen* (1945) which recounts Stein's experiences in France during the two world wars. From Virago has come a reprint of a curious 1948 'thriller', *Blood on The Dining-Room Floor*[79], with an introduction by Janet Hobhouse which relates the novel to the writer's block Stein suffered after *The Autobiography of Alice B. Toklas*, and which discusses the relation between detective fiction and modernism. Further Gertrude Stein reprints are promised from both presses.

The year 1984 has also seen two major critical examinations of Gertrude Stein's work. Jayne L. Walker's *The Making of a Modernist*[80] analyses her

---

77. *An Amateur Laborer*, by Theodore Dreiser, intro. by Richard W. Dowell. UPenn (1983). pp. iv + 207. pb $9.95.

78. *Paris France*, by Gertrude Stein, intro. by Jean Strauss. Brilliance (1983). pp. [iii] + 120. pb £2.50. *Wars I Have Seen*, by Gertrude Stein, intro. by Jacqueline Morreau. Brilliance. pp. xxiv + 259. pb £3.95.

79. *Blood on the Dining-Room Floor*, by Gertrude Stein, intro. by Janet Hobhouse. Virago. pp. xvii + 73. pb £2.50.

80. *The Making of a Modernist*, by Jayne L. Walker. UMass. pp. xix + 167. $17.50.

writings from 1905 (*Three Lives*) to 1912 (*Tender Buttons*), and steers a middle course between abstract and mimetic readings of her work. Walker relates changes in narrative discourse to shifts in Stein's attitude to perception and representation. The study is particularly informative on the respective influences of William James, Cézanne, and Picasso. It sheds considerable new light on Stein's use of repetition, discontinuity, continuous verb-forms, and collage methods. Whereas Walker sees a variety of styles in Stein's work, Randa Dubnick's *The Structure of Obscurity*[81] locates two stylistic extremes – 'prose', based on syntax and the sentence (e.g. *The Making of Americans*), and 'poetry', based on the word (e.g. *Tender Buttons*). Drawing on structuralist analyses of discourse, Dubnick confronts stylistically the central problem of Stein's obscurity and argues that the difficulty of her work can be attributed to specific features such as her suppression of pictorial cues in her 'portraits' or her lack of connectives in her lists. Dubnick too highlights the influence of Picasso. These two books nicely complement each other in scope and approach. Walker tends to cover a specific period while Dubnick surveys Gertrude Stein's whole *oeuvre*, noting a return to clarity and syntactic orthodoxy in her later work.

The Sun and Moon Press and Virago are jointly issuing Djuna Barnes's works. The first of the series, *Smoke and Other Early Stories*[82], has now appeared in Britain with an excellent introduction by Douglas Messerli which relates the methods of these stories (published between 1914 and 1916 but never collected) to the journals where they appeared. Alyce Barry has now edited the second volume[83] of the series (so far only available in America), this time a collection of forty-one interviews conducted between 1913 and 1931 with celebrities of the times, mostly in the performing arts. The volume includes Flo Ziegfeld, Yvette Guilbert, and also writers such as Donald Ogden Stewart and James Joyce. As Douglas Messerli points out in his foreword, the interviews are non-biographical and rather examine posture, appearance, and image to find the personality behind the public reputation. The last item of the book is an interesting exception. This time it is Djuna Barnes who is interviewed by Guido Bruno, the famous Greenwich Village charlatan. Two other Virago reprints from this period deserve mention. The first is Emily Holmes Coleman's powerful novel, *The Shutter of Snow*[84] (1930), which she wrote after the birth of her son had triggered off a breakdown. The second is a first novel by another better-known member of the Paris expatriates, Kay Boyle. *Plagued by the Nightingale*[85] (1931) carries a new preface by the author, who retrospectively criticizes her weakness for victimized characters and who admits that her American publisher forced her to make major additions to the novel.

As Ian Bell has pointed out in the poetry section of this chapter, 1984 is a major year for H.D. studies. Not only have her poems been collected, but

81. *The Structure of Obscurity*, by Randa Dubnick. UIll. pp. xvii + 161. £17.50.

82. *Smoke and Other Early Stories*, by Djuna Barnes, intro. by Douglas Messerli. Virago (1985). pp. 184. pb £2.95.

83. *Interviews*, by Djuna Barnes, ed. by Alyce Barry. S&M. pp. 396. hb $16.95, pb $10.95.

84. *The Shutter of Snow*, by Emily Holmes Coleman, intro. by Carmen Callil and Mary Siepmann. Virago. pp. [viii] + 219. pb £2.95.

85. *Plagued by the Nightingale*, by Kay Boyle. Virago. pp. 190. pb £2.95.

several of her prose works have been re-issued, and a major biography has appeared. Virago has issued two early novels, *Bid Me To Live* and *Her*[86] (published in America under the title *HERmione*), which draw in varying degrees on H.D.'s own life (particularly her relationship with Pound and her failing marriage to Richard Aldington) to dramatize their protagonists' struggles to create an identity for themselves. New introductions to these novels by Helen McNeil admirably examine their range of symbolic and narrative techniques. Also from Virago comes *The Gift*[87], an autobiographical memoir still only available in a truncated version. It explores H.D.'s Moravian family past as a means of locating spiritual origins and coping with the war (it was written in 1943). All three volumes carry a biographical afterword by H.D.'s daughter, Perdita Schaffner. Barbara Guest's *Herself Defined*[88] performs a remarkable job of disentangling the many complex relationships formed by H.D. during her life. Guest argues convincingly that her Moravian childhood gave H.D. a lifelong yearning for the transcendental which manifests itself, for instance, in her spiritualist activities at the end of the Second World War. Guest also does justice to the dominant influences in H.D.'s life of Pound, Lawrence, and the writer Bryher. This biography demonstrates again and again how H.D. transformed her experiences into poetry or fiction, and might promote the view that her works have a primarily biographical value. In spite of this risk we certainly have in *Herself Defined* an exceptionally well-informed and lucid account of H.D.'s relationships.

Two substantial articles have appeared in the same number of the *SoQ* on James Branch Cabell. In the one Donald Pizer surveys Cabell's multivolume serial *Life of Manuel* set in the legendary realm of Poictesme. Pizer sees the series as held together by man's search for an ideal, and notes similarities and divergences from Cabell's own life. He also touches on sexual themes and the treatment of the dream-life, concluding that Cabell combines epic with a satire on contemporary beliefs and practices. James D. Riemer argues that Cabell's fantasies are unusual because they parody the high fantasy traditions. This element of parody is in turn related to the contrasts between the ideal and the mundane in Cabell's work. Both articles cogently demonstrate that Cabell is a witty and far more serious writer than his reputation as a mannered stylist would suggest. In the same period Jim Elledge (*SSF*) has examined the parallels between the Paolo-Francesca segment of Dante's *Inferno* and the story 'Hands' from Sherwood Anderson's *Winesburg, Ohio*.

Willa Cather's 1935 novel *Lucy Gayheart*[89] has been re-issued with a new afterword by A. S. Byatt who discusses the love themes, imagery, character-symbolism, and the general treatment of the protagonist's vitality. Patrick W. Shaw (*AL*) gives a lively and intelligent reading of the motif of the subterranean life in *My Ántonia*, showing that emergence is a repeated action by both animals and humans. In this context the imagery of light and darkness has an obviously important role to play. Shaw has interesting insights to offer on Cather's treatment of childhood as a time of sexual guiltlessness, and on the

86. *Bid Me to Live*, by H.D., intro. by Helen McNeil. Virago. pp. xix + 194. pb £3.50.
Her, by H.D., intro. by Helen McNeil. Virago. pp. xi + 239. pb £3.50.
87. *The Gift*, by H.D., ed. by Griselda Ohanessian. Virago. pp. xxvii + 142. pb £3.50.
88. *Herself Defined: The Poet H.D. and Her World*, by Barbara Guest. Collins. pp. xv + 360. £15.
89. *Lucy Gayheart*, by Willa Cather. Virago. pp. 240. pb £3.50.

contrasts between Jim and Antonia who, he suggests, represent different sides of Willa Cather's psyche. Beth Bowling has shown (*WAL*) that John Pavelka is the prototype of both Anton Luzak in *My Ántonia* and Anton Rosicky in the story 'Neighbour Rosicky', but it is difficult to see how this discovery sheds much new light on the texts in question.

In spite of Matthew J. Bruccoli's massively documented *Some Sort of Epic Grandeur* (1981), Scott Fitzgerald continues to attract biographers as if some hidden dimension to his life were continually eluding his readers. André Le Vot's Life[90] probes carefully behind the Fitzgerald legend, scrutinizing the conflicting accounts of the novelist's career by friends and associates. Le Vot does not limit himself to straight biography, but also explores the nature of periodical publishing in the 1910s and 1920s, the many influences on Fitzgerald from Mencken and others, and finally gives a tactful account of Fitzgerald's relationship with Zelda. Apart from biographical information, Le Vot's study contains an interesting discussion of colour symbolism in Fitzgerald's fiction. James R. Mellow's *Invented Lives*[91] takes a rather different tack. He is primarily concerned with how Fitzgerald and Zelda demonstrated a constant compulsion to transform their experiences into fiction, even using their fiction to engage in a covert dialogue with each other. Like Le Vot, Mellow demonstrates a healthy scepticism towards the Fitzgeralds' and others' accounts of their doings, and he draws on documents like Alec McKaig's diaries to clear up factual ambiguities (like Fitzgerald's affair with the English actress Rosalinde Fuller, for example). In spite of its title, *Invented Lives* is mainly about Scott Fitzgerald.

Jackson R. Bryer[92] has now produced a supplement to his original Fitzgerald bibliography of 1967 (*YW* 48.383), following the same chronological arrangement. He has expanded his original work in a number of areas: there are now reviews listed of Fitzgerald's play *The Vegetable* (1923), and also a section of reviews of *Save Me the Waltz*. Reviews are included of Fitzgerald's books published between 1964 and 1966. This supplement demonstrates that interest in the Fitzgeralds is showing no sign of flagging. Between 1967 and 1981 forty-five new books about them have appeared, to say nothing of collections like *Bits of Paradise* or new editions. All Bryer's entries are meticulously annotated in this essential bibliographical aid to Fitzgerald studies. Rose Adrienne Gallo has produced a general introduction to Fitzgerald's work[93] in Ungar's Literature and Life Series which will be of use mainly to a first-time reader. The book follows the pattern of the series in dealing with the novels chronologically, and for the most part goes over familiar ground. Gallo's emphasis on myth is interesting, however, and she notes the use of Diana in *Tender is the Night*, and a 'solar figure' in *The Last Tycoon*. Leonard A. Podis briefly looks at parallels between 'Rappaccini's Daughter' and 'The Diamond as Big as the Ritz' (*SSF*), arguing that the similarities suggest that Fitzgerald was probably familiar with Hawthorne's story. Curtis Dahl has investigated Fitzgerald's use of American architectural styles in *The Great*

90. *F. Scott Fitzgerald* by André Le Vot. Lane. pp. xiv + 393. £14.95.

91. *Invented Lives*, by James R. Mellow. Souvenir. pp. xxi + 569. £15.95.

92. *The Critical Reputation of F. Scott Fitzgerald. A Bibliographical Study – Supplement One through 1981*, by Jackson R. Bryer. Archon. pp. xvi + 542. £41.55.

93. *F. Scott Fitzgerald*, by Rose Adrienne Gallo. Literature and Life Series. Ungar. pp. ix + 166. $12.95.

Gatsby (*AmerS*) and has made out a very convincing case for their centrality. The feudal style of Gatsby's mansion relates the novel to the Gothic tradition, but also, because it is an imitation, embodies the ambivalent stature of Gatsby. This house contrasts forcibly with the Buchanans' which evokes a 'dignified old American aristocratic tradition'. Dahl does a good job of demonstrating Fitzgerald's accurate sense of style and the crucial role architecture plays in defining the social structure of the book.

Other writers from the 1920s and 1930s whose works have been reprinted include Ring Lardner, a selection of whose pieces has been issued by Dent under the editorship of David Lodge[94]. This selection contains such classics as 'Haircut', 'Some Like Them Cold', and Lardner's spoof essay 'How To Write Short Stories'. Lodge's introduction is brief but characteristically interesting on the kind of careful reading Lardner's colloquial style demands. Philip J. Klukoff[95] has translated and edited a selection of stories by Berl Botwinik, a major contributor to Abraham Cahan's *Daily Forward* and a significant Yiddish writer. His stories deal with the life of the *shtetl* and of the New York tenements. Carroll & Graf have reprinted Michael Gold's classic proletarian novel, *Jews Without Money*[96] (1930). Leslie Field has tackled the controversial topic of Thomas Wolfe's attitude towards Germany and the Jews (*JML*) and takes the visits of 1935 and 1936 as a turning point for Wolfe. Thanks to personal contacts Wolfe had access to more information about Hitler's activities than was being made public and after 1937 he became explicitly anti-German. Field's biographical article will perform a useful function in correcting a vague impression of pro-Teutonic bias in Wolfe.

As usual Faulkner and Hemingway dominate the critical scene. Cleanth Brooks has produced an ideal volume for the first-time reader, *William Faulkner: First Encounters*[97]. Brooks admits that he has not been fair to Faulkner's later career but nevertheless he provides good introductions to the better-known stories and novels. In his discussions he skilfully extrapolates the main themes and argues against seeing Faulkner as a provincial writer. Eric J. Sundquist[98] has a different tack to follow. He sets out to counter what he sees as a formalist bias in Faulkner criticism by examining three major novels before racial themes became explicitly central, and three after. Not that he ignores form. On the contrary, he has plenty to say about metaphor, doubling, and structure; but he relates these aspects of the novel to their themes and to American history – hence his title-phrase from Lincoln. *Sanctuary* is linked to the hard-boiled fiction of the 1920s, *Go Down, Moses* is a 'serial history' of the South, and so on. Sundquist sets his critical discussions within the historical context of the debate over race. Doreen Fowler[99] argues from the texts themselves that Faulkner's view of the human situation was constantly changing and being revised. The early works show conflicts between idealism and

94. *The Best of Ring Lardner*, ed. by David Lodge. Dent. pp. xvi + 213. pb £2.95.
95. *Lead Pencil*, by Berl Botwinik, trans. and ed. by Philip J. Klukoff. WSU. pp. 163. $12.95.
96. *Jews Without Money*, by Michael Gold. C&G. pp. 309. pb $7.95.
97. *William Faulkner: First Encounters*, by Cleanth Brooks. Yale. pp. x + 230. £19.50.
98. *Faulkner: The House Divided*, by Eric J. Sundquist. JHU. pp. xi + 183. $16.95.
99. *Faulkner's Changing Vision: From Outrage to Affirmation*, by Doreen Fowler. UMIRes. pp. 94. £29.50.

materialism, and put an emphasis on flux. After *Sanctuary* a rejection of empiricism paves the way for a new hospitality to spiritual affirmation. The extreme generality and piety which to a certain extent disables Fowler's study is avoided by Gail L. Mortimer who now directs her attention to language in *Faulkner's Rhetoric of Loss*[100]. As her title suggests, she sets out to explain how formal idiosyncrasies reflect a certain view of the world. This involves partly a stylistic analysis and partly an application of the theories of identity-formation. *Light in August* demonstrates Faulkner's Manichean polarization of the world between male and female, for instance. Subsequent chapters treat the relation of perception to transience (hence the importance of the river in *The Sound and the Fury*), Faulkner's 'dualistic depiction of the past', and the interplay between myth and ritual in his works. Although it is only of article length, Karl F. Zender's 'Faulkner and the Power of Sound' (*PMLA*) covers a lot of ground, suggesting that in his early works Faulkner exploits sound to express romantic yearning for reconciliation with the world. Sound gradually becomes a hostile force to struggle against. The winter issue of *ArQ* is a special Faulkner number which begins with an overdocumented piece by Francis S. Heck finding a source for Eula Varner (*The Hamlet*) in Zola's *Nana*. Doreen Fowler proposes that the interplay between light and darkness in *Light in August* helps Faulkner's portrayal of social misery. Terry Heller argues that the projected reader in *Sanctuary* is subjected to psychological violence in having expectations constantly disrupted. And Dexter Westrum puts forward an interesting argument about the pairing of characters in *Flags in the Dust*.

Two books have tackled Faulkner's beginnings with very different results. Martin Kreiswirth[101] cursorily surveys Faulkner's poetry in an opening chapter but dismisses it as mere exercises. He sees *The Sound and the Fury* as the culmination of Faulkner's early career, a novel which draws extensively on the writings which precede it. In the course of his discussion Kreiswirth identifies some important influences from Huxley (*Mosquitoes*), Joyce, and James Cabell (*Mayday*). Judith L. Sensibar[102], however, refuses to dismiss Faulkner's poetry and provides an excellent account of how the techniques of the poems feed directly into the techniques of the fiction. Taking 1918–1924 as the pivotal period, she looks at *The Marble Faun*, 'The Lilacs', and *Vision in Spring* (which she has edited – see p. 614), identifying influences from T. S. Eliot, Conrad Aiken, and the 1890s, and demonstrating how the adoption of pierrot-like masks and of large formal sequences anticipates the methods of his early fiction. After Sensibar's excellent exposition it will no longer be possible to deny the formative importance of Faulkner's poetry.

UMI has published three studies of particular aspects of Faulkner's work. Carl E. Rollyson Jr[103] builds on the critical accounts of Warren Beck and R. P. Adams to explain the historical process in several of Faulkner's novels. He deals with the past as family legend and reminiscence in *Flags in the Dust* and *The Unvanquished*, and two chapters relate dissolution to the play of historical

100. *Faulkner's Rhetoric of Loss*, by Gail L. Mortimer. UTex. pp. 153. $17.50.

101. *William Faulkner. The Making of a Novelist*, by Martin Kreiswirth. UGeo. pp. 193. $15.

102. *The Origins of Faulkner's Art*, by Judith L. Sensibar. UTex. pp. xxi + 290. $22.50.

103. *Uses of the Past in the Novels of William Faulkner*, by Carl E. Rollyson Jr. UMIRes. pp. 224. £45.25.

points of view in *Absalom, Absalom!*. Rollyson's readings are closely detailed and involve useful comparisons with Scott, Thackeray, and Conrad. A final chapter on Yoknapatawpha County argues that its history became more explicit as Faulkner's career developed. Rollyson's agile and scholarly arguments contrast rather with Jesse McGuire Coffee's survey of biblical allusions in Faulkner[104]. Strictly speaking hers is a double study, the first part of which identifies biblical patterns such as the patriarchal bequest. Coffee shows that allusion is flexible, designed to support theme and motif. The second part gives a concordance to specific biblical allusions in the fiction with an explanatory comment on each entry, and thereby amply demonstrates the extent of Faulkner's familiarity with the Bible. Joan M. Serafin also produces a tabulation, this time of classical allusions[105], with an introductory essay which rather blandly relates these allusions to the Southern idealization of the classics. They underpin, she suggests, a rhetoric of decline to clarify mythic themes and strengthen structure. Three indexes make up the bulk of her volume; the first collates classical allusions and quotations, the second classical names, and the third arranges Faulkner's classical allusions in alphabetical order. Martin Kreiswirth engages with the absence of centres in Faulkner, openings *in medias res*, and closure (*AL*), but the article is mainly confined to demonstrating these features rather than showing their importance.

On individual texts James G. Watson directs our attention to the series of interior monologues which Faulkner contributed to the New Orleans *Double Dealer* in 1925 (*AL*). He surveys critical opinion on these pieces and claims a greater importance for them since they mark Faulkner's transition from poetry to prose fiction. The imagistic and metaphorical techniques he spots point to a probable influence from Hemingway. David Krause makes out a good case that the letter read in Chapter 4 of *Absalom, Absalom!* is entangled in uncertainties, and as such sheds light on the problematic nature of reading the novel as a whole. He connects this letter with other cases of invention and reading in the novel, and relates them in turn to the problem of understanding history. Two articles on *Go Down, Moses* concentrate on history and greed, respectively. In the first Thomas C. Foster (*CentR*) takes as starting-point the reader's entanglement in genealogy through the complexities of the syntax. One story might fit into the syntactic gap of another and certainly draws on preceding stories. Where Foster enterprisingly interlocks theme and style, Richard Pascal concentrates exclusively on moral theme (*ArielE*), seeing racism as inseparable from characters' rapacious greed to appropriate the wilderness. Love is distorted again and again into racism and violence by a greed which makes a community virtually impossible. John Tucker (*TSLL*) goes outside *As I Lay Dying* to explain its peculiarities which, we are told, stem from cubism. The pictogram of the coffin which appears in the text indicates Faulkner's interest in the geometry of form. On the whole Tucker's application of artistic terminology works quite well in showing the interrelation of form and content in this novel. John L. Skinner (*JNT*) rehearses the critical accounts of 'A Rose for Emily' and identifies inconsistencies. His answer is to

104. *Faulkner's Un-Christlike Christians: Biblical Allusions in the Novels*, by Jesse McGuire Coffee. UMIRes. pp. xi + 155. £29.50.

105. *Faulkner's Use of the Classics*, by Joan M. Serafin. UMIRes. pp. ix + 198. £29.25.

work from basics and to produce an explanation of the story which highlights the associative logic of the narrator. It is the narrator, he concludes, and not Emily who is the real protagonist of the story.

Turning from criticism to bibliography, the major contribution in this area is undoubtedly O. B. Emerson's painstaking compilation, *Faulkner's Early Literary Reputation in America*[106]. He surveys Faulkner's critical reception from 1924 (*The Marble Faun*) to 1954 (*A Fable*), demonstrating that recognition was delayed until 1939 when articles by George O'Donnell and Conrad Aiken consolidated the signs of praise which had been growing steadily through the 1930s. Emerson charts the fluctuations in Faulkner's reputation through left-wing attacks and hostile journalistic reviews to his 1950 Nobel Prize which predictably triggered off a fresh wave of favourable critical discussion. The careful documentation in Emerson's survey means that it will usefully complement the Critical Heritage volume on Faulkner. Keen Butterworth's monograph on *A Fable*[107] details the process of composition from 1943 to 1953 (delayed by numerous interruptions), and then embarks on a chapter-by-chapter explication of the novel, pointing out its structure, use of Christian parallels, and borrowing from Humphrey Cobb's *Paths of Glory*. An appendix collates textual variants and gives a summary of criticism. Louis Daniel Brodsky has published detailed accounts in *SB* of two stories – 'Wash' and 'The Wishing Tree'. In the case of the former Brodsky compares the various manuscripts to show that Faulkner had his narrative clear from the very start. He composed the story in segments which Faulkner would halt and then begin again on separate sheets, retaining only as much of the earlier version as was useful. Brodsky makes this working method clearer by printing in parallel the holograph working draft and the revised complete holograph. Brodsky's second article shows that Faulkner typed out two individual presentation copies of 'The Wishing Tree' in 1928 and further copies in 1948. In each case the recipient thought the copy was unique! The two main versions are printed in parallel with full documentation of the texts and Brodsky argues that Faulkner pared down the narrative to suit the child who was to receive that copy.

Ernest Hemingway has been the focus of as much critical attention as Faulkner, but the publications have been spread rather differently. The most original study of Hemingway this year is undoubtedly John Raeburn's *Fame Became of Him*[108]. Raeburn analyses the public image which Hemingway projected during his literary career, which emerges as a continuous performance or adoption of shifting roles. Achieving early fame in the mid 1920s, Hemingway was quickly labelled the spokesman for a generation. After 1930 he began actively projecting various roles in his non-fiction (as war hero, aficionado, etc.). Raeburn interprets these roles as self-protective but argues that they were so effective in the postwar period they persisted under their own momentum, even surviving Hemingway's death. *Fame Became of Him* suggests a new way of reading Hemingway's non-fiction and convincingly shows how his self-promotion shifted according to the changes in his career. J. F.

106. *Faulkner's Early Literary Reputation in America*, by O. B. Emerson. UMIRes. pp. ix + 420. £41.75.

107. *A Critical and Textual Study of Faulkner's 'A Fable'*, by Keen Butterworth. UMIRes. pp. xii + 122. £29.50.

108. *Fame Became of Him*, by John Raeburn. IndU. pp. xiii + 231. $21.88.

Kobler[109] also deals with Hemingway's whole career, this time in connection with journalism. He attacks the conventional attitude that Hemingway's early journalism was just hack-work but suggests instead that there was an alternation between fiction and journalism right through his career. Although Kobler does not take up the issue of referentiality involved in Hemingway's revision, for instance of his Thrace sketches into his fiction, his thesis is an important one. He also summarizes the themes to be found in the journalism, denying that Hemingway ever produced propaganda.

Two studies examine the position of women in Hemingway's fiction and in his life. Roger Whitlow's *Cassandra's Daughters*[110] confronts what he sees as a crude division of Hemingway's female characters into aggressive bitches or passive daydreamers. His close scrutiny of the major novels leads him to conclude that the 'Hemingway Woman' is a stereotype created by critics borrowing the attitudes of the novels' male characters. Hemingway's women are in fact more varied, more authoritative, and more life-affirming than critics have recognized. Like Whitlow, Bernice Kert[111] sets out to redress a distorted impression – this time biographical – that Hemingway was antagonistic to women. Drawing extensively on unpublished letters and interviews, she gives an interestingly different account of Hemingway's life from the angle of his lovers and wives. She counters Hemingway's own projected image of his mother as hatefully oppressive by showing her to be both genteel and vigorous, i.e. altogether more complex than Hemingway would have us believe. Prototypes for Catherine Barkley, Margot Macomber, and others are identified, but this is not an exercise in source-spotting. In fact Kert demonstrates that Hemingway's characters are often assembled out of qualities selected from various individuals. Both of these books have a straightforward but none the less effective point to make: that the roles of women in Hemingway's fiction and life are far more complex than we tend to assume.

James Nagel's collection *Ernest Hemingway. The Writer in Context*[112] presents twelve papers originally delivered at the 1982 Hemingway conference at Northeastern University. There are four groupings. First come 'personal comments and reminiscences' including Charles Scribner's interesting account of Hemingway's dealings with his company, and a memoir by Hemingway's son Patrick. The second group consists of a detailed description of how Hemingway composed *Death in the Afternoon* by Robert W. Lewis and an account of the origins of 'Ten Indians' by Paul Smith. The former should go a long way towards redressing the critical neglect of this crucial text. A third section relates to the areas covered by Roger Whitlow and Bernice Kert, touching variously on Hemingway's mother, the biographical dimension to *A Farewell to Arms* (by Millicent Bell), and the position of women in Hemingway's mythology. Lastly, Hemingway's relation to four other writers is discussed. Peter L. Hays gives a useful and sometimes amusing description of the rivalry between Hemingway and Faulkner; Adeline R. Tintner argues

109. *Ernest Hemingway: Journalist and Artist*, by J. F. Kobler. UMIRes. pp. 174. £40.

110. *Cassandra's Daughters*, by Roger Whitlow. Contributions to Women's Studies. Greenwood. pp. xii + 148. £23.95.

111. *The Hemingway Women*, by Bernice Kert. Norton. pp. 555. £15.75.

112. *Ernest Hemingway. The Writer in Context*, ed. by James Nagel. UWisc. pp. xvii + 246. $27.50.

judiciously that Hemingway had a love–hate relationship with Henry James; Jacqueline Tavernier-Courbin adds little to our knowledge of the connection with Ezra Pound; and finally James D. Brasch examines the 'literary conversation' between Hemingway and Malcolm Cowley.

Donald R. Noble's *Hemingway: A Revaluation*[113] assembles four general essays which usefully survey the state of Hemingway criticism (by Jackson J. Benson), the reception of his works, and the importance of painting and travel in his writings. Then follow nine pieces on specific works. The themes of *In Our Time* are dealt with, as is the pilgrimage-landscape of *The Sun Also Rises*, and revaluations are offered of *Islands in the Stream* and *Across the River and into the Trees*. Philip Young gives a general description of Hemingway's decline into self-obsession. Inevitably there is some overlap between these two volumes and even with the other Hemingway criticism of this year (see below), but two of the most interesting essays in Noble's collection are a comparison between the manuscripts and final versions of *The Sun Also Rises* by Michael S. Reynolds – although this is now superseded by Svoboda's monograph on this very subject (again see below) – and a challenging piece by F. Allen Josephs called 'Hemingway's Poor Spanish'. Josephs identifies so many errors that he puts Hemingway's self-styled role of aficionado in a very ironic perspective indeed.

Several articles have attempted to locate Hemingway in relation to earlier writers and painters. Kenneth G. Johnson shows that Cézanne influenced Hemingway's composition of place in his early stories (*AL*), and Mark Spilka (*Novel*) has produced a detailed account of Hemingway's admiration for Captain Marryat. Marryat was both a man of action and a man of letters; as such he helped to authorize directions Hemingway was already taking in defining his own roles, presenting women, and depicting warfare. Jeffrey Meyers looks again at Hemingway's friendship with 'Chink' Dorman-Smith (the dedicatee of *In Our Time*) and proposes him as a model for Richard Cantwell in *Across the River and into the Trees* (*JML*). Rather more important are his explanations of Kipling's influence, again channelled largely through Dorman-Smith (*AL*), and an excellent account of Hemingway's coverage of the 1920–2 Greco-Turkish war (*MFS*). Spilka's piece is the third in a series of 'Victorian keys' to Hemingway, and Meyers's also seem to grow out of a continuing interest in Hemingway's origins. It is to be hoped that both writers will collect these articles into books in due course.

Frederic Joseph Svoboda[114] has produced what will surely stay the definitive account of how Hemingway composed *The Sun Also Rises*. He locates three stages in the process: the initial notebook draft, the typescript, and the galley proofs. At the suggestion of Scott Fitzgerald, Hemingway deleted the first one and a half chapters from the latter, thus cutting out considerable information about Brett. Svoboda notes that Hemingway began his composition in a journalistic way, using the actual names of friends, but then very quickly changed both events and characters into fiction. Further into the process he then tried to reduce literary signs and discursive or commentating passages.

113. *Hemingway: A Revaluation*, ed. by Donald R. Noble. Whitston (1983). pp. 282. $22.50.

114. *Hemingway & 'The Sun Also Rises'. The Crafting of a Style*, by Frederic Joseph Svoboda. UKan (1983). pp. xi + 148. $19.95.

Deletion was thus an important factor in composition although Hemingway did add clarificatory details, particularly on the bull-fighting episodes. Svoboda's study is invaluable for demonstrating Hemingway's working methods so clearly. Nina Schwartz has also tackled *The Sun Also Rises* (*Criticism*), and focused particularly on Jake's exploitation of silence. He rescues war, for instance, from cliché by not naming it and this becomes a recurring tactic in his narration and in his dialogues with Brett. Schwartz suggests that the bull-fight could stand as an analogy for Jake's mastery of Brett, in depending similarly on secrecy and ritualism. This agile piece contrasts with slighter articles and notes on the stories. Neal B. Houston (*AN&Q*) had compared the tale told to the old lady in *Death in the Afternoon* with the manuscript story 'There's One in Every Town', noting similarities and suggesting that Hemingway reduced the homosexual motifs for publication. Kenneth G. Johnston (*SSF*) examines 'The Snows of Kilimanjaro' and offers the biographical reading that Hemingway wrote it to purge his guilt at neglecting his serious fiction.

Although partial biographies of John Dos Passos have appeared, Virginia Spencer Carr's[115] is the first thorough treatment of the subject and the result is a splendid achievement. She does full justice to the versatility of Dos Passos, who emerges from her account as a poet, painter, inveterate polemicist, and political activist as well as a writer of novels. Not only was he personally involved in an astonishingly broad series of political events, but he demonstrated a constant compulsion to record his impressions and opinions in print. Carr tactfully describes Dos Passos's shifts in political allegiance and places an appropriate emphasis on his studies in American history which were, she suggests, an exercise in self-definition which persisted right up to his death in 1970. Dos Passos's fiction still receives inexplicably brief criticism, and this excellent biography should rectify that situation. Robert James Butler (*TCL*) has taken up the theme of movement in Dos Passos's life and applied it to the methods of *U.S.A.* which, he suggests, defines modern America in centrifugal terms. *1919* shows a 'vision of outward unification but inward disintegration' and *The Big Money* consists of claustrophobic and static narratives. Butler argues against seeing *U.S.A.* as nihilistic, finding signs of hope in the Camera Eye sections and the picaresque openness of 'Vag'. David Seed (*JNT*) concentrates on the Newsreels to explore their rhetoric and to extrapolate Dos Passos's anxieties over the media as means of political control. The Newsreels in this respect relate closely to the careers of certain characters, especially of J. Ward Morehouse.

Pride of place in this year's Steinbeck criticism must also go to a major biography, Jackson J. Benson's *The True Adventures of John Steinbeck, Writer*[116]. This meticulous study will certainly stand as the definitive biography for years. Benson demonstrates the gap between Steinbeck's private sense of himself and the public images he displayed. Many simplistic attitudes are disposed of once and for all by this book, such as the belief that Steinbeck was an anti-intellectual writer. Benson shows that this was certainly not the case but rather that Steinbeck became so interested in scientists like Harold Brown

115. *Dos Passos, A Life*, by Virginia Spencer Carr. Doubleday. pp. xix + 624. $24.95.

116. *The True Adventures of John Steinbeck, Writer*, by Jackson J. Benson. Heinemann. pp. xiv + 116. £28.

that his fiction became 'ecological parables'. Benson relates Steinbeck to the naturalistic tradition of American literature but also recognizes his variety. He charts the attacks levelled against Steinbeck by the Left in the postwar years, arguing that this was based on a misunderstanding of the early fiction and of, for instance, Steinbeck's support for Johnson's Vietnam policy. Brian St Pierre's *John Steinbeck. The California Years*[117] covers some of the same ground as Benson but far less intensively. This outline critical biography portrays Steinbeck as a single-minded hard-working writer but only takes us up to the 1940 Sea of Cortez expedition, thereby giving an impression of regionalism which might otherwise not appear. Thomas Fensch[118] has recorded one specific friendship between Steinbeck and his publisher Pascal Covici. The volume presents a selection from their correspondence from 1937 to 1963 and makes clear what important advice Covici gave Steinbeck on his writing (about the ending of *The Grapes of Wrath*, for instance). The help was not just professional but personal as well since Covici eased Steinbeck through his divorces. Covici's answers to Steinbeck's letters about *East of Eden* were deleted from *Journal of a Novel* which the present volume nicely complements.

Robert J. DeMott[119] has provided us with a catalogue of books referred to by Steinbeck in his writings, both published and unpublished. *Steinbeck's Reading* demonstrates – and DeMott has made this explicit in his introduction – how far other literature influenced Steinbeck's fiction. Books are listed alphabetically with explanatory notes and relevant quotations from his writings. A selective primary and secondary bibliography concludes the volume, which will perform an important critical function in disproving that Steinbeck wrote directly from experience. Three articles should be noted from this year's *StQ*, one number of which contains a supplement by DeMott to his bibliography. Stanley Renner argues that the garden–wilderness contrast is important in the story 'The White Quail' because it symbolically suggests different treatments of sexuality. Louis D. Owens also considers a story – this time 'The Murder' – and argues that it is about chivalric illusion. Finally, Roy S. Simmonds gives an impressively full account of the composition of *The Moon Is Down* which was originally to be set in America. This novel is located in Steinbeck's various wartime activities: writing dispatches for the *New York Herald-Tribune*, producing the script for Hitchcock's film *Lifeboat*, and so on.

A number of Southern writers have received critical attention. Joan Givner's biography of Katherine Anne Porter[120] sympathetically narrates a life racked by illness and marital misfortune. Givner discusses Porter's early poverty in Texas and traces the various stages of her career through journalism to her spells of postwar university teaching. Again and again she shows how the fiction draws on Porter's life. Particularly valuable is the documentation of Porter's involvement with the Sacco-Vanzetti case, Mexican politics, and desegregation in the South, but Givner also does justice to the main relationships in Porter's life, particularly with Josephine Herbst and Hart Crane.

117. *John Steinbeck. The California Years*, by Brian St Pierre. Chronicle. pp. 120. pb $7.95.
118. *Steinbeck and Covici: The Story of a Friendship*, by Thomas Fensch. Eriksson. pp. 248. pb $9.95.
119. *Steinbeck's Reading*, by Robert J. DeMott. Garland. pp. lxxiii + 239. $47.
120. *Katherine Anne Porter, A Life*, by Joan Givner. S&S. pp. 572. $10.95.

D. H. Unrue has argued briefly (*AL*) that an early story, 'The Martyr', sheds light on Porter's methods of composition and grew out of her misgivings over the Mexican revolution. Katherine Snipes has written a general introduction to the work of Robert Penn Warren[121], dealing with his fiction, poetry, and criticism. A useful opening chapter considers his membership of the Agrarians and his whole complex relation to the South. Alternating chapters then discuss his poetry (showing a shift from postlapsarian gloom to the lighter lyricism of the 1950s) and his novels. In the case of the latter the discussion is mainly thematic, stressing the recurrence of alienation. Ellen M. Caldwell has tackled the connections between Ellen Glasgow and the Agrarians (*AL*), locating a shift in her emphasis on history and myth from 1925 onwards. This was partly due to influence from Allen Tate and the Agrarians. Where Glasgow had previously satirized the disintegration of aristocratic values, she now paid more explicit attention to the Southern heritage and tradition. J. E. Bunselmeyer (*CentR*) defends Glasgow's mixing of tones and narrative modes, drawing partly on her own positions in *A Certain Measure*. Three syntactic patterns are identified: ironic (based on the balancing of opposites), realistic description (focused through a unified point of view), and sentimental (exploiting repetition). The latter is the least successful. Lynette Carpenter (*SSF*) has given a very narrative reading of 'Dare's Gift', arguing that Dare's legacy is a 'female commitment to something beyond personal loyalty'.

Ray McIver has selected twenty-two stories by Erskine Caldwell[122] which revolve around interracial relationships in the South during the Depression. These stories provide excellent examples of Caldwell's apparently noncommittal narrative style. Under the rather unfortunate title of 'Portrait of an American Primitive' (*SAQ*) D. G. Kuehl has interviewed Caldwell with illuminating comments on journalism, his Southern contemporaries, and his narrative methods. Twenty-six interviews with Eudora Welty[123] have been collected and edited by Peggy Whitman Prenshaw; these date from 1942 to 1982, although the majority took place after 1970. In spite of her anxieties over interviews Eudora Welty makes many valuable comments on her own fiction and working methods (she revises as she copies), and she predictably expresses admiration for Faulkner. Equally predictably, her Southern background figures very prominently here although she is reluctant to be labelled a regional writer. She does, however, admit a debt of gratitude to friends like Cleanth Brooks and Katherine Anne Porter who helped her career significantly. Patricia S. Yaeger analyses what she calls Welty's 'dialogic imagination' (*PMLA*), applying Bakhtin's theories to *The Golden Apples*. Some of these stories draw on Yeats's poems but the variety of their styles shows that Welty is revising Yeats's mythology of gender. Lorraine Liscio (*SSF*) also notes the influence of Yeats on 'The Bride of the Innisfallen', arguing that the narrative language becomes more poetical once the journey to Ireland has been achieved. Jefferson Humphries[124] applies gnostic doctrine to three writers – Proust, Flannery O'Connor, and Villon – and presents O'Connor's fiction as a

121. *Robert Penn Warren*, by Katherine Snipes. Ungar. pp. ix + 195. $12.95.

122. *The Black and White Stories of Erskine Caldwell*, ed. by Ray McIver. Peachtree. pp. x + 189. $12.95.

123. *Conversations with Eudora Welty*, ed. by Peggy Whitman Prenshaw. UMissip. pp. xii + 356. pb $9.95.

124. *The Otherness Within*, by Jefferson Humphries. LSU. pp. 184. £25.

'catalog of the unbeliever in his many incarnations'. Humphries concentrates mainly on violence in general and the story 'The Enduring Chill' (from *Everything That Rises Must Converge*). The latter is used to shed light on the relation of art to delusion. Sura Prasad Rath (*SSF*) has used Northrop Frye's theories to give a generic reading of *Wise Blood*, showing that the characters resemble comic archetypes. And Jane Marston (*SSF*) concentrates on one story, 'Greenleaf', to argue that the senses are too untrustworthy to make nature an unambiguous medium of grace. There is, she declares, a tension between the natural and the supernatural in this story.

It is gratifying to see that criticism is being devoted to American detective fiction although attention seems to focus mainly on the hard-boiled school. Zomba Books have reprinted four works by a founder of this fiction, William Riley Burnett[125]. The novels included comprise *Little Caesar* (1929), *The Asphalt Jungle* (1949), *High Sierra* (1940), and *Vanity Row* (1952). The first three are well known partly through their successful film adaptations. Burnett soon moved away from the hard-boiled style to investigate the roots of criminality, and *Vanity Row* is rather the odd one out in this collection, dealing with political manipulation and political passion. Diane Johnson (herself a novelist) has written a biography of Dashiell Hammett[126] which puts flesh on the bones of a comparatively familiar story. Hammett began his working life with Pinkerton's and during this period was first introduced to industrial unrest. His first story was accepted in 1922 and by 1929 he had become a famous writer. Then followed several years in Hollywood, years of increasing political activity which had already caused Hammett trouble during his wartime military service. His last years are a grim story of struggles with illness, the inland revenue, and the communist witch-hunts when he was briefly imprisoned. Johnson rightly gives prominence to Hammett's long-standing relationship with Lillian Hellman which lasted from 1930 until his death in 1961. Macmillan have now issued Frank MacShane's valuable selection of Chandler's letters (first published in 1981) in paperback[127]. The letters cover the period 1937–59 and, unlike the transcripts used for the miscellany *Raymond Chandler Speaking*, are mostly from originals. Chandler wrote at length partly to cope with his chronic insomnia and ranges over the subjects of his own writings, criticism of Agatha Christie and Erle Stanley Gardner, and of course Hollywood which he described as 'poison to any writer'. Ernest Fontana (*WAL*) notes that Chandler uses allusions to chivalry and romance in *The Big Sleep* to define Marlowe's relation to place. Romance fails, thwarted by city corruption. Matthew J. Bruccoli has written a life of Ross Macdonald[128] to introduce the new series of HBJ Album Biographies. Kenneth Millar wrote numerous detective stories under his famous pen-name, being directly influenced by Hammett and Chandler. He is particularly remembered for his private detective Lew Archer. Apart from detailing Macdonald's working methods, Bruccoli also shows that he had strong links with literature, studying under Auden, complet-

125. *Four Novels*, by William Riley Burnett. Zomba. pp. x + 588. hb £9.95, pb £5.95.

126. *The Life of Dashiell Hammett*, by Diane Johnson. C&W. pp. xxi + 344. hb £12.95. Picador (1985). pp. xvii + 344. pb £3.95.

127. *Selected Letters of Raymond Chandler*, ed. by Frank MacShane. Macmillan. pp. xx + 501. pb £6.95.

128. *Ross Macdonald*, by Matthew J. Bruccoli. HBJ Album Biographies. HBJ. pp. xxi + 147. pb $7.95.

ing a doctoral thesis on Coleridge, and teaching creative writing at Santa Barbara. In *Crit* Donald J. Greiner declares that Robert B. Parker is the only surviving practitioner of the hard-boiled school, doing research on Hammett, Chandler, and Macdonald before he embarked on his series of twelve novels.

Turning to black American fiction Nellie Y. McKay has written a particularly intelligent study of Jean Toomer[129]. Part biography, part criticism, she has drawn extensively on unpublished writings and declares Toomer's besetting problem was a 'lack of harmony between his mind, his emotions, and his body'. His impulse to write was thus part of a drive towards personal integration. In spite of the success of *Cane* (1923) Toomer very quickly felt alienated from it and turned to Gurdjieff and later scientology. The restlessness evident in his works emerges from a deep-rooted ambivalence about his own racial identity. Something of a revival of interest is taking place in Zora Neale Hurston's fiction and the latest reprints to appear are *Moses Man of the Mountain* (1939) and her autobiography *Dust Tracks on a Road* (1942)[130]. A new introduction to the former relates her novel to the Harlem Renaissance and points out that her avid interest in black folk-lore has fed her treatment of the biblical story of Moses. When her autobiography first appeared shortly after Pearl Harbor it had some passages excised which were critical of Western imperialism. These have now been restored in the present edition. Although its factual details are notoriously unreliable, Robert E. Hemenway argues in his introduction that *Dust Tracks on a Road* sheds light on the evident tension Hurston felt between furthering racial equality and not alienating her white readership. Vashti Crutcher Lewis (*CLAJ*) points out that the mulatto is the main figure in novels by black American women writers but asserts that this character becomes far less stereotyped in Hurston's fiction since she is more interested in qualities than appearances. Mary Ellen Williams Walsh takes up an acknowledgement by Ralph Ellison that Eliot influenced him, and identifies numerous parallels between *The Waste Land* and *Invisible Man*, suggesting that the novel contains a ritual landscape. The final major publication in this area is undoubtedly the autobiography of Leroi Jones/Amiri Baraka[131]. This work revolves around a series of journeys which accumulate into a metaphor of the learning process Baraka identifies as central to his life. The narrative is shaped by turning-points – his discovery of modern literature, his commitment to black activism in the mid 1960s and so on. The culmination to this autobiography is a simultaneous recognition that Newark is Baraka's home and that he has become a Marxist. This account sets up an indispensable context for Baraka's poems, plays, and prose.

Two new works by Henry Miller have been published. The first is a collection of contributions he made to the New York magazine *The Striker* between 1978 and 1980[132]. These were some of the last things Miller wrote and include letters, short fictions, essays (attacking the film *Bonnie and Clyde*, for instance), and memoir-articles on the New York theatre and Brooklyn. They contain brief but valuable comments on Hesse, Grosz, Isaac Singer, and

129. *Jean Toomer, Artist*, by Nellie Y. McKay. UNC. pp. xiv + 262. £27.

130. *Moses Man of the Mountain*, by Zora Neale Hurston. UIll. pp. xix + 351. pb $6.95. *Dust Tracks on a Road*, by Zora Neale Hurston. UIll. pp. xxix + 348. hb $22.95, pb $8.95.

131. *The Autobiography of Leroi Jones/Amiri Baraka*. Freundlich. pp. 329. $16.95.

132. *From Your Capricorn Friend*, by Henry Miller. ND. pp. xix + 101. pb $6.25.

others. The second work is a piece of erotica entitled *Opus Pistorum*[133] which Miller wrote for the Hollywood bookseller Milton Luboviski in 1941–2 shortly after he returned from Greece. The novel dates from the same period as *The Air-Conditioned Nightmare* and sheds a suggestive light on the erotic themes of his other fiction. Anais Nin also produced erotica under similar circumstances in the same period, and Smaro Kamboureli (*JML*) points out interestingly that she avoids pornographic terminology. She brings the theories of Foucault and Bataille to bear here and concludes that Nin does not by any means produce conventional pornography because the works (*Delta of Venus* and *Little Birds*) are so intricate artistically and because they exploit a feminine point of view. Peter Owen has published the third volume of Anais Nin's legendary early diary (*Journal of a Wife*) which covers the years 1923–7[134]. The book revolves around her newly married life with Hugh Guiler, first in America and then in Paris. She describes her attempts at writing and demonstrates the pressure which Paris exerted on her aesthetic idealism.

Edward Halsey Foster has produced a booklet on William Saroyan[135] which follows the pattern of the University of Minnesota booklets in surveying Saroyan's most famous works, examining his use of San Francisco and his treatment of American materials. As well as pointing out his strengths, Foster admits that Saroyan had a weakness for improbable plots. Arnold Beichman was given unique access to archives at Columbia University for his biography of Herman Wouk[136]. The result is a brief but well-informed study which places Wouk in a line of social realism (he is a fervent admirer of Fielding and Balzac) without making exaggerated claims for his novels. A practising Orthodox Jew, Wouk is constantly concerned with moral issues such as the clash between authority and right in *The Caine Mutiny*. His religious beliefs are fuelled by an interest in philosophy but Wouk did not treat the Jewish milieu directly in his fiction until *Marjorie Morningstar* (1955).

Matthew J. Bruccoli has edited the air force diaries and Pentagon memos of James Gould Cozzens[137]. That these documents form the raw material for *Guard of Honor* (1948) hardly justifies such a lavish edition, however. George Garrett has written a life of another novelist to use war materials – James Jones[138]. This professional study has consulted the Jones archives at Yale and the University of Texas, and makes out a good case for treating Jones as a serious novelist. His interest in writing was stimulated by reading Thomas Wolfe, and his wartime service in the Pacific supplied Jones with his raw materials. *From Here to Eternity* (1951) was a famous success but from then onwards, Garrett argues, Jones fell foul of a current in American taste which separated the intelligentsia from the general public. Jones's subsequent works were neither best sellers exactly, nor were they granted the critical recognition

133. `Opus Pistorum*, by Henry Miller. Allen. pp. 286. £9.95.

134. *Journal of a Wife*, by Anais Nin. Owen. pp. xv + 297. £12.95.

135. *William Saroyan*, by Edward Halsey Foster. Western Writers Series. BoiseU. pp. 51. pb $2.

136. *Herman Wouk: The Novelist as Social Historian*, by Arnold Beichman. Transaction. pp. 100. £14.95.

137. *A Time of War: Air Force Diaries and Pentagon Memos 1943–45*, by James Gould Cozzens, ed. by Matthew J. Bruccoli. BClark. pp. xiii + 407. $29.95.

138. *James Jones*, by George Garrett. HBJ Album Biographies. HBJ. pp. xxi + 218. pb $10.95.

Garrett suggests they should receive. Roy S. Simmonds has written the first study of the little-known writer William Robert Campbell (1893–1954)[139], who under the pen-name of William March produced stories, novels, and fables. He combined writing with a career in a steamship company and has been hailed by Alistair Cooke as a 'connoisseur of morbidity'. Simmonds gives full biographical details, closely analyses March's fiction, and shows how his lifelong interest in psychology fed his narrative techniques. To move from William March to James A. Michener is to step from the wings into a floodlit centre stage. John P. Hayes has produced the first biography of this best-selling novelist[140], describing his Quaker background, his teaching in the 1930s, and his wartime service. As with Jones, Cozzens, and Mailer the war acted as a springboard to Michener's writing career which began – slowly it must be admitted – with *Tales of the South Pacific* (1947). From then on he developed a knack of timing, of producing novels about contemporary issues (*The Bridge of Andau* after the Hungarian invasion, *The Drifters* about the alienated youth of the late 1960s, etc.) which brought him an enormous readership but also charges of 'dramatized journalism' from the reviewers. Hayes says very little about the methods of Michener's fiction and seems to understate his subject's evident enormous drive to succeed. Nevertheless Michener is revealed as more varied than one might expect. He reported on sport, wrote journalistic pieces, was active in Democratic politics, and even wrote one of the reports on the notorious shootings at Kent State University.

Interest in Paul Bowles's fiction continues with Peter Owen's reprinting of *Let It Come Down* (1952)[141], a brilliant study in disorientation revolving around an American clerk who comes to Tangiers to start a new life and is swept into a web of smuggling. Peter Owen has also issued the collected works of his wife Jane Bowles[142], an important author in her own right. This is the first British edition of her works and includes her one novel *Two Serious Ladies*, a collection of short stories (*Plain Pleasures*), and her play *In the Summer House*. Moreover, six stories were found among Jane Bowles's papers after her death in 1973 and are now published here for the first time. Truman Capote's rather dated introduction to the 1966 American edition of her works has been retained where he notes Jane Bowles's blending of tragedy and comedy.

New Directions has issued a collection of thirteen 'doctor stories' by William Carlos Williams from *The Farmers' Daughters*, six poems on medical subjects, and a section of his autobiography in one volume[143]. All these works have been published before but it is useful to have them brought together with an introduction by Robert Coles, who examines the relation of medicine to writing in Williams's career as a whole. His son supplies an afterword. James R. Bettinger (*RCF*) examines Williams's treatment of European influences on

139. *The Two Worlds of William March*, by Roy S. Simmonds. UAla. pp. xviii + 367. $30.

140. *James A. Michener: A Biography*, by John P. Hayes. Allen. pp. xiv + 276. £10.95.

141. *Let It Come Down*, by Paul Bowles. Owen. pp. 318. £8.95.

142. *The Collected Works of Jane Bowles*, intro. by Truman Capote. Owen. pp. ix + 476. £10.95.

143. *The Doctor Stories*, by William Carlos Williams, intro. by Robert Coles. ND. pp. xvi + 142. hb $13.50, pb $4.95.

American life. He pays especial attention to the themes and language of *White Mule* and *The Great American Novel*. Robert Creeley's *Collected Prose*[144] has now been published in Britain and consists only of his fictional works, bringing together *The Gold Diggers* (1954), *The Island* (1963), *Listen* (a tape improvisation of 1972), and *Mabel. A Story* (1976). This is a necessary act of consolidation for a major American writer whose prose deserves to be better known. Creeley has written an introduction for this volume where he discusses the unity of a writer's *oeuvre* and notes his particular admiration for Turgenev. The Dalkey Archive Press has been established to revive neglected modern works of fiction and has so far published Douglas Woolf's novel *Wall to Wall* and Gilbert Sorrentino's Rimbaud-inspired alphabetic meditation *Splendide-Hotel* with a new afterword by Robert Creeley[145].

John W. Aldridge has written a memoir-article in *CentR* on Vance Bourjaily's *The End of My Life* (1947) basically to confirm his position in *After the Lost Generation* that post-World-War-II novelists were fundamentally different from the 1920s postwar writers. He finds an ambivalence about causes and a fear of authoritarian systems in Bourjaily's novel which suggests that he is a forerunner of later novelists of conspiracy such as Heller or Pynchon. James W. Bittner has explored the interconnections between the novels of Ursula K. Le Guin[146]. He suggests that she uses story as a means of discovery and exploration, and looks in turn at the dialectical plots of her romances, the relation of realism to fantasy, and of myth to science in her works. Eberhard Alsen[147] has ambitiously tried to demonstrate that Salinger's Glass stories should be considered as one sequence, as a 'composite novel'. Firstly he examines the stories in their order of publication from 1948 to 1965, and shows that it was only in 1955 that Salinger had formed a definite plan for the series. He neither completed this plan nor gave the stories a definitive arrangement. The second section assembles a biography of Seymour, outlining his search for God, spiritual deterioration, and final suicide. In the course of this discussion Alsen adds to our knowledge of Salinger's interest in eastern religions. Linda W. Wagner (*JNT*) identifies the ways in which Sylvia Plath makes the protagonists of her stories special. They are usually lonely, divorced from familiar contexts, or faced with specifically female choices. This article bears usefully on the question of characters' freedom in Plath's fiction.

Three books have appeared on Nabokov's fiction, eloquent testimony to critical fascination with his narrative intricacies for all their dangers. Alan Levy's *Vladimir Nabokov: The Velvet Butterfly*[148] is mainly addressed to those encountering the fiction for the first time. It is the third in the series and follows the general pattern of interviews with Nabokov, followed by quotations from texts and other interviews, a discursive chapter on the experience of reading

144. *The Collected Prose*, by Robert Creeley. Boyars. pp. 432. £16.95.

145. *Wall to Wall*, by Douglas Woolf. Dalkey. pp. 190. pb $4.50. *Splendide-Hotel*, by Gilbert Sorrentino, afterword by Robert Creeley. Dalkey. pp. 64. pb $3.95.

146. *Approaches to the Fiction of Ursula K. Le Guin*, by James W. Bittner. UMIRes. pp. xvii + 161. £28.50.

147. *Salinger's Glass Stories as a Composite Novel*, by Eberhard Alsen. Whitston (1983). pp. xiv + 271. $22.50.

148. *Vladimir Nabokov: The Velvet Butterfly*, by Alan Levy. Permanent Press Portrait Books. Permanent. pp. x + 163. pb $9.95.

Nabokov, and a selective bibliography. David Rampson[149] engages in a lively antistructuralist polemic in his study of Nabokov. He directs scorn against those critics who reduce Nabokov's fiction to self-reflexive exercises and, after taking up Nabokov's critical statements on Dickens and others, he proceeds to underline the ostensible subjects of the novels. According to him Nabokov is a satirist treating totalitarianism as farce in his early works, taking his bearings from Russian literature in *The Gift*, and testing out the human cost of narrating in *Lolita*. In short Rampson makes out a pleasing and convincing case that Nabokov is a novelist of issues. Michael Long has attempted a peculiarly arbitrary *tour de force* in juxtaposing Marvell and Nabokov[150], working through a series of alternating chapters on each writer (see also p. 291 for another notice of this book). The comparison is further forced by giving the Nabokov chapters titles appropriate to Marvell, and vice versa. While Long makes out an argument that there is a recurrent nostalgia for a lost arcadian childhood in Nabokov, he only achieves this through simplistic readings which, apart from a few token gestures, scarcely even begin to cope with Nabokov's formal complexities. Michael Seidel (*ELH*) takes as his subject 'supplemental vision-making' in *Pale Fire*, comparing Kinbote's narrative to the descent into the underworld in the *Aeneid*. This is an interesting article mainly about imaginative projections but also touching on retrospection, doubling, etc. John Haegert (*TSLL*) proposes that we should take the indeterminacy and disorder of the novel at face value and not try to harmonize poem and commentary, the latter being a critical work not a work of art. Shade and Kinbote are similar rather than opposites since both work clearly in excess of the facts. The real focus of the novel is what Haeggert calls the 'art of reading'.

William Burroughs still occupies a curiously anomalous position in having achieved critical status without a substantial body of criticism to support that status. It is therefore welcome that *The Job*[151], a collection of interviews first published in 1974, has now appeared in Britain. It includes an article, 'Playback from Eden to Watergate', and contains extensive materials inserted into the basic interview format. Many of his main statements are gathered here, on control mechanisms, scientology, narcotics, and his famous 'cut-up' methods of composition. *RCF* has produced a special Burroughs issue which contains two short prose pieces and a 1974 interview with him as well as a 1982 interview with his manager James Grauerholz. Although there is an emphasis on *The Naked Lunch*, the articles consider diverse areas of his whole output. Among others the following topics are covered: his ambivalence towards an audience (Michael Leddy), parallels between his mythology and gnosticism (Gregory Stephenson), his 'cut-up' and cinematic methods of composition, the influence of Wilhelm Reich (Allan Johnston), and the mythology of the post-Nova fiction (Jennie Skerl). This excellent number also contains memoir-articles by Alan Ansen and David Ohle.

Unlike Burroughs, Jack Kerouac still receives mainly biographical

149. *Vladimir Nabokov: A Critical Study of the Novels*, by David Rampson. CUP. pp. xi + 233. hb £20, pb £7.50.

150. *Marvell, Nabokov: Childhood and Arcadia*, by Michael Long. Clarendon. pp. xvi + 270. £19.50.

151. *The Job*, by William Burroughs. Calder. pp. 224. pb £4.95.

attention. Chris Challis's *Quest for Kerouac*[152] is part travelogue and part memoir with only the slightest dash of criticism added. He narrates a series of journeys to the former haunts of the Beats and the results of interviews with surviving writers. In spite of the title Challis is interested in the Beat movement as a whole and his work consists of a gesture of piety rather than research, intended to re-emphasize familiar characteristics of the writers in question, although he does have some useful new details to add about Ferlinghetti, Clellon Holmes, and others. Tom Clark's life of Kerouac[153] makes a thorough study of the published material and, while not introducing much new information, manages to avoid the pitfalls in the subject. Clark never sinks into mere adulation and avoids restrictive categories like drop-out.

New Directions has issued a John Hawkes reader[154] which puts together a sequence of stories and excerpts from the novels from 1949 through to *Adventures in the Alaskan Skin Trade* with an introduction by William H. Gass. Hawkes has added valuable glosses on each section which clarify his themes and relate his fiction to his own biography. Mary F. Robertson has given an impressive textual analysis of *Second Skin* (*TSLL*) which exemplifies a general risk in Hawkes's fiction: his ideas (in this novel identity, authority, and paternity) are always threatened with extinction by their very means of expression. She compares Skipper's tale with *The Ambassadors* and argues that Hawkes does not just delay but actually denies revelation through the discrepancies in his language. Steven Moore is continuing his admirable work on William Gaddis. His reader's guide to *The Recognitions* (*YW* 63.457–8) is now followed by a collection of critical essays which Moore has co-edited with John Kuehl[155]. An introduction rehearses the known facts of Gaddis's life and then seven essays deal with different aspects of *The Recognitions*: its composition (David Krenig), an excellent account of its moral vision by John Leverence, its use of *Peer Gynt* (Moore), debt to Eliot (Miriam Fuchs), etc. The next group turns to *J.R.*, specifically to the themes of order, time, and activity as exchange in that novel. Finally, three articles discuss the two novels together, concentrating on the relation between monetary and literary discourse (a particularly penetrating piece by Steven Weisenburger) and Gaddis's depiction of America as a corporate empire (Joel Dana Black). Moore has also supplemented his reader's guide with additional sources (*AN&Q*), mainly from the *Oxford Dictionary of Quotations*.

Charles B. Harris[156] gives a new reading of John Barth's fiction up to *LETTERS* (1979) which closes off a phase in his career. In spite of its variety Barth's writing constantly returns to a desired unity between words and the world, which it seeks through a series of epistemic exercises. The first two novels deal with a split between mind and body; *The Sot-Weed Factor* treats the disruptions of a new world-view historically; and *Giles Goat-Boy* sets up a

152. *Quest for Kerouac*, by Chris Challis. Faber. pp. 238. pb £3.95.

153. *Jack Kerouac*, by Tom Clark. HBJ Album Biographies. HBJ. pp. xviii + 254. pb $10.95.

154. *Humors of Blood and Skin. A John Hawkes Reader*, intro. by William H. Gass. ND. pp. xvi + 298. $22.50.

155. *In Recognition of William Gaddis*, ed. by John Kuehl and Steven Moore. Syracuse. pp. xiii + 209. $25.

156. *Passionate Virtuosity. The Fiction of John Barth*, by Charles B. Harris. UIll. pp. xi + 217. £16.

novel as a metaphor of a unified cosmos. *Lost in the Funhouse* relates language to sexuality, *Chimera* relates myth to daily reality, and finally *LETTERS* deconstructs traditional novelistic forms to discover history. Harris's *Passionate Virtuosity* presents a lucid, well-argued view of Barth which does ample justice to the conceptual frameworks of his fiction. Robert P. Winston has briefly traced debts to the Reeve's and Miller's Tales in *The Sot-Weed Factor* (*AL*), and Max F. Schulz (*ConL*) believes that the character Thalia (in *Lost in the Funhouse*) embodies a double perspective on reality. Instead of taking this work as evidence of Barth's decline we should treat it as an interlude in his career where he plays with the duplicity involved in story-telling.

Although no new book has appeared on Pynchon this year, *PNotes* 14 is a special number on deconstructing *Gravity's Rainbow* under the guest editorship of Bernard Duyfhuizen. Louis Mackey places Pynchon in a line of failed efforts by American writers to escape the negations of Puritanism. *Gravity's Rainbow* is both suspicious of the law but at the same time undermines any notion of an outside refuge. Joel D. Black sees the novel as a 'de-centered metafiction' which keeps undermining itself. Terry Caesar and Stephen P. Schuber take the critics to task for oversystematizing the novel, extrapolating a meaning that the text appears to work against, but do not offer much in the way of alternative readings. Steven Weisenburger tabulates the novel's external chronological references and thereby demonstrates that Pynchon has carefully worked out a circular structure. Terry Caesar has also examined monstrosity in *Gravity's Rainbow* (*Novel*), adeptly extending this notion from literal monsters to include systems in general. The monstrous both articulates characters' responses to the war and also hints at a more positive possibility beyond language and nearer to the sacred. David Marriott (*JAmS*) also touches on the sacred in this novel but compares its narrative formation to the creation of a gospel. 'Pynchon wants', he declares, 'to write a commentary on History which is not subject to History's distortions.' Marriott's argument illuminates the textuality of *Gravity's Rainbow* and the transformation of Tyrone Slothrop into myth. Still with the same novel John M. Muste (*MFS*) locates *Gravity's Rainbow* within the genre of war fiction, noting that Pynchon blurs the differences between war and peace, and presents war as a 'manifestation of economic and social control'.

The title of Judie Newman's *Saul Bellow and History*[157] seems self-explanatory but her book proves to be even broader in scope, examining religion, myth, and philosophy as well as history in Bellow's work. *The Adventures of Augie March* is tied to historical specifics and theories of history, particularly to those of Ortega y Gasset, as Judie Newman explains elsewhere (*DUJ*). The theories of Reich and Freud prove to be particularly relevant to *Henderson the Rain King* and *Herzog*. Global history is the subject of *Mr Sammler's Planet* and contrasting historical viewpoints in *Humboldt's Gift*. *SLitI* has devoted a whole issue to 'Philosophical Dimensions of Saul Bellow's Fiction'. Once again the emphasis is heavily intellectual. Allan Chavkin locates Bellow's roots in Romanticism, while M. Gilbert Porter concentrates specifically on the American Transcendentalists who, he argues, have influenced the polarities of Bellow's fiction. Stanley Trachtenberg, however, finds Schopenhauer a more decisive presence and accordingly gives a much darker

---

157. *Saul Bellow and History*, by Judie Newman. Macmillan. pp. 208. £20.

reading of the fiction. Daniel Fuchs discusses Bellow's ambivalence towards Freud and declares that he rejects the latter's determinism. For Fuchs, Bellow is a humanist with a 'religious tendency'. For L. H. Goldman it is more than a question of tendency since he argues that Bellow writes like an Old Testament prophet. Eusebio Rodriguez warns us against fitting Bellow's fiction into rigid philosophical patterns, and Judie Newman concludes the volume with an examination of nihilism in *The Dean's December*. Allan Chavkin has also explained the importance of Dostoevskian humanism in shaping Bellow's attitude to suffering (*CLS*), comparing *Herzog* with *The Brothers Karamazov* and concluding that Bellow is a 'secular humanist'. Matthew C. Roudané has interviewed Bellow (*ConL*) and elicited useful statements about the import-ance of Chicago, the 'slippage of self-valuation' in his protagonists, and on *The Dean's December*.

Hilary Mills's *Mailer, A Biography*[158] has now come out in paperback. It is a fascinating examination of Mailer's public career and of his capacity to invent new roles for himself. Mills recognizes the importance of Mailer's Jewish background but also rightly emphasizes his drive to excel Hemingway as a literary celebrity. Although this ambition has been realized primarily in novels Mills also examines Mailer's interests in film, theatre, sport, and journalism. Far from being the result of whim, she shows that Mailer's shifts in role and style are closely tied to public events in America. A 1965 interview with Mailer to promote *An American Dream* has been included in David Leitch's collected journalism, *Deadline* (Harrap). Penguin have issued a *Philip Roth Reader*[159] which contains the complete revised version of *The Breast*, excerpts from eight novels, an essay, and one short story. Martin Green's introduction discusses Roth's particular susceptibility to literary influence, not only from the classics but from contemporaries such as Bellow. George J. Searles[160] has attempted with varying success to compare Roth's fiction with that of John Updike. To do so he has approached both writers as social realists and then run through a series of contrasts: Roth examines Jewishness, Updike the world of the WASP; Roth uses urban settings, Updike draws on New England. These themes unfortunately overlap with each other and necessitate a lot of plot summary to make comparatively small points about character-patterns, etc. In spite of two chapters on the subject, the stylistic intricacies of Roth and Updike receive rather superficial treatment and recognition of *The Breast* really ques-tions Searles's opening premise of social realism. H. H. Nilson (*ES*) has written an unnecessary article on *Portnoy's Complaint* pointing out the ob-vious: that there is a conflict between ethnic heritage and secular environment in Roth. Steven G. Kellman (*CLS*) has more fruitfully built on Roth's declared admiration for Kafka to explore the history of his interest. He scans Roth's essays, analyses (though surprisingly briefly) *The Breast*, and points out that Roth's visit to Prague was incorporated into *The Professor of Desire*.

Stephen W. Potts has very briefly surveyed Joseph Heller's fiction[161], noting redundancy and non-linear chronology in *Catch-22*, the articulation of insecur-

158. *Mailer, A Biography*, by Hilary Mills. NEL. pp. 463. pb £4.95.

159. *A Philip Roth Reader*, intro. by Martin Green. Penguin. pp. xxiii + 483. pb £4.95.

160. *The Fiction of Philip Roth and John Updike*, by George J. Searles. SIU. pp. ix + 197. $16.95.

161. *From Here to Absurdity*, by Stephen W. Potts. Borgo (1982). pp. 64. pb $3.95.

ity in *Something Happened*, and the expression of disgust with political parties in *Good as Gold*. None of this is particularly new but the booklet would make a serviceable introduction to Heller's works. Lindsey Tucker (*ConL*) has produced an outstanding article on *Something Happened* which, she demonstrates, is packed with references to problems on language which seems to be in entropic decline. The reader's problem is how to cope with this verbal disorder and the same problem is experienced by the protagonist who tries to retreat into his own closed system. Bruce Jay Friedman has collected eighteen stories[162], mostly from the 1960s, which continue his early treatments of urban black comedy. And Jerome Charyn's Isaac Quartet (*Marilyn the Wild, Blue Eyes, The Education of Patrick Silver*, and *Secret Isaac*) has now been issued in one volume[163]. Charyn explains in his introduction that his discovery of Ross Macdonald's fiction in 1973 changed the direction of his own writings towards crime and simple narrative lines. In spite of this change Robert L. Patten (*Novel*) still finds complexities in *Pinocchio's Nose* (1983) which he describes as charged with a 'personal and desperate hunt for an origin'. He explains Charyn's blending of Carlo Collodi's story with the novel's Oedipal triangle, and points out allusions to both Joyce and Melville.

The Southern novelists have been dealt with in several articles. Robert Siegle (*ConL*) has discussed Truman Capote's 'Handcarved Coffins' (from *Music for Chameleons*) in relation to the non-fiction novel. He points out Capote's descriptive strategies, his evocation of mystery, and his complex use of interpretative frames. William Styron, whose essays have also appeared this year (see p. 657), is described by Samuel Coale (*Crit*) as a Southern Gothic novelist who exploits dualisms in his fiction. These dualisms undermine Christian norms and quest-patterns. The article deals mainly with *Set This House on Fire* and *Sophie's Choice*, but sheds a general light on Styron's works. Michael K. Glenday (*AL*) uses a 1973 interview with James Dickey to explain the role of Ed Gentry in *Deliverance*, and to ask whether he survives by virtue of his skills as a graphic artist.

This year's articles on John Updike have focused on his stories and novels. Bruce H. Tracy (*SSF*) pleads for a more favourable reading of the protagonist in 'The Music School', insisting that we must distinguish between his character and the story as a whole. The ultimate subject of this narrative is the causal connections between events. Randall H. Waldron (*AL*) looks at the reasons made by Updike for the 1964 Penguin edition of *Rabbit, Run* when much of the sexual language was restored. A final and detailed revision of the text was made for the 1970 reprinting. Miriam Youngerman (*ArQ*) takes up the issue of Updike's regionalism and suggests that his New England settings should be taken literally. They are both historically accurate and important for their metaphorical connotations. James Purdy's 1967 novel *Eustace Chisholm and the Works*[164] has now been reprinted with a new introduction by Paul Binding which points out the importance of the Depression for the book's characterization. Binding sees this novel as a watershed in Purdy's career because it now makes homosexuality an overt and central issue.

162. *Let's Hear It for a Beautiful Guy*, by Bruce Jay Friedman. Fine. pp. 252. $15.95.
163. *The Isaac Quartet*, by Jerome Charyn. Zomba. pp. x + 548. hb £9.95, pb £5.95.
164. *Eustace Chisholm and the Works*, by James Purdy, intro. by Paul Binding. GMP. pp. vi + 241. £7.95.

The intellectual substance of Walker Percy's fiction[165] has now been amply demonstrated by Patricia Lewis Poteat who proposes that the novels and the essays (*The Message in the Bottle*) engage in a continuous anti-Cartesian polemic. The novels which start with a predicament to be explored are more successful than the essays because in the latter 'Percy himself falls victim to the very incoherence of modern philosophy he intends to criticize'. Although Poteat praises the novels for their poised wit, her discussion really concentrates on more abstract questions – on linguistic theory, behaviourism, etc. She presents Percy as an impressively broad thinker, if not always a successful one. A. Lawson looks to the protagonist's father for an explanation of alienation in *The Moviegoer* (*RMR*). Failing to maintain a sense of universal reality, the protagonist yields to the passive role of watching movies even though he knows they are deceptive. Lawson too draws our attention to the allusiveness of this novel, identifying references to contemporary science, Plato, etc. Better known as a naturalist, it is often forgotten that Peter Matthiessen (one of the founders of the *Paris Review*) also writes fiction and Bert Bender has tried to place *Far Tortuga* (1975) in a general context of American sea fiction (*AL*). He proposes Captain Raib as a thematic focus and draws contrasts with Melville and Hemingway. Torborg Norman has tackled the daunting problem of how character is revealed in the short stories of Joyce Carol Oates from 1963 to 1980[166]. Three separate behavioural groups are identified: the individual set against an institutional background; the family; and a contrast between idea and reality. The analyses of tone, statement, and verbal action are businesslike and thorough.

Equally thorough is Robert A. Morace's *John Gardner. An Annotated Secondary Bibliography*[167]. This work lists interviews and speeches, and in its second section lists reviews of Gardner's thirty-one published works up to 1983. Section 3 lists reviews of works to which Gardner contributed and Section 4 surveys articles and essays about his writings. The concluding section provides an addendum of primary works to John Howells's 1980 Gardner bibliography. For most of the 1600 items listed Morace gives helpful summaries of the contents of his entries. Robert Merrill (*AL*) attempts to reconcile *Grendel* with Gardner's attacks on the 'cult of cynicism and despair'. Drawing incidental comparisons with Barth, Heller, and Vonnegut, he agrees that Grendel is the hero, but adds that he also represents a negative example of nihilistic rationalism. *Mickelsson's Ghosts* gives Craig Barrow his subject (*Crit*). He discusses Gardner's theorizing about the morality of fiction and applies these ideas to the novel, concluding that Mickelsson learns feeling not thought. Arthur M. Saltzman has interviewed William Gass in *ConL* and has followed the usual high standard of that journal in eliciting full comments on Gass's own latest novels, on varieties of realism and the nature of representation, and on his interest in the French and in Kafka.

Charles Berryman (*Crit*) surveys Kurt Vonnegut's recent fiction and finds it

165. *Walker Percy and the Old Modern Age*, by Patricia Lewis Poteat. LSU. pp. xi + 177. £20.

166. *Isolation and Contract. A Study of Character Relationships in Joyce Carol Oates' Short Stories, 1963–1980*, by Torborg Norman. GSE 57. AUG. pp. 261. Skr 105.

167. *John Gardner. An Annotated Secondary Bibliography*, by Robert A. Morace. Garland. pp. xiv + 364. $45.

to be very uneven in quality, but is at his most interesting when he identifies autobiographical elements in these works. He notes, for instance, the recurring images of massacre and argues that Vonnegut repeatedly appears in his own works, either as narrator or as character. Beverly Gross (*JNT*) takes a similarly psychoanalytical tack in her reading of Robert Pirsig's *Zen and the Art of Motorcycle Maintenance*. The book takes its structure from the narrator's mind. 'Phaedrus' (i.e. the narrator's former self) gradually surfaces and the narrator sinks into despair. She concludes that Pirsig is projecting a negative view of institutionalized sanity. Jerry Andrew Varsava (*SSF*) briefly discusses the fragmentation of narrative in Robert Coover's 'Spanking the Maid'. Frames are left unresolved and the proliferation of interpretative possibilities suggests that this is a postmodern fiction. Two articles in *Critique* deal with Donald Barthelme. In one Lee Upton considers the theme of failure in *Sixty Stories*, noting narrative absences and suggesting that Barthelme uses failure as a 'working principle'. In the other Robert A. Morace surveys criticism of *Snow White* and suggests that the book analyses contemporary language. It is thus a comic critique of society, not just a symptom of a trend. Gina Wisker (*Over Here*) finds a pattern of increasing alienation in Jerzy Kosinski's novels and argues that he deconstructs the popular formulae he has based his novels on to expose the contradiction in those formulae.

Four book-length studies of contemporary best-selling authors have been published this year. *The Ayn Rand Companion*[168] is the first book to cover her whole career. The opening chapter discusses her life (1905–82). Then Mimi Reisel Gladstein turns to the novels and plays which Rand used to develop her doctrine of objectivism, to her non-fiction from the 1960s and 1970s, and finally gives the reader a comprehensive primary and secondary bibliography of this proponent of 'rugged individualism and titanic self-assertion'. Kim Stanley Robinson[169] shows that Philip K. Dick (1928–82) was a novelist *manqué*, never completely happy with science fiction. Although Dick wrote at least eight realistic novels only one was ever published. He channelled his activities mainly into science fiction, exaggerating aspects of contemporary America for satirical purposes. Robinson charts his career from its beginning in the 1950s to its peak in the next decade and subsequent decline. Edgar L. Chapman contributes a pamphlet on Philip José Farmer[170] to the Milford Popular Writers of Today series, outlining his life and prodigious output since 1952. He points out the clear influence of Edgar Rice Burroughs and discusses the series of 'fictional author' tales, one of which was published under the name of Vonnegut's Kilgore Trout. Douglas E. Winter has wasted no time in putting together a study of Stephen King[171] who operates within the genres of science fiction and Gothic horror. Winter's book is a guide rather than a critical analysis, and as such is useful for the bibliographical details it provides.

168. *The Ayn Rand Companion*, by Mimi Reisel Gladstein. Greenwood. pp. xii + 130. £23.95.

169. *The Novels of Philip K. Dick*, by Kim Stanley Robinson. UMIRes. pp. xii + 150. $24.95.

170. *The Magical Labyrinth of Philip José Farmer*, by Edgar L. Chapman. Popular Writers of Today. Borgo. pp. 96. pb $4.95.

171. *Stephen King: The Art of Darkness*, by Douglas E. Winter. NAL. pp. xix + 252. $14.95.

To conclude this section a number of articles should be noted on lesser-known contemporary novelists. John G. Parks (*TCL*) discusses Shirley Jackson's own particular variations on the Gothic mode, particularly the ways in which a disintegrating world forces her female protagonists into fantasy or madness. Charles H. Adams (*Crit*) chooses a rather older novel – W. M. Kelley's *A Different Drummer* (1962) – and finds gloom there about the possibility of a black community. Natalie Maynor and Richard F. Patteson (*Crit*) look at Russell Hoban's creation of a postholocaust dialect in *Riddley Walker* (1980) to evoke a regression to the primitive. The novels of Toni Morrison attract three critics. Peter B. Erickson surveys patterns of imagery in *The Tar Baby* (*CLAJ*), locating preoccupations with female sexuality and motherhood as the sources of narrative momentum. Elizabeth B. House (*AL*) also looks for patterns in the fictions but her preferences go to the repeated contrasts between idyllic dreams and the 'competitive acquisition of power or money'. Robert James Butler (*CentR*) relates Morrison's *Song of Solomon* to the tradition of mobility in American literature. He identifies a dialectical structure in the novel 'between the possibilities of space and the securities of place'.

4. Non-fictional Prose

Two equally important studies have been published of that scourge of provincialism, H. L. Mencken. Charles Scruggs gives an extremely well-documented account of Mencken's relations with black writers in the 1920s[172]. His call for naturalism predicted and even influenced the direction of the Harlem Renaissance, and his abrasive articles set a satirical pattern to be followed by writers like George Schuyler. During his editorship of the *American Mercury* (1924–33) Mencken opened its pages to Negro writers and joined others in pleading for a Great Negro Novel. Thanks to various different factors this hope (and Mencken's general confidence in Negro writing) waned considerably. Although Scruggs concentrates mainly on Mencken he also has much to say about Jean Toomer, Claude McKay, and Langston Hughes. Edward A. Martin sets Mencken in the broader context of 1920s satire[173]. Starting with an explanation of 'debunk' (coined in 1923), Martin traces Mencken's shift from progressivism towards harsher satire and examines both his subjects and his literary tactics. In this way he relates Mencken to Sinclair Lewis, Don Marquis, Ring Lardner, *The New Yorker*, and even to Nathaniel West whose attitudes and methods grew out of 1920s satire.

The year 1984 was the fiftieth anniversary of *PR* and to celebrate the occasion a special number of the journal has been produced with retrospective articles by William Phillips, Sidney Hook, *et al*. Excerpts from Lionel Trilling's notebooks are included, as are a play by Nabokov and an interview with Dwight Macdonald. Edith Kurzweil and William Phillips have put together an anthology of pieces from the same journal entitled *Writers and Politics*[174]. This gives a number of theoretical pieces by Camus, Trotsky, and others. The most

172. *The Sage in Harlem*, by Charles Scruggs. JHU. pp. viii + 213. $21.50.

173. *H. L. Mencken and the Debunkers*, by Edward A. Martin. UGeo. pp. 251. $22.50.

174. *Writers and Politics: A 'Partisan Review' Reader*, ed. by Edith Kurzweil and William Phillips. RKP. pp. x + 326. £8.95.

important articles in the present context are a commentary on the predicament of the American intellectual by Irving Howe, an examination of Hemingway's politics by Dwight Macdonald, and a survey of the American 1950s by Morris Dickstein. Given this anniversary, it is fitting that the cofounder with Philip Rahv of *PR*, William Phillips, should publish his memoirs[175]. Established in 1937, the journal was briefly affiliated with the John Reed Club until it broke away and under Phillips's editorship set a tradition of left-wing (but anticommunist) writing. It only survived with great difficulty during the war and during litigation with Rutgers when sponsorship was shifting to Boston University. Phillips includes in the course of this history thumb-nail sketches of a huge range of authors and shows the major developments in American intellectual life from the 1930s to the 1960s counterculture.

A selection of John Crowe Ransom's letters[176] has now been edited by T. D. Young and George Core with a definite thesis to put forward: that Ransom's formal and logical public mask hid his private feelings. His 'attitude toward sentiment' is the theme of this collection, most of the letters being written to his family of friends or long standing. In every case the letters are printed in their entirety with full biographical and explanatory notes. They range from 1911 (when Ransom was in Oxford), through the 1940s when he was involved with *KR*, to 1968. His two main correspondents were Robert Penn Warren, a lifelong friend, and Allen Tate, with whom he maintained a more formal professional relationship. This year has also seen the appearance of Elizabeth Bishop's *Collected Prose*[177] which brings together, among other writings, nine non-fictional pieces which were found among her papers after her death in 1979. They consist of memoir-articles on her childhood, Florida and Brazil, and her close friend Marianne Moore. The only piece which was published in her lifetime was her introduction to the Brazilian journal-novel, *The Diary of 'Helena Morley'*. Also included are eight stories dating as far back as 1937.

Two novelists, William Styron and Harlan Ellison, have both published collections of essays. Styron's *This Quiet Dust*[178] (1983), now in paperback, collects essays mostly from the 1960s and 1970s on such diverse topics as the death penalty, *Holocaust*, and the 1968 Democratic convention. The majority deal with literary topics, one of the most interesting being retrospective reflections on the furore over *The Confessions of Nat Turner* (1967) set in the context of historians' disputes over American slavery. Styron distrusts professional criticism (with its 'greasy little toolkits') so many of his articles read like memoirs or impressions. Nevertheless, his accounts of Faulkner's funeral, Peter Matthiessen, James Jones, and other contemporaries have a special value from being first-hand. Apart from being a leading practitioner of science fiction, Harlan Ellison has also made a name, through works like *The Glass Teat*, as a cultural critic, and *Sleepless Nights in the Procrustean Bed*[179] divides its attention between contemporary fiction and the commercialism of

175. *A Partisan View: Five Decades of the Literary Life*, by William Phillips. S&D. pp. 312. $19.95.

176. *Selected Letters of John Crowe Ransom*, ed. by T. D. Young and George Core. LSU. pp. 430. £32.55.

177. *The Collected Prose*, by Elizabeth Bishop. C&W. pp. xxii + 278. £12.95.

178. *This Quiet Dust and Other Writings*, by William Styron. BS. pp. 344. pb £4.95.

179. *Sleepless Nights in the Procrustean Bed*, by Harlan Ellison. Borgo. pp. 192. hb $14.95, pb $7.95.

the television networks. These essays show a shrewd awareness of the technological and even political aspects of the entertainment industry.

Sylvia Beach, Mabel Dodge Luhan, and James Agee all have in common a close involvement with literary production and experimentation without being major writers themselves. Noel Riley Fitch[180] has done a masterly job of rescuing Sylvia Beach from her own modesty and setting on record her prodigious entrepreneurial and promotional activities in Paris. Under her direction Shakespeare & Co. became an institution – variously a shop, salon, or simple gathering-place for writers. These activities have inevitably been overshadowed by her offer to publish *Ulysses*, a thankless and exhausting task which she came to regret. She also performed an important ambassadorial role between French and American culture, taking a prominent part in a Whitman exhibition among others. Fitch has used unpublished as well as published memoirs to give a uniquely full picture of Sylvia Beach's life. Mabel Dodge Luhan had a completely different personal style, coming from a wealthy Victorian background. Lois Palken Rudnick[181] describes her establishment of a Greenwich Village salon in the 1910s which became an important meeting-place for artists and radicals like John Reed. Seized with a primitivistic utopian dream Mabel Luhan then established her famous household community in Taos, New Mexico. As well as being a base for supporting the Pueblo Indians, from the 1920s until the Second World War, Taos became an obligatory place to visit for a whole range of figures from Lawrence and Jung to Georgia O'Keefe and Robinson Jeffers. Lois Rudnick has admirably documented the career of one of the most versatile and dynamic figures in modern American letters. James Agee[182], according to Laurence Bergreen, was also dynamic but in a curiously uncontrolled fashion. He moved from crisis to crisis, haunted by the memory of his father's early death. Agee too diversified his activities, writing poetry, screenplays (most famously for *The African Queen*), and articles and reviews for *Time*, *Fortune*, and *The Nation*. It is characteristic of his disorganized energy that his one major novel *A Death in the Family* should be published (unfinished) two years after his death. Bergreen gives a thorough and incisive account of Agee's documentary report on the share-croppers (*Let Us Now Praise Famous Men* is arguably a masterpiece of reportage) and his abiding fascination with the cinema in the 1940s and 1950s.

Four autobiographical memoirs, this time by quite diverse writers, have also appeared. Carl Sandburg's *Ever the Winds of Chance*[183] was written in 1955 when he was planning to extend his autobiography, but was left unfinished. Accordingly what we have before us is only a draft. It covers his years at Lombard College, Illinois, from 1898 to 1902 and details his reading enthusiasms (Browning, Lamb, etc.) During this period he became involved with the *Lombard Review*, trying his hand at editorials and poems. The final chapters of this volume take us up to 1905. Sandburg had decided to become a writer but drifted around the country hopping trains. Finally, when he moved to Chicago, he took up a post as advertising manager for *The Lyceumite* and first began to develop his interest in radical literature and politics. Mary

180. *Sylvia Beach and the Lost Generation*, by Noel Riley Fitch. Souvenir. pp. 447. £14.95.
181. *Mabel Dodge Luhan*, by Lois Palken Rudnick. UNM. pp. xvi + 384. $19.95.
182. *James Agee, A Life*, by Laurence Bergreen. Dutton. pp. xii + 467. $20.
183. *Ever the Winds of Chance*, by Carl Sandburg. UIll (1983). pp. xiii + 172. £12.25.

Barnard's *Assault on Mount Helicon*[184] would be the memoir of an obscure minor poet had it not been for the friends she made. In 1933 she submitted some poems to Ezra Pound for his comments and this marked the beginning of a long friendship with him, William Carlos Williams, and Marianne Moore, many of whose letters are published here for the first time. Eventually Mary Barnard's major work *Sappho. A New Translation* was published in 1959. *Assault on Mount Helicon* gives important and revealing views of the Yaddo Summer School, the beginnings of the New Directions publishing house, and of the general difficulties of getting published in the 1930s and 1940s. Lionel Abel's *The Intellectual Follies*[185] is a totally different kind of book, being a cross between a memoir and commentary on American intellectual life from the 1930s by a noted New York playwright and essayist. Abel thus covers some of the same ground as William Phillips. He participated in the WPA Writers Project and reflects generally on left-wing radicalism in the 1930s; and is also particularly incisive on André Breton and the Surrealists, and on the rise of 'off-Broadway' drama in the 1950s. The Greek-American novelist Harry M. Petrakis has brought together two books in one, simply entitled *Reflections*[186]. The first, *Stelmark*, narrates Petrakis's early life in Chicago up to the point where he started writing and supplies one more significant account of the immigrant writer's clash of allegiances to the old and the new. The second, *Journal of a Novel*, follows Steinbeck's model in charting Petrakis's research from 1972 to 1975 for *The Hour of the Bell*, his novel about the Greek War of Independence.

Humour is the other important area to receive consideration. The English Department of Barcelona University has produced a volume of proceedings from the sixth conference of the Spanish Association of Anglo-North American Studies[187]. The theme of the volume is humour and a significant proportion of the papers deal with American culture. David Royot looks at ethnic humour, Brigitte Scheer-Schaezler discusses the relation of comedy to history in Bellow's fiction, and Kevin Power the Nietzschean humour of Ed Dorn's *Gunslinger*. Lastly, Paul Witkowsky takes up the unlikely but, as it turns out, surprisingly important topic of plumbing in *Babbitt*. In 1932 a satirical but non-aligned periodical called *Americana* was founded in New York. It had an uneasy and very brief existence, running through less than twenty monthly issues, but it numbered among its contributors George Grosz, Kenneth Burke, and Gilbert Seldes. Clive Giboire[188] has now performed an important service in reprinting a selection of pieces from this journal, including items by e. e. cummings and Nathaniel West. *Lightest Blues* has a double literary and historical interest in compiling contemporary comments on America during the Depression.

The circle of humorists which includes Thurber, Robert Benchley, and E. B.

184. *Assault on Mount Helicon: A Literary Memoir*, by Mary Barnard. UCal. pp. xviii + 332. £18.30.

185. *The Intellectual Follies*, by Lionel Abel. Norton. pp. 304. $17.95.

186. *Reflections*, by Harry M. Petrakis. Lake View (1983). pp. 252. hb $16.95, pb $9.95.

187. *Literary and Linguistic Aspects of Humour*, ed. by Doireann MacDermott. UBarcelona. pp. 311.

188. *Lightest Blues, Great Humor from the Thirties*, ed. by Clive Giboire. Imago. pp. 239. hb $25, pb $14.95.

White has been well served by reprints, biographies, and critical studies. Scott Elledge has written the first life of E. B. White[189], using the White archive at Cornell University. He joined *The New Yorker* when it was founded in 1925 and became a regular contributor to its 'Notes and Comments' section. He also wrote light verse, collaborated with Thurber on their comic look at psychiatry, *Is Sex Necessary?* (1929), and began a series of 'preposterous parables' in 1928. During the postwar years he published several children's books and a 1954 miscellany entitled *The Second Tree from the Corner*. Elledge's biography shows White to have been a many-sided writer – not only a humorist but also a naturalist (he was a fervent admirer of Thoreau) and political commentator. An anthology of pieces by Robert Benchley, *The Benchley Roundup*[190], first published in 1954, has been re-issued. This volume gathers together sketches written between 1915 and 1945 for periodicals like *Vanity Fair* and *The New Yorker*, and was selected by Benchley's son. Thurber reprints continue to appear regularly, notably *Thurber's Dogs*[191] and his 1959 memoir of *The New Yorker, The Years with Ross*[192]. Thurber has much to say on its founding editor Harold Ross, but also surveys contributors to the periodical such as E. B. White, Benchley, and Ogden Nash. C. M. Kenney[193] has analysed Thurber's whole output, whether fables, drawings, or poems, and summed it up as a 'systematic study of chaos'. She suggests that Thurber used humour therapeutically as an anodyne to anxiety. Borrowing some of Thurber's own terms (like Twain he distinguished firmly between comedy and humour), she examines his treatment of the mechanical, the prominence of animals in his work, and the games he plays with readers' expectations. Thurber emerges as a complex stylist strongly influenced by James, and Kenney endorses the recurring vein of melancholy in his work which was first spotted by E. B. White.

5. Drama

It is hardly necessary to say so, but Gerald Bordman's *The Oxford Companion to American Theatre*[194] is, in the true meaning of an overworked adjective, indispensable. Not only is it massively researched and comprehensive, but it is written with sheer pleasure and a lightness of style that take it beyond the plain worthiness of the customary standard reference work. Bordman is alert to the need to operate within the 'mainstream' of American theatrical activity, and although the more experimental theatre of the 1960s and 1970s is not covered as fully as one might have wished, the author refuses to be confined by the enduringly familiar or the canonically significant. He is thus also responsive to the genuinely popular aspects of his subject and includes entries on musicals as well as on minstrelsy, vaudeville, circuses, and

189. *E. B. White: A Biography*, by Scott Elledge. Norton. pp. xv + 400. £19.95.

190. *The Benchley Roundup*, by Robert Benchley. UChic. pp. x + 333. £8.25.

191. *Thurber's Dogs*, by James Thurber. S&S. pp. xvii + 288. pb $7.95.

192. *The Years with Ross*, by James Thurber. HH. pp. 274. pb £4.95.

193. *Thurber's Anatomy of Comparison*, by C. M. Kenney. Archon. pp. xii + 235. £22.75.

194. *The Oxford Companion to American Theatre*, by Gerald Bordman. OUP. pp. vi + 704. £35.

wild west shows. Additionally, it is extremely useful to have the occasional entry devoted to the ideas of theatre – to 'Blacks in American Theatre and Drama' or to 'Little Theatre in America', for example. Thoroughly in keeping with its substantive matter, this is one of the most entertaining reference works around – to be read as well as merely consulted.

The second volume of C. W. E. Bigsby's impressive survey of the American theatre, *A Critical Introduction to Twentieth-Century American Drama*[195], examines its major postwar practitioners: Tennessee Williams, Arthur Miller, and Edward Albee. Williams and Miller in particular are rendered acutely responsive to the shifts from New Deal liberalism towards postwar conservatism with its new claims for conformity upon the individual, and its concomitant disturbances of the self's possibilities for transformative private fictions and for authentic public behaviour. Bigsby views both playwrights as engaged within a move (engendered by a recognition of the inadequacies of the political stances available during the 1930s) from the social to the metaphysical through a reconstructed romanticism. Albee, whose first works were staged as the careers of the earlier two seemed to be faltering, is seen as centralizing their concerns with the nature of the 'real' by a struggle 'to fictionalise the world as it attempts to fictionalise him'. All three, despite their involvement (inevitably so, within a different mode of critical discourse) in forms of acquiescence with the very issues they deplore, are regarded as sharing a belief in some final redemptive possibility. For Bigsby, this belief marks theirs as, with the exception of O'Neill, 'the outstanding achievement of the American theatre' because of their capacity to address the anxieties of their age: 'They lament the decline of the moral self and the slow fading of a vision but in doing so they implicitly make a case for the possibility of change and indeed see in the theatre itself a principal agent of transformation and a paradigm of the social, moral and spiritual community whose decline they regret.'

The Macmillan Modern Dramatists series continues with Bernard F. Dukore's *American Dramatists 1918–1945*[196], a volume which deliberately excludes O'Neill because of Normand Berlin's study in the same series, and also because of a wish to remove the playwrights treated here from under O'Neill's shadow to suggest 'the intrinsic value of their work'. Dukore chooses to chart the period when 'America's first wave of major dramatists came of age'. After a breezy introductory chapter on the conditions of (essentially, New York) theatre of the 1910s and the intervention of O'Neill, the author deals in turn with selected moments from the works of Elmer Rice, e. e. cummings, George S. Kaufman and Moss Hart, Maxwell Anderson, Clifford Odets, Thornton Wilder, Lillian Hellman, and William Saroyan. Dukore conducts his survey briskly, and if, on occasion, it threatens to become a descriptive listing of major plays, it redeems itself invariably by a freshness of perspective and a liveliness of discussion which generate, for example, strong claims for the importance of less familiar works such as cummings's *Him*.

The revised edition of James Roose-Evans's *Experimental Theatre from*

195. *A Critical Introduction to Twentieth-Century American Drama*, Vol. II, by C. W. E. Bigsby. CUP. pp. viii + 355. hb £25, pb £7.95.

196. *American Dramatists 1918–1945*, by Bernard F. Dukore. MMD. Macmillan. pp. xiv + 191. hb £15, pb £4.95.

Stanislavsky to Brook[197] is roughly twice the length of the original 1970 publication. While its main attention remains directed towards the English and European avant-garde, the author chooses, interestingly in view of his selectiveness, to locate America's contribution in the choreography of Martha Graham and Alwin Nikolais, the Dancers' Workshop of Anna Halprin, and in those theatre groups (such as the Living Theatre, the Open Theatre, the Squat, the Bread and Puppet Theatre) and those directors (such as Richard Foreman and Robert Wilson) whose 'commitment is primarily to the non-professional'. As an experimental director of fringe activities himself, the author's selectiveness goes beyond the putative sneers of perverseness from academic critics and stresses precisely those theatrical activities on the margins which sustain the book's opening premise: 'To experiment is to make a foray into the unknown – it is something that can be charted only after the event.'

Gertrude Stein wrote seventy-seven plays, twenty-three of which have actually reached the stage. Betsy Alayne Ryan's study, *Gertrude Stein's Theatre of the Absolute*[198], is, by its very existence, a rarity whose originality is further sustained by a detailed account of Stein's dramaturgical aesthetic and techniques, a listing of the plays' traits whereby they may most fruitfully be analysed, and a powerful argument for Stein's effect within the contemporary avant-garde theatre. From a scholarly point of view, Ryan's deployment of a vast range of unpublished material is extremely impressive, and what are simply of great practical use are the catalogues with which she concludes: a first chronology of the plays by composition and by production, and a bibliography of reviews of those productions. Ryan's entire project is convened through a consideration of Stein's more general aesthetic of the 'now', predominantly via her concerns with notions of time and entity, to substantiate a view of 'immediate dynamic, and self-contained theatre' which disrupts the 'alternate reality' and relational context of traditional drama by keeping the focus of the spectator upon the present moment of theatre itself. Ryan has produced an excellent account of her subject, a book whose absence from any subsequent consideration of the field would be unimaginable.

William Carlos Williams wrote few plays, for which we should be grateful. They have generated two recent commentaries: David A. Fedo's *William Carlos Williams: A Poet in the American Theatre*[199] and Steven Ross Loevy's *William Carlos Williams' 'A Dream of Love'*[200]. Fedo is engagingly sensible in that, while wanting to challenge what he views as the unjustified critical neglect of Williams's excursions into the theatre, he resists overstating his case for the quality of those excursions. Although Williams's plays evinced uncertainties both of control and a sense of dramatic resolution, they did provide opportunities for exploring one of his most fundamental beliefs, the testing of language's capacities to be 'swung': as Fedo remarks of *A Dream of Love*, 'the drama pushes from the language itself'. The author successfully

197. *Experimental Theatre from Stanislavsky to Brook*, by James Roose-Evans. Rev. edn. RKP. pp. x + 210. pb £6.95.

198. *Gertrude Stein's Theatre of the Absolute*, by Betsy Alayne Ryan. Studies in Modern Literature. UMIRes. pp. xiv + 232. $39.95.

199. *William Carlos Williams: A Poet in the American Theatre*, by David A. Fedo. Studies in Modern Literature. UMIRes (1983). pp. x + 203. £33.25.

200. *William Carlos Williams' 'A Dream of Love'*, by Steven Ross Loevy. Studies in Modern Literature. UMIRes (1983). pp. ix + 82. £25.

distributes his attention between the plays considered in their own terms and, through their concern with issues of history, locality, love, autobiography, and language, their relationships within the more familiar canon of Williams's work. Loevy's study has no pretence to scholarship. He places what is generally acknowledged to be Williams's best play, *A Dream of Love*, in the context of his two prior compositions for the theatre, *The First President* and *Many Loves*, and, while refusing the play's autobiographical dimensions, proceeds to offer a reading on behalf of an imagined director, providing a 'conceptual framework by which to design the overall impact' and explaining 'how to speak the lines'. These imaginings add sturdiness to an appreciative and sensitive account of the play's concerns with issues of love and utterance.

In 'The Theatre of Metaphor' (*PR*) Robert Brustein essays a general account of the relationship between politics and the arts in the theatre, finding the key to lie in a capacity for metaphor and that, contemporaneously, such a capacity is most prevalent in the *American* theatre. In an interesting chronicle of contemporary activity, 'The Medicine Show Log: Reconstructing a Traditional American Entertainment' (*DRev*), Brooks McNamara gives a first-hand account of Steve Zeitlin's restaging of a medicine show at the Smithsonian Institute's Summer 1979 Folklife Festival in Washington, its repeat for the documentary film *Free Show Tonight* in 1980 at Bailey, North Carolina, its further repeat for the Folklife Festival in 1981, and again, under the name of the 'Vi-Ton-Ka Medicine Show' in New York in 1983. McNamara concludes with a printing of one of the most popular medicine show comedy sketches, 'Niagara Falls'.

Susan L. Carlson's stimulating 'Comic Textures and Female Communities, 1937 and 1977: Clare Boothe and Wendy Wasserstein' (*MD*) analyses Boothe's *The Women* and Wasserstein's *Uncommon Women and Others* to 'disclose the kinds of female characters and communities comedy encourages or discourages'. While Boothe's play exposes the limitations imposed by comedy upon its female characters, Wasserstein creates 'a comic world where women can work within a female community to challenge social roles'. In ' "The Will to Live": An Interview with Arthur Miller' (*MD*) Steven R. Centola records a largely uneventful conversation of 1982 with Miller.

Sam Shepard attracts two fairly ordinary essays. In 'Mythic Levels in Shepard's *True West*' (*MD*) Tucker Orbison argues that even though Shepard has moved from a relatively mysterious, mythic, surreal theatre to one that is more realistic and conventional, he continues to draw upon the resources of myth at the sociohistorical, artistic, and psychological levels, while amidst a general complaint about the absence of an active literary environment in the theatre, Herbert Blau's 'The American Dream in American Gothic: The Plays of Sam Shepard and Adrienne Kennedy' (*MD*) selects the talents of Shepard and Kennedy as exemplifying 'the persistence of desire in language to overcome the failed promise' of America itself.

In the general context (only briefly alluded to) of an argument for the drama of the last thirty years being 'antilanguage', Kathleen Gregory Klein, in 'Language and Meaning in Megan Terry's 1970s "Musicals" ' (*MD*), examines *Tommy Allen Show, Babes in the Bighouse, Brazil Fado*, and *American King's English for Queens* unremarkably as challenges to 'the perceptions moulded by language itself and the clichés about language as a vehicle for communication', and affirmations of a faith that language 'is never without meaning or power'.

Posing the question 'Has Williams' effectiveness as a playwright suffered a recent decline?' Ruby Cohn, in 'Late Tennessee Williams' (*MD*), nominates by way of an implicit answer three 'major' plays from the last decade of Williams's life: *The Two-Character Play*, *Vieux Carre*, and *Clothes for a Summer Hotel*. More interesting and more sophisticated on Williams is Jack E. Wallace's 'The Image of Theatre in Tennessee Williams' *Orpheus Descending*' (*MD*). Wallace notes the limitations of readings of *Orpheus Descending* which centre on Val, and, sustaining his argument by a careful consideration of Williams's extensive revisions, claims that Williams's adjustment to commercial America occasioned a concept of theatre which is more clearly reflected in the rebellion of Lady and Carol than in the fugitive role of Val.

African, Caribbean, Indian, Australian, and Canadian Literature in English

JAMES BOOTH, SUSHEILA NASTA, PRABHU GUPTARA, JOHN THIEME, and CHARLES STEELE

This chapter has the following sections: 1. Africa, by James Booth; 2. The Caribbean, by Susheila Nasta; 3. India, by Prabhu Guptara; 4. Australia, by John Thieme; 5. Canada, by Charles Steele.

1. Africa

(a) General

In 'Bibliographies on African Literature since 1970' (*RAL*) Yvette Scheven provides titles of a selection of bibliographies devoted to particular countries, individual authors, and those of general scope. Particularly useful is the quarterly *African Book Publishing Record*, edited by Hans M. Zell. The title of Ezenwa-Ohaeto's 'Studies in African Literature in a Nigerian University: A Bibliographical Checklist of B.A. Theses in the Department of English, University of Nigeria, Nsukka (1977–1982)' (*RAL*) is self-explanatory. The standard length for these undergraduate theses is forty typed pages. A new, excellently produced journal, *Wasafiri*, published by ATCAL, made its debut in 1984. Its first issue carries an essay by Anne Walmsley, which recounts the specific intrusions of censorship on ATCAL to date. Dennis Brutus could not attend its 1980 conference since he could not leave the United States without losing his right of re-entry; Micere Githae-Mugo who spoke at the 1981 conference was later to flee into exile from Kenya; Lauretta Ngcobo, president of ATCAL at the time of writing, has been in exile from South Africa since 1963 and her novel is banned there. Walmsley goes on to define various forms of censorship, from the formally explicit systems of South Africa and Malawi to the 'unrecorded' harassment and suppression in Kenya. The essay is most eloquent in its sober recital of facts.

Although Neil McEwan opens his book *Africa and the Novel*[1] with the statement 'I mean to put a case of interest to everyone who reads new novels', his book will be most valuable to a particular kind of British reader, one with little knowledge of Africa and some characteristic prejudices. Other readers,

1. *Africa and the Novel*, by Neil McEwan. Macmillan (1983). pp. x + 179. £22.50.

particularly Africans, may be disconcerted by his attempts to 'put a case of interest' for their national literatures, which continually places them in a context defined by Kingsley Amis, John Barth, Anthony Burgess, George Watson, and other representatives of the British and American literary establishment of the 1950s and 1960s. McEwan's first chapter, 'Modern Africa', argues vigorously that 'Achebe, Ngugi, Soyinka and others have been writing fiction which is fully contemporary', and sets out to refute 'the false hypothesis that Africa's present state can be equated with Europe's past'. The second chapter, 'Colonial Africa', offers expositions of novels by Achebe, Ferdinand Oyono, and Camara Laye, including a lucid analysis of the shifting register of *Things Fall Apart* from that of an unquestioning member of 1890s Igbo society to that of a sophisticated observer of the 1950s. Chapter Three, 'Independence', treats works by Soyinka, Achebe, and Armah. *The Interpreters* is described as 'a bright satire, full of good sense and good humour which are African and contemporary', and is related to Kingsley Amis's *One Fat Englishman* and Anthony Burgess's *Inside Mr Enderby*. A miscellaneous fourth chapter, 'Stories, Themes and Impressions in Recent African Fiction', treats Ngugi, Farah, Mwangi, and La Guma, and the final chapter, 'Outsiders?', focuses on Nadine Gordimer and Laurens van der Post. The limitation of McEwan's liberal, common-sense, British approach is seen in the confident tone in which he prescribes a satisfactory role to the white writer in South Africa: 'a quiet, persevering, intelligent dissent is the best policy for a white novelist'. He later remarks that van der Post risks scenes which most writers would avoid as too sentimental, but 'we accept them because we come to respect the narrator'. The confident 'we' here clearly does not include those to whom van der Post's brand of paternalist emotionalism has become unacceptable.

Some of the essays on general topics explore familiar territory, attacking Eurocentric notions of Africa from various viewpoints, or surveying its literature in terms of culture conflict and postcolonial crisis. Other essays however attempt more conceptual dynamism, offering revisionist critiques of these orthodoxies, or alternatively adopting the newer theoretical positions of structuralism or feminism. In Willfried F. Feuser's 'Reflections of History in African literature' (*WLWE*) some familiar abuse of Hugh Trevor-Roper is followed by a wide-ranging account of postcolonial political developments: 'the messianism of the early leadership often turns into caesarism, the new millennium into a scene of murderous megalomania, the dream into nightmare'. Brief analyses are given of some selected works, the 'classic' historical novels, *Things Fall Apart*, *Arrow of God*, and *The River Between* being inexplicably ignored. Solomon Plaatje's *Mhudi* is treated, and Mazisi Kunene's *Emperor Shaka the Great* is persuasively accused of failing to reconcile the image-laden language of epic with the conceptualized language of political analysis. A brief discussion of Soyinka's *A Dance of the Forests* follows, and Feuser goes on to express a preference for the second of Armah's two historical romances, *The Healers*, in which he detects 'perfect localization and greater proximity to historical truth' than in *Two Thousand Seasons*. Christophe Dailly's 'The Coming of Age of the African Novel' (*PA*) summarizes the plots of *Petals of Blood*, *Two Thousand Seasons*, and *In the Fog of the Season's End*, and concludes that Ngugi, Armah, and Alex La Guma 'endeavour to bridge the past and the present in order to arrive smoothly into the future'. The African novel has, Dailly feels, come of age in these novels because they show 'the common man as the shaper of African history' and include no white liberal or Asian allies of the blacks. Dailly's judgement is ideologically simplistic and his thematic focus ignores all complexities of style and tone: 'These three novelists', he tells us, 'have discarded romanticism to write objectively about African history.' This may be true enough of La Guma, but both the other writers (Armah quite deliberately) frequently project an ideal precolonial harmony. Dailly is mistaken when he asserts that we are here 'very far from the Negritude movement and its everlasting tendency to beautify the African past'. Juliet Okonkwo's focus in 'The Intellectual as Political Activist: A Character Type in Recent African Fiction' (*PA*) falls on novels of the 1960s and early 1970s, in which she detects a new political positivism 'which transcended the novels of disillusion and offered solutions to the ills they exposed'. She treats Robert Serumaga's *Return to the Shadows*, Soyinka's *Season of Anomy*, and Armah's *Two Thousand Seasons*. Unfortunately her approach, like Dailly's, is reductively thematic, and under her analysis these complex, uneven, and often ambiguous works of literature become diagrammatic manuals of ideological instruction. The muddled authorial stance in Serumaga's novel is ignored, and the Dentist in Soyinka's novel and Isanusi in Armah's are presented as unambiguously successful portrayals of positive heroism. The essay has little to offer those interested in literature as a sensitive register of real imaginative and ideological issues.

Ken Goodwin's 'Political Power and Social Flexibility in African and Australian Novels' (*WLWE*) offers 'a comparative study of how conflict is dealt with in the work of six novelists, three African, three Australian'. Goodwin contrasts the flexibility of the Asante society portrayed in Yaw M. Boateng's *The Return* with the rigid convict regime in Thomas Keneally's *Bring Larks and Heroes*. He compares Achebe's *Arrow of God* at various points with Roger McDonald's *1915*, and contrasts Ngugi's tone of apocalyptic vision in *Petals of Blood* with David Ireland's sceptical fatalism in *The Unknown Industrial Prisoner*. Some limited general conclusions are ventured: for example, that West African society, as portrayed by Boateng and Achebe, is more flexible in some respects than parliamentary democracy, and that the two novels (African and Australian) dealing with 'the past about to fade' are more optimistic in tone than those dealing with either the past proper or the immediate present. Goodwin offers no explanation apart from chronological parallelism and a general 'colonial' association between the two continents, as to why this particular asssortment of novels should have invited comparison. And it is difficult not to feel that quite different, even opposite, implications could easily have been drawn simply by choosing six different works from Africa and Australia. Also somewhat miscellaneous in effect, though quite theoretically stimulating, is 'The African Short Story Written in English: A Survey' (*ArielE*) by Jean de Grandsaigne and Gary Spackey. A comparison between Poe's well-turned stories and the 'open form' preferred by some later writers is followed by a thematic diagnosis of the African short story, stressing its concern with present-day situations and its depiction of a perpetual unresolved conflict between the old and the new. Mphahlele's threefold classification of the 'romantic-escapist' story, 'the protest story', and the 'ironic short story' is mentioned, but is rejected in favour of 'a purely textual approach'. Possible connections between the art of the oral tale and that of the written story are tentatively suggested; they may perhaps share the same 'evocative African imagery' and allude to the same 'intertext'. More theoretically cogent is Mineke Schipper's interdisciplinary exercise in literature and anthropology, 'Eurocentrism and Criticism: Reflections on the Study of Literature in Past and Present' (*WLWE*). Schipper notes that although 'cultural evolutionism', which sees society as evolving from primitivism to Western complexity, has long been subject to attack in anthropological circles, such Eurocentrism still flourishes in literary criticism. Schipper rejects Wellek's evaluative approach, recognizes that the cultural relativism of Herskovits can be equally ethnocentric in encouraging an apartheid distinction between cultures, and approves Bernard Mouralis's notion of 'counter-literatures'. She wishes to see an openness in critics towards other cultures, and an attempt to transcend the polarity between evaluative absolutism and cultural separatism.

The question of language is a recurrent element in several essays, including F. Odun Balogun's 'The African Novel: A Developmental Assessment' (*CNE*). Balogun argues that ultimately all fiction, including the European novel, derives from oral tales, 'which all over the world exhibit essentially the same characteristics'. Africa thus has as much claim to the 'Western' novel form as Europe. Balogun defends fiction in 'Africanized' European languages and refuses to endorse Obiajunwa Wali's pronouncement 'that any true African literature must be written in African languages'. Nevertheless he agrees with Ngugi that language can be a powerful imperialist instrument of acculturation, and notes that the modern European nations threw off the yoke of Latin and Greek by translating them, while Russian 'was a language relegated to the background in Russia up till the nineteenth century'. He predicts that the literatures already well established in Swahili, Yoruba, and Ibo will flourish, though he recognizes that 'for the foreseeable future they will still have to co-exist as a less-favoured partner with African literature in foreign languages'. Balogun's useful essay ends by tracing the generic development of the African novel from its oral beginnings, and its thematic development from the slavery period, through colonialism to the present day.

Two essays seem almost designed to illustrate the extremes of Eurocentric and Afrocentric criticism, particularly in relation to the language issue. Albert S. Gérard's 'Literary Tradition and Literary Change in Black Africa' (*JCL*) is refreshingly blunt in its refusal to be impressed by the return to preliterate roots. Oral tradition is in his view irrelevant to the complex modern world: 'It has never been the purpose of oral art to question premises or encourage heresy.' Gérard develops an extended parallel between Rome's early and complete conquest of the Celts and the thorough French *assimilation* of its colonial subjects. Thus, just as the Celts adopted the Latin language and their vernaculars were not reduced to writing until more than six centuries after the fall of the Roman Empire, so does French dominate the literate élites in former French territories, while the vernaculars are scarcely cultivated yet. In the former British Empire, Gérard argues, the situation is more akin to that beyond the *limes* of the later Roman Empire, where writing was brought not by conquest, but by Christian missionaries. Thus Irish and Germanic literatures developed as an early alternative to that in Latin long before the Romance languages came to be written down; and similarly the African in a former British colony already has a real choice of his own language as an alternative to English. Gérard is unmoved by the 'shrill denunciation of

European literary supremacy' which has recently developed in relation to literature in the colonial languages, and which he relates to the coming to maturity of a generation educated wholly within Africa. 'To the European reader using cultured standards, their work is certainly a mediocre sample of English- or French-language fiction. But in the African context it may come to be regarded as signifying the real birth of a genuine African tradition of writing . . . Only time (meaning not decades but centuries) will tell us which of today's novelties will go to the making of a tradition.' He guesses that vernacular literature will only prosper in the Anglophone territories. Gérard's leisurely historical overview is in sharp contrast to the urgent immediacy of Ngugi wa Thiong'o's approach in 'The Tension Between National and Imperialist Culture' (*WLWE*). In this essay, originally presented at a conference on Commonwealth literature in West Germany, Ngugi attacks the neo-imperialist conception of a 'Commonwealth' identity, grouping together as it does 'literatures and cultures . . . whose basis of coherence is their relationship to the British throne'. He rejects the conference's formulation: 'the tension between indigenous and metropolitan cultures and literatures'. The real tension in his view is between 'national democratic' cultures and 'imperialist' cultures. The attempt of the imperialist powers to destroy indigenous language was an attempt to destroy indigenous culture, and the minority who continue to use European languages see 'through the eyeglasses of imperialism'. Ngugi goes on to tell the story of his involvement with the Kamiriithu Educational and Cultural Centre, for which he wrote his first play in Gikuyu. It was suppressed after nine performances and Ngugi was imprisoned. While in prison he wrote his Gikuyu novel, on coarse toilet paper, which 'although it was very bad for the body . . . was very good writing material'. His second Gikuyu play, scheduled for performance at the National Theatre, was again suppressed, and the Kamiriithu Centre was razed to the ground by the police. The coercion and harassment Ngugi has attracted since he started to appeal to the vernacular audience should perhaps be borne in mind when assessing Gérard's Olympian perspective.

The question of language also figures in a methodical and dispassionate essay by A. N. Ebeogu, 'African Literature: Regional, National and Ethnic Imperatives' (*ArielE*, 1983). African literature can, as Ebeogu shows, be treated as a unity; regional divisions however, between West, East, South, and North, are increasingly important; and the familiar European focus on national literature is well advanced in some cases, particularly that of Nigeria. Ethnic literatures in vernacular languages form natural units, but European languages have also been naturalized in new ethnic contexts. Following Achebe, for instance, a thorough 'Igboization' of English has been effected. A more hard-hitting and sceptical overview of African literary criticism is given by David Attwell in 'The British Legacy in Anglophone African Literary Criticism' (*EinA*). From a distinctively South African perspective Attwell criticizes the 'undisguised essentialist concepts' which characterize much literary criticism in independent black Africa: 'African taste, African culture and aesthetics, African standards, Africanness.' He feels that this stridency betrays an uneasiness in the critics about the influence in Africa of European critical and theoretical traditions. Upon Independence the choice lay between building upon the British legacy ('literature from Chaucer to Achebe') or 'Africanizing' the syllabus, and cultural nationalism ensured that it was the second option that was largely adopted. Attwell points out that the literary culture was in fact 'becoming increasingly academicized', and that the inevitable retention of the English language in higher education further insulated the academic literary establishment from the populace. 'Intellectually, the relationship of African criticism to the British heritage is a provincial one', Attwell concludes. Attwell ends by convicting Abiola Irele's 'sociological imagination' of irrelevance to the real social complexities of Africa, and diagnosing the provincialisms of Romanus Egudu, Emmanuel Ngara, and Ali Mazrui. His argument is cogent and persuasive; but its unrelieved destructiveness is somewhat oppressive. Less ideologically sceptical, but more sympathetic, is Robert Green's attempt to revise the excesses of Afrocentrism in 'African Literary Criticism: The Banality of Cannibalism' (*JCL*). He, like Attwell, laments the insularity and parochialism of much African criticism, referring to its 'startling absence of theoretical sophistication', and he also attributes this backwardness to the preoccupation with 'relevance', which though inevitable and necessary, entails some negative consequences. As European syllabuses have been rejected, so the complex critical history attendant on the European classics has vanished with them. There is a danger of new 'instant classics' being created in Africa, which, lacking any context of accumulated perspectives, are at once subject to a reverential bromide of analysis. In this situation literary criticism becomes a mere service to the system. Green attacks such 'cultural protectionism', and argues that a novel by Balzac set in Paris in the last century can tell the contemporary black reader 'more about his own capital, Lagos or Nairobi, than an African novel superficially more "relevant"'. Indeed, Green looks forward to the possibility of a reversal of the cultural traffic between the continents, whereby valuable new critical insights may be offered by African critics into the distant literature of Shakespeare, Brecht, and Sophocles. Green ends with a defence of the 'battered and bruised' concept of universality which, though often justifiably suspect, is still in his view necessary and valuable.

The appearance of three essays by West Africans in an anthology of criticism intended to stress the problematic relation between 'black texts' and the canon of 'Western literary criticism'[2] may perhaps suggest that Green's perception of the theoretical poverty of African criticism is a little out of date. The contribution by Wole Soyinka, 'The critic and society: Barthes, leftocracy, and other mythologies', is a characteristically original piece accusing critics of African literature of 'building up c.v.s at the expense of the condemned productivity', and adopting 'the *langue* of the assessors of the Appointments and Promotions Committee or of the learned journals' while neglecting '*l'engage* of social signification' (he freely admits the awfulness of the ungrammatical pun). 'In short', he asks, 'is the excursion into Onitsha Market Literature or alias Majority music ever different from opportunism, an appropriation of proletarian production by a member of the bourgeoisie for its small erudite coterie?' Soyinka is particularly concerned with those 'leftocrats' who attack the works of African writers, including himself, for lacking 'relevance' to the masses. In his view the sociology of such critics invites examination itself; Barthes was only too aware of the paradox of the bourgeois critic setting out to demythologize the bourgeoisie. Soyinka next turns to different targets in the literary

2. *Black Literature and Literary Theory*, ed. by Henry Louis Gates Jr. Methuen. pp. 328. £15.

establishment, convicting Gerald Moore of inventing a spurious 'Yoruba-Mooreland', and accusing Bernth Lindfors's oft-reprinted essay on his (Soyinka's) earliest writing (see *YW* 64.538) of 'the lucrative business of juvenile hagiography of everything that moves on two feet, from pop stars to syndicated criminals'. This, he says, 'is very much the lifestyle of American letters. It is to be hoped that it never becomes a way of life in Nigeria.' Soyinka's summary of the abusers of African literary criticism will strike a familiar note with those who have read this section of *YWES* in previous years: 'the self-seekers, the opportunists, the radical chic and the starkly ideological illiterate'. It is interesting that, when Soyinka leaves such crisp demystification for a defence of his own work against the charge of essentialist idealism, his style becomes contorted and overheated, and his references to Barthes seem a mere excuse for rhapsodies on the *metalangue* of music and the 'ahistorical' permanence of the emotion of love.

The two other relevant essays in Gates's collection take opposing views on structuralism. Sunday O. Anozie in 'Negritude, structuralism, deconstruction' denies that the search for 'internal coherence', which characterizes structuralism, is incompatible with Irele's 'sociological imagination'. Indeed 'no adequate sociological theory of African literature, the novel in particular, can be formulated outside a framework of structuralism'. Anozie analyses Senghor's poem 'Le Totem' in an attempt to reconcile structuralism with negritude. Anthony Appiah's 'Strictures on structures: the prospects for a structuralist poetics of African fiction' mounts an elegant attack on Anozie's *Structural Models and African Poetics*, accusing it of being 'threateningly hermetic' and jargon-ridden. The essay, which includes a patient and lucid account of the theories of Saussure, is essentially an empiricist critique of the 'privileged' status of linguistics in structuralist thought, which 'seems to derive only from the scientism of our culture and its times'. Appiah concludes that Anozie's book will only serve to confirm the view of many 'that literary study is a matter not of the development of theory but of a sensitive understanding of literary texts'. Willy A. Umezinwa's 'Une Théorie Semiotique de la Ligne Vectorielle dans le Romain Africain' (*Neoh*) gives a compendious overview of Francophone and Anglophone writers, including Armah, Achebe, Dillibe Onyeama, Ngugi, Peter Abrahams, Es'kia Mphahlele, and Paton.

'Titles, Names and Themes in African Literature' (*QQ*) by Carroll Lasker and Kwaku Amoabeng discusses the onomatology of African literature. It includes some interesting information: that Baako means 'a solitary figure' and Onipa 'a person' for instance; that Ikemefuna means 'let my power/labour not go to waste'; and that Okonkwo is a combination of *okoro* meaning 'a man' and *nkwo* which is a name given to a person born on the day preceding the *nkwo* market day. Some of the examples, particularly this last, scarcely seem to support the authors' sweeping contention that 'the name is the sum total of the African character'. The last part of the essay moves on to explore the literary significance of the titles *The Beautyful Ones Are Not Yet Born*, *Blade Among the Boys*, *The Grass Is Singing*, and *Too Late the Phalarope*.

In 'Masks and Marx: the Marxist Ethos *vis à vis* African Revolutionary Theory and Praxis' (*PA*) Ayi Kwei Armah defends his right as an artist to speak about political revolution: 'As far back as our written and unwritten records go, it has been the prime destiny of the serious African artist to combine the craft of creativity with the search for regenerative values.' He

offers methodical revisions of Marxism, expurgating its racism and
Eurocentric arrogance, and attacking such specific elements as the doctrine of
abundance as a precondition for communism, the notion of proletarian
rationality, the dogma of peasant stupidity, the fable of Oriental stagnation,
and the absence of Africa. He feels that 'an accurate, integral view of the
world' is essential as a corrective to the Western hegemonism of Marx, and
attacks the neocolonial élites of Africa with Fanonesque acerbity and passion.

Two essays adopt a feminist perspective. Kirsten Holst Petersen's 'First
Things First: Problems of a Feminist Approach to African Literature' (*Kunapipi*) is quite brilliant. Feminism, Petersen notes, is often seen as problematic
in a postcolonial context: 'Whereas Western feminists discuss the relative
importance of feminist versus class emancipation, the African discussion is
between feminist emancipation versus the fight against neo-colonialism.' She
cites as an extreme a poem by Malawian, Felix Mnthali:

> When Africa
> at home and across the seas
> is truly free
> there will be time for me
> and time for you
> to share the cooking
> and change the nappies –
> till then,
> first things first!

Such blunt sexism is perhaps an easy target, but the problem is none the less
real and complex. Early African creative writers were concerned to see their
past in positive terms, and inevitably woman's place in traditional society was
lent more dignity than reality warranted. Sexism, as an issue, was simply
suppressed. For Achebe the inequality of the sexes is 'the subject of mild
amusement', while Okot p'Bitek's *Song of Lawino* shows 'a male writer
deliberately misusing the persona of a female character to extol a grossly sexist
system, which is obviously completely to his satisfaction'. The problem is that
drawing attention to such sexism (particularly in the case of a celebrated poem
like *Lawino*) can easily be seen as 'tearing away the carpet from under the feet
of the fighter against cultural imperialism'. Petersen turns next to the modern,
urbanized woman, crisply dismissing Ekwensi and contrasting the views of
Armah and Ngugi, both Marxists. Armah is a 'misogynist' (there may be a
certain simplification here), while Ngugi is progressive, but afflicted by residual romantic stereotyping and allegorical clumsiness. Buchi Emecheta,
Petersen feels, writes more effectively than Ngugi, being inspired not by an
ideological programme, but by 'a sense of outrage'. In comparison with Ngugi,
however, she could be accused of 'ignoring the African dilemma'. Equally rich
in insights is Katherine Frank's 'Feminist Criticism and the African Novel'
(*ALT*), a review of the different schools of feminist literary theory, with some
judicious speculation as to their possible application in Africa. Stereotypical or
'image' criticism, in the tradition of Kate Millett, Frank considers useful, but
of limited relevance to the best or most complex literature. Generic and
archetypal criticism (Gilbert and Gubar) can be usefully applied to African
women writers, many of whom 'seem to be recapitulating the literary history of
their Victorian women predecessors'. Thus Buchi Emecheta and Flora Nwapa

practise 'domestic realism', while Rebeka Njau and Bessie Head concern themselves with 'the madwoman in the village' or the buried slave girl. Sociological and historical criticism, whose feminist practitioners, such as Elaine Showalter, attempt to re-evaluate tradition and unearth 'lost women', could also be of use. Adelaide and Gladys Casely-Hayford and Mabel Dove Danquah are mentioned as candidates for rediscovery. Frank concludes by summarizing the dilemma facing the contemporary African fictional heroine, 'torn between two antagonistic identities: her communally-bred sense of herself as an African, and her feminist aspirations for autonomy and self-realization as a woman'. In her view only Mariama Bâ successfully resolves this issue in fiction. Frank will no doubt welcome the appearance of Charlotte H. Bruner's anthology *Unwinding Threads: Writing by Women in Africa*[3], which includes in its geographically and chronologically wide selection delightful pieces by both Adelaide Casely-Hayford and Mabel Dove Danquah.

Two essays concern themselves with Achebe's celebrated attack on Conrad, made in Massachusetts in 1977. The eminent Conrad scholar, Cedric Watts, in '"A Bloody Racist": About Achebe's View of Conrad' (*YES*, 1983), shows that 'far from being a "purveyor of comforting myths", Conrad most deliberately and incisively debunks such myths'. Indeed, *Heart of Darkness* 'probes the very assumptions Achebe says it endorses'. Watts concedes that Conrad does occasionally express the casual racism of his day in his letters, but his fiction consistently transcends this. Indeed, the attitudes of his characters towards race constitute a reliable indicator of their true moral worth. Reinhardt Kuesgen in 'Conrad and Achebe: Aspects of the Novel' (*WLWE*) also defends Conrad, citing Ngugi wa Thiong'o's view that the skulls outside Kurtz's house are 'a powerful indictment of colonialism'. He goes on to discuss the question of the naturalization of the Western novel form in Africa. Though it originated in Europe, the form now 'belongs to the general cultural repertoire', he concludes. Conrad is also placed in the wider colonial perspective in an essay by Robert Hamner, 'Colony, Nationhood and Beyond: Third World Writers and Critics Contend with Joseph Conrad', included in an issue of *WLWE* devoted to the proceedings of a conference held in Canada on the theme: 'Beyond Nationalism: The Literary Context'.

Kole Omotoso's 'Trans-Saharan Views: Mutually Negative Portrayals' (*ALT*) is a sharp little piece highlighting a large and neglected issue. Omotoso argues that since Arabs and sub-Saharan Africans are today equally the victims of Western colonialism and neocolonialism, they 'need to fight together to win freedom'. However, the mutual respect necessary for this co-operation is nowhere in evidence. Omotoso entertainingly mocks recent Arab attempts to represent their historical role in Africa as a civilizing, non-imperialist one, remarking that the Arab slave trade is estimated to have removed fourteen million Africans over a period of twelve centuries. He also convicts modern Arab fiction of crude racism borrowed from Europe in its portrayal of black Africans.

(b) West Africa

In a thought-provoking preface to Daniel Britz's bibliographical instalment

---

3. *Unwinding Threads: Writing by Women in Africa*, sel. and ed. by Charlotte H. Bruner. Heinemann. pp. xv + 208. pb £2.60.

in *JCL*, 'Africa: Western', Bernth Lindfors notes that at least sixty per cent of the titles listed were published in Nigeria, 'some of them by fledgling presses that do not yet have the means to market their books effectively abroad'. Indeed, Nigeria dominates the compilation, with a small Ghanaian representation; 'but where', Lindfors asks, 'are the Cameroonians, the Sierra Leonians, the Liberians, the Gambians?' Though he detects increasing depth in recent literary criticism, in the realm of fiction 'Trash is becoming increasingly commonplace'. 'Adolescent Literature in Contemporary Nigeria' (*WLWE*) by Osayimwense Osa briefly outlines 'the Nigerian junior novel', from its beginning in Cyprian Ekwensi's *The Drummer Boy* (1960) to the current immense success of Macmillan's Pacesetters series. Osa feels that the overt didacticism of much of this material may soon succumb before the growing sophistication of the Nigerian readership.

In 'Creative Tension in West African Drama in English: The Linguistic Dimension' (*WLWE*) Alex C. Johnson gives a lucid and strictly objective account of the modifications of English usage observable in J. P. Clark, Ola Rotimi, Achebe, and Soyinka. He focuses on the tension between their various West African languages (WAL) and their second language, English (EL2), which has a distinctively different 'lexis, syntax, morphology, phonology' from that of native-speaker's English (EL1). In dramatic performance different variants of EL2 are used by different characters, and sometimes EL2 stands for WAL, in which case it adopts appropriate proverbs, figurative expressions, and imagery. Johnson's descriptive analysis offers no literary insights, claiming only to indicate 'the surface configuration of the linguistic dimension of the corpus'. Beyond this surface he declines to go. Altogether more vigorous is 'The Strangling Hold of Zurrjir: Nigerian Writers and the Burden of the "Half-Bodied Baby"' (*ArielE*) by Emeka Okeke-Ezigbo. Okeke-Ezigbo depicts the English language as an incubus on the Nigerian spirit similar to the child born from the protagonist's wife's thumb in Tutuola's *The Palm-Wine Drinkard*, which 'constitutes a serious psychosomatic [*sic*] danger to his parents'. He argues, with some persuasiveness, that literary or creative language needs to be used 'instinctively and unconsciously', and this rarely happens in the case of a second language. Much of the essay is concerned to show, not always so convincingly, how Christopher Okigbo, Michael Echeruo, Gabriel Okara, Achebe, and Soyinka reject élitist virtuosity in their use of English, in favour of language with a more popular appeal. The assertion that Professor's sign in *The Road*, 'AKSIDENT STORE – ALL PART AVAILEBUL', represents a 'sincere and functional' use of language, and a return from grammatical pedantry to 'the fresh, well-ventilated, home-made speech of his own people' is ingenious rather than illuminating.

S. E. Ogude's scholarly and authoritative essay 'Olaudah Equiano and the Tradition of Defoe' (*ALT*) argues that *The Interesting Narrative* is essentially a fiction, and that in all important respects its protagonist is as ignorant of the African continent as Defoe's Captain Singleton or Robinson Crusoe. There are compelling similarities in presentation and treatment between Equiano's work and *Robinson Crusoe* (even in the layout of its title-page). Indeed, it could be retitled, without strain, *The Strange, Surprizing Adventures of Olaudah Equiano*. Like Defoe's heroes, Ogude points out, 'Equiano' is a lonely man in a hostile environment, but resourceful enough to overcome all odds. He also is 'a particular favourite of heaven', and enjoys providential escapes from accident. On a deeper level the protagonist clearly shares current European attitudes to Africa, being astonished at its exotic fecundity. Moreover, like Colonel Jack, he poses as that popular literary type of the day, 'the model planter', who by being kind to his slaves makes greater profits out of their willing labour. Equiano, Ogude points out, even argues, as Defoe had done, that Britain could maximize its profit by colonizing Africa, rather than transporting its inhabitants across the Atlantic.

Raoul Granqvist, in 'The Early Swedish Reviews of Chinua Achebe's *Things Fall Apart* and *A Man of the People*' (*RAL*), offers an interesting account of the reception accorded to the Swedish translations of these works, which appeared during the Nigerian Civil War (in 1967 and 1968). Not surprisingly Swedish reviewers revealed a lack of real knowledge of traditional Africa. They were concerned primarily with the sociological and political information which could be gleaned from the books, *A Man of the People* being treated 'less as "literature" than as a political handbook that might provide insights into the preludes of the war'. In the context of the war the novel's light tone was felt by reviewers to make it 'somewhat unreal' and 'frivolous'. Charles E. Nnolim's 'The Form and Function of the Folk Tradition in Achebe's Novels' (*ArielE*, 1983) explores with nerveless elegance the familiar theme of the novelist's skill in 'subtly and cunningly' working 'the African folkways' into his narrative. He points out that the folk-tale of Tortoise and the birds in *Things Fall Apart* is 'a paradigm for the entire novel. It is the story of the sudden rise and fall of Tortoise, just as *Things Fall Apart* is the story of the rise and fall of Okonkwo ... Tortoise survives, a patchwork of himself, just as Igbo clanship survives, half pagan (who adheres to the ancestral ways) and half Christian (iconoclasts all)'. Nnolim goes on to treat the central place of the *Egwugwu* in traditional Igbo society, a subject 'entirely neglected by critics'. Very different in tone and style is Abdul Jan Mohamed's 'Sophisticated Primitivism: The Syncretism of Oral and Literate Modes in Achebe's *Things Fall Apart*' (*ArielE*). Jan Mohamed argues that the style and structure of the novel 'encode the phenomenology of oral cultures and thereby create a new syncretic form and contribute to the negative dialectics by deterritorializing, to some extent, the English language and the novelistic form'. His point (always itself suitably 'encoded') is that the narrative technique of the novel moves from one appropriate to an oral culture to one appropriate to a literate culture as the whites begin to dominate the development of the plot. Jan Mohamed's delight in elaborate academic diction ('noetic', 'chirographic', 'homeostatic', 'phenomenology', 'valorize', etc.) makes his essay difficult to follow. The same critic's book, *Manichean Aesthetics: The Politics of Literature in Colonial Africa* (UMass, 1983) was not seen.

In 'Beginning: Christopher Okigbo's "Four Canzones"' (*WLWE*) James Wieland argues that although the poet's first serious writing is certainly apprentice work, it is nevertheless important, 'offering an introduction both to the metaphysic that underpins his work and to his thematic and formal preoccupations'. Wieland gives a sympathetic account of Okigbo's philosophy of flux and process, through which he sought to place his 'elemental heritage' in relation to the postcolonial present, and concludes that 'such explorations of traditional and contemporary Western form and traditional Nigerian form and presentation provide access to a mind struggling to find its way, and to a poetry seeking a form'. S. A. Gingell treats the more legible imagery of a less problematic poet in 'His River's Complex Course: Reflections on Past, Present and Future in the Poetry of Gabriel Okara' (*WLWE*). With a sensitive lucidity appropriate to his subject, Gingell draws out the symbolism of Europe *versus* Africa in 'Piano and Drums', explores the motif of a man at a riverside which recurs frequently in Okara's work as a symbol of cultural indecision, and shows how fire is used to suggest African passion smothered by European coldness and technology. In 'The Fisherman's Invocation' all these image-strands are seen united in a basically optimistic 'grand orchestration combining old and new, past and present'. Gingell feels that Okara's abandonment of his idiosyncratic Ijaw style with the trauma of the civil war leaves his work 'regrettably, if understandably, impoverished'. For an essay treating Ola Rotimi's *Ovonramwen Nogbaisi* in conjunction with Ngugi's *The Trial of Dedan Kimathi* see below, p. 684.

Two of the five essays on Soyinka concern themselves with the question of European influences on his plays. The simpler of the two (in every sense) is Catherine Obianuju Acholonu's 'A Touch of the Absurd: Soyinka and Beckett' (*ALT*), which lists some obvious similarities between the playwrights without developing any real argument: 'Like Vladimir and Estragon in Beckett's play, Soyinka's tramps stink'; 'Soyinka's rhetorical devices are akin to those of Samuel Beckett though sometimes more acidic'; 'Like Beckett, Soyinka uses water in *The Swamp Dwellers* as a symbol of death ...' The conclusion is that 'Wole Soyinka has not escaped the touch of the magic staff of that great writer'. James Gibbs's '"Grafting is an Ancient Art": The Relationship of African and European Elements in the Early Plays of Wole Soyinka' (*WLWE*) is more assured and engaging in tone. Gibbs devotes much space to explaining why he prefers the metaphor of grafting to those of integration, fusion, or marriage, to describe Soyinka's combination of elements from European and African traditions. He supposes it likely that Soyinka had Joyce Cary's *Mister Johnson* in mind when he created the village in *The Lion and the Jewel*, and invites us to observe how Soyinka 'cuts the stock' of Cary's novel 'right back to the root and firmly implants his scion'. But there is no evidence in the play that Soyinka did have Cary specifically in mind, nor would Gibbs's metaphorical flights take us very far, even if he had. Gibbs's hunt for 'sources' is beset by such tenuousness. Soyinka has, he notes, denied being influenced by Wycherley. He 'may have been acquainted with the annual Edi festival'; 'it is just possible' that he read a particular Pirandello play in England. One wonders why, if Gibbs thinks these things of importance, he cannot simply ask Soyinka for the answers.

Two of the essays treat the more metaphysical aspect of Soyinka's genius, with different degrees of critical composure. David Richards's '*Òwe l'esin òrò*: Proverbs like horses – Wole Soyinka's *Death and the King's Horseman*' (*JCL*) concentrates on the aphoristic wisdom of the proverb: 'Proverbs are horses for searching for the truth; when the truth is missing, proverbs are used to discover it.' That the Yoruba characters speak largely in proverbs makes the speech of the British characters seem flat and uninteresting in comparison. After his failure to sacrifice himself, Elesin 'grapples desperately with a devalued language', 'since he has lost the right to utter the linguistic summations of "the Yoruba mind"' which proverbs express'. Richards's heady enthusiasm for the profundities of Yoruba communal wisdom and human sacrifice leads him on occasion into a kind of hectic melodrama of expression, as when he asserts that the line, 'It takes an Elesin to die the death of death', 'internally generates semantic tensions which leap like a spark across the words as their sense-polarities change and reverse themselves'. This makes a great exotic meal of a life-through-death paradox familiar in many cultural traditions (including the Christian). Phyllis Pollard's 'Myth, Literature and Ideology – a reading of Wole Soyinka's *Season of Anomy*' (*JCL*) takes a less ingenuous view of Soyinka's metaphysics. She traces the uneasy attempt of Soyinka's second novel to marry the archetypal and mythic notion of regeneration familiar from Jung and Joseph Campbell with Fanon's political notion of the third, 'fighting', or revolutionary phase of colonial development. The romance element in the novel, and its 'labyrinthine imagery', invite the reader to view Ofeyi (Orpheus) as Campbell's 'creative hero', travelling through the three stages of his rite of passage: separation, initiation, and return. However, the alliance between the Dentist and Ofeyi shows Soyinka attempting to combine this mythic pattern with Marxist theory – and action. Ultimately in Pollard's view the 'over-blown wit' of the novel serves to betray that the mixture of myth and Marx has failed: '*Season of Anomy* is a novel about the writer's dilemma rather than a work of ideological commitment'; 'There is more of the private quest of an Orpheus in it than the public *agon* of an Ogun.' Pollard shows a refreshing ability to connect literary analysis with ideology, without reducing either. James Olney's review-article '*Aké*: Wole Soyinka as Autobiographer' (*YR*, 1983) offers complex meditations on the nature of autobiography in terms derived from Aristotle. His drift is that autobiography should be seen as the imaginative product of its author's personality at a particular time, rather than as a reliable history or a definitive summing up of his or her life. In a coda to his essay Olney takes Nadine Gordimer to task for her 'conceptually inadequate' criticism of the first part of *Aké*, which she feels is 'reworked' and not true to the emotions of a child, as child. She thinks that the second half rings truer. Gordimer's reservations seem to the present writer to be natural and justified, and Olney's position a tenuous sophistication.

Obi Maduakor's 'On the Poetry of War: Yeats and J. P. Clark' (*ALT*) argues, persuasively enough, that Clark's *Casualties* (1970) fails to achieve the gravity and effectiveness of Yeats's poetry on the same theme. The animal characters in Clark's poems, with their folk-tale resonances, are inadequate as vehicles for a tragic experience. Clark's language 'is frequently descriptive, affirmative and declamatory and does not evoke a mood, or order emotions'. Maduakor exempts 'Dirge', 'The Casualties', and 'Night Song' from these strictures, but still concludes that Soyinka's and Okigbo's poems on this theme are more likely to outlive their time than Clark's – though none of them can match the technical expertise of Yeats's. More theoretically ambitious is Chidi Amuta's 'History, Society and Heroism in the Nigerian War Novel' (*Kunapipi*). Amuta claims to be participating in an attempt to give the 'critical discourse of African literature . . . the identity of a rigorous discipline' by delving 'deeper into the ontological configurations of the very literary works in order to decipher the truth value of the texts as systems of aesthetic signification of meanings that ultimately derive from history'. In Europe 'the heroic institution' inherited from the last century, has fallen victim to the 'unbridled angst, ennui and general self-doubt' induced by advanced capitalism and two destructive wars. Underdeveloped Africa, however, is still confronting 'historical challenges requiring urgent heroic intervention'; the hero is still dynamic, a '*problematic* being'. This is an intriguing and plausible idea, but it is scarcely borne out by Amuta's critical analyses. The 'heroism' of Eddie Iroh's Chumah in *Forty-Eight Guns for the General* is, as he demonstrates, merely of the Hollywood type (which is as popular in the West as ever); the heroism of Chukwuemeka Ike's Dr Kanu in *Sunset at Dawn* is undercut by the author's radical cynicism and irony; and there is, as he admits, no real heroism in John Munonye's *A Wreath for the Maidens* at all. Despite his reference to 'aesthetic signification', Amuta seems unconcerned by the absence of literary complexity or merit in the works he treats, drawing parallels with Balzac, Flaubert, and Dostoevsky.

Although insisting that, since Flora Nwapa never intended to write feminist tracts, an evaluation of her work should not use feminist aesthetics as a frame of reference, Chidi Ikonné's 'The Society and Woman's Quest for Selfhood in Flora Nwapa's Early Novels' (*Kunapipi*) does in fact adopt such a feminist perspective. This theoretical ambiguity aside, the essay is vigorous and discriminating. Nwapa, it is argued, holds up 'a near perfect mirror' to the patriarchy of traditional Igbo society, in which women are undervalued chattels, the birth of a girl is a disappointment, and females are ritually castrated by 'circumcision' in order to reduce their superiority 'in matters coital'. Ikonné quotes Masters and Johnson on women's superior powers of orgasm to underline the injustice of polygamy and clitoridectomy, attributing these practices to the jealous inadequacy of men, abetted by the propensity of women themselves to internalize the ideology of male supremacy. Ikonné goes on to show how, in portraying rebellions against social norms, Nwapa does produce potential feminist documents. But the potential remains unrealized, and 'male supremacy is intact from beginning to end'. Ikonné's subtle conclusion is that Nwapa is not, as she might seem, a sycophant to male ego. She is 'a sociologist almost to a fault, . . . trying to document, albeit in fictional form, the way it was in a particular Igbo community at a particular point in time. Her characters' penchant for conformity derives not from the novelist's ideological stance, but from the dictates of her art'. Whether one agrees with this lucid separation of art and ideology or not, Ikonné has canvassed the issues with vigour and discrimination.

The title of G. Ojong Ayuk's essay 'The Lust for Material Well-Being in *The Beautyful Ones Are Not Yet Born* and *Fragments* by Ayi Kwei Armah' (*PA*) promises few profound or original insights, and the essay amply fulfils this lack of promise. Ayuk recounts the main drift of Armah's first two novels in order to come to such banal conclusions as: 'His fictional axe is aimed at those leaders whose thinking has unfortunately been distorted by current materialism', and 'In a sense, this society despises the poor and the foolish'. Apparently Armah tries to show us that 'it is the post-independence materialistic society that is out of step and not the protagonists'. Out of step with what remains unexplained. More interesting is Sara Chetin's 'Armah's Women' (*Kunapipi*), which relates the female characters in *Fragments* to the determinist stereotypes indicated by the novel's protagonist, Baako: 'Women destroying, women saving.' Naana is a sympathetic sufferer but nevertheless sucks Baako into her resigned passivity. Juana is more complex, being related to the Mame Water myth of the fated poet. Chetin intriguingly relates the progress of her relationship with Baako to the phases of the lunar year and the tides. Juana 'represents the sea goddess and, despite her characterization as a sympathetic healer, Armah also depicts her as destructive due to the very impotence of her healing power'. (There seems to be something forced about the argument here.) Like all Armah's women, Chetin says, Juana is seen as powerful, 'always driving, always in control'. She concludes, perhaps a little too sweepingly, that 'Armah has a distorted concept of female strength', and is unable to see women except in terms of stereotypes.

In 'E pluribus Unum? The language for a National Literature in a Multilingual Community' (*ArielE*) Loreto Todd champions Pidgin English as a candidate for literary expression in Cameroon. French and English are, she says, associated with privilege and education. Hausa is associated with Islam; and the other vernaculars are associated with Christianity. Only Pidgin English transcends these divisive associations. Moreover, it is 'a flexible, evocative language capable of expressing cultural and literary aspirations'. She cites some examples (with translations), and discusses problems of orthography, regional variation, the poor reputation of 'bastard' English, and the small potential audience for Pidgin.

(c) East and Central Africa

R. N. Ndegwa contributes a section, 'Africa: East and Central', to the continuing bibliography in *JCL*. His introduction notes the mushrooming of new publishing companies in Kenya, records a slight increase in English-language publishing in Tanzania, and regrets that Ugandan writing has not stabilized.

G. D. Killam's anthology of criticism, *The Writing of East and Central Africa*[4], is something of a landmark, providing in one volume excellent general surveys of the literature of each country, together with essays on the more important individual writers. Malawi unfortunately had to be omitted. Various authors agreed to provide a chapter on that country, but they all concluded that any serious account of the subject would attract the malign attention of the Banda regime, and would, as one of them remarked, 'have dangerous consequences to authors whose names and writings would inevitably have to appear in the survey'. Peter Nazareth's chapter, 'Waiting for Amin: Two Decades of Ugandan Literature', remarks on the difficulty of defining his fragmented subject. A critic of Ugandan literature 'has first to act as a retriever of the literature: he has to track down the writers and their work and he has to record the existence of the work before beginning to analyse it'. This essential task Nazareth carries out most impressively, and his chapter will certainly be an invaluable basic reference point for future readers. He surveys the older, more established writers: Okot p'Bitek, David Rubadiri, himself, John Ruganda, Robert Serumaga, Jagit Singh, Okello Oculi, and Richard Ntiru; then briefly introduces the 'new voices' of those who began writing under Amin: Nuwa Sentongo, Cliff-Lubwa p'Chong, Grace Akello, Mukotani Rugyendo, and John Nagenda. His account is necessarily bitty and discontinuous since he is called upon to treat writers of very different talents and achievement. But this is no defect, and the essay is certainly not lacking in stimulus to serious critical thought. Nazareth makes an eloquent appeal on behalf of Rubadiri's 'brilliant novel', *No Bride Price*, which he considers

4. *The Writing of East and Central Africa*, ed. by G. D. Killam. Heinemann. pp. x + 274. £8.50.

underrated. He criticizes Serumaga's Englishness and Pinteresque affecta-
tions, and praises S. Joshua L. Zake's exciting thriller, *Truckful of Gold*, while
acknowledging its second-hand Americanness. Altogether Nazareth's is a
most valuable introduction to the subject. Jacqueline Bardolph's contribution,
'The Literature of Kenya', which follows, stresses that 'well-known writers
like Ngugi wa Thiong'o and Meja Mwangi do not stand isolated like lone trees
on a plain, they emerge from a thriving forest'. She surveys the literature from
its beginnings in Kenyatta's *Facing Mount Kenya* and the *Origin East Africa*
anthology, and discusses the two central themes of 'culture conflict' and the
Emergency. The distinctive qualities of the more 'serious' writers she identifies as a 'rather sombre' self-critical tone, a lack of any great experimentation,
and a sense of moral urgency. She speculates on the future of literature in
Gikuyu and considers whether a truly popular literature (as opposed to
'mechanically produced potboilers') may develop from the westernized 'pop'
style of Charles Mangua, Mwangi Ruheni, and David Maillu. Her perceptive
analyses make clear that many central issues of Kenyan literature still remain
in the melting-pot.

The next chapter, 'Writing in English from Tanzania' by Ismael R. Mbise, is
rather different. Partly this is a result of the subject-matter, literature in
English being so relatively insignificant in Tanzania, compared with its posi-
tion in other East African countries: 'The history of Kiswahili literature in
Tanzania dates back about three hundred years,' Mbise tells us, 'that of
English literature dates back only three decades.' The difference is also,
however, a matter of Mbise's approach, as a representative of official Tanza-
nian cultural policy. He quotes approvingly one of his colleagues at the
University of Dar Es Salaam: 'The prime function of the study of literature in
Tanzania must ... be to contribute to the development of a revolutionary
consciousness.' Mbise's own ideological (and literary) consciousness seems
questionable, however, in the light of his remarks on Nyerere's translation of
The Merchant of Venice into Kiswahili. He explains that Nyerere's plural (lit.
The Capitalists of Venice) must be meant to indicate that many Shylocks
threaten the growth of socialism. That Antonio and Bassanio are also capitalists seems to have escaped his notice, though not, of course, Nyerere's. In the
second part of his essay Mbise ponderously contrasts the introspective individualism of Peter Palangyo's *Dying in the Sun* with the more external, socially
orientated treatment of Gabriel Ruhumbika's *Village in Uhuru*. He goes on to
echo Wole Soyinka's appeal that Kiswahili be adopted as the *lingua franca* of
Africa, noting that in 1978 it was used for the first time as the medium of
communication at an international conference (in Dar Es Salaam). John
Reed's chapter in Killam's collection, 'Zambian Fiction', is very different
again. Reed charts the early history of the country 'on the outer rim of the
South African sphere of influence', which gives it its unique cultural identity:
'Northern Rhodesia experienced European culture as the colony of a colony,
but the realities of modern industrial life more directly than anywhere further
north.' No strong 'Africanist' anticolonial literature has developed in Zambia,
nor does the fiction aspire to European models of high art. 'All Zambian
fiction so far has been quite free of literary pretension and self-consciousness.'
Reed surveys fiction from *New Writing from Zambia* and *Voices of Zambia*,
through Fwanyanga Mulikita and Andreya Masiye, to Dominic Mulaisho's
The Tongue of the Dumb, which he considers 'a symbolic novel of depth and

resonance' despite its lack of clarity and realism. Gideon Phiri's *That Ticklish Sensation* is felt to be schoolboyish in its crudeness but shows 'a sharp ear for the varieties of Zambian English, spoken and written'. Reed ends his invaluable essay by reviewing a group of works published by Neczam in 1979, singling out William Saidi's *The Hanging* for its convincing social seriousness (blended however with unconvincing melodrama), and Storm Banjayomoyo's *Sofiya*, which though weak, brilliantly evokes the specific geography of Lusaka, and furthermore, 'completely captures, like a poignant background music to the action, that sense of life itself as an aching, unstanchable outflowing of money'.

Danielle Quet's 'Mauritian Voices: A Panorama of Contemporary Creative Writing in English (Part Two)' (*WLWE*) gives a fascinating and sympathetic account of the culture of this small Indian Ocean island. She notes that English is on the defensive against the aggressive Francophone lobby and the movement to have Creole adopted as the national language. She comments on 'the small number and the disappointing brevity of most publications', and their almost total absence from the best British libraries (she could, however, locate only eleven such works in the bookshops of Port Louis). Nevertheless, fourteen writers, four previously unpublished, produced work in English in 1980–2. She briefly reviews the poetry of Karl Vadamootoo and Shakuntala Hawoldar, the plays of Gian Aubeeluck and Bhisma Dev Seebaluck, and the work of the 'only true Mauritian novelist in English', Deepchand Beeharry, who in her view 'forcefully conveys the terrible solitude of the coloured immigrant in an indifferent or racist environment'. The checklist which follows the essay supplements that published in 1980 by Michel Fabre. Angela Smith's 'Mauritian Literature in English' treats the same topic with different emphases. Many Mauritians, she observes, look to India rather than to Africa or Europe for their literary perspectives; English is a natural language for protest, as against the dominant Indian languages and French; and self-publication is a practice attracting considerable status. Of those poets who manage to get their work printed, she concedes, 'few . . . attain a level of basic competence'. She quotes some execrable examples, extending limited praise to Hossenjee Edoo and the Indian-born Shakuntala Hawoldar. Deepchand Beeharry she condemns for his 'flat didacticism'.

Killam's collection of essays ends with three devoted to the major literary *genres*. Ken Goodwin gives a workmanlike introduction to East African poetry, dividing it in 'crude outline' into three phases: first, the localized version of British Victorianism; second, poetry influenced by Western modernism but often expressing anticolonial sentiment (David Rubadiri); and third, poetry drawing inspiration 'from the oral poetry and song of one or more African languages' (Okot p'Bitek). He analyses the last two phases in detail, giving brief verdicts on Henry Barlow, Jonathan Kariara, Richard Ntiru, Jared Angira, Amin Kassam, Okello Oculi, and David Maillu. Taban lo Liyong he admits resists 'any kind of taxonomy'. He concludes that though publication on a small scale is easier to achieve nowadays, 'opportunities for widespread regional publication and distribution are no less tenuous than they were ten years ago'. He feels that East African poetry could easily 'fragment into local schools'. Simon Gikandi's chapter, 'The Growth of the East African Novel', is sharp and discriminating. Gikandi relates the formal uninventiveness of the East African novel, when compared with poetry and drama, to the lack of the native traditions which feed the other *genres*. His historical survey takes up Ngugi's point that colonial literature contains a full literary celebration of the settler culture, and should not be disregarded as irrelevant. Blixen's intense landscapes and Huxley's stereotypical Africans create a powerful imaginative pattern which the nationalist novel is concerned to break. *The River Between* is thus beset by 'an ambivalence born out of the need to defeat the colonialist by using his own tool'. Nationalism, Gikandi acutely observes, 'is not a creed nor an ideology, hence the prominence of spirit, sentiment, mood and feeling, rather than criticism and analysis in the archetypal nationalist novel'. A more advanced stage is reached in *A Grain of Wheat* and the works of Peter Palangyo, Robert Serumaga, Leonard Kibera, and even Meja Mwangi, whose novels reflect various facets of a more complex state of culture. Perhaps, Gikandi speculates, *Petals of Blood*, as a consciously 'political' novel, introduces a more positive and constructive phase, though, with nice intellectual precision, he hastens to add 'that literary evolution does not imply literary improvement'. Very different from Gikandi's is L. A. Mbughini's contribution, 'The Development of English Drama in East Africa', in which again official Tanzanian policy looms large (Mbughini is Director of Arts and National Culture in the Government). He remarks that 'English theatre and drama have thrived greatly between 1960 and 1980, notwithstanding the nationalistic pressures and programmes to revive, develop and promote the indigenous theatre and drama'. He attributes this state of affairs partly to the international status of English, Kiswahili not having yet been adopted as the national language in Kenya and Uganda. But more important, he feels, is the appearance since independence of Marxist literature in English, and the subsequent publication of 'African plays in English with Marxist or socialist inclinations'. Mbughini gives a useful survey of playwrights, grouped according to popularity. Ebrahim Hussein, Ngugi wa Thiong'o, Robert Serumaga, and John Ruganda make up the first group; Mukotani Rugyendo, Benjamin L. Leshoai, and Rebeka Njau the second. The third consists of the younger playwrights included in the anthology *Short East African Plays in English* (1970) edited by David Cook and Miles Lee. Mbughini's literary perceptions are unreliable. His verdict that Ngugi's *The Trial of Dedan Kimathi* is 'daring and mature', and ranks with the plays of Athol Fugard and Soyinka, is a transparent case of ideological approval mistaking itself for aesthetic judgement.

Still in Killam, Bernth Lindfors's 'The Songs of Okot p'Bitek' locates the poet's importance in the fact that 'when he sang, no European echoes could be heard in the background. His *Song of Lawino* was the first long poem in English to achieve a totally African identity.' Lindfors is careful not to mistake Lawino for a mouthpiece of the poet. Sometimes the satire is 'reflexive', and it is she who is criticized for her cultural chauvinism, though the central thread of the poem remains a satire on Ocol's 'apemanship' of Europe. Although *Song of Ocol* ostensibly redresses the balance of the debate, Lindfors feels that it asserts basically the same position as *Lawino*. 'Nothing Ocol says wins our sympathy.' Some will feel that Lindfors underestimates the complexity of Ocol's (and Okot's) tone in this poem. His treatment of *Song of Prisoner* resolves the apparent contradictions of the work by interpreting it as 'a medley of various voices', while *Song of Malaya* is said to provide 'boisterous comic relief'. Lindfors makes no mention of the *machismo* and offensive sexism which is beginning to preoccupy other critics of Okot's work (see Petersen above, p. 672). He sums up Okot as 'a serious clown who provoked regenerative laughter'. Following Lindfors's essay is Peter Nazareth's entertaining 'Bibliyongography, or Six Tabans in Search of an Author', which distinguishes, with a mixed tone of amusement and exasperation, six quite different Tabans, ranging from the singer or 'bard', through the champion of individual freedom, to the 'legislator', and even the rooted traditionalist. The 'egoist' is the most problematic incarnation. This Taban can rave like an Amin, telling us how the world can be set to rights, with no sense of practical possibilities, and no regard to the consequences in misery and bloodshed. Taban excuses his own multiplicity by reference to his transitional position, which inevitably involves a synthesis of widely varying cultural strands. Nazareth cites his joke derivation of his own name, from Caliban and Li Po (the Chinese philosopher), as a typically Tabanesque expression of this.

Killam himself contributes a somewhat neutral-sounding chapter on Ngugi wa Thiong'o, stressing the coherence of his writing career: 'The thematic interests Ngugi displays remain the same throughout his writing . . . and are broadened and deepened as his writing career advances.' Ngugi's development can be seen in terms of a series of rejections: of Christianity, of the foreign English language, and ultimately of all British values and standards. Killam sees *A Grain of Wheat* as his 'most finished piece of writing in conventional fictional terms', and excuses the 'simplistic format' of *I Will Marry When I Want* by reference to 'the intentions of the authors and the audience at whom the information in dramatized form is directed'. The popularity of *Devil on the Cross* proves that Ngugi 'has found his legitimate audience'. The undercurrent of critical qualification which is detectable in Killam's studied phrasing ('information in dramatized form') comes close to the surface only in the last paragraph, which hints at the problematic elements of Ngugi's work around which the essay has carefully skirted. Killam acknowledges that Ngugi's work will 'exercise the critical sensibilities of some readers', but he himself will venture no further than a non-commital tautology: 'Readers will make what they will out of his art now that it has been given to them.' Joyce Johnson's 'Character and Circumstance in Ngugi wa Thiong'o's *A Grain of Wheat*' (*CNE*) contains no such nuances. Its laborious and oversimplified exposition of the novel leads to the conclusion that 'the types of characters appearing in *A Grain of Wheat* are types which are continually ranged opposite each other in major African novels – traditionalists, collaborators, revolutionaries and pragmatists'. All four central male characters, she notes, 'are related to Mumbi in some way', but she fails to point out the religious significance of Mumbi's name. She explains Kihika's version of Christianity as basically self-contradictory: 'He is attempting to free his society from foreign domination but relies on symbolism derived from a foreign culture to convey his purpose.' Such a crudely schematic reading ignores not only the political brilliance of Kihika's deliberate adaptation of theology for the purposes of liberation, but also Ngugi's deep and persistent emotional attachment to Christian imagery and rhetoric.

In 'Ngugi wa Thiong'o and the Question of Language and Literature in Kenya' (*WLWE*) Dieter Riemenschneider returns to the ubiquitous debate about language choice, arguing that, though it seemed to have run into a sterile dead end, the question has been revived again by Ngugi's adoption of his mother tongue. Ngugi's change of language represents a move from an idealistic but 'anaemic' dedication to national culture, to the more practical involvement entailed in addressing himself to the workers and peasants of his nation in their own language. 'Although he sometimes slips into repetition, even propaganda, the seriousness of his struggle makes it difficult to criticize him for this.' Riemenschneider compares Ngugi's last play in English, *The Trial of Dedan Kimathi*, with *Ngaahika Ndeenda*, his first play in Gikuyu, detecting a fundamental shift in technique to a more 'collective' approach, less programmatically directed *at* the audience. The same kind of comparison is then made between *Petals of Blood* and *Caitaana Mutharaba-ini* (*Devil on the Cross*). '*Petals of Blood* is a highly sophisticated novel which requires a great deal of attention to detail by the reader'. *Devil on the Cross*, on the other hand, gives prominence to the oral narrator figure and has a 'paradigmatic meaning' expressed through a 'simple story which ends on a rather melodramatic note'. It shows a 'masterful combining of the allegorical and the realistic'. Whether or not one agrees with all Riemenschneider's critical judgements, his is a persuasive account of the critical and ideological issues involved. More sceptical is Brian Crow's searching essay, 'Melodrama and the "Political Unconscious" in Two African Plays' (*ArielE*, 1983). Crow treats the hypothesis 'that melodrama expresses both the pervasive anxiety and the desire for ethical certitude in modern, or "modernizing", societies'. He notes that both Ola Rotimi's *Ovonramwen Nogbaisi* and Ngugi's *The Trial of Dedan Kimathi* polarize absolutes of good and evil in simplified characters. Ovonramwen represents right, embodied in a vaguely defined traditional hierarchy, and the British are simple villains. Dedan Kimathi is depicted as virtuous and composed, while the whites are 'hysterically racist', a polarity reinforced by the play's Christian imagery of betrayal and crucifixion. Crow detects in both plays a 'political unconscious' behind the melodrama. In Rotimi's play the rampantly corrupt Nigerian élite 'is reassured, through its empathy with Oba Ovonramwen, that it is the innocent inheritor of an historical legacy, not the guilty because willing participant in neo-colonialism'. In Ngugi's play the rhetorical excess 'is in proportion to the absence of any mass-based political movement in Kenya capable of realizing successfully the political objectives advocated by the play'.

In 'Jared Angira and East African Poetry of Social Testimony' (*WLWE*) Abdul R. Yesufu argues that East African poets as a group 'are didactic in the tradition of the achievement of a harmonious marriage of art and ideas'. He gives straightforward explications of the thematic import of various poems to support his view that Angira's work is 'an acutely ideologized poetry put to the maximum service of society'.

Angus Calder's 'Meja Mwangi's Novels'[4] presents a well-considered critical analysis of 'the most interesting and exciting writer of fiction to emerge in East Africa since Ngugi wa Thiong'o'. Mwangi's, Calder says, is a 'natural' talent, little influenced by 'serious' writing either from Africa or Europe, and taking inspiration from popular thrillers. He is less 'African' than Achebe; less committed and earnest than Ngugi. But despite this he possesses 'a degree of talent for carrying the reader breathlessly forward from page to page which not even fervent admirers would claim for either of those elder writers'. Moreover, his work does generate serious symbolic resonances, and he could be seen as offering us 'visions of life as Hell, in all his novels'. Calder also presents the case against Mwangi: his free use of the conventions of American movies;

his complete failure to 'keep faith with complex linguistic reality' which results in his Mau Mau fighters in *A Carcase for Hounds* speaking 'movie-dialogue English'; and, worst of all, his use of easy determinist stereotypes, particularly that of the hard-bitten loner with his faithful male 'buddy'. Calder ends by arguing that *The Cockroach Dance* shows signs of transcending these limitations. Mwangi is, in his view, 'clearly driving in the right direction, trying to write about urban Kenya in a fashion both entertaining and socially responsible'.

No less than four essays on the work of Nuruddin Farah are to be treated. D. R. Ewen's contribution to Killam's collection[4] offers convincing insights into the uneasy relation between author and reader in Farah's increasingly sombre novels. Ewen's critical tone, however, is a little uncertain. He is perhaps too ready to enthuse about, or even himself to imitate, Farah's 'outlandish and carefree' puns and eclectic literary references, rather than analysing their effectiveness. He speculates extravagantly whether it is too much to hope that Farah is 'rewriting the entire history of the English Novel in the Somali context'. Ebla in *From a Crooked Rib* can be compared with Pamela and Moll Flanders; *A Naked Needle* combines Fielding and Smollett; *Sweet and Sour Milk* is 'a mystery novel, spanning Wilkie Collins to Agatha Christie; and *Sardines* is the novel of social commitment'. This is tenuously intriguing, but forced. Ian Adam in 'Nuruddin Farah and James Joyce: Some Issues of Intertextuality' (*WLWE*) shows a similar enthusiasm for Farah's literariness. The obvious direct influence of Joyce on Farah is not surprising, Adam says, since a 'marginal' writer from the metropolis is a natural choice of 'sibling' for a third-world author (the 'central' metropolitan writers are 'stepfathers'). Thus the learned and brooding, antitraditional hero of *A Naked Needle* can be compared with Stephen Dedalus. Adam is not so much concerned with direct echoes however, as with 'intertextuality', a formulation 'capacious enough to allow for terms suggesting like-mindedness or even autonomy'. (Here is an academic *langue* indeed!) It is difficult to see what significant literary 'issues' are raised by 'intertextuality', so capaciously defined, though Adam does point out some undoubted examples of it: the daring verbal experimentation of both writers, for example, their 'capacity to discern seemingly endless parallels', and their 'autonomous' choices of – totally different – attitudes towards political commitment. A tiny suspicion arises that, illuminating though Adam's essay is in some ways, his omnivalent 'intertextuality' is, in reality, no more than an ingenious invention designed to provide unlimited grist to the mill of the c.v.-conscious academic.

Two essays by Juliet Okonkwo concern themselves with Farah. 'Nuruddin Farah and the Politics of Somalia' (*PA*) detects a balance in Farah's work between 'ideological fervour' and 'artistic aesthetics' (*sic*): 'Although his novels manifest a deep political consciousness, he is careful not to adopt an ideological stance as Ngugi, Armah, Soyinka or Sembène Ousmane have done.' Rather Farah mirrors society. His concern in *Sweet and Sour Milk* and *Sardines* is to assert a 'true record of history' against the propaganda of a fascist state, which has 'reassembled' traditional values into a 'bogus structure'. Okonkwo criticizes Farah's treatment of the democratic resistance, arguing that 'Farah's inconsistency in depicting the development of a definite point of view obscures the resolution that he seems to be striving after'. This comes dangerously close to demanding that Farah re-assemble his attitude towards the weak and divided Somali opposition in order to achieve a specious revolutionary coherence. Okonkwo's second essay on Farah, 'Nuruddin Farah and the Changing Roles of Women' (*WLT*) is more completely persuasive. She provocatively compares women in early African novels written by men with the blacks in colonial novels, who 'functioned merely as props for the actual performance of the master group'. Even the most celebrated of African writers 'have been unable to conceive of a woman except in terms of an appendage to man (in the case of Achebe) or as a prostitute, disguised or undisguised (in the case of Soyinka)'. This is telling criticism. Exceptions to the rule, in her view, are Ngugi, John Munonye, Sembène Ousmane, and Armah, who do make the attempt to portray women fully. Also important is the testimony of female writers such as Ama Ata Aidoo, Grace Ogot, Buchi Emecheta, Mariama Bâ, and Rebeka Njau. However, these 'have so far succeeded only in delineating the woman in her subjection'. Farah, Okonkwo argues, is 'virtually alone among African writers in depicting the progress which women have made within the constricting social landscape', by demythologizing the 'glorified' African past and showing how women can take active part in various forms of life around them. Okonkwo ends by illustrating this dynamism in Farah's portrayal of women within three distinct categories: the traditional African; the modern emancipated African; and the foreigner or West European.

(d) Southern Africa

Dorothy Driver's introduction to her bibliographical contribution 'South Africa' in *JCL* declares local publishing to be in a healthy state, and detects 'a gathering sense that the country is experiencing the start of a literary renaissance to match the output of the 50s and 60s'. Recent works by Sipho Sepamla, Achmat Dangor, Njabulo Ndebele, Stephen Watson, Menan du Plessis, and Jeremy Cronin, together with the growing international recognition of J. M. Coetzee, Nadine Gordimer, and Athol Fugard, show that 'a literary tradition is gradually being built'. The huge critical output to be treated in the present section may perhaps be taken as supporting her optimism, though a strong impression of dislocation is also given by the weird compartmentalization of the literary traditions treated. Apartheid has been only too successful so far in crippling South Africa's cultural development, and one cannot but wonder whether it is possible at this stage to talk of a merely literary renaissance, separate from the impending political resolution.

Two usefully compendious surveys of different broad areas of South African literature have appeared. Jacques Alvarez-Péreyre, the author of *The Poetry of Commitment in South Africa*[5], is a professor of politics in Grenoble and his 'half-literary, half-sociological outline' was first published in French in 1979. It is divided into three sections, the first of which explores the general issue of commitment and identifies the different focuses of the various language and culture groups. Alvarez-Péreyre points up well the gulf between the old-fashioned, white approach epitomized by Guy Butler's very European sense of having 'to fill, or abolish or redeem the culturally empty centuries' of Africa before the white man, and the new black South Africa of the townships, 'bursting with vitality'. The second section, 'The Liberal Conscience and

5. *The Poetry of Commitment in South Africa*, by Jacques Alvarez-Péreyre, trans. by Clive Wake. Heinemann. pp. ix + 278. pb £9.50.

White Power' gives a businesslike if somewhat prolix account of white poetry from Thomas Pringle, through the liberal evasions of Paton and Anthony Delius, to the 'total commitment' of Hugh Lewin and David Evans, and beyond. Throughout there is information and political perspective in abundance, but the literary judgements are unconvincing. Delius, Hugh Lewin, and David Evans, for instance, seem to be grossly overrated by Alvarez-Péreyre, at least on the evidence of the poems which he quotes (many of them by the last two unpublished). The third chapter, 'The Black Poets and the Struggle for Power', moves from the adaptations of *izibongo* made by Xhosa poets in the early part of the century, through the first generation of commitment represented by Dennis Brutus, Cosmo Pieterse and Arthur Nortje, to the growing confidence of Black Consciousness in Oswald Mtshali, Wally Serote, and Don Mattera. The approximateness of Alvarez-Péreyre's literary critical perspectives can be illustrated from his treatment of Pieterse. This poet, who also writes in Afrikaans, is said to use 'an English that he seems to gather from its beginnings, an English that is very close to its original meanings and its many roots'. In the absence of any actual analysis of the poet's use of the 'original' (Anglo-Saxon? Latin? Norman-French?) meanings and 'roots' of English, it is difficult to assess the validity of this judgement. The passage on Pieterse ends with a jumble of emotive but trite metaphor: 'Of all the present committed poets, he has the best talent for choral symphonies. It is on these large canvasses that those artists who have at heart the progress of mankind best express themselves.' Subheadings multiply as the book progresses, and its prosiness becomes oppressive. It is, however, valuable for its information and broad (rather than ideologically alert) sociopolitical summary.

Ursula A. Barnett's *A Vision of Order: A Study of Black South African Literature in English (1914–1980)*[6] gives the impression of being rather closer to its subject than Alvarez-Péreyre's book. Barnett includes in 'black' literature that by 'Coloureds' and Indians since, as she remarks, apartheid has united these groups in 'a common black South African literature'. The first chapter offers a history of black writing in English, from the pioneers R. R. R. Dhlomo and Solomon Plaatje, through the 'golden age' of *Drum* magazine in the 1950s and the repression and bannings following Sharpeville, to the present. Barnett documents the 'literary scramble for Africa' of the 1960s and 1970s, as European publishers picked up the growing number of exiles. Thus the new mood of Black Consciousness which grew up in South Africa in the 1970s owed little to the previous generations. Barnett remarks as a most encouraging sign the rise of *Staffrider* magazine, and of independent South African publishers willing to brave banning orders, such as Renoster Press, David Philip, Ravan Press, and Ad Donker. The second chapter is a compendious account of black poetry, with most space being devoted to poets of the 1970s: Oswald Mtshali, Mongane Serote, Sipho Sepamla, James Matthews, and Christine Douts. Poetry which falls 'outside the current trend of protest', but which inevitably reflects the political situation, such as that of Jennifer Davids, Adam Small, and Arthur Nortje, is also treated. The third chapter is concerned with the novel, and the fourth with short stories, Mphahlele being quoted on the reasons for the importance of the genre in South Africa: 'It is

6. *A Vision of Order: A Study of Black South African Literature in English (1914–1980)*, by Ursula A. Barnett. Browne (1983). pp. 336. £15.

impossible for a writer who lives in oppression to organize his whole personality into writing a novel . . . The short story is used as a short cut [to get] some things off one's chest in quick time.' A nine-page chapter on autobiographical writing is followed by chapters on drama and critical writing. Overall the book is a useful and lucid survey, though sometimes the long succession of analyses of different writers, loosely strung together and introduced by somewhat limp connectives, becomes mechanical. It is a book for dipping into rather than reading at length.

Olive Schreiner and After: Essays on Southern African Literature edited by Malvern van Wyk Smith and Don Maclennan[7] is a sumptuously produced *Festschrift*, marking both the retirement of Guy Butler, the poet and professor who saw the South African writer's task as to 'redeem . . . the culturally empty centuries behind us', and also the centenary of the publication of *The Story of an African Farm*. All its contributors, and *almost* all the topics treated belong to liberal white South Africa, or to the colonial parent-country, England. Though it contains some invaluable essays, as a whole it exudes a safe academic respectability which, in the context of an apartheid state, seems in bad taste. How long will it be, one is compelled to wonder, before a similarly lavish send-off will be possible for a *black* South African poet-professor, focusing perhaps on the respectably classic works of Solomon Plaatje? Eleven of the contributions are devoted to Olive Schreiner herself, and taken in sequence, they create some fascinating ideological and aesthetic contrasts. Patricia Morris opens with 'Biographical Accounts of Olive Schreiner', an entertainingly acerbic treatment of Schreiner's biographers, from those who (like Vera Buchanan-Gould) see her as a transcendant and magnificent soul, to those who (like Marion Friedmann) use her as a quarry for Freudian excavations. Ruth First and Ann Scott emerge as the most reliable, since their perspective is flexible enough to cope with Schreiner's contradictions without reductivism. Morris suggests intriguingly that at the next centenary Afrikanerdom may have claimed Schreiner for its own, while English-speakers will see her as 'that primitive phenomenon, a racist feminist'. After such incisiveness it is disappointing that Morris falls back on a limp relativism in her conclusion: 'There are as many Olive Schreiners as there are her biographers. The definitive biography exists only in each reader's reading.' A fine review of First's and Scott's biography by Nadine Gordimer follows, praising the surprisingly successful blend of English feminist and South African radical approaches provided by its dual authorship. Gordimer is brutally emphatic on the relative importance of white feminism and black liberation: 'Olive Schreiner seems not to have seen that her wronged sense of self, as a woman, *her* liberation, was a secondary matter within her historical situation.' With the next essay in the volume, 'Forms of Dependence and Control in Olive Schreiner's Fiction' by Cherry Clayton, we enter a very different ideological landscape. Clayton seeks to show that Schreiner, 'by exercising her narrative imagination and fusing its creations into an autonomous structure, achieved in the artefact a freedom and control inaccessible to her in real life'. References to Trotsky and Lukacs fail to disguise the essay's unadventurous formalism, which succeeds in reaching

7. *Olive Schreiner and After: Essays on Southern African Literature in Honour of Guy Butler*, ed. by Malvern van Wyk Smith and Don Maclennan. David Philip (1983). pp. xvii + 233. £12.25.

such conclusions as that *The Story of an African Farm* is patterned on antitheses: of characterization (Waldo and Lyndall); and of narrative mode (comedy/tragedy, realism/allegory); and that it abounds in 'internal artistic analogues and narratives'.

Alan Paton's contribution, on *Trooper Peter Halket of Mashonaland*, wears its ideology on its sleeve. There is a distinct air of bad faith about Paton's tone: 'When I consider the problems of the future of our own country, one of the things which I can never get out of my mind is the terribleness of our colonial heritage.' To whom is this portentous banality addressed? Paton goes on to declare that 'unless the new future is brought about by a violent and pitiless revolution' Schreiner's *novella* will remain an enduring part of 'our literature'; but 'if our future is determined by violence and destruction, it is difficult to foresee what would happen to the writings of people like Olive Schreiner'. There is something grotesque about a white South African today fearing that a 'pitiless' black revolution might disregard Olive Schreiner, when the whole purpose of that revolution would be to overthrow the continuing pitiless white violence which her *novella* attacks. It is impossible to miss Paton's nostalgia for the stability of the earlier phase of colonialism, to which Olive Schreiner and he himself belong, when the lone patrician liberal could salve his conscience by ineffective protests, secure in the certainty that the white hegemony which protected him would not be threatened thereby. Another sudden shift of perspective follows Paton's essay in Ridley Beeton's 'Olive Schreiner's Fiction Revisited', a piece of cosy *belles-lettrism*, which roundly asserts that '*The Story of an African Farm* takes its rightful place at the summit or centre of Olive Schreiner's creative work'. With heady pugnacity Beeton informs us that he has 'gone beyond the stage of defending' his view that this is 'a truly great novel': 'The flame of its art never falters, and the farm is always at the mysterious and actual centre, as "Wuthering Heights", the dwelling, is at the centre of the tempests of Cathy and Heathcliff and all their satellite characters.'

In the same volume, Arthur Ravenscroft's 'Literature and Politics: Two Zimbabwean Novels' has much wider critical perspectives. Ravenscroft illustrates the powerful atmosphere of the opening of *Trooper Peter Halket* and argues persuasively that this literary strength, at least in part, redeems the work's faults of sermonizing and 'biblicality'. He then turns to Stanlake Samkange's *On Trial for My Country*, excusing its 'transparently political' intent on the grounds that 'it was important in 1966 that the outside world . . . should have a different, an African, version of how Rhodesia had come into existence'. Ravenscroft's wider topic, the relation between politics and art, is a rich and complex one, but his ideological innocence precludes him from saying anything significant about it. He tells us, for instance, 'I used to believe that literature is produced wholly by linguistic activity', a statement both baffling and incredible. And by the end of this essay he has, very cautiously, brought himself to the point where he can concede that (in the Third World at any rate) 'fictive procedures can legitimately be used for suasive purposes'. If he wishes to modify Orwell's 'All art is propaganda', or to refute Sartre and Barthes, he really needs to apply more intellectual grit to the issue than this. In contrast to Ravenscroft's, Christopher Heywood's essay 'Olive Schreiner and Literary Tradition' is, if anything, too intellectually gritty. It is a very 'brilliant' piece, packed with elliptical allusions to a host of cultural figures of all kinds: Roger

Fry, J. S. Mill, Bachelard, Lévi-Strauss, Konrad Theodor Preuss, Goethe, Jessie Weston, F. R. Leavis, Auguste Comte, 'Nietzsche and Virginia Woolf, Tylor and Hardy' (sic), Chinua Achebe, William Golding, Kant, Hawthorne, Bishop Colenso, Lord David Cecil, and many, many more. Is Heywood perhaps aiming for a place in *The Guinness Book of Records* for name-dropping. Actually his essay *does* develop a profound, if also very subtle, argument. Offering his own version (in which Schreiner is central) of the modern rejection of exploitative Western 'enlightenment', Heywood posits a shift in the late nineteenth and early twentieth century away from the dualism of civilized versus primitive, to a triad, in which a third term is added, inherited from palaeolithic culture. 'The destruction of palaeolithic settlements in Australasia, the American West and in southern Africa', he says, 'were signals for a revulsion of conscience and a new appraisal of values.' Thus Waldo's concern with Bushman paintings in Schreiner's novel is connected with profound philosophical elements in the book, such as its contradiction of the usual negative value of death.

Laurence Lerner's 'Olive Schreiner and the Feminists' expresses some surprise that *The Story of an African Farm* should have seemed so important to early feminists. Lerner re-examines the text in order to suggest that its implications are not so unambiguously feminist as those of *Women and Labour* or *From Man to Man*. Lyndall, for instance, the focus of the woman issue in the novel, is 'curiously absent' during her all-important education, and there is something 'most unfeminist' about her death. Schreiner's later unconvincing attempts to distance herself from Lyndall (insisting that she is 'a child of seventeen when she dies') betrays an uneasiness with the novel's fundamentally pessimistic and defeatist import. It projects a 'belief in the moral value of suffering, and the superiority of women because they suffer more', which is 'pure Victorian orthodoxy'. The attraction of the novel to feminists was partly because of association with Schreiner's later, more actively reformist work, and partly because they had so little to choose from. Lerner argues that the characters of Rebekah and Bertie in *From Man to Man* are 'more interesting and profound' in conception than their parallels, Lyndall and Em, in *The Story of an African Farm*. This is a most illuminating and persuasive essay. Two essays concerning Schreiner's historical context follow. Alan Bishop's ' "With suffering and through time": Olive Schreiner, Vera Brittain and the Great War' focuses mainly on Brittain, arguing, in a similar vein to Lerner's, that the 'masochistic fantasy and fatalism' of *The Story of an African Farm* actually fed Brittain's immature jingoism during the Great War. Her feminism came rather from *Women and Labour*. Rodney Davenport's 'Olive Schreiner and South African Politics' gives a detailed account of Schreiner's changing relations with Rhodes, the Bond, and Smuts, remarking on her prophetic insight in forecasting that the whites would inevitably, 'in fifty or a hundred years', be brought to book for their treatment of the blacks. This section of the Guy Butler *Festschrift* ends with Geoffrey Haresnape's 'The *Voorslag* Movement and Olive Schreiner', which shows how her work was an inspiration to the three *Voorslagers*, and, to some extent, a model also. Her influence is particularly strong in William Plomer's *Portraits in the Nude*, which, like Schreiner's novel, exploits 'the motif of a farm in its empty landscape as a symbol for the isolation of each individual human being'.

Three other essays in this *Festschrift*, on various topics, can be conveniently dealt with here. A. E. Voss's 'The Hero of *The Native Races*: The Making of a Myth' explores unpublished material in the University of Witwatersrand relating to George William Stow (born 1822), the geologist, poet, and anthropologist who developed the idea that the Bushmen ('these wonderful little people') were of quite different origin from the 'obnoxious tribes' of the region. John Povey's 'Landscape in Early South African Poetry' surveys the 'myriad examples of rhymed reaction to the environment' to be found in early colonial verse, stressing their significance, despite technical ineptitudes, since 'place defines nationality'. Marshall Walker's 'Ennobling Interchange: Some Thoughts on English in South Africa' attacks crude notions of 'relevance', contending that *Othello* may gain new meaning in the context which produced Fugard, and that *The Prelude* will speak more eloquently to a South African, familiar with the wilds of the Hogsback or the Drakensberg, than to an English reader, who knows only the 'tourist-encrusted national monument' of the Lake District. In 'A Sense of Place in New Literatures, Particularly South African English' (*WLWE*) Stephen Gray enlarges entertainingly on a similar topic: 'The big ship that knew where it was going – English literature – has gone down, and dispersed little replicas of itself that have put ashore at harbourages around the world.' In the earliest colonial days the spirit of place is a 'life-boat' to be clung to, but this new feeling is swiftly recuperated by the metropolis in 'The Scenic Special' brand of literature, which stresses the exoticism and entertainment value of 'far-flung' places (a tradition still going strong in Laurence Durrell). Later comes a rebellion by some of the colonials, who begin to depict their environment from *within* (Olive Schreiner, Miles Franklin). But this bid for independence is also defused by the metropolis. The third phase is self-referential, the colony now producing its own 'great works', possessing its own publishing houses and journals, and conceiving of place as 'a shared, felt milieu, a familiar and meaningful backdrop' (Fugard, Sepamla). Jeremy Cronin's 'Turning Around: Roy Campbell's "Rounding the Cape"' (*EinA*) treats one colonial poet's attempt to come to terms imaginatively with the African environment. Cronin presents a subtle analysis of one of the poet's most concentrated pieces, focusing on the ambiguities of its lyric treatment of the Adamastor figure, inherited from Camoens's epic. Through the imagery of darkness versus light, and of blood, Adamastor and Africa emerge as both victim and threat to the European adventurer. More personally, Campbell's poem 'celebrates an individual "revolt", . . . and like so much contemporary English-language literature in South Africa, a delight in leaving behind it a certain dark threat'.

Three essays on Pauline Smith are to be mentioned. Dorothy Driver in 'Pauline Smith: "A Gentler Music of Her Own"' (*RAL*) offers a sensitive re-assessment of *The Beadle* and the short stories, focusing on Smith's treatment of English–Afrikaner relations (she once referred to herself as 'a "pro-Boer" at heart'), and more importantly, her specifically feminist aspect. Smith, in Driver's view, 'makes a significant contribution to the literature of the female tradition: in her imagery of sexual awakening and in her evaluation of female sensibility'. Driver gives bold and imaginative interpretations of Smith's sexual landscapes and her images of enclosure and entrapment, arguing that, although she does project 'the stereotypical image of the woman as angel or redeemer', she is original in the respect with which she treats women's sensibility. Charles Ponnuthurai Sarvan's 'Pauline Smith: A Gentle

Rebel' (*WLWE*) is similarly appreciative, but less adventurous. He discusses various aspects of *The Beadle*: its wagon imagery, its attitudes towards women, and, most important, its complex religious imagery. He concludes that 'Pauline Smith was individualistic and iconoclastic. She was a rebel but gentle.' Sheila Roberts in 'A Confined World: A Rereading of Pauline Smith' (*WLWE*) refuses, with persuasive iconoclasm, to join in the chorus of approval. Smith's attempts to render Afrikaans into English, she says, produce a 'rhythmic yet cumbrous style' which 'can prove unremittingly intrusive'. More important is 'the way her works contribute towards upholding certain myths about the Afrikaner'. The virtual exclusion of black characters from her picture is an important defect in her claim to do the lives of the Afrikaners full justice, and 'write about them as I had known them'. Comparing Schreiner's and Plaatje's less idealized pictures of the Boers, Roberts rejects Smith's myth of 'the Afrikaner as Israelite, as the Chosen of God', though she does pay tribute to Smith's insight into the tension between Old and New Testament in Afrikaner religion, which leads her to create a world 'devoid of villains'. Roberts finds a rigid temperamental narrowness in Smith's characters. Andrina's well-trained servant role would, she feels, be almost comic 'were it not for the reader's irritation at her unquestioning subservience'. And she also points out simple weaknesses of characterization (Nind), and of plot. Tony Voss contributes a sharp and entertaining review article on *Pauline Smith* (ed. Dorothy Driver, 1983) to *EinA*.

Robert Ross's 'A New Time for the Fiction of Sarah Gertrude Millin and Olive Schreiner' (*WLWE*) welcomes the re-appearance in print of Millin's *Mary Glenn* and three important works by Schreiner. He argues that these two writers should not be dismissed simply as 'darlings of the feminists, thus inconsequential to students of world literature written in English': a strange piece of logic which seems to assume that feminism precludes literary value. Ross wishes to see a re-assessment of Millin, who 'whatever her racial aberrations' (scarcely aberrant surely in the context of white South Africa), is an important figure in Commonwealth literature, and 'a writer for whom every word and action count', judgements which seem preposterous to the present writer. Muriel Bradbrook's ' "A dome of many-coloured glass": The Lyric Poetry of Guy Butler'[7] is a classic of its misbegotten *genre*, the politely complimentary *Festschrift* appreciation. With adjectives of the greatest judiciousness Bradbrook builds her subject's shrine. Butler's poetry offers a rare blending of 'attentiveness' and 'serenity'; it is characterized by 'discretion and reticence'; and its 'composure' witnesses to a 'habit of discipline'. 'Alertness and repose, keenness and stillness . . . complement each other; contraries, not opposites.' The impression of competent insipidity would be difficult to improve upon. Her other strategy (again characteristic of the *genre*) is to insert references to the great tradition to which her subject is a not unworthy addition. Thus Eliot, Arnold, Yeats, Owen, and Wordsworth are woven in to reinforce the flattering Shelley reference in the essay's title. In deference to Butler's colonial origins the metropolitan critic detects 'perhaps a memory of a cadence from Zulu' in one poem, while at another point she quotes Butler's characteristic view of his native land: 'I must go back . . . / To soil still savage, in a sense still pure: / My loveless, shallow land of artless shapes.' Butler's poetry deserves a more serious analysis than is offered here, one which recognizes his ideological and historical limitations, and seeks out any literary virtues which transcend them. Bradbrook offers only a familiar kind of academic bad faith. A select bibliography of Butler's publications is included in the *Festschrift* dedicated to him[7].

On a very different level from this is *Literature and Society in South Africa*, edited by Landeg White and Tim Couzens[8]. Here, in sharp contrast to much of the material in the Butler volume, we find ideological literacy and a concern to understand the objective relation between art and society. In their introduction the editors note that their book contains chapters on Xhosa and Zulu-Ndebele praise poetry, on the 'colonial novel' in English and Afrikaans, and on black writing in the vernaculars and in English. 'Is there, then, a single South African "literature"? Are there not at least five literatures operating alongside each other . . .?' Their answer is that all these literatures are united by their relation to the same sociopolitical context: 'a capitalist state with, by and large, a unified and dominating economy'. 'The criticism of literature', they insist, 'has everything to do with the criticism of society', and lament that literary criticism in South Africa has become 'a stagnant discipline', critics often setting themselves 'no larger task than simple exposition – a mixture of plot summary and praise'. Simple concepts dominate, such as the 'traditional African way of life', and the 'corruption following independence', 'concepts which must seem strangely innocent to the historian or to the social or political scientist'. The essays in their book are intended to inject the needed social and political realism into literary criticism. In the event invaluable insights into the sociology of South African literature do emerge, though whether this in itself constitutes literary criticism is another matter. Tim Couzens's essay in the volume, 'Widening Horizons of African Literature, 1870–1900', for example, gives an excellent impression of the activities of the Lovedale Training Society and the Lovedale Literary Society in the 1870s, documents the new, more radical movement centred on the secular Native Educational Association founded in 1879 and the newspaper *Imvo Zabantsundu*, founded in 1884. And Couzens goes on to give figures from the 1921 Census Report to show how literary activity spread inexorably from the conservative religious élite into more popular political manifestations, as the literacy rate grew. The essay thus indicates the growth of the social conditions essential to the development of black literature. But this is not, as the introduction seemed to promise, a more rigorous kind of literary *criticism* – it is literary *history*. Stephen Gray's contribution to the volume, 'The Theatre of Stephen Black: An Example of Cultural Discontinuity in South Africa', is also an essay in socioliterary documentation, tracing the career of a man who 'was for over two decades South Africa's only actor-manager, very widely regarded as the "first South African dramatist"'. It covers the same ground as Gray's earlier essay in *Kunapipi* (*YW* 63.475). Ian Steadman's chapter in the book, 'Alternative Theatre: Fifty Years of Performance in Johannesburg', focuses first on H. I. E. Dhlomo, whose play *The Girl Who Killed to Save* (1936) takes 'a conscious stand against the established norms'. After a fallow period in the 1940s and 1950s musical theatre constituted the next break-through, culminating in the 'township musical' *King Kong*. Steadman goes on to review the different protest strands of Athol Fugard and Gibson Kente, arguing that Kente, though 'less politically

8. *Literature and Society in South Africa*, ed. by Landeg White and Tim Couzens. Longman. pp. 220. £5.95.

conscious than the radical political playwrights of Black Consciousness . . . was the first playwright in Soweto to create a popular theatre which reflected the ambience of black life'.

The only black critic included in White's and Couzens's volume (they apologize for this) is Mbulelo Vizikhungo Mzamane, whose essay 'The Uses of Traditional Oral Forms in Black South African Literature' argues that oral tradition is not 'residual', and still exerts a great influence on written literature. The *izibongo* or *lithoko* (praise poetry) *genre*, for example, with its concentration on the heroic figure, is useful in the struggle against apartheid: 'So that whether it is Dennis Brutus writing about Luthuli or Mongane Serote paying homage to the role of the African woman in the struggle, there is in all these poets a common urge to turn to *izibongo*.' Mzamane briefly discusses the mixture of traditional and modern elements in the poetry of B. W. Vilikazi, H. I. E. Dhlomo, A. C. Jordan, and Wally Serote. When he turns his attention to prose, the argument loses itself for a while in a long summary of Thomas Mofolo's *Chaka*, and ends awkwardly (but interestingly) by summarizing an analysis by Brian Willan of his own (Mzamane's) trilogy, *The Children of Soweto*, in which work he claims to be following his ancestors in recording history with 'the community as a whole' as the hero. Mzamane also contributes a related essay, 'Colonial and Imperial Themes in South African Literature: 1820–1930', to *YES*, surveying the early history of black writing from Ntsikana's Great Hymn in Xhosa, through Citashe, to Samuel Mqhayi's famous ironic praise poem addressed to the Prince of Wales (1925). Up until 1930, Mzamane comments, indigenous languages carried the main developments; after that 'the white settlers tightened the screws of oppression' and English, perforce, became more important. Mzamane concludes with a useful introduction to the works of Solomon Plaatje.

In 'Alan Paton: Anachronism or Visionary?' (*CNE*) Russell J. Linnemann attacks an easy target with great vigour. He notes that Paton's latest novel, *Ah, But Your Land is Beautiful* has essentially the same impulse as *Cry, the Beloved Country*. Paton, in Linnemann's view, is in 'a time warp', having totally failed 'to accommodate either new realities or an altered political commitment'. His 'anachronistic vision is paternalist to the core'. Two sharply contrasted essays on Doris Lessing are to be noticed. Eve Bertelsen's 'Doris Lessing's Rhodesia: History into Fiction' (*EinA*) argues that criticism should aim to 'reveal the *multiplicity* of the text rather than its single germ of truth, and rather than its organic coherence, its very *incompleteness*'. Bertelsen identifies three 'normative' readings which are frequently imposed on Lessing's work: documentary, personal developmental, and archetypal, which relate to 'at least three distinct layers of discourse in the texts themselves'. Bertelsen contends that the principle of composition is the real key to the meaning of a work of literature, 'and there is more "to be got out of it" than is dreamed of by its author!' Antony Beck in 'Doris Lessing and the Colonial Experience' (*JCL*) certainly gets more out of Lessing than she dreamed of, but not at all in the way that Bertelsen means. He carefully places Lessing in the social class background to which she was born, the undercapitalized and inexperienced immigrant farming community encouraged by the British government after the Great War. It is from the social aspiration she acquires from this background that, in Beck's view, her dislike of outspoken Afrikaners and working-class immigrants derives. Like other educated 'English' radical socialists of her day, she shows little interest in the question of the franchise for blacks. Her hostility to European colonialism derives not from an ideologically coherent socialism but from 'the metaphysics of liberal individualism'. The SRLP, of which she was an active member, never countenanced autonomous black political initiatives, though it did establish a separate black branch. Lessing herself saw the problem as one of integrating blacks within European culture, writing in 1944 about the difficulties encountered by people 'just emerging from primitive communalism' into the capitalist phase of development. Once in London 'there is noticeably little sign of any radical alienation from the values and attitudes of the English colonial establishment'. Beck's brilliant re-interpretation offers valuable insights into the novels, particularly into Lessing's portrayal of black politics. He suggests also that the strangely exaggerated sense of alienation at the end of *Landlocked* may be the result of Lessing's inner realization that the only way forward for her society lay with black development; but 'for "Martha Quest" and Doris Lessing a mobilization of the blacks as an independent political force would have cost them everything'. An essay by Adrian Adams, '*Le cercueil dans la valise:* l'Afrique et l'avenir des Européens dans les romans de Doris Lessing', appears in *CEAfr.*

Like Beck, David Maughan Brown also detects a liberal subtext in a supposed work of the radical Left, in '"Like a Leaf on the Stream"': Harry Bloom's *Transvaal Episode*' (*EinA*). Brown remarks on Bloom's crucial position as a member of the SACP, 'on the radical fringe of white politics in the 1950s', and summarizes his 'limited but surprisingly diverse' work, ranging from the lyrics for *King Kong* to a thriller, *Whittaker's Wife*. Brown's reading of *Transvaal Episode* demonstrates that its ideology 'is predominantly liberal not Marxist'. Though explicitly identifying the police as the source of oppression, the novel's descriptions of black violence are particularly horrific and powerful. Indeed, Bloom comes 'ominously close to the colonial myths about blacks having "no restraint" in general and a propensity to violence in particular'. Brown suggests that the unbanning of the novel in 1982 may partly have come about because it draws on fears of the primitive savagery of the black mob. Moreover, Bloom's wider political analysis is evasive, identifying a generalized 'bureaucracy' as the source of oppression, rather than specific socio-economic forces. Bloom's view of the world emerges as surprisingly similar in imaginative essentials to that of Paton.

In 'Brutus and Shakespeare' (*RAL*) Colin Gardner provides a sensitive reading of Dennis Brutus, 'a traditional poet, nourished in the classic English tradition, in a way that is largely foreign to the poets of Soweto'. Brutus's work echoes earlier English poets, particularly the meditative sonnets of Shakespeare and his soliloquies (hence the essay's somewhat forced title). Gardner disagrees, however, with Brutus's own assertion that the protest element is 'incidental' to his verse. Even in his love poems 'the interaction between personal and political, between the inward and the outward, is complete . . .' Gardner sees Brutus's 'universality', with which some critics are impatient, not as a weakness but a strength, since it always finds concrete and specific expression. Gardner perhaps overstates Brutus's poetic virtues and ignores his vices, but he illustrates his argument well. Jacques Berthoud's 'Poetry and Exile: The Case of Arthur Nortje' (*EinA*) offers a persuasive defence of one of Africa's most considerable poets, who has been similarly attacked for 'irrelevant' aestheticism. Berthoud quotes Romanus Egudu's attack on Nortje as one of those who 'merely sung their sorrows' in 'a weak-limbed dirge', sapping the will to action. He counters with careful readings of specific poems. In 'Waiting', he argues, 'community and the self are involved in each other at the deepest level'. Far from abstracting his experience from history in sensitive egotism, Nortje shows himself in poems like 'Autopsy' as very much the accurate register of his particular time, the 1960s, when liberalism had collapsed and Black Consciousness had not yet risen. It is important also, as Berthoud points out, to realize the unusual nature of exile in Nortje's case: not an amputation 'from a healthy body to which he longs to be re-attached', but flight from a diseased homeland. Nortje's 'neurosis has public resonances'. Berthoud also stresses Nortje's sheer delight in the masterful use of words, which gives his work its 'efficacy as a preserver', despite its despair. It is clear that such delicate and authentic poetry as Nortje's has little to fear from the attacks of philistine utilitarians such as Egudu. In a cumbrously titled essay 'Culturally Derived Motifs and Symbols as Structural Features in Es'kia Mphahlele's *Chirundu*' (*Kunapipi*) Joyce Johnson offers an exhaustive exploration of themes and imagery, focusing on 'the motif of marriage' and 'the python as a symbol'. Much of what she indicates will already have been obvious to readers of Mphahlele's explicit and thin-textured novel, but she does show interestingly that, in identifying his protagonist symbolically with the python, 'Mphahlele is clearly adapting one of the methods and motifs of Bantu oral narrative to the purpose of characterization'.

In his book *Athol Fugard*[9] Dennis Walder quotes Kenneth Tynan's critical review of *The Blood-Knot*: 'to people who would not be horrified if their daughter married a negro, it seems drably unadventurous'. This is the key critical issue treated in this well-written and useful introduction to the play-wright's work. Fugard is very much 'a white South African talking to other white South Africans', Walder concludes. More than this, he possesses a 'naive faith in the reforming potential of personal moral pressure, associated with a failure to recognize the real centres of power'. Walder deals first with 'Career and Influences', stressing Fugard's (in South African terms) 'mixed' white descent. The next chapter concerns the Sophiatown plays, which establish Fugard's basic (and very 'universal') theme: 'the cost of survival under extreme conditions'. Walder notes that the immediate political themes of *No-Good Friday* and *Nongogo*, the pass laws and apartheid, are curiously muted and seem to have been introduced by Fugard's black actors. His lack of involvement with the actual politics of the play perhaps explains why 'his depiction of Tobias is severely limited, even sentimental'. Walder turns his incisive analysis next on the Port Elizabeth plays, in which resonances from Beckett become audible; but 'it is Beckett domesticated, localized'. Here Walder begins to pinpoint the key to Fugard's real successes: his own involvement, both as performer, and as theatrical stimulus for other actors. Walder is somewhat doubtful about the future survival of the plays once divorced from the personal dynamism of their creator and the small, talented group of actors he has gathered together. In the *Statements* plays, treated in Chapter Five, improvisation becomes even more crucially important. Walder relates Fugard's approach here to the innovations of Peter Brook, and Jerzy Grotowski's notion of 'Poor Theatre'. *Dimetos* Walder pronounces a revealing

9. *Athol Fugard*, by Dennis Walder. Macmillan. pp. x + 142. hb £14, pb £4.95.

failure, the protagonist being 'a small man' with none of the stature Fugard evidently wishes to suggest. The universalism of its style is meretricious. Dimetos 'is a white South African, not a mythical Greek; indeed, an Afrikaner'. Walder welcomes Fugard's recent return, in *A Lesson from Aloes* and *'Master Harold' . . . and the Boys*, to the specific South African setting which he evokes so well. Walder's account is well conceived, but he perhaps understates the sexual dimension to Fugard's imagination. He says for instance that *'Dimetos'*s first audiences did not know what to make of the play'. As a spectator at one of the first Edinburgh performances, I detected little sense of puzzlement at this embarrassingly obvious fantasy of patriarchal glamour and potency.

Chris Wortham's 'A Sense of Place: Home and Homelessness in the Plays of Athol Fugard'[7] focuses on another aspect of Fugard's work not greatly emphasized by Walder. Wortham argues that it is invariably the sense of place which marks his best work: 'in Johannesburg Fugard was a sojourner; Port Elizabeth has always been his home'. Wortham's analyses prove his point well, though his insistence on Fugard's universality may seem to some to smack of the familiar liberal evasion: 'If Port Elizabeth is a paradigm for, or a microcosm of, South Africa, so is South Africa for the world: the inhumanity of man is a constant quality.' Derek Cohen's subtle defence of Fugard's novel in 'Beneath the Underworld: Athol Fugard's *Tsotsi'* (*WLWE*) refuses this recourse to universality. In South Africa, Cohen insists, to be white is to be privileged, whatever one's personal views: 'the worldly success of Fugard, Paton, Gordimer, Brink and Coetzee is a condition and function of their whiteness as much as their merit'. The danger to the writer's work arises from the intense perception of pathos, which may lead to a missionary, change-of-heart message supplanting a more objective view of reality. Although Fugard's book is certainly marred by facile Christian liberalism, Cohen argues, its realism and empathy still give it the power to move: 'we take the characters and their lives seriously enough to believe in them and thus to feel that the author has diminished them by the application of an arbitrary moral system upon them'. Cohen's subtlety succeeds on the whole in rescuing Fugard from the charge of crudely poetic existentialism, though one might feel that the 'we' in the last-quoted sentence is still ideologically presumptuous.

Paul Rich's wide-ranging and insightful 'Romance and the Development of the South African Novel'[8] summarizes the critical orthodoxy that literary realism is at the centre of the South African novel, and that this conventional realism undergoes a crisis of confidence marked by Nadine Gordimer's *The Conservationist*. After this crisis the previous 'cultural hubris' is increasingly abandoned, to be replaced by a sense of marginalization and a disillusion with liberal individualism. However, Rich argues, there has always existed another, non-realist undercurrent in South African fiction, deriving from the romance *genre* of Haggard and Buchan, and projecting onto the landscape romantic interpretations of settlerdom derived from the Eden of the Bible, late-nineteenth-century medievalism, viking sagas, etc. With this kind of perspective in mind the reputation of Paton's *Cry, the Beloved Country* as a novel reflecting the growing maturity of South African literary realism seems questionable. Ndotsheni is surely the idyllic world of the pastoral; Johannesburg is a hell which destroys tribal values. The pattern retains its potency even in the postmodernist world of Gordimer and Coetzee. Indeed, in view of the parody idyll of Mehring ('a jet-age Alan Quartermain') in *The Conservationist*, and the reverse-pastoral in *In the Heart of the Country*, 'the crisis in realism may be said to have brought out the romance idiom even more clearly'. Christopher Heywood's WTW booklet, *Nadine Gordimer*[10], supplies a most useful basic introduction to the novelist's work. Characteristically, Heywood is concerned to place the cultural crisis which Gordimer reflects in the widest context of ideas. In this case, however, unlike the essay on Schreiner treated above, the references to Matthew Arnold, Conrad, Herbert Marcuse, Fanon, Achebe, and (most frequently) D. H. Lawrence and Olive Schreiner, are lucidly introduced and always serve to illuminate the argument. The novels are treated chronologically and the last of the three chapters treats the short stories (as selected in *Some Monday for Sure*), which Heywood considers in general more assured than the novels.

Several essays are preoccupied with the 'post-modernist' phase of white fiction represented in particular by the recent work of Nadine Gordimer and John Coetzee. In 'The Seventies and After: The Inner View in White, English-language Fiction'[7] Rowland Smith incisively compares two different ways of confronting the 'rawness' of the postliberal 1970s. Sheila Fugard and John Coetzee turn inwards and become preoccupied with the monologues of often deranged protagonists, whose 'bizarre psychological states are paradigms of the bizarre reality in the apartheid state'. In Smith's view a basic evasion is involved in this kind of 'emotional camouflage'. In *The Castaways* and *In the Heart of the Country* the author dissociates him or herself from the mad prophetic personae of the protagonists, and can even be felt to be jeering uneasily at their inadequacies. Though Coetzee may produce an imaginatively effective 'grim absurd' by this approach, at bottom 'the oblique method is cloying. A diet of Sibylline utterances, however deftly presented, becomes over-portentous.' In contrast, Nadine Gordimer's use of the inner monologue in *The Conservationist* and *Burger's Daughter* is more imaginatively courageous: 'The author never slips into a knowing, explanatory comment. The situation is vivid, real and doomed'. She refuses to let herself and the reader off the hook by withdrawing empathy from her self-projective creations. Smith develops from this insight a fine and illuminating comparison between *Waiting for the Barbarians* and *July's People*. The same two novels are compared in Paul Rich's 'Apartheid and the Decline of the Civilization Idea' (*RAL*). Rich's ambitious and brilliant argument sums up Western civilization in Mumfordian terms as rejecting the 'polytechnics' of early society in favour of an 'enlightened' and manipulative 'monotechnics', South Africa being a classic and extreme example. The problem for liberals in that country has been that they share this idea of civilization, and are unable to replace it with anything more ideologically powerful than the privatized individual self. Gordimer illustrates the difficulty in her 'somewhat idealized portrayal of a humanistic African peasantry' in terms of a familiar 'pastoral idiom'. Also there is, in the depiction of Maureen's relation with July's wife, too easy an assumption 'that female gender association can transcend class divisions between bourgeois white and working class or peasant blacks'. Gordimer is unable to move beyond a negative reaction against urban civilization to any

10. *Nadine Gordimer*, by Christopher Heywood. WTW. Profile (1983). pp. 50. pb £1.95.

'positive new culture'. Rich nevertheless finds her novel fascinating and suggestive when compared with Coetzee's *Waiting for the Barbarians*. Coetzee consigns his barbarians to 'the traditionally shadowy, background idiom of the conventional colonial novel, lacking any depth of character or historical meaning'. Where Gordimer shows an awareness of the problem, Coetzee has absolutely no conception of any positive values outside his own 'civilization'. His allegorical method exempts him from the need to attempt 'any understanding of the historical forces that produce actual imperial systems at particular phases of history; failing, above all, to have any understanding of *capitalist* economic processes'. There is a huge unintended irony in the magistrate's words, 'the barbarians will wipe their backsides on the town archives. To the last we will have learned nothing.' In fact it is the white imported colonial culture which has shown a lack of historical understanding in South Africa, while the forces of African nationalism have attempted to cultivate historical awareness. In any case every historian knows that barbarians rarely wipe their backsides on the imperial civilization they replace. Usually they cultivate it carefully. Rich's is a definitive debunking of Coetzee's self-indulgent and grossly overrated work. Rich's book, *White Power and the Liberal Conscience* (Ravan), has not yet been seen.

In comparison with Smith's and Rich's essays, André Brink's contribution to an issue of *WLT* marking Orwell's prophetic year, 'Writing against Big Brother: Notes on Apocalyptic Fiction in South Africa', seems simple – even naive. Brink notices that apocalyptic fiction has generally increased in volume since Orwell wrote, but in South Africa it has been the particular province of white writers: 'Black writers, most notably since the liberation of Mozambique, Angola and Zimbabwe, have reason to look forward to Genesis, not Apocalypse.' Many of the works Brink considers are in Afrikaans, but he includes praise for Coetzee's 'magnificent' *Waiting for the Barbarians* and Gordimer's 'poignant and often incisive' *July's People*. Brink feels the apocalyptic novel in South Africa reaches its culmination in Coetzee's *The Life and Times of Michael K*, whose protagonist offers 'the ultimate reply to Big Brother'. Brink's ideological naïveté expresses itself in heady, romantic rhetoric: 'the only factor which can in the long run change the world is the word'. He should go tell that to the marines. An interview between Coetzee and Folke Redin appears in *Kunapipi*, in which he shows himself uneasy at his immense popularity among 'a fairly middle-of-the-road literary establishment'. He wishes he could work in a more formally inventive way, but this is difficult because of South Africa's isolation from wider artistic developments. Nancy Bailey's 'Living Without the Future: Nadine Gordimer's *July's People*' (*WLWE*) offers a subtle and stimulating analysis, which may be felt to force the novel on occasions. Bailey finds Bram's adaptation to the new situation 'remarkable and hopeful' and relates it to his ability to return to primary motivations rather than socially determined ones. He adopts 'what Jung suggests is the feminine mode (necessary for both males and females) of relatedness, as well as the masculine one (equally necessary for both sexes) of action and thought'. Maureen, in contrast, is seen as discovering 'that she has no substance and no self'. Bailey draws from the novel the lesson that the 'only hope for the future, for South Africa as a nation, and for each of us as individuals' is an 'androgynous balance' – a middle-class liberal nostrum perhaps inadequate to the grimly complex inconclusiveness of the novel.

Stephen Clingman's essay 'Writing in a Fractured Society: The Case of Nadine Gordimer'[8] seems more clear-sighted, quoting Gordimer's own perception that 'my consciousness has the same tint as my face', and her recognition of the 'unscalable limitations' confronting the writer's imagination under apartheid. Clingman notes how Gordimer in *The Conservationist* is unable to project the black future in anything other than 'formalistic and transcendental' terms, in the image of the 'resurrection' of the black corpse. He returns to the beginning of Gordimer's career, noting how liberalism is still an imaginative possibility in *A World of Strangers* (1958), and develops a complex defence of her individual 'ideological traversal' within the determined world of race and class identities. Gordimer cannot actually write *for* blacks, but she can and does write *towards* this 'virtual audience', addressing the question of its oppression, the justice of its cause, and the eventuality of its triumph. F. M. Birbalsingh's 'Urban Experience in South African Fiction' (*PA*) also traces the collapse of liberal Christian ethics in South Africa. He covers familiar ground, briefly treating Abrahams, Paton, Lessing, and La Guma, and presenting apartheid as an extreme representative of the alienation of industrialization, which threatens the whole world. There are some mistakes; Olive Schreiner was not of Dutch descent as Birbalsingh states.

One of the 1984 issues of *EinA* takes the form of a tribute to the work of Sydney Clouts, whose *Collected Poems* (including much new material) have now been published by David Philip. Guy Butler contributes an opening memoir, reviewing Clouts's life and work, in which he asserts that 'like all original poets, Clouts forces his readers to rethink their beliefs about poetry'. Various interviews and statements made by Clouts follow, and 'The Critical Reception: 1955–83' collects together reviews and comments from a variety of sources. The issue ends with two longer essays: 'On Sydney Clouts' by Guy Butler, and 'Some Poems by Sydney Clouts' by Ruth Harnett.

In an interview with Robert Bush in *Wasafiri* Lauretta Ngcobo talks of the painful decision to leave South Africa with her children in 1963, and discusses 'the psychology of oppression': 'It assaults so much of your dignity that you feel somehow you deserve it, you have earned it in some unknown way – you wear the humiliation secretly.' She goes on to discuss her novel, *Cross of Gold*, and the mutual contempt between rural and city blacks which impedes the liberation struggle. Significantly, she reveals that the hopeful epilogue was added to the book at the publisher's insistence, and she would like to see it omitted in a future edition. Had there been a possibility that her novel could have been published in South Africa she would have written it in Zulu rather than English. She also comments on the balance between antiracism and feminism. Black women she admits are peculiarly disadvantaged in South Africa, at the bottom of the chain of oppressions. 'But is this the time to fight our men?' There is something moving and eloquent about Ngcobo's quiet dignity which makes the contortions of Brink, Coetzee, and Fugard seem pathological.

Michael Vaughan's '*Staffrider* and Directions within Contemporary South African literature'[8] questions the contradiction between, on the one hand, the collective, Black Consciousness solidarity of the magazine's non-hierarchical layout and regional grouping of contributions, and, on the other, the individualist, neoliberal revolt implied by the anarchic staffrider symbol ('with a certain inevitability, male'), and the personalized heroes of a contributor such

as Mtutuzeli Matshoba. Though he welcomes the rapprochement in the magazine between the writers' perspectives and popular agitation, Vaughan hopes
that the social and economic realities of exploitation will not be diffused in the
mere raising of 'consciousness'. One of *Staffrider*'s most acclaimed contributors, Njabulo S. Ndebele, gives his own lively view of current developments in
an interview with Kirsten Holst Petersen in *Kunapipi*. Ndebele takes issue
with Mphahlele over the reasons for the popularity of the short story in South
Africa, seeing it as a matter merely of the lack of publishing opportunities for
blacks. The recent expansion of publishing in the country has produced a
corresponding increase in black fiction, even sometimes of an experimental
kind. On the broader aesthetic level he insists that literature must be 'mediated
by the complex resonances of language', and cannot be simply reportage or
political exposition. The poetic results of Ndebele's approach are considered
in Colin Gardner's 'A Poem about Revolution'[7], which offers a sensitive
analysis of his finely wrought poem 'The Revolution of the Aged'. Gardner
notes the 'almost surrealistic evocations of dreams and seemingly mythical
events' which characterize Ndebele's work, and 'his habit of projecting himself
into a persona', going on ingeniously to parallel the ambiguities of the poem
with the political debate between Lenin and Kautsky about whether revolution should be made by force or should be left to develop organically until ripe.

   Two thoughtful essays on Zimbabwean literature are to be noticed, both by
T. O. McLoughlin. 'Black Writing in English from Zimbabwe'[4] compares the
English version of Solomon M. Mutswairo's *Feso* with Charles Mungoshi's
Waiting for the Rain, to suggest two poles of writing in the country, the one
concerned with understanding historical, social, and political forces in external
action, the other with the exploration of internal awareness. His survey is
preoccupied with the Zimbabwean writer's attempts to come to grips with the
nation's recent past, complicated as it has been by censorship, UDI, and the
war. He praises Samkange's 'moral protest against history' in *Year of the
Uprising* for its creative but authentic remodelling of events, and analyses
Dambudzo Marechera's 'hyperactive verbal iconoclasm that leaves nothing
standing but its fictions about itself'. Charles Mungoshi, in McLoughlin's
view, offers surer imaginative foundations on which to build beyond the
present disillusion. McLoughlin also offers a survey of poetry, preferring
Eddison Zvogbo's 'sureness of tone' and 'sharpness of language' to the 'sentimentality and forced metaphors' of many less mature poets. McLoughlin's
'The Past and the Present in African Literature: Examples from Contemporary Zimbabwean Fiction' (*PA*) enlarges on the problem of imaginative fragmentation. Zimbabwean writers have not (with the exception of Samkange)
been concerned much with relating past to present. They seem 'less interested
in the processes than in the manifestations of history'. He illustrates this point
with reference to Solomon Mutswairo's *Feso*, Geoffrey Ndhlala's *Jikinya*,
Charles Mungoshi's *Waiting for the Rain*, and Stanley Nyamkufudza's *After-
maths*. Zimbabwe's best writing, he concludes, has not been in the celebratory
and idealizing vein of *Feso*, but has treated (in Mungoshi's words) the 'blind
alley of disintegration' of the colonial period. McLoughlin is hesitant about
predicting a future positive and constructive phase. For the moment the
writers see their task as helping the country 'be honest with itself about the
present'.

2. The Caribbean

(a) General

Apart from the references noted in *YWES* (1983), no comprehensive bibliography of primary and secondary sources has been published during this review period. Reference bibliographies produced serially in the various English-speaking territories and which contain substantial background information were listed in last year's chapter. While *Kunapipi*'s annual survey of Caribbean literature in 'The Year That Was' is always welcome, its publication is erratic; *JCL*'s annual bibliography has sadly been similarly delayed.

Other potentially fruitful sources for scholars are the growing number of little magazines and journals which publish material in this field. A listing of some of their titles follows since many of them are relatively unknown and are often difficult to locate. *ACOLIT* (Germany) carries a selected listing of primary and secondary works; the *ACLALS Bulletin* publishes conference papers given by the Association of Commonwealth Literature and Language Studies; *Antilia* (recently inaugurated by the University of the West Indies, Trinidad) covers Caribbean arts, creative writing, and reviews; *Bim* (Barbados), one of the earliest magazines to publish creative writing and critical essays by Caribbean writers and academics, continues to appear; *Caribbean Review* has a useful subject index; *The Trinidad and Tobago Review* is a topical monthly arts magazine. *Art Rage* (the publication of the Minority Arts Advisory Service) covers some significant material. *Wasafiri* (the journal of the Association for the Teaching of Caribbean and African Literature) was launched in Britain this year; it will be of particular use to teachers of Caribbean, African, and Asian Literature. Robert Bensen's special issue of *PQy* (1983) focuses on 'New Writing from the Caribbean'. It provides an illuminating sample of the range of West Indian writing in English including major figures such as Derek Walcott, E. K. Brathwaite, and Jean Rhys. In addition, the issue surveys Francophone writing and Caribbean poetry.

More specialized bibliographical aids have continued to appear. E. K. Brathwaite's annotated bibliography to *History of the Voice*[11] (a study of the development of nation language in Anglophone Caribbean poetry), is particularly interesting as it encompasses both traditional critical frameworks – the social/political influences, for instance, and the relationship between African, Caribbean, and New World cultures – as well as containing important listings of recorded performances by various of the poets.

The Association for the Teaching of Caribbean and African Literature has also produced some useful and unusual reference material for the teacher involved in multicultural studies. A series of annotated reading-lists cover Caribbean texts for the primary and secondary classroom; in addition there is a Caribbean discography and a bibliography of black British literature.

Author bibliographies of three major Caribbean writers add to the growing body of research material now available. The vast range of C. L. R. James's creative, critical, and political writings are included in a bibliography at the end of a recently published collection of his essays, *At the Rendezvous of*

---

11. *History of the Voice: The Development of Nation Language in Anglophone Caribbean Poetry*, by Edward Kamau Brathwaite. NBB. pp. 87. pb £2.40.

Victory[12]. V. S. Naipaul scholarship is updated by Harveen Sachdeva Mann's post-1977 checklist of his primary and secondary writings (*MFS*). Prior to 1977, R. D. Hamner's 'An Annotated Bibliography' in *Critical Perspectives on V. S. Naipaul* (1977) provided a near-comprehensive listing. The most distinguished publication this year is Elgin W. Mellown's definitive bibliography of Jean Rhys[13]. The bibliography contains an introduction with a concise biography and an outline of her critical reception; the six sections of the book are very clearly divided into the novels, contributions to other books, contributions to periodicals, translations, adaptations by Rhys, and writings about her. The material is annotated throughout and Section F (Writings about Rhys) stands out for its lucid assessment of Rhys's current critical status.

One of the most noteworthy and distinguished general publications this year is the new collection of essays by C. L. R. James, *At the Rendezvous of Victory*[12]. The third volume in a series of selected writings (*The Future in the Present* appeared in 1977, and *Spheres of Existence* in 1980), the book brings together essays spanning the entire range of this remarkable writer's career. From James's early articles in *The Beacon* during the 1930s one moves through history, politics, the art of cricket to a recent essay revealing his current commitments to Poland. The extraordinary versatility of James's imagination and intellect (he is often described as the black Plato of our generation), is clearly documented in Margaret Busby's biographical introduction. One of the most striking essays in the collection deals with Rohan Kanhai, a Guyanese batsman of East Indian extraction. Angus Calder's lively review-article, 'An Audience with C. L. R. James' (*TWR*), illustrates the breadth of his imaginative vision and its ability to bridge several worlds. James is able to relate his discussions of cricket both to historical tendencies and to the Ancient Greeks. 'In Kanhai's combination of Apollonian discipline and Dionysian abandon' we have a 'premonition of the rebirth in the West Indies, of the glories of Athenian democracy, philosophy and art'. James's impressive output as a black man of letters is recorded for the first time in the bibliography to the book. While it does not claim to be exhaustive, it covers a wide sweep of James's writings from *The Black Jacobins* (1938), the well-known historical study of Toussaint L'Ouverture, to *Mariners, Renegades and Castaways* (1953), an appraisal of the works of Herman Melville.

The appearance of a new paperback edition of George Lamming's seminal work *The Pleasures of Exile*[14] marks its continuing centrality in the history of Caribbean literary criticism. First published in 1960, *The Pleasures of Exile* was originally conceived as an examination of the predicament of that group of writers who first migrated to the metropolis of London in the 1950s. Lamming powerfully registers the mood of those formative years prior to Federation and Independence when Caribbean literature first made a substantial impact in international literary circles. The book focuses primarily on the experiences of the writer-in-exile and raises crucial questions concerning the relationship between language, politics, and a history of colonialism. The ambivalent dialogue between Caliban and Prospero in *The Tempest* is used as

12. *At the Rendezvous of Victory*, by C. L. R. James. A&B. pp. vii + 303. hb £13.95, pb £4.95.

13. *Jean Rhys: A Descriptive and Annotated Bibliography of Works and Criticism*, by Elgin W. Mellown. Garland. pp. 256. $47.

14. *The Pleasures of Exile*, by George Lamming. A&B. pp. 232. pb £3.50.

a metaphorical frame for a discussion of the ex-colonial writer's relationship to the 'Mother-Country'. The new preface to this edition notes that while things in the 1980s have changed ('no one argues any longer [for instance] about the racist character of the United Kingdom'), the central issues dominating debate in the 1960s are still very much in evidence. Moreover, after twenty years and a 'considerable sharpening' of perspective, Lamming *remains* with this theme. Only now:

> three decades of migration from Asia and the Caribbean have set the scene . . . for a repetition of the American experience . . . young Blacks . . . in London are closer in feeling and language to their equivalent in New York than they are to the same generation in any Caribbean Island.

This review period has been a prolific one in terms of general criticism and new research. The significance of the role of the little magazine is explored by Stewart Brown in his essay 'Little Magazines: Big Achievements' (*Bim*). Brown notes (in a paper originally delivered during the Carifesta literary symposium in 1981) that the emergence of the little magazine during the interwar period was a crucial influence on the development of a literary consciousness in Africa and the Caribbean. Bibliographers, however, will find them hazardous to catalogue; an informative list of titles and addresses is included for interested readers. Mervyn Morris develops this topic in his historical and regional survey 'Little Magazines in the Caribbean' (*Bim*). Morris also outlines the careers of several of the major literary figures involved with these publications such as Frank Collymore, (one of the early editors of *Bim*) and E. K. Brathwaite, founder of *Savacou*. Apart from Reinhard Sander's original study of the prewar period in Caribbean writing, *From Trinidad* (1978), little substantial research has been completed on the subject. Yet these little magazines provided the first platform for writers to get their work recognized in an essentially hostile environment. As George Lamming says, many West Indian writers used *Bim* as an 'avenue' by which they might reach a 'literate and sensitive reading public'.

In 'Literature and Transitional Politics in Dominica' (*WLWE*) Elaine Campbell stresses the dangers of simply seeing the island as a 'banana republic'. The historical and literary background of Dominica is worthy of more credence than the superficial 'journalese' which frequently describes it. She refers to less dismissive accounts of the island by Trollope, Froude, and Alec Waugh and directs us to its imaginative potential in the literary works of Jean Rhys, Phyllis Allfrey, and Elma Napier. David Dabydeen also adopts a historical approach in his essay 'Race and Community in Anglophone Caribbean Fiction' (*CJE*); Dabydeen surveys the multilayered history and culture of the Caribbean and stresses the dangers of placing one's emphasis on an oversimplified Afro-Caribbean perspective. The racial influence of the East Indian community should not be underestimated in terms both of politics and the 'fundamental ambivalence of Caribbean literature, which is its simultaneous celebration of the local community' and its 'looking beyond the boundaries of history and geography'. The need for holding several perspectives concurrently is also considered by Louis James in 'The Transforming Glass: Identity and Alienation in Caribbean Writing in English'[15]. The mirror

15. *A Sense of Place: Essays in Post-Colonial Literatures*, ed. by Britta Olinder. UGoth. pp. 230. pb £8.

appears frequently as a dominant symbol in Caribbean literature for it is an image that can transform the 'crisis of Caribbean history'. It also reflects the complex relationship of different cultures – Africa, Europe, India, and the U.S.A. Wolf Kindermann's analysis in 'From Babylon to Eden: Afro-Caribbean Responses to Metropolitan Culture' (*WLWE*) develops this theme further. Kindermann considers the strong influence of a consistent sense of exile or alienation in Caribbean writing. Attitudes towards the metropolis have shifted from a full adaptation of its values to an outright rejection, a change of vision from a 'mercantile Eden' to a 'rickety Babylon'. The triangular relationship between Africa, the Caribbean, and Britain is investigated by an assessment of Equiano's odyssey in 1789, in *The Interesting Narrative of Olaudah Equiano, or Gustavus Vassa, the African*, to George Lamming's *The Emigrants* (1954), While different motives inform the work of Caribbean writers, characters created by several writers in the 1970s seem to be more or less 'caught in a British Babylon'.

In 'Literary Criticism and Aesthetics in the Caribbean: E. K. Brathwaite' (*WLWE*) Martini Jurgen provides one of the first critical surveys of the arguments and ideas expounded in literary and cultural essays by Caribbean scholars over the years. Jurgen focuses his attention on the informative theories of Caribbean aesthetics expressed by the poet and historian E. K. Brathwaite. Another valuable historical perspective is provided by Dennis Sardinha in 'Literature of the Caribbean: The Spanish Connection' (*Bim*). Sardinha stresses the high degree of cultural homogeneity in countries of the Caribbean and notes important correspondences between the works of Spanish-speaking writers (Alejo Carpentier of Cuba, Fernando Ortiz who represents the 'Negro' element of Cuban society and Puerto Rican writers), and Anglophone Caribbean literature. John Thieme's essay, 'Alternative Histories: Narrative Modes in West Indian Literature', in *A Sense of Place: Essays in Post-Colonial Literatures*[15], emphasizes the importance of the 'need to overcome a deracinated past'. Beginning with Derek Walcott's rejection of servitude to the 'muse of history' and of the assumptions of western historical discourse in *Another Life* (1973), Thieme compares Walcott's literary strategies with V. S. Reid's alternative vision in *New Day* (1949). Thieme's analysis reveals the dangers of shackling literature in a 'strait-jacket' of 'old forms'. New modes of expression are imperative and can be witnessed in the art of E. K. Brathwaite, Samuel Selvon, Earl Lovelace, Erna Brodber, Wilson Harris, and Faustin Charles.

In the first issue of *Wasafiri*, Anne Walmsley examines the powerful influences of political history and censorship on the works of African and Caribbean authors. 'Put This Man in Jail' also makes the important point that censorship takes many forms. While direct censorship can be imposed by 'forced exile, detention [and] book-banning', more insidious methods exist from 'writers' lack of access to a publisher, or theatre, to barriers of language and literacy'.

(b) The Novel

Wilson Harris has frequently been received as one of the most complex and original novelists of the twentieth century. In 1975 a major critical study by Michael Gilkes appeared, *Wilson Harris and the Caribbean Novel*, which assessed Harris's oeuvre up to the publication of *Black Marsden* (1973). Hena

Maes-Jelinek's recent study[16] updates Harris criticism and is the culmination of several years of familiarity with Harris's methods. Maes-Jelinek's book provides an extensive and comprehensive analysis of Harris's use of language and his original uses of form and time in his fiction. The complexity of Harris's work – its aim to modify contexts and meanings of images – is described in her preface as 'one narrative canvas, at once spiritual autobiography and unrelenting quest for a new art of fiction, . . . exploring the multilevelled inner space of human consciousness'. While Maes-Jelinek acknowledges the difficulties involved in reading Harris, she stresses that this miscomprehension can arise from the reader's reluctance to 'relinquish conventional expectations in art'.

Wilson Harris's theories of the relationship between this inner universe of the imagination and the physical and temporal world have frequently been expressed in his own critical essays. In *The Womb of Space*[17] Harris states his passion for a transformation of the inner and outer worlds. And as Joyce Adler notes in her review-essay (*Kunapipi*), 'never before has his perception of universal images central to myths of many places and . . . novels . . . been so richly demonstrated'. Harris's conviction that the past, the present, and the future are all intertwined and can speak creatively to each other across cultures and across metaphorical boundaries is illustrated in his analysis of the fundamental unity of the human community. Harris compares and contrasts the 'mythical currents of texts' from the American, Latin American, and European literary traditions including Faulkner, Ralph Ellison, Juan Rulfo, Raja Rao, Paule Marshall, Patrick White, and Djuna Barnes. His reasons for selecting the authors mentioned also indicate his main purpose; they are seen as signposts or gateways into the largely submerged territory of the imagination. The works Harris explores develop correspondences, not only through the realm of myth, folk-lore and visual art, but 'are continually related . . . to each other through cross-cultural images' and form a 'cross-cultural web' that reflects his vision of a 'cross-cultural loom'. A similar theme informs Harris's more recent essay entitled 'Character and Philosophic Myth'; here again Harris draws parallels between the mythological foundations of many cultures and stresses the power of language to unlock cultural barriers and stereotypes.

Jean Pierre Durix has been extremely prolific this year in his critical essays on Harris's art. In 'An Introduction to Wilson Harris's Discursive Strategies'[15], Durix points out that many essays so far published on Harris tend to deal with individual novels and focus primarily on the unravelling of the complex metaphorical layers of his fictional world. He therefore looks at Harris's work more broadly and provides perceptive material on the organization of the more explicit and formal features – epigraphs, titles, subdivisions – of Harris's art. Durix, however, has also published articles on specific novels. In 'Paradoxes of Creation: Wilson Harris's *The Secret Ladder*' (*ArielE*) Durix attempts to decode the creative conflicts at the heart of Harris's fourth novel. And in 'Through Tension to Metamorphosis: *The Angel at the Gate*' (*WLWE*) we are shown how Harris concentrates on the creative possibilities of 'catastrophe' and the 'weakness' of humanity. Harris illustrates a radically new form of perception – angels figure in the novel as 'catalysts of discovery'; in many senses the narrative becomes a dream journey and represents an important

16. *Wilson Harris*, by Hena Maes-Jelinek. Twayne (1982). pp. 191. $17.95.
17. *The Womb of Space*, by Wilson Harris. Greenwood (1983). pp. xx + 151. $29.95.

development in Harris's metafictional enterprise. Also on *Angel at the Gate* (1982), is Hena Maes-Jelinek's piece, '"Altering Boundaries": The Art of Translation in *Angel at the Gate*' (*WLWE*). Jelinek suggest that many critics who attempt definitions of 'Commonwealth Literature' set up oppositions (such as national/international, indigenous/metropolitan, 'high' versus 'low' culture, or European versus national societies), thereby transferring to literature their own social and political distinctions or even antagonisms. The essay highlights the pitfalls of these kinds of categorizations and focuses on a comparative study of Patrick White, the Australian-born novelist, and Harris. Both writers have 'delved deeply into the roots of their respective countries and translated into art the experience of their people' but neither has limited the experience to the restrictive definition of a crude national identity. Both have used myth as a 'medium of transformation' and Harris's *Angel at the Gate* involves the reader in a revision of the 'whole landscape of the metropolitan world'.

At last some substantial critical essays are beginning to appear on the work of Earl Lovelace, the Trinidadian novelist and dramatist. While Lovelace has published several remarkable works of fiction, and is a leading literary figure in Trinidad, few scholars have so far analysed his writing. In 'Engaging the World' (*Wasafiri*) Lovelace provides many insights into the nature and purpose of his fiction. Like Wilson Harris, Lovelace condemns rigid categorization in the 'labelling' of Caribbean writing; for future growth a 'multi-cultural vision' is critical as is the need to depart from the self-enclosing 'oppressor-victim' mentality. Three impressive essays have been published on Lovelace's third novel. Harold Barratt explores the use of 'Metaphor and Symbol in *The Dragon Can't Dance*' (*WLWE*). Barratt argues that Lovelace takes Calvary and the Christian celebration of the Eucharist as his 'sacred liturgy' of dominant symbols in the novel. When combined with the Trinidadian ritual of Carnival, Lovelace succeeds in capturing the ambivalent essence of his society. Lovelace's dramatization of this fictional world becomes parodic representation of the Crucifixion and Redemption, the 'Carnival and the Rebellion being at once a quest for form and a form of escapism'. Angelita Reyes pursues a complementary theme in 'Carnival: Ritual Dance of the Past and Present in Earl Lovelace's *The Dragon Can't Dance*' (*WLWE*). Reyes suggests that Lovelace uses Carnival as a means of portraying the effects of social change and history; Carnival becomes an 'unconscious continuation of ritualised resistance and spiritual fulfilment in the New World'. It is exemplified in the novel as a 'rite of passage', a means by which 'characters reactualize their past in an attempt at understanding and changing their present circumstance'. And Louis James, in 'Making the Dragon Dance' (*Wasafiri*), suggests that Carnival and calypso are explored as the expression of the inner life of the people. The Dance of Carnival (which takes place around the time of Eric Williams's government) becomes both an 'affirmation and a question, an enrichment and a probing' into the failure of Trinidad society to 'overcome the burden of its history'.

Mention of the significance of little magazines was made in the general section of this chapter. Alfred Mendes played an important role with C. L. R. James in the formation of *The Beacon* group (a magazine first published during the 1930s). *Pitch Lake*, Mendes' first novel, was published in 1934: *Black Fauns* appeared in 1935 and has been reprinted this year with an informative introduction by Rhonda Cobham[18]. Cobham stresses the centrality of writing produced in the interwar years – its concern with social history and political issues for instance – and shows how female characters were seen as the 'economic and emotional' pivots of the West Indian lower classes despite the fact that the majority of the novels were written by male writers such as Claude McKay, H. G. de Lisser, and Ralph de Boissière.

V. S. Naipaul continues, perhaps because of the controversial nature of some of his writings, to attract the largest amount of journal space. Two major publications have added meat to critical responses to Naipaul's work. *Finding the Centre: Two Narratives*[19], however, is only marginally a new publication as its two main essays, 'Prologue to an Autobiography' and 'The Crocodiles of Yamoussoukro', have both in part been presented previously in journal form. The narratives nevertheless are 'personal' documents and will be illuminating to scholars, as both, so Naipaul tells us in his foreword, are about 'the process of writing'. The first, as its title suggests, unravels the 'imaginative promptings' of Naipaul's literary background. It is 'an account, with the understanding of middle age, of the writer's beginnings'. Naipaul expands on the importance of his Trinidadian childhood and the literary influence of his father's short stories; we also gain details of the background to the creation of one of his first fictional characters, 'Bogart' of *Miguel St* (1959). Naipaul adds a revealing account of a trip he made to Venezuela in search of the man on whom he based his character:

> There was much in that first call of 'Bogart' that had to be examined. It was spoken by a Port of Spain Indian, a descendant of a nineteenth-century indentured immigrant from South India: as Bogart was linked in a special Hindu way with my mother's family . . . There was my Hindu family . . . there was India itself . . . there was Trinidad . . . once part of Venezuela . . . and there was my own presence in England, writing.

Valuable autobiographical detail is provided in Naipaul's precise descriptions of his childhood home – a house bearing close similarities to Anand's house in *A House for Mr Biswas* (1961). The second narrative is a piece of travel writing set on the Ivory Coast of Africa. It reveals surprisingly that Naipaul felt almost at home there amidst what he describes as an 'exotic Community'; he instructs himself in 'Ivorian mysteries' and sees the new nation (*Ex Africa semper aliquid novi*) as what one reviewer has called 'an ancient heartland, a centre'; *not* as we might expect from several of Naipaul's other published commentaries on 'Third World' countries, as one of the many global 'suburbs' of the world.

A new edition of Naipaul's classic novel *A House For Mr Biswas*[20] has also appeared during this review period. In the foreword to this edition, Naipaul stresses the autobiographical significance of this major novel: 'it is the most personal, created out of what I saw and felt as a child'. Naipaul's own introduction to the republication of his fourth novel harmonizes well with the tone of the two narratives in *Finding the Centre*. He recalls that the two years spent

18. *Black Fauns*, by Alfred Mendes, intro. by Rhonda Cobham. NBB. pp. xvi + 328. pb £4.50.

19. *Finding the Centre: Two Narratives*, by V. S. Naipaul. Deutsch. pp. 189. £7.95.

20. *A House For Mr Biswas*, by V. S. Naipaul. Deutsch. pp. 531. £9.95.

writing this novel while living in Streatham Hill, London, 'remain the most consuming, the most fulfilled, the happiest years of my life'. They were his 'Eden'.

True to form, Naipaul has contributed an essay on recent political events in Grenada. In 'Grenada: An Island Betrayed' (*Harper's*) Naipaul describes his responses to a visit he made seventeen days after the American invasion in 1984. Stating that the 'revolution depended on language', Naipaul caustically notes that 'it never got beyond slogans and texts', for 'amid the heat and torpor, language and intentions blurred'. The words were too big and confusing, the revolution 'blew away and what was left in Grenada was a murder story'.

A special issue of *MFS* is devoted entirely to Naipaul. The essays here cover the entire span of Naipaul's creative output from his early social comedies, *The Mystic Masseur* (1957) and *The Suffrage of Elvira* (1958), to more recent novels such as *Guerillas* (1975) and *A Bend in the River* (1979). There is also a perceptive assessment by Amin Malak of Naipaul's study of Islamic culture in *Among the Believers: An Islamic Journey* (1981). Malak sees Naipaul's concerns as focused centrally on the 'fate and affairs of man' and from the conglomeration of Naipaul's observations of the Believers he meets, a pattern of three major characteristics emerges: 'the absurd, the cruel and the contradictory'. The essays in this collection serve to chart the development of Naipaul's literary career over the last twenty-four years. Paul Theroux, an early disciple and an old friend of the writer, provides an engaging portrait of the development of his relationship with Naipaul, the man. In contrast, Bibhu Padhi discusses the relevance of some of Naipaul's own observations about himself as a writer. Several major themes and modes of discourse in Naipaul's fiction are examined including Mimicry and Performance by Harveen Sachdeva Mann, Tabulation in *Mr Stone and the Knight's Companion* (1963) – a little-known and important novel of exile – by John Thieme, and Hinduism and Colonization by Hana Wirth-Nesher. While several of these approaches are not entirely surprising in Naipaul criticism, the essays offer a lively, diverse, and revaluative perspective; they compose, as the editor Leon Gottfried points out, a workable 'portrait of [Naipaul's] subtle metonymic face'.

In 'Jonathan Swift and *Miguel St*' (*WLWE*) William F. Belcher pinpoints Naipaul's Swiftian debts. The 'complex allusiveness' of this first novel makes it a more 'impressive achievement than a superficial reading might suggest' for Naipaul uses the character and stance of an 'exiled satirist of the past' to deal with the modern problems of a history of colonialism. And in 'V. S. Naipaul: The Irrelevance of Nationalism' (*WLWE*) Victor Ramraj considers Naipaul's attitudes towards his colonial background and makes some important observations on the nature of Naipaul's uncommitted political standpoint. Ramraj concludes that Naipaul's consciousness is cosmopolitan and internationalist; it 'surveys encompassingly the human condition, not restrictively the political, the racial or the national'. John Thieme's 'Introduction to *A House for Mr Biswas*' in *A Sense of Place*[15] develops the significance of the human in the Naipaul canon. Drawing parallels between H. G. Wells's *Mr Polly* and Naipaul's novel, Thieme notes that both books are pervaded by 'the myth of the Fall'; the novel functions simultaneously on the level of naturalism and of allegory. Finally, Louis Simpson's 'Disorder and Escape in the fiction of V. S.

Naipaul' (*HudR*) evaluates Naipaul's fiction in the light of disorder and break-down. According to Simpson, Naipaul's protagonists are always struggling to escape. While much of his fiction is set in the Caribbean or Africa, the novels gain their compelling quality by the psychological states of the main character rather than any 'machinery of action'. These protagonists reveal 'areas of darkness' behind their exteriors; they seek to escape but do not 'hope to arrive'.

Jean Rhys died in May 1979; she left instructions in her will that no biogra-phy of her should be written unless authorized in her lifetime. *The Jean Rhys Letters, 1931–1966*[21] in many senses take the place of that life she so much dreaded. Francis Wyndham, one of the editors of this remarkable collection of letters and Rhys's literary executor, calls her a 'fiercely private person' who believed firmly 'that an artist's work should be assessed in separation from the facts of her life'. Rhys's dread of biographical inaccuracy – 'the falsity she detected in books written about people and places she had known' – resulted in her attempt to write *Smile Please* (an unfinished autobiography) which was published after her death. The letters selected by the editors, Francis Wyndham and Diana Melly, take up Rhys's life after her childhood in Domini-ca (recounted in *Smile Please*) from about 1930 and frame the development of the slow and protracted creation of her last novel *Wide Sargasso Sea* (1966). Printed in chronological order, the letters end on 9 March 1966; the corres-pondence discloses an impressive self-portrait of a dedicated artist. Most importantly, they provide valuable insights for scholars into the turbulent process of literary creation and the 'single-minded seriousness' with which Rhys approached her work. They also illustrate, as Francis Wyndham points out, 'the symptoms if not the cause, of her chronic sadness and deep dissatis-faction'. The editors were both close associates and personal friends of Rhys; the letters are scrupulously edited with tact and vision.

Andre Deutsch have also published a collection of Rhys's early novels[22]. Introduced by Diana Athill, one of Rhys's literary editors, the novels reveal the undeniably important relationships between the raw material of her own life and the world of her fiction. Diana Athill discusses Rhys's various heroines within an autobiographical context but makes the critical point that while Rhys never denied that much of the material in her novels came from her own life, she was a self-conscious artist, 'not a woman . . . brooding over her own experience'. As a result, her novels do not say, ' "This is what happened to me" ', but ' "This is how things happen" '.

In 'Jean Rhys and the Dutch Connection' (*JML*), Martien-Kappers-den Hollander brings to light several important biographical factors concerning Rhys's links with the Netherlands through her first marriage to the Dutch writer and journalist Willem Johan Marie (often called Jean Lenglet). Hollander makes the important point that Lenglet is often misrepresented in critical discussions of *Quartet* (1928): it is lamentable that Rhys's fictional character Stephan Zelli (who is portrayed as a swindler, a robber even) has been 'superimposed upon the real man'. Important too is the discovery of an early Dutch translation of *Voyage in the Dark* (1934) – called *Melodie in Mineur* with

21. *The Jean Rhys Letters, 1931–1966*, ed. by Francis Wyndham and Diana Melly. Deutsch. pp. 315. £9.95.
22. *Jean Rhys: The Early Novels*, intro. by Diana Athill. Deutsch. pp. 476. £8.95.

a third-person narration rather than a first-person narrative. And Marsha Z. Cummins examines the shift in narrative focus in Rhys's fiction in her essay, 'Point of View in the Novels of Jean Rhys: The Effect of a Double Focus' (*WLWE*). Rhys's technique of conveying intense emotional states, her technical facility in creating an extraordinary intimacy between her narrators and her readers, is heightened by her shift in narrative perspective. It is a focus which expresses a 'divided state of mind'; it also expresses Rhys's own state as a female colonial writer finding a voice against a 'predominantly male English tradition'.

Samuel Selvon's writing continues to be appreciated and Heinemann have re-issued *Moses Ascending*[23]. First published in 1975, *Moses Ascending* was the second in a trilogy of novels concerned with the central figure of the black immigrant Londoner, Moses Aloetta, who first appeared in *The Lonely Londoners* (1956). The novel has been out of print for some time and is sensitively introduced by the poet Mervyn Morris, who examines Selvon's use of subversive, literary burlesque. And the sequel *Moses Migrating*[24] (winner of the Writer's Guild of Alberta Howard O'Hagan Award for the best fiction in 1984) has been published in the Longman Drumbeat series. Jeremy Poynting's review-article (*WLWE*) aptly describes the novel as a 'comedy of impersonation' in which Moses, who has returned to Trinidad for Carnival, becomes a vehicle for Selvon to 'satirise both mental colonialism and the myth of Britain as a welcoming society'. A related theme is approached by Victor Ramraj in 'Selvon's Londoners: From the Centre to the Periphery'[25]. According to Ramraj, Selvon's immigrant characters are trapped on the edges of two societies: 'Their exposure in the Caribbean to the English language and to British culture . . . gives them a shaky sense of belonging'; they half possess a modified form of English which only creates 'recurring feelings of alienation'. Selvon treats his subject with artistic integrity and vision.

(c) Poetry

E. K. Brathwaite's lecture, delivered at Harvard University in 1979, has recently been published in book form. Entitled *History of the Voice: The Development of Nation Language in Anglophone Caribbean Poetry*[11], the essay defines the historical influences on the creation of various modes of oral discourse in Caribbean poetic expression. Brathwaite distinguishes what he calls 'nation language' from 'dialect' which has often carried pejorative overtones of 'bad English'. Nation language has grown out of a submerged sensibility, a sensibility which co-existed with that of 'standard, imported . . . English'; it is a sensibility which is 'increasingly coming to the surface and influencing the perception of contemporary Caribbean people'. This underground language, which stemmed originally from cultures of the African slaves, constantly transformed itself into new forms; in addition, the pluralism of these societies created a need for constant adaptations – from a form which was African to a new language suited to the new environment and the cultural imperatives of European languages. It is this forceful movement in language patterns – its

23. *Moses Ascending*, by Samuel Selvon, intro. by Mervyn Morris. Caribbean Writers Series. Heinemann. pp. xviii + 141. pb £2.50.
24. *Moses Migrating*, by Samuel Selvon. Drumbeat. Longman. pp. 185. pb £1.75.
25. *Language and Literature*, ed. Satendra Nandan. Fiji: Proceedings of *ACLALS* conference (1980). pp. xvii + 390.

fundamentally oral character and its revitalization through poetic expression –
which is the main theme of Brathwaite's study. It places the development of
language in Caribbean literature within a specific historical framework and
provides a splendid background bibliography of thirty-six pages.

When it first appeared in 1978, Lloyd W. Brown's comprehensive study of
West Indian Poetry was an important milestone in Caribbean criticism. Heinemann's new paperback edition[26] enforces its significance; the book provides a
meticulous and thorough analysis of the origins of Caribbean poetry from 1760
to the present day. The main focus is on the works of Claude McKay, Derek
Walcott, and Edward Brathwaite; however, these major figures are placed
within the context of several others who also face the dilemma of defining a
specifically Caribbean reality with the tools of a partially inherited colonial
language. The written tradition is deftly linked to, and integrated with, the
significant oral poetry of Louise Bennett and the calypsonian, Sparrow. The
major objective of the study is to reflect a movement from the 'derivativeness
and colonial "conversions" ' of the early years to the 'more imaginative and
complex "transformations" of the contemporary period'.

Valerie and Douglas Bloom's survey of 'The Development of Caribbean
Dialect Poetry' (*CJE*) is a welcome addition. The authors point to the recent
upsurge in dialect poetry both in Britain and in the Caribbean itself. While
there was very little use of 'dialect' in early anthologies (such as *Caribbean
Voices* edited by John Figneroa or *Caribbean Verse* edited by O. R.
Dathorne), recent publications reflect a significant shift in focus. *News for
Babylon*[27] edited by James Berry, for instance, illustrates the modifications in
attitudes to language over the past twenty years. Berry includes in this new
anthology dub poets such as Benjamin Zephaniah, Linton Kwesi Johnson, and
other young writers who are sensitive to the shifting nuances of oral language
such as John Agard, Fred D'Aguiar, and Grace Nichols. In his introduction
Berry briefly traces the historical background to Caribbean poetry and makes
the important point that along with political independence came the search for
new art forms: 'An uncharted and unwritten experience had to be external-
ised.' *News for Babylon* represents a landmark in contemporary poetry. And
W. S. Milne draws parallels between the problems of language facing the
Caribbean and the Scottish poet. In 'The Country's Music' (*Agenda*) Milne
points out that nationalism is central to the adequate definition of a culture's
particular vision; it is important for writers to create a language that will *fight*,
to 'iterate over and over again the unique truths' that language expresses.
These expressions are not simply 'dialect' or 'derivations' of Standard English.

An edition of *Selected Poems*[28] by Louise Bennett has been edited by
Mervyn Morris. A central element in the history of 'folk' poetry, Louise
Bennett's work has been well known to Jamaicans for over forty years. Mervyn
Morris opens her world to a wider audience with his seventeen-page introduction, the publication of eighty-one poems subdivided into sixteen semantically
related sections, forty-five pages of notes, a glossary, and several imaginative
suggestions for discussion. While the poems are written in the main in a

26. *West Indian Poetry*, by Lloyd W. Brown. Heinemann. pp. 202. pb £5.95.
27. *News for Babylon*, ed. by James Berry. C&W. pp. xxvii + 212. pb £4.95.
28. *Selected Poems*, by Louise Bennett, ed. by Mervyn Morris. Jamaica: Sangsters
(1982). pp. 230. pb.

creolized Jamaican tongue, the orthography employed is based on the conventions and spelling of Standard English.

In 'The Death and Rebirth of African Deities in Edward Brathwaite's *Islands*' (*WLWE*) Funso Aiyejina examines the survival of African attitudes to religion in the New World. Contrary to Derek Walcott who once claimed that 'no one in the New World whose one God is advertised as dead can believe in innumerable gods of another life', Aiyejina argues that Brathwaite's *Islands* represent an explicit expression of the importance of these gods; furthermore, such gods are 'active in the shaping of the New World African's contemporary psyche'.

David Dabydeen's first collection of poems, *Slave Song*[29], was winner of the Commonwealth Poetry Prize this year. Born and raised on a sugar plantation in Guyana, Dabydeen writes in Creole and concentrates on a recreation of the primal urges of the life of slaves in the Guyanan cane fields. The book is sensitively introduced, contains fourteen poems, six illustrations, notes, and translations for each poem by the author. The previous year's prize-winner Grace Nichols won the award with *I is a long memoried woman*[30]. The sequence of fifty-one poems relates in mythic terms to the experiences of a Caribbean woman reclaiming her African past and affirming her distinctive New World identity. Maggie Butcher in a review (*CJE*) points to the central purpose of the collection: 'The brutality of the middle passage, the degradation of slave labour and plantation life', is evoked by Nichols from the perspective of 'generations of Caribbean women'.

(d) Drama

While there are many prolific Caribbean dramatists, few critical studies have been published. *Theatre in the Caribbean*[31] (with an introduction by Trevor Rhone, Jamaica's leading dramatist) is therefore a useful background work; it outlines the historical origins of dramatic activity in the islands – its ethnic, religious, and cultural roots – as well as providing a refreshing overview of contemporary development. Importantly, Caribbean theatre is 'helping to restore the spirit of Caribbean man – it helps to topple old negative images and set in place more meaningful ones'.

In 'A Caribbean Don Juan: Derek Walcott's *Joker of Seville*' (*WLWE*) John Thieme shows how Walcott reworks the Don Juan legend in his play; it is a legend, 'redolent with echoes of European culture'. Walcott creolizes the Spanish original and transforms the folk elements to create a 'supra-national currency' resulting in a 'metatheatrical piece which investigates the traditions in West Indian drama'.

Finally, it is worth mentioning the publication by Heinemann of Earl Lovelace's three plays set in Trinidad. In *Jestina's Calypso and Other Plays*[32] Lovelace characteristically makes use of the complex ambiguities of calypso and the suggestive possibilities of a carnival freedom; each play moves between a stylized and a realistic presentation.

29. *Slave Song*, by David Dabydeen. Dangaroo. pp. 72. pb £2.95.

30. *I is a long memoried woman*, by Grace Nichols. Karnak (1983). pp. 78. pb £2.25.

31. *Theatre in the Caribbean*, by Ken Corsbie, intro. by Trevor Rhone. H&S. pp. vi + 58. pb £2.50.

32. *Jestina's Calypso and Other Plays*, by Earl Lovelace. Caribbean Writers Series. Heinemann. pp. 118. pb £1.95.

3. India

(a) General Studies

Indian publishing is very vigorous; in English alone, India produces more books than any other country in the world except the United States and Britain. Some 12,000 Indian publishers produce an estimated 25,000 English language titles each year. Though the country now exports books worth approximately R250 million to over eighty countries, its system for publicizing and distributing titles is still quite basic. Thanks are, therefore, due once again to the Indian publishers who have supplied review copies, and to Mr Ronald Warwick, South Asia Librarian of the Commonwealth Institute, London. Without their assistance, this section could not have been prepared.

However, I have not come across as many notable works this year as usual. There is a fascinating bibliography of 'South Asian Canadian Fiction in English (–1982)' by Suwanda Sugunasiri (*TSAR*, 1983). Reed Way Dasenbrock's stimulating essay, 'The Politics of Stylistic Experimentation' (*JIWE*), argues that while there is a tradition of 'serious stylistic experimentation', some authors, such as Desani and Rushdie, do not contribute to it as much as they seek to escape it.

Two books by eminent literary critics have also appeared. The first is Professor C. D. Narasimhaiah's *Moving Frontiers of English Studies in India*[33], consisting of five lectures, three of them delivered at various Indian universities as part of a series with this title when the author was National Lecturer in 1973–4. As a member of the original audience it was not clear to me then (and it remains obscure to me now) why the author chose to inaugurate the series by a lecture on Nehru and Chaudhuri as autobiographers; a good lecture, but autobiography is not exactly the acme of Indian writing, nor are Nehru and Chaudhuri the best regarded of Indian English writers. The second lecture, 'India and the Literature of the Commonwealth', is a plea for extending the traditional Eng. Lit. syllabus beyond its usual province to literature in English from the Commonwealth. The third lecture, 'The Indian Critical Heritage: Its Relevance Today', argues that notions of criticism from traditional Indian aesthetics can illuminate our understanding of literatures both Indian and English – though the author concedes that 'we have today neither theories, canons nor shared assumptions to which we can appeal . . . as much in our criticism of our literature as that of the West' (*sic*). To the three lectures in the series, Professor Narasimhaiah has added two others 'as they reinforce the theme of the National Lectures'. The fourth in the book, 'Search for Values in Literary Criticism', was in fact delivered three years earlier than the preceding three, and amplifies the concerns of the third; and although the date of the book's last lecture, 'An Indian Footnote to T. S. Eliot Scholarship', is not revealed, it repeats some of the points made by Professor Narasimhaiah in his earlier essay, 'Notes Towards an Indian Response to T. S. Eliot's Poetry'[34]. Though he provides a very full account of the background to the Indian references in Eliot's poems, he does not address himself to the fundamental

33. *Moving Frontiers of English Studies in India*, by C. D. Narasimhaiah. Chand (1977). pp. v + 109. Rs 30.
34. In *Indian Response to American Literature*, Anon. United States Educational Foundation in India. pp. 248.

question of how those references function in Eliot's poetry. Professor Narasimhaiah suggests that Eliot was not merely eclectic but actually syncretistic in the usual Indian manner. I remain unconvinced: could Eliot's rigorously analytical Anglo-Catholicism have permitted him to go so completely against one of the cardinal philosophical premises of all Semitic religions? Rather, is it not self-evidently the case that Eliot's use of Indian references subserves Christian purposes in a manner similar to that in which Milton used classical references? However, Professor Narasimhaiah's main points in the book are well worth considering. One last matter: the lectures 'repeat certain ideas and expressions', so an index is necessary and should have been considered essential by the author and his publishers.

The second notable book on the field as a whole is M. K. Naik's *Dimensions of Indian English Literature*[35], a collection of miscellaneous articles written over several years. The book is divided into four sections, each section including a lead article on the achievement, respectively, of Indian English poetry, prose, fiction, and drama, followed, in each case, by three articles – on an individual author, subgroup, or work within the genre. For example, 'The Achievement of Indian English Poetry' precedes articles on A. K. Ramanujan, on Arun Kolatkar's *Jejuri*, and on 'The Tale in the Sting: An Analysis of Nissim Ezekiel's "Night of the Scorpion"'. In spite of this scheme, the book retains the appearance of a somewhat haphazard collection, covering well-known authors and works as well as relatively unimportant areas: there are pieces, for example, on Srinivasa Sastri as a biographer (arguing that Sastri was a biographer who was both serious and thoughtful), and on Tagore's English plays. Naik places Tagore's English versions in the context of the Bengali originals, compares Tagore's plays to those of Yeats, and concludes that Tagore's plays 'forged a new form', combining traditional Indian drama with modern elements.

R. C. P. Sinha's *The Indian Autobiographies in English*[36] takes a breathtakingly wide view of its subject, covering the self-portraits of literary as well as historical and political figures. Another doctoral thesis, this is the first published book-length study of Indian autobiographies. Sinha concedes that the philosophical and religious traditions of ancient India were opposed to autobiographical concerns, and then goes on to consider the autobiographical fragments that do exist in ancient Indian texts. He does not inquire about the implications of such a flat contradiction between the theories propounded by Indian religion and philosphy and what actually obtains in practice. His consideration of autobiographies in the medieval (Muslim) period is objective and thorough, and he then proceeds to a historical survey of Indo-Anglian autobiography, before examining in some detail, separately, the works of religious people, of people in politics, and of litterateurs. Sinha's argument is that Indian English autobiographies are a result of 'the happy union of the native tradition and the tradition of the West'. Incontrovertibly, elements of the two traditions are combined in Indian autobiographies, whatever the language in which they are written. The fact remains, however, that if autobiographies

35. *Dimensions of Indian English Literature*, by M. K. Naik. Sterling; available through Books from India, London. pp. 208. £4.95.
36. *The Indian Autobiographies in English*, by R. C. P. Sinha. Chand (1978). pp. v + 223. Rs 40.

assume the value of individuals and individuality, of place, and of time, and that if these contradict the assumptions of mainstream Indian traditions on these points, then the increasing practice of autobiography cannot be a 'happy' one from the viewpoint of a conservative, or indeed of anyone who is concerned about cultural imperialism and indigenous traditions. This is not my own position, but it is a position that Sinha might have taken into account in a country such as India.

Rama Jha's *Gandhian Thought and Indo-Anglian Novelists*[37] argues that the spread of Gandhian thought made a profound difference to Indian writers, especially those writing in English. Gandhi provided writers such as Mulk Raj Anand, Raja Rao, R. K. Narayan, and Bhabani Bhattacharya, for the first time, with 'a national context and a vision of a society on the move towards political freedom and socio-political reconstruction'. Jha's first three chapters attempt a typology of Gandhian thought and show how these are reflected in the fiction of the period. She pins her case on the fact that there was a sudden efflorescence of Indian fiction in English during the 1930s, when Gandhi first began to influence the country. However, this exposes her to the weakness of the scientific method, which C. S. Lewis once called 'nothing buttery'; if one proposes a thesis, tests it, and finds it true, that does not mean that alternative or additional theses on the same or on overlapping areas might not, if tested, also be found true. The question remains, is it entirely inconceivable that the impact of Gandhian thought and the surge of the writing were not causatively related, but perhaps both due to an entirely different factor, such as a sudden rise in the number of disaffected English-educated young people in the country? Was it not the case that Gandhi's thought appealed to a detraditionalized class of Indians, because Gandhi was himself a part of that class? Jha devotes a chapter to examining the work of each of the four writers to try and trace the nature of the presence of Gandhian thought in them. Her conclusion is that Gandhian thought has been 'the main inspiration behind post-independence Indo-Anglian novelists as well'. Again, it is undoubtedly the case that contemporary Indian novelists, of all languages, share certain assumptions with Gandhi; but Jha does not ask whether these assumptions were uniquely or even distinctively Gandhi's, rather than those of a large part of the Western-educated middle class to which both Gandhi and these writers belong.

P. K. Rajan's 'Patterns of Cultural Orientation in the Approach to Indian Reality' (*Littcrit*, 1982) examines what effects cultural backgrounds have on the ways in which reality is perceived and presented; it is based on a study of the writings of V. S. Naipaul, E. M. Forster, Nirad C. Chaudhuri, and Mulk Raj Anand.

Stella Sandhal's 'India and its Critics' (*TSAR*, 1983) is a discussion of the image of India in books by Indians and others. After discussing dirt, poverty, disease, Gandhi, independence, concepts of individual identity, Freudian approaches to Indian philosophy, and so on, Sandhal concludes that the majority of India's population must be traumatized.

John Oliver Perry, in 'English Poems Responding to the Emergency in India (1975–77)' (*TSAR*) quotes and comments on several English-language poems by Indian writers protesting at, or concerned about, the National Emergency

37. *Gandhian Thought and Indo-Anglian Novelists*, by Rama Jha. Chanakya (1983); available through Books from India, London. pp. vi + 209. £9.95.

declared by the late Mrs Gandhi. The poems considered include Keshav Malik's 'Good Friday', S. Balu Rao's 'This Many-Splendoured Freedom' and 'The Woodpecker and the Tamarind Tree', Kamala Das's 'Tomorrow', Dhiren Bhagat's 'need i say it?', Nissim Ezekiel's 'Toast', and Jayanta Mahapatra's 'Someday I'll Know What I'm Searching For', 'A Fear of Falling', and 'Stand By, Memory'.

(b) Individual Writers

Pride of place must go to T. V. Philip's study *Krishna Mohan Banerjea*[38] which is the first attempt to investigate the contribution of this seminal but completely neglected dramatist, translator, encyclopaedist, and educationalist. Philip looks at Banerjea from the standpoint of his contribution to the fierce debate which was raging then between Indian and Western Christians on the one hand, and non-Christian Indians on the other. He locates Banerjea within the context of the Bengal Renaissance, and there is a full list of Banerjea's published English works.

Izzat Yar Khan's *Sarojini Naidu: The Poet*[39] is one of the few detailed studies of the most well known of pre-Independence Indian poets, who is often called the 'Nightingale of India'. She is perhaps the only pre-Independence poet who continues to be popular, but academic criticism on her work has been infrequent and scattered. Khan's book is based on thorough research of all previous work, and he has even turned up several unknown poems and letters by Naidu; he sketches her social, political, and literary background, her poetic outlook, and her place among other Indian English poets, before considering each of her four published volumes. Khan, is, however, descriptive rather than genuinely evaluative.

Anisur Rahman's *Form and Value in the Poetry of Nissim Ezekiel*[40] is part of his doctoral thesis, and assesses the work of the poet, starting with his first volume, *A Time to Change* (1952) and coming up to *Hymns in Darkness* (1976). Rahman examines Ezekiel's themes, images, symbols, metre, diction, and poetic principles, and argues that the poetry achieves 'objective form' through Ezekiel's technique of 'objective detachment'. Ezekiel is one of India's most substantial English-language poets. In his awareness of the lost dimensions of faith and hope at the individual, racial, and national levels, Ezekiel turns to language – the right word, 'the exact name' – to celebrate as well as to try to reach beyond the 'unfinished' nature of modern man, to quest for wholeness. Rahman sees Ezekiel's central metaphors as being the pagan woman, the putrid city and the moral self, and argues that the poems are accomplished, authentic, and vital.

The work of Arvind Mehrotra is little known in the West, but he is very highly regarded in India, in spite of the limited amount of poetry he has published. Bibhu Padhi, in 'A Wonderland of Riddles and Fantasies: The Poetry of Arvind Mehrotra' (*TSAR*, 1983) shows that Mehrotra is 'an extremely conscious writer, aware of the exact nature of the goods he is to deliver and cautious about the methods through which he would do it'. She argues that

38. *Krishna Mohan Banerjea*, by T. V. Philip. Christian Literature Society (1982). pp. 201. Rs 20.

39. *Sarojini Naidu: The Poet*, by Izzat Yar Khan. Chand (1983). pp. vii + 276. Rs 100.

40. *Form and Value in the Poetry of Nissim Ezekiel*, by Anisur Rahman. Abhinav (1981); available through Books from India, London. pp. viii + 94. £5.95.

though the superficial reader may miss this through a preoccupation with the fantastic moods of Mehrotra's poems, his poetry is marked by a remarkable sense of precision and order, arising from his view of poetry as 'gesture', and from his belief that a poem comprises 'games, riddles and accidents ... and [that] the poet creates as many accidents as he can'. Padhi examines the nature of the difficulty of Mehrotra's poems and their ballast of hard facts, and offers the explanation that the basis of all of Mehrotra's experiments is protest: 'his analogies are meant to be a radical answer to his failures on ... other, less artistic frontiers of life'.

John Persaud Ramphal analyses the neglected dimension of 'Religious Satire in V. S. Naipaul's *A House for Mr Biswas*' (*TSAR*). Examining biographical information as well as other sources, Ramphal suggests that Naipaul is not so much taking refuge from psychological and philosophical problems in satire, as 'demonstrating satirically one of the great weaknesses of West Indian society, its religious rootlessness'.

Lettie A. Myers's ' "Bring Memory to Silence": The Celebratory Nature of V. S. Naipaul's *A House for Mr Biswas*' (*JIWE*) goes some way towards explaining the violence with which Naipaul denounces societies of the Third World. Myers suggests that Naipaul holds memory in particularly high respect as a primary means of access to self-knowledge; 'a man's past, not only his particular but also his cultural past, cannot be forgotten or he will become one of a "culturally destitute" people like the Mayans'. Myers portrays *A House for Mr Biswas* as an act of reverence for Naipaul's East Indian community, because it honours an individual who, while only haltingly aware of the larger forces in his world, did not hesitate to pursue the path of self-knowledge with the powerful but now perhaps superseded tools that his culture gave him.

K. M. Chandar's essay 'R. K. Narayan's *The Guide*: A Psychological Study' (*JIWE*) shows that Narayan is primarily concerned in the novel with a psychological study of the protagonist, Raju; questions which do not accept this are pointless or even misconceived. These include questions which have underlain a great deal of criticism on the novel, such as whether, at the end of the novel, it really rains or whether Raju dies. In Chandar's view, Narayan did not intend us to ask whether the novel is supportive or subversive of tradition, a question that is implicit in discussions of a causative connection between the rain, if it comes, and Raju's genuine fast.

G. S. Balarama Gupta's 'Marco, the Partial Man' (*JIWE*) proposes that Narayan's *The Guide*, in spite of its widespread popularity, fails to attain the stature of an enduring classic because the strength of Narayan's essentially comic genius is quick observation and ironic recording of human oddities and eccentricities; it is inadequate for the sustained task of handling tragic characters and their enervating conflicts and dilemmas.

Inder Nath Kher takes a rather different view in 'Reality and Myth in R. K. Narayan's *The Guide*' (*TSAR*, 1983). Kher sees the novel as encompassing the various polarities and inconsistencies of human nature and generating a sensibility that responds, through the novel's action, setting, and characterization, to the contraries in existence with equanimity and acceptance: 'Blending the average and the extraordinary, the comic and the ... tragic, the profane and the ... scared, the realistic and the poetic (mythic) dimensions of our *being*, Narayan achieves a comprehensive (inclusive) view of reality, and thus succeeds in preserving a poetic view of life without sacrificing its opposite' and resolves or transcends the seeming or real contradictions of character or circumstance.

A. N. Dwivedi finds himself 'deeply impressed' by the predominance of the love theme in 'A. K. Ramanujan as a Poet of Love' (*JIWE*), but discovers that Ramanujan remains *sans* sex, that his treatment of love 'displays a sort of detachment, a certain puritan attitude'. K. Chellappan and Kanaka Bhashyam in 'Encounter and Synthesis in the Poetry of A. K. Ramanujan' (*JIWE*) find Ramanujan to be torn between two worlds – the Eastern and the Western – and see him exploring his memories of childhood in a language that keeps him 'apart from them but still near. While he is searching for roots in an alien idiom, he achieves a synthesis which results in enhancement of both his vision and language.'

'Aspects of Mythic Form and Style in Raja Rao's *The Serpent and the Rope*' are explored by Paul Sharrad (*JIWE*). Rao criticism often finds itself in an impasse: the novel's central character is seen as the embodiment of the author's views and of the character's own pronouncements, and all these are then admired or vilified according to the cultural and philosophical preconceptions of the critic concerned. Sharrad suggests that examination of the novel's form and style may help us to assess the novel more objectively. He feels that the drama of the novel may be discovered not so much in an interpretation of the novel as an idiosyncratic thesis about 'Indianness' and orthodoxy, nor in an investigation of the antithesis of Europe and heresy, but in the mental and literary attempts of the protagonist and the author to span the divides between the two. Sharrad suggests that the novel builds its myths by enabling style and structure to circle around and enact the tensions between history and eternity, dualism and monism.

Cecil Nelson's 'Syntactic Creativity and Intelligibility' (*JIWE*) explores the title problem with reference to Rao's *Kanthapura*. A detailed stylistic analysis leads Nelson to conclude that

> intelligibility is a function of both the writer's presentation and of the reader's effort, whether in leaps of intuition or in delving into dictionaries or notes. . . . Reassigned features of meaning and of collocational possibilities in Indian English are exploited by the Indian writer in English to set his characters in times and places of his own choosing.

Salman Rushdie probably dislikes being seen in relation to a 'regional' literature such as Indian English and would prefer to see himself in relation to mainstream world literature. However, Uma Parameswaran in 'Salman Rushdie in Indo-English Literature' (*JIWE*) takes her cue from Ruth Prawer Jhabvala's statement on the ideal Indian novel as consisting of 'bits of prose-poetry, anecdotes, lots of philosophizing and musing, . . . oblique kinds of wit, and an ultimate self-surrender, a sinking back into formlessness'. On the basis of a comparison of Rushdie's linguistic and formal experiments with those of other Indian writers such as Rao, Parameswaran places him firmly in the 'stream' of Indian English literature.

Feroza Jussawalla, in 'Beyond Indianness: The Stylistic Concerns of *Midnight's Children*' (*JIWE*), feels that Rushdie's impulse towards stylistic experiments has come from two different sources. One is that of modern English fiction, the second is that of modern Indian critics who 'favour any style that seems experimental and different'. Both impulses have led, in Jussawalla's view, to experiments that have been unsuccessful. Accusing writers such as Rushdie and G. V. Desani of building a 'Chinese wall of language', she suggests that works such as theirs are celebrated by academic critics on the basis of 'abstract critical criteria' which are out of touch with the reality of readers' tastes. 'English can be a creative language for Indians only if they are able to break from formulaic abstractions such as Indianness, experimentation, innovativeness, and modernism', she says, and finds the work of Indian poets and of novelists such as R. K. Narayan much more satisfactory, because they are readable and because they persuade their reader that they are Indian without making that an item on the agenda.

4. Australia

(a) General Studies

ALS provides a comprehensive annual bibliography of critical books and articles on Australian literature and also includes selective coverage of new creative writing, reviews, prefaces, and books on Australian language. Entries for both creative and critical books are immediately, and very conveniently, followed by listings of major reviews. The bibliography for 1983, compiled by Marianne Ehrhardt under the direction of the journal's editor, Laurie Hergenhan, includes over three hundred main items, plus subsidiary reviews. *Australian National Bibliography*, published four times monthly, and the Australian Information Service's *A Subject Guide to Current Literature*, published monthly, provide the very latest information on new work, but their literature listings are subsequently subsumed by *ALS*. *ABR*, published ten times a year, is another valuable guide to recent work.

JCL's annual primary and secondary bibliography is most useful in the area of new creative work, since it is considerably more selective than *ALS* with regard to criticism. Compiled by Van Ikin, Brenda Walker, and John Maddocks, it includes an introduction which reviews the previous year's output and highlights trends, again mainly in the area of new creative writing. The entry for 1983 sees the year as belonging to Elizabeth Jolley, who published three works of fiction and was the subject of considerable critical attention, praises Nigel Krauth's first novel *Matilda, My Darling* as a work unlucky to have been passed over by the judges of the Miles Franklin award when they decided not to confer it, and says women's writing seems to have been the area which received most recognition from critics. Mark Macleod's survey of 'The Year That Was' in *Kunapipi* concurs that 1983 was Jolley's year and praises Les Murray's *The People's Otherworld* and Nigel Roberts's *Steps for Astaire* as the outstanding poetry collections of the year.

The most welcome bibliographies of the year are Horst Priessnitz's 'Australian Literature: A Preliminary Subject Checklist' (*ALS*) and Maureen Mann's bibliography of 'Printed Sources for the study of the Australian stage to 1980', which appears in Harold Love's *The Australian Stage: A Documentary History* (see below). Priessnitz's bibliography fills a gap left by the excellent serial bibliographies in *ALS* and *JCL*, in which all general items are lumped together. With a growing preponderance of criticism which is neither author- nor text-based, the need for this kind of aid has increased. Priessnitz employs twelve main categories: Regionalism; Australian Themes; the Jindyworobaks;

Interdependence and Comparisons; Intellectuals and Australian Literature; Women and Australian Literature; Aborigines; Other Minorities; War Literature; Children's Literature; Landscape; and Fiction. By far the largest section is that on Interdependence and Comparisons. It comprises almost half of the total bibliography, and subdivisions of subsections within it (twelve listings of D. H. Lawrence contacts and comparisons as part of the Australia–Great Britain section) can run to as many items as are included in the whole of another category. It is not difficult to find fault with the choice of categories. Only eight items are listed on the Jindyworobaks and these might reasonably have been included as a subsection of the Aborigine category. 'Women and Australian Literature' firmly shifts the emphasis away from the notion of mateship, as put forward in works like Russel Ward's *The Australian Legend*, as a crucial aspect of the national myth, but leaves one wondering whether 'Gender' might not have been a more valuable category. Similarly, it seems rather arbitrary to single out Fiction for special attention and to divide this category into four very specific subsections: Convict Narratives; City Fiction; Science Fiction; and 'New Writing'. But such criticism should not obscure the very real contribution that this selective bibliography makes. It is a preliminary bibliography, which is both useful in its own right and in paving the way for further subject bibliographies.

One of the items Priessnitz lists under 'Other Minorities' is the '4th. rev. and extended edition' of Lolo Houbein's bibliography *Ethnic Writings in English from Australia*[41]. In point of fact this is the third edition and the compiler says it is likely to be the last, since the notion of 'ethnic' writing (which has replaced that of 'migrant' writing since the first edition) is nearing the end of its usefulness. Certainly the term is becoming a woolly one in Australia, because of the variety of ways in which it is employed. Houbein's own usage is, however, unexceptionable: the authors she includes were all born abroad in countries other than Great Britain or Ireland. This is a full and fascinating bibliography which describes itself as 'the last of the primitive ones' in the age of the computer, a comment that points to both its strengths and weaknesses. It both charms and exasperates because of its inconsistencies. Information is given under the headings of date of birth, date of arrival in Australia, education and career, and works (by genre). These are followed by sections in parentheses which give other information and here haphazardness appears to have taken over. It will, one suspects, be some time before the new technology produces annotated bibliography of the order of 'Vytautas Janavicius had a short story fragment published in the U S A and a story in a Lithuanian periodical, but lost both copies and references to them' or the unattributed quotation 'Just to fill you in on Kosti's background: he's been writing more or less full time for fifteen years. . . .'

The first volume of Dorothy Green's revised edition of H. M. Green's classic *A History of Australian Literature*[42], covering the period 1789–1923 has appeared, with Volume II, which continues the story up to 1950, to follow in 1985. As originally conceived, the new edition was to revise the work and

41. *Ethnic Writings in English from Australia: A Bibliography*, by Lolo Houbein. Third revised and extended edn. Adelaide Australian Literary Studies Working Papers. Department of English Language and Literature, UAdelaide. pp. 124. pb A$3.

42. *A History of Australian Literature*. Vol. 1: *1789–1923*, by H. M. Green, revised by Dorothy Green. A&R. pp. xlviii + 917. A$50.

extend it up to 1973. A different plan has, however, been adopted: Volume I *is* a revised version of the 1961 original; Volume II reprints H. M. Green's text, with minimal corrections in an appendix; and there is to be a third volume, which will be Dorothy Green's independent work and which will cover the years 1950–80. When H. M. Green first published his *History*, the critical climate was very different and there was little awareness of Australian literature as a whole. That it is a flourishing discipline today may in part be attributed to his work, which helped establish some of the parameters, but it means that the *History* now reads very differently. Specialist work has now superseded its commentary in virtually every area. Yet there are few subjects to which it does not still provide a valuable introduction. So it is of far more than historical interest. In her foreword Dorothy Green speaks of the dilemma of trying to remain faithful to both her 'primary source' and her own age. She finds, however, that occasions which bring these two impulses into conflict are comparatively rare, since by and large her late husband's judgements stand the test of time. Consequently her revisions are minor: the discussion of William Forster's plays is rewritten and adjustments are made to the sections on Henry Kendall and Henry Handel Richardson, but for the most part the text of the first edition is reprinted without alterations. On the whole this seems justified, but there are passages when the original cries out for updating. One such comes in the chapter on the bush song, which begins apologetically by acknowledging its dependence on a single source, Banjo Paterson's *Old Bush Songs*, and says 'when a larger collection becomes available the opinions here expressed will no doubt need amplification and revision'. Dorothy Green provides a dutiful footnote, mentioning two subsequent collections and a discussion of the origins of folk-song, but does not see the need to rewrite the chapter. More seriously, she justifies H. M. Green's total omission of Aborigine writing on the grounds that his concern was with *written* literature, a position which the bush song chapter calls into question. In general, however, her instinct seems right: the *History* does not need revisions to remain a seminal reference-work and more changes might have compromised the tone of the writing.

The Music of Love[43], a collection of her own essays and reviews provides a better show-case for Dorothy Green's talent as a critic. Like the *History*, it is criticism which is very much concerned with the relationship between text and context, between literature and social thought. Green emerges as out of sympathy with postmodernism, feminism of the Germaine Greer variety, permissiveness, and the commercialization of the arts. Yet, whether she is writing about Colleen McCullough's 'porn birds', Greer's *The Obstacle Race*, or the 'hectic rococo style' of Manning Clark's biography of Henry Lawson, she never dismisses the works she discusses without detailed and reasoned analysis. A strong sense of her belief in the moral dimension of literature is evident, but these are not conservative essays. Rather, as Drusilla Modjeska's introduction argues, they represent the struggle for a radical cultural critique of an independently minded woman, intent on highlighting connections between literature and politics. The essays are urbane, discriminating, and polished and are among the best of the work of the older generation of

43. *The Music of Love: Critical Essays on Literature and Life*, by Dorothy Green. PenguinA. pp. 228. pb A$7.95.

Australian critics. Green is at her strongest when writing about authors she admires and the outstanding pieces in the collection are three fine Patrick White reviews and major re-assessments of Martin Boyd, E. L. Grant Watson, and Louis Stone's *Judah*.

At first glance the only similarities between John Docker's *In a Critical Condition*[44] and *The Music of Love* would seem to be that they are both wide-ranging discussions of Australian literature and culture published by Penguin. *In a Critical Condition* is a polemic which takes as its central thesis the premise that Australian literature has been controlled by a cartel of individuals, characterized at one point as 'sensibility police' who act as jailers of Australian writers (shades of the penal colony days?). These individuals, based mainly at the universities of Sydney and Melbourne, are seen as, intentionally or otherwise, being involved in a conspiracy to pass off Australian variants of New Critical and Leavisite assumptions as universals. However, Docker is like Green in that he is concerned with the interrelationship of texts and contexts and attacks critical movements which ignore this: Russian Formalism and the 'new formalism' of Roland Barthes, as well as New Criticism. The crux of his book comes in two chapters, 'The Metaphysical Ascendancy' and 'The Gloom Thesis', in which the focus on specific debates about Australian literature is sharpest. He argues that the dominant New Critical hegemony in Australia has championed 'metaphysical' writers and themes at the expense of virtually everything else and this has led to the replacement of the radical nationalist account of Australian literature, with its emphasis on 'the legend of the Nineties', by the 'Gloom Thesis' in which the 1890s, far from being regarded as a golden age, are assigned the problematic status that typifies so many New Critical readings. Women, Aborigines, labour, and popular culture are all seen as having been marginalized by this orthodoxy. *In a Critical Condition* contains comparatively little positive advocacy, nor is it finally theoretically sophisticated: Docker insists on the essential sameness of Russian Formalism and New Criticism and gives an extremely reductive account of semiotic theory. Yet the book has already elicited a considerable amount of commentary and, written as it is in a very accessible style, it is likely to play a major role in advancing debate on the issues it addresses. As such it is an important document of cultural history itself. Graeme Turner's *ALS* review (May 1985) points to a number of problematic areas in the work and does a good job of contextualizing Docker's text.

Geoffrey Dutton's *Snow on the Saltbush*[45] completes a trio of general works published by Penguin Australia. Dutton describes his book as a 'history of the Australian literary environment' and his main concern is with the effect of Anglo-Saxon culture on this environment, how English snow fell on the saltbush of the Australian imagination. Like Green and Docker, he views literature in a broad, social context. His study begins with a brief account of the attempt to establish an Australian literature and goes on to discuss writers' needs for both national and international sustenance. He examines various kinds of subliterary writing – school readers, Australian correspondence

44. *In a Critical Condition: Reading Australian Literature*, by John Docker. PenguinA. pp. x + 246. pb A$9.95.

45. *Snow on the Saltbush: The Australian Literary Experience*, by Geoffrey Dutton. PenguinA. pp. xii + 311; 18 illus. pb A$9.95.

courses, and school and university magazines – to see how they have reflected and shaped notions of cultural identity. An especially interesting chapter records some of the responses he received to a questionnaire sent out to forty writers, asking them about the part played by Australian literature and culture in their upbringing. Subsequent discussion of 'the mechanics of literature' includes chapters on particular booksellers, patrons, publishers, and editors. Dutton concludes by stressing the importance of the English language as the 'dominant strain' in Australian culture and by arguing for a completion of the country's 'intellectual decolonization and de-insularization', for a nationalism which is not parochial.

Ross Gibson's *The Diminishing Paradise*[46] is an outstanding study of literary perceptions of Australia up to 1850 and is likely to become the definitive work on this subject. Gibson's main concern is with English literature which deals with Australia and a wide range of source-material is surveyed in a scholarly and discriminating way. 'Literature' is understood in a broad, general way to include Dampier's Voyages, the writings of the First Fleet annalists and the earliest colonists, and the journals of the explorers of the 1830–50 period, as well as the work of Defoe, Swift (whose *Tale of a Tub* is seen as anticipating both the establishment of the penal colony and the later European image of Australia as a kind of purgatory), Southey, and others. Gibson finds two main strands in the early responses of outsiders; a matter-of-fact 'objectivity', in which some of those who actually visited Australia tried to record neutrally their impressions of an environment they often found depressing; and a more imaginative style in which writers in Europe, as well as some of those who journeyed to the Antipodes, constructed an image of the continent which was derived from European mythologies of paradisal realms. From this he arrives at his central theme, that the dominant image of Australia in this period was that of the diminishing paradise. The encounter with the actualities of the new landscape gradually forced the European imagination to abandon the notion of an Edenic continent and later a paradisal heartland for a vision of the land, shaped by another Old World mythology, as a purgatory in which some kind of salvation might be attained through suffering. This image is seen as the dominant pattern informing the journals of the explorers Sturt, Mitchell, and Eyre (one regrets the omission of Leichhardt, presumably on the grounds that he was German), in which the attempt at objective reconstruction and imaginative response are seen as coming together, and Gibson's readings of these works are the high point of his study. A final chapter considers two novels by Patrick White, *Voss* and *A Fringe of Leaves*, which have their origins in the historical period 1835–50. This is designed to illustrate the contemporary resonance of the 'proto-myths' which Gibson has been discussing and their enduring significance.

European responses to Australia and general discussions of interaction between the two continents are also much in evidence in articles and essays. Anna Rutherford's essay 'The Land as Protagonist with Specific Reference to Exploration', published in Britta Olinder's *A Sense of Place*[15], a collection of papers from the 1982 Gothenburg University Congress of Commonwealth Language and Literature, covers similar terrain to *The Diminishing Paradise*

46. *The Diminishing Paradise: Changing Literary Perceptions of Australia*, by Ross Gibson. A&R. pp. xvi + 295; 7 illus. pb £6.95.

in a witty and accessible style and with a variety of well-chosen illustrations. Randolph Stow's 'Wilderness and Garden' in the same volume is a complementary piece which, like Rutherford's essay, looks at the 'mythic prehistory' of Australia, in which belief in the existence of the yet-to-be-discovered Antipodes was deemed heretical by most theologians, and also discusses a variety of later attempts to come to terms with the land. A. P. Riemer's 'This World, the Next and Australia – the Emergence of a Literary Commonplace' (*Southerly*) provides another perspective on the idea of Australia as a kind of purgatory. Taking its cue from a joke in *The Importance of Being Earnest*, it examines the '*topos*' of 'Australia, Land of the Living Dead' in novels by Angus Wilson, D. H. Lawrence, Anthony Burgess, Christina Stead, Shirley Hazzard, Patrick White, Morris Lurie, Elizabeth Jolley, and David Foster.

CE&S, the journal of the French Société d'Etude des Pays du Commonwealth, devotes a special issue to 'Australia and Continental Europe'. A section on 'Early Literary Relationships' includes Elizabeth Webby's brief survey of 'Literary and Theatrical Connections between Australia and Europe: 1788–1850', Sylvia Lawson on J. F. Archibald (material developed more fully in her book, *The Archibald Paradox* – see below), and Nelson Wattie's essay on Henry Handel Richardson, which examines her work in relation to the *Bildungsroman* and provides a fresh viewpoint on material which has been worked over several times by relocating the genre in its original German context. Discussions of 'Contemporary Literary Responses' include two essays which focus on the work of George Johnston, Gareth Griffiths on the plays of Louis Nowra, and André Dommergues's account of how Australian, European, and Chinese cultures are fused together in Randolph Stow's *To the Islands*. David English's 'The Cultural Cringe?' looks at some of the implications which the study of contemporary European critical theory has for Australian literature in a modest and non-prescriptive way. A section entitled 'A New Identity' includes papers by Rudolf Bader and Ariane Blindt on recent Australian migrant writing, as well as two less literary pieces on the same subject, and the volume concludes with essays on aspects of Australian cinema by David Wills, Peter Quartermaine, and J. D. Clancy.

Another volume which attests to European interest in Australian literature and which is also centred on Australian–European cultural relations is Mirko Jurak's *Australian Papers*[47], a collection of pieces from a 1982 Symposium on Australian Literature and Culture held at Bled, Yugoslavia. To the uninitiated it comes as something of a surprise to find that the most substantial section of this book, comprising a dozen essays, deals with Yugoslav–Australian cultural relations. This becomes less surprising when one learns from Ian McArthur's opening essay that there are now nearly 150,000 Yugoslav-born migrants living in Australia, a figure only surpassed by immigrants from the United Kingdom, Ireland, and Italy. Literary discussions in this section include pieces on writing by Slovenes in Australia, Patrick White in Serbo-Croat literary criticism, and Macedonian literature in and about Australia. A more general section on European–Australian cultural relations includes essays on a Spanish contribution to Western Australia, the image of the Greek in Australian literature, and a report on Australian writing published in Czechoslovakia. Commendable though many of the articles in these first two sections are, the finest pieces come in a more general section on Australian literature. Bernard Hickey provides an overview of Miles Franklin's work and argues for more critical attention to be paid to her 1954 novel, *Cockatoos*. Michel Fabre discusses the metafictional aspects of David Ireland's work with particular reference to *The Flesheaters*. Vida Jankovic finds echoes of Emerson in the work of Katharine Susannah Prichard. Barry Andrews offers a stimulating reading of Roger McDonald's *1915*, which argues that the novel is less concerned with national identity than 'fragmentation, disintegration, the search ... for shapeliness, a wholeness in human existence'. Brian Kiernan discusses the work of Louis Nowra and Stephen Sewell, and Adi Wimmer provides a general analysis of the New Wave in Australian drama. R. F. Brissenden assesses the overall coherence of David Campbell's poetic achievement. Georges Denis Zimmerman gives a preliminary account of some interrelationships between Irish and Australian ballads. The outstanding essay in this section is Werner Arens's 'The Image of Australia in Australian Poetry', another exploration of changing literary perceptions of the Antipodes. It is a very fully documented piece, ranging from the early nineteenth century to the present day and discussing, among other things, the subjective image of Australia as a landscape of the mind that emerged in the 1930s and 1940s and the recent Aboriginal and ethnic image of 'an antagonistic, (ecologically) suicidal, dismembered and heartless Australia'. The volume concludes with a symposium on Patrick White (see below) and interesting essays on aspects of Australian literary studies in Italy and England, by Claudio Gorlier and Peter Quartermaine, respectively.

Tasmanian Literary Landmarks[48] by Margaret Giordano and Don Norman and *A City in the Mind: Sydney – Imagined by Its Writers*[49], edited by Patricia Holt, are literary topography of another kind. The former is an engaging small press book which provides biographies of about 1500 words each of twenty-nine writers, who were either Tasmanian-born or who lived there and had strong connections with the state. Those who only visited briefly are omitted, as are all living writers; those included range from Henry Savery and Charles Rowcroft, pioneer figures in the Australian novel, to James McAuley, argu-ably the most significant writer discussed in the book. The title proves to be something of a misnomer, since the essence of the entries is biographical, but details and illustrations or photographs of the Tasmanian houses where the writers lived and of places associated with them are provided. *A City in the Mind* is a more lavishly produced volume with an attractive cover design that suggests the way ink constructs images of cities. Basically it is an anthology of fictional and autobiographical writing about Sydney, but, like *Tasmanian Literary Landmarks*, it offers biographical information and topographical and personal photographs, which in this case are contemporary with the antholo-gized extracts. In her introduction Patricia Holt says that she hopes the anthology 'will serve as a re-introduction to some outstanding Australian literature that has, for various reasons, been ignored or forgotten'. She is

48. *Tasmanian Literary Landmarks*, by Margaret Giordano and Don Norman. Shearwater. pp. 202; 29 illus. pb A$13.95.
49. *A City in the Mind: Sydney – Imagined by Its Writers*, ed. and intro. by Patricia Holt. A&UA. pp. 131; 56 illus. £11.95.

particularly at pains to rehabilitate social realist writers (who naturally 'concentrated on cities, where ordinary people lived and worked') and sees such writers as having been neglected or undervalued by academe, as exemplified by Leonie Kramer's *Oxford History of Australian Literature*. So her selection is informed by similar principles to those for which John Docker argues in *In a Critical Condition*. Among the writers she includes from this neglected tradition are Jack Lindsay, Norman Lindsay, Marjorie Barnard, Dymphna Cusack, Eleanor Dark, and Ethel Turner. Many of the authors are still alive and several are from the younger generation. Holt says that her publisher requested that fifty per cent of the book be composed of extracts from women novelists' work, but her problem was to find sufficient males for the remaining fifty per cent. In the finished product thirteen of the twenty-eight writers included are men.

The *Australian Stage: a documentary history*[50], edited by Harold Love, has its origins in a conference held at the University of New South Wales in 1978 to discuss the possibility of a comprehensive history of Australian theatre. The conference decided against the idea of the comprehensive history on the grounds that it was too ambitious and resolved to produce a basic source-book of documents instead. *The Australian Stage* is the result. It is an impressive volume which, in fact, comes close to providing the history originally envisaged, albeit in a discontinuous way, through the accretion of the various documents. In all 146 documents are included in four main sections: from first settlement to the gold rush (1788–1853); stock companies, travelling stars, and the birth of the 'firm' (1854–1900); the struggle for an Australian theatre (1901–50); and new paths since 1950. Each of these sections is prefaced by a summary of theatrical events in the period, which, in addition to putting the documents in context, provides an outline history of the Australian theatre. In addition there are six essays on aspects of theatre in these four periods. The volume also contains a forty-page section of 'Pictorial Documents', covering theatre, audience, and performers, and an excellent bibliography of 'Printed Sources for the Study of the Australian Stage to 1980'. Compiled by Maureen Mann, this lists over nine hundred items and, like the book as a whole, puts the emphasis on writings about theatre and not drama in the wider sense. *The Australian Stage* is a scholarly work with an emphasis on recording rather than evaluating and an encyclopaedic approach that should pave the way for the comprehensive history. Steadfastly eclectic, it ranges from the high-brow to vaudeville and satire, from nineteenth-century productions of *Hamlet* to Roy Rene as Mo and Barry Humphries as Edna Everage; it discusses international imports as well as local drama, recording what has been performed on the Australian *stage* rather than attempting a history of Australian *drama*; and it moves between mainstream and fringe theatre, offering specific essays on the state theatre companies and alternative theatre in the fourth section. It is an indispensable work for students of Australian theatre and a valuable introduction for newcomers to the field.

Other general discussions of theatre concentrate mainly on the contemporary period. Louis Nowra (*ADS*) finds Australian theatre 'At the Crossroads' with the liberal opponents of the conservative establishment of a decade ago

---

50. *The Australian Stage: a documentary history*, ed. by Harold Love. NSWUP. pp. xx + 383; 29 illus + 44 pp. 'pictorial documents'. A$29.95.

having now come to represent a new status quo. Arlene Sykes, writing in an *NLRev* special issue devoted to Theatre of the New Literatures in English, sees the success of the drama of the late 1960s and early 1970s as 'a hard act to follow' and fails to detect a dominant style in the theatre of the 1980s, but argues that it has this in common with recent Australian fiction, which has received more critical acclaim. She provides a useful account of recent plays by immigrants and women, and of developments in musical comedy and the revue. Katharine Brisbane's 'Looking Out from Australia: New Directions in the Australian Theatre' (*Island*) also addresses herself to the supposed decline in the quality of Australian drama over the last decade. She locates the cause of the problem in the financial success of the theatre industry, which has brought about greater professionalism without an increase in sensitivity to basic dramaturgical issues. Like Sykes, she comments on the increasingly multicultural nature of the theatre. A *Meanjin* special issue on Performing Arts in Australia keeps the emphasis primarily on performance rather than stage history or criticism and includes pieces on youth theatre, actor training, women's theatre, community theatre, and drama reviewing.

Brian McFarlane's *Words and Images*[51] is a study of recent film adaptations of Australian novels. Although its central focus is not literary, it aims to identify and relate the distinctive qualities of both book and film versions and so provides readings of the novels discussed. Thus, *The Getting of Wisdom* is illuminatingly discussed as a portrait of the artist as a young woman, structured around a series of episodes that reveal the protagonist's early obsession with fiction-making, while Bruce Beresford's film of Henry Handel Richardson's novel is seen as ignoring this element without substituting anything comparable to provide artistic unity. McFarlane's opening chapter promises formal comparisons between the versions in the two media and introduces semiotic elements into its discussion. Most of the ensuing chapters are, however, mainly concerned with thematic issues. Peter Weir's film of C. J. Koch's *The Year of Living Dangerously* is seen as changing the emphasis from the political to the romantic; Weir's film of Joan Lindsay's *Picnic at Hanging Rock* is viewed as superior to the novel as a result of the unity achieved by the director's concentration on the theme of sexual repression. In each case the approach is based on modernist notions of artistic unity rather than semiotic analysis. Other works examined include *The Chant of Jimmie Blacksmith* (where McFarlane finds a particularly close correspondence between Keneally's novel and Fred Schepisi's film), *My Brilliant Career*, and *Monkey Grip*. The book also discusses the film version of Patrick White's short story 'The Night the Prowler' and television adaptations of Martin Boyd's novels, *Lucinda Brayford* and *Outbreak of Love*. It includes numerous stills from the films and a filmography which lists ninety items, dating back to 1907.

Persistence in Folly[52] by Les Murray and *Three Absences in Australian Writing*[53] by Chris Wallace-Crabbe are both prose volumes by major poets. *Persistence in Folly* is Murray's second collection of prose articles and brings

51. *Words and Images: Australian Novels into Film*, by Brian McFarlane. Heinemann. pp. vi + 210; 70 illus. pb A$14.25.

52. *Persistence in Folly: Selected Prose Writings*, by Les Murray. A&R. pp. vi + 183. £4.95.

53. *Three Absences in Australian Writing*, by Chris Wallace-Crabbe. Foundation for Australian Literary Studies, James CookU, Monograph No. 7 (1983). pp. iv + 44. pb.

together pieces written between 1977 and 1982. Like its predecessor, *The Peasant Mandarin*, it shows its author's commitment to the vernacular Australian experience operating in a range of contexts. Some of the articles have specifically literary subjects, but a majority approach culture more generally; several of them subsume autobiographical and critical elements in broad, probing explorations of aspects of Australianness. A piece called 'The Bonnie Disproportion' takes its title from Murray's observation that a disproportionately large number of Australians of Scottish extraction have become poets, but, although poetry is mentioned, it is not of major importance in an essay which blends personal reminiscence and commentary on the Scottish experience, both in Australia and Britain, to provide a brilliantly illuminating discussion of the topic. The articles in this volume tend to be longer than those in *The Peasant Mandarin* and several have been revised and extended for book publication. Other major pieces include 'The Human Hair-Thread', which relates Murray's attempts to incorporate Aboriginal elements into his own poetry, 'Some Religious Stuff I Know about Australia', which includes witty and perceptive remarks on 'Strine Shinto' and 'Rallies' (pop and political), an account of his years as editor at *Poetry Australia* and 'On Being Subject Matter', which records his sufferings at the hands of academics and schoolchildren. Among the shorter articles are notes on his novel sequence *The Boys who Stole the Funeral* and reviews of Bruce Dawe, C. J. Koch, *The Macquarie Dictionary*, and Lévi-Strauss's *The Origin of Table Manners*. *Persistence in Folly* is unquestionably one of the major volumes of the year.

Three of the essays in *Persistence in Folly* were originally delivered as lectures at the James Cook University of North Queensland and Chris Wallace-Crabbe's monograph *Three Absences in Australian Writing* had similar origins. Wallace-Crabbe's volume is more overtly concerned with literature than Murray's and yet finally offers less insights. The three 'absences' he examines are those of romantic love, fully developed metaphysical views, and the forging of radically new forms in prose or verse. He argues from literature and declines to make large generalizations about Australian life and values from his evidence, though he concedes it is 'probable' that his findings may point to strains of puritanism, pragmatism, and conservatism in Australian social life. Each of the three sections is problematic. Wallace-Crabbe's discussion of romantic love utilizes two epigraphs from Freud rather uncritically and since the basic thesis being developed here is that Australia lacks something that is a staple of European mores, it seems unfortunate, if not a contradiction in terms, to quote the Viennese quack's theories as if they had universal validity. His second 'absence' is equally hard to accept, not only because he finds developed metaphysical views in writers as diverse as Christopher Brennan, Judith Wright, and John Tranter, but also because, as John Docker points out in *In a Critical Condition*, the 'metaphysical ascendancy' has long held sway in Australian criticism. And there is a similar problem when he discusses the 'absence' of formal innovation. This section concentrates on talking about works which *do* exhibit this quality and by the time Wallace-Crabbe has argued for the oral nature of Lawson's narrative art, the Aboriginal elements in the writings of the Jindyworobaks and Les Murray, and the metafictive aspects of Joseph Furphy's *Such is Life*, the case against this part of his thesis seems to have been made convincingly. Chris Wallace-Crabbe also writes interestingly on his own poetry in the inaugural issue of *BASAM* and offers reflections on the 1940s, in 'The Surreal Decade' (*Westerly*). In a *JCL* article, 'Mixed Motives, Mixed Diction: Recent Australian Poetry', by way of side-stepping some of the recent controversies and 'guerrilla warfare' that have surrounded contemporary Australian poetry, he attempts to draw attention to 'a few of the more arresting poets of the past thirty years', who have not yet received much critical attention outside Australia.

The Younger Australian Poets[54], an anthology of recent poetry selected by two further practitioners, Robert Gray and Geoffrey Lehmann, also claims to be an attempt to transcend the fierce partisanship which has characterized debates about the subject. In the introduction it outlines its aim, to mediate between the avant-garde poetry of 'the generation of 68', who rejected the aesthetic assumptions of most earlier Australian poetry, and the group of poets published in *Poetry Australia* by Les Murray, which saw the poetic of 'the generation of 68' as élitist and excessively influenced by the work of the New York school. This is a fine anthology, including a considerable amount of what is best in recent Australian poetry, but the selection is less impartial than the preliminary comments suggest. Gray and Lehmann are, on the whole, hostile to the avant-garde. Consequently, when they come to choose poems to represent a writer like John Tranter, against whose anthology, *The New Australian Poetry*, this collection defines itself, they plump for pieces that illustrate his 'acknowledged humanity' and 'real perceptiveness about people' rather than those concerns that have more generally been seen to typify his work. The collection includes poems by twenty-nine writers, all but five of them born in the 1940s. It is arguably the best anthology of its kind, but by totally excluding 'abstractionist' poems, it falls a long way short of the representative survey it promises.

Barry O'Donohue's *Place and Perspective: Contemporary Queensland Poetry*[55] follows *Dots over Lines* (1980) and *Soundings* (1976), from South Australia and Western Australia, respectively, in providing an anthology of the poetry of a specific region. It aims to show how poets living in Queensland are linked demographically without wishing to suggest that the state's literary development can be separated off from that of Australia as a whole. The poems included are all work written since 1980 by poets living in Queensland at the time of the anthology's compilation. While the emphasis is thus on the contemporary, poets of all generations and persuasions are included. There are well-known names such as Bruce Dawe and Thomas Shapcott, as well as poets who are beginning to ·gain recognition and several unknowns. The introduction attempts to discountenance the myth of Queensland's not being a very healthy environment for writers. It lists prominent poets born in the state, as well as those who 'lived and developed' their writings there and it draws attention to the role played by Queensland presses and Queenslanders in the production of important poetry anthologies over the last two decades. This evidence and that provided by the selection itself seem to justify the introduction's conclusion that the 'Cinderella state' has indeed been dancing in glass slippers all along.

54. *The Younger Australian Poets*, ed. by Robert Gray and Geoffrey Lehmann. H&I. pp. 207. hb A$12.95, pb A$7.95.
55. *Place and Perspective: Contemporary Queensland Poetry*, ed. by Barry O'Donohue. Jacaranda. pp. xiv + 225. pb A$15.50.

Six essays on Australian poetry in *Poetry of the Pacific Region*[56], proceedings of the 1983 CRNLE/SPACLALS Conference at Flinders University edited by Paul Sharrad, also make a significant contribution to the debate about contemporary poetics. Keith F. Pearson argues that the real 'new Australian poetry' is that of the Canberra poets and not 'the generation of 68', here referred to as 'the Durwell/Tranter group of Sydney regionalists' (*sic*). He identifies the characteristic concerns of the work of Kevin Hart, Alan Gould, and Mark O'Connor. Adrian Caesar attempts to chart the directions taken by contemporary poetry by surveying the work published in six magazines in 1982. Two practising poets tackle more general topics: Philip Martin argues for a return to character and narrative, traditional resources of poetry which, he suggests, are frequently neglected today; Andrew Taylor offers a stimulating semiotic discussion of the problematics attaching to the notion of 'A Book of Australian Poetry' and relates poetry to such discourses as historiography and cartography with passing reference to Bloom, Showalter, Althusser, and Culler. Lyn Jacobs gives an account of Vincent Buckley's 'Growth into Uncertainty', his movement from the 'conviction of a Catholic intellectual towards the more catholic appreciation of his own personal, immediate natural and cultural environment'. Bruce Bennett provides one of the best general accounts of the poetry of Peter Porter to have appeared to date. *Poetry of the Pacific Region* is the second volume of the CRNLE Essays and Monographs Series and an appendix gives the text of Bruce Dawe's address at the launching of its predecessor, *Myth and Metaphor*, edited by Robert Sellick.

Andrew Taylor's essay in *Poetry of the Pacific Region* makes the point that anthologies, like critical studies, are 'signifiers' which work 'by exclusion'. Kerryn Goldsworthy's *Australian Short Stories*[57] excludes certain classics of the genre, while including a number of comparatively obscure pieces. Goldsworthy says that her aim has been 'to steer a middle course between the idiosyncratic and the predictable'. She is at pains to take nothing as given, and both her introduction and selections question traditional definitions of the short-story form. The opening three 'stories' are the first chapter of Catherine Helen Spence's *Clara Morrison* (chosen on the grounds that it has narrative self-containment and provides an ideal introduction to the rest of the anthology), Marcus Clarke's 'An Up-Country Township', a sketch with no real plot, and Price Warung's polemic, 'The Crime of Convict Cunliffe'. In all there are thirty-two stories by twenty-six writers, pieces ranging from the 1850s to the present day. Goldsworthy identifies three 'roughly identifiable short-story "booms"': the 'Bulletin' school of the 1890s and early 1900s; the social realism of the 1940s and 1950s; and the 'formal and stylistic' innovation of the 1970s. Each is well represented and, throughout, the selection attempts to establish and maintain interrelationships and continuity: there is a particular concentration on stories which contrast Australia with other countries. The intention behind this is to shift emphasis away from the Lawson tradition of what Michael Wilding has called 'formula bush tales' and it is successfully realized. In the end, though, this collection achieves a good balance between received

56. *Poetry of the Pacific Region*, ed. by Paul Sharrad. CRNLE Essays and Monographs Series No. 2. FlindersU. pp. x + 144. pb.

57. *Australian Short Stories*, ed. and intro. by Kerryn Goldsworthy. DentA (1983). pp. xxx + 375. pb A$9.95.

orthodoxies and iconoclasm and is sometimes closer to the former than the introduction might suggest. Thus Goldsworthy claims to have avoided the standard anthology-pieces of Henry Lawson and Barbara Baynton, but in Lawson's case 'The Union Buries Its Dead' is included along with the less well-known 'Telling Mrs. Baker'. Her selection also works towards a re-assessment of gender mythologies, and the traditional male focal-points of the bushman, the Anzac, and the sporting hero are frequently replaced by female protagonists. Other stories are chosen for the insights they can offer into the exclusion of women, and these range from 'Telling Mrs. Baker', where the wife is seen as existing beyond the male world of action about which she must be 'told', to Frank Moorhouse's postmodernist 'Audition for Male Voice', where, as Goldsworthy sees it, the absence of female characters is central to the point of the story.

Moorhouse's own collection, *The State of the Art: The Mood of Contemporary Australia in Short Stories*[58] includes forty-one stories by as many authors. They are grouped in five sections: Marriage, Parenthood, Ancestors; Low Life; Travelling About, Bumming Around, In Transit; Games, Fantasies, Lyricism; and Growing, Ageing. Moorhouse excludes all permanent expatriates and master practitioners of the genre such as Hal Porter, John Morrison, Thea Astley, and Marjorie Barnard, but he includes well-known writers like Murray Bail, Peter Carey, and Michael Wilding, a procedure that raises unanswered questions about his principles of selection. Could it be that these writers are allowed entry, not because they are not considered 'masters', but because they help to form a new canon and present a particular view of 'the mood of contemporary Australia'? The collection does not, however, champion postmodernist fiction to the exclusion of other modes. As the title suggests, the anthology has a twofold aim: to offer a view of the state of the contemporary short story and to see it as a reflector of Australian society today. On the one hand, Moorhouse seems fascinated by postmodernist notions of literature as play; on the other, he is happy to allow the dimension of social referentiality a fair hearing. He finds 'stories from a journey' the most successful subvariety of the genre in Australia – accounting for about twenty per cent of the best of the 2700 stories from which his selection has been drawn – and perceptively sees such stories as about encounters with one's nationality. He observes that 'political life as a narrative site' is hardly evident at all and that the redefinition of gender roles is very prominent. He says that about a third of the stories take issue with conservative conventions, while the remainder are written from within the conservative culture, and concludes that contemporary Australia is a non-spiritual nation, characterized by 'a robust hedonism'. The volume was originally intended to appear with biographical notes on the authors, and in '*State of the Art* Contributors: A Survey' (*ALS*) Moorhouse explains how this failed to happen and gives a statistical summary of the answers he received from the bulk of the anthology's contributors to a questionnaire which he sent them.

Other general articles include some interesting discussions of regionalism. Two *Westerly* pieces, from the Australian and New Zealand Association for Canadian Studies Conference held at the University of Canterbury in 1984,

58. *The State of the Art: The Mood of Contemporary Australia in Short Stories*, ed. by Frank Moorhouse. PenguinA. pp. 282. pb A$9.95.

examine possible applications of North American work on regional aesthetics to the study of Australian literature. Bruce Bennett looks at 'Concepts of "the West"', while Gillian Whitlock discusses 'the last frontier' of Queensland. Whitlock's article cites a passage in Hugh MacLennan's 1967 novel *Return of the Sphinx*, in which the distinctive cultural identity of Quebec appears to be threatened by a bulging 'cloud shaped like Australia'. The implication is that Australia is a monolith, lacking any regional variation, a fate which threatens culturally diverse (and here, more specifically, Francophone) Canada. However, these two articles and Trevor James's 'From Exploration to Celebration: Writers and Landscape in Australia's Northern Territory' (*ArielE*) provide clear evidence, not only that there is resistance to homogeneous definitions of Australia in the marginalized regions today, but also that each of the three states discussed has a literature stretching back some distance.

A group of articles on ethnic minority writing also argues for the recognition of heterogeneity in Australian literature and society. In the second issue of *Outrider*, a new magazine whose policy is 'to extend the concept of Australian literature by presenting the work of ethnic writers', June Factor discusses 'Writing about Immigrants', Serge Liberman writes on 'The Place of Ethnic Minority Writing in the Mainstream of Australian Literature' and contributes two pieces on Jewish-Australian Writing, and Alexandra Karakostas looks at 'Forty Years of Greek Writing in Australia, 1943–83'. Sneja Gunew, who prefers the term 'migrant' to 'ethnic minority', has two British conference papers published in European magazines. Her 'Migrant Writing: promising territory' (*Kunapipi*) is a succinct, theoretically stimulating discussion of migrants as characters, writers, and readers. In comparison, 'Migrants in Silver City' (*BASAM*), which appears to attempt to simplify her structuralist approach to issues of cultural identity, seems rather reductive.

Several *WLWE* articles, most of them originally papers delivered at the Association of Commonwealth Literature and Language Studies Conference held in Guelph, Ontario in 1983, compare aspects of Australian literature with other New Literatures in English. Ken Goodwin discusses 'Political Power and Social Flexibility' in Thomas Keneally's *Bring Larks and Heroes*, Roger McDonald's *1915*, and David Ireland's *The Unknown Industrial Prisoner* in relation to three comparable African texts. Coral Ann Howells compares the way in which *1915* renders history a mythic discourse with a similar procedure in the Canadian Timothy Findley's *The Wars*. Bruce Nesbitt looks at early attitudes to literary nationalism in Canada, Australia, and New Zealand. Terry Goldie writes on 'An Aboriginal Present: Canadian and Australian Literature in the 1920s' with specific Australian reference to works by Katharine Susannah Prichard and Vance Palmer. Dorothy Jones provides an account of women writers' responses to the world of nature and, while incorporating references to a wide range of female mythologies, offers specific discussion of works by Christina Stead and Kylie Tennant.

Bruce Clunies Ross and Peter Quartermaine both, in *Kunapipi* articles, examine attitudes to place expressed by Australian city-dwellers. Clunies Ross's 'The Paradise Tram' is a valuable survey of writing about suburbia that helps to correct the unsympathetic image created by Patrick White, Barry Humphries, and others. Quartermaine's 'Bury me behind the Mountains: the Australian Aborigines, the City and the 1988 Bicentennial' looks at city-dwellers' attitudes to the past and present in the period leading up to the country's first centennial, 1888. Both pieces have interesting illustrations.

General articles on gender relations include Nicholas Jose's 'Possibilities of Love in Recent Australian Short Stories' (*Island*), which argues that love plays a more important part in contemporary Australian fiction than is generally conceded, but finds writers 'uneasy about the relationship between individual bonds and the larger social world'. Shirley Walker's 'Towards an Australian Male Aesthetic' (*Island*) identifies characteristic male attitudes in the work of three poets, John Shaw Neilson, Christopher Brennan, and Kenneth Slessor, and is not, as the title might suggest, concerned with analysing trends that might point towards a change in the future. Geoffrey Dutton (*Quadrant*) surveys a broad range of female types in his 'Australian Women, Woman and Love', but does not admit the possibility of altering stereotypes into his discussion.

Miscellaneous general articles include two *Quadrant* pieces by Noel Macainsh, on 'Australian Poets after the Revolution of 1968' and the pursuit of 'Beauty' in early Australian poetry with particular reference to the work of Christopher Brennan, Kenneth Slessor, and A. D. Hope. David Carter (*WLWE*) looks at the impact of modernism on Australian literature. Alan Shoemaker (*Westerly*) writes on 'Sex and Violence in the Black Australian Novel'. John Barnes (*Quadrant*) gives an account of Edward Garnett's attempts to promote such Australian writers as Henry Lawson, Barbara Baynton, and Joseph Furphy in Britain. Last but very definitely not least, two outstanding *ALS* articles: Helen Tiffin discusses Asia in the contemporary Australian novel, arguing that it has become a territory for the exploration of the Australian psyche and discussing works by Christine Townend, Bruce Grant, Robert Drewe, Blanche D'Alpuget, Ian Moffitt, C. J. Koch, and Randolph Stow. Graeme Turner analyses the way character is constructed in Australian fiction and finds a tension between the codes of mateship and individualism informing narrative procedures.

(b) Individual Authors, 1789–1920

There are a number of notable books on individual authors in this period, but the volume of essays and articles is not proportionate. The outstanding works are five studies, in which the main thrust is biographical.

J. S. D. Mellick's *The Passing Guest: A Life of Henry Kingsley*[59] is a scholarly biography of an English writer who has always been allowed a place in the canon of Australian literature. It is a very fully researched work which shows that, although Kingsley only spent four years in Australia, they were years which were crucial in shaping his sensibility. A thorough account of the whole of Kingsley's life is given, but there is a particular emphasis on his Australian period which gave rise to *The Recollections of Geoffry Hamlyn* and influenced all his subsequent fiction. The alleged 'roughness' of his style which his brother, the clergyman and novelist Charles, tried to temper is seen as a particularly colonial trait and one which proved both a strength and a weakness in the eyes of differing segments of the Victorian reading public. Moreover, his subsequent involvement in Australian debates, such as that which

59. *The Passing Guest: A Life of Henry Kingsley*, by J. S. D. Mellick. UQueen (1983). pp. xii + 211; 30 illus. £16.95.

surrounded the former Australian explorer Eyre after the Morant Bay uprising of 1865 in Jamaica, where he was then Governor, is given prominence. This is a book which is to be commended for its high production standards, typical of recent volumes from the University of Queensland Press. Its fine illustrations include colour reproductions of some of the watercolours painted by Kingsley while in Australia. If the study has a fault, it is its tendency to extrapolate details about Kingsley's life from supposedly autobiographical passages in the fiction. Problematic at the best of times, such an approach becomes especially so in this instance, since Mellick argues against those who have attributed sentiments expressed in *Geoffry Hamlyn* to its author, saying 'what Kingsley wrote did not represent his personal beliefs'. Nevertheless *The Passing Guest* will become a standard work and deservedly so. It includes an excellent bibliography, which gives details of Kingsley's twenty-four books, his shorter works, manuscript sources in Britain, Australasia, and the United States, and a full listing of secondary sources.

Xavier Pons's *Out of Eden: Henry Lawson's Life and Works*[60] is more a study in personality than a conventional biography. It attempts to explain some of the apparent paradoxes in Lawson's character by means of a psychoanalytic approach and its material is organized into a series of thematically structured chapters. It sees an oral fixation (leading to alcoholism), a dependence on his mother, and a lifelong quest for a father figure as the key determinants of Lawson's psychological make-up. As this suggests, the method employed is primarily Freudian and, while there is occasional reference to later theorists such as Lacan and Laing, Pons takes the view that there is a basic unitary Lawson self, which is at times obscured by role-playing, rather than arguing for the notion of a series of constructed or divided selves. This is an absorbing study that throws light on many aspects of Lawson's thought and writings, not least his socialism and belief in mateship, which had such important consequences in the shaping of a national mythology. The suggestion that these were a product of repressed homosexuality and Lawson's response to his cultured mother provokes various speculations, especially when Lawson's role in the formation of Australian gender stereotypes is taken into account. Pons examines a broad range of issues and goes far beyond the obvious: he shows how Lawson's nationalism (his idea of Australia as *mother*-land) and his racism emanated from his inner conflicts and how his attitude to Empire changed with the passing of the Victorian Age and the replacement of the matriarchal monarch by the son who had so long existed in her shadow. His method also yields valuable insights into Lawson's ideas about literary production and his response to specific genres and modes. He provides a particularly interesting and plausible account of why Lawson excelled as a short-story writer, but failed to achieve the same level of artistry in poetry, which he regarded as an alien and artificial medium. While the book's casting of Louisa Lawson, the writer's mother, as the villainess of the piece is by no means original (one wonders how long it will be before there is a full feminist rebuttal of this view), the argument is sustained with flair and vitality. All in all, *Out of Eden* is a fascinating interpretation of Lawson's life and development as a writer, which, if read as a case study of the literary psyche in the period, helps

60. *Out of Eden: Henry Lawson's Life and Works – A Psychoanalytic View*, by Xavier Pons. A&R. pp. viii + 315. pb £7.95.

to explain the apparent conflict between 'the legend of the nineties' and 'the gloom thesis', to show how nationalist constructs can co-exist with individual traumas.

A. B. Paterson, who along with Lawson did much to create 'the legend of the nineties', is the subject of Clement Semmler's *The Banjo of the Bush*[61], a welcome reprint of the second edition of a work that originally appeared in 1966. It stands up well and remains the definitive biography. Another interesting item of Patersoniana is *Banjo Paterson's Old Bush Songs*[62], a selection from the bush songs collected by Paterson and published in seven editions between 1905 and 1931. It includes thirty-nine songs and, unlike the original editions, prints their melodies, usually following the 'Banjo's' indications as to which tune is to be used. The selection ranges from familiar titles such as 'On the Road to Gundagai' and 'The Wild Colonial Boy' to less well-known pieces. The songs are annotated and there is a short introduction, bibliography, and discography by Graham Seal. It comes with a cassette which offers recordings of twelve of the songs by the bush band, Speewah. These bring the music alive and could be a valuable teaching aid.

Sylvia Lawson's *The Archibald Paradox*[63] is biography with a difference. It is less the life-story of J. F. Archibald, the legendary editor of the *Bulletin*, than an account of how his personality and temperament made this extraordinary colonial newspaper possible. While the early chapters are comparatively unmemorable, those which deal with Archibald's editorship of the *Bulletin*, and in particular Chapter 7, 'The Great Print Circus', offer illuminating insights, not only into the production forces that went into this seminally important creator of Australian mythologies, but also into the 'paradox' of the book's title, which is the paradox of being colonial. In her introduction Lawson writes that 'Metropolis, the centre of language, of the dominant culture and its judgements, lies away in the great Elsewhere; but the tasks of living, communicating, teaching, acting-out and changing the culture must be carried on not Elsewhere but Here'. So the colonial is viewed as existing at the interface of the twin pulls of national and international forces. Unlike most earlier commentators who have written on the *Bulletin*, Lawson eschews an approach that focuses on the strictly 'literary' or the explicitly political aspects of the newspaper, and readers looking for a full account of the contributions of Henry Lawson, Banjo Paterson, or Steele Rudd will be disappointed, since any such information is only incidental here. Instead, the approach is to regard the *Bulletin* as a vast collective text, whose characteristic mode is that of a circus, breaking down distinctions between élite and masses and between writers and readers. Archibald himself is seen as a circus-master who made his own editorial role 'a source of play'.

Michael Noonan's *A Different Drummer*[64] is a biography of E. J. Banfield, author of *The Confessions of a Beachcomber*. Written in an accessible style

61. *The Banjo of the Bush: The Life and Times of A. B. "Banjo" Paterson*, by Clement Semmler. UQueen. pp. xx + 263; 14 illus. £16.95.

62. *Banjo Paterson's Old Bush Songs*, ed. by Graham Seal. A&R. pp. xii + 153; 31 illus; audio cassette, 12 songs by Speewah. boxed pb and cassette set A$24.95.

63. *The Archibald Paradox: A Strange Case of Authorship*, by Sylvia Lawson. LaneA. pp. xii + 292. A$29.95.

64. *A Different Drummer: the Story of E. J. Banfield, the Beachcomber of Dunk Island*, by Michael Noonan. UQueen. pp. xii + 263; 26 illus. £11.95.

that should appeal to general readers, it provides a useful introduction to the life of a figure who occupies a small, but significant place in the annals of Australian writing. Noonan's account of how, after the collapse of his health in his mid-forties, Banfield found a new identity, living a *Walden*-like existence on Dunk Island off the Queensland coast for the rest of his life, will undoubtedly stimulate a renewed interest in his four books, but it is essentially the story of his life, not his work. It does, however, demonstrate how his nightly reading was an integral part of his beachcombing *modus vivendi* and how the persona he constructed for the latter part of his life was a product of his enthusiasm for the work of the American Transcendentalists (the title of Noonan's book is taken from Thoreau) and the island fiction of Defoe and Stevenson. *A Different Drummer* is an attractive volume and the text contains illustrations, maps, and documents.

Christopher Brennan[65], edited by Terry Sturm, the latest volume in the Portable Australian Authors Series, is a valuable selection of the writer's poetry and prose. It contains previously unpublished material, as well as a number of short prose pieces that have been printed, but have hitherto only been available in specialist reference libraries. The edition includes most of Brennan's poetry and reprints his *magnum opus*, *Poems [1913]* in its entirety. Where the prose is concerned, the format of the series in which this edition appears has meant that anything approaching comprehensiveness has been impossible. Consequently, the volume cannot reasonably be expected to compete with A. R. Chisholm and J. J. Quinn's 1962 edition of Brennan's prose, but, like all good selections, it helps to redefine the parameters of the subject. The emphasis is placed on pieces written between 1897 and 1904, the period in which most of *Poems [1913]* was composed, and on writings on Australian art and letters. Brennan's 'Curriculum Vitae', a twenty-page account of his life written in 1930, is printed in full for the first time and there is a generous selection of material from his critical essays and notes for *From Blake to Arnold*, the poetry anthology that he co-edited at the turn of the century. The effect of choosing these pieces is to shift the emphasis from Brennan's well-known absorption with European literature, and in particular French Symbolism, to his interests in Australian and English literature. Sturm provides a fine introduction to Brennan's work, which highlights his commitment to self-definition through art and his fascination with the Lilith figure. The edition has notes, which give details of dates and sources for all the selections and full explanatory information on the new material. There is an excellent review of it by Brennan's biographer, Axel Clark, in *ALS* (May 1985).

Noel Macainsh's 'Chris Brennan's Poetic' (*Southerly*) also argues against the pre-eminence accorded to French Symbolist influences in Brennan studies and advances the view that the enthusiasm that he developed for German neoromanticism during his years in Berlin provided him with a theoretical standpoint from which he was able to interpret the course of Western literature as 'an ever repeated striving for the ideal of Symbolic literature'. Other articles on writers from this period include three pieces by Michael Ackland on Charles Harpur: in *Westerly* he writes on Harpur's republicanism; 'God's

---

65. *Christopher Brennan*, ed. by Terry Sturm. Portable Australian Authors Series. UQueen. pp. xxxii + 477. hb £16.95, pb £9.95.

Sublime Order in Harpur's "The Creek of Four Graves" ' (*ALS*) argues that Harpur's best-known work belongs in the tradition of prophetic blank-verse narrative of the poet's two great English mentors, Milton and Wordsworth; 'Charles Harpur for a New Generation' (*Quadrant*) takes a similar line by attempting to locate the poet in the tradition of Romantic meditative verse rather than the descriptive tradition in which his work has generally been placed. Marcus Clarke's *For the Term of His Natural Life* comes under existentialist scrutiny in Avis G. McDonald's ' "Men in Fetters . . . a Picture of Man's State" ', a *WLWE* piece that compares the novel's treatment of exile and bondage with that of the West Indian writer, Orlando Patterson, in his novel *Die the Long Day*. P. D. Edwards's 'Charles Reade, Wilkie Collins, and Marcus Clarke' (*ALS*) discusses letters to Clarke from the two prominent Victorian sensation novelists which are held in the Mitchell Library, Sydney.

Elizabeth Webby also analyses manuscript material in the Mitchell Library in her discussion of 'Barbara Baynton's Revisions to "Squeaker's Mate" ' (*Southerly*), a piece that reprints the text of the manuscript version of the story, which differs considerably from the printed one. Lois Hoffman (*ALS*) provides a full annotated checklist of Joseph Furphy's contributions to periodicals. This comprises seventy-one items and is prefaced by an account of Furphy's stories and articles for the *Bulletin*. Noel Macainsh's 'Point-of-View and Consequent Naturalism in the Novels of Henry Handel Richardson' (*Westerly*) sees Richardson as a novelist in the tradition of Flaubert and James and argues that her exclusion of authorial presence from her fiction makes for 'a sense of the unmistakable individuality of the consciousness of her figures'. Hanna K. Bock (*ALS*) uses epistolary evidence to give an account of Richardson's responses to reviews of her two translations.

(c) Individual Authors, 1920–.

Predictably, Patrick White is the writer in this period whose work attracts most attention. His popularity with non-Australian critics is demonstrated by the appearance of three book-length studies and a Yugoslav symposium. Peter Wolfe's *Laden Choirs*[66] and John Colmer's *Patrick White*[67] are both general introductions to White's work. Wolfe's rather expensively priced study offers a leisurely tour through White's work, structured around a chronological approach to the novels and the critic's own impressionistic response. While it examines all the novels, from *The Happy Valley* to *The Twyborn Affair*, the dust-jacket's claim that it deals with a broader range of White's writing than any previous volume is palpably absurd since the plays are neglected. Wolfe puts particular stress on White's 'growing affirmation' and his blending of Victorian earnestness with a modernist moral and artistic vision. Several commonplaces of White criticism, such as his absorption with 'the mystery of unity', are rehashed, but frequently carry less conviction than in earlier studies. So this is a book that is unlikely to be of great value to White scholars. It is, however, equally problematic as an introduction. Its half-dismissal of *Riders in the Chariot* as a rhetorical failure, its categorization of *Voss* as a 'period-piece' and a host of similar comments all suggest that the prospective

66. *Laden Choirs: The Fiction of Patrick White*, by Peter Wolfe. UKen (1983). pp. 248. £27.50.
67. *Patrick White*, by John Colmer. Contemporary Writers Series. Methuen. pp. 94. pb £2.05.

reader would be better off going straight to the novels themselves. More seriously, Wolfe's style often obfuscates issues, and the study is likely to disappoint those who prefer disciplined and sustained analysis.

John Colmer's book is a more modest volume, both in price and length, but it is a better general introduction than *Laden Choirs*. Colmer blends personal evaluation with the kind of exegesis that has characterized most previous White studies. Like Wolfe, he can be impressionistic, but since he readily admits to the subjective quality of some of his judgements and, since the amount of useful information conveyed is considerably greater, this is altogether more acceptable here. Colmer views White's work as a departure from the liberalism of the Great Tradition and sees his affinities as lying with such writers as Dickens, Hawthorne, Melville, Dostoevsky, and the British Modernists. Unlike earlier books which stress the quest for unity in White's fiction and the religious impulse behind it, this volume regards him as a secular salvationist, dividing his characters into saved and damned, and argues that his universe is pre-eminently dualistic, with only the elect achieving visions of unity. Biography is used productively and, given the restricted amount of space that can be devoted to it in a work of this scope, Colmer does a good job of identifying the central formative influences of White's life and writing. He shows how the roots of his fiction can be found in the imaginative sets of his early upbringing: 'a symbolic house, distorting mirrors, a wild garden and a privileged visionary whose life has been moulded by an ineffective father and a dominant mother'. Succinct, illuminating discussions of each of the novels are given and, while the format of the Methuen series means that a work like *A Fringe of Leaves* is allowed only four pages, it is hard to imagine a treatment of this length that could go much further in pin-pointing the novel's main concerns. The book also contains a valuable chapter on White's plays and short stories, which are seen as sharing the novels' preoccupation with solitary vision. All in all, this is a richer and more discriminating introduction than *Laden Choirs*; it is an excellent White primer for students and a work that should not be overlooked by scholars.

Karin Hansson's *The Warped Universe*[68] is a very different kind of White study. Originally a doctoral thesis, it is a dense and heavily annotated piece of writing, which is certainly not intended as a critical introduction. Yet its opening chapter, which gives a brief account of White's life and writing and surveys the critical reception of his work, is extremely useful in this respect. Subsequently the book enters deeper waters. Hansson describes her approach as an attempt to illustrate and analyse 'connections between style and theme, meaning and form, in the widest sense of these words . . . from a structuralistic point of view, based on the function of "foregrounded" elements as represented by the Czech scholar Jan Mukărovský'. If this suggests a primarily linguistic or formalist model, the detailed discussion that follows is in fact more general, and at the end Hansson concludes that 'a flexible, openminded interpretative pluralism is called for'. 'Foregrounded' elements prove to be any aspects of texts, stylistic or thematic, which stand out from the background, often with a disjunctive effect, and much of the study is taken up with the analysis of themes and symbols. Ultimately, the distance between

68. *The Warped Universe: A Study of Imagery and Structure in Seven Novels by Patrick White*, by Karin Hansson. LSE 69. Gleerup. pp. 271. pb.

Hansson's approach and those of the writers of two earlier major works of White criticism, Patricia Morley and Peter Beatson, both of whom, as Hansson indicates in her introduction, borrow the tools of Northrop Frye's mythic method, is not very great. Indeed, when she examines metaphysical and psychological influences on White's work in the second section of the book, her commentary on his debt to Jung, Blake, and Schopenhauer has much in common with Morley's *The Mystery of Unity* (1972). But *The Warped Universe* is a fine study and the depth of research behind it breathes new life into some of the commonplaces of White criticism. Thus, while the discussion of Jungian influences on White's work follows a well-trodden path in examining how elements such as the anima, mandala, and individuation process inform his fiction, Hansson's remarks on the relationship between Jung's treatment of the Antichrist figure and White's Faustian heroes are extremely interesting. Similarly, the significance of Schopenhauer's influence is extended from his discussion of the Will into such areas as his distinction between phenomenon and noumenon and his metaphysics of music. The main focus of *The Warped Universe* is on White's middle seven novels – his first two and his most recent two are seen as having essentially different concerns – but there is a brief note on *A Fringe of Leaves*, which draws attention to 'discrepancies' between this novel and those that have been the book's main subject. An appendix provides plot summaries of the seven novels in question.

Karin Hansson's '"The Terrible Nostalgia of the Desert Landscape": Reflections on Patrick White's Australia from a European Point of View', which incorporates material from her book, is included in both Britta Olinder's *A Sense of Place*[15] and Mirko Jurak's *Australian Papers*[47]. In the Yugoslav volume it forms part of a short symposium on White's work. Other contributions are a fairly basic essay on *Voss*, a specialist piece on the problems of translating White's 'graphemic sign' and two fine comparative articles: Laurie Hergenhan considers how the past is 'the present rendered fabulous' by examining the way European origins are confronted in *A Fringe of Leaves* and Thomas Keneally's *Bring Larks and Heroes*; and Werner Senn discusses the struggle of the self to come to terms with disintegration and fragmentation, which are seen as the basis of the human condition, in *A Fringe of Leaves* and *The Twyborn Affair* and Randolph Stow's *Visitants* and *The Girl Green as Elderflower*.

White and Stow are also brought together in Paul Sharrad's *WLWE* article, '*Pour mieux sauter*: Christopher Koch's Novels in Relation to White, Stow and the Quest for a Post-Colonial Fiction'. The three novelists are seen as sharing a concern to extend the boundaries of Australian fiction in the 1950s beyond what Koch refers to as 'flat, dreary naturalism' and into the realms of the poetic, mythic, and symbolic. While this article mainly deals with Koch's fiction – and is one of the best discussions of his work to have yet appeared – it provides a valuable context for consideration of the 1950s novels of the other two writers. *WLWE* also includes several other White items. Norbert H. Platz writes on 'The Western Consciousness of Novel Writing and the Image of Australia in Patrick White's *Voss*'. Karin Hansson contrasts the treatment of the indigenous and the metropolitan in *A Fringe of Leaves*, examining a broad range of White's work. Jennifer Strauss writes on his 'versions of pastoral', which are seen as being mainly associated with the bush. Hena Maes-Jelinek compares the way *The Twyborn Affair* breaks down traditional cultural and gender boundaries with the Guyanese Wilson Harris's similar approach in *The Angel at the Gate*. Finally, Terry Goldie also detects affinities between White and a writer from another part of the Commonwealth: his 'Comparative Views of an Aboriginal Past' looks at correspondences between *A Fringe of Leaves* and the Canadian Rudy Wiebe's *The Temptations of Big Bear*. Other discussions of White's work include a fascinating account of the significance of the Byzantine references in *The Twyborn Affair* by John Coates in *ALS*, and some remarks on Voss's attempt 'to acquire the knowledge needed to penetrate the logic of another culture' in Lloyd Fernando's *Westerly* article 'Re-Defining the Self in South-East Asia'.

After White, the writer who receives most critical attention is Shirley Hazzard. Nancy Dew Taylor, in a *WLWE* introduction to *The Transit of Venus*, laments that, although the novel won the 1980 PEN Faulkner Award for Fiction and the American National Book Critics Circle Award, it has yet to receive the attention it merits. The year's crop of articles does much to remedy this. Taylor's own discussion examines how Hazzard's attempt to make the development of her fable seem 'preordained' leads to the novel's having a very careful structure that puts particular emphasis on the beginning and the end. John Colmer (*JCL*) argues that *The Transit of Venus* extends the range of her earlier fiction, with its emphasis on the fusion of poetry and reason and the co-existence of happiness and sorrow in love, to accommodate a commentary on the social and political changes of the last thirty years. Susan Moore (*Quadrant*) examines the novel's problematic treatment of conventional moral responses and considers the dissatisfaction felt by many readers with its ending. James Wieland (*CNE*) looks at the differing responses of the men and women in *Transit* to 'going through with things', to showing 'willingness or reluctance to signal a difference from the established power elite'.

Paul M. St Pierre's 'Martin Boyd: The Last Years' (*Southerly*) evaluates Boyd as a precursor of the postnationalist movement in literature and the ecumenical movement in religion. Dennis Robinson in 'David Campbell's Poetic Mind' (*ALS*) argues that Campbell's verse fuses disparate elements of his experience – among them personal and family history, sex and love, classical mythology, Aboriginal rock paintings, features of the modern urban landscape, and literary references – as 'part of a wider quest for unity within creation itself'. Peter Cowan discusses J. M. Harcourt's three novels of the 1930s in *Westerly*. Andrew Taylor's 'Dorothy Hewett as Poet' (*Southerly*) examines the confessional aspect in Hewett's verse, claiming that instead of transforming reality into language, her procedure has the effect of making it seem that 'language has been transformed into reality: it has surrendered its linguistic nature as a system of signifiers to become concrete, immediate, the very thing itself, real life'. *Southerly* also prints an interview with Dorothy Hewett by Paul Kavanagh and in *Westerly* May-Brit Akerholt compares the female figures in Hewett's better-known plays with those in the plays of Patrick White. In *TN/DU*, an interesting new magazine from Vancouver Island which is devoted to Canadian and Australian writing and interrelationships between the two literatures, Colin Partridge examines David Ireland's Australia, viewing it as an urban world of distraught behaviour and repressed violence that can suddenly erupt into life. Garry Kinnane's 'The Reconstruction of Self: Background and Design in George Johnston's Meredith Trilogy' (*ALS*) looks at the way Johnston has incorporated and departed from autobiography in *My Brother Jack* and the two subsequent volumes of the trilogy. Dorothy Jones's 'The Goddess, the Artist and the Spinster' (*Westerly*) is an account of how Elizabeth Jolley's *Miss Peabody's Inheritance* uses the triple image of the goddess Diana – Artemis, Lucina, and Hecate – as a focus for the novel's themes and charts an interesting parallel between Diana Hopewell's turning Miss Peabody's world upside down and the similar inversion that occurs in *Great Expectations* when Magwitch re-enters Pip's life. Jolley's work is also discussed in John Kirkby's 'The Nights Belong to Elizabeth Jolley' (*Meanjin*). Norman Bartlett's 'Mollie Skinner and *The Boy in the Bush*' (*Quadrant*) is less an account of the novel than of the relationship between Skinner and D. H. Lawrence. Also in *Quadrant* is Michael Sharkey's account of Geoffrey Lehmann's *Nero Poems*, which puts the emphasis on the way the sequence has cast Nero as an artist.

James McAuley is the subject of three articles: Noel Rowe (*Quadrant*) discusses the Catholic element in his poetry; Peter Kirkpatrick's 'Patience and Despair: James McAuley's Pessimism' (*Southerly*) questions this received version of the poet's beliefs, arguing that there is a strong agnostic strain in his later work and indicating 'some of the ways in which the ceremonial vision becomes impaired by a conscious poetic acquaintance with the harsh, unconsecrated spaces of the real world'; Noel Macainsh's 'Music in Mirabell' (*Quadrant*) follows a very different line in discussing McAuley's affinities with the Austrian poet George Trakl, whose work he translated.

ALS publishes the text of talks given by David Malouf, Les Murray, and David Rowbotham at the Warana Writers' Weekend in Brisbane in 1983. The same issue of *ALS* includes Laurie Hergenhan's 'Discoveries and Transformations: Aspects of David Malouf's Work', which argues that Malouf's fiction is based on a series of oppositions. Murray's work is discussed in Carmel Gaffney's *Quadrant* review-article on *The People's Otherworld*, which is also the subject of Dennis Haskell's 'Bringing the C20 to Bay' (*Westerly*). James Tulip's 'Les Murray in the 1980s' (*Southerly*) keeps the focus firmly on his recent work, finding 'a new religious equanimity' in this poetry. *Southerly* also includes an interview with Murray by Paul Kavanagh and Peter Kuch.

Overland has a full obituary of Alan Marshall by John Morrison, which could serve as an introduction to the writer's work and, in the same issue, prints the text of the last interview Marshall gave. Xavier Herbert and Hal Porter, who both died in 1984, are also the subject of obituaries in several leading Australian journals. C. J. Koch's 'In Memoriam: Hal Porter' (*Quadrant*) is a particularly noteworthy tribute to the latter author by a fellow-writer who considered him Australia's 'finest contemporary writer'. *Quadrant* also includes an excellent introduction to Hal Porter's Asian stories by Jean Hawley-Crowcroft, a discussion that was originally delivered as a paper at the Polytechnic of North London's Australian Literature and Arts Week in 1984. The expatriate Peter Porter's work has attracted an increasing amount of attention in Australian circles in recent years and, in addition to pieces mentioned above, this year sees Peter Steele's 'The Radiations of Peter Porter' (*Westerly*), which discusses the qualities that he sees as animating Porter's poetry: 'expatriation, negotiation, intervention and radiation'. Porter is interviewed by Martin Harrison in *ALS* and his recent work is discussed by David Williams in *CritQ*.

One of the benefits of the recent upsurge of feminist publishing in Britain has been the re-issue of several classic novels by Australian women writers. This year *Golden Miles*[69] and *Winged Seeds*[70], the second and third volumes of Katharine Susannah Prichard's goldfields trilogy, follow *The Roaring Nineties* into the Virago Modern Classics series. Both come with fine introductions from Drusilla Modjeska, which succinctly place the novels in context and give an account of their critical reception, as well as a brief literary evaluation. In *Kunapipi* Prichard's son, Ric Throssell, discusses her response to the Australian landscape.

Rudolf Bader examines the *Bildungsroman* aspect of the work of another Virago author, Christina Stead, in *WLWE*. Jennifer McDonnell writes on Stead's *The Man Who Loved Children* in *Southerly*, a journal that devotes a special issue to previously unpublished writings by Stead, edited by R. G. Geering. These represent a first sifting of her literary and personal papers which she left to the National Library of Australia, undertaken by Geering in his capacity of literary trustee. The pieces chosen come from all periods of Stead's career; short stories predominate, but there are also some non-fictional prose and a short play.

Arlene Sykes and Keith Richards analyse the revisions which Alan Seymour made to his renowned Anzac play *One Day of the Year* in a full and scholarly *ADS* discussion which includes the text of some of the revised passages. John McCallum's 'A New Map of Australia: The Plays of David Williamson' (*ALS*) attempts to reconcile Williamson's appeal to the democratic popular audience with the conservative reputation given to him by Australian drama and theatre critics. He does so by examining Williamson's ability to create a recognizable social and personal world, his naturalistic style, and the autobiographical element in his work. Hans Hauge's 'Michael Wilding, Post-Modernism and the Australian Literary Heritage' (*Overland*) is a more modest piece than its title might suggest: it is a brief discussion of postmodernism, which initially takes little for granted and then focuses almost exclusively on Wilding's novel *The Short Story Embassy*.

Finally a number of further interviews: Thea Astley and Roland Robinson are interviewed in *NoP*, a welcome magazine from Darwin; Sumner Locke Elliott in *Quadrant*; and Fay Zwicky in *Westerly*.

5. Canada

(a) General

JCL continues its coverage of criticism and scholarship on Canadian literature in its 'Annual Bibliography of Commonwealth Literature' prefaced by a general overview from W. H. New. *UTQ*'s 'Humanities' section of its 'Letters in Canada' annual survey offers brief reviews by several hands of books of literary criticism and scholarship written or edited by Canadian scholars, and about two dozen of those noted in the August 1984 issue have particular application to Canadian literature. Criticism of Canadian poetry is noted by Mary Ann Jameson in a section of *CP* entitled 'The Year's Work in Canadian

69. *Golden Miles*, by Katharine Susannah Prichard, intro. by Drusilla Modjeska. Virago. pp. xi + 384. pb £3.95.

70. *Winged Seeds*, by Katharine Susannah Prichard, intro. by Drusilla Modjeska. Virago. pp. xvi + 388. pb £3.95.

Poetry Studies', with valuable accompanying summaries and abstracts of many of the books and journal articles noted. *Fiddlehead*, in two of its 1984 issues, provides 'A Checklist of Recent Literary Publications of Atlantic Canada' which notes criticism and bibliographies in addition to its lists of creative works. Volume Five has been added to *The Annotated Bibliography of Canada's Major Authors*[71]; it provides extensive listings of primary and secondary sources up to June 1982 of publications (in various media) by and about Morley Callaghan, Mavis Gallant, Hugh Hood, Alice Munro, and Ethel Wilson. ECW Press also published a bibliographical study of John Glassco[72] which provides information on works by and about Glassco up to his death in January 1981. It follows the normal ECW bibliographical patterns, though it does not attempt completeness because of the many problems raised by Glassco's habits of anonymous and pseudonymous publication and by the widespread pirating of some of his pornographic works. Also, its editor provides a biocritical essay covering the major outlines of Glassco's life and career, commenting on his literary activity in its various genres, and calling the reader's attention especially to Glassco's statements of literary theory.

Barry McKinnon has published a bibliography of his 'Caledonia Writing Series' from Prince George, British Columbia, with an accompanying essay outlining its genesis, history, and conclusion, and with 'A Selection from the Archive' (*line*). The reader's position in the publication matrix is addressed by David Staines in 'Moving Away from Disbelief: The Rise of a Canadian Reading Public' (*ARCS*).

Research devoted to exploring the backgrounds of Canadian literature were few in 1984. G. A. Rawlyk's *Ravished by the Spirit*[73] addresses the religio-socio-cultural ethos of late-eighteenth-century Maritimes and New England. The historical contexts of literature also figure largely in essays on Metis culture by Thomas Flanagan and Wolfgang Klooss. Flanagan's 'Louis Riel and Metis Literature' (*WLWE*) reflects that in different historical circumstances Riel might have been the father of a Metis literature, but that his youthful promise as a versifier was betrayed by an overweening didacticism and moralism, and that from the more than five hundred pages of verse soon to be published, only a slim volume of any literary interest could ensue. Flanagan's persistent vision of Riel as a madman is consistent with the stereotypical representations of him and his people which are surveyed in Kloos's 'Canada's Forgotten People: The Metis in Nineteenth-century Fiction and Drama' (*WLWE*).

Two other notable volumes of literary scholarship appeared in 1984. Both will be indispensable reference texts. Solomon J. Spiro has mustered an impressive amount of research on the Judaic allusions in the poetry and fiction of A. M. Klein[74], giving references not only for explicit allusions, but also for those which are general, suffused, or submerged. He includes also valuable

71. *The Annotated Bibliography of Canada's Major Authors*, Vol. Five, ed. by Robert Lecker and Jack David. ECW. pp. 480. C$48.

72. *John Glassco: An Essay and Bibliography*, by Fraser Sutherland. ECW. pp. 121. C$8.95.

73. *Ravished by the Spirit: Religious Revivals, Baptists, Henry Alline*, by G. A. Rawlyk. The 1983 Hayward Lectures. Mc-Q. pp. xiv + 176. C$8.95.

74. *Tapestry for Designs: Judaic Allusions in the Poetry and 'The Second Scroll' of A. M. Klein*, by Solomon J. Spiro. UBC. pp. ix + 236. C$45.

appendixes on allusions of content and form in *The Second Scroll*, on the 'passenger's theory' of Jewish history, and on the poet of Tiberias. Chris Ackerley and Lawrence J. Clipper perform a similar service for readers of Malcolm Lowry's *Under the Volcano*. Their *Companion*[75] is a thorough and generally trustworthy source not only of the novel's extratextual references, but of its intertextual allusions as well.

Though neither critical nor scholarly in a strict sense, interviews with writers are significant sources of information and commentary for critics, and they have become a popular feature of both criticial and creative journals, as the following list will prove. Interviews were published with Brian Moore (*Gamut*), Marian Engel (*ROO*), Eli Mandel (*line*), Pat Lane (*WCR*), Claire Harris (*Waves*), Roo Boorson (*Waves*), Edna Alford (*Descant*), Lorna Crozier (*PJCL*), Michael Bullock (*CFM*), Graeme Gibson (*WLWE*), and a joint interview of Barry McKinnon and David Phillips (*CapR*). The importance of the interview has, in fact, been acknowledged by the criticial community's interviewing one of its own (Malcolm Ross in *SCL*) and by that journal's decision to undertake a series of interviews with figures significant to Canada's intellectual history. The interview with Ross, on his education and his pedagogical career as much as on his critical writing, confirms the declared approach.

Ross's interview is, in fact, a sort of memoir. And the special issue of *CanL* to celebrate its one hundredth number presents another three brief memoirs. Irving Layton's 'Waiting for the Messiah' focuses on his childhood years, and such events as his 'miraculous' circumcision, his grandmother's miraculous self-sacrifice just before his birth, a semideliberate self-conflagration at the age of four, and neighbourhood hostilities. Clark Blaise's 'Mentors' also discusses childhood, but as it is reflected in his fiction. Otherwise, Blaise's attention is devoted to the beginnings of his writing career, under Paul Bennet's tutelage at Denison College, and an encounter with Bernard Malamud at Harvard. Finally, Anthony Bukowski records first-hand reflections upon the experience of present Canadian writers at the University of Iowa from 1948 to the 1980s. Blaise is included, as are also Robert Kroetsch, Rudy Wiebe, Robert Harlow, W. D. Valgardson, W. P. Kinsella, Christopher Wiseman, and others.

From memoir to autobiography is but a short step, and the question of autobiography does arise in 1984. George Woodcock's 'Don't Ever Ask for the True Story; Or, Second Thoughts on Autobiography' (*ECW*) takes up the debate over whether autobiography is a descriptive or inventive art, and agrees with what has now become conventional wisdom that 'autobiography depends on the form and the style that enable it to evoke a world and a personality rather than on the sensational nature of its contents'. This conception of autobiography also underlies Ira Bruce Nadel's consideration of Norman Levine in '*Canada Made Me*: and Canadian Autobiography' (*CanL*), as he presents Levine's text as an exercise which allows re-entry to Canada to discover limitations and possibilities of self, to 'locate himself and his home'. The pattern, Nadel asserts, associates Levine's autobiography with those of Frederick Philip Grove and Glassco, though also with those of Orwell and Henry Miller. Morley Callaghan responded, too, to an international model in

75. *A Companion to Under the Volcano*, by Chris Ackerley and Lawrence J. Clipper. UBC. pp. xv + 476. C$45.

composing one of his autobiographical works, or so Paul Miller argues in 'Callaghan's *That Summer in Paris*: A Portrait of the Artist as a Young Man' (*CanL*). Callaghan rejected the American model of Hemingway because the latter turned on friends, but he did accept to some extent the model of Joyce because he saw in him more human compassion. But even this acceptance was only partial because Callaghan's aesthetic was more socially oriented than that of either Joyce or Hemingway, and he consequently rejected Paris as a place of habitation though not as a place of the mind. The autobiographical exercise is envisioned by Miller as liberating for Callaghan, as Nadel similarly suggested it was for Levine, and K. P. Stich's 'Painter's Words: Personal Narratives of Emily Carr and William Kurelek' (*ECW*) agrees. His analysis of Carr's *Growing Pains* and *Hundreds and Thousands* and of Kurelek's *Someone With Me* indicates ways in which their autobiographical writings enabled these two painters to 'see meaning in their roles as artistic diviners in and of the New World'.

Travel literature, like autobiography, has lately benefited from the expansion of critical attention – though almost as a one-person industry in 1984. I. S. MacLaren published *four* essays on the subject. His 'David Thompson's Imaginative Mapping of the Canadian Northwest 1784–1812' (*ArielE*) convincingly contends and illustrates that Thompson 'writes at his best when his multi-level perception of the world is operative', when he gives both the foreign and indigenous perspectives on a scene, the latter probably made possible by his arrival in Canada at the early and still formative age of fourteen and by the Hudson's Bay Company's practice of having its men live among the natives to absorb their language, customs, and outlook. MacLaren's 'Samuel Hearne and the Landscapes of Discovery' (*CanL*) emphasizes the explorer's European cultural baggage as it cogently traces the sublime and picturesque taxonomies which Hearne brought to the landscapes of the Canadian north. These taxonomies are also the focus of MacLaren's 'Retaining Captaincy of the Soul: Response to Nature in the First Franklin Expedition' (*ECW*) and his 'The Grandest Tour: The Aesthetics of Landscape in Sir George Back's Explorations of the Eastern Arctic 1833–1837' (*ESC*), the latter of which indicates how nature's aesthetically repulsive qualities 'denied the consummation of generic conventionality' to Back's journals.

While Back was forced by nature to see more clearly than he wished, Anna Jameson, argues Leslie Monkman in 'Primitivism and a Parasol: Anna Jameson's Indians' (*ECW*), should receive more credit than has hitherto been accorded her as a clear-eyed literary anthropologist. Neither explorer nor tourist, she was a traveller (*à la* Paul Fussell) who struggled with the 'violent dualities' which characterize every response to cultures in conflict, and which have so preoccupied writers and critics throughout Canadian literary history.

A different kind of prose endeavour is acknowledged by Gwendolyn Davies's 'James Irving: Literature and Libel in Early Nova Scotia' (*ECW*). She comments on Irving's serial contribution to *The Acadian Recorder* in the 1820s of 'Letters on the Present State of English Poetry', and on the controversy stirred with the conservative rival publisher Edmund Ward which centred upon Irving's comments on Swift and Byron and which eventually led to a libel trial.

With Davies's essay on Irving we move into that region, becoming progressively more inhabited, where criticism and the critic become themselves the subject of the critical endeavour. In Canada that inevitably occasions commentary on Northrop Frye – and, perhaps just as inevitably, commentary by Frye's foremost scholar, Robert D. Denham, whose 'An Anatomy of Frye's Influence' (*ARCS*) covers some old ground. Also inevitably, come the attacks on Frye, and his presumably pernicious influence on Canadian literature and criticism – at least pernicious in the view of Paul Steuwe and B. W. Powe. The former's *Clearing the Ground: English–Canadian Literature After Survival*[76], journalistic in its sweeping assertions, scanty evidence, and repetitiousness, attacks Frye for his presumed reliance on the 'statistical fallacy', for his exclusivity, and his metaliterary system, but most for his theoretical buttressing of thematic criticism. Steuwe's assertion that much thematic criticism is a mask for superficial thinking and superficial analysis is accurate, and the approach does deserve corrective challenge. But Steuwe's attack is too querulous and facile. His familiarity with the subject of current Canadian criticism is certainly suspect when he claims that Malcolm Ross, Ernest Buckler, Hugh MacLennan, and Ethel Wilson do not already enjoy, or surpass, the critical stature of Callaghan. B. W. Powe's essays in *A Climate Changed*[77] are stylistically better than Steuwe's work, but the whole is similarly flawed by oversimplification and misrepresentation, and by a too obvious, too laboured, effort to be controversial. When he claims that Frye 'eliminates the moral dimension of art without a whimper' he is simply wrong. As he is also when he dismisses Margaret Laurence as an undemanding writer, parochial, and uncomfortable with ideas. He credits Margaret Atwood with intelligence and technical accomplishment, though he finds her a poor creator of character, and dislikes her fashionability. He dismisses Leonard Cohen as solipsistic. But he likes Robertson Davies's moralism, and in fact throughout reveals his own (not unworthy) critical bias in favour of moral writing.

Both Steuwe and Powe attack the academic hegemony of contemporary criticism and offer themselves in the roles of public critics. Alan R. Knight, on 'The Dilemma of the Public Critic; or, Does George Bowering Have *A Way With Words*' (*SCL*), asserts that Bowering fails as a public critic because he does not recognize that the public critic's apparent free rein is restrained by his answerability to the academic critic's theories. In practice, this failure is exemplified by Bowering's forcing his Black Mountain theory, by his using questionable or inappropriate etymology, and his contradictory employment of metaphor instead of phenomenological language.

At least one critic was feted in 1984 however. Clara Thomas was the subject of a special issue of *ECW* in which, in addition to critical essays by former students which are individually noted throughout this chapter, appear encomiums to her by Margaret Laurence and Brandon Conron, a brief review of her academic career by editors Michael Darling and John Lennox, a bibliography of her works by Darling, and a baccalaureate address by Thomas herself.

But less attention has been paid, appropriately, to the critics than to theory. Commentary on the latter has varied substantially. Andrew Payne and Steve McCaffrey's 'Nothing Is Forgotten But the Talk of How to Talk' (*line*) focuses

---

76. *Clearing the Ground: English-Canadian Literature After Survival*, by Paul Steuwe. Proper Tales. pp. 112. C$5.95.
77. *A Climate Changed. Essays on Canadian Writers*, by B. W. Powe. Mosaic. pp. 196. C$9.95.

especially on linguistic theory. Linda Hutcheon's 'The "Postmodernist" Scribe: The Dynamic Stasis of Contemporary Canadian Writing' (*UTQ*) uses the categories of poststructuralist theory to elucidate the narrative strategies of several contemporary Canadian writers such as Robert Kroetsch, Timothy Findley, Rudy Wiebe, and Jack Hodgins, as well as Cohen, Michael Ondaatje, and Atwood. *Driving Home*[78] also employs contemporary literary theory but not to address texts, rather to address the genesis and reception of texts. In a series of papers given at a summer workshop in 1982, writers such as D. G. Jones, Aritha van Herk, E. D. Blodgett, Myrna Kostash, Peter Stevens, and Christopher Wiseman examine polarities such as desire and memory, fiction and non-fiction, writer and author, national and universal, place and person.

Place is a favourite consideration of Canadian critics. Aritha van Herk's 'Stranded Bestride in Canada' (*WLWE*) reflects on the tension in Canada between the indigenous and the metropolitan, and attributes to it the Canadian's consequent recourse to, and delight in, disguise and in being a trickster. In 'Space and Landscape. A Personal Mapping'[15] van Herk repeats the message that place forms the writer but adds that the writer then trans/forms place by imposing upon it language which is partly the language of that place. John Moss's 'Landscape, Untitled' (*ECW*) also queries the relationship of language and place, though in more historical parameters, as he suggests that one of the characteristics of Canadian colonialism was its use of a language inappropriate and inadequate to the place and culture it attempts to define. This is by now a truism.

Ramsay Cook (*CanL*) suggests that Canadians were in fact slow to choose their place. Unlike Americans, in Cook's somewhat dubious scheme, Canadians initially chose history and Europe rather than nature, later with the confederation poets did choose nature, and still later with F. R. Scott and others began to attempt to reconcile nature and history, to reintegrate Europe into North American art. The scheme has interest, but the essay is guilty of oversimplification (as when it proposes that John Richardson suggests that morality will be found only within the garrison) and misrepresentation (as when quotations from Richardson and Catharine Parr Traill are presented without acknowledging severely qualifying contexts).

Considerations of regional space/place are also popular in Canadian criticism and are to be found again in 1984. Attempts to define the regional distinctiveness of the literature of British Columbia are made by W. H. New and Allan Pritchard. New's 'A Piece of the Continent, A Part of the Main: Some Comments on B.C. Literature' (*BCS*) finds the consistent factor in this literature to be a 'tension between continental and isolating impulses', and examines the various guises in which it is represented. Pritchard's 'West of the Great Divide: Man and Nature in the Literature of British Columbia' (*CanL*) asserts that the major themes in B.C. writing have been those of paradise, land despoliation, the noble savage, the hero/villain logger, and urban corruption, and sees these as emanating from a dominantly Anglican vision.

Aritha van Herk's 'Women Writers and the Prairie: Spies in an Indifferent Landscape' (*Kunapipi*) simultaneously addresses regionalism and feminism.

---

78. *Driving Home: A Dialogue Between Writers and Readers*, ed. by Barbara Belyea and Estelle Dansereau. WLU for the Calgary Institute for the Humanities. pp. xii + 102. C$7.50.

van Herk points out that the images which have dominated prairie literature have been masculine, characterized geometrically by straight lines and consequently denied entrance because the landscape itself is feminine in its curves and undulations and therefore more susceptible to a feminine vision. Feminism is more extensively taken up in *Tessera*, a special issue of *ROO* collectively edited by Barbara Godard, Daphne Marlatt, Kathy Mezei, and Gail Scott, and containing essays primarily of a theoretical cast. Lorraine Weir calls for rejection of the patriarchal, bourgeois, critical illusions of closure, completion, stasis, and perfection and for the embrace of the 'possibility of an open text, the so-called "fragment" as utilized by a writer like Alice Munro'. Daphne Marlatt reflects on the potentially liberating implications of conceiving language as female body. Barbara Godard argues that women writers in Canada have played a central, pioneer role by subverting conventional lexical laws and literary forms to demonstrate how a colonial, marginalized role may be transformed. Modulating theory with critical practice, Wendy Keitner interprets the poet/artist figure in the poetry of Audrey Alexandra Brown and Anne Wilkinson to be stereotypically male, and Jennifer Waelti-Walters discusses the discrepancy between a conventional male reading of Atwood's *Bodily Harm* and her own which sees the novel as misogynist. Finally, Andrea Lebowvitz warns that contemporary feminist critics are in danger of being élitist, exclusive, obscure, inaccessible – in short, of continuing to follow, subordinately, the lead of contemporary male theorists.

Feminism is subjected to male scrutiny by Frank Davey in *Margaret Atwood: A Feminist Poetics*[79]. Davey offers an intriguing and incisive analysis of textual detail and generic form in support of his contention that Atwood employs various deconstructive strategies in her attempt to subvert conventional male literary patterns and so find room for a feminine voice and perspective which can demythologize women. Davey seems to stumble only in his failure to accord sufficient attention to the metaphorical character of *Survival*, which leads him to conclude, erroneously I think, that it repudiates Atwood's injunctions against naming and categorization.

The other two volumes published thus far in the Talonbooks series are of mixed quality. Leslie Mundwiler's *Michael Ondaatje: Word, Image, Imagination*[80] pays only occasional attention to Ondaatje's work; there is minimal engagement with textual particulars. Instead, Mundwiler indulges himself with his interest in theory: making distinctions between 'amusement' art and 'significant' art, flirting with reception theory, talking about 'logical interrogation', reviewing theories of the imagination, and discussing the episteme of modernism. Stephen Scobie's *bp Nichol: What History Teaches*[81] is better. Though similarly fascinated by theory, Scobie keeps his subject constantly in view. When he does digress to Gertrude Stein and cubism or to Julia Kristeva and her definition of experimental as 'writing which violates grammatical convention, thereby preventing normal reading', he does so to explicate Nichol. Theory is subordinated to craft rather than, as with Mundwiler, craft

79. *Margaret Atwood: A Feminist Poetics*, by Frank Davey. NCC. Talonbooks. pp. 198. C$8.95.

80. *Michael Ondaatje: Word, Image, Imagination*, by Leslie Mundwiler. NCC. Talonbooks. pp. 160. C$8.95.

81. *bp Nichol: What History Teaches*, by Stephen Scobie. NCC. Talonbooks. pp. 153. C$8.95.

to theory. Consequently, Scobie's depiction of Nichol's move towards self-generating texts which remain fundamentally humanist, while occasionally exaggerated, is creditable.

Creditable too, in a far less pretentious way, and despite being afflicted with a very poorly proofed text, is Anthony Robertson's *Above Tide*[82]. Robertson surveys the life of naturalist/essayist/fiction writer/judge Roderick Haig-Brown from his English origins through immigration and settlement in British Columbia and subsequent devotion to both natural and human communities. Robertson delineates how Haig-Brown sought, sometimes with a difficulty that is represented in the tensions of his fiction, to reconcile these communities, and how he did so through his concept of the interdependence of all things.

Not very creditable is David Stouck's *Major Canadian Authors*[83]. Intended 'to introduce to a wide audience Canada's most important authors writing in English', Stouck's book is given to paraphrase and overgeneralization, is generally simplistic, and is, at times, quite misleading as, for example, when he contends that 'the first indigenous literary activity in English Canada appeared . . . in the 1830s'. Canada's major authors are indeed mentioned at some point or another in the volume, but the criteria which assign Al Purdy to the level of biocritical essay and relegate Atwood, Kroetsch, Mavis Gallant, Wiebe, or Mordecai Richler to the level of biobibliographical note must be questionable. I would not recommend this book as an introductory text for Canadian literature.

(b) Fiction

The year 1984 saw little expression of fictional theory untrammelled by practical criticism. Geoff Hancock, in an afterword to an issue of *CFM* which he edits, expatiates briefly on the difference between story and fiction, the latter of which he sees as dominating in Canada in the last fifteen years. In the same issue Michael Bullock celebrates surrealist writing as 'a weapon of liberation under all circumstances'; sociology, he contends, has made naturalism unnecessary. If his definition of naturalism includes realism, he might not have the agreement of Matt Cohen whose 'Realism in Modern English Canadian Fiction'[15] insists that the mainstream of English–Canadian fiction, despite some exceptions, has always been and still is, realistic. And Larry MacDonald, in 'Psychologism and the Philosophy of Progress: The Recent Fiction of MacLennan, Davies, and Atwood' (*SCL*), clearly regards the subjectivism advocated by Bullock as wrong-headed and dangerous. He condemns the contemporary obsession with subjectivity, and shrilly excoriates the 'collective refusal' of his three subjects 'to imagine a *single* positive image of active rebellion against the mad and spiritless society they portray, which amounts to an uncritical promotion of political resignation and psychological adaptation'. Sylvia Soderlind, in 'Identity and Metamorphosis in Canadian Fiction Since the Sixties'[15], is more positive. She sees writers such as Atwood, Godfrey, Kroetsch, and Cohen answering the absence of a native mythology

82. *Above Tide: Reflections on Roderick Haig-Brown*, by Anthony Robertson. Harbour. pp. 136. C$8.95.

83. *Major Canadian Authors: A Critical Introduction*, by David Stouck. UNeb. pp. xii + 308. C$22.95.

and a native idiom with metamorphic strategies which produce 'language of
... "pure magic", an insignificant language of pure intensity liberated from
the "colonization" of the Other'.

To some Canadian writers and critics the colonizing Other is central
Canada, as Stanley S. Atherton argues in 'Fighting Back: The Regional
Renaissance in Recent Canadian Fiction' (*WLWE*). Atherton insists that
the shift from centralism to regionalism in the last two decades has produced
in the fiction of such writers as Horwood, Richards, van Herk, Maillard, and
Musgrave an emphasis on the contemporary and the antitraditional, rural or
working class, urban settings, rebellious central characters searching for personal or communal definition in isolated or semi-isolated surroundings, and an
emphasis on daily ritual and small ceremony. Jon Carlsen's perspective on
prairie regionalism is much milder. In 'Canadian Prairie Fiction: Towards a
New Past (Margaret Laurence, Robert Kroetsch, Rudy Wiebe)'[15], Carlsen
contends that these writers are simply attempting to correct past views of
prairie history and identity. George Bowering's 'Home Away: A Thematic
Study of Some British Columbia Novels' (*BCS*) mostly ignores the question of
Other and concentrates, somewhat apologetically, on home as the central
unifying and informing symbol of British Columbia culture.

The Other seems to be preferred by Stanley Fogel in his *A Tale of Two
Countries*[84], and the specific other to be preferred is the United States with
whose outlook, he feels, Canadian writers should associate themselves rather
than with that of British writers. Fogel offers close readings of the American
metafictionists Gass and Coover, of the Canadian modernists Atwood and
Davies, and of Robert Kroetsch whom he unsurprisingly casts as a mediator
between the two approaches. This *schema* conveniently supports Fogel's
essentially Romantic discrimination of contemporary American fiction as
antagonistic to a rigidified and monolithic cultural identity from contemporary
Canadian fiction as nurturing an 'inchoate' Canadian identity. The former
finds deconstructive criticism and metafictional technique to be effective
strategies of cultural subversion which the latter should be employing to
combat the isolationism and complacency occasioned by its ontological
modernism.

Such opinions would not please Thomas Haliburton, as Katherine
Morrison's 'In Haliburton's Nova Scotia: *The Old Judge or Life in a
Colony*' (*CanL*) makes clear. That novel, she indicates, rejects American
belief in nature and its repudiation of the past, and also registers a dislike of
the trend towards individualism. But it similarly rejects British aristocracy;
it insists instead upon the necessity of community, thereby belying the claims
that Haliburton's writings are not in the mainstream of Canadian literary
tradition.

T. D. MacLulich's 'The Colonial Major: Richardson and *Wacousta*' (*ECW*)
clearly disagrees with the stature accorded that author and work in Canadian
literary tradition. MacLulich concurs with the dismissive opinions of Dennis
Duffy and Desmond Pacey, especially with the latter's judgement that
Richardson was a pornographer. He blithely dismisses the interpretations of
Richardson's biographer, David Beasley, but without ever seriously engaging

84. *A Tale of Two Countries. Contemporary Fiction in Canada and the United States*,
by Stanley Fogel. ECW. pp. 143. C$9.95.

the specific details of Richardson's life or offering evidence of a substantial or specific nature to refute Beasley. Meanwhile, Beasley is one of the contributors to *Recovering Canada's First Novelist*[85], a collection of conference papers which assume but also argue cogently for Richardson's significance. Beasley's paper, which recounts some of the considerations, the difficulties, and the serendipities of biographical research, concludes with a statement of affection for an admittedly difficult man, and Carl Klinck refutes the suggestion that John Norton was the model for Morton/Wacousta. Douglas Cronk details the changes in the pirated American edition of *Wacousta* that has influenced all subsequent editions, changes that radically alter plot, character, theme, and dramatic effect, and that have prevented a proper reading of the text even today. I. S. MacLaren compares *Wacousta* with several other Gothic conventions to effect more extreme outcomes and to root the narrative more firmly in place. Jay Macpherson establishes numerous connections between Richardson's work and that of writers ranging from Shakespeare to Bulwer-Lytton, M. G. Lewis, Scott, Young, and many others, while Michael Hurley examines the geometrical patterns of Richardson's fiction to support his claim that Richardson produced a unified corpus with a consistent vision. Richardson's relationship to Sir Walter Scott is also the subject of a paper by David Richards in *Re-visions of Canadian Literature*[86], but Richards concludes that their work is significantly different in that Scott can resolve past conflicts by means of present pragmatic compromises and of 'the timeless dissolving of the Romantic Image' whereas for Richardson 'Canadian literary culture in the 1830s offer[ed] no satisfactory alternative aesthetic to the hour of cultural confrontation and destruction'.

No other nineteenth-century Canadian fiction writer received as much attention as did Richardson. Mrs Moodie is the subject of Margot Northey's 'Completing the Self-Portrait: Moodie's *Rachel Wilde*' (*ECW*) which reads the novel as an expression of desire for self-revelation and self-justification, and as an indication that Moodie's sense of exile predicted her experience of recording *Roughing It in the Bush*. Michèle Lacombe in 'Frying Pans and Deadlier Weapons: The Immigrant Novels of Mary Ann Sadlier' (*ECW*) offers for examination the hitherto ignored life and work of a prolific writer and sometime publisher. Camille R. Le Bossière's 'The Mysterious End of James de Mille's Unfinished *Strange Manuscript*' (*ECW*) gives a good defence of the adequacy of the novel's abrupt conclusion by judiciously sifting criticism of the novel and by comparing it fruitfully with Samuel Butler's contemporaneous *Erewhon*. Eva-Marie Kröller takes us back to the game of influence and parallel in 'George Eliot in Canada: *Romola* and *The Golden Dog*' (*ARCS*).

Turn-of-the-century fiction writers received scant attention in 1984. Peter Allen's 'Narrative Uncertainty in Duncan's *The Imperialist*' (*SCL*) argues weakly that the novel's inconsistent narrative control bespeaks the ambiguity of Canadian identity at the century's turn. Gerald Lynch's 'Sunshine Sketches: Mariposa Versus Mr. Smith' (*SCL*) presents a more intriguing case in oppos-

85. *Recovering Canada's First Novelist*, ed. by Catherine Sheldrick Ross. Porcupine's Quill. pp. 101. C$10.95.

86. *Re-visions of Canadian Literature*. Papers presented at a Seminar in Canadian Literature held at the University of Leeds, April 1984. IBIC. pp. 102.

ing Smith's individualism to the community and suggesting that the community is affirmed over Smith. Judith Miller claims, in 'Montgomery's Emily: Voices and Silences' (*SCL*), that Montgomery uses the fragmentary *Emily Climbs* to articulate indirectly through the superficial appearance of 'an idyllic novel of girlhood' a 'curiously contemporary' feminine struggle.

Of the modern pre-Second World War writers only Martha Ostenso received individual critical attention. Rosalie Murphy Baum provides some interesting generic insight in her 'Martha Ostenso's *Wild Geese*: More Insight into the Naturalistic Sensibility' (*JCC*). Sinclair Ross might also squeeze into this category, though *As for Me and My House* appeared during the war. Several of his stories appeared before, however, and they do occasion some comment. Paul Comeau's 'Sinclair Ross's Pioneer Fiction' (*CanL*) propounds the banal argument that Ross's movement from tragedy to irony to comedy in his writing career 'broadly parallel[s] human emotional development from the expectancy of youth through the disillusionment of middle years to the acquiescence of old age'. Marilyn Chapman is far more persuasive in 'Another Case of Ross's Mysterious Barn' (*CanL*) in contending that the story, 'One's A Heifer', is deliberately inconclusive, a study in illusion, perhaps even of the reader's. David Williams, in his 'The "Scarlet" Rompers: Toward a New Perspective in *As for Me and My House*' (*CanL*) intriguingly, but not conclusively, insists not only that the novel is profoundly ironic in its presentation of its narrator, Mrs Bentley, as a self-deluded woman who needs to find her husband flawed, but even that Paul is the actual father of Judith's child. In ' "Its Better Nature Lost": The Importance of the Word in Sinclair Ross's *As for Me and My House*' (*CanL*) Lorraine M. York, on the other hand, takes a far safer and far less interesting course in tracing patterns of the verbal and the non-verbal throughout the novel to suggest that both poles are positive *and* negative and that they are ultimately fused in the child (the word made flesh) of the novel's conclusion.

Much of this year's critical effort on Canadian fiction is concentrated on the postwar period. The *Companion To Under the Volcano* has already been mentioned, but Lowry is the subject of several other efforts. Elizabeth D. Rankin's 'Malcolm Lowry's Comic Vision: "Elephant and Colosseum" ' (*CanL*) contends that this short story reveals Lowry's use of the artist-theme as an unexpressed metaphor in which he is suggesting that man can direct his life towards meaning and fulfilment as Cosnahan does after his coincidental meeting with his old friend, the elephant Rosemary, or towards tragedy as the Consul does in *Under the Volcano*. This novel is really a religious book, argues Michael Cripps in 'Lost in the Wilderness: The Puritan Theme in *Under the Volcano*' (*ESC*). It presents in Geoffrey Firmin the ultimately self-destructive dimensions of Puritan individualism. Keith Harrison suggests, in 'Allusions in *Under the Volcano*: Function and Pattern' (*SCL*), that Lowry sees that past and present are alike in human disorder, and that he therefore employs allusions differently from Joyce, Eliot, and Pound.

Ethel Wilson also dissents from cultural importation, or at least her *Swamp Angel* heroine Maggie Vardoe does, according to Brent Thompson in 'Ethel Wilson, Wary Mythologist' (*CanL*). Maggie seeks to escape the revolutionary monotheism of Christianity, the geometric power of mathematics and the Cartesian egocentric consciousness, all represented in Eddie, by pursuing a relativistic, subjective universe of symbol and myth. What Maggie pursues,

Sheila Watson assumes in *The Double Hook*. Stephen Putzel, in 'Under Coyote's Eye: Indian Tales in Sheila Watson's *The Double Hook*' (*CanL*), contends that her use of the Indian trickster figure from an outsider's perspective is not a limitation, but permits her to recognize that her white characters have transformed Coyote into a bogey man, a figure of evil and death, and to use him simultaneously as a figure of hope. Angela Bowering's 'Figures Cut in Sacred Ground: *Illuminati* in *The Double Hook*' (*line*) brings a postmodern perspective to the same text to delineate the strategies whereby Watson teases out the articulation and exemplification of her view that language is not representation but creation, that the text is not *mimesis* but *praxis*. The importance of language is addressed in a different way in Marco LoVerso's 'Language Private and Public: A Study of [Adele] Wiseman's *Crackpot*' (*SCL*). LoVerso avers that Hoda's story is that of someone who is never given a proper public language and therefore a conventional morality, because her tutors (parents, teachers, etc.) are engrossed in their own narrow verbal worlds with dire consequences for her until Lazar begins to enable her to move into the public sphere (not into madness) at the novel's end.

Robertson Davies's critical popularity continues. Shirley Chew suggests that triptych is a more accurate word than trilogy to acknowledge the balance in the relationship of the Deptford novels and to account for their open-endedness[86]. Paul W. Miller's 'Pursuit of the Heroic Self in Davies' Deptford Trilogy' (*ARCS*) offers a more conventional perspective. Nancy Bailey examines the same texts in 'The Role of Dunstan Ramsay, the "Almost" Saint of Robertson Davies' Deptford Trilogy' (*JCL*), questioning the trilogy's coherence and connection, and concluding that Ramsay ultimately fails to confront the self fully and that the trilogy offers his character, therefore, as a warning rather than as a model. R. D. MacDonald focuses on only one of these novels in 'Small Town Ontario in Robertson Davies' *Fifth Business*: Mariposa Revised?' (*SCL*), and presses a rather narrow and unconvincing thesis that Ramsay is presented as a sly and vindictive person who precipitates the accident to Mrs Dempster and deliberately brings about Boy's death.

Margaret Laurence was especially popular in 1984 among international scholars of Canadian Literature. Two papers in *Re-visions of Canadian Literature*[86] were devoted to her work. Peter Easingwood comments on the relationship of Laurence's work to the ideas of W. L. Morton, especially as regards the acceptance of place. Arthur Ravenscroft suggests that the influence of African culture can be discerned in Laurence's minimalist view of life, in her reverence for life and the process of making, and in her Yoruba-like physical conception of history and healing. Pierre Spriet unfortunately misunderstands as solipsistic the two novels examined in 'A Retrospective Reading of *The Stone Angel*, in the light of *The Diviners*' (*WLWE*). To support his dubious contention, he emphasizes love-denying elements which seem to valorize independence and resistance over social integration. Michael Darling, a native critic, analyses a Laurence short story in ' "Undecipherable Signs": Margaret Laurence's "To Set Our Home in Order" ' (*ECW*), focusing on the tension between order and disorder and finding its resolution in the affirmation of the capacity of the narrative consciousness to order and thereby to understand experience.

Perhaps the most popular subject of critical scrutiny among fiction writers in

1984 is Robert Kroetsch. A special issue of articles on his work was published by *OL*. The issue also contains a travel commentary by Kroetsch, an article on American literature by him, and an interview with him by his wife Smaro Kamboureli, but there are a dozen critical treatments of his work covering his criticism as well as his fiction and poetry and giving evidence, both by the content of their exegeses and by the postmodernist critical strategies employed, of the influential stature which Kroetsch presently enjoys in Canadian literature. One of the articles compares Kroetsch's work with that of Sinclair Ross. This comparative approach also characterizes the two articles on him in *Re-visions of Canadian Literature*[86]. John Thieme compares *Badlands* with Atwood's *Surfacing* and sees both novels as attempts to journey back to a state v. here 'the dualities of history have been unwritten'. John Moss compares *Badlands* with Bowering's *Burning Water* and claims that they demonstrate the ultimate solipsism of realistic fiction by either reducing 'the word-world to words' (*Burning Water*) or reducing 'the concept of reality to a text' (*Badlands*). In a different place (*SCL*), Stanley Fogel addresses the theme of language as worked out by Kroetsch, particularly in *Alibi* and *Gone Indian*, and concludes that in the former Dorf is aware of the illusory quality of language as a transparent medium and writes out his story knowing that it is alibi, catachresis. Finally, Arnold E. Davidson's 'Intimations of Eliot in Robert Kroetsch's *Gone Indian*' (*JCC*) offers some mildly interesting parallels between the work of the two writers.

Kroetsch's prairie compatriot, Rudy Wiebe, was the subject of two essays by Coral Ann Howells. In 'Re-Visions of Prairie Indian History in Rudy Wiebe's *The Temptations of Big Bear* and *My Lovely Enemy*'[86] she finds 'a developmental pattern of progressively closer imaginative engagement' in Wiebe's movement from rewriting history from a different angle to recreating history by reliving it. In 'Silence in Rudy Wiebe's *The Mad Trapper*' (*WLWE*) she says that Wiebe employs the trapper's almost complete silence to focus on his fundamental humanity, and to affirm thereby Wiebe's own faith in the possibilities of language while admitting its fragility as a medium for human communication.

Like Kroetsch, Marian Engel was the subject of a special issue of a literary journal, but most of the entries in *ROO* are personal rather than analytical. Alice Munro, Timothy Findley, and Sara Stambaugh offer statements of friendship and appreciation. Jane Rule provides some analysis of Engel's short-story collection of 1975, *Inside the Easter Egg*, Annette Wengele provides a short bibliography of Engel's writings, and George Woodcock makes substantial claims for the artistic worth of *The Glassy Sea*. In *A Sense of Place*[15] Dorothy Jones indicates how Engel uses the motifs of Gothic fantasy in *Bear* to effect her heroine's release through an acceptance of her physical, sexual, nature and of the otherness of the bear.

Alice Munro also had an entire volume of papers devoted to her in 1984. *The Art of Alice Munro*[87] publishes papers given at a conference at the University of Waterloo, and an interview with Munro conducted by fellow-novelist Harold Horwood. The nine articles range from a discussion of archival concerns about the arrangement of Munro's papers at the University of Calgary,

87. *The Art of Alice Munro: Saying the Unsayable*, ed. by Judith Miller. Waterloo. pp. vi + 135. C$9.95.

to analyses of individual and groups of stories, to a comparison with the work of Clark Blaise, and to a discussion of the quality of her imagination. Elsewhere, Susan J. Warwick's 'Growing Up· The Novels of Alice Munro' (*ECW*) compares *Lives of Girls and Women* and *Who Do You Think You Are?* (with greater attention to the latter) and concludes that for Munro maturity seems to bring despair, but narrative voice affirms the possibility of authentic communication. In *A Sense of Place*[15] Lars Hartveit finds that the same two novels present the three-stage process of survival (adaptation, rebellion, reconciliation) necessary to small-town life. They both present this process through the strategy of memoir which permits the simultaneous retention of a core of factual reality and a translation of the ordinary. L. M. Eldredge concentrates on 'A Sense of Ending in *Lives of Girls and Women*' (*SCL*) and finds there a tension between the True and the Real which is resolved in favour of neither, but throughout evoking the concept of an incomprehensible language. Of more general, contextual, interest is Robert Thacker's 'Connection: Alice Munro and Ontario' (*ARCS*).

Anne Archer's 'Real Mummies' (*SCL*) considers the work of Munro's friend, Audrey Thomas, and finds its personal nature problematic, provoking the thought that she may have only one story to tell. Pauline Butling's 'Thomas and Her Rag-Bag' (*CanL*) is more sanguine, seeing Thomas as one who deconstructs the traditional images of women by shifting to an autobiographical base and reconstructing, from the shards separated from myth and story, new models.

Among other writers receiving individual critical attention in 1984 may be found David Godfrey, John Metcalf, David Adams Richards, Naim Kattan, John Mills, and Richard Rohmer. Lorraine M. York in ' "River Two Blind Jacks": Dave Godfrey's Chaucerian Allegory' (*SCL*), thinks Godfrey is torn between tradition and contemporary relevance, protest and responsibility and that he plays with the motifs and structures of 'The Pardoner's Tale' in order to move towards the realization of a collective fate. Keith Garebian's '*General Ludd*: A Satire on Decadence' (*CanL*) depicts Metcalf's novel as bitterly comic, attacking especially the decadence of language and the myth of progress. H. W. Connor, in 'Coming of Winter, Coming of Age: The Autumnal Vision of David Adams Richards' First Novel' (*SCL*), argues cogently the promising stature of Richards's work by pointing out that *The Coming of Winter* is not merely an example of regional realism or rural naturalism as reviewers seem to think, but that it exemplifies, in a simpler form than he would subsequently utilize, Richards's use of 'symbolic dialectics', defined primarily through imagery of nature and time, 'to reflect the thematic implications of the action, especially to define a basic tension between internal intensity and external barrenness'. Nell Waldman, in 'A Tudor in Lotusland: The Writings of John Mills' (*ECW*), surveys Mills's work, praising his erudition, humour, linguistic gifts, and grace, and identifies *Skevington's Daughter* as his most successful. Michael Greenstein's 'The Desert, the River, and the Island' (*CanL*) asserts that Naim Kattan's fiction deserves more critical attention, but it fails itself to provide that attention in anything more than a very cursory manner. Finally, Lorna Irvine's 'Canada Counsel: Richard Rohmer's Political Best Sellers' (*JCC*) affords that writer's work more attention than it deserves.

(c) Poetry
  Index to Canadian Poetry in English[88] is 1984's major addition to the reference collection on Canadian poetry. It can be a useful text if one keeps in mind its considerable limitations. It indexes some 7000 poems in fifty-one anthologies, including some French-Canadian poems in translation, but of course falls far short of being a complete index to English-Canadian poetry. Its materials are arranged in three main sections: title and first-line index, author index, and subject index. 'The Year's Work in Canadian Poetry Studies' has been mentioned earlier. Of passing interest might be Douglas Barbour's eccentric 'Canadian Poetry Chronicle' (*Quarry*) which is an omnibus review of poetry books, poorly organized, and uneven in judgement. A more valuable addition to poetry scholarship is *A Literary Friendship*[89], an edition of sixty-four letters that passed between Ralph Gustafson and W. W. E. Ross from 1940 to 1964. The letters provide valuable insights into Canadian modernist poetry and the literary history of the 1940s and 1950s.
  Survey treatments of Canadian poetry are few and focus predictably on the Confederation poets. *CP* devoted an issue to them with editor D. M. R. Bentley's 'Prefaces to Minor Poets of a Superior Order' pointing out that they 'achieved more of a presence in American, English, and Canadian literatures than is often realized' and illustrating this point by means of a quick glimpse at some of the particulars of notice by their British and American contemporaries and by modern Canadian writers. In the same issue, Les McLeod contributes a lengthy essay, 'Canadian Post-Romanticism: the Context of Late Nineteenth Century Canadian Poetry', proposing, as the title suggests, new nomenclature to replace the misleading and unsatisfactory titles of 'Romantic', 'Victorian', and 'Confederation'.
  Little of an exclusively theoretical nature on Canadian poetry appeared in 1984. Douglas Barbour's 'Lyric/Anti-Lyric: Some Notes About a Concept' (*line*) argues the formal subversion of conventional lyric by modern and contemporary poets who use the outward forms of lyric to do so.
  Few pre-Confederation poets enjoyed critical attention. James de Mille, more noted for his fiction, had his 'Class Poem of 1854' edited and introduced by Patricia Monk in *CP*; she indicates that it is a well-organized narrative. D. M. R. Bentley's 'Through Endless Landscapes: Notes on Charles Sangster's *The St. Lawrence and the Saguenay*' (*ECW*) analyses the poem in detail and at length, explicating its central, cohering theme of love, pointing out its influences from Dante and Spenser to Byron and Wordsworth, and concluding that the poem 'has moments of originality, success, and fitness ... for all its facile borrowings and dismaying failures'.
  Of the Confederation, or post-Romantic, contemporaries Isabella Valancy Crawford and William Henry Drummond were written about. Robert Alan Burns makes the credible contention in 'Crawford and Gounod: Ambiguity and Irony in *Malcolm's Katie*' (*CP*) that Gounod's *Mireille* is a likely source for Crawford's poem. He goes on to claim that it 'is also a poem about destructiveness, self-deception, exploitation, greed, and the futility of human aspiration

---

88. *Index to Canadian Poetry in English*, comp. and ed. by Jane McQuarrie, Anne Mercer, Gordon Ripley. Reference. pp. 367. C$45.
  89. *A Literary Friendship. The Correspondence of Ralph Gustafson and W. W. E. Ross*, ed. with intro. by Bruce Whiteman. ECW. pp. 248. C$22.

and endeavour, all of which contribute to the dark, ironic undercurrent of the poem'. Burns's reading is perhaps the darkest ever given the poem, but he undermines it by rendering Alfred more virtuous than Max and Katie, and moreover, than the poem allows. Gerald Noonan's 'Perceptions of Drummond Cet Idiome Batarde' (*CP*) notices some contemporary responses to Drummond and argues unconvincingly that his portraits of the habitant were nicely balanced.

Among the Confederation poets themselves, 1984 especially favoured Roberts. Two collections of papers devoted to him and his work were published. *The Proceedings of the Sir Charles G. D. Roberts Symposium*[90] held at Mount Allison in the fall of 1982 contains nine papers – on his poetry (D. M. R. Bentley, David Jackel, W. J. Keith), on his fiction (Joseph Gold, John Moss), on preparing a collected edition of the poems (Graham Adams), on bibliography (Donald Conway), on the American reception of his work (James Doyle), and a personal overview (Fred Cogswell). The Ottawa conference in the spring of 1983 was a larger affair and so *The Sir Charles G. D. Roberts Symposium*[91] covers Roberts's work more extensively, albeit by some of the same scholars. The volume contains fifteen papers, a panel discussion, and a preliminary bibliography of Roberts. His poetry, appropriately, receives the greatest attention, though there are also papers on his fiction, his international literary contexts, his criticism, his letters, and his acquaintanceships. In addition to these two volumes can be found a very good analysis of the subtle and complex coherence of one of Roberts's volumes of poetry in Glennis Stephenson's 'The Bitter-Sweet Rose: The Conception of Woman in Roberts' *The Book of the Rose*' (*CP*), and a critical curiosity in an essay on Roberts's mysticism prepared in 1937 by the husband of Roberts's niece, August R. Leisner, who writes 'Charles G. D. Roberts: Mystical Poet', which is edited by Laurel Boone with Dorothy Roberts Leisner in *SCL*.

Roberts's post-Romantic colleagues, Bliss Carman, Archibald Lampman, and D. C. Scott remain objects of critical activity. In the vein of scholarship H. Pearson Gundy edited and introduced a memoir of Carman written by his friend and sometime room-mate Mitchell Kennerley which, among other things, confirms for any who remain doubtful the sexual nature of Carman's relationship with Mary Perry King (*CP*). Tracy Ware's 'The Integrity of Carman's *Low Tide on Grand Pré*' (*CP*) attacks the question of that volume's unity and maintains weakly, after some interesting reflections on individual poems, that its integrity is to be found in 'multeity in unity'. L. R. Early is the best scholar of Lampman at the moment. He provides a very valuable dating (probably not exact) for more than 350 of Lampman's published poems in 'A Chronology of Lampman's Poems' (*CP*). Early also writes on the relationship of the poet to Katherine Waddell in 'Lampman's Love Poetry' (*ECW*), asserting that the impact of this relationship on his poetry 'can be hardly overestimated', and reviews several poems from the appropriate period to prove the assertion. A rather specialized subject is presented in R. S. Kilpatrick's 'Scott's "Night Hymns on Lake Nipegon": "Matins" in the Northern Mid-

90. *The Proceedings of the Sir Charles G. D. Roberts Symposium*, ed. by Carrie MacMillan. Anchorage Series 1. MtAllisonU. pp. 129.
91. *The Sir Charles G. D. Roberts Symposium*, ed. with intro. by Glenn Clever. Reappraisals: Canadian Writers 10. UOttawa. pp. xiv + 249. C$10.35.

night' (*CP*). Kilpatrick suggests that Scott's reference in the poem to ancient hymns and Latin may have been provoked by his familiarity with Gregory's matin, *Nocte surgentes*.

The first volume of David G. Pitt's eagerly awaited biography of E. J. Pratt has at last appeared and justifies expectation. *E. J. Pratt: The Truant Years 1882–1927*[92] is a thoroughly researched, sympathetic, but sensitive and cogent treatment of Pratt's first forty-five years. It elucidates important issues such as the poet's relationship with his parents, and his consequently curious relationship with Methodism. It details as well the problematic years from about 1910 to the mid-1920s when Pratt completed his formal education, married, but seemed without any certain career direction. Pitt clarifies but does not simplify his subject. Volume Two will now be awaited with even greater anticipation. Meanwhile, the Pratt editorial project continues and in 'The "Blue Pencil" Revisions of E. J. Pratt: Editorial Procedures for Modern Canadian Texts' (*ECW*), one of its editors, R. G. Moyles, declares the editorial principles guiding the project. James F. Johnson's '*Brebeuf and His Brethren* and *Towards the Last Spike*: The Two Halves of Pratt's National Epic' (*ECW*) unfortunately offers no advance upon Frye's long-ago designation of Pratt as an epic writer and these two poems as his tragic and comic epic, respectively.

Solomon J. Spiro's book on allusions in the work of A. M. Klein was mentioned above. William Walsh's paper in *Re-visions of Canadian Literature*[86] also deals with Klein's Jewishness, insisting that it permeates all of Klein's work, even *The Rocking Chair* poems. In 'Personality and Authority: A. M. Klein's Self-Portrait' (*CP*) J. M. Kertzer also attends to this problem but presents its complexity more fully and convincingly as he details how Klein fails to define an authoritative, authentic, poetic self because he cannot accept the traditional religious, romantic, or existential assurances of personality. This articulation of the darker dimensions of Klein's work is continued in D. M. R. Bentley's 'A Nightmare Ordered: A. M. Klein's *Portrait of the Poet As Landscape*' (*ECW*).

Andrew Stubbs and Jeannette Stein, in 'Anne Marriott: Frontier Poet' (*CP*), insinuate a sinister dimension to her outlook too as they insist that 'her journeys are circular, inevitably leading back to their original starting points, where they turn in on themselves or dissolve'. The argument is not fully convincing. But Shirley Neuman's 'Allow Self, Portraying Self: Autobiography in *Field Notes*' (*line*), an award-winning essay missed in our 1983 survey, is convincing as she analyses the ways in which Kroetsch uses the first-person pronoun as a release from *I* by moving away from solipsism and from the convention of the poem as speech utterance to the idea of the poem as intertext. Linguistic indeterminacy and the textuality of nature are the anti-humanistic concepts which Smaro Kamboureli attributes to the work of 'Fred Wah: A Poetry of Dialogue' (*line*).

R. F. Gillian Harding, in 'Ironic Mythopoeia in MacEwen's *The T. E. Lawrence Poems*' (*SCL*), an essay dominated by J. E. Cirlot, presents an ultimately incoherent list of MacEwen's images in terms of 'icons' and their clustered and particular significations. Daphne Marlatt's brief 'Distance and

92. *E. J. Pratt: The Truant Years 1882–1927*, by David G. Pitt. UTor. pp. xix + 415. C$14.95.

Identity: A Postscript to *Steveston*' (*line*) is a none the less valuable reflection on the relationship of the book's poems and photographs. Robert Billings, in 'Discovering the Sizes of the Heart: The Poems of Mary Di Michele' (*ECW*), provides an interesting introduction to the work of a relatively new poet, surveying her principal formal and thematic preoccupations.

(d) Drama

The most considerable attempt at drama scholarship in 1984 is E. Ross Stuart's *The History of Prairie Theatre*[93]. His subject is immense and amorphous but he does a creditable job of covering it with some measure of coherence. There will be inevitable complaints about omissions but Stuart's materials are at least representative. His first section on prairie pioneer theatre covers not only early theatre in cities such as Winnipeg, Regina, Saskatoon, Edmonton, and Calgary, but also offers some account of touring activities, stock companies, and vaudeville. His second section on amateur theatre proceeds from the Chautauqua, Earl Grey competitions, small town and ethnic amateur theatre, amateur theatre in each of the major prairie cities, to provincial drama organizations, the Dominion Drama Festival, and amateur playwrights. Section Three is on educational theatre, principally at the universities, but also in the primary and secondary schools, and at the Banff School of Fine Arts and summer theatre schools. The fourth and final section examines, albeit sketchily, the new professional theatre such as the Manitoba Theatre Centre, Winnipeg's Rainbow Stage, Edmonton's Citadel and Theatre 3, and professional theatre in Saskatchewan and Calgary, as well as a section on modern prairie playwrights.

With Robert C. Nunn's 'Performing Fact: Canadian Documentary Theatre' (*CanL*) we move from theatre documentary to documentary theatre. Nunn argues that the latter, as exemplified by *Paper Wheat*, *The Komagata Maru Incident*, and *1837: The Farmers' Revolt*, is significant to the growth of Canadian drama because of a 'dual focus on the actual world and on the actuality of performance' which makes the performance a political/social event in and of itself. Drama's fundamentally social character is also an assumption of Richard Paul Knowles in '*Homo Ludens*: Canadian Theatre, Canadian Football, Shakespeare and the NHL' (*CanD*), which contends that good theatre can only happen when the audience thinks of players as 'us' as in spectator sports, and that this happens most frequently with small companies. Patrick B. O'Neill continues his examination of new-found drama documents in the British Museum, and gives us 'Reflections in a Cracked Mirror: Canadian Drama and World War I' (*CanD*), which asserts that playscripts from the first quarter of this century reveal considerable dramatic activity and of a higher quality than our traditional impression of the period suggested. Harry Lane's 'CBC Radio Drama and Scandinavian Literature' (*CanD*) reveals that between 1939 and 1982 CBC produced more than 150 radio dramas using Scandinavian literature: plays, fiction, legends, sagas, and autobiographical materials. And continuing this documentary thrust, Jonathan Rittenhouse provides an account of the history of 'Festival Lennoxville: An All-Canadian

---

93. *The History of Prairie Theatre. The Development of Theatre in Alberta, Manitoba and Saskatchewan*, by E. Ross Stuart. Canadian Theatre History No. 2. S&P. pp. 292. C$24.95.

Story' (*CanD*) with a calendar of its activities from 1975 to 1982, during which it produced plays by most of Canada's notable contemporary playwrights. And finally, Chris Johnson, in 'Amerindians and Aborigines in English Canadian and Australian Drama' (*CanD*), documents the movement from the presentation of the indigenes as part of the wilderness (in both nations) to his presentation as an unwelcome and threatened intruder in the wilderness of the white man's urban world (in Canada only).

The comparative approach is also employed by Paulette Collet and Richard Perkyns. Collet's 'Fennario's *Balconville* and Tremblay's *En pièces détachées*: A Universe of Backyards and Despair' (*CanD*) concentrates primarily on the similarities of the two plays, especially their common attempt to provoke audiences to action. Perkyns's 'PIONEERS: Two Contrasting Dramatic Treatments' (*CanD*), reprinted from his *Major Plays of the Canadian Theatre 1834*, depicts Herman Voaden's *Hill-Land*, as a Dionysic version of the pioneer, and Robertson Davies's *At My Heart's Core* as its Apollonian counterpart.

Several essays were devoted to the work of individual playwrights. Kathleen Garay provides a detailed account of John Coulter's 1950s London sojourn with some valuable incidental glimpses of the theatre scene in both London and Canada in ' "Highest Hopes and Deepest Disappointments": John Coulter's London Diaries 1951–1957' (*CanD*). In 'A Literary Perspective on the Plays of W. O. Mitchell' (*CanD*) Diane Bessai concludes that W. O. Mitchell is really a dramatist manqué, a writer for whom the stage has a particular suitability. Christopher Innes's 'The Many Faces of Rita Joe: The Anatomy of a Playwright's Development' (*CanD*) presents a history of the play from its germination in George Ryga's earlier work through its various productions. Ann Messenger's 'Imagination in the Cellar: Rex Deverell's *Boiler Room Suite*' (*CanD*) admits that Deverell sometimes falls into the role of sentimentalist and/or sociologist but that he transcends these in this play. Rota Herzberg Lister's 'Beverley Simons and the Influence of Oriental Theatre' (*CanD*) presents *Leela Means to Play* as an amalgam of Eastern and Western traditions. Peter Copeman's 'Rick Salutin and the Popular Dramatic Tradition: Towards a Dialectical Theatre in Canada' (*CanD*) discusses several Salutin plays, pointing out that he has worked at both the literary and popular levels but that *Les Canadiens* is his most successful attempt at dialectical theatre to date, comprehensively reflecting current social reality. Dennis W. Johnston's 'George F. Walker: Liberal Idealism and the "Power Plays" ' (*CanD*) depicts Walker as still a playwright in process whose progressively greater accessibility indicates a fulfilling, not a betrayal, of his dramatic promise.

Literary Theory

NICK ROYLE, LAURA MARCUS, RACHEL BOWLBY,
TONY CROWLEY, and RONALD MACDONALD

This chapter has the following sections: 1. General; 2. Narrative Theory; 3. Reception-theory and Semiotics; 4. Rhetoric and Deconstruction; 5. Feminist Criticism; 6. Marxist, Historical, and Discursive Criticism; and 7. Psychoanalytic Critical Theory. Nick Royle has contributed sections 1 and 4, Laura Marcus sections 2 and 3, Rachel Bowlby section 5, Tony Crowley section 6, and Ronald Macdonald section 7.

1. General

It may not yet be entirely correct to suggest, as Edward Said does, in a short piece in *MLN* entitled 'The Future of Criticism', that 'the barriers between discourses, rhetorically and actually, are down'; but there is certainly a continuing sense of the need for greater interdisciplinary and political awareness. One of the most potentially consequential aspects of this concerns important shifts in the question, place, and value of subjectivity and individuality. Here the contributions of feminism and of work on black and other literatures are crucial. There are also signs of an increasing Anglo-American and French responsiveness to critical theory in Germany; the important appearance of Manfred Frank's *Was ist Neostrukturalismus?*[1], which provides clear and extensive accounts of such writers as Deleuze, Derrida, Foucault, and Lacan, demonstrates a corresponding responsiveness in Germany. Frank is particularly stimulating in dealing with the work of Derrida, arguing against the notion of 'différance' in so far as it is or might be taken to account for everything we understand by the term 'consciousness'. (Of related interest here is a special issue of *Boundary* on 'The Criticism of Peter Szondi', which includes Frank's 'The Text and Its Style: Schleiermacher's Hermeneutic Language' and Rainer Nägele's 'Text, History and the Critical Subject: Notes on Peter Szondi's Theory and Praxis of Hermeneutics'.) From a rather different perspective, there are the implications for notions of subjectivity and individuality of Jacques Derrida's *Signsponge* and related work (see section 4 below).

Subjectivity is isolated as the central issue by William E. Cain in his lively study, *The Crisis in Criticism*[2]. He proposes that ' "Subjectivity" has always

1. *Was ist Neostrukturalismus?*, by Manfred Frank. Suhrkamp. pp. 480. DM30.
2. *The Crisis in Criticism: Theory, Literature, and Reform in English Studies*, by William E. Cain. JHU. pp. xx + 307. £21.80.

been perceived as the major threat to the legitimacy of English studies, and the fear of subjectivity lies behind many of the most fervent calls for order and authority in the discipline'. Cain views 'the interpreter's self, the individual subject' as constituting the recurrent 'crisis in criticism', and advocates a move away from the reader as 'the solitary individual' confronting a text, towards seeing 'each "subject" as social actor and agent'. This position is reached through sharp and informative critiques of the work of E. D. Hirsch (whose 'Meaning and Significance Reinterpreted' appears this year in *CritI*), J. Hillis Miller, and Stanley Fish (whose exchange with Walter A. Davis, also in *CritI*, is itself concerned with subjectivism and responsibility in 'the profession').

The Crisis in Criticism also maps the emergence of New Criticism and its institutionalization, showing how New Criticism has been 'transformed into "criticism"', the essence of what we do as teachers and critics'; and, in a section entitled 'Reviewing the State of Criticism', Cain ranges over a large number of critics and critical texts, from Trilling, Leavis, Burke, and Blackmur, to Said, Gerald Graff, and Christopher Norris. Cain's attention to the 'radical' elements of Leavis's work is refreshing, as is the stress he gives to Burke and Blackmur, two American critics still deserving greater consideration in Britain. Most energetic, however, is Cain's conclusion which, partly inspired by Foucault, argues for 'the formation of counter-traditions, the critique of literary and cultural monuments, the study of educational practices and techniques, and the historical investigation of the discipline's origins'. This is illustrated by reference to *Moby Dick* – to 'the critical terms, tactics, and values that made the growth of Melville's reputation possible' – and, more generally, by focusing on the question and status of black literature.

The latter is importantly and extensively treated in *Black Literature and Literary Theory*[3], a collection of essays edited and with a very stimulating and helpful introduction by Henry Louis Gates Jr. The collection is in two parts: 'Theory: on structuralism and post-structuralism' and 'Practice'. The former contains 'The critic and society: Barthes, leftocracy and other mythologies' by Wole Soyinka; 'Repetition as a figure of black culture' by James A. Snead; 'Structural analysis of the Afro-American trickster tale' by Jay Edwards; 'Negritude, structuralism, deconstruction' by Sunday O. Anozie; 'Strictures on structures: the prospects for a structuralist poetics of African fiction' by Anthony Appiah; and 'I yam what I am: the topos of un(naming) in Afro-American literature' by Kimberly W. Benston. 'Practice' comprises individual analyses of writers such as Frederick Douglass, Jean Toomer, Zora Neale Hurston, Ralph Ellison, Gwendolyn Brooks, and Toni Morrison.

The Crisis in Criticism is admirable for the priority it gives to the 'practical', pedagogical dimensions of criticism and theory, though this does involve kinds of reductiveness which Cain elsewhere criticizes. The question of subjectivity is explicitly left 'unresolved' and this is apparent, for example, in Cain's humanist appropriation of Foucault – an appropriation which necessarily ignores Foucault's treatment of the human subject. The question of subjectivity presents evidently fewer problems for Paul H. Fry, whose *The Reach of Criticism: Method and Perception in Literary Theory*[4] stresses the

3. *Black Literature and Literary Theory*, ed. and intro. by Henry Louis Gates Jr. Methuen. pp. xiii + 328. pb £8.95.

4. *The Reach of Criticism: Method and Perception in Literary Theory*, by Paul H. Fry. Yale (1983). pp. xi + 239. £21.

importance of the Sublime and 'distraction' in preference to that of method in interpretation. Enlightening and often evocative accounts of Aristotle, Longinus, Dryden, Shelley, and Walter Benjamin allow Fry to conclude with the argument that 'if personality and self-expression are bound to appear in criticism, they may as well be admitted'. Fry's penchant is thus towards 'a personable but philologically keen, densely allusive criticism that takes *more* and more diverse cues from its text than is customary'.

Humanist appropriations of Foucault are likely to persist although, in the year which has sadly witnessed his death, we can at least welcome the publication of Mark Cousins and Athar Hussain's *Michel Foucault*[5]. This is an invaluable book, without doubt the most scrupulous and sustained exposition of Foucault's work yet to appear. Terry Eagleton's *The Function of Criticism: From 'The Spectator' to Post-Structuralism*[6] is a loosely Foucauldian study offering salient perspectives on the history of literary criticism, particularly in Britain. Eagleton argues that 'modern criticism was born of a struggle against the absolutist state'. He starts with the 'English bourgeois public sphere of the early eighteenth century, of which Steele's *Tatler* and Addison's *Spectator* are central institutions', and moves through to the nineteenth in order to focus on that 'interestingly allusive term', the 'man of letters'. Eagleton argues that 'the general "amateur" humanism of the man of letters could less and less provide a plausible centre of coherence for the conflictual discursive formation of late Victorian England'. For, as he focuses on the twentieth century and the significance of *Scrutiny* with 'its shoddily imprecise metaphysics (Lawrentian vitalism)', the 'classical public sphere' has disintegrated. This disintegration is linked to the most fundamental problem with this study, namely the author's own place in it, and the place of his reader(s). Eagleton is here exemplary in displaying an acute awareness of this problem himself. The penultimate section drifts away from Britain and goes from New Criticism to deconstruction. Eagleton then deals with the work of Raymond Williams. On the one hand he sees Williams's 'field' as being 'the space constituted by the interaction of social relations, cultural institutions and forms of subjectivity'. On the other he provocatively specifies what he regards as 'the major problem confronting all socialist intellectual work today: that it is in some sense addressed to an absent counterpublic sphere, one based upon those very institutions of popular culture and education which failed to emerge in post-war Britain'. A few pages later Eagleton invokes 'a new counterpublic sphere: that of feminist discourse and practice'; modern criticism, though, 'has ended up, in effect, as a handful of individuals reviewing each other's books'. (See also pp. 790–1 for another notice of this volume.)

The Function of Criticism is an invigorating work which, with its indebtedness to the work of Jürgen Habermas and the notions of consensus and the public sphere, can be read, with Fredric Jameson, alongside Jean-François Lyotard's *The Postmodern Condition: A Report on Knowledge*[7] (*La*

5. *Michel Foucault*, by Mark Cousins and Athar Hussain. Theoretical Traditions in the Social Sciences. Macmillan. pp. 278. pb £6.95.

6. *The Function of Criticism: From 'The Spectator' to Post-Structuralism*, by Terry Eagleton. Verso. pp. 133. pb £3.95.

7. *The Postmodern Condition: A Report on Knowledge*, by Jean-François Lyotard, trans. by Geoff Bennington and Brian Massumi. THL 10. UMinn. pp. xxv + 110. pb £7.50.

LITERARY THEORY 765

Condition postmoderne (1979)). The distinctiveness of this book is marked from the start, in having a foreword (by Jameson) in many respects antagonistic to what follows it. Employing Wittgenstein's notion of language games, as in earlier work (see *YW* 62.56 and 64.588–9), Lyotard considers the legitimation of knowledge in terms of narratives: 'the grand narratives of legitimation – the life of the spirit and/or the emancipation of humanity –' have perhaps already ceased to be relevant. His analysis is opposed to what it sees as the 'search for universal consensus' and the 'dialogue of argumentation' encouraged by Habermas. For Lyotard, 'consensus is a horizon that is never reached'; it 'has become an outmoded and suspect value'.

The Postmodern Condition is a powerful and controversial text which has already elicited a number of responses. As part of a continuing concern (see *YW* 62.63), *NGC* has an issue on 'Modernity and Postmodernity', which contains interesting essays by Andreas Huyssen ('Mapping the Postmodern'), Jameson ('The Politics of Theory: Ideological Positions in the Postmodernism Debate'), Hal Foster ('(Post)Modern Polemics'), Habermas ('The French Path to Postmodernity: Bataille between Eroticism and General Economics'), and Seyla Benhabib ('Epistemologies of Postmodernism: A Rejoinder to Jean-François Lyotard'). The differences between Habermas and Lyotard are usefully outlined by Martin Jay in 'Habermas and Modernism', in *Praxis*; *Praxis* also contains a piece by Richard Rorty, entitled 'Habermas and Lyotard on Postmodernity'.

Matters are complicated by the fact that Lyotard's work has taken new directions since *La Condition postmoderne*. *Diac* this year has a special issue on Lyotard, which includes a clarifying interview between himself and Georges Van Den Abbeele. Abbeele is struck, in Lyotard's work, by 'its heterogeneity, its diversity, its relentless questioning of previously advanced categories'. One of these categories is 'language games', which in Lyotard's more recent work (in particular, *Le différend* (1984), parts of which are translated in *Diac*) has been replaced by 'phrases'. This special issue of *Diac* also contains 'Talks', a translation of Philippe Lacoue-Labarthe's contribution to the 1982 Cerisy conference, itself devoted to the work of Lyotard.

A number of publications this year are, in different degrees and ways, concerned with resituating poststructuralism. *The Theory of Reading*[8] is a collection of essays which, in the words of its editor, Frank Gloversmith, addresses 'the possibility of defining a text' and wishes to stress that, *pace* Derrida's 'anti-concept [*sic*] of *différance*', 'things can get said, reference is made, language and history speak in and through one another'. The essays comprise Valentine Cunningham's 'Renoving That Bible: The Absolute Text of (Post) Modernism', which is taken up with, among other things, 'what logocentrism really means' [*sic*] and a curiously misplaced defence of 'history'; David Morse's 'Author–Reader–Language: Reflections on a Critical Closed Circuit'; Homi Bhabha's 'Representation and the Colonial Text: A Critical Exploration of Some Forms of Mimeticism', which is a deeply absorbing elaboration of reading colonial literature 'otherwise'; Allon White's 'Bakhtin, Sociolinguistics and Deconstruction', which offers a clear introduction to Bakhtin's work; Frank Gloversmith's 'Autonomy Theory:

8. *The Theory of Reading*, ed. by Frank Gloversmith. Harvester, pp. xvii + 246. hb £18.95, pb £7.95.

Ortega, Roger Fry, Virginia Woolf'; Alistair Davies's 'Contexts of Reading: The Reception of D. H. Lawrence's *The Rainbow* and *Women in Love*'; and finally Stuart Laing's 'Making and Breaking the Novel Tradition', which focuses on the 'decanonization' of 1950s 'provincial realist' writers such as Alan Sillitoe, John Braine, David Storey, and Stan Barstow.

The attempt to produce a critique of the work of Derrida on the basis of a critique of the work of his 'followers' (Cunningham) or of 'most popular forms of deconstruction' (White) has evidently not yet exhausted itself. This is also a weakness of some of the essays in *Criticism and Critical Theory*[9], edited by Jeremy Hawthorn. One purpose of this collection is, as Hawthorn states in his preface, 'to draw attention to tensions, points of conflict, contradictions and disagreements within literary studies and in contiguous areas'. This volume includes Colin Mercer's 'Paris Match: Marxism, Structuralism and the Problem of Literature', which is worth remarking for its attention to the importance of nationalism; P. D. Juhl's 'Playing with Texts: Can Deconstruction Account for Critical Practice?', which is an attempt to show 'that deconstructionist theory of literary interpretation is untenable'; Iain Wright's 'History, Hermeneutics, Deconstruction', which proposes that 'whatever we think of the sillinesses and excesses of American deconstruction, a genuine anti-positivist and anti-empiricist revolution has taken place in philosophical and social scientific thought' – but fails to deal with Derrida's work as such; Maud Ellmann's 'Blanche', which is a highly original account of Chaucer's *The Book of the Duchess*, making use of Derrida and psychoanalysis; and finally Christopher Butler's 'The Pleasures of the Experimental Text', which employs notions of pleasure and enjoyment based not so much on an understanding of psychoanalytic theory as on what he refers to as 'irrefutable subjective authority'.

From a more pervasively sociological perspective, *The Structural Allegory: Reconstructive Encounters with the New French Thought*[10] is a group of essays generally intended to question and move 'beyond' what the editor, John Fekete, in his introduction calls 'the language paradigm'. Structuralism and poststructuralism are hardly to be distinguished here and are taken as 'models': 'The structural allegory is now in its second stage, having passed through "structuralism" proper to the currently dominant model of "poststructuralism"'. Poststructuralism is characterized in terms of 'nihilism', 'anarchism', and 'play'; Fekete wants, among other things, 'to provide a charter of rights for a materialized *cogito*' and 'to draw from the antiobjectivist implications of the new physics a *participatory* theory of the universe in order to promote self-conscious reprogrammings of social and individual life and to reimprint the radical imagination'. As well as serving to introduce readers to the work of Cornelius Castoriadis ('The Imaginary Institution of Society') and Jean Baudrillard ('The Structural Law of Value and the Order of Simulacra'), this volume also contains Arthur Kroker's 'Modern Power in Reverse Image: The Paradigm Shift of Michel Foucault and Talcott Parsons', which argues that Parsons and Foucault share the 'recognition that power now justifies itself on

9. *Criticism and Critical Theory*, ed. by Jeremy Hawthorn. SUAS, Second Series. Arnold, pp. xiii + 146. pb £6.95.
10. *The Structural Allegory: Reconstructive Encounters with the New French Thought*, ed. and intro. by John Fekete. THL 11. ManU. pp. xxiv + 269. hb £29.50, pb £9.95.

the basis of an appeal to a biological ethos'; György Márkus's 'The Paradigm of Language: Wittgenstein, Lévi-Strauss, Gadamer', which is a clear and direct account of how each of these three writers 'finds in language the universal paradigm of all forms of social interaction and objectivation [sic]'; Andrew Wernick's 'Structuralism and the Dislocation of the French Rationalist Project', which gives attention to theological and nationalistic aspects of French thought; Marc Angenot's 'Structuralism as Syncretism: Institutional Distortions of Saussure', which attempts to get around 'smokescreens spread by structuralist verbiage' and contends that 'French structuralism never existed as an *episteme*'; Robert D'Amico's 'Text and Context: Derrida and Foucault on Descartes', which is a thoughtful account ultimately more sympathetic to Foucault; John O'Neill's 'Breaking the Signs: Roland Barthes and the Literary Body' which focuses on the 'political and sociological implications' of 'the antiestablishment pathos of Barthes' theory and practice of literary pleasure and its post-structuralist direction'; Charles Levin's 'La Greffe du Zèle: Derrida and the Cupidity of the Text', which tries to argue that 'while remaining within the abstraction of the opposition of speech and writing by "deconstructing" it, Derrida fails to see that he could move outside it by challenging *the structural model of language that establishes the privilege of the opposition itself*, and not just one of its terms'; and John Fekete's own contribution, 'Modernity in the Literary Institution: Strategic Anti-Foundational Moves', which sees 'an overpoliticization of discourse' in the work of Foucault and Derrida and urges an 'anti-foundationalist program' that 'moves beyond the matrix of the language paradigm'. Even if one considers such a notion tenable, the preoccupation with 'language paradigm' finds a weird and ironic reflection in the language of some of the contributors. Perhaps the finest example, and taken from the final essay in the volume, is the following sentence: 'Although both the regulatory proceduralism of structuralist relativism and the potentiating deconstructionism of post-structuralist relativism can serve to effect a certain anti-empiricist de-naturalization of the phenomenal event, neither escapes the limiting – and, ultimately, the reifying [sic] – frame of the language paradigm, which excludes evolutionary, axiological, and praxical dimensions of human agency that are germane to the future of the human community with respect to real options at the levels of communication and social organization.'

Gillian Rose's *Dialectic of Nihilism: Post-Structuralism and Law*[11] is a dense and original study, which uses a framework of Roman, Greek, Hebrew, and Germanic law, and the work of Kant and Hegel, in order to argue that poststructuralism's 'claims that it has surpassed metaphysics, dialectics and universal history are grounded and presented by reinstating a fundamental category or schema – a mathesis'. Poststructuralism is viewed as being concerned with 'the nihilistic identity and non-identity of law and metaphysics'. Rose's aim is to show how 'the case beyond nihilism' yields 'to an historical dialectic which it claims to surpass'. The first part of the book provides accounts of Kant, and of the Marburg and Heidelberg schools of neo-Kantianism and writers such as Emile Lask, Rudolf Stammler, Rudolf von Ihering, and Herman Cohen, before moving on to consider Heidegger. In

11. *Dialectic of Nihilism: Post-Structuralism and Law*, by Gillian Rose. Blackwell. pp. viii + 232. hb £25, pb £8.50.

the second part Rose discusses the work of Deleuze ('The New Bergsonism'), Saussure and Lévi-Strauss ('Structuralism and Law'), Derrida ('Law and Writing'), and Foucault ('Legalism and Power'). The account of Deleuze is based largely on *Le Bergsonisme* (1966) and *Différence et répétition* (1972): other and more recent work is not covered. (This is perhaps an appropriate moment to mention that *Substance* has a special issue on Deleuze, which includes his 'Image-Movement and Its Three Varieties: Second Commentary about Bergson' and a useful ten-page bibliography of Deleuze and Félix Guattari.) Rose's account of Derrida is similarly based on 'early' work – *The Origin of Geometry*, *Of Grammatology*, and *Writing and Difference*. Rose's argument assumes a reading of Derrida's use of 'writing' and 'metaphor' as 'transcendental'; but it is to be welcomed for its detail, especially in discussing the relation of Hegel to Derrida's formulation of 'différance'. Her analysis of Foucault stresses his 'indiscriminate separation of politics and knowledge' and uncovers what is apparently seen as the key term in his work: ' "Life" is the overarching, absolute concept which unifies his *oeuvre*, whether the individual works are organized as studies of *episteme*, or, later, of "power" '.

If one of the more obvious reservations about *Dialectic of Nihilism* is its failure to discuss the place and importance of psychoanalysis in relation to 'post-structuralism and law', a subtler one might be made regarding its resolute avoidance of the 'literary'. Hazard Adams's *Philosophy of the Literary Symbolic*[12] takes off from Vico and Blake and provides straightforward and helpful expositions of Kant, Goethe, Schelling, Coleridge, Carlyle, Hegel, Baudelaire, Mallarmé, Yeats, Wilde, Freud, Jung, Bachelard, Croce, Hans Vaihinger, Ernst Cassirer, Susanne Langer, Eliseo Vivas, Joseph Campbell, Mircea Eliade, Philip Wheelwright, and Northrop Frye. In this way Adams elaborates his 'philosophy': it requires 'a concept of language as "creative" ' and 'as fundamentally poetic'. Less satisfactory when dealing with more recent work, this is nevertheless a lucid and extensive, pedagogically useful study, especially enjoyable for the attention it gives to Cassirer and twentieth-century mythography.

William Ray's *Literary Meaning: From Phenomenology to Deconstruction*[13] is also an instructive and clearly written expository work, particularly for its coverage of phenomenological criticism (Poulet, Sartre, Maurice Blanchot, Mike Dufrenne, Ingarden, Iser) and of the work of Norman Holland, David Bleich, and E. D. Hirsch. Consideration is then given to the work of Culler (the Culler, however, of *Structuralist Poetics* rather than *On Deconstruction*), Eco, Fish, Barthes, and de Man. The title and subtitle of Ray's study may be misleading: 'literary meaning' is confined to 'meaning in prose reading'; Derrida is dealt with in just over eight pages, ostensibly because 'most of his work does not fall within the tradition of literary criticism that here concerns us'. Finally, it is difficult to see why Ray continues to valorize a theory/practice distinction and a notion of dialectics while at various points bearing witness to their highly questionable status in the writings of Derrida, Barthes, and de Man.

PMLA this year has a centennial issue containing a series of essays and

12. *Philosophy of the Literary Symbolic*, by Hazard Adams. UFlorS. pp. xiv + 466. hb $37.50, pb $17.50.

13. *Literary Meaning: From Phenomenology to Deconstruction*, by William Ray. Blackwell. pp. vi + 228. hb £17.50, pb £5.95.

addresses on the MLA, its history, and literary studies. It includes, most significantly, Geoffrey Hartman's 'The Culture of Criticism'. This is an eloquent, highly informative, and wide-ranging account of Anglo-American and European culture – specifically in relation to criticism – from Dilthey, Arnold, and Schleiermacher to de Man and Derrida. The essay closes with a trenchant remark about English culture: 'The culture of criticism in England has a philosophical thinness that essays by Sartre, Ortega, Benjamin, Adorno, and Burke never display.' If this has been so, a corresponding observation might be made of British philosophy regarding *its* lack of attentiveness to developments in the past two decades or so, in continental philosophy and literary criticism and theory.

Philosophy and Literature[14], which brings together a number of lectures delivered at the Royal Institute of Philosophy in 1981–2, is a case in point. Here we find 'Solitude in Philosophy and Literature', by Hywel D. Lewis; 'Death and Fulfilment, or Would the Real Mr. Dostoevsky Stand Up?', by Stewart Sutherland; 'Aristotle and Agamemnon', by Renford Bambrough; '"Reality" in Early Twentieth-Century German Literature', which is an absorbing analysis of the word 'Wirklichkeit' and of the emergence of *'the ideology and literature of "reality"'*, by J. P. Stern; 'Literary Examples and Philosophical Confusion', by R. W. Beardsmore; 'Thematic Concepts: Where Philosophy Meets Literature', by Stein Haugom Olsen; 'Dostoevsky: Psychology and the Novelist', by Ilham Dilman; 'The End of the Road: The Death of Individualism', which is an examination of the work of Sartre and John Barth, by Jacquelyn Kegley; 'The Noble', by John Casey; 'When Do Empirical Methods By-pass "The Problems Which Trouble Us"?', by Frank Cioffi; 'Philosophical Autobiography: St Augustine and John Stuart Mill', by Martin Warner; and 'Philosophy, Interpretation, and *The Golden Bowl*', by Peter Jones. These essays in general simply presuppose, or set out to re-affirm, the traditional boundaries and distinctions between 'literature' and 'philosophy'. As such they are scarcely representative of what constitutes contemporary literary theory. Uncomfortably lodged among them is Derrida's 'Devant la loi' which, although delivered in English, appears here, markedly truncated, in French. 'Devant la loi' focuses on Kafka's short story *Vor dem Gesetz* (*Devant la loi*), and on 'la double question (qui décide, et à quel titre, de l'appartenance à la littérature?)' This essay, even in its shortened form, has fascinating implications for notions of law and could very interestingly be placed alongside (or 'before') Gillian Rose's *Dialectic of Nihilism*.

Remaining with questions of the literary we have Patricia Waugh's *Metafiction: The Theory and Practice of Self-Conscious Fiction*[15], an animated and engaging introduction to 'fictional writing which self-consciously and systematically draws attention to its status as an artefact in order to pose questions about the relationship between fiction and reality'. This is a very illuminating survey of such writing, both in Britain and in the United States, though there is an unresolved difficulty in the 'or' of Waugh's thesis that 'metafiction is a tendency or function inherent in *all* novels'. More generally, the status of the concept of self-consciousness is never examined as such. One might suggest

14. *Philosophy and Literature*, ed. by A. Phillips Griffiths. Royal Institute of Philosophy Lecture Series 16. Supplement to *Philosophy* 1983. CUP. pp. 233. pb £9.95.

15. *Metafiction: The Theory and Practice of Self-Conscious Fiction*, by Patricia Waugh. Methuen. pp. ix + 176. pb £3.95.

that 'metafiction' is not so much 'ensuring the survival through adaptability of the novel itself' as inadvertently attesting to a more disturbing and more powerful 'trembling' (Derrida's word in *Positions*, 1981), signalled in earlier work such as Blanchot's or, for example, Philippe Sollers's essay, 'The Novel and the Experience of Limits' (*YW* 64.589).

Waugh gives repeated attention to the idea of reality as construct: as is indicated by its subtitle, the same could hardly be said of Kathryn Hume's *Fantasy and Mimesis: Responses to Reality in Western Literature*[16], a survey (without bibliography) of critical approaches to fantasy and of fantastic literature as 'illusion', 'vision', 'revision', and 'disillusion'. Recently issued as a paperback and also worth mentioning here is Dorrit Cohn's *Transparent Minds: Narrative Modes for Presenting Consciousness in Fiction*[17] (see also *YW* 60.347). Cohn supplies very lucid and thorough coverage of many different modes of narration, dividing these into two parts: 'Consciousness in Third-Person Context' and 'Consciousness in First-Person Texts'.

Finally, we have two books on somewhat heterogeneous topics perhaps: John R. Abercrombie's *Computer Programs for Literary Analysis*[18], which serves as 'a textbook to augment classroom instruction' and provides help with everything from morphological analysis to index and concordance compilation; and Don E. Wayne's *Penshurst: The Semiotics of Place and the Poetics of History*[19], a charming and thought-provoking study of the house and of Ben Jonson's poem, 'To Penshurst'.

2. Narrative Theory

In *Reading for the Plot: Design and Intention in Narrative*[20], Peter Brooks defines his text as an attempt to 'move beyond strict allegiance to the various formalisms that have dominated the study of narrative in recent decades'. Brooks perhaps exaggerates the extent and contemporaneity of this allegiance, although this theme recurs in a number of the studies of narrative fiction published this year. Marxism, or at least its metaphors – commodification, use, and exchange – and psychoanalysis are employed and deployed in the critical endeavour to return history and the subject to the field of narratology. Earlier versions of most of the chapters in *Reading for the Plot* have previously appeared in periodicals. The text does not, however, appear essayistic, primarily because Brooks has produced a powerful linking structure and two excellent introductory chapters, in which he defines his two major areas of concern, the nature of 'plotting' and of 'narrative desire'. The second of these chapters also includes a valuable formulation of the distinction between the hermeneutic and the proaireutic codes of narrative, worked through

16. *Fantasy and Mimesis: Responses to Reality in Western Literature*, by Kathryn Hume. Methuen. pp. xvi + 213. hb £16, pb £6.95.

17. *Transparent Minds: Narrative Modes for Presenting Consciousness in Fiction*, by Dorrit Cohn. Princeton (1983). pp. x + 331. hb £28.40, pb £8.80.

18. *Computer Programs for Literary Analysis*, by John R. Abercrombie. UPenn. pp. 203. pb £12.30.

19. *Penshurst: The Semiotics of Place and the Poetics of History*, by Don E. Wayne. Methuen. pp. xv + 228. £20.

20. *Reading for the Plot: Design and Intention in Narrative*, by Peter Brooks. OUP. pp. 363. £17.50.

Conan Doyle's 'The Musgrave Ritual' and Rousseau's *Confessions* in ways which illuminate both texts.

Brooks defines plot as the logic and dynamic of narrative, 'the organizing dynamic of a specific mode of human understanding'. Narratology, formalism, and poetics, he states, have failed to take into account the transformative and the temporal elements within narratives, either by confining their analyses to the minimal units of discourse, or by failing to see that plot, defined here as the transformation from story to discourse, is an active, dynamic, and temporal process.

Brooks calls upon a specific version of psychoanalysis as an extraliterary narrative model upon which to structure his analyses of nineteenth- and twentieth-century narratives: the energetic, dynamic, and transformative model which emerges in Freud's *Beyond the Pleasure Principle*. However, it remains a structural model rather than an interpretative or explanatory system in Brooks's analyses of *Le Rouge et Le Noir*, *L'Education sentimentale*, *La Peau de Chagrin*, *Great Expectations*, *The Wolf-Man*, *Heart of Darkness*, and *Absalom, Absalom! Reading for the Plot* remains a work of narrative theory rather than becoming psychoanalytic literary criticism. Particularly stimulating are Brooks's chapters on *Great Expectations*, in which, as in his analysis of 'The Musgrave Ritual', he turns the multiple meanings of 'plot' to full advantage, and on *L'Education sentimentale* as a commentary on the nature of narration itself – although history does not become an absence in Brooks's reading of Flaubert. *Reading for the Plot* is an important critical work, which provides valuable reformulations of narrative theory, together with highly informative and insightful textual analysis. It is not least commendable for its lucidity.

By comparison, the introductory chapters of Ross Chambers's *Story and Situation: Narrative Seduction and the Power of Fiction*[21] emerge as a ransacking, rather than an articulation, of theoretical positions and critical discourses. Wlad Godzich provides a generous foreword, in which he endorses the eclecticism of Chambers's approach, while giving a short but lucid exposition of his sources and influences, including an account of Walter Benjamin's writing on story and narrative. Chambers himself defines his interest in story-telling as a concern with its performative function, the communicational situations and contexts which texts produce within their narrative structures. His criticism of narratology is that it has neglected 'those textual indices of contractual and transactional understandings', thus ignoring the 'point' of literature. He turns to the nineteenth century 'art tale' – never clearly defined but exampled by Balzac's *Sarrasine*, Flaubert's *Un Coeur Simple*, James's 'The Figure in the Carpet' and Joyce's 'The Dead' – as representative of literary narrative, although at other times the 'art tale' is imbued with the special properties of foregrounding models of narrative exchange, contract, and context – as in Poe's 'The Purloined Letter'. Chambers's methodology revolves around a set of metaphors, the most central of which is 'seduction', less as theme than as the *modus operandi* of narratives of the last two centuries and related 'most probably' to Benjamin's distinction between the story-teller and novelistic narrative. Chambers's substitution of 'narrative' for Benjamin's 'narrator' is significant; the text itself must be seen

21. *Story and Situation: Narrative Seduction and the Power of Fiction*, by Ross Chambers. ManU. pp. 255. pb £8.50.

to exert its own 'seductive' powers at the historical point at which the story-teller loses his status. The 'ideology of the subject', which Chambers ostensibly critiques, is thus transferred to the text, conceived as capable of desiring and seducing in its own right.

Given the frequency with which the term 'seduction' occurs, it is strange that Chambers does not define its usage more clearly; he disregards its original meaning of 'leading astray' and avoids its implications as a primarily masculine fantasy of sexual power and manipulation. The issue is important, in that it highlights a regrettable critical tendency to employ metaphors whose resonances are already assured, and on which the critic has to do little work. Reification and alienation are significant examples in *Story and Situation* of terms which operate as little more than figures for Chambers, but which bring with them the giant edifice of Marxism, thus offering an illusory effect of critical totalization. Chambers's readings of the 'art tales' themselves are both more modest and more enlightening than the theoretical apparatus outlined in the book's opening chapters. His analysis of 'The Figure in the Carpet', for example, offers a close and careful reading of the relationship between narrator and reader, critic and text in James's short story. This is good textual criticism, however, rather than the stuff from which significant narrative theory is made.

Whereas Peter Brooks's concern is with the temporality of narrative, Susan Stewart examines its spatial aspects. *On Longing: Narratives of the Miniature, the Gigantic, the Souvenir, the Collection*[22] is a highly idiosyncratic text, which blurs the distinction between books as objects and literary oddities (miniature and gigantic), variable size as literary theme (the extensive use of *Gulliver's Travels* as exemplum leads one to suspect that Swift himself created an oddity rather than a narrative paradigm), and historical accounts of very small and very large people. Stewart's theoretical positions range engagingly, if arbitrarily, between Kristeva (maternal body), Bakhtin (grotesque body), and Baudrillard (fetishized body and object). *On Longing* contains some interesting reflections on our relationship to size and the meaning of exaggeration in literature, Victorian miniaturization, and postmodern expansionism, but its theorizations of narrative resemble too loose a version of Jean-François Lyotard's 'grand Narratives', the legitimizers of knowledge, to make a useful contribution to narrative theory.

Stewart's extensive use of Bakhtin leads me to brief mention of a new edition of *Rabelais and his World*[23], Bakhtin's study of folk culture, carnival, and the grotesque, but also a seminal contribution to the poetics of the novel and an analysis of the relations between language, politics, and the body. Another welcome reprint is Vladimir Propp's *Theory and History of Folklore*[24], a collection of Propp's essays on folk-lore, the 'wondertale', and heroic poetry. Also included in this edition is Claude Lévi-Strauss's essay 'Structure and Form', a critique of Propp's *Morphology of the Folktale*, and, more broadly, of the formalist enterprise, for its failure to recognize the

22. *On Longing: Narratives of the Miniature, the Gigantic, the Souvenir, the Collection*, by Susan Stewart, JHU. pp. 213. $20.
    23. *Rabelais and his World*, by Mikhail Bakhtin. IndU. pp. 484. hb. $29.50, pb. $10.95.
    24. *Theory and History of Folklore*, by Vladimir Propp. ManU. pp. 251. pb £11.50.

interdependence of form and content and of the complementarity of signifier and signified. A lengthy and very useful introduction by Anatoly Liberman contextualizes the argument between Propp and Lévi-Strauss, formalism and structuralism.

One effect of formalist criticism has been to allow for the creation of an increasing number of distinctions, subsets, and categorizations within the narrative genre. Clayton Koelb's *The Incredulous Reader*[25] is concerned with the 'literature of disbelief', and with the question of what happens when we read things we do not and cannot believe. Koelb defines his object against that of Tzvetan Todorov; 'the fantastic' involves an 'hesitation' between natural and supernatural explanations of events, whereas Koelb is concerned with texts in which there is no hesitation – in which events are clearly 'incredible' though not necessarily supernatural. Qualifying his narrative category yet further, Koelb defines the objects of his study as 'apistic fictions', those we disbelieve because our disbelief is solicited, and 'lethetic fictions', which present words that are oblivious of the world of things, and which involve a process of 'forgetting' the demands of the real on the part of the reader. In other words, the lethetic fiction gains the reader's assent, though not his/her belief. Texts analysed include Aristophanes' *The Birds*, Poe's 'The Tell-Tale Heart', and Gogol's *The Nose*.

Koelb combines reader-response theory, as articulated by Wolfgang Iser and Stanley Fish, with an exposition and analysis of a number of literary and rhetorical figures and tropes which he sees as formative of states of readerly disbelief, held in play rather than suspended. The application of figures to texts is less convincing as in his treatment of 'syllepsis' in Oscar Wilde's *The Importance of Being Earnest* which is based solely on the strength of Wilde's punning on name and adjective. Despite its title and subject matter, *The Incredulous Reader* exhibits a degree of critical literal-mindedness.

Finally, a critical text which is not ashamed to define its field as 'narratology': F. K. Stanzel's *A Theory of Narrative*[26] describes a triad of basic analytic categories – person, mode, and perspective – which are then applied to a broad spectrum of European novels. Henry James is the informing voice in *A Theory of Narrative*, in particular his theory of narrative 'reflectors', expounded most fully in the preface to *The Ambassadors*. The distinction between telling and showing, describing and narrating, formalized in Anglo-American narrative theory by Wayne Booth's *The Rhetoric of Fiction* is also extensively employed by Stanzel. This is a curiously old-fashioned work, which earnestly debates the relationships between narrator and reader (person), narrator and character (mode), and point of view (perspective). According to Stanzel, the central task of a theory of narrative is to systematize the various kinds and degrees of 'mediacy' that result from the shifting relationship between the story and how it is being told. To this end, Stanzel maps out a 'typological circle', a narrative 'programme' which is both deduced from his sample of a hundred novels and exists, curiously, as an indication of the 'possibilities' for the development of narrative fiction, in its 'realization of the ever-increasing possibilities of narration'. Stanzel's progressive

25. *The Incredulous Reader. Literature and the Function of Disbelief*, by Clayton Koelb. CornU. pp. 240. $19.50
26. *A Theory of Narrative*, by F. K. Stanzel. CUP. pp. 308.

programme for the novel is unconnected with a history, a politics, or a philosophy; the nature of its aims thus remains unclear.

3. Reception-theory and Semiotics

The cross-fertilizations between hermeneutics, reception-theory, and semiotics during the last two decades often make it difficult to draw clear lines of demarcation between these critical fields. Robert Holub provides a valuable introduction to reception-theory which also links this critical movement to traditional and contemporary hermeneutics and defines its allegiances to semiotic analysis. *Reception Theory*[27] is both a historical and a critical account which succeeds admirably in balancing explanation and argument.

Holub begins by acknowledging the difficulty of creating clear distinctions between 'reception theory' and 'reader-response theory'. His working premises are that 'reader-response criticism' is a term loosely applied to a number of critical positions, often disparate and linked only by a shared concern among its exponents with the text-reader pole of literary theory. Reception-theory, by contrast, is defined as a more cohesive undertaking, primarily associated with the University of Constance, and initiated by reactions against social, intellectual, and literary developments in West Germany during the late 1960s. Such contextualization is useful, although in itself it does not offer a theoretical definition, while the connections between reception and reader-response theory are perhaps worth more investigation than Holub allows for.

None the less, *Reception Theory* offers an extremely lucid and thorough account of its chosen area. The work of its most influential exponent, Hans Robert Jauss, is explored in detail: Holub's support throughout *Reception Theory* tends to be for theorists who provide historical and social contexts for literary reception; in a later chapter he also devotes some time to the Marxist and G.D.R. criticisms of an overly aestheticized and hermetic account of literature and its reception. The second chapter gives an extremely helpful account of reception-theory's influences and precursors, including Russian Formalism, Prague Structuralism, Phenomenology and the work of Roman Ingarden, Gadamer's hermeneutics, and the sociology of literature. The strength of this chapter is that it selects those features pertinent to the development of reception-theory without seeing these as the only significant methodological principles of five disparate theoretical areas, and then moves to a very detailed description of the more recent work of Jauss and Wolfgang Iser. Holub uses Iser's work to structure a set of crucial arguments pertaining to reception and reader-response theory, including the distinctions between real and implied readers and textual determinacy and indeterminacy. These are pursued in an account of the debate between Iser and Stanley Fish, the major American exponent of reader-response theory. Holub concludes with a brief but suggestive chapter which contrasts the theoretical premises informing poststructuralist criticism with those of reception-theory; he does not dismiss the centrality of the concept of the subject in the latter, but argues that it could

---

27. *Reception Theory: A Critical Introduction*, by Robert Holub. New Accents. Methuen. pp. 189. hb £7.95.

learn from theories which question the stability of the reading subject as well as of the text.

Much of the argument within reception and reader-response theory has centred upon the nature and constitution of the collectivities of readers invoked in order to avoid an overly subjectivized and individualized concept of the reader. The debate rages again in an exchange between Stanley Fish and Walter Davis. In 'The Fisher King: *Wille zur Macht* in Baltimore' (*CritI*) Davis launches an *ad hominem* attack on Fish, while claiming to see the latter merely as a representative, albeit an influential one, of the declining standards of literary studies in American universities. Holub points to the problems in Fish's concept of the 'interpretive community'; the text may disappear in Fish's account, but the interpretive community, although it is never defined, becomes a determinate structure controlling interpretation. Moreover, to accept Fish's position, we must accept his metacritical assumptions about conventions and communities – a further level of the determinacy which is ostensibly being denied. Davis is also concerned with these issues, but in his account, Fish becomes a critical despot reigning over subjects trained in his particular critical methodology.

Davis's arguments are familiar ones; the denial of the existence of a text not wholly dependent for its construction on interpretative strategies is a denial of both history and literature. More than this, however, Davis sees Fish's turn to the community rather than the reader as produced by a naïve belief that an appeal to sociology will resolve the epistemological problems of understanding and interpretation. Holub suggests this also, but Davis's further charge is that Fish is simply unaware of the philosophical arguments which it would be necessary to invoke to defend his own position credibly, a blindness which Davis sees as characteristic of the academic literary profession at this time. Splenetic as Davis's account is, he makes a number of telling points about the ways in which European political and philosophical debate is rendered 'harmless' in its American literary critical versions. The only arena for power struggles becomes the academic profession itself. The 'interpretive community' of reader-response theory loses all social and political contextualization and becomes a way of defining the dominant literary critical movement within English studies. Fish counters these charges rather weakly, or perhaps consciously evasively, by defending a single textual point in *Is There a Text in This Class?*; and by re-asserting the relativism of his critical assumptions. Davis's rebuttal is fuelled yet more fiercely by his reconfirmed belief that this claim to critical relativism is at once duplicitous and wholly representative of the general academic refusal to conceptualize and argue through literary and philosophical problems. It must be said that Davis's account possesses a degree of plausibility.

A far more benign interchange on the subject of literary interpretation occurs in *NLH*. The colloquium on *The Interrelation of Interpretation and Creation* brings together Richard Wollheim, René Girard, Umberto Eco, Norman Holland, and Wolfgang Iser. Eco's essay on 'Metaphor, Dictionary, and Encyclopedia' is a semiotic analysis of metaphor which aligns the Aristotelean model of metaphor with the forms of definition offered by dictionary-structures, and creates as a supplement to this a more complex analysis of metaphor akin to the structures of knowledge afforded by an encyclopaedia – 'the basis of a universe of content that is already organized into networks of interpretants, which decide (semiotically) upon the identities and differences of properties'. The hallmark of metaphor becomes its process of unlimited semiosis. Eco concludes by stating that although metaphor is structured by encyclopaedia, it also restructures encyclopaedia by opening up hitherto unforeseen modes of similarities and dissimilarities. This is a rigorous and fascinating essay.

Wolfgang Iser, in his role as discussant, draws the essays together in this *NLH* issue with remarkable clarity, and produces from them a new formulation of the relationship between creation and interpretation. His main point is that these are not so much epistemological as anthropological issues, the interplay between creation and interpretation 'reflects something inherent in the human situation'. Iser, following Girard, sees creation as both more destructive and more liberating than its conventional definitions allow; it acts as a 'decomposition' within an interpreted world which stands in need of constant re-arrangement in order to prevent it from lapsing into immobility. Interpretation becomes a means of processing creation's new arrangements. Iser is not clear as to whether creation is the activity of reader or author/artist; his formulations are suggestive but perhaps overly utopian.

Several of the essays in *The Structure of the Literary Process*[28] combine reception-theory with semiotics and poetics. Iser and Jauss appear again with essays on 'Spenser's Arcadia: The Interrelation of Fiction and History' and 'Norwid and Baudelaire as Contemporaries', respectively. Prague School poetics are also well represented, with a valuable analysis of the work of Mukarovsky and Felix Vodicka by Lubomir Dolozel, in which the relationship between structural and historical poetics is particularly well analysed. Janice Radway also discusses Mukarovsky as the foundation for a reception-theory-based study of popular fiction. In 'The Aesthetic in Mass Culture: Reading the "Popular" Literary Text', Radway uses the Gothic romance to explore the co-existence of aesthetic and non-aesthetic functions within the popular novel. Her main contention is that popular texts deny the productive aspect of the reading process and thus present meaning as a thing to be consumed; the distinction she formulates between production and consumption by the reader is an excellent corrective to less politically acute forms of reader-response theory. It is also extremely encouraging to see reception-theory which engages with the role of gender in the reader–text relationship.

Other essays in this volume include Jan van der Eng's 'The Effectiveness of the Aesthetic Function', an examination of the poetic 'devices' foregrounded by the Russian Formalists in which the author states that it is not novelty that constitutes 'literariness' but the versatile and multifarious application of old devices. The essay, although suggestive, combines formal and semiotic analysis with an emotive sense of literature in a curious admixture. Peter Steiner's essay on 'The Semiotics of Literary Reception' is more rigorous in its methodology; this is an excellent analysis of the relationship between literary and non-literary discourse – the latter to include legal, rhetorical, and scientific communication. Steiner uses the 'asymetric model' of the linguistic sign advanced by the Prague School Structuralists both to discuss the absolutist–relativist controversy central to reception-theory and to define the specific

28. *The Structure of the Literary Process*, ed. by P. Steiner, M. Cervenka, and R. Vroon. Benjamins (1982). pp. 613. $66.

nature of literary communication. The value of this essay springs, however, from the attention Steiner pays to non-literary communication; the rhetorical forms and linguistic modes of scientific and legal discourse, in particular, are all too rarely analysed. *The Structure of the Literary Process* contains several excellent essays; the volume would benefit, however, from an editorial preface and general introduction. In its present form, it will appear *in vacuo* to all but a very specialized audience. This is regrettable, in that a number of the essays raise issues of interest to those working outside the field of East European semiotics. Its present price and presentation will ensure its arcane status.

The writings of the semiotician Alexander Zholkovsky are translated into English in *Themes and Texts: Towards a Poetics of Expressiveness*[29]. Zholkovsky helped to rehabilitate the Formalists in the Soviet Union in the 1960s; he takes from Formalist poetics a focus on verbal 'devices' and formulates from this concern a 'Soviet generative poetics' or a 'poetics of expressiveness'. The main components of this poetics are 'expressive devices', defined as universal elementary transformations responsible for the gradual heightening of expressiveness on the way from the theme to the text. Zholkovsky's emphasis on the necessity for a 'scientific poetics', a literary criticism to 'compete with Einstein, not Shakespeare' is fully enacted in his analyses; this is formalism of a rigour and exactitude undreamed of by the Formalists themselves. There is a fascination in his production of networks of productive meaning from the most mimimal of literary units: an aphorism of Bertrand Russell's, a Somali proverb, the image of the window in Pasternak's writing. Image-location is, of course, used in very different forms of literary criticism; Dorothy van Ghent's essay on window-imagery in *Wuthering Heights* comes to mind in this context. The crucial difference is that van Ghent employs imagery for antithetical ends; Zholkovsky wholly refuses symbolic readings in favour of functionalist analysis. There are moments, however, when Zholkovsky's analyses set up the expectation of the form of fruitful conjuncture between functionalism and cultural codings that occur in Barthes' *S/Z*. Zholkovsky ultimately refuses the move into cultural readings, re-asserting the lexical and linguistic nature of his codes. As a critical tour-de-force, *Themes and Texts* resembles *S/Z*; it cannot, however, take us as far in an understanding of the relationship between language and social meaning.

4. Rhetoric and Deconstruction

How deconstruction relates to the ethical and political remains a fundamental issue. It is treated, if obliquely, by Christopher Butler in his *Interpretation, Deconstruction, and Ideology*[30], a study of linguistic, structuralist, deconstructive, and Marxist approaches to literary texts. Butler's concern with 'pragmatic ends that are important within the theory of interpretation' is clarified only at the end of the book, where he finally testifies to 'the radical–liberal position from which the foregoing argument has been conducted'. It is from within this context, then, that kinds of deconstructive criticism are to be judged useful and significant, or not. Butler's study can be

29. *Themes and Texts: Towards a Poetics of Expressiveness*, by Alexander Zholkovsky. CornU. pp. 300. $35.

30. *Interpretation, Deconstruction, and Ideology: An Introduction to Some Current Issues in Literary Theory*, by Christopher Butler. OUP. pp. x + 159. pb £5.95.

contrasted with an article by Nancy Fraser in *NGC*, entitled 'The French Derrideans: Politicizing Deconstruction or Deconstructing the Political?' This is an important and impressive account of the Center for Philosophical Research on the Political, set up in the wake of the 1981 Cerisy conference. It concentrates, in particular, on the work of Jean-Luc Nancy and Philippe Lacoue-Labarthe and on the idea of the ethical and political as 'the practical effectuation of the philosophical'. In this essay Fraser also urges 'French postmarxists to develop links with German Critical Theory and Anglo-American socialist feminism'.

The politics of Paul de Man's work have consistently been a subject of debate and disagreement. Barbara Johnson's 'Rigorous Unreliability', in *CritI*, is a succinct and very cogent introduction to his work. It is especially admirable for its close reading and careful exposition of de Man's 'Semiology and Rhetoric' (in *Allegories of Reading*, 1979). Besides posing such splendidly rhetorical questions as, 'Couldn't subjectivity be defined as a grammatical mistake?', Johnson argues that 'the "real mystery" for de Man would seem to be the eternal return of the moral imperative to resist reading'. This 'real mystery' is one, she suggests, 'about which no moral imperative to leap from textuality to subjectivity or history can tell us more than de Man's stubborn labyrinths of rigor, resistance, and profoundly meaningful unreliability'.

De Man's *The Rhetoric of Romanticism*[31], a posthumously published collection of essays written between 1956 and 1983, is in keeping with Johnson's characterization. Two of these essays, 'Intentional Structure of the Romantic Image' and 'Shelley Disfigured', are already justly famous. 'The Image of Rousseau in the Poetry of Hölderlin' (1965) and 'Wordsworth and Hölderlin' (1966) appear here for the first time in English: 'Wordsworth and Hölderlin' is a particularly remarkable meditation on the historical nature and conception of Romanticism. 'Autobiography As De-Facement' (1979) focuses on Wordsworth's *Essays upon Epitaphs* and elaborates a captivating account of autobiography in relation to prosopopeia. 'Wordsworth and the Victorians' takes Wordsworth as 'a poet of sheer language', exploring the idea that 'it is as if his language came from a region in which the most carefully drawn distinctions between analytic rigor and poetic persuasion are no longer preserved, at no small risk to either'. 'Symbolic Landscape in Wordsworth and Yeats' (1962) offers close and innovative readings of Wordsworth's 'Composed by the Side of Grasmere Lake' and Yeats's 'Coole Park and Ballylee, 1931'. This essay complements 'Image and Emblem in Yeats' which, taken from de Man's Ph.D. dissertation (1960), is the longest and earliest piece in the book. It is especially interesting for its lucid and analytically thorough treatment of Yeats's work as a whole.

The final two essays in *The Rhetoric of Romanticism* are also the most recent. 'Anthropomorphism and Trope in the Lyric' moves from Nietzsche's *On Truth and Lie* to Baudelaire's 'Correspondances' and 'Obsession', concluding with the powerful assertion that 'generic terms such as "lyric" (or its various sub-species, "ode", "idyll", or "elegy") as well as pseudo-historical period terms such as "romanticism" and "classicism" are always terms of resistance and nostalgia, at the furthest remove from the materiality of actual history'. 'Aesthetic Formalization: Kleist's *Über das Marionettentheater*'

31. *The Rhetoric of Romanticism*, by Paul de Man. ColU. pp. ix + 327. £17.30.

LITERARY THEORY 779

provides excellent illustrations of 'rigorous unreliability' as well as general observations about the relation of politics and education to the aesthetic which is here viewed as 'one of the most powerful ideological drives to act upon the reality of history'; de Man also observes that 'the politics of the aesthetic state are the politics of education'.

One of the most striking features of *The Rhetoric of Romanticism* is the general absence of the term 'deconstruction': in his preface, de Man refers to the 'rhetorical analysis of figural language', a phrase which of course embraces both literary and philosophical discourse. Distinctions between deconstruction in 'philosophical' and in 'literary' contexts are considered by Ralph Flores in the opening pages of his *The Rhetoric of Doubtful Authority*[32]. The introductory chapter, 'Questioning the Question of Authority', ranges over a number of topics – history, genealogy and filiation, dissemination as 'rhetoricity', the nature of questions, of authority, and of monstrosity. Of the general import of Derrida's work Flores suggests that 'the Derridean dislocation may be powerful precisely to the extent of its unpredictability, its strangeness, and above all, its slowness'. Flores goes on, in the chapters which follow, to provide a series of engaging and forceful 'deconstructive readings of self-questioning narratives' – from St Augustine and Descartes to *Don Quixote, Tristram Shandy*, and *Absalom, Absalom!* These readings are described as 'of doubtful authority (there can be no "pure" deconstruction) and are offered only as possible readings among others'. In fact, they are also a little disappointing: the introductory chapter is wide-ranging and has a potency and freshness which, while admirable in themselves, make the succeeding chapters seem by comparison rather narrow.

Jeffrey Mehlman comments on what he regards as 'the general interpretative effort called "deconstruction"' in his original and characteristically acute study, *Legacies of Anti-Semitism in France*[33]: 'The discovery and valorization of the marginal, that is, and its intricate displacement to a strategic (near-)center from which a chiasmic shift in the values of a *corpus* may be effected strike me as among the most difficult and rewarding gestures that reading at present allows.' *Legacies of Anti-Semitism in France* is indeed an intricate work, and chiasmus its recurring and predominant figure. The 'marginal' here is anti-Semitism which, 'by dint of Europe's recent history, is one of the few taboo regions of speculation in our secularized democracies'. Mehlman's aim is to demonstrate 'a lost anti-Semitic tradition' running through twentieth-century French literature. He achieves this through extremely subtle and persuasive close readings of (often little known) texts by Blanchot, Lacan, Giradoux, and Gide. *Legacies of Anti-Semitism in France* is at another level pursuing certain readings of Freud and Derrida; in this respect it has interests broadly analogous to the Jewish 'heretic hermeneutics' outlined in Susan Handelman's *The Slayers of Moses* (*YW* 64.591). Mehlman's study is written explicitly 'under the aegis of the later Freud – and his liberating articulation of repetition, interpretation, and masochism'. One of its least expected conclusions, supported by a reading of

32. *The Rhetoric of Doubtful Authority: Deconstructive Readings of Self-Questioning Narratives, St. Augustine to Faulkner*, by Ralph Flores. CornU. pp. 175. $17.50.
33. *Legacies of Anti-Semitism in France*, by Jeffrey Mehlman. UMinn (1983). pp. 141. hb $25, pb $10.95.

Glas (1974), is that Derrida 'has turned his work into a protracted meditation on the institution of circumcision'. An appendix on the work of Julien Gracq moves away from specific questions about Judaism and anti-Semitism, however, and is concerned with the idea of literature as 'blackgracq' and with 'the transition between the poetic effect *per se* and the author's signature or name'. In current literary theory this concern is perhaps more predictable and more significant.

For it is clear that in many ways the literary theoretical preoccupation with deconstruction is being displaced onto an involvement with the notions of signature and proper name. This movement is neatly illustrated by Mehlman's provocative and ingenious study. It is also evident in *The Rhetoric of Doubtful Authority*, proceeding from a remark Flores makes in his opening chapter: 'If signs are undecidably other, however, we may be unable to master our representations; who, in that case, can be a singular writing agent, and by what authority?'

Derrida's engagement with the notions of signature and proper name is of long standing; but it is nowhere more sustained, more difficult, and more compelling than in *Signéponge / Signsponge*[34], published in French in 1976–7, parts of which earlier appeared in English in *OLR* (1982). It now appears as a bilingual text, finely translated by Richard Rand. Described in Rand's preface as 'the most irruptive essay on literature to have come before the English-speaking public since Mallarmé's *La Musique et les lettres* [1894]', *Signsponge* meditates on the work of 'Francis Ponge' and displays a singularity consistently found in Derrida's work: it is a text disorientatingly by 'Derrida' and by the 'author' under analysis (here Ponge, hence signé Ponge); and simultaneously by neither. It is doubly exemplary: it is the 'classical' contemporary text concerned with the signature and proper name, opening the way for other work in this field; and yet it is at the same time singular – inextricably binding or absorbing the name of Francis Ponge (as example) with the theoretical elaboration of the structure and operation of the signature (as sponge, éponge, et ponge, est ponge, etc.) in general.

Signsponge moves off from Derrida's observation that literary critics and philologists

> may wonder whether a certain piece of writing is indeed assignable to a certain author, but as regards the event of the signature, the abyssal machinery of this operation, the commerce between the said author and his proper name, in other words, whether he signs when he signs, whether his proper name is truly his name and truly proper, before or after the signature, and how all this is affected by the logic of the unconscious, the structure of the language, the paradoxes of name and reference, of nomination and description, the links between common and proper names, names of things and personal names, the proper and the non-proper, no question is ever posed by any of the regional disciplines which are, as such, concerned with texts known as literary.

In fact, since this essay's appearance in French, work has been done – most notably by the translator, Richard Rand, on Coleridge ('Geraldine' in *Untying*

34. *Signéponge / Signsponge*, by Jacques Derrida, trans. by Richard Rand. ColU. pp. xi + 160. £24.

the Text, edited by Robert Young (1981)) and on Keats ('o'er-brimm'd' in *OLR* (1982)). And, of course, there is Derrida's own work on, for example, the proper name of Freud in *La Carte postale* (1980) (see *YW* 62.32–3). But, in part as a response to *La Carte postale*, 1984 has seen a marked increase in the number of essays in this area.

One may place 'signature' in the non-synonymic chain which includes terms such as 'deconstruction', 'différance', 'trace', 'hymen', and so on. Yet it must also be evident that the notion of signature in Derrida's work functions as a powerful equivalent (at the same time as being radically heterogeneous) to that of narcissism in psychoanalytic discourse. There are perhaps dangers of a broad appropriation, however paradoxical or impossible, of this work on the signature in a manner similar to the U.S. 'domestication' of deconstruction. In both cases there remains the possibility that a classical model of self-reflexivity, and linked assumptions concerning the status of the human subject, will neither be abandoned nor exceeded.

One of the implications of *Signsponge* is that signature-effects, whether manifest as a 'good' or a 'bad' signing, whether conscious or unconscious, etc., operate across all discourses: they represent a spanner in works in general, not only literary ones, but psychoanalytical, philosophical, and so on. The issues at stake here are considerable and of considerable excitement. Work on the signature and proper name has already taken several directions. Derrida's 'Fors', the preface to Nicolas Abraham's and Maria Torok's *Cryptonymie* (1976), marked the opening of the very strange question of how one proper name or signature might incorporate, haunt, or 'live' on (the text of) another. Derrida's 'Télépathie', published in *Furor* in 1981, involves a bizarre 'correspondance' with Freud; a stimulating collection of essays (by Hélène Cixous, Stephen Heath, Jacques Aubert, Jean-Michel Rabaté, André Topia, and Daniel Ferrer, with an introduction by Derek Attridge and Ferrer), entitled *Post-structuralist Joyce*[35], also contains Derrida's 'Two words for Joyce', in which he speaks of his 'feeling about Joyce' and, in particular, '*being in memory of him*'. A special issue of *MLN*, commemorating the death in September last year of Eugenio Donato, contains an essay by Derrida entitled 'An Idea of Flaubert: "Plato's Letter"' and another by Donato himself, entitled 'Who Signs "Flaubert"?'. These two essays complement and supplement each other. Donato's epigraph is from 'Fors': 'The Self: a cemetery guard'. In both essays there is a concern with autobiography as 'always a thanatography'; as Donato concludes, 'if the proper name "Flaubert" remains illegible, it is partly because it is engendered by another proper name which could almost be said to be that of "Loulou-Le Poittevin"; however, "Loulou-Le Poittevin", being a name of a dead person, itself remains illegible except through the proper name "Flaubert", which it renders possible by its own encryptment (*mise en crypte*)'.

In so far as the work of the signature involves 'the desire for the proper joined with the most utterly assumed phallocentrism', *Signsponge* might appear of only negative or very dubious interest to feminism. However, Gayatri Chakravorty Spivak's brilliant 'Love Me, Love My Ombre, Elle', which appears in *Diac*, offers an extremely suggestive account of the signature and proper name of Derrida in relation to the special importance given to the

35. *Post-structuralist Joyce: Essays from the French*, ed. by Derek Attridge and Daniel Ferrer. CUP. pp. xi + 162. hb £20, pb £6.95.

name of 'woman' in his texts. Of Derrida, Spivak also writes, 'It is surely significant that, even today, the men who take to him take everything from him but his project of re-naming the operation of philosophy with the "name" of woman.' Spivak's article can be juxtaposed to David Wills's 'Post / Card / Match / Book / *Envois* / Derrida', in *Substance*. Wills examines the 'Envois' section of *La Carte postale* 'in the light of narrative and its relations with communication theory'. Like Spivak, Wills provides careful readings of parts of *La Carte postale*, while indicating a certain dissatisfaction or scepticism, allied to a consideration of the inscription and significance of Derrida's own signature and proper name. Derrida's postcards, Wills suggests, 'are to my mind trying to lay one on me while at the same time hedging their bets'.

   Taking Chances: Derrida, Psychoanalysis, and Literature[36] represents an important unsettling of the ways in which one might conceive of chance, risk, play, bets and debts, and, again, the signature and proper name. In their introduction Joseph H. Smith and William Kerrigan outline one of the main issues addressed by the contributors to this volume: 'Is psychoanalysis willing to say that it is literature? If it does, will scientists be willing to say that literature / psychoanalysis is a science?' *Taking Chances* opens with Derrida's 'My Chances / *Mes Chances*: A Rendezvous with Some Epicurean Stereophonies'. This dynamic essay proceeds from an observation about the ' "worlds" of science, literature, the arts, or the humanities': 'Their frontiers are those of "contexts" and justificatory procedures currently undergoing rapid transformation.' The supposition or imposition of limits and boundaries is crucial: 'deliberate self-limitation gives psychoanalysis its only chance as a science'. 'What is the difference', Derrida also asks, 'between superstition or paranoia on the one hand, and science on the other, if they all mark a compulsive tendency to interpret random signs in order to reconstitute a meaning, a necessity, or a destination?' Experiences and events ascribed to chance by Freud are analysed and rewritten by Derrida: the resulting indeterminacy regarding the place and status of chance in relation to psychoanalysis, science, and literature is exhilarating indeed.

   Samuel Weber's contribution to *Taking Chances* is 'The Debts of Deconstruction and Other Related Assumptions'. This essay, in many respects Weber's most challenging and intriguing to date, operates very much at the level of suggestion or implication – of the '*perhaps*' which he isolates as of particular interest in Derrida's reading of Freud's *Beyond the Pleasure Principle*, in *La Carte postale*. Weber moves elegantly across texts by Nietzsche, Freud, Heidegger, and Derrida and considers the notions of 'debt' and 'assumption' with especial care. The proper name is of fundamental importance here. Focusing on Derrida's reading of *Beyond the Pleasure Principle*, Weber is concerned with 'the manner in which an irresistible process of repetition *assumes* the aspect and the allure of a *proper name*'. This leads him to ask, '*who* is repeating *whom*: Freud Derrida or Derrida Freud?', and at least to imply that what in some way exceeds 'deconstruction' is the proper name.

   The final essay in the volume, '*Goethezeit*' by Avital Ronell, compares with work such as Mehlman's and Weber's in its combining intricacy and inventiveness with a formidable and uncanny sense precisely of 'taking chances'. This is

---

   36. *Taking Chances: Derrida, Psychoanalysis, and Literature*, ed. and intro. by Joseph H. Smith and William Kerrigan. JHU. pp. xvi + 191. £17.80.

the movement of discourse into a space where the logic of demonstration and verification, of proof and truth, has lost its former 'proper' place. 'Goethezeit' is a deeply thought-provoking account of textual relations between 'Goethe' and 'Freud', working around the extraordinary notion that the manner of Freud's death is essentially related to the effects of the texts of Goethe.

Taking Chances also contains 'The Double Game: An Introduction', by Alan Bass; 'Atoms Again: The Deaths of Individualism', by William Kerrigan; 'Institutional Authority vs. Critical Power, or the Uneasy Relations of Psychoanalysis and Literature', by David Carroll; and 'Thomas Hardy, Jacques Derrida, and the "Dislocation of Souls"', by J. Hillis Miller. Of these David Carroll's is the most significant: it forms an excellent complement to Nancy Fraser's 'The French Derrideans', this time on questions of the domestication and political implications of Derrida's work in the U.S.A. It ends by advocating 'a healthy pessimism concerning authority, especially one's own, . . . in order to resist the inevitable attempts to institutionalize all potentially critical and disruptive forces'.

Carroll's essay is useful also for its coverage of Derrida's 'Géopsychanalyse: "and the rest of the world"' (1981), still unpublished in translation; Hillis Miller's performs a similar service in giving an account of 'Télépathie'. That such important essays remain as yet unavailable in translation is indicative of the volume and diversity of Derrida's writing. This year has also seen the publication of his 'Of an Apocalyptic Tone Recently Adopted in Philosophy' in *OLR* (see *YW* 62.56). *Boundary 2* publishes 'voice ii', an exchange of letters between Derrida and Verena Conley, of particular interest to feminists because it elaborates on issues raised in the exchange between Derrida and Christie V. McDonald in 'Choreographies', in *Diac* (1982). 'Where there is voice,' writes Derrida, 'sex becomes undecided.' This fascination with voice can be related to 'Of an Apocalyptic Tone' and especially to its astonishing 'rendition' of the word 'Come'. *Diac*'s 'Nuclear Criticism' is a special issue concerned with 'the application of literary critical procedures to the logic and rhetoric of nuclear war', together with 'the interpretation of canonical texts through the perspective of nuclear criticism'. Included here are Frances Ferguson's 'The Nuclear Sublime', which sees 'the nuclear as the unthinkable to be the most recent version of the notion of the sublime'; Michael McCanles's 'Machiavelli and the Paradoxes of Deterrence', which argues persuasively that 'unmasking the paradoxes of deterrence is . . . a vital role that the resources peculiar to literary criticism, particularly of the deconstructive variety, can play in our present situation'; and Derrida's 'No Apocalypse, Not Now (full speed ahead, seven missiles, seven missives)', which is in some respects his most overtly 'political' essay published in English to date. With 'Of an Apocalyptic Tone', it offers a superb and complex description of the apocalyptic, especially with reference to the present historical conjuncture. In the meantime we await with interest developments in the new field of nuclear criticism.

Finally it is worth observing that work published this year has indicated an increasing awareness of the relations between the texts of Derrida and Heidegger. The appearance of Heidegger's *The Metaphysical Foundations of Logic*[37]

37. *The Metaphysical Foundations of Logic*, by Martin Heidegger, trans. and intro. by Michael Heim. IndU. pp. xii + 241. $25.

(with a useful introduction by the translator, Michael Heim) will no doubt add to this. An issue of *YFS* entitled 'Concepts of Closure' contains Eugenio Donato's 'Ending / Closure: On Derrida's Edging of Heidegger'. This fine essay begins by noting that 'the task of reading Derrida's relation to Heidegger is, at the present crossroads of critical theory, urgent and necessary yet probably impossible' (in part because of the enormous amount of Heidegger's work not yet available), but goes on to argue that it is 'literariness' which differentiates Heidegger from Derrida (and also Nietzsche). 'Derrida's philosophical enterprise implies the practice of a literary idiom', suggests Donato and he concludes by asking, 'is not the quest for the literariness of literature, for the "thing" literature which grounds our literary reading/writing as literary critics the very quest, the always/already improbable future, of our impossible practice?' By contrast, in an article in *CritI* entitled 'Deconstruction and Circumvention', Richard Rorty focuses on similarities between Heidegger and Derrida, arguing among other things that their shared claim 'that the "ontotheological" tradition has permeated science, literature, and politics – that it is central to our culture – is a self-deceptive attempt to magnify the importance of an academic speciality'. More specific and more detailed, a short piece by John Sallis, 'Heidegger / Derrida – Presence', which appears in *JP*, suggests that Derrida's reading of Heidegger's formulation of 'presence' is rather limited to the 1927 text of *Being and Time*. *JP* also contains 'Origin(s) in (of) Heidegger / Derrida', by Edward S. Casey.

Heidegger's work is one of the topics covered by Robert Magliola in his *Derrida on the Mend*[38]. This is the most exhaustive study to date focusing on the theological dimensions and/or analogues of Derrida's work. In the first part Magliola provides a stimulating account of Derrida's work, and of différance in particular; in the second part attention switches to Heidegger. The third consists of a clear and extremely interesting exposition of Nagarjuna and argues for its importance alongside and indeed 'beyond Derrida'. Following on from this, the final part is concerned with a 'differential' Christianity. 'God' here becomes 'differential but Divine *mise-en-abyme*'.

5. Feminist Criticism

Popular fiction for women has become one of the central areas of research and debate in feminist criticism. One reason for this is the striking sociological fact of the success in recent years of mass-market romances produced by publishers like Harlequin and Mills & Boon. Feminists have sought, on the one hand, to account for the appeal of such fiction to its readers, and, on the other, to counter the prevailing tendency to dismiss it as unworthy of serious attention. Rather than assume that romances simply reflect and reinforce familiar forms of patriarchal and capitalist oppression of women in a way that requires no further explanation, critics have set about analysing in detail what romances can reveal about the structuring and mechanisms of that oppression, and how the reading of them may also function as a means, or a symptom, of indirect resistance to it.

Three books on romances have appeared this year, as well as a number of articles. Tania Modleski's suggestive and compact study, *Loving with a*

---

38. *Derrida on the Mend*, by Robert Magliola. PurdueU. pp. xiv + 238. $18.

Vengeance: Mass-produced Fantasies for Women[39] covers romances, gothics, and soap operas. Modleski uses psychoanalytic and narrative theory to argue that romances both expose and temporarily allay the psychic conflicts inherent in the contemporary determinations of femininity. Janice A. Radway's *Reading the Romance: Women, Patriarchy and Popular Literature*[40] is equally sophisticated and wide-ranging in its use and interrogation of theoretical approaches. The study takes its opening from the probable disparity between the textual analyses of academic critics and those of the romances' regular readers. In a detailed working through of Stanley Fish's concept of the 'interpretive community', the book is then based on a sociological investigation of the responses of one group of women to the novels and of their understanding of how romance reading functions in their daily lives. From this, via structural analyses of the texts specifically preferred or disliked by the readers, and psychoanalytic postulates derived from Nancy Chodorow, Radway proceeds to concluding hypotheses not dissimilar from Modleski's. Where Modleski argues that mass 'art simultaneously challenges and reaffirms traditional values, behaviour and attitudes', Radway suggests that romance reading possibly 'supplies vicariously those very needs and requirements that might otherwise be formulated as demands in the real world and lead to the potential restructuring of sexual relations'. But the case, for Radway, is far from proven given the so far limited scope of empirical research and given an apparent shift within the genre to narratives of a quasi-feminist cast.

Margaret Ann Jensen in *Love's Sweet Return: The Harlequin Story*[41] is much more sanguine both about the significance of the new type of plot and about the facility of establishing criteria for determining this: 'Will some of the positive trends that have emerged recently continue, or will the genre backtrack?' Less concerned than the other two with theoretical questions, Jensen's book, like Radway's, supplies much background information on the institutional history and structure of the romance publishing business, and includes reports of interviews with readers as well as descriptions of novels.

In an article in *FR* which focuses on one of the best-selling romances ever, Daphne du Maurier's *Rebecca*, Alison Light demonstrates, like Modleski and Radway, how the genre both raises and provisionally resettles questions of female sexuality and identity. But Light extends the social analysis in terms of patriarchy to address the problem of class-specific constructions of femininity. In this case the narrative invites and then tries to suppress a pleasurable identification on the part of the reader with a Rebecca whose strong sexuality must ultimately give way to the safely middle-class gentility of her husband's second wife.

Two strong essays in the collection *Popular Fiction and Social Change*[42] also interrogate the relations between particular forms of romance and their tacit ideological implications. In 'True To Me Always', a study of 1930s magazine

39. *Loving with a Vengeance: Mass-produced Fantasies for Women*, by Tania Modleski. Methuen. pp. 140. pb £4.95.
40. *Reading the Romance: Women, Patriarchy and Popular Literature*, by Janice A. Radway. UNC. pp. x + 274. hb £25, pb £7.95.
41. *Love's Sweet Return: The Harlequin Story*, by Margaret Ann Jensen. WP. pp. 188. pb £4.95.
42. *Popular Fiction and Social Change*, ed. by Christopher Pawling. Macmillan. pp. vii + 241. hb £14, pb £4.95.

fiction, Bridget Fowler is concerned not so much with class-based definitions of sexuality as with the promotion of a bourgeois ideology of 'possessive individualism' to the working-class readers of these stories. Rosalind Brunt's piece on Barbara Cartland succeeds in revealing the 'Queen of Romance' to be nothing less or more than an 'inadvertent feminist'. Cartland's public pronouncements and the narrative structure of her novels turn out to reveal the precise determinations of female oppression in a patriarchal capitalist society, in that they stress the value of a 'virginity' whose sole attribute is that of a priceless commodity.

In a volume of essays on gender, youth, and popular culture[43], Valerie Walkerdine's 'Some Day My Prince Will Come' looks at the precarious formation of female subjectivity in and through stories in girls' comics. Walkerdine's lucidly written piece draws on the feminist reading of Lacan to show the inadequacy of popular fiction studies which assume that subjectivity, including the terms of sexual difference, is straightforwardly imprinted on a passively receptive reader. Rather, like the writers discussed above who are interested in analysing the structuring of the desires to which romances partially answer, Walkerdine is against the view that romances should be seen as simply or successfully oppressive in relation to hypothetically pristine, unmarked consumers.

Other work in this growing field of feminist criticism includes Rosalind Coward's *Female Desire: Women's Sexuality Today*[44]. Written in a deliberately accessible style, this book consists of a series of short pieces analysing representations of femininity, sexuality, and desire in popular media ranging through advertising, television, fashion, and popular fiction.

Questions of femininity and fantasy are explored from many angles in *Pleasure and Danger*[45], a vast anthology which bears witness to the diversity of disciplinary and non-disciplinary approaches that can usefully be combined and compared in addressing feminist questions. The book includes autobiographical, historical, and theoretical material and is particularly directed towards the interpretation of the recent history of debates in the women's movement about sexuality.

Several contributions, especially those by Bette Gordon and Kaja Silverman, engage questions of cinematic representation. Gordon's essay concerns problems of female pleasure in looking addressed through her own film, *Variety*. Silverman sets out, via a Foucauldian reading of Pauline Réage's *Histoire d'O*, to analyse the construction of the female subject in terms which avoid either taking the body as a 'pre-cultural given' (Irigaray, Montrelay, Kristeva), or treating it as simply a floating signifier (the *m/f* position). Teresa de Lauretis's *Alice Doesn't: Feminism, Semiotics, Cinema*[46] draws particularly on the work of Stephen Heath. She blends semiotics, psychoanalysis, and narrative theory to analyse, through the paradigm of filmic representation,

43. *Gender and Generation*, ed. by Angela McRobbie and Mica Nava. Macmillan. pp. xii + 228. hb £15, pb £6.95.
44. *Female Desire: Women's Sexuality Today*, by Rosalind Coward. Paladin. pp. viii + 253. pb £2.95.
45. *Pleasure and Danger: Exploring Female Sexuality*, ed. by Carole S. Vance. RKP. pp. xix + 462. hb £12.95, pb £6.95.
46. *Alice Doesn't: Feminism, Semiotics, Cinema*, by Teresa de Lauretis. Macmillan. pp. ix + 220. hb £20, pb £6.95.

the ways in which women do and don't find an identity under the patriarchal sign of 'woman'. Also working within questions of cinema and psychoanalysis, and utilizing especially the questions raised by the Lacanians Jean Laplanche and J.-B. Pontalis, Elizabeth Cowie's *m/f* piece 'Fantasia' both summarizes and interrogates the terms of the current feminist debate on fantasy.

Verena Andermatt Conley's book on Hélène Cixous[47] presents the work of a French feminist writer who moves between fiction, philosophy, psychoanalysis, and literary criticism in order to challenge the coherence and fixity of masculine categories from the position of a 'feminine border'. Cixous' work, like that of Luce Irigaray and Julia Kristeva, has been influential for British and American literary critics in suggesting a feminist critique and re-orientation of French poststructuralist philosophy and psychoanalysis. Conley's book, in addition to making available passages of previously untranslated writings, supplies a valuable exposition of Cixous' projects, showing their changing relation to the cultural and historical situation from which she writes.

Virago's volume of essays by Juliet Mitchell[48] collects a range of work by the author of *Woman's Estate* and *Psychoanalysis and Feminism*, including the influential 1966 article 'Women: The Longest Revolution', which gives the book its title. Moving between politics, literature, and psychoanalysis, and mediated by her own introductions, the essays show the shifts and continuities in Mitchell's questions and priorities and also, indirectly, cast light on the history of feminist debates over the past twenty years.

K. K. Ruthven's *Feminist Literary Studies: An Introduction*[49] does not fall so easily into a generic classification as the title might suggest. The author declares himself anxious to defend the credentials of a man undertaking such an enterprise; yet at the same time he points out that 'it is easier for men . . . to object to the more ridiculous manifestations of feminist criticism', since 'a woman might feel diffident about having herself represented as a patriarchally brainwashed traitor to her own sex simply for saying that women don't always see eye to eye with one another'. Rhetoric of this kind makes fascinating reading for anyone who needs convincing of the need for feminist literary studies. The book has the advantage of providing many references to articles in Australian and American journals not well known in Britain.

Written from a rather different standpoint, Hester Eisenstein's *Contemporary Feminist Thought*[50] offers a succinct analytical synopsis of the past fifteen years of feminist theory. Eisenstein traces the development from an initial moment of challenge to patriarchal forms, through a separatist phase of 'woman-centred' criticism based on distinctively female values, to argue that the present stage of feminist engagement requires a politics and theory that take account of cultural as well as sexual differences.

47. *Hélène Cixous*, by Verena Andermatt Conley. UNeb. pp. x + 181. $16.95.
48. *Women: The Longest Revolution: Essays in Feminism, Literature and Psychoanalysis*, by Juliet Mitchell. Virago. pp. xi + 335. pb £5.95.
49. *Feminist Literary Studies: An Introduction*, by K. K. Ruthven. CUP. p. viii + 152. hb £16.50, pb £4.95.
50. *Contemporary Feminist Thought*, by Hester Eisenstein. A&U. pp. xviii + 216. hb £9.95, pb £3.50.

6. Marxist, Historical, and Discursive Criticism

The work of the Frankfurt school continues to hold an important position within Marxist criticism and Adorno's elevation to the status of a 'Modern Master' is evidence of this. Martin Jay's *Adorno*[51] is an attempt to introduce the difficult work of this major cultural theorist to a non-specialized audience. In so doing, however, Jay risks the possibility of simplifying the work of a theorist who would have been appalled at such a prospect: Adorno once commented that 'the splinter in your eye is the best magnifying glass'. In fact, Jay resists the temptation to simplify and gives an accurate account of Adorno's work by arranging his exposition around five principal themes: Marxism, aesthetic modernism, mandarin cultural conservatism, the 'Jewish impulse', and 'the anticipation of deconstruction'. His account starts with a short biography followed by an examination of the essay 'Subject–Object' outlining Adorno's work on subjectivity and consciousness. Jay then proceeds to look at Adorno's rejection of economistic Marxism and his critical use of psychoanalysis in order to analyse 'culture and the individual psyche'. The conclusion offers a consideration of Adorno's own musical, literary, and critical works and attempts to relate them to Adorno's attitudes to both 'high' and 'popular' culture.

Perhaps this is also the place to note the important publication of Adorno's *Against Epistemology*[52]. In this work Adorno cites Husserl's phenomenology as the most advanced form of bourgeois idealism and therefore as the form that has to be subjected to a rigorous materialist critique. Instead of simply attacking Husserl's phenomenology from without, Adorno attempts an immanent critique from within; that is, by exposing and confronting the logic of the phenomenologic, Adorno attempts to reveal the social and political foundations of the bracketing of history in Husserl's search for transcendental first principles. This is a welcome translation of an important text in the field of Western Marxism.

Moving to the earliest major figure in Western Marxism, J. M. Bernstein's *The Philosophy of the Novel*[53] is an extended account and analysis of Lukács's essay, 'The Theory of the Novel'. Bernstein argues that although the importance of Lukács's essay has been recognized (by writers as diverse as Adorno and Harry Levin), there has been, as yet, no rigorous evaluation of the claims of the theory; this work is an attempt to rectify that omission. The work proceeds by presenting a philosophical reconstruction of Lukács's argument followed by a defence of it and a claim that in spite of the author's aim (since the essay was a pre-Marxist work), the essay contains the rudiments of a Marxist theory of the novel. The book opens with a delineation of Lukács's conception of philosophical analysis, with particular reference to the problems of representation and the status of a Marxist hermeneutic. Chapter Two traces affinities between the thought of Kant and the early Lukács in specifying Lukács's explication of both the internal workings of the novel and the cultural significance of the novel. Then follows an account of Lukács's concepts of

51. *Adorno*, by Martin Jay. Fontana Modern Masters. pp. 192. pb £2.50.

52. *Against Epistemology: A Metacritique*, by Theodor W. Adorno, trans. by Willis Domingo. Blackwell (1982). pp. vii + 248. hb £22.50, pb £7.95.

53. *The Philosophy of the Novel: Lukács, Marxism and the Dialectics of Form*, by J. M. Bernstein. Harvester. pp. xxiii + 296. hb £28.50.

'form' and 'life' and an analysis of the process whereby a category or concept serves to unite diverse events. Chapter Four examines the relations between narrative and temporal forms in Lukács's essay, by referring to the comments on Flaubert's *Sentimental Education*; and Chapter Five assesses the problem of transcendenttal subjectivity and how that concept arises and is deployed in the 'Cartesian novel'. This analysis is continued in Chapter Six in an examination of Lukács's claim for irony as the structural principle of the novel. Finally Bernstein extends the theory of the classical realist text in order to examine its worth in relation to the texts of modernism. In an interesting and provocative book, Bernstein offers a number of new ways of considering this early essay of Lukács; not the least interesting aspect of the book is Bernstein's use of the novel to act as a commentary on Kantian philosophy.

Pauline Johnson's *Marxist Aesthetics*[54] links the older and more recent works of Western Marxists in a critique of 'the foundations within everyday life for an enlightened consciousness'. Maintaining that all Marxist theories of aesthetics accord an enlightening potential to art, Johnson outlines the major problem facing Marxist aestheticians: how to determine the possibilities for the realization of such enlightenment. Arguing against Perry Anderson's account of the Western Marxist 'turn to aesthetics' as a 'pessimistic retreat', Johnson claims instead that the aesthetic turn was an attempt to come to terms with a changed situation. Thus, Johnson runs through most of the major Marxist critics of the century – Lukács, Benjamin, Brecht, Adorno, Marcuse, Althusser, Macherey, and Eagleton – in order to evaluate their contribution to the problem that she sees for Marxist aesthetics. Such a run-through can become rather repetitious at times and occasionally reads as a guide to the good and bad twentieth-century Marxists: Lukács, Benjamin (to an extent), and Marcuse good; Brecht, Adorno, Althusser, Macherey, and Eagleton bad. The mode of evaluation is roughly along the lines of the pro- and antihumanists; Johnson's own position is revealed to be one that considers 'the study of the art work and its emancipatory impact [to] provide a particularly suitable forum for a humanistic critique of an alienated life experience'. No doubt such claims will meet with no more than a lukewarm response in the present antihumanist period.

The major modern Marxist critic not featuring in Johnson's work is Fredric Jameson. However, Jameson is the subject of William C. Dowling's *Jameson, Althusser, Marx*[55]. Dowling's work is 'unabashedly' an introduction to a single text of Jameson: 'not a study, not a critique, not a survey of contemporary Marxism or Jameson's place in it', but an attempt to make the argument of Jameson's *The Political Unconscious* more accessible. There are clear problems with such a project: the work needs no introduction (since it was written by Jameson), and yet it does need an introduction (since it was written by Jameson). That is, the text is familiar but difficult. Moreover, there are problems in attempting to simplify the argument since 'for Jameson the question of style as enactment is the Marxist question of theory and practice' and 'the plain style is the limpid style of bourgeois ideology where there is no

54. *Marxist Aesthetics: The Foundations within Everyday Life for an Enlightened Consciousness*, by Pauline Johnson. RKP. pp. viii + 168. hb £13.95.
55. *Jameson, Althusser, Marx: An Introduction to the Political Unconscious*, by William C. Dowling. Methuen. pp. 147. pb £4.95.

need for obscurity because all truths are known in advance'. Dowling's good intentions run aground on this paradox; his simple introduction is ruled out of play in advance by the master.

There are, of course, no such problems with one of Jameson's own texts, and thus we turn to a significant essay in *NLR* on the question of postmodernism. Jameson's essay, 'Postmodernism, Or the Cultural Logic of Capital', is a dazzling display of cultural critique ranging over a number of different fields (architecture, painting, film, the novel, poetry, and contemporary theory), in an interrogation of the status and function of 'postmodernism'. Jameson begins by noting the increasing number of declarations of 'the end': 'the end of ideology, art, or social class; the crisis of Leninism, social democracy, or the welfare state, etc., etc.' (though the 'end' of global capitalism seems nowhere in sight). Drawing a possible definition of postmodernism from this tendency, Jameson poses the question: is postmodernism a fundamental break with modernism, or is it simply a periodic and stylistic innovation within the discourse of modernism? This question forms the basis of the essay. Having noted the rise of 'aesthetic populism' in the postmodern period, Jameson argues that such a shift is not a 'purely cultural affair' but a political question. Thus, for Jameson, the analyses of modernism and postmodernism are to be founded upon the recognition of their differential 'meaning and social function' within their respective economic periods. That is, Jameson argues, postmodernism differs from modernism precisely and most significantly in its position in the economic system of late capitalism and in the changed role of culture in that system. Following from this analysis, Jameson moves to a set of brilliant critiques of cultural forms in order to uncover the constitutive features of the postmodern period. Thus, in Warhol's 'Diamond Dust Shoes', Cage's music, the Language Poets, the Los Angeles Bonaventura hotel, and much contemporary theory, there appear the features of postmodernism: 'a new depthlessness', and 'a consequent weakening of historicity'; 'a new type of emotional ground tone'; and, of course, the new technologies figuring in the new economic world system. Such an argument leads Jameson to the conclusion that postmodernism is a significant historical development, not a new style or optional choice, but 'the cultural dominant of the logic of late capitalism'. Drawing from that, Jameson ends by suggesting the political and cultural problems posed by postmodernism and potential radical responses to them.

Returning to the literary field, Terry Eagleton's latest book asks the very reasonable question: what is *The Function of Criticism*[56]? One way to answer that question is to put it in the past and to pluralize it: what were the functions of criticism? And it is that route that Eagleton takes. Using a flexible interpretation of Habermas's notion of 'the public sphere', Eagleton gives a drastically selective history of the institution of criticism in order to show the changing functions of criticism since the eighteenth century. In the final chapter Eagleton argues that criticism only has a significant function when it becomes more than literary criticism. One example of such achieved significance is the work of Raymond Williams; however, Eagleton points to the enforced isolation of much of Williams's work and argues for the creation

---

56. *The Function of Criticism from 'The Spectator' to Post-Structuralism*, by Terry Eagleton. Verso. pp. 133. hb £15, pb £3.95.

of a counter-public sphere (as, for example, in the discourse and practice of feminism). Eagleton concludes by asserting that Marxist criticism is the most traditional form of criticism in its desire to return all critique to the public sphere 'defined by an engagement in the cultural politics of late capitalism'. Although the argument ranges sketchily over an extended historical terrain, this text carries the provocative and sustained critique that one would expect from this highly productive Marxist critic. (See also pp. 764 for another review of this book.)

Moving from the literary to the philosophical, there is the chance to note a work unavailable last year for review: Alex Callinicos's *Marxism and Philosophy*[57], which takes up many of the themes of his earlier *Is There a Future for Marxism?* (1982). Although Marx turned his back not just on a particular philosophical school but philosophy itself, Callinicos justifies his work by asserting that Marxists have 'to confront critically, and seek to appropriate the positive elements of the most advanced forms of bourgeois thought'. Thus, in Chapter 1 he explores the two traditions – (i) from Kant to Hegel, and (ii) from Kant to Gottlob Frege – in order to gain some perspective on the historical predecessors of the Marxist and analytical traditions. Chapter 2 deals with the intellectual development of Marx, treating issues such as Marx's view of human nature on the way. Chapter 3 analyses the returns to philosophy made by later Marxists, principally Lukács, Adorno, and Althusser. Chapters 4 and 5 deal with Marxism and various interpretations of 'Naturalism' and 'Realism'. And Chapter 6, the most interesting for theorists, treats the subject of 'language and ideology'. The chapter begins by noting the importance of the concept of ideology for Marxists, and exploring various Marxist theories of ideology. This is followed by an analysis of 'two concepts of language', the Fregean and the Saussurian, which holds that Marxism has more to learn from the former. Then follows a review of theories of 'truth and communication', analysing Austin, Searle, and Habermas; and a concluding section, 'discourse and practice', that continues Callinicos's attack on both analytical and continental philosophy. Clearly Callinicos is an uncompromising Marxist thinker and his two books amount to a significant critique of many positions in contemporary theory.

Another text dealing with language and politics is the fascinating collection of that title edited by Michael J. Shapiro[58]. The theme of the collection is 'the issue of politicising language', and this theme is explored by bringing together both Anglo-American and continental traditions in the philosophy of language. In this project, the first chapter of Jameson's *The Prison House of Language* ('The Linguistic Model') is used as a central overview of the differences in both traditions, and a constant stress is laid upon the similarities evinced in the work of Wittgenstein and Derrida. The first chapter is an early essay by C. Wright Mills which offers a sociological critique of statements of motive, considering the meanings of such statements in the light of the social functions they perform and the historically constructed vocabularies upon which they depend. J. G. A. Pocock's essay uses Austin's speech act theory to

57. *Marxism and Philosophy*, by Alex Callinicos. OUP (1983). pp. 177. hb £10.95, pb £3.95.
58. *Language and Politics*, ed. by Michael J. Shapiro. Blackwell. pp. 261. hb £18.50, pb £6.95.

attack the idea of the subject's control over his or her meaning; and Murray Edelman demonstrates how particular meanings can be dictated by a particular register beyond the control of a language-user, in this case the terms of 'the language of the helping professions'. Kenneth Burke focuses upon rhetorical structures in a review of *Mein Kampf*; and this is followed by Tracy Strong's account of Nietzsche's view of language that stresses the similarities between Nietzsche and Wittgenstein in their view of language as a field of human practices. Following that is Foucault's essay, 'The Order of Discourse'; this is followed in turn by William Connolly's 'The Politics of Discourse', a critical confrontation of Anglo-American and Continental positions concentrating upon the problems posed by the differing views of the subject and the consequences of such views. After Jameson's insight into the blindness of the Anglo-American tradition, we move to de Man's essay, 'The Epistemology of Metaphor'. This is a reading of Locke, Condillac, and Kant which demonstrates that each writer ends up as a rhetorician despite himself. The collection is an excellent survey of distinctive approaches to language and can serve as an introduction to many contemporary critical problems.

Mark Poster's *Foucault, Marxism and History*[59] is an attempt to concentrate on specific areas of the relations between Marxist theory and the theories presented in the work of Foucault. Poster argues that a Foucauldean analysis of the 'mode of information' ('the new language experiences of the twentieth century brought about for the most part by advances in electronics and related technologies') has to replace the Marxist analysis of the 'mode of production' as a means of understanding the deployment of power in contemporary capitalism. Thus, Poster appears to be arguing that Foucault is 'more Marxist' than Althusser, that he is 'continuing the work of western Marxists by other means', that 'Marxism itself may be an obstacle to social criticism' and 'a relic out of the past'. However, despite these ambitious claims, Poster spends only the final five pages of the book specifying the modes of information that have arisen in the course of the twentieth century and then asserts that he is 'not arguing that the mode of information completely replaces the mode of production: society could not continue without the uninterrupted production of commodities'. The text presents an interesting comparison of Foucault and Sartre, a useful introduction to Foucault's historical technique, and basic surveys of Foucault's work on prisons and sexuality; however, the contradiction between the claims for the mode of production and the mode of information that can be found within Poster's argument makes the text ultimately unsatisfying.

The deployment of power within the academic and institutional teaching of literature has been a major concern of the *LTP* group. This is reflected in their latest *Journal* which is again an interesting collection of essays that is wide-ranging in scope, yet precise in its focus. Kiernan Ryan has a stimulating article on the possibilities of 'reclaiming the canon', and both Gina Wisker and James McGeachie are concerned with pedagogical practice: Wisker with 'the experience of a contemporary women's writing seminar' and McGeachie with the curricula of secondary education. Michael Moriarty reviews a recent film through a Barthesian analysis, and Steve Watts and Steve Xerri consider one

---

59. *Foucault, Marxism and History: Mode of Production Versus Mode of Information*, by Mark Poster. Polity. pp. x + 173. hb £16.50, pb £5.95.

of the most undertheorized areas of contemporary cultural production, pop-music. Andrew Bowie has a careful and interesting look at debates between 'Marxists' and 'Deconstructionists', and this is repeated in a review by Geoff Bennington of Michael Ryan's *Marxism and Deconstruction* (see *YW* 63.530). T. J. Cribb returns to the problem of mimesis, and Peter Middleton has a lively and assured attack on 'The Con in Contemporary Literature'. The pick of the essays is, however, Julia Swindells's 'Falling Short with Marx: Some Glimpses of Nineteenth Century Sexual Ideology'. Through a careful reading of the language of specific texts of Marx, Swindells argues for the need to think again about relations between Marxism and Feminism.

Popular Fiction and Social Change[60] attempts to analyse some of the theoretical problems posed for radical critics by popular fiction. The editor, Christopher Pawling, notes that although there has been a growth of interest in this field (though it is significantly not on the curricula of most schools or colleges), there has not been a sustained critical project working with it. Much of the work on popular literature has as yet been untheorized and eclectic; therefore the aim of this study is to stimulate interest in the field and in a critical response to it. Problems examined in this work include the distinction between 'popular' and 'elite' culture and the differing views of popular fiction as crass ideology or utopian form. This latter theme is taken up in the last three chapters of the book with an examination of the relations between popular fiction and cultural politics in specific texts in the postwar period. Methodological problems are also analysed with a consideration of 'genre analysis' in relation to both science fiction and thrillers. And the work of three major theorists is deployed in an attempt to see if their work is useful in comprehending popular fiction. Both Macherey and Goldmann are used in examinations of science-fictional texts, and Gramsci's concept of 'common sense' is used in feminist readings of both Barbara Cartland and women's magazine fiction. The collection is a useful introduction to this field, combining theory with careful analysis.

Popular fiction is also the subject of Ken Worpole's *Reading by Numbers*[61]. The text, claims Worpole, 'aspires to some of the qualities of a good pub discussion' and achieves them. This is an irreverent, amusing, yet rigorously serious critique of the culture industry and its productions. The analysis starts by arguing (against contemporary trends) that reading still occupies a major position in British leisure time and this, combined with the fact that printing and publishing is London's largest manufacturing sector, means that publishing has to be at the forefront of market capitalism. The book then examines what that means for the forms, means, and content of the works published. Thus, by taking both a historical and analytical survey, Worpole considers what publishers publish and why, the role of women as popular writers and readers, the crime novel, contemporary poetry (from nineteenth-century dialect poetry to West Indian 'dub' poetry), children's fiction, and more formal concerns such as the dissemination of texts and the significance of this for independent publishers. Worpole amusingly cites the Arts Council's

60. *Popular Fiction and Social Change*, ed. by Christopher Pawling. Macmillan. pp. vii + 246. pb £4.95.

61. *Reading by Numbers: Contemporary Publishing and Popular Fiction*, by Ken Worpole. Comedia. pp. 119. pb £3.95.

The Glory of the Garden, a recent policy statement on the arts, as an example of reactionary cultural policy: if the arts in Britain *are* a garden, then they are surrounded by an enormous fence (the politics of landscape). Perhaps the absence of popular fiction on courses in schools and colleges (and particularly in universities) is understandable only in the light of the observation of the Kenyan novelist Ngugi wa Thiong'o that it is part of the mystification of literature that it always starts with that which is furthest from the student. This book is an attack on the cultural politics of the literary establishment; it is all the more welcome for that.

7. Psychoanalytic Critical Theory

It is scarcely surprising that psychoanalysis – the 'talking cure' – and modern narratology have joined forces. Anna O. might just as well have called the new therapy that Breuer and Freud were evolving 'the telling cure', that process in which the patient recovers, reconstructs, or simply constructs his story. The presence of Jacques Lacan has vastly enriched (and complicated) the alliance, not least of all by calling into radical question the notion of the integrity of the subject. Narratives in the Lacanian view tend to be traversed by voices from elsewhere: they are echo-chambers, sites, or loci infiltrated by a variety of alien discourses, machines for constructing the 'I' (the pronoun reduced to a purely deictic function, designating no specifiable structure, but rather a pure position) which the ego psychologist confidently takes as his starting point. All six of the books under review speak in whole or in part to the alliance of psychoanalysis and narratology and to its difficult, puzzling, but nearly always intriguing Lacanian aftermath. The case of the purloined *l'être* seems far from closed.

In *Reading for the Plot*[20] Peter Brooks presents an argument richly informed by the psychoanalytic perspective. Two chapters in particular, 'Freud's Masterplot' and 'Fictions of the Wolf Man' (the former first appeared in *YFS* in different form and the latter in *Diac*), engage in symmetrical procedures. In 'Freud's Masterplot' Brooks reads fictional plots as versions of Freud's itinerary of the instincts set forth in *Beyond the Pleasure Principle*; in 'Fictions of the Wolf Man' he reads Freud's case-study as a version of fictional plotting and shows how the Wolf Man (both the man and the study of the man) is implicated at every level with the fictional. Thus Freud reads narrative, but narrative also reads Freud, an egalitarian gesture, which, among many other similar moves, puts the argument well beyond vulgar Freudianism.

Brooks's argument is a constant turning away from notions of plot as structure to notions of plot as structuration: he is not talking of plot so much as of plotting, and he thus moves beyond the relatively static models of structuralism (e.g. Lévi-Strauss's 'atemporal matrix structure') to a consideration of the dynamic relationship between *histoire* and *récit*, or in Barthesian terms, the 'overcoding' of the proairetic code by the hermeneutic. The movement of plot becomes in Freud's terms a dialectic of continuing and ending, a postponement of the end so that a story may die in its own fashion: as we live *in order* to die (in the right manner), so we have the arabesque, the detour of plot *in order* to reach the end, we pursue in a story the metonymic chain of the signifier *in order* to attain the metaphoric coherence of the end. The book also contains a number of provocative specific readings of stories as diverse as *La Peau de chagrin*, *Great Expectations*, and *Absalom, Absalom!*

Steven Marcus's *Freud and the Culture of Psychoanalysis*[62] similarly brings the study of narrative to bear on the Freudian text, in particular on the case studies of Dora and the Rat Man. While the case of Dora, Marcus argues, reveals much about the central place of narrative in Freud's thinking, the much more complex case of the Rat Man studies an 'entirely psychological neurosis' (there were no somatic conversions in this instance of obsessive compulsion) 'which does not reduce itself to coherent narrative form or structure'. The argument here must of necessity deal with the 'strategies of understanding, therapy, and writing Freud took to when he was confronted with a case or a case history that did not easily, naturally, inevitably, or eventually turn itself out as or into a story'. One may doubt that *any* case history 'naturally' turns into a story. There is something rather *ad hoc* and perfunctory in a number of literary analogies Marcus actually does adduce, something disturbingly impressionistic in being told, for instance, of one of the Rat Man's muddled memories and his evident confusion of Freud with the dreaded Captain N., that the episode is 'Gogolian in detail', that it 'reminds one of some of Dostoevsky's early descriptions of the bizarre behavior of small bureaucrats', or that 'it is Kafka-like in tone'. Somewhat later the Rat Man in the grip of a murderous fantasy is described as 'Raskolnikov on the Ringstrasse'.

One of Freud's strategies of writing the case of the Rat Man, Marcus argues, is postponement, a kind of 'crab-like' way of advancing the narrative. There is an interesting, though unremarked, analogy to what might be called the 'strategies' of the neurosis itself here, to the way Freud himself described the displaced impulse to act as 'a sort of *regression*': 'preparatory acts become substituted for the final decision, thinking replaces acting, and, instead of the substitutive act, some thought preliminary to it asserts itself with all the force of compulsion'. There is a further analogy to Marcus's own style of argumentation, which frequently circles back ('I shall retreat from these abstrusenesses and begin . . .'; 'But before we do this we will have to take several steps backwards') and approaches the point with extreme obliquity. *Freud and the Culture of Psychoanalysis* is a well informed and repeatedly interesting argument, but its implications for literary theory are finally small.

The collection of essays *Lacan and Narration*[63] is a reprint of part of a recent special issue of *MLN*. Contributions range from Régis Durand's discussion of the 'dramaturgy' of the subject in narration, its constitution in the act of vanishing or *aphanisis*, through Juliet Flower MacCannell's meditation on Stendhal and the Lacanian Real, Jerry Aline Flieger on the joke as textual paradigm, to Shoshana Felman's masterly 'Beyond Oedipus: The Specimen Story of Psychoanalysis'. Flieger's argument is an intriguing superimposition of various intersubjective triangles (Oedipal and textual, particularly the recurrent configurations of 'The Purloined Letter') upon the basic situation of the tendentious joke as Freud described it. Her insistence on the *successive* character of such triangles, with the listener to the joke in the first instance becoming the jokester in the next, along with her understanding of gender as 'position' rather than as biological necessity, is what gives her discourse a

62. *Freud and the Culture of Psychoanalysis: Studies in the Transition from Victorian Humanism to Modernity*, by Steven Marcus. A&U. pp. 268. $24.95.
63. *Lacan and Narration: The Psychoanalytic Difference in Narrative Theory*, ed. by Robert Con Davis. JHU. pp. v + 220. $10.95.

Lacanian stamp and leads to her teasing out of the paradoxes of desire in the joking triangle. Here each 'player' is at once active *and* passive: if roles switch from one successive staging of the joking triangle to another, they are nevertheless coincidental or superimposed *within* each such staging.

Felman's argument is directed not so much at Lacanian analysis *and* narration as at Lacanian analysis *as* narration, an interminable story always demystifying the sense of an ending. She speculatively expands Lacan's strategy of reversal in attempting not a reading of the literary Oedipus in terms of Freud's theory, but a rereading of Freud's theory in terms of the literary Oedipus. This leads to multiple 'beyonds': we move beyond *Oedipus the King* (where ego psychology came to rest in an act of self-blinding) to *Oedipus at Colonus*; beyond *The Interpretation of Dreams* to Freud's rethinking of wish-fulfilment and pleasure in *Beyond the Pleasure Principle*; even beyond the International Psychoanalytic Association to Lacan's 'exile'. We are given, Felman argues, in *Oedipus at Colonus* the gift of speech, the chance to assume our histories to the point where our life-histories (the discourse of the Other) may more nearly coincide with our life-stories, those 'misrecognized' versions of ourselves which we tell and retell in gestures of bad faith. The central instance of bad faith is perhaps for Felman the attempt to dispense summarily with *Beyond the Pleasure Principle*, a move analogous to the refusal to follow Oedipus beyond Thebes to his death at Colonus.

The essays collected in *Interpreting Lacan*[64] are not for the most part concerned with literary narration, although the collection ends with a fine reading of *Bleak House* by Christel van Boheemen-Saaf in which she argues that the novel tells two family romances, the first the unriddling of Esther's origins, the second the resolution of the Jarndyce–Esther–Woodcourt triangle. If the first raises the spectre of the Other in the form of the Mother, female sexuality, the disease of illicit and tainted desire, the second manages to excommunicate the threat of the Other from the surface level of the text. This is not a false move in van Boheemen-Saaf's view: it is Dickens's way of supplying his audience on an unconscious level with the reassuring myth it needs to pull through.

But the bulk of the essays in this volume are concerned with explicating the Lacanian text and suggesting the rich philosophical context out of which that text arises. William J. Richardson's two contributions, 'Lacan and the Subject of Psychoanalysis' and 'Psychoanalysis and the Being-question', are exemplary of both modes, the first a lucid discussion of the Other, the barred signifier, the insistence of meaning in the signifying chain, and the droll game of peek-a-boo in which the self and the Other are engaged. Richardson is even amusing on the subject of the larcenous forays of the unconscious into consciousness, the piratical raids that can be known only by their traces, the gaps and derangements they leave behind. His second contribution, a study of Lacan and Heidegger, is necessarily more difficult, but none the less an exciting account, among other things, of the ambiguous genetive in the phrase 'desire of the Other', where in Heideggerian fashion we must understand the preposition to designate the Other as both destination and origin, a desire that belongs to the Other and a desire *for* the Other. There is much else in

64. *Interpreting Lacan*. Vol. 6: *Psychiatry and the Humanities*, ed. by Joseph H. Smith and William Kerrigan. Yale. pp. xvii + 289. $28.50.

Interpreting Lacan – Julia Kristeva on borderline speech, André Green on the difficult logic of the Lacanian *objet a*, Wilfried Ver Eecke on Lacan and Hegel – that the literary theorist will find most certainly interesting and possibly useful.

Language and Interpretation in Psychoanalysis[65] is a re-issue of Marshall Edelson's argument attempting to reground psychoanalytic interpretation in the transformational linguistics of Noam Chomsky rather than in the structural linguistics of Saussure and Jakobson favoured by Lacan and Lacanians. Each psychic agency has a set of transformations peculiar to it, Edelson argues, and the operation of the dream-work and the mechanisms of defence may be viewed as canons of transformation. It is the analyst's familiarity with such canons that constitutes his listening competence, his ability to posit the deep structure of the analysand's discourse. Interpretation (and Edelson makes a firm distinction between 'interpreting' and 'explaining', the latter being the procedure of the physical sciences) consists finally in nothing but this positing of deep structures, kernel sentences, pretransformational material in an attempt to disambiguate and otherwise clarify the surface structure of the stream of discourse. Above all, says Edelson, 'the aim of a theory of interpretation is to specify what the psychoanalyst must know – wittingly or unwittingly – to perform such acts of interpretation'. But much that is interesting in Edelson's argument is not really so at odds with Jakobsonian categories. Thus interpreting resistance and defence depends on the analyst's awareness of the phatic properties of utterances, those elements that have to do with the code and the channel of communication, the redundancies, the mobilizers and maintainers of attention, the suppression of potentially disruptive lexical items, all of which are designed to keep a socially interactive system functioning. This certainly raises the possibility of a phatic pathology, but it is not clear that it depends on transformational linguistics. The phatic is, of course, one of Jakobson's six functions of verbal communication, and it does not seem to be used here in a materially different sense. Close to the last half of Edelson's book is taken up with a minutely circumstantial reading of Wallace Stevens's 'The Snowman' according to transformational principles. Much of this is intriguing, particularly the section on syntax, but, again, the long concluding section on sound sometimes looks remarkably like the kind of thing Jakobson and Lévi-Strauss did with Baudelaire.

Finally, Elizabeth Wright's *Psychoanalytic Criticism: Theory in Practice*[66], a contribution to Methuen's Landmark series, is an adroit overview of psychoanalytic theory from classical analysis to poststructuralism and the schizoanalysis of Gilles Deleuze and Félix Guattari. It would be difficult to imagine a better short introduction of the work of Derrida bearing on psychoanalysis or of Sylvère Lotringer's reading of Wilhelm Jensen's *Gradiva*. The initiated may not find much new here, but the lucidity with which the exposition is conducted, the evident control of a large and complicated body of material, makes this a valuable reference.

65. *Language and Interpretation in Psychoanalysis*, by Marshall Edelson. UChic. pp. xv + 243. $9.

66. *Psychoanalytic Criticism: Theory in Practice*, by Elizabeth Wright. Methuen. pp. xii + 208. hb $19.95, pb $8.95.

Books Received

Chapter I. Literary History and Criticism

Abrams, M. H., ed., *The Norton Anthology of English Literature*. Fifth edn. Two vols. Norton, 1986. pb £12.95 each.

Alexander, Michael, *'The Miller's Tale' by Geoffrey Chaucer*. Macmillan, 1986. pb £0.99.

Backhouse, Janet, *Book of Hours*. BL, 1985. pb £4.95.

Belsey, Catherine. *The Subject of Tragedy: Identity and Difference in Renaissance Drama*. Methuen, 1985. hb £13.95. pb £6.95.

Benn, Caroline, and John Fairley, *Challenging the MSC on Jobs, Training and Education*. Pluto, 1986. pb £5.95.

Bold, Alan, *Longman Dictionary of Poets: The Lives and Works of 1001 Poets in the English Language*. Longman, 1985. £9.95.

Bowers, Fredson, ed., *Studies in Bibliography*, Vol. 38. Virginia, 1985.

Braun, Rene, ed., *Hommage à Jean Granarolo: Philologie, Littératures et Histoires Anciennes*. Annales de la Faculté des Lettres et Sciences Humaines de Nice. Les Belles Lettres, 1985.

Butts, Dennis, *'Bleak House' by Charles Dickens*. Macmillan, 1986. pb £0.99.

Chainey, Graham. *A Literary History of Cambridge*. Pevensey P, 1985. £14.95.

Cole, Susan Letzler, *The Absent One: Mourning Ritual, Tragedy, and the Performance of Ambivalence*. UPenn, 1985. £18.95.

Collie, Michael, *George Gissing: A Bibliographical Study*. StPB, 1985. £25.

Commire, Anne, ed., *Something About the Author*, Vols 39, 40, 41 (1985), Vols 42, 43 (1986). Gale. $64 each.

Conrad, Peter, *The Everyman History of English Literature*. Dent, 1985. £16.

Deane, Seamus, *A Short History of Irish Literature*. Hutchinson, 1986. pb $6.95.

Draper, R. P., *Lyric Tragedy*. Macmillan, 1985. £25.

Eagle, Dorothy, ed., *The Concise Oxford Dictionary of English Literature*. OUP, 1985. pb £4.95.

Estes, Glenn E., ed., *American Writers for Children before 1900*. DLB 42. Gale, 1985. $88.

Fadiman, Clifton, ed., *The Faber Book of Anecdotes*. Faber, 1985. £15.

Ficino, Marsilio, *Commentary on Plato's Symposium on Love: An English Translation by Sears Jayne*. Spring Publications, 1985.

Gaur, Albertine, *A History of Writing*. BL, 1984. £15.

Gibson, James, *'Tess of the D'Urbervilles' by Thomas Hardy*. Macmillan, 1986. pb £0.99.

Gilbert, V. F., and D. S. Tatla, *Women's Studies: A Bibliography of Dissertations 1870–1982*. Blackwell, 1985. £57.50.

Grambs, David, *Literary Companion Dictionary: Words without Words.* RKP, 1984. £14.95.

Hall, H. W., ed., *Science Fiction and Fantasy Book Review Index, 1980–1984.* Gale, 1985. $160.

Harris, Laurie Lanzen, and Charles D. Abbey, eds, *Nineteenth-Century Literature Criticism,* Vol. 11. Gale, 1986. $88.

Harris, Laurie Lanzen, and Emily B. Tennyson, eds, *Nineteenth-Century Literature Criticism,* Vols 9, 10. Gale, 1985. $88 each.

Hawthorn, Jeremy, *Studying the Novel: An Introduction.* Arnold, 1985. pb £2.95.

Jennings, Humphrey, *Pandaemonium 1660–1886: The Coming of the Machine as seen by Contemporary Observers.* Deutsch, 1985. £12.95.

Jones, R. T., *Studying Poetry: An Introduction.* Arnold, 1986. pb £2.95.

Kabbani, Rana, *Europe's Myths of Orient: Devise and Rule.* Macmillan, 1986. £25.

Kavanagh, P. J., and James Michie, *The Oxford Book of Short Poems.* OUP, 1985. £9.50.

Kelsall, Malcolm, *Studying Drama: An Introduction.* Arnold, 1985. pb £2.95.

LeFanu, William, *A Bibliography of Edward Jenner.* Second edn. StPB, 1985. £24.

Lodge, David, *Working with Structuralism: Essays and Reviews on Nineteenth- and Twentieth-Century Literature.* Ark, 1986. pb £3.95.

McKitterick, David, *Four Hundred Years of University Printing and Publishing in Cambridge 1584–1984: Catalogue of the Exhibition in the University Library Cambridge.* CUP, 1984. £17.50.

Makepeace, Christopher, *Ephemera: A Book on its Collection, Conservation and Use.* Gower, 1985. £17.50.

Marigny, Jean, *Le Vampire dans la Littérature Anglo-Saxonne.* Didier, 1985.

Martin, Stoddard, *Art, Messianism and Crime: A Study of Antinomianism in Modern Literature and Lives.* Macmillan, 1986. £25.

Menasce, Esther, *La Camera di Barbablu: Studi sull'evoluzione del mito di Faust in Gran Bretagna.* Liviana, 1983. L20,000.

Morris, Helen, *'Henry IV Part I' by William Shakespeare.* Macmillan, 1986. pb £0.99.

Ormond, Leonee, *'St Joan' by George Bernard Shaw.* Macmillan, 1986. pb £0.99.

Oxbury, Harold, *Great Britons: Twentieth-Century Lives.* OUP, 1985. £14.95.

Parsons, Nicholas, *The Book of Literary Lists: A Collection of Annotated Lists of Fact, Statistic and Anecdote Concerning Books.* S&J, 1985. £9.95.

Partridge, Eric, *A Dictionary of Catch Phrases British and American from the Sixteenth Century to the Present Day,* ed. by Paul Beale. RKP, 1985. £14.95.

The Penguin Reference Dictionary. Penguin, 1985. pb £4.95.

Person, James E., ed., *Literature Criticism from 1400 to 1800,* Vol. 3. Gale, 1986. $85.

Poupard, Dennis, ed., *Literature Criticism from 1400 to 1800,* Vol. 2. Gale, 1985. $82.

Profumo, David, and Graham Swift, *The Magic Wheel: An Anthology of Fishing in Literature.* Heinemann, 1986. £15.

Ranger, Paul, 'The School for Scandal' by Richard Sheridan. Macmillan, 1986. pb £0.99.

Rawson, C. J., ed., Anglo-French Literary Relations. YES 15. MHRA, 1985.

Reilly, John M., ed., Twentieth-Century Crime and Mystery Writers. Second edn. St James Press, 1985. £37.50.

Roberts, Marie, British Poets and Secret Societies. CH, 1986. £17.95.

Robson, W. W., A Prologue to English Literaure. Batsford, 1986. pb £4.95.

Ross, Jean W., ed., Dictionary of Literary Biography Yearbook: 1984. Gale, 1985. $92.

Rowe, Jeremy, 'The Rivals' by Richard Sheridan. Macmillan, 1986. pb £0.99.

Sampson, Anthony and Sally. The Oxford Book of Ages. OUP, 1985. £8.95.

Sarkissian, Adele, ed., Something About the Author: Autobiography Series, Vol. 1. Gale, 1986. $50.

Scott, Norman A., Jr, The Poetics of Belief: Studies in Coleridge, Arnold, Pater, Santayana, Stevens and Heidegger. UNC, 1985. £24.

Smallwood, P. J., A Concise Chronology of English Literature. CH, 1985. £17.95.

Smith, Eric, A Dictionary of Classical Reference in English Poetry. Brewer, 1985. pb £9.95.

Smith, Leonard, 'The Crucible' by Arthur Miller. Macmillan, 1986. pb £0.99.

Smith, Margaret M., and Penny Boumelha, Index of English Literature Manuscripts. Vol. 3: 1700–1800. Part 1: Addison–Fielding. Mansell, 1986. £120.

Smith, Thomas, Catalogue of the Manuscripts in the Cottonian Library 1696, ed. by C. G. C. Tite. Brewer, 1984. £65.

Spear, Hilda D., 'A Passage to India' by E. M. Forster. Macmillan, 1986. pb £0.99.

Stephen, Martin, Longman Exam Guides: English Literature. Longman, 1986. pb £5.95.

Thomson, Peter, and Gāmini Sālgādo, The Everyman Companion to the Theatre. Dent, 1985. £15.

Thornley, G. C., and Gwyneth Roberts, An Outline of English Literature. Longman, 1984. pb £4.30.

van Emden, Joan, The Metaphysical Poets. Macmillan, 1986. pb £0.99.

Vinson, James, and D. L. Kirkpatrick, eds, Contemporary Poets. Fourth edn. St James Press, 1985. $70.

Westmancoat, John K., Newspapers. BL, 1985. pb £4.95.

Whalley, George, Studies in Literature and the Humanities: Innocent of Intent. Macmillan, 1985. £27.50.

Williams, John, Reading Poetry: A Contextual Introduction. Arnold, 1985. pb £3.95.

Williams, Moelwyn I., A Directory of Rare Books and Special Collections in the United Kingdom and the Republic of Ireland. LA, 1985. £75.

Wilson, Raymond, 'Lord of the Flies' by William Golding. Macmillan, 1986. pb £0.99.

Chapter II. English Language

Allan, Keith, Linguistic Meaning. Two vols. RKP, 1986. hb £17.95 each; pb £8.95 each.

Anderson, John M., *Case Grammar and the Lexicon*. Ulster, 1984. pb.

Attridge, Derek, and Daniel Ferrer, eds, *Post-Structuralist Joyce*. CUP, 1985. hb £20, pb £6.95.

Auroux, Sylvain, *et al.*, eds, *La Linguistique Fantastique*. Joseph Clims & Denoël, 380 Ffr.

Bammesberger, Alfred, ed., *Problems of Old English Lexicography: Studies in Memory of Angus Cameron*. Pustet, 1985. DM 74.

Brumfit, Christopher, *Language and Literature Teaching*. Pergamon, 1985. £6.90.

Brumfit, Christopher, Rod Ellis, and Josie Levine, *English as a Second Language in the United Kingdom: Linguistic and Educational Contexts*. Pergamon, 1985. pb £5.50.

Burchfield, R. W., ed., *A Supplement to the Oxford English Dictionary. IV: Se–Z*. Clarendon, 1986. £90.

Burchfield, Robert M., *The English Language*. OUP, 1985. £9.50.

Burton-Roberts, Noel, *Analysing Sentences: An Introduction to English Syntax*. Longman, 1986. pb £6.95.

Bybee, Joan L., *Morphology: A Study of the Relation between Meaning and Form*. Benjamins, 1985. hb Fl 90, pb Fl 55.

Carrington, Lawrence D., *St. Lucian Creole: A Descriptive Analysis of its Phonology and Morpho-syntax*. Helmut Buske, 1984. pb DM 32.

Chilton, Paul, ed., *Language and the Nuclear Arms Debate: Nukespeak Today*. Pinter, 1985. £17.50.

Comrie, Bernard, *Tense*. CUP, 1985. hb £17.50, pb £5.95.

Cottle, Basil, *The Language of Literature: English Grammar in Action*. Macmillan, 1985. hb £16, pb £5.95.

Cruttenden, Alan, *Intonation*. CUP, 1986. pb £7.95.

Crystal, David, *A Dictionary of Linguistics and Phonetics*. Second edn, updated and enlarged, Blackwell/Deutsch, 1985. hb £25, pb £7.95.

Crystal, David, *What is Linguistics?* Fourth edn. Arnold, 1985. pb £2.95.

Dahl, Östen, *Tense and Aspect Systems*. Blackwell, 1985. £22.50.

Davies, Eirlys, *The English Imperative*. CH. 1986. £25.

Dolezal, Frederic, *Forgotten but Important Lexicographers: John Wilkins and William Lloyd*. Niemeyer, 1985. DM 42.

Dutz, Klaus D., and Ludger Kaczmarek, eds, *Rekonstruktion und Interpretation*. Narr, 1984. hb DM 120, pb DM 68.

Enkvist, Nils Erik, ed., *Coherence and Composition: A Symposium*. Åbo, 1985.

Enright, D. J., ed., *Fair of Speech: The Uses of Euphemism*. OUP, 1985. £9.95.

Fisher. Ulla Thagg, *The Sweet Sound of Concord: :* ... Gleerup, 1985.

Freeborn, Dennis, with David Langford and Peter French, *Varieties of English: An Introduction to the Study of Language*. Macmillan, 1986. hb £18, pb £5.95.

Gazdar, Gerald, Ewan Klein, Geoffrey K. Pullum, and Ivan Sag, *Generalized Phrase Structure Grammar*. Harvard/Blackwell, 1985. hb £25, pb £8.50.

Giegerich, Heinz J., *Metrical Phonology and Phonological Structure: German and English*. CUP, 1985. £27.50.

Greenbaum, Sidney, ed., *The English Language Today*. Pergamon, 1985. pb £12.50.

Halliday, M. A. K., *An Introduction to Functional Grammar*. Arnold, 1985. pb £14.95.

Hansen, Erik, and Hans Frede Nielsen, *Irregularities in Modern English*. OdenseU, 1986. pb Dkr 220.

Hawthorn, Jeremy, ed., *Narrative: From Malory to Motion Pictures*. Arnold, 1985.

Howard, Philip, *The State of the Language: English Observed*. HH, 1984. £8.95.

Johns-Lewis, Catherine, ed., *Intonation in Discourse*. CH, 1986. £21.

Jones, Daniel, *Our Changing Speech*, ed. by Arne Juul and Hans Frede Nielsen. With a Supplement, *Daniel Jones—his Life and Contribution to Phonetics*, by Beverley Collins. National Institute for Educational Media, Copenhagen, 1985.

Kirk, John M., Steward Sanderson, and J. D. A. Widdowson, eds, *Studies in Linguistic Geography*. CH, 1985. £35.

Large, Andrew, *The Artificial Language Movement*. Blackwell, 1985. £19.50.

Latre, Guido, *Locking Earth to the Sky: A Structuralist Approach to Philip Larkin's Poetry*. Peter Lock, 1985. Sfr 81.

Linnarud, Moira, *Lexis in Composition: A Performance Analysis of Swedish Learners' Written English*. Gleerup, 1986.

McLelland, Ben W., and Timothy R. Donovan, eds, *Perspectives on Research and Scholarship in Composition*. MLA, 1985.

Mather, James Y., and Hans H. Speitel, *The Linguistic Atlas of Scotland*. Scots Section, Vol. III: *Phonology*. CH, 1986. £135.

Maubrey-Rose, Victoria, *The Anti-Representational Response: Gertrude Stein's Lucy Church Amiably*. AUU, distr. by A&W, 1985. Skr 118.

Michael, Ian, *English Grammatical Categories and the Tradition* (1970). CUP, 1985. £20.

Milroy, James and Lesley, *Authority in Language*. RKP, 1985. £16.95.

Nash, Walter, *English Usage: A Guide to First Principles*. RKP, 1986. £12.95.

Noordegraaf, J., *Norm, Geest en Geschiedenis*. Foris, 1985. Fl 85, $42.50.

Petyt, Kenneth M., *Dialect and Accent in Industrial West Yorkshire*. Benjamins, 1985. hb Fl 120, pb Fl 44.

Pomorska, K., and S. Rudy, eds, *Roman Jakobson: Verbal Art, Verbal Sign, Verbal Time*. Blackwell, 1985. £19.50.

Riffaterre, Michael. *Text Production*. ColU, 1985. pb $12.50.

Ringbom, Håkan, ed., *Foreign Language Learning and Bilingualism*. Åbo, 1985.

Riquelme, Jean-Paul, ed., *Fritz Senn: Joyce's Dislocations: Essays on Reading as Translation*. JHU, 1984. £20.35.

Rohlfing, Helmut, *Die Werke James Elphinstons (1721–1809) als Quellen der englischen Lautgeschichte*. CWU, 1985. hb DM 82, pb DM 56.

Smith, Thomas, Sir, *Literary and Linguistic Works*. Part 3, ed. by Bror Danielsson. A&W, 1985.

Standop, Ewald, *Englische Wörterbucher unter der Lupe*. Niemeyer, 1985. pb DM 32.

Stein, Dieter, *Natürlicher syntaktischer Sprachwandel: Untersuchungen zur Entstehung der englischen 'do'-periphrase in Fragen*. TUDUV, 1985. pb DM 58.80.

Stein, Gabriele, *The English Dictionary before Cawdrey*. Niemeyer, 1985. DM 140.

Tajima, Matsuji, *The Syntactic Development of the Gerund in Middle English*. Nan'un-do, Tokyo, distr. Benjamins, 1985. $35.

Todd, Loreto, *Modern Englishes: Pidgins and Creoles*. Blackwell/Deutsch, 1984. hb £22.50, pb £8.50.

Tosi, Arturo, *Immigration and Bilingual Education*. Pergamon, 1984. hb £6.80, pb £4.50.

Trudgill, Peter, and Jean Hannah, *International English: A Guide to Varieties of Standard English*. Second edn. Arnold, 1985. pb £4.50.

van Dijk, Teun A., *Discourse and Literature*. Benjamins, 1985. hb $37, pb $21.

van Peer, W., and J. Renkema, eds, *Pragmatics and Stylistics*. Acco, 1984. pb Bfr 790.

Verdonk, Peter, ed., *Literary Stylistics*. University of Amsterdam English Dept., 1985. hb £22.50, pb £7.95.

Vestergaard, Torben, and Kim Schroder, *The Language of Advertising*. Blackwell, 1985.

Wekker, Herman, and Liliane Haegeman, *A Modern Course in English Syntax*. CH, 1985. hb £17.95, pb £8.95.

Wires, Richard, *Terminology of the Third Reich*. BSU, 1985. pb.

Chapter III. Old English

Aldhelm, *The Poetic Works*, trans. by Michael Lapidge and James L. Rosier, Appendix by Neil Wright. Brewer, 1985. £25.

The Anglo-Saxon Chronicle: A Collaborative Edition. Vol. 17: *'The Annals of St Neots' with 'Vita Prima Sancti Neoti'*, ed. by David Dumville and Michael Lapidge. Brewer, 1985. £27.50.

Bammesberger, Alfred, ed., *Problems of Old English Lexicography: Studies in Memory of Angus Cameron*. Pustet, 1985. DM 74.

Bjork, Robert E., *The Old English Verse 'Saints' Lives': A Study in Direct Discourse and the Iconography of Style*. UTor, 1985. $29, £18.75.

Hoover, David L., *A New Theory of Old English Meter*. Lang, 1985. $24.

Howe, Nicholas, *The Old English Catalogue Poems*. R&B, 1985. Dkr 290.

John of Glastonbury, *The Chronicle of Glastonbury Abbey: An Edition, Translation and Study of John of Glastonbury's 'Cronica sive Antiquitates Glastoniensis Ecclesie'*, ed. by James P. Carley, trans. by David Townsend, Boydell, 1985. £29.50.

Lapidge, Michael, and Helmut Gneuss, eds, *Learning and Literature in Anglo-Saxon England: Studies Presented to Peter Clemoes on the Occasion of His Sixty-fifth Birthday*. CUP, 1985. £45.

Ogilvy, J. D. A., *Books Known to the English 597–1066: Addenda et Corrigenda*. CMERS, 1985. $3.

Olsen, Alexandra Hennessey, *Speech, Song, and Poetic Craft: The Artistry of the Cynewulf Canon*. Lang, 1984. Sfr 55.60.

Page, R. I., *Anglo-Saxon Aptitudes: An Inaugural Lecture Delivered Before the University of Cambridge on 6 March 1985*. CUP, 1985. pb £1.95.

Robinson, Fred C., *'Beowulf' and the Appositive Style*. UTenn, 1985. $12.50.

Rosenthal, Joel T., *Anglo-Saxon History: An Annotated Bibliography 450–1066*. AMSP, 1985. $34.50.

Sawyer, Peter, ed., *Domesday Book: A Reassessment*. Arnold, 1985. £25.

Smith, Andrea B., *The Anonymous Parts of the Old English Hexateuch: A Latin–Old English/Old English–Latin Glossary*. Brewer, 1985. £25.

Stafford, Pauline, *The East Midlands in the Early Middle Ages*. ULeics, 1985. hb £25. pb £9.75.

Szarmach, Paul E., ed., *Studies in Earlier Old English Prose: Sixteen Original Contributions*. SUNY, 1986. hb $39.50, pb $19.50.

Walsh, Katherine, and Diana Wood, eds, *The Bible in the Medieval World: Essays in Memory of Beryl Smalley*. Ecclesiastical History Society. Blackwell, 1985. £25.

Chapter IV. Middle English: Excluding Chaucer

Barber, Richard, ed., *Arthurian Literature*, Vol. 3. Brewer/B&N, 1984. £17.50.

Barber, Richard, ed., *Arthurian Literature*, Vol. 4. Brewer/B&N, 1985. £17.50.

Barber, Richard, ed. *Arthurian Literature*, Vol. 5. Brewer/B&N, 1985. £19.50.

Beadle, Richard, and Pamela King, eds, *York Mystery Plays: A Selection in Modern Spelling*. OUP, 1984. £17.

Bevington, D., H. Diehl, R. K. Emmerson, R. Herzman, and P. Sheingorn, *Homo, Memento Finis: The Iconography of Just Judgment in Medieval Art and Drama*. MIP, 1985.

Boffey, Julia, *Manuscripts of English Courtly Love Lyrics in the Later Middle Ages*. Brewer, 1986. £29.50.

Bunt, G. H. V., *William of Palerne*. Bouma's Boekhuis (Groningen), 1985. Fl 125.

d'Avray, D. L. *The Preaching of the Friars: Sermons diffused from Paris before 1300*. Clarendon, 1985. £25.

Ebin. Lois, *John Lydgate*. Twayne, 1985. $19.95.

Ebin, Lois, ed., *Vernacular Poetics in the Middle Ages*. MIP, 1984. hb $24.95, pb $14.95.

Fowler, David C., *The Bible in Middle English Literature*. UWash, 1985. $25.

Gray, Douglas, ed., *The Oxford Book of Late Medieval Verse and Prose*. Clarendon, 1985. £15.

Kennedy, B., *Knighthood in the Morte d'Arthur*. Brewer, 1985. £29.50.

Lindberg, Conrad, *The Middle English Bible*. Vol. 2: *The Book of Baruch*. UOslo, 1983. £20.

Pearsall, D., ed., *Manuscripts and Readers in Fifteenth-Century England*. Brewer, 1983. £22.50.

Scheps, Walter and J. Anna Looney, *Middle Scots Poets: A Reference Guide*. Hall, 1986. $60.

Turville-Petre, T., *The Alliterative Revival*. Brewer/R&L, 1977. £19.50.

Tydeman, William, *English Medieval Theatre 1400–1500*. RKP, 1986. £25.

Vantuono, William, ed., *The Pearl Poems: An Omnibus Edition*. Vol. 1: *Pearl and Cleanness*. Garland, 1984. $60.

Whitaker, M., *Arthur's Kingdom of Adventure*. Brewer/B&N, 1984. £19.50.

Chapter V. Middle English: Chaucer

Aers, David, ed., *Medieval Literature: Criticism, Ideology and History.*
Harvester, 1986. £28.50.

Ames, Ruth M., *God's Plenty: Chaucer's Christian Humanism.* LUP, 1984.
$12.95.

Arn, Mary-Jo, Henneke Wirtjes and Hans Jensen, *Historical and Editorial
Studies in Medieval and Early Modern English for Johan Gerritsen.* W-N,
1985. Fl 60.00.

Birney, Earle. *Essays on Chaucerian Irony,* ed. by Beryl Rowland. UTor,
1985. hb £18.75, pb £9.50.

Blake, N. F., *The Textual Tradition of the Canterbury Tales.* Arnold, 1985.
£25.

Donaldson, E. Talbot, *The Swan at the Well: Shakespeare Reading Chaucer.*
Yale, 1985. £15.

Ferster, Judith, *Chaucer on Interpretation.* CUP, 1985. £19.50.

Heffernan, Thomas J., ed., *The Popular Literature of Medieval England.*
UTenn, 1985. $28.50.

Heffernan, Thomas, J., ed., *Studies in the Age of Chaucer,* Vol. 7. New
Chaucer Society/UTenn, 1985.

Lawton, David, *Chaucer's Narrators.* Brewer, 1985. £29.50.

Leyerle, John, and Anne Quick, *Chaucer: A Bibliographical Introduction.*
UTor, 1986. hb £24.50, pb £12.

Machan, Tim William. *Techniques of Translation: Chaucer's 'Boece'.* Pilgrim,
1985. $31.95.

Payne, Robert O., *Geoffrey Chaucer.* Second edn. Twayne, 1986. $15.95.

Pearsall, Derek. *The Canterbury Tales.* A&U, 1985. hb £25, pb £9.95.

Ransom, Daniel J., *Poets at Play: Irony and Parody in the Harley Lyrics.*
Pilgrim, 1985. $31.95.

Ross, Thomas W., and Edward Brooks, Jr, eds, *English Glosses from British
Library Additional Manuscript 37075.* Pilgrim, 1984. $39.95.

Sandved, Arthur O., *Introduction to Chaucerian English.* Brewer, 1985.
£22.50.

Wallace, David, *Chaucer and the Early Writings of Boccaccio.* Brewer, 1985.
£27.50.

Wasserman, Julian N., and Robert J. Blanch, eds, *Chaucer in the Eighties.*
Syracuse, 1986. hb $37.50, pb $17.50.

Weiss, Alexander, *Chaucer's Native Heritage.* Lang, 1985. Sfr 67.30.

Wright, David, *Geoffrey Chaucer: The Canterbury Tales: a Verse Translation.*
OUP, 1985. £15.

Chapter VI. The Sixteenth Century: Excluding Drama after 1550

Harner, James L., *English Renaissance Prose Fiction 1500–1660.* Hall, 1985.
$45.

Jack, R. D. S., *Alexander Montgomerie.* SAP, 1985. £4.50.

Keene, Dennis, ed., *Henry Howard Earl of Surrey.* Carcanet, 1985. £3.95.

Marius, Richard, *Thomas More.* Dent, 1985. £16.95.

Martines, Lauro, *Society and History in English Renaissance Verse*. Blackwell, 1985. £17.50.

Spearing, A. C. *Medieval to Renaissance in English Poetry*. CUP, 1985. hb £27.50, pb £9.95.

Trevor-Roper, Hugh, *Renaissance Essays*. S&W, 1985. £15.

Wilson, K. J., *Incomplete Fictions: The Formation of English Renaissance Dialogue*. Catholic U of America P, 1985. $19.95.

Chapter VII. Shakespeare

Brockbank, Philip, ed., *Players of Shakespeare: Essays in Shakespearean Performance by Twelve Players with the Royal Shakespeare Company*. CUP, 1985. £12.50.

Dessen, Alan C., *Shakespeare and the Late Moral Plays*. UNeb, 1986.

Devlin, Diana, *'The Winter's Tale'*. Macmillan, 1985. pb £0.99.

Dodsworth, M., *'Hamlet' Closely Observed*. Athlone, 1985. £18.

Donaldson, E. T., *The Swan at the Well: Shakespeare Reading Chaucer*. Yale, 1985. £15.

Drakakis, John, ed., *Alternative Shakespeares*. Methuen, 1985. pb £4.95.

Edwards, Philip, *Shakespeare: A Writer's Progress*. OUP, 1986. £12.50.

Haring-Smith, Tori. *From Farce to Metadrama: A Stage-History of 'The Taming of the Shrew' 1594–1983*. Greenwood, 1985. £35.

Harris, A., *Night's Black Agents: Witchcraft and Magic in Seventeenth-Century English Drama*. ManU, 1980. $19.50.

Harris, L. L., and M. W. Scott, eds, *Shakespearean Criticism*. Gale. Vol. 2, 1985, $80. Vol. 3, 1986, $82.

Hawkins, Harriett, *The Devil's Party: Critical Counter-Interpretations of Shakespearian Drama*. OUP, 1985. £15.

Jorgensen, Paul A., *William Shakespeare: The Tragedies*. Twayne, 1985. $15.95.

Kennedy, Dennis, *Granville-Barker and the Dream of Theatre*. CUP, 1985. £25.

Levin, Bernard, *A Shakespeare Mystery*. EA, 1985. pb £0.60.

MacCary, W. Thomas, *Friends and Lovers: The Phenomenology of Desire in Shakespearean Comedy*. ColU, 1985. $36.

Marienstras, Richard, *New Perspectives on the Shakespearean World*. CUP, 1985. £27.50.

Metz, G. Harold, *Four Plays Ascribed to Shakespeare: An Annotated Bibliography*. Garland, 1982. £36.

Mills, J. A., *Hamlet on Stage: The Great Tradition*. Greenwood, 1985. £37.50.

Muir, Kenneth, sel. *Interpretations of Shakespeare*. OUP, 1985. £15.

Neely, Carol Thomas, *Broken Nuptials in Shakespeare's Plays*. Yale, 1985. £24.

Peck, John, and Martin Coyle, *How to Study a Shakespeare Play*. Macmillan, 1985. £4.95.

Rhoads, Diana Akers, *Shakespeare's Defense of Poetry*. UPA. pb $13.75.

Rowse, A. L., *Prefaces to Shakespeare's Plays*. Orbis, 1985. £10.

Salingar, L., *Dramatic Form in Shakespeare and the Jacobeans*. CUP, 1986. £27.50.

Saxo-Grammaticus, *History of the Danes*, trans. by P. Fisher, with a commentary by Hilda Ellis Davidson. Two vols. Brewer, 1979. $38.50.

Shakespeare, William, *Coriolanus*, ed. by Tony Parr. Macmillan, 1985. pb £1.95.

Shakespeare, William. *Hamlet*, ed. by Philip Edwards. CUP, 1985. hb £15. pb £3.50.

Shakespeare, William, *Shakespeare's 'Sonnets' and 'A Lover's Complaint'*, ed. by Stanley Wells. OUP, 1985. £8.95.

Shakespeare, William, *Twelfth Night*, ed. by Elizabeth Story Donno. CUP, 1985. hb £15, pb £2.95.

Sher, Antony, *The Year of the King*. C&W, 1985. £10.95.

Sherwood, H. C., *Shakespeare: The Tempest* (1973). Blackwell, 1983.

Srigley, Michael, *Images of Regeneration: A Study of Shakespeare's 'The Tempest' and Its Cultural Background*. Uppsala, 1985.

Steinberg, Micheline, ed., *Flashback: A Pictorial History, 1879–1979, 100 Years of Stratford-upon-Avon and the Royal Shakespeare Company*. RSC, 1985. £6.95.

Taylor, Gary, *Moment by Moment by Shakespeare*. Macmillan, 1985. £25.

Wakefield, G. P., *Shakespeare: Othello*. Blackwell, 1983.

Chapter VIII. Renaissance Drama: Excluding Shakespeare

Bale, John, *The Complete Plays of John Bale*, ed. by Peter Happé. Two vols. Brewer, 1985. £27.50, £25.

Barroll, J. Leeds, III, ed., *Medieval and Renaissance Drama in England*, Vol. 2. AMSP, 1985. $42.50.

Beaumont, Francis, and John Fletcher, *The Dramatic Works in the Beaumont and Fletcher Canon*, Vol. 6, ed. by Fredson Bowers. CUP, 1985. £55.

Bhattacharyya, Jibesh, *The Dramatic Art of John Ford*. Maya Prakashan, 1984. Rs 110.

Braden, Gordon, *Renaissance Tragedy and the Senecan Tradition: Anger's Privilege*. Yale, 1985. £21.

Brandt, Bruce Edwin, *Christopher Marlow and the Metaphysical Problem Play*. USalz, 1985.

Bristol, Michael D., *Carnival and Theater: Plebeian Culture and the Structure of Authority in Renaissance England*. Methuen, 1985. £21.

Bryant, James C., *Tudor Drama and Religious Controversy*. Mercer UP, 1984. $14.50.

Cohen, Walter, *Drama of a Nation: Public Theater in Renaissance England and Spain*. CornU, 1985. $38.50.

Cornelius, R. M., *Christopher Marlowe's Use of the Bible*. Lang, 1984. Sfr 73.60.

Edward III, ed. by George Parfitt. NDT, 1985. pb £2.50.

Foakes, R. A., *Illustrations of the English Stage 1580–1642*. Scolar, 1985. £35.

Ford, John, *The Fancies, Chast and Noble, by J. Ford: A Critical Edition*, ed. by Dominick J. Hart. Garland, 1985. $40.

Ford, John, *The Lover's Melancholy*, ed. by R. F. Hill. ManU, 1985. £25.

Galloway, David, ed., *Records of Early English Drama: Norwich 1540–1642*. UTor, 1984. $85.

Grant, Patrick, *Literature and the Discovery of Method in the English Renaissance*. Macmillan, 1985. £25.

Haselkorn, Anne M., *Prostitution in Elizabethan and Jacobean Comedy*, Whitston, 1983. $15.

Heywood, Thomas, *A Woman Killed with Kindness*, ed. by Brian Scobie. Black, 1985. pb £3.95.

Hinchliffe, Arnold P., *Volpone: Text and Performance*. Macmillan, 1985. pb £3.95.

Honigman, E. A. J., ed., *Shakespeare and His Contemporaries: Essays in Comparison*. ManU, 1986. £25.

Howard, Douglas, ed., *Philip Massinger: A Critical Reassessment*. CUP, 1985. £22.50.

Jones, Robert C., *Engagement with Knavery: Point of View in 'Richard III', 'The Jew of Malta', 'Volpone', and 'The Revenger's Tragedy'*. DukeU, 1986. $22.50.

Jonson, Ben, *Volpone*, ed. by Peter Hollindale. Longman, 1985. pb £1.60.

Kistner, A. L., and M. K. Kistner, *Middleton's Tragic Themes*. Lang, 1984. Sfr 53.

Limon, Jerzy, *Gentleman of a Company: English Players in Central and Eastern Europe 1590–1660*. CUP, 1985. £22.50.

Marlowe, Christopher, *Christopher Marlowe: Dr Faustus: The A-Text*, ed. by David Ormerod and Christopher Wortham. Western Australian UP, 1985. £5.75.

Maus, Katherine Eisaman, *Ben Jonson and the Roman Frame of Mind*. Princeton, 1984. £19.

Munday, Anthony, *Pageants and Entertainments of Anthony Munday: A Critical Edition*, ed. by David M. Bergeron. Garland, 1985. $30.

Orrell, John, *The Theatres of Inigo Jones and John Webb*. CUP, 1985. £25.

Pavel, Thomas G., *The Poetics of Plot: The Case of English Renaissance Drama*. ManU/UMinn, 1985. hb £25, pb £7.50.

Rozett, Martha Tuck, *The Doctrine of Election and the Emergence of Elizabethan Tragedy*. Princeton, 1984. £23.40.

Schuman, Samuel, *John Webster: A Reference Guide*. Hall, 1985. $55.

Sweeney, John Gordon, III, *Jonson and the Psychology of Public Theater: To Coin the Spirit, Spend the Soul*. Princeton, 1985. £26.90.

Underdown, David, *Revel, Riot, and Rebellion: Popular Politics and Culture in England 1603–1660*. OUP, 1985. £17.50.

Waage, Frederick O., *The White Devil Discover'd: Backgrounds and Foregrounds to Webster's Tragedy*. Lang, 1984. Sfr 37.45.

A Yorkshire Tragedy, ed. by A. C. Cawley and Barry Gaines. ManU, 1986. £25.

Chapter IX. The Earlier Seventeenth Century: Excluding Drama

Bacon, Francis, *The Essayes or Counsels, Civill and Morall*, ed. by Michael Kiernan. Clarendon, 1985. £35.

Bacon, Francis, *The Essays*, ed. by John Pitcher. Penguin, 1985. pb £3.95.

Hill, Christopher, *Collected Essays*. Vol. 1: *Writing and Revolution in Seventeenth-Century England*. Harvester, 1985. £28.50.

Hill, Christopher, *Collected Essays.* Vol. 2: *Religion and Politics in Seventeenth-Century England.* Harvester, 1986. £28.50.

Jonson, Ben, *Ben Jonson,* ed. by Ian Donaldson. OA. OUP, 1985. pb £7.95.

Martines, Lauro, *Society and History in English Renaissance Verse.* Blackwell, 1985. £17.50.

Otten, Charlotte F., *Environ'd With Eternity: God, Poems, and Plants in Sixteenth- and Seventeenth-Century England.* Coronada Press (Kansas), 1985. $19.95.

Roberts, John R., ed., *Richard Crashaw: An Annotated Bibliography of Criticism 1632–1980.* UMiss, 1985. £38.

Salzman, Paul, *English Prose Fiction 1558–1700: A Critical History.* Clarendon, 1985. £25.

Smith, A. J., *The Metaphysics of Love: Studies in Renaissance Love Poetry from Dante to Milton.* CUP, 1985. £25.

Stocker, Margarita, *Apocalyptic Marvell: The Second Coming in Seventeenth-Century Poetry.* Harvester, 1986. £32.50.

Chapter X. Milton

Brown, Cedric C., *John Milton's Aristocratic Entertainments.* CUP, 1985. £25.

Budick, Sanford, *The Dividing Muse: Images of Sacred Disjunction in Milton's Poetry.* Yale, 1985. £18.

Lewalski, Barbara Kiefer, *'Paradise Lost' and the Rhetoric of Literary Forms.* Princeton, 1985. £22.60.

Martindale, Charles, *John Milton and the Transformation of Ancient Epic.* CH, 1986. £22.50.

Miller, Leo, *John Milton & The Oldenburg Safeguard: New Light on Milton and His Friends in the Commonwealth from the Diaries of Hermann Mylius, Agonist in the Early History of Modern Diplomacy.* Lowenthal Press, 1985. $45.

Milton, John, *Poems,* ed. by Laurence D. Lerner. Penguin, 1985. pb £1.95.

Shawcross, John T., ed., *The Collection of the Works of John Milton and Miltoniana in the Margaret I. King Library. University of Kentucky.* UKen Libraries. $15.

Shoaf, R. A., *Milton, Poet of Duality: A Study of Semiosis in the Poetry and the Prose.* Yale, 1985. £17.

Sterne, Laurence, and Harold H. Kollmeier, eds, *A Concordance to the English Prose of John Milton.* MRTS 35. CMERS, 1985. $96.

Chapter XI. The Later Seventeenth Century

Congreve, William, *The Comedies of William Congreve,* ed. by Eric S. Rump. Penguin, 1985. pb £4.95.

Dryden, John, *Poems and Prose,* sel. by Douglas Grant. Penguin, repr. 1985. pb £2.50.

Dunn, John, *Locke.* OUP, 1984. hb £7.75, pb £1.95.

D'Urfey, Thomas, *Butler's Ghost (1682).* SF&R, 1984. $45.

Gibbons, Brian, intro., *Five Restoration Comedies*. Black, 1984. £5.95.

Harwood, John T., *Critics, Values and Restoration Comedy*. SIU, 1982. $17.95.

Highfill, Philip H., Jr, Kalman A. Burnim, and Edward A. Langhans, *A Biographical Dictionary of Actors, Actresses, Musicians, Dancers, Managers and Other Stage Personnel in London, 1660–1800*, Vols 9 and 10. SIU, 1984.

Hopkins, David, *John Dryden*. CUP, 1986. hb £25, pb £7.50.

James, Eugene Nelson, *George Farquhar: A Reference Guide*. Hall, 1986.

Kenny, Virginia C., *The Country House Ethos in English Literature 1688–1750*. Harvester, 1984. £28.50.

László, Földényi F., *A Dramaturgia Csapdája*. Magvető Könyvkiadó, 1983.

Lawrence, Robert G., ed., *Restoration Plays*. Dent, 1985. pb £3.50.

Lindley, David, ed., *The Court Masque*. ManU, 1984. £22.50.

Markley, Robert and Laurie Finke, eds, *From Renaissance to Restoration: Metamorphoses of the Drama*. Bellflower, 1984. $16.

Myers, William, ed., *Restoration and Revolution*. CH, 1986. pb. £11.95.

Parfitt, George, *English Poetry of the Seventeenth Century*. Longman, 1985. hb £13.95, pb £5.95.

Pix, Mary, *The Inhumane Cardinal (1696)*. SF&R. 1984. $45.

Powell, Jocelyn. *Restoration Theatre Production*. RKP, 1984. £19.95.

Schleifer, Ronald, and Robert Markley, eds, *Kierkegaard and Literature: Irony, Repetition and Criticism*. UOkla, 1984. $22.95.

Stone, Lawrence, and Jeanne C. Fawtier Stone, *An Open Elite? England 1540–1880*. Clarendon, 1984. £24.

Wasserman, George, *Samuel Butler and the Earl of Rochester: A Reference Guide*. Hall, 1986. $49.

Weiss, Wolfgang, ed., *Die Englische Satire, Wege der Forschung*. Band 4 562. WB, 1982.

Zwicker, Steven N., *Politics and Language in Dryden's Poetry*. Princeton, 1984. £20.90.

Chapter XII. The Eighteenth Century

Ayling, Stanley, *A Portrait of Sheridan*. Constable, 1985. £9.95.

Battestin, Martin, ed., *British Novelists 1660–1800*. Gale, 1985. $170.

Bell, Ian A., *Defoe's Fiction*. CH, 1985. £17.95.

Black, Jeremy, *The British and the Grand Tour*. CH, 1985. £19.95.

Brown, Laura, *Alexander Pope*. Blackwell, 1985. pb £3.95.

Burney, Fanny, *Cecilia*, intro. by Judith Simons. Virago, 1986. pb £6.95.

Burns, Robert, *Letters of Robert Burns*, ed. by J. De Lancey Ferguson. Second edn, by G. Ross Roy. Clarendon, 1985. £90.

Burrow, J. W., *Gibbon*. OUP, 1985. pb £1.95.

Byrd, Max, *Tristram Shandy*. A&U, 1985. £15.

Clark, J. C. D., *English Society 1688–1832*. CUP, 1985. £10.95.

Cleland, John, *Fanny Hill or Memoirs of a Woman of Pleasure*, ed. by Peter Sabor. OUP, 1985. pb £2.95.

Cleland, John, *Fanny Hill or Memoirs of a Woman of Pleasure*, ed. by Peter Wagner. Penguin, 1985. pb £2.95.

Cole, Richard Cargill, *Irish Booksellers and English Writers 1740–1800*. Mansell, 1986. £27.50.

Davison, Peter, ed., *Sheridan: Comedies: A Selection of Critical Essays*. Macmillan, 1986. hb £20, pb £6.95.

Doody, Margaret Anne, *The Daring Muse: Augustan Poetry Reconsidered*. CUP, 1985. pb. £8.95.

Ellis, Frank H., ed., *Swift vs. Mainwaring: The Examiner and The Medley*. Clarendon, 1985. £48.

Farquhar, George, *The Recruiting Officer*, ed. by Peter Dixon. ManU, 1986. £27.50.

Feather, John, *The Provincial Book Trade in Eighteenth-Century England*. CUP, 1985. £22.50.

Goldsmith, M. M., *Private Vices, Public Benefits: Bernard Mandeville's Social and Political Thought*. CUP, 1985. £20.

Griffin, Dustin, *Regaining Paradise: Milton and the Eighteenth Century*. CUP, 1986. £25.

Grundy, Isobel, *Samuel Johnson and the Scale of Greatness*. ULeics, 1986. £27.

Houston, R. A., *Scottish Literacy and the Scottish Identity*. CUP, 1985. £27.50.

Ingram, Allan, *Intricate Laughter in the Satire of Swift and Pope*. Macmillan, 1986. £25.

Kenshur, Oscar, *Open Form and the Shape of Ideas*. AUP, 1986. £16.95.

King, James, *William Cowper: A Biography*. DukeU, 1986. $35.

Larsen, Lyle, *Dr. Johnson's Household*. Archon, 1985. £20.25.

Lock, F. P., *Burke's Reflections on the Revolution in France*. A&U, 1985. £18.

Mack, Maynard, *Alexander Pope: A Life*. Yale, 1985. £15.95.

Marshall, David, *The Figure of Theatre: Shaftesbury, Defoe, Adam Smith and George Eliot*. ColU, 1985. $27.

Meehan, Michael, *Liberty and Poetics in Eighteenth-Century England*. CH, 1985. £17.95.

Morwood, James, *The Life and Works of Richard Brinsley Sheridan*. SAP, 1985. £12.50.

Nokes, David, *Jonathan Swift: A Hypocrite Reversed*. OUP, 1985. £14.95.

Patey, D. L., and T. Keegan, eds, *Augustan Studies: Essays in Honour of Irvin Ehrenpreis*. AUP, 1986. £24.50.

Percy, Thomas, *The Percy Letters: The Correspondence of Thomas Percy and John Pinkerton*, ed. by Harriet Harvey Wood. Yale, 1985. £25.

Phillips, Patricia, *The Adventurous Muse: Theories of Originality in English Poetry 1650–1760*. Uppsala, 1984. pb £8.75.

Pocock, J. G. A., *Virtue, Commerce, and History*. CUP, 1985. pb £7.95.

Powell, David, *Tom Paine: The Greatest Exile*. CH, 1985. £18.95.

Ranger, Paul, *'She Stoops To Conquer' by Oliver Goldsmith*. Macmillan, 1985. pb £0.99.

Rawson, Claude, *Order from Confusion Sprung: Studies in Eighteenth-Century Literature*. A&U, 1985. £27.50.

Richardson, Samuel, *Clarissa, or the History of a Young Lady*, ed. by Angus Ross. Penguin, 1985. pb £9.95.

Rippey, Francis Mayhew, *Matthew Prior*. Twayne, 1986. $23.95.

Rogers, Pat, *Eighteenth Century Encounters: Studies in Literature and Society in the Age of Walpole*. Harvester, 1985. £20.

Sambrook, James, *The Eighteenth Century: The Intellectual and Cultural Context of English Literature 1700–1789.* Longman, 1986. pb £7.95.

Schofield, Mary Anne, *Eliza Haywood.* Twayne, 1985. $20.95.

Scott, Sarah, *Millenium Hall*, intro. by Jane Spencer. Virago, 1986. pb £4.95.

Sher, R. B., *Church and University in the Scottish Enlightenment: The Moderate Literati of Edinburgh.* EdinU, 1985. £27.50.

Simpson, K. G., ed., *Henry Fielding: Justice Observed.* Vision, 1985. £14.95.

Tipton, Ian, *Reason and Experience: Locke.* OpenU, 1983.

Chapter XIII. The Nineteenth Century: Romantic Period

Aske, Martin, *Keats and Hellenism.* CUP, 1985. £22.50.

Austen, Jane, *The Manuscript Chapters of 'Persuasion'.* Athlone, 1985. £10.50.

Austen, Jane, *Selected Letters.* OUP, 1985. pb. £2.95.

Austen, Jane, *The Watsons.* Athlone, 1985. £10.95.

Baker, Jeffrey, *John Keats and Symbolism.* Harvester, 1986. £25.

Bracher, Mark, *Being Form'd: Thinking Through Blake's Milton.* Station Hill, 1985. pb $9.95.

Burns, Bryan, *The Novels of Thomas Love Peacock.* CH, 1985. £16.95.

Burns, Robert, *The Kilmarnock Poems*, ed. by Donald A. Low. Dent, 1985. £10.95.

Bygrave, Stephen, *Coleridge and the Self: Romantic Egotism.* Macmillan, 1986. £25.

Byron, George Gordon, *The Complete Poetical Works*, Vol. 4, ed. by Jerome J. McGann. Clarendon, 1986. £50.

Byron, George Gordon, *Selected Works*, ed. by Jerome J. McGann, OUP, 1986. hb £22.50, pb £7.95.

Chilcott, Tim, *'A Real World and a Doubting Mind': A Critical Study of John Clare.* UHull, 1985. £13.95.

Christensen, Inger, *The Shadow of the Dome: Organicism and Romantic Poetry.* UBergen, 1985. Nkr 120.

Crompton, Louis, *Byron and Greek Love.* Faber, 1985. £17.50.

Fraistat, Neil, *The Poem and the Book: Interpreting Collections of Romantic Poetry.* UNC, 1985. £19.95.

Galt, John, *The Member.* SAP, 1985. pb £3.75.

Gittings, Robert, and Jo Manton, *Dorothy Wordsworth.* Clarendon, 1985. £12.50.

Harding, Anthony John, *Coleridge and the Inspired Word.* Mc-Q, 1985. $27.50.

Hogg, James, *Tales of Love and Mystery.* Canongate, 1985. £9.95.

Jackson, J. R. de J., *Annals of English Verse, 1770–1835: A Preliminary Survey of the Volumes Published.* Garland, 1985. $76.

Jordan, Frank, ed., *The English Romantic Poets: A Review of Research and Criticism.* MLA, 1985. pb $22.50.

King-Hele, Desmond, *Erasmus Darwin and the Romantic Poets.* Macmillan, 1986. £27.50.

McGann, Jerome, J., *The Beauty of Inflections: Literary Investigations in Historical Method and Theory.* Clarendon, 1985. £19.50.

Menascé, Esther, *Il tragico errare di Faust: Melmoth*. Olschki, 1983.
Mendilow, Jonathan, *The Romantic Tradition in British Political Thought*. CH, 1985. £22.50.
Modiano, Raimonda, *Coleridge and the Concept of Nature*. Macmillan, 1985. £25.
Newlyn, Lucy, *Coleridge, Wordsworth and the Language of Allusion*. Clarendon, 1986. £22.50.
Scott, Sir Walter, *Redgauntlet*. OUP, 1985. pb £3.95.
Shelley, Mary, *The Last Man*. Hogarth, 1985. pb £3.95.
Shelley, Percy Bysshe, *'Zastrozzi' and 'St Irvyne'*. OUP, 1986. pb £2.95.
Thompson, James R., *Thomas Lovell Beddoes*. Twayne, 1985. $18.95.
Turner, John, *Wordsworth: Play and Politics*. Macmillan, 1986. £25.
Vassallo, Peter, ed., *Byron and the Mediterranean*. UMalta, 1986.
Watson, J. R., *English Poetry of the Romantic Period 1789–1830*. Longman, 1985. pb £7.50.
Witke, Joanne, *William Blake's Epic: Imagination Unbound*. CH, 1986. £18.95.

Chapter XIV. The Nineteenth Century: Victorian Period

Agajanian, Shaakeh S., *Sonnets From The Portuguese and the Love Sonnet Tradition*. Philosophical Library, 1985. pb $9.95.
Archer, John H. G., ed., *Art and Architecture in Victorian Manchester*. ManU, 1985. £29.95.
Arnold, Matthew, *Poems*, ed. by Kenneth Allott. Penguin, 1985. pb £1.95.
Arthurs, H. W., *Without the Law: Administrative Justice and Legal Pluralism in Nineteenth-Century England*. UTor, 1985.
Barnes, Malcolm, *Augustus Hare: Victorian Gentleman*. A&U, 1985. £20.
Billcliffe, Roger, *The Glasgow Boys*. Murray, 1985. £35.
Bindman, David, ed., *Thames and Hudson Encyclopaedia of British Art*. T&H, 1985. £10.50.
Blaikie, Thomas, ed., *Victorian Love Poetry*. Macmillan, 1985. pb £3.95.
Bloom, Harold, ed., *Alfred Lord Tennyson*. Chelsea House, 1985. $24.50.
Bloom, Harold, ed., *Robert Browning*. Chelsea House, 1985. $19.95.
Bronte, Anne, Branwell, Charlotte, and Emily, *Selected Bronte Poems*, ed. by Edward Chitham and Tom Winnifrith. Blackwell, 1985. pb £5.95.
Bronte, Anne, Charlotte, and Emily, *Poems By The Bronte Sisters*, ed. by M. R. D. Seaward. Black, 1985. pb £3.50.
Bronte, Anne, Charlotte, and Emily, *The Brontes: Selected Poems*, ed. by Juliet Barker. Dent, 1985. pb £2.50.
Bronte, Charlotte, *The Poems of Charlotte Bronte: A New Text and Commentary*, ed. by Victor A. Neufeldt. Garland, 1985. $65.
Bronte, Charlotte, *The Professor; Emma: A Fragment*, intro. by Anne Smith. Dent, 1985. pb £2.95.
Browning, Elizabeth and Robert, *The Brownings' Correspondence*, Vol. 3, ed. by Philip Kelley and Ronald Hudson. Wedgestone, 1985. $47.50.
Browning, Robert, *More Than Friend: The Letters of Robert Browning to Katharine de Kay Bronson*, ed. by Michael C. Meredith and Rita S. Humphrey. Wedgestone, 1985. $25.
Campbell, James L., *Edward Bulwer-Lytton*. Twayne, 1986. £19.95.

Carpenter, Edward, *Towards Democracy*. GMP, 1985. pb £5.95.

Chapman, Raymond, *The Sense of the Past*. CH, 1985. £22.50.

Charles, Edna Kotin, *Christina Rossetti: Critical Perspectives 1862–1982*. AUP, 1985. £18.50.

Chitham, Edward, *The Brontes' Irish Background*. Macmillan, 1986. £25.

Colee, Fulton, *Union List of Victorian Serials*. Garland, 1985. $103.

Collie, Michael, *George Gissing: A Bibliographical Study*. StPB, 1985. £28.

Connor, Steven, *Charles Dickens*. Blackwell, 1985. hb £12.50, pb £3.95.

Cook, Ramsay, *The Regenerators: Social Criticism in Late Victorian Canada*. UTor, 1985. £24.50.

Cooter, Roger, *The Cultural Meaning of Popular Science: Phrenology and the Organization of Consent in Nineteenth-Century Britain*. CUP, 1985. £25.

Coustillas, Pierre, and Colin Patridge, eds, *Gissing: The Critical Heritage*. RKP, 1985. pb £8.95.

Crawford, Alan, *C. R. Ashbee: Architect, Designer & Romantic Socialist*. Yale, 1985. £35.

Cross, Nigel, *The Common Writer: Life in Nineteenth-Century Grub Street*. CUP, 1985. £25.

Crump, R. W., *Charlotte and Emily Bronte: 1916–54: A Reference Guide*. Hall, 1985. $35.

Culler, A. Dwight, *The Victorian Mirror of History*. Yale, 1986. £22.50.

Danon, Ruth, *Work in the English Novel: The Myth of Vocation*. C-H, 1985. £17.95.

Darwin, Charles, *Correspondence*. Vol. 1: *1821–36*. ed. by F. Burkhardt and S. Smith. CUP, 1985. £30.

Dave, J. C., *The Human Predicament in Hardy's Novels*. Macmillan, 1985. £22.50.

Demers, Patricia, *The Creating Word*. Macmillan, 1986. £25.

Denvir, Bernard, *The Late Victorians: Art, Design and Society 1852–1910*. Longman, 1986. pb £7.50.

Dickens, Charles, *Selected Letters of Charles Dickens*, ed. by David Paroissien. Macmillan, 1985.

Downes, David Anthony, *Ruskin's Landscape of Beatitude*. Lang, 1984.

Eliot, George, *Scenes of Clerical Life*, ed. by Thomas Noble. Clarendon, 1985. £32.

Eliot, George, *Some George Eliot Notebooks*, Vol. 2, ed. by William Baker. USalz, 1984.

Eliot, George, *Some George Eliot Notebooks*, Vol. 4, ed. by William Baker. USalz, 1985.

Engels, Friedrich, *The Origins of the Family. Private Property and the State*. Penguin, 1985. pb £3.95.

Engen, Rodney K., *A Dictionary of Victorian Wood Engravers*. C-H, 1985. £45.

Ermath, Elizabeth D., *George Eliot*. Twayne, 1985. $14.95.

Flint, Kate, *Dickens*. Harvester, 1986. hb £16.95, pb £5.95.

Fraser, Hilary, *Beauty and Belief: Aesthetics and Religion in Victorian Literature*. CUP, 1986. £25.

Fredeman, William, and Ira B. Nadel, eds, *Victorian Poets After 1850*. Gale, 1985. $85.

Golding, Robert, *Idiolects in Dickens*. Macmillan, 1985. £25.

Goodin, George, *The Poetics of Protest: Literary Form and Political Implication in the Victim-of-Society Novel.* SIU, 1985. $19.95.

Green, Vivian, *Love in a Cool Climate: The Letters of Mark Pattison and Meta Bradley.* OUP, 1985. £12.95.

Handley, Graham, *'Middlemarch' by George Eliot.* Macmillan, 1985. pb £0.99.

Hardman, Malcolm, *Ruskin and Bradford: An Experiment in Victorian Cultural History.* ManU, 1986. £27.50.

Hardy, Emma, *Diaries*, ed. by Richard Taylor. MidNAG/Carcanet, 1985. £14.95.

Hargrove, Anne C., and Maurine Magliocco, eds, *Portraits of Marriage in Literature.* UWIll, 1984. pb $8.50.

Holderness, Graham, *Wuthering Heights.* OpenU, 1985. hb £12.50, pb £3.50.

Honri, Peter, *John Wilton's Music Hall.* Ian Henry Publications, 1985. £17.45.

Horstman, Allen, *Victorian Divorce.* CH, 1985. £17.95.

Howe, Irving, *Thomas Hardy.* Macmillan, 1985. hb £25, pb £7.95.

Hudson, W. H., and George Gissing, *Landscapes and Literati: Unpublished Letters of W. H. Hudson and George Gissing*, ed. by Dennis Shrubsall and Pierre Coustillas. Michael Russell, 1985. £12.95.

James, Jerry D., and Rita B. Bottoms, *The Norman and Charlotte Strouse Lectures on Carlyle and His Era.* UCal, 1985.

Janson, H. W., *Nineteenth-Century Sculpture.* T&H, 1985. £35.

Kavanagh, James H., *Emily Bronte.* Blackwell, 1985. hb £12.50, pb £3.95.

King, Mary C., *The Drama of J. M. Synge.* Fourth Estate, 1985. £17.50.

Kinzer, Bruce L., *The Gladstonian Turn of Mind.* UTor, 1985. £24.50.

Kipling, Rudyard, *Kipling's India: Uncollected Sketches, 1848–88*, ed. by Thomas Pinney. Macmillan, 1986. £25.

Knott, John, *Popular Opposition to the 1834 Poor Law.* CH, 1985. £19.95.

Landow, George P., *Ruskin.* OUP, 1985. pb £2.25.

Leatherdale, Clive, *Dracula: The Novel and the Legend.* Aquarian, 1985. pb £6.95.

Magnet, Myron, *Dickens and the Social Order.* UPenn, 1985. £29.95.

Maitland, F. W., *G. R. Elton.* W&N, 1985. £12.95.

Martin, Graham, *'Great Expectations'.* OpenU, 1985, hb £12.50, pb £3.50.

Martin, Robert B., *With Friends Possessed: A Life of Edward Fitzgerald.* Faber, 1985. £17.50.

Melchiori, Barbara Arnett, *Terrorism in the Late Victorian Novel.* C-H, 1985. £19.95.

Messinger, Gary S., *Manchester in the Victorian Age.* ManU, 1985. £4.50.

Midgeley, Mary, *Evolution as a Religion.* Methuen, 1985. £12.95.

Mill, John Stuart, *Essays on French History and Historians.* UTor, 1985. £55.

Monod, Sylvere, *'Martin Chuzzlewit'.* A&U, 1985. £18.

Morgan, Margery, *August Strindberg.* Macmillan, 1985. hb £15, pb £4.95.

Munsell, F. D., *The Unfortunate Duke: Henry Pelham, Fifth Duke of Newcastle 1811–1864.* UMiss, 1985. £15.95.

Newman, Louise Michele, ed., *Men's Ideas/Women's Realities: Popular Science, 1870–1915.* Pergamon, 1984. hb $32.50, pb $13.50.

Noakes, Vivien, *Edward Lear 1812–1888.* W&N, 1985. hb £16.95, pb £8.95.

Norman, Edward, *The English Catholic Church in the Nineteenth Century.* OUP, 1984. £8.95.

Norrman, Ralph, *Samuel Butler and the Meaning of Chiasmus*. Macmillan, 1986. £27.50.

Oliphant, Margaret, *Selected Stories of the Supernatural*, ed. by Margaret K. Gray. SAP, 1985. £8.50.

Oppenheim, Janet, *The Other World: Spiritualism and Psychic Research in England 1850–1914*. CUP, 1985. £25.

Page, Norman, *'Hard Times' by Charles Dickens*. Macmillan, 1985. pb £0.99.

Page, Norman, ed., *Thomas Hardy Annual*, No. 3. Macmillan, 1985. £30.

Page, Norman, ed., *Wilkie Collins: The Critical Heritage*. RKP, 1985. pb £8.95.

Palgrave, F. T., *Selected Poems*, ed. by Brian Louis Pearce. Brentham, 1985. pb £3.50.

Perth, Earl of, ed., *A Tour of Scotland in 1863*. The Roxburghe Club, 1984.

Peterson, William S., *A Bibliography of the Kelmscott Press*. OUP, 1984. £25.

Planché, James Robinson, *Plays by James Robinson Planché: 'The Vampire'; 'The Garrick Fever'; 'Beauty And The Beast'; 'Fortunio And His Seven Gifted Servants'; 'The Golden Fleece'; 'The Camp At The Olympic'; 'The Discreet Princess'*, ed. by Donald Roy. CUP, 1986. hb £27.50, pb £11.95.

Read, Jack, *Empires, Palaces & Hippodromes*. Alderman Press, 1985. £12.50.

Rosenberg, John D., *Carlyle and the Burden of History*. OUP, 1985. £19.50.

Sawyer, Paul L., *Ruskin's Poetic Argument: The Design of the Major Works*. CornU, 1985. £27.50.

Schafer, Werner, *Komik in Den Romancen George Eliots*. Gruner, 1985. Fl 50.

Schlicke, Paul, *Dickens and Popular Entertainment*. A&U, 1985. £21.

Schulz, Max F., *Paradise Preserved: Recreations of Eden in Eighteenth- & Nineteenth-Century England*. CUP, 1986. £58.

Shelston, Alan, ed., *Dickens' 'Dombey and Son' and 'Little Dorrit': A Casebook*. Macmillan, 1985. hb £20, pb £6.95.

Sinfield, Alan, *Alfred Tennyson*. Blackwell, 1986. pb £4.95.

Slater, Michael, *Dickens and Women*. Dent, 1986. pb £5.95.

Smiles, Samuel, *Self-Help*, ed. by K. Joseph. Penguin, 1986. pb £3.95.

Stansky, Peter, *Redesigning the World: William Morris, the 1880's and the Arts and Crafts*. Princeton, 1985. £29.60.

Stevenson, Robert Louis, *A Child's Garden of Verses*. Gollancz, 1985. pb £6.95.

Stewart, Robert, *Henry Brougham: His Public Career 1778–1868*. Bodley, 1986. £18.

Swindells, Julia, *Victorian Writing and Working Women*. Polity, 1985. pb £6.95.

Taylor, Tom, *Plays by Tom Taylor: 'Still Waters Run Deep'; 'The Contested Election'; 'The Overland Route'; 'The Ticket-Of-Leave Man'*, ed. by Martin Banham. CUP, 1985. £27.50.

Temblett-Wood, Colin, *'Far From the Madding Crowd' by Thomas Hardy*. Macmillan, 1985. pb £0.99.

Tennyson, Alfred, *Poems*, ed. by W. E. Williams. Penguin, 1985. pb £1.95.

Thomas, Gillian, *Harriet Martineau*. Twayne, 1985. £18.50.

Vance, Norman, *The Sinews of the Spirit: The Ideal of Christian Manliness in Victorian Literature and Religious Thought*. CUP, 1985. £22.50.

Vann, J. Don, *Victorian Novels in Serial*. MLA, 1985. $50.

Vernon, John, *Money and Fiction: Literary Realism in the Nineteenth and Early Twentieth Centuries*. CornU, 1984. $19.95.

Vogeler, Martha S., *Frederic Harrison: The Vocations of a Positivist*. OUP, 1984. £27.50.

Westwater, Martha, *The Wilson Sisters: A Biographical Study of Upper Middle-Class Victorian Life*. OhioU, 1984. £30.

Wilde, Oscar, *More Letters of Oscar Wilde*, ed. by Rupert Hart-Davis. Murray, 1985. £12.50.

Williams, Ioan, ed., *Meredith: The Critical Heritage*. RKP, 1985. pb £8.95.

Wilson, Charles, *First with the News: the History of W. H. Smith 1792–1972*. Cape, 1985. £16.

Young, Robert M., *Darwin's Metaphor: Nature's Place in Victorian Culture*. CUP, 1985. £9.95.

Chapter XV. The Twentieth Century

al-Raheb, Hani, *The Zionist Character in the English Novel*. Zed Books, 1985. hb £16.95, pb £6.50.

Amos, William, *The Originals: Who's Really Who in Fiction*. Cape, 1985. £12.95.

Asquith, Margot, *The Autobiography of Margot Asquith*, intro. by Mark Bonham Carter, Methuen, 1985. £4.95.

Ayling, Ronald, ed., *O'Casey: the Dublin Trilogy: A Casebook*. Macmillan, 1985. hb £20, pb £6.95.

Baker, Paul, *A Reassessment of D. H. Lawrence's 'Aaron's Rod'*. UMIRes, 1985. £33.75.

Balbert, Peter, and Philip L. Marcus, eds, *D. H. Lawrence: A Centenary Consideration*. CornU, 1985. $25.

Batchelor, John, *H. G. Wells*. CUP, 1985. £6.50.

Beckett, Samuel, *Collected Shorter Plays*. Faber, 1985. pb £3.95.

Beckett, Samuel, *Collected Shorter Prose 1945–80*. Calder, 1984. £9.95.

Beckett, Samuel, *The Complete Dramatic Works*. Faber, 1986. £12.50.

Beer, John, ed., *'A Passage to India': Essays in Interpretation*. Macmillan, 1985. hb £25, pb £7.95.

Behan, Brian, *Mother of All the Behans*. Arena, 1985. pb £2.95.

Beja, Morris, ed., *Critical Essays on Virginia Woolf*. Hall, 1985. £35.

Bellorini, Maria Grazia, Gianfranca Balestra, Margherita Giulietti, and Domenico Pezzini, *W. H. Auden: Riti della Parola*. Biblioteca del Dipartimento di Lingue e di Letterature Straniere 1. Vita e Pensiero. Pubblicazioni della Universita Cattolica Milano, 1985. L 26,000.

Bennett, Alan, *A Private Function*. Faber, 1984. pb £3.95.

Bennett, Alan, *The Writer in Disguise*. Faber, 1985. pb £3.95.

Berger, John, *The White Bird: Writings by John Berger*, ed. by Lloyd Spencer. C&W, 1985. £10.95.

Bergonzi, Bernard, *The Myth of Modernism and Twentieth Century Literature*. Harvester, 1986. £22.50.

Berkoff, Steven, *'West' and Other Plays*. Faber, 1985. pb £3.95.

Black, Michael, *D. H. Lawrence: The Early Fiction*. Macmillan, 1986. £27.50.

Bold, Alan, ed., *W. H. Auden: The Far Interior*. Vision/B&N, 1985. £15.95.

Bowker, Gordon, *Malcolm Lowry Remembered*. BBC, 1985. £4.25.

Brivic, Sheldon, *Joyce the Creator*. UWisc, 1985. $21.50.

Broderick, John C., ed., *George Orwell and 'Nineteen Eighty-Four'*. LC, 1985. $3.50.

Brown, Richard, *James Joyce and Sexuality*. CUP, 1985. £19.50.

Bufkin, E. C., ed., *The Twentieth Century Novel in English: A Checklist*. UGeo, 1984. $20.

Burt, Forrest D., *W. Somerset Maugham*. Twayne, 1985. $16.95.

Callow, Simon, *Being an Actor*. Penguin, 1985. pb £3.95.

Carter, Michael, *George Orwell and the Problem of Authentic Existence*. CH, 1985. £17.95.

Chesterton, G. K., *The Bodley Head G. K. Chesterton*, ed. by P. J. Kavanagh. Bodley, 1985. £12.95.

Clareson, Thomas, and Thomas Wymer, eds, *Voices for the Future: Essays on Major Science Fiction Writers*. Popular, 1984.

Clews, Hetty, *The Only Teller: Readings in the Monologue Novel*. SonoNis, 1985. $14.

Connolly, Cyril, *The Condemned Playground*. Hogarth, 1985. pb £4.95.

Cooper, Andrew, ed., *D. H. Lawrence: 1885–1930: A Celebration*. DHL Soc., 1985. pb £2.75.

Cornish, Roger, and Violet Ketels, intro., *Landmarks of Modern British Drama*. Vol. 1: *The Plays of the Sixties*. Methuen, 1985. pb £4.95.

Cornish, Roger, and Violet Ketels, intro., *Landmarks of Modern British Drama*. Vol. 2: *The Plays of the Seventies*. Methuen, 1986. pb £4.95.

Costa, Richard Hauer, *H. G. Wells*. Twayne, 1985. $13.95.

Creighton, Joanne, *Margaret Drabble*. Methuen, 1985. pb £2.75.

Dabydeen, David, ed., *The Black Presence in English Literature*. ManU, 1985. hb £19.95, pb £5.95.

Davey, Charles, *D. H. Lawrence: A Living Poet*. Brentham, 1985. pb £2.50.

Davidson, Arnold E., *Conrad's Endings: A Study of Five Major Novels*. UMIRes, 1985. £28.50.

Davin, Dan, sel., *Short Stories From the Second World War*. OUP, 1984. pb £3.50.

Davis, Elizabeth, *Graham Greene: the Artist as Critic*. YorkP, 1985. hb $12.95, pb $6.95.

Dawe, Gerald, and Edna Longley, eds, *Across a Roaring Hill: The Protestant Imagination in Modern Ireland*. Blackstaff, 1985. £10.95.

Deane, Seamus, *Celtic Revivals: Essays in Modern Irish Literature*. Faber, 1985. £15.

Dervin, Daniel, *A Strange Sapience: The Creative Imagination of D. H. Lawrence*. UMass, 1984. $23.50.

Donaldson, Frances, *Evelyn Waugh: Portrait of a Country Neighbour*. W&N, 1985. hb £9.95, pb £4.95.

Douglas, Keith, *Keith Douglas: A Prose Miscellany*, ed. by Desmond Graham. Carcanet, 1985. pb £8.95.

Duplessis, Rachel Blau, *Writing Beyond the Ending*. IndU, 1985. hb $27.50, pb $12.95.

Elgin, Don D., *The Comedy of the Fantastic: Ecological Perspectives on the Fantasy Novel*. Greenwood, 1985. £29.95.

Fido, Martin, *Rudyard Kipling*. Hamlyn, 1985. £6.95.

Finney, Brian, *The Inner I: British Literary Autobiography of the Twentieth Century.* Faber, 1985. £14.95.

Fisher, Margery, *The Bright Face of Danger: An Exploration of the Adventure Story.* H&S, 1985. £12.95.

Fitzgibbon, Theodora, *Love Lies a Loss: An Autobiography 1946–1959.* Century, 1985. £10.95.

Fletcher, Beryl S. and John, *A Student's Guide to the Plays of Samuel Beckett.* Second rev. and expanded edn. Faber, 1985. hb £10, pb £4.95.

Ford, Ford Madox, *The Ford Madox Ford Reader,* ed. by Sondra M. Stang. Carcanet, 1986. £18.95.

Ford, James Allan, *The Brave White Flag.* Richard Drew, 1985. pb £3.95.

Gardner, Averil, *Angus Wilson.* Hall, 1985. $15.95.

Gardner, Philip, ed., *E. M. Forster: Commonplace Book.* Scholar, 1985. £25.

Garstenauer, Maria, *A Selective Study of English History Plays in the Period between 1960 and 1977.* USalz, 1985.

Gidal, Peter, *Understanding Beckett.* Macmillan, 1986. £29.50.

Gifford, Douglas, *The Dear Green Place? The Novel in the West of Scotland.* Third Eye Centre (Glasgow), 1985. pb £1.50.

Golding, William, *An Egyptian Journal.* Faber, 1985. £12.95.

Gould, Warwick, ed., *Yeats Annual,* No. 4. Methuen, 1986. £30.

Gray, Simon, *An Unnatural Pursuit.* Faber, 1985. hb £10.95, pb £4.95.

Greene, Graham, *Author's Choice: Four Novels by Graham Greene.* Penguin, 1985. pb £5.95.

Greene, Graham, *Collected Essays.* Penguin, 1985. pb £3.95.

Gunn, Neil, *The Silver Bough.* Richard Drew, 1985. pb £3.95.

Hadfield, John, sel. and intro., *Modern Short Stories to 1940.* Dent, 1984. pb £1.95.

Haffenden, John, *Novelists in Interview.* Methuen, 1985. hb £11.95, pb £5.95.

Hamilton, Ian, ed., *The New Review Anthology.* Heinemann, 1985. £12.95.

Hampton, Christopher, *Les Liaisons Dangereuses.* Faber, 1985. pb £3.95.

Harding, James, *Agate.* Methuen, 1986. £12.95.

Hardy, George, and Nathaniel Harris, *A D. H. Lawrence Album.* Moorland, 1985. £8.95.

Hare, David, *Plenty.* Methuen, 1986. pb £3.95.

Hare, David, *Wetherby.* Faber, 1985. pb £3.95.

Harmon, Maurice, ed., *The Irish Writer and the City.* Smythe, 1984. £12.50.

Harmon, Maurice, *Sean O'Faolain: A Critical Introduction.* Wolfhound, 1984. £5.95.

Harris, John, *Fury Never Leaves Us: A Miscellany of Caradoc Evans.* UWales, 1985. pb £4.50.

Hart, F. R., and J. B. Pick, *Neil Gunn: A Highland Life.* Polygon, 1985. pb £5.95.

Harvey, David, *The Song of Middle-Earth: J. R. R. Tolkien's Themes, Symbols and Myths.* A&U, 1985. £10.95.

Higdon, David Leon, *Shadows of The Past in Contemporary British Fiction.* Macmillan, 1985. £25.

Hignett, Sean, *Brett: From Bloomsbury to New Mexico.* H&S, 1984. £14.95.

Hinchliffe, Arnold P., ed., *T. S. Eliot: Plays: A Casebook.* Macmillan, 1985. hb £20, pb £6.95.

Hirst, David L., *Edward Bond.* Macmillan, 1985. hb £15, pb £4.95.

Hubbard, Francis A., *Theories of Action in Conrad.* UMIRes, 1985. £28.50.
Hutcheson, Linda, *A Theory of Parody: The Teachings of Twentieth Century Art Forms.* Methuen, 1985. hb £12.95, pb £5.95.
John, Brian, *Thomas Carlyle and D. H. Lawrence.* Carlyle Society, 1985.
Jones, Michael P., *Conrad's Heroism: A Paradise Lost.* UMIRes, 1985. £40.
Jones, Nesta, comp., *File on O'Casey.* Methuen, 1986. hb £7.95, pb £3.50.
Kiberd, Declan, *Men and Feminism in Modern Literature.* Macmillan, 1985. £25.
Kiell, Norman, ed., *Blood Brothers: Siblings as Writers.* IntUP. 1983. $40.
Kilroy, James F., ed., *The Irish Short Story: A Critical History.* Twayne, 1984. $17.95.
Kohfeldt, Mary Lou, *Lady Gregory.* Deutsch, 1985. £12.95.
Kosok, Heinz, *O'Casey the Dramatist.* Smythe, 1985. £19.50.
Lake, Carlton, ed., *No Symbols Where None Intended: A Catalogue of Books, Manuscripts and Other Material Relating to Samuel Beckett in the Collections of the Humanities Research Center.* UTex, 1984. $20.
Laurence, Dan H., and Martin Quinn, eds, *Shaw on Dickens.* Ungar, 1985. $12.95.
Lawrence, D. H., *Sons and Lovers*, ed. by Geoffrey Halson. Longman, 1985. pb £2.50.
Lawrence, D. H., *Study of Thomas Hardy and Other Essays*, ed. by Bruce Steele. CUP, 1985. hb £25, pb £12.50.
Lea, F. A., *Lawrence and Murry: A Twofold Vision.* Brentham, 1985. pb £2.95.
Leclercq, Florence, *Elizabeth Taylor.* Hall, 1985. $17.95.
Lee, Hermione, sel. and intro., *The Secret Self: Short Stories by Women.* Dent, 1985. pb £3.95.
Lehmann, John, and Roy Fuller, eds, *The Penguin New Writing 1940–50.* Penguin, 1985. pb £4.95.
Lemon, Lee T., *Portraits of the Artist in Contemporary Fiction.* UNeb, 1985. £22.50.
Lewis, Peter, *John le Carré.* Ungar, 1985. $13.95.
Lewis, Gifford, *Somerville and Ross: The World of the Irish R.M.* Viking, 1985. £12.95.
Liddell, Robert, *Elizabeth and Ivy.* Owen, 1985. £10.50.
Linklater, Eric, *The Merry Muse.* Richard Drew, 1985. pb £3.95.
Lloyd Evans, Gareth and Barbara, eds, *Plays in Review 1956–1980.* Batsford, 1985. £7.95.
Loveday, Simon. *The Romances of John Fowles.* Macmillan, 1985. £25.
Lowe, Stephen, sel. and intro., *Peace Plays.* Methuen, 1985. £3.95.
Lowery, Robert G., ed., *O'Casey Annual*, No. 4. Macmillan, 1985. £25.
Lowry, Malcolm, *Selected Letters of Malcolm Lowry*, ed. by Harvey Breit and Margerie Bonner-Lowry. Penguin, 1985. pb £5.95.
Lucas, John, *Moderns and Contemporaries.* Harvester, 1985. £22.50.
Mac Colla, Fionn, *The Albannach.* Souvenir, 1984. £8.95.
McDonald, Jan, *The 'New Drama' 1900–1914.* Macmillan, 1986. hb £15, pb £4.95.
McEwan, Ian, *The Ploughman's Lunch.* Methuen, 1985. pb £3.95.
MacInnes, Colin, *Absolute MacInnes: the Best of Colin MacInnes*, ed. by Tony Gould. A&B, 1985. pb £4.95.

MacInnes, Colin, *The Colin MacInnes Omnibus*. A&B, 1986. hb £12, pb £6.95.

MacLeod, Sheila, *Lawrence's Men and Women*. Heinemann, 1985. £12.95.

Martin, Bruce K., *British Poetry Since 1939*. Twayne, 1985. £18.95.

Matthias, Roland, *A Ride Through the Wood: Essays on Anglo-Welsh Literature*. PWP, 1985. £12.95.

Measham, Donald, ed., *D. H. Lawrence and the Real England*. Staple, 1985. pb £2.50.

Metzger, Linda, ed., *Contemporary Authors*. Gale, 1985. $88.

Meyers, Jeffrey, ed., *D. H. Lawrence and Tradition*. Athlone, 1985. £20.

Miller, Henry, *The World of D. H. Lawrence: A Passionate Appreciation*. Calder, 1985. £14.95.

Miller, Jonathan, *Subsequent Performances*. Faber, 1986. £15.

Mitchison, Naomi, *Among You Taking Notes ... The Wartime Diary of Naomi Mitchison 1939–45*, ed. by Dorothy Sheridan. Gollancz, 1985. £12.95.

Monaghan, David, *The Novels of John Le Carré*. Blackwell, 1985. £12.50.

Murfin, Ross C., *Conrad Revisited: Essays for the Eighties*. UAla, 1985. $17.50.

Musgrave, P. W., *From Brown to Bunter: The Life and Death of the School Story*. RKP, 1985. £12.95.

Nardin, Jane, *Barbara Pym*. Twayne, 1985. $15.95.

Nichols, Peter, *Feeling You're Behind*. Penguin, 1985. pb £3.95.

Nigam, Alka, *F. T. Prince: A Study of His Poetry*. USalz, 1983.

O'Casey, Sean, *Seven Plays*, sel. with intro. and notes by Ronald Ayling. Macmillan, 1985. hb £27.50, pb £9.95.

O'Connor, Frank, sel. and intro., *Classic Irish Short Stories*. OUP, 1985. pb £2.95.

Owen, Wilfred, *The Poems*, ed. by Jon Silkin. Penguin. pb £1.95.

Page, Norman, *A Conrad Companion*. Macmillan, 1986. £25.

Page, Norman, ed., *William Golding: Novels 1954–67: A Casebook*. Macmillan, 1985. hb £20, pb £6.95.

Patai, Daphne, *The Orwell Mystique: A Study in Male Ideology*. UMass, 1984. hb £28.50, pb £14.25.

Peters, John, *C. S. Lewis: The Man and His Achievement*. Paternoster Press, 1985. £4.95.

Pinter, Harold, *Collected Poems and Prose*. Revised edn. Methuen, 1986. pb £3.95.

Pinter, Harold, *One for the Road*. Rev. edn, with illus. and intro. Methuen, 1985. pb £3.95.

Plimpton, George, ed., *Writers at Work*. S&W, 1985. £12.50.

Porush, David, *The Soft Machine: Cybernetic Fiction*. Methuen, 1985. hb £15, pb £6.95.

Pritchett, V. S., *A Man of Letters: Selected Essays*. C&W, 1985. £12.95.

Punter, David, *The Hidden Script: Writing and the Unconscious*. RKP, 1985. £14.95.

Purtill, Richard L., *J. R. R. Tolkien, Myth, Morality and Religion*. Harper, 1985. £9.95.

Pym, Barbara, *A Very Private Eye: An Autobiography in Letters and Diaries*. Granada, 1985. pb £2.95.

Quigley, Austin E., *The Modern Stage and Other Worlds*. Methuen, 1985. hb £20, pb £7.95.

Rai, Ramda Nand, *W. B. Yeats: Poetic Theory and Practice*. USalz, 1983.

Rattigan, Terence, *Plays: Two*, intro. by Anthony Curtis. Methuen, 1985. pb £2.95.

Raval, Suresh, *The Art of Failure: Conrad's Fiction*. A&U, 1986. £25.

Reilly, Catherine W., *English Poetry of the Second World War: A Bibliography*. Mansell, 1986. £35.

Reilly, Patrick, *George Orwell, The Age's Adversary*. Macmillan, 1986. £27.50.

Reilly, Robert, ed., *The Transcendent Adventure: Studies of Religion in Science Fiction/Fantasy*. Greenwood, 1985. £35.

Rieselback, Helen Funk, *Conrad's Rebels*. UMIRes, 1985. £40.

Rose, Ellen Cronan, ed., *Critical Essays on Margaret Drabble*. Hall, 1985. $29.95.

Rusinko, Susan, *Tom Stoppard*. Twayne, 1986. $14.95.

Russell, Willy, *Educating Rita; Stags and Hens; and Blood Brothers*. Methuen, 1986. pb £3.95.

Salwak, Dale, *A. J. Cronin*. Twayne, 1985. $15.95.

Samuel, Raphael, Ewan MacColl, and Stuart Cosgrove, *Theatres of the Left 1880–1935*. RKP, 1985. £8.95.

Sanders, Dennis, and Len Lovallo, *The Agatha Christie Companion*. Allen, 1985. £10.95.

Sandison, Alan, *George Orwell: After 1984*. Macmillan, 1986. £8.95.

Schlossman, Beryl, *Joyce's Catholic Comedy of Language*. UWisc, 1985. £25.

Schneider, Daniel J., *D. H. Lawrence: The Artist as Psychologist*. UKan, 1984.

Schofield, Stephen, ed., *In Search of C. S. Lewis*. Bridge, 1983. $4.95.

Schulkind, Jeanne, ed., *Virginia Woolf: Moments of Being*. Hogarth, 1985. £12.95.

Scott, Paul, *Staying On*, ed. by Tim Pearce. Longman, 1985. pb £1.95.

Sharp, Alan, *A Green Tree in Gedde*. Richard Drew, 1985. £3.95.

Shaw, Bernard, *Caesar and Cleopatra*, ed. by Frances Frazer. Longman, 1985. £8.95.

Sherry, Vincent B., Jr, ed., *Poets of Great Britain and Ireland Since 1960*. Part 1: *A–L*. Part 2: *M–Z*. Gale, 1985. $176.

Shires, Linda M., *British Poetry of the Second World War*. Macmillan, 1985. £25.

Sicher, Efraim, *Beyond Marginality: Anglo-Jewish Literature After the Holocaust*. SUNY, 1985. hb $34.50, pb $10.95.

Simons, Kenneth, *The Ludic Imagination: A Reading of Joseph Conrad*. UMIRes, 1984. $34.95.

Smith, Graham, *The Achievement of Graham Greene*. Harvester, 1986. £18.95.

Smith, Janet Adam, *John Buchan: A Biography*. OUP, 1985. £4.95.

Smith, Stan, *W. H. Auden*. Blackwell. hb £12.50, pb £3.95.

Spalding, Peter, *Drama in Practice*. Macmillan, 1985. hb £20, pb £5.95.

Spender, Dale, and Carole Hayman, sel. and intro., *How the Vote was Won: and Other Suffragette Plays*. Methuen, 1985. pb £3.95.

Spice, Nicholas, ed., *London Reviews*. C&W, 1985. £5.95.

Squier, Susan Merrill, *Virginia Woolf and London: The Sexual Politics of the City*. UNC, 1985. £19.95.

Squires, Michael, and Dennis Jackson, *D. H. Lawrence's 'Lady': A New Look at 'Lady Chatterley's Lover'*. UGeo, 1985. $24.

Stead, C. K., *Pound, Yeats, Eliot and the Modernist Movement*. Macmillan, 1986. £27.50.

Stourac, Richard, and Kathleen McCreery, *Theatre as a Weapon*. RKP, 1986. £30.

Sykes, Christopher, *Evelyn Waugh: A Biography*. Penguin, 1985. pb £5.95.

Thomas, Dylan, *Collected Letters*, ed. by Paul Ferris. Dent, 1985. £20.

Thompson, Raymond H., *The Return from Avalon: A Study of the Arthurian Legend in Modern Fiction*. Greenwood, 1985. $29.95.

Tomlin, Ruth, ed., *W. H. Hudson: Far Away and Long Ago*. Dent, 1985. pb £2.95.

Torchiana, Donald T., *Backgrounds for Joyce's Dubliners*. A&U, 1986. £25.

Vanatta, Dennis, ed., *The English Short Story 1945–1980*. Twayne, 1985. $18.95.

Velicu, Adrian, *Unifying Strategies in Virginia Woolf's Experimental Fiction*. Uppsala, 1985.

von Rosenberg, Ingrid, *Alan Sillitoe: Saturday Night and Sunday Morning*. Fink, 1984. DM 14.80.

Waugh, Evelyn, *Remote People*. Penguin, 1984. pb £2.95.

Waugh, Evelyn, *A Tourist in Africa*. Methuen, 1985. pb £3.95.

Webb, Kaye, ed., *Lilliput Goes to War*. Hutchinson, 1985. £10.95.

Weiss, Timothy, *Fairy Tale and Romance in Works of Ford Madox Ford*. UPA, 1984. £11.50.

West, Thomas, *Ted Hughes*. Methuen. pb £2.75.

West, W. J., ed., *Orwell: The War Broadcasts*. Duckworth, 1985. £12.95.

West, W. J., ed., *Orwell: The War Commentaries*. Duckworth, 1985. £14.95.

Wilcox, Michael, sel. and intro., *Gay Plays*. Methuen, 1985. pb £3.50.

Wilson, Angus, *Reflections in a Writer's Eye*. S&W, 1986. £7.50.

Chapter XVI. American Literature to 1900

Allen, Elizabeth, *A Woman's Place in the Novels of Henry James*. Macmillan, 1984. £25.

Allen, Michael, *Emily Dickinson as an American Provincial Poet*. USussex, 1985. pb £1.95.

Ashley, Perry J., ed., *American Newspaper Journalists 1690–1872*. DLB 43. Gale, 1985. $88.

Baym, Nina, *Novels, Readers, and Reviewers: Responses to Fiction in Antebellum America*. CornU, 1984. $27.45.

Brown, Charles Brockden, *Edgar Huntly*, ed. by Sydney J. Krause and S. W. Reid. Kent State UP, 1985. $35.

Cameron, Sharon, *Writing Nature: Henry Thoreau's Journal*. OUP, 1985. £15.

Carton, Evan, *The Rhetoric of American Romance: Dialectic and Identity in Emerson, Dickinson, Poe, and Hawthorne*. JHU, 1985. $25.

Clark, Robert, ed., *James Fenimore Cooper: New Critical Essays*. Vision, 1985. £15.95.

Davidson, Cathy N., *The Experimental Fictions of Ambrose Bierce: Structuring the Ineffable*. UNeb, 1984. £15.95.

Donohue, Agnes McNeill, *Hawthorne: Calvin's Ironic Stepchild*. Kent State UP, Ohio, 1985. $27.50.

Elliott, Emory, ed., *American Colonial Writers 1606–1734*. DLB 24. Gale, 1984. $80.

Ferlazzo, Paul J., *Critical Essays on Emily Dickinson*. Hall, 1984. $32.50.

Fryer, Judith, *Felicitous Space: The Imaginative Structures of Edith Wharton and Willa Cather*. UNC, 1986. pb £9.95.

Goetz, William R., *Henry James and the Darkest Abyss of Romance*. LSU, 1986. £25.

Jones, Vivien, *James the Critic*. Macmillan, 1985. £22.95.

Kaston, Carren, *Imagination and Desire in the Novels of Henry James*. Rutgers, 1984. $22.50.

Kolodny, Annette, *The Land Before Her: Fantasy and Experience of the American Frontiers 1630–1860*. UNC, 1985. pb £9.95.

Lenz, William E., *Fast Talk and Flush Times: The Confidence Man as a Literary Convention*. UMiss, 1985. $21.

Levernier, James A., and Douglas R. Wilmes, eds, *American Writers before 1800: A Biographical and Critical Reference Guide*, 3 vols. Greenwood, 1984. $195.

Lubin, David M., *Act of Portrayal: Eakins, Sargent, James*. Yale, 1986. £20.

Martin, Jean-Pierre, and Serge Ricard, *Une Institution Particulière: Aspects de l'Esclavage aux Etats-Unis*. UProvence, 1986.

Martin, Wendy, *An American Triptych: Anne Bradstreet, Emily Dickinson and Adrienne Rich*. UNC, 1984. $24.

Myerson, Joel, ed., *The Transcendentalists: A Review of Research and Criticism*. MLA, 1984. $30.

Perosa, Sergio, *American Theories of the Novel 1793–1903*. NYU, 1984. $43.

Pocock, Ross, *Henry James and the Problem of Robert Browning*. UGeo, 1985. $24.

Reynolds, Larry J., *James Kirke Paulding*. Twayne, 1984. $16.95.

Riddle, Mary-Madeleine Gina, *Herman Melville's Piazza Tales: A Prophetic Vision*. AUG, 1985.

Robinson, Douglas, *American Apocalypses: The Image of the End of the World in American Literature*. JHU, 1985. £20.35.

Sattelmeyer, Robert, and J. Donald Crawley, eds, *One Hundred Years of 'Huckleberry Finn': The Boy, His Book, and American Culture*. UMiss, 1985. $29.

Todorov, Tzvetan, *The Conquest of America*, transl. by Richard Howard. Harper, 1984. $17.26.

Wagenknecht, Edward, *The Tales of Henry James*. Ungar, 1984. $16.50.

Chapter XVII. American Literature: The Twentieth Century

Abbot, Dorothy, ed., *Mississippi Writers: Reflections of Childhood and Youth*. Vol. 1: *Fiction*. UMissip, 1985. hb $35, pb $14.95.

Agee, James, *Selected Journalism*, ed. by Paul Ashdown. UTenn, 1985. $17.95.

Anderson, Sherwood, *Letters to Bab: Sherwood Anderson to Marietta D. Finley, 1916–1933*, ed. by William A. Sutton. UIll, 1985. £27.50.

Andrews, Bruce, and Charles Bernstein, eds, *The Language Book*. SIU, 1984. pb $12.95.

Arnold, Marilyn, *Willa Cather's Short Fiction*. OhioU, 1985. £30.35.

Asch, Sholem, *The Apostle*. C&G. 1985. $10.95.

Ashberry, John, *Selected Poems*. Carcanet, 1986. £16.95.

Bakker, J., *Ernest Hemingway in Holland 1925–1981*. Costerus. Rodopi, 1985. Fl 40.

Baldwin, James, *Evidence of Things Not Seen*. Joseph, 1986. £8.95.

Baldwin, James, *Notes of a Native Son*. Pluto, 1985. pb £3.95.

Baldwin, James, *The Price of a Ticket: Collected Non-Fiction 1948–1985*. Joseph, 1985. £14.95.

Barlow, Judith E., *Final Acts: The Creation of Three Late O'Neill Plays*. UGeo, 1985. $22.50.

Bassett, John Earl, *Faulkner: An Annotated Checklist of Recent Criticism*. Kent State UP, 1984.

Baym, Nina, *et al.*, eds, *The Norton Anthology of American Literature*. Second edn. 2 vols. Norton, 1985. $37.90.

Beaver, Harold, *The Great American Masquerade*. Vision, 1985. £16.95.

Benchley, Robert, *Benchley at the Theatre: Dramatic Criticism 1920–1940*, ed. by Charles Getchell. Ipswich, 1985. $14.95.

Bird, Roy K., *Wright Morris: Memory and Imagination*. Lang, 1985. Sfr 46.60.

Bishop, Elizabeth, *The Complete Poems 1927–1979*. Hogarth, 1984. pb £6.95.

Blumenthal, Eileen, *Joseph Chaikin*. CUP, 1984. £18.50.

Bowlby, Rachel, *Just Looking: Consumer Culture in Dreiser, Gissing and Zola*. Methuen, 1985. hb £10.95, pb £4.95.

Bowles, Jane, *Out in the World: Selected Letters of Jane Bowles 1935–1970*, ed. by Millicent Dillon. Black Sparrow, 1985. hb $20, pb $12.50.

Bowles, Paul, *Midnight Mass*. Owen, 1985. £8.95.

Bowles, Paul, *She Woke Me Up So I Killed Her*. Cadmus, 1986. $7.95.

Boyd, Brian, *Nabokov's 'Ada': The Place of Consciousness*. Ardis, 1985. hb $22.95, pb $7.50.

Boyle, Kay, *Words That Must Somehow Be Said: The Selected Essays of Kay Boyle 1927–1983*, ed. by Elizabeth S. Bell. North Point, 1985. $16.50.

Braham, Jeanne, *A Sort of Columbus: The American Voyages of Saul Bellow's Fiction*. UGeo, 1984. $15.

Brodsky, Louis Daniel, and Robert W. Hamblin, eds, *Faulkner: A Comprehensive Guide to the Brodsky Collection*. Vol. 2: *The Letters*. Vol. 3: *The De Gaulle Story*. UMissip, 1984, 1985. £37.95, £15.40.

Bruccoli, Matthew J., *James Gould Cozzens: A Life Apart*. HBJ, 1985. $9.95.

Bruccoli, Matthew J., *Nelson Algren: A Descriptive Bibliography*. UPitt, 1985. $29.95.

Burges, Anthony, *Ernest Hemingway*. T&H, 1986. £3.25.

Burroughs, William S., *The Adding Machine: Collected Essays*. Calder, 1985. £10.95.

Burroughs, William S., *The Burroughs File*. City Lights, 1985. $8.95.

Burroughs, William S., *Queer*. Viking, 1985. $14.95.

Butterick, George, ed., *Charles Olsen and Robert Creeley*. Black Sparrow, 1985. £9.95.

Byerman, Keith E., *Fingering the Jagged Grain: Tradition and Form in Recent Black Fiction*. UGeo, 1986. £30.

Callard, D. A., *Pretty Good for a Woman: The Enigmas of Evelyn Scott*. Cape, 1985. £9.95.

Canfield, Dorothy, *Her Son's Wife*, intro. by Dorothy Goldman, Virago, 1986. pb £3.95.

Capellan, Angel, *Hemingway and the Hispanic World*. UMIRes, 1985. £51.50.

Carothers, James B., *William Faulkner's Short Stories*. UMIRes, 1985. $39.95.

Carpenter, Frederic I., *Eugene O'Neill*. Twayne, 1985. pb $5.95.

Carver, Raymond, *Fires*. Collins, 1985. £8.95.

Castronovo, David, *Edmund Wilson*. Ungar, 1985. $15.50.

Chandler, Raymond, *Playback*. Harrap, 1986. £8.95.

Clark, Randall, ed., *American Screenwriters: Second Series*. Gale, 1986. $88.

Coale, Samuel Chase, *In Hawthorne's Shadow*. UKen, 1985. £21.75.

Conder, John J., *Naturalism in American Fiction: The Classic Phase*. UKen, 1984. $21.

Conover, Robert L., ed., *Mina Loy: The Last Lunar Baedeker*. Carcanet, 1985. pb £7.95.

Conrad, Peter, *The Art of the City*. OUP, 1984. £15.

Cooke, Michael G., *Afro-American Literature in the Twentieth Century*. Yale, 1985. £18.50.

Cookson, William, *A Guide to the Cantos of Ezra Pound*. CH, 1985. pb £4.95.

Cowart, David, *Arches and Light: The Fiction of John Gardner*. SIU, 1985. $19.95.

Crane, John Kenny, *The Root of All Evil: The Thematic Unity of William Styron's Fiction*. USC, 1984. $17.95.

D[oolittle] H[ilda], *Tribute to Freud*, intro. by Norman Holmes Pearson. Carcanet, 1985. £5.95.

Dasenbrock, Reed Way, *The Literary Vorticism of Ezra Pound and Wyndham Lewis*. JHU, 1985. £24.

Davenport, Guy, *Thasos and Ohio: Poems and Translations 1950–1980*. Carcanet, 1985. pb £4.95.

Davis, Thadious M., *Faulkner's 'Negro': Art and the Southern Context*. LSU, 1985. hb £25, pb £10.95.

Davis, Thadious M., and Trudier Harris, eds, *Afro-American Writers After 1955: Dramatists and Prose Writers*. Gale, 1985. $85.

Dawson, Fielding, *Tiger Lilies: An American Childhood*. DukeU, 1984. hb £20.10, pb £12.90.

Dikty, Thaddeus, and R. Reginald, *The Work of Julian May: An Annotated Bibliography and Guide*. Borgo, 1985. hb $19.95, pb $9.95.

Donaldson, Scott, *Critical Essays on F. Scott Fitzgerald's 'The Great Gatsby'*. Hall, 1984. $31.

Donoghue, Denis, *Conoisseurs of Chaos: Ideas of Order in Modern American Poetry*. ColU, 1983. $34.

Dreiser, Theodore, *Selected Magazine Articles*, ed. by Yoshinobu Hakutani. AUP, 1985. £28.95.

Dugan, Alan, *New and Collected Poems 1961–1983*. EccoP (New York), 1985. pb $9.50.

Eastlake, William, *Jack Armstrong in Tangiers and Other Escapes.* Bamberger, 1985. pb $6.50.

Edwards, Anne, *The Road to Tara.* Coronet, 1985. pb £2.50.

Elkin, Stanley, *Early Elkin.* Bamberger, 1985. hb $15, pb $6.50.

Fabre, Michel, *The World of Richard Wright.* UMissip, 1985. £25.

Falk, Signi L., *Tennessee Williams.* Twayne, 1985. pb $6.95.

Fante, John, *1933 was a Bad Year.* Black Sparrow, 1985. hb $14, pb $8.50.

Fante, John, *Ask the Dust.* Granada, 1985. pb £2.50.

Fante, John, *The Road to Los Angeles.* Black Sparrow, 1985. hb $17.50, pb $10.

Fante, John, *Wait Until Spring, Bandini.* Granada, 1985. pb £2.50.

Fante, John, *The Wine of Youth.* Black Sparrow, 1985. £9.95.

Faulkner, William, *The Penguin Collected Stories of William Faulkner.* Penguin, 1985. pb £6.95.

Fauset, Jessie Redmon, *Plum Bun*, intro. by Deborah E. McDowell. Pandora, 1985. pb £4.95.

Fine, David, ed., *Los Angeles in Fiction.* UNM, 1985. hb $24.95, pb $9.95.

Fowler, Doreen, and Ann J. Abadie, *New Directions in Faulkner Studies.* UMissip, 1985. hb $25, pb $14.95.

Fraistat, Rose Ann C., *Caroline Gordon as Novelist and Woman of Letters.* LSU, 1984. £24.

French, Warren, ed., *American Literary Scholarship 1983.* DukeU, 1985. $37.75.

Friedman, Alan Warren, *William Faulkner.* Ungar, 1985. $15.50.

Friedman, Melvin, J., and Beverly Lyon Clark, eds, *Critical Essays on Flannery O'Connor.* Hall, 1985. $38.

Froula, Christine, *To Write Paradise: Style and Error in Pound's Cantos.* Yale, 1985. £18.95.

Gaddis, William, *The Recognitions.* Penguin, 1985. pb £7.95.

Gass, William H., *Habitations of the Word: Essays.* S&S, 1985. $17.95.

Geherin, David, *The American Private Eye: The Image in Fiction.* Ungar, 1985. pb $7.95.

Gellhorn, Martha, *The Face of War*, Virago, 1986. £10.95.

Gellhorn, Martha, *A Stricken Field.* Virago, 1986. pb £3.95.

Gelpi, Albert, *Wallace Stevens: The Poetics of Modernism.* CUP, 1986. £19.50.

Gerber, Philip L., *Robert Frost.* Twayne, 1984. pb $6.95.

Giles, Paul, *Hart Crane: The Contexts of 'The Bridge'.* CUP, 1986. £25.

Glasgow, Ellen, *Barren Ground*, intro. by Paul Binding. Virago, 1986. pb £4.50.

Gold, Herbert, *Stories of Misbegotten Love.* Capra, 1985. pb $7.50.

Goodman, Paul, *Parents' Day.* Black Sparrow, 1985. hb $14, pb $10.

Gordon, Caroline, *The Southern Mandarins: Letters of Caroline Gordon to Sally Wood, 1924–1937*, ed. by Sally Wood. LSU, 1984. £30.

Greiner, Donald J., *Understanding John Hawkes.* USC, 1985. hb $19.95, pb $7.95.

Gresset, Michel, *A Faulkner Chronology.* UMissip, 1985. pb $7.95.

Gresset, Michel, and Noel Polk, eds, *Intertextuality in Faulkner.* UMissip, 1985. £17.95.

Griffin, Peter, *Along With Youth: Hemingway, the Early Years*. OUP, 1986. £12.95.

Grimes, Larry E., *The Religious Design of Hemingway's Early Fiction*. UMIRes, 1985. £45.50.

Grobel, Lawrence, *Conversations with Truman Capote*. Hutchinson, 1985. £10.95.

Gysin, Brion, *Here To Go*. Quartet, 1985. £12.50.

Gysin, Brion, *Stories*. Inkblot, 1984. pb $7.95.

Hardwick, Elizabeth, *The Ghostly Lover*. Virago, 1986. pb £3.95.

Harris, Trudier, and Thadious M. Davis, eds, *Afro-American Poets Since 1955*. Gale, 1985. $88.

Hass, Robert, *Twentieth Century Pleasures: Prose on Poetry*. EccoP, 1985. pb $9.50.

Headings, Philip R., *T. S. Eliot*. Twayne, 1985. pb $6.95.

Heller, Joseph, *Catch-22*, intro. by Anthony Burgess. Black Swan, 1985. pb £4.95.

Helterman, Jeffrey, *Understanding Bernard Malamud*. USC, 1985. hb $19.95, pb $7.95.

Hemingway, Ernest, *The Dangerous Summer*. HH, 1985. £9.95.

Hemingway, Ernest, *The Dangerous Summer*. CSS, 1985. $17.95.

Hemingway, Ernest, *Ernest Hemingway on Writing*, ed. by Larry W. Phillips. Granada, 1985. pb £7.95.

Hemingway, Ernest, *Selected Letters 1917–1961*, ed. by Carlos Baker. Granada, 1985. pb £5.95.

Henry, Dewitt, ed., *The Ploughshares Reader: New Fiction for the Eighties*. Pushcart, 1985. $24.95.

Herbst, Josephine, *Rope of Gold*, intro. by Alice Kessler-Harris. Feminist, 1986. pb £6.95.

Hirshberg, Edgar E., *John D. MacDonald*. Twayne, 1985. $14.95.

Hughes, Langston, *The Big Sea*. Pluto, 1986. pb £4.95.

Hughes, Langston, and Roy De Carava, *The Sweet Flypaper of Life*. Howard, 1984. $24.95.

Huncke, Herbert, *The Evening Sun Turned Crimson*, intro. by Allen Ginsberg. Cherry Valley, 1986. pb £3.95.

Hunt, George W., *John Cheever: The Hobgoblin Company of Love*. Eerdmans, 1984. $7.20.

Hurston, Zora Neale, *I Love Myself When I Am Laughing . . .*, intro. by Mary Helen Washington. Feminist, 1986. £9.95.

Hurston, Zora Neale, *Their Eyes Were Watching God*, intro. by Holly Eley. Virago, 1986. pb £3.95.

Jackson, Richard, *Acts of Mind: Conversations with Contemporary Poets*. UAla, 1984. pb $9.95.

Jay, Gregory S., *T. S. Eliot and the Poetics of Literary History*. LSU, 1984. $27.50.

Jemie, Onwuchekma, *Langston Hughes: An Introduction to the Poetry*. ColU, 1985. pb $10.

Johnson, Joyce, *Minor Characters*. Picador, 1985. pb £2.50.

Johnston, John H., *The Poet and the City*. UGeo, 1985. $25.

Kempf, James Michael, *The Early Career of Malcolm Cowley: A Humanist Among the Moderns*. LSU, 1985. £17.50.

Keyssar, Helene, *Feminist Theatre: An Introduction to the Plays of British and American Women*. Macmillan, 1984. hb £15, pb £4.95.

Kinney, Arthur F., ed., *Critical Essays on William Faulkner: The Sartoris Family*. Hall, 1985. $38.

Kinney, Arthur F., *Flannery O'Connor's Library: Resources of Being*. UGeo, 1985. $25.

Klinkowitz, Jerome, *Literary Subversions: New American Fiction and the Practice of Criticism*. SIU, 1986. $18.95.

Krassner, Paul, ed., *Best of 'The Realist'*. RunningP, 1984. pb $8.95.

Kroes, Rob, ed., *Nineteen Eighty-Four and the Apocalyptic Imagination in America*. Free UP, 1985. Fl 30.

Kronick, Joseph G., *American Poetics of History*. LSU, 1984. $30.

Lawson, Lewis A., *Another Generation: Southern Fiction Since World War II*. UMissip, 1985. $7.95.

Lawson, Lewis A., and Victor A. Kramer, eds, *Conversations and Walker Percy*. UMissip, 1984. hb $17.95, pb $9.95.

Lehrer, Sylvia, *The Dialectics of Art and Life: A Portrait of Sylvia Plath as Woman and Poet*. USalz, 1985.

Levine, Paul, *E. L. Doctorow*. Methuen, 1985. pb £2.25.

Lewis, Sinclair, *Main Street*, intro. by Malcolm Bradbury. Penguin, 1985. pb £4.95.

Libby, Anthony, *Mythologies of Nothing: Mystical Death in American Poetry 1940–1970*. UIll, 1984. £20.75.

London, Jack, *The Cruise of the Snark*, intro. by Kaori O'Connor. RKP, 1986. pb £6.95.

London, Jack, *The Star Rover*. Alan Sutton, 1986. pb £3.95.

London, Jack, *Youth Wolf: The Early Adventure Stories of Jack London*, ed. by Howard Lachtman. Capra, 1984. pb $8.95.

Long, Elizabeth, *The American Dream and the Popular Novel*. RKP, 1985. £15.

Long, Robert Emmet, *Nathaniel West*. Ungar, 1985. $13.95.

McBridge, Dic, *Cometh With Clouds*. Cherry Valley, 1985. pb £3.50.

McCarthy, Mary, *Occasional Prose*. W&N, 1985. £14.95.

McConachie, B. A., and D. Friedman, eds, *Theatre for Working-Class Audiences in the U.S. 1830–1980*. Greenwood, 1985. £35.

McHaney, Thomas L., ed., *Faulkner Studies in Japan*. UGeo, 1985. £20.

MacShane, Frank, *The Life of Raymond Chandler*. HH, 1986. pb £5.95.

Manso, Peter, *Mailer: His Life and Times*. Viking, 1985. £16.95.

Martinez, Julio A., and Francisco A. Lomeli, eds, *Chicano Literature: A Reference Guide*. Greenwood, 1985. £49.95.

Meyers, Jeffrey, *Hemingway: A Biography*. Macmillan, 1986. £16.95.

Miller, Henry, *A Henry Miller Reader*, ed. by John Calder. Picador, 1985. pb £3.95.

Miller, Henry, *The World of Lawrence*. Calder, 1985. £14.95.

Miller, Jeffrey, *Paul Bowles: A Descriptive Bibliography*. Black Sparrow, 1986. $50.

Mitchell, Margaret, *A Dynamo Going to Waste: Letters to Allen Edee 1919–1921*. Peachtree, 1985. $12.95.

Munson, Gorham, *The Awakening Twenties: A Memoir – History of a Literary Period*. LSU, 1985. $19.95.

Murphy, John J., ed., *Critical Essays on Willa Cather*. Hall, 1985. $38.

Nelson, Gerald B., and Glory Jones, *Hemingway: Life and Works*. Facts on File, 1986. hb £12.95, pb £6.95.

Newman, Charles, *The Post-Modern Aura: The Act of Fiction in an Age of Inflation*. Northwestern, 1985. hb $18.95, pb $7.95.

Nicosia, Gerald, *Memory Babe: A Critical Biography of Jack Kerouac*. Viking, 1985. £16.95.

Nierman, Judith, *Floyd Dell: An Annotated Bibliography of Secondary Sources, 1910–1981*. Scarecrow, 1984. $15.

Nin, Anais, *The White Blackbird and Other Writings*, ed. by Rupert Pole. Capra, 1985. pb $7.50.

O'Hara, John, *Appointment in Samarra*. Faber, 1985. pb £3.95.

Orlovsky, Peter, and Steven Taylor, *Allen Ginsberg on Tour*. S Press, 1985. pb £4.95.

Orr, Gregory, *Stanley Kunitz: An Introduction to the Poetry*. ColU, 1985. $29.50.

Owens, Louis, *John Steinbeck's Re-Vision of America*. UGeo, 1985. $22.50.

Pack, Robert, Sydney Lea, and Jay Parini, eds, *The Bread Loaf Anthology of Contemporary American Poetry*. UPNE, 1985. pb £11.

Parker, Robert Dale, *Faulkner and the Novelistic Imagination*. UIll, 1985. £18.75.

Parkinson, Kathleen, *F. Scott Fitzgerald: Tender Is the Night: A Critical Study*. Penguin, 1986. pb £1.50.

Patke, Rajeev S., *The Long Poems of Wallace Stevens: An Interpretative Study*. CUP, 1985. £25.

Pauly, Thomas H., *An American Odyssey: Elia Kazan and American Culture*. Temple, 1985. $12.95.

Pennell, Joseph Stanley, *The History of Rome Hanks and Kindred Matters*. Second Chance, 1985. hb $16.95, pb $10.95.

Perelman, S. J., *The Most of S. J. Perelman*, intro. by Dorothy Parker. Methuen, 1985. pb £5.95.

Perloff, Marjorie, *The Dance of the Intellect*. CUP, 1986. £22.50.

Peters, Robert, *The Peters Black and Blue Guide to Current Literary Journals*. Cherry Valley, 1985. pb £3.95.

Peters, Robert, *The Second Peters Black and Blue Guide to Current Literary Journals*. Cherry Valley, 1985. pb £4.50.

Phillipson, John S., ed., *Critical Essays on Thomas Wolfe*. Hall, 1985. $38.

Pinsker, Sanford, *Conversations with Contemporary American Writers*. Rodopi, 1985. Fl 20.

Pound, Ezra, *A Quinzaine for this Yule*. StPB, 1986. pb £9.

Pound, Ezra, and John Theobold, *Ezra Pound/John Theobold: Letters*, ed. by Donald Pearce and Herbert Schneidau. BS, 1984. $22.50.

Prenshaw, Peggy Whitman, *Elizabeth Spencer*. Twayne, 1985. $18.95.

Prenshaw, Peggy Whitman, ed., *Women Writers of the Contemporary South*. UMissip, 1985. $20.

Purdy, James, *Narrow Rooms*, intro. by Paul Binding. GMP, 1985. hb £9.95, pb £3.95.

Putzel, Max. *Genius of Place: William Faulkner's Triumphant Beginnings*. LSU, 1985. hb £32.55, pb £14.95.

Pynchon, Thomas, *Slow Learner*. Cape, 1985. £8.50.

Quartermain, Peter, ed., *American Poets, 1880–1945: First Series*. Gale, 1985. $88.

Rae, Catherine M., *Edith Wharton's New York Quartet*. UPA, 1984. hb $16.50, pb $8.

Rainwater, Catherine, and William J. Scheick, eds, *Contemporary American Women Writers: Narrative Strategies*. UKen, 1986. £14.95.

Ranald, Margaret Loftus, *The Eugene O'Neill Companion*. Greenwood, 1985. £61.25.

Reynolds, Michael, *The Young Hemingway*. Blackwell, 1986. £14.95.

Richter, Conrad, *The Rawhide Knot and Other Stories*, intro. by Harvena Richter. UNeb, 1985. pb £6.50.

Rickman, Gregg, *Philip K. Dick: The Last Testament*. Fragments West, 1985. $9.95.

Roth, Philip, *Reading Myself and Others*. Penguin, 1986. pb £3.95.

Ruas, Charles, *Conversations with American Writers*. Knopf, 1985. $17.95.

Samuelson, Arnold, *With Hemingway*. Severn House, 1985. £10.95.

Sanford, John, *The Winters of that Country*. Black Sparrow, 1985. hb $20, pb $12.50.

Saroyan, Aram, *William Saroyan*. HBJ, 1984. pb $8.95.

Saroyan, William, *The New Saroyan Reader*, ed. by Brian Darwent. Creative Arts, 1984. $11.50.

Sarton, May, *As We Are Now*. WP, 1984. pb £2.95.

Sarton, May, *Journal of a Solitude*. WP, 1985. hb £7.95, pb £3.95.

Sarton, May, *A Reckoning*. WP, 1984. pb £3.95.

Sayre, Henry M., *The Visual Text of William Carlos Williams*. UIll. 1983. £14.25.

Sayres, Sohnya, *et al.*, eds, *The 60s Without Apology*. UMinn, 1985. hb $29.50, pb $12.95.

Schlueter, Paul and Jane, eds, *Modern American Literature*. Second supplement to 4th edn. Ungar, 1985. $65.

Schwartz, Sandford, *The Matrix of Modernism: Pound, Eliot and Early 20th Century Thought*. Princeton, 1986. £18.

Schweitzer, Darrell, ed., *Exploring Fantasy Worlds: Essays on Fantastic Literature*. Borgo, 1985. hb $14.95, pb $6.95.

Seller, Maxine Schwartz, ed., *Ethnic Theatre in the United States*. Greenwood, 1985. £49.95.

Sexton, Anne, *No Evil Star*. UMich, 1985. pb $8.95.

Sinclair, Upton, *Boston*. 2 vols. Scholarly, 1985. $59.

Sinclair, Upton, *The Flivver King*, intro. by Stephen Meyer. Kerr, 1984. pb $5.95.

Sinclair, Upton, *The Jungle*. Penguin, 1985. pb £2.50.

Skei, Hans H., *William Faulkner: The Short Story Career*. OUP, 1985. £10.50.

Skei, Hans H., *William Faulkner: The Novelist as Short Story Writer*. OUP, 1986. £22.50.

Skinner, Robert E., *The Hard-Boiled Explicator*. Scarecrow, 1985. $13.50.

Smart, Robert Augustin, *The Nonfiction Novel*. UPA, 1985. $19.50.

Smith, Dave, *The Giver of Morning: On the Poetry of Dave Smith*. F-B, 1984. hb $9.95, pb $5.95.

Smith, Dave, *Local Assays: On Contemporary American Poetry*. UIll, 1985. £20.95.

Snyder, Gary, *Good Will Sacred*. Five Seasons P, 1985. pb. £3.

Spurr, David, *Conflicts in Consciousness: T. S. Eliot's Poetry and Criticism*. UIll, 1985. £16.50.

Stearns, Harold, *Confessions of a Harvard Man*. Paget, 1985. £12.95.

Stein, Gertrude, *Everybody's Autobiography*, intro. by Janet Hobhouse. Virago, 1985. pb £3.95.

Stein, Gertrude, *Lectures in America*, intro. by Wendy Steiner. Beacon, 1985. hb $21, pb $10.95.

Stein, Gertrude, *Picasso: The Complete Writings*, intro. by Leon Katz and Edward Burns. Beacon, 1985. hb $16.95, pb $7.95.

Stengel, Wayne B., *The Shape of Art in the Short Stories of Donald Barthelme*. LSU, 1985. £22.50.

Stitt, Peter, *The World's Hieroglyphic Beauty: Five American Poets*. UGeo, 1985. $30.

Sublette, Jack R., *J. D. Salinger: An Annotated Bibliography, 1938–1981*. Garland, 1984. $42.

Sukenick, Ronald, *In Form: Digressions on the Act of Fiction*. SIU, 1985. $16.95.

Swearingen, Bethany C., *Eudora Welty: A Critical Bibliography, 1936–1958*. UMissip, 1985. $10.

Symons, Julian, *Dashiell Hammett*. HBJ, 1985. $12.95.

Tani, Stefano, *The Doomed Detective*. SIU, 1984. $17.95.

Tapscott, Stephen, *American Beauty: William Carlos Williams and the Modernist Whitman*. ColU, 1984. $36.

Tate, Allen, *The Fathers*, intro. by Arthur Mizener. Swallow, 1984. pb $8.95.

Tate, Claudia, ed., *Black Women Writers at Work*. Oldcastle, 1985. pb £4.95.

Taylor, Carole Anne, *The Poetics of Seeing: The Implications of Visual Forms of Modern Poetry*. Garland, 1985. $40.

Terrell, Carrol F., ed., *Robert Creeley: The Poet's Workshop*. National Poetry Foundation, 1985. pb $9.50.

Theroux, Paul, *Sunrise With Seamonsters: Travels and Discoveries 1964–1984*. HH, 1985. £12.50.

Toklas, Alice B., *What Is Remembered*. NPP, 1985. pb $9.50.

Updike, John, *Hugging the Shore*. Penguin, 1985. pb £7.95.

Waggoner, Hyatt H., *American Visionary Poetry*. LSU, 1984. $20.

Walker, Alice, *In Search of Our Mothers' Gardens*. WP, 1984. hb £12.95, pb £4.95.

Walsh, Joy, *Jack Kerouac: Statement in Brown*. Textile Bridge, 1985. pb $6.

Ward, J. A., *American Silences*. LSU, 1985. £20.

Weales, Gerald, *Odets the Playwright*. Methuen, 1985. pb £4.95.

Weber, Tom, *John Steinbeck's Cannery Row: A Time to Remember*. Orenda/Unity, 1985. pb $7.95.

Weigl, Bruce, ed., *The Giver of Morning: On the Poetry of Dave Smith*. F-B, 1984.

Weigl, Bruce, and T. R. Hummer, eds, *The Imagination as Glory: The Poetry of James Dickey*. UIll, 1984. £19.25.

Weld, John, *Young Man in Paris*. Academy (Chicago), 1985. $14.95.

Welty, Eudora, *Losing Battles*. Virago, 1986. pb £3.95.

Welty, Eudora, *One Writer's Beginnings*. Faber, 1985. pb £2.95.

Wharton, Edith, *The House of Mirth*, intro. by Cynthia Griffin Wolff. Penguin, 1985. pb £4.50.

Wharton, Edith, *Hudson River Bracketed*. Virago, 1986. pb £4.95.

Wharton, Edith, *The Mother's Recompense*. Virago, 1986. pb £3.95.

Wiget, Andrew, *Native American Literature*. Twayne, 1985. $35.50.

Wilder, Thornton, *The Journals of Thornton Wilder, 1939–1961*, ed. by Donald Gallup. Yale, 1985. £22.50.

Wilhelm, J. J., *The American Roots of Ezra Pound*. Garland, 1985. $19.95.

Williams, Mance, *Black Theatre in the 1960s and 1970s: A Historical-Critical Analysis of the Movement*. Greenwood, 1985. £27.95.

Williams, Tennessee, *Collected Stories*, intro. by Gore Vidal. ND, 1985. $19.95.

Williams, William Carlos, and John Sanford, *A Correspondence*. Capra, 1984. hb $17, pb $8.

Wilson, Edmund, *Memoirs of Hecate County*. Hogarth, 1986. pb £3.95.

Wilson, Jonathan, *On Bellow's Planet*. FDU, 1985. £16.95.

Woll, Allen, *Dictionary of the Black Theatre: Broadway, Off-Broadway, and Selected Harlem Theatre*. Greenwood, 1985. £39.95.

Yardley, Jonathan, *Ring: A Biography of Ring Lardner*. Atheneum, 1985. $13.95.

Yezierska, Anzia, *Bread Givers*, intro. by Alice Kessler. WP, 1984. pb £3.95.

Chapter XVIII. African, Caribbean, Indian, Australian and Canadian Literature in English

Africa

Gibbs, James L., *Wole Soyinka*. Macmillan, 1986. hb £15, pb £4.95.

Maughan-Brown, David, *Land, Freedom and Fiction: History and Ideology in Kenya*. Zed, 1985. hb £18.95, pb £6.95.

Ngara, Emmanuel, *Art and Ideology in the African Novel*. Heinemann, 1985. pb £7.50.

Schipper, Mineke, ed., *Unheard Words*, trans. by Barbara Potter Fasting. A&B, 1985. pb £4.95.

Sotto, Wiveca, *The Rounded Rite: A Study of Wole Soyinka's Play 'The Bacchae of Euripides'*. LSE. Gleerup, 1985.

The Caribbean

Angier, Carole, *Jean Rhys*. Penguin, 1985. pb £3.95.

Berry, James, *Chain of Days*. OUP, 1985. pb £4.95.

Brown, Stewart, ed., *Caribbean Poetry Now*. H&S, 1984. pb £2.95.

Burnett, Paula, ed., *Caribbean Poetry Now*. Penguin, 1986. pb £4.95.

D'Aguiar, Fred, *Mama Dot*. C&W, 1985. pb £3.95.

Dalphinis, Morgan, *Caribbean and African Languages*. Karia P. £16.95.

Hill, Errol, ed., *Plays for Today*. Longman, 1986. pb £2.95.

Johnson, Amryl, *Long Road to Nowhere*. Virago, 1985. pb £2.95.

Khan, Ismith, *The Jumbie Bird*. Longman, 1985. pb £2.50.

King, Bruce, ed., *Literatures of the World in English*. RKP, 1985, pb £4.95.

Lovelace, Earl, *The Dragon Can't Dance*. Longman, 1985. pb £2.95.

Lovelace, Earl, *While Gods Are Falling*. Longman, 1985. pb £1.95.
McKay, Claude, *A Long Way From Home*. Pluto, 1985. pb £4.95.
Mahabir, Noor Kumar, *The Still Cry*. Calaloux Pubns, 1985. pb £4.95.
Markham, E. A., *Human Rites*. Anvil, 1984. pb £4.95.
Monar, Rooplall, *Backdam People*. Peepal Tree P, 1985. pb £2.95.
Ormerod, Beverley, *An Introduction to the French Caribbean Novel*. Heinemann, 1985. pb £6.95.
Pearn, Julie, *Poetry in the Caribbean*. H&S, 1985. pb £4.95.
Rhys, Jean. *Tales of the Wide Caribbean*. Heinemann, 1985. pb £2.95.
Roy, Namba, *Black Albino*. Longman, 1986. pb £2.95.
Selvon, Samuel, *A Brighter Sun*. Longman, 1986. pb £2.95.
Selvon, Samuel, *The Lonely Londoners*. Longman, 1986. pb £2.50.
Selvon, Samuel, *Ways of Sunlight*. Longman, 1986. pb £2.95.
Senior, Olive, *Summer Lightning*. Longman, 1986. pb £2.50.
Williams, Milton, *Years of Fighting Exile*. Peepal Tree P, 1986. pb £2.95.
Wynter, Sylvia, *The Hills of Hebron*. Longman, 1984. pb £1.95.

India

Chavan, Sunanda P., *The Fair Voice: A Study of Indian Women Poets in English*. Sterling ND, 1984. Rs 75.
Dwivedi, A. N., ed., *Studies in Contemporary Indo-English Verse: A Collection of Essays on Male Poets*. Prakash Book Depot (Bareilly, India), 1984. Rs 65.
Jussawalla, Feroza F., *Family Quarrels: Towards a Criticism of Indian Writing in English*. Lang, 1985. Sfr 58.40.
Labru, G. L., *Indian Newspaper English*. B. R. Pub. (Delhi), 1984. Rs 100.
Mohan, Narendra, *The Eternal NO: Dimensions of Protest in Literature*. Ajanta (Delhi), 1985. Rs 60.
Yule, Henry, and A. C. Burnell, *Hobson-Jobson: A Glossary of Colloquial Anglo-Indian Words and Phrases*. RKP. £18.95.

Australia

Anderson, Don, ed., *Transgressions: Australian Writing Now*. PenguinA, 1986. pb A$8.95.
Blackford, Jenny, Russell Blackford, Lucy Sussex, and Norman Talbot, *Contrary Modes: Proceedings of the World Science Fiction Conference, Melbourne, Australia 1985*. Ebony Books (Newcastle, N.S.W.), 1985.
Cook, Michael, *Thomas Keneally's 'The Chant of Jimmie Blacksmith'*. Little Hills P (St Peters, N.S.W.), 1985. pb A$4.95.
English, Audrey, *Peter Kenna's 'A Hard God': A Critical Study*. Little Hills P (St Peters, N.S.W.). pb A$4.95.
Ferrier, Carole, ed., *Gender, Politics and Fiction: Twentieth Century Australian Women's Novels*. UQueen, 1985. £24.95.
Goodwin, Ken, *A History of Australian Literature*. Macmillan, 1986. hb £27.50, pb £8.95.
Hassall, Anthony J., *Strange Country: A Study of Randolph Stow*. UQueen, 1986. £19.95.
Hewett, Dorothy, *Bobbin Up*. Virago, 1985. pb £3.50.

Hickey, Bernard, *Lines of Implication: Australian Short Fiction from Lawson to Palmer.* Cafoscarina (Venice), 1984.

Hickey, Bernard, *Statements.* Cafoscarina (Venice), 1984.

Kalechofsky, Robert and Roberta, eds, *Jewish Writing from Down Under.* Micah Publications (Marblehead, Massachusetts), 1984. $10.

Kramer, Leonie, and Adrian Mitchell, eds, *The Oxford Anthology of Australian Literature.* OUPM, 1985. £15.

Michel, Christine, ed., *Aspects de la Poésie Australienne.* Sud (Marseilles), 1985. Ffr 120.

Strahan, Lynne, *Just City and the Mirrors: Meanjin Quarterly and the Intellectual Front 1940–1965.* OUPM, 1984. A$25.

Thompson, Tom, ed., *The View from Tinsel Town.* PenguinA/Southerly, 1985. pb A$6.95.

Wilde, William H., Joy Hooton, and Barry Andrews, eds, *The Oxford Companion to Australian Literature.* OUPM, 1985. A$50.

Canada

Keith, W. J., *Canadian Literature in English.* Longman, 1985. hb £14.95, pb £6.95.

Kroepsch, Robert, and Reingard M. Nischik, eds, *Gaining Ground: European Critics on Canadian Literature.* NeWest, 1985.

Solecki, Sam, ed., *Spider Blues: Essays on Michael Ondaapje.* Vehicule, 1985. pb $15.

Chapter XIX. Literary Theory

Altizer, Thomas J. J., *History as Apocalypse.* SUNY, 1985. $10.95.

Auerbach, Nina, *Romantic Imprisonment.* ColU, 1985. $25.

Bal, Mieke, *Narratology: Introduction to the Theory of Narrative.* UTor, 1985. pb $8.95.

Barker, Francis, *et al.*, *Confronting the Crisis: War, Politics and Culture in the Eighties.* UEssex, 1984. £6.50.

Barthes, Roland, *The Grain of the Voice: Interviews 1962–1980.* Cape, 1985. £25.

Barthes, Roland, *The Responsibility of Forms: Critical Essays on Music, Art and Representation.* Blackwell, 1985. £19.50.

Bataille, Georges, *Visions of Excess: Selected Writings 1927–1939.* ManU, 1985. £8.50.

Bersani, Leo, *A Future for Astyanax: Character and Desire in Literature.* ColU, 1984. $9.95.

Bersani, Leo, and Ulysse Dutoit, *The Forms of Violence: Narrative in Assyrian Art and Modern Culture.* Schocken, 1985. $19.95.

Brownmiller, Susan, *Femininity.* Grafton, 1986. pb £2.95.

Burgin, Victor, *The End of Art Theory: Criticism and Postmodernity.* Macmillan, 1986. £20.

Caplan, Jay, *Framed Narratives: Diderot's Genealogy of the Beholder.* ManU, 1985. pb £7.95.

Corngold, Stanley, *The Fate of the Self: German Writers and French Theory.* ColU, 1986. $28.50.

Couzyn, Jeni, ed., *The Bloodaxe Book of Contemporary Women Poets*. Bloodaxe, 1985. hb £12.95, pb £5.95.

Danto, Arthur C., *Narrative and Knowledge*. ColU, 1985. $12.50.

Davidson, Harriet, *T. S. Eliot and Hermeneutics: Absence and Interpretation in 'The Waste Land'*. LSU, 1985. £17.50.

Duchen, Claire, *Feminism in France*. RKP, 1986. pb £6.95.

Dyson, A. E., *Poetry Criticism and Practice: Developments Since the Symbolists*. Macmillan, 1986. £20.

Eagleton, Terry, *Against the Grain: Essays 1975–85*. Verso, 1986. pb £5.95.

Felperin, Howard, *Beyond Deconstruction: The Uses and Abuses of Literary Theory*. OUP, 1985. £15.

Fisch, Harold, *A Remembered Future: A Study in Literary Mythology*. IndU, 1985. $22.50.

Fischer, Michael, *Does Deconstruction Make Any Difference? Poststructuralism and the Defence of Poetry in Modern Criticism*. IndU, 1985. $20.

Goldberg, Jonathan, *Voice Terminal Echo: Postmodernism and English Renaissance Texts*. Methuen, 1986. pb £7.95.

Graham, Joseph F., ed., *Difference in Translation*. CornU, 1985. pb £9.50.

Hartman, Geoffrey H., *Easy Pieces*. ColU, 1985. $20.

Hawkes, Terence, *That Shakespeherian Rag: Essays on a Critical Process*. Methuen, 1985. pb £3.95.

Hollander, John, *Vision and Romance: Two Senses of Poetic Form*. Yale, 1985. £10.95.

Hollingdale, R. J., *Nietzsche*. Ark, 1985. pb £3.95.

Hutcheon, Linda, *A Theory of Parody: The Teachings of Twentieth-Century Art Forms*. Methuen, 1985. pb £5.95.

Innes, Robert E., ed., *Semiotics: An Introductory Reader*. Hutchinson, 1986. pb £9.95.

Jardine, Alice, *Gynesis*. CornU, 1985. $29.95.

Kuhn, Annette, *The Power of the Image*. RKP, 1985. pb £5.95.

Lindley, David, *Lyric*. Methuen, 1985. pb £2.75.

MacCabe, Colin, ed., *High Theory/Low Culture: Analysing Popular Television and Film*. ManU, 1986. pb £6.50.

MacCabe, Colin, *Theoretical Essays: Film, Linguistics, Literature*. ManU, 1985. £17.50.

McNaron, Toni A. H., ed., *The Sister Bond*. Pergamon: Athene, 1985. pb £8.

Merquior, J. G., *From Prague to Paris: A Critique of Structuralist and Post-Structuralist Thought*. Verso, 1986. pb £6.95.

Merquior, J. G., *Western Marxism*. Paladin, 1986. pb £3.95.

Merrell, Floyd, *Deconstruction Reframed*. PurdueU, 1985. $18.50.

Miller, Jane, *Women Writing about Men*. Virago, 1986. hb £10.95, pb £5.50.

Miller, Karl, *Doubles: Studies in Literary History*. Clarendon, 1985. £19.50.

Moi, Toril, *Sexual/Textual Politics*. Methuen, 1985. pb £5.95.

Nietzsche, Friedrich, *Selected Letters*. Soho Book, 1985. pb £6.95.

Norris, Christopher, *The Contest of Faculties: Philosophy and Theory after Deconstruction*. Methuen, 1985. pb £6.95.

Ragland-Sullivan, Ellie, *Jacques Lacan and the Philosophy of Psychoanalysis*. CH, 1985. £25.

Rajchman, John, *Michel Foucault: The Freedom of Philosophy*. ColU, 1985. $22.

Rose, Phyllis, *Writing of Women*. Wesleyan, 1985. £8.95.

Schmidt, James, *Maurice Merleau-Ponty: Between Phenomenology and Structuralism*. Macmillan, 1985. pb £6.95.

Schror, Naomi, *Breaking the Chain*. ColU, 1985. $32.50.

Schwarz, Daniel R., *The Humanistic Heritage: Critical Theories of the English Novel from James to Hillis Miller*. Macmillan, 1986. £27.50.

Selden, Raman, *A Reader's Guide to Contemporary Literary Theory*. Harvester, 1985. pb £4.95.

Shapiro, Gary, and Alan Sica, *Hermeneutics: Questions and Prospects*. UMass, 1984. $24.

Showalter, Elaine, ed., *The New Feminist Criticism*. Virago, 1986. hb £11.95, pb £5.95.

Simon, Richard Keller, *The Labyrinth of the Comic: Theory and Practice from Fielding to Freud*. UFlorS, 1986, $27.95.

Smart, Barry, *Michel Foucault*. Tavistock, 1985. pb £4.25.

Staten, Henry, *Wittgenstein and Derrida*. Blackwell, 1985. £19.50.

Sternberg, Meir, *The Poetics of Biblical Narrative: Ideological Literature and the Drama of Reading*. IndU, 1985. $45.

Warren, Joyce W., *The American Narcissus: Individualism and Women in Nineteenth-Century American Fiction*. Rutgers, 1984. $23.

Welby, Victoria, *Significs and Language*. Benjamins, 1985. £33.

York, R. A., *The Poem as Utterance*. Methuen, 1986. pb £5.95.

Index I. Critics

Authors such as Chinua Achebe and Paul de Man, who are both authors of criticism and subjects of discussion by critics, are listed in whichever index is appropriate for each reference; a page number in bold indicates a chapter or part of a chapter written by a contributor to the volume.

Index II. Authors and Subjects Treated

Authors such as Chinua Achebe and Paul de Man, who are both authors of criticism and subjects of discussion by critics, are listed in whichever index is appropriate for each reference; a page number in bold represents the main entry for a particular author or subject; numbers in brackets e.g. 346(2) indicate the number of times the author or subject is referred to on a particular page.

poetry, 399; poetry attributed to, 399;
satire in, 413; *Childe Harold's
Pilgrimage*, 399; *The Prisoner of
Chillon*, 399; 'To Barbara', 399
Byron, H.J.: *The Babes in the Wood*,
492; *The Gaiety Gulliver*, 492; *The
Lancashire Lass*, 492; *Our Boys*, 492
cabaret, 579
Cabbala: in 16th C Europe, 35
Cabell, James Branch, 633; and
Faulkner, 636; *Life of Manuel*, 633
Cable, George Washington: and Grace
King, 630; *The Grandissimes*, 630
Cabot, James: and Emerson, 595
Caesar: *Bellum Gallicum*, 81
Cage, John, 527; and postmodernism,
790
Cahan, Abraham, 628, 635
Caird, John, 203
Calderón de la Barca, Pedro, 342
Caldwell, Erskine, **643**; interview, 643
Calgary: theatre in, 760
Callaghan, Morley, 744, 747;
autobiography, 745–6; *That Summer
in Paris*, 746
Calsada, David (illustrator), 612
Calvinism, 257, 269, 287, 505, 559
calypso: Caribbean, 707, 712, 713
Cambert, Robert, 346
Camden, William, 302
Cameron, Julia Margaret: poems, 433;
'On a Portrait', 433; 'On Receiving a
Copy of Arthur Clough's Poems at
Fresh Water Bay', 433
Cameroon literature, 679
Camoens, Luis de: and Campbell, 691
Campbell, David, 726, 741
Campbell, Joseph, 677, 768
Campbell, Mrs Patrick, 495
Campbell, Roy, 17–18; 'Rounding the
Cape', 691
Campbell, William Robert, 647
Campion, Thomas, 177
Camus, Albert, 656
Canada: cultural identity, 732–3;
Shakespeare productions in, 203
Canadian English, 36
Canadian historical writing: and Scott,
405
Canadian literature, **743–61**; and
Australian literature, 733; South
Asian Canadian fiction, 714
Canadian theatre: documentary, 760
Canetti, Elias, 10; and Murdoch, 559
cannibalism: Melville, 598

canon, 792
Canterbury: AS church in, 74
Capgrave, John: *Abbreuiacion of
Chronicles*, 129
capitalism: in English literature, 319; and
women's reading, 784–5
Capote, Truman: 'Handcarved Coffins',
653; *Music for Chameleons*, 653
Carcanet Press, 564
Carew, Thomas, 289; and visual arts,
279; *Coelum Britannicum*, 272
Carey, Henry: and *Bounce to Fop*, 357;
Ballad of Sally in Our Alley, 356
Carey, John, 304, 330
Carey, Peter, 732
Caribbean English, 37
Caribbean literature, **702–13**; censorship,
665
Caribbean poetry, 793; British West
Indians, 565
caricature: and drama, 368; and T.S.
Eliot, 570; theatrical, 498
Carleton, Mary, 344; *The Case of Madam
Mary Carleton*, 344
Carlyle, Thomas, 445, 459, **478–9**, 768;
and Bulwer Lytton, 450; and Conrad,
518; and Dickens, 457; and Conan
Doyle, 479; and Fitzgerald, 484; and
Frithiof's saga, 478–9; and Homer,
478; and epic, 478; and history, 478;
and stylistic dualism, 476; and
Sweden, 479; essays on history, 478;
letters, 478, 484; marginalia, 479;
'Chaos and Cosmos', 478; *Cromwell*,
479; *Frederick the Great*, 478; *The
French Revolution*, 478; 'The Hero as
Divinity', 445; *Latter Day Pamphlets*,
478; *Past and Present*, 478(2); *Sartor
Resartus*, 478, 518; *Signs of the Times*,
478
Carman, Bliss, 758; *Low Tide on Grand
Pré*, 758
Carmichael, Gershom, 353
carnival, 772; Caribbean, 713; in
Lovelace, 707
carnivalization: theory of, and 18th C
novels, 376
Carpenter, Edward, 525
Carpentier, Alejo, 705
Carr, Emily: and autobiography, 746;
Growing Pains, 746; *Hundreds and
Thousands*, 746
Carr, J.L., 547, 558
Carr, John Dickson: and Chesterton, 523
Carroll, Lewis, **466**; and Stoppard, 587;

German: germanisms, in English, 56; influence on English language, 56, 57

German aesthetics, 389

German criticism, 389, 762, 774; and French criticism, 778

German Neoromanticism: and Brennan, 737

Germanic literatures, 668

Germany: English actors in, 248; Shakespeare productions in, 201, 202–3, 208

Gerritsen, Johan, 44

ghost stories: and Dickens, 459; in Edwardian period, 500

Gibbon, Edward: and Greece, 19

Gibbon, Lewis Grassic, 505, **549**; letters, 549; manuscripts, 549; *A Scots Quair*, 502, 505, 549; and MacDiarmid, *Scottish Scene*, 505

Gibbs, James, 353–4; *Book of Architecture*, 354

Gibson, Colin, 191

Gibson, Graeme, 745

Gide, André, 19, 779

Gielgud, John, 202, 576

Gifford, Don, 527

The Gifts of Men, 83

Gikuyu literature, 680; Ngugi, 669, 684

Gil, Alexander, 308

Gilbert, Sandra M., 672

Gilbert, Stuart, 526, 530

Gilbert, W.S. and Sullivan, 497; *Ruddigore*, 497; *Trial by Jury*, 497

Gildas, 73–4

Gilpin, John: and Austen, 410; *Observations*, 410

Ginsberg, Allen, 14, 608

Giorgione, Giorgio Barbarelli: and Sidney, 169

Giradoux, Jean, 19, 779

Giraldi, Lilio Gregorio, 314

Girard, René, 776

Gismond of Salerne, 268

Gissing, George, **469–70**; and Dickens, 469; and James, 469–70; and Johnson, 469; and Wells, 519; essays, 469; *Born in Exile*, 470; *A Life's Morning*, 469; *New Grub Street*, 469–70; *The Odd Women*, 470

Githae-Mugo, Micere, 665

Glanvill, Joseph: and Locke, 344

Glasgow, Ellen, **643**; language, 643; *A Certain Measure*, 643; 'Dare's Gift', 643

Glassco, John, 744; autobiography, 745

Glossa Ordinaria, 122

glossaries, 80

glosses, 80; and Chaucer, 139; ME, 105; OE, 54, 79, 83, 101(2)

glottogenesis, 34

Glover, Richard, 350

Gluck, Louise, 626

gluttony, 119; and Chaucer, 150

gnosticism, 643–4; and Burroughs, 649

God: nature of, and poetry, 611

Godfrey, David, 750–1, 756; 'River Two Blind Jacks', 756

Godwin, Mary: and children's literature, 352

Godwin, William, **386**, 389, 397; and children's literature, 352; biography, 376; diaries, 386; novels, 386; political writing, 386; *Caleb Williams*, 386; *Damon and Delia*, 386; *Fleetwood*, 386, 413; *Imogen*, 386; *Italian Letters*, 386; *Mandeville*, 386, 413; *Political Justice*, 376, 386; *St. Leon*, 386; *Things as They Are*, 386

Goethe, Johann Wolfgang von, 389, 690, 768, 782–3; and Arnold, 421–2; and Freud, 783; and Marlowe, 259; and Scott, 407; and Tennyson, 435; and Greece, 19; *Dichtung und Wahrheit*, 421; *Faust*, 259, 390; *Werther*, 421

Goffman, Erving, 198

Gogol, Nicolai, 10, 795; *The Nose*, 773

Gold, H.L., 627

Gold, Michael, 628; *Jews Without Money*, 635

Golding, Arthur, 222

Golding, William, **557–8**, 690; essays, 557; reviews, 557; travel writing, 557; *Darkness Visible*, 557; *The Hot Gates*, 557; *The Inheritors*, 558; *Lord of the Flies*, 557–8; *The Paper Men*, 557; *Pincher Martin*, 515; *The Pyramid*, 557; *Rites of Passage*, 557; 'The Scorpion God', 557; *The Spire*, 557

Goldmann, Lucien: and popular fiction, 793

Goldoni, Carlo, 257

Goldring, Douglas: and Lawrence, 538–9

Goldsmith, Oliver, **364–5**, **375**; and cosmopolitanism, 598; poetry, **364–5**; politics, 375; prose, 375; *Bee*, 364; *The Citizen of the World*, 375; *The Deserted Village*, 364; *The Vicar of Wakefield*, 382

Gollancz, Israel, 83

Gollancz, Victor: and Orwell, 543–4